Encyclopedia of Internet Technologies and Applications

Mario Freire
University of Beira Interior, Portugal

Manuela Pereira
University of Beira Interior, Portugal

INFORMATION SCIENCE REFERENCE

Hershey · New York

Acquisitions Editor:	Kristin Klinger
Development Editor:	Kristin Roth
Senior Managing Editor:	Jennifer Neidig
Managing Editor:	Sara Reed
Copy Editor:	Larissa Vinci and Mike Goldberg
Typesetter:	Amanda Appicello and Jeffrey Ash
Cover Design:	Lisa Tosheff
Printed at:	Yurchak Printing Inc.

Published in the United States of America by
Information Science Reference (an imprint of IGI Global)
701 E. Chocolate Avenue, Suite 200
Hershey PA 17033
Tel: 717-533-8845
Fax: 717-533-8661
E-mail: cust@igi-global.com
Web site: http://www.igi-global.com/reference

and in the United Kingdom by
Information Science Reference (an imprint of IGI Global)
3 Henrietta Street
Covent Garden
London WC2E 8LU
Tel: 44 20 7240 0856
Fax: 44 20 7379 0609
Web site: http://www.eurospanonline.com

Library of Congress Cataloging-in-Publication Data

Encyclopedia of Internet technologies and applications / Mario Freire and Manuela Pereira, editors.
    p. cm.
  Summary: "This book is the single source for information on the world's greatest network, and provides a wealth of information for the average Internet consumer, as well as for experts in the field of networking and Internet technologies. It provides the most thorough examination of Internet technologies and applications for researchers in a variety of related fields"--Provided by publisher.
  Includes bibliographical references and index.
  ISBN 978-1-59140-993-9 (hardcover) -- ISBN 978-1-59140-994-6 (ebook)
  1. Internet--Encyclopedias. I. Freire, Mário Marques, 1969- II. Pereira, Manuela.
  TK5105.875.I57E476 2007
  004.67'803--dc22
                            2007024949

British Cataloguing in Publication Data
A Cataloguing in Publication record for this book is available from the British Library.

Editorial Advisory Board

List of Contributors

Contents
by Volume

Preface

Before the invention of the World Wide Web, computer communications were mainly associated with the data transmission and reception among computers. The invention of the Web by Tim Berners-Lee in 1989, led to a deep change of this paradigm, imposing the share of information over the data transmission. After the invention of the Web, Internet refers to the global information system that is logically linked through a global unique address space based on the Internet Protocol (IP) and is able to support communications using the Transmission Control Protocol / Internet Protocol (TCP/IP) architecture and/or other IP-compatible protocols, and provides, uses or makes accessible information and communication services world wide.

The World Wide Web, also known as WWW, Web or W3, represents the greatest networked repository of human knowledge accessible worldwide. The Web contains billions of objects and documents, which may be accessed by hundreds of million of users around the world and it became indispensable for people, institutions or organizations. The search of information in the current Web is based on the use of robust and practical applications known as search engines and directories. However, the fast and unorganized growth of the Web is making difficult to locate, share, access, present or maintain on-line trustful contents for an increasing number of users. Difficulties in the search of web contents are associated to the use of non-structured, sometimes heterogeneous information, and to the ambiguity of Web content. Thus, one of the limitations of the current Web is the lack of structure of its documents and the information contained in them. Besides, information overload and poor aggregation of contents make the current Web inadequate for automatic transfers of information. As a consequence, the current Web may evolve for a new generation Web called Semantic Web, in which data and services are understandable and usable not only by humans but also by computers. Moreover, in the future, the Semantic Web may further evolve to a Sentient Web, which is a further new generation of Web with capabilities for sentience.

If, by one hand, the invention of the Web led to the fact that the TCP/IP architecture, which is the support of Internet, is being used in applications for which it was not designed for, by other hand, a large number of new applications have been developed, which led to the rise of new communication protocols that have been incorporated into the TCP/IP architecture. Besides scientific and technological challenges in the development of Web and its evolution, in the framework of W3C (World Wide Web Consortium), in order to explore all its potential, research and development activities have also been observed towards the development of new multimedia applications over the Internet and towards the ubiquity and autonomic systems. The development of these new applications and systems, by their side, require the research of new protocols and technologies, or the integration of existing technologies used in other fields. A strong research effort is also observed in the transport and network layers in order to cope with mobility, guarantee the quality of service or security and privacy for networked applications, and new forms of group communications in the scenario of the exhaustion of the address space at network layer. Besides, intense research activities also have been observed for the discovery of new solutions that led to an increase of the link bandwidth and the throughput of routers and switches.

The functioning principle of Internet is based on the client-server paradigm, in which the client has an active role and the server has a passive role answering to the queries made by the client. Besides the research activities that are being carried out in each layer of the TCP/IP architecture, it may be also observed intense research activities towards a new kind of networks, called peer-to-peer (P2P) networks. The term P2P refers to a class of systems and applications that use distributed resources to execute some function in a decentralized way, in which each machine may act as a client or a server. Although P2P networks present some problems regarding security and legality, they represent the most advanced stage, in terms of scalability and fault tolerance, in the evolution of distribution multimedia services.

The purpose of the Encyclopedia of Internet Technologies and Applications is to provide a written compendium for the dissemination of knowledge and to improve our understanding in the area of Internet technologies and applications. The encyclopedia presents carefully selected articles from 232 submission proposals, after a double blind review process. It also provides a compendium of terms, definitions and explanation of concepts, technologies, applications, issues and trends in the area of Internet technologies and applications.

The projected audience is broad, ranging from simple Internet users (Internet consumers), which would like to learn more about Internet, to experts working in the areas of networking and Internet technologies and applications. This encyclopedia will be of particular interest to teachers, researchers, scholars and professionals working in these areas, who may require access to the most current information, about concepts, technologies, applications, issues and trends in these areas. The encyclopedia also serves as a reference for engineers, consultants, IT professionals, managers, and others interested in the latest knowledge on Internet technologies and applications.

Mario Freire and Manuela Pereira
Editors

Acknowledgment

The editors thank all the authors who submitted valuable articles to the encyclopedia and are also grateful to the members of the editorial advisory board and to the reviewers. Without their support, the organization of such a high-quality encyclopedia would not have been possible. The editors are also indebted to many individuals and organizations that made possible this encyclopedia, namely to IGI Global and University of Beira Interior, Portugal.

About the Editors

Mário Freire received a 5-year BS degree (licentiate) in electrical engineering and an MSc in systems and automation (1992 and 1994, respectively), from the University of Coimbra, Portugal. He received a PhD in electrical engineering from the University of Beira Interior, Covilhã, Portugal (2000). He is an associate professor of computer science at the University of Beira Interior and is the leader of the Network and Multimedia Computing Group. Presently, he is the head of the Department of Computer Science of University of Beira Interior, where he is also director of the PhD programme in computer science and engineering and teaches courses at the MSc and PhD levels on network architectures and protocols and multimedia networks. His main research interests include: high-speed networks, network security, Web technologies and applications, and medical informatics. He was the co-editor of two books in the LNCS book series of Springer, co-editor of three proceedings in IEEE Computer Society Press, and has authored or co-authored around 100 papers in international refereed journals and conferences. He served as a technical program committee member for some tens of international conferences. He was the general chair of IEEE HSNMC2003, general co-chair of ECUMN2004, the TPC chair of ICN2005, the TPC co-chair of ICIW2006, co-chair of IS2006 and IS2007, track co-chair of the ACM SAC 2007 and ACM SAC 2008, general co-chair of GOBS2007 and of HPC-Bio2007. He is also an associate editor of the Wiley journal *Security and Communication Networks*, a member of the editorial board of the *Journal of Computer Systems, Networks and Communications*, a member of the editorial board of the *IEEE Communications Surveys and Tutorials*, a member of the editorial review board of the *International Journal of Business Data Communications and Networking*, and a member of the editorial advisory board of the IGI Advances in Business Data Communications and Networking (ABDCN) book series. He also served as a guest editor of a Feature Topic on "Security in Mobile Ad Hoc and Sensor Networks" of *IEEE Communications Magazine* (February 2008) and a guest editor of the special issue on "Service, Security and Data Management for Ubiquitous Computing" of the *International Journal of Ad Hoc and Ubiquitous Computing* (Second Issue of 2008). He is a licensed professional engineer by the Order of Engineers – Informatics Engineering College (Portugal) and he is a member of IEEE Computer Society and IEEE Communications Society, a member of the ACM (Association for Computing Machinery) and of the Internet Society. He is also the chair of IEEE Computer Society – Portugal Chapter.

Manuela Pereira received a 5-year BS degree (licentiate) in mathematics and computer science in 1994 and an MSc in computational mathematics in 1999, both from the University of Minho, Braga, Portugal. She received a PhD in signal and image processing (Groupe CREATIVE du laboratoire I3S, CNRS/UNSA) from the University of Nice Sophia Antipolis, France (2004). She is an assistant professor with the Department of Computer Science of the University of Beira Interior, Portugal, and a member of the Network and Multimedia Computing Group. Presently, she is the vice-head of the Department of Computer Science, where she is also director of the MSc programme in computer science and engineering and teaches courses on multimedia technologies, image communication, and multimedia processing and communication. Her main research interests include: multiple description coding, joint source/channel coding, image and video coding, wavelet analysis, information theory, image segmentation and real-time video streaming. She served or serves as a technical program committee member for several international conferences in the areas of multimedia and communications.

Active Queue Management

Michele Mara de Araújo Espíndula Lima
Federal University of Pernambuco, Brazil

Nelson Luís Saldanha da Fonseca
State University of Campinas, Brazil

INTRODUCTION

Congestion is the state of a network in which the offered load exceeds the network capacity for a certain period of time. Under congestion conditions, network performance deteriorates; resources are wasted, delays and jitters increase, and predictability of services is reduced. Moreover, the occurrence of congestion almost always results in the degradation of the quality of service to end users.

In order to avoid congestion, the transmission control protocol (TCP) modifies the transmission rate as a function of the estimated available bandwidth. The idea is to probe the available bandwidth and then adjust the transmission rate accordingly. Such adjustment is governed by the reception of acknowledgements (ACKs) sent by the receiver upon the reception of a packet. When an ACK is received, the congestion window is increased; this continues until a packet loss is detected. If three ACKs for the same packet are received, the next packet in sequence is considered lost and the transmission window is reduced to half of its size. Moreover, upon expiration of a period of time set for the reception of the acknowledgment of a packet, the packet is retransmitted (Retransmission TimeOut, RTO). The transmission window is then drastically reduced to a single packet, and the TCP sender is forced to enter in its initial phase. When congestion is intense, bursts of losses occur, the number of RTO's increases, and consequently, the performance of TCP degrades.

Although powerful and necessary to prevent network collapse, the congestion control mechanism of the TCP is not sufficient to avoid congestion. Since TCP sources exert a limited control of the network and unresponsive flows, which do not slow down their sending rates when congestion occurs, may be present, the efficacy of end-to-end congestion control also relies on queue mechanisms at the routers.

BACKGROUND

The simplest scheme for routers to manage queue length is called tail drop. With this mechanism, arriving packets are admitted into queues as long as there is empty space. When the number of packets arriving during a certain period of time exceeds the available buffer space, overflow occurs, and packets are lost.

Tail drop present two major drawbacks: (1) a small set of flows can monopolize the queue, while packets from others will be dropped; (2) it is detrimental to bursty traffic. These two drawbacks can also lead to the global synchronization problem, which is the synchronization of packet loss from most of the flows, with the consequent reduction in window size and a potentially low network utilization. Under tail drop, queues at the routers are generally full, which yields high loss rates, as well as long delays.

To overcome these problems, packets should be dropped randomly for notifying end nodes about the beginning of congestion; these nodes can then reduce their transmission rate before queue overflows occur. The congestion control mechanism that allows routers to control when and which packets should be dropped is called active queue management (AQM). The main action of AQM is the early notification of incipient congestion by dropping/marking of packets.

AQM OBJECTIVES

In order to use buffer space efficiently, AQM policies must achieve certain objectives. Global synchronization must be avoided by selective discard of packets, as well as by limiting the number of flows affected.

The loss of packets belonging to specific flows under the same network conditions should be proportional to the queue utilization of those flows. Furthermore, even when multiple losses in the same flow are unavoidable, AQM policies should minimize the occurrence of bursts of losses so that the number of RTO's can be reduced.

Hollot, Misra, Towsley, and Gong (2002) have formulated additional performance goals for AQM policies: efficient queue utilization, assurance of low delay, and delay variation. Efficient queue use means that unnecessary periods of overflow and emptiness will be avoided. The former results in loss of packets, undesired retransmissions, and the penalization of bursty traffic, whereas the latter leads to buffer underutilization. Low delay values are a result of the queue lengths, although such a situation can lead to link underutilization. Moreover, queue size variations should be avoided to prevent jitter, which is detrimental to certain real time applications.

AQM policies should also be robust and keep the queue length stable, despite unfavorable network condition such as variations in RTT and traffic fluctuation. Moreover, they must be simple to avoid unnecessary overhead in packet processing.

RED POLICY

The random early detection policy (RED) (Floyd & Jacobson, 1993) estimates average queue size and compares it to two thresholds. If the average queue size is less than the lower threshold, no packets are marked or dropped, but in the interstice, arriving packets are marked/dropped according to a certain probability. Above the upper threshold all arriving packets are dropped. RED was originally proposed to avoid congestion, ensure an upper bound on average queue size, avert global synchronization, and prevent bias against bursty traffic. The Internet engineering task force (IETF) recommends RED as the AQM policy to be deployed on the Internet.

Although simple and relatively efficient, RED reaches its optimal operational point only when threshold values are correctly defined. If not, RED may perform even worse than the traditional Tail Drop policy. Moreover, with a large number of flows, RED reacts slowly to sudden variations in queue length, and fails to mark/drop packets proportionally. Another drawback of RED is unfairness, as it is biased against short-lived TCP flows (i.e., flows with small windows).

AQM POLICIES BASED ON RED

Various algorithms have been proposed to overcome the drawbacks of RED. The adaptive random early drop algorithm, ARED, (Feng, Kandlur, Saha, & Shin, 1999) provides a dynamic setting of RED parameter values. The underlying idea behind is to determine when RED should be more or less aggressive. With a small number of active flows, RED should be more conservative to avoid link underutilization, but when this number is high, RED should be more aggressive.

A second algorithm is flow random early drop (FRED) (Lin & Morris, 1997), which was designed principally to reduce RED unfairness. FRED indicates the existence of congestion by marking/dropping packets from flows, which have a larger number of packets in queue.

A third algorithm, flow proportional queuing (FPQ) (Morris, 2000), deals with problems involving a large number of active flows. FPQ tries to maintain loss rates fixed by varying the RTT proportionally to the number of active flows, as well as by keeping the queue length proportional to the number of active flows.

AQM POLICIES BASED ON OPTIMIZATION THEORY

In general, AQM policies based on optimization theory represent the control of congestion as an optimization problem widely known as Kelly's system problem (Kelly, Maulloo, & Tan, 1998). In this approach, a utility function value is associated with each flow, and the utility function of the system as a whole maximized, subject to link capacity constraints. Congestion control schemes try to reach optimum or suboptimum solutions to this maximization problem (Basar & Srikant, 2003).

In the Kelly's approach, source rates are seen as primal variables whereas congestion measures functions as dual variables; a primal-dual problem is then formulated so that aggregate source utility is maximized. In the primal problem, source rates are dynamically adapted on the basis of route costs, and links are selected according to their offered load (Kunniyur & Srikant, 2004). On the other hand, in the dual problem, their costs are adapted on the basis of link rates. Source rates are then determined by route costs and source parameters (Low, 2003; Srikant, 2004). Primal-dual algorithms involve dynamic adaptations of links at the

Figure 1. System for congestion control

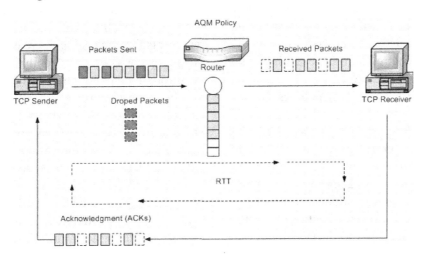

user end (Paganini, Wang, Doyle, & Low, 2005). In this case, source dynamics are similar to those of primal algorithms, although the link dynamics are similar to those of dual algorithms.

Special policies have been proposed for implementing approaches based on optimizations theory. One solution for the primal problem is the use of a virtual queue with a lower capacity than that of the corresponding real queue. The idea here is to drop packets from the real queue when the virtual queue overflows. Gibbens and Kelly (1999) used a static virtual queue, whereas Kunniyur et al. (2004) used a dynamic one, with size and capacity varying as a function of the characteristics of the arriving flow, to develop the adaptive virtual queue (AVQ) AQM policy.

The random exponential marking policy (REM), which has been presented as the solution for the dual problem formulation (Athuraliya, Low, Li, & Yin, 2001), expresses measures of congestion as costs, which are calculated for each link on the basis of local information. Sources are then informed of these costs when their packets are dropped/marked. One possible policy for the solution of the dual-primal problem is E-RED (Basar et al., 2003).

AQM POLICIES BASED ON CONTROL THEORY

AQM policies based on control theory consider the feedback, which exists in congestion control systems.

In such systems, transmission rates of the sources are adjusted according to the level of congestion. This level, in turn, is determined by the queue occupancy (Figure 1). Controllers are responsible for determining the appropriate values for the minimum rate of drop/mark probability, which will ensure maximum transmission rates as well as the stabilization of the queue size, regardless of network conditions (Srikant, 2004).

The great majority of AQM policies based on control theory have used classical controllers such as proportional (P), integral (I), proportional-integral (PI), proportional-derivative (PD), or proportional-integral-derivative (PID) controllers. Some of them are discussed next.

Loss-ratio-based RED (LRED) is an AQM policy developed using a controller of type P (Wang, Li, Hou, Sohraby, & Lin, 2004). This policy dynamically adjusts the mark/drop probability value as a function of the loss rate in conjunction with queue length.

The dynamic RED (DRED) policy tries to stabilize the queue size in the neighborhood of a reference value independent of the number of active flows (Aweya, Ouellette, & Montuno, 2001). To achieve such a goal, DRED adjusts the dropping probability as a function of the difference between the queue level and the queue reference level. Although presented as a proportional controller, it is actually an integral controller.

The proportional integrator (PI) AQM controller used the TCP dynamic model presented by Hollot et al. (2002) to simplify the control model. Its design concentrates on the nominal behavior (low frequency) of window dynamics so that the high frequency residual can be determined. The procedure involves simplification to isolate the contribution of the delay of the residuals, which is treated as an unmodeled dynamic. In this approach, the controller ensures stability of the system by stabilizing the residual.

Among the proposals for AQM policies that use proportional-integral-derivative controller are VCR AQM (Park, Lim, Park, & Choi, 2004), Receding Horizon AQM (RHA–AQM) (Kim & Low, 2002), and the one presented in Agrawal and Granelli (2004). The VCR AQM policy (Park et al., 2004) was designed to stabilize both the input rate and the queue length at their approximate target levels. It uses the notion of a virtual target value, as originally presented in AVQ policy. The difference between them is that AVQ uses a virtual queue, while VCR uses virtual rates. The RHA-AQM policy explicitly compensates for delays in congestion measure by using a memory control structure. Finally, in Agrawal et al. (2004), a linear quadratic regulator is used to design a robust PID controller.

A PD AQM with goals similar to the ones of DRED has been presented by Sun, Chen, Ko, Chan, Zukerman, and Chan (2003). The difference is that DRED is based on the instantaneous queue length whereas the PD controller is based on the average queue length. As does DRED, this PD policy has its parameters determined empirically.

Modern control theory has also been used to design AQM controllers. Some controller designs use feedback compensation, but only a few use optimal or robust control (Fengyuan, Chuang, Xunhe, & Fubao, 2002; Lima, Fonseca, & Geromel 2004; Yan, Gao, & Ozbay, 2005).

Heying, Baohong, and Wenhua (2003) used feedback compensation techniques to derive the algorithm called proportional integral-based series compensation, and the positional feedback compensation (PIP AQM). The idea is to choose appropriate feedback compensation parameters so that they help achieve system desired performance.

Most of AQM policies based on control theory use only current information about the dynamics of the queue and do not explicitly compensate for long delays. The novelty of the H2-AQM policy presented by Lima et al. (2004) is the use of non-rational controllers. Furthermore, stability and performance objectives are expressed as linear matrix inequalities (LMIs) so that the parameters of the controller can be computed by solving a single convex problem. Although the model used to derive H2-AQM was the same model used to derive PI AQM, the plant used in the H2-AQM design represents the congestion in greater detail. Moreover, the policy considered the equilibrium that maximizes the throughput and minimizes the packet loss.

The algorithm based on sliding mode variable structure control (SMVS) constitutes the basis for the variable structure AQM (Fengyuan et al., 2002). The structure of SMVS control is not constant, but is varied during the control process so that the controller is insensitive to system dynamic parameters. VS-AQM is another AQM policy based on SMVS control (Yan et al., 2005). The difference is that VS-AQM was designed considering a non-linear model of the congestion control system.

FUTURE AND EMERGING TRENDS

Recently, several variants of TCP for high-speed networks have been proposed to overcome the scalability deficiency of TCP-Reno, which is not capable to take advantage of the huge bandwidth availability in high capacity links. One of the questions that needs to be addressed is whether these TCP variants are effective when deployed in networks with AQM mechanisms at the routers. Another open problem is the design of AQM policies for such variants.

CONCLUSION

Under conditions of congestion, the performance of a network deteriorates; resources are wasted, delays and jitters increase, and the predictability of network services is reduced. Therefore, minimization of congestion and its consequences is of paramount importance in the efficacy of a network. This text introduced mechanisms, which can be used to control congestion using active queue management. The purpose of these mechanisms is the early notification of incipient congestion by dropping/marking packets so that TCP senders can reduce their transmission rate before queue overflows and sustained packet losses occur. RED, the AQM policy recommended by the IETF for deployment on the Internet, presents various drawbacks, including difficulty in the tuning of parameters. Various other policies based on heuristics have been proposed to overcome this problem. Nevertheless, these studies neither assure that an equilibrium point can be reached nor guarantee stability of queue length. In the past few years, significant progress has been made towards a precise mathematical modeling for the control of congestion. This has led to the development of AQM policies, which do ensure stability in the neighborhood of an equilibrium point. Results indicate that this non-heuristic mathematical approach is very useful in improving existing control and feedback mechanisms, as well as in making them scalable to networks that operate at very high speeds.

REFERENCES

Agrawal, D., & Granelli, F. (2004). Redesigning an active queue management system. In *Proceedings of IEEE Global Telecommunications Conference* (Vol. 2, pp. 702-706).

Athuraliya, S., Low, S., Li, V., & Yin, Q. (2001). REM: Active queue management. *IEEE Networks*, *15*(3), 48-53.

Aweya, J., Ouellette, M., & Montuno, D. Y. (2001). A control theoretic approach to active queue management. *Computer Networks*, *36*(2), 203-235.

Basar, S. L., & Srikant, T. (2003). Controlling the Internet: A survey and some new results. In *Proceedings of the 42nd IEEE Conference on Decision and Control*, *3*(12), 3048-3057.

Feng, W., Kandlur, D. D., Saha, D., & Shin, K. G. (1999). A self-configuring RED gateway. In *Proceedings of IEEE INFOCOM 1999* (Vol. 3, pp. 1320-1328).

Fengyuan, R., Chuang, L., Xunhe, Y., & Fubao, X. S. W. (2002). A robust active queue management algorithm based on sliding mode variable structure control. In *Proceedings of IEEE INFOCOM 2002* (Vol. 1, pp. 13-20).

Floyd S., & Jacobson, V. (1993). Random early detection gateways for congestion avoidance. *IEEE/ACM Transactions on Networking*, *1*(4), 397-413.

Heying, Z., Baohong, L., & Wenhua, D. (2003). Design of a robust active queue management algorithm based on feedback compensation. In *Proceedings of the 2003 Conference on Applications, Technologies, Architec-tures, and Protocols for Computer Communications* (pp. 277-285). ACM Press.

Hollot, C. V., Misra, V., Towsley, D., & Gong, W. (2002). Analysis and design of controllers for AQM routers supporting TCP flows. *IEEE Transaction on Automatic Control*, *47*(6), 945-959.

Kelly, F., Maulloo, A., & Tan, D. (1998). Rate control in communication networks: Shadow prices, proportional fairness, and stability. *Journal of the Operational Research Society*, *49*, 237-252.

Kim, K. B., & Low, S. H. (2002). Analysis and design of AQM for stabilizing TCP. California Institute of Technology, Tech. Rep. CSTR:2002.009, 03 2002.

Kunniyur, S. S., & Srikant, R. (2004). Analysis and design of an adaptive virtual queue algorithm for active queue management. *IEEE/ACM Transactions on Networking*, *4*, 286-299.

Lima, M. M. de A. E., Fonseca, N. L. S., & Geromel, J. C. (2004). An optimal active queue management controller. In *Proceedings of IEEE International Conference on Communications 2004* (pp. 2261-2266).

Lin, D., & Morris, R. (1997). Dynamics of random early detection. *Proceedings of SIGCOMM'97* (pp. 127-137).

Low, S. H. (2003). A duality model of TCP and queue management algorithms. *IEEE/ACM Transactions on Networking*, *11*(4), 525-536.

Morris, R. (2000). Scalable TCP congestion control. In *Proceedings of INFOCOM 2000* (pp. 1176-1183).

Paganini, F., Wang, Z., Doyle, J., & Low, S. (2005). Congestion control for high performance, stability, and fairness in general networks. *IEEE/ACM Transactions on Networking*, *13*(1), 43-56.

Park, E. C., Lim, H., Park, K. J., & Choi, C. H. (2004). Analysis and design of the virtual rate control algorithm for stabilizing queues in TCP networks. *Computer Networks*, *44*(1), 17-41.

Srikant, R. (2004). Models and methods for analyzing Internet congestion control algorithms. In C. Abdallah, J. Chiasson, & S. Tarbouriech (Eds.), *Advances in communication control networks in the series lecture notes in control and information sciences (LCNCIS)*. Springer-Verlag.

A

Sun, J., Chen, G., & Ko, K. T., Chan, S., & Zukerman, M. (2003). PD-controller: A new active queue management scheme. In *Proceedings of Global Telecommunications Conference 2003* (Vol. 12, pp. 3103-3107).

Wang, C., Li, B., & Hou, T., Sohraby, K., & Lin, Y. (2004). LRED: A robust active queue management scheme based on packet loss ratio. In *Proceedings of IEEE Infocom 2004*.

Yan, P., Gao, Y., & Ozbay, H. (2005). A variable structure control approach to active queue management for TCP with ECN. *IEEE Transactions on Control Systems Technology*, *13*(2), 203-215.

KEY TERMS

Active Queue Management (AQM): Congestion control mechanism for the early notification of incipient congestion pursued by dropping/marking packets.

Congestion: State of the network characterized by the demand of traffic transmission exceeding its transport capacity.

Congestion Avoidance: Traffic control mechanisms that attempt to avert the occurrence of network congestion.

Congestion Control: Traffic control mechanisms that remedy the consequences of congestion problems that have already occurred.

Congestion Window: Range of packets that can be transmitted by a sender without leading to network congestion.

Global Synchronization Problem: A phenomenon that happens when most of active TCP flows lose packets, reducing their sending rates, which can lead to network underutilization.

Random Early Detection Policy (RED): An AQM policy recommended by the Internet task engineering force for deployment on the Internet.

Round Trip Time: Time elapsed between the transmission of a packet and the reception of the corresponding acknowledgement.

Tail Drop: A policy, which admits packet into the router buffer whenever there is available space.

Transmission Window: Range of packets that can be transmitted by a sender.

Adaptive Routing Quality of Service Algorithms for Internet's Irregular Traffic

Abdelhamid Mellouk

LISSI/SCTIC, University of Paris XII – Val de Marne, France

INTRODUCTION

Networks, such as the Internet, have become the most important communication infrastructure of today's society. It enables the worldwide users (individual, group, and organizational) to access and exchange remote information scattered over the world. Currently, due to the growing needs in telecommunications (VoD, video-conference, VoIP, etc.) and the diversity of transported flows, the Internet network does not meet the requirements of the future integrated-service networks that carry multimedia data traffic with a high quality of service (QoS). The main drivers of this evolution are the continuous growth of the bandwidth requests, the promise of cost improvements, and finally the possibility of increasing profits by offering new services. First, the Internet network does not support resource reservation which is primordial to guarantee an end-to-end QoS (bounded delay, bounded delay jitter, and/or bounded loss ratio). Second, data packets may be subjected to unpredictable delays and thus may arrive at their destination after the expiration time, which is undesirable for continuous real-time media. In this context, for optimizing the financial investment on their networks, operators must use the same support for transporting all the flows. Therefore, it is necessary to develop a high quality control mechanism to check the network traffic load and ensure QoS requirements (Strassner, 2003; Welzl, 2003). It's clear that the integration of these QoS parameters increases the complexity of the used algorithms. Anyway, there will be QoS-relevant technological challenges in the emerging hybrid networks which mix several different types of networks (wireless, broadcast, mobile, fixed, etc.), especially in the routing process, which is central to improve performances in the hybrid networks. Constraints imposed by QoS requirements, such as bandwidth, delay, or loss, are referred to as QoS constraints, and the associated routing is referred to as QoS routing, which is a part of constrained-based routing (CBR).

In this article, we focus our attention on the problem of the integration of QoS parameters in the process of decision routing. After discussing the traditional routing approaches, the QoS-based routing schemes are given. We developed essentially some special kinds of algorithms based on reinforcement learning techniques called state-dependent QoS routing.

BACKGROUND

A lot of different definitions and parameters for the concept of quality of service can be found. For the ITU-T E.800 recommendation, QoS is described as "the collective effect of service performance which determines the degree of satisfaction of a user of the service." This definition is completed by the I.350 ITU-T recommendation, which defines more precisely the differences between QoS and network performance. Relative QoS concepts on the Internet are focused on a packet-based, end-to-end, edge-to-edge, or end-to-edge communication. QoS parameters referring to this packet transport at different layers are: availability, Bandwidth, delay, jitter, and loss ratio.

In the literature, we can find the usage of QoS in three ways:

- **Deterministic:** QoS consists in sufficient resources reserved for a particular flow in order to respect the strict temporal constraints for all the packages of flow. No loss of package or extending beyond expires is considered in this type of guarantee. This model makes it possible to provide an absolute terminal in the time according to the reserved resources.
- **Probabilistic:** QoS consists in providing a long-term guarantee of the level of service required by a flow. For time-reality applications tolerating the loss of a few packages, or going beyond some expires, the temporal requirements as well as the

rates of loss are evaluated on average. The probabilistic guarantee makes it possible to provide a temporal terminal with a certain probability, which is given according to the conditions of the network load.

- **Stochastic:** QoS which is fixed beforehand by a stochastic distribution.

Because the problem of routing is a relevant issue for maintaining good performance and successfully operating in a network, many types of routing algorithms have been proposed, such as shortest-path, centralized, distributed, flow-based, etc., for optimally using the network resources. The resolution of this problem, considered as a necessary condition in a high-performance network, is naturally formulated as a dynamic programming problem, which, however, is too complex to be solved exactly. Making globally optimal routing decisions requires that as the load levels, traffic patterns and topology of the network change; the routing policy also adopts a decision's router in the goal to take into account the dynamic change in communication networks.

Various techniques have been proposed to take into account QoS requirements. By using inband or outband specific control protocols, these techniques may be classified into two directions: QoS routing and traffic engineering. QoS routes by constraint-based routing for better delivery to the flow customer while Traffic Engineering aims to optimize the policy management of the traffic distribution in order to minimize congestions and optimize resource utilization. We can mention here some of these techniques:

- Congestion control (Slow Start: Welzl, 2003), weighted random early detection (Welzl, 2003), etc.).
- Traffic shaping, which include all the integrated services architecture: Leaky Bucket (Adamovic, 2004), Token Bucket (Adamovic, 2004), integrated services architecture, RSVP (Zhi, 2004), etc. RSVP is employed to reserve the required resources.
- Differentiated services based on several policies: DiffServ (Zhi,2004), policy-based management, etc.). DiffServ scales well by pushing complexity to network domain boundaries.
- QoS based routing which integrates QoS in the choice of path followed by the transported flow.

In this survey paper, we focus our attention on QoS dynamic routing policies based on reinforcement learning paradigms. We can just mention here that the traffic engineering-based algorithms have the goal to facilitate efficient and reliable network operations, and optimize the utilization of network resources. Traffic engineering objectives can be divided into traffic-oriented and resource-oriented objectives. The first aims to improve the QoS characteristics of traffic stream. The second refers to the efficient use of network resources, especially bandwidth. Resource objectives should prevent congestion in one part of the network, while other parts of the network provide alternate paths that are under-used. One important technique by traffic engineering is load balancing, which aims to minimize maximum resource utilization (Strassner, 2003; Pujolle, 2003).

CLASSICAL ROUTING ALGORITHMS

Traditionally, a network is divided into multiple autonomous systems (AS). An AS is defined as a set of routers that use the same routing protocol. An interior gateway protocol (IGP) is used to route data traffic between hosts or networks belonging to the same AS (e.g., RIP and OSPF). An exterior gateway protocol (EGP) is used to route traffic between distinct AS (e.g., BGP and IDRP).

In the two cases, a routing algorithm is based on the hop-by-hop shortest-path paradigm. The source of a packet specifies the address of the destination, and each router along the route forwards the packet to a neighbor located "closest" to the destination. The best optimal path is chosen according to given criteria. When the network is heavily loaded, some of the routers introduce an excessive delay while others are under-utilized. In some cases, this non-optimized usage of the network resources may introduce not only excessive delays but also high packet loss rate. Among routing algorithms extensively employed in the same AS routers, one can note: a distance vector algorithm, such as RIP (Grover, 2003) and the link state algorithm, such as OSPF (Grover, 2003). These kinds of algorithms do take into account variations of load leading to limited performances.

Distance Vector Approach

Also known as Belman-Ford or Ford-Fulkerson, the heart of this type of algorithm is the routing table maintained by each host. With the distance-vector (DV) routing scheme (e.g., RIP and IGRP), each node exchanges with its neighbouring nodes its distance (e.g., hop count) to other networks. The neighbouring nodes use this information to determine their distance to these networks. Subsequently, these nodes share this information with their neighbours, etc. In this way the reachability information is disseminated through the networks. Eventually, each node learns which neighbour (i.e., next hop router) to use to reach a particular destination with a minimum number of hops. A node does not learn about the intermediate to the destination. These approaches suffer from a classic convergence problem called "count to infinity." It also does not have an explicit information collection phase (it builds its routing table incrementally). DV routing protocols are designed to run on small networks.

Link State Approach

With link-state (LS) routing (e.g., OSPF), each node builds a complete topology database of the network. This topology database is used to calculate the shortest path with Dijkstra's algorithm. Each node in the network transmits its connectivity information to each other node in the network. This type of exchange is referred to as flooding. This way each node is able to build a complete topological map of the network. The computational complexity cost used here is lower than the DV protocol. However, LS algorithms trade off communication bandwidth against computational time.

QoS-BASED ROUTING ALGORITHMS

Interest in QoS-based routing has been steadily growing in the networks, spurred by approaches like ATM PNNI, MPLS, or GMPLS. A lot of study has been conducted in a search for an alternative routing paradigm that would address the integration of dynamic criteria. The most popular formulation of the optimal distributed routing problem in a data network is based on a multicommodity flow optimization whereby a separable objective function is minimized with respect to the types of flow subject to multicommodity flow

constraints (Gallager, 1977; Ozdaglar, 2003). However, due their complexity, increased processing burden, a few proposed routing schemes could been accepted for the Internet. We list here some QoS-based routing algorithms proposed in the literature:

- **QOSPF (Quality Of Service Path First)** (Armitage, 2003) is an extension of OSPF. Combined with a protocol of reservation, this protocol of routing with quality of service makes it possible to announce to all the routers the capacity of the links to support QOS constraints.
- **The MPLS (Multiprotocol Label Switching)** (Adamovic, 2004; Zhi, 2004) is often regarded as a technique resulting from Traffic Engineering approaches. This technology has emerged from the need to integrate high-speed label-swapping ATM switches into IP routing networks. It introduces a connection-oriented label-switching mechanism in a connectionless IP network. MPLS is a protocol which allows the assignment of a fixed path to the different flows toward their destination. It is based on the concept of label switching. A traffic characterization representing the required QoS is associated to each flow. MPLS Traffic Engineering allows overriding the default routing protocol (e.g., OSPF), thus forwarding over paths not normally considered.
- **Wang-Crowcroft algorithm** (Wang, 1996) consists of finding a bandwidth-delay-constrained path by Dijkstra's shortest path algorithm. First, all links with a bandwidth less than the requirements are eliminated so that any path in the resulting graph will satisfy the bandwidth constraint. Then, the shortest path in terms of delay is found. The path is feasible if and only if it satisfies the delay constraint.

QoS-ROUTING REINFORCEMENT LEARNING APPROACHES

For a network node to be able to make an optimal routing decision, according to relevant performance criteria, it requires not only up-to-date and complete knowledge of the state of the entire network but also an accurate prediction of the network dynamics during propagation of the message through the network. This, however, is impossible unless the routing algorithm is capable of adapting to network state changes in almost real time. So, it is necessary to develop a new intelligent and adaptive routing algorithm. This problem is naturally formulated as a dynamic programming problem, which, however, is too complex to be solved exactly. Reinforcement learning (RL), introduced by Sutton (1997), is used to approximate the value function of dynamic programming.

Algorithms for reinforcement learning face the same issues as traditional distributed algorithms, with some additional peculiarities. First, the environment is modeled as stochastic (especially links, link costs, traffic, and congestion), so routing algorithms can take into account the dynamics of the network. However, no model of dynamics is assumed to be given. This means that RL algorithms have to sample, estimate, and perhaps build models of pertinent aspects of the environment. Second, RL algorithms, unlike other machine-learning algorithms, do not have an explicit learning phase followed by evaluation.

The Reinforcement Learning Paradigm

The RL algorithm, called the reactive approach, consists of endowing an autonomous agent with a correctness behavior guaranteeing the fulfillment of the desired task in the dynamics environment (Sutton, 1997). The behavior must be specified in terms of perception-decision-action loop (Figure 1). Each variation of the environment induces stimuli received by the agent, leading to the determination of the appropriate action. The reaction is then considered as a punishment or a performance function, also called reinforcement signal.

Thus, the agent must integrate this function to modify its future actions in order to reach an optimal performance. Reinforcement learning is different from supervised learning, the kind of learning studied in most current researches in machine learning, statistical pattern recognition, and artificial neural networks. Supervised learning learns from examples provided by some knowledgeable external supervisor. This is an important kind of learning, but alone it is not adequate for learning from interaction. In interactive problems, it is not often practical to obtain examples of desired behavior that are both correct and representative of all the situations in which the agent has to act. Thus, RL seems to be well-suited to solve QoS-routing problems.

In other words, a RL Algorithm is a finite-state machine that interacts with a stochastic environment, trying to learn the optimal action the environment offers through a learning process. At any iteration, the automaton chooses an action, according to a probability vector, using an output function. This function stimulates the environment, which responds with an answer (reward or penalty). The automaton takes into account this answer and jumps, if necessary, to a new state using a transition function. It is necessary for

Figure 1. Reinforcement learning model

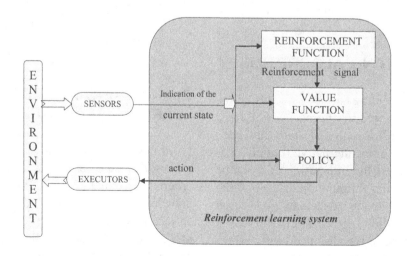

the agent to gather useful experience about the possible system states, actions, transitions, and rewards actively in order to act optimally. Another difference from supervised learning is that online performance is important: The evaluation of the system is often concurrent with learning.

Recently, RL algorithms have attracted the attention of many researchers in the field of dynamic routing, through communication networks justified by the statistical nature of these problems and the necessity to "predict" the effects of the multiplexed traffic in the networks. Resulting routing algorithms should be robust to face dynamically and irregular network changes. To make our discussion concrete, we present in the next section the main approaches of adaptive routing based on RL paradigm.

Q-Routing Approach

One of pioneering works related to this kind of approach concerns the Q-Routing algorithm (Boyan, 1994) based on the Q-learning technique (Watkins, 1989). In order to implement regular adaptive routing, there is a need for a training signal to evaluate or improve the routing policy, which cannot be generated until the packet reaches the final destination. However, using reinforcement learning, the updates can be made more quickly, using only local information.

To explain the principle, let $Qx(y,d)$ be the time that a node x estimates it takes to deliver a packet P bound for node d by way of x's neighbor node y, including any time that P would have to spend in node x's queue. Upon sending P to y, x immediately gets back y's estimate for the time remaining in the trip. Each node keeps a large routing table which contains Q-values of the form $Qx(d,y)$, representing the estimate delay cost from x to d via neighbor y. The reinforcement signal T employed in the Q-learning algorithm can be defined as the minimum of the sum of the estimated $Qy(x,d)$ sent by the router x neighbor of router y and the latency in waiting queue q_y corresponding to router y.

$$T = \min_{x \in \text{neighbor of } y} \{q_y + Qy(x,d)\}$$

Once the choice of the next router is made, router y puts the packet in the waiting queue and sends back the value T as a reinforcement signal to router s. It can therefore update its reinforcement function as:

$$\Delta Qs(y,d) = \eta\,(\alpha + T - Qs(y,d))$$

So, the new estimation $Q's(y,d)$ can be written as follows:

$$Q's(y,d) = Q's(y,d)(1 - \eta) + \eta(T + \alpha)$$

α and η are, respectively, the packet transmission time between s and y and the learning rate.

In this approach, each node makes its routing decision based on the local routing information, represented as a table of Q values which estimate the quality of the alternative routes. These values are updated each time the node sends a packet to one of its neighbors. However, when a Q value is not updated for a long time, it does not necessarily reflect the current state of the network, and hence, a routing decision based on such an unreliable Q value will not be accurate. The update rule in Q-Routing does not take into account the reliability of the estimated or updated Q value because it's depending on the traffic pattern and load levels; only a few Q values are current, while most of the Q values in the network are unreliable. For this purpose, other algorithms have been proposed, like confidence-based Q-routing (CQ-routing) (Kumar, 1998) or dual reinforcement Q-routing (DRQ-routing) (Kumar, 1999).

- DRQ-routing combines Q-routing with dual reinforcement learning. Dual reinforcement learning adds the backward exploration to the forward exploration of Q-routing, making DRQ-routing twice as good as Q-routing in terms of speed of adaptation (at low loads) and average packet delivery time (at high loads).
- CQ-routing improves over Q-routing by incorporating a confidence measure (C value) with each Q value. The C value denotes how closely the corresponding Q value represents the current state of the network. As the time since the last update of a Q value increases, its C value decreases exponentially.

All these routing algorithms use a table to estimate Q values. However, the size of the table depends on the number of destination nodes existing in the network. Thus, this approach is not well suited when we are concerned with a state-space of high dimensionality.

Ants-Routing Approach

Inspired by the dynamics of how ant colonies learn the shortest route to food sources using very little state and computation, Ants-routing algorithms proposed initially by Dorigo (2004) are described as follows: Instead of having fixed next-hop value, the routing table will have multiple next-hop choices for a destination, with each candidate associated with a possibility, which indicates the goodness of choosing this hop as the next hop in favor of forming the shortest path. These possible values are initially equal and will be updated according to the ant packets that pass by.

Given specified source and destination nodes, the source node will send out some kind of ant packets based on the possible entries on its own routing table. Those ants will explore the routes in the network. They can memorize the hops they have passed. When an ant packet reaches the destination node, the ant packet will return to the source node along the same route. Along the way back to the destination node, the ant packet will change the routing table for every node it passes. The rules of updating the routing tables are: increase the possibility of the hop it comes from while decreasings the possibilities of other candidates.

Compared with the real ant foragers, changing the routing table is just like laying down some virtual pheromone on the way, and thus affects the route of the subsequent ant packets. Since the route with higher possibility is always favored, so more ants will pick up that route, and further increase its possibilities and, in turn, attract more ants. With this positive feedback loop, we can expect a best path will quickly emerge. With the changing of network load, when a new best solution comes up, we also expect that it could be identified and enforced by ant packets too. So ant routing is much more dynamic, robust, and scalable.

The Ants approach is immune to the sub-optimal route problem since it explores, at all times, all paths of the network, although the traffic generated by ant algorithms is more important than the traffic of the concurrent approaches.

Cognitive Packet Approach

The random neural network (RNN) model (Haykin, 1998) has been the basis of theoretical efforts and applications during the last decade. It has been proven to be successful in a variety of applications when used either in a feed-forward or a fully recurrent architecture. In most problems, RNN yields strong generalization capabilities, even when training data sets are relatively small compared to the actual testing data. Cognitive packet networks (CPNs) proposed in Gelenbe (2002) are based on random neural networks. These are store-and-forward packet networks in which intelligence is constructed into the packets, rather than at the routers or in the high-level protocols.

CPN is, then, a reliable packet network infrastructure which incorporates packet loss and delays directly into user QoS criteria and uses these criteria to conduct routing. Cognitive packet networks carry three major types of packets: smart packets, dumb packets, and acknowledgments (ACK). Smart or cognitive packets route themselves, they learn to avoid link and node failures and congestion and to avoid being lost. They learn from their own observations about the network and/or from the experience of other packets. They rely minimally on routers. When a smart packet arrives at a destination, an acknowledgment (ACK) packet is generated by the destination and the ACK heads back to the source of the smart packet along the inverse route. As it traverses successive routers, it is used to update mailboxes in the CPN routers, and when it reaches the source node, it provides source routing information for dumb packets. Dumb CPN packets of a specific QoS class use successful routes which have been selected in this manner by the smart packets of that class.

The major drawback of algorithms based on cognitive packet networks is the convergence time, which is very important when the network is heavily loaded.

Q-Neural Routing Approach

In Mellouk (2006), we have presented an adaptive routing algorithm based on the Q-learning approach; the Q-function is approximated by a reinforcement learning-based neural network (NN). In this approach, NNs ensure the prediction of parameters depending on traffic variations. Compared to the approaches based on a Q-table, the Q-value is approximated by a reinforcement learning-based neural network of a fixed size, allowing the learner to incorporate various parameters, such as local queue size and time of day, into its distance estimation. Indeed, a neural network (NN) allows the modelling of complex functions with good precision along with a discriminating training and a taking into account of the context of the network. Moreover, it can be used to predict non-stationary or irregular traffic. In this approach, the objective is to minimize the average packet delivery time. Consequently, the reinforcement signal which is chosen corresponds to the estimated time to transfer a packet to its destination. Typically, the packet delivery time includes three variables: the packet transmission time, the packet treatment time in the router, and the latency in the waiting queue.

The input cells in NN use correspond to the destination and the waiting queue states. The outputs are the estimated packet transfer times passing through the neighbors of the considered router. The algorithm derived from this architecture can be described according to the following steps:

When receiving a packet of information:

1. Extract a destination IP address
2. Calculate Neural Network outputs
3. Select the smallest output value and get an IP address of the associated router
4. Send the packet to this router
5. Get an IP address of the precedent router
6. Create and send the packet as a reinforcement signal

At the reception of a reinforcement signal packet:

1. Extract a Q-estimated value computed by the neighbor
2. Extract a destination IP address
3. Update neural network using a retro-propagation algorithm based on gradient method
4. Destroy the reinforcement packet

This approach offers advantages compared to standard DV routing policy and Q-routing algorithm, like the reduction of the memory space for the storage of secondary paths and a reasonable computing time for alternative-paths research. The Q-value is approximated by a reinforcement learning-based neural network of a fixed size. Results given in [19] show better performances of the proposed algorithm comparative to standard DV and Q-routing algorithms. In fact, at a high load level, the traffic is better distributed along the possible paths, avoiding the congestion of the network.

K Best Path Q-Routing Algorithm

All these routing algorithms explore all the network environment and do not take into account loop problems in a way leading to long times for algorithm convergence. To address this drawback and reduce computational time, we have presented (Mellouk, 2007) an improvement of our earlier Q-Neural Routing algorithm called "K Best Path Q-Routing algorithm."

Q-neural routing needs a rather large computational time and space memory. In the goal of reducing the complexity of this algorithm, Mellouk (2007) proposed a hybrid approach combining neural networks and reducing the search space to K-Best no loop paths in terms of hops number. This approach requires each router to maintain a link state database, which is essentially a map of the network topology. When a network link changes its state (i.e., goes up or down, or its utilization is increased or decreased), the network is flooded with a link state advertisement (LSA) message (Yanxia, 1999). This message can be issued periodically or when the actual link state change exceeds a certain relative or absolute threshold. Obviously, there is tradeoff between the frequency of state updates (the accuracy of the link state database) and the cost of performing those updates. In this model, the link state information is updated when the actual link state changes. Once the link state database at each router is updated, the router computes the K-Best optimal paths and determines the best one from the Q-routing algorithm. This solution is based on a label-setting algorithm (based on the optimality principle and being a generalization of Dijkstra's algorithm). Simulation results (Mellouk, 2007) show better performances of the K-Best Path Q-routing approach comparative to standard Q-routing algorithms. To improve the mechanism of multipath routing used in our algorithm, we add a new module in order to compute dynamically a probabilistic traffic path distribution. This module takes into account the capacity of the queuing file in the router and the average packet delivery time.

FUTURE TRENDS

QoS management in networking has been a topic of extensive research in the last decade. As the Internet network is managed on best effort packet routing, QoS assurance has always been an open issue. Because the majority of past Internet applications (e-mail, Web browsing, etc.) do not have strong QoS needs, this issue have beenmade less urgent in the past. Today, with the development of Internet real-time applications, and the convergence of voice and data networks, it is necessary to develop a high quality control mechanism to check the network traffic load and ensure QoS requirements. It's clear that the integration of these QoS parameters increases the complexity of the used algorithms. Anyway, there will be QoS-relevant technological challenges in the emerging hybrid networks which mix several different types of networks (wireless, broadcast, mobile, fixed, etc.) especially in the routing process which is central to improve performances in the hybrid networks. Many of the future services proposed on networks like video-on-demand, Web services, Grid computing, etc., require the immediate and efficient provisioning of network resources to meet the demand, a wide range of effective QoS-aware network operations, and the accurate runtime information on network QoS conditions.

This paper provides a survey for QoS routing based on reinforcement learning approaches. However, extensions of the framework for using these techniques across hybrid networks to achieve end-to-end QoS needs to be investigated. Another challenging area concerns the composite metric used in routing packets (residual bandwidth, loss ratio, waiting queue state, etc.) which is quite complex, and the conditioning of different models in order to take into account other parameters like the information type of each packet (voice, video, data, etc.).

CONCLUSION

QoS-based routing can improve the probability of the successful establishment of a path, satisfying the QoS requirements. The deployment of QoS-based routing will increase the dynamics of path selection. Several methods have been proposed to solve this problem. However, for a network node to be able to make an optimal routing decision according to relevant performance criteria, it requires not only up-to-date and complete knowledge of the state of the entire network, but also an accurate prediction of the network dynamics during propagation of the message through the network. This problem is naturally formulated as a dynamic programming problem, which, however, is too complex

to be solved exactly. Reinforcement learning (RL) is used to approximate the value function of dynamic programming. In these algorithms, the environment is modeled as stochastic, so routing algorithms can take into account the dynamics of the network. However no model of dynamics is assumed to be given.

REFERENCES

Adamovic, L., & Collier, M. (2004). A new traffic engineering approach for IP networks. *Proceedings of CSNDSP* (pp. 351-358).

Armitage, G.L. (2003). Revisiting IP QoS: Why do we care, what we have learned? ACM SIGCOMM 2003 RIPQOS Workshop Report. *ACM/SIGCOMM Computer Communications Review, 33*, 81-88.

Boyan, J.A., & Littman, M.L. (1994). Packet routing in dynamically changing networks: A reinforcement learning approach. In Cowan, Tesauro, & Alspector (Eds.), *Advances in Neural Information Processing Systems, 6*, 671-678.

Dorigo, M., & Stüzle, T. (2004). *Ant colony optimization.* MIT Press.

Gallager, R.G. (1977). A minimum delay routing algorithm using distributed computations. *IEEE Transactions on Communications, 25*(1), 73-85.

Grover, W.D. (Ed.). (2003). *Mesh-based survivable transport networks: Options and strategies for optical, MPLS, SONET and ATM networking.* Prentice Hall PTR.

Haykin, S. (1998). *Neural networks: A comprehensive roundation.* Mcmillan College Publishing.

Mellouk, A., Hoceini, S., Amirat, Y. (2006). Adaptive Quality of Service Based Routing Approaches: Development of a Neuro-Dynamic State-Dependent Reinforcement Learning Algorithm. In *International Journal of Communication Systems*, ed. Wiley InterSciences Online. September 2006,

Mellouk, A., Hoceini, S., Cheurfa, M. (2007). Reinforcing Probalistic Selective Quality of Service Routes in Dynamic Heterogeneous Networks. In *Journal of Computer Communication*, ed. Elsevier Online. March 2007.

Kumar, S. (1998). Confidence-based Q-routing: An On-Line Adaptive Network Routing Algorithm. Master's Thesis, Department of Computer Sciences, The University of Texas at Austin, Austin, TX-78712. USA Tech. Report AI98-267.

Kumar, S., & Miikkualainen, R. (1999). Confidence based dual reinforcement Q-routing: An adaptive online network routing algorithm. *Proceedings of the Sixteenth International Joint Conference on Artificial Intelligence* (IJCAI-99, Sweden, Stockholm) (pp. 758-763). San Francisco: Kaufmann.

Ozdaglar, A.E., & Bertsekas, D.P. (2003, June). Optimal solution of integer multicommodity flow problem with application in optical networks. *Proceedings Of Symposium on Global Optimisation* (pp. 411-435).

Pujolle, G., Koner, U., & Perros, H. (2003). Resource Allocation in the New Fixed and Mobile Internet Generation. *Journal Of Network Management, 13*(3), 181-185.

Sutton, R.S., &. Barto, A.G. (1997). *Reinforcement learning.* MIT Press.

Gelenbe, E., Lent, L., & Xu, Z. (2002). Networking with cognitive packets. *Proceedings of ICANN 2002,* Madrid, Spain (pp. 27-30).

Strassner, J. (2003). *Policy-based network management: Solutions for the next generation?* Morgan-Kaufmann.

Wang, Z., & Crowcroft, J. (1996). QoS routing for supporting multimedia application. *IEEE Journal on Selected Areas in Communications, 14*(7), 1228-1234.

Watkins, C.J., & Dayan, P. (1989). Q-learning. *Machine Learning, 8,* 279-292.

Welzl, M. (2003). *Scalable performance signalling and congestion avoidance.* Kluwer Academic Publishers.

Yanxia, J., Ioanis, N., & Pawel, G. (2001, June). Multiple paths QoS routing. *International Conference on Communications* (pp. 2583-2587).

Zhi, L., & Mohapatra, P. (2004). QRON: QoS-aware routing in overlay networks. *IEEE Journal on Selected Areas in Communications, 22*(1), 22-40.

Adaptive Transmission of Multimedia Data over the Internet

Christos Bouras
Research Academic Computer Technology Institute and University of Patras, Greece

Apostolos Gkamas
Research Academic Computer Technology Institute and University of Patras, Greece

Dimitris Primpas
Research Academic Computer Technology Institute and University of Patras, Greece

Kostas Stamos
Research Academic Computer Technology Institute and University of Patras, Greece

INTRODUCTION

Internet is a heterogeneous network environment and the network resources that are available to real time applications can be modified very quickly. Real time applications must have the capability to adapt their operation to network changes. In order to add adaptation characteristics to real time applications, we can use techniques both at the network and application layers. Adaptive real time applications have the capability to transmit multimedia data over heterogeneous networks and adapt media transmission to network changes. In order to implement an adaptive multimedia transmission application, mechanisms to monitor the network conditions, and mechanisms to adapt the transmission of the data to the network changes must be implemented.

Today, the underlying infrastructure of the Internet does not sufficiently support quality of service (QoS) guarantees. The new technologies, which are used for the implementation of networks, provide capabilities to support QoS in one network domain but it is not easy to implement QoS among various network domains, in order to provide end-to-end QoS to the user. In addition, some researchers believe that the cost for providing end-to-end QoS is too big, and it is better to invest on careful network design and careful network monitoring, in order to identify and upgrade the congested network links (Diot, 2001).

In this article, we concentrate on the architecture of an adaptive real time application that has the capa-

bility to transmit multimedia data over heterogeneous networks and adapt the transmission of the multimedia data to the network changes. Moreover in this article, we concentrate on the unicast transmission of multimedia data.

BACKGROUND

The subject of adaptive transmission of multimedia data over networks has engaged researchers all over the world. During the design and the implementation of an adaptive application special attention must be paid to the following critical modules:

- The module, which is responsible for the transmission of the multimedia data
- The module, which is responsible for monitoring the network conditions and determines the change to the network conditions
- The module, which is responsible for the adaptation of the multimedia data to the network changes
- The module, which is responsible for handling the transmission errors during the transmission of the multimedia data

A common approach for the implementation of adaptive applications is the use of UDP for the transmission of the multimedia data and the use of TCP for the transmission of control information (Parry & Gangatharan,

2005; Vandalore, Feng, Jain, & Fahmy, 1999). Another approach for the transmission of the multimedia data is the use of RTP over UDP (Bouras & Gkamas, 2003; Byers et al., 2000). Most adaptive applications use RTP/RTCP (real time transmission protocol / real time control transmission protocol) (Schulzrinne, Casner, Frederick, & Jacobson, 2003) for the transmission of the multimedia data. The RTP protocol seems to be the de facto standard for the transmission of multimedia data over the Internet and is used both by mbone tools (vit, vat, etc.) and ITU H.323 applications. In addition RTCP offers capabilities for monitoring the transmission quality of multimedia data.

For the implementation of the network monitoring module, a common approach is to use the packet loss as an indication of congestion in the network (Bouras et al., 2003; Byers et al., 2000). One other approach for monitoring the network conditions is the use of utilization of the client buffer (Rejaie, Estrin, & Handley, 1999; Walpole et al., 1997). An important factor that can be used for monitoring the network conditions, and especially for indication of network congestion, is the use of delay jitter during the transmission of the multimedia data.

For the implementation of the adaptation module, some common approaches are the use of rate shaping (Byers et al., 2000; Bouras et al., 2003), the use of layered encoding (Rejaie et al., 1999), the use of frame dropping (Walpole et al., 1997) or a combination of the previous techniques (Ramanujan et al., 1997). The implementation of the adaptation module depends on the encoding method that is used for the transmission of the multimedia data. For example, in order to use the frame dropping technique for the adaptation of a MPEG video stream, a selective frame dropping technique must be used, due to the fact that MPEG video

uses inter-frame encoding and some frames contain information relative to other frames. In Vandalore et al. (1999), a detailed survey of application level adaptation techniques is given.

It is important for adaptive real time applications to have "friendly" behavior to the dominant transport protocols (TCP) of the Internet (Floyd & Fall, 1998). In Widmer et al. (2001), a survey on TCP-friendly congestion control mechanisms is presented.

ADAPTIVE TRANSMISSION OF MULTIMEDIA DATA OVER THE INTERNET

The Architecture of an Adaptive Streaming Application

This section presents a typical architecture for an adaptive streaming application, based on the client server model. Figure 1 displays the architecture of such an adaptive streaming application.

The server of the adaptive streaming architecture consists of the following modules:

- **Video archive:** Video archive consists of a set of hard disks in which the video files are stored. The adaptive streaming application may support various video formats (for example MPEG, JPEG, H.263, etc.). It is possible for one video file to be stored in the video archive in more than one format in order to serve different target user groups. For example, it is possible to store the same video in MPEG format in order to serve the users of the local area network (who have faster network

Figure 1. System architecture

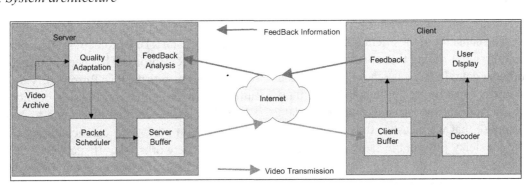

connection with the server) and in H.263 format in order to serve distant users with slow network connections. In this article, we do not investigate the problem of video storage in video archives in order to achieve the optimal performance of the server.

- **Feedback analysis:** This module is responsible for the analysis of feedback information from the network. The role of this module is to determine the network condition mainly based on packet loss rate and delay jitter information, which are provided by RTCP receiver reports. After the examination of network condition, the feedback analysis module informs the quality adaptation module, in order to adapt the transmission of the video to current network conditions.

- **Quality adaptation:** It is responsible for the adaptation of the video transmission quality in order to match with the current network conditions. This module can be implemented using various techniques (rate shaping, layered encoding, frame dropping, etc.).

- **Packet scheduler/Server buffer:** This module is responsible for the encapsulation of multimedia information in the RTP packets. In addition, this module is responsible for the transmission of the RTP packets in the network. In order to smooth accidental problems to the transmission of the multimedia data from the server to the network, an output buffer is used on the server.

The client of the adaptive streaming architecture consists of the following modules:

- **Client buffer:** The use of the buffer on the client for the implementation of streaming applications is very important. The client application stores the incoming data to the buffer before starting to present data to the user. The presentation of the multimedia data to the user starts only after the necessary amount of the data is stored in the buffer. The capacity of the client buffer depends to the delay jitter during the transmission of the multimedia data. In any case the capacity of the client buffer must be greater than the maximum delay jitter during the transmission of the data (we suppose that we measure the buffer capacity and the delay jitter in the same units, e.g. in seconds).

- **Feedback:** This module is responsible of monitoring the transmission quality of the data and informing the server. The monitoring of the transmission quality is based on RTCP receiver reports that the client sends to the server. RTCP receiver reports include information about the packet loss rate and the delay jitter during the transmission of the data. With the previous information, the feedback analysis module of the server determines the network's condition.

- **Decoder:** This module reads the data packets from the client buffer and decodes the encoded multimedia information. Depending on the packet losses and the delay during the transmission of the packets, the quality of the multimedia presentation can vary. The decoding and the presentation of the multimedia data can stop, if the appropriate amount of data does not exist in the buffer.

- **User display:** It is responsible for the presentation of the multimedia data to the user.

In the following paragraphs, we give a detailed description of the most important modules of the previously described architecture.

Transmission of Multimedia Data

The transmission of the multimedia data is based on the protocols RTP/RTCP. The protocol RTP is used for the transmission of the multimedia data from the server to the client and the client uses the RTCP protocol, in order to inform the server of the transmission quality.

The RTP/RTCP protocols have been designed for the transmission of real time data like video and audio. Although the RTP/RTCP protocols were initially designed for multicast transmission, they were also used for unicast transmissions. RTP/RTCP can be used for one-way communication like video on demand or for two-way communication like videoconference. RTP/RTCP offers a common platform for the representation of synchronisation information that real time applications needs. The RTCP protocol is the control protocol of RTP. The RTP protocol has been designed to operate in cooperation with the RTCP protocol, which provides information about the transmission quality.

RTP is a protocol that offers end to end transport services with real time characteristics over packet switching networks like IP networks. RTP packet headers include information about the payload type of the data, numbering of the packets and timestamping information.

RTCP offers the following services to applications:

- **QoS monitoring:** This is one of the primary services of RTCP. RTCP provides feedback to applications about the transmission quality. RTCP uses sender reports and receiver reports, which contain useful statistical information like total transmitted packets, packet loss rate and delay jitter during the transmission of the data. This statistical information is very useful, because it can be used for the implementation of congestion control mechanisms.
- **Source identification:** RTCP source description packets can be used for identification of the participants in a RTP session. In addition, source description packets provide general information about the participants in a RTP session. This service of RTCP is useful for multicast conferences with many members.
- **Inter-media synchronisation:** In real time applications, it is common to transmit audio and video in different data streams. RTCP provides services like timestamping, which can be used for inter-media synchronisation of different data streams (for example synchronisation of audio and video streams).

More information about RTP/RTCP can be found in RFC 3550 (Schulzrinne et al., 2003).

Feedback from the Network

The presentation quality of real time data depends on the packet loss rate and the delay jitter during the transmission over the network. In addition, packet losses or rapid increases of delay jitter may be considered as an indication of problems during the transmission of data over the network. In such a case, the adaptive streaming application must adapt the transmission of the data in order to avoid phenomenon like network congestion. Real time applications have upper bounds to the packet loss rate and to the delay jitter. If packet loss rate or jitter gets to be over these upper bounds, the transmission of real time data can not be continued.

Packet loss rate is defined as the fraction of the total transmitted packets that did not arrive at the receiver. Usually the main reason of packet losses is congestion.

It is difficult to define delay jitter. Some researchers define delay jitter as the difference between the maximum and the minimum delay during the transmission of the packets for a period of time. Some other researchers define delay jitter as the maximum difference between the delay of the transmission of two sequential packets for a period of time. According to RFC 3550 (Schulzrinne et al., 2003), delay jitter is defined to be the mean deviation (smoothed absolute value) of the difference D in packet spacing at the receiver compared to the sender for a pair of packets. This is equivalent to the difference in the "relative transit time" for the two packets. The relative transit time is the difference between a packet's timestamp and the receiver's clock at the time of arrival. If s_i is the timestamp from packet i and R_i is the time of arrival for this packet, then for two packets i and j, D is defined as: $D(i,j) = (R_j - R_i) - (S_j - S_i) = (R_j - S_j) - (R_i - S_i)$. The delay jitter is calculated continuously as each packet i arrives, using the difference D for that packet and the previous packet, according to the following formula:

$$J_i = J_{i-1} + (|D(i-1,j)| - J_{i-1})/16$$

The previous formula states that the new value of delay jitter depends on the previous value of the delay jitter and on a gain parameter, which gives good noise reduction.

Delay jitter occurs when sequential packets encounter different delays in the queue of the network devices. The different delays are related to the serve model of each queue and the cross traffics in the transmission path.

Sometimes delay jitter occurs during the transmission of real time data, which does not originate from the network but is originated from the transmission host (host included delay jitter). This is because during the encoding of the real time data, the encoder places a timestamp in each packet, which gives information about the time that the packet's information, must be presented to the receiver. In addition, this timestamp is used for the calculation of the delay jitter during the transmission of the real time data. If a notable time passes from the encoding of the packet and transmission of the packet in the network (because the CPU of the transmitter host is busy) the calculation of the delay jitter is not valid. Host included delay jitter can lead to erroneous estimation for the network conditions.

We can conclude that delay jitter can not lead to reliable estimation of network condition by itself. Delay jitter has to be used in combination with other parameters, like packet loss rate, in order to make reliable estimations of the network conditions. In Bouras et al. (2003), it is shown that the combination of packet loss rate and delay jitter can be used for reliable indication of network congestion.

Quality Adaptation

Quality adaptation module is based on the rate shaping technique. According to the rate shaping technique, if we change some parameters of the encoding procedure, we can control the amount of the data that the video encoder produces (either increase or decrease the amount of the data) and as a result, we can control the transmission rate of the multimedia data.

The implementation of rate shaping techniques depends on the video encoding. Rate shaping techniques change one or more of the following parameters:

- **Frame rate:** Frame rate is the rate of the frames, which are encoded by video encoder. Decreasing the frame rate can reduce the amount of the data that the video encoder produces but will reduce the quality.
- **Quantizer:** The quantizer specifies the number of DCT coefficients that are encoded. Increasing the quantizer decreases the number of encoded coefficients and the image is coarser.
- **Movement detection threshold:** This is used for inter-frame coding, where the DCT is applied to signal differences. The movement detection threshold limits the number of blocks which are detected to be "sufficiently different" from the previous frames. Increasing this threshold decreases the output rate of the encoder.

Error Control/Packet Loss

The packet loss rate is depends on various parameters and the adaptive transmission applications must adapt to changes of packet losses. Two approaches are available to reduce the effects of packet losses:

- **APQ (Automatic Repeat Request):** APQ is an active technique where the receiver and ask the sender to retransmit some lost packets.
- **FEC (Forward Error Correction):** FEC is a passive technique where the sender transmits redundant information. This redundant information is used by the receiver to correct errors and lost packets.

FUTURE TRENDS

The most prominent enhancement of the adaptive real time applications is the use of multicast transmission of the multimedia data. The multicast transmission of multimedia data over the Internet has to accommodate clients with heterogeneous data reception capabilities. To accommodate heterogeneity, the server may transmit one multicast stream and determine the transmission rate that satisfies most of the clients (Byers et al., 2000; Rizzo, 2000; Widmer et al., 2001), and may transmit multiple multicast streams with different transmission rates and allocate clients at each stream or may use layered encoding and transmit each layer to a different multicast stream (Byers et al., 2000). An interesting survey of techniques for multicast multimedia data over the Internet is presented by Li, Ammar, and Paul (1999).

Single multicast stream approaches have the disadvantage that clients with a low bandwidth link will always get a high-bandwidth stream if most of the other members are connected via a high bandwidth link and the same is true the other way around. This problem can be overcome with the use of a multi-stream multicast approach. Single multicast stream approaches have the advantages of easy encoder and decoder implementation and simple protocol operation, due to the fact that during the single multicast stream approach there is no need for synchronization of clients' actions (as is required by the multiple multicast streams and layered encoding approaches).

The subject of adaptive multicast of multimedia data over networks with the use of one multicast stream has engaged researchers all over the world. During the adaptive multicast transmission of multimedia data in a single multicast stream, the server must select the transmission rate that satisfies most the clients with the current network conditions. Three approaches can be found in the literature for the implementation of the adaptation protocol in a single stream multicast mechanism: equation based (Rizzo, 2000; Widmer et al. (2001), network feedback based (Byers et al., 2000), or based on a combination of the previous two approaches (Sisalem & Wolisz, 2000).

CONCLUSION

Many researchers urge that due to the use of new technologies for the implementation of the networks, which offer QoS guarantees, adaptive real time applications will not be used in the future. We believe that this is not true and adaptive real time applications will be used in the future for the following reasons:

- Users may not always want to pay the extra cost for a service with specific QoS guarantees when they have the capability to access a service with good adaptive behaviour.
- Some networks may never be able to provide specific QoS guarantees to the users.
- Even if the Internet eventually supports reservation mechanisms or differentiated services, it is more likely to be on per-class than per-flow basis. Thus, flows are still expected to perform congestion control within their own class.
- With the use of the differential services network model, networks can support services with QoS guarantees together with best effort services and adaptive services.

REFERENCES

Bouras, C., & Gkamas, A. (2003). Multimedia transmission with adaptive QoS based on real time protocols. *International Journal of Communications Systems, Wiley InterScience, 16*(2), 225-248

Byers, J., Frumin, M., Horn, G., Luby, M., Mitzenmacher, M., Roetter, A., & Shaver, W. (2000). FLID-DL: Congestion control for layered multicast. In *Proceedings of NGC* (pp. 71-81).

Cheung, S. Y., Ammar, M., & Xue, L. (1996). On the use of destination set grouping to improve fariness in

multicast video distribution. In *Proceedings of INFO-COM 96*, San Francisco.

Diot, C. (2001, January 25-26). On QoS & traffic engineering and SLS-related work by Sprint. *Workshop on Internet Design for SLS Delivery*, Tulip Inn Tropen, Amsterdam, The Netherlands.

Floyd, S., & Fall, K. (1998, August). Promoting the use of end-to-end congestion control in the Internet. In *IEEE/ACM Transactions on Networking*.

Li, X., Ammar, M. H., & Paul, S. (1999, April). Video multicast over the Internet. *IEEE Network Magazine*.

Parry, M., & Gangatharan, N. (2005). Adaptive data transmission in multimedia networks. *American Journal of Applied Sciences, 2*(3), 730-733.

Ramanujan, R., Newhouse, J., Kaddoura, M., Ahamad, A., Chartier, E., & Thurber, K. (1997). Adaptive streaming of MPEG video over IP networks. In *Proceedings of the 22nd IEEE Conference on Computer Networks*, 398-409.

Rejaie, R., Estrin, D., & Handley, M. (1999). Quality adaptation for congestion controlled video playback over the Internet. In *Proceedings of ACM SIGCOMM '99*, 189-200. Cambridge.

Rizzo, L. (2000) pgmcc: A TCP-friendly single-rate multicast congestion control scheme. In *Proceedings of SIGCOMM 2000*, Stockholm.

Schulzrinne, H., Casner, S., Frederick, R., & Jacobson, V. (2003). *RTP: A transport protocol for real-time applications*, RFC 3550, IETF.

Sisalem, D., & Wolisz, A. (2000). LDA+ TCP-friendly adaptation: A measurement and comparison study. The *Tenth International Workshop on Network and Operating Systems Support for Digital Audio and Video*, Chapel Hill, NC.

Vandalore, B., Feng, W., Jain, R., & Fahmy, S., (1999). A survey of application layer techniques for adaptive streaming of multimedia. *Journal of Real Time Systems (Special Issue on Adaptive Multimedia)*.

Vickers, B. J., Albuquerque, C. V. N., & Suda, T. (1998). Adaptive multicast of multi-layered video: Rate-based and credit-based approaches. In *Proceedings of IEEE Infocom*, 1073-1083.

A

Walpole, J., Koster, R., Cen, S., Cowan, C., Maier, D., McNamee, D., et al. (1997). A player for adaptive mpeg video streaming over the Internet. In *Proceedings of the 26th Applied Imagery Pattern Recognition Workshop AIPR-97*, SPIE, (Washington DC), 270-281.

Widmer, J., Denda, R., & Mauve, M., (2001). A survey on TCP-friendly congestion control mechanisms. *Special Issue of the IEEE Network Magazine Control of Best Effort Traffic, 15*, 28-37.

Widmer, J., & Handley, M. (2001). Extending equation-based congestion control to multicast applications. In *Proceedings of the ACM SIGCOMM* (San Diego, CA), 275-285.

KEY TERMS

Adaptive Real Time Applications: Adaptive real time applications are application that have the capability to transmit multimedia data over heterogeneous networks and adapt media transmission to network changes.

Delay Jitter: Delay jitter is defined to be the mean deviation (smoothed absolute value) of the difference in packet spacing at the receiver compared to the sender for a pair of packets.

Frame Rate: Frame rate is the rate of the frames, which are encoded by video encoder.

Movement Detection Threshold: The movement detection threshold is a parameter that limits the number of blocks which are detected to be "sufficiently different" from the previous frames.

Multimedia Data: Multimedia data refers to data that consist of various media types like text, audio, video, and animation.

Packet Loss Rate: Packet loss rate is defined as the fraction of the total transmitted packets that did not arrive at the receiver.

Quality of Service (QoS): Quality of service refers to the capability of a network to provide better service to selected network traffic.

Quantizer: Quantizer specifies the number of DCT coefficients that are encoded.

RTP/RTCP: Protocol which is used for the transmission of multimedia data. The RTP performs the actual transmission and the RTCP is the control and monitoring transmission.

Addressing the Credibility of Web Applications

Pankaj Kamthan
Concordia University, Canada

INTRODUCTION

The Internet, particularly the Web, has opened new vistas for businesses. The ability that anyone using (virtually) any device could be reached anytime and anywhere presents a tremendous commercial prospective.

In retrospect, the fact that almost *anyone* can set up a Web application claiming to offer products and services raises the question of credibility from a consumers' viewpoint. If not addressed, there is a potential for lost consumer confidence, thus significantly reducing the advantages and opportunities the Web as a medium offers. Establishing credibility is essential for an organization's reputation (Gibson, 2002) and for building consumers' trust (Kamthan, 1999).

The rest of the article is organized as follows. We first provide the motivational background necessary for later discussion. This is followed by the introduction of a framework within which different types of credibility in the context of Web applications can be systematically addressed and thereby improved. Next, challenges and directions for future research are outlined. Finally, concluding remarks are given.

BACKGROUND

In this section, we present the fundamental concepts underlying credibility and present the motivation and related work for addressing credibility within the context of Web applications.

Basic Credibility Concepts

For the purposes of this article, we will consider credibility to be synonymous to (and therefore interchangeable with) believability (Fogg & Tseng, 1999). Since trust indicates a *positive* belief about a person, object, or process, we do not consider credibility and trust to

be synonymous but we do consider trust to be a sufficient condition for credibility.

A taxonomy of credibility helps associating the concept with a specific user class. A user could consider a Web application to be credible based upon direct interaction with the application (*active credibility*), or consider it to be credible in absence of any direct interaction but based on certain pre-determined notions (*passive credibility*). Based on the classification of credibility in computer use (Fogg et al., 1999) and adapting them to the domain of Web applications, we can decompose these further. There can be two types of *active credibility*: (1) *surface credibility*, which describes how much the user believes the Web application based on simple inspection, and (2) *experienced credibility*, which describes how much the user believes the Web application based on first-hand experience in the past. There can be two types of *passive credibility*: (1) *presumed credibility*, which describes how much the user believes the Web application because of general assumptions that the user holds, and (2) *reputed credibility*, which describes how much the user believes the Web application because of a reference from a third party.

The Problem of Web Credibility

The credibility of computer systems is a critical issue in its own right (Fogg et al., 1999). However, the credibility of Web applications deserves special attention for the following reasons:

*   **Delivery:** Web applications as opposed to desktop software are delivered, not installed and the delivery context in a changing environment of user agents and devices is nontrivial. The services that Web applications offer are usually remote. This non-proximity or "facelessness" although may not in itself instill doubt, the absence of a human component raises a variety of emotions

(uncertainty, perplexity, or anxiety), particularly in the time of crisis.

- **Legality:** The stakeholders of a Web application need not be co-located. For example, they may be in different jurisdictions in the same country or in different countries. Therefore, the laws that govern the provider and the user of that Web application may be different. The possibilities of personal harm such as theft of computer domain name or user identity theft and misuse of information provided by users with proportionally little legal repercussions for the perpetrators is high in a networked environment. News of mishaps only worsens presumed credibility, particularly if the user is not aware of the provider.

- **Expertise:** The Internet and the Web provide the freedom to everybody for providing a service with minimal cost, time, and effort, and basic expertise. Unfortunately, not all Web sites conform to the quality and ethical standards expected by a user.

- **Maturity:** The Web is a bit more than 10 years old during which it has notably matured. In spite of the exponential growth in its use and rapid ascent in related technologies, this time period is seen "young" by many, particularly when compared to other public services.

- **Privacy:** There are Web portals that require a user to submit personal information, at times, in the name of personalization. The provision for personalization in the light of respecting privacy leads to both an ethical and a legal issue. Managing this dichotomy is a constant struggle for businesses where the benefits of respecting one can adversely affect the other, thereby impacting their credibility in the view of their customers.

- **Reliability:** Experiences of users with technologies of the Web have not always been positive. The instability of the user agents and extensions (say via plug-ins or ActiveX controls) and errors in client-side scripts, have impacted the user's system (system crash) at times. This has shaken customer confidence and created negative perceptions about the Web as a medium for communication.

- **Security:** There are a variety of security-related vulnerabilities that get amplified in a networked environment and can lead to uncertainty and fear among users.

A set of guidelines for addressing credibility of Web applications have been presented in Fogg (2003). However, it is limited by the following issues. The approach toward ensuring and/or evaluating credibility is not systematic. The proposed means for ensuring credibility is singular (only guidelines), these guidelines can be open to broad interpretation and are stated at such a high-level that they may not always be practical or may be difficult to realize by a novice user, and the issue of feasibility of the means is not addressed.

ADDRESSING THE CREDIBILITY OF WEB APPLICATIONS

In this section, we consider approaches for understanding and improving active and passive credibility.

A Framework for Addressing Active Credibility of Web Applications

In order to address the active credibility of Web applications, we first take the appropriate steps to separate the concerns involved:

1. View credibility as a qualitative aspect and address it indirectly via quantitative means.
2. Select a theoretical basis for communication of information (semiotics), and place credibility in its setting.
3. Address semiotic quality in a systematic and practical manner.

Using this as a basis, we propose a framework for active credibility of Web applications from the perspective of semiotic quality (Table 1). The external attributes (denoted by E) are extrinsic to the software product and are directly user's concern, while internal attributes (denoted by I) are intrinsic to the software product and are directly an engineer's concern. Now, not all attributes corresponding to a semiotic level are on the same echelon, and the different tiers are denoted by "Tn."

We now describe each of the components of the framework in detail.

Table 1. A semiotic framework for active credibility of Web applications

Semiotic Level	Quality Attributes		Means for Credibility Assurance and Evaluation	Decision Support
Social	**Credibility**		• "Expert" knowledge (principles, guidelines, patterns) • Inspections • Testing • Metrics • Tools	Feasibility
	Aesthetics, legality, privacy, security, (provider) transparency [T5;E]			
Pragmatic	Accessibility, usability [T4;E]			
	Interoperability, portability, reliability, robustness [T3;E]			
Semantic	Completeness and validity [T2;I]			
Syntactic	Correctness [T1;I]			

Semiotic Levels

The first column of Table 1 addresses semiotic levels. Semiotics (Stamper, 1992) is concerned with the use of symbols to convey knowledge.

From a semiotics perspective, a representation can be viewed on six interrelated levels: physical, empirical, syntactic, semantic, pragmatic, and social, each depending on the previous one in that order. The physical and empirical levels are concerned with the physical representation of signs in hardware and communication properties of signs and are not of direct concern here. The syntactic level is responsible for the formal or structural relations between signs. The semantic level is responsible for the relationship of signs to what they stand for. The pragmatic level is responsible for the relation of signs to interpreters. The social level is responsible for the manifestation of social interaction with respect to signs.

Quality Attributes

The second column of Table 1 draws the relationship between semiotic levels and corresponding quality attributes. We contend that the quality attributes we mention are necessary but make no claim of their sufficiency.

Credibility belongs to the social level and depends on the layers beneath it. The external quality attributes legality, privacy, security, (provider) and transparency also at the social level depend upon the external quality attributes, accessibility, and usability, at the pragmatic level, which in turn depend upon the external quality

attributes, interoperability, portability, reliability, and robustness also at the pragmatic level. We discuss in some detail only the entries in the social level. The sensitivity part of visual perception is strongly related to aesthetics as it is close to human senses. The artistic expression plays an important role in making a Web application "attractive" to its customers beyond simply the functionality it provides. It is critical that the Web application be legal (e.g., is legal in the jurisdiction it operates and all components it makes use of are legal), takes steps to respect user's privacy (e.g., does not abuse or share user-supplied information without permission), and takes steps to secure itself (e.g., in situations where financial transactions are made). The provider must take all steps to be transparent with respect to the user (e.g., not include misleading information such as the features of products or services offered, clearly label promotional content, make available their contact information including physical address, policies regarding returning/exchanging products, etc.).

The internal quality attributes for syntactic and semantic levels are inspired by Fenton and Pfleeger (1997) and Lindland, Sindre, and Sølvberg (1994). At the semantic level, we are only concerned with the conformance of the Web application to the domain(s) it represents (that is, semantic correctness or completeness) and vice versa (that is, semantic validity). At the syntactic level, the interest is in conformance with respect to the languages used to produce the Web application (that is, syntactic correctness).

The definitions of each of these attributes can vary in the literature, and therefore it is important that they be adopted and followed consistently.

Means for Credibility Assurance and Evaluation

The third column of Table 1 lists (in no particular order) the means for assuring and evaluating active credibility.

- **"Expert" body of knowledge:** The three types of knowledge that we are interested are (in order of decreasing abstraction and increasing practicality) principles, guidelines, and patterns. Following the basic principles (Ghezzi, Jazayeri, & Mandrioli, 2003) underlying a Web application enables a provider to improve quality attributes related to T1-T3 of the framework. The guidelines such as for addressing accessibility (Chisholm, Vander-heiden, & Jacobs, 1999) and usability (Nielsen, 2000) of Web applications encourage the use of conventions and good practice, and could serve as a checklist with respect to which an application could be evaluated. However, guidelines tend to be less useful for a novice to whom they may seem rather general. Patterns are reusable entities of knowledge and experience aggregated by experts over years of "best practices" in solving recurring problems in a domain including Web applications (Van Duyne, Landay, & Hong, 2003). However, there is a cost involved in adaptation of patterns to new contexts.

- **Inspections:** Inspections (Wiegers, 2002) are a means for *static* verification of software artifacts that can address quality concerns at both technical and social levels (T1-T5), and help improve the credibility of Web applications. Inspections could for example, determine "sufficiency" of contact information, decide what information is and is not considered "promotional," help improve the natural language-based labels used (say, in a navigation system), or assess the readability of documents or images. In spite of their usefulness, inspections do involve an initial overhead cost from training each participant in the structured review process, and the logistics of checklists, forms, and reports.

- **Testing:** Testing is a means for *dynamic* verification of (executable) software artifacts and an integral part of most development models of Web applications (Nguyen, Johnson, & Hackett, 2003). However, testing due to its very nature

addresses quality concerns only at some of the technical and social levels (T1, T3, T4, subset of T5). A full-scale accessibility or usability testing requires setting up an environment (hiring real users, infrastructure with video monitoring, and subsequent analysis of data) that can prove to be prohibitive for small-to-medium size enterprises.

- **Metrics:** Metrics provide a quantitative means to make qualitative judgments of quality concerns at technical levels. For example, metrics of size or structure can help compare and make a choice between two designs, which could then (given the identical network) be used to evaluate download times. Similar arguments can be made for reliability and robustness. There are budget and resource constraints to any activity including addressing credibility concerns: the metrics for cost (time, effort) estimation can also help the providers address the Web application quality concerns in a feasible manner.

- **Tools:** There are various tools that can help improve quality concerns at technical and social levels, manually, semi-automatically, or automatically. For example, they can help us detect security breaches, inform us of absence of privacy metadata, report violations of accessibility guidelines, find non-conformance to markup language syntax, suggest image sizes favorable to the Web, or find broken links. However, state-of-the-art tools can be expensive. They also cannot address some of the social concerns at all (like provider intent) and therefore should be used in perspective.

Decision Support

The providers of Web applications take into account organizational constraints of time and resources (personnel, infrastructure, budget, etc.) and external forces (market value, competitors, etc.), which compels them to make quality related decisions that, apart from being sensitive to credibility, must also be feasible. Indeed, the last column of Table 1 acknowledges that with respect to any assurance and/or evaluation, and includes feasibility as an all-encompassing consideration on the layers to make the framework practical.

There are well-known techniques such as analytical hierarchy process (AHP) and quality function deployment (QFD) for carrying out feasibility analysis and further discussion of this aspect is beyond the scope of this article.

Addressing Passive Credibility of Web Applications

In this section, we briefly look into the case of passive credibility, specifically reputed credibility. In the real world, the assurance for credibility is often provided by a third party such as approval of a drug by the national medical association or certification of degree granting programs by a recognized body. We discuss two relevant initiatives in the direction of addressing reputed credibility, namely WebTrust and TRUSTe.

In response to the concerns related to business-to-consumer e-commerce and to increase consumer confidence, the public accounting profession has developed WebTrust principles and criteria and a WebTrust seal of assurance. Independent and objective certified public or chartered accountants, who are specifically licensed by the American Institute of Certified Public Accountants (AICPA) or Canadian Institute of Chartered Accountants (CICA), can provide assurance services to evaluate and test whether a particular Web application meets these principles and criteria. The WebTrust seal of assurance is a symbolic representation of a practitioner's objective report. The VeriSign encryption and authentication technology and practices help assure the consumer that the seal on a Web application is authentic and that the provider is entitled to display it.

The TRUSTe program enables companies to develop privacy statements that reflect the information gathering and dissemination practices of their Web applications. The program is equipped with the TRUSTe "trustmark" seal that is awarded only to those that adhere to TRUSTe's established privacy principles and agree to comply with ongoing TRUSTe oversight and resolution process. The privacy principles embody fair information practices approved by the U.S. Department of Commerce, Federal Trade Commission, and prominent industry-represented organizations and associations.

Finally, the perceptions related to presumed credibility may be one of the most difficult to deal with (by virtue of the old adage of there being no cure for doubt). There are no absolute guarantees for presumed credibility assurance but personalizing the application to user context, providing an informative frequently asked questions (FAQ), and in general, a user-oriented approach to application development can help.

The nature of content of a Web application could be labeled appropriately as per the platform for internet content selection (PICS)/resource description framework (RDF), and conforming to the requirements of the Internet content rating association (ICRA).

FUTURE TRENDS

To control and manage the increasing size and complexity of Web applications has led to a systematic approach to creating them and is termed as *Web engineering* (Ginige & Murugesan, 2001). If credibility is important to an organization, it needs to be taken as a first-class concern *throughout* the development process. For that, incorporating credibility as a mandatory non-functional requirement in Web engineering specifications would be essential.

It is known (Schneidewind & Fenton, 1996) that, when applied judiciously, standards can contribute toward quality improvement. Indeed, credibility has recently being seen as a topic of interest for Web applications standards (Carduci & Isaak, 2003). However, awareness and broad use of these standards among providers remains a challenge.

A natural extension of the discussion on credibility of the preceding section would be in context of the next generation Web applications, namely semantic Web applications, Web services, and semantic Web services.

CONCLUSION

The Web provides both opportunities and challenges to a provider. Although there have been many advances toward enabling the technological infrastructure of the Web in the past decade, there is much to be done in addressing the social challenges, including user perceptions and expectations. Addressing credibility of Web applications in a systematic manner is one step in that direction.

Credibility is a social concern that is not always amenable to a purely technological treatment. Still, by decomposing it into quantifiable elements and approaching them in a feasible manner, we can make improvements toward its establishment.

Web applications belong to an ecosystem where both the people and the product play a role in its evolution. If the success of a Web application is measured by use of its services, then establishing credibility with the users is critical for the providers. By making efforts to improve upon the criteria that affect credibility, the providers of Web applications can change the user perception in their favor.

REFERENCES

Carduci, M., & Isaak, J. (2003, October 22-24). Standards and Web site credibility. *The 3rd IEEE Conference on Standardization and Innovation in Information Technology (SIIT2003)*, Delft, The Netherlands.

Chisholm, W., Vanderheiden, G., & Jacobs, I. (1999). *Web Content Accessibility Guidelines 1.0*. W3C Recommendation. World Wide Web Consortium (W3C).

Fenton, N. E., & Pfleeger, S. L. (1997). *Software metrics: A rigorous & practical approach*. International Thomson Computer Press.

Fogg, B. J. (2003). *Persuasive technology: Using computers to change what we think and do*. Morgan Kaufmann Publishers.

Fogg, B. J., & Tseng, S. (1999, May 15-20). The elements of computer credibility. *The ACM CHI 99 Conference on Human Factors in Computing Systems*, Pittsburgh, Pennsylvania, USA.

Gibson, D. A. (2002). *Communities and reputation on the Web*. PhD Thesis, University of California, Berkeley, CA.

Ghezzi, C., Jazayeri, M., & Mandrioli, D. (2003). *Fundamentals of software engineering* (2nd ed.). Prentice-Hall.

Ginige, A., & Murugesan, S. (2001). Web engineering: An introduction. *IEEE Multimedia, 8*(1), 14-18.

Lindland, O. I., Sindre, G., & Sølvberg, A. (1994). Understanding quality in conceptual modeling. *IEEE Software, 11*(2), 42-49.

Kamthan, P. (1999). E-commerce on the WWW: A matter of trust. internet related technologies (IRT.ORG).

Nguyen, H. Q., Johnson, R., & Hackett, M. (2003). *Testing applications on the Web: Test planning for mobile and Internet-based systems* (2nd ed.). John Wiley & Sons.

Nielsen, J. (2000). *Designing Web usability: The practice of simplicity*. New Riders Publishing.

Schneidewind, N. F., & Fenton, N. E. (1996). Do standards improve product quality? *IEEE Software, 13*(1), 22-24.

Van Duyne, D. K., Landay, J., & Hong, J. I. (2003). *The design of sites: Patterns, principles, and processes for crafting a customer-centered Web experience*. Addison-Wesley.

Wiegers, K. (2002). *Peer reviews in software: A practical guide*. Addison-Wesley.

KEY TERMS

Delivery Context: A set of attributes that characterizes the capabilities of the access mechanism, the preferences of the user and other aspects of the context into which a resource is to be delivered.

Personalization: A strategy that enables delivery that is customized to the user and user's environment.

Quality: The totality of features and characteristics of a product or a service that bear on its ability to satisfy stated or implied needs.

Quality Model: A set of characteristics and the relationships between them that provide the basis for specifying quality requirements and evaluating quality of an entity.

Semantic Web: An extension of the current Web that adds technological infrastructure for better knowledge representation, interpretation, and reasoning.

Semiotics: The field of study of signs and their representations.

Web Engineering: A discipline concerned with the establishment and use of sound scientific, engineering and management principles and systematic approaches to the successful development, deployment, and maintenance of high quality Web applications.

ADSL2+ Technology

D. Kagklis
Hellenic Telecommunications Organization S.A., Greece

S. Androulidakis
Hellenic Telecommunications Organization S.A., Greece

G. Patikis
Hellenic Telecommunications Organization S.A., Greece

T. Doukoglou
Hellenic Telecommunications Organization S.A., Greece

INTRODUCTION

Recent reports on market trends indicate that half the households in the United States intend to subscribe to next-generation broadband access in the immediate future, marking a shift to data rates in the range between 20Mbps to 100Mbps, as Seals (2006) states. According to the same studies, broadband penetration will rise to 75% by 2010, while at the same time, 10 to 20% of U.S. households will have subscribed to the highest access speeds. This data reflects the general tendency toward an increasing demand for more bandwidth, keeping pace with increasing computing power and memory/storage capacity.

The growing demand for higher speed broadband access connections is definitely connected to the emergence of high-quality bandwidth-consuming services such as massive-scale IP video transmission or multi-point video-conference. Examining the trends in the European market, Seals (2006) claims that it is evident that an increasing number of network access providers have already launched or plan to launch TV services over their respective IP networks (IPTV service). It is estimated that 40% of households in the U.S and Europe will have access to IPTV by 2010, while as much as 20% will have access to High-Definition IP-TV (HDTV quality video). To meet the inflated bandwidth needs at the network access, standard residential connections should be able to offer between 20 to 30Mbps in the downstream direction, which translates into supporting two HDTV compressed streams concurrently or a range of standard-definition channels, together with high-speed Internet access and voice over IP (VoIP).

At the present time, ADSL is the most widely deployed DSL flavor in the world. It is however incapable of supporting the necessary speeds for offering IPTV and HDTV services, as it can only offer up to 8Mbps broadband connectivity, subject to subscriber loop conditions. A newly proposed standard, the ADSL2+ technology, providing greater reach, higher bit rates, and added quality of service facilities, is now emerging as a possible solution, as new equipment implementing this ITU standard is being deployed in commercial networks. Furthermore, the ADSL2+ technology also implements the reach extension model (ITU-T G.992.3 Annex L, 2002), as well as the increased upstream option (ITU-T G.992.3 Annex J, 2002), referred to as ADSL2+ Annex J/M (ITU-T G.992.5 Annex J/M, 2003). Thus, the main advantages of the new technology are its potential for greater reach and higher speed. The increased rates enable the so-called triple-play service concept, consisting of converged Internet-access, telephone, and TV/VoD services over a standard telephone line. In this context, access rate offerings above the standard ADSL range of 3-6 Mbps downstream are gradually becoming available, while in certain countries access rates above 20 Mbps are already becoming the norm. The greater reach allows more customers to enjoy such services over their local loop. However, just as in the case of standard ADSL, the actually achievable rate is subject to the condition of the subscriber loop.

This chapter presents and evaluates the ADSL2+ technology with respect to its physical layer performance, which provides the foundation for supporting high-quality residential triple-play services on a massive scale.

BACKROUND

Over the past few years, there has been a substantial increase in the use of the Internet and its numerous applications by an ever swelling and ever more demanding residential user community. The widespread adoption of the Internet among non business/corporate users has been powered by the emergence of low-cost high-speed residential broadband access and the great popularity of a number of related high-end applications as Androulidakis, Kagklis, Doukoglou, and Skenter (2004a) stated.

To support the extra traffic generated by the numerous residential clients, backbone network infrastructures have evolved to a level capable of sustaining high volumes of traffic belonging to bandwidth-intense applications. On the other hand, however, the currently mass-deployed residential broadband access technologies are considered inadequate for supporting the increased needs of high-end multimedia/audiovisual services.

Since it first became available, the ADSL technology (ITU-T G.992.1, 1999) has become the dominant technology for residential broadband access, deployed on a massive scale in order to address the Internet-access needs of the majority of residential end users. The data rates supported by ADSL and currently offered by most access service providers typically fall in the range of 512Kbps up to 8Mbps for the downstream direction, and 128Kbps up to 768Kbps for the upstream direction, with the actual figures depending on a variety of technology- and business-specific considerations. Even though such speeds represent a significant improvement over typical PSTN/ISDN-based connectivity (i.e., 56/128Kbps), a typical ADSL line is unable to provide users with enough bandwidth for upstream-intense services (e.g., peer-to-peer networking) and ultra-high-quality audio-visual content access (e.g., HDTV). Indeed, it is a fact established by monitoring current network usage practices that the majority of residential users (i.e., "mainstream" users) require quasi-symmetric access, with high upstream and downstream bitrates, in order to enjoy such services as bi-directional video conferencing, peer-to-peer networking, or online entertainment. Furthermore, Wolfe (2003) claims that the emergence of HDTV-based applications is expected to give rise to a category of "power" residential users, who will require very high downstream access rates in order to enjoy premium services. In this context, the ADSL

technology as it stands today is not a suitable choice for addressing the needs of both "mainstream" and "power" users and their respective "profile" services.

With this in mind, enhancements were made to the original ADSL technology that produced ADSL2 as an immediate successor (ITU-T G.992.3, 2002). ADSL2 offered higher bitrates in both the downstream and upstream directions by using a more efficient G.DMT-based modulation mechanism, as described in the Aware White Paper (2003). The new modulation scheme was applied to the same frequency band as in the original ADSL standard (i.e., up to 1,1MHz), thus ensuring backward-compatibility with existing equipment. However, ADSL2 never achieved prominence and has come to be considered a transitional technology.

Consequently, further improvements to the original ADSL specification have produced the next successor standard referred to as ADSL2+ (ITU-T G.992.5, 2003). This technology will be the focus of the present chapter, in which ADSL2+ will be described with reference to its predecessors. In the course of the description, the new features, improvements, and advantages of this new technology will be presented, while physical-layer performance measurements will be used to provide a better understanding of what ADSL2+ has to offer.

FEATURES, IMPROVEMENTS, AND ADVANTAGES OF ADSL2+

This section is organized in two sub-sections, the first one describing and the second one evaluating the ADSL2+ technology.

The technology description offers an overview of functions, features, and improvements incorporated in the ADSL2+ specification. The evaluation is based on a performance and quality comparison between ADSL2+ and its predecessor technologies, on the basis of experimental results.

The Components of the ADSL2+ Technology

The ADSL2+ technology was specifically designed to offer almost three times the downstream rate offered by ADSL, as well as a substantially increased upstream rate. At the same time, backward compatibility with existing customer premised equipments, providing reduced-speed connectivity, was also a prime concern in formulating the new standard. To achieve these goals, ADSL2+ employs a dual approach; firstly, by adopting the improved modulation mechanism of the ADSL2 standard (ADSL-compatible), it improves the bit carrying efficiency per sub-carrier frequency; secondly, by doubling the downstream spectrum bandwidth[1] of the ADSL/ADSL2 specifications, it effectively doubles the downstream bitrate it can offer. Both these choices are intended to endower ADSL2+ with greatly improved access rates, while maintaining compatibility with both the ADSL and ADSL2 standard.

Furthermore, ADSL2+ has included the reach extension model described in the ADSL2 Annex L standard (studied by Ouyang, Duvaut, Moreno, & Pierrugues, 2003), as well as the increased upstream option introduced in the ADSL2 Annex J standard. The latter feature has been included as the Annex J/M of the ADSL2+ standard (ITU-T G.992.5, 2003). The importance of these two features is demonstrated by Bong, Taek, Ginis, and Cioffi (2002) and Androulidakis, Kagklis, Doukoglou, and Skenter (2004b) in their respective work. The former has shown that an ADSL2+ Annex L transceiver can deliver an improvement in reach for distances beyond 5.5km, allowing for broadband connectivity even in remote areas. The latter has demonstrated how an ADSL2+ Annex J/M transceiver can offer the necessary high upstream rates for customers needing low-cost symmetric broadband access similar to a G.SHDSL service (ITU-T, G.991.2, 2001).

The ADSL2+ standard has incorporated other improvements, including:

- Better diagnostic methods such as SELT described in the Texas Instruments White Paper (2003), or DELT, (ITU-T G.992.5, 2003)
- Improved power management capabilities (the L0/L2/L3 power management scheme) as well as
- Line bonding functionality based on an ATM IMA layer, similar to the method described by the Aware White Paper (2004) and evaluated by Androulidakis, Kagklis, Doukoglou, and Sykas (2005)

All these features indicate that the new standard holds much promise, especially in view of the move to bandwidth-intense multimedia-based services targeted at the residential market. Given the rising demand for advanced "triple play" services, which the current ADSL technology cannot fully support, and the fact that many content providers seek entrance into new markets (e.g., DVD- or HDTV-quality video broadcasts) through IP-based networks, the move to ADSL2+ technology seems perfectly justified. It is expected that deploying ADSL2+ on a massive scale for residential broadband access will address the inflated bandwidth requirements in the access network at a low cost per customer.

Evaluation of the ADSL2+ Technology

The following evaluation of the ADSL2+ technology is based on actual performance measurements regarding the synchronization of ADSL2+ ATU-R/ATU-C transceiver pairs in a noise-free environment. The performance of ADSL2+ is assessed according to increasing subscriber loop length, with respect to bitrates offered in both the downstream and upstream directions.

All measurements were performed in-lab, using a Globespan-based ADSL2+-compliant DSLAM (Ericsson, 2003) and two modems; a Broadcom chipset ADSL2+-compliant modem (Ericsson 410, supporting Annexes A, L, J/M through configuration) and a Globespan Virata chipset standard ADSL modem (Lancom 821). Therefore two combinations were tested: an "ADSL2+ ATU-R/ATU-C" (ADSL2+) link and an "ADSL ATU-R/ADSL2+ ATU-C" (ADSL) link. A Telebyte Inc. 458-LM-HDE 0.4mm copper line emulator was used to observe the behaviour of the test links according to increasing subscriber loop lengths, ranging from 300m up to 6600m in steps of 300m. For each individual loop length, the corresponding bitrate values, for both the downstream and upstream directions of both test links, were recorded. These measurements were then crosschecked for validity, by performing a second set of measurements on real 0.4mm copper line lengths. The ATU-R/ATU-C training process had a fixed target SNR of 6dB (DSLAM equipment default) applicable to all measurement cases. This threshold represents a minimum for maintaining a low bit error rate and acceptable communication quality on the DSL access link.

The measurement results are presented in the following figures, documenting the values acquired from the line emulator measurements, corroborated by the values acquired from measurements on the real 0.4mm copper loops (max divergence ~5%). Figures 1 and 2 demonstrate the decrease of downstream and upstream bitrates according to increasing loop length.

Figure 1. Downstream bitrate performance

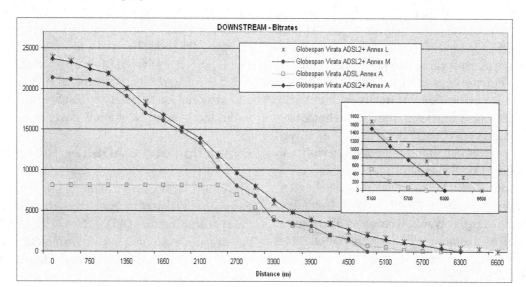

Figure 2. Downstream bitrate performance

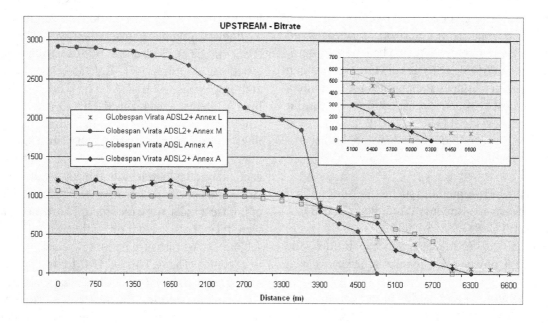

The results in Figure 1 relate to the downstream bitrates for the ADSL2+ and ADSL test links. It clearly shows that the ADSL2+ technology consistently delivers higher rates than ADSL, regardless of subscriber loop length. The ADSL2+ technology (in Annex A, L and J/M modes) almost triples the bitrate offered by the older ADSL at short loops. Moreover, at loop-lengths over 3500m, the ADSL2+ technology consistently offers between 50% and 100% more bandwidth than ADSL. At the same time, ADSL2+ manages to sustain an active link over a longer subscriber loop, exceeding the ADSL loop length limit by a further 300m for ADSL2+ Annex A and 750m for ADSL2+ Annex L, respectively.

Similarly, the results of the upstream performance measurements on the test links show that the upstream bitrates offered by ADSL2+ (Annexes A and L) exceed those offered by ADSL, which is in accordance to their respective specifications (Figure 2). The same figure indicates that the Annex J/M link can reach up to 3Mbps in the upstream direction, thus offering about 225% more upstream bandwidth than the ADSL2+ Annex A and Annex L links, or almost three times more upstream bandwidth than the ADSL link. This means that ADSL2+ Annex J/M can be used to support customers needing a symmetric broadband access service, even being able to substitute for the G.SHDSL technology for corporate access.

The upstream measurements also reveal that when connecting a standard ADSL modem to an ADSL2+-compliant DSLAM port, even when the latter is operating in standard ADSL mode, the upstream link capacity will clearly exceed the upper limit of ~800Kbps of a pure "ADSL ATU-R/ATU-C" link. In fact, the upstream bitrate was measured consistently above 900Kbps at loop lengths up to 3300m, possibly achieving an up to 32% increase over the pure ADSL link, as calculated by Androulidakis et al. (2004a).

FUTURE TRENDS

Today ADSL2+ can be considered a mature technology as more and more ADSL2+ chipsets are developed and marketed by the leading manufacturers, including Globespan, Broadcom, and others. Almost all major access equipment manufacturers, including Alcatel, Ericsson, Paradyne, UTstarcom, Huawei, Siemens, and others, have made available ADSL2+-compliant DSLAMs and modems, continuously expanding the range of available products and incorporating more sophisticated features (e.g. Annex B for access over ISDN lines or and Annex J/M for symmetric services).

As "triple play" services become commonplace among residential customers, directly competing against traditional media networks (e.g., high-quality video broadcast over terrestrial or satellite), ageing ADSL-based broadband access networks will be upgraded to ADSL2+. However, the adoption of ADSL2+ as the access technology of choice does not immediately enable high-end multimedia-rich services for all. The measurement-based evaluation of the technology has shown that the performance of ADSL2+ is highly

dependant on the loop length, just as all the various flavours of the DSL family. Even the extended-reach feature, specifically developed to counter the adverse effects of increased loop lengths, only offers about 500m of extra coverage. Furthermore, even though HDTV-based services can (marginally) be offered over ADSL2+ broadband access, even more advanced future Super HDTV- and Ultra HDTV-based services can certainly not. The bandwidth needed by the latter two may exceed by a large margin the ADSL2+ limits and indeed the limitations of copper-based broadband access.

In the short term and in view of the limitations of ADSL2+, a new DSL access technology has been developed as an alternative to a full Fibre-to-the-Home access solution, namely the VDSL2 technology. Its short distance reach however requires a supporting Fibre-to-the-Curb network, which, in most countries, is only now beginning to materialise.

CONCLUSION

This chapter studies the new ADSL2+ technology, describing the new functionality it offers and comparing its performance against the older ADSL technology. The comparison is based on a set of physical layer measurements, conducted in a controlled laboratory environment. The physical layer speeds achieved by each technology were measured at increasing loop lengths without the presence of noise. At the same time the corresponding SNR values were also measured in each case. The charts plotting the measured bitrates and SNR values according to length, for both the ADSL technology and three different flavours of ADSL2+, offer a visual perspective of ADSL2+ performance and how it relates to ADSL. Comparing the results in these charts, it can be concluded that ADSL2+ offers higher access rates as loop length increases.

All in all though, the greatest advantage of ADSL2+ is the high downstream rate it can offer over a single copper loop. With 24Mbps of downstream bitrate, ADSL2+ is ideal for offering bandwidth-intense multimedia services on a massive scale. Furthermore, ADSL2+ in the Annex J/M flavour can support symmetric connections at speeds up to 3Mbps, which is better than the G.SHDSL technology. However, HDTV or better services may not be effectively offered over ADSL2+, mainly due to coverage issues. Even though it is expected that ADSL2+ will be the next dominant broadband access technology for the residential market, ultra-high-quality audio-visual services will have to be offered through VDSL2 (either cell-mode or frame-mode) access connections, studied by Walko (2005), which offers backward compatibility with all previous DSL flavours, or an all optical access network (passive or active optical networks).

ACKNOWLEDGMENT

The authors would like to thank the Research Department of the Hellenic Telecommunications Organization S.A. (OTE) for allowing the use of the Broadband Access Laboratory as well as the use of the equipment used for the measurements.

REFERENCES

ADSL2 and ADSL2+: The New ADSL Standards, Revision 3. (2003). *Aware White Paper.*

Androulidakis, S., Kagklis, D., Doukoglou, T., & Skenter S. (2004a). ADSL2: A sequel better than the original? *IEE Communication Engineer Magazine, 2*(3), 22-27.

Androulidakis S., Kagklis D., Doukoglou T., & Skenter S. (2004b). ADSL2 vs. SHDSL for symmetric broadband access networking. *IEE Electronic Letters, 40*(16), 1027-1029.

Androulidakis S., Kagklis D., Doukoglou T., & Sykas E. (2005). Bonding techniques for symmetric services over ADSL and ADSL2/2+. In *Proceeding of the IEEE Eurocon Conference* (Vol. 2, pp. 1770-1773).

Bonded ADSL2+ New Standards for Multi-Line Services. (2004). *Aware White Paper.*

Bong, S. K., Taek, C. S., Ginis, G., & Cioffi, J. M. (2002). Dynamic spectrum management for next-generation DSL systems. *IEEE Communications Magazine, 40*(10), 101-109.

Ericsson EDN-110 IP DSLAM. (2003). Retrieved 15th March 2003 from http://www.ericsson.com/

ITU-T G.992.1. (1999). *Asymmetrical Digital Subscriber Line (ADSL) Transceivers.* ITU-T standard Series G: Transmission Systems and Media, Digital Systems and Networks, Digital transmission systems—Digital sections and digital line system—Access networks.

ITU-T G.991.2 (2001). *'Single-Pair High-speed Digital Subscriber Line (SHDSL) Transceivers'.* ITU-T standard Series G: Transmission Systems and Media, Digital Systems and Networks, Digital transmission systems—Digital sections and digital line system—Access networks.

ITU-T G.992.3. (2002). *Asymmetric Digital Subscriber Line (ADSL) transceivers 2 (ADSL2).* ITU-T standard Series G: Transmission Systems and Media, Digital Systems and Networks, Digital transmission systems—Digital sections and digital line system—Access networks.

ITU-T G.992.5. (2003). *Asymmetrical Digital Subscriber Line (ADSL) transceivers—Extended bandwidth ADSL2 (ADSL2+).* ITU-T standard Series G: Transmission Systems and Media, Digital Systems and Networks, Digital transmission systems—Digital sections and digital line system—Access networks.

Ouyang, F., Duvaut, P., Moreno, O., & Pierrugues, L. (2003). The first step of long-reach ADSL: Smart DSL technology, READSL. *IEEE Communications Magazine, 41*(9), 124-131.

Seals, T. (2006). *Expanding the value of copper.* Xchange Magazine. Retrieved January 2, 2006, from http://www.xchangemag.com

Single-Ended Loop Testing (SELT) Expectations and Realities. (March 2003). *Texas Instruments White Paper.*

Walko, J. (2005). Click here for VDSL2. *IEE Communications Engineering Magazine, 3*(4), 9-12.

Wolfe, A. (2003). HDTV—Ready for the long drive? *IEEE Spectrum, 40*(6), 13-15.

KEY TERMS

ADSL: Asymmetrical digital subscriber line.

ATU-C : ADSL transceiver unit--centre.

ATU-R: ADSL transceiver unit--remote.

DELT: Dual ended line test.

DSLAM: Digital subscriber line access multiplexer.

HDTV: High-definition TV.

SELT: Single-ended loop testing.

SHDSL: Single-pair high-speed DSL.

SNR: Signal to noise ratio.

VDSL: Very-high-bit-rate digital subscriber line.

ENDNOTE

[1]   The downstream band of ADSL2+ ends at 2,2MHz instead of 1,1MHz of the older technologies. The upstream band remains unaltered in the basic standard (i.e., Annex A operation).

A

Advanced Techniques for Web Content Filtering

Elisa Bertino
Purdue University, USA

Elena Ferrari
Università degli Studi dell'Insubria, Italy

Andrea Perego
Università degli Studi dell'Insubria, Italy

Gian Piero Zarri
Université Paris IV, France

INTRODUCTION

Web content filtering concerns the enforcement of mechanisms able to inform users about the content and characteristics of the Web resources they access. The former application of such techniques focused on blocking access to resources was considered inappropriate to given users (e.g., children). Nonetheless, its possible applications are not limited to such issue since it can be effectively used in order to notify users about the "quality" of a resource (i.e., the fact of satisfying given requirements), which may concern the authoritativeness and/or authenticity of the provided information, the treatment of personal data, and so on.

In this chapter, besides discussing the current strategies for Web content filtering, and outlining their advantages and drawbacks, we present an approach, formerly developed in the framework of the EU project EUFORBIA, which, besides addressing the main drawbacks of the existing systems, can be applied for purposes comprising both users' protection and quality assurance. The main features of such an approach are the support for multiple metadata vocabularies for the rating and filtering of Web resources, and the possibility of specifying policies, which allow the system to decide whether a resource is appropriate or not for a given user based on his or her preferences and characteristics.

BACKGROUND

Classification of Web resources based on their content emerged as a need as soon as online information exponentially grew in quantity and heterogeneity during the 1990s. Search engines were designed in order to simplify to users the task of finding what they were looking for. Nonetheless, another issue to be addressed was (and still is) making users able to realize whether a Web resource satisfies a given set of requirements concerning its content and/or characteristics. An example of such requirements concerns protecting children from possible harmful contents. Search engines are not suitable for this purpose since they cannot ensure users of having correctly rated a resource (i.e., they provide only a probabilistic classification of Web resources) and, consequently, they may consider as appropriate resources that are, by contrast, inappropriate. For this reason, this issue has been addressed by building tools able to filter Web content, which adopted two main strategies. The former is based on the manual classification of resources in order to build white and/or black lists, which are then used in order to verify whether the user is requesting access to an appropriate or inappropriate resource. The latter follows the PICS approach (*PICS*, 2005; Resnick, & Miller, 1996), where resources are rated by associating with them labels containing a formal description of their content/characteristics. Based on such labels and on the user profile, the filtering tool is then able to decide whether a requested resource should be considered as appropriate or not.

Both such approaches have a main drawback in that they focus mainly on filtering efficiency. As a result, they adopt strategies that enforce a very restrictive access to online resources, with the consequence that users' navigation is limited to a very narrow subset of the Web. The label-based approach has been designed to solve such problem. Nonetheless, the supported metadata vocabularies are semantically poor, and they are not suitable for supporting policies more flexible and expressive than those used in the list-based approaches. This is why, so far, Web content filtering has been applied mainly for minors' protection purposes, although it may have other relevant applications that can help in improving users' confidentiality in using the information and services available in the Web. In particular, in recent years, it emerged the need of designing technologies able to ensure the "quality" of the Web. The P3P W3C standard (Cranor, Langheinrich, Marchiori, Presler-Marshall, & Reagle, 2002) has been one of the first outcomes of such research trend; thanks to this technology, users can be aware of how their personal data will be used by a Web service, and thus they can decide whether to use it or not. Nonetheless, besides privacy protection, the quality of Web resources can be ensured with respect to a variety of requirements, which may help users in being more confident with the Web. Suppose, for instance, that a user accesses a medical Web site, providing information about diseases, their symptoms, and the corresponding treatments; currently, such user cannot be sure if such information is reliable and accurate, and thus he or she must avoid considering it for addressing his or her needs. The availability of more sophisticated filtering systems may also help in addressing such issues.

THE EUFORBIA APPROACH TO WEB CONTENT FILTERING

In this section, we illustrate a filtering framework, formerly developed in the context of the EU project EUFORBIA (*EUFORBIA*, 2004), which addresses the main drawbacks of existing filtering systems; on one hand, by supporting both the list- and metadata-based approaches, and, on the other hand, by allowing the specification of policies taking into account the characteristics of both users and resources. The main com-

ponents of our framework are a cross-domain ontology, allowing an accurate description of Web resources, a new format for labels, which describe both the content and the structure of Web sites, and two integrated systems, specifically designed in order to address the needs of both home and institutional users.

THE EUFORBIA ONTOLOGY AND EUFORBIA LABELS

To make it possible to apply Web content filtering for purposes not limited to users' protection, it is necessary to have the proper tools for describing resources from different points of view. This can be obtained by supporting multiple domain-dependent metadata vocabularies, focusing on a specific usage of Web resources.

Besides supporting such features, we designed a cross-domain ontology, which can be extended with concepts pertaining to new content domains. More precisely, the EUFORBIA ontology has been obtained by extending the general class hierarchy (HClass) of NKRL (Zarri, 2003) with concepts pertaining to the domain of users' protection (e.g., pornography). Figure 1 depicts a portion of the upper level of the HClass hierarchy.

The main difference between NKRL and the usual ontology paradigm is the support for an ontology of events in addition to the traditional ontology of concepts. In an ontology of events, nodes represent multiadic structures called *templates* obtained by combining quadruples consisting of the template name, a predicate, and the arguments of the predicate, which consist of a structured set of concepts.

The NKRL ontology of events is a hierarchy of templates (HTemp), which correspond to classes of elementary events such as move a physical object, be present in a place, produce a service, send/receive a message, build up an Internet site, and so forth. Currently, HTemp provides about 180 templates, which can be instantiated in order to represent an actual event (e.g., "Mr. Smith has created a new Web site having the URL ..."). Templates represent, in short, all sort of *dynamic relationships* between basic concepts, and are then of vital importance for the correct rendering of *narratives*—in the widest meaning of this term, including also, the semantic content of Web sites.

Note that there is no real contradiction between NKRL and the ontological languages such as OWL

Figure 1. An abridged representation of the HClass hierarchy

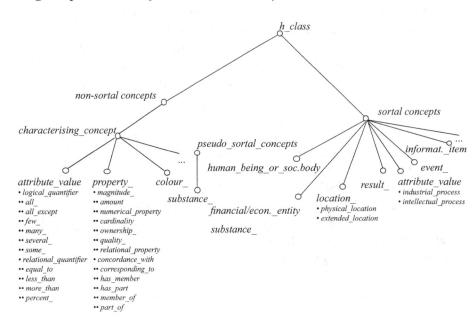

Box 1.

```
c73) (COORD c76 c77)
c76) OWN   SUBJ SNOOP_DOGG_INTERNET_SITE (www.snoop-dogg.com)
       OBJ property_
       TOPIC (SPECIF dedicated_to SNOOP_DOGG)
// instance of: Own:CompoundProperty
c77) BEHAVE SUBJ SNOOP_DOGG (www.snoop-dogg.com)
       MODAL rap_star
// instance of: Behave:Role
```

(McGuinness & Harmelen, 2004). This is due mainly to the fact that the ontology of events (HTemp) of NKRL works strictly in conjunction with an NKRL standard ontology of concepts (HClass)—as already stated, the arguments of the predicate in the templates are built up from concepts or combination of concepts. Moreover, translators from/to XML (Bray, Paoli, Sperberg-McQueen, Maler, & Yergeau, 2006) and RDF(s) (Brickley & Guha, 2004; Klyne & Carroll, 2004) exist for NKRL. Extensions to RDF have been developed in order to preserve all the NKRL power when NKRL structures are converted into RDF (e.g., by securing full compatibility between RDF containers and NKRL expansion operators).

NKRL and the EUFORBIA ontology are the tools on which EUFORBIA labels are based. More precisely,

labels are expressed in NKRL, using the set of concepts provided by the EUFORBIA ontology. A EUFORBIA label consists of three main sections: the first (aims) describes the Web site purposes, the second (properties) provides information about some relevant characteristics of a Web site, whereas the third (sub-sites) illustrates the structure of the Web site.

A very simple example of the aim section of a EUFORBIA label is reproduced in Box 1. Such set of assertions can be translated as follows: "The site is devoted to an individual named Snoop Dogg; this individual is a rap star." Statement c73 specifies that this section of the labels consists of two "predicative occurrences," c76 and c77, that must take place together (COORD = coordination). Statements c76 and c77 are instances of two different NKRL templates, respectively, Own:

Box 2.

```
Name: Behave:Role
Father: Behave
Position: 1.1
NL description: "A Human Being or a Social Body Acts in a Particular Role"

BEHAVE SUBJ var1: [(var2)]
  *OBJ
  [SOURCE    var3: [(var4)]]
  [BENF      var5: [(var6)]]
  MODAL      var7
  [TOPIC     var8]
  [CONTEXT   var9]
  [ modulators ]


var1 = <human_being_or_social_body>
var2 = <geographical_location> | <premise_>
var3 = <human_being_or_social_body>
var5 = <human_being_or_social_body>
var7 = <role_>
var8 = <entity_>
var9 = <situation_> | <symbolic_label>
var4, var6 = <geographical_location>
```

Compound Property and Behave:Role. A representation of the latter is depicted in Box 2.

As can be seen, the arguments of the predicate are expressed through variables (**var***i*) and constraints on the variables, like *human_being_or_social_body* for **var1**.

THE MFilter PROTOTYPE

The first EUFORBIA prototype, referred to as MFilter (Bertino, Ferrari, & Perego, 2003, 2006), is based on a filtering model where policies are specified on either the identity or characteristics of users and resources. Resources' characteristics are described by labels, which may use different metadata vocabularies (thus, also the EUFORBIA ontology). Metadata vocabularies are also used for describing user profiles. In such a case, the adopted vocabulary depends on the context (e.g., a user profile in a school context will be different with the profiles adopted in companies). An example of a hierarchy of user profiles in a school context is depicted in Figure 2.

This is a relevant improvement with respect to the available filtering systems where users are grouped into one or more static classes, taking into account only a given parameter (e.g., age). By contrast, in our model the classes of resources and users to which a policy applies are determined dynamically in policies by expressing constraints on their properties. Thus, we can specify a policy stating that the sexual content is inappropriate for students of less than 15 years old.

Two other relevant features of our model are the support for both negative and positive policies, and the support for a policy propagation mechanism. Thanks to the former feature, we can specify policies stating not only which resources are inappropriate (negative sign), but also those that are appropriate (positive sign) for a given user. The latter feature is related to the fact that metadata vocabularies may be hierarchically organized (as the EUFORBIA ontology, and the user profiles in Figure 2). Thus, we can exploit such hierarchy according to the principle that a policy applying to a given, say, user profile, is inherited by all its children.

Although such features improve the expressivity of our model, they may cause conflicts between policies (e.g., two policies applying to the same user and the same resource, but with different sign). For this reason, our model supports also a conflict resolution mechanism, based on the principle of stronger policy, according to which the prevailing policy is the more specific one wrt the hierarchy. In case the policies are

Figure 2. An example of user profile hierarchy

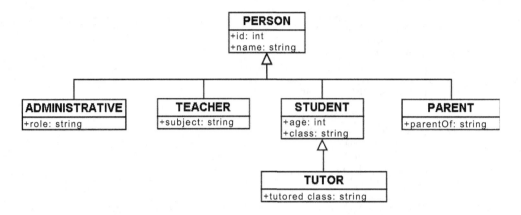

Figure 3. MFilter architecture

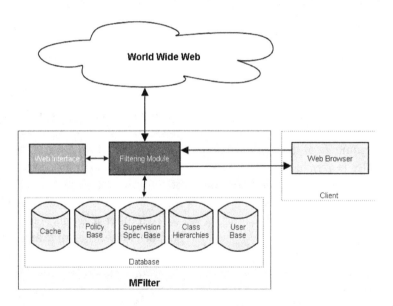

incomparable with respect to the hierarchy, the prevailing policy is the one with the stronger sign, which may be either the positive or the negative one, depending on the specific context.

Finally, our model provides support for concurrent policy specification (i.e., it allows different classes of supervisors, with possibly different authority levels) to specify policies applying to the users of whom they are responsible. This feature is useful since it may often be the case that the responsibility of deciding what is appropriate or not for a user is shared among different persons (e.g., in a school context, teachers and parents). In case two supervisors specify conflicting policies, their authority level is taken into account in order to determine the prevailing policy.

The architecture of MFilter, depicted in Figure 3, consists of three main components: a database, storing all the data needed by the system, a Web interface, for managing the system, and the filtering module, which is in charge of processing all the access requests and verifying whether they are appropriate or not based on the policies stored in the database.

Since the filtering module must evaluate a high number of access requests and, for each of them, identify the set of policies applying to the requesting user and the requested resource, this may affect both the efficiency and effectiveness of filtering. It is in fact fundamental that the response delay is not perceived by users. For this purpose, pre-computational strategies and caching

Figure 4. Web browser module of the NKRL-based EUFORBIA prototype

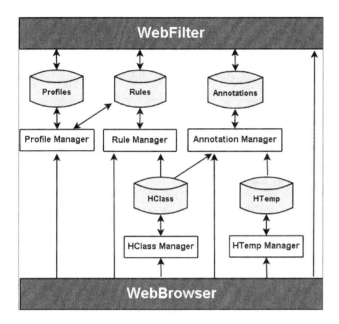

Finally, the MFilter Web interface allows the SA to insert, edit, and/or delete data stored in the database. It is structured into three main sections: the administration interface, for the management of the filtering system; the supervision interface, for validating the policies specified by the SA; the user interface, the aims of which are (a) to perform user authentication, (b) to supply some general information about the prototype and its use, and (c) to provide a tool for editing the user's password.

THE WebBrowser AND THE INFERENCE RULES

The architecture of the second EUFORBIA prototype, depicted in Figure 4, consists of two main components, namely the *WebBrowser* and *WebFilter*. Such software, installed on a Proxy server or on the user's machine, performs the basic filtering actions of this prototype.

By using the *ProfileManager* module, the user can specify the categories of resources that he or she considers as appropriate and inappropriate. Such "user profile" is stored in the "profile" repository. The "rules" repository stores the existing filtering rules expressed in NKRL. Whenever a EUFORBIA label is retrieved, it is unified with the left-hand side of the rules applying to the requesting user. If the label can be unified with the rules, the system returns a response corresponding to "resource r is inappropriate for user u."

The information provided by EUFORBIA labels allows us to enforce filtering with a granularity finer than the whole Web site. In other words, we may have different evaluation results depending on the possible presence of Web pages or Web site sub-sections different with respect to their content.

In Box 3, the NL transcription of some simple filtering rules is provided. The actual code of RULE2 is reported in Box 4.

Note that in spite of the (apparently) different knowledge representation formalisms used, the concrete deductive power of these rules does not seem to be very different from that of other rule systems proposed recently in a Semantic Web contex (Shadbolt, Berners-Lee, & Hall, 2006; SW, 2006) as SWRL (Horrocks et al., 2004).

The particular inference engine used in the NKRL-based prototype of EUFORBIA is a simplified version of the standard NKRL inference engine, based on a

mechanisms are enforced by the filtering module. More precisely, the filtering module stores the results of the evaluations already carried out in the MFilter database (see below) so that they can be re-used whenever the corresponding access requests are submitted again, thus avoiding to perform the filtering procedure.

The main components of the MFilter database schema are depicted in Figure 3. The rating system, user, and policy bases store all the corresponding data directly inserted by the system administrator (SA). Currently, MFilter supports all the PICS-based rating systems and the EUFORBIA ontology. The resource base stores the URIs and metadata concerning the already requested resources as previously mentioned. Yet, since Web page content is dynamic and may change with a frequency depending on the Web page type, all the metadata concerning online resources are associated with an expiring time set by default or possibly specified by the SA. Moreover, the cache component stores all the pre-computed data regarding the policies, but also all the access requests already submitted along with the identifier of the users and the corresponding (negative or positive) responses. All this information is accessed and managed by the SA through the Web interface.

Box 3.

Only one condition (*IF cond1* ⇒ deny access)
RULE1: *IF* a given site/site section praises topics like racism, violence, sexuality, etc.
　　THEN the site/site section must be refused
(see, e.g., the sub-section lyrics.shtml of www.snoop-dogg.com site that advocates sexuality, violence and drug legalization).

Two conditions (*IF cond1* ∧ *cond2* ⇒ deny access)
RULE1: *IF* a given site/site section is devoted to spreading information over the Internet
　　AND this information concerns sexuality, violence, racism, etc.
　　THEN the site/site section must be refused
(see, e.g., the site www.textgais.com, devoted to the diffusion of short stories about homosexuality).

Three conditions (*IF cond1* ∧ *cond2* ∧ *cond3* ⇒ deny access)
RULE1: *IF* a given site does not contain explicit nudity
　　AND this site includes sections
　　AND some of these show photos of women/teenagers dressed in bras or undewears
　　THEN the site (or site sections, according to the chosen strategy) section must be refused
(see, e.g., sections "mixed-sheer-bras" and "mixed-teen-bras" of softcoregp.com/bracity).

Box 4.

RULE2:COND1) OWN SUBJ **var1**
　　OBJ *property_*
　　TOPIC (SPECIF *dedicated_to* (SPECIF *internet_publishing* **var2**))
RULE2:COND2) OWN SUBJ **var2**
　　OBJ *property_*
　　TOPIC **var3**

var1 = *site_ | internet_site_section*
var2 = *information_item*
var3 = *sexuality_ | violence_ | racism_*

---

classical backward chaining approach with chronological backtracking. The differences with respect to other well-known examples of use of this approach (Mycin, PROLOG, etc.) are mainly linked with the complexity of the NKRL data structures. This complexity implies the execution of difficult operations of reconstruction of the program environment whenever, after a deadlock, it is necessary to return to the previous choice point to try a new way of pursuing with the processing.

FUTURE TRENDS

We are currently investigating how our approach can be enforced in the framework of the semantic Web and in the W3C Web services architecture (Booth et al., 2004), where the possible applications of Web content filtering will play a relevant role in customizing the Web to the needs and preferences of end users. A first step toward this use of Web content filtering has been established in the framework of the EU project QUATRO (QUATRO, 2006), where a standard RDF format for content labels and trust marks has been defined. Besides enhancing the metadata-based approach to Web content rating and filtering, QUATRO addresses one of the major issues in such field, namely, verifying the accuracy and trustworthiness of content labels. This is obtained by applying flexible strategies for labels' authentication and validation, which can be tailored to the labeling policy of the organization which released the labels. Moreover, an integrated system architecture has been designed and implemented, consisting of a set of Web services, in charge of labels' retrieval and validation, and two front-end tools, namely, ViQ and LADI, which notify to end users the evaluation results concerning labels' content and validity (Karkaletsis et al., 2006).

A relevant outcome of the project has been the establishment of a W3C incubator activity (Web Content Label Incubator Group, 2006), aiming at proposing a W3C standard for Web content labels, starting from the QUATRO experience.

CONCLUSION

Web content filtering aims at analyzing the content/characteristics of Web resource in order to verify whether they satisfy the preferences and requirements expressed by end users. In this chapter, we discussed the possible applications of Web content filtering, and how it is currently enforced, outlining the advantages and drawbacks of both the list- and metadata-based approaches.

As an example of how Web content filtering can be enhanced, we illustrated the EUFORBIA filtering approach, the main features of which are the support for both list- and metadata-based approaches, the support for multiple metadata vocabularies for the rating and filtering of Web resources, and the possibility of specifying policies, which allow the system to decide whether a resource is appropriate or not for a given user, based on his or her preferences and characteristics.

Finally, we briefly presented a novel approach developed in the context of the QUATRO project, where Web content filtering is enforced by using a metadata-based approach based on Semantic Web technologies. Such an approach indicates the future trends of Web content filtering, namely, its integration into the Semantic Web and Web services frameworks, where it will play a relevant role in customizing the Web to the needs and preferences of end users.

REFERENCES

Bertino, E., Ferrari, E., & Perego, A. (2003, November). Content-based filtering of Web documents: The MaX system and the EUFORBIA project. *International Journal of Information Security, 2*(1), 45-58.

Bertino, E., Ferrari, E., & Perego, A. (2006). Web content filtering. In E. Ferrari & B. Thuraisingham (Eds.), *Web and information security* (pp. 112-132). Hershey, PA: Idea Group Publishing.

Booth, D., Haas, H., McCabe, F., Newcomer, E., Champion, M., Ferris, C., et al. (2004, February). *Web services architecture* (W3C Working Group Note). Retrieved from http://www.w3.org/TR/ws-arch

Bray, T., Paoli, J., Sperberg-McQueen, C. M., Maler, E., & Yergeau, F. (2006, August). *Extensible markup language (XML) 1.0. Fourth Edition* (W3C Recommendation). Retrieved from http://www.w3.org/TR/xml

Brickley, D., & Guha, R. (2004, February). *RDF vocabulary description language 1.0: RDF Schema* (W3C Recommendation). Retrieved from http://www.w3.org/TR/rdf-schema

Cranor, L., Langheinrich, M., Marchiori, M., Presler-Marshall, M., & Reagle, J. (2002, April). *The Platform for Privacy Preferences 1.0 (P3P1.0) specification* (W3C Recommendation). Retrieved from http://www.w3.org/TR/P3P

The EUFORBIA project (Project Web Site). (2004, September). (http://semioweb.msh-paris.fr/euforbia)

Horrocks, I., Patel-Schneider, P. F., Boley, H., Tabet, S., Grosof, B., & Dean, M. (2004, May). *SWRL: A Semantic Web rule language combining OWL and RuleML* (W3C Member Submission). World Wide Web Consortium. Retrieved from http://www.w3.org/Submission/SWRL)

Karkaletsis, V., Perego, A., Archer, P., Stamatakis, K., Nasikas, P., & Rose, D. (2006). Quality labeling of Web content: The QUATRO approach. In *Proceedings of the WWW'06 Workshop on Models of Trust for the Web (MTW 2006)*. Retrieved from http://www.l3s.de/~olmedilla/events/MTW06_papers/paper11.pdf

Klyne, G., & Carroll, J. J. (2004, February). *Resource description framework (RDF): Concepts and abstract syntax* (W3C Recommendation). Retrieved from http://www.w3.org/TR/rdf-concepts

McGuinness, D. L., & Harmelen, F. van (2004, February). *OWL Web ontology language overview* (W3C Recommendation). Retrieved from http://www.w3.org/TR/owl-features

Platform for Internet Content Selection (PICS) (W3C Initiative Web Site). (2005, July). (http://www.w3.org/PICS)

The QUATRO project (Project Web Site). (2006, December). (http://www.quatro-project.org)

Resnick, P., & Miller, J. (1996, October). PICS: Internet access controls without censorship. *Communications of the ACM, 39*(10), 87-93.

Semantic Web (W3C Activity Web Site). (2006, October). (http://www.w3.org/2001/sw)

Shadbolt, N., Berners-Lee, T., & Hall, W. (2006). The Semantic Web revisited. *IEEE Intelligent Systems, 21*(3), 96-101.

Web Content Label Incubator Group (W3C Incubator Activity Web Site). (2006, July) (http://www.w3.org/2005/Incubator/wcl)

Zarri, G. P. (2003). A conceptual model for representing narratives. In R. Jain, A. Abraham, C. Faucher, & B. van der Zwaag (Eds.), *Innovations in knowledge engineering*. Adelaide: Advanced Knowledge International.

KEY TERMS

List-Based Web Rating: A classification of Web resource with respect to their content and/or characteristics, into two distinct groups, corresponding to resources considered as appropriate (white lists) or inappropriate (black lists) for a given set of end users.

Metadata Vocabulary: A formal definition of a set of descriptors to be used for denoting the characteristics of resources (e.g., an ontology is a metadata vocabulary). Usually, metadata vocabularies are domain-specific.

Metadata-Based Web Rating: A manual or semi-automatic description of Web resources with respect to their content and/or characteristics, based on a set of descriptors defined by a *metadata vocabulary*.

Web Content Filtering: The analysis of the content and/or characteristics of Web resource with respect to the preferences expressed by end users. Such analysis is performed based on the resource classification carried out either by a *list-* or *metadata-based Web rating* approach.

Web Content Label: A formal description of the content and/or characteristics of Web resources, by using descriptors defined in one or more *metadata vocabularies*. Currently, content labels are encoded by using two W3C standards, namely, PICS and RDF/OWL.

Web Content Rating: The classification of Web resources with respect to their content and/or characteristics. Resource classification is performed by using two orthogonal strategies, namely, *list-based Web rating* and *metadata-based Web rating*.

Web Trust Mark: A third-party certification that a resource satisfies a given set of requirements (e.g., the VeriSign seal is a Web trust mark). A trust mark may be just a graphical symbol attached to the resource or even a *Web content label*.

Agent–Based Web Services

Larbi Esmahi
Athabasca University, Canada

Ylber Ramadani
Athabasca University, Canada

OVERVIEW OF WEB SERVICES TECHNOLOGY

Web services have become a significant technology in the evolution of the Web and distributed computing. Web services represent a set of related standards that allow any two applications to communicate and exchange data via the Internet. The main components of these standards are the general architecture, the delivery protocol (SOAP), the description language (WSDL), and the discovery directory (UDDI):

- **Architecture:** Web services are currently based on the triad of functionalities (Huhns, 2002).
- **Publish:** The Web services description language (WSDL) describes the services in a machine-readable form, where the names of functions, their required parameters, and their results can be specified.
- **Find:** Universal description, discovery, and integration (UDDI) gives clients, users, and businesses a way to find needed services by specifying a registry or "yellow pages" of services.
- **Bind:** Finally, the simple object access protocol (SOAP) provides the common protocol systems need to communicate with each other so that they can request services, such as to schedule appointments, order parts, and deliver information.

Simple Object Access Protocol (SOAP)

SOAP is one of the common standards used to deliver Web services. The purpose of SOAP is to enable data transfer between distributed systems. When an application communicates with a Web service, SOAP is the most commonly used standard through which data is exchanged. A SOAP message that is sent to a Web service invokes a method that is provided by that service, which means that the message actually requests that the service execute a particular task. The service uses information that is provided by the SOAP message to perform its action. If needed, the Web service can return the result back via another SOAP message.

SOAP is not the only protocol that can enable Web services. For example, XML-RPC is an older technology that provides similar functionality. It is important to mention that most major software vendors have already chosen to support SOAP over other similar technologies.

Web Services Description Language (WSDL)

An important feature of Web services is that they are self-describing. This means that every Web service is accompanied by information that enables developers to invoke that service. These descriptions typically are written in WSDL, which is an XML-based language through which a Web service can expose to other applications the methods that the service provides and how those methods can be accessed.

A WSDL document defines different types of messages a Web service can send and receive, as well as specifies the data that a calling application must provide for the Web service to perform its task. WSDL documents also provide specific technical information that informs applications about how to connect to and communicate with Web services over HTTP or another communications protocol.

Universal Description, Discovery, and Integration (UDDI)

The third major Web services standard, UDDI, enables developers and businesses to publish and locate Web services on a network. UDDI is originally designed by Microsoft, IBM, and Ariba, and it initially started as a way for companies to share information about their businesses and business processes with potential partners and affiliates (Korzeniowski, 2002). UDDI specification allows companies to describe their own services and electronic processes, discover those of other companies and also integrate others services into their systems.

AGENT-BASED SOFTWARE DEVELOPMENT

An agent-based system is a system in which the key abstraction used is that of an agent. Agent-based systems may contain a single agent (as in the case of user interface agents or software secretaries), but arguably the greatest potential lies in the application of multi-agent systems. Agent-based system is a system that enjoys the following properties:

- **Autonomy:** Agents encapsulate some state (that is not accessible to other agents), and make decisions about what to do based on this state, without the direct intervention of humans or other agents (Castelfranchi, 1995).
- **Reactivity:** Agents are situated in an environment (which may be the physical world, a user via a graphical user interface, a collection of other agents, the Internet, or perhaps many of these combined), are able to perceive this environment, and are able to respond in a timely fashion to changes that occur in it (Ferber, 1996).
- **Pro-activeness:** Agents do not simply act in response to their environment; they are able to exhibit goal-directed behavior by taking the initiative.
- **Sociability:** Agents interact with other agents (and possibly humans) using an agent communication language, and typically have the ability to engage in social activities (such as cooperative problem solving or negotiation) in order to achieve their goals (Castelfranchi, 1990).

An obvious question to ask is why agents and multi-agent systems are seen as an important new direction in software engineering. There are several reasons:

- **Natural metaphor:** Just as the many domains can be conceived of consisting of a number of interact-

ing but essentially passive objects, so many others can be conceived as interacting, active, purposeful agents. For example, a scenario currently driving a lot of research activity in the agent field is that of software agents capable of buying and selling goods via the Internet on behalf of clients. It is natural to view the software participants in such transactions as semi-autonomous agents.

- **Distribution of data or control:** For many software systems, it is not possible to identify a single point of control. Instead, overall control of the systems is distributed across a number of computing nodes, which are frequently distributed geographically. In order to make such systems work effectively, these nodes must be capable of autonomously interacting with each other. These nodes must be implemented as agents.
- **Legacy systems:** A natural way of incorporating legacy systems into modern distributed information systems is to provide another abstraction layer on top of them, which can be done by wrapping them with an agent layer that will enable them to interact with other agents.
- **Open systems:** Many systems are open in the sense that it is impossible to know at design time exactly what components the system will be comprised of, and how these components will be used to interact with each other. To operate effectively in such systems, the ability to engage in flexible autonomous decision-making is critical.

The area of Web services offers real interest to the software agent community, mainly because of similarities in system architectures, powerful tools, and the focus on issues such as security and reliability. Similarly, techniques developed in the agent research community promise to have a strong impact on this fast growing technology.

To realize the potential of agents to manage interactions with Web services, a number of research efforts are under way to bring semantics to Web service descriptions that will sit at layers above what is being offered commercially. A number of approaches have been offered to provide Web services with agent-like behavior through the use of agent wrappers. Some approaches use wrappers so that Web sources can be queried in a similar manner to databases (Buhler & Vidal, 2003).

SOFTWARE AGENTS TO THE RESCUE OF WEB SERVICES

While a Web service does not have to possess all characteristics of an agent, the Web services approach to building complex software systems bears many similarities to the engineering process of a collection of software agents.

Based on this match between agents and Web services, these later can be engineered to encompass properties such as cooperation, autonomy and other agent capabilities. Using these agent's capabilities, Web services will be able to integrate some complex functionalities such as context awareness, personalization, automatic composition, and semantic content.

Cooperation

Web services as we know them today cannot cooperate among each other without a manual (human) intervention or request. Cooperation among Web services would not be needed if all the services offered could do the job on their own without any help from other services. In reality, this is rarely the case. Let us examine a simple situation where a Web service books an airline ticket. Without cooperation, the Web service will only do what it is programmed to do, which in this case is booking a ticket. If we implement this service by using agents and their cooperative nature, we can provide a much more robust service to clients. In this example, an agent-based service could automatically request information from other agent-based services about different flights available, prices, nearby hotels and rates, car rental availability and cost, attractions, currency exchange, weather forecast for the time the client will be away, and many other services. This smart service can act as a multi-purpose broker for clients.

Autonomy

A Web service, as currently defined and used, is not autonomous. Autonomy is a characteristic of agents, and it is also a characteristic of many envisioned Internet-based applications. One of the major drawbacks of the Web services infrastructure is its lack of semantic information.

The fact that current Web services infrastructures do not support automatic Web service reconfiguration creates an infrastructure that is inflexible, brittle, and expensive to maintain.

To overcome this brittleness, Web services need more autonomy, which will let them reconfigure their interaction patterns as needed. Any increase in autonomy will let Web services react to potential changes in the environment while minimizing developer's direct intervention.

Autonomy can be achieved by using DAML-S, which is both a language and ontology for describing Web services (Martin, 2003). DAML-S attempts to close the gap between the semantic Web and current Web services.

Context Awareness

We humans are context-aware. We are able to use implicit situational information, or context, to increase our conversational bandwidth (Brown, Davies, Smith, & Steggles, 1999). This ability allows us to act in advance and anticipate other's needs based on three valuable capabilities:

- **Ontology sharing:** Humans are able to share communication languages and vocabularies.
- **Sensing:** Humans are able to perceive their environment through sensory organs.
- **Reasoning:** Humans are able to make sense out of what they have perceived based on the knowledge that they posses.

Ontology sharing, sensing, and reasoning are not only crucial to human context-awareness, but also significant to the realization of context-aware applications. Because current Web services do not posses all three capabilities, they cannot offer context-awareness. Research community has proposed several context managers that track the user as its temporal and spatial location changes. Similarly, user profiles maintain static and dynamic information about the user. Static information is pre-registered while dynamic information is learnt by studying user behavioral patterns.

Personalized Services/ Dynamic Adaptation

Personalization describes the process of using customer information in order to optimize business relationships

Figure 1. Service description with ACL process ontology

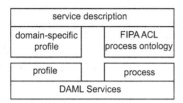

with them. Traditionally, personalization technology has focused on a service's interactions with the customer. The main goal of this technology has been to use information about a customer so as to better serve the customer by anticipating their needs, make the interaction efficient and satisfying for both parties, and build a relationship that encourages the customer to return for subsequent purchases.

Web services promise a lot of potential in providing personalization, which is tightly linked with dynamic adaptation and context-awareness. The problem is that current standards on which Web services are based do not support any type of personalization. This means that there is no way that a Web service can be aware of who is invoking it or keep track about client who invoked it in the past.

Research community has proposed several personalized service architectures that involve agent technology. For example, Kuno and Sahai (2002) came up with an architecture that uses personalization component to provide interaction between user devices and Web services.

Semantic Web

One general characterization of the technologies used for service discovery in the Web services world can be made by studying the difference between approaches, which could be considered semantically poor, and those, which are semantically rich. In the former case, services are often referred to by opaque names or function signatures, which give little or no indication of the nature of the services being managed. In the latter, however, service descriptions are more complex expressions, which are based on terms from, agreed vocabularies, and which attempt to describe the meaning of the service, rather than simply assigning a

name to it. A key component in the semantically rich approach is the ontology, the formal, agreed vocabulary whose terms are used in the construction of service descriptions. An ontology is a conceptualization of an application domain in a human understandable and machine readable form, and typically comprises the classes of entities, relations between entities and the axioms which apply to the entities which exist in that domain. Ontologies are currently a fast growing research topic, with interest from several communities, including agent-based computing, Semantic Web and knowledge management communities, because they offer a more formal basis for characterizing the knowledge assets held by software agents, Semantic Web services or organizations (Guarino & Giaretta, 1995).

The division of service descriptions into a profile and a process component, as in DAML Services, provides a means to compartmentalize Web services in a manner similar to that found in agent systems. It therefore makes sense to describe the pragmatics of message types in the process component, giving an abstract ontology of message types that corresponds to the agent communication language, while the more application-specific details of the abilities of a particular agent (expressed as constraints on the content of messages) are expressed in the profile component, as shown in Figure 1 (FIPA, Oct. 2002).

Automatic Composition of Services

The automatic composition of Web services is a recent trend that focuses on simplifying the process of composition of Web services and allowing services to automatically acquire related services so they can perform the task together (Berners-Lee, 2001). This section presents a short overview of Semantic Web centered approach for the automatic composition of Web services (Medjahed, Bouguettaya, & Elmagarmid, 2003). One of the proposed approaches builds on the semantic description framework and composability model (Medjahed, 2004). It consists of three conceptually separate phases: specification, matchmaking, and generation.

The specification phase (phase 1) enables high-level descriptions of composition requests. For that purpose, a composition specification language (CSL) is defined. CSL extends UML activity diagrams with an ontological description of the composition request (Object Management Group, 1999). Using CSL, composers specify the what part of the desired composition but will not concern themselves with the how part.

The matchmaking phase (phase 2) uses the composability model to generate composition plans that conforms to composer's specifications. One or several composition plans are generated for each composer's sub-request. By composition plan, we refer to the list of imported operations to be outsourced, their orchestration order, and the way they interact with each other (plugging operations, mapping messages, etc.) in order to implement the corresponding sub-request. In the generation phase (phase 3), detailed descriptions of the composite service are generated. The quality of composition (QoC) model is specified to assess the quality of the generated descriptions.

Web-Services, Agents, and Grid Computing

Grid technologies have evolved through at least three distinct generations: early ad hoc solutions, de facto standards based on the Globus Toolkit (GT), and the current emergence of more formal Web services based standards within the context of the open grid services architecture (OGSA) (Foster, Kesselman, Nick, & Tuecke, 2002). The grid community has participated in, and in some cases led, the development of Web services specifications that address other grid requirements. The Web services resource framework (WSRF) defines uniform mechanisms for defining, inspecting, and managing remote state, a crucial concern in many settings. WSRF mechanisms underlie work on service management (WSDM, in OASIS) and negotiation (Web services agreement, in GGF), efforts that are crucial to the grid vision of large-scale, reliable, and interoperable grid applications and services. Other relevant efforts are aimed at standardizing interfaces to data, computers, and other classes of resources.

A core unifying concept that underlies grids and agent systems is that of a service: an entity that provides a capability to a client via a well-defined message exchange (Booth et al., 2003). Within third generation grids, service interactions are structured via Web service mechanisms, and thus all entities are services. However, while every agent can be considered a service (in that it interacts with other agents and its environment via message exchanges), we might reasonably state that not every grid service is necessarily an agent (in that it may not participate in message exchanges that exhibit flexible autonomous actions).

While grid technologies provide the means for describing and grouping services, these higher level matchmaking, and discovery capabilities are not currently part of grid infrastructure (Foster et al., 2002). Fortunately, this is an area where much work has been done in the space of agents, and incorporation of this technology would help a lot to improve this situation. This integration may have an impact on how state is represented and how services are organized.

CONCLUSION

Current Web services, without any support from agents, still do provide the capability to seamlessly integrate different platforms. They provide an excellent choice for implementing distributed applications because they are architecturally neutral. Web services operate using open, text-based standards, such as WSDL, UDDI, and SOAP, which enable components written in different languages and for different platforms to communicate.

Agent technology provides several advantages, which can be easily incorporated in existing Web services. The capability of agents to be autonomous, cooperate with other agents, be aware of the context in which they are invoked, and dynamically adapt to changes in the environment are some of the main advantages that agents have compared to current Web services. Agent-based Web services would provide clients with a fast, personalized, and intelligent service. This in turn will increase the percentage of returned customers because of higher satisfaction from services provided.

Instead of focusing on Web services separately from the agent technology, both technologies should be considered together. This approach makes it simpler to implement standards that organizations will have to follow which will lead to services that can be provided and consumed seamlessly.

REFERENCES

Berners-Lee, T. (2001). *Services and semantics: Web architecture*. Retrieved January 15, 2006, from http://www.w3.org/2001/04/30-tbl

Booth, D., Haas, H., McCabe, F., Newcomer, E., Champion, M., Ferris, C., & Orchard, D. (2004). *Web services architecture.* Retrieved January 15, 2006, from W3C, http://www.w3.org/TR/ws-arch/

Brown, P. J., Davies, N., Smith, M., & Steggles, P. (1999, September). Towards a better understanding of context and context-awareness. H.-W. Gellersen (Ed.), Handheld and ubiquitous computing: First International Symposium, HUC'99, Karlsruhe, Germany (LNCS 1707, pp. 304-307).

Buhler, P. A., & Vidal, J. M. (2003). Semantic Web services as agent behaviors. In B. Burg, J. Dale, T. Finin, H. Nakashima, L. Padgham, C. Sierra, et al. (Eds.), *Agentcities: Challenges in open agent environment* (LNAI, pp. 25-31). Springer-Verlag.

Castelfranchi, C. (1995). Guarantees for autonomy in cognitive agent architecture. In M. Wooldridge, & N. R. Jennings (Eds.), *Intelligent agents: Theories, architectures, and languages* (LNAI 890, pp. 56-70). Springer-Verlag: Heidelberg, Germany.

Castelfranchi, C. (1990). Social power: A point missed in multiagent, DAI and HCI. In Y. Demazeau & J. P. Muller (Eds.), *Decentralized AI—Proceedings of the First European Workshop on Modelling Autonomous Agents in a Multi-Agent World (MAAMAW-89)* (pp. 49-62). Amsterdam, The Netherlands: Elsevier Science Publishers B.V.

Ferber, J. (1996). Reactive distributed artificial intelligence: Principals and applications. In G. O'Hare & N. Jennings (Eds.), *Foundations of distributed artificial intelligence* (pp. 287-314). Wiley Inter-Science.

FIPA. (2002, October). *FIPA communicative act library specification.* Technical Report SC00037J, Foundation for Intelligent Physical Agents. Retrieved January 15, 2006, from http://www.fipa.org/specs/fipa00037/SC00037J.html

Foster, I., & Kesselman, C. (2001). The anatomy of the grid: Enabling scalable virtual organizations. *International Journal of Supercomputer Applications, 15*(3), 200-222.

Foster, I., Kesselman, C., Nick, J. M., & Tuecke, S. (2002). Grid services for distributed systems integration. *IEEE Computer, 35*(6), 37-46.

Guarino, N., & Giaretta, P. (1995). Ontologies and knowledge bases: Towards a terminological clarification. In N. Mars (Eds.), Towards very large knowledge bases: Knowledge building and knowledge sharing (pp. 25-32), Amsterdam, NL: IOS Press.

Huhns, M. N. (2002). Agents as Web services. *IEEE Internet Computing, 6*(4), 93-95, July 2002.

Korzeniowski, P. (2002, February 4). A little slice of the UDDI pie. *eWeek*, 50-51.

Kuno, H., & Sahai, A. (2003). My agent wants to talk to your service: Personalizing Web services through agents. In B. Burg, J. Dale, T. Finin, H. Nakashima, L. Padgham, C. Sierra, et al. (Eds.), *Agentcities: Challenges in open agent environments* (pp. 25-31). Springer-Verlag.

Martin, D. (2003). DAML-S: Semantic markup for Web services. Retrieved January 15, 2006, from http://www.daml.org/services/daml-s/2001/05/daml-s.html

Medjahed, B. (2004). Semantic Web enabled composition of Web services. Dissertation submitted to the Faculty of the Virginia Polytechnic Institute and State University in partial fulfillment of the requirements for the degree of Doctor of Philosophy in Computer Science and Applications. Retrieved January 15, 2006, from http://citeseer.ist.psu.edu/medjahed04semantic.html

Medjahed, B., Bouguettaya, A., & Elmagarmid, A. (2003). Composing Web services on the Semantic Web. *The VLDB Journal, 12*(4), 333-351.

Object Management Group. (2005). *Unified modeling language specification (Version 2.0).* Retrieved January 15, 2006, from http://www.omg.org/technology/documents/formal/uml.htm

KEY TERMS

Agent-Based System: An agent-based system is a system in which the key abstraction used is that of an agent. Agent-based system enjoys the following properties: autonomy, reactivity, pro-activeness, and sociability.

Grid: Grids provide an infrastructure for federated resource sharing across trust domains. Much like the Internet on which they build, current Grids define protocols and middleware that can mediate access provided by this layer to discover, aggregate, and harness resources.

Java WSDP Registry Server: An implementation of the UDDI version 3.0. The Java WSDP Registry Server serves the purpose of testing applications written using Java API for XML Registries (JAXR).

Java WSDP: Java WSDP contains libraries for generating XML and SOAP, processing XML, accessing service registries, and calling RPC-based Web services. Java WSDP provides Java developers with a one-stop API solution for the development of Java Web service applications.

Java XML Pack: An architectural solution toolkit that is intended to ease software development by providing a set of high level APIs and reference implementations that abstract the complexities behind XML processing.

OGSA: The open grid services architecture is a set of core capabilities and behaviors that address key concerns in grid systems. OGSA uses most of Web service technologies, notably WSDL and SOAP, but it aims to be largely agnostic in relation to the transport-level handling of data upon the grid.

Ontology: An ontology can be defined as "an explicit formal specification of how to represent the objects, concepts, and other entities that are assumed to exist in some area of interest and the relationships that hold among them." (Dictionary.com, 2003). Basically, this means that an ontology is a collection of domain concepts and their relationships.

OWL-S/DAML-S: Both a communication language and ontology for describing Web services. OWL-S supplies Web service providers with a core set of markup language constructs for describing the properties and capabilities of their Web services in unambiguous, computer-interpretable form.

SOAP: SOAP is one of the common standards used to deliver Web services. Initially developed by DevelopMentor, Userland Software, and Microsoft, SOAP was conceptualized in 1998 and published as SOAP 0.9 in 1999. After several versions released from above companies, the protocol was submitted to the W3C.

UDDP: UDDI enables developers and businesses to publish and locate Web services on a network. UDDI is originally designed by Microsoft, IBM, and Ariba, but has acquired significant industry backing. UDDI version 2.0 was released in June 2001 while UDDI 3.0.1, the latest version, was released in October 2003.

WSDL: The WSDL specification emerged when Microsoft and IBM decided to combine their description technologies into a universal standard. In March 2001, Microsoft, IBM, and Ariba submitted WSDL 1.1 to the W3C. Currently the W3C is working on a version 2.0 of the language.

A

ALBA Cooperative Environment for Scientific Experiments

Andrea Bosin
Università degli Studi di Cagliari, Italy

Nicoletta Dessì
Università degli Studi di Cagliari, Italy

Maria Grazia Fugini
Politecnico di Milano, Italy

Diego Liberati
Consiglio Nazionale delle Ricerche, Italy

Barbara Pes
Università degli Studi di Cagliari, Italy

INTRODUCTION

Scientific experiments are supported by activities that create, use, communicate, and distribute information and whose organizational dynamics is similar to processes performed by distributed cooperative enterprise units. The aim of this chapter is to describe the approach undertaken in the *Advanced Lab for Bioinformatics Agencies (ALBA)* project to the design and management of cooperative scientific experiments (Bosin, Dessì, Fugini, Liberati, & Pes, 2006a). A framework is used that defines the responsibility of computational nodes in offering services and the set of rules under which each service can be accessed by networked nodes through invocation mechanisms in the service-oriented style of computing and collaborating (COOPIS, 2005).

The ambition of the ALBA project is to be able to support a wide range of service platforms useful for scientific experiments, encompassing Web service platforms, centralized and grid platforms, and specialized platforms able to execute orchestrated and coordinated workflows of activities. Another ambition is to be able to integrate new service platforms as they appear or when they need to be integrated (Estublier & Sanlaville, 2005). ALBA currently proposes a *conceptual model*, in terms of classes and their behavior/methods distributed in a networked environment. The methods, corresponding to experiment steps, are captured, sent to an orchestration layer that, analyzing the experiment context (such as

the scientific area, domain), and determines the flow of needed steps (activities) to be invoked to perform the scientific experiment. The orchestration in ALBA coordinates the needed local services pertaining to the service implementation platforms, using an abstract service machine (ALBA machine).

The aim of ALBA is to apply the technologies of services and of the grid to one of this century's major research and development efforts, that is, to the area of biological and health sciences. It has been anticipated (Knuth, 1993) that scientists will continue working on biological changes, while Adleman (1998) has argued that biological life can be equated with computation. These views suggest that future directions in computer science will significantly influence biological experiments. Modelling and data analysis are of central importance when tackling problems in medicine and human biology, as it is the biomedical researcher's aim to uncover the biological structures and mechanisms underlying biological processes. Their high complexity, their common non-linear mathematical nature, and the efforts required in collecting biomedical data makes it hard, if not often impossible, to describe biomedical mechanisms with traditional manual tools. E-science is the term usually applied to the use of advanced computing technologies to support scientists (VV AA, 2004).

High-performance computing, Internet applications, and cooperative technologies can enable computational scientists, or *e-scientists*, to study and better understand complex systems and share information in a Web based and cooperative applications style (Brown, 2003). Global-scale experimental networking initiatives have been developed in the last years: the aim is to enhance cyber-infrastructure for e-scientists through the collaborative development of networking tools, and advanced services based on the technologies of cooperation, of communication over heterogeneous platforms through peer to peer computation, interoperability objects, and through the grid (De Fanti et al., 2003; Newman et al., 2003; Taylor, 2004).

ALBA is based on *cooperative systems*, denoting Web-based information systems to be employed by users of different organizations under a common goal (COOPIS, 2005). In particular, we refer to an extension of the cooperative paradigm, referred to as *e-applications,* which is becoming more and more frequent since e-applications allow the dynamic composition of e-services (Singh & Huhns, 2005). Hence, a problem is the integrated use of heterogeneous applications and software tools that were not designed specifically to promote interaction and cooperation, but still are inherently suitable for the cooperation support. This scenario is similar to that of enterprise environments, whose progress requires large-scale collaboration and efficient access to very large data collections and computing resources (Pollock & Hodgson, 2004). We will be using the "*e*"-terms to denote elements that *collaborate* in a computer supported way ("*electronically*"). Examples are e-scientists, e-nodes, and e-services.

Assuming the *service-oriented architecture (SOA)* (Singh et al., 2005) as the enacting paradigm, the purpose of this chapter is to illustrate the application of existing cooperative, service-based models to the context of supporting distributed scientific experiments. The environment supporting a *distributed scientific processes* is regarded in ALBA as a network of cooperative e-nodes (e.g., the research laboratories, the hospitals, the analysis centres) having a local configuration and a set of shared resources, as preliminary discussed in Bosin et al., 2006a).

BACKGROUND

The genetic and molecular studies of the last three or four decades and more recently the high-throughput technologies that measure the concentration of different cell components on a global scale (for instance transcripts, proteins, and metabolites) in various physiological conditions have made available a wealth of biological data that could previously only be dreamed of (Russell, 2002; Werner, 2004; Willett, 2002). Starting from raw data, statistical methods allow the generation of molecular profiles, that is snapshots of the presence or absence of each transcript, protein, or metabolite in a given condition, giving indications on their modulation by genetic and/or environmental factors. But since only crude pictures of the regulatory circuits of most cellular processes are available (cell signalling, cell cycle, apoptosis, differentiation, transformation, etc.), it is often an unmet task to give a logic structure to molecular profiles and to gain from them predictive ability.

Technologies are thus necessary to perform dynamic and integrated studies of the gene expression (analysis of the transcriptional profile or transcriptome) of the protein expression, accumulation, and post-translational modifications (proteome), and of the metabolic profile (metabolome) (Collins, Green, Guttmacher, & Guyer, 2003; Vidal, 2001) allowing the highly parallel, genome-wide analysis of a cell population transcriptome and proteome in specific experimental conditions.

Such scientific revolution supplies new powerful tools allowing access to the information content of a cell (Brent, 2000) and facilitates an information and communication technology (ICT) approach to biomedical research.

On the side of ICT, Internet technologies and applications are the enabling concepts to obtain a distributed information system that can be employed by researchers of different organizations under a common goal. In particular, e-applications (applications executing on the network) allow the composition of services provided by different organizations. A classical approach to e-applications is based on registries, of which one of the most common is UDDI (Universal Description, Discovery, and Integration), allowing publication, and discovery of services on the Web. Other proposed architectures for e-services and workflow-based environments are presented in the literature, starting from the concept of cooperative process (Hsieh, Shi, & Yang, 2003). Methods are not yet completely defined in the literature to specify the sequence and conditions for a correct execution of distributed services. Proposals have been submitted by the W3C consortium (W3C, 2004).

Thus, in a bioinformatics post-genomic context, the capability of performing experiments across scientific distributed and trans-disciplinary groups, each one with its own expertise, will enable to improve the speed of data analysis. It will also support easier, and possibly semi-automatic, assembly of models, which incorporate data of different nature, deriving from different laboratories.

THE ADVANCED LAB FOR BIOINFORMATICS AGENCIES (ALBA)

The ALBA project aims at going beyond the existing virtual laboratory platforms—that essentially enable information sharing and distributed computations—by offering to the researchers more complex and, possibly, semi-automated ways of conducting experiments, by exploiting and composing services offered by different institutions.

More specifically, the ALBA project assumes the Internet, the Web, and the grid for experiments formalization in terms of sets of tasks to be executed on various computational nodes of a network of labs. ALBA specifies models, languages, and support tools for realizing a network infrastructure that defines the organizational responsibility of the global experiments, the framework of e-nodes and the set of rules under which each node can execute local services to be accessed by other e-nodes in order to achieve the whole experiment's results. A knowledge network is being studied to enable data and service sharing, as well as expertise and competences to allow the team of scientists to discuss representative cases or data. It exploits the approach of UDDI to make services and experiment portions available, through discovery and invocation, as services in a collaborative environment, under specific privacy rules to be agreed upon by the participants.

Setting the ALBA Cooperative Framework

In the ALBA approach, scientific experiments are modelled as e-processes that operate on, and manipulate, data sources and physical devices on the Internet. Each e-service is attributed to, and associated with, a set of specific experimental tasks; workflows are employed to control these tasks.

This modelling approach is assumed as an enactment paradigm to conceive an experiment, at least for certain application domains; an experiment is regarded as an application whose tasks can be decomposed and made executable as (granular) services individually. The decomposition is based on appropriate modelling of the experiment as a set of components that need to be mapped to distinct services. The decomposition offers good opportunities for achieving an open, scalable, and cooperative environment for scientific experiments.

The framework for modelling the experiments is a network of cooperative e-nodes having a local configuration and a set of shared resources. Services correspond to different functionalities across several research domains, and encapsulate problem solving and simulation capabilities. All services have an e-node that is responsible for offering the service and setting the rules under which the service can be accessed by other e-nodes through invocation. An experiment involves multiple e-nodes interacting with one another in order to offer or to ask for services.

The researcher has the following possibilities:

1. Selection of the experiment of interest and of the information sources he or she wants the experiment be carried on
2. Acquisition and collection of local data
3. Surveillance/monitoring of local experiments, which are part of a cooperative experiment
4. Definition of new experiments; this implies that the global workflow of the experiment must be designed
5. Inspection of remote data sources and experiment results (e.g., by mining in a data warehouses)
6. Cooperation with users of other e-nodes, for example to co-design experiments and jointly evaluate results

The local information sources collect the experimental data related to the activities assigned to the e-node. Their granularity can vary from the file to the database or data warehouse level. Parts of local information sources can be declared as public by the e-node and hence become part of the network (i.e., remotely accessible).

The local services map granular experimental tasks performed by the e-node or other local control activities. The services organize their activity on the basis of both local and network information sources. They are related to a particular experimental context by a workflow describing the tasks to be executed and the context knowledge applied to solve a problem, to enact a decision, or to achieve a goal.

Classes of Experiments

Four main classes of methodological approaches to the experiments can be identified:

- Process simulation and visualization on the already available information sources.
- Supervised or unsupervised classification of observed events without inferring any correlation nor causality such as in clustering (Garatti, Bittanti, Liberati, & Maffezzoli, 2007), and neural networks (Drago, Setti, Licitra, & Liberati, 2002).
- Machine Learning: Rule inference (Muselli & Liberati, 2002) and Bayesian Networks (Bosin, Dessì, Liberati, & Pes, 2006b) able to select and to link salient involved variables in order to understand relationships and to extract knowledge on the reliability and possibly causal relationships among related cofactors via tools like logical networks and Cart-models.
- Identification of the process dynamics (Ferrari-Trecate, Muselli, Liberati, & Morari, 2003).

Such classes, listed in increasing order of logical complexity, might have an impact on the design of the experiment and of its execution modality in terms of execution resources, even requiring recursive approaches and hence intense computation either on a single specialized node or in a grid structure.

Modeling Scientific Experiments

According to the presented approach adopted in ALBA, the overall goal of an experiment has to be decomposed into a set of tasks (the *experiment life cycle*), each accomplished by an appropriate class of e-services. From a methodological point of view, we observe that heterogeneous services can provide similar capabilities, but the chief scientist is in charge of choosing the most suitable methods to accomplish each task, that is, he is in charge of designing the workflow of the experiment.

What remains open, however, are many questions about the evaluation of such a approach. Since the realization of a distributed general-purpose scientific environment is not immediate, the evaluation effort described here involves a prototypical environment based upon emerging Web service technology and applied to the previously mentioned four classes of experiments.

The prototype we are implementing at various sites of our organizations is intended to help scientists to extract increasingly complex knowledge from data, promoting information reuse in well-defined experimental patterns. The general architecture of the prototype implements a set of basic data mining tasks as widely accessible Web services. Planning and composition of all the tasks that make up an experiment are not addressed here in detail since their best implementation is still under investigation.

The current implementation is based on the J2EE (Armstrong et al., 2004) and Oracle platforms, but the use of standard technologies (HTTP, XML, SOAP, WSDL) and languages (Java, SQL) makes it flexible and easily expandable. Data mining services are organized according to a multi-tier architecture whose abstract layers are client, service, data mining, and data repository. While the tier separation can be purely logical, our prototype allows the physical separation of tiers, where each one is located on a separated and networked hardware resource.

The client tier represents the consumers of data mining services. Clients located across the Internet (i.e., on the e-nodes of the experiment which requires the data mining service) invoke the data mining services provided by the service layer. Clients are implemented by standalone Java applications that make use of existing libraries (J2EE application client container) in charge of the low-level data preparation and communication (HTTP, SOAP, WSDL).

Executing Scientific Experiments

The ALBA architecture encompasses the following main modules for executing scientific experiments:

1. **Experiment engine:** The experiment engine interfaces with the Matlab environment and executes the code related to clustering methods. The core of the computation is a Matlab function, activated by Java code through a suitable JMatLink[1] interface. The whole Java code is exposed as a Web service. Single functions can also be isolated as

Figure 1. The ALBA modules

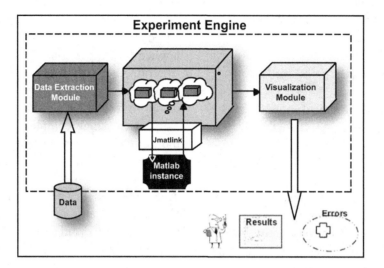

independent Web services and allocated on different nodes for reuse purposes. The creation and deploy of Web services is based on Apache Axis on the Apache Tomcat[2] Web container.

2. **Data extraction module:** Almost the totality of DNA-microrrays data is currently present in three formats, each coming in different variants. A wide choice of data is available for example on the Cancer Program Data Set of the Broad Institute, MA. The Data Extraction Module is a Java module that maps different kinds of formats into a unique, uniform representation. The module is exposed as a Web service.

3. **Visualization module:** The visualization module of ALBA deals with the suitable visualization of experiment results. The results can be returned as graphs or as textual descriptions; they are reversed into an HTML page accessible from any Web browser. Also the Visualization Module is a virtual resource and, as such, can be (re)used in subsequent experiments as an independent module to be included in the experiment workflow of other organizations.

The three modules are depicted in Figure 1. They implement an integrated environment where experiments can be executed as workflows of services on heterogeneous platforms.

FUTURE TRENDS

In future works, the classes of experiments of interest could be extended, to implement the proposed structure in specific application fields where its need looks of primary relevance, and of course to detail the sequences of interaction among actors in the specific use cases. The approach should be deeper investigated by enlarging the scope of the experiments of interest, such as, for instance, brain dynamics investigation, geo-informatics, drug discovery.

CONCLUSION

We have illustrated the elements of the ALBA project, aimed at defining models and tools for scientific cooperative services to be designed and executed in a distributed manner over the Internet. The proposed cooperative framework for distributed experiments is quite general and flexible, being adaptable to different contexts.

Given the challenge of evaluating the effects of applying emerging Web service technology to the scientific community, the evaluation performed up to now takes a flexible and multi-faceted approach: it aims at assessing task-user-system functionality and can be extended incrementally according to the continuous evolution of scientific cooperative environment.

REFERENCES

Adleman, L. (1998). Computing with DNA. *Sci. Am. 279*(2), 54-61, August.

Armstrong, E., Ball, J., Bodoff, S., Bode Carson, D., Evans, I., Ganfield, K., et al. (2004, December 16). *The J2EE 1.4 Tutorial.*

Bosin, A., Dessì, N., Fugini, M., Liberati, D., & Pes B. (2006a, September 15). Applying enterprise models to design cooperative scientific environments. In *Proceedings of the 6ᵗʰ International Conference on Enterprise and Networked Enterprises Interoperability (ENEI'2005)*, Nancy, France (LNCS 3812, pp. 281-292).

Bosin, A., Dessì, N., Liberati, D., & Pes, B. (2006b). *Learning Bayesian classifiers from gene-expression microarray data.* (LNCS 3849, pp. 297-304). Springer-Verlag,

De Fanti, T., de Laat, C., Mambretti, J., Neggers, K., & St. Arnaud, B. (2003). Translight: A global-scale LambdaGrid for e-science. *Communications of the ACM, 46*(11). New York: ACM Press.

Brent, R. (2000). Genomic biology. *Cell, 100*(1), 169-83.

Brown, M. (2003). Blueprint for the future of high-performance networking. *Communications of the ACM, 46*(11).

Collins, F. S., Green, E. D., Guttmacher, A. E., & Guyer, M. S. (2003). A vision for the future of genomics research. *Nature, 422*, 835-47.

COOPIS. (2005, November). *Proceedings 6ᵗʰ International Conference on Cooperative Information Systems (CoopIS)*, Cyprus. Springer Verlag.

Drago, G. P., Setti, E., Licitra, L., & Liberati, D. (2002). Forecasting the performance status of head and neck cancer patient treatment by an interval arithmetic pruned perceptron. *IEEE T Bio-Med Eng, 49*(8), 782-787.

Estublier, J., & Sanlaville, S. (2005, December). Extensible process support environments for Web services orchestration. *International Journal of Web Services Practices (IJWSP).*

Ferrari-Trecate, G., Muselli, M., Liberati, D., & Morari, M. (2003). A clustering technique for the identification of piecewise affine systems. *Automatica, 39*, 205-217.

Garatti, S., Bittanti, S., Liberati, D., & Maffezzoli, P. (2007). An unsupervised clustering approach for leukaemia classification based on DNA micro-arrays data. *Intelligent Data Analysis, 11*(2), 175-188.

Hsieh, Y., Shi, M., & Yang, G. (2003). CovaModeler: A multi-user tool for modelling cooperative processes. *International Journal of Computer Application in Technology 2003, 16*(2/3), 67-72.

Knuth, D. (1993). *Computer literacy interview.* Retrieved from http://www.literateprogramming.com/clb93.pdf

Muselli, M., & Liberati, D. (2002). Binary rule generation via Hamming Clustering. *IEEE Transactions on Knowledge and Data Engineering, 14*(6), 1258-1268.

Newman, H., Ellisman, M., & Orcutt, J. (2003). Data-intensive for e-science frontier research. *Communications of the ACM, 46*(11).

Pollock, J. T., & Hodgson, R. (2004). *Adaptive information: Improving business through semantic interoperability, grid computing, and enterprise integration (Wiley Series in Systems Engineering and Management).* Wiley-Interscience.

Russell, R. B. (2002, September 24). Genomics, proteomics, and bioinformatics: All in the same boat. *Genome Biology, 3*(10).

Singh, M., & Huhns, M. (2005). *Service-oriented computing: Semantics, processes, agents.* Wiley.

Taylor, I. J. (2004, August). *From P2P to Web services and grids: Peers in a client/server world.* Springer Verlag.

VV AA. (2004). Special issue on e-science. *IEEE Intelligent Systems, 19*(1).

Vidal, M. (2001). A biological atlas of functional maps. *Cell, 104*(3), 333-339.

Werner, T. (2004). Proteomics and regulomics: The yin and yang of functional genomics. *Mass Spectrometry Reviews, 23*(1), 25-33.

Willett, J. D. (2002). Genomics, proteomics: What's next? *Pharmacogenomics, 3*(6), 727-8. Review.

A

W3C. (2004, March). WS choreography model overview (Working Draft 24). Retrieved from http://www.w3.org/TR/2004/WD-ws-chor-model-20040324/

KEY TERMS

Bioinformatics: The application of the ICT tools to advanced biological problems, like transcriptomics and proteomic, involving huge amounts of data.

Clustering: Automatic aggregation of data in classes according to a given distance (usually Euclidean). It is supervised if a subset of data is used in order to learn the classification embedded rule to be applied to the rest of the data; otherwise unsupervised.

Cooperative Information Systems: Independent, federated information systems that can either autonomously execute locally or cooperate for some tasks toward a common organizational goal.

Drug Discovery: Forecasting of the properties of a candidate new drug on the basis of a computed combination of the known properties of its main constituents.

E-Experiment: Scientific experiment executed on an ICT distributed environment centred on cooperative tools and methods

E-Science: Modality of performing experiments in silico in a cooperative way by resorting to information and communication technology (ICT)

Grid Computing: Distributed computation over a grid of nodes dynamically allocated to the process in execution.

Interoperability: Possibility of performing computation in a distributed heterogeneous environment without altering the technological and specification structure at each involved node.

Web Services: Software paradigm enabling peer-to-peer computation in distributed environments based on the concept of "service" as an autonomous piece of code published in the network.

ENDNOTES

[1]   http://jmatlink.sourceforge.net/

[2]   http://tomcat.apache.org/

Analysis of TCP–Friendly Protocols for Media Streaming

A

Gábor Hosszú
Budapest University of Technology and Economics, Budapest

Dávid Tegze
Budapest University of Technology and Economics, Budapest

INTRODUCTION

This chapter presents various congestion control schemes for transport protocols together with a number of metrics for the evaluation of these protocols with special emphasis on fairness-related measures. The paper analyzes some properties of the TFRC algorithm, which provides applications with congestion control mechanisms that can be applied for streaming media. Streaming media is a delivery method of media content, which is simultaneously received by, and displayed to, the end-user while it is being delivered by the provider. It is hard to explore the various protocol mechanisms implemented in various protocols in a uniform manner; therefore the SimCast (simulator for multicast) simulator has been developed for traffic analysis of the unicast (one-to-one) and multicast (one-to-many) streams. This article evaluates some TCP and other transport protocol metrics based on results from the *SimCast* simulator (Orosz & Tegze, 2001). The simulated results are presented along with the evaluated measures. Due to spreading of traffic lacking end-to-end congestion control, congestion collapse may arise in the Internet (Floyd & Fall, 1999). This form of congestion collapse is caused by congested links that are sending packets to be dropped in the network later. The fundamental factor behind this form of congestion collapse is the absence of end-to-end feedback. On the one hand, an *unresponsive flow* fails to reduce its offered load at a router in response to an increased packet drop rate, and on the other hand, a *disproportionate-bandwidth flow* uses considerably more bandwidth than other flows in time of congestion. In order to achieve accurate multicast traffic simulation—being not so TCP-friendly yet—the effects of the flow control of the TCP protocol should be determined (Postel, 1981).

However, there are many different kinds of TCP and other unicast transport protocol implementations with various flow control mechanisms, which make this investigation rather difficult (He et al., 2005).

Up to now, a lot of comparisons have been done. For example, Wang et al., reviewed the TCP-friendly congestion control schemes in the Internet (Wang et al., 2001). They differentiated two groups of the TCP-friendly congestion control algorithms as follows: (1) *end-to-end* and (2) *hop-by-hop* congestion control mechanisms. The end-to-end mechanisms are grouped into (i) AIMD-based schemes (AIMD: additive increase multiplicative decrease) with the window- and rate-adaptation schemes, (ii) modeling-based schemes, including equation-based congestion control schemes and the so-called model-based congestion schemes, and (iii) a combination of AIMD-based and modeling-based mechanisms. Wang's classification is mostly used in our discussion, too.

Yu proposes another important approach to the survey on TCP-friendly congestion control protocols for media streaming applications (Yu, 2001), in which several TCP-friendly congestion control protocols were discussed via a comparison of many important issues that determine the performance and *fairness* of a protocol.

It is an important advantage of the simulator *SimCast* that it implements recent congestion control mechanisms. In this way, the simulator is capable of the examination of cooperation among different TCP protocol entities, or various other transport level protocols (Shalunov, 2005).

This chapter presents the basic congestion control mechanisms of TCP, then it demonstrates the way media streams control their sending rate to avoid congestion. After this, a couple of metrics for various transport layer attributes are defined. Then some fairness measures of concurrently running flows are evaluated, based on sending rate traces of simulated TCP and TFRC protocol entities. Lastly, conclusions are drawn, and work to be done identified.

OVERVIEW OF THE TCP CONGESTION CONTROL

The Basic Control Mechanisms

TCP congestion control is based on the use of a *sliding window*. Its main concept is that the sender can only send a limited number of unacknowledged segments to the receiver (Van Jacobson, 1988). The number of segments to be sent without receiving acknowledgement is determined by the *congestion window* (**Cwnd**). The *Cwnd* is given in bytes, which is the total length of the segments that belong to the congestion window (Floyd, 2001).

TCP congestion control is based on *additive increase multiplicative decrease (AIMD)*, halving the *Cwnd* for every window containing a packet loss, and increasing the *Cwnd* by roughly one segment size per **round trip time** (**RTT**) otherwise.

Retransmit timers are of fundamental importance in highly congested systems, which have exponential backoff of the retransmit timer when a retransmitted packet itself is dropped.

The *slow-start* mechanism is for initial probing of available bandwidth, instead of initially sending it at a high rate that might not be supported by the network (Stevens, 1997). At the beginning of the *Slow-Start* state, the *Cwnd* equals one segment size. During *slow-start,* the *Cwnd* is increased with a squared function in time.

ACK-clocking is the mechanism that uses the arrival of acknowledgements at the sender to clock out the transmission of new data.

CONGESTION CONTROL OF MEDIA STREAMS

TCP-friendly rate control (TFRC) is proposed for equation-based congestion control that explicitly adjusts the sending rate as a function of the measured rate of loss events (Handley et al., 2003). The TFRC

is a receiver-based congestion control mechanism, with calculation of the loss event rate performed in the data receiver rather than in the data sender. This is appropriate for an application where the sender is a large server handling many concurrent connections. Therefore, this is suitable as a building block for multicast congestion control. The TFRC is not a complete protocol; it is a congestion control mechanism only. It could be implemented in a transport protocol like *real-time transport protocol* (Schulzrinne, 1996) or in an application incorporating end-to-end congestion control at the application level.

TFRC uses the following throughput equation directly to determinate the allowed sending rate as a function of the loss event rate and the RTT. This equation is a simplified version of the throughput equation for the Reno-TCP (Padhye et al., 1998).

$$T = \frac{s}{R \cdot \sqrt{\frac{2bp}{3}} + t_{RTO}\left(3\sqrt{\frac{3bp}{8}}\right)p\left(1 + 32p^2\right)}, \qquad (1)$$

where T is the transmit rate in bytes/second, s is the packet size in bytes, R is the RTT in seconds, p is the loss event rate, t_{RTO} is the TCP retransmission timeout value in seconds, and b is the number of packets acknowledged by a single TCP ACK. For simplicity, $t_{RTO} = 4R$ and $b = 1$ in most cases, however, if the competing TCP implementations use "*delayed ACKs*," $b = 2$ is a more appropriate value.

During operation, the TFRC receiver measures the loss event rate and feeds this information back to the data sender. Then the sender uses timestamp fields in feedback messages to measure the RTT and feeds these measured values into the throughput equation (1) to get the acceptable transmit rate. The sender then adjusts its transmit rate to match the calculated rate.

The TFRC is reasonably fair when competing for bandwidth with TCP flows, but has a much lower variation of throughput over time compared with TCP, making it more suitable for applications such as streaming media, where a relatively smooth sending rate is of importance. The flow is "reasonably fair" if its sending rate is generally within a factor of two of the sending rate of a TCP flow under comparable conditions (Handley et al., 2003).

The drawback of smoother throughput than TCP while competing fairly for bandwidth is that TFRC responds slower to changes in available bandwidth than TCP. Thus, TFRC should only be used when the application has a requirement for smooth throughput, in particular, avoiding TCP's halving of the sending rate in response to a single packet drop.

METRICS OF THE CONGESTION CONTROL

In order to study the advantages and downsides of existing congestion control mechanisms, we need some well-defined metrics to classify the properties of transport layer protocols. We also need to identify the relationships between the effects of these mechanisms, which makes it easier to do some trade-offs in the design phase of transport protocols. Such trade-offs lie, for example, between the throughput and the delay. Some metrics are defined on the aggregate traffic and some are per-flow metrics.

Different applications have different needs, so they should choose the most appropriate transport protocol. Bulk data transfer applications need high throughput, and interactive traffic requires low delay. In the case of wireless communication, robustness has a very important role. Various applications often pose conflicting requirements for the underlying transport protocol. In our survey, we focus on the fairness properties of different transport layer protocol entities. There are several interpretations of the term fairness in the literature, since one could keep various goals in mind; in this paper we only demonstrate the most important approaches.

One can consider fairness between flows of the same type, and between flows of different protocols. Since the most prevalent source of Internet traffic is the various types of TCP, the fairness of newly designed transport protocols should be compared with TCP to prove their TCP-friendliness.

There are a number of different fairness measures. A loose definition of fairness says that the long-term mean sending rate of a protocol is approximately the same as that of TCP under the same conditions of round-trip time and packet loss rate. There are some fairness-related properties of transport protocols. One such property is *smoothness*, which is the extent of sending rate variations over time for a particular flow in a stationary environment; another isr *responsiveness,* the deceleration speed of the protocol-sending rate when there is a step increase of network congestion.

Aggressiveness of a flow is defined as the acceleration of the protocol-sending rate to improve network utilization when there is a step increase in the available bandwidth.

There are a number of strict measures of protocol fairness. These include: *Pareto-efficiency, max-min fairness*, the *fairness index*, and the *product measure*. Some of these terms define network-based metrics; others are per-flow measures.

A resource allocation is said to be *Pareto-efficient* if all resources are consumed in the sense that the bit rate allocated to one flow cannot be increased without decreasing the bit rate allocated to another flow. This is an important term, since most of the common fairness definitions are also *Pareto-efficient*.

The principle of *max-min fairness* is to allocate network resources in such a way that the bit rate of a flow cannot be increased without decreasing the bit rate of a flow having a smaller bit rate. In this way, *max-min fairness* maximizes the allocation of the most poorly-treated sessions. *Max-min fairness* is a unique allocation of resources that can be produced by the water-filling procedure:

- At first sending, rate of all flows are set to zero
- Increase the bit rate of all flows at the same speed until the bit rate of some flows is limited by the capacity of a network link; fix the bit rate of these flows
- Repeat previous step on non-fixed flows until no sending rate could be increased

Note that *Max-min fairness* shows the *Pareto-efficient* property.

The above fairness definitions could be used to determinate a fair allocation of network resources, given the link capacities of the network. The below-mentioned methods will show how the measured or simulated sending rate trace data of different protocol entities could be used to evaluate the fairness of some concurrently running flows. Some methods qualify the steady-state behavior of protocols; others examine the reaction to some transient event.

In order to evaluate the *smoothness* of a flow, we examine sending rate traces in the steady state. To quantify the smoothness, we can calculate the coefficient of variation for a particular flow against the ideally fair bandwidth allocation. The value of **coefficient of variation (CoV)** depends on measurement timescale:

The longer the timescale, the smaller the CoV is. For the calculation of short-term fairness sending rate, traces of the round trip time timescale are used, however the long-term fairness is determined by multiple round-trip-times long sending rate traces.

Some methods use the *fairness index,* which is defined in equation (2). This metric qualifies the fairness of competing flows, not the time series of bandwidth samples:

$$F = \frac{(\sum x_i)^2}{K \sum x_i^2}$$

(2)

where K is the number of samples and x_i is the sending rate sample of the i-th flow.

During our simulations, we experienced that increased loss rates resulted in worse smoothness and fairness values for a particular flow.

Other evaluation tools are concerned with the transient behavior of competing flows; aggressiveness of a flow could be estimated as the time needed to utilize newly available bandwidth for a flow; conversely, responsiveness could be characterized as the time needed to halve the sending rate in response to durable network congestion.

SIMULATION RESULTS

This simulation demonstrates the concurrent execution of TCP-friendly flows. The competing flows are of type TCP-Tahoe and TFRC. The sending rate traces of the simulated protocol entities allow us to evaluate some fairness-related measures.

Figure 1 shows the network topology used in our simulations. The network endpoints are connected by two LAN links and a WAN link. In the course of

the simulations, we managed bulk data transfer from host *H02* to *H01* using simple file transfer application protocols on the top of TCP. We implemented TFRC as a transport layer protocol, and we operated simple streaming applications over it between the same hosts with the same data transfer direction as in the case of TCP simulations. We applied a *drop tail* queuing policy and we generated congestion events using *Bernoulli* packet drops on the network links to simulate high multiplexing environments. In the *Bernoulli loss model,* each packet is lost with probability p, which is independent and identically distributed (i.i.d.) for all packets. We consider this model as a representative for high multiplexing environments. By a high multiplexing environment, we mean that loss is relatively insensitive to the sending rate of the flow under study. Our TFRC implementation applies the *WALI algorithm* (Floyd et al., 2000) for *loss event* calculation.

Table 1 shows a couple of interesting fairness related measures of the examined flows. The granularity of the bandwidth logger was set to two seconds for both flows. We set the *Bernoulli* packet drop rate of the WAN link in the topology to seven percent. The standard deviation values of the sending rate samples show clearly that TFRC has a much lower variation of bandwidth. The values of flows' calculated coefficient of variation denotes that the large part of the sending rate variation is caused by TCP, while TFRC remains relatively smooth. The *fairness index* value in Table 1 is calculated as the average of fairness indices calculated using equation (2) for each traced time interval. The equation produces fairness values between 0 and 1, where perfectly fair bandwidth allocation gives the value of one for fairness index.

In the subsequent simulation, all parameters remained unchanged except that the probability of the Bernoulli losses was increased to 10 percent. Figure 2 plots the fairness indices for the both simulations as the function of time. The figure shows that higher loss

Figure 1. Simulation topology

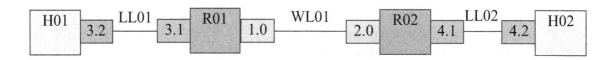

Table 1. Some fairness metrics of the simulated flows

Metrics of fairness of data flows	Evaluated results
Standard deviation of TCP sending rate samples	28.577
Standard deviation of TFRC sending rate samples	1719.981
CoV TCP-average	1126822.157
CoV TFRC-average	193461.058
Average fairness index	0.958

Figure 2. Time function of fairness indices

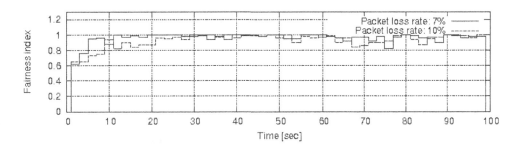

rate results in slower convergence of flows to a fair state, and even in the steady-state, the bandwidth-share remains somewhat less fair than in the first simulation; the average of fairness indices in this simulation was 0.927, which is slightly worse than in the first simulation scenario.

CONCLUSION AND FUTURE DEVELOPMENTS

Our primary goal is the development of an evaluation framework, which can be used to classify various transport layer protocols from the TCP-Friendliness standpoint. The qualifying process should provide us with the maximum amount of information about the investigated protocols running the minimum amount of simulation.

Our simulations confirmed that TFRC is more suitable for multimedia applications than TCP implementations because of its smoother sending rate, and it is also justified that TFRC can be stated as TCP-friendly because the examined protocols' long-term throughput

and other relevant parameters do not differ significantly from that of TCP. For this reason, the protocols implemented in *SimCast* can be used as the basis of such an evaluation framework.

Future development plans of the simulator include dynamic fine-tuning of TFRC protocol entities to adapt to the changing network conditions. We also intend to create real network traffic using the current simulator code. In this way we can execute our protocol implementations with real world transport protocols in parallel. This makes it possible to fit our model to real protocol entities.

REFERENCES

Floyd, S. (April, 2001). A report on some recent developments in TCP congestion control. *IEEE Communications Magazine, 39*(4), 84-90.

Floyd, S., & Fall, K. (1999). Promoting the use of end-to-end congestion control in the Internet. In *Proceedings of IEEE/ACM Trans. Networking* (Vol. 7, pp. 458-472).

Floyd, S., & Henderson, T. (1999). *The NewReno modification to TCP's fast recovery algorithm.* IETF RFC 2582.

Floyd, S., Handley, M., Padhye, J., & Widmer, J. (2000, August). Equation-based congestion control for unicast applications. In *Proceedings of ACM SIGCOMM 2000*, 34-56. Stockholm, Sweden: ACM Press.

Grieco, L.A., & Mascolo, S., (2004). Intraprotocol fairness and interprotocol friendliness of TFRC congestion control algorithm. *IEEE Journal, 40*, 354-355.

Handley, M., et al. (Jan. 2003). *TCP friendly rate control (TFRC): Protocol specification.* IETF RFC 3448.

He, E., Vicat-Blanc Primet, P., & Welzl, M. (2005) A survey of transport protocols other than "standard" TCP. *Global Grid Forum Document GFD-I.055,* Data Transport Research Group.

Li, Q., and Chen, D. (2005, September 23-26). Analysis and improvement of TFRC congestion control mechanism. In *Proceedings of the Conference on Wireless Communications, Networking and Mobile Computing (WiCOM 2005)*, Vol. 2, 1149-1153. Wuhan, China.

Mathis, M., Mahdavi, J., Floyd, S., & Romanow, A. (1996). *TCP selective acknowledgement options.* IETF RFC 2018.

Orosz, M., & Tegze, D. (2001, September 19-20). The SimCast multicast simulator. In *Proceedings of the International Workshop on Control & Information Technology, IWCI'01*, Ostrava, Czech Republic (pp. 66-71).

Padhye, J., et al. (1998). Modeling TCP throughput: A simple model and its empirical validation. In *Proceedings of ACM SIGCOMM '98*, Vancouver (pp. 303-314).

Postel, J.B. (Ed.). (1981, September). *Transmission control protocol, DARPA Internet program, protocol specification.* IETF RFC 793.

Schulzrinne, H., et al. (1996, January). *RTP: A transport protocol for real-time applications.* IETF RFC 1889.

Shalunov, S., Dunn, L.D., Gu, Y., Low, S., Rhee, I., Senger, S., et al. (2005). *Design space for a bulk transport tool.* Internet2 Bulk Transport Working Group Report.

Stevens, W. (1997, January). *TCP slow start, congestion avoidance, fast retransmit, and fast recovery algorithms.* IETF RFC 2001.

Van Jacobson (1988). TCP congestion avoidance control, In *Proceedings of ACM SIGCOMM*, Stanford (Vol 18, No. 4, pp. 314-329).

Wang, Q., et al. (2001). TCP-friendly congestion control schemes in the Internet, In *Proceedings of 2001 Inernational. Conference on Information Technology and Information Networks (ICII2001)* (Vol. B, pp. 205-210). Beijing, China.

Yu, B. (2001). *Survey on TCP-friendly congestion control protocols for media streaming applications.* Retrieved 2 August, 2007 from from http://cairo.cs.uiuc.edu/~binyu/writing/binyu-497-report.pdf

KEY TERMS

Congestion Control: A mechanism that can be built into a protocol. Its main goal is to help the data transmission avoid the buffer overflow in the network routers.

Data Stream Applications: The class of large receiver set, low bandwidth real-time data applications.

Goodput: The bandwidth of the useful packets at the receiver side, which is also called *the effective receiving rate*.

Max-Min Fairness: The principle of max-min fairness allocates network resources in such a way that the bit rate of a flow cannot be increased without decreasing the bit rate of a flow having a smaller bit rate.

Pareto Efficiency: A resource allocation is said to be Pareto efficient if all resources are consumed in the sense that the bit rate allocated to one flow cannot be increased without decreasing the bit rate allocated to another flow.

Port Handling: From the network, the processes running in a computer that can be addressed with an integer number between 0...65535 is called a port. Some port numbers are mapped steadily to important applications. They are called *well-known port numbers*. E.g., the Web server typically uses the port number 80.

Reliability: The improved quality of data transmission. Different types of reliability exist, including data accuracy, or real-time delivery.

Round Trip Time (RTT): The time period that is necessary for sending a packet from the sender to the receiver and for sending it from the receiver back to the sender.

TCP (Transmission Control Protocol): Widely used for bulk data transmission. It is suitable for file transfer, but not for streaming media transmission.

Transport Layer: This is an abstraction; the protocol belonging to the transport layer is responsible for the *port handling* and sometimes the improved reliability of the transmission.

Autonomic Computing

Kevin Curran
University of Ulster, Ireland

Maurice Mulvenna
University of Ulster, Ireland

Chris Nugent
University of Ulster, Ireland

Matthias Baumgarten
University of Ulster, Ireland

INTRODUCTION

Modern networks offer end-to-end connectivity however, the increasing amount of traditional offered services may still not fulfill the requirements of ever demanding distributed applications and must therefore be enriched by some form of increased intelligence in the network. This is where the promise of autonomous systems comes into play. Paul Horn of IBM Research first suggested the idea of autonomic computing on October 15, 2001 at the *Agenda* Conference in Arizona. The need centers around the exponential growth of networking complexity. Autonomous systems are capable of performing activities by taking into account the local environment and adapting to it. No planning is required hence autonomous systems simply have to make the best of the resources at hand. Locality in this scenario is no longer geographical but rather the information and applications on the boundary of the autonomic communicating element, which may be distributed over a wide area. The most common definition of an autonomic computing system is one, which can control the functioning of computer applications and systems without input from the user, in the same way that the autonomic nervous system regulates body systems without conscious input from the individual. Thus, we attempt here to more clearly identify the need for autonomous systems, their architecture, the path of evolution from traditional network elements, and the future of such systems.

BACKGROUND

Autonomous systems are capable of performing activities by taking into account the local environment and adapting to it. No planning is required hence autonomous systems simply have to make the best of the resources at hand. Locality in this scenario is no longer geographical but rather the information and applications on the boundary of the autonomic communicating element, which may be distributed over a wide area. The key aim of autonomous communication systems is that they exhibit self-awareness properties, in particular self-contextualisation, self-programmability and self-management (i.e., self-optimisation, self-organisation, self-configuration, self-adaptation, self-healing, and self-protection). One of the main drivers indeed behind autonomous computing is that industry is finding that the cost of technology is decreasing, yet IT costs are not. Autonomic systems are designed to be self-protecting, able to detect hostile or intrusive acts as they occur and deal autonomously with them in real time. They can take actions to make themselves less vulnerable to unauthorized access. Self-protected systems will anticipate problems based on constant reading taken on the system, as well as being able to actively watch out for detailed warnings of attacks from internet sources. They will take steps from such reports to avoid or mitigate them. These characteristics previously stated all come to together to help a system run more efficiently while reducing costs due to less human input. An autonomic system for instance can help IT administrators deal with software installation by being aware of what is needed to run and to install those components, which need installing. It should obviously also be aware of what applications are installed on the system already and how to avoid or resolve any conflicts that would arise once installed. This type of system would constantly monitor itself for problems and should a problem arise, then the fault is sought and corrected. The Internet with its multiple standards and interconnection of components such as decoders, middleware, databases, and so forth, deserves more than a plug, try, and play mentality. A key goal for the next generation Internet is to provide a principled means of allowing the underlying infrastructure to be adapted throughout its lifetime with the minimum of effort, thus, the principles of autonomic computing provides a means of coping with change in a computing system as it allows access to the implementation in a principled manner. We attempt here to more clearly identify the need for autonomous systems, the role of middleware, and the future of such systems.

AUTONOMIC COMPUTING

The Internet is comprised of close to a billion daily users, each of which can potentially communicate. Hosts can be anything from desktop computers and WWW servers, to non-traditional computing devices such as mobile phones, surveillance cameras, and Web TV. The distinction between mobile phones and personal device assistants (PDA's) has already become blurred with pervasive computing being the term coined to describe the tendency to integrate computing and communication into everyday life. New technologies for connecting devices like wireless communication and high bandwidth networks make the network connections even more heterogeneous. Additionally, the network topology is no longer static, due to the increasing mobility of users. Ubiquitous computing is a term often associated with this type of networking (Tanter, Vernaillen, & Piquer, 2002). Thus, a flexible framework is necessary in order to support such heterogeneous end-systems and network environments.

The Internet is built on the DARPA protocol suite transmission control protocol/Internet protocol (TCP/IP), with IP as the enabling infrastructure for higher-level protocols such as TCP and the user datagram protocol (UDP). The Internet protocol is the basic protocol

of the Internet that enables the unreliable delivery of individual packets from one host to another. It makes no guarantees about whether or not the packet will be delivered, how long it will take, or if multiple packets will arrive in the order they were sent. Protocols built on top of this add the notions of connection and reliability. One reason for IP's tremendous success is its simplicity. The fundamental design principle for IP was derived from the "end-to-end argument," which puts "smarts" in the ends of the network—*the source and destination network hosts*—leaving the network "core" dumb. IP routers at intersections throughout the network need do little more than check the destination IP address against a forwarding table to determine the "next hop" for an IP datagram (where a datagram is the fundamental unit of information passed across the Internet). However, the protocols underlying the Internet were not designed for the latest generations of networks especially those with low bandwidth, high error losses, and roaming users, thus many "fixes" have arisen to solve the problem of efficient data delivery (Saber & Mirenkov, 2003). Mobility requires adaptability meaning that systems must be location-aware and situation-aware taking advantage of this information in order to dynamically reconfigure in a distributed fashion (Solon, Mc Kevitt, & Curran, 2005). However, situations, in which a user moves an end-device and uses information services can be challenging. In these situations, the placement of different cooperating parts is a research challenge. The heterogeneity is not only static but also dynamic as software capabilities, resource availability, and resource requirements may change over time. The support system of a nomadic user must distribute, in an appropriate way, the current session among the end-user system, network elements, and application servers. In addition, when the execution environment changes in an essential and persistent way, it may be beneficial to reconfigure the co-operating parts. The redistribution or relocation as such is technically quite straightforward but not trivial. On the contrary, the set of rules that the detection of essential and persistent changes is based on and indeed the management of these rules is a challenging research issue which to date has not been solved by the traditional "smarts in the network" approach (Chen, Ge, Kurose, & Towsley, 2005).

A bare bones traditional communication system can be seen as consisting of three layers, as illustrated in Figure 1. End systems inter-communicate through layer T, the transport infrastructure. The service of layer

Figure 1. 3 layer model

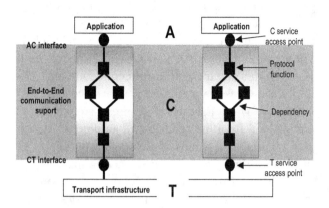

T is a generic service corresponding to layer 2, 3, or 4 services in the OSI reference model. In layer C, the end-to-end communication support adds functionality to the services in layer T. This allows the provision of services at the layer A for distributed applications (A-C interface). Layer C is decomposed into protocol functions, which encapsulate typical protocol tasks such as error and flow control, encryption and decryption, presentation coding, and decoding among others. A protocol graph is an abstract protocol specification, where independence between protocol functions is expressed in the protocol graph. If multiple T services can be used, there is one protocol graph for each T service to realize a layer C service. Protocol functions (modules) can be accomplished in multiple ways, by different protocol mechanisms, as software or hardware solutions with each protocol configuration in a protocol graph being instantiated by one of its modules. Layering is a form of information hiding where a lower layer presents only a service interface to an upper layer, hiding the details of how it provides the service. A traditional network element such as the previous could form part of the architecture of an adaptable middleware. Here the flexible protocol system could allow the dynamic selection, configuration, and reconfiguration of protocol modules to dynamically shape the functionality of a protocol in order to satisfy application requirements or adapt to changing service properties of the underlying network. Some uses that these dynamic stacks may be used for could include increasing throughput where environmental conditions are analyzed and heuristics applied to decide if change would bring about optimal performance (Bradshaw, Kurose, Shenoy, & Towsley, 2005).

Many such dynamically reconfigurable conventional middleware systems exist (Becker, Schiele, Gubbels, & Rothermel, 2003; Blair, Coulson, & Andersen, 2001; Curran & Parr, 2004; Gill et al., 2004), and which enable systems to adapt their behavior at runtime to different environments and applications requirements. The resource restrictions on mobile devices prohibit the application of a full-fledged middleware system therefore one traditional approach is to restrict existing systems and provide only a functional subset (e.g., OMG, 2002; Schmidt, 2004), which leads to different programming models or a subset of available interoperability protocols. Another option is to structure the middleware in multiple components, such that unnecessary functionality can be excluded from the middleware dynamically. One such example is the Universally Interoperable Core UIC (Roman, Kon, & Campbell, 2001), which is based on a micro-kernel that can be dynamically extended to interact with various middleware solutions but the protocol is determined prior to communication and dynamic reconfiguration is not possible. However, even in the case of most existing dynamically reconfigurable middleware, which concentrate on powerful reconfiguration interfaces—the domain that they are applied in is simply too narrow (e.g., multimedia streaming). It seems that *future proofing* for future uses is not built in (Fry & West, 2004). It must be noted that the authors are not claiming that this is trivial rather that an alternative approach for handling change in complex networks seems called for.

Autonomic computing systems will manage complexity, possess self-knowledge, continuously tune themselves, adapt to unpredictable conditions, prevent and recover from failures, and provide a safe environment (Murch, 2004):

- The autonomic nervous system frees our conscious mind from self management and is the fundamental point of autonomic computing thus "freeing" up system administrators and normal users from the details of system operation and maintenance. If a program can deal with these aspects during normal operation, it is a lot closer to providing users with a machine what runs 24x7 and its optimal performance. The autonomic system will change anything necessary so as to keep running at optimum performance, in the face of changing workloads, demands and any other external conditions it faces. It should be able to cope with software and or hardware failures whether they are due to an unforeseen incident or malicious acts.

- Installing and configuring systems can be extremely time consuming, complex, and can be open to human error no matter how qualified the administrator is. Autonomic systems could configure themselves automatically by incorporate new components seamlessly (Tanter et al., 2002).
- Modern systems may contain large amounts of different variables/options/parameters, which a user can change to optimize performance. Few people, however, know how to use these and even fewer know how to get them exactly right to get 100% performance. An autonomic system could continually monitor and seek ways of improving the operation efficiency of the systems in both performance and/or cost. It is faster at this than a person and is able to dedicate more time to finding ways of improving performance.
- Autonomic systems are designed to be self-protecting, able to detect hostile or intrusive acts as they occur, and deal autonomously with them in real time. They can take actions to make themselves less vulnerable to unauthorized access. Self-protected systems will anticipate problems based on constant reading taken on the system, as well as being able to actively watch out for detailed warnings of attacks from internet sources. They will take steps from such reports to avoid or mitigate them (Murch, 2004).

The characteristics stated above all come to together to help a system run more efficiently while reducing costs due to less human input.

The IBM autonomic computing toolkit[1] enables developers to add self-configuring and other autonomic capabilities to their software. The autonomic computing toolkit is a collection of technologies, tools, scenarios, and documentation that is designed for users wanting to learn, adapt, and develop autonomic behavior in their products and systems. Microsoft aims to develop self-healing, autonomic computing under its Visual Studio product line, and presently claim to be in the process of software releases designed to reduce data centre complexity.

FUTURE TRENDS

As systems become more advanced, they tend to become more complex and increasingly difficult to maintain. To complicate matters further, there has been and for the foreseeable future, will be a scarcity of IT professionals to install, configure, optimize, and maintain these complex systems. Therefore, the aim of autonomic computing is to reduce the amount of maintenance needed to keep systems working as efficiently as possible, as much of the time as possible (i.e., it is about making systems self-managing). Future trends in network design, which will support the need for more "open networks," include the increasing popularity of component architectures that reduce development time and offer freedom with choice of components. This allows alternative functionality to be deployed in various scenarios to combat differing QoS needs. Another trend is introspection, which provides run-time system information allowing applications to examine their environment and act accordingly. Autonomic computing systems can provide an infrastructure for building adaptive applications that can deal with drastic environment changes. The Internet with its various standards and interconnection of components such as decoders, middleware, and databases deserve more than a plug, try, and play mentality. The introduction of mobility will also increase the complexity due to the proliferation in possible actions. A key goal for next generation networks is to provide a principled means of allowing the underlying infrastructure to be adapted throughout its lifetime with the minimum of effort thus the principles of autonomic computing provides a means of coping with change in a computing system as it allows access to the implementation in a principled manner

CONCLUSION

Modern networks offer end-to-end connectivity, however, the increasing amount of traditional offered services may still not fulfill the requirements of ever demanding distributed applications and must therefore be enriched by some form of increased intelligence in the network. This is where the promise of autonomous systems comes into play. One of the main drivers indeed behind autonomous computing is that Industry is finding that the cost of technology is decreasing, yet IT costs are not. Autonomous systems are capable of performing activities by taking into account the local environment and adapting to it. The key aim of autonomous communication systems is that they exhibit self-awareness properties, in particular self-contextualisation, self-programmability and self-management (i.e., self-optimisation, self-organisation, self-configuration, self-adaptation, self-healing, and self-protection). Autonomic computing refers to the ability of a system to self-diagnose without the need for operator intervention. Traditionally, systems management has focused on monitoring and measurement, with an emphasis on end-to-end management but autonomic computing focuses on the self-managing capabilities of the infrastructure itself.

REFERENCES

Becker C., Schiele, G., Gubbels, H., & Rothermel, K. (2003, July). BASE—A micro-broker-based middleware for pervasive computing. In *Proceedings of the IEEE International Conference on Pervasive Computing and Communication (PerCom)*, Fort Worth.

Blair, G. S., Coulson, G., & Andersen, A. (2001). The design and implementation of OpenORB version 2. *IEEE Distributed Systems Online Journal, 2*(6), 45-52. Bradshaw, M., Kurose, J., Shenoy, P., & Towsley, D. (2005, June). Online scheduling in modular multimedia systems with stream reuse. In *Proceedings of NOSSDAV*, Skamania, Washington.

Chen, W., Ge, Z., Kurose, J. , & Towsley, D. (2005). Optimizing event distribution in publish/subscribe systems in the presence of policy-constraints and composite events. *IEEE ICNP 2005.*

Curran, K., & Parr, G. (2004, October 20-22). Introducing IP domain flexible middleware stacks for multicast multimedia distribution in heterogeneous environments. In *MATA 2004—International Workshop on Mobility Aware Technologies and Applications*, Florianopolis, Brazil (LNCS, pp. 313). Springer-Verlag Heidelberg.

Fry, G., & West, R. (2004, May 25-28). Adaptive routing of QoS constrained media streams over scalable overlay topologies. In *Tenth IEEE Real-Time and Embedded Technology and Applications Symposium*, Le Royal Meridien, Toronto, Canada.

Gill, C. M., Gossett, J., Corman, D. P., Loyall, J. E., Schantz, R., Atighetchi, M., et al. (2004, May 25-28). Integrated adaptive qos management in middleware: An empirical case study. Submitted to the *Tenth Real-Time Technology and Application Symposium*, Le Royal Meridien, Toronto, Canada.

Murch, R. (2004). *Autonomic computing*. IBM Press, Prentice Hall PTR.

Object Management Group. (2002, July). The common object request broker: Architecture and specification, Revision 3.0.

Roman, M., Kon, F., & Campbell, R. (2001, July). Reflective middleware: From your desk to your hand. *IEEE Distributed Systems Online Journal*. Special issue on Reflective Middleware.

Saber, M., & Mirenkov, N. (2003, September 24-26). A multimedia programming environment for cellular automata systems. In *Nineth International Conference on Distributed Multimedia Systems (DMS'2003)*, Florida International University Miami, Florida, USA (pp. 104-110).

Solon, A., McKevitt, P., & Curran, K. (2005, February). TeleMorph: Bandwidth determined mobile multimodal presentation. *Information Technology and Tourism, 7*(1), 33-47.

Tanter, E., Vernaillen, M., & Piquer, J. (2002). Towards transparent adaptation of migration policies. Position paper submitted to *EWMOS 2002*, Chile (pp. 34-39).

KEY TERMS

Autonomic: Relating to, or controlled by the autonomic nervous system.

Closed Control Loop: This technique stems from process control theory. A closed control loop in a self-managing system monitors some resource and autonomously tries to keep its parameters within a desired range.

Distributed Computing: A system where tasks are divided among multiple computers rather than having all processes originating from one main central computer. Client/server systems are one type of distributed computing. It can also be described as a system in which services are provided by teams of computers collaborating over a network.

Grid Computing: A computing model that provides the ability to perform higher throughput computing by taking advantage of many networked computers to model a virtual computer architecture that is able to distribute process execution across a parallel infrastructure. GRID Computing is basically taking a number of inexpensive personal computers and connecting them via a network to build a supercomputer, which can utilize the idle processing time on each machine to carry out tasks that would have previously required an expensive mainframe. One comparison that is often used to describe a computational GRID is that of the electrical GRIDs responsible for providing electricity.

Pervasive Computing: This is the trend toward increasingly ubiquitous connected computing devices in the environment and particularly, wireless technologies and the Internet. Pervasive computing devices are not broadly speaking personal computers as we tend to think of them, but rather small (often micro like)—electronic mobile embedded devices in almost any type of real world object, including cars, tools, household appliances, clothes, and so forth—all communicating through increasingly interconnected networks.

Self Healing: Having the power or property of healing one's self or itself. Autonomic computing refers to the ability of systems to self-diagnose and self-heal without the need for operator intervention.

Self-Management: The process by which computer systems manage their own operation without human intervention.

ENDNOTE

[1]   http://www-03.ibm.com/autonomic/

Autonomic Networking

Pantelis N. Karamolegkos
Telecommunications Laboratory School of Electrical and Computer Engineering, NTUA, Greece

Charalampos Patrikakis
Telecommunications Laboratory School of Electrical and Computer Engineering, NTUA, Greece

Emmanuel Protonotarios
Telecommunications Laboratory School of Electrical and Computer Engineering, NTUA, Greece

INTRODUCTION

The term "autonomic networking" refers to a recently emerged communications paradigm that uses distributed techniques (swarm intelligence-based methods) and distributed hash tables to implement traditional functionalities of networking, including among others, routing, service and resource discovery, addressing, load balancing, etc. The shift of interest toward the autonomic networking approach has been mainly motivated by the pervasion of novel algorithms into relevant fields of computer communication science. These innovative techniques have been greatly alleviated by their fusion with already established solutions and applications (i.e., agent-based systems, network middleware development, etc.) so as to form a new ever-evolving landscape in networking.

BACKGROUND

As computers and networks become an integrated part of a constantly increasing number of human activities, the inherent complexity of such a process becomes a significant drawback toward the road to a ubiquitous networking environment. From the first simple to use and manage telephone networks to the latest advances in fixed and wireless multimodal platforms, there has been a long technological distance covered. This is clearly reflected in the variety of protocols, applications, and architectures that compose the current status in telecommunication networks. Information dissemination, network management, and service and resource discovery have become intrinsically complex tasks, due to both the heterogeneity of the technologies and to the explosive growth of the networked users.

Traditional models of networking and legacy protocols have been unable to scale efficiently so as to meet the complexity introduced by the modern communication environments. Therefore, the need for a new approach resulted into the creation and proliferation of novel algorithms, being mainly attributed by decentralization of tasks and abstraction of the underlying networking and/or hardware infrastructure.

This need has also been emphasized by the abundance of a new generation of mobile devices that encompass a large variety of functionalities and networking interfaces. Smartphones, PDAs, and mini PCs are essential elements to the currently perceived notion of ubiquitous networking, and their ever growing penetration rate to mobile users makes the demand for self-organized communication modes more substantial than ever. Quoting from Kutzner, Cramer, and Fuhrmann (2005): "... as the number of networked devices increases, so does system complexity," while "the required amount of management and human intervention increases more and more, both slowing down the growth rate and limiting the achievable size of ubiquitous systems."

Apart from the growth in size and complexity however, new challenges have been introduced by specific recently emerged forms of networking such as peer-to-peer (P2P), ad-hoc, and sensor networks. Currently, there is an ongoing worldwide research activity spanning the range of traditional and modern thematic fields of computer communications, including, but not limited to the aforementioned areas.

Autonomic Networking Concepts

In an effort to track down the main scientific and technological contributions of the autonomic networking research concept, one would identify the following areas.

Epidemic/Gossip Protocols

The recent growth of P2P systems and of similar communication substructures, as for example sensor networks, has created the emergence of fast and efficient information dissemination techniques. The distributed nature of such topologies raises the need for more sophisticated approaches than the ones adopted in traditional forms of networks. These approaches should adequately address the issue of reliable data multicast, resource discovery, routing, and other application specific issues in a way that scales efficiently with communicating group size, while at the same time addresses other constraints imposed by the transient topologies characterizing these communication infrastructures.

Epidemic protocols (Kermarrec, Massoulie, & Ganesh, 2003; Vogels, Renesse, & Birman, 2003) comprise a family of algorithms that imitate the spread of infectious diseases among populations to implement networking solutions that scale efficiently with network size, while on the other hand are very robust to topology changes and node or communication link failures. The main motivation for the emergence of this kind of protocols was given by already existing solutions used for consistency management on replicated databases (Demers et al., 1987) and by the legacy USENET protocol. The common characteristic of this group of protocols is the use of randomized algorithms in the message exchange process between network members comprising a physical or logical neighborhood. The relevant implementations usually differ in the way the randomized algorithm is implemented, the neighbor selection criteria, group membership management, and message buffering between nodes.

A distinguishing feature of epidemics is the probabilistic approach regarding algorithm's success guarantees. Quoting from Birman et al. (2003, p. 45):

... our protocol can be configured to have a very small probability of delivering to a small number of destinations (counting failed ones), an insignificant risk of delivering to "many" but not "most" destinations, and a very high probability of delivering the message to all or almost all destinations.

This is a clear and concise demonstration of epidemic protocols applicability, in terms of fine tuning probabilistic guarantees, which usually sums up to a trade off between scalability and reliability.

One of the first attempts to provide a thorough definition of a protocol that will support reliable multicast over large groups of processes was scalable reliable multicast (Floyd, Jacobson, Liu, McCanne, & Zhang, 1997), which reduced traffic flow among members of the multicast group by alleviating the task of retransmissions from the sender, and initiating a P2P like message exchange between the receivers in case of lost messages. Membership management was performed by the exchange of low frequency session messages between group members.

In bimodal multicast (Birman, et al., 1999), a two-tier approach is implemented in which messages are randomly and unreliably propagated between processes—members of the networks using IP multicast functionality wherever available, or any other similar protocol replicating this technique. Each process/group member that wishes to initiate a multicast transmission, it does so through pseudo-randomly generated spanning trees. Each message sent through these trees, bears a relevant tree identifier. This first level of information dissemination is complemented by a so called anti-entropy protocol, which runs periodically and concurrently with the normal message exchange process previously described. During execution of the anti-entropy protocol, each process randomly selects a subset of other processes (preferably the closest ones in terms of network proximity) and sends to them a digest of the messages that are in its possession while soliciting from them any messages it discovers to be lacking.

The scientific team that has developed bimodal multicast has conducted a large-scale research effort within the area of epidemic protocols, putting together some of the most noteworthy relevant frameworks such as Astrolabe (Renesse, Birman, & Vogels, 2003) and Isis (Birman, 1985), which was a pioneering work regarding the field of epidemics (although more akin to the distributed computing paradigm) and served as the framework for the implementation of highly critical applications such as the Swiss and New York stock exchanges, the French Air Traffic Control System, and the U.S. Navy's AEGIS warship. The same group has also proposed an alternative approach to increase the reliability and availability of Web services transactions using an epidemic approach. (Birman, Renesse, & Vogels, 2004).

In lightweight probabilistic broadcast (Eugster, Guerraoui, Handurukande, Kermarrec, & Kouznetsov, 2001), periodical non-synchronized gossip messages are used to provide membership management and event dissemination. Processes subscribe and unsubscribe to groups through the exchange of these messages, providing a framework for information dissemination in large scale, unstructured systems. In lightweight probabilistic broadcast, a gossip message is exchanged in four distinct occasions: in *subscriptions* of processes entering the group, in *unsubscription* of processes leaving the group, as notifications of events received since the last outgoing gossip (*event notifications*), and as digests of received events (*event notification identifiers*).

Directional gossip, developed by Lin and Marzullo (1999), uses representative values of neighboring processes' connectivity called *weights,* so as to perform a topology-based optimization regarding the message dissemination. This protocol is a WAN-based gossip implementation that is designed in a way so as to incorporate provision for message exchange between more than one LANs in which case gossiping takes place through dedicated gossip servers.

Finally, in terms of routing, a related approach that targets ad-hoc networks is proposed by Vahdat and Becker (2000), in which case the epidemic framework is used to deliver specific messages to specific destinations, while at the same time optimizing the network resource utilization by limiting the intermediate hosts carrying the message to the recipient. For this purpose, each node stores messages it has recently sent in a hash table as also the ones he is buffering as an intermediate, and when the message exchange process initiates, each node is in position of requesting messages it has not yet received. The proposed algorithm also incorporates the option of the message delivery acknowledgment, either as a stand-alone message or piggybacked in data packets.

Overlay Networking in P2P Systems

This group of algorithms that have as common denominator the use of distributed hash tables (DHTs) as elementary routing entities, provide the substrata for members of a P2P network to self-organize in resilient overlay topologies, and to self-manage issues regarding resource discovery, addressing, routing, scalable indexing, etc. The main objectives of such schemes that are usually middleware-based implementations, is average hop distance and object (services, files) lookup time minimization, overcoming the intricacies of the highly transient morphology of the unstructured P2P networks.

These algorithms surfaced mainly as a resolution to the centralization and poor scaling capabilities encountered in the early P2P implementations. For example, Napster (www.napster.com) used centralized lookup architecture as peer user's queries were directed to a central server, which subsequently returned the query's results providing a direct P2P connection between the file exchange parties. At the same time, Gnutella used a flooding-based query architecture that scaled inefficiently with the number of participants in the P2P network. DHT-based P2P systems therefore, emerged as a modest solution balanced between centralization and complete lack of overlay structure that provided upper bounds to the number of hops that a query will traverse until it reaches the node with the relevant content.

What all DHT systems actually implement is a key-based routing algorithm. Every file to be stored is associated through a hash function with a relevant key; this file/key is subsequently assigned to and stored by one of the currently active nodes of the overlay network, while there is usually an association between the node identifier and the file key. This association is the cornerstone of most of the DHT implementations since it allows for efficient routing and resource discovery that is guaranteed to take place within limited query hops.

Another common aspect characterizing this form of P2P systems is their provision for load balancing due to the inherent tendency of hash functions to assign keys and subsequently files to all network nodes with uniform probability. This feature significantly limits the probability of a node becoming overloaded with content, guaranteeing fairness in file storage and hence in network traffic.

Among the most widespread DHT-based platforms within the context of the research community are the following.

Content addressable networks (Ratnasamy, Francis, Handley, Karp, & Schenke, 2001) is a DHT implementation that uses a logical d-dimensional torus coordinate space mapping keys onto values. Each node forming the CAN overlay, maintains its own space within the coordinate system in a way that the sum of nodes spans the entire coordinate space. Each key-value pair is assigned to a node by mapping through a deterministic hash function the key to a point in the coordinate space. The key is therefore stored in the node that owns the space that this points belongs to. In terms of performance, in a CAN overlay comprising N nodes and using a d-dimensional system, each node needs to maintain O(d) state, while routing is performed in an average of

$$\frac{dn^{\frac{1}{d}}}{4}$$

hops. The obvious advantage is that the state maintained by each node does not depend on the size of the network.

In *Pastry* (Rowstron & Druschel, 2001), each node joining the network is randomly assigned a unique node identifier which ranges from 0 to $2^{128} - 1$; fairness is achieved by using a uniform distribution in terms of random node id assignment. An architectural aspect that significantly differentiates Pastry from the other DHT systems is the fact that the former takes into account the actual underlying network topology, in an effort to optimize its efficiency in terms of routing time. Each Pasty node keeps track of L (application – specific parameter) logically adjacent nodes, which are called the "leaf set." Efficient routing in the Pastry framework is guaranteed unless $\lfloor |L|/2 \rfloor$ nodes with adjacent identifiers fail simultaneously. Assuming again a network of N nodes, average length of forwarding path is O(logN), which is also the average routing table size maintained by a Pastry node.

Nodes in a *Chord* overlay structure (Stoica, Morris, Karger, Kaashoek, & Balakrishnan, 2001) form a conceptual circle, since all of their identifiers fall within the range of 0 to $2^m - 1$, with the parameter m varying according to the specific protocol instantiation; the node identifier is the result of hashing its IP address. Hashed key files are assigned to the first node whose id is equal to or follows the key of the file in the identifier space. In Chord, each node is responsible for an almost equal portion of the total number of files stored in the distributed overlay, while in a network of N nodes, each one of them maintains O(log(N)) states; this is also the average hop count encountered by a routing message within Chord.

Tapestry (Zhao et al., 2004) resembles Pastry in the exploitation of the underlying local network information for message routing optimization. Other commonalities shared between Tapestry and the aforementioned systems is the use of a consistent hashing for even distribution of node identifiers as also the node state and average hop distance during experienced by a message routed through this network (O(logN) in both cases, N being the number of network nodes). The Tapestry's algorithm is based on the longest-prefix routing concept, which in this case is implemented through the maintenance by each node of multi-level local routing maps (neighbor maps).

Currently there is a variety of applications being developed and running on DHT-based infrastructures. To name a few, *OpenDHT* (www.opendht.org), a project supported by Intel, IBM, and National Research Foundation is a public service open to any user that wants to store or retrieve files from publicly available DHT nodes. *UsenetDHT*, developed at MIT by Sit, Dabek, and Robertson (2004), uses a DHT infrastructure to run a distributed Usenet server by keeping the data shared across the service participants. *OceanStore* (Kubiatowicz et al., 2000) is a data storage system developed at the University of California at Berkeley and built over the Tapestry framework.

Swarm-Based Network Protocols

Algorithms inspired by nature have served as a valuable tool for the modeling and simulation of complex problems addressing a broad range of applications and research areas. The list of these algorithms that have been commonly attributed by the term "evolutionary algorithms" includes genetic algorithms, evolutionary programming, evolution strategies, classifier systems, and genetic programming. Artificial populations, sometimes represented as strings of bits (bitstrings), evolve during the execution of the simulation program according to certain operations that imitate biological life (i.e., selection, reproduction, and mutation).

Recently, a new genre of distributed techniques, which was also inspired by biological phenomena has been gaining interest in the research field of computer communications, bringing forth a new generation of networking protocols that are based on modeling and implementations of swarming methods (i.e., foraging strategies, nesting, etc.). This work has been mainly motivated by recent relevant studies on ant colony optimization (Bonabeau, Dorigo, & Theraulaz, 1999; Dorigo & Stützle, 2004), a novel algorithm that models the basic underlying concepts of the self-organization that is omnipresent in many insect colonies.

In telecommunications and computer networking implementations, ant colony optimization is mostly used for routing, load balancing, and resource discovery purposes. Ants are replicated by simple software agents that follow simple sets of rules governing their interactions and manage to solve difficult and complex tasks through the emergence of sophisticated patterns of global system behavior.

Ant-based control (ABC) (Schoonderwoerd, Holland, & Bruten, 1997) is a swarm-based algorithm designed for telephone networks. Routing tables that are composed of entries that have the form of probabilities are updated by software agents (ants), which are periodically launched within the network and provide implicit reports (through table records modification) on its status. The software ants move within the network in a probabilistic mode, while real data follow the path designated by the highest probability entries of the tables. AntNet follows a similar approach that uses two kinds of ants-agents, forward ants and backward ants. Routing tables are organized as in the distance-vector algorithms, modified to contain probability values. A complementary data structure maintained in each node holds parametric values regarding the traffic load in each direction as perceived by the node itself. Forward ants are launched at regular intervals to various destinations gathering statistical information regarding the paths they traverse during their trip to the final node. As soon as they arrive, backward ants start traveling at the exact opposite direction modifying nodes contents according to the information collected by their forward counterparts.

Lately, significant attention has been given to exploit ant colony optimization techniques within the area of mobile ad-hoc networking applications (Di Caro & Dorigo, 1998; Di Caro, Ducatelle, & Gambardella, 2004) whose distributed and transient nature is strongly reminiscent of P2P systems.

FUTURE TRENDS

All of the three aforementioned fields are currently highly active areas of research covering many aspects of the networking paradigm. Regarding the area of epidemic protocols, the focus is mainly on the efficient self-organization of sensor network applications (Günes & Spaniol, 2003) and in innovative algorithms for information dissemination in novel applications based on ad-hoc networks. The latter field is also attracting a lot of interest in the context of swarm-based routing, since new proposals for routing techniques in ad-hoc networks (Di Caro et al., 2004) keep emerging. On the other side, DHT-based overlay networks continue to provide a reliable framework for the design and development of many legacy applications such as file services, indexing services, and cooperating mirroring within the context of this new distributed approach.

CONCLUSION

Autonomic networking concept has emerged through a constructive merge of existing techniques (e.g., agents) with sophisticated distributed algorithms and infrastructures (e.g., DHTs) some of which are largely inspired or influenced by many natural phenomena (foraging ants, spread of a disease among populations). Novel solutions that keep emerging throughout the current landscape of telecommunications are demonstrating a significant shift of interest toward these new techniques, which will eventually play a significant role in the formation of the networking paradigm in the years to come.

REFERENCES

Birman, K. P. (1985). Replication and fault tolerance in the ISIS system. In *Proceedings of ACM Symposium on Operating Systems Principles*, Orcas Island, Washington.

Birman, K. P., Hayden, M., Ozkasap, O., Xiao, Z., Budiu, M., & Minsky, Y. (1999). Bimodal mutlicast. *ACM Transactions on Computer Systems*, *17*(2), 41-88.

Birman, K. P., Renesse R. V., & Vogels, W. (2004). Adding high availability and autonomic behavior to Web services. In *Proceedings of the 26th International Conference on Software Engineering*, Edinburgh, Scotland.

Bonabeau, E., Dorigo, M., & Theraulaz, G. (1999). Swarm intelligence: From natural to artificial systems.

In *Santa Fe Institute Studies in the Sciences of Complexity Proceedings*, Oxford University Press.

Demers, A. Greene, D., Hauser, C., Irish, W., Larson, J., Shenker, S., et al. (1987). Epidemic algorithms for replicated data management. In *Proceedings of the 6th Annual ACM Symposium on Principles of Distributed Computing*, Vancouver *(PODC)* (pp. 1-12).

Di Caro, G., & Dorigo, M. (1998). AntNet: Distributed stigmergetic control for communications networks. *Journal of Artificial Intelligence Research*, *9*, 317-365.

Di Caro, G., Ducatelle, F., & Gambardella, L. M. (2004). *AntHocNet: An adaptive nature-inspired algorithm for routing in mobile ad hoc networks*. Technical Report No. IDSIA-27-04-2004, IDSIA/USI-SUPSI.

Dorigo, M., & Stützle, T. (2004). *Ant colony optimization*. Bradford Books, The MIT Press.

Eugster, P., Guerraoui, R., Handurukande, S., Kermarrec, A. M., & Kouznetsov, P. (2001). Lightweight probabilistic broadcast. In *Proceedings of the 2nd International Conference on Dependable Systems and Networks* (pp. 443-452). Los Alamitos, CA: IEEE Computer Society Press.

Floyd, S., Jacobson, V., Liu, C., McCanne, S., & Zhang, L. (1997). A reliable multicast framework for lightweight sessions and application level framing. *IEEE/ACM Transactions on Networking*, *5*(6), 784-803.

Günes, M., & Spaniol, O. (2003). Ant-routing-algorithm for mobile multi-hop ad-hoc networks. *Network control and engineering for Qos, security and mobility*, *2*, 120-138.

Kermarrec, A. M., Massoulie, L., & Ganesh. A. (2003). Probabilistic reliable dissemination in large-scale systems. *IEEE Trans. Par. Distr. Syst.*, *14*(3), 248-258.

Kubiatowicz, J., Bindel, D., Chen, Y., Czerwinski, S., Eaton, P., Geels, D., et al. (2000). OceanStore: An architecture for global-scale persistent storage. In *Proceedings of the ACM ASPLOS*.

Kutzner, K., Cramer, C., & Fuhrmann, T. (2005, March 14-17). Towards autonomic networking using overlay routing techniques. In *Proceedings of the 18th International Conference on Architecture of Computing Systems (ARCS '05)—System Aspects in Organic*

and Pervasive Computing, Innsbruck, Austria (LNCS 3432).

Lin, M. J., & Marzullo, K. (1999). Directional gossip: Gossip in a wide area network. In *Proceedings of the European Dependable Computing Conference* (pp. 364-379).

Napster. (n.d.). Retrieved from http://www.napster.com

OpenDHT: A Publicly Accessible DHT Service. (n.d.). Retrieved from http://www.opendht.org

Ratnasamy, S., Francis, P., Handley, M., Karp, R., & Schenke, S. (2001). A scalable content-addressable network. In *Proceedings of the 2001 Conference on Applications, Technologies, Architectures, and Protocols for Computer Communications*, San Diego, USA.

Renesse, R .V., Birman, K. P., & Vogels, W. (2003). Astrolabe: A robust and scalable technology for distributed system monitoring, management, and data mining. *ACM Transactions on Computer Systems (TOCS)*, *21*(2), 164-206.

Rowstron, A., & Druschel. P. (2001). Pastry: Scalable, distributed object location, and routing for large-scale peer-to-peer systems. *IFIP/ACM International Conference on Distributed Systems Platforms (Middleware)*, Heidelberg, Germany.

Schoonderwoerd, R., Holland, O., & Bruten, J. (1997). Ant-like agents for load balancing in telecommunication networks. In *Proceedings of the 1st International Conference on Autonomous Agents*. Marina del Rey, California.

Sit, E., Dabek, F., & Robertson, J. (2004). UsenetDHT: A low overhead usenet server. *Proceedings of the 3rd IPTPS*.

Stoica, I., Morris, R., Karger, D., Kaashoek, M. F., & Balakrishnan, H. (2001). Chord: A scalable peer-to-peer lookup service for Internet applications. In *Proceedings of the 2001 Conference on Applications, Technologies, Architectures, and Protocols for Computer Communications*, San Diego, USA.

Vahdat, A., & Becker, D. (2000). *Epidemic routing for partially connected ad hoc networks*. Technical Report CS-200006, Duke University.

A

Vogels, W., Renesse R. V., & Birman, K. (2003). The power of epidemics. *ACM SIGCOMM Computer Communication Review*, *33*(1).

Zhao, B. Y., Huang, L., Stribling, J., Rhea, S. C., Joseph, A. D., & Kubiatowicz, J. D (2004). Tapestry: A resilient global-scale overlay for service deployment. *IEEE Journal on Selected Areas in Communications*, *22*(1), 41-53.

KEY TERMS

Ad-Hoc Network: A term characterizing mostly wireless networks in which nodes become members just during the process of a specific communication session, or while they are in the physical range of the network.

Ant Colony Optimization (ACO): Recently emerged optimization algorithm that is inspired by techniques used by swarms of ants. At each iteration of an ACO algorithm, each agent (ant) of the swarm builds a solution of the problem based on both it is own estimation and information the indirect form of communication (stigmergy) he attains with the other agents, through an artificial hormone (pheromone).

Distributed Hash Tables (DHT): Distributed platforms that assigns keys (usually representing real life objects such as files) onto nodes of a network, providing the basic infrastructure for the implementation of basic networking functionalities such as routing and resource discovery

Epidemic Protocols: Protocols that imitate the spread of a disease among a (usually homogeneous) population in order to provide the algorithmic substructure for reliable information dissemination in large and transient groups of users processes

Evolutionary Algorithms: Optimization algorithms that imitate processes of life such as mutation, selection, and reproduction. Genetic algorithms, evolutionary programming, evolution strategies, classifier systems, and genetic programming are considered part of this category of optimization techniques.

Overlay Networks: Networks created by creating virtual interconnections between nodes, on top of the physical structure of the original network.

Peer to Peer (P2P): Networking concept that contradicts the traditional client-server model by assigning to participating nodes equal roles. P2P based applications include among others file sharing systems, streaming platforms, and so forth.

Cfengine Configuration Management Agent

C

Mark Burgess
Oslo University College, Norway

INTRODUCTION

Cfengine is a policy-based configuration management system (Burgess, 1995). Its primary function is to provide automated configuration and maintenance of computers, from a policy specification. The cfengine project was started in 1993 as a reaction to the complexity and non-portability of shell scripting for Unix configuration management and continues today. The aim was to absorb frequently used coding paradigms into a declarative, domain-specific language that would offer self-documenting configuration. Cfengine is estimated to run on millions of Unix, MacOSX, and Windows computers all around the world. It is used in both large and small companies, as well as in many universities and government institutions. Sites as large as 11,000 machines are reported, while sites of several thousand hosts running under cfengine are common. Cfengine falls into a class of approaches to system administration, which is called policy-based configuration management (Sloman & Moffet, 1993).

BACKGROUND

The problem of mass configuration of workstations and servers (henceforth called "hosts") has led to a plethora of solutions. Many of these have been schemes for cloning a basic configuration; some using package management. One of the problems with cloning is that one is limited to a fixed configuration for all hosts. Zwicky (1992) introduced the notion of classes of machines for operating system installation; Anderson (1994) has similar ideas. Previous approaches had simply cloned a "master" disk requiring all users to have the same configuration. Typecast allowed different configurations based on the type of the user. Cfengine also returned to the idea of class-based typing in Burgess (1995).

Language-based tools for automatic system configuration have appeared from the outset. Apart from procedural scripting tools such as Perl, Tcl, and Scheme, more declarative languages were introduced in Hage-mark and Zadeck (1989). Rouillard and Martin (1994) designed a language for checking the configuration of systems using the Unix utility "rdist" to perform updates from a master version-control repository. They used Tripwire to check whether the configuration was changing unexpectedly. This contrasts with the approach of Cfengine, which allows the system to approach a policy-defined state voluntarily. Cfengine differs from similar approaches to configuration management in that it embraces a stochastic model of system evolution (Burgess, 2003). Rather than assuming that transitions between states of its model occur only at the instigation of an operator or at the behest of a protocol, like SNMP or NETCONF, cfengine imagines that changes of state occur unpredictably at any time as part of the environment to be discovered. Cfengine holds to a set of principles referred to as the immunity model (Burgess, 2004b). These embody the following features:

- Policy-based specification using an operating system independent language
- Distributed agent-based action; each host agent is responsible for its own maintenance
- Convergent semantics encourage every transaction to bring the system closer to an "ideal" average-state, like a ball rolling into a potential well.
- Once the system has converged, action by the agent desists. In an analogous way to the healing of a body from sickness, cfengine's configuration approach is to always move the system closer to a "healthy" state (Burgess, 1998), or oppose unhealthy change, hence the name "immunity model." This idea shares several features with the security model proposed in refs. (D'haeseleer, Forrest, & Helman, 1996; Somayaji, Hofmeyr, & Forrest, 1997). Convergence is described further next. A "healthy state" is defined by reference to a local policy. When a system complies with policy, it is healthy; when it deviates, it is "sick." Cfengine makes this process of maintenance into an error-correction channel for messages belong-

Figure 1. Cfengine components

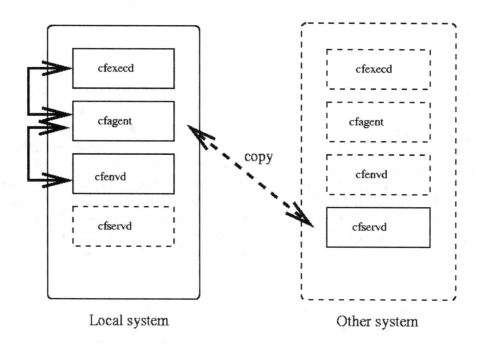

Local system   Other system

ing to a fuzzy alphabet (Burgess, 2002), where error-correction is meant in the sense of Shannon (Shannon & Weaver, 1949). In Burgess (2003), it was shown that a complete specification of policy determines an approximate configuration of a software system only approximately over persistent times. There are fundamental limits to the tolerances a system can satisfy with respect to policy compliance in a stochastic environment. The main components of cfengine are shown in Figure 1.

- A repository of policy files for each host in a domain; this can be either common or individual
- A declarative policy interpreter (cfengine is not an imperative language but has many features akin to Prolog (Couch & Gilfix, 1999)
- An active agent, which executes intermittently on each host in a domain
- A secure server, which can assist with peer-level file sharing and remote invocation, if desired
- A passive information-gathering agent, which runs on each host, assisting in the classification of host state over persistent times; setting configuration policy for distributed software and hardware is a broad challenge, which must be addressed both at the detailed level and at the more abstract en-

terprise level; cfengine is deployed throughout an environment and classifies its view of the world into overlapping sets so that systems can be customized according to membership in these sets; those tasks, which overlap with a particular agent'sworld view, are performed by the agent

Each host, which runs a cfengine agent, therefore builds up a list of its own attributes (called the classes to which the host belongs). Some examples include:

1. The identity of a machine, including hostname, address, network
2. The operating system and architecture of the host
3. An abstract user-defined group to which the host belongs
4. The result of any proposition about the system
5. A time or date
6. A randomly chosen strategy element
7. The logical combination of any of the previous, with AND (.), OR (|), NOT (!) and parentheses

A command or action is only executed if a given host is in the same class as the policy action in the configuration program. There is no need for other formal decision structures; it is enough to label each statement with classes. For example:

linux:: linux-actions

solaris:: solaris-actions

More complex combinations can perform an arbitrary covering of a distributed system (Comer & Peterson, 1989):

AllServers.Hr22.!exception_host:: actions

where AllServers is an abstract group, and exception host is a host, which is to be excluded from the rest. Classes thus form any number of overlapping sets, which cover the coordinate space of the distributed system (h, c, t), for different hosts h, with software components c, over time t. Classes sometimes become active in response to situations which conflict with policy. Each host can be characterized by many different classes or attributes, recognizing the multiple functions of each node in the virtual community, and the distributed nature of software systems.

Some classes are automatically evaluated based on the state of the host in relation to earlier times. This is accomplished by the additional cfenvd daemon, which learns and continually updates a database of system averages, which characterize "normal" behavior. This allows integrated anomaly detection.

A cfengine state is defined by policy. The specification of a policy rule is like the specification of a coordinate system (a scale of measurement) that is used to examine the compliance of the system. The full policy is a patchwork of such rules, some of which overlap. They are regular language classes (Lewis & Papadimitriou, 1997), often represented in the form of a regular expressions that place bounds on:

- Characterizations of the configuration of operating system objects (cfagent digital comparisons of fuzzy sets)
- Numerical counts of environmental observations (cfenvd counts or values with real-valued averages)
- The frequency of execution of closed actions (cfagent locking)

Figure 2 illustrates schematically how a state can be a fuzzy region consisting of values that are "as good as one another." This is called internal stability in the language of graph transitions (Burgess, 2004a). If the value of an object strays outside of the set of internally stable values, it is deemed to be a different state. A cfengine operator is then required to restore the value of the object to any one of the values in the stable set.

For example, given the cfengine rule:

files:

/etc/passwd mode=a+r,o-w owner=root

Figure 2. A Cfengine state is a potentially fuzzy region (i.e., it is a constrained region rather than a necessarily unique point)

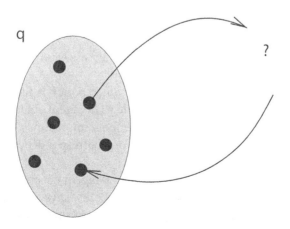

Figure 3. A schematic view of the management model

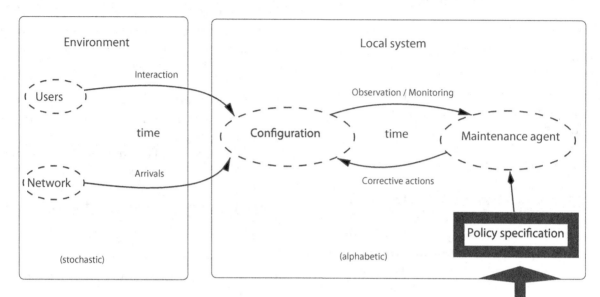

Note: We define host and environment. The environment leads to randomness in the configuration of a host as it "propagates" into the future. The maintenance agent responds in a finite time to repair the changes that are contrary to policy.

we see that this is not a unique specification of file permissions, but a set of acceptable "equally good" values. The mode specification says that the acceptable state must be readable by all and must not be writable by any other than the owner of the file or its group owner.

The maintenance model, underpinning cfengine, was outlined in Burgess (2000) and is fully described in Burgess (2003, 2004b). Although a precise description of the cfengine viewpoint is involved, the idea is rather simple. Each computer system that is to be managed by cfengine is treated as an autonomous system embedded in an environment. (see Figure 3). All hosts participate in a policy voluntarily and can opt out at any time.

Policy is a description of how we define normal (i.e., what we would like to be true on average). A policy as a description of normality is thus a decision about how we define "errors" or noise. The Shannon communication model of the noisy channel has been used to provide a simple picture of the maintenance process (Burgess, 2002). Maintenance is the implementation of corrective actions (i.e., the analogue of error correction in the Shannon picture). Maintenance appears more complex than Shannon error correction, however. What makes the analogy valid is that Shannon's conclusions are independent of a theory of observation and measurement. For alphabetic strings, the task of observation and correction is trivial. To view policy as digital, one uses the computer science idea of a language (Lewis et al., 1997). One creates a one-to-one mapping between the basic operations of cfengine and a discrete symbol alphabet, for example:

A -> ``file mode=0644"

B -> ``file mode=0645"

C -> ``process email running"

Since policy is finite, in practice, this is denumerable. The agent interprets and translates the policy symbols into actions through operations, also in one to one correspondence:

1. Cfagent observes : X
2. Policy says : X ! A
3. Agent says : A -> Ofile(passwd, 0644, root)

Although the space of all possible policies is potentially very large (though never truly infinite due to finite memory etc), only a small fraction of the possibilities is ever realized on a real system and this problem is not a limitation. Cfengine operations fall into the following categories: file attribute correction, file content correction (file contents are modeled as a line-based regular language), file distribution management, process management, interface attribute management, and software package management. The presumed and observed states of the system feed into the definition of the policy (Burgess, 2004c; Couch & Sun, 2004). However, if one defines the operations into classes O1, O2, ... etc, then these form a strict alphabet of "black box" objects. The fuzziness in the operations can be eliminated by introducing a new symbol for each denumeration of the possible parameters. Here is an example operation, simplified for the purpose of illustration:

```
files:
```

```
/etc/passwd mode=0644 owner=root
```

This is actually a special instance of files:

```
<filename> mode=<permissions>
```

```
owner=<username>
```

which tells the agent to assert these properties of the named file object. Since there is a finite number of files, permissions, and users, there is no impediment to listing every possible permutation of these and assigning a different alphabetic symbol to them. In operator language, the previous action might be written:

```
Ofile(name, mode, owner)
```

Let us suppose that the previous examples evaluate the alphabetic symbol "A." When the agent observes these properties of the named object, it comes up with a symbol value based upon what it has measured. Suppose now that a user of the system (who is formally part of the environment) accidentally changes the permissions of the password file from mode=0644 to mode=0600. Moreover, we can suppose that this new value evaluates to the alphabetic character "X."

Cfengine operators use the idea of convergence to an ideal state (Burgess, 2004b). This means that no matter how many times the same operations are applied, state will only get closer to the ideal configuration, for example:

$$Oq = q0$$
$$Oq0 = q0.$$

If two operations are orthogonal, it means that they can be applied independently of order without affecting the final state of the system. Using a linear representation of vectors and matrix-valued operators, this is equivalent to requiring their commutativity. The construction of a consistent policy compliant configuration has been subject to intense debate since it was understood that cfengine actions are not generally order dependent (Burgess, 2004c; Couch et al., 2004; Traugott, 2002).

Uniqueness of ordering is not required as long as operations are orthogonal. We require there only to be absorbing states, or for operations to behave like semi-groups (Burgess, 2004a);

FUTURE TRENDS

Promise theory has been developed as a way of modeling policy using autonomous agents like cfengine (Burgess, 2005). This is a graph theoretical model, which has led to a greater understanding of the issues surrounding configuration management in an autonomous setting and has spawned a complete redesign of cfengine, emphasizing its principles more clearly. Promise theory also ties into game theory, which has been suggested as a way of optimizing decisions about system policy (Burgess, 2003, 2004a).

The main challenges in cfengine today include integrating feedback from monitoring data in order to react to alarm situations automatically. Work in this area is being pursued on a number of fronts. Cfengine uses a rather pragmatic declarative language to describe policy at a relatively low level. Most researchers accept cfengine policy as the "assembler language" of system configuration and are pushing for higher level abstractions that build on the low level properties.

CONCLUSION

The key points to understanding cfengine management are:

- The stochastic nature of change and the environment
- The discrete nature of host configuration by constraint
- Classification of environmental changes into a patchwork of sets
- Policy constraints on the desired state of hosts
- Convergence of configuration operations. Cfengine is an on-going project and, at present, it is being re-written to more directly reflect the theoretical model that has emerged in tandem with its development and extended to allow more general software control of robotic systems.

REFERENCES

Anderson, P. (1994). Towards a high-level machine configuration system. In *Proceedings of the 8th Systems Administration Conference (LISA VIII)* (p. 19). Berkeley, CA: USENIX Association.

Burgess, M. (2005). An approach to understanding policy based on autonomy and voluntary cooperation. In *IFIP/IEEE 16th International Workshop on Distributed Systems Operations and Management (DSOM)* (LNCS 3775, pp. 97-108).

Burgess, M. (2004a). *Analytical network and system administration—Managing human computer systems.* Chichester, UK: J. Wiley & Sons.

Burgess, M. (2004b). Configurable immunity for evolving human-computer systems. *Science of Computer Programming, 51*, 197.

Burgess, M. (2004c). Configurable immunity model of evolving configuration management. *Science of Computer Programming, 51*, 197.

Burgess, M. (2003). On the theory of system administration. *Science of Computer Programming, 49*, 1.

Burgess, M. (2002). System administration as communication over a noisy channel. In *Proceedings of the 3rd International System Administration and Networking Conference (SANE2002)* (pp. 36).

Burgess, M. (2000). Theoretical system administration. *Proceedings of the 14th Systems Administration Conference (LISA XIV)* (p. 1). USENIX Association: Berkeley, CA.

Burgess, M. (1998). Computer immunology. In *Proceedings of the 12th Systems Administration Conference (LISA XII)* (p. 283). USENIX Association: Berkeley, CA.

Burgess, M. (1995). A site configuration engine. *Computing systems, 8*, 309. Cambridge MA: MIT Press.

Comer, D., & Peterson, L. (1989). Understanding naming in distributed systems. *Distributed Computing, 3*, 51.

Couch, A., & Gilfix, M. (1999). It's elementary, dear Watson: Applying logic programming to convergent system management processes. In *Proceedings of the 13th Systems Administration Conference (LISA XIII)* (p. 123). USENIX Association: Berkeley, CA.

Couch, A., & Sun, Y. (2004). On observed reproducibility in network configuration management. *Science of Computer Programming, 53*, 215-253.

D'haeseleer, P., Forrest, S., & Helman, P. (1996). An immunological approach to change detection: Algorithms, analysis, and implications. In *Proceedings of the 1996 IEEE Symposium on Computer Security and Privacy*.

Hagemark, B., & Zadeck, K. (1989). Site: A language and system for configuring many computers as one computer site. In *Proceedings of the Workshop on Large Installation Systems Administration III* (p. 1). USENIX Association: Berkeley, CA.

Lewis, H., & Papadimitriou, C. (1997). *Elements of the theory of computation* (2nd ed.). New York: Prentice Hall.

Rouillard, J., & Martin, R. (1994). Config: A mechanism for installing and tracking system configurations. In *Proceedings of the 8th Systems Administration Conference (LISA VIII)* (p. 9). USENIX Association: Berkeley, CA.

Shannon, C., & Weaver, W. (1949). *The mathematical theory of communication.* Urbana, IL: University of Illinois Press.

Sloman, M., & Moffet, J. (1993). Policy hierarchies for distributed systems management. *Journal of Network and System Management, 11*(9), 1404.

Somayaji, A., Hofmeyr, S., & Forrest, S. (1997, September). Principles of a computer immune system. *New*

Security Paradigms Workshop (pp. 75-82). ACM.

Traugott, S. (2002). Why order matters: Turing equivalence in automated systems administration. In *Proceedings of the 16th Systems Administration Conference (LISA XVI)* (pp. 99). USENIX Association: Berkeley, CA.

Tripwire. (n.d.). *Security scanner*. Retrieved from http://www.tripwire.com

Zwicky, E. (1992). Typecast: Beyond cloned hosts. In *Proceedings of the 6th Systems Administration Conference (LISA VI)* (pp. 73). USENIX Association: Berkeley, CA.

KEY TERMS

Autonomic: Refers to a self-regulating system.

Classes: A way of slicing up and mapping out the complex environment into discrete set-like regions that can then be referred to by a symbol or name. They are formally constraints on the degrees of freedom available in the system parameter space. They are an integral part of specifying rules. They describe where something is to be constrained. Cfengine classes are not to be thought of in an object-oriented sense.

Cfengine: Refers to a configuration management software agent for autonomic maintenance.

Configuration Management: Refers to controlling the change of system components throughout their life-cycle, reporting the status, and verifying the completeness and correctness of items.

Convergence: Refers to the property that policy states should be absorbing (i.e., the system only gets closer to the policy state under the action of the agent).

Operators (^O): Or primitive skills are the commands that carry out maintenance checks and repairs. They form the basic sentences of a cfengine program. They describe what is to be constrained.

Policy (P): A description of the average, desired host configuration. It comprises a partially ordered list of operations or tasks for an agent to check and a schedule for maintenance.

States: Are fuzzy regions within the total system parameter space (i.e., coarse grained observables).

A Clustering Model of the Application-Level Multicast

Gábor Hosszú
Budapest University of Technology and Economics, Budapest

Raymond Pardede
Budapest University of Technology and Economics, Budapest

INTRODUCTION

This chapter reviews the most important fact of the application-level multicast (**ALM**) and then describes a novel concept of modeling relative density of members called **bunched mode** and a proposed host-end multicast routing protocol called shortest tunnel first (**STF**). The bunched mode is based on the thematic multicast concept (**TMC**), which means that it is a typical multicast scenario where there are a lot of interested hosts in certain institutions, relatively far from each other. This situation is called bunched mode, in which the members of a multicast group are locally in the dense mode, and globally their situation is similar to the sparse mode because these spots are far from each other. The developed analysis tool, *NetSim,* and the implementation of the *TMC, PardedeCAST,* are also presented as the tools of this research.

OVERVIEW OF THE APPLICATION LEVEL MULTICAST

Currently there is a fast increasing need for scalable and efficient group communication technology. The multicast is theoretically optimal for such purposes. It can be realized in the Data-link Level, IP level, and Transport/Application level (Hosszú, 2005). However, the IP Multicast has a slow deployment; it has been implemented in the most Operating Systems (OS) and routers, but not widely enabled. That is why the end-host based multicast is emerging, in which each member host duplicates and forwards packets. That solution is called application-level multicast (**ALM**). ALM is easy to deploy, but less efficient. In the following, the various solutions for the ALM are listed.

The special type of the ALM is the **host multicast**, which is a hybrid approach. Its goal is to reach a ubiq-uitous multicast. One of its design requirements is that it should be deployable on the current Internet, which means that the installation of a user-space program is done at end hosts and there is no support required from OS, routers, or servers to enable multicast services. The client applications can create a virtual network called *overlay network* (shortly *overlay*) on the top of the Internet. However, the hybrid approach has another design requirement, which is the compatibility with IP multicast to the furthest extent. For that reason, it should use the IP multicast where available, keep the IP Multicast service model, and provide incentive to the future deployment.

Another type of the ALM is the *mesh-based* protocol. This type creates a mesh for the control plane at first with a redundant topology of the connections between members. After creating the mesh, the algorithm starts to construct a multicast tree. Such protocols are the *Narada* (Chu et al., 2000), or the *Gossamer* (Chawathe, 2000).

The opposite of the mesh-based type are the *tree-based* protocols, where the multicast delivery tree is formed first and then each member discovers others that are not neighboring members and creates control links to these hosts. This solution is suitable for data transferring applications, which need high bandwidth, but are not efficient for real-time purposes. Such protocols are the *Yoid* (Francis, 2000) and the **host multicast tree protocol** (**HMTP**) from Zhang et al. (2002).

APPLICATION-LEVEL MULTICAST PROPERTIES

The goodness of the ALM system can be measured by some parameters, such as *control overhead*, *robustness of the overlay*, *stress,* and *stretch*.

Control overhead means the ratio of the necessary control messages sent by the clients to each other and the amount of the data traffic on the ALM system. In other words, the control overhead is a metric to examine the scalability of the overlay to large groups. Each member on the overlay exchanges refresh messages with all its peers on the overlay. Those messages build the control overheads at different routers, different links, and different members of the multicast group. For efficient use of network resources, the control overhead should be low (Banerjee et al., 2002).

Robustness of the overlay of the ALM protocols is measured by quantifying the extent of the disruption in data delivery when various members fail, and the time it takes for the protocol to restore delivery to the other members. Since hosts are potentially less stable than routers, it is important for ALM protocols to decrease the effect of host failures.

Stress means the number of identical packages sent through a certain link. In the case of IP-Multicast, the stress is one, but in the case of the ALM, the stress is possibly higher than one. The total amount of the necessary network resources of an ALM system can be measured by the following expression:

$$\sum_{i=1}^{L} d_i \cdot s_i,$$

where L is the number of active links in the data or control message transmission, d_i is the propagation delay of the link, and s_i is the stress of the link.

Stretch measures the ratio of length of the path from the sender to the receiver in the case of the ALM, and path length in the case of the pure unicast transmission for each receiver. For the IP-Multicast, the stretch equals to one for every receiver; for ALM the stretch is possibly higher than one.

AD-HOC MULTICAST

There are a lot of various protocols and implementations of the Application Layer Multicasting. Not only that, the communication over the wireless networks also enhances the importance of the ALM. The reason is because that in the case of mobile devices, the importance of the *ad-hoc networks* is increasing. Ad-hoc is a network that does not need any infrastructure. Such networks are the **Bluetooth** (Haartsen, 1998) and mobile ad hoc network (**MANET**), which comprise a set of wireless devices that can move around freely and communicate in relaying packets on behalf of one another (Mohapatra et al., 2004).

In computer networking there is a weaker definition of this ad-hoc network. It says that ad-hoc is a computer network that does not need routing infrastructure. It means that the mobile devices that use base stations can create an *ad-hoc computer network*. In such situations, instead of *IP-multicast*, the usage of application-level networking (**ALN**) technology is more practical. In order to support this group communication, various multicast routing protocols are developed for the mobile environment. The multicast routing protocols for ad-hoc networks differ in terms of state maintenance, route topology, and other attributes.

The simplest ad-hoc multicast routing methods are *flooding* and *tree-based routing*. *Flooding* is very simple, which offers the lowest control overhead at the expense of generating high data traffic. This situation is similar to the traditional IP-Multicast routing. However, in the wireless ad-hoc environment, the *tree-based routing* fundamentally differs from the situation in the wired IP-Multicast, where the tree-based multicast routing algorithms are obviously the most efficient ones, such as in the multicast open shortest path first (**MOSPF**) routing protocol (Moy, 1994). Though tree-based routing generates optimally small data traffic on the overlay in the wireless ad-hoc network, the tree maintenance and updates need a lot of control traffic. That is why the simplest methods are not scalable for large groups.

A more sophisticated ad-hoc multicast routing protocol is the core-assisted mesh protocol (**CAMP**), which belongs to the mesh-based multicast routing protocols (Garcia-Luna-Aceves & Madruga, 1999). It uses a shared mesh to support multicast routing in a dynamic ad-hoc environment. This method uses cores to limit the control traffic needed to create multicast meshes. Unlike the core-based multicast routing protocol as the traditional protocol independent multicast-sparse mode (**PIM-SM**), multicast routing protocol (Deering et al., 1996), CAMP does not require that all traffic flow through the core nodes. CAMP uses a receiver-initiated method for routers to join a multicast group. If a node wishes to join to the group, it uses a standard procedure to announce its membership. When none of its neighbors are mesh members, the node either sends a join request toward a core or attempts to reach a group member using an expanding-ring search process. Any mesh member can respond to the join request with a join **ACK** (**ack**nowledgement) that propagates back to the request originator.

Contrary to the mesh-based routing protocols, which exploit variable topology, is the so-called ***gossip-based*** multicast routing protocols that exploit randomness in communication and mobility. Such multicast routing protocols apply gossip as a form of randomly-controlled flooding to solve the problems of network news dissemination. This method involves member nodes to talk periodically to a random subset of other members. After each round of talk, the gossipers can recover their missed multicast packets from each other (Mohapatra et al., 2004). As opposed to the deterministic approaches, this probabilistic method will better survive a highly dynamic ad hoc network because it operates independently of network topology and its random nature fits the typical characteristics of the network.

A type of gossip-based protocol is *anonymous gossip routing*. This method does not require a group member to have any information of the other members of the same group. The procedure has two phases: In the first phase a host sends multicast packets to the group. In the second phase, periodic anonymous gossip takes place in the background as each group member recovers any lost data packets from other group members that might have received it.

Another interesting type of ad-hoc multicasting is ***geocasting***. The host that wishes to deliver packets to every node in a certain geographical area can use such a method. In such cases, the position of each node with regard to the specified geocast region implicitly defines group membership. Every node is required to know its own geographical location. For this purpose they can use a **g**lobal **p**ositioning **s**ystem (**GPS**). The geocasting routing method does not require any explicit join and leave actions. The members of the group tend to be clustered both geographically and topologically. The geocasting routing exploits the knowledge of location.

Geocasting can be combined with flooding; such methods are called ***forwarding-zone*** methods, which constrain the flooding region. The *forwarding zone* is a geographic area that extends from the source node to cover the geocast zone. The source node defines a *forwarding zone* in the header of the geocast data packet. Upon receiving a geocast packet, other machines will forward it only if their location is inside the *forwarding zone*. The **l**ocation-**b**ased **m**ulticast (**LBM**) is an example of such geocasting-limited flooding (Ko & Vaidya, 2002).

THE THEMATIC MULTICAST CONCEPT AND SHORT TUNNEL FIRST

The **t**hematic **m**ulticast **c**oncept (**TMC**) is an example of the current research works in the field of ALM: a novel concept of modeling relative density of members called **bunched mode**. The bunched mode means a typical multicast scenario, where there are a lot of interested hosts in certain institutions but these institutions are relatively far from each other. The members of a multicast group are locally in the dense mode; however, these spots are far from each other. Globally, their situation is similar to the sparse mode. The bunch can be a *local-area network (LAN)* or just an *autonomous system (AS)*. This situation is typical in the case when one collaborative media application has a special topic. That is why this model of communication is called *thematic multicast concept*.

The **s**hortest **t**unnel **f**irst (**STF**) is an ALM routing protocol, which is optimal for bunched mode delivering. Every group of member hosts in a bunch locally elects their designated member (DM). All DMs after elected calculate the shortest unicast IP tunnels among them, see Figure 1.

The DMs exchange their IP addresses and the information of shortest unicast paths among them. The path is a series of IP links from one host to another. In this way, all know each of the shortest possible unicast paths and calculate the same topology of the inter-bunch IP tunnels. This mechanism is similar to the *multicast open shortest path first (MOSPF)* routing at network level (Moy, 1994). The STF does not require any global rendezvous point for creating the inter-bunch delivery tree, however, supposing that there is only one source per group and a unidirectional tree is constructed.

The list of the DMs is maintained by the source application, and the new DM registers here and receives a copy of the current list. Every DM sends IP packets periodically to every other DM and a keep-alive message to the source if a DM is not available. If a DM is not reported to the source, it is deleted from the list.

Figure 1. The STF multicast architecture

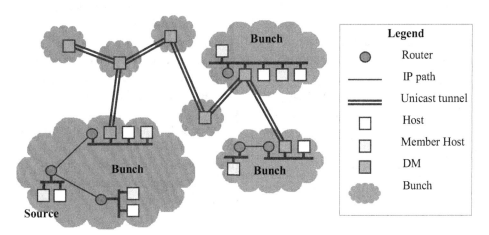

The source periodically sends the list to the DMs. If the source is not available, the group state is timed out in the DMs.

The STF, similar to the MOSPF protocol (Moy, 1994), uses the Dijkstra algorithm (Dijkstra, 1959) for calculating the shortest path, which, in its case, is composed of IP tunnels. But the MOSPF uses the underlying open shortest path first (OSPF) protocol, in which the routers exchange the link-state information about their neighbors, while in the case of the STF, the designated member hosts (DMs) exchange the path information to each other, since there are IP paths to every other DM.

The STF protocol constructs an almost similar optimal tree to the IP-multicast; however, it does not require any inter-domain multicast routing mechanism in the routers. It belongs to the mesh-first class. It is optimal for relatively small groups, but due to the TMC method, the topological size of the group does not limit its scalability.

IMPLEMENTATION AND RESULTS

The thematic mode multicast concept and the shortest tunnel first (STF) Application-Level routing protocol

Figure 2. Optional routing protocols in the PardedeCAST software

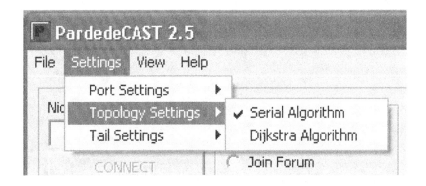

are being implemented in the PardedeCAST software. The current version of the software is able to create the P2P overlay where the clients use the STF routing protocol for creating the multicast distribution tree. In the software, a simpler routing algorithm can optionally be chosen, too, as *Figure 2* shows.

The current version of the software, however, has not yet used the IP-multicast. Therefore, in the future such features are going to be built in, since the native multicast in the IP-multicast islands is theoretically and practically the fastest form of transmission.

The implemented software can help in the analysis of the quality parameters introduced before. *Figure 3* shows an example for the analysis screen of the test network topology (Pardede et al., 2002).

Figure 3 shows the link delays of the test topology. Based on the topology data, the analysis software **Net-Sim** (**net**work **sim**ulator) can calculate the efficiency of the various routing algorithms (Pardede, 2002). *Figure 4* presents the graphical editor screen of *NetSim*.

The analyzer interface of the NetSim software is presented in *Figure 5*. By using NetSim, various ALM multicast routing and transporting protocol mechanisms can be tested and compared.

Figure 3. The network analysis screen of the software

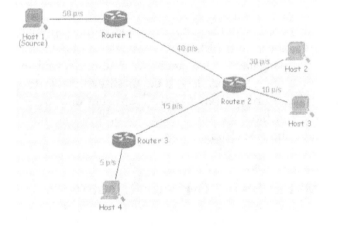

CONCLUSION

This chapter presented an overview of the emerging application-level multicast protocols, and focused on the novel thematic multicast concept method. It is intended to describe a typical multicast scenario, where the interested members are located in a restricted number of institutions, far from each other. For modeling the delivery in this situation, the bunched mode delivery is introduced. The novel STF multicast routing protocol is applicable for this bunched mode multicast. In each bunch (LAN or AS), designated members are elected. In order to avoid a globally available rendezvous point for the designated members, an inter-bunch tunneling protocol called shortest tunnel first is developed.

Figure 4. An example network topology created with network scheme editor

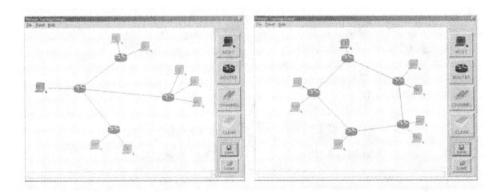

Figure 5. The analyzer interface of NetSim software

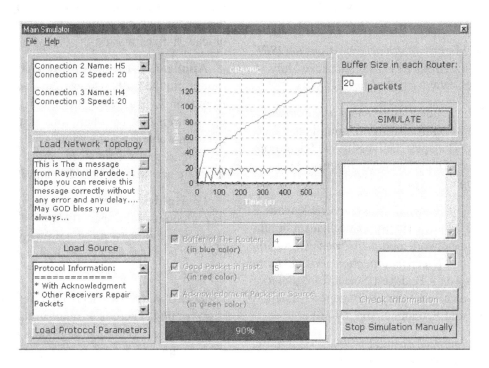

REFERENCES

Banerjee, S., Bhattacharjee, B., & Kommareddy, C. (2002). Scalable application-layer multicast. In *Proceedings of ACM SIGCOMM 2002,* 205-220. Pittsburgh, Pennsylvania, Association for Computing Machinery.

Chawathe, Y. (2000). *Scattercast: An architecture for Internet broadcast distribution as an infrastructure service.* PhD Thesis, University of California, Berkeley.

Chu, Y.-H., Rao, S.G., Seshan, S., & Zhang, H. (2002). A case for end system multicast. *IEEE Journal on Selected Areas in Communications, 20*(8), 1456-1469.

Deering, S.E., Estrin, D., Farinacci, D., Jacobson, V., Liu, C-G., & Wei, L. (1996). The PIM architecture for wide-area multicast routing. *IEEE/ACM Transactions on Networking, 4*(2), 153-162.

Dijkstra, E.W. (1959). A note on two problems in connection with graphs. *Numerische Mathematik, 1,* 269-271.

Francis, P. (2000). *Yoid: Extending the multicast Internet architecture.* Technical Report, *ACIRI.* Retrieved August 7, 2006, from http://www.aciri.org/yoid

Garcia-Luna-Aceves, J.J., & Madruga, E.L. (1999). The core-assisted mesh protocol. *IEEE Journal of Selected Areas in Communications, 17*(8), 1380-1394.

Haartsen, J. (1998). Bluetooth: The universal radio interface for ad hoc, wireless connectivity. *Ericsson Review, 3,* 110-117. Retrieved August 7, 2006, from http://www.ericsson.com/review

Hosszú, G. (2005). Mediacommunication based on application-layer multicast. In S. Dasgupta (Ed.), *Encyclopedia of virtual communities and technologies* (pp. 302-307). Hershey, PA: Idea Group Reference.

Ko, Y-B., & Vaidya, N.H. (2002). Flooding-based geocasting protocols for mobile ad hoc networks. In *Proceedings of the Mobile Networks and Applications, 7*(6), 471-480.

Mohapatra, P., Gui, C., & Li, J. (2004). Group communications in mobile ad hoc networks. *Computer, 37*(2), 52-59.

Moy, J. (1994, March). *Multicast extensions to OSPF*, Network Working Group RFC 1584. Retrieved July 31, 2006, from http://www.ietf.org/rfc/rfc1584.txt

Pardede, R.E.I. (2002). *Development a classification methodology for multicasting*. Unpublished MSc Project Thesis. Budapest University of Technology and Economics, Department of Electron Devices, Budapest, Hungary.

Pardede, R.E.I., Szilvássy, G., Hosszú, G., & Kovács, F. (2002). NetSim: Multicast transport mechanism simulator for simplified network model. In *Proceedings of the Meeting Advanced Telecommunication and Informatic Systems and Networks*. Budapest, Scientific Association for Infocommunications Hungary, Budapest University of Technology and Economics (pp. 59-60).

Zhang, B., Jamin, S., & Zhang, L. (2002). Host multicast: A framework for delivering multicast to end users. In *Proceedings of INFOCOM 2002, Twenty-First Annual Joint Conference of the IEEE Computer and Communications Societies* (Vol. 3, pp. 1366-1375). New York: IEEE Computer Society Press.

KEY TERMS

Ad Hoc Network: A network which does not need any infrastructure. Bluetooth is such a network.

ALM Routing Protocol: Members of the host's construct delivery tree using similar algorithms to those of the *IP-multicast* routing protocols.

Application Level Multicast (ALM): A multicast technology which does not require any additional protocol in the network routers, since it uses the traditional unicast IP transmission.

Application-Level Network (ALN): Applications running in the hosts that can create a virtual network from their logical connections. This is also called an *overlay network*. The operations of such software entities are not able to be understood without the knowledge of their logical relations. In most cases these ALN software entities use the *P2P model*.

IP-Multicast: Network-level multicast technology which uses the special class-D IP-address range. It requires multicast routing protocols in the network routers. It is also known as *network-level multicast (NLM)*.

Local Area Network (LAN): Network where there is no routing. There is a router in the LAN acting as a gateway and the remaining nodes are usually hosts without any routing functionality.

Multicast Island: A multicast-capable network, where all routers have multicast routing protocols and *IP-multicast* is available. One of the main problems of IP-multicast is connecting the multicast islands into an Internet-wide network.

Multicast Routing Protocol: In order to forward multicast packets, routers have to create multicast routing tables using multicast routing protocols.

Peer-to-Peer (P2P): A communication method where each node has the same authority and communication capability. The nodes create a virtual network overlaid on the Internet. Its members organize themselves into a topology for data transmission.

Collaborative Support for Graphical-Based Design Tools

Wong Kok Seng
Multimedia University, Malaysia

Sellappan Palaniappan
Malaysia University of Science and Technology, Malaysia

Nor Adnan Yahaya
Malaysia University of Science and Technology, Malaysia

INTRODUCTION

In today's information and communication technology (ICT) era, the need for real-time collaboration over the Internet is increasing. Due to ongoing corporate globalization and geographic dispersion of project operations, collaborative becomes a key for supporting these distributed corporate operations. Current electronic design automation (EDA) and computer-aided software engineering (CASE) tools typically do not support collaborative work. In a geographically dispersed environment, designers from different companies or locations are finding it difficult to communicate with each other. Several studies have been done on collaborative environment; however, all studies are still in the research level and not yet commercialized. In order to support collaborative work, few concerns must be taken into consideration. Network architecture is the main concern when designing a network-based collaborative environment. Client-server architecture and peer-to-peer architecture are two possible architecture designs that can be used for a collaborative graphical-based design environment.

Architects, practitioners, designers, and researchers alike are all interested in how computer technology may help them to improve effectiveness in the collaborative works. The technological advances in computing and networking in recent years have enabled collaborative work among members of a project team. Collaborative technology is used to improve the speed and efficiency of project implementation as well as its operations. Creating, maintaining, and evolving social interaction in communities are concerned for collaboration. As described by McCullough (2004), interaction design needs to be concerned with how people interact with each other in situations where technology should be part of the environment.

Collaborative work is also aimed at supporting groups of people engaged in a common task and pursuing a common goal. There were several types of solutions that enable users to work in a collaborative environment. Two competing solutions are peer-to-peer (P2P) and client-server architecture. Both architectures allowed data sharing among collaborators within a single environment—collaborative environment.

According to Xu (2000), "Collaboration is primarily concerned with creating, maintaining, and evolving social interaction in communities, and it is aimed at supporting groups of people engaged in a common task and pursuing a common goal." Projects that involved a team of people often supported by basic needs of enabling communication tools such as e-mail, Web-based file sharing, and chat programs. There is a need for these components to support collaborative environment so that collaborators will feel that they are working together on a daily, hourly, or even continuous basis (Agarwal, Sachs, & Johnston, 1998). Both client-server and peer-to-peer architecture can be used to support graphical-based design tools such as EDA and CASE. However, the usage of these architecture designs is based on the functionality and requirement from the collaborative team. The framework with either architecture design is comprehensive enough to support the development of a collaborative design environment, particularly one that uses graphical-based design tools. In this article, we will examine the usage of the previously mentioned architecture to support graphical-based tools (e.g., EDA). A design overview and the salient features of such a collaborative environment or system will be presented.

BACKGROUND

Collaborative support for graphical-based designed tools is relatively new. There are only few projects that are carried out at research level. The first identified project is Web-based electronic design (WELD, 1999), which is currently running at the Department of Electrical Engineering and Computer Sciences University of California at Berkeley. This project is the first operational prototype in IC design for the U.S. electronic industry. It aims to provide a reliable, scalable connection and communication mechanisms for a distributed environment that consist of users, EDA tools, and services. The Internet-based distributed VHDL design (IVE) project is another similar project that focuses on VHDL design tool. IVE as described in Yang, Windisch, Schneider, Mades, and Ecker (1999), helps developers to distribute VHDL related design data, software components, and services over the networks. It is applicable in distributed, concurrent design, teamwork develop, and provisions of IPs. The main advantage of the proposed system in this project is platform independence. The system is implemented in JAVA and supports multi platforms.

PROBLEM STATEMENT

According to Jeffrey and Tony (2001), collaborative interactions can be divided into four categories, which include face-to-face, asynchronous, distributed asynchronous, and distributed synchronous. There are many collaborative tools that are now available in the market to support these collaborative interactions. There are also many studies conducted in universities and organizations that focus on collaborative design. The success of collaborative computing depends on many factors including protocols used, the architecture style used, the level of need, and performance of network system. Currently, graphical-based design tools were used in most of the industries. Industries from different domains apply such tools into their business operations. Collaborative works become a trend for most of the companies especially projects that involve multi-parties. The study on existing graphical-based tools and techniques are not efficient enough to support the growing technology nowadays. Graphical-based design tools are of significant importance to system architecture design, electronic circuit design, and other forms of design. The usage of these tools is becoming increasingly important to help designers in monitoring their work. Unfortunately, there is no standard framework that enables such tools to be used in a collaborative environment.

Graphical-based design tools such as EDA, CASE, and CAD are commonly used nowadays. These tools are important because they can accelerate the design cycle. Software industry needs CASE tool to help in their software design (e.g., use case modeling can help the designers or developers to produce quality design. EDA tool is a new design tool for electronic industry. This tool is developed and designed for electrical circuit design, schematic capture, simulation, prototyping, and production. There are many electronic companies looking for EDA tools because it can increase productivity and shorten the design circle time for electronic circuit design. EDA tool helps the electronic industry to speed up their complex circuit design. The electronic design automation industry supplies services, products, and tools used by electronic engineers. Engineers who develop today's highly complex computer chips and the larger electronic systems in which they reside require EDA tools and services.

Many problems will occur if there is no collaborative support for designers. Significant research efforts have been devoted to the area of sharing information through computers and the Internet. However, limited attention has been devoted to the basic communication mechanisms and the encoding of these mechanisms as discussed in Pena-Mora and Hussein (1998). If only one designer controls the entire design, it is hard for another project member to understand the existing design. This problem becomes worse when the person who controls the design process leaves the company or quits the project. All these problems occur because there are no features from existing design tools that enable collaborative work among designers. Current design tools do not support information sharing among collaborators. All information is available locally to the team or organization. There is no central repository to store files and information. During the collaboration process of large-scale projects, the design is separated into sub modules and distributed to several project teams. Unfortunately, the current design environment assumes that the design is a product that belongs to their company and minimizes information and idea sharing. The lack of collaboration between all project teams might cause the project to fail as all teams think only of their own benefits and decline to share information and resources.

MOTIVATION FOR COLLABORATIVE SUPPORT

This section will discuss a sample scenario for motivation toward collaborative support for graphical-based design tools. Company A is an international company. They have a team of designers working on a project, but team members are from dispersed locations. The project is then divided into different modules and each designer is responsible for a particular module. The work of each designer might depend on work completion from other designers. Due to this, there must be some communications among the team members. The project manager is responsible for managing the project and he or she needs to track and review all the works.

Designers are able to access information or files at any location. He or she will expect modifications made to any of these files on one device to be automatically reflected on another, even when the devices are geographically far apart and connected to physically separate networks. He or she also wants all files to be accessible even when his or her system is in disconnected mode. Designers will need to share their work with other team members. Each of the designers would like to read and view the group's files, and also be able to modify the files, delete, and add a new file.

The collaboration system must be able to support different network environments such as machines connected via intranet and shielded by firewall, wireless network such as 802.11 or 802.11b, or machines connected to an ISP via an ADSL or dialup and have dynamically assigned IP addresses. A designer may work in online or off-line mode. For example, during working hours, designer X's laptop is connected to the corporate intranet. Modifications made to any of the files are replicated to other designers of the group. At the end of the working day, designer X may disconnect his or her laptop and continue to work on some of the shared files at home. Thus, he or she is working in off-line mode. Any modifications are stored in the local

drive of his or her laptop, and hence may be uploaded to the network when designer X reconnects to the network in the following morning. He or she boots up the notebook and reconnects to the P2P-C system. After he or she has logged in, the system will fetch the changes and update to other members automatically. From the discussed sample scenario, it brings up the motivation to setup an environment that allows collaborators to work under a same virtual environment.

DESIGN CONSIDERATIONS

In 1999, Fastie (1999) defined the concept of client-server architecture as one or more machines (client) accessing a powerful computer (server) to store and process data. In this case, a client is an individual user's computer or a user application that does a certain amount of processing on its own. The client can be any machine within the network that is connected to the server. However, peer-to-peer architecture has been introduced and used in many applications such as KaZaA, Gnutella, Mojo Nation, and Freenet. According to Mauthe and Hutchison (2003), "Napster was the first major system enabling the direct exchange and sharing of content. While the actual exchange of content in Napster is between peers, the discovery of the peers, however, is highly centralized." According to Barkai (2001), "There are many types of applications that employ P2P technologies compared to client-server architecture.

A matter of great interest to architects, practitioners, and researchers alike is how computer technology might affect the way they think and work. The concern is not about the notion of "support" alone, but about ensuring that computers do not disrupt the design process and collaborative activity already going on (Finholt, Sproull, & Kiesler, 1990). Architecture style that can be used to support collaborative works for graphical-based design tools included client-server architecture, peer-to-peer architecture, as well as distributed object architecture.

There are some criterions to be considered in order to choose the best architecture style for the collaborative framework. Feasibility is one of the main concerns for the selected architecture. As the number of nodes on the collaborative network increase very fast, the architecture used must be able to support large number of users

Figure 1. Shared workspaces without lock mechanism

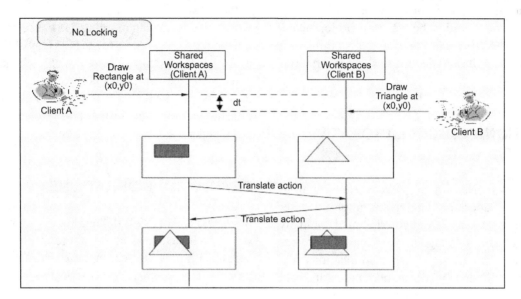

simultaneously. In the collaborative environment, there might be more than 10 or even 100 users collaborating together for a same project at the same time.

Data transfer rate is another important feature that must be provided by the network architecture. All data must be transferred securely between the nodes in the network. File sharing is essential because it is the primary requirement for collaborative work (Agarwal & Perry, n.d.). In terms of scalability, architecture used must allow the creation of additional nodes or services anytime, anywhere. It has to support simultaneous users and provide a reasonable performance.

Workspaces locking algorithms or locking mechanisms are concerned when concurrent operations occur. It is used to prevent conflicts and inconsistencies of the collaborative design. The coordination of group members' activities in the shared workspaces is crucial because any inconsistency will bring the big impact to the design. Problems might occur if there are two or more clients working at the same time within the same environment without having locking mechanisms. An example is shown in Figure 1.

In this example, peer-to-peer (P2P) architecture is selected. Client A draws a rectangle at (x0, y0), while client B on the other hand draws a triangle at (x0, y0). Assuming that both clients drawing at the same time or within a small different of time. Thus, this may result in having two different drawings as shown in Figure 1.

P2P uses a locking mechanism for workspace to solve this problem. The locking mechanism is shown in Figure 2. When client A is drawing a rectangle, a message is sent to client B to lock the workspace. Client B can only view the workspace and no modification is allowed. The workspace is unlocked after client A has finished drawing and this action is translated to client B's workspace.

The locking operation is done transparently from the user and it uses implicit floor control mechanisms. When users draw an object on the screen, the workspace is temporarily locked until the operation is completed. Other users are not able to draw on the workspace in the mean time.

Collaborative environments for graphical-based design tools use transmission control protocol (TCP) to transmit information across the Internet. TCP is the Internet standard transport protocol that provides the reliable, two-way connected service that allows an application to send a stream of data end-to-end between two computers across a network (definitions of transmission control protocol). It uses the Internet protocol (IP) as the underlying protocol. In addition to TCP, there is another transport level protocol called user datagram protocol (UDP). The UDP provides a connectionless service for application level procedures. However, UDP does not guarantee delivery, preservation of sequence and protection against duplication.

Figure 2. Shared workspaces with locking mechanism

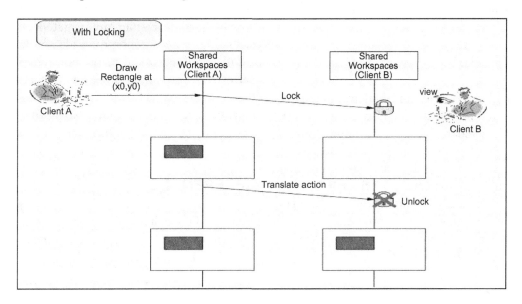

TCP uses the concept of port numbers to identify sending and receiving applications. Each side of a TCP connection has an associated 16-bit unsigned port number assigned to the sending or receiving application. The port numbers are divided into three ranges: well known (0 to 1023), registered (1024 to 49151) and private (49152 to 65535) ports. Well known are ports that are listening for connections, such as HTTP (80), FTP (21), and TELNET (23). Registered ports are named services that have been registered by a third party. Private ports are those used by end user applications. We can use 8888 as listening ports and use random port numbers to accept connection.

IMPLEMENTATION

The implementation of collaborative support into graphical-based designed tools is a daunting task. The design can be different from one tool to another tool. However, collaborators in the workspace should be able to use and share the same components from the server.

According to Maziloglou, Scrivener, and Clark (1994), workspace can be defined as both interpersonal space and shared workspace. In this section, we will discuss the implementation by using peer-to-peer approach as discussed by Minar and Hedlund (2001).

The client logs on to the centralized server and publishes local information. Published information includes the client's IP address, listen port, and firewall status. The server verifies the client's username and password. If it is a valid client, a log file is added into the database. The server then sends a list of active peers who are in the same group as the client. The list includes nodes' IP address, listen port, and firewall status. The client receives the list and proceeds to work through it, attempting to establish connection between the group members.

The client requests for a direct point-to-point connection by sending connection request messages. The peer needs to accept the connection request to establish a direct point-to-point connection. In the initial state, the central server is needed to manage and integrate the connection because in the current design it is not possible to establish and maintain connectivity between clients without connecting to the central server. Therefore, central server is needed for peer discovery and peer joining. Clients that connect to the server need authentication from the server such as username and password checking. Clients register with the server to announce their availability in the network. The central server acts as a common user directory service to locate group members at anytime, and also resolves the issue of node discovery for joining clients. A periodic update to this status is tracked so that the server knows whether the node is still online or no longer available by using a connection checker.

FUTURE TRENDS

Future work includes research and implementation improvements. In future, the data transfer over the network would use XML standard. XML is a common standard used to structure information and exchange data using markup tags. Users would need to exchange information in a collaborative environment, even though they are not online simultaneously. A relay server is required to solve the intermittent connectivity problem.

Authentication and authorization process applied in the prototype might not be perfectly secure for distributed environment as discussed by Parashar, Agarwal, Arbeeny, Bhat, and Chowdhury (2001). The research on security itself can be complicated because there are many factors that have to be taken into consideration. Public key infrastructure (PKI) is a method of allowing users of networks such as the Internet to securely and privately exchange messages using public key cryptography. Voice over Internet protocol is a way of IP telephony. It involves the transmission of telephone calls over a network or Internet. VoIP may be used as voice communication tool, which is cheaper than the telephone line. Video conferencing allows team members to hold a meeting with team members in a virtual conference room.

CONCLUSION

Overall, there are many concerns for graphical-based design tools over the collaborative environment. Real-time information and files exchange among group members will increase the productivity of the final work. Meetings among project members from dispersed system will not required traveling to target office or destination. Real-time data repository can be used to allow group members to access shared documents easily. A project may be divided into several modules, and implemented or developed by several group members who are dispersed in different geographical locations. Even though each member may be working on different modules independently, some modules have to be incorporated together at some point. Therefore, a Web-based collaborative tool is required to allow all

of them to collaborate and coordinate their tasks and allow the transfer of information between the group members. This article investigated collaboration technologies and proposed an idea on how to setup a collaboration system to provide reliable and high performance communication for collaborative works. It used P2P architecture as the sample architecture. A more complex collaborative design can be developed based on idea presented in this article.

REFERENCES

Agarwal, D., Sachs, S. R., & Johnston, W. E. (1998). The reality of collaboratories. *Computer Physic Communications, 110*(1-3), 134-141.

Agarwal, D., & Perry M. (n.d.). *Supporting collaborative computing and interaction.* Retrieved April 21, 2006, from http://dsonline.computer.org/collaborative/events/iwces-5/PerryAgarwal.pdf

Barkai, D. (2001). Technologies for sharing and collaborating on the net. The *First International Conference on Peer-to-Peer Computing* (pp. 13-28).

Definitions of Transmission Control Protocol (TCP). (n.d.). Retrieved January 20, 2006 from http://www.google.com.

Fastie, W. (1999, February). Understand client server computing. *PC Magazine: "Enterprise Computing",* 229-230.

Finholt, T., Sproull, L., & Kiesler, S. (1990). *Communication and performance in ad hoc task groups* (pp. 291-325), Hillsdale, NJ: Lawrence Erlbaum Associates.

Jeffrey, H., & Tony, L. (2001). Collaborative computing. *IEEE Computer, 7*(44), 79-85.

Mauthe, A., & Hutchison, D. (2003). *Peer-to-peer computing: Systems, concepts, and characteristics.* Retrieved February 18, 2006, from http://www.efinancelab.de/pubs/pubs2003/PeerComputing.pdf

Maziloglou, Scrivener, M., & Clark, S. M. (1994). *Proceedings of the Delft Protocols Workshop in Analyzing Design Activity.*

Minar, N., & Hedlund, M. (2001). A network of peers: Peer-to-peer models through the history of the Internet.

In A. Oram (Ed.), *Peer-to-peer: Harnessing the benefits of a disruptive technology* (pp. 8-18). Sebastopol, CA: O'Reilly & Associates.

McCullough, M. (2004). *Digital ground: Architecture, pervasive computing, and environmental knowing.* Cambridge.

Parashar, M., Agarwal, M., Arbeeny, S., Bhat, V., & Chowdhury, R. (2001). *Evaluating security mechanisms in peer-to-peer applications.* Retrieved January 14, 2006, from http://www.cs.ucr.edu/~csyiazti/courses/cs260-2/gnutella/p2psecurity.pdf

Pena-Mora, F., & Hussein, K. (1998). Interaction dynamics in collaborative civil engineering design discourse: Applications in computer mediated communication. *Journal of Computer Aided Civil and Infrastructure Engineering, 14,* 171-185.

Slater, M., Sadagic, A., Usoh, M., & Schroeder, R. (2000). Small group behaviour in a virtual and real environment: A comparative study. *Presence: Teleoperators and Virtual Environments, 9*(1), 37-51.

WELD: Web-Based Electronic Design. (1999). Retrieved March 21, 2006 published in http://www-cad.eecs.berkeley.edu/Respep/Research/weld

Xu, C. (2000). *Interaction and collaboration mechanisms for distributed communities and groups in educational settings.* Retrieved March 3, 2006, from http://tumb1.biblio.tu-muenchen.de/publ/diss/in/2000/xu.pdf

Yang, K., Windisch, A., Schneider, T., Mades, J., & Ecker, W. (1999). *An environment for Internet-based distributed.* Retrieved March 20, 2006 from www.iftp.or.at/con2000/icda2000/icda-16-3.pdf

KEY TERMS

Computer-Aided Design (CAD): Computer-aided design is a system with the combination of hardware and software that enables designer to design their works.

Computer-Assisted Software (CASE): Computer-assisted software engineering is a category of software used to provides a development environment for programmers.

Client-Server: One or more machines (client) accessing a powerful computer (server) to store and process data.

Client-Server Collaborative Environment (CSCE): An environment that serves as the virtual workspace for collaborators. It was implemented using client server architecture.

Electronic Design Automation (EDA): Electronic design automation is a software used to design electronic circuit. It is an automation tool that can simplify the design work as well as speed up the required time for a design.

Integrated Circuit (IC): A small electronic device made up by semiconductor materials.

IVE: Internet-based distributed VHDL design is a tool used to help developers to distribute VHDL related design data, software components, and services over the networks.

NAPSTER: An application that gives individual access to media files such as MP3 by creating a file sharing system over the Internet.

Web-Based Electronic Design (WELD): Web-based electronic design is a system used to provide a reliable, scalable connection and communication mechanisms for a distributed environment that consist of users, EDA tools, and services.

Comparison of Multipath Schemes for Hybrid Models in MPLS

Kyeongja Lee
Ecole Centrale de Lille, France

Armand Toguyeni
Ecole Centrale de Lille, France

Ahmed Rahmani
Ecole Centrale de Lille, France

INTRODUCTION

Congestion is derived from insufficient network resources and unbalanced traffic distribution. To treat today's greedy applications, adding more bandwidth to networks is not the solution for solving the congestion problems in the long term. There are two main approaches to improve quality of service (QoS) of actual network: QoS routing and traffic engineering (Wang, 2001). QoS routing searches the paths by constraint-based routing for better delivery of traffic and is serviced to attract more customers, while traffic engineering aims to reduce congestions and to improve resource utilization through the network by carefully managing the traffic distribution inside a network (Wang, 2001).

In order to engineer the traffic effectively in IP networks, network administrators must be able to control the complete paths of packets instead of hop-by-hop. This requires some kinds of connections in the connectionless IP networks. MPLS (multi-protocol label switching) enables you to distribute network traffic more evenly than best effort service and the probability of network congestion can be reduced (Xiao, 2000).

In this article, we focus on traffic engineering and more specifically on multipath routing that routes demands on multiple paths simultaneously for balancing the load in the network instead of routing all the traffic on the shortest path as current Internet service. In literature, there are a lot of proposed algorithms for multipath routing. Each algorithm is declared very efficient by its authors but generally with respect to restricted conditions. This study aims to compare some recent MPLS-based routing algorithms both with regard to their respective model and to the scalability and the stability of each solution in order to verify if it is efficient. Based on this comparison, we propose new hybrid approaches.

BACKGROUND

There are basically two main stages in a multipath routing algorithm (Figure 1): computation of multiple paths and traffic splitting among these multiple paths.

In the first stage, it computes the set of candidate paths, which is a subset of all the paths between a pair of considered routers. According to the nature of a cost function, different algorithms can be applied to determine these candidate paths. The authors consider various static criteria such as bandwidth, hop count, delay, error ratio, and so on for a cost function. This problem of a cost function definition is typically a multi-criteria problem (T'kindt, & Billaut, 2002):

Cost of Path Selection = f (Bandwidth, Hop-Count, Delay, Error Ratio)

The second stage consists of splitting traffic among multiple candidate paths from the first stage. These paths are qualified of candidate paths because not all of them are necessary to be used at a given time. The utilization ratio of selected paths depends on the evaluation of dynamic criteria such as blockages, the packet loss ratio, the measured delay, the jitter, and so on. This also requires the definition of a cost function based on dynamic criteria what is still a multi-criteria problem (T'kindt et al., & Billaut, 2002).

Cost of Traffic Splitting = g (Blockage, Packet Loss Ratio, Measured Delay, Jitter)

If multiple criteria must be optimized simultaneously, the complexity of the algorithms usually becomes very high (Chen, 1999). A lot of heuristic algorithms are proposed to solve this problem.

To obtain the routing that gives an average QoS for different type of applications, we think that the good criterion consists in minimizing the maximum utilization ratio of the most heavily used link in the network. When the maximum link utilization minimizes, naturally the rejection rate for demand is reduced. If it is assumed that traffic grows in proportion to the current traffic pattern, this minimization objective will ensure that the extra traffic causes minimum congestion. This study focuses on four load-balancing models that respect this requirement. Consequently, our problem is to determine if the corresponding routing algorithms are scalable and efficient to be deployed in a large network.

Owing to this functional model of multipath routing (Figure 1), the possibility of cross combination of two steps from different algorithms is possible and notably one example of such a combination is given after four multipath algorithms' comparison in this study.

ALGORITHMS COMPARISON WITH REGARD TO COMPLEXITY AND STABILITY

Among the propositions for **multipath routing** algorithms that we found, we have selected four algorithms, which fit our expectations in terms of architecture: WDP (widest disjoint paths), MATE (MPLS adaptive traffic engineering), multipath-AIMD (additive increase multiplicative decrease), and LDM (load distribution over multipath). Behind the respective objective function expressed by the authors of each algorithm, we find a common objective that is to minimize the maximum link utilization ratio of the network. These propositions are all based on MPLS and they use local or infrequent updates of the network state, contrary to approach such as SWP (shortest widest path) (Wang & Crowcroft, 1996) or WSP (widest shortest path) (Guerin, Orda, & Williams, 1997).

WDP (Nelakuditi & Zhang, 2001)

WDP is not a full multipath-routing algorithm, but focuses on the selection of good paths. This approach is mainly based on two concepts: path width and path distance. Path width is defined as the residual bandwidth of its bottleneck link. This concept avoids sending too much traffic to the path with the smallest width, if possible. Path distance is original because contrary to most approaches, it is not a hop-count measure but it is indirectly dependent on the utilization ratio of each link defining the path. This approach is very promising when considering a practical implementation with numerous ingress-egress router pairs.

WDP algorithm performs candidate paths selection based on the computation of the width of the good disjoint paths with regard to bottleneck links. A path is added to the subset of good paths if its inclusion increases the width of this subset. At the opposite, a path is deleted if this does not reduce the width of the subset of good paths. The complexity of WDP is in $O(n^2)$. This allows using WDP online.

MATE (Elwalid, Jin, Low, & Widjaja, 2001)

The MATE article presents a traffic engineering scheme, which uses a constant monitoring of the links using probe packets to evaluate link properties such as packet delay and packet loss. Using these statistics the MATE algorithm is able to optimize packets splitting among paths to avoid link congestion.

Contrary to other algorithms compared here, there is no selection of candidate paths in MATE: all available paths are considered. Anyway, another step is required before proceeding to the load distribution: the incoming packets are regrouped into a fixed number of bins. The number of bins determines the minimum amount of data that can be shifted. The splitting of the packets among the bins can be done by different approaches, as shown in Elwalid et al. (2001). These approaches differ in their complexity and the way they handle packet sequencing. The better splitting method is "Using flow hash" because its complexity is $O(n)$ (with n the number of bins) and this method preserves packet sequencing.

The load balancing stage splits the content of the bins among LSPs, by using a technique such as the gradient algorithm. The complexity of this algorithm is $O(n^2)$ where n is the number of LSPs between an ingress-egress pair of nodes. Finally, since the two stages are in sequence and if we assume that the numbers of bins and the number of LSPs are comparable, MATE complexity is in $O(n^2)$. The designers of MATE have proved that MATE's algorithm converges to an optimal routing when specific conditions are verified (see Theorem 2 page 4 in Elwalid et al., 2001).

Multipath-AIMD (Wang, Patek, Wang, & Liebeherr, 2002)

In the multipath-AIMD article, the authors present an algorithm based on the notion of primary path. A primary path is a preferred path associated to each source. The data are sent mainly on the primary path, but can also use other LSPs when the bandwidth of the primary path is not sufficient.

The selection of paths in multipath-AIMD consists in selecting n LSPs equal to the number of current sources. This can be done by sorting the LSPs using its own metric and then extracting the better paths. For a set of n sources, the complexity of the treatment is in $O(n \ln(n))$. There is no stability issue in this step of the routing procedure. The traffic splitting stage uses an Additive Increase/Multiplicative Decrease: starting on an average splitting, the iterative process increases the data to be sent to a path with a constant value if the link is not saturated (additive increase) and divides the amount of data to be sent to a path by a certain value if the path is saturated (multiplicative decrease). This approach is done in $O(n)$ complexity for n chosen paths. Wang et al. (2002) also present a modified AIMD algorithm that is closer to PPF (primary path first)-optimality. This solution, called *multipath-AIMD with PPF correction*, is better in the way it comes closer to the expectations of the authors in terms of behavior, but it is also more expensive in resources. Its complexity is in $O(n^2)$ for n chosen paths.

LDM (Song, Kim, & Lee, 2003)

The LDM algorithm has the particularity to use a flow-based approach in multipath routing. This particularity is interesting to avoid some problems encountered with lower-level load distribution by preserving packet sequencing.

The algorithm tries to find a minimal set of good paths. The set is built on two criteria: the metric hop-count associated to each path must be as low as possible while maintaining links utilization inferior to a certain parameter ρ. This is done in $O(n^2)$ time in the worst case, the number of iterations growing with the utilization of the network. Here n refers to the number of paths available for the considered ingress-egress pair of nodes. In terms of convergence, the number of iterations has an upper limit defined by a given parameter δ, so the number of iterations is bounded and stability issues avoided.

The traffic splitting is then done using a heuristic to determine a splitting policy for incoming flows. Each path is adjoined a probability of selection using formula (1). Once probabilities are defined, each incoming flow is directed to the route with the highest probability. The $h(l)$ and $d(l)$ functions refer to the length and the remaining capacity of link l, while C_0 and C_1 are constants computed to make $P(l)$ a probability. The a_0 and a_1 factors are to be defined by the administrator to fit its needs:

$$P(l) = a_0 \frac{C_0}{h(l)} + a_1 \frac{d(l)}{C_1} \quad \text{with} \quad a_0 + a_1 = 1 \qquad (1)$$

The complexity of the whole procedure is clearly $O(n)$. Here n refers to the number of paths selected at the end of the previous step. However, our experiments show that LDM suffers potential stability issues. The next section will propose an improvement of LDM selection step.

HYBRID APPROACH WITH TWO STEPS COMBINATION FROM THE DIFFERENT ALGORITHMS

In this section, we aim to propose new hybrid algorithms built by combining steps of the four algorithms presented in the previous section. We begin this section by proposing an improvement of LDM selection part.

Our Proposition of a Modified LDM with Two Thresholds

LDM suffers potential stability issues. LDM algorithm for selecting candidate paths converges necessarily to a solution in a finite delay because of the limitation of the number of extra-hops that is admissible to augment the number of selected paths. In the path selection algorithm given in Song et al. (2003), this is expressed by the condition "m > δ" that allows stopping the first loop. However, the real problem of stability that can have LDM can be caused by oscillations derived from candidate path selection. Each time there are changes in path utilization values, the whole algorithm is applied without taking account of previous selections. Let us assume first that $\eta(t) < \rho$ and that the load of the network becomes too important and the utilization rate of candidate path set, $U(A_{ij})$, becomes superior to ρ. The computation at $t+\Delta T$ will give more candidate paths than at time t. Consequently the load will be distributed on new paths (with length superior to shortest paths) implying the decrease of the utilization of each path. If the load of shortest paths decreases under $\eta(t)$, the set of computed candidate paths will come back to the situation of the time t and so on.

Our idea is that the path selection algorithm can be improved by using two thresholds. The first threshold ρ_1 allows adding new paths in candidate path set. If the minimum of candidate path utilization goes under the second threshold ρ_2, this enables to reset the candidate paths selection by restarting the whole algorithm (Figure 2). The second threshold must be lower than the first one.

Construction of Hybrid Algorithms

The theoretical complexity study of MPLS-based multipath algorithms shows that each of them has its advantages and its drawbacks depending on the considered stage (see the study summarized in Table 1). This leads us to consider the possibility of building a hybrid algorithm composed of WDP and the splitting part of LDM.

To start, this hybrid calculates candidate paths using WDP algorithm in all possible paths from source to destination nodes every link state update time. For each candidate path, its selection probability value using each candidate path's hop-count and link utilization is calculated according to LDM's method (see equation 1). On arrival of a new demand to send, it selects one path with the highest probability among candidate paths. At that time, it deletes the paths, which have an insufficient capacity to assign the current traffic from the candidate paths set. If all paths in the candidate

paths set have insufficient capacity, it recalculates new candidate path set except the previous ones. On selecting one path to assign the current demand, it sends the traffic through that path. This algorithm performs better than original LDM owing to WDP's disjointed paths to avoid congestion.

To be able to perform credible comparison, traffic bifurcation (TB) problems (Lee, Seok, Choi, & Kim, 2002) and MATE are also evaluated using the linear programming solver, MATLAB. TB gives an optimal bound of the network utilization rate. LDM algorithm is also simulated with *ns-2* (DARPA, 1995) and *MNS 2.0* (Ahn & Chun, 2000) and compared with our proposed hybrid algorithm.

Figure 3 is our simulation topology with MPLS-based IP network. The bandwidths between two routers are marked on the link between them. There are 50 Poisson traffics to the egress node, LSR9, from the ingress node, LSR1. The demand of 200 Kbits/s is sent every 2s. The use of the Poisson distribution traffic for simulations is justified by its similar characteristics with real Internet traffic. Flow duration time is decided randomly in an Exponential distribution with an average of 15. Link state update period is 10s.

Figure 4 depicts the simulations' results of these algorithms with regard to the maximum link utilization. It shows that our proposed hybrid algorithm, WDP with LDM, is more efficient for load balancing than the classic LDM and it does not have a big difference with the result of MATE with MATLAB with regard to the maximum link utilization rate in the whole network.

FUTURE TRENDS

New hybrid algorithms using already existing or improved parts of multipath routing can be proposed. For example, LDM's splitting part can be improved by comparing the effective splitting ratio of each LSP with the planned one, and then it can be combined with good path selection algorithm (see Lee et al., 2006).

We are also researching new DS-TE (differentiated service MPLS traffic engineering) (Le Faucheur & Lai, 2003) mechanisms to meet the customers' various requirements using hybrid approach of this study. The idea is as follows: after balancing the load with regard to maximum link utilization using good multipath routing algorithm as shown in this study, DiffServ model is suitable to prioritize the different traffics according to specific criteria such as measured delay, jitter, and so on. By mapping the traffic from a given DiffServ class of service on a separate path in MPLS, the integration of MPLS and DiffServ in backbone networks can meet engineering constraints, which are specific to the given class. Additionally as presented in this study, different types of hybrid schemes for specific classes can be adapted in the multi-model approach.

Our proposed algorithms must be estimated in the physical test-bed using more realistic traffic models for the Internet.

CONCLUSION

We propose a functional framework that allows comparing different contributions for load balancing in ISP network. Following this framework, we have studied and compared four recent propositions to obtain a real adaptive model. The goal of this study is to identify actual routing algorithms that are efficient.

Our study shows that the stability of original LDM path selection is not guaranteed and proposes a modified algorithm to correct this aspect of LDM.

Based on our functional framework and four algorithms' comparison, hybrid approaches can be envisaged instead of developing a new routing algorithm. It consists of building a hybrid approach that combines the candidate path selection step and the traffic-splitting step from the different algorithms. Of the possible combinations, one example combination, WDP for the first step and LDM for the second step, is proposed and simulated. The simulation result shows that hybrid approach can get the better performance than original one with regard to the maximum link utilization rate that must be the main criteria for network performance evaluation.

REFERENCES

Ahn, G., & Chun, W. (2000, September). Design and implementation of MPLS network simulator supporting LSP and CR-LDP. The *8th IEEE International Conference on Networks*, Singapore.

Chen, S. (1999). *Routing support for providing guaranteed end-to-end quality-of-service*. Unpublished doctoral dissertation, University of Illinois at Urbana-Champaign, Chicago, USA.

DARPA & NSF. (1995). *The network simulator ns-2*. Retrieved from http://www.isi.edu/nsnam/ns/

Elwalid, A., Jin, C., Low, S., & Widjaja, I. (2001, April). MATE: MPLS adaptive traffic engineering. The *20th Annual Joint Conference of the IEEE Computer and Communications Societies (INFOCOM'2001)*, Alaska, USA.

Guerin, R., Orda, A., & Williams, D. (1997, November). QoS routing mechanisms and OSPF extensions. In *Proceedings of the Global Internet Miniconference*, Arizona, USA.

Lee, K., Toguyeni, A., & Rahmani, A. (2006, April). Hybrid multipath routing algorithms for load balancing in MPLS based IP network. *AINA2006* (pp. 165-170), Vienna, Austria.

Lee, Y., Seok, Y., Choi, Y., & Kim, C. (2002, April). A constrained multipath traffic engineering scheme for MPLS networks. *IEEE International Conference on Communications*, USA.

Le Faucheur, F., & Lai, W. (2003, July). *Requirements for support of differentiated services-aware*. RFC 3564. Retrieved from http://www.rfc-archive.org/

Nelakuditi, S., & Zhang, Z. L. (2001, June). On selection of paths for multipath routing. In *Proceedings of the 9th IEEE International Workshop on Quality of Service*, Karlsruhe, Germany.

Song, J., Kim, S., & Lee, M. (2003, February). Dynamic load distribution in MPLS networks. *International Conference on Information Networking 2003* (LNCS 2662, pp. 989-999). Cheju, Korea.

T'kindt, V., & Billaut, J. C. (2002). *Multicriteria scheduling: Theory, models, and algorithms*. Springer.

Wang, J., Patek, S., Wang, H., & Liebeherr, J. (2002, April). Traffic engineering with AIMD in MPLS networks. In *Proceedings of 7th International Workshop on Protocols for High-Speed Networks* (LNCS 2334, pp. 192-210), Berlin, Germany.

Wang, Z. (2001). *Internet QoS: Architectures and mechanisms for quality of service*, Morgan Kaufmann Publishers, Lucent Technology.

Wang, Z., & Crowcroft, J. (1996). Quality-of-service routing for supporting multimedia applications. *IEEE Journal of Selected Areas in Communications*, *14*, 1228-1234.

Xiao, X. (2000). *Providing quality of service in the Internet.* Unpublished doctoral dissertation, Michigan state University, USA.

KEY TERMS

Complexity: In computer science, complexity measures the number of cycles to achieve an algorithm.

Congestion: Congestion occurs when the offered load exceeds the capacity of a data communication path.

DiffServ: Differentiated Services is architecture for providing different types or levels of service for network traffic. Flows are aggregated in the network, so that core routers only need to distinguish a comparably small number of aggregated flows.

Exponential Distribution: In probability theory and statistics, the exponential distribution is a class of continuous probability distribution. It is often used to model the time between events that happen at a constant average rate.

Ingress Router: Routers on the incoming edge of the MPLS network.

LSP: Label Switched Paths is a set of hops across a number of MPLS nodes.

MPLS (Multi-Protocol Label Switching): A method used to increase the speed of network traffic flow by inserting information about a specific path the packet is taking to its destination. This saves the time needed for a router to look up the address for the next node that the packet is supposed to be sent to.

Oscillation: A periodic movement back and forth between two extreme limits.

Traffic Engineering: Traffic engineering uses statistical techniques such as queuing theory to predict and engineer the behavior of telecommunications networks such as telephone networks or the Internet.

Congestion Control in Multicast Networks

Miguel Rodríguez Pérez
Universidade de Vigo, Spain

Cándido López-García
Universidade de Vigo, Spain

Sergio Herrería-Alonso
Universidade de Vigo, Spain

INTRODUCTION

Multicast is a transmission service that simultaneously delivers packets from a sender to a group of receivers. The set of receivers form a *multicast group* logically identified by a unique *multicast address*. In a network with network level multicast support (e.g., IP), a copy of each packet is transmitted once on each link of a directed tree rooted at the sender with the receivers as leaves. In the public Internet, IP multicast is an extension to the basic routing and forwarding model, endowed with its own address space, signaling (IGMP), and routing protocols (MOSPF, DVMRP, PIM).

Bandwidth is shared in a communications link among different flows, and a link to which more traffic than its physical capacity is offered is said to be congested. Congestion, even at a moderate level, causes higher packet loss rates, longer transit delays, and unequal share of bandwidth among users. Thus, congestion control is the set of rules affected to adapt properly the flows' rates to the available bandwidth in every link, ensuring further that overloaded resources are distributed fairly among competing flows. On the Internet, the congestion control algorithm is embodied into TCP. It consists of a feedback-based, dynamic adaptation of a transmission window, with packet losses as an implicit congestion indication.

BACKGROUND

The problem of congestion control can be formulated on a sound theoretical basis, which allows you to analytically understand the key issues of stability and fairness. The framework borrows tools from optimization theory and sets congestion control as a resource allocation problem--bandwidth is the resource—with selfish participants (flows or users). The network is modeled as a set of directed links with fixed (but different) capacities, and every flow transmits at a given rate x along a subset of links (its route). Then, the aggregate rate of a link is the sum of rates of all sessions using such link. Each flow is characterized by a *utility function, $u(x)$*, which represents its value of bandwidth. Hence, utility functions grasp the notion of transmission rate as an economic asset. From a network wide perspective, the congestion optimization problem is that of maximizing the *sum of aggregate utility* of all flows, subject to the constraint that traffic on each link must not exceed its capacity. Provided some general and intuitive conditions on the utility functions are met (continuity and concavity), there always exists an optimal rate allocation. The choice of the utility function ultimately determines the equilibrium point and therefore is bound to some formal definition of fairness (Bonmariage & Leduc, 2006).

For multicast networks, it suffices to appropriately define the flow's utility. In fact, it should be a *receiver-oriented* utility because otherwise the multicast flows, which potentially use many links, receive unfair rates compared to unicast flows (Shapiro, Towsley, & Kurose, 2002).

In designing congestion control protocols, the main concern is finding a solution with a decentralized and iterative rate adaptation algorithm, which lends itself to a distributed implementation. So, it becomes essential that individual users need only locally available information to set its own rate. In the previous model, the network condenses such information into a *link price* sent periodically to the sources. The price is interpreted as a measure of the level of congestion in a link, and a source reacts by maximizing its individual utility minus the cost of sending x units of bandwidth, the unit price being the sum of link prices along the route. By studying different algorithms for adjusting prices, convergence to the optimal rate allocation and stability results can be firmly established in some cases (Kelly, Maullo, & Tan, 1998; Deb & Srikant, 2004). In practice, the link prices are simply congestion signals in the form of marked packets, packet drops, or delay measurements.

MULTICAST CONGESTION CONTROL

For multicast networks, congestion control poses a number of challenges over the unicast case. Firstly, since source adaptation is the response to the feedback from receivers, there should be some means to limit the so called *feedback implosion* problem (the accumulation of congestion signals on the sender) in order to support large groups. Secondly, the multicast tree can have different levels of congestion in each link, and the receivers could demand heterogeneous rates. As a last requirement, well-behaved protocols should achieve some form of fairness between unicast and multicast flows, particularly with TCP, the predominant traffic in the current Internet. We shall review these issues in turn.

TCP-COMPATIBILITY

To ease deployment of a multicast congestion control solution, the issue of fairness with TCP is of paramount importance. This goal has been addressed so far in a variety of ways. A first step has been to properly define the notion of fairness in diverse multicast contexts, which is more involved than its unicast counterpart because to reach n receivers, a packet must traverse n different paths (Rubenstein, Kurose, & Towsley, 2002; Wang & Schwartz, 1998). Another concern has been how to ensure that multicast sessions compete fairly for bandwidth with regular TCP sessions. Many multicast protocols are equation-based, which means that the receivers use a simple throughput formula for TCP in order to compute their fair share of bandwidth. Thus, the aim is that every receiver behaves as if an ordinary point-to-point TCP session would be running between the sender and itself (e.g., Widmer and Handley, 2001 or Luby, Goyal, Skaria, and Horn, 2002). Generally, equa-

tion-based protocols show slow reaction. Furthermore, since round trip times and packet loss probabilities have to be incorporated into the formula, measurement errors make difficult to obtain good accuracy. Instead of that, other protocols emulate directly, at every receiver, the congestion window of a hypothetical TCP flow along the path from the sender (Rizzo, 2000). The dynamics of the congestion window are well understood, less prone to measurement errors, and yields faster convergence to the fair rates.

Though fair in some definite sense, compatibility with TCP by the previous methods imply a behavior under the classical additive increase-multiplicative decrease (AIMD) dynamics for the rate or the congestion window. As it is well known, AIMD tends to produce sharp variations in the instantaneous rate. Yet for multicasting multimedia content (loss tolerant but usually delay stringent traffic), it would be desirable a smoother rate adaptation. To this end, the solution is to replace AIMD with a different algorithm, such as the one of TCP-Vegas (which uses delay rather than packet loss as a congestion signal) or a nonlinear algorithm (Rodríguez Pérez, Herrería Alonso, Fernández Veiga, & López García, 2005).

Receiver Heterogeneity

The simplest case in multicast transmission arises when the set of links in the multicast tree and the set of receivers are homogeneous. In such context, single-rate multicast protocols can be used, those in which the same rate is used in every link. Consequently, the rate for the entire session is necessarily limited by the most bandwidth-constrained receiver. Thus, severe congestion episodes, though isolated on a single link, impact jointly all the receivers in the group. In single-rate protocols, rate adaptation is performed by the sender in response to receiver feedback, usually mimicking some point-to-point congestion control algorithm. The risk of feedback implosion is handled differently in several protocols, ranging from not to counteract feedback implosion at all (Liang & Cheriton, 2002; Sisalem & Wolisz, 2000) to randomizing the congestion signals (Wang et al., 1998).

In the so-called *multiple-rate* protocols, the rate is allowed to vary on each link depending on the bandwidth available to downstream receivers and on their demands. To this end, the sender splits the information in a series of *layers*, each one transmitted via a different multicast group. Receivers subscribe to a subset of those layers according their current conditions, and adapt the rates with support from the network. The class of multiple-rate protocols can be classified along three axes: the layering scheme, the subscription policy followed by the receivers, and the dynamics of the transmission rate in each layer. The great majority of multiple-rate protocols adhere to a *cumulative layering scheme* in which the different layers are ordered and the subscription to one layer implies belonging to all the lower ones (Byers, Horn, Luby, Mitzenmacher, & Shaver, 2002; McCanne, Jacobson, & Vetterli, 1996; Rizzo, Vicisano, & Crowcroft, 1998). This flexible approach naturally suits the applications that use loss tolerant, incremental data encoding techniques (e.g., multimedia applications), because the data stream is degraded only along the congested paths but is delivered without impairment to uncongested receivers. Note that, with cumulative layering, every link in the subtree rooted at any given node transmits a subset of the layers passing through the node. Nevertheless, since partial subscription to a given layer is forbidden, cumulative layering imposes some rigidity and coarseness upon the finite set of accumulated rates eligible by a receiver. For such reason, another class of protocols advocate a scheme where receivers can join freely to any subset of layers (Byers, Luby, & Mitzenmacher, 2001), so as to obtain a finer-grained control over the rate. Therefore, in these non-cumulative albeit incremental layering schemes, the same total rate can be achieved with different combinations of layers. However, this comes at the cost of more complexity in the encoding process and diminished efficiency in the usage of network resources, as now the receivers downstream to a congested link could use disjoint sets of layers. Finally, a hybrid subscription scheme is also possible, relying on a cumulative scheme to approximate the reception rate and on a set of complementary layers transmitting at lower rates, which a receiver could independently choose from to get a fine adjustment of its rate (Byers & Kwon, 2001).

Another division in multiple-rate protocols concerns how receivers join and leave the layers. Some protocols are purely passive in that receivers modify their subscriptions only in response to changes in the measured congestion. Thus, upon a congestion episode, generally inferred by one or more packet losses, a particular receiver cautiously leaves one of its current layers—with cumulative layering, the highest one.

When no congestion is detected, a *subscription probe* is launched to seek available bandwidth (Byers et al., 2002; McCanne et al., 1996). There exists some risk of synchronization between probes from different receivers, and consequently they must be coordinated. In contrast, the active protocols anticipate the appropriate receiving rate—usually a TCP-compatible rate—before deciding to join a new layer. This rate can be approximated either with a known TCP model (Liu, Li, & Zhang, 2004) or simulating the evolution of a fictitious congestion window at the receivers (Rodríguez Pérez, Fernández Veiga, López Ardao, López García, & Herrería Alonso, 2003).

The last dimension to classify multiple-rate protocols is the dynamism in the transmission rates. The simplest possibility is to use a fixed transmission rate in each layer, as in McCanne et al. (1996) and Rodríguez Pérez et al. (2003), but there are some benefits in letting the rate vary over time. For example, it can compensate for the high signaling latency of IGMP, especially when leaving a group (Byers et al., 2002); or it may be useful to get better adaptation to the receiver demands, changing the transmission rates sporadically (Liu et al., 2004); or even to provide a richer set of transmission rates to the receivers, at the expense of more frequent subscription changes (Luby et al., 2002).

A third approach to manage heterogeneity is represented by the class of *hybrid protocols*, a sort of blend between single-rate and multiple-rate concepts. Hybrid protocols also use multiple layers, but the transmission rate of each layer is established by an isolated single-rate protocol run by the receivers currently subscribed to it. This artifact suppresses most of the join and leave operations that happen with multiple-rate protocols to adapt the reception rate, because now each layer offers some degree of flexibility in the rate that can be used to accommodate for light congestion. The practical differences lay on the rules that dictate to which layers a receiver must subscribe to comply with its TCP-compatible rate. It can be a fixed range for every group (Kwon & Byers, 2004), a minimum transmission rate (Rodríguez Pérez et al., 2005), or a minimum difference between the TCP-compatible rate and the transmission rate in other group (Li & Kalyanaraman, 2003).

Scalability

It is commonly known that processing congestion feedback from all the receivers leads to unscalable multicast protocols. Protocol designs have therefore employed various ad hoc mechanisms to limit the set of receivers sending congestion signals to the source. One option is using some variant of randomized feedback, where a receiver only notifies its state with a given probability after a random waiting time (Wang et al., 1998). An alternative approach appoints a single receiver to send regular feedback on behalf of the entire group. This special receiver, known as *the leader*, is always the most congested receiver at any given time, so it changes during the session lifetime (Rizzo, 2000; Widmer et al., 2001). Then, the path between sender and leader can be thought of as a unicast session used to establish the transmission rate. However, it is not always easy to pick the correct leader, and frequent leader changes could generate substantial overhead traffic. Yet another possibility is to conduct a random poll on the group members, bounding the number of responses in each round (Rodríguez Pérez et al., 2005).

Scalability issues also arise related to the architecture of a congestion control mechanism. If congestion control is performed end-to-end, and TCP-compatibility is a requirement, it has been demonstrated that the throughput of the multicast session decreases with the logarithm of the number of receivers under very optimistic assumptions (homogeneous settings) (Chaintreau, Bacelli, & Diot, 2002). This result indicates that there are fundamental limits on the group size beyond which multicast with end-to-end congestion will not scale. One escape from this limitation is to use an overlay network for congestion control where transmissions between adjacent overlay nodes are decoupled and could progress at a rate determined only by the conditions in the path between them. A particularly appealing form of overlay is that of P2P overlays for multimedia multicast communications, either with end-to-end or with hop-by-hop congestion control.

FUTURE TRENDS

Despite numerous attempts and several breakthroughs, the issue of multicast congestion control has not yet been resolved in a satisfactory way. On the theoretical side, deriving conditions for stability, and characterizing fairness, in networks with unicast and multicast traffic is an essential problem. Further, modeling the interaction between multicast traffic and AQM (active queue management) algorithms may shed new light on the dynamics of the congestion control algorithms proposed so far. Also, recently, a completely new approach for multicast communications has appeared. Network coding uses an algebraic framework to exploit the full multicast capacity of any network. Packets are interpreted as symbols from a discrete alphabet and the routers perform a certain (linear) encoding of the packets they receive before forwarding them. Whether network coding has implications on the multicast congestion control problem, and whether it can be practically applied, are still open problems.

For the networking practitioner, it is worth mentioning that some single-rate TCP-compatible approaches (PGMCC (Rizzo, Iannaccone, Vicisano, & Handley, 2004) and TFMCC (Widmer & Handley, 2006)) are currently in the process of being standardized. In heterogeneous scenarios, where single-rate protocols are less adequate, hybrid protocols are expected to provide better efficiency and smoother rate adaptation, so it is likely that they enter the track of standardization soon. As a final statement, it is still needed a large scale testbed to demonstrate that multicast, and multicast congestion control, is a robust technology. Perhaps the incentives might be driven by new bandwidth intensive multimedia applications, such as video or TV on demand.

CONCLUSION

In addition to reliable transmission, congestion control is a key issue to foster the adoption of multicast communications. The congestion control mechanisms must be able to scale up to large groups and, in view of the prevalence of TCP traffic, must achieve a fair share of bandwidth with TCP sessions. In homogeneous environments, single-rate protocols guarantee TCP compatibility, but exhibit usually low bandwidth efficiency. In heterogeneous environments, many proposals are receiver-based and partition the data into multiple layers, to which receivers dynamically join. Despite the differences in the management of layers, multiple-rate protocols overload the routers due to the frequent join and leave operations and show slow convergence. Hybrid protocols leverage the existence of several multicast groups with the ability of the receivers to adapt their transmission rate within each layer. They appear the most promising approach for future multicast communications.

REFERENCES

Bonmariage, N., & Leduc, G. (2006, February). A survey of optimal network congestion control for unicast and multicast transmission. *Computer Networks, 50*(3), 448-468.

Byers, J. W., & Kwon, G. I. (2001, September). STAIR: Practical AIMD multirate multicast congestion control. In *Proceedings of the 3ʳᵈ International COST264 Workshop on Networked Group Communication* (Vol. 2233, pp. 100-112). London, UK: Springer-Verlag.

Byers, J. W., Horn, G., Luby, M., Mitzenmacher, M., & Shaver, W. (2002, October). FLID-DL: Congestion control for layered multicast. *IEEE Journal on Selected Areas in Communications, 20*(8), 1558-1570.

Byers, J. W., Luby, M., & Mitzenmacher, M. (2001, April). Finegrained layered multicast. In *Proceedings of the IEEE INFOCOM*, Anchorage, AK, USA (Vol. 2, pp. 1143-1151).

Chaintreau, A., Bacelli, F., & Diot, C. (2002). Impact of network delay variation on multicast sessions performance with TCP-like congestion control. *IEEE/ACM Trans. on Netw.*, 500-512.

Deb, S., & Srikant, R. (2004, April). Congestion control for fair resource allocation in networks with multicast flows. *IEEE/ACM Trans. on Netw., 12*(2), 274-285.

Kelly, F., Maullo, A., & Tan, D. (1998). Rate control in communication networks: Shadow pricing, proportional fairness, and stability. *J. Oper. Res. Soc., 49*, 237-252.

Kwon, G. I., & Byers, J. W. (2004, December). Leveraging single rate schemes in multiple rate multicast congestion control design. *IEEE Journal on Selected Areas in Communications, 22*(10), 1975-1986.

Li, J., & Kalyanaraman, S. (2003, September). Generalized multicast congestion control. In *Proceedings of the 5ᵗʰ COST264 International Workshop on Network Group Communications (NGC 2003) and ICQT* (pp. 155-167). Springer-Verlag.

Liang, S., & Cheriton, D. (2002, June). TCP-SMO: Extending TCP to support medium-scale multicast applications. In *Proceedings of the IEEE INFOCOM* (Vol. 3, pp. 1356-1365).

Liu, J., Li, B., & Zhang, Y. Q. (2004, February). An end-to-end adaptation protocol for layered video multicast using optimal rate allocation. *IEEE Transactions on Multimedia, 6*(1), 87-102.

Luby, M., Goyal, V. K., Skaria, S., & Horn, G. B. (2002). Wave and equation based rate control using multicast round trip time. *ACM SIGCOMM Computer Communication Review, 32*(4), 191-204.

McCanne, S., Jacobson, V., & Vetterli, M. (1996). Receiver-driven layered multicast. *ACM SIGCOMM Computer Communication Review, 26*(4), 117-130.

Rizzo, L. (2000). pgmcc: A TCP-friendly single-rate multicast congestion control scheme. *ACM SIGCOMM Computer Communication Review, 30*(4), 17-28.

Rizzo, L., Iannaccone, G., Vicisano, L., & Handley, M. (2004, July). *PGMCC single rate multicast congestion control: Protocol specification*. Internet Draft. Retrieved from http://tools.ietf.org/wg/rmt/draftietf-rmt-bb-pgmcc/draft-ietf-rmt-bb-pgmcc-03.txt

Rizzo, L., Vicisano, L., & Crowcroft, J. (1998, March). TCP-like congestion control for layered multicast data transfer. In *Proceedings of the IEEE INFOCOM*, San Francisco, CA, USA (Vol. 3, pp. 996-1003).

Rodríguez Pérez, M., Fernández Veiga, M., López Ardao, J. C., López García, C., & Herrería Alonso, S. (2003, December 1-5). An open-loop multicast layered congestion control protocol for real-time multimedia transmission. In *Proceedings of the IEEE GLOBECOM*, San Francisco, CA, USA (Vol. 5, pp. 2855-2859).

Rodríguez Pérez, M., Herrería Alonso, S., Fernández Veiga, M., & López García, C. (2005, November). An auto-configurable hybrid approach to multicast congestion control. In *Proceedings of the IEEE GLOBECOM*, St. Louis, MO, USA (Vol. 2, pp. 657-661).

Rubenstein, D., Kurose, J., & Towsley, D. (2002). The impact of multicast layering on network fairness. *IEEE/ACM Transactions on Networking, 10*(2), 169-182.

Shapiro, J. K., Towsley, D., & Kurose, J. F. (2002, September). Optimization-based congestion control for multicast communications. *IEEE Comm. Mag., 40*(9), 90-95.

Sisalem, D., & Wolisz, A. (2000, May). MLDA: A TCP-friendly congestion control framework for heterogeneous multicast environment. *IWQOS*, Pittsburgh, KS, USA (pp. 65-74).

Wang, H. A., & Schwartz, M. (1998). Achieving bounded fairness for multicast and TCP traffic in the Internet. *ACM SIGCOMM Computer Communication Review*, 28(4), 81-92.

Widmer, B., & Handley, M. (2001). Extending equation-based congestion control to multicast applications. *ACM SIGCOMM Computer Communication Review*, 31(4), 275-285.

Widmer, J., & Handley, M. (2006, March). *TCP-friendly multicast congestion control (TFMCC): Protocol specification*. Internet Draft. Retrieved from http://tools.ietf.org/wg/rmt/draft-ietf-rmt-bbtfmcc/draft-ietf-rmt-bb-tfmcc-06.txt

KEY TERMS

Feedback Implosion: In a multicast protocol, when a large group of receivers sends information nearly simultaneously to the sender, possibly overwhelming the capacity of the network links near the sender.

Join Experiment: Attempt done by a receiver in a multiplerate protocol to increase the reception rate by joining an additional layer.

Layered Multicast: A multicast transmission in which information is divided in segments carried over different multicast groups.

Leader: In a single-rate protocol, it is the receiver responsible for sending regular feedback to the sender.

Multiple-Rate Protocol: A congestion control protocol that can provide diverse transmission rates to different receivers.

Single-Rate Protocol: A congestion control protocol that delivers the same flow of data to all receivers simultaneously.

TCP-Compatible: Protocol said of a congestion control protocol that obtains the same throughput that a conforming TCP implementation would obtain under identical circumstances.

Content–Aware Caching for Cooperative Transcoding Proxies

Kyungbaek Kim
University of California, Irvine, USA

Byungjip Kim
Korea Advanced Institute of Science and Technology, Korea

Daeyeon Park
Korea Advanced Institute of Science and Technology, Korea

INTRODUCTION

In recent years, the technologies of the network and the computer have enormously developed diverse devices such as PDAs, mobile phones, TVs, and so forth, which are connected to the network with various ways such as wired or wireless interfaces. These diverse devices have been able to use the Web contents, but some clients can not use the Web contents directly because their capabilities differ from those of the Web content provider's expectation. For these clients, the content adaptation, called the transcoding, is needed. This transcoding transforms the size, quality, presentation style, and so forth, of the Web resources to meet the capabilities of the clients. The main features of the transcoding can be summarized with two. First is that multiple versions exist for the same Web content due to the diverse client demand. Second is that the transcoding is a very computational task. These two features of the transcoding bring many issues to design a transcoding system.

The existing approaches of the transcoding system can be classified into three categories broadly, depending on the entity that performs the transcoding process: client-based, server-based, and intermediary-based approaches. In the client-based approaches, the transcoding is performed in client devices and the transcoder has direct access to the capabilities of the various devices. However, these approaches are extremely expensive due to the limited connection bandwidth and computing power of clients. Conversely, in the server-based approaches (Knutsson, Lu, & Mogul, 2002), the content server transforms objects into multiple versions online or offline. These approaches preserve the original semantic of the content and reduce the

transcoding latency during the time between the client request and the server response. However, keeping the multiple versions of an object wastes too much storage and the content providers actually cannot provide all kinds of versions of content for the diverse clients. In the intermediary-based approaches (Cardellini, Yu, & Huang, 2000), edge servers or proxy servers can transform the requested object into a proper version for the capability of the client before it sends the object to the client. These approaches need additional infrastructures in the network and the additional information (e.g., client capability information, semantic information of contents). Although these additional needs exist, these intermediary-based approaches address the problems of the client-based and server-based approaches and many researches have been emerged.

Although the intermediary-based approaches are considered most appropriate due to their flexibility and customizability, they have some system issues to be addressed. Because the costly transcoding has to be performed on demand in proxy servers, the scalability problem arises. To address the scalability problem and improve the system performance, researchers have proposed caching the transcoding results. Because of the cached results, we can reduce repeated transcoding tasks and the system performance can be improved. Recently, the cooperative transcoding proxy architecture is proposed to improve the system performance (Maheshwari, Sharma, Ramamritham, & Shenoy, 2002; Singh, Trivedi, Ramamritham, & Shenoy, 2002). However, applying the traditional cooperative caching directly to the transcoding proxy architecture is not efficient due to inherent problems of the content transcoding such as multiple versions of contents (Canali, Cardellini, Colajanni, Lancellotti, & Yu, 2003; Cardellini, Colaja-

Figure 1. The discovery process of the cooperative transcoding proxies

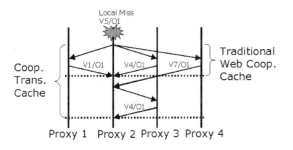

nni, Lancellotti, & Yu, 2003). Because of the multiple versions, the communication protocol of cooperative caches is more complex than existing protocols such as ICP (Chankhunthod, Danzig, Neerdaels, Schwartz, & Worrell, 1996) and causes additional delay, which is incurred by finding a more similar version of an object during the time for discovering the object in cooperative caches. Additionally, each cooperative cache consumes too much storage to store redundant multiple versions for the same object. These hurdles decrease the system performance and utilization.

BACKGROUND

In recent years, some proposals have exploited both transcoding and caching to reduce the resource usage at the proxy server, especially for transcoding time. The main idea of these approaches is that caching the transcoding results improves the system performance by reducing the repeated transcoding operation. Moreover, some studies extend a stand-alone transcoding proxy to cooperate each other to increase the size of the community of clients. This cooperative caching increases the hit ratio of the cache system by cooperating with each other caches for discovery, transcoding, and delivery. As a result of the increased hit ratio of system, it reduces not only the repeated transcoding operations, but also the user perceived latency for an object.

The transcoding proxy should manage the multiple version of an object because the transcoding results depend on the various capabilities of clients. According to the multiple versions, there are two types of hit: exact hit and useful hit. The exact hit means the proxy

cache contains the exact version required by the client, and the useful hit means the proxy cache does not have the exact version of the requested object but contains a more detailed and transcodable version of the requested object that can be transformed to obtain a less detailed version that meets the client request.

These two types of hits make the communication protocol of cooperative caches, especially the discovery protocol, more complex than existing protocols such as ICP. Figure 1 shows the difference of the discovery process between the cooperative transcoding proxies and the traditional Web proxies. Proxy 2 gets a request for an object, O1, whose version is the version 5, V5, and misses the object, then proxy 2 sends queries to other proxies to find the object. If we use the traditional Web proxies, the discovery process is over after getting any object from any proxy. In this figure, proxy 1 or 3 returns the O1 to proxy 2 and the process is over. However, if we use the transcoding proxies, we should consider not only the object but also the version, then we have to wait for the best version that minimizes the transcoding operation. In this figure, though proxy 1 and 3 return the objects with versions V1 and V4, proxy 2 does not know that proxy 4 has the exact version and has to wait for the responses from proxy 4. After proxy 2 gets all responses from all proxies, it chooses the proxy that has the best version, in this figure proxy 3, and sends a query to get the object itself. This behavior takes a long time to determine the best version that minimizes the transcoding operation because a local transcoding proxy has to wait for a potentially better version. Also, it generates enormous query messages to discover an object. That is, each transcoding proxy has to process redundant query messages for every discovery request.

CONTENT-AWARE CACHING

Overview

We mentioned the problems of the query-based discovery protocol of the cooperative transcoding proxy in the previous section. A cause that a proxy waits for a potentially better version is that each version of the same content resides irregularly at different proxies. In this situation, a proxy should send queries to every proxy to discover the best version because it does not know which proxy has the best version of the content. However, if the different versions of content are cached together at the designated proxy, a proxy can determine the best version of content with only one query message.

Each proxy has to store transcoded versions of an object at designated proxy being aware of the object. We would refer to this caching scheme as content-aware caching. In content-aware caching, a transcoding proxy stores its transcoded results at a designated proxy according to the URL of objects. Then, every version of the same URL is stored at a designated proxy. We would refer to this designated proxy as a home proxy of an object. Each URL is mapped into its home proxy by using URL hashing. The 128bit ID space is generated by the hash function, which balances the ID with high probability such as SHA-1, and each proxy, which is the participant of the system, manages the partial ID space, which is determined by the proxy node ID that is computed by hashing the unique value of node such as an ip address. Each object has the object ID that is obtained by hashing the URL of the object and is stored at the home proxy that manages the object ID.

This content-aware caching has several advantages. First, a proxy can discover the best version of an object deterministically. A proxy can find the best version of an at home proxy with only one query and does not wait for a potentially better version after it receives an exact or useful hit message. Second, the redundant query processing is reduced significantly. In the previous system, a proxy sends a query to every peer proxy, and each proxy, which receives a query, performs the query processing to find a proper version of an object. However, in the content-aware caching system, only a home proxy performs query processing. Third, the network traffic is reduced because the number of query messages is reduced significantly.

Figure 2. Overall of the content-aware caching system

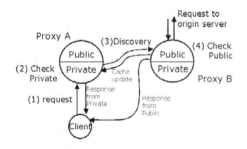

Prevention of Hot Spot

When we use the content-aware caching, the request for an object is always forwarded to the home proxy. If the hot spot for an object occurs, the home proxy, which has the responsibility for the object, has to deal with every request and the home proxy is overloaded and out of order. To prevent this case, we divide a cache storage into two: public storage and private storage. The public storage is used to store every version of an object for the content-aware caching and the private storage is used to store the hot objects of the local clients. That is, a proxy stores the clusters of version for objects whose object IDs are managed by itself in the public storage and caches the frequently requested objects from the local clients in the private storage.

Figure 2 shows the overall of the cache architecture and the cooperation mechanism. When a proxy receives a request: (1), it first checks its private storage. (2) If a exact hit occurs, the proxy returns the object to the client. However, if either a local useful hit or a local miss occurs, the proxy tries to discover a matched transcoded object at the home proxy of the requested object. (3) Then, the home proxy checks its public storage for the object. (4) If there is the object, which is exact or useful, the home proxy transforms the object into the exact version and returns the object to the client, and updates the private storage of the local proxy if the home proxy decides that the object is frequently requested. Otherwise, if a miss occurs, this proxy gets the new object from the origin server. According to this behavior, the hot objects reside at the local private storage with high probability and we can reduce the excessive load of the home proxies of the hot objects.

Cooperation Mechanism

There are mainly three cooperation processes: the discovery process, the transcoding process, and the delivery process. First, the discovery process takes advantages of the content-aware caching. In our proposed system, different versions of the same content are cached together at the public storage of the home proxy. If a proxy gets a request and a miss occurs at the private storage, it does not need to send queries to every peer proxies but send only one query to a home proxy of the requested URL. Therefore, in the discovery process, we can reduce not only the query messages but also

Figure 3. The comparison on the system response time

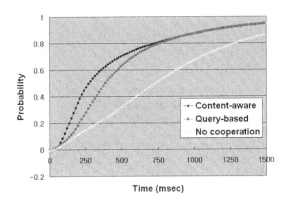

(a) Cumulative distribution

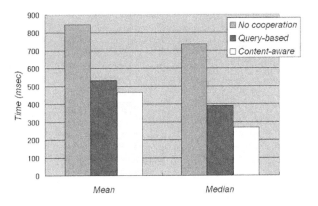

(b) Mean and Median

the waiting time for finding a potentially better version. Moreover, because the home proxy could have almost versions of an object, the exact hit ratio increases and the system performance would increase.

When we find the useful object in the public storage of the home proxy, we should decide the location of the transcoding. If the local proxy, which gets the request from the client, performs the transcoding, it has to update the public storage of the home proxy because the home proxy manages the whole version of an object. That is, we preserve the advantage of the discover process by using this redundant traffic. According to this, we performs transcoding task for the requested object at the home proxy to eliminate the redundant transmission.

After the transcoding task, the new version of the object is stored at the public storage of the home proxy. If the home proxy returns the new object to the local proxy and the local proxy returns it to the client, this indirect transmission causes the redundant object transmission that generally makes the response time long. To prevent this redundant traffic and reduce the response time, the home proxy redirects the response to the client, which requests the object. When the local proxy forwards the request to the home proxy, the forwarding message includes the redirection information. However, this redirection mechanism can cause the hot spot problem at the home proxy. To cope with this problem, the home proxy has to update the private storage of the local proxy. If the exact hit occurs at the public storage, the home proxy checks how frequently

the object is requested. If the object is decided as a hot object, the home proxy sends this object to the local proxy, which requests it, and the local proxy stores it at the private storage. This cache update policy compensates the effect of the hot objects with the local private storage.

Simulation Setup

We simulate the cooperative transcoding proxy architecture to evaluate its performance. We use Simjava to simulate the architecture. Simjava is a toolkit for building working models of complex systems. It is based around a discrete event simulation kernel (Howell & McNab, 1998).

We try to reflect the real environment in our simulation as accurate as possible. We examine the previous papers on the cooperative caching to extract the simulation parameters (Lindemann & Waldhorst, 2001). The size of cache storage is 300MB and 30% of the total storage is assigned to the public storage. We use four caches, which cooperate with each other and use the LRU replacement policy. The establishing HTTP connection takes three msec and the cache lookup needs 1.5 msec. The processing the ICP query need 0.3 msec and the hashing calculation for the content-aware caching takes 0.6 msec. The transmission time to content server takes 300 msec as average and the transmission time in local backbone network takes 40 msec as average. The simulation parameters about the transcoding operation are extracted from the previous paper (C. Canali 2003).

Figure 4. The comparison on the cache hit ratio

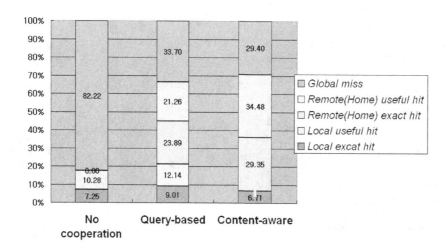

The transcoding takes 150 msec as the mean value and 330 msec as the 90th percentile.

We use a trace file of IRCache (IRCache project 2003). The trace date is October 22, 2003 and the total duration is 1 day. The total number of requests is 416,015 and the mean request rate is 4.8 requests per second. We assume that the 100 clients use one proxy cache and consider a classification of the client devices on the basis of their capabilities of displaying different objects and connecting to the assigned proxy server. The classes of devices range from high-end workstations/PCs, which can consume every object in its original form, to mobile phones with very limited bandwidth and display capabilities. We introduce five classes of clients.

System Response Time

The system response time is the time between sending requests of clients and receiving of responses of clients and it is generally used as a criterion of system performance. Figure 3 shows the comparison on the system response time. It shows clearly that the cooperative architecture provides better performance than the stand-alone architecture. Also, it shows that the content-aware cooperation architecture provides better performance than the query-based cooperation architecture. The 90th percentile of the response time is similar between the content-aware architecture and the query-based architecture. However, the median of

the response time is much better in the content-aware architecture.

The main reason of the different response times is the cooperative discovery protocol. The query-based discovery protocol has a problem of a long decision time due to the two-phase lookup. To address this problem, we proposed a content-aware caching mechanism and this significantly reduces the decision time in the multiple-version lookup. Therefore, the performance of the system increases.

However, the 90th percentile is similar because the global cache miss causes the long round-trip time to the original server. This long round-trip time is the system bottleneck for both architectures. Although the content-aware cooperative architecture provides fast decision in multiple-version lookup, the dominant factor of the long transmission time from content server to a proxy server causes long user response time. Therefore, high hit ratio of a proxy cache is important.

Cache Hit Ratio

Cache hit ratio is the important factor that affects the system performance of the transcoding proxy. A cache in the multiple-version environment has three different event: an exact hit, a useful hit, and a miss. The high exact hit ratio improves the system performance by eliminating the transcoding overhead that generally involves a long processing time. The high useful hit ratio improves the system performance by reducing the redundant transcoding process. The high cache miss ratio degrades the system performance since this case needs the content transmission from a content sever to a transcoding proxy and the complete transcoding task.

Figure 4 shows the cache hit ratio of each scheme. The cooperation schemes provide much higher ratio of both an exact hit and a useful hit. The hit ratio of the content-aware scheme is slightly higher than the query-based scheme. In the query-based scheme, the exact hit ratio of the local cache is 9.01% and the exact hit ratio of the remote cache is 23.89%. In the content-aware scheme, the exact hit ratio in the private storage is only 6.71%, which is smaller than the query-based, but the exact hit ratio of the public storage is 29.35%, which is much bigger than the query-based. Even if the local exact hit ratio of the content-aware scheme is smaller, the main factor of high exact hit ratio is the remote exact hit ratio for both schemes. In this case, the global lookup process of the query-based scheme causes the long decision time due to two-phase lookup in the multiple-version environment mentioned in the BACKGROUND section. However, the content-aware scheme finds the exact object with the simple discovery process, which takes only one query to the home proxy. Therefore, the content-aware scheme can provide better performance than the query-based scheme.

We can see that the useful hit ratio is increased in case of the content-aware cooperation architecture. The reason is that each useful version is clustered to be discovered directly in the content-aware cooperation architecture and they use the cache storage more efficiently without the redundant copies. Additionally, in the content-aware scheme, the local useful hit ratio is zero because the private storage is used to find the exact objects only.

FUTURE TRENDS

The transcoding proxies help each other and achieve high performance. However, there is room for enhancement of the trancoding performance. Some researches (Chang & Chen, 2003; Lum & Lau, 2002) explore the efficient methods such as cache replacement and content adaptation to increase the performance of transcoding in the proxy cache and these methods can be used with the cooperative transcoding proxy caches. These studies are motivated by the various heterogeneous environment of internet. Moreover, because of a increasing in the ubiquitous computing, the content-aware approaches are more important to support the various devices and users. The middleware to support the ubiquitous computing should concern not only the content-awareness but also the cooperation of the servers to share the data.

CONCLUSION

In this article, we propose the efficient cooperative transcoding proxy architecture, which uses the content-aware caching. We cope with the problem that is caused by the multiple version environments by using the content-aware caching, which means that every version for an object is stored at one designated proxy together. The proposed architecture makes the communication protocol between each proxy simpler, especially the discovery process and reduces the number of messages, which are used to maintain the cache system such as ICP queries and object responses. Moreover, because of gathering all versions of an object at one proxy, the exact hit ratio increases and the performance of the system increases too. This architecture has an improvement of 20 percentage points of response time, an increase of 10 percentage points of cache hit ratio, and improved scalability on bandwidth consumption. Though the many advantages exist, the hot spot problem can be appeared. We prevent this problem by using the private cache and the cache update policy.

REFERENCES

Canali, C., Cardellini, V., Colajanni, M., Lancellotti, R., & Yu, P. S. (2003). Cooperative architectures and algorithms for discovery and transcoding of multi-version content. *Proceedings of the 8th International Workshop on Web Content Caching and Distribution.*

Cardellini, V., Colajanni, M., Lancellotti, R., & Yu, P. S. (2003). A distributed architecture of edge proxy servers for cooperative transcoding. *Proceedings of the 3rd IEEE Workshop on Internet Applications*, San Jose.

Cardellini, V., Yu, P. S., & Huang, Y. W. (2000). Collaborative proxy system for distributed Web content transcoding. *Proceedings of the 9th ACM International*

Conference on Information and Knowledge Management (pp. 520-527).

Chang, C. & Chen, M. (2003). On exploring aggregate effect for efficient cache replacement in transcoding proxies. *IEEE Transactions on Parallel and Distributed Systems, 14*(6), 611-624.

Chankhunthod, A., Danzig, P. B., Neerdaels, C., Schwartz, M. F., & Worrell, K. J. (1996). A hierarchical Internet object cache. *Proceedings of the 1996 Usenix Technical Conference,* San Diego.

Howell, F., & McNab, R. (1998). SimJava: A discrete event simulation package for Java with applications in computer systems modeling. *Proceedings of the 1st International Conference on Web-based Modelling and Simulation,* San Diego.

IRCache project (2003) http://www.irchache.net

Knutsson, B., Lu, H., & Mogul, J. (2002). Architectures and pragmatics of server-directed transcoding. *Proceedings of the 7th International Workshop on Web Content Caching and Distribution.*

Lindemann, C., & Waldhorst, O. P. (2001). Evaluating cooperative Web caching protocols for emerging network technologies. *Proceedings of International Workshop on Caching, Coherence and Consistency.*

Lum, W. Y., & Lau, F. C. M. (2002). On balancing between transcoding overhead and spatial consumption in content adaptation. *Proceedings of the 2002 ACM MOBICOM Conference.*

Maheshwari, A., Sharma, A., Ramamritham, K., & Shenoy, P. (2002). TransSquid: Transcoding and caching proxy for heterogeneous e-commerce environments. *Proceedings of the 12th IEEE International Workshop on Research Issues in Data Engineering* (pp. 50-59).

Singh, A., Trivedi, A., Ramamritham, K., & Shenoy, P. (2002). PTC: Proxies that transcode and cache in heterogeneous Web client environments. *Proceedings of the 3rd International Conference on Web Information Systems Engineering.*

KEY TERMS

Home Proxy: A proxy which is responsible for a target object key.

Node ID: A unique and hashed value to identify a node.

Object ID: A unique and hashed value to identify an object.

Private Storage: A storage on a proxy cache for the clients which are only on this proxy cache.

Proxy Cache: A server which locates on the border of ISP or institution and helps the original server by intercepting the user request.

Public Storage: A storage on a proxy cache for the group of clients which are on the cooperative proxy caches.

Transcoding: Transform the size, quality, presentation style, etc., of objects to meet the capabilities of clients.

Context-Aware Service Discovery in Ubiquitous Computing

Huaqun Guo
Institute for Infocomm Research and National Univerity of Singapore, Singapore

Daqing Zhang
Institute for Infocomm Research, Singapore

Lek-Heng Ngoh
Institute for Infocomm Research, A*STAR, Singapore

Song Zheng
Institute for Infocomm Research, Singapore

Wai-Choong Wong
National University of Singapore, Singapore

INTRODUCTION

The decreasing cost of networking technology and network-enabled devices is driving the large scale deployment of such networks and devices so as to offer many new and innovative services to users in ubiquitous computing. For example, when you carry your mobile laptop or personal digital assistant (PDA) around, or drive on the road, various services have been made available, ranging from finding a local printer to print a file, to instantaneously knowing about the traffic situation from traffic-cameras and other sensors along a highway.

To achieve the above, every participating network-enabled end-device must solve an interesting technical problem, i.e., to locate a particular network service or device out of hundreds of thousands of accessible services and devices. Such service advertising and discovery is important as mobile devices and mobile wireless devices proliferate on networks. For this reason, a service discovery and advertising protocol is an important tool to help these devices find services on the network wherever they connect, and to let other network users know about the services they are offering.

Context-aware service discovery, on the other hand, would help users to find services that are most appropriate based on fast-changing client conditions, such as location. For example, most laptops are statically configured to print to dedicated office printers. With the help of the context-awareness, a laptop could find the nearest accessible printer attached to the network that the laptop is currently plugged into.

SERVICE DISCOVERY PROTOCOLS

As new services are made available, clients would be able to obtain services based on a set of client-defined keywords or attributes. These attributes would allow the client to narrow the scope of the search so that only those services that pertain to its needs would be discovered. Furthermore, the client would be able to automatically start interacting with the newly discovered services without any programming (Intel).

For the past few years, competing industries and standards communities have been hotly pursuing the technologies for service discovery. E-speak (HP, 2002), UDDI (Universal Description, Discovery, and Integration), Sun's Jini (Arnold, ed. 2001), Microsoft's Universal Plug and Play (UPnP), IBM's Salutation (Salutation Architecture Specification), Service Location Protocol (SLP) of IETF (Guttman, 1999), and Bluetooth's Service Discovery Protocol (SDP) (Helal, 2002) are among the front-runners in this new race. E-speak and UDDI are designed specifically for discovering Web services. On the other hand, Jini, UpnP, and Salutation are geared toward services furnished by hardware devices such as printers, faxes, etc. We elaborate each of these in detail next.

- **E-speak** is an open software platform designed by HP (Hewlett-Packard Co.) to facilitate the delivery of e-services (electronic services) over the Internet. Based on Extensible Markup Language (XML), the E-speak Service Framework Specification makes it possible for e-services to advertise, discover, negotiate, and form contracts, learn each other's interfaces and protocols, and invoke each other's services, all without human intervention.

- **UDDI** protocol is one of the major building blocks required for successful Web services. UDDI creates a standard interoperable platform that enables companies and applications to quickly, easily, and dynamically find and use Web services over the Internet. UDDI is a cross-industry effort driven by major platform and software providers, as well as marketplace operators and e-business leaders within the OASIS (Organization for the Advancement of Structured Information Standards) consortium.

- **Jini** is a distributed service discovery and advertisement architecture that relies on mobile code and leverages the platform independent of Java language. Jini entities consist of services, lookup servers that catalog available services, and clients that require services. All service advertisements and requests go through the lookup servers. To register service availability or to discover services, a service or client must first locate one or more lookup servers by using a multicast request protocol. This request protocol terminates with the invocation of a unicast discovery protocol, which clients and services use to communicate with a specific lookup server. A lookup server can use the multicast announcement protocol to announce its presence on the network. When a lookup server makes an announcement, clients and services that have registered interest in receiving announcements of new lookup services are notified.

- **UPnP** is considered at some levels to be a natural extension of Microsoft Plug and Play to the networking scenario. The UPnP specification describes device addressing, service advertisement and discovery, device control, event, and presentation. AutoIP (Troll, 2000) protocol is used to allow devices to dynamically claim IP addresses in the absence of a DHCP server. UPnP uses simple service discovery protocol (SSDP) for service discovery. SSDP uses HTTP over multicast (HTTPMU) and unicast UDP (HTTPU) to announce a device's presence to others and discover other devices and services. Each service can be searched by any of its three associated IDs—service type, service name, and location. An UPnP service description includes a list of actions to which the service responds and a list of variables that model the service's state at runtime. After discovery, a control point sends a message to the service's specified control object URL (Uniform Resource Locator) according to the Simple Object Access Protocol (SOAP). The device or service returns action-specific values. A control point can also subscribe to receive event notifications which are updates of services' state in a format of General Event Notification Architecture (GENA).

- **Salutation** is an architecture for service advertisement, discovery, and invocation among devices and services of dissimilar capabilities. The architecture is composed of three fundamental components: functional units, Salutation managers, and transport managers. In Salutation, the concept of a "service" is broken down into a collection of functional units with each unit representing some essential feature. A service description is then a collection of functional unit descriptions, each having a collection of attribute records (name, value, etc.). These records can be queried and matched against during the service discovery process. The Salutation manager contains a registry to keep information about services, and a client can register or un-register itself. An ensemble of Salutation managers can coordinate with one another to exchange registration information, even with those on different transport media. Communication between Salutation managers is based on remote procedure call (RPC). A discovery request is sent to the local Salutation manager, which in turn will be directed to other Salutation managers. This cooperation among Salutation managers forms a conceptually similar lookup service to Jini. One difference, though, is that it is distributed over the network. The transport manager isolates the implementation of the Salutation managers from particular transport-layer protocols and hence gives Salutation network transport independence.

- **SLP** is an Internet Engineering Task Force (IETF) standard for decentralized, lightweight, and extensible service discovery. It uses service URLs, which define the service type and address for a particular service. For example, "service: printer:lpr://hostname" is the service URL for a line printer service available at hostname. Based on the service URL, users (or applications) can browse available services in their domain and select and use the one they want. SLP establishes a framework for resource discovery that includes three "agents" that operate on behalf of the network-based software: User Agents (UA), Service Agents (SA), and Directory Agents (DA). UAs perform service discovery on behalf of client software. SAs broadcast the advertisement of the location and attributes on behalf of services. As a centralized service information repository, the DA caches advertisements from SAs and processes discovery queries from UAs.

- **Bluetooth SDP** is specific only to Bluetooth devices (Specification of the Bluetooth System). It defines a very simple service discovery mechanism for peer-to-peer type networks. It does not provide access to services, brokering of services, service advertisements, or service registration, and there is no event notification when services become unavailable (Helal, 2002). Since there is no centralized directory for service registration, the attributes about a service are stored in the local service discovery server in each mobile device. Clients can search for available services either by service classes, which correspond to unique 128-bit identifiers and uniquely identify types of devices, or by matching attributes. The server replies whether a service is available on the queried platform only and a higher level protocol must provide specific actions to utilize the service.

All of the above mentioned discovery mechanisms have their pros and cons and are valuable within their own infrastructures. The comparison of service discovery protocols is shown in Table 1. Most of them promise similar functionalities which are targeted at

reducing configuration hassles, improving device cooperation, and automating discovery of required services. However, due to the lack of a widely adopted service discovery mechanisms, these different products have different APIs and do not work together. In addition, current service discovery frameworks do not consider important context information. Therefore, none of them offer a universal solution to context-aware service discovery.

CONTEXT-AWARE SERVICE DISCOVERY

The basic areas we need to address in order to create a context-aware service discovery architecture are:

1. **Interoperability:** Our proposed architecture can interoperate with and provide value added functionality to existing service discovery mechanisms.

2. **Context-awareness:** It will acquire and search for context, and carry out context reasoning to find the most appropriate services for users/applications.

3. **Security, privacy, and trust:** All of this must be done in a manner that provides a sufficient level of security, privacy, and trust to meet the customer's needs.

Based on the above requirements, we propose a context-aware service discovery architecture as shown in Figure 1. In order to interoperate with existing service discovery mechanisms, we adopt OSGi (Open Service Gateway Initiative) architecture (Marples, 2001; Dobrev, 2002; Kim, 2001) to accommodate the different service collaboration.

Founded in March 1999, the OSGi creates a set of open specifications for the delivery of a wide array of services to end users. The OSGi mission is to enable the deployment of services over wide area networks to local networks and devices (Marples, 2001). The key benefits of OSGi are the following:

- Platform independent. Based on Java technologies, the OSGi gateway can run on most operating systems.
- Multiple network technology support. Home network technologies, such as Jini and UPnP,

Table 1. Comparison of service discovery protocols

	E-Speak	UDDI	Jini	UPnP	Salutation	SLP	Bluetooth SDP
Developer	HP	OASIS standards consortium	Sun Microsystems	Microsoft	Salutation consortium	IETF	Bluetooth SIG
Service type	Web services	Web services	Hardware devices with JVM (Java Virtual Machine)	Hardware devices	Hardware devices	Hardware devices	Only Bluetooth devices
Central cache repository	Yes	Yes	Yes (lookup server)	No	Yes	Yes	No
Operation w/o directory	-	-	Lookup table required	No	Yes	Yes	Yes
Network transport	TCP/IP	TCP/IP	Independent	TCP/IP	Independent	TCP/IP	Bluetooth communication
Programming language	XML	Independent	Java	Independent	Independent	Independent	Independent
OS and platform	Independent	Dependent	JVM	Dependent	Dependent	Dependent	Dependent

Figure 1. Context-aware service discovery architecture

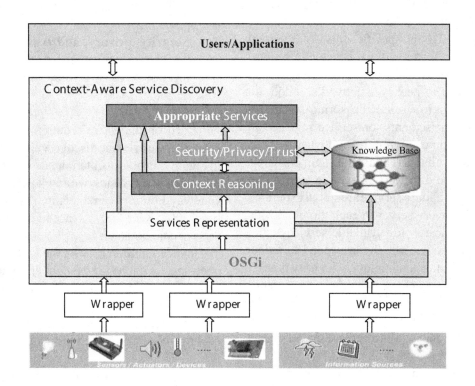

facilitate device and service discovery in the OSGi gateway (Dobrev, 2002).

- Multiple services support and service collaboration. Multiple applications from different service providers are able to run on a single service platform and provide functionality to other services.

Interoperability

The benefits of OSGi provide a feasible interoperation platform for different service discovery mechanisms. Each of the existing service discovery mechanisms has a wrapper to communicate with the OSGi. Wrappers transform the functions of those entities into the form of services and publish those services in the OSGi framework service registry. In the OSGi framework, entities discovered by existing service discovery protocol are represented in the form of services in a standardized way. As the functions of every entity are described using common convention, entities can thus understand each other and collaborate to achieve a certain goal.

Context-Awareness

Context information plays an important role in making the physical spaces "smart." Users and applications often need to be aware of their surrounding context and adapt their behaviors to context changes. Context-awareness involves the use of context to provide relevant services to the user, where relevancy depends on the user's task (Dey, 2000).

An appropriate model should address different characteristics of context information, such as dependency and uncertainty. Context acquisition is closely coupled with sensors to acquire context data from physical or virtual sensors. In our earlier work, we have proposed an ontology-based context model to describe context information in a semantic way, which exhibits features such as expressiveness, extensibility, ease of sharing and reuse, and logic reasoning support (Zhang, 2006). Context search provides users and applications both synchronous context query service and asynchronous context event notification service. A context processing and management engine called Semantic Space has also been implemented to support context reasoning (Wang, 2004). Context reasoning uses context to carry out logical reasoning to provide the most appropriate services to the users/applications.

Security, Privacy, and Trust

In the service discovery, the interaction and information exchange between clients and services must be secure, private, and trustworthy. OSGi defines SSL (Secure Sockets Layer) service for secure network communication and enforces policy-based fine-grained control mechanisms to permit local resource access. The relevant techniques will be exploited and the research works in this area are still ongoing as shown in orange color in Figure 1. We will elaborate more in the future trends.

FUTURE TRENDS

The pervasive availability of embedded devices in the environment imposes significant technical and research challenges in service cooperation and interaction. One aspect that captures more attention at the present is security, privacy, and trust which are explained briefly next.

Security includes the three main properties of confidentiality, integrity, and availability (Stajano, 2002). **Confidentiality** is concerned with protecting the information/service from unauthorized access; **Integrity** is concerned with protecting the information/service from unauthorized changes; and **Availability** is concerned with ensuring that the information/service remains accessible.

Privacy is the claim of individuals, groups, or institutions to determine for themselves when, how, and to what extent information is communicated to others. Privacy is about protecting users' personal information. Privacy control relates not only to the process of setting rules and enforcing them, but also to the way privacy is managed/controlled adaptively according to changes in the degree of disclosure of personal information or user mobility from one space to another (Cook, 2005).

Trust management is to develop a trust specification that can be analyzed and evaluated before appropriate interactions/transactions really start. As clients and services often interact and collaborate with each other in an ad-hoc manner, those clients and services may come from unfamiliar administrative domains and therefore be completely unknown to each other. To safely take advantage of all the possibilities, it is essential to assess the confidence level of involved parties, estimate the likely behavior of entities, and recommend a certain level for interactions, which is so called trust management. Trust management involves the trust model, the trust and recommendation specifications for different entities from different certified authorities, and risk thresholds. The trust management service uses the trust model to compute the trust value for each interaction. The trust value indicates the degree of confidence and is used as a parameter to determine the access level of services or degree of information interaction or exchange.

From the above elaboration, we may predict that the future trends for context-aware service discovery will involve addressing the issues related to security, privacy, and trust. The techniques related to authentication, authorization, cryptography, and trust management will be exploited for the interaction and information exchange between clients and services.

CONCLUSION

This paper surveys the existing service discovery protocols, such as E-speak, UDDI, Jini, UPnP, Salutation, SLP, and SDP, and discusses the different mechanisms. All of the above mentioned mechanisms have their pros and cons, but none of them offer a universal solution to context-aware service discovery. Next, we identified the requirements of service discovery mechanisms and described a context-aware service discovery architecture to support the interoperability and context-awareness which are required in ubiquitous computing. Finally, the future trends for context-aware service discovery will involve addressing the issues related to security, privacy, and trust.

REFERENCES

Arnold, K. (Ed.). (2001). *The Jini specifications* (2nd edition). Addison-Wesley.

Cook, D. J., & Das, S.K. (2005). *Smart environments technologies, protocols and application*. NJ: John Wiley & Sons.

Dey, A.K. (2001). *Understanding and using context. Personal and ubiquitous computing*. Special issues on Situated Interaction and Ubiquitous Computing.

Dey, A.K., & Abowd, G.D. (2000). Towards a better understanding of context and context-awareness. *CHI 2000 Workshop on the What, Who, Where, When and How of Context-Awareness*, April.

Dobrev, P., et al. (2002). Device and service discovery in home networks with OSGi. *IEEE Communication Magazine*, 86-92.

Guttman, E., Perkins, C., Veizades, J., & Day, M. (1999). *Service location protocol Version 2*. IETF RFC 2608, June. http://www.rfc-editor.org/rfc/rfc2608.txt

Helal, S. (2002). Standards for service discovery and delivery. *IEEE Pervasive Computing,* July/September.

HP. (2002). E-speak. Retrieved from http://searchcio. techtarget.com/sDefinition/0,,sid19_gci503994,00. html

Intel, Dynamic Service Discovery Executive White Paper (UDDI Enhancement Proposal). Retrieved from http://www.intel.com/cd/ids/developer/asmona/eng/20409.htm?page=1

Kim, J.-H., Yae, S.-S., & Ramakrishna R.S. (2001). Context-aware application framework based on open service gateway. *International Conference on Info-tech and Info-net* (pp. 200-204).

Marples, D., & Kriens, P. (2001). The open services gateway initiative: An introductory overview. *IEEE Communication Magazine*, December, 110-114.

Salutation Architecture Specification. http://www.salutation.org/specordr.htm

Sen, R., Handorean, R., Roman, G.C., & Gill, C. (2005). *Service oriented computing imperatives in ad hoc wireless settings, service oriented software engineering: Challenges and practices*. Hershey, PA: Idea Group Publishing.

Specification of the Bluetooth System. http://www.bluetooth.com/developer/specification/specification. asp

Stajano, F. (2002). *Security for ubiquitous computing*. Wiley.

Troll, R. (2000). Automatically choosing an IP address in an ad-hoc IPv4 network. IETF Draft Draft-ietf-dhc-ipv4-autoconfig-05.txt. http://ftp.gnus.org/internet-drafts/draft-ietf-dhc-ipv4-autoconfig-05.txt

UDDI (Universal Description, Discovery and Integration). http://www.uddi.org/

UPnP, Universal Plug and Play specification v1.0. http://www.upnp.org/

Wang, X.H., Zhang, D.Q., Dong, J.S., Chin, C.Y., & Hettiarachchi, S.R.. (2004). Semantic space: A semantic Web infrastructure for smart spaces. *IEEE Pervasive Computing*, *3*(2).

Zhang, D.Q., Cheng, H.S., Gu, T., Zhu, M.L., Guo, H.Q., & Leong, M.K.. (2006). A scalable and trusted middleware for smart spaces. Accepted in *Fourth International Conference On Smart homes and health Telematics (ICOST 2006)*, Northern Ireland, UK.

KEY TERMS

Client: An application that is interested in or requires some other application to perform some type of work for the client (Intel).

Context: Any information that can be used to characterize the situation of an entity. An entity is a person, place, or object that is considered relevant to the interaction between a user and an application, including the user and the application themselves (Dey, 2001).

Context-Awareness: To use context to provide relevant services to the user, where relevancy depends on the user's task (Dey, 2000). A **service** is a component or application that performs the work on behalf of a requesting application or client (Intel).

Service Advertisement: Is responsible for advertising a given service description on a directory service or directly to other hosts in the network. The effectiveness of an advertisement is measured as a combination of the extent of its outreach and the specificity of information it provides up front about a service (Sen, 2005).

Service Description: Is responsible for describing a service and the type of context information in a comprehensive, unambiguous manner that is machine interpretable to facilitate automation and human readable to facilitate rapid formulation by users (Sen, 2005).

Service Discovery: Is the keystone and carries out three main functions. It formulates a request, which is a description of the needs of a service consumer. This request is formatted in a similar manner to the service description. It also provides a matching function that pairs requests to services with similar descriptions, so that the service which can best fulfill service consumer's needs on peer devices is selected. Finally, it provides a mechanism for the service consumer to communicate with the service provider (Sen, 2005).

Service Invocation: Is responsible for facilitating the use of a service. Its functions include transmitting commands from the service consumer to the service provider and receiving results. It is also responsible for maintaining the connection between the consumer and the provider for the duration of their interaction. A good invocation mechanism abstracts communication details from the service consumer and, in the case of network failure, redirects requests to another provider or gracefully terminates (Sen, 2005).

Ubiquitous Computing (ubicomp, or sometimes ubiqcomp): Integrates computation into the environment, and enables people to move around and interact with information and computing naturally and casually. One of the goals of ubiquitous computing is to enable devices to sense changes in their environment and to automatically adapt and act based on these changes according to user needs and preferences.

Creative Information Systems

Vitor Santos
Microsoft, Portugal

Henrique São Mamede
Universidade Aberta, Portugal

INTRODUCTION

There are many definitions about creativity from different schools of thought. Coming from distinct environments there are two different approaches, for example the cases presented by Kao (1996) and Gryskiewicz (1993). The first defines creativity as the process through which ideas are generated, developed, and transformed into value. The second defines creativity as a useful newness.

There is a great diversity of techniques that support the creativity thinking and huge panoply of tools, which performs some of those techniques (http://www.mycoted.com/creativity/techniques/, http://www.brainstorming.co.uk/tutorials/creativethinkingcontents.html). All the creativity techniques have strong and weak points and can be more or less useful depending on the kind of problem.

Considering that the capacity to innovate is more and more a decisive factor in the enterprise competition and also in personal, the study and conception of systems that helps to innovate it has increasing importance (Bennetti, 1999).

In this context, the hypothesis to appeal to the capacity of computer systems, based in knowledge or in adaptations of creativity techniques in order to help to produce new combinations and to give unexpected, original, useful, and satisfactory answers, focus in one specific context is presented as something extremely challenging. In this article, we consider the concept of "creative information system," which introduces us to a proposal of a concrete architecture fact to a creative information system based in the technique of creativity named brute thinking (Michalko, 1991).

BACKGROUND

During the inquiry about creativity, we came across a variety of theories and models that explain the creative thought and its mental procedures (Koestler, 1964). The most known is the concept of the divergent thought of the American J. P. Guilford (Arieti, 1993; Gardner, 1998), decisive theory in the inquiry of the creativity in the United States between 1960s and 1970s, and the theory of the lateral thought, developed by Edward De Bono (Baxter, 2000; Binnig, 1997) between 1970 and 1980.

Later in a conference about "design thinking," Nigel Cross criticized those creators that have frequent difficulties to abdicate from an initial idea and choose a new way for the search of a new solution (Binnig, 1997), calling the attention for the necessity of a bigger use of a lateral thought in creativity.

Other aspects not considered by Guilford and De Bono are the personal characteristics and the cognitive styles of the individual, the bio-social conditions (work structures, communication styles, conflict management, hierarchies), and environment (colours and shapes in-house, temperature, light, noise, etc.) where individuals work. All these aspects had been already identified by one of the most recent theories that explain the creativity—the theory of the systems (Cardoso de Sousa, 1998).

The systemic vision of the creativity is based on the general theory of the systems of biologist Ludwig von Bertalaffy who applied this term in the 1970s to frequently describe points of the biological, physical, and social systems. Previously, systemic theories had been developed within the cybernetics (Wiener), to whom the objectives were to dominate the complexity of technical and economic systems (Bono, 1994). On the base of the Bertalaffy and Wiener's work, a theory of systems was largely developed and it leads us to the explanation, simulation, and manipulation of the nature process evolution. Currently, the main goal is to find a universal theory on the common systemic principles to different sciences (Jonas, 1994).

The majority of the investigators in creativity agree with the three main faculties that characterize a creative person: the fluidity, the flexibility, and the originality of the thought, being these three pointers, the criteria of evaluation in many creativity tests (Cross, Dorst, & Roozenburg, 1992). The fluidity of the thought points out the easiness to produce ideas in quantity within a limited time. This is about a non-critic thought, which can be stimulated by techniques such as brainstorming or brainwriting (Guilford, 1986).

The flexibility of the thought is characterized by the easiness not only to produce ideas in quantity, but also in quality and to find answers that allow different classifications. In opposition to flexibility, there is rigidity, immobility, and incapability to change attitudes, behaviours, or points of view, the impossibility to offer other alternatives, or to change an already applied method. When a proposal is created, if it is different from the existing one within a certain context for being uncommon or unusual, then is considered the originality of the thought.

The analytical thought is the process to recognize, classify, and describe the elements of a problem. Man describes itself to the others and to the world as an analytical being that studies and decomposes everything in parts. The conclusions of the analysis can give us tracks to the accomplishment of a hypothesis, an analogy, or a new synthesis. Since the traditions of the occidental thought are based on analysis and logical reasoning, analysis is one of the abilities of the creative thought each time more used; however, difficulties are noticed in many students to accomplish functional and morphological analyses problems (Ferreras, 1999).

The accomplishment of hypotheses is another procedure of the creative thought. It is the ability to assume and to establish. In the experimental sciences, a reasonable explanation of the facts is provisionally adopted with the aim to submit it to a methodical verification for the experience. It is the search of causes and consequences. An important procedure of the hypothetical thought is the divergent interrogation. Divergent questions allow some valid answers. Inducing because they are open stimulating a diversity of ideas, images, feelings, and immediate reactions.

To understand relations and interconnections it is necessary to compare and relate. Another elementary operation to solve a problem in a creative way is the analogical-comparative thought. It is about a mental process of bi-association of ideas (Smith, 1990), which allow establishing a new and uncommon relation between objects and situations. The ideas are bi-associations; to create is to recombine the available knowledge. The development of the analogical thought demands imagination training and the use of metaphors.

The synthetic thought is a combinational thought that carries through new syntheses in an individual or group base. It is the dispersed integration of fragmentary elements and information in a new combination. To create an innovative product through an original synthesis, it is necessary to have an open attitude to different stimulations in order to have the maximum possible choice. Finally, but not less important, the mental procedure to process creation is the intuition. It is linked with the direct and immediate contemplation of the reality or a problem for which is search a different solution from the one that could be get by a logical reasoning. It is an unconscious thought, where the procedure is not explainable. According to the physicist Gerd Binnig, the intuition is a kind of analysis or synthesis that is not processed logically when the problem is too much complex (Smith, 1990). Thus, the intuitive thought helps the designer to take a decision if the situation is not well defined and not very clear, and data is contradictory, incomplete, or too much subjective, which is the majority of the situations concerning design projects.

To the creativity process, one or more available technique is appealed for the effect. Overall there are hundreds of techniques published in works by Michalko, Van Gundy, Higgins, Dilip Mukerjea, among other authors (Michalko, 2000). These techniques are tools in a workshop to suit different tools for different creative parties. For example, techniques for the definition of existing problems, to explore attributes of a problem, to generate alternatives for visual explorations, metaphors, analogies and evaluation, and implementation of ideas. A few groups of techniques will be presented to be followed as a small example. In this sense, we have the technique of random word or image, false rules, random Web site, the SCAMPER, research, and the reusing and role-play.

The technique of random word, also called brute thinking, appeals to the random generation of a word that will work as an initial stimulation, extracting its underlying principles and applying them to the problem. The technique of the random image is in everything similar to the previous one but with resource to an image in detriment of a word. The technique of false rules applies rules to the problem that previously was not considered as possible. That is why the name of "false." Getting the false rule and forcing its use in the new situation though for differentiated directions of which normally they would be followed.

The technique of random Web site consists of finding and consulting a site in a random way, collecting ideas, which are used there, generating new ideas, and getting the answer to our problems. The SCAMPER technique is a good example of a much elaborated technique that appeals to direct questions to which answers are given taking into account the problem, in order to lead to the generation of new ideas. The stimulation comes from the creation of answers to questions that would not be asked. The technique of research and reutilization implies a look to a stimulation searching for in other areas of knowledge to find a process that has decided a similar problem.

The technique of role-play allows changing the perspective of the problem, acting like another person, and trying to determine the way he or she would face the question.

More information and hyperlinks for related Web pages with techniques of creative thought can be found in http://members.optusnet.com.au/~charles57/Creative/Techniques/, the Web site of Andy Beckett, which is promotes a work of compilation of techniques (http://www.mycoted.com/creativity/techniques/).

THE CREATIVE INFORMATION SYSTEM

We could define "creative information system" (CIS) as an information system that faces a concrete problem in a certain context and uses an adjusted creativity technique and is able to automatically generate a set of answers that are potentially innovative for the solution of a problem.

The information system that we consider does not cover all the development cycles of the creative process, but allows relying on the computer system with all the direct creativity techniques application, with a bigger or smaller sophistication degree.

To be able to work, the information system has to receive as a starting point the necessary minimum inputs, namely the specification of the problem, the context, and the restrictions to the generated solutions. The answers are generated through the application of one or more techniques of creativity or by the combi-

nation of the same ones adapted in order to be able to be implemented through computer applications, with a bigger or smaller sophistication degree.

As far as we are able to see, all the known techniques of creativity can be implemented with bigger or smaller adaptation without restrictions.

The generated answers or solutions can be direct or indirect proposal solutions. We understand as a direct solution when the answer possesses an immediate applicability for the resolution of the problem. We understand as an indirect solution when the answer cannot immediately be applied but has potential to lead to the appearance of a direct solution. The degree of sophistication of the system can be measured by supplied answers than can be more or less direct.

AN EXAMPLE FOR THE ARCHITECTURE OF A CIS

The architecture for a creative information system that we consider in this section is based on a technique from Michalko named brute thinking. This technique, very simply, has a very simple process as a base, which is developed in four steps, as follows:

- **Step 1:** Choose a word randomly.
- **Step 2:** Choose things/elements associated with the random word obtained.
- **Step 3:** Force links between the word and the problem and also between the associations and the problem.
- **Step 4:** List the obtained ideas and analyze them.

The construction strategy of a CIS based on this technique goes through the conception of an automatic system, assisted by a certain number of tools able to generate a set of phrases that, after analyzed by a user, can lead to the creation of a new idea.

In order to become possible, a context is supplied to the system by the user. This context will be used later in the final phase of the sentences composition, attempting to generate a new idea based on the user's context. Simultaneously, a whole of words representing tangible or intangible objects is generated in a perfectly random form. For each one of these objects, a whole of key characteristics are associated with it's determined.

Figure 1. General scheme of a creative information system

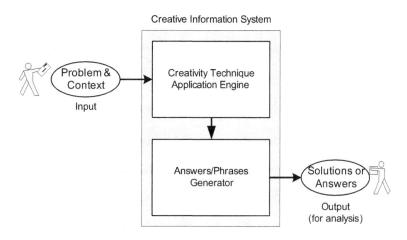

Figure 2. Global architecture of a creativity information system based in brute thinking

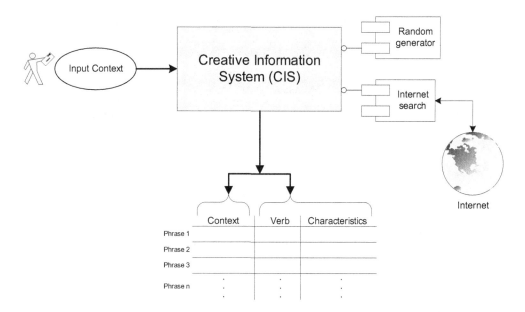

For this determination, a dictionary of characteristics from the Internet can be used.

Once owner of all these elements, the system is in a condition to be able to pass on to the generator of phrases, which will also have a predetermined structure. Then they are constituted of context—the verb that will be also randomly generated and one of the key characteristics that had been determined. The sentences will go on being generated and presented to the user for analysis; we estimate that only a very small percentage can have some meaning for the user. However, this will

be the result of the exclusively random combinations without any base in other previously existing ideas, which could restrict the generator.

Thus, for the implementation of this architecture, it becomes possible to determine which of the elements will constitute the central core of our creative information system. We will need a random generator of words, an element capable to determine the characteristics of the objects, and a module with capacity to combine all these elements with the keywords that describe the context generating phrases.

Figure 3. Detailed architecture of a CSI

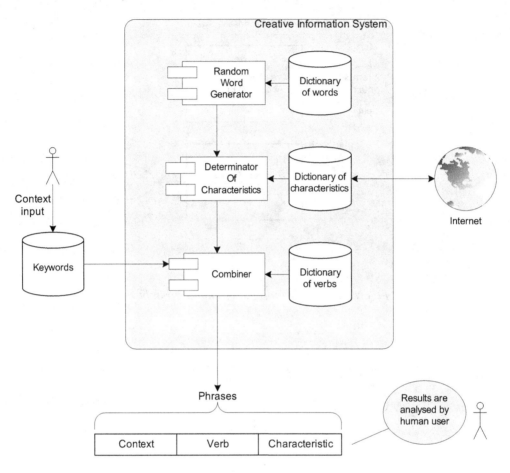

In this document, the element, which composes the architecture proposal, is represented in Figure 2. The central element of the system architecture is a module capable to combine the objects and its characteristics with words, which describe the context where the generation of new ideas is demanded and the verb giving origin to a phrase that might be or not considered a new idea. For the determination of the use of the characteristics the system carries out the creation of objects, based in a dictionary. For each one of these objects there are some characteristics, which are common to all having as base or support a dictionary that searches it in the Internet and stores it for later reference. These are transferred into the combiner that conjugates them with the keywords that describes the context of the user and with a verb which is get in turn from a proper dictionary. With the capacity to combine these ele-

ments, a set of phrases is generated and then analyzed by the user who will collect those that are capable to effectively represent a new idea or proposal and will discard the remains.

CONCLUSION

It becomes possible the use of an information system that supports most automatic functions of the creative process by implementing different techniques. The final part always will be processed by a human user because generated solutions will have the lack of an analysis which allows determining between the generated solutions from those that effectively can be used as solutions for the problem and the ones that can consist exactly as new chances.

REFERENCES

Adams, J. L. (1986). *Guía y juegos para superar bloqueos mentales* (2nd ed.), Editorial Gedisa, Barcelona.

Arieti, S. (1993). *La creatividad, La síntesis mágica.* Fondo de Cultura Económica, México.

Baxter, M. (2000), *Projeto de produto. Guia prático para o design de novos produtos* (2nd ed.), Editora Edgard Blücher, S. Paulo.

Bennetti, P. (1999). *O Uso de Técnicas do Pensamento Criativo Facilita a Participação e o Comprometimento do Corpo Gerencial de uma Empresa com o Planejamento Estratégico.* Tese de Mestrado em Criatividade Aplicada Total, Universidade de Santiago de Compostela.

Binnig, G. (1997). *Aus dem Nichts. Über die Kreativität von Natur und Mensch* [Desde o Nada. Sobre a Criatividade da Natureza e do Homem], Piper Verlag München.

Bono, Edward de. (1994), *De Bono's Thinking Course.* London: BBC Books..

Bono, Edward de. (1998), *El pensamiento lateral, Manual de creatividad*, Paidós Plural, Barcelona, Buenos Aires, México.

Bono, Edward de. (1999), *El pensamiento creativo, El poder del pensamiento lateral para la creación de nuevas ideas*, Paidós Plural, Barcelona, Buenos Aires, México.

Cardoso de Sousa, F. (1998). *A criatividade como disciplina científica, Colecção de Monografias "Master de Creatividad."* Servicio de Publicacións da Universidade de Santiago de Compostela, Santiago.

Cross, N., Dorst, K., & Roozenburg, N. (1992). *Research in design thinking.* Delft: Delft University Press.

Ferreras, A. P. (1999). *El cerebro creador, "Psicologia."* Alianza Editorial, Madrid.

Gardner, H. (1998). *Mentes Creativas, una anatomía de la creatividad*, Paidós, Barcelona, Buenos Aires, México.

Gryskiewicz, S. (1993). *Discovering creativity.* CCL Press.

Guilford, J. P. (1986). *Creative talents; Their nature, uses, and development.* Buffalo, NY: Bearly Limited.

Kao, J. (1996). *Jamming* (1st ed.). New York: HarperBusiness.

Koestler, A. (1964). *The act of creation.* London: Arkana Penguin Books.

Michalko, M. (2000). *Los secretos de los genios de la creatividad*, Ed. Gestión 2000, Barcelona.

Michalko, M. (1991). *Thinkertoys: A handbook of business creativity for the 90s.* Ten Speed Press.

Smith, F. (1990). *Pensar, "Epigénese e Desenvolvimento."* Instituto Piaget, Lisboa.

Lista de técnicas de criatividade, http://www.mycoted.com/creativity/techniques/

Técnicas de pensamento criativo e pensamento lateral,

http://www.brainstorming.co.uk/tutorials/creative-thinkingcontents.html

Técnicas para pensamento criativo,

http://members.optusnet.com.au/~charles57/Creative/Techniques/

Data Caching in Web Applications

Tony C. Shan
Bank of America, USA

Winnie W. Hua
CTS Inc., USA

INTRODUCTION

Nowadays, the e-commerce business models demand increasingly higher performance of information systems that support various business processes. Higher levels of service at a lower cost must be provided by the information technology (IT) group to help the business compete and succeed in a global economy. IT has to find a way to extend the current infrastructure in an organization and get the most out of the existing investments by applying innovative solutions. One of the most valuable innovations is scalable data management.

BACKGROUND

Definition

A data cache, in its simplest terms, is a data block that contains frequently accessed data in a text or binary format. The data block either may be saved to a persistent storage at the client or server side, or is persistent in memory for the lifetime of a process, a client session, or a user request. Caching is a general technique used to improve data access performance. In the case of transient data, the data retrieved from the data source is stored in a memory buffer. When an application needs to access a particular data element, the data cache is first checked to see if the data has been already stored. If there is a match, the application will use the data directly from the cache, rather than querying the data source again. This results in a drastic performance gain, because the data access in RAM is much faster than that to a disk or external resource over the network. Moreover, the cached data is typically in a form that needs little or no transformation and initialization, which yields higher performance in the application.

Why Caching

In general, a simple solution to many performance challenges is horizontal or vertical scaling. Either more servers are added or the existing machines are upgraded with additional and faster processors, extra RAM, bigger hard drives, and/or higher-speed LAN connection. In today's competitive environment, however, the ultimate challenge is how to make our application designs perform and scale well to satisfy the capacity demand while at the same time reducing the total cost of ownership. Even though investing more on hardware alone may alleviate the pain points for a short period of time, it usually does not fix the root cause. This means that the architectural problems still remain and should be resolved by handling the data access in a more disciplined way. The best solution to systematically address this issue is usually an aggressive use of data caching technology.

DATA CACHING TECHNIQUES

Various types of caching technologies can be utilized as a means to improve Web application performance. Each technique has its own specific merits and resolves a certain set of data access issues. There are a number of ways to classify the data caching techniques, depending on the criteria used. For example, they may be categorized into the groups of class, component, application, API, protocol, language, platform, and device. They may also be grouped as creational, structural, or behavioral.

Virtually all Web applications developed today in either Java or .NET are based on an n-tier architecture, which consists of a series of logical/physical tiers—client, Web, application, integration, and enterprise information. Accordingly, a taxonomic scheme is designed in Figure 1 to sort various caching techniques

Figure 1. Data caching techniques

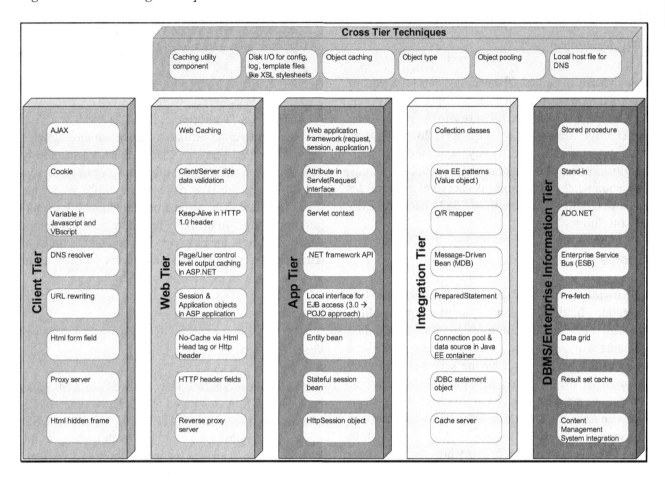

into appropriate tiers. In addition, some techniques are applicable in multiple tiers, which are consequently grouped in the cross-tier category.

Client Tier

Proxy Server

A proxy server is a software or hardware device that enables applications to indirectly connect to other network resources. It is a commonly used complementary technology that reduces network bandwidth consumption by sending only changed blocks of data of a dynamically constructed Web page.

HTML Form Field

Hidden fields in an HTML form are used to store session-related data. The advantages of this approach are

that this technique is independent from the server-side technology, and the data elements may be used by Web sites other than the original site that set the data. The primary downside is that the same data block has to be sent back and forth between the browser and server in each communication exchange. Binary data has to be encoded and decoded using algorithms like *Base 64*. Further, the name and value of the hidden input fields may have to be encrypted to protect the data elements.

HTML Hidden Frame

A hidden frame in an HTML page is used to cache data on the client browser, avoiding the roundtrips to the server that are inherent in the hidden field technique. The data contained in a hidden frame can be accessed locally using the client-side scripting. No server resources are needed in this method as the data fields in the hidden frame are stored and read directly from the page at the client side.

URL Rewriting

URL rewriting embeds the caching data as a part of the URL request string in a session. The restriction is that a request can only be submitted to the server using HTTP GET. Moreover, although RFC 2616 (Fielding et al., 1999) does not specify any requirement for URL length, most browsers impose a cap on the URL length. For example, the Microsoft Internet Explorer browser has a maximum URL length of 2083 characters (Microsoft Support, 2006).

Cookie

Client-side cookies may serve as a data cache just like the hidden fields. Data can be persistent on the client machine via a cookie. For a session cookie, the data contents will need to be set once, unlike the hidden fields that have to be set by the server-side in each response. In the scenario where multiple systems collaborate to provide a service by transferring controls between each other, a cookie is the best choice to store the session data. However, the cookie data is sent to the server from a browser in every http request, which still creates a great deal of network traffic. Cookie data may not be accessible to other Web sites if the originator sets the domain. In addition, if a user opts to turn off the cookie in the browser settings, this technique becomes useless.

RFC 2109 (Kristol et al., 1997) recommends the implementation limits of at least 4096 bytes per cookie, which is the size limit placed by most browsers today. Support for 8192-byte size cookies is emerging in the new versions of browsers.

DNS Resolver

The DNS entries may be cached to avoid DNS lookup calls. Client DNS resolvers are implemented with cache in popular Web browsers. DNS lookups are cached for 15 minutes in Mozilla, while Internet Explorer caches the DNS host entries for 30 minutes (Microsoft Support, 2004).

Script Variable

Cache data may be stored in variables in the JavaScript or VBscript embedded in a HTML page.

Ajax

Asynchronous JavaScript and XML (Ajax) is a Web development technique that exchanges small chunks of data with the Web server in XML format asynchronously behind the scene. This results in a more responsive interaction on the Web page as the entire Web page is not reloaded every time a user clicks a link or button on the page. In the Ajax model, a great amount of data is cached at the browser side, and other blocks of data can be retrieved from the servers on demand or proactively in an asynchronous fashion.

Web Tier

Web Caching

Caching at the presentation layer called Web caching has been successfully leveraged to accelerate the delivery of static contents such as HTML files, images, CSS, scripts, and multimedia contents. Web caching at the Web layer can optimize the use of the view elements generated at the application tier. This type of caching significantly enhances the delivery of non-dynamic contents.

Reverse Proxy Server

A reverse proxy acts as a cache for different backend servers, which enables Web pages to be delivered in a single URL space from Web servers of drastically different architectures or systems. It is noteworthy that a reverse proxy always terminates a SSL/TLS connection (i.e., a SSL connection cannot transparently extend across a reverse proxy). As a result, it has full control over the connection including authentication header fields. Additionally, reverse proxy servers are not designed for optimized caching, so they may not scale well when network loads grow significantly, although they can be used to replicate content to geographically dispersed areas or for load balancing.

Client/Server-Side Data Validation

Input data validation is virtually a prerequisite before the business logic is invoked. Performing data validation is a type of caching method, which avoids unnecessary hits to the backend server if the input data is invalid. Microsoft .NET technology (Microsoft .NET, 2005) enables the IIS server to detect at run time whether to push the data validation logic to the client side. For rich client applications, the data validation logic and reusable data block are generally sent to the client side in favor of performance enhancement. This also applies to partner applications using Web services communications.

However, this translates to a tremendous amount of duplication for a large client base. Additionally, it is most likely that there is insufficient space to cache a large portion of data in pervasive computing devices like Blackberry.

ASP

Active server page (ASP) technology (Microsoft Knowledgebase, 2004) provides two objects, which enables storing key/value pairs in memory, namely *session* and *application*. The *session* object is used to store per-user data across multiple requests, whereas the *application* object is used to store per-application data for use by requests from multiple users.

ASP.NET

The ASP.NET technology adds two types of caching—output caching at the page level, and user-control level (fragment caching).

Keep-Alive in Http Header

The socket connection between a Web browser and a Web server may be preserved for subsequent hits after the first request.

HTTP Header Field

Under certain circumstances, an HTTP header field may be exploited to store cache data in a session. However, it is not recommended to use the header to contain business logic-related data, to mandate loose coupling between tiers.

No-Cache via HTML Head Tag

In some scenarios like stock quotes, the output should not be cached at a browser. The HTML specification (Fielding et al., 1999) defines a way to notify the browser that it should not cache the information so that it requests the information from the server each time, and displays it.

To enforce no caching, include the following code segment between the <Head> and </Head> tags in a HTML page:

```
<meta HTTP-EQUIV="Pragma" CONTENT="no-cache">
<meta HTTP-EQUIV="Cache-Control" CONTENT="no-cache">
```

The first line is for HTTP Version 1.0, while the second line is for Version 1.1. This ensures that the data is not cached, so that fresh data is always retrieved from the server before serving the client's request.

No-Cache via Http Header

The no-caching information can be alternatively transmitted in the Http header. The following code is for ASP applications:

```
<% Response.CacheControl = "no-cache" %>
<% Response.AddHeader "Pragma", "no-cache" %>
<% Response.Expires = -1 %>
```

The last line prevents caching at the proxy server. In Java EE applications, this task can also be accomplished programmatically, by using the setHeader(), addHeader(), and setDateHeader() method in the Response Class in the JSP and Servlet code, for example:

```
<% response.setHeader("Cache-Control", "no-cache");
response.setHeader("Pragma", "no-cache");
response.setDateHeader ("Expires", 0); %>
```

Edge Side Includes

A Web-tier cache is also generally used to cache JSP fragments. More and more applications are moving toward JSP fragment caching. Some vendors provide custom tags for caching JSP fragments, which enables the caching content produced within the body of the tag. The contents cached can be the final view of the content, or simply the values calculated for variables. The latter is useful when the presentation is independent of the computed data. The JSP Tag Library for Edge Side Includes, or JESI (JSR-128 2004), is a specification of a custom tag library that uses the JSP syntax to automatically generate ESI code. ESI is a markup language that enables partial page caching for HTML fragments (ESI 2001).

Application Tier

HttpSession

In a Java EE application, an HttpSession object (JSR-154, 2006) can store very complex data structures with a rich set of APIs. This data cache is tied to a particular browser session. In reality, most containers implement the HttpSession by means of either an in-memory replication or a separate database as persistence storage. The data can be retrieved much more rapidly from the HttpSession object than from the original data source.

One pitfall that one needs to be cautious about is that only one HttpSession object exists between a browser and a Servlet engine that persists for a period of time. If some values are placed to represent data objects in the HttpSession, this object will exist for every Servlet-based application on the server. If there are multiple Servlet applications running on the same server, they may use the same values to store data values with HttpSession. If, during the same session, the user of that session visits another Servlet application in the same container that uses the same values in HttpSession, a collision will occur.

The session time-out value, typically 60 minutes, triggers the invalidation of caching items and garbage collection. In order to save the cache space, one needs to invalidate the session and clear the cache manually, rather than relying on the container's garbage collection, which takes longer cycles than needed.

Stateful Session Bean

Stateful session beans can store a relatively small chunk of data as cache in addition to the state data

for a particular user session. One of the advantages of this technique is that cross-server data replication is automatically implemented by the containers in a clustered environment. However, the stateful session beans do not scale well, and could become a bottleneck for high-volume Web applications, as the container has to manage a large number of beans with the state information.

Entity Bean

Whereas a session bean is typically used to realize the business logic, an entity bean represents an instance of a persistent object. If the EJB components are deployed to a single instance of an application server, the caching of entity beans is taken full advantage of. However, the clustering and load-balancing features of the application servers are often used in most high-end applications. In the case of multiple instances deployed, it is possible that the cached entity bean is updated by another copy of this entity bean in another instance. Consequently, the ejbLoad() method should always be invoked at the beginning of a transaction to load the current state and ensure data integrity in a clustered environment. Additionally, the entity bean is replaced by the Entity class in Java Persistence API in Java EE 5.

Read-Only Entity Bean

Some container vendors offer EJBs classified as read-only entity beans. This allows caching of entity beans that were marked as read-only. The configurations of caching attributes are provided via the vendor-specific deployment descriptor. Vendors also provide a proprietary API for invalidating cached data. This solution is vendor specific and therefore not portable. Read-only entity beans are not supported in the latest EJB 3.0 specification (JSR-220, 2005).

Accessing EJB Using Local Interface

Access to EJBs in early Java EE specifications had to be implemented through a remote interface, which is implemented via RMI. The later EJB versions (EJB 2.0 above) provide the ability to access EJBs through a local interface, which should be used unless an application needs to access a remote client.

Servlet Context Singleton

The Servlet context implements the singleton design pattern. It can cache for all Servlet requests. The downside is that this resource is not managed by the container. Singleton caches are usually designed via a Hashtable object with no limitation in size, but it leads to a similar collision issue as seen in the HttpSession object.

Attribute in ServletRequest Interface

The ServletRequest interface provides a mechanism to store an attribute in the request. The attributes are in the form of name-value pairs, where the value is a generic Java object. The *setAttribute()* and *getAttribute()* methods are invoked to manage attributes in the request that is forwarded to another handler or Servlet. Be aware that the attributes are reset between requests. They are often used in conjunction with *RequestDispatcher*.

Web Application Frameworks

Most popular Java EE Web application frameworks such as Struts (2006), JavaServer Faces (JSR-252, 2006), and Spring (2006) all provide caching capability of the client session data at different levels: request, session, and application. If an application is developed based on one of these frameworks, these built-in features can be taken advantage of.

.NET Framework API

Microsoft .NET framework includes a rich set of data caching APIs, which provides an in-memory, application-scoped, thread-safe space that can hold any serializable object or object collection. The .NET data caching API consists of two classes in the System.Web. Caching namespace. The first class, *Cache*, is used to insert and delete data elements from the cache. The second class, *CacheDependency*, is used to specify a cache dependency to a data element in the cache.

The time-based expiration is built in the method *Insert()*. The time for invalidation can be either absolute or sliding. A callback function to a cached item can be implemented to be executed when that item is removed form the cache.

Web Services

In the Web services space, WS-resource framework (WSRF) and WS-addressing are emerging as the de facto mechanism for stateful Web services invocations, which caches the state data during a session.

Integration Tier

Cache Server

Some ecommerce systems use a dedicated integration server or middleware like message queues for application/business integration. Business integration servers are usually used for process orchestration and long-lived transactional processes. Both volatile and non-volatile data may be cached in this layer. A standalone cache server is also utilized. This is particularly useful when implementing a distributed cache. A cache server also serves as a stand-in to backend databases and legacy systems.

Connection Pool

A connection pool is a widely used practice to reuse expensively created connections such as SSL and database connections. Application servers that are Java EE 1.3 and above compliant all have the data source built-in, which should be used for database access, rather than writing custom connection pooling. Alternatively, the Apache Jakarta Commons package has a component supporting database connection pooling (Apache Jakarta Commons, 2005).

O/R Mapper

Object-relational mapping packages usually provide common caching services. For example, the Hibernate product (Hibernate, 2006) supports four different caching services—EHCache, OSCache, SwarmCache, and TreeCache—with the cache data stored in memory, disk, or cluster.

Prepared Statement

Many Java EE application servers provide caching of prepared statements. Creating prepared statements is

137

an expensive operation and transactional Java EE applications often repeatedly execute many of the same SQL statements with different parameters. Ensure that the application makes use of prepared statements whenever possible.

JDBC Statement Object

The JDBC statement objects can be cached and reused in the application code.

Collection Classes

Appropriate collection classes should be used as data structures in a Java application. Misuse of the standard collections is a classic resource waster. For example, if thread-safe is not needed, Hashmap should be used in place of Hashtable, which will significantly improve the performance. One should always pick the attribute collection that has the narrowest scope to meet the technical requirements.

Java EE Patterns

Value object (Alur, Crupi, & Malks, 2003) is a very useful Java EE pattern to reduce *get()* method calls to obtain attribute values from an enterprise bean. A value object class is an arbitrary serializable Java object, which provides a constructor that accepts all the required attributes to create the value object. By offering no methods to set the values, a value object is virtually read-only after its creation. The value object pattern is also known as a transfer object pattern.

Fast lane reader pattern should be used for read-only data access such as an online catalog. Read-only access to large quantities of tabular data should not use entity beans.

DBMS/Enterprise Information Tier

ADO.NET

The latest ADO.NET version adds a new signaling feature called query notifications for refreshing the cache of read-mostly lookup tables.

Stored Procedure

One may also consider using stored procedures for a complex set of database operations and leverage the optimized processing in DBMS to produce the result sets in the most efficient way. However, using stored procedures splits the business logic over two tiers, which is not a preferred practice from the maintenance and OO design perspectives.

Pre-Fetch

Pre-fetch is a technique to retrieve the required data sets from data sources by predicting that a user may well need the data in the subsequent interactions with a system. This may be used in combination with other asynchronous technologies like Ajax to accelerate performance.

Cross Tier

DNS

The DNS entries may be cached to minimize DNS lookup calls to the DNS servers. A machine may also take advantage of the local hosts file, which contains the mappings of IP addresses to domain names. Further, the IPs of the most frequently used partner servers can be cached in the memory after the first-time lookup in the local hosts file or the DNS server.

A pre-compiler concept is introduced for caching purpose. All static data that is stored in a dynamic fashion, say in a configuration file, is plugged in at the place where the data is used, when the deployable build is constructed. This is similar to the inline function in C++ applications. Alternatively, the IP addresses may be centralized in a file that is updated and cached at deployment time and runtime, while keeping the keys that are static in a configuration or properties file for the application to use.

Object Pooling

Object pools allow an application to recycle objects of the same type, to avoid unnecessary instantiation and garbage collection. Quite a bit of special handling is required to make it work. The performance can be improved and better control over certain resources can be gained at the cost of adding complexity to the code. For example, a thread pool provides reusable threads that can be used interchangeably.

Object Caching

Object caching is useful for objects that take a relatively long time to instantiate. In a Java EE environment, this includes objects like the JNDI resources such as EJB home interfaces, data sources, JMS connection factories, and LDAP. Caching can be applied to complex components or objects at the application level that make use of other external resources that involve disk I/O, networking, marshalling/unmarshalling, or other relatively expensive operations. In object caching, all objects must be made thread-safe for concurrent access by multiple callers. For example, the ThreadLocal class enables local variables to be created for individual threads only. Another efficient way of object caching is object cloning.

Object Type

Every object instance created in a running process takes up some memory on the heap, as compared with primitive data types on the memory stack. And the garbage collector has to deal with every object instantiated, either to determine whether it is still referenced by an active process or to release it.

A common example of this occurs when string objects are used carelessly. Unlike in C, strings in Java are objects. Consequently, each string object brings overheads. Even simple operations like text processing can become slow if string objects are used too much. A solution to this is to utilize the StringBuffer class, which makes an application use fewer objects.

Disk I/O

The amount of file reads/writes in an application should be minimized. For example, a configuration file for application metadata should be read once at startup and cached in the application. Audit and log data may be buffered and written to the hard drive asynchronously to keep the disk hits to the minimum. Other template files are usually cached, such as XSL stylesheets.

Caching Utility Component

Several innovative caching utility components are available for data caching (Shan, 2004). OSCache (OpenSymphony, 2005) is a tag library that supports cache in the session and application scope. It caches post-processed JSP fragments in the Web-tier. Duration may be specified as an attribute in the cache tag.

The OSCache tag library implementation includes a properties file that is installed in the /WEB-INF/classes directory, which allows the user to set attributes for operational preferences. The *cache.path* property points to the location where the cache files are placed. The *cache.debug* property specifies if the debugging messages will be produced, and the *cache.unlimited* property may be set to ensure that the cache disk space is unlimited.

Another interface is the CacheFilter, which is a Servlet 2.3 filter that caches entire responses with both text and binary content. OSCache can be configured to use memory persistence as well as disk caching, where cache entries are written to disk to survive a server crash and restart.

Design Patterns

Flyweight and Façade are two powerful design patterns in caching implementations. For example, accessing entity beans from a Servlet can be very inefficient and difficult to maintain. Session Façade pattern is an effective method to encapsulate entity bean access in a session bean that accesses the entity bean through a local interface to avoid excessive remote calls.

Other well-known design patterns (Broemmer, 2002) may be leveraged in the application design such as proxy, lazy instantiation, etc.

FUTURE TRENDS

As new technologies emerge at an unprecedented pace and application development is migrating from a component-based method to a service-oriented paradigm, the convergence of different techniques and approaches is expected, and consequently consolidated engineering patterns will be standardized. Future work includes how to effectively combine data caching methods in related tiers and treat the caching design as an aspect in the overall application technology stack. Collaborative global optimization of data caching among dependent applications is also of interest to achieve the best response time and throughput for a set of Web-based partner systems. Dedicated caching servers or appliances are promising to provide the distributed caching capability as a common service. Data caching services tend to integrate seamlessly with other technologies such as grid services, enterprise services bus, and content management services.

CONCLUSION

Data caching is a critical design element in distributed system development. Data caching not only improves the application performance, but also provides the application-level scalability in addition to the vertical and horizontal scaling at the hardware level. The justification of the requirements and benefits of data caching is presented. A variety of effective data caching techniques are evaluated in this article to cope with the complexity of the caching design solution in an n-tier architecture. The caching implementations are classified to the client, Web, application, integration, and database/enterprise information tiers. A broad range of data caching technologies are analyzed: network appliance, HTML hidden field/frame, Http header, URL rewriting, cookie, HttpSession, stateful session bean, entity bean, Servlet context singleton, ServletRequest attribute, .NET API classes, application frameworks, DNS caching, design patterns, object caching, object pooling, disk I/O, as well as open-source distributed cache utilities. Other important considerations and limitations are articulated in the context. Future trends are also discussed.

REFERENCES

Alur, D., Crupi, J., & Malks, D. (2003). *Core J2EE patterns: Best practices and design strategies* (2nd ed.). California: Prentice Hall.

Apache Jakarta Commons. (2005). *Commons DBCP component*. Retrieved from http://jakarta.apache.org/commons/dbcp

Broemmer, D. (2002). *J2EE best practices: Java design patterns, automation, and performance*. Indiana: Wiley Publishing.

ESI. (2001). *ESI standard*. Retrieved from http://www.esi.org

Fielding, R., Gettys, J., Mogul, J., Frystyk, H., Masinter, L., Leach, P., and Berners-Lee, T. (1999). RFC 2616: Hypertext Transfer Protocol—HTTP/1.1.

Hibernate. (2006). *Hibernate framework*. Retrieved from http://www.hibernate.org

JSR-128. (2004). *JESI—JSP tag library for edge side includes (ESI)*. Retrieved from http://www.jcp.org/en/jsr/detail?id=128

JSR-154. (2005). *Java Servlet 2.4 and 2.5 Specification*. Retrieved from http://www.jcp.org/en/jsr/detail?id=154

JSR-220. (2005). *Enterprise JavaBeans 3.0*. Retrieved from http://www.jcp.org/en/jsr/detail?id=220

JSR-252. (2006). *JaveServer Faces 1.2*. Retrieved from http://www.jcp.org/en/jsr/detail?id=252

Kristol, D., and Montulli, L. (1997). RFC 2109: HTTP State Management Mechanism.

Microsoft .NET. (2005). *.NET framework 2.0*. Retrieved from http://msdn.microsoft.com/netframework

Microsoft Knowledgebase. (2004). *Article 300883*. Retrieved from http://support.microsoft.com/default.aspx?scid=kb;en-us;300883

Microsoft Support. (2006). *Article 208427*. Retrieved from http://support.microsoft.com/default.aspx?scid=KB;en-us;q208427

Microsoft Support. (2004). *Article 263558*. Retrieved from http://support.microsoft.com/kb/263558/en-us

OpenSymphony. (2005). *OSCache component*. Retrieved from http://www.opensymphony.com/oscache

Shan, T. (2004). Building a service-oriented ebanking platform. In *Proceedings of 1st IEEE Conference on Services Computing*.

Spring. (2006). *Spring application framework*. Retrieved from http://www.springframework.org

Struts. (2006). Struts framework. Retrieved from http://struts.apache.org

KEY TERMS

Ajax: Asynchronous JavaScript and XML.

Connection Pool: A cache of connections maintained in memory so that the connections can be reused.

Data Cache: A data block that contains frequently accessed data in a text or binary format, which may be either saved to a persistent storage at the client or server side, or is persistent in memory for the lifetime of a process, a client session, or a user request.

Design Patterns: Common solutions to common problems in software design.

Edge Side Includes: A markup language that enables partial page caching for HTML fragments.

Http Cookie: A message given to a Web browser by a Web server, and the text is sent back to the server each time the browser accesses a page from the server.

O/R Mapper: A technology that integrates object-oriented programming language capabilities with relational databases.

Proxy Server: A software or hardware device that enables applications to indirectly connect to other network resources.

Web Application: A server-based application that is accessed with a Web browser over a network.

Web Application Framework: A reusable, skeletal, semi-complete modular platform that can be specialized to produce custom Web applications, which commonly serve the Web browsers via the Http(s) protocol.

Data Extraction from Deep Web Sites

Hadrian Peter
University of the West Indies, Barbados

Charles Greenidge
University of the West Indies, Barbados

INTRODUCTION

Traditionally a great deal of research has been devoted to data extraction on the Web (Crescenzi, Mecca, & Merialdo, 2001; Embley, Tao, & Liddle, 2005; Laender, Ribeiro-Neto, da Silva, & Teixeira, 2002; Hammer, Garcia-Molina, Cho, Aranha, & Crespo, 1997; Huck, Frankhauser, Aberer, & Neuhold, 1998; Ribeiro-Neto, Laender, & Soares da Silva, 1999; Wang & Lochovsky, 2002, 2003) from areas where data is easily indexed and extracted by a **search engine**, the so-called *Surface Web*. There are, however, other sites that are greater and potentially more vital, that contain information, which cannot be readily indexed by standard search engines. These sites, which have been designed to require some level of direct human participation (for example, to issue queries rather than simply follow hyperlinks), cannot be handled using the simple link traversal techniques used by many Web crawlers (Cho & Garcia-Molina, 2000; Cho, Garcia-Molina, & Page, 1998; Edwards, McCurley, & Tomlin, 2001; Rappaport, 2000). This area of the Web, which has been operationally off-limits for crawlers using standard indexing procedures, is termed the *deep Web* (Bergman, 2001; Zillman, 2005). Much work still needs to be done as deep Web sites represent an area that is only recently being explored to identify where potential uses can be developed.

BACKGROUND

The deep Web comprises pages, which are not normally included in returned results by the conventional search engines. These Deep Web sites' pages are easily accessible to people with domain specific information through the use of some user interface and may include dynamic Web pages returned as a query response.

The problem arises when, due to design limitations, common spidering programs utilized by search engines to harvest pages from the surface Web, may be unable to perform the tasks needed to formulate and send the user query, thus hampering the search engines' efforts at accessing the information. These search engine design barriers make the information appear to be "deep," "hidden," or "invisible"—hence the terms "deep Web," "hidden Web," or, less frequently, "invisible Web."

Advances in search engine technology has changed the outer boundaries of the deep Web which once included non-text document formats such as the popular Word (.doc), postscript, and .pdf formats. Nevertheless, it is clear that information stored in dynamically accessed online databases is still increasing, thus making future deep Web querying an attractive prospect.

Determining whether a retrieved page belongs to the deep Web or surface Web is, as shown in Figure 1, a difficult problem, as dynamically generated pages can sometimes point to static pages in the deep Web or other dynamic pages, which may not be visible from the surface Web. It has been estimated (Bergman, 2001) that the deep Web is more than 500 times the size of the surface Web.

In this article, we propose a method that uses deep Web sites to automate the discovery and extraction of numeric data from HTML-encoded tables. In our research, we focus on numeric tables, which arise in the banking domain and show how step-by-step analysis can be performed to disambiguate labels, headings, and other information in a table. The cells containing labels will (in this case) vary significantly from the central data content of a table due to their predominantly non-numeric values.

Our method takes into account the HTML <table> tag in particular and parses this structure to derive data cells. Due to the flexible nature and usage of HTML tables, not every region of data encoded using the

Figure 1. The surface Web and the deep Web

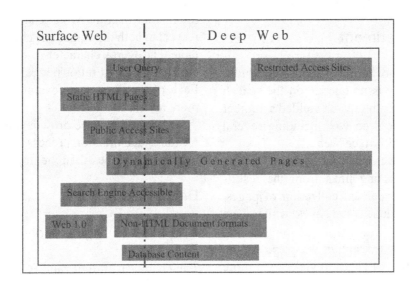

<table> tag is identified as a table—it may be purely a document-formatting construct. Using a combination of heuristics and standard statistical techniques, we differentiate between genuine and non-**genuine table** characteristics.

The issue of general table recognition is a complex one, and several researchers (Chen, Tsai, & Tsai, 2000; Hu, Kashi, Lopresti, Wilfong, & Nagy, 2000; Hu, Kashi, Lopresti, & Wilfong, 2001) have developed a number of approaches in recent years. The identification of tables in HTML has also been studied and various methods applied with some success. Determining the presence of labels encoded in a table is also a very important activity, as these may suggest the presence of data attributes which can further be used to categorize and bring structure to the otherwise unstructured or semi-structured data found in Web pages.

One of the aims of our research is to identify methods, which will allow table data encoded using the HTML <table> tag to be automatically structured using the identification of potential labels in the structure of the table itself.

We focus on both the benefits and limitations of the <table> tag and its associated <td> and <tr> tags. Unlike other previous research approaches, our approach intends to take into account the presence of sub-cells, row spanning, and column spanning. We also look at a broad spectrum of other tags which may be found in a typical HTML table document (such as <B>, <P> and <BR>) and use these to augment our research investigations.

Previous research (Chen et al., 2000; Embley et al., 2005; Hu et al., 2000, 2001) has also focused on the physical structure of tables. However, we focus on both physical characteristics (row and column information) and the formatting structure, tag structure, and content. In particular we seek to make use of the broad spectrum of HTML tags available to perform our analysis.

MAIN THRUST

It is important to note that today many large data producers such as the U.S. Census Bureau, Securities and Exchange Commission, and Patent and Trademark Office, along with many new classes of Internet-based companies, choose the deep Web as their preferred medium for commerce and information transfer.

In the deep Web, databases contain information stored in tables created by such programs as Access, Oracle, SQL Server, and DB2. A significant amount of valuable information on the Web is generated from these databases. This therefore provides the motivation for the title of our article in which we focus on extracting data in numeric HTML tables.

In our approach, we gather HTML files from predominantly numeric deep Web sites through the use of deep Web indexes such as profusion.com and brightplanet.com. We then run a <table> tag cell data extraction and parsing engine to lift cell data from HTML files. For each cell we record key features such as alphabetic character content, digit content, and various other internal cell HTML tag content parameters.

Methodology/Experiment

We used the interfaces of profusion.com and bright-planet.com to manually issue queries on the **search key** "bank rates." This initial search yielded a number of links to pages on the deep Web including several Web sites visible on the surface Web.

These initial links were then further exploited by programmatically extracting links from the results pages to produce an expanded collection of pages, care being taken to exclude some pages, which were not HTML-based.

The process of **link extraction** was repeated on the expanded collection of pages to yield a yet more diverse collection of URLs, all loosely related to our initial query term.

From this last diverse collection of URLs, we downloaded the corresponding Web pages, being careful to exclude pages that were not HTML-based. We noted that this diverse collection of URLs contained the names of many international banking Web sites. Efforts were made to restrict the number of URLs utilized from an individual Web site, for example royalbank.com/rates/mortgage.html and royalbank.com/ were recognized as having the same basic Web site name.

The diverse collection also initially contained a number of links to search engines and directories, as well as links to news sites, popular downloading sites, and advertising sites, but these were filtered out.

The final set of links used for our experiments contained in excess of 380 URLs from which we retrieved Web pages for our analysis.

Extraction of Data

We utilized the Perl 5 (Christiansen & Torkington, 2003) scripting language for both the initial **harvesting** of deep Web sites as well as for the parsing-intensive data extraction process.

Each HTML document in the diverse collection was read and parsed using the Perl HTML::TableContent-Parser and HTML::Parse modules. The parsing allowed the HTML table to be broken into its constituent cells, which were then organized into rows and columns. Processing on each cell was carried out to allow **cell content**-based data such as HTML format tags, digits

counts, and alphabetic character counts to be performed. Statistics, including the mean, standard deviation, and minima and maxima, were generated for each table with respect to both the alphabetic characters and digits in a table. The overall character-to-digit ratios per table and character-to-digit ratios per cell were also computed. Each of the documents examined contained zero or more tables.

In Algorithm 1 we provide a high-level algorithm for the data extraction process. The in-line comments in the algorithm explain the important steps.

Design Issues

Character-to-Digit Ratio

The character-to-digit ratio (CDR) is defined as follows:

$$CDR = \begin{cases} 0 & \text{if } C_n = 0 \\ C_n & \text{if } D_n = 0 \\ C_n/D_n & \text{otherwise} \end{cases}$$

Where, C_n is the total number of alphabetic characters (A-Z) in a cell, and D_n is the total number of digits (0-9) in a cell.

Cells with high CDR values have a predominance of alphabetic characters, while CDRs between 0 and 1 indicate a preponderance of numeric digits. Tables with a majority of cells with CDRs between 0 and 1 are termed *numeric*.

Heuristics for Numeric Regions

The following rules can be used to characterize cells and tables:

- **Rule #1:** If there were digits found in a cell and the CDR for that cell was substantially below the average for that table then the cell was designated "numeric data region."
- **Rule #2:** If the digit total for a table was greater than 10 and at least 60% of the cells were designated as predominantly numeric by a ratio of 2:1 (i.e. CDR < 0.5), then the table was designated as a "numeric table."
- **Rule #3:** Tables in which more than 60% of the cells were alphabetic and the total characters for

Algorithm 1.

```
/* The HTML Table Data Extraction Algorithm Utilises TML::TableContentParser
      and HTML::Parser                                                        */
/* (1) Extracts data from cells in HTML Tables where each cell lies in a
          <TD></TD> pair of HTML tags.                                        */
/* (2) Builds a 4-D array recording data points for each cell in the HTML Table. */
/* ****************************************************************** */

 INITIALISE local variables;
INCLUDE Perl Modules HTML::TableContentParser and HTML::Parse;
CREATE TableParserObject;
SETUP FILE HANDLES;
DECLARE HASH_TYPE 4D_Array[File_elem][TableID_elem][row][column];

FOR EACH HTML INPUT FILE
BEGIN
    FOR EACH TABLE IN CURRENT HTML FILE utilise Parsing Object
    BEGIN
       /* Need to record table width, borders etc. */
       SELECT TABLE ATTRIBUTES
       FOR EACH ROW IN CURRENT TABLE
       BEGIN
          /*record row info using <TR> tag */
          SELECT ROW ATTRIBUTES
          FOR EACH COLUMN IN THE ROW
          BEGIN
             /*record cell info using <TD> tag */
             EXTRACT DATA FROM CURRENT CELL
             PROCESS DATA /*record digits & characters counts*/
             UPDATE 4D_Array with Processed Data
             TAKE CELL SPANNING INTO ACCOUNT
          END

       END
    END

END
```

the table was greater than 30 were titled as "non-numeric tables."

Results

HTML Tag Occurrences in Table Cells

The top four HTML tags found inside cells in the sample documents examined were the anchor <A>, image <IMG>, break <BR>, and font <FONT> tags, in that order. Over 14,000 anchors were found and around 10,000 image tags. The break tag occurred more than 5,000 times, and the font tag just below 5,000. Relatively rare tags out of the sample were the meta <META>, map <MAP> and form <FORM> tags which together occurred less than 250 times. The information is contained in Figure 2.

Histogram of Anchor Tag

Results show that of the 4779 tables examined, approximately 2500 contained no anchors. Of the tables containing anchors, few contained more than 20 anchors, and over 1500 of these tables contained 1-10 anchors. We can conclude therefore that anchors are concentrated in a minority of tables, and in these tables, the number of anchors is relatively small. Figure 3 shows the results.

Program Generated Categories

From the sample investigated, 3% of tables were identified as "numeric," 19% as "non-numeric," but a majority (78%) was not identified with either category.

Figure 2. HTML tag occurrences in table cells over all documents

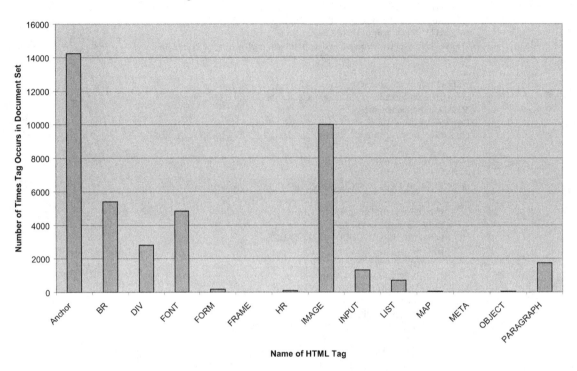

Figure 3. Distribution of anchor tags in tables

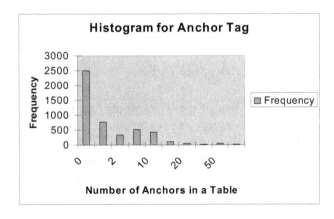

Figure 4. Distribution of the character-to-digit ratios

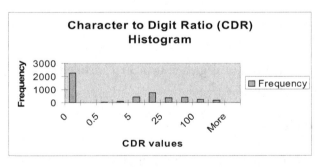

of digits relative to alphabetic characters. Figure 4 contains these results.

CDR—Histogram

Of the total of 4779 tables, over 2200 recorded a CDR of zero, indicating that no alphabetic characters were present in their cells. The number of tables with CDRs between 5 and 50 was in excess of 1800. CDRs between 0 and 1 but nearer to 0 indicate a high concentration

Table Digits Totals Distribution

Figure 5 indicates that digits are distributed evenly among files and many tables have less than 50 digits present. It should be noted that in instances where the digit count was zero, the CDR was computed using the character count alone.

Figure 5. Number of digits in different tables

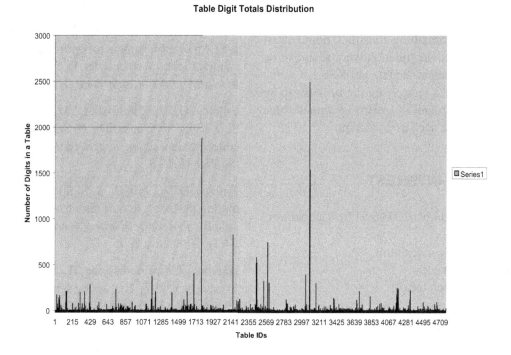

Table Digit Totals Distribution

HTML Tables Distributed Among Files

From our sample of 389 files (with 4779 tables), 25% of the documents examined contained no HTML tables. The other major categories were 23%, which contained 1 to 5 HTML tables and 21%, which contained 11 to 20 HTML tables.

FUTURE TRENDS

The deep Web remains an intriguing area, which needs to be further investigated, especially in domains where numeric data is found. This initial research has raised a number of important questions such as the relative prevalence of numeric tables in HTML documents in general, the use of javascript and other HTML-enabled technologies in table construction, and the use of HTML content in cells to identify potential labels.

We are also interested in encoding some key features identified by our data extraction efforts in an XML-based format so that we can standardize findings across domains. The development of this XML described meta-data may aid future researchers.

In our attempts at identifying tables, we also intend to take into account the presence of sub-cells, row spanning, and column spanning.

CONCLUSION

In this article, we have introduced a method that uses deep Web sites to automate the discovery and extraction of numeric data from HTML-encoded tables. Our method extends previous approaches in a number of respects. In particular, our method focuses on physical characteristics, formatting structure, tag structure, and content.

Our research has shown that the character type content predominates in a minority of cells across our sample Web documents. Even more surprising we found that numeric tables proved to be extremely rare, even though the domain ("banking") should have been biased in favour of numeric content.

The existence of over 2200 tables with CDRs of 0 shows that approximately 50% of the tables did not register any character content. This is significant and may be due to the fact that the <TABLE> tag is often used as a document formatting construct. Some unusable documents upon examination were found to be in an XML format such as the popular RSS 1.0, some contained HTML links redirecting the browser to an alternative Web document, and others contained some type of scripting code such as javascript.

WEB SITES OF INTEREST

http://www.perl.com/pub/a/2003/09/17/perlcookbook.html
http://perldoc.perl.org/index.html
www.completeplanet.com
www.deepWebresearch.info
www.tpj.com
http://en.wikipedia.org/wiki/Deep_Web

REFERENCES

Bergman, M. (August 2001). The deep Web: Surfacing hidden value. BrightPlanet. *Journal of Electronic Publishing*, *7*(1). Retrieved from http://beta.brightplanet.com/deepcontent/tutorials/DeepWeb/index.asp

Chen, H. H., Tsai, S. C., & Tsai, J. H. (2000). Mining tables from large-scale html texts. In *Proceedings of the 18ᵗʰ International Conference on Computational Linguistics*, Saabrucken, Germany.

Cho, J., & Garcia-Molina, H. (2000). The evolution of the Web and implications for an incremental crawler. In *Proceedings of 26ᵗʰ International Conference on Very Large Databases*.

Cho, J., Garcia-Molina, H., & Page, L. (1998). Efficient crawling through URL ordering. In *Proceedings of 7ᵗʰ World Wide Web Conference (WWW7)*.

Christiansen, T., & Torkington, N. (2003). *Perl cookbook* (2ⁿᵈ ed.). O'Reilly Media, Inc.

Crescenzi, V., Mecca, G., & Merialdo, P. (2001, September 2001). ROADRUNNER: Towards automatic data extraction from large Web sites. In *Proceedings of the 27ᵗʰ International Conference on Very Large Databases*, Rome, Italy (pp. 109-118).

Edwards, J., McCurley, K., & Tomlin, J. (2001, May 1-5). An adaptive model for optimizing performance of an incremental Web crawler. In *Proceedings of the 10ᵗʰ World Wide Web Conference (WWW10)*, Hong Kong.

Embley, D. W., Campbell, D. M., Jiang, Y. S., Liddle, S. W., Ng, Y., Quass, D., & Smith, R. D. (1998). A conceptual modeling approach to extracting data from the Web. *ER'98*.

Embley, D. W., Tao, C., & Liddle, S. W. (2005). Automating the extraction of data from HTML tables with unknown structure. *Data & Knowledge Engineering*, *54*(1), 3-28, July 2005.

Hammer, J., Garcia-Molina, H., Cho, J., Aranha, R., & Crespo, A. (1997). Extracting semistructured information from the Web. In *Proceedings of the Workshop on the Management of Semistructured Data*.

Hu, J., Kashi, R., Lopresti, D., Wilfong, G., & Nagy, G. (2000). Why table ground-truthing is hard. In *Proceedings of the 6ᵗʰ International Conference on Document Analysis & Recognition* (Vol. 11, pp. 127-163).

Hu, J., Kashi, R., Lopresti, D., & Wilfong, G. (2001, January). Table structure recognition and its evaluation. In *Proceedings of Document Recognition and Retrieval VIII*, San Jose, CA (Vol. 4307, pp. 44-55).

Huck, G., Frankhauser, P., Aberer, K., & Neuhold, E. J. (1998). Jedi: Extracting and synthesizing information from the Web. *CoopIS'98*.

Laender, A. H. F., Ribeiro-Neto, B. A., da Silva, A. S., & Teixeira, J. S (2002). A brief survey of Web data extraction tools. *SIGMOD Record*, *31*(2), 84-93, June 2002.

Rappaport, A. (2000). *Robots & spiders & crawlers: How Web and Internet search engines follow links to build indexes*. (White paper; Search Tools Consulting).

Ribeiro-Neto, B. A., Laender, A., & Soares da Silva, A. (1999). Extracting semistructured data through examples. *CIKM'99*.

Wang, J., & Lochovsky, F. H. (2003). Data extraction and label assignment for Web databases. *WWW2003 Conference*, Budapest, Hungary.

Wang, J., & Lochovsky, F. (2002). Data-rich section extraction from HTML pages. In *Proceedings of the 3rd Conference on Web Information Systems Engineering* (pp. 313-322).

Zillman, M. P (2005). *Deep Web research 2005*. Retrieved from http://www.llrx.com/features/deep-Web2005.htm

KEY TERMS

Cell: A region with a HTML-encoded table, which is delimited by a HTML <TD> tag. Cells may contain rich variety of HTML tags and markup in addition to raw data in the form of text.

Character Content: In our context, this refers to the presence of alphabetic characters (A-Za-z) within a cell.

Character-to-Digit Ratio (CDR): This is a narrowly defined ratio obtained by dividing the number of characters by the number of digits. In the case where there are no digits the CDR is set to the number of characters, and in the case where there are no characters the CDR is set to zero. It gives a sense of the character content versus digit content of a cell.

Deep Web: A largely untapped region of cyberspace in which Web data is indirectly accessible through the use of query-type human readable interfaces. Typically, the user must enter log-on information or select options before being granted access to the information from the Web site. The need for human interaction restricts the ability of search engines and Web bots to index these sites. The terms *invisible Web* and *hidden Web* are also loosely used to describe these regions of cyberspace.

Digit Content: In our context, this refers to the presence of digit characters (0-9) within a cell.

Dynamic Web Page: A Web page that is created on-the-fly from a back-end database when a user interactively issues a query on a Web site. Sometimes the presence of a question mark "?" in the body of a URL indicates that dynamic content will be sent instead of a static HTML page.

General Table Recognition: A complex field of study, which seeks to identify tables within documents, typically by a pixel by pixel analysis of an image file. The presence of borders and other repeating regions of distinctions may indicate the presence of a table.

HTML-Encoded Tables: Sections of HTML code, which are delimited by the HTML <TABLE> tag. The data within these sections are not always tables in the logical sense of the word.

HTML Tag: HTML consists of elements, which control how HTML encoded data is displayed. Tags start with a "<" and end with a ">." For example <HTML>, <P>, and <A> are three distinct tags in HTML. Tags may also contain information, which modify the default behaviour of the tag called attributes. For example the tag <TABLE BORDER="0"> contains the border attribute for this table. The lettering inside the angle brackets is not case sensitive.

Perl Module: This is a special-purpose pre-built section of Perl code, which is freely available from the CPAN.org or other standard Perl-coding Web sites. Modules act as code libraries and allow extended functionality to be added simply and easily to Perl programs. For example the HTML::TableContentParser module.

The Differentiated Services Architecture

Sergio Herrería-Alonso
Universidade de Vigo, Spain

Manuel Fernández Veiga
Universidade de Vigo, Spain

Andrés Suárez González
Universidade de Vigo, Spain

Miguel Rodríguez Pérez
Universidade de Vigo, Spain

Cándido López-García
Universidade de Vigo, Spain

INTRODUCTION

IP networks only offer **best-effort service** to all kinds of traffic. This means that IP tries to deliver each packet as quickly as possible, but makes no service guarantees. However, as the diversity of applications increase, this simple model with no service guarantees cannot satisfy all of them. For example, novel interactive applications such as Internet telephony, video conferencing, or networked games expect some performance guarantees to operate right. The growing importance of these recent applications with stringent constraints behooves network service providers to differentiate among various types of traffic and provide a new range of service models able to accommodate heterogeneous application requirements and user expectations.

Along the past years, the *Internet Engineering Task Force* (IETF) has standardized two frameworks to meet the demand for quality of service (QoS) support: the *Integrated Services* (IntServ) (Braden, Clark, & Shenker, 1994) and *Differentiated Services* (DiffServ) (Blake et al., 1998) architectures. DiffServ defines an architecture for implementing scalable service differentiation on the Internet. The differentiated service is obtained through **traffic conditioning** and packet marking at the edge of the network along with simple differentiated forwarding mechanisms at the core. DiffServ achieves scalability by aggregating traffic at network boundaries and marking accordingly each packet header with an adequate **DiffServ codepoint**. Packets containing the same codepoint receive an identical forwarding treatment on nodes along their path, thus eliminating the need of state or complex forwarding decisions within the network core. In the following, we will briefly describe the DiffServ model and its several components.

BACKGROUND

The IntServ model (Braden et al., 1994) was the earliest architecture for QoS support emanating from the IETF. It was designed to provide per-flow QoS guarantees to individual application sessions. With IntServ, when a host application needs a specific QoS level, it uses the RSVP signaling protocol (Braden, Zhang, Berson, Herzog, & Jamin, 1997) to reserve the required network resources at each node on the entire path. Such a framework implies the storage of state information for every flow across their routes. Since Internet core routers forward thousands of flows, maintaining and managing their associated state information would consume an excessive amount of resources. In contrast to the fine-grained IntServ model, DiffServ provides different levels of network service without maintaining per-flow state and signaling at every hop. The mechanisms proposed for DiffServ are derived from a model that considers aggregate traffic streams instead of individual flows. This architecture applies forwarding behaviors to aggregated traffic which has been appropriately marked at network boundaries and, therefore, per-flow state need not be maintained at core nodes.

DiffServ codepoints are similar to labels in the Frame Relay (ANSI T1S1, 1990), ATM (ATM Forum, 1996) or MPLS (Rosen, Viswanathan, & Callon, 2001) technologies. In these technologies, aggregates are associated with a label-switched path (LSP) at ingress nodes, and packets belonging to each LSP are marked with a forwarding label that is used to lookup the next-hop node, the forwarding behavior, and the replacement label at each hop. This model permits finer granularity resource allocation to traffic streams than DiffServ, since label values are not globally significant. However, extra management and configuration operations to establish and maintain the LSPs are required.

DIFFSERV ARCHITECTURE

A DiffServ domain (Figure 1) consists of boundary nodes and interior nodes. Boundary nodes interconnect the DiffServ domain to other domains, while interior nodes only connect to other nodes within the same DiffServ domain.

At the boundary of a domain, service providers and customers negotiate the QoS level to be met. The agreements contracted are known as **service level agreements** (SLAs), and prescribe the overall performance that the customer should expect. In particular, SLAs may include packet classification rules and traffic conditioning actions to traffic streams. The required performance level is specified on a packet-by-packet basis by marking the DiffServ field in the IP header of each packet (or the ToS field in IPv4) with the adequate codepoint (Nichols, Blake, Baker, & Black, 1998). This field tells the routers how packets should be treated, so each packet marked with the same codepoint receives identical forwarding treatment at the core. Additionally, boundary nodes can also perform traffic conditioning functions to ensure that the traffic entering the DiffServ domain conforms to SLAs.

DiffServ defines a set of packet-forwarding criteria called **per hop behaviors** (PHBs). A PHB is the forwarding behavior applied to a particular collection of packets with the same codepoint. PHBs are combined with several policing strategies at the boundary nodes to provide a range of multiple services. Many different PHBs can be defined, but the following two have been standardized by the IETF: the **expedited forwarding** PHB, also known as premium service, and the **assured forwarding** PHB group, also known as assured ser-

Figure 1. DiffServ domain

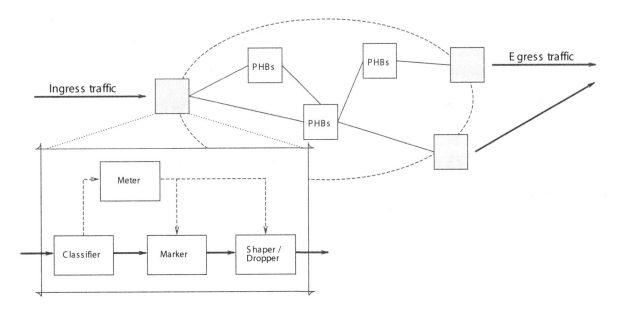

vices. The premium service is aimed at high priority traffic that requires low loss, low delay, and bandwidth assurance through the DiffServ domain, while assured services can provide different levels of performance to IP packets. The best-effort forwarding behavior should also be available. The network will send best-effort packets as soon as possible and as much as possible, but no guarantee is provided to them. This behavior is used as the default service.

A PHB is selected at a node by a mapping of the DiffServ codepoint in a received packet. Standardized PHBs have a recommended codepoint. However, the total space of codepoints is larger than the space required for standardized PHBs, leaving some codepoints available for experimental or local use.

PHBs are implemented in nodes by means of buffer management and packet scheduling mechanisms. In general, a variety of implementation mechanisms may be suitable for implementing a particular PHB. DiffServ does not standardize any particular mechanism. The vendors may use anyone they prefer, as long as the observable behavior meets the PHB specification.

Traffic Classification and Conditioning

Packets received at the boundary of a DiffServ domain are first classified by a classifier module. The job of **packet classification** is to identify the subsets of traffic which may receive a differentiated service within the DiffServ domain. Two types of classifiers are supported: The BA (behavior aggregate) classifier distinguishes packets based on the DiffServ codepoint only; the MF (multi-field) classifier selects packets based on the value of multiple header fields, such as addresses, port numbers, and codepoints.

Once the classification process is complete, packets are passed onto a traffic conditioner for more processing. A traffic conditioner may contain the following elements: **marker**, **meter**, **shaper**, and **dropper**. The marker sets the DiffServ field of a packet to a particular codepoint so that the packet receives the appropriate PHB in subsequent nodes. A meter is used to monitor a packet stream and to determine its level of conformance with the negotiated traffic profile. The results of the metering process may be used to mark, shape, or drop the traffic, based on its level of conformance with the SLA contract. For example, in-profile packets may be allowed to enter the DiffServ domain without further

conditioning. In contrast, out-of-profile packets may be passed to a shaper or a dropper, or marked with a new codepoint. Shapers introduce some delay in order to bring the stream into compliance with its traffic profile. Shapers have limited buffer, and packets may be discarded if there is not enough buffer space to hold them. A dropper simply discards the packets that are out-of-profile. It is a special instance of a bufferless packet shaper. Traffic conditioners are usually located within boundary nodes, but may also be placed within nodes in the core of the DiffServ domain.

Premium Service

The *expedited forwarding* (EF) (Davie et al., 2002) behavior is provided for applications which require a service with low loss, low delay, and low jitter. Such a service (also known as premium service) is intended for traffic that requires departure rates from any DiffServ node greater than a configurable rate. The EF traffic must receive this rate irrespective of the load of any other traffic attempting to transit the node.

To minimize delay and jitter, EF-marked packets should encounter short or empty queues, so they will have a dedicated high-priority queue at the routers. The details of how to build this service are not defined by the IETF specification, but **scheduling disciplines** such as *priority queue* or *weighted round robin* can be employed to implement it. Since EF traffic is not allowed to preempt other traffic, the implementation has to include some means to limit the damage EF traffic could inflict on other traffic. Therefore, this service must be also characterized by a desired peak rate that EF traffic should not exceed. If the traffic rate exceeds the peak rate, this will cause packet discards.

Assured Services

The *assured forwarding* (AF) (Heinanen, Baker, Weiss, & Wroclawski, 1999) PHB group provides a means to offer different levels of forwarding assurances for IP packets. These assured services are appropriate for applications requiring better reliability than best effort service. Assured services must guarantee a minimum throughput even during periods of congestion. In addition, more bandwidth should be provided to these kinds of packets if the network load allows it. Therefore, users may exceed their subscribed profiles with the understanding that the excess traffic is not forwarded with as high a probability as the traffic that is within the profile.

AF distinguishes four classes of delivery for IP packets and three levels of **drop precedence** per class. Each AF class has a certain amount of buffer space and bandwidth reserved in each node. To distribute router resources among the different classes, scheduling disciplines such as *weighted round robin*, *deficit round robin* (Shreedhar & Varghese, 1995) or *weighted fair queueing* (Demers, Keshav, & Shenker, 1989) can be used.

Within each AF class, IP packets are marked with one of three possible drop precedence values. In case of congestion, the drop precedence of a packet determines its relative importance within the class. A congested node tries to protect packets with a lower drop precedence by preferably discarding packets with a higher drop precedence value. Thus, the level of forwarding assurance of a packet depends on:

1. The router resources allocated to the AF class that the packet belongs to
2. The current load of the AF class
3. In case of congestion within the class, the drop precedence value of the packet

To provide assured services, AF has to introduce a packet marking mechanism at boundary nodes and an **active queue management** scheme at interior nodes. Among the most popular packet marking mechanisms, we can highlight the *token bucket-based* markers (Heinanen & Guerin, 1999a, 1999b) and the *time sliding window three color marker* (TSWTCM) (Fang, Seddigh, & Nandy, 2000). Token Bucket-based markers assign the drop precedence level (color) of a packet by using a token bucket traffic policer. Under these mechanisms, marking is based on a *Committed Information Rate* (CIR) and two associated burst sizes: a *committed burst size* (CBS), and an *excess burst size* (EBS). The size of the token bucket is incremented at the CIR rate and its maximum size is the EBS. A packet is marked with the lowest drop precedence if the number of tokens in the bucket is greater than the CBS (green packets). If the number of tokens is greater than zero, but at most the CBS, packets are marked with a higher drop precedence (yellow packets). The highest drop precedence is assigned to a packet when

the bucket is empty (red packets). Another interesting packet marking mechanism is the TSWTCM algorithm. In this algorithm, two target rates are defined: the *committed information rate* (CIR), and the *peak information rate* (PIR). Under TSWTCM, the aggregated traffic is monitored and when the measured traffic is below its CIR, packets are marked green. If the measured traffic exceeds its CIR but falls below its PIR, packets are marked yellow. Finally, when traffic exceeds its PIR, packets are marked red.

At the core of the network, the different drop probabilities can be achieved with the *weighted RED* (WRED) (Cisco, 1998) or the *RED with in/out* (RIO) (Clark & Fang, 1998) schemes. WRED is an active queue management scheme that extends RED gateways (Floyd & Jacobson, 1998) to provide service differentiation. In RED, incipient congestion is detected by computing a weighted average queue size, since a sustained long queue is an evidence of network congestion. WRED is configured with three different sets of RED parameters, one for each of the priority markings (Figure 2). These different RED parameters cause packets marked with lower drop precedence to be discarded less frequently during periods of congestion than packets marked with higher drop precedence. RIO is similar to WRED, but while WRED calculates a single average queue size that includes arriving packets of all priority markings, RIO uses a different queue size for each one. In RIO, the average queue size for packets of different colors is calculated by adding their average queue size to the average queue sizes of colors of lower drop precedence. The basic reason to maintain separate queue sizes is to isolate in-profile traffic from bursts of out-of-profile traffic during congestion.

DiffServ Regions

Multiple contiguous DiffServ domains constitute a DiffServ region. These regions support differentiated services along paths which span the domains within the region. DiffServ domains in the region are allowed to support different PHB groups. However, they must each establish a peering SLA which specifies how the traffic that flows between the DiffServ domains is conditioned at the boundary between them. In any event, several DiffServ domains may adopt a common set of PHB groups and codepoint mappings, thus eliminating the need for traffic conditioning between those domains.

Figure 2. WRED drop probability

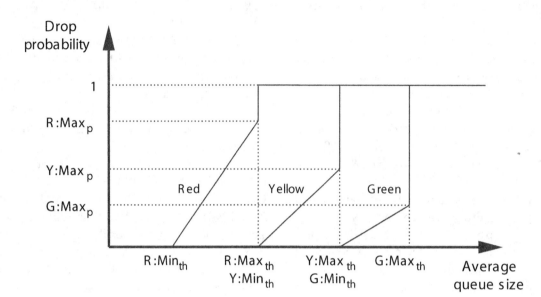

FUTURE TRENDS

Several matters have threatened the deployment of the DiffServ architecture into TCP/IP networks. For example, regular IP access is a difficult environment in which to deploy this architecture because of inter-provider issues. In order to provide end-to-end DiffServ service, all the ISPs between the end systems not only must provide this service, but also must cooperate and establish inter-provider QoS agreements. Therefore, mechanisms need to be in place for smooth transfer of traffic among different ISPs. In addition, Diff-Serv does not offer any explicit resource reservation mechanism and thus, only some level of qualitative service differentiation can be provided. To effectively support quantitative QoS guarantees, DiffServ networks can be equipped with a new class of network agents named bandwidth brokers (Nichols, Jacobson, & Zhang, 1999). The bandwidth broker is the server in charge of managing the access to each resource in the DiffServ network, so it has to deal with all the session requests to its domain. Unfortunately, due to the centralized processing nature of bandwidth brokers, DiffServ would exhibit the same lack of scaling as IntServ. New approaches propose the use of the NSIS

(Next Steps in Signaling) protocol for QoS signaling (Manner, Karagiannis, & McDonald, 2006) to provide quantitative guarantees in DiffServ networks while still preserving their simplicity and scalability.

In any case, there is a thriving deployment of the DiffServ architecture in the context of private networks. For example, this architecture can be commonly deployed by ISPs supporting customers who have high expectations of mixing voice over IP (VoIP) and usual IP traffic over shared links running at very high utilizations (Davie, 2003). These scenarios are easily tractable because they avoid the issues of maintaining QoS across inter-provider boundaries.

CONCLUSION

The DiffServ architecture provides scalable service discrimination in the Internet without the need for per-flow state and signaling at every hop. It is composed of a number of functional elements implemented in network nodes, including a set of traffic conditioning functions and per-hop forwarding behaviors. A wide variety of services can be implemented on top of these building blocks. Services currently defined include premium service for customers requiring low loss, low delay, and low jitter, and assured services, for those requiring better reliability than best effort service.

REFERENCES

ANSI T1S1. (1990). DSSI core aspects of frame relay.

ATM Forum. (1996). ATM traffic management specification, version 4.0.

Blake, S., Black, D., Carlson, M., Davis, E., Wang, Z., & Weiss, W. (1998*). An architecture for differentiated services*. RFC 2475.

Braden, B., Clark, D., & Shenker, S. (1994). *Integrated services in the Internet architecture: An overview*. RFC 1633.

Braden, B., Zhang, L., Berson, S., Herzog, S., & Jamin, S. (1997). *Resource reSerVation Protocol (RSVP)—Version 1 functional specification*. RFC 2205.

Cisco. (1998). *Distributed weighted random early detection*. Retrieved 19 July, 2006 from http://www.cisco.com/univercd/cc/td/doc/product/software/ios111/cc111/wred.pdf

Clark, D., & Fang, W. (1998, August). Explicit allocation of best effort packet delivery. *IEEE/ACM Transactions on Networking, 6*(4), 362-373.

Davie, B. (2003, March). Deployment experience with differentiated services. In *Proceedings of ACM SIGCOMM workshops* (pp. 131-136).

Davie, B., Charny, A., Bennet, J., Benson, K., Boudec, J. I. L., Courtney, B., et al. (2002). *An expedited forwarding PHB*. RFC 3246.

Demers, A., Keshav, S., & Shenker, S.(1989, September). Analysis and simulation of a fair queueing algorithm. In *Proceedings of ACM SIGCOMM* (pp. 1-12).

Fang, W., Seddigh, N., & Nandy, B. (2000). *A time sliding window three colour marker (TSWTCM)*. RFC 2859.

Floyd, S., & Jacobson, V. (1998, August). Random early detection gateways for congestion avoidance. *IEEE/ACM Transactions on Networking, 1*(4), 397-413.

Heinanen, J., Baker, F., Weiss, W., & Wroclawski, J. (1999). *Assured forwarding PHB group*. RFC 2597.

Heinanen, J., & Guerin, R. (1999a). *A single rate three color marker*. RFC 2697.

Heinanen, J., & Guerin, R. (1999b). *A two rate three color marker*. RFC 2698.

Manner, J., Karagiannis, G., & McDonald, A. (2006). *NSLP for quality-of-service signaling*. Internet draft.

Nichols, K., Blake, S., Baker, F., & Black, D. (1998). *Definition of the differentiated services field (DS field) in the IPv4 and IPv6 headers*. RFC 2474.

Nichols, K., Jacobson, V., & Zhang, L. (1999). *A two-bit differentiated services architecture for the Internet*. RFC 2638.

Rosen, E., Viswanathan, A., & Callon, R. (2001). *Multiprotocol label switching architecture*. RFC 3031.

Shreedhar, M., & Varghese, G. (1995, October). Efficient fair queueing using deficit round robin. *ACM Computer Communication Review, 25*(4), 231-242.

KEY TERMS

Active Queue Management: Queue management algorithms that control the length of packet queues by dropping packets when necessary or appropriate, usually before the queue becomes full so that end nodes can respond to congestion before buffers overflow.

Assured Forwarding (AF): A PHB group intended to offer different levels of forwarding assurances for IP packets.

Differentiated Services (DiffServ): An IETF proposal to provide a framework that enables deployment of scalable service distinction in IP networks.

Expedited Forwarding (EF): A PHB intended to provide low loss, low delay, and low jitter services.

Internet Engineering Task Force (IETF): A large open international community of network designers, operators, vendors, and researchers concerned with the development and promotion of Internet standards. It is organized into a large number of working groups, each dealing with a specific topic (e.g., routing, transport, security, etc.).

Integrated Services (IntServ): An IETF proposal to provide a framework that enables per-flow QoS guarantees to individual application sessions in IP networks.

Per Hop Behavior (PHB): The forwarding treatment applied to a particular collection of packets with the same codepoint at a DiffServ node.

Scheduling Discipline: An algorithm intended to distribute network resources among parties which simultaneously and asynchronously request them.

Service Level Agreement (SLA): A service contract between a customer and a service provider that specifies the forwarding service a customer should receive.

Traffic Conditioning: Control functions typically performed on boundary nodes to enforce rules specified in a SLA. These functions may include measuring the temporal properties of a traffic stream, marking packets with appropriate codepoints, shaping traffic streams, and discarding packets.

DNS–Based Allocation of Multicast Addresses

Mihály Orosz
Budapest University of Technology and Economics, Budapest

Gábor Hosszú
Budapest University of Technology and Economics, Budapest

Ferenc Kovács
Budapest University of Technology and Economics, Budapest

INTRODUCTION

Despite the efficiency of the IP-multicast it has not been deployed in the whole Internet. The main reason is that the wide-area multicasting among the different *autonomous systems* (**AS**) has not been solved perfectly. The global address allocation is especially a problematic part of Internet-wide multicasting. This article addresses such problems in order to review the existing methods and the emerging research results (Hosszú, 2005).

IP-multicasting uses a shared IPv4 address range. In Internet-wide applications the dynamic allocation and reuse of addresses is essential. Recent Internet-wide IP-multicasting protocols (MBGP/MSDP/PIM-SM) have scalability or complexity problems (McBride, et al., 2004). This article introduces the existing solution for the wide-area multicasting and also proposes a novel method, which overcomes the limitations of the previous approaches.

Current wide-area multicasting is based on the PIM-SM multicast routing protocol, which was developed and maintained by the *Internet Engineering Task Force* (**IETF**) *Protocol Independent Multicast* (**PIM**) *Working Group*. This working group is chartered to standardize and promote the *Protocol Independent Multicast Version 2* (**PIMv2**), *Sparse Mode* and *Dense Mode*, as a scalable, efficient, and robust multicast routing protocol, capable of supporting thousands of groups, different types of multicast applications, and all major underlying layer-2 subnetwork technologies (PIM Charter, 2006).

BACKGROUND

The advantages of the multicast are especially the effective bandwidth usage and the dynamic nature of the multicast delivery tree. The alternative of the IP-multicast is the *application-level multicast* (**ALM**), where the multiplication point of the multicast distribution tree is the hosts and not the routers, as in case of the IP-multicast (Banerjee et al., 2002). The ALM methods are inherently less efficient than the IP-multicast, since the hosts in the case of the ALM generate duplicated traffic around the hosts; furthermore, the distribution tree of the ALM methods is less optimal than the multicast tree constructed by the IP-multicast, since the ALM protocols generally do not take into account the real topology of the network, but use a virtual network, called an *overlay*. The third disadvantage of the ALM is the inherent unreliability of its multiplication points, since these are hosts, which are run by users without any responsibility for the whole communication.

The well-elaborated IP-multicast routing protocols, the most widely-used *Protocol Independent Multicast— Sparse Mode* (**PIM-SM**) (Fenner et al., 2006), and the experimental *Bi-directional Protocol Independent Multicast* (**BIDIR-PIM**) (Handley et al., 2005) ensure that building and ending the multicast distribution trees has already been solved inside a routing domain, where all the routers are under the same administration (or a strict hierarchy of the administrators), where there is a homogenous infrastructure for registering the sources and the receivers. The sophisticated multicast routing protocols work efficiently inside a *multicast routing domain*, however, the Internet is composed of several ASs and wide-area multicasting needs the inter-AS (inter-domain) routing as well (Savola, 2006).

Unluckily, the cooperation of the ASs in transmitting the multicast traffic has not been completely solved yet. One of its problems is the *address allocation* (to reliably choose a unique multicast IP address from the existing address range). There are existing solutions for address allocation (Johnson & Johnson, 1999), but they are not scalable and not reliable enough.

Another barrier of wide-area IP-multicasting is the *source discovery*. It arises at the network level, when in a certain routing domain a multicast address has been allocated, and a new host in another domain should want to join to this multicast group address. The intra-domain multicast routing protocols do not announce the allocated multicast addresses to other domains, so this host has no chance to join the existing multicast session from a remote domain. Since the address allocations and the source discovery are strongly related problems, the solution proposed in this article will be discussed together.

In the case of the intra-domain multicast, the problems above are solved. The multicast addresses are allocated dynamically and they are registered at router level, e.g., in the case of the popular PIM-SM multicast routing protocol, the *Rendezvous Point* (**RP**) router is responsible to register all the used multicast addresses (Kim et al., 2003). The dynamic allocation of the multicast IP-addresses is easy to manage, as *Figure 1* shows.

In the case of inter-domain multicasting, the *Multiprotocol BGP* (**MBGP**) multicast inter-domain routing protocol is used in order to make routes among the ASs (Bates, et al., 1998), where every router exchanges routing information with its neighboring peers (Rajvaidya & Almeroth, 2003) regularly.

In order to solve the source discovery problem, the *Multicast Source Discovery Protocol* (**MSDP**) was developed and standardized, which makes it possible to use independent multicast routing methods inside the domains while the multicast sessions originating from or to another domains reach all the participants. Every separate PIM-SM domain uses its own *Rendezvous Point* (**RP**) independently from other PIM-SM domains. The information about active sessions (sources) is replicated between the domains by the MSDP protocol, which means a flooding among them. Every MSDP host informs its peers about the multicast sources known by it. The new information is downloaded to the database of its local RP. The native multicast routing between the domains (inter-domain routing) is done by the MBGP protocol. The advantage of the MSDP is that it solves the problem of the Internet-wide resource discovery, however, due to the periodical flooding, its scalability is limited. That is why the MSDP-based inter-domain multicast is named short-term solution, since some researchers state that a more scalable system (see below) should have been used.

In order to obtain a solution for the address allocation problem, an address allocation method called *GLOP* is developed (Meyer & Lothberg, 2000), which statically assigns multicast IP-address ranges to the ASs. The protocol encodes the AS-number into the multicast addresses, namely the second and third segments of the IP-address are the coded AS-number. GLOP uses the 233/8 address range from the whole 224/4 (224.0.0.0... 239.255.255.255) range, which is dedicated for the IP-multicast. The main problem of this method is that every AS uses only a small amount of an address (the fourth segment of the IP-address), which means there are only 256 different addresses.

Another solution for the address allocation, which solves the source discovery as well, is the *Multicast Address Allocation Architecture* (**MAAA**). The MAAA is a three-level architecture, including the *Inter-domain level*, the *Intra-domain level*, and the *Host-to-network level*. The implementation of the top level of the archi-

Figure 1. The scenario of the multicast in a PIM-SM multicast routing domain

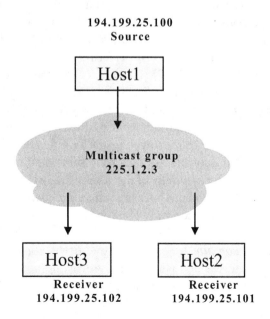

Figure 2. Inter-domain routing example

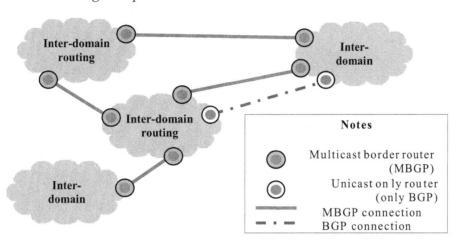

tecture of the MAAA is the *Multicast Address Set Claim* (**MASC**), a hierarchical address allocation protocol that interoperates with the inter-domain routing protocols. It uses a hierarchical address allocation method.

The MAAA architecture handles the address allocation and source discovery for multicast inter-domain routing. The entities of the *Address Allocation Protocol* (**AAP**) are an intra-domain address allocation protocol and the *Multicast Address Dynamic Client Allocation Protocol* (**MADCAP**), run on the hosts and communicating with the *Multicast Address Allocation Server* (**MAAS**) when a new multicast address is needed. The MAAA is a scalable and dynamic system for an Internet-wide multicast, however, its architecture is very complicated therefore this is not deployed on the Internet (Savola, 2006).

For wide-area multicasting, the MBGP/MSDP/PIM-SM protocols are applied, which use a local copy of the all active multicast source address set; therefore, it is not well-scalable for Internet-wide usage, only in smaller sets of domains or small numbers of sources. The proposed novel address allocation method, named *Dynamic Allocation of Multicast Addresses* (**DAMA**), is targeted to give a simple and scalable solution for the dynamic allocation of the addresses and the resource discovery as well. It is designed to improve the MBGP/MSDP/PIM-SM architecture, since, based on the current practice of the multicast technology, this solution can be used longer than it was supposed before (Savola, 2006).

The proposed address allocation method DAMA is a robust addressing infrastructure for multimedia one-to-many applications (audio, video-on-demand, etc.). Other recent protocols do not make it possible to start an IP-multicast-based multimedia application Internet-wide quickly. DAMA is an easy, ready to run address allocation protocol that makes it possible to start multicast streams over the Internet, but only sessions with single source are allowed by the protocol today.

THE NOVEL METHOD

In the DAMA project, a protocol was constructed from the idea about using an existing well-tried *domain name system* (**DNS**) for communication needs of multicast address allocation and service discovery, and implemented (Orosz & Tegze, 2001). DAMA is an operating system software library for applications and a DNS extension communicating with each other as described in *Figure 3*.

The transmission control of the communication is done by IP-level multicasting. The application uses the operating system extension, the **DAMA Library,** to allocate multicast addresses and for service discovery. The operating system extension offers the following services to the application:

- Obtaining new (free) multicast addresses for the service
- Releasing unused multicast addresses after usage
- Finding services on definite hosts

Figure 3. The DAMA architecture

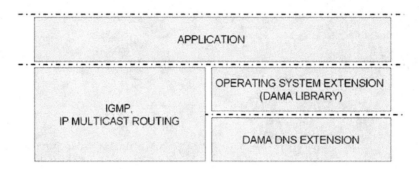

Table 1. DAMA library services

- Requesting and reserving available IP -multicast addresses
- Freeing them after use
- Querying assigned multicast IP addresses for gi ven se rvices and host s
- Querying sources of sessions related to g iven I P-multicast address es

Table 2. Mechanisms for DNS servers

- Allocating IP multicast address ran ges fro m upper serv ers
- Freeing I P multicast address ran ges
- Managing IP multicast address- range mappin g for slav e serv ers
- Managing I P multicast address m apping for hosts and serv ices

- Finding sources of multicast sessions based on multicast addresses (querying multicast address-related source unicast addresses)

The DAMA Library uses the **DAMA DNS Extension** as its distributed database system; therefore, the database functions are similar to the services the library offers. DAMA DNS Extension uses normal DNS protocol (Mockapetris, 1987) for communication, but in order to extend DNS functionality, new methods are necessary. The database records for address allocation are stored in normal DNS Resource Records. The functions of the DNS extension are listed in the *Table 1*.

In addition, the system DAMA offers algorithms for DNS servers as listed in *Table 2*.

For starting a multicast session (session initialization), a prior server needs a multicast address. It asks the DAMA library for it. Every host has an IP-multicast address table with 256 addresses for unicast addresses.

The DAMA library asks the local name server to allocate an address from the unicast reverse zone name server. If the name server has unmapped IP-multicast addresses, it maps to the unicast address of the host (in the host map, every unicast address has 256 slots for multicast addresses). If there is no unmapped address, it asks for an address range from the upper DNS server in the reverse mapping. If it gets a new address range, it then allocates an address from it. If there is an error, or no more addresses available, then it returns an error to the DAMA library. The DAMA library allocates the offered address for the unicast address, and returns it to the applications or signals the error. When the multicast session finishes (session termination) the application sends the freed message to the DAMA library, which sends the unmapped messages to the name server. If a name server has too many unmapped addresses or has a query from an upper server to free addresses, it tries to unallocate unmapped entries, and give them back to the upper server.

Table 3. Requirements for using DAMA based applications

- IP multicast enabled operating system (Windows, Unix, etc.)
- IP multicast routing enabled in routers within the autonomous systems
- IP multicast routing (packet forwarding) enabled in border routers (native multicast)
- DAMA extension implemented in source-related reverse zone DNS servers

Table 4. The authentication schemes

- *Public:* any source can join the group freely up to the max source limit
- *First source controlled:* only the first source of the session can register additional sources

Table 5. The necessary modification in the case of new opcodes for accessing information

- Separate structures for DAMA informations
- Opcode for Allocating IP multicast address for host "get_mca_address(inet addr_addr, int slot)"
- Opcode for Freeing IP multicast address for host "release_mca_address(inet_addr addr, int slot) "
- Opcode for Allocating IP multicast address ranges from upper servers "get_mca_address_range()"
- Opcode for Freeing IP multicast address ranges "release_mca_address_range(mca_range range)"
- Opcode for DAMA compatibility "get_mca_zoneinfo(zone)"

Every allocated and mapped address has a timeout assigned. Within the timeout, a keepalive message must arrive to renew the allocation (session holding). Every keepalive message must be acknowledged. If a keepalive message has not been acknowledged or its renewal refused, the application must finish sending to the related multicast address (session failure).

The requirements of the usage of the DAMA-based application are listed in *Table 3*.

The main features of the system DAMA are the usage of the source-routed shared trees, however, it recently has not supported multi source sessions. Every host can use a maximum of 256 multicast addresses for its unicast addresses.

The base concept is using the existing DAMA DNS extension to store additional information about sources. A mechanism to allow joining and leaving sources to the session is needed. For security reasons, the first source to set up the session can choose one of the two authentication schemes that are listed in *Table 4*.

In the first source controlled case, if the first source leaves the session, the session is closed, even if addition sources are left. An application-level mechanism is necessary to handle the requests from the additional sources implementing the authentication functionality.

There are two versions of the DNS extensions; the first one uses new opcodes for accessing information, and the second uses specially formatted zones. *Table 5* presents the necessary modifications for the first version.

In the case of the second version, we use definite domain name syntax identifying multicast address allocation information. In this case, only simpler extensions are necessary, and the older name servers can be used with dynamic *DNS* update. For the second version, a prototype application was implemented and a test network was set up. Performance tests have been running by then in order to refine the protocol based on the results of the test.

FUTURE TRENDS

The protocol called DAMA is a solution for the Internet-wide IP-multicast problem. It allows starting IP-multicast-based applications Internet-wide with minimum configuration needs. It offers scalable dynamic address allocation and service discovery, while the transmission control relies on the IP and higher-level protocols. In a simple situation, a native IP level multicasting can be used, for reliable communication, a reliable multicast transport level protocol (Orosz & Tegze, 2001) is the appropriate selection. DAMA uses an existing domain name system as the distributed database for storing address and service information. This hierarchical, distributed system makes the protocol scalable, and redundancy of the system ensures robustness. The existing infrastructure means there is no need to invest in new infrastructure, and makes the services based on DAMA protocol ready to run with minimal configuration.

In a multicast environment, the multicast routing is one of the main elements of the **traffic management** (Yu, 2001), therefore, the stability and scalability of the multicast routing must be guaranteed. The aim of the introduced DAMA project is to create an algorithm and software for multimedia applications using IP-multicasting to let them easily connect to multicasting environments. DAMA is Internet-wide scalable and uses low communication overhead. The entities of the DAMA algorithm run on name servers, and under client-side operating systems as extensions. DAMA offers service registration, discovery, and multicast address allocation in a distributed hierarchical infrastructure. The use of the existing domain name system makes DAMA robust, easy, and scalable.

CONCLUSION

The IP-multicast gives the theoretically optimal solution for local- and the wide-area media streaming. Its serious problem, the lack of Internet-wide deployment, can be facilitated by applying the proposed multicast address allocation method called DAMA. The implementation and testing of the DAMA multi-source extension is in progress. The following steps required are simulation and measurement of the properties in order to refine the protocol parameters.

The relatively simply solution for the wide-area multicast, which the method DAMA provides, gives an efficient way to reach desired global IP-multicasting. The DAMA can help the Internet-wide deployment of the IP-multicast, since it is easy to deploy and does not require fundamental changes in the IP infrastructure.

Despite of the relative success of the *Application-Level Multicast* (**ALM**), the Internet can be used as a mass medium if the IP-multicast is available. In recent years, the bandwidth of the Internet has dramatically increased, however, the demands were similarly enhanced. For small party conferences, the ALM solutions are perfect and easy to deploy. However, the current capability of the Internet gives the possibility of applications with multimillions of users. In the latter case, the ALM was inherently not scalable enough, but the IP-multicast gives a scalable and powerful solution. The proposed DAMA addressing infrastructure is a logical and smooth extension of the earlier IP-multicast address allocations and the traditional unicast-based *Domain Name System* (**DNS**).

REFERENCES

Banerjee, S., et al. (2002). Scalable application-layer multicast, *ACM SIGCOMM*.

Bates, T., Chandra, R., Katz, D., & Rekhter, Y. (1998, Febr.). *Multiprotocol extensions for BGP-4*. Internet Engineering Task Force, Network Working Group, Request for Comments (RFC) 2283.

Fenner, B., Handley, M., Holbrook, H., & Kouvelas, I. (2006). *Protocol independent multicast—Sparse mode (PIM-SM): Protocol Specification (Revised)*, Internet Engineering Task Force, PIM Working Group, draft-ietf-pim-sm-v2-new-12.txt, work-in-progress.

Handley, M., Kouvelas, I., Speakman, T., & Vicisano, L. (2005). *Bi-directional protocol independent multicast (BIDIR-PIM)*. Internet Engineering Task Force, PIM Working Group, draft-ietf-pim-bidir-08.txt, work-in-progress.

Hosszú, G. (2005). Current multicast technology. In M. Khosrow-Pour (Ed.), *Encyclopedia of information science and information technology Vol. I-V* (pp. 660-667). Hershey, PA: ISR.

Johnson, V., & Johnson, M. (1999). *IP multicast APIs & protocols: The IP multicast channel at Stardust.com.* Retrieved 2004 from, http://www.stardust.com/multicast/whitepapers/apis.htm

Kim, D., Meyer, D., Kilmer, H., & Farinacci, D. (2003). *Anycast rendezvous point (RP) mechanism using protocol independent multicast (PIM) and multicast source discovery protocol (MSDP).* Internet Engineering Task Force, Network Working Group, Request for Comments (RFC) 3446.

McBride, M., Meylor, J., & Meyer, D. (2004). *Source discovery protocol (MSDP) deployment scenarios.* Internet Engineering Task Force, draft-ietf-mboned-msdp-deploy-06.txt, work-in-progress.

Meyer, D., & Lothberg, P. (2000). *GLOP addressing in 233/8.* Internet Engineering Task Force, Network Working Group, Request for Comments (RFC) 2770.

Mockapetris, P. (1987). *Domain names—Implementation and specification,* STD 13, Request for Comments (RFC) 1035.

Orosz, M., & Tegze, D. (2001). The SimCast multicast simulator. In *Proceedings of the International Workshop on Control & Information Technology, IWCIT'01* Ostrava, Czech Republic (pp. 66-71).

PIM Charter. (2006). *IETF protocol independent multicast (pim) working group charter.* Retrieved April 20, 2006, from http://www.ietf.org/wg-dir.html

Rajvaidya, P., & Almeroth, K. (2003). Analysis of routing characteristics in the multicast infrastructure. In *Proceedings of the IEEE INFOCOM* (p. 12).

Savola, P. (2006). *Lightweight multicast address discovery problem space.* Internet Engineering Task Force, MBONE Deployment, draft-ietf-mboned-addrdisc-problems-02.txt, work-in-progress.

Savola, P. (2006). *Overview of the Internet multicast addressing architecture.* Internet Engineering Task Force, draft-ietf-mboned-addrarch-04.txt, work-in-progress.

Savola, P. (2006). *Overview of the Internet multicast routing architecture.* Internet Engineering Task Force, draft-ietf-mboned-routingarch-03.txt, work-in-progress.

Yu, B. (Dec. 2001). *Survey on TCP-friendly congestion control protocols for media streaming applications.* Retrieved May 20, 2005 from, http://cairo.cs.uiuc.edu/~binyu/writing/binyu-497-report.pdf

KEY TERMS

Address Allocation: The problem of choosing an unused IP-multicast address before starting a multicast session; when the session has been finished, this address should be released.

Application-Level Multicast (ALM): A multicast technology which does not require any additional IP-multicast routing protocol in the network routers, since it uses the traditional one-to-one unicast IP transmission. This technology is the alternative of the IP-multicast (see below).

Autonomous System (AS): A network where the main routers are in common administration. The Internet is composed of peering ASs, which are independent from each other.

Domain Name System (DNS): A hierarchical distributed database for mapping the IP addresses to segmented name structure and vice versa.

Inter-Domain Routing Protocol: IP-level routing protocol in order to create paths through the border-routers of the Autonomous Systems (ASs).

IP-Multicast: Network-level multicast (one-to-many) technology, which uses the special class-D IP-address range. It requires multicast routing protocols in the network routers. This technology is an alternative to the Application-Level Multicast (ALM, see above). Its other name is Network-level Multicast (NLM).

Multicast Routing Protocol: In order to forward the multicast packets, the routers have to create multicast routing tables using multicast routing protocols. An example of the multicast routing protocol is the Protocol Independent Multicast (PIM).

Multicast Source Discovery Protocol (MSDP): This protocol makes it possible to use independent multicast routing inside the domains, while the multicast sessions originated from or to other domains reach all the participants. In each AS (*see above*), there is at least an MSDP protocol entity in order to exchange the information about the active sources among them.

Rendezvous Point (RP): A router acts as a RP which uses PIM-SM multicast routing protocol and is responsible to register all the used multicast addresses in the domain.

Source Discovery: This problem arises when a host sends a join message to a router. The router can forward this join message toward the source of the multicast group if it has information about the source. This problem is more difficult, if the joining host and the source of the group are in different ASs (see above). In this situation, the MSDP (see above) can be used in order to exchange the information about the active sources among the ASs.

E-Collaboration Concepts, Systems, and Applications

Christos Bouras
Research Academic Computer Technology Institute and University of Patras, Greece

Eri Giannaka
Research Academic Computer Technology Institute and University of Patras, Greece

Thrasyvoulos Tsiatsos
Aristoleian University of Thessaloniki and Research Academic Computer Technology Institute, Greece

INTRODUCTION

The need to support collaboration among users for the facilitation of everyday tasks, communication, work, and training has been identified since the early stages of computer usage. This need became more critical when computer networking became available. The wide expansion of computer networks, the Internet, and the World Wide Web are some of the main reasons that have accelerated the creation of applications, technologies, standards, and systems that can support communication and e-collaboration. These technologies along with the wide expansion of the Internet led the application designers to rethink the way of exploiting information and communication technologies (ICT) for supporting groups of users. This fact has affected the design and the provision of e-collaboration services, which allows geographically dispersed users in companies and/or organizations to communicate and collaborate in order to learn (computer supported collaborative learning—CSCL) or to work (computer supported collaborative work—CSCW) together.

Today there are many tools, standards, and technologies available that could be used for developing collaborative systems and applications according to the end users' requirements and specific needs.

E-collaboration is an important research topic with a great number of researchers contributing on many aspects. The main reason for this major research activity is the broad topic's scope, which involves not only technological but also social and psychological issues. As a result, there are multiple interpretations about what e-collaboration is. More specifically, we definitely can say that e-collaboration has been defined in many ways in the past, and the number of definitions has grown recently. The next section presents the main terms in this area.

BACKGROUND

With the development of new technologies, and particularly ICTs, teams have evolved to encompass new forms of interaction and collaboration. This team could be called virtual teams. As defined by Lipnack and Stamps (1997) a **virtual team**, like every team, is a group of people who interact through interdependent tasks guided by a common purpose. Unlike conventional teams, a virtual team work across space, time, and organizational boundaries with links strengthened by webs of communication technologies. The members of virtual teams can collaborate and cooperate in order to interact with each other. Collaboration and cooperation are very similar terms and they are often used interchangeably. **Collaboration** is the act of working together on a common task or process. **Cooperation** is the joint operation toward a common goal or benefit. Biuck-Aghai (2003) stated that we can better understand the difference between collaboration and cooperation by considering their antonyms: the antonym of collaboration is "working independently," while that of cooperation is "competition." Therefore, we think that collaboration is a better term to describe the mode of interaction among the members of virtual teams.

According to the previous, we can consider the broad and descriptive term of **virtual collaboration** introduced by Biuck-Aghai (2003), which is defined as collaboration, which is conducted without face-to-face interaction, enabled by technology.

A similar definition has been introduced by Kock, Davison, Ocker, and Wazlawick (2001), who stated that e-collaboration is "collaboration among individuals engaged in a common task using electronic technologies."

This broad definition regards e-collaboration as a term, which is not limited to computer-mediated communication (CMC) or CSCW. **CSCW** is computer-assisted coordinated activity carried out by groups of collaborating individuals. So it should be clear that CSCW is a generic term, which combines the understanding of the way people work in groups with the enabling technologies of computer networking and associated hardware, software, services, and techniques. Until the introduction of CSCW, the majority of computer systems were based on the wrong hypothesis that the persons work alone and there is no reason to use systems that could support their collaboration. Kock and Nosek (2005) believe that e-collaboration should be a broad term because many other electronic technologies that are not (strictly speaking) computers and that can be used to support collaboration among individuals engaged in a common task. According to this definition, e-collaboration may take place without any CMC or CSCW.

We could agree with this definition. However, we can say that today we observe a trend where the communication devices are (in a broad sense) computers—either they are personal computers (PC), mobile phones, or embedded systems and portable devices. Furthermore, the most instances of e-collaboration involve computers and computer networks and also the trend today in tele-communication networks is to go on all-IP networks.

Therefore, in this article we focus on **e-collaboration** defined as "collaboration, which is conducted without face-to-face interaction among individuals or members of virtual teams engaged in a common task using ICT."

Groupware (or collaborative software) refers to application software that integrates work on a single project by several concurrent users at separated workstations. Groupware is software that accentuates the multiple user environments, coordinating and orchestrating things so that users can "see" each other, avoiding the conflicts with each other. Groupware is distinguished from common software by the basic as-

sumption it makes: groupware makes the user aware that he or she constitutes a member of a group, while the majority of other software seeks to hide and protect users from each other.

E-COLLABORATION CONCEPTS, SYSTEMS, AND APPLICATIONS

As implied from the definitions presented in the previous section, e-collaboration is a very complex topic and there is a definite need to shape e-interaction to avoid chaos and failure in virtual teams. The shaping of e-interaction in order to support e-collaboration involves not only technological but also social and psychological issues. This issues, useful concepts and as well as useful architectures, systems, protocols, and standards for the development and the support of e-collaboration are presented in this section.

Concepts and Issues for E-Collaboration

Collaboration, with respect to information technology, seems to have many aspects. Understanding the differences in human interactions is necessary to ensure the appropriate technologies are employed to design and develop groupware systems that could support e-collaboration effectively. As presented in Wikipedia (2006), there are three primary ways in which humans interact: conversational interaction, transactional interaction, and collaborative interaction:

- Conversational interaction is an exchange of information between one or many participants where the primary purpose of the interaction is discovery or relationship building. Communication technology such as telephones, instant messaging, and e-mail are generally sufficient for conversational interactions.
- Transactional interaction involves the exchange of transaction entities where a major function of the transaction entity is to alter the relationship between participants. Transactional interactions are most effectively handled by transactional systems that manage state and commit records for persistent storage.
- In collaborative interactions, the main function of the participants' relationship is to alter a collaboration entity. The collaboration entity is in a

relatively unstable form. Examples include the development of an idea, the creation of a design, and the achievement of a shared goal. Therefore, real collaboration technologies deliver the functionality for many participants to augment a common deliverable. Record or document management, threaded discussions, audit history, and other mechanisms designed to capture the efforts of many into a managed content environment are typical of collaboration technologies.

Research on e-Collaboration in order to satisfy the need for collaboration and collaborative work tries to resolve the following key issues: group awareness, multi-user interfaces, concurrency control, communication and coordination within the group, shared information space, and support of a heterogeneous, open environment, which integrates existing single-user applications.

Biuck-Aghai (2003) refers that two main challenges of e-collaboration are the following:

- How can one know how to carry out collaboration virtually?
- How can one know what is, and has been, "going on" during virtual collaboration?

These challenges could be satisfied by the features of collaborative software presented by Cerovsek and Turk (2004) in order to support sharing. These features are the following:

- Information sharing, which includes different types of information that must be interpreted by human
- Knowledge sharing, which is one of the processes in knowledge management framework apart from knowledge creation, knowledge organization/storage, and knowledge application
- Application sharing, which implies sharing of code or making applications available: categories of sharing are: code, components, applications, services, computing
- Workspace sharing, which provides a virtual space (shared workspace) allocated for employees' work (as in an office) and may include the sharing of several all previous levels of sharing
- Resource sharing, which includes all kinds of sharing previously listed, as well as the sharing

of other resources such as computing resources, processor time, equipment, and so forth

E-collaboration systems are often categorized according to the time/location matrix using the distinction between same time (synchronous) and different times (asynchronous), and between same place (face-to-face) and different places (distributed). Another categorization of the collaboration technologies has been introduced by Poltrock (2002) and it is based on time-interaction criterion (i.e., synchronous and asynchronous). According to this categorization, groupware can be divided into three categories depending on the level of collaboration:

- Communication tools, which send messages, files, data, or documents between people and hence facilitate the sharing of information; examples of synchronous tools in this category are audio/video conferencing, telephone, textual chat, instant messaging, and broadcast video; examples of asynchronous tools in this category are e-mail, voice mail, and fax
- Collaboration/conferencing tools that also facilitate the sharing of information, but in a more interactive way; examples of synchronous tools in this category are whiteboards, application sharing, meeting facilitation tools, and collaborative virtual environments; examples of asynchronous tools in this category are document management tools, threaded discussions, hypertext, and team workspaces.
- Collaborative management (coordination) tools, which facilitate and manage group activities; examples of synchronous tools in this category are floor control and session management; examples of asynchronous tools in this category are workflow management, case tools, project management tools, as well as calendar and scheduling tools

Architectures for E-Collaboration Systems

As previously mentioned, e-collaboration systems can be either asynchronous or synchronous. Regarding the tools and architectures for asynchronous systems of collaboration from distance, the tendency nowadays is the use of technologies of Web-based systems in which asynchronous services and tools such as electronic

Figure 1. Peer-to-peer topology

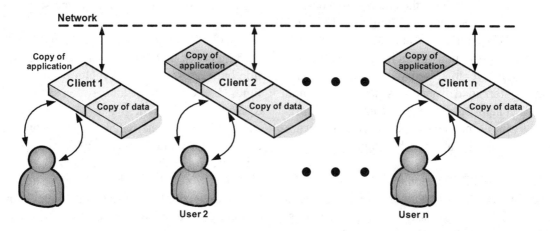

Figure 2. Client-server topology

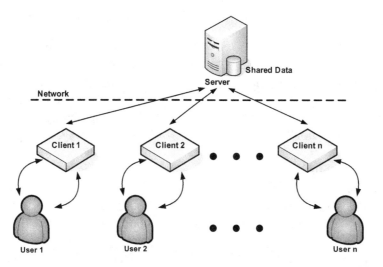

post, group calendars, and forums are incorporated. In particular, nowadays the tendency turns to the direction of developing collaborative portals. The basic technological solutions for the development of Web-based systems are (a) 3-tier architectures with use Web server, a database, and a scripting language; and (b) N-tier architectures with the use application servers, databases, and modules that allow the development of presentation independent applications in multiple levels.

As far as it concerns the synchronous e-collaboration systems, it should be noted that these systems present great interest due to the advanced sense of realism they aim to achieve. Generally speaking, the communication among participating workstations in a collaborative session could be supported by using various network architectures with different characteristics. To this direction the architectures that support these types of systems usually fall into one of the following cases: (a) **client-server architectures** (Figure 2), where the clients communicate their changes to one or more servers and these servers, in turn, are responsible for the redistribution of the received information to all connected clients and (b) **peer-to-peer architectures** (Figure 1), where the clients communicate directly their modifications and updates of the world to all connected clients. The case of the client-server model is the most simple but it is cannot support high scalability as there is a central point of failure, the server. As far as it concerns the peer-to-peer model, the scalability is restricted by the network. Greenberg and Roseman (1999) refer to the previous network topologies also as replicated (peer-to-peer) and centralized (client-server).

Technologies and Standards for E-Collaboration Systems

This section presents useful technologies, standards, and protocols for the development and support of e-collaboration systems. These standards and systems could be categorized in the following categories:

- **Standards and technologies for peer-to-peer systems:** The main standards are: (a) instant messaging and presence protocol (IMPP) (http://www.ietf.org) and JXTA (http://www.jxta.org).
- **Standards and technologies for videoconference applications:** The main standards and protocols for supporting tele-conference and voice over IP (VoIP) services are: (a) eXtensible messaging and presence protocol (XMPP) for supporting text chat functionality; (b) T.120 (http://www.itu.int) series of recommendations which collectively define a multipoint data communication service for use in multimedia conferencing environments; (c) H.323 (http://www.itu.int), which describes terminals and other entities that provide multimedia communications services; and (d) session initiation protocol (SIP), which supports user sessions that involve multimedia elements such as video, voice, instant messaging, online games, and virtual reality.
- **Real time protocols:** They support real time multimedia transmission, multimedia transmission over the Internet, and quality of services. Examples are RSVP (resource reservation protocol) and RTP/RTCP (real-time transport protocol/real-time transport control protocol).
- **Protocols for collaborative virtual environments:** They are protocols that can support the communication in collaborative virtual environments. Examples are DWTP (distributed worlds transfer and communication protocol) (Broll, 1998; Diehl, 2001), ISTP (interactive sharing transport protocol) (Waters, Anderson, & Schwenke, 1997), VIP (VRML interchange protocol) (Teraoka & Tokoro, 1993), VRTP (virtual reality

transfer protocol) (Brutzman, Zyda, Watsen, & Macedonia, 1997), and DIS (distributed interactive simulation) (Zeswitz, 1993).

Integrated E-Collaboration Systems

According to Mandviwalla and Khan (1999, p. 245), a collaborative technology is integrated if it combines support for more than one mode (e.g., synchronous or asynchronous), medium (e.g., text, graphic, audio, video, shared whiteboard, etc), and structure (i.e., the support provided by the application for group development and productive outcomes). Following this definition, Munkvold & Zigurs (2005) presented seven categories of e-collaboration systems (collaborative product suites, collaborative portals, desktop conferencing systems, Web-based team/project rooms, collaboration peer to peer systems, electronic meeting systems, and e-learning systems). We propose to add another one category titled: collaborative virtual environments, which refers to 3D-based e-collaboration tools.

According to the previous categorization, the following paragraph presents examples of collaborative tools included in each category as well as products and research prototypes that could be categorized there:

- Collaborative product suites include tools such as e-mail, group calendar, threaded discussions, document management, and workflow. Examples are Lotus Notes/Domino, Microsoft Exchange, and GroupWise (Novell).
- Collaborative portals include tools such as instant messaging, presence awareness, team workplaces, people finder, e-meetings, and document management. Examples are IBM Websphere portal, and MS Sharepoint.
- Desktop conferencing systems include tools such as instant messaging/chat, audio conferencing, presence awareness, videoconferencing, application sharing, shared whiteboard, polling, voting, and recording of meeting information. Examples are MSN Messenger, Interwise, Centra 7, WebEx Meeting, Microsoft Live Meeting, and Virtual Room Videoconferencing System (VRVS).
- Web-based team/project rooms include tools such as group calendar, contacts, notes, tasks, file sharing, e-mail, chat, pinboard, project management, document management, threaded discussions, brainstorming, voting, time sheets, telegram,

evaluation, and scheduler. Examples are Team-Space, Documentum eRoom, ConferenceXP, and Lotus Workplace Team Collaboration.

- Peer to peer systems include tools such as include tools such as instant messaging/chat, presence awareness, threaded discussion, file sharing, project management, group calendar, group outliner, and meeting management. An example is the Groove Virtual Office.

- Electronic meeting systems include tools such as include tools such as agenda, brainstorming, categorization & organizing, voting and prioritizing, action planning, surveys, shared whiteboard, meeting log, and chat. Examples are GroupSystems, Facilitate.com, and Meetingworks.

- E-Learning systems include tools such as e-mail, instant messaging, presence awareness, calendar, threaded discussion, learning objects repository, and course administration. Examples are Blackboard, Centra 7, Aspen, Lotus Workplace Collaborative Learning, WebEx Training Center and Moodle.

- Collaborative Virtual Environments include tools such as user representation by avatars, presence awareness, text chat, audio chat, intelligent agents, bubble chat, 3D representation of the collaborative space. Examples are Flash Communication Server MX, Blaxxun, ActiveWorlds, Parallel Graphics, and Adobe Atmosphere.

FUTURE TRENDS

The new e-collaboration systems tend to be integrated in at least four dimensions: users and group members, collaboration processes, technologies, and application areas, in order to lead into a suitable e-collaboration platform, which will provide support and openness for all mentioned aspects as explained next:

- From a user-centric point of view, next generation e-collaboration environments have to deliver "quality of experience" and support the presence of other users.

- New e-collaboration environments tend to provide seamless integration of synchronous and asynchronous communications and maintain the user experience in both connected and disconnected modes.

- From a technique-centric point of view, next generation e-collaboration environments should be based on flexible service components which will allow adaptability and scalability. Furthermore, haptic devices and augmented reality platforms will be used the next years for supporting e-collaboration.

- From the application-centric and process-oriented point of view, collaborative ICT technologies have to be customizable to different communities.

CONCLUSION

Recent trends in computing research and the availability of inexpensive computing and communication technology have encouraged the development of e-collaboration environments. Such distributed collaboration is already changing the way business and research is conducted. Nowadays, there is a variety of tools available based on different technologies and offering a wide variety of functionality. The next years we can say that the new e-collaboration systems will be integrated in at least four dimensions: users and group members, collaboration processes, technologies, and application areas, in order to lead into a suitable e-collaboration platform, which will provide support and openness.

REFERENCES

Biuck-Aghai, R. (2003). *Patterns of virtual collaboration*. PhD Thesis, University of Technology, Sydney, Australia. Retrieved May 8, 2007, from http://www.sftw.umac.mo/~robertb/publications/thesis/thesis.pdf

Broll, W. (1998, February 16-19). DWTP—An Internet protocol for shared virtual environments. In S. N. Spencer (Ed.), *VRML '98, Virtual Reality Modeling Symposium*, Monterey, CA (pp. 49-56). New York: ACM, S.

Brutzman, D., Zyda, M., Watsen, K., & Macedonia, M. (1997). Virtual reality transfer protocol (vrtp) design rationale. In *Proceedings of WETICE '97, Distributed System Aspects of Sharing a Virtual Reality Workshop* (pp. 179-186). IEEE Computer Society, Cambridge, MA.

Cerovsek, T., & Turk, Z. (2004). *Working together: ICT infrastructures to support collaboration.* Retrieved from http://e-pub.uni-weimar.de/volltexte/2004/212/

Diehl, S. (2001). *Distributed virtual worlds, foundations, and implementation techniques using VRML, Java, and CORBA.* Berlin, Heidelberg, Germany: Springer-Verlag.

Greenberg, S., & Roseman, M. (1999). Groupware toolkits for synchronous Work. In M. Beaudouin-Lafon (Ed.), *Computer-supported cooperative work (Trends in Software 7).* John Wiley & Sons Ltd.

Kock, N., & Nosek J. (2005). Expanding the boundaries of e-collaboration. *IEEE Transactions on Professional Communication, 48*(1), March 2005.

Kock, N., Davison R., Ocker R., & Wazlawick, R. (2001). E-collaboration: A look at past research and future challenges. *Journal of Syst. Inform. Technol., 5*(1), 1-9.

Lipnack, J., & Stamps, J. (1997). *Virtual teams: reaching across space, time, and organizations with technology.* John Wiley & Sons, Inc.

Mandviwalla, M., & Khan, S. (1999). Collaborative object workspaces (COWS): Exploring the integration of collaboration technology. *Decision Support Systems, 27*(3), 241-254.

Munkvold, B., & Zigurs, I. (2005, April-June). *Integration of e-collaboration technologies. International Journal of E-Collaboration, 1*(2), 1-24.

Poltrock, S. (2002). *Mapping collaboration technology requirements to human social structure. mathematics & computing technology phantom works.* The Boeing Company.

Waters, R. C., Anderson, D. B., & Schwenke, D. L. (1997). Design of the interactive sharing transfer protocol. In *Proceedings of WETICE '97, IEEE 6th Workshops on Enabling Technologies: Infrastructure for Collaborative Enterprises.* Los Alamitos, CA: IEEE Computer Society Press.

Wikipedia. (2006). *Collaborative software.* Retrieved March 9, 2006, from http://en.wikipedia.org/wiki/Groupware

Zeswitz, S. (1993, September). *NPSNET: Integration of distributed interactive simulation (DIS) protocol for communication architecture and information interchange.* Master's Thesis, Naval Postgraduate School, Monterey, California. Retrieved May 8, 2007, from http://gamepipe.usc.edu/~zyda/Theses/Michael.Canterbury.pdf

KEY TERMS

Collaboration: Collaboration is the act of working together on a common task or process.

Cooperation: Cooperation is the joint operation toward a common goal or benefit.

CSCW: Computer-supported cooperative work or CSCW is computer-assisted coordinated activity carried out by groups of collaborating individuals.

E-Collaboration: E-collaboration defined as "collaboration, which is conducted without face-to-face interaction among individuals or members of virtual teams engaged in a common task using information and communication technologies."

Groupware: Groupware is software that accentuates the multiple user environments, coordinating and orchestrating things so that users can "see" each other, yet do not conflict with each other.

Integrated Collaborative Technology: A collaborative technology is integrated if it combines support for more than one mode (e.g., synchronous or asynchronous), medium (e.g., text, graphic, audio, video, shared whiteboard, etc.), and structure (i.e., the support provided by the application for group development and productive outcomes).

Virtual Collaboration: Virtual collaboration is defined as collaboration, which is conducted without face-to-face interaction, enabled by technology.

Virtual Team: Virtual team, like every team, is a group of people who interact through interdependent tasks guided by a common purpose. Unlike conventional teams, a virtual team work across space, time, and organizational boundaries with links strengthened by Webs of communication technologies.

Efficient and Scalable Client–Clustering for Proxy Cache

Kyungbaek Kim
University of California, Irvine, USA

Daeyeon Park
Korea Advanced Institute of Science and Technology, Korea

INTRODUCTION

The recent increase in popularity of the Web has led to a considerable increase in the amount of Internet traffic. As a result, the Web has now become one of the primary bottlenecks to network performance and Web caching has become an increasingly important issue. Web caching aims to reduce network traffic, server load, and user-perceived retrieval delay by replicating popular content on caches that are strategically placed within the network. Browser caches reside in the clients' desktop, and proxy caches are deployed on dedicated machines at the boundary of corporate network and Internet service providers.

By caching requests for a group of users, a proxy cache can quickly return documents previously accessed by other clients. Using only one proxy cache has limited performance because the hit rate of the proxy is limited by the cache storage and the size of the client population. That is, if a cache is full and needs space for new documents, it evicts the other documents and it will retrieve the evicted documents from the Internet for other requests. In Figure 1(a), if the square object is evicted, the proxy cache obtains it from the Internet. But if the near proxy cache has a square object like that in Figure 1(b), Proxy 1 can obtain it from Proxy 2 and reduce the latency and the Internet traffic. According to this procedure, multiple proxies should cooperate with each other in order to increase the total client population, improve hit ratios, and reduce document-access latency; that is the cooperative caching (Chankhunthod, Danzig, Neerdaels, Schwartz, & Worrell, 1996; Cohen, Phadnis, Valloppillil, & Ross, 1997; Rodriguez, Spanner, & Biersack, 1999; Wolman et al., 1999).

BACKGROUND

Cooperative Web Caching

The basic operation of the Web caching is simple. Web browsers generate HTTP GET requests for Internet objects such as HTML pages, images, mp3 files, etc. These are serviced from a local Web browser cache, Web proxy caches, or an original content server depending on which cache contains a copy of the object. If a cache closer to the client has a copy of the requested object, we reduce more bandwidth consumption and decrease more network traffic. Hence, the cache hit rate should be maximized and the miss penalty, which is the cost when a miss occurs, should be minimized when designing a Web caching system.

The performance of a Web caching system depends on the size of its client community. As the user community increases in size, so does the probability that a cached object will soon be requested again. Caches sharing mutual trust may assist each other to increase the hit rate. A caching architecture should provide the paradigm for proxies to cooperate efficiently with each other. One approach to coordinate caches in the same system is to set up a caching hierarchy. With hierarchical caching, caches are placed at multiple levels of the network. Another approach is a distributed caching system, where there are only caches at the bottom level and there are no other intermediate cache levels.

Internet cache protocol (ICP) (Chankhunthod et al., 1996) is a typical cooperating protocol for a proxy to communicate with other proxies. If a requested object is not found in a local proxy, the proxy sends ICP queries to neighbor proxies, sibling proxies, and parent proxies.

Figure 1. Cooperative caching: request and response path when Client A requests the square (a) initial situation; (b) after square is evicted from Proxy 1

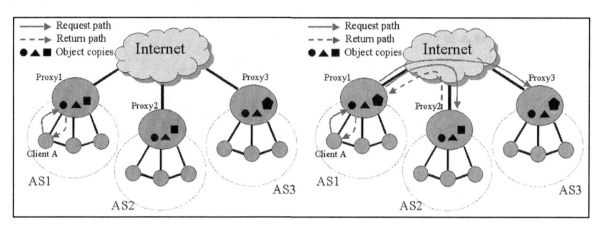

Each neighbor proxy receives the queries and sends ICP replies without the existence of the object. If the local proxy receives an ICP reply with the object, it uses that reply. Otherwise, the local proxy forwards the request to the parent proxy. ICP wastes expensive resources--core-link and cache storage. Even if the neighbor caches do not have the requested object, ICP uses the core-links between proxies, which are used for many clients and are bottlenecks of the network bandwidth. Another protocol for cooperative caching is the cache array routing protocol (CARP) (Cohen et al., 1997), which divides the URL-space among an array of loosely coupled caches and lets each cache store only the objects whose URL are hashed to it. For this feature, every request is hashed and forwarded to a selected cache node. In this scheme, clients must know the cache array information and the hash function, making the management of CARP difficult. Additionally, there are other issues such as load balancing and fault tolerance.

Another problem of CARP, as well as ICP, is scalability of management. Large corporate networks often employ a cluster of machines, which generally must be overprovisioned to handle burst peak loads. A growth in user population creates a need for hardware upgrades. This scalability issue cannot be solved by ICP or CARP.

Peer-to-Peer Lookup

Peer-to-peer systems are distributed systems without any centralized control or hierarchical organization, where the software running at each node is equivalent in

functionality; this includes redundant storage, selection of nearby servers, anonymity, search, and hierarchical naming. Among these features, lookup for a data is an essential functionality for peer-to-peer systems.

A number of peer-to-peer lookup protocols have been recently proposed, including Pastry (Rowstron & Druschel, 2001), Chord (Stoica, Morris, Karger, Kaashoek, & Balakrishnan, 2001), CAN (Ratnasamy, Francis, Handley, Karp, & Shenker, 2001), and Tapestry (Zhao, Kubiatowicz, & Joseph, 2001). In a self-organizing and decentralized manner, these protocols provide a distributed hash-table (DHT) that reliably maps a given object key to a unique live node in the network. Because DHT is made by a hash function that balances load with high probability, each live node has the same responsibility for data storage and query load. If a node wants to find an object, a node simply sends a query with the object key corresponding to the object to the selected node determined by the DHT. Typically, the length of routing is about O(log n), where n is the number of nodes. According to these properties, peer-to-peer systems balance storage and query load, transparently tolerate node failures and provide efficient routing of queries.

PEER-TO-PEER CLIENT-CLUSTERING

Overview

As we described in the previous section, the use of only a proxy cache has a performance limitation because of potential growth in client population. Even

Figure 2. Backup storage: Client C stores and services the evicted square from Proxy 1

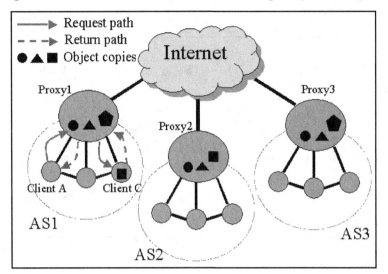

if proxy caches cooperate with each other to enhance performance, high administrative cost, and scalability issues still exist. To improve the performance of the cache system and solve the scalability issues, we exploit the residual resources of clients for a proxy cache. That is, any client that wants to use the proxy cache provides small resources to the proxy and the proxy uses these additional resources to maintain the proxy cache system. This feature makes the system resourceful and scalable.

We use the residual resources of clients as a backup storage for the proxy cache, like Figure 2. While a conventional proxy cache drops evicted objects, our proxy cache stores these objects to the backup storage, which is distributed among the client-cluster. When a client sends a GET request to a proxy cache, it checks its local storage. If a hit occurs, it returns the requested object; otherwise, it sends a lookup message to the backup storage and this message is forwarded to the client that has responsibility for storing the object. If the client has the object, it returns the object to the proxy; otherwise, the proxy gets the object from the original server or other proxy caches. This interaction between the proxy cache and the backup storage decreases the probability of sending requests outside the network, reduces the usage of inter-proxy links, and increases the performance of the proxy cache.

Client-Cluster Management

In our scheme, a proxy cache uses the resources of clients that are in the same network. Generally, if a peer wants to use other peers, it should have information about those. This approach is available when the other peers are reliable and available. However, the client membership is very large and changes dynamically. If the proxy cache manages the states of all clients, too much overhead is created to manage the client information and complex problems such as fault-tolerance, consistency, and scalability arise. In consideration of these issues, we establish the proxy cache such that it has no information for the clients and the client-cluster manages itself.

We design the client-cluster by using DHT-based peer-to-peer protocol. To use this protocol, each client needs an application whose name is *station*. A station is not a browser or a browser cache, but a management program to provide clients' resources for a proxy cache. A client cannot use resources of a station directly, while a proxy cache sends requests issued from clients to stations in order to use resources of a client-cluster. When a station receives requests from a proxy cache, it forwards requests to another station or checks whether it has the requested objects. Each station has a unique node key and a DHT. The unique node key is generated by computing the SHA-1 hash of the client identifier,

Figure 3. Two types of backward ICP message

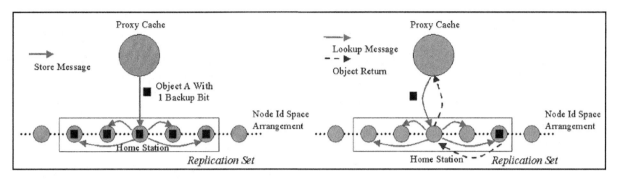

such as an IP address or an Ethernet address, and the object key is obtained by computing the SHA-1 of the corresponding URL. The DHT describe the mapping of the object keys to responsible live node keys for efficient routing of request queries. It is similar to a routing table in a network router. A station uses this table with the key of the requested object to forward the request to the next station. Additionally, the DHT of a station has the keys of *neighbor stations,* which are numerically close to the station, like the leaf nodes in PASTY or the successor list in CHORD. When a proxy cache sends a request query to one station of a client-cluster, the station gets the object key of the requested object and selects the next station according to the DHT and the object key. Finally, the *home station,* which is a station having the numerically closest node key to the requested object key among all currently live nodes, receives the request and checks whether it has the object in local cache. If a hit occurs, the home station returns the object to the proxy cache; otherwise, it only returns a null object. The cost of this operation is typically O(log n), where n is the total number of stations. If 1000 stations exist, the cost of lookup is about 3, and if 100000 Stations, the cost is about 5.

The client-cluster can cope with frequent variations in client membership by using this protocol. Though the clients dynamically join and leave, the lazy update for managing the small information of the membership changes does not spoil the lookup operation of this protocol. When a station joins the client-cluster, it sends a join message to any one station in the client-cluster and gets new DHT and other stations to update their DHT for the new station lazily. On the other hand, when a station leaves or fails, other stations, which have a DHT mapping with the departing station, detect the

failure of it lazily and repair their DHT. According to this feature, the client-cluster is self-organizing and fault-tolerant.

The proxy cache stores the evicted objects to a particular station in the client-cluster by using this lookup operation. All stations have roughly the same amount of objects because the DHT used for the lookup operation provides a degree of natural load balance. Moreover, the object range, which is managed by one station, is determined by the number of live nodes. That is, if there are few live nodes, the object range is large; otherwise, it is small. According to this, when the client membership changes, the object range is resized automatically and the home stations for every object are changed implicitly.

As described, the routing information and the object range are well managed by this protocol. Consequently, after updating the information for variation in the client membership, future requests for an object will be routed to the station that is now numerically closest to the object key. If the objects for the new home station are not moved, subsequent requests miss the objects. According to these misses, the performance of a client-cluster decreases remarkably. We can replicate the objects to neighbor stations to prevent such misses. This approach ensures the reliability of the objects, but leads to serious traffic overhead and inefficient storage usage. To reduce this overhead and use the storage efficiently, we store and lookup objects using the *Backward ICP.* This is described in the next section.

Backward ICP

The backward ICP, which is a communication protocol between the proxy cache and the client-cluster, is similar

175

Figure 4. Hit rate and byte hit rate comparison between only proxy cache and client-cluster

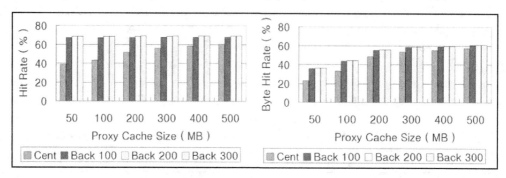

to the ICP used between the proxy caches. However, the backward ICP uses a local area network rather than an inter-proxy link.

There are two types of messages in the backward ICP as shown in Figure 3. One is a *store* message and the other is a *lookup* message. A store message is used to store evicted objects from a proxy cache. The proxy cache sends a store message and the evicted object to the home station and the home station replicates the objects to the replication set, which is composed of neighbor stations. Before sending a store message for an evicted object, the proxy cache checks the *backup bit* of the evicted object. This backup bit is used to prevent duplicated storage of an object that is already in the client-cluster. If the backup bit is set to 1, the proxy cache knows that the client-cluster has this evicted object and drops this object immediately. If the bit is set to 0, the proxy cache backs up the evicted object to the client-cluster. When the proxy cache gets the object from the client-cluster, this bit is set to 1. When the object is refreshed or returned from the original server, this bit is set to 0.

A lookup message is used to find objects in the client-cluster. When the proxy cache sends a lookup message to the home station, this station returns the object to the proxy cache if it has the requested object. Otherwise, if a miss occurs, it sends lookup messages to the replication set simultaneously and waits for a response from any station. If the object is somewhere among the replication set, the home station stores this object and returns this to the proxy cache; otherwise, it returns a null object. Following this, the home station replicates the object to the replication set, except the responding station.

This protocol replicates objects only at the time when they are stored or a lookup miss occurs. It reduces traffic overhead incurred by object replications.

Moreover, it uses storage efficiently by giving more opportunities to retrieve popular objects. The first time when any object is stored, the object is replicated to increase the probability of accessing the object. As time goes by, popular objects are requested more than other objects and they are replicated again to increase the probability.

Comparison of Hit Rate and Byte Hit Rate

In our trace-driven simulations, we use traces from KAIST, which uses a class B IP address for the network. The trace from the proxy cache in KAIST contains over 3.4 million requests in a single day. We have run our simulations with traces from this proxy cache since October 2001.

Figure 4 shows a comparison of the *hit rate* and the *byte hit rate*. By the hit rate, we mean the number of requests that hit in the proxy cache as a percentage of total requests. A higher hit rate means the proxy cache can handle more requests and the original server must deal with proportionally lighter load of requests. The byte hit rate is the number of bytes that hit in the proxy cache as a percentage of total number of bytes requested. A higher byte hit rate results in a greater decrease in network traffic on the server side.

In the figures, cent means using only a proxy cache and back n means using the client-cluster with n hundreds clients. The hit rate of only the proxy cache is greatly affected by the cache size, but the hit rate of using the client-cluster achieves nearly an infinite-hit rate without any relationship to the proxy cache size. This is achieved by the plentiful resources provided by the clients. That is, though the proxy cache size is limited, the storage of the client-cluster is sufficient to store evicted objects and the proxy cache gets almost all requested objects from the client-cluster.

Table 1. Summary of client loads for trace 1 with the 200MB proxy

Client No.	Mean Req.	Max Req.	Dev.	Mean Byte Req. (KB)	Max Byte Req. (KB)	Dev.
100	1024	1369	2.2	13422	316805	11.1
200	602	733	2.4	6711	315158	12.1
300	401	510	2.5	4474	314197	12.9

For the byte hit rate, we can obtain a similar result as that for the hit rate. However, in this case, using the client-cluster does not yield infinite-byte hit rate, particularly with a small proxy cache size. The reason for this result is the different byte size of the object range, which is roughly the same for each client, because of the different sizes of the objects. Thus some clients that usually have large objects cannot store many objects, and the hit rate and the byte hit rate decrease. In particular, large size objects whose size is bigger than that of one client storage, which is the Station's storage, 10MB, are not stored on the client-cluster and the byte hit rate decreases remarkably.

Client Load

We examine the client loads, which include the request number, storage size, stored objects, hit rate, etc, to verify that the client-cluster balances the storage and request queries. Table 1 shows a summary of the request number and the sizes of the requested objects. Each client receives roughly the same load, and when the client number increases the load of each client decreases. The properties of DHT-base peer-to-peer protocols account for these findings. For the byte request, we again see the effect of the different sizes of the objects, which we strongly believe account for the performance degradation.

FUTURE TRENDS

Some peer-to-peer approaches for Web caching appear including our approach (Iyer, Rowstron, & Druschel, 2002; Kim & Park, 2003; Xiao, Zhang, & Xu, 2002; Xu, Hu, & Bhuyan, 2004). These approaches distribute the requests and the loads to the client by using the p2p manner. The only difference of them is the storing method of the Web object. Some approaches store the index of the object on the proxy or the clients to share

the object in the storage of client. The others store the object itself to the storage and find the location with the p2p protocol.

In these days, the Web becomes more complicate because of the dynamic pages, the large objects(audio/video) and so on. Moreover, the p2p networks are very heterogeneous. The computing power, the bandwidth, the storage, etc., of the participant nodes are very various. These facts need the well-adapted p2p support for Web caching.

CONCLUSION

In this article, we propose and evaluate peer-to-peer client-cluster, which is used as a backup storage for the proxy cache. The proxy cache with this client-cluster is highly scalable, more efficient, and has low administrative cost. Even if the clients take the load, this load has been verified on a range of real workloads to be low. Moreover, the utility of the client-cluster can be improved by managing objects according to their properties such as size, popularity, and update frequency. We can extend the usage of the client-cluster to other proxy systems. If a proxy performs demanding jobs such as encoding/decoding and complex calculation for many clients, it can use the residual resources of the clients to accomplish these tasks.

REFERENCES

Chankhunthod, A., Danzig, P. B., Neerdaels, C., Schwartz, M. F., & Worrell, K. J. (1996). A hierarchical Internet object cache. *Proceedings of the 1996 Usenix Technical Conference,* San Diego.

Cohen, J., Phadnis, N., Valloppillil, V., & Ross, K. W. (1997). *Cache array routing protocol v1.0.* Retrieved from http://www.ietf.org/internet-drafts/draft-vinod-carp-v1-03.txt

Iyer, S., Rowstron, A., & Druschel, P. (2002). Squirrel: A decentralized peer-to-peer Web cache. *Proceedings of the 21st ACM SIGACT-SIGOPS Symposium on Principles of Distributed Computing*, Monterey.

Kim, K., & Park, D. (2003). Efficient and scalable client clustering for Web proxy cache. *IEICE Transaction on Information and Systems, E86-D*(9), 1577-1585.

Ratnasamy, S., Francis, P., Handley, M., Karp, R., & Shenker, S. (2001). A scalable content-addressable network. *Proceedings of the 2001 ACM SIGCOMM Conference*, San Diego.

Rodriguez, P., Spanner, C., & Biersack, E. W. (1999). Web caching architectures: Hierarchical and distributed caching. *Proceedings of the 4th International Web Caching Workshop*, San Diego.

Rowstron, A., & Druschel, P. (2001). Pastry: Scalable, decentralized object location, and routing for large-scale peer to-peer systems. *Proceedings of the 18th International Conference on Distributed Systems Platforms*, Heidelberg.

Stoica, I., Morris, R., Karger, D., Kaashoek, M. F., & Balakrishnan, H. (2001). Chord: A scalable peer-to-peer lookup service for Internet applications. *Proceedings of the 2001 ACM SIGCOMM Conference*, San Diego.

Wolman, A., Voelker, G. M., Sharma, N., Cardwell, N., Karlin, A., & Levy, H. M. (1999). On the scale and performance of cooperative Web proxy caching. *Proceedings of the 17th ACM symposium on Operating Systems Principles* (pp. 16-31), Kiawah Island Resort.

Xiao, L., Zhang, X., & Xu, Z. (2002). On reliable and scalable peer-to-peer Web document sharing. *Proceedings of the 16th International Parallel and Distributed Processing Symposium* (pp. 228), Fort Lauderdale, IEEE CS.

Xu, Z., Hu, Y., & Bhuyan, L. (2004). Exploiting client cache: A scalable and efficient approach to build large Web. *Proceedings of the 18th International Parallel and Distributed Processing Symposium* (pp. 55a), Santa Fe, IEEE CS.

Zhao, B. Y., Kubiatowicz, J., & Joseph, A. (2001). Tapestry: An infrastructure for fault-tolerant wide-area location and routing. *UCB Technical Report UCB/CSD-01-114.*

KEY TERMS

Backward ICP: A communication protocol between a proxy cache and a client-cluster.

Client-Cluster: A well organized group of clients, which communicate with the p2p protocol.

Cooperative Proxy Cache: A proxy cache, which trusts and cooperates with each other proxy cache.

Distributed Hash Table: A hash table, which is distributed to many other components with the specific mechanism.

Home Node: A node, which is responsible for a target object key.

Node Key: A unique and hashed value to identify a node.

Object Key: A unique and hashed value to identify an object.

Peer-to-Peer: A communication method between clients. cf. client-to-server

Proxy Cache: A server, which locates on the border of ISP or institution and helps the original server by intercepting the user request.

Station: An application or daemon to help the communication of the client-cluster.

E-Learning

Gregory R. Gay
University of Toronto, Canada

Paola Salomoni
University of Bologna, Italy

Silvia Mirri
University of Bologna, Italy

INTRODUCTION

The evolution of an information society has transformed many activities in our everyday lives, including how we work, communicate, entertain, teach, and learn. More recently widespread Internet connectivity together with the development of new Web-based multimedia technologies, has strongly encouraged educational uses for information and communication technology (ICT).

Activities that require network technologies to deliver learning and training programs can be considered forms of "e-learning." In the not too distant past, before the broad use of Internet-based learning technologies became commonplace, a variety of technological solutions had been used to support teaching and learning activities, generally referred as computer assisted instruction (CAI). With CAI, people started using a computer as a means of teaching, providing tutorials, simulations, or games. CAI was generally learning activities that did not require network connectivity. E-learning today more often refers to systems and activities that go well beyond interactions with a single computer.

ICT naturally fueled the spread of e-learning, forcing the emergence of a society in which economic and social performance are largely judged by a continuous distribution of information and knowledge (Sloman, 2002). After a complex and long experimental phase in the latter decades of the 20ᵗʰ century, current e-learning technologies support cost effective, just-in-time, customized education that is delivered effectively in a variety of educational scenarios including schools, post secondary education, and professional skills training. Easy access to learning content and learning technologies provides greater opportunity for people and communities to develop new skills and improve their knowledge, minimizing the effects of socio-economic status, geographic location, and other ethnographic characteristics.

BACKGROUND

E-learning currently represents the most widespread form of "*distance education*," which generally refers to educational activities that involve teachers and students remotely located both in time and space. Current distance education is based on a wide range of delivery methods, including traditional correspondence, as well as books, audio/video tapes, interactive TV, CD-ROM, and DVD, as well as services that can be offered through the Internet (Rosenberg, 2000). More generally "*e-learning*" can be defined as the delivery of education or training programs through electronic means. Beyond this general definition, are terms or phrases used synonymously with e-learning or its specific forms. One such frequently used term is "*computer-based training*" (CBT), its main unique distinction being its focus on the computer instead of a more general association with ICT. Another broadly used term is "*online learning*," which emphasizes the presence of the Internet as a means for conducting learning activities. An additional specialization is termed "*Web-based education*," which more specifically refers to the use of Web-based applications that support educational activities.

E-learning activities can be classified according to their time dependence as (Clark & Mayer, 2002):

- **"*Synchronous*" e-learning:** Where teachers and students are involved in learning activities at the same time; they have to synchronize their activities; examples include video conferencing, chats, and real-time video lectures

- **"Asynchronous" e-learning:** In which teachers and students are involved in learning activities at different times; they "do not" have to synchronize their activities; examples include content delivery, cooperation through a forum, a blog, or a wiki, as well as e-mail communication and file sharing; new asynchronous e-learning applications are emerging based on archived podcasting and Webcasting content.

The more common approach is asynchronous e-learning. Its main benefit is its freedom from time and space requirements, thus supporting an "anytime" dimension of e-learning. On the other hand, synchronous activities give e-learning more appeal, involving people interacting directly with each other in real-time activities. A typical e-learning scenario might involve components of both.

E-LEARNING TECHNOLOGIES

From a technological point of view, today's e-learning is rooted primarily in Web-based delivery of educational multimedia content, coupled with synchronous and asynchronous communication features that allow students and teachers to interact (Sloman, 2002). There are several types of systems that assist with e-learning activities. Perhaps, the most common type of e-learning application, the so called *learning management system* (LMS), is devoted to managing learning activities and, more specifically, to keeping track of what learners do and learn, following both their activities within the system, and their progress mastering learning materials. A second category of applications, called a *learning content management systems* (LCMS), aim primarily at managing the delivery of course content, but such systems are frequently extended to include communication tools and user management features often found in an LMS (Jacobsen, 2002).

Often used interchangeably with LMS (and often with LCMS) is the *virtual learning environment* (VLE), with its focus on the "*virtuality*" of the learning space and on the idea of a platform that supports the whole range of learning activities as a stand alone integrated "virtual environment."

A very different role is played by "*e-learning content repositories,*" applications that are used to store, distribute, and share learning content. Often content repositories are linked into an LMS so instructors, and often students, can search and retrieve learning materials, export content from the repository in a standard format, import or link that content into an LMS as part of a course lesson, and often transfer content from an LMS into the repository to be shared with others.

The nature of e-learning content allows it to be reused in many contexts, and to be redistributed as standardized packaged educational materials (Horton & Horton, 2003). Pieces of learning material in a "content package" are often referred to as "*learning objects*" (LO). A content package is a collection of learning objects assembled together with a document, generally XML based, that defines association and sequencing rules used to organize the content within an e-learning system.

E-LEARNING STANDARDS

A standard description of content structure is needed to make content interoperable across different e-learning platforms. Several interoperability specifications have been developed by international organizations such as:

- **The Institute of Electrical and Electronics Engineers (IEEE):** With a specific working group, the Learning Technology Standards Committee, that is working on e-learning standardization (IEEE, 2006)
- **The Instructional Management System Global Learning Consortium (IMS Global Learning Consortium):** A collaboration of government organizations that are defining specifications to ensure interoperability across e-learning systems (IMS Global Learning Consortium, 2006b)

The goal of such standards is to define metadata, data structures, and communication protocols that will make learning content work across platforms, providing guidelines for designing, developing, and delivering electronic learning content.

Another similar project is the advanced distributed learning (ADL) initiative, lead by the U.S. Department of Defence. It has developed the *shareable content object reference model* (SCORM) standard, one of the more widely used e-learning specifications. ADL has based its work on that of IEEE and IMS, and has created a more encompassing interoperability standard that takes into consideration recommendations from those and other standards (ADL, 2004). The collected standards can be applied to learning content and to learning platforms (e.g., LMS, LCMS, VLE) with the aim to fully support the reuse of content across systems and standardize the delivery e-learning content. SCORM includes a de-facto standard for defining a sharable content object (SCO). An SCO is a learning resource that can be presented in any SCORM compliant system, displaying and sequencing content, and tracking student progress. Each SCO is made up of one or more assets or resources, which are generally electronic media (e.g., text, images, sound, video), Web pages, or other types of data. SCOs can be described with metadata, and often retrieved from online content repositories by searching for terms in the metadata, thereby encouraging their re-use.

Metadata and structural information about a unit of learning content is usually contained within a *"manifest,"* an XML file that describes the learning content in a standard manner. A SCORM manifest generally contains the content semantic description (metadata), together with its navigation or structural description (organizations), and the locations of each of the contained assets (resources). The SCORM main specifications are (ADL, 2004):

- The content aggregation model (CAM) that defines the structure or arrangement of learning materials, and describes the content or topics it contains with metadata (based on the IMS content packaging specification)
- The run-time environment (RTE), a JavaScript Application Programming Interface (API) that delivers to a LMS or LCMS real time information about user actions within a SCO, including exercise solving and tracking through resources
- The sequencing and navigation (SN) specification describes rule-based definitions of possible paths through learning content

PEDAGOGICAL APPROACHES

We will now consider e-learning from a pedagogical perspective. Teaching methodologies in e-learning have been widely discussed, starting from perhaps an obvious observation that the introduction of a new (electronic) means of teaching and learning requires changes in the way instruction and learning materials are delivered (Khan, 2005). First, education and training programs may be conducted *"fully online."* In this case all learning activities, including interactions among staff and students, assessments, and tutoring, are all conducted without any face-to-face interaction. A second approach has emerged in recent years that combines the positive effects of e-learning with effective classroom-based instruction. This hybrid approach that combines online learning with more traditional classroom-based forms of training, is often referred to as *"blended learning."* It can be implemented in many ways (e.g., by using electronic services to teach theoretical aspects of a discipline, and face-to-face activities for practical aspects). The adaptability of e-learning strategies provides potential support for a wide range of pedagogical approaches by implementing a variety of Web-based teaching methods (Driscoll & Carliner, 2005).

The main theoretical pedagogical perspectives are now beginning to drive the design of e-learning systems ranging from emotional and social human interaction approaches, to more cognitive information processing approaches. From a social perspective (e.g., *social constructivism*) e-learning systems are being designed to support group-based construction of knowledge, where students interact, often in small groups, through discussion forums, wikis, blogs, chats, and file sharing applications, to assemble knowledge about a topic area they are learning. From a cognitive perspective (e.g., *cognitivism*) learning content can be presented through multiple modalities, duplicating information in visual, auditory, and kinaesthetic forms, and structuring information so it can be absorbed in sequence, in a hierarchical form, or in a more global exploratory manner. Learning occurs by absorbing information through multiple senses, and by storing information in memory in multiple structures, so knowledge is more easily retrieved later. From an experiential perspective (e.g., *behaviourism*), learning can occur by interacting with the learning content itself, through interactive activities, simulations, and hands on practice. E-learning environments are beginning to evolve into systems that will accommodate these, as well as a full range of other pedagogical approaches to teaching and learning.

FUTURE TRENDS

Despite the benefits and motivating factors for educational institutions and business, e-learning has not yet reached its full potential. This may be due to a variety of factors, including institutional and social constraints on innovation, limitations of current technologies, or the limited accommodation by most current e-learning systems for diverse teaching methods and learning styles. Factors include:

- **Customization (flexibility, adaptability):** E-learning content and services need to be tailored to the knowledge level, context, culture, goals, and the interests of individual learners. Current technologies partially address this factor, though with a new generation of systems and standards emerging, future e-learning scenarios will accommodate a much broader range of pedagogical methodologies, and individual learning styles. E-learning will be designed around peoples' needs, considering how each individual is able to learn.
- **Accessibility:** E-learning materials are often used with a specific technology or configuration, making them less available to people who have limited access capabilities or are using non-standard computer equipment. Learners with disabilities using assistive technologies can benefit greatly from e-learning, not just because it allows distance and flexible learning activities, but also because it helps students with disabilities to access resources, which would otherwise present significant barriers for them (IMS Global Learning Consortium, 2006a). Future developments will focus on how assistive technologies and the Internet could be improved to enhance e-learning experiences for people with disabilities.
- **Mobility:** A new form of e-learning is emerging with the broad adoption of mobile terminals (e.g., cell phones, PDAs), sometimes called "m-learning" (Metcalf, 2006). The opportunity to browse learning materials everywhere, outside places that are traditionally devoted to learning, will have a strong impact on all aspects of training and education, and will present a great challenge for educators from both methodological and technological perspective. Current support of m-learning is limited, though with recent advances in mobile terminals, the possibility for "anywhere" e-learning is on the verge of reality. In the coming years m-learning may once again force us to rethink the strategies used to deliver electronic learning.

These future trends have a common theme: new e-learning paradigms will consider each student's individual abilities and learning goals, where learning is occurring, and through which particular device learning is taking place. Learning will be adapted for each individual learner. The IMS Global Learning Consortium has developed two specifications that attempt to address the personalization or transformation of e-learning content:

- The IMS Accessibility for Learner Information Package (ACCLIP) (IMS Global Learning Consortium, 2002b), describes a personal profile of preferences (e.g., preferred/required input devices or preferred content alternatives) used to tailor the presentation of learning content (e.g., visual, aural, textual) to the individual. An ACCLIP profile would be presented to an e-learning application by a learner, perhaps using a smart card, a memory stick, or perhaps automatically retrieved from a database. The system in turn would serve up the appropriately customized content adapted specifically for that person.
- The IMS AccessForAll Meta-data (ACCMD) specification (IMS Global Learning Consortium, 2002a) describes adaptable learning content by specifying, for example, what form the content will be presented in. The ACCMD specification might be implemented in an LMS. The LMS would receive an ACCLIP profile from a user, then based on that profile use an ACCMD application in the LMS to retrieve content appropriate for that person's needs. ACCMD is a mirror of ACCLIP, providing an interpreter for ACCLIP profiles and choosing the appropriate content based on that interpretation.

The AccessForAll Meta-data specification is intended to make it possible for systems to identify resources that match a user's stated preferences or needs. ACCMD describes the adaptability of learning content by specifying alternative formats for each content element, such as text alternatives for images, descriptive audio for video content, transcripts or captioning for audio tracks, visual alternatives for text, colour alternatives to increase contract, reduced alternatives for small screens, and a variety of other potential alternate formats.

CONCLUSION

There are many benefits associated with e-learning, cited in countless publications. E-learning opportunities are now found in a great many schools, colleges and universities, professional organizations, as well as government and business (Forman, 2002). Some of the primary benefits are:

- **E-learning is available anytime and anywhere:** People can instantly access services at their convenience, 24 hours a day, seven days a week, from any location they choose.
- **E-learning is easily scaled:** Both fully online and blended e-learning are easier to scale than traditional face-to-face education.
- **E-learning enlarges educational opportunities:** People can easily access a wide variety of learning services and materials, removing geographical and physical barriers.
- **E-learning is adaptable:** Learners of a wide variety can be accommodated with learning materials that adapt to their specific needs.

E-learning technologies and standards are evolving rapidly and are taking into consideration advances in our understanding of human learning, pedagogical methodologies, and systems interoperability. Future developments will require a coordinated effort between educators and information science experts. Efforts will focus on new teaching scenarios opened by advances in, and widespread use of, a range of information technology. Efforts will focus on adapting systems to accommodate a full range of pedagogical needs, adjusting, revising, improving, and sometimes reinventing technologies to support an ever growing number of e-learning communities.

REFERENCES

ADL. (2004). *Sharable content object reference model (SCORM) 2004 2ⁿᵈ Edition Document Suite*. Retrieved from http://www.adlnet.org/downloads/70.cfm

Clark R. C., & Mayer, R. E. (2002). *E-learning and the science of instruction: proven guidelines for consumers and designers of multimedia learning*. Pfeiffer.

Driscoll, M., & Carliner, S. (2005). *Advanced Web-based training strategies: Unlocking instructionally sound online learning*. Pfeiffer.

Forman, D. (2002). Cultural change for the e-world. In *Proceedings of the International Conference on Computers in Education* (Vol. 2, pp. 1412-1413).

Horton, W., & Horton, K. (2003). *E-learning tools and technologies: A consumer's guide for trainers, teachers, educators, and instructional designers*. John Wiley & Sons.

IEEE. (2006). *IEEE Learning Technology Standards Committee Home page*. Retrieved from http://ieeeltsc.org/

IMS Global Learning Consortium. (2006a). *IMS guidelines for developing accessible learning applications*. Retrieved from http://www.imsglobal.org/accessibility/

IMS Global Learning Consortium. (2006b). *IMS global learning consortium home page*. Retrieved from http://www.imsglobal.org/.

IMS Global Learning Consortium. (2002a). *IMS AccessForAll Meta-data Specification*. Retrieved from http://www.imsglobal.org/specificationdownload.cfm

IMS Global Learning Consortium. (2002b). *IMS learner information package accessibility for LIP*. Retrieved from http://www.imsglobal.org/specificationdownload.cfm

Jacobsen, P. (2002). *LMS vs. LCMS*. Retrieved from http://www.elearningmag.com/ltimagazine/article/articleDetail.jsp?id=21264

Khan, B. H. (2005). *Managing e-learning strategies: Design, delivery, implementation and evaluation*. Hershey, PA: Information Science Publishing.

Metcalf, D. S. (2006). *M-learning: Mobile e-learning*. HRD Press, Inc.

Rosenberg, M. J. (2000). *E-learning: Strategies for delivering knowledge in the digital age*. McGraw-Hill.

Sloman, M. (2002). *The E-learning revolution: How technology is driving a new training paradigm.* American Management Association.

KEY TERMS

Content Package: Content packages are collections of electronic learning materials assembled in a standard manner so they can be used across different e-learning systems. A common standard for assembling these learning units is the IMS content packaging specification. A content package will contain a manifest file that has in it a metadata section to semantically describe the content, an organizations section that describes the structure of the content, and a resources section that describes the location of files that make up the content package. Included with the manifest will be the resource files themselves. The pieces of a content package are usually distributed as a zip archive.

E-Learning Content Repository: A content repository is a storage system used to archive and manage learning content. Content repositories generally include search and retrieve features, metadata authoring and editing features, intellectual property controls, and often content authoring tools. Through a Web services interface, instructors and sometimes students are often able to search, retrieve, and edit content in the repository directly from within an LMS/LCMS.

Learning Content Management System (LCMS): Initially an LCMS referred to a system for managing learning content, though current LCMS tools include many of the administrative and course management features that might be found in a standard LMS. The primary difference is the management of content in an LCMS, which often includes tools for authoring, versioning, and archiving content, features that are less commonly found in a traditional LMS. An LMS might be used in conjunction with an LCMS when the primary function of the LCMS is the authoring and archiving of content (e.g. when acting as a content repository).

Learning Management System (LMS): The term LMS generally refers to systems that support the management of learning activities as well as course related administrative activities. Common features include discussion or chat space, test creation and delivery tools, file sharing tools, student and course management features, and assignment and grade management utilities, among others. The term LMS is frequently confused with LCMS, the two are often difficult to distinguish as they have over time, come to include many of the same features.

Learning Object (LO): IEEE defines a learning object as *"any entity, digital or not-digital, which can be used, re-used, or referenced during technology supported learning."* Many other definitions have been published that generally consider a learning object as a unit of reusable learning content that may range from a single file, to a collection of files that make up a lesson, to the content of an entire course.

Sharable Content Object (SCO): A SCO is similar to a content package, infact they will both include a manifest file that is much the same. The primary difference between a content package and a SCO is the interactivity found in a SCO. In addition to metadata, organizations, and resources found in the manifest of content packages, SCOs will also contain dependencies or sequencing rules. A SCO can then have multiple paths through the content based on the results of a quiz, or exercise for example. If a student fails a quiz, a dependency for advancing is not met, so they might be guided through a remedial section of the SCO before being allowed to continue on to the next level. A SCO is viewed or played in a SCORM Run Time Environment (RTE).

Virtual Learning Environment (VLE): Used synonymously with LMS and sometimes LCMS, a VLE is a system that provides learning content and course management services.

Ethernet to the Doorstep of Metropolitan Area Networks

E

Lampros Raptis
National Technical University of Athens, Greece

D. Kagklis
Hellenic Telecommunications Organization S.A., Greece

Yiorgos Patikis
Hellenic Telecommunications Organization S.A., Greece

INTRODUCTION

Ethernet has become the predominant technology in the Local Area Networks (LANs) due to its simplicity and cost effectiveness. It has been evolved over the past years from a simple shared medium protocol to a full duplex switched networking solution, from which originates almost 90% of the overall IP traffic that flows throughout the Internet. Its dominance has led many players in the telecommunication market (equipment manufacturers, network and service providers, end users, etc.) to consider Ethernet also as a candidate networking solution to the MAN (Metropolitan Area Networks) and WAN (Wide Area Networks) environment. Already several efforts are underway by international standardization bodies and forums like the Institute of Electrical and Electronics Engineers (IEEE), Internet Engineering Task Force (IETF), International Telecommunications Union (ITU), and Metro Ethernet Forum (MEF) to extend Ethernet into the MAN environment. The focus of this article is to provide a concise overview of these initiatives and analyze the challenges that must be faced for the transformation of Ethernet into a carrier-class networking solution capable of providing telecommunication services (Ethernet services) into the MAN.

BACKGROUND

The early Ethernet specification (IEEE 802.3, 2004) family standards were mostly concerned with the problems faced in a LAN environment. Ethernet's simplicity and price/performance advantages have made it the ultimate winner, thus **displacing other** once-promising technologies such as Token Ring, FDDI, and ATM. At the same time, those advantages make it a very attractive candidate for the MAN environment, which is the part of the network between the end-users' network (LAN) and the network and service providers' backbone network. Serrat (2003) states that currently the MAN environment is entrenched with legacy time-division multiplexing (TDM) based solutions (i.e., SONET/SDH technology) that were primarily designed for traditional voice and leased-line services. These legacy technologies have proven to be inadequate for providing the necessary resources for modern bandwidth hungry applications. Apart from the cost, there are several other key reasons for employing Ethernet-based technologies in the MAN network. Most notably, the fact that they are better suited for carrying the bursty Internet-based services, which nowadays constitute the vast majority of the overall traffic. Traditional TDM interfaces, on the other hand, do not cope as well in the same area, as they do not allow for statistical multiplexing of the data flows. The alternative of transporting Ethernet frames over legacy SDH infrastructure for combining the advantages of each technology leads to suboptimal hub and spoke topologies that are not as efficient as a native Ethernet solution. To displace these legacy technologies from the MAN environment, a new series of mechanisms and services must be introduced that will provide functionalities similar to that provided by the legacy networking solutions. The efforts of various standardization bodies and international forums to define such mechanisms are further described and analysed in the following sections.

ENHANCING ETHERNET FOR THE METRO ENVIRONMENT

The prospect of Ethernet's expansion in the metro environment has attracted the interest of several international standardization bodies and forums that are already in the process of defining key mechanisms that will enable Ethernet to resemble to a carrier class networking technology. IEEE, ITU-T, IETF, and Metro Ethernet Forum have already formed working groups that focus on the following areas:

- Ethernet services
- Scalability
- Survivability
- Network management

The following paragraphs provide a brief overview of each one of these enhancements of metro Ethernet. Raptis, Manousakis, and Bau (2006) provide a detailed analysis from a real case scenario of deploying an advance metropolitan Gigabit Ethernet network, whereas Allan, Bragg, McGuire, and Reid (2006) discuss what enhancements are required in order to transform existing Ethernet infrastructure into a carrier transport infrastructure.

Ethernet Services

The term Ethernet services is generally used to described a Layer 2 "connectivity" service, which allows the "connection" of geographically separated LANs utilizing Ethernet as a core protocol. The Ethernet traffic (frames) are agnostic of the underlying network infrastructure and can transported over different transport technologies like MPLS, SDH, WDM, etc. The motivation for adopting the Ethernet services comes from the desire to have a converged network that delivers multiple services that are currently provided by parallel or overlay networks. In the literature, different terms and names are used and a common terminology has not been agreed upon yet. From a topological point of view, three categories of Ethernet services can be defined, namely point-to-point (P2P) Ethernet connectivity service, point to multi-point (P2MP), and multi-point to multi-point (MP2MP). In the rest of the document, according to *Metro Ethernet Forum Technical Specification (2005),* the term E-Line service will be used for P2P and P2MP services and the term

E-LAN will be used for MP2MP service. Zier, Fischer, and Brockners (2004) provide a detailed comparison between different services and technologies.

Figure 1a and Figure 1b depict the basic reference model. More specifically, E-Line is a P2P Layer 2 connectivity service, which allows the transparent interconnection between two remote PoPs (point of presence). The CPE (customer premise equipment) of each PoP can be any device with a standard Ethernet interface from an unmanaged Layer-2 Ethernet switch up to a Layer 3 router. The demarcation point of the E-Line service is the UNI (user to network interface) port. For each E-Line service, different service characteristics can be defined like bandwidth, class of service (IEEE 802.1p bits), and so forth. The P2MP service is a special case of multiple P2P services, which are terminated in the same UNI port. For example in Figure 2a, the two E-Line services are terminated in the same UNI (UNI-2) allowing the creation of a hub-and-spoke topology. Finally, the E-LAN service is a MP2MP Layer 2 connectivity service, which allows the transparent interconnection between three or more remote PoPs. The connected PoPs belong to the same Layer 2 broadcast domain.

Scalability

For the delivery of different Ethernet services over a Metro Ethernet Network, a mechanism is needed in order to distinguish the services. Currently, there are three different approaches namely IEEE 802.1Q (VLANs), IEEE 802.1ad Q-in-Q (IEEE 802.1ad, 2005), and IEEE 802.1ah (MAC-in-MAC). Bottorf, Sajassi, and Suzuki (2006) and Chiruvolu, Ge, Elie-Dit-Cosaque, Ali, and Rouyer (2004) discuss and compare in-depth the different approaches.

Figure 1a. E-Line services

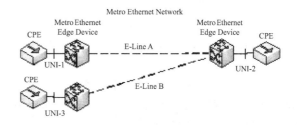

Figure 1b. E-LAN service

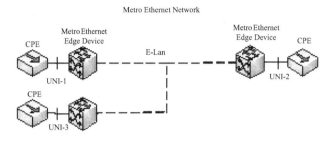

IEEE 802.1Q (VLAN)

IEEE 802.1Q was originally specified as a mechanism, which allows the creation of different logical LAN over the same physical LAN infrastructure. The creators of this mechanism had not anticipated the fact that Ethernet may one day used in the Metro environment as a networking technology; therefore scalability was not their main concern at that time. The main issue with IEEE 802.1Q is the small number of supported Virtual LAN Identifiers (VLAN Ids). Even if an agreement between the network provider and its customer regarding the VLAN Ids can be achieved in order to avoid VLAN Ids overlaps between different customers, the maximum number of customers is equal to the maximum number of VLANS, which is 4096.

IEEE 802.1ad (Q-in-Q)

Due to the 4096 VLAN Ids limitation, different vendors propose the duplication of the VLAN tags into the Ethernet frame. This addition partially solved the scalability issue and providers can easily deliver different Ethernet services (i.e., an E-Line service can be simply implemented by mapping the customers tagged Ethernet frames into a specific service provider VLAN). However, when it comes to more complex cases (i.e., E-LAN services), VLAN stacking reaches its limits. In that case, customer's and provider's Ethernet control frames, which are identified only by their destination MAC address and do not have a VLAN tag associated with them cannot be separated. A loop within a customer's LAN will be then disastrous since the Spanning Tree Protocol (STP) will be initiated to

resolve the loop leading to network reconfiguration of the network operator's network.

IEEE 802.1ah (MAC-in-MAC)

In tackle order with the limitation of the VLAN stacking mechanisms, IEEE has defined the MAC-in-MAC technology (IEEE 802.1ah). MAC-in-MAC is an alternative tunnelling technology, which extends the VLAN stacking concept by duplicating in the Ethernet frame not only the VLAN tag but also the source and destination MAC address including also additional fields (i.e., service provider label field). The service provider label field is a new field in the Ethernet frame, which allows the provider to tunnel the customer Ethernet frames throughout its network, based on the value of the service provider label and not on the provider VLAN tag. This approach allows the creation of a complex hierarchy, where customer frames could be encapsulated into the provider frames using the provider VLAN tags, which could be further encapsulated into the MAC-in-MAC frames using the service provider label. The main advantages of the MAC-in-MAC approach is subscriber/provider MAC addresses separation, subscriber control protocol transparency (i.e., STP, etc) and scalable Ethernet services up to 16 Million (2^{24}) using the service provider label. Figure 2 depicts a high-level overview of the Ethernet frame for the three different approaches.

Figure 2. A high-level overview of the Ethernet frame for the three different approaches

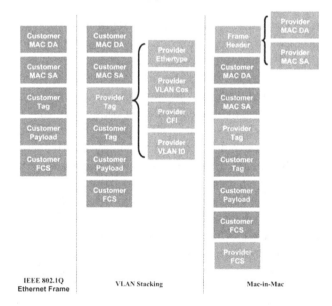

Table 1. Overview of the different Ethernet recovery mechanisms

Recovery Mechanisms	Advantages	Disadvantages
IEEE 802.3ad Link Aggregation	All links are active	Applicable only for point to point topologies between 2 nodes
STP	Supports any topology	Poor convergence time (from 4 sec up to 50 sec)
RSTP	Supports any topology.	Poor convergence time (from 2 sec up to 5 sec)
MSTP	Supports any topology. Not all the VLANs are affected in case of a network failure.	Poor convergence time (from 4 sec up to 50 sec)
IEEE 802.17 RPR	Provides 50msec protection	Not standardised implementation

Survivability

The term survivability is a general term, which refers to the mechanisms that can be used to recover a network from failures. Table 1 includes an overview of the different Ethernet recovery mechanisms.

Ethernet was originally designed for deployment in the LAN environment, which from a topological point of view is completely different than the MAN. LANs are built based on the bus topology or a combination of bus and star topologies. In order to eliminate loops in the network, the STP protocol was defined as a mean to avoid loop creation in the network. In case of a failure, the STP protocol was triggered in order to create a new tree topology of the network, therefore recovering, as a "side effect" the network from the failure. However, the recovery functionality was not the primary purpose of the STP protocol which had not been optimized in terms of convergence time. The rapid STP (RSTP) protocol was a more efficient protocol compared to the STP achieving convergence of the network in 2-5 seconds depending of course on the topology (the more complex the topology, the more time was required). An enhancement of the RSTP protocol was the MSTP (multiple VLAN instances STP) protocol that allows the definition of different trees topology, one for every VLAN. In case of a failure, MSTP reconfigures only the VLANs that are affected by the failure.

All those variances of the STP protocol suffer from the same native weakness. They were not designed having in mind the ring topologies, which are very common topologies in the MAN environment and therefore they cannot be used to provide carrier class survivability (50 msec). In order to cope with this requirement, vendors implement solutions optimized for ring topologies based mainly on the SDH/SONET framing. Those solutions achieve protection in 50 msec, however they are proprietary and inter-working between different vendors' Ethernet switches cannot be achieved. Moreover, minor issues like multiple rings interconnection or double failures in the rings are not always coped with success due to the immatureness of the different implementations. In order to merge all those solutions into a standardised one, IEEE defined the 802.17 RPR standard (IEEE 802.17, 2005) that provides a 50ms ring resiliency protocol for Ethernet transport *as* stated by Davik, Yilmaz, Gjessing, and Uzun (2004).

Finally, it should be mentioned that especially for point-to-point topologies and only between 2 nodes, the IEEE 802.3ad link aggregation protocol (IEEE P802.3ad, 2005) can be used as a recovery mechanism. IEEE 802.3ad allows grouping of multiple ports into the same Ethernet logical link. In case of a failure, traffic converge is less than 1 second.

Network Management

The term network management includes all the functions and actions that are required for the configuration of the network, the analysis and resolution of possible faults, as well as the monitoring of the provided services with respect to the agreed quality of service (QoS). Existing Ethernet Network Management Systems (NMSs) cover primarily the network element management layer of the telecommunication management network (TMN) architecture (ITU-T M.3100, 2005) and partly the network management layer. The provided functionality includes functions that allow the manual configuration of Ethernet services through graphical device managers, the alarm and performance monitoring of the network in term of network access points (ports) and links, and finally the authorization, authentication, and access control. In the next paragraphs, special attention is given to configuration, fault, and performance management, which are three out of the five FCAPS areas.

Configuration management includes the functionality of provisioning in an automatic way, end-to-end Ethernet services. Existing Ethernet NMSs are lacking such functionality and Ethernet vendors only provide tools and applications that allow the provisioning of Ethernet services by means of manual configuration of each node across the path. Moreover, due to the fact that Ethernet does not have advance call admission control functions, such functionality should be implemented in the NMS. The physical speed of the Ethernet ports combining with the rate limiting functionality, supported by the majority of the Ethernet vendors, are not adequate parameters when admission control decisions should be taken. Detailed knowledge of the utilization of all links as well as of the already provided services is required in order to accept or reject a new Ethernet service request with guarantee QoS.

With regard to *fault management*, Ethernet NMSs support real time alarm monitoring as well as graphical representation of faulty network managed entities. However, this alarm monitoring functionality does not directly permit the identification of the affected services and workarounds are needed for such association. For example, when a fiber cut occurs, the Ethernet NMS receives only a SNMP trap from the affected port. The association between the port and the affected services should be done manually by the operator.

Finally, Ethernet NMSs implement basic *performance management* functions like performance monitoring. However, the monitoring parameters (i.e., end-to-end delay, throughput, and availability) are not directly associated with the provided services. This non-service-oriented monitoring significantly increases the network operator operation expenses since additional third party applications and tools are needed in order to associate the native Ethernet network parameters (i.e., ports utilization) with the provided Ethernet services.

FUTURE TRENDS

Even if the current metro Ethernet solutions achieve end-to-end connectivity between separate LAN segments, utilizing the E-Line and E-LAN services, still network and service providers need to further consider some crucial revenue generating elements in Ethernet Metro networks. Such elements, to mention a few, are the ability to guarantee QoS for the various services (E-Line and E-LAN) and the exploitation of resiliency mechanisms that will give Ethernet robustness similar to existing carrier class technologies (i.e., SDH/SONET).

According to Cavendish (2004) and McFarland, Salam, and Checker (2005), OAM protocols are expected to be a key component in ensuring conformance to the agreed Service Level Agreements (SLAs) by implementing the necessary operations and maintenance functions in the Ethernet layer. These mechanisms will provide the ability to determine connectivity and measure traffic parameters like jitter, which are crucial to the service provisioning. Furthermore, they will implement the necessary functionality for alarm notification and performance measurements thus enhancing Ethernet with characteristics that are crucial for the operation in a Metro environment.

Finally, the adoption of the Ethernet technology in the metro is expected to rise considerably with the increased penetration of broadband technologies like FTTH (Fibber to the Home) and VDSL2 (Very High Speed Digital Subscriber Line) that use Ethernet framing for the data transport. The adoption of Ethernet in the access networks, besides metro networks, will elevate it from a LAN technology to a ubiquitous networking technology.

CONCLUSION

The motivation for deploying Ethernet in the MAN comes from the need to recreate the characteristics of a Layer 2 network across a service provider infrastructure.

This article discussed the different approaches that are available to achieve this by extending Ethernet beyond LANs. Using standard Ethernet interfaces, end-users acquire the ability to connect their sites utilizing the E-Line or the E-LAN services. With these services, Metro Ethernet installations can support a wide area of applications easier and more cost effectively than the existing network infrastructures. Despite the fact that there are still some open issues, it is expected that Metro Ethernet deployments will be increased in the next years.

REFERENCES

Allan, D., Bragg, N., McGuire, A., & Reid, A. (2006). Ethernet as carrier transport infrastructure. *IEEE Communications Magazine, 44*(2), 134-140.

Bottorf, P., Sajassi, A., & Suzuki, M. (2006). *IEEE 802.1ah—Provider Backbone Bridges 802.1ah, Draft 2.01 comment dispositions*. Retrieved January 2006, from http://www.ieee802.org/1/pages/802.1ah.html

Cavendish, D. (2004). Operation, administration, and maintenance of Ethernet services in wide area networks. *IEEE Communications Magazine, 42*(3), 72-79.

Chiruvolu, G., Ge, A., Elie-Dit-Cosaque, D., Ali, M., & Rouyer, J. (2004). Issues and approaches on extending Ethernet beyond LANs. *IEEE Communications Magazine, 42*(3), 80-86.

Davik, F., Yilmaz, M., Gjessing, S., & Uzun, N. (2004). IEEE 802.17 Resilient packet ring tutorial. *IEEE Communications Magazine, 42*(3), 112-118.

IEEE 802.17 Resilient Packet Ring Working Group. Retrieved July 2005, from http://www.ieee802.org/17/

IEEE 802.1ad—Provider Bridges (QinQ). Retrieved March 2005, from http://www.ieee802.org/1/pages/802.1ad.html

IEEE 802.3 CSMA/CD (ETHERNET) Working Group. Retrieved December 2004, from http://www.ieee802.org/3/

IEEE P802.3ad Link Aggregation Task Force Retrieved July 2005, from http://www.ieee802.org/3/ad/index.html

ITU-T Recommendation M.3100. (2005). *Generic network information model*. ITU-T standard Series M: Maintenance Telecommunications Management Network.

McFarland, M., Salam, S., & Checker, R. (2005). Ethernet OAM: Key enabler for carrier class metro Ethernet services. *IEEE Communications Magazine, 43*(11), 152-157.

Metro Ethernet Forum Technical Specification. *Metro Ethernet Network Architecture Framework - Part 1: Generic Framework*. Retrieved from January 2005, http://www.metroethernetforum.org/

Raptis, L., Manousakis, M., & Bau, D. (2006). Deployment of an advance metropolitan gigabit Ethernet network: Experience from the Attica Telecom case. *Journal of Optical Networking, 5*(2), 107-121.

Serrat, J., & Galis, A. (2003). *Deploying and managing IP over WDM networks* (pp. 7-30). Boston: Artech House.

Zier, L., Fischer, W., & Brockners, F. (2004). Ethernet-based public communication services: Challenge and opportunity. *IEEE Communications Magazine, 42*(3), 88-95.

KEY TERMS

LAN: The term local area network (LAN) is used mainly to describe a network of computers, servers, switches and other network devices that are located in a small geographical area like an office or a building. In some cases, the term is also used to describe the network of a campus.

MAC Address: The media access control (MAC) address is a unique address identifier allowing the identification of a network device attached to a network. The MAC address is assign to every device by its manufacturer and is a 48 bit hexadecimal number.

MAN: Metropolitan area network (MAN) is a network connecting different LANs and is usually located in a large geographical area, which can be a city.

SDH: Synchronous digital hierarchy, the European counterpart to SONET, is a networking technology based on time division multiplexing allowing the transmission of data in speeds of STM-1 (155 Mbps), STM-4 (622 Mbps), STM-16 (2.5 Gbps), or STM-64 (10 Gbps).

SLA: Service level agreement is the contract between the user and the service provider and describes technical parameters of the service. The most common parameter of a SLA is the latency, packet loss and network availability.

UNI: User network interface is the demarcation point between the user's network and the network provider's network.

VLAN: The virtual LAN is a logical segregation of a physical LAN into many different logical LANs. A computer connected to one Virtual LAN cannot communicate directly with a computer connected to a different virtual LAN, even if they are both connected to the same physical LAN.

WAN: Wide area network (WAN) is the network covering a large geographical area connecting different LANs and MANs.

E

Extend the Building Automation System through Internet

Kin Cheong Chu
Hong Kong Institute of Vocational Education (Tsing Yi), Hong Kong

INTRODUCTION

All buildings have some forms of mechanical and electrical services in order to provide the facilities necessary for maintaining a comfortable working environment. Building management systems (BMS) are used in buildings for automatic monitoring and control of services such as lighting, plumbing, fire services, security and access control, heating, ventilation, and air conditioning systems (Mustafa & Bansal, 2002a, 2002b). Basic BMS controls take the form of manual switching, time clocks, or temperature switches that provide the on and off signals for enabling pumps, fans, or valves etc. This traditional BMS is now migrating to building automation system (BAS). This trend can reduce the manpower, be easier for management, reduce the chance for making mistakes due to human errors, increase the operation efficiency of the building, and reduce the operation expenses (Tang, 2000).

The remote operation of BMS offers true duplex operation with identical duplicate screens on both controller and computer. It indicates that every event on the controller or action on the remote computer is immediately reproduced on the other screen. This unique feature is particularly useful for remote monitoring, operator training, and troubleshooting (Tang & O, 2000).

There are several different ways to connect to the remote controller, each being adapted to specific situations such as location and availability of communications equipment. Among these methods, Internet is one of the best choices for remote control as no telephone line is required, high data transfer rate is possible and technical support from dealer or manufacturer through Internet connection. This article is going to describe the current BMS and its extension through the Internet.

BUILDING MANAGEMENT SYSTEMS (BMS)

The term BMS refers to a system that uses sensors, controls, and activators (Mustafa & Bansal, 2002b). All of these use computers or processors to implement control algorithms and have the capability of communicating with other controls. Actually, BMS provides a building centralized monitoring and control, which facilitate to obtain information such as temperatures, pressure, and equipment status from a single location. Usually, BMS can be under automatic controlled and also known as building automated system (BAS).

Reducing energy consumption cost effectively is easy when controlled by BMS (Wimalaratne, 2005). Special climate control of the Grace Hotel in Sydney included the installation of a fully integrated direct digital control BMS to control air conditioning and lighting. The hotel also installed variable speed drives for air handling units and exhaust fans, and fine tuned the chiller set points on the BMS to program the chillers to cycle on and off as per set chilled water return temperature.

Digital control can also be integrated with BMS to provide operators and engineers with information to identify maintenance and operational issues within the mechanical systems, through comprehensive alarming and reporting capabilities (Mairah, 2004).

BMS does not limit to a building in a city; the building management system (BMS) installed at Munich airport can serve 160 buildings and provides comfort and safety for the 12,000 employees and 15 million passengers who use the airport each year (Ancevic, 1997). The system has the capacity to serve power plants, runway lights, and terminal's people-moving equipment. It has the advantage of taking all energy saving opportunities with power management, lighting control, and comfort optimisation.

Actually, BMS has a trend to interconnect different networked accessed equipment within a control panel through Ethernet (Stasiek & Thomas, 2006), wireless link (Hartman, 2001), or Internet (Ehrlich, 2006). The concept of intelligent building is to develop building automation and management systems (BAS/BMS) for building management staff who can gain access to any building system via the BAS/BMS to accomplish the goals of monitoring, real-time control, and condition-based maintenance inside the shift duty room (Mc-Gowan, 2006; So & Leung, 2004). Such information has been confined within the building or at a specified remote control station. With the help of the Internet, all critical data of a BAS/BMS can be made available to any authorized user around the world, who can then monitor and control the building systems even thousands of miles away (Sharpe, 2001).

Modern BMS allows a building manager to better handle his resources, improving operational efficiency and reducing costs in the control room. These BMS systems cost less, are faster and more reliable, offer more features, have a more user-friendly interface, and are easier to learn and use. They have been installed successfully in facilities of all sizes and types, making them practically an essential requirement to the successful management of operating costs. With today's data communication technology and sophisticated computer software, an intelligent building can be managed and monitored centrally through a computerized building management system. With the concept of combining intelligent building and green living, it will be a catalyst for major changes in the housing industry (Thompson, 2001). The "integer" is an action research network based in the UK, which promotes innovation in building using intelligent and green technologies. It will:

- Minimize the use of energy, water, and the waste.
- Address issues of air quality, noise, etc.
- Be better communications, control, and metering.
- Safer, faster, and better quality of life.

CURRENT BUILDING AUTOMATION SYSTEM (BAS)

Figure 1 shows a building automation system currently installed in a modern commercial building in the Hong Kong. The purpose of this building automation system is to monitor and control other building E&M, security, and communication subsystem. Each subsystem has its own system server, control console, and client console. The subsystem's server, client console, control console, peripheral are connected via a network switch, which provide a platform to exchange data among them. Data

Figure 1. Building automation system infrastructure

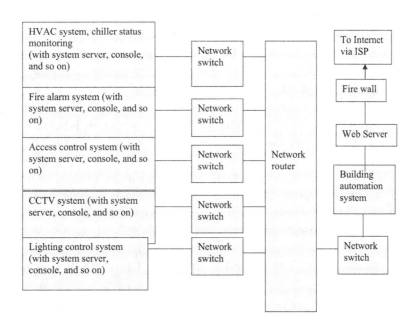

Figure 2. Block diagram of building automation system

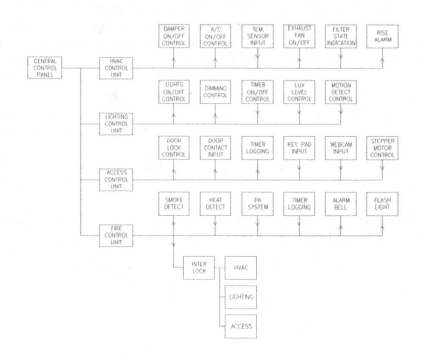

between subsystems are exchanged via the network router, where network router provides the function of filtering and security control. Router can use the "access control list" to allow the approved type of data only to transmit from one system to another and avoid data transmission congestion and security control.

Building automation system will be receiving data from sub-system via the network router. It provides an integrated monitor and control of all system (except fire alarm system). The building automation system will connect to the ISP via Web server and firewall to facilitate this function.

National Instruments LabVIEW software (Bishop, 2004) is used to develop the building automation system as it is easily controlled hardware found in the equipment room of a building and can access the Internet without any problem.

The Internet allows building automation system to become integrated with enterprise functions, eliminating geographic restrictions, easing access to all data from any site, and making it easier to use and support building systems operation. It should be the future trend of remote control and monitoring for a building automation system.

Figure 2 shows the main block diagram of this BAS, which consists of four units (HVAC control, lighting control, access control, and fire alarm) and are interconnected together.

HVAC Control Unit

Figure 3 shows one of the control panels of HVAC. When fire occurs, the "override from fire" function will automatically interrupt this control program and turn on the exhaust fan, open the damper, and turn off the A/C. When the room temperature is over the preset temperature (e.g., 22°C), it will turn on the exhaust fan and open the damper to cool down the room temperature. If room temperature is below the preset temperature, it will turn off all equipment function, but excludes the "override from fire" function. When damper is open and exhaust fan is turned on but the room temperature still remains over predefined temperature (e.g., 28°C), it will control the A/C turn on and turn off the damper and exhaust fan. In case the room temperature is rising continually over the maximum defined temperature (e.g., 38°C), it will turn on the alarm. All the panel signal conditions and status can be monitored through the Internet and displayed in the remote site.

Figure 3. HVAC control panel

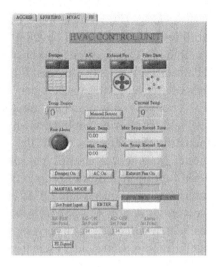

Figure 4. Lighting control panel

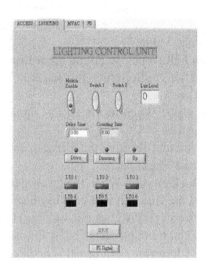

Lighting Control Unit

Figure 4 shows one of the lighting control panels for the equipment room. There is a motion detector inside the equipment room of the building to check any motion (people) inside this room. If no motion is detected within a fixed time, it will turn off the lightings. The photocell inside this equipment room is implemented to detect the brightness level inside the equipment room and then control the brightness of a group of lighting. When the brightness in this room is high, the software will dim the corresponding group of lighting to lower level or even turn them off. When any fire occurs, the "override from fire" function will interrupt the control program and directly turn on all lighting. Again, all the panel signal conditions and status can be monitored through the Internet and displayed in the remote site.

Access Control Unit

Figure 5 shows one of the access control panels. A camera is used to monitor the people going into and out of an entrance. The camera is equipped with stepper motor for easily monitoring wider area. Other functions of this panel are listed as follows:

- **Password check:** Distinguish the key code entered is correct and open the door of an entrance
- **Manual open:** Manually remote control to open the door of an entrance

Figure 5. Access control panel

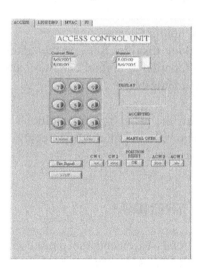

- **Override from fire:** When fire occurs, the "override from fire" function will interrupt the program and open the door of an entrance.

Again, all the panel signal conditions and status can be monitored through Internet and displayed in the remote site.

Fire Control Unit

The last unit is fire control and its major functions are listed as follows:

- **Smoke & heat detector:** Detection of smoke and heat condition in this room to check either the smoke or temperature exceeded a predetermined maximum value
- **Alarm bell:** When receiving the warning signal from other control units, the alarm bell will be turned on.
- **Flash light:** When receiving the signal, a light will flash on.
- **Reset switch:** Resume the alarm or fault signal to normal condition.
- **Inter lock enable:** When the fire occurs and receiving the signal, it will transfer the signal to 3 sub-systems (HVAC, access, lighting) to operate the special functions as listed as follows:
- **HVAC:** Interrupt the normal schedule, turn off the A/C, turn on the exhaust fan, and open the damper in any condition.
- **Access:** Interrupt the normal schedule and open the door lock in any condition.
- **Lighting:** Interrupt the normal schedule and turn on the lighting in any condition.
- **Inter lock disable:** Resume the "inter lock enable" function to normal condition and turn off alarm and flashlight.

Again, all the panel signal conditions and status can be monitored through the Internet and displayed in the remote site.

FUTURE TRENDS

There are trends to extend the remote control and monitoring BAS based on existing network:

- **Wireless link:** There is great potential in wireless technology such as Bluetooth. Field service technicians will be able to take advantage of this technology through handheld computers wirelessly connected to the Internet. Moreover, a wireless approach has the advantages of allowing the comfort system to follow occupants through the building and to automatically adjust occupancy, ventilation, lighting, and thermal levels to meet personal preferences wherever the occupant travels through the building.
- **PDA remote control from LabVIEW:** The LabVIEW PDA module is an add-on module

for LabVIEW that programmers can easily build applications that run on personal digital assistant (PDA) devices. The PDA module extends the capabilities of LabVIEW to develop and build executable PDA applications on a host computer for a Palm OS or Pocket PC devices. Together with wireless LAN technology, users can freely use the PDA device to download and run the remote control and monitoring application anywhere.

- **Defocusing the servers:** Since the BAS can integrate equipment from different manufacturers used for different purposes on to the intranet or Internet, there is a possibility of defocusing the servers. It is now possible to provide small boxes, which will act as Web servers, which can gather the required data and present it direct to the Web. If all the data can be presented in this way, it removes the need for large numbers of PC's to act as Web servers. The servers are devices, which can sit within data network distribution units away from expensive office space.

CONCLUSION

Nowadays buildings are equipped with a number of independent systems, including energy management, fire safety, security, lighting, and maintenance management. There is often a need to share information between the systems. Sharing information through systems integration will reduce installation and operating cost, improve building efficiency, and the productivity of facility staff will increase.

The Internet solves the information sharing problem by allowing BAS/BMS to become integrated with enterprise functions, eliminating geographic restrictions, easing access to all data from any site and making it easier to use and support building systems operation.

Integrated and interoperable systems are the wave of the future. One of the most significant recent developments in the BAS/BMS field is the implementation of interoperability standards. Two standards to govern how systems communicate between devices are in place: ASHRAE's BACnet, and LonMark's LonWorks. Managers who buy a system that conforms to one of the standards are no longer locked into one manufacturer for components and devices. There is huge competition and development between manufacturers in this area and finally maintains the price of equipment in reasonable standard.

REFERENCES

Ancevic, M. (1997). Intelligent building system for airport. *ASHRAE Journal*, *39*(11), 31-35.

Bishop, B. H. (2004). *Learning with LabVIEW 7 Express*. Upper Saddle River, NJ: Prentice Hall.

Ehrlich, P. (2006, January). *The time is now for intelligent buildings*. AutomateBuildings.com. Retrieved January 29, 2006, from www.automatedbuildings.com

Hartman, T. (2001, March). *Occupant connectivity for building controls*. AutomateBuildings.com. Retrieved January 29, 2006, from www.automatedbuildings.com

Mairah, J. P. (2004, July). Commissioning controls for energy efficiency. *EcoLibrium* (*July 2004*), 20-24.

McGowan, J. (2006). *Blazing a new trail to intelligent buildings?* AutomateBuildings.com, Jan issue. Retrieved January 30, 2006, from www.automatedbuildings.com

Mustafa, H., & Bansal, P. K. (2002a). Intelligent buildings: Necessity or an option? *IRHACE Journal*, *14*(3), 22-24.

Mustafa, H., & Bansal, P. K. (2002b). Building management systems: Beyond electronics. *AIRAH Journal*, *1*(4), 22-27.

Sharpe, L. (2001, July). Setting a standard for building control. *IEE Review 47*(4), 35-39.

So, T. P. A., & Leung, A. Y. T. (2004). Survey on attitudes towards buildings in three Chinese cities: Hong Kong, Shanghai, and Taipei. *Facilities*, *22*(3/4), 100-108.

Stasiek, J., & Thomas, G. (2006, February). *Building automation system Ethernet switch selection*. AutomateBuildings.com. Retrieved February 2, 2006, from www.automatedbuildings.com

Tang, P. (2000). *A simple and pragmatic solution for the automation of building services*. Paper presented at CUS-EPSA 16th Conference, Hong Kong.

Tang, P., & O, B. (2000). *A building services automation prototype using LonWorks technology*. Paper presented at Advances in Building Services Joint Annual Symposium of HKIE- BSD, Hong Kong.

Thompson, N. C. (2001). Climbing up a magic mountain—The story of Integer. *Hong Kong Engineer*, *29*(11), 13-19.

Wimalaratne, J. (2005). A greener stay in Sydney. *EcoLibrium* (*Feb. 2005*), 16-18.

KEY TERMS

BACnet: It is one of the most high level protocols used in the BMS industry that can be used to integrate building automation and control products from different manufacturers into a single cohesive system.

Building Automated System (BAS): Usually, BMS can be under automatic controlled and also known as building automated system (BAS).

Building Management Systems (BMS): BMS are used in buildings for automatic monitoring and control of services such as lighting, plumbing, fire services, security and access control, heating, ventilation, and air conditioning systems. The term refers to a system that uses sensors, controls, and activators. All these use an electronic digital processor to implement control algorithms and have the capability of communicating with other controls. The BMS term covers all control elements, including hardware, controllers, any linking network and central controllers.

Intelligent Building: The concept of intelligent building is to develop building automation and management systems (BAS/BMS) for building management staff who can gain access to any building system via the BAS/BMS to accomplish the goals of monitoring, real-time control, and condition-based maintenance inside the shift duty room.

HVAC: Short form of heating, ventilation, and air conditioning.

LabVIEW: LabVIEW is the graphical development environment for creating flexible and scalable test, measurement, and control applications. With LabVIEW, users can interface with real-world signals, analyze data for meaningful information, and share results and applications.

LonWorks: Another high level protocols used in the BMS industry that can be used to integrate building automation and control products from different manufacturers into a single cohesive system.

Hackers, Hacking, and Eavesdropping

Kevin Curran
University of Ulster, Ireland

Peter Breslin
University of Ulster, Ireland

Kevin McLaughlin
University of Ulster, Ireland

Gary Tracey
University of Ulster, Ireland

INTRODUCTION

Eric Raymond, compiler of *The New Hacker's Dictionary* (Raymond, 1996) defines a hacker as a clever programmer. According to Raymond, a "*good hack*" is a clever solution to a programming problem and *hacking* is the act of doing it. Hacker is a slang term for a computer enthusiast. Among professional programmers, the term hacker implies an amateur or a programmer who lacks formal training. Depending on how it is used, it can be either complimentary or derogatory, although it is developing an increasingly derogatory connotation in recent years. Raymond lists five possible characteristics that qualify one as a hacker:

1. A person who enjoys learning details of a programming language or system
2. A person who enjoys actually doing the programming rather than just theorizing about it
3. A person capable of appreciating someone else's hacking
4. A person who picks up programming quickly
5. A person who is an expert at a particular programming language or system, as in "Unix hacker"

Raymond, like many hackers condemns someone who attempts to crack someone else's system or otherwise uses programming or expert knowledge to act maliciously. This type of person, according to most hackers, would better be described as a *cracker*. A cracker is someone who illegally breaks into someone else's computer or network by bypassing passwords and licences and so forth. A cracker could be doing this for purposes of maliciously making a profit. On the other hand, a hacker (according to a hacker) would break into a system to supposedly point out sites security problems. Therefore, we must carefully distinguish between a hacker and a cracker (Wright, 2003).

"Access" is defined in Section 2(1)(a) of the Information Technology Act[1] as "gaining entry into, instructing, or communicating with the logical, arithmetical, or memory function resources of a computer, computer system, or computer network." Unauthorised access would therefore mean any kind of access without the permission of either the rightful owner or the person in charge of a computer, computer system, or computer network. Thus not only would accessing a server by cracking its password authentication system be unauthorised access, switching on a computer system without the permission of the person in charge of such a computer system would also be unauthorised access.

BACKGROUND

Although hacking according to many hackers themselves is beneficial to the development of systems security, it is still known as a crime under the computer misuse act. Categories of misuse under this act include:

*   Computer fraud
*   Unauthorized access to information
*   Computer hacking
*   Eavesdropping
*   Unauthorized use for personal benefit

- Unauthorized alteration or destruction of data
- Preventing access to system by original authorized user
- Unauthorized removal of data (Harris, Harper, Eagle, Ness, & Lester, 2005)

Crackers use various methods to maliciously attack a computer systems security, one such method is a "virus." A virus a software program capable of reproducing itself and usually capable of causing great harm to files or other programs on the same computer. A *computer virus* attaches itself to a program or file so it can spread from one computer to another, leaving infections as it travels. The severity and effects of a computer virus can range much the same as a human virus. Some viruses have only mild affects simply to annoy the host, more severe viruses can cause serious damages to both hardware and software. Almost all viruses are attached to an executable file, which means the virus may exist on your computer but it cannot infect your computer unless you run or open the malicious program. A virus needs the host program to be executed. It does not have to be executed by a human. For example, a virus in a MIME attachment to an innocuous looking e-mail might be automatically executed by an e-mail client, without any human action. People continue the spread of a computer virus, mostly unknowingly, by sharing infecting files or sending e-mails with viruses as attachments in the e-mail.

Another method is to use a worm, which is similar to a virus in both design and in the damage it can cause. Worms spread from system to system similar to a virus. Worms have the capability of replicating themselves on many other systems, so rather than your computer sending out a single worm, it could send out hundreds or thousands of copies of itself, creating a huge devastating effect. It does this by delivering its payload. For example, it is common for a worm to be sent through e-mail; if you receive a worm via e-mail, it is possible for the worm to use the information in your e-mail address book to send duplicates of itself to your contacts and their contacts etc. Due to the copying nature of a worm and its ability to travel across networks, the end result in most cases is that the worm consumes too much system memory (or network bandwidth) causing Web servers, network servers, and individual computers to stop responding.

In more recent worm attacks such as the much talked about Ms.Blaster Worm., the worm has been designed to tunnel into a system and allow malicious users to control a computer remotely. Another example was the Santy.a worm, which targeted vulnerability in some versions of the phpBB bulletin board system application to damage content on Web sites. This was done by simply creating an automated search in a Google query string. Google was able to stop the worm quickly once they figured out what was going on by blocking any searches used for malicious purposes. The most common Google hacks involve queries that call up user names and passwords on unsecured servers. Log files for these particular users were put in jeopardy by not placing security measures and access privileges on important documentation (Gilmer, 2006).

EAVESDROPPING

Eavesdropping can be thought of as another form of hacking. In a lot of cases, it involves unlawfully accessing a computer system in order to listen to (gather) information. It is achieved by intercepting packets on the network (i.e., snooping). This is invasion of privacy. Eavesdropping can be used by a hacker to gain information on the victim such as passwords and bank account details, although not all forms of eavesdropping is used for malicious purposes .Some governments look to use computer eavesdropping as a way of surveillance. They use this to catch paedophiles and other people who could be holding illegal information on their computers. Some employers have invested in surveillance software (eavesdropping software) that allows them to monitor or eavesdrop on everything their employee's type on their computers, be it e-mail, Web site surfing, or even word processing. Therefore, not all forms of eavesdropping may be illegal.

This kind of surveillance (eavesdropping) software is very similar to so-called Trojan software already used illegally by some hackers and corporate spies. Trojan software is a very common hacking and eavesdropping tool used by a lot of hackers. Trojan horse software would allow the hacker to enter your system and even take control of it in some cases although this is more commonly known as a backdoor. The Trojan horse at first glance will appear to be useful software but will actually do damage once installed or run on your computer. Those who are at the receiving end of the Trojan will have to activate (by opening it) it for the Trojan horse to do it's work. They are normally tricked into doing so because they appear to be receiving legitimate software or files from a legitimate source. The affects of the Trojan can vary much like a virus; sometimes the affects can be more annoying than malicious (like changing your desktop, adding silly active desktop icons) and sometimes they affects can be severe as Trojans can cause serious damage by deleting files and destroying information on your system (Harris et al., 2005).

Key Loggers

Another method of computer systems eavesdropping is to use what is know as a key logger. A key logger is a program that runs in the background recording all the keystrokes. Once keystrokes are logged, they are hidden in the machine for later retrieval or sent automatically back to the attacker. The attacker can use the information gained by the key logger to find passwords and information like bank account details. It is important to remember that a key logger is not just used as a hacking tool. Many home users and parents use key logger such as Invisible Key logger to record computer and Internet activities. These key loggers are helpful in collecting information that will be useful when determining if your child is talking to the wrong person online or if your child is surfing inappropriate Web site content and it again can be used by businesses to monitor employees' work ethics. Normally there may be many files to key loggers and this means that it can be difficult to manually remove them; it is best to use anti-virus software or try to use methods such as firewalls to prevent them from getting onto the system in the first place.

On Thursday March 17th 2005, it was revealed that one of the largest bank robberies in Britain was foiled by police in London. The target was the London branch of the Japanese bank "Sumitomo Mitsui." The bank robbers planned to steal an estimated £220 million pounds. The stolen money was to be wired electronically from the bank into 10 different offshore bank accounts. This planned robbery was unlike any traditional bank robbery in Britain's history. It didn't involve running into the bank with handguns, taking hostages, and leaving in a getaway car. This bank robbery was much more high-tech[2]. The bank robbers uploaded a program onto the bank's network that recorded every keystroke made on a keyboard. This type of program is known as "keylogging software." The program recorded the Web sites

that were visited on the network, the passwords, bank account numbers, and PIN numbers that were entered on these Web sites and saved them to a file. This file was accessed by the robbers and when they visited the same sites as the people in the bank, they could use their login information to logon. The site wouldn't have any reason to think that the person logging on wasn't authorised to do so. Keylogging software can record all sorts of computer operations not just keystrokes. It can also record e-mails received and sent, chats, and instant messages, Web sites, programs accessed, peer-to-peer file sharing, and it also takes screen snapshots (Vines, 2002). Keylogging can occur in two ways. A specially coded program can be uploaded onto a network from anywhere in the world. The other is a piece of hardware that is about the size of a battery. This piece of hardware is plugged into the computer from the keyboard and records the keystrokes made. This has to be physically installed onto the machine by a person and in order to retrieve the information gathered by the mini-hard drive the person also has to physically remove the hardware.[3] The keylogging software was uploaded to the network more than 6 months prior to the planned robbery. It was first noticed that the keylogging software was on the network in October 2004. It was then that the National Hi-Tech Crime Unit (NHTCU) kept a close eye on the situation. This was the biggest and most high profile coup in the unit's short history.

Spyware

The most common form of computer systems eavesdropping is the adware and spyware software. Spyware can be defined as software that covertly gathers user information through the user's Internet connection without his or her knowledge, usually for advertising purposes. Spyware applications send the user's browsing habits to an ad-serving company, which then targets adverts at the user based on their interests. Kazaa and eXeem are popular file-sharing programs that deliver target ads to their users. Spyware applications are typically bundled as a hidden component of freeware or shareware programs that can be downloaded from the Internet; however, it should be noted that the majority of shareware and freeware applications do not come with spyware. Once installed, the spyware monitors user activity on the Internet and transmits that information in the background to someone else. Spyware can also gather information about e-mail addresses and even passwords and credit card numbers (Briere, 2005). Spyware software is quite similar to a Trojan horse in that the user will unknowingly install the software themselves. The software can also cause a decrease in bandwidth as it runs in the systems background sending and receiving information from the software's home base. The most common way in which spyware software is installed to a machine is when the user has downloaded certain free-ware peer-to-peer file swapping software such as "WarezP2p" or "Kazaa." Spyware software can be used by companies for advertising purposes as well as being used by hackers to gain incriminating information.

Adware is extremely similar to spyware. It affects your computer in much the same way, the main difference being that adware is used more for advertising purposes. Adware is software integrated into or bundled with a program and generally is seen by the programmer as a way to recover programming development costs, and in some cases it may allow the program to be provided to the user free of charge or at a reduced price. The advertising income may allow or motivate the programmer to continue to write, maintain and upgrade the software product. Adware can cause a lot of pop ups to appear once you have connected to the internet, also it can allow icons to be added to your desktop and add Web sites to your internet favourites. A number of software applications are available to help users search for and modify adware programs to block the presentation of advertisements and to remove spyware modules

System Backdoors

System backdoors are used to gain access usually acting in an illegal manner. Access is achieved by researching the best way to secure a site by reading through different security manuals to establish the recommendations they offer, and why these are necessary. When the hacker gains access to a system, they often attempt to gain administrative privileges, which would make the attack worthwhile. This also gives them the freedom, which a basic user will not experience, for example, when it comes to privileges the system administrator is at the top of the hierarchy, so access to such capabilities give the attacker major advantages such as access to all types of files, whereas the basic user with set basic privileges can only access the files associated with the work that the particular employee carries out

(McClure, Scrambray, & Kurtz, 2003). The attacker is also capable of editing the computer logs of the system in order to cover up their tracks and these capabilities could be used to set up bogus user accounts allowing the attacker to gain easy access to the system upon re-entry. An important aspect of hacking into a system is the ability to cover up any trace of the intrusion. This is possible via a variety of methods, the most important of course being, that the cracker approaches the attack cautiously (Dr-K, 2000).

Password Cracking

To crack a password means to decrypt a password, or to bypass a protection scheme. When the UNIX operating system was first developed, passwords were stored in the file "/etc/passwd." This file was readable by everyone, but the passwords were encrypted so that a user could not figure out what a person's password was. The passwords were encrypted in such a manner that a person could test a password to see if it was valid, but couldn't decrypt the entry. However, a program called "crack" was developed that would simply test all the words in the dictionary against the passwords in "/etc/passwd." This would find all user accounts whose passwords where chosen from the dictionary. Typical dictionaries also included people's names since a common practice is to choose a spouse or child's name. Password crackers are utilities that try to "guess" passwords. One way, also known as a dictionary attack, involves trying out all the words contained in a predefined dictionary of words. Ready-made dictionaries of millions of commonly used passwords can be freely downloaded from the Internet. Another form of password cracking attack is "brute force" attack. In this form of attack, all possible combinations of letters, numbers, and symbols are tried out one by one until the password is found out. Brute force attacks take much longer than dictionary attacks (Nakhjiri, 2005). There are also many other ways of obtaining passwords illicitly such as social engineering, wiretapping, keystroke logging, login spoofing, identity management system attacks, and compromising host security. However, cracking usually designates a guessing attack (Cole, 2003).

Wireless Hacking

Wireless networks, broadcast signals throughout an area, which allow hackers easy connection to their network by simply being physically within their range. A hacker will initially locate the wireless device using either the passive method of listening for access points and broadcast beacons or the aggressive method of transmitting client beacons in search of a response. Wired-based network hacking requires the hacker to have an in depth knowledge so that they can apply the most appropriate tools, know what to look for, and how to cover their tracks. In contrast to other systems, however, wireless networks are easily located and poorly protected (Gavrilenko, 2004). One method of security, which is applied widely, is WEP (wired equivalent protocol). By using a key it encrypts the data shared by all users of the network, however, with the correct software WEP can be easily bypassed (Hardjono & Lakshminath, 2005). Another method involves MAC address filtering, which allows only specific wireless network adaptors to connect to the networks. This is facilitated by using a unique identifier; however, this method is both time consuming and requires greater networking knowledge. To overcome this type of obstacle, hackers have been known to monitor the traffic of packets within the network to capture an approved MAC address. This is then imitated to gain access (Imai, 2005). Wireless routers commonly come with firewalls to control access to the computer from outside. However, anyone with the ability to access the wireless portion of the network will be able to bypass the firewall.

FUTURE TRENDS

We can also expect to see more use of advanced hiding techniques in steganography tools. The word steganography means "covered or hidden writing." The object of steganography is to send a message through some innocuous carrier (to a receiver while preventing anyone else from knowing that a message is being sent at all). Computer-based stenography allows changes to be made to what are known as digital carriers such as images or sounds. The changes represent the hidden message but result if successful in no discernible change to the carrier (Bailey, Curran, & Condell, 2004). Unfortunately, it can be used by terrorists to communicate with one another without anyone else's knowledge. Other trends include mobile malware being successfully monetized, the anonymous and illegal hosting of

(copyrighted) data, rise in encryption, and packers and hijacking botnets and infected PCs (Danchev, 2006).

CONCLUSION

Unauthorized access can be described as an action in which a person accesses a computer system without the consent of the owner, this may include using sophisticated hacking/cracking software tools to gain illegal access to a system, or it could simply be a case of a person guessing a password and gaining access. There are a lot of methods to be taken in an attempt to prevent unauthorized computer access, such as regularly changing your password, ensuring anti-virus software is up to date and ensuring that an up-to-date firewall exists on each system.

REFERENCES

Bailey, K., Curran, K., & Condell, J. (2004, September). An evaluation of pixel-based steganography and stegodetection methods. *The Imaging Science Journal, 52*(3), 131-150.

Briere, D. (2005, October). *Wireless network hacks and mods for dummies* (For Dummies S.), Hungry Minds Inc, U.S.

Cole, E. (2003). *Hacking—What the future holds. Computer and Hacker Exploits*. Philadelphia: SANS Publishers.

Danchev, D. (2006). Malware—future trends, Mind streams of information security knowledge Blog, January 9th 2006

Dr-K. (2000). *Complete hacker's handbook*. London: Carlton Book Limited.

Gavrilenko, K. (2004). *WI-FOO: The secrets of wireless hacking*. London: Addison Wesley, June 2004.

Gilmer, C. (2006). *Worms prey on Google for victims*. The unofficial Google weblog, February 15, 2006.

Hardjono, T., & Lakshminath R. D. (2005, July). *Security in wireless LANs and MANs*. Artech House Books.

H

Harris, S., Harper, A., Eagle, C., Ness, J., & Lester, M. (2005, January). *Gray hat hacking: the ethical hacker's handbook*. McGraw-Hill Publishing Co.

Imai, H. (2005, December). *Wireless communications security*. Boston: Artech House Books, December 2005.

McClure, S., Scrambray, J., & Kurtz, G. (2003). *Hacking exposed Network security secrets & solutions* (4th ed.). London: McGraw-Hill/Osborne.

Nakhjiri, M. (2005). *AAA and network security for mobile access: Radius, diameter, EAP, PKI, and IP mobility*. New York: John Wiley and Sons, September 2005.

Raymond, E. (1996). *The new hacker's dictionary* (3rd ed.). Boston: MIT Press, October 1996.

Vines, R. D. (2002). *Wireless security essentials, defending mobile systems from data piracy*. Indianapolis: Wiley Publishing.

Wright, J. (2003). *Detecting wireless LAN MAC address spoofing*. Retrieved from http://home.jwu.edu/jwright/papers/wlan-mac-spoof.pdf

KEY TERMS

Back Door: In the security of a system, this is a hole deliberately left in place by designers or maintainers. May be intended for use by service technicians. However, it is more commonly used now a days to refer to software, which has been maliciously loaded by persons remotely in order to allow them to enter the system through a 'back door' at an opportune time.

Cracker: This was coined by hackers in defence against journalistic misuse of the term "hacker." The term "cracker" reflects a strong revulsion at the theft and vandalism perpetrated by cracking rings.

Eavesdropping: Eavesdropping is the intercepting of conversations by unintended recipients. One who participates in eavesdropping is called an eavesdropper.

Hacking: Hacking is commonly used today to refer to unauthorized access to a computer network. Breaking into a computer system or network is simply one of many forms of hacking.

Rootkit: The primary purposes of a rootkit are to allow an attacker to maintain undetected access to a compromised system. The main technique used is to replace standard versions of system software with hacked version, and install backdoor process by replacing one or more of the files, such as ls, ps, netstat, and who.

Trojan: A Trojan (aka Trojan horse) is a software program in which harmful or malicious code is contained within another program. When this program executes, the Trojan performs a specific set of actions, usually working toward the goal of allowing itself to persist on the target system.

Virus: A virus is a piece of software which is capable of reproducing itself and causing great harm to files or other programs on the same computer. A true virus cannot spread to another computer without human assistance.

Worm: A worm is a software program capable of reproducing itself that can spread from one computer to the next over a network. Worms take advantage of automatic file sending and receiving features found on many computers.

ENDNOTES

[1] http://www.stpi.soft.net/itbill2000_1.html

[2] http://news.bbc.co.uk/2/hi/technology/4357307.stm

[3] http://searchsecurity.techtarget.com/sDefinition/0,,sid14_gci962518,00.html

Handheld Computing and Palm OS Programming for Mobile Commerce

Wen-Chen Hu
University of North Dakota, USA

Lixin Fu
The University of North Carolina at Greensboro, USA

Hung-Jen Yang
National Kaohsiung Normal University, Taiwan

Sheng-Chien Lee
University of Florida, USA

INTRODUCTION

It is widely acknowledged that mobile commerce is a field of enormous potential. However, it is also commonly admitted that the development in this field is constrained. There are still considerable barriers waiting to be overcome. One of the barriers is most software engineers are not familiar with handheld programming, which is the programming for handheld devices such as smart cellular phones and PDAs (personal digital assistants). This article gives a study of handheld computing to help software engineers better understand this subject. It includes three major topics:

- **Mobile commerce systems:** The system structure includes six components: (1) mobile commerce applications, (2) mobile handheld devices, (3) mobile middleware, (4) wireless networks, (5) wired networks, and (6) host computers.
- **Handheld computing:** It includes two kinds of computing: client- and server-side handheld computing.
- **Palm OS programming:** The Palm OS Developer Suite is used to develop applications for palm devices by handheld programmers.

This article focuses on Palm OS programming by giving a step-by-step procedure of a palm application development. Other client-side handheld computing is also discussed.

BACKGROUND

With the introduction of the World Wide Web, electronic commerce has revolutionized traditional commerce and boosted sales and exchanges of merchandise and information. Recently, the emergence of wireless and mobile networks has made possible the extension of electronic commerce to a new application and research area: *mobile commerce*, which is defined as the exchange or buying and selling of commodities, services, or information on the Internet through the use of mobile handheld devices. In just a few years, mobile commerce has emerged from nowhere to become the hottest new trend in business transactions. To explain how the mobile commerce components work together, Figure 1 shows a flowchart of how a user request is processed by the components in a mobile commerce system, along with brief descriptions of how each component processes the request (Hu, Lee, & Yeh, 2004).

1. **Mobile commerce applications:** Electronic commerce applications are numerous, including auctions, banking, marketplaces and exchanges, news, recruiting, and retailing to name but a few. Mobile commerce applications not only cover the electronic commerce applications, but also include new applications, which can be performed at any time and from anywhere by using mobile computing technology, for example, mobile inventory tracking.

Figure 1. A flowchart of a user request processed in a mobile commerce system

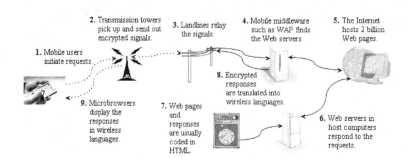

2. **Mobile handheld devices:** An Internet-enabled mobile handheld device is a small general-purpose, programmable, battery-powered computer that is capable of handling the front end of mobile commerce applications and can be operated comfortably while being held in one hand. It is the device with which mobile users interact directly with mobile commerce applications (Hu, Yeh, Chu, Chu, Lee, & Lee, 2005).

3. **Mobile middleware:** The term middleware refers to the software layer between the operating system and the distributed applications that interact via the networks. The primary mission of a middleware layer is to hide the underlying networked environment's complexity by insulating applications from explicit protocols that handle disjoint memories, data replication, network faults, and parallelism (Geihs, 2001). The major task of mobile middleware is to seamlessly and transparently map Internet contents to mobile stations that support a wide variety of operating systems, markup languages, microbrowsers, and protocols. WAP (Open Mobile Alliance Ltd., n.d.) and i-mode (NTT DoCoMo Inc., 2006) are the two major kinds of mobile middleware.

4. **Wireless and wired networks:** Wireless communication capability supports mobility for end users in mobile commerce systems. Wireless LAN, MAN, and WAN are the major components used to provide radio communication channels so that mobile service is possible. In the WLAN category, the Wi-Fi standard with 11 Mbps throughput dominates the current market. However, it is expected that standards with much higher transmission speeds, such as IEEE 802.11a and 802.11g,

will replace Wi-Fi in the near future. Compared to WLANs, cellular systems can provide longer transmission distances and greater radio coverage, but suffer from the drawback of much lower bandwidth (less than 1 Mbps). In the latest trend for cellular systems, 3G standards supporting wireless multimedia and high-bandwidth services are beginning to be deployed.

5. **Host computers:** A user request such as database access or updating is actually processed at a host computer, which contains three major kinds of software: (1) Web servers, (2) database servers, and (3) application programs and support software.

MAIN FOCUS OF THE CHAPTER

Handheld computing is a fairly new computing area and a formal definition of it is not found yet. Nevertheless, the authors define it as follows:

Handheld computing is to use handheld devices such as smart cellular phones and PDAs (personal digital assistants) to perform wireless, mobile, handheld operations such as personal data management and making phone calls.

Again, handheld computing includes two kinds of computing: client- and server- side handheld computing, which are defined as follows:

- **Client-side handheld computing:** It is to use handheld devices to perform mobile, handheld operations, which do not need the supports from server-side computing. Some of its applications are (a) address books, (b) video games, (c) note pads, and (d) to-do-list.

- **Server-side handheld computing:** It is to use handheld devices to perform wireless, mobile, handheld operations, which require the supports from server-side computing. Some of its applications are (a) instant messages, (b) mobile Web contents, (c) online video games, and (d) wireless telephony.

Client- and Server-Side Handheld Computing

Some popular mobile environments/languages for client-side handheld computing are listed below:

- **BREW (Binary Runtime Environment for Wireless):** It is an application development platform created by Qualcomm Inc. for CDMA-based mobile phones (Qualcomm Inc., 2003).
- **J2ME (Java 2 Platform, Micro Edition):** J2ME, developed by Sun Microsystems Inc., provides an environment for applications running on consumer devices, such as mobile phones, PDAs, and TV set-top boxes, as well as a broad range of embedded devices (Sun Microsystem Inc., 2002).
- **Palm OS:** Palm OS, developed by Palm Source Inc., is a fully ARM-native, 32-bit operating system running on handheld devices. Using Palm OS to build handheld applications will be introduced later.

- **Symbian OS:** Symbian Ltd. is a software licensing company that develops and supplies the advanced, open, standard operating system—Symbian OS—for data-enabled mobile phones (Symbian Ltd., 2005).
- **Windows Mobile:** Windows Mobile is a compact operating system for mobile devices based on the Microsoft Win32 API. It is designed to be similar to desktop versions of Windows (Microsoft Corp., 2005).

They apply different approaches to accomplishing handheld computing. Table 1 shows the comparison among these five handheld-computing languages/environments.

Most applications of server-side handheld computing such as instant messaging require network programming such as TCP/IP programming will not be covered in this article. The most popular application of server-side handheld computing is database-driven mobile Web sites, whose structure is shown in Figure 2. A database-driven mobile Web site is often implemented by using a three-tiered client/server architecture consisting of three layers.

A database-driven mobile Web site is often implemented by using a three-tiered client/server architecture consisting of three layers:

1. **User interface:** It runs on a handheld device (the client) and uses a standard graphical user interface (GUI).

Table 1. A comparison among five handheld-computing languages/environments

	BREW	J2ME	Palm OS	Symbian OS	Windows Mobile
Creator	Qualcomm Inc.	Sun Microsystems Inc.	PalmSource Inc.	Symbian Ltd.	Microsoft Corp.
Language/ Environment	Environment	Language	Environment	Environment	Environment
Market Share (PDA) as of 2005	N/A	N/A	3rd	4th	1st
Market Share (Smartphone) as of 2006	?	N/A	4th	1st	5th
Primary Host Language	C/C++	Java	C/C++	C++	C/C++
Target Devices	Phones	PDAs & phones	PDAs	Phones	PDAs & phones

Figure 2. A generalized system structure of a database-driven mobile Web site

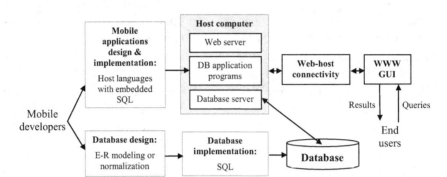

2. **Functional module:** This level actually processes data. It may consist of one or more separate modules running on a workstation or application server. This tier may be multi-tiered itself.
3. **Database management system (DBMS):** A DBMS on a host computer stores the data required by the middle tier.

The three-tier design has many advantages over traditional two-tier or single-tier designs, the chief one being: The added modularity makes it easier to modify or replace one tier without affecting the other tiers.

Palm OS

Palm OS is a fully ARM-native, 32-bit operating system designed to be used on palm handhelds and other third-party devices. Its popularity can be attributed to its many advantages such as its long battery life, support for a wide variety of wireless standards, and the abundant software available. The plain design of the Palm OS has resulted in a long battery life, ap-

proximately twice that of its rivals. It supports many important wireless standards including Bluetooth and 802.11b local wireless and GSM, Mo-bitex, and CDMA wide-area wireless networks (PalmSource Inc., 2002). Two major versions of Palm OS are currently under development:

*   **Palm OS Garnet:** It is an enhanced version of Palm OS 5 and provides features such as dynamic input area, improved network communication, and support for a broad range of screen resolutions including QVGA.
*   **Palm OS Cobalt:** It is Palm OS 6, which focuses on enabling faster and more efficient development of smartphones and integrated wireless (WiFi/Bluetooth) handhelds.

Palm OS Programming

The *Palm OS Developer Suite*, which is the official development environment and tool chain from Palm-Source, is intended for software developers at all

Table 2. Palm OS SDK documentation

Document	Description	URLs
Palm OS Programmer's API Reference	An API reference document that contains descriptions of all Palm OS function calls and important data structures.	http://www.palmos.com/dev/support/docs/palmos/PalmOSReference/ReferenceTOC.html
Palm OS Programmer's Companion, Vol. I & II	A multi-volume guide to application programming for the Palm OS. This guide contains conceptual and "how-to" information that complements the reference.	http://www.palmos.com/dev/support/docs/palmos/PalmOSCompanion/CompanionTOC.html and http://www.palmos.com/dev/support/docs/palmos/PalmOSCompanion2/Companion2TOC.html
Constructor for Palm OS	A guide to using constructor to create Palm OS resource files.	http://www.palmos.com/dev/support/docs/constructor/CGRTOC.html
Palm OS Programming Development Tools Guide	A guide to writing and debugging Palm OS applications with the various tools available.	http://www.palmos.com/dev/support/docs/devguide/ToolsTOC.html

Figure 3. A screenshot of the Palm OS Developer Suite

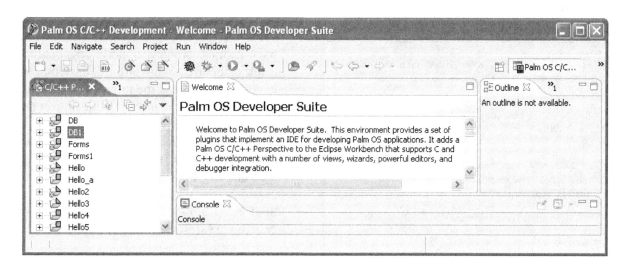

levels. It is a complete IDE (integrated development environment) for:

- Protein applications (all ARM-native code) for Palm OS Cobalt and
- 68K applications for all shipping versions of the Palm OS.

The following steps show how to develop a Palm OS application, a simple "Hello, Mobile world!" program, under Microsoft Windows XP:

1. Download and install the Palm OS Developer Suite at http://www.palmos.com/dev/tools/dev_suite.html.
2. Activate the Eclipse Workbench IDE as shown in Figure 3 under the Windows environment by selecting the following options:

   Start ► All Programs ► PalmSource ► Palm OS Developer Suite

   May select a default workspace at "C:\Program Files\PalmSource\Palm OS Developer Suite\ workspace."

3. Create a new project by selecting a wizard. There are three Palm OS application types as shown in Figure 4:
   - Palm OS 68K Application
   - Palm OS 68K Application with PACE Native Objects
   - Palm OS Protein Application

There are also two kinds of *make files*:
- **Standard make:** It provides a generic set of makefiles that you can modify and tailor for your specific application build.
- **Managed make:** It dynamically generates your makefile based on the contents of your project folders.

4. Create a Palm OS C/C++ program and put it in the directory "C:\Program Files\PalmSource\Palm OS Developer Suite\workspace\HelloWorld\." Figure 5 gives a Palm example, which displays

Figure 4. A screenshot showing Palm OS application and make types

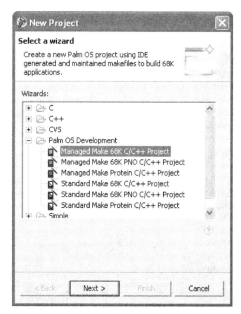

Figure 5. An example of a Palm OS HelloWorld program

```
C:\Program Files\PalmSource\Palm OS Developer Suite\workspace\
Hello\HelloWorld.c

// This header is from the Palm SDK and contains the needed reference
// materials for the use of Palm API and its defined constants.
#include <PalmOS.h>

// The following IDs are from using Palm Resource Editor.
#define Form1 1000
#define OK  1003

// --------------------------------------------------------------------
// PilotMain is called by the startup code and implements a simple
// event handling loop.
// --------------------------------------------------------------------
UInt32 PilotMain( UInt16 cmd, void *cmdPBP, UInt16 launchFlags ) {
short  err;
EventType e;
FormType *pfrm;

if ( cmd == sysAppLaunchCmdNormalLaunch ) {
 // Displays the Form with an ID 1000.
 FrmGotoForm( Form1 );

 // Main event loop
 while( 1 ) {
  // Doze until an event arrives or 100 ticks are reached.
  EvtGetEvent( &e, 100 );
  // System gets first chance to handle the event.
  if ( SysHandleEvent( &e ) ) continue;
  if ( MenuHandleEvent( (void *) 0, &e, &err ) ) continue;

  switch ( e.eType ) {
  case ctlSelectEvent:
   if ( e.data.ctlSelect.controlID == OK )
               goto _quit;
   break;
  case frmLoadEvent:
   FrmSetActiveForm( FrmInitForm( e.data.frmLoad.formID ) );
   break;
  case frmOpenEvent:

pfrm = FrmGetActiveForm( );

FrmDrawForm( pfrm );

break;
        case menuEvent:

break;
        case appStopEvent:

goto _quit;
   break;
           default:
   if ( FrmGetActiveForm( ) )
    FrmHandleEvent( FrmGetActiveForm( ), &e );
   break;
  }
 }
_quit:
 FrmCloseAllForms( );
}
```

the text "Hello, Mobile world!" an image, and a button "OK" on a Palm device.

For how to create Palm OS applications, check Palm OS Developer Documentation at http://www.palmos.com/dev/support/docs/. In order to display the current status on the Eclipse, may need to constantly refresh the project *HelloWorld* by right clicking on the mouse on the project name as shown in Figure 6.

If the project includes resources (with an .xrd filename extension) such as buttons and images, the *Palm OS Resource Editor* at

Start ► All Programs ► PalmSource ► Tools ► Palm OS Resource Editor

could be used to create the resources as shown in Figure 7.

5. Build the project *HelloWorld*.
6. Activate a Palm OS emulator by selecting

Start ► All Programs ► PalmSource ► Tools ► Palm OS Emulator

7. Drag the icon of Hello.prc (Palm Application file) at "C:\Program Files\PalmSource\Palm OS Developer Suite \workspace\Hello5\Debug\Hello.prc" to the Palm OS emulator. Figure 8 shows the execution result of the project HelloWorld.
8. If the application is finalized, synchronize the application to handheld devices by selecting

Start ► All Programs ► Palm Desktop ► Palm Desktop

after downloading and installing the Palm Desktop at http://www.palmos.com/dev/tools/desktop/.

Palm References

Since this article is not intended to be a comprehensive Palm programming guide, this section provides more palm information for further references for interested readers. Table 2 shows four documents for Palm OS SDK (software development kit). Details of the two documents *Palm OS Programmer's API Reference* and *Palm OS Programmer's Companion* are given next.

The *Palm OS Programmer's Companion* (PalmSource Inc., 2004b, 2004c) provides extensive con-

Table 3. An overview of the Palm OS Programmer's Companion

Volume	Description
I	Gives fundamental knowledge of Palm OS programming such as event loop and user interface.
II	Describes the handheld's communications capabilities such as Bluetooth and network communication.

ceptual and "how-to" development information, and official reference information of Palm OS 68K functions and data structures. Table 3 gives an overview of the Palm OS Programmer's Companion.

Table 4 gives an overview of the *Palm OS programmer's API* (Application Programming Interface) reference of Palm OS 68K SDK (PalmSource Inc., 2004a). It includes four major sections (1) user interface, (2) system management, (3) communications, and (4) libraries.

FUTURE TRENDS

A number of mobile operating systems with small footprints and reduced storage capacity have emerged to support the computing-related functions of mobile devices. For example, Research In Motion Ltd's Black-Berry 8700 smartphone uses RIM OS and provides Web access, as well as wireless voice, address book, and appointment applications (Research In Motion Ltd., 2005). Because the handheld device is small and has limited power and memory, the mobile OSes' requirements are significantly less than those of desk- or lap- top OSes. Although a wide range of mobile handheld devices are available in the market, the operating systems, the hub of the devices, are dominated by just few major organizations. The following two lists show the operating systems used in the top brands of

smart cellular phones and PDAs in descending order of market share:

- **Smart cellular phones:** Symbian OS, Linux, RIM OS, Palm OS, Windows Mobile-based Smartphone, and others (Symbian Ltd., 2006).
- **PDAs:** Microsoft Pocket PC, RIM OS, Palm OS, Symbian OS, Linux, and others (Gartner Inc., 2005).

The market share is changing frequently and claims concerning the share vary enormously. It is almost impossible to predict which will be the ultimate winner in the battle of mobile operating systems.

CONCLUSION

Using Internet-enabled mobile handheld devices to access the World Wide Web is a promising addition to the Web and traditional e-commerce. Mobile handheld devices provide convenience and portable access to the huge information on the Internet for mobile users from anywhere and at anytime. However, most software engineers are not familiar with programming for handheld devices. Handheld computing is the programming for handheld devices such as smart cellular phones and PDAs. This article gives a study of handheld computing by including three major topics:

Figure 6. A screenshot of the Palm OS Developer Suite after the HelloWorld project is created

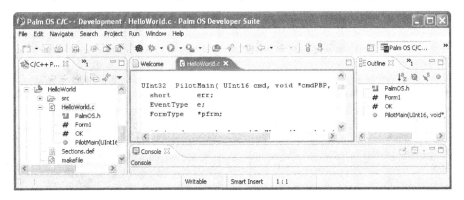

Table 4. An overview of the Palm OS programmer's API reference

Function	Description
User Interface	User interface APIs include events, notifications, attention, control, dialogs, forms, lists, menus, scroll bars, and so forth.
System Management	Provides largest number of functions such as alarm, debug, file streaming, graffiti, I/O, memory, pen, sound, time, windows, etc. for system management.
Communications	Provide various communication functions such as IR, modem, network, telephony, and so forth.
Libraries	Include miscellaneous libraries such as Internet, Bluetooth, cryptography, and so forth.

- **Mobile commerce systems:** Mobile commerce is defined as the exchange or buying and selling of commodities, services, or information on the Internet through the use of mobile handheld devices. The system structure includes six components: (1) mobile commerce applications, (2) mobile handheld devices, (3) mobile middleware, (4) wireless networks, (5) wired networks, and (6) host computers.
- **Handheld computing:** It includes two kinds of computing:
  - **Client-side handheld computing:** It is to use handheld devices to perform mobile, handheld operations, which do not need the supports from server-side computing.
  - **Server-side handheld computing:** It is to use handheld devices to perform wireless, mobile, handheld operations, which need the supports from server-side computing.
- **Palm OS programming:** Two major versions of Palm OS are currently under development:
  - **Palm OS Garnet:** It is an enhanced version of Palm OS.
  - **Palm OS Cobalt:** It is the Palm OS 6.

This article focuses on Palm OS programming by giving a step-by-step procedure of a palm application development. The Palm OS Developer Suite is used to develop applications for palm devices by handheld programmers.

REFERENCES

Gartner Inc. (2005). Gartner says Worldwide PDA shipments increased 32 percent in the second quarter of 2005. Retrieved January 13, 2006, from http://www.gartner.com/press_releases/asset_133230_11.html

Geihs, K. (2001). Middleware challenges ahead. IEEE Computer, 34(6), 24-31.

Hu, W. C., Lee, C. W., & Yeh, J. H. (2004). Mobile commerce systems. In S. Nansi (Ed.), *Mobile commerce applications (pp.* 1-23). Hershey, PA: Idea Group Publishing.

Figure 8. A screenshot of the execution results of the HelloWorld project

Figure 7. A screenshot of the Palm OS Resource Editor

Hu, W.-C., Yeh, J.-h., Chu, H.-J., & Lee, C.-w. (2005). Internet-enabled mobile handheld devices for mobile commerce. *Contemporary Management Research, 1*(1), 13-34.

Microsoft Corp. (2005). What's new for developers in Windows Mobile 5.0? Retrieved December 21, 2005, from http://msdn.microsoft.com/mobility/windowsmobile/howto/documentation/default.aspx?pull=/library/en-us/dnppcgen/html/whatsnew_wm5.asp

NTT DoCoMo Inc. (2006). i-mode technology. Retrieved October 2, 2005, from http://www.nttdocomo.com/technologies/present/imodetechnology/index.html

Open Mobile Alliance Ltd. (n.d.). WAP (wireless application protocol). Retrieved July 21, 2005, from http://www.wapforum.org/

PalmSource Inc. (2004a). Palm OS programmer's API reference. Retrieved December 15, 2005, from http://www.palmos.com/dev/support/docs/palmos/PalmOS-Reference/ReferenceTOC.html

PalmSource Inc. (2004b). Palm OS programmer's companion, Vol. I. Retrieved February 21, 2006, from http://www.palmos.com/dev/support/docs/palmos/PalmOSCompanion/CompanionTOC.html

PalmSource Inc. (2004c). Palm OS programmer's companion, Vol. II. Retrieved February 21, 2006, from http://www.palmos.com/dev/support/docs/palmos/PalmOSCompanion2/Companion2TOC.html

PalmSource Inc. (2002). Why Palm OS? Retrieved June 23, 2005, from http://www.palmsource.com/palmos/Advantage/index_files/v3_document.htm

Qualcomm Inc. (2003). BREW and J2ME—A complete wireless solution for operators committed to Java. Retrieved February 12, 2005, from http://brew.qualcomm.com/brew/en/img/about/pdf/brew_j2me.pdf

Research In Motion Ltd. (2005). BlackBerry application control—An overview for application developers. Retrieved January 05, 2006, from http://www.blackberry.com/knowledgecenterpublic/livelink.exe/fetch/2000/7979/1181821/832210/BlackBerry_Application_Control_Overview_for_Developers.pdf?nodeid=1106734&vernum=0

Sun Microsystem Inc. (2002). Java 2 Platform, Micro Edition. Retrieved January 12, 2006, from http://java.sun.com/j2me/docs/j2me-ds.pdf

Symbian Ltd. (2006). Fast facts. Retrieved June 12, 2006, from http://www.symbian.com/about/fastfacts/fastfacts.html

Symbian Ltd. (2005). Symbain OS Version 9.2. Retrieved December 20, 2005, from http://www.symbian.com/technology/symbianOSv9.2_ds_0905.pdf

KEY TERMS

Client-Side Handheld Computing: It is used by handheld devices to perform mobile, handheld operations, which do not need the supports from server-side computing. Some of its applications are (a) address books, (b) video games, (c) note pads, and (d) to-do-list.

Handheld Computing: It is used by handheld devices such as smart cellular phones and PDAs (personal digital assistants) to perform wireless, mobile, handheld operations such as personal data management and making phone calls.

Mobile Commerce: It is defined as the exchange or buying and selling of commodities, services, or information on the Internet through the use of mobile handheld devices.

Mobile Handheld Devices: They are small general-purpose, programmable, battery-powered computers, but they are different from desk- or lap- top computers mainly due to the following special features: (1) limited network bandwidth, (2) small screen/body size, and (3) mobility.

Palm OS: Palm OS, developed by PalmSource Inc., is a fully ARM-native, 32-bit operating system running on handheld devices. Two major versions of Palm OS are currently under development: Palm OS Garnet and Palm OS Cobalt.

Palm OS Developer Suite: It is the official development environment and tool chain from PalmSource Inc. and is intended for software developers at all levels. It is a complete IDE (Integrated Development Environment) for (1) Protein applications (all ARM-native code) for Palm OS Cobalt and (2) 68K applications for all shipping versions of the Palm OS.

Server-Side Handheld Computing: It is used by handheld devices to perform wireless, mobile, handheld operations, which need the supports from server-side computing. Some of its applications are (a) instant messages, (b) mobile Web contents, (c) online video games, and (d) wireless telephony.

Impact of Portal Technologies on Executive Information Systems

Udo Averweg
Information Services, eThekwini Municipality & University of KwaZulu-Natal, South Africa

Geoff Erwin
Cape Peninsula University of Technology, South Africa

Don Petkov
Eastern Connecticut State University, USA

INTRODUCTION

Internet portals may be seen as Web sites which provide the gateway to corporate information from a single point of access. Leveraging knowledge—both internal and external—is the key to using a portal as a centralised database of best practices that can be applied across all departments and all lines of business within an organisation (Zimmerman, 2003). The potential of the Web portal market and its technology has inspired the mutation of search engines (for example, Yahoo®) and the establishment of new vendors in that area (for example, Hummingbird® and Brio Technology®). A portal is simply a single, distilled view of information from various sources. Portal technologies integrate information, content, and enterprise applications. However, the term portal has been applied to systems that differ widely in capabilities and complexity (Smith, 2004). A portal aims to establish a community of users with a common interest or need.

Portals include horizontal applications such as search, classification, content management, business intelligence (BI), **executive information systems** (EIS), and a myriad of other technologies. Portals not only pull these together but are also absorbing much of the functionality from these complementary technologies (Drakos, 2003). When paired with other technologies, such as content management, collaboration, and BI, portals can improve business processes and boost efficiency within and across organisations (Zimmerman, 2003). This article investigates the level of impact (if any) of portal technologies on EIS. It proceeds with an overview of these technologies, analysis of a survey on the impact of Web-based technologies on EIS implementation, and conclusions on future trends related to them.

BACKGROUND ON PORTAL TECHNOLOGIES AND EIS

Gartner defines a portal as "access to and interaction with relevant information assets (information/content, applications and business processes), knowledge assets and human assets, by select target audiences, delivered in a highly personalized manner" (Drakos, 2003). Drakos (2003) suggests that a significant convergence is occurring with portals in the centre. Most organisations are being forced to revisit their enterprise-wide Web integration strategies (Hazra, 2002). A single view of enterprise-wide information is respected and treasured (Norwood-Young, 2003). Enterprise Information Portals are becoming the primary way in which organisations organise and disseminate knowledge (PricewaterhouseCoopers, 2001).

EIS grew out of the development of information systems (IS) to be used directly by executives and used to augment the supply of information by subordinates (Srivihok, 1998). For the purposes of this article, an Executive Information System is defined as "a computerized system that provides executives with easy access to internal and external information that is relevant to their critical success factors" (Watson et al., 1997). EIS are an important element of the information architecture of an organisation. Different EIS software tools and/or enterprise resource planning (ERP) software with EIS features exist.

EIS is a technology that is emerging in response to managers' specific decision-making needs (Turban et al., 1999). Turban (2001) suggests that EIS capabilities are being "embedded in BI." All major EIS and information product vendors now offer Web versions of their tools, designed to function with Web servers and browsers (PricewaterhouseCoopers, 2002). With EIS established in organisations and the presence of portal technologies, there is thus a need to investigate the link (if any) between EIS and portal technologies.

Web-based technologies are causing a reexamination of existing information technology (IT) implementation models, including EIS (Averweg, 2003). Web-based tools "are very much suited" to executives key activities of communicating and informing (Pijpers, 2001). With the emergence of global IT, existing paradigms are being altered, which is spawning new considerations for successful IT implementation. Challenges exist in building enterprise portals as a new principle of software engineering (Hazra, 2002). Yahoo® is an example of a general portal. Yahoo® enables the user to maintain a measure of mastery over a vast amount of information (PricewaterhouseCoopers, 2001). Portals are an evolutionary offshoot of the Web (Norwood-Young, 2003). The Web is "a perfect medium" for deploying decision support and EIS capabilities on a global basis (Turban et al., 1999).

As the usage of IT increases, Web-based technologies can provide the means for greater access to information from disparate computer applications and other information resources (Eder, 2000). Some Web-based technologies include: intranet, Internet, extranet, e-commerce business-to-business (B2B), e-commerce business-to-consumer (B2C), wireless application protocol (WAP), and other mobile and portal technologies. The portal has become the most-desired user interface in Global 2000 enterprises (Drakos, 2003).

SURVEY OF WEB-BASED TECHNOLOGIES' IMPACT ON EIS

The technology for EIS is evolving rapidly and future systems are likely to be different (Sprague & Watson, 1996). EIS is now clearly in a state of flux. As Turban (2001) notes, "EIS is going through a major change." There is therefore both scope and need for research in the particular area of EIS being impacted by portal technologies as executives need systems that provide access to diverse types of information. Emerging (Web-based)

technologies can redefine the utility, desirability, and economic viability of EIS technology (Volonino, et al., 1995). There exists a high degree of similarity between the characteristics of a "good EIS" and Web-based technologies (Tang et al., 1997). With the absence of research efforts on the impact of portal technologies on EIS implementations, this research begins to fill the gap with a study of thirty-one selected organisations in South Africa which have implemented EIS.

A validated survey instrument was developed and contained seven-point Likert scale statements (anchored with (1) Not at all and (7) Extensively) dealing with how an interviewee perceives specific Web-based technologies impacted his organisation's EIS implementation. The selected Web-based technologies were: (1) intranet; (2) Internet; (3) extranet; (4) e-commerce: business-to-business (B2B); (5) e-commerce: business-to-consumer (B2C); (6) wireless application protocol (WAP) and other mobile technologies; and (7) any other Web-based technologies (for example, portal technologies). The questionnaire was administered during a semi-structured interview process. A similar approach was adopted by Roldán and Leal (2003) in their EIS survey in Spain.

The sample was selected using the unbiased "snowball" sampling technique. This technique was also used by Roldán and Leal (2003). The sample selected included organisations with actual EIS experience with representatives from the following three constituencies: (1) EIS executives/business end-users; (2) EIS providers; and (3) EIS vendors or consultants. These three constituencies were identified and used in EIS research by Rainer and Watson (1995). A formal extensive interview schedule was compiled and used for the semi-structured interviews. Those were conducted during May-June 2002 at organisations in the large eThekwini Municipal Area (EMA) in the eastern part of South Africa, including Durban, which is the most populous municipality in the country, with a geographic area size of 2,300 km² and a population of 3.09 million citizens (Statistics South Africa, 2001).

The number of surveyed interviewees and associated percentages per constituency for the three EIS constituencies are reflected in Table 1.

The respondents in the organisations surveyed reported a wide range of available commercially purchased EIS software tools and/or ERP software with EIS features. These included Cognos®, JDEdwards BI®, Oracle®, Hyperion®, Lotus Notes®, Business

Table 1. EIS constituencies and number of interviewees surveyed per constituency

Stakeholder groups (constituencies)	Number of interviewees surveyed and associated percentage of total sample
EIS executives/business end-users	20 (64.5%)
EIS providers	7 (22.6%)
EIS vendors or consultants	4 (12.9%)
SAMPLE SIZE	**31 (100%)**

Table 2. Tally and associated percentage of the degree to which specific Web-based technologies impacted respondent's current EIS implementation

Web-based technology	The degree to which Web-based technologies impacted respondent's EIS implementation (N=31)						
	Not at all	Very little	Somewhat little	Uncertain	Somewhat much	Very much	Extensively
Intranet	17 (54.8%)	2 (6.5%)	2 (6.5%)	0 (0.0%)	3 (9.7%)	4 (12.9%)	3 (9.6%)
Internet	21(67.7%)	1 (3.2%)	1 (3.2%)	0 (0.0%)	2 (6.5%)	3 (9.7%)	3 (9.7%)
Extranet	24 (77.4%)	1 (3.2%)	2 (6.5%)	1 (3.2%)	1 (3.2%)	2 (6.5%)	0 (0.0%)
E-Commerce: (B2B)	28 (90.4%)	1 (3.2%)	0 (0.0%)	0 (0.0%)	0 (0.0%)	1 (3.2%)	1 (3.2%)
E-Commerce: (B2C)	26 (83.9%)	1 (3.2%)	1 (3.2%)	0 (0.0%)	2 (6.5%)	0 (0.0%)	1 (3.2%)
WAP and other mobile technologies	29 (93.6%)	1 (3.2%)	0 (0.0%)	0 (0.0%)	0 (0.0%)	0 (0.0%)	1 (3.2%)
Portal technologies	26 (83.8%)	0 (0.0%)	0 (0.0%)	0 (0.0%)	2 (6.5%)	2 (6.5%)	1 (3.2%)

Objects®, and Pilot®. Cognos® was the most popular EIS software tool, comprising 60% of the sample surveyed.

From the data gathered through the authors' survey instrument, a tally and associated percentage of the perceived degree to which specific Web-based technologies impacted the respondent's current EIS implementation in the organisations surveyed is reflected in Table 2. Table 2 shows that only seven (22.5%) organisations surveyed report that the Intranet significantly impacted their EIS implementation. Intranets are usually combined with and accessed via a corporate portal (Turban, et al., 2005). The level of impact by the Internet on EIS implementation is slightly lower with six (19.4%) organisations surveyed reporting that the Internet has significantly impacted their EIS implementation. While 24 (77.4%) organisations surveyed report that the Extranet had no impact on their organisation's EIS implementation, the balance of the data sample (22.6%) reports different degrees of impact.

The results in Table 2 show that the vast majority (90.4%) of respondents reports that e-commerce: (B2B)

has not impacted EIS implementation in organisations surveyed. A slightly lower result (83.9%) was reported for e-commerce: (B2C). One possible explanation for the e-commerce (B2B) and (B2C) low impact levels is that the software development tools are still evolving and changing rapidly.

WAP and other mobile technologies have no (93.6%) or very little (3.2%) impact on EIS implementations. Of the seven Web-based technologies given in Table 2, WAP and other mobile technologies have the *least* impact (combining "Somewhat much," "Very much," and "Extensively") on EIS implementation in organisations surveyed. Only one respondent (3.2%) reported that WAP and other technologies had extensively impacted the EIS implementation in her organisation. A possible explanation for this result is that the EIS consultant was technically proficient in WAP technologies. The potential benefits of mobile access to portals are numerous and self-evident. PricewaterhouseCoopers (2002) notes that organisations must first establish the benefits of mobile access to its portal and assess the

Table 3. Descending rank order of impact levels of Web-based technologies on current EIS implementation

Rank	Web-based technology	Tally and level of impact on EIS implementations (N=31)
1	Intranet	10 (32.2%)
2	Internet	8 (25.9%)
3	Portal technologies	5 (16.2%)
4	Extranet	3 (9.7%)
4	E-Commerce: (B2C)	3 (9.7%)
6	E-Commerce: (B2B)	2 (6.4%)
7	WAP and other mobile technologies	1 (3.2%)

value of providing those benefits via mobile access to the organisation.

According to Table 2, three interviewees reported that their organisation's EIS implementations were significantly impacted ("Very much" and "Extensively") by portal technologies. At first this may appear to be noteworthy as the portal technology impact on EIS implementations (9.7%) is higher than that on the extranet (6.5%), e-commerce: (B2B) (6.4%), e-commerce: (B2C) (6.4%), and WAP and other technologies (3.2%) impacts. However, it should be noted that the impact levels of all the Web-based technologies assessed are fairly low. This still means that after the Intranet and Internet, portal technologies have the third highest impact on EIS implementations in organisations surveyed. Combining the results ("Somewhat much," "Very much," and "Extensively") for each of the seven

Web-based technologies, Table 3 gives a descending ranking order of the levels of impact of different Web-based technologies on EIS implementations.

A tally and associated percentage of the perceived degree to which specific Web-based technologies will impact a respondent's future EIS implementation is given in Table 4. These are obtained from the data gathered using the authors' survey instrument.

Table 4 reflects that only two (6.4%) organisations surveyed reported that it is unlikely that the Intranet will impact future EIS implementations. The unlikeliness of impact by the Internet on future EIS implementations is somewhat higher (16.1%). While seven (22.6%) respondents indicated that is unlikely that the Extranet will impact their future EIS implementations, eight (25.8%) respondents were unsure of future impact levels by the extranet. Twelve (38.7%) respondents indicated

Table 4. Tally and associated percentage of the expected degree to which specific Web-based technologies will impact respondent's future EIS implementations

Web-based technology	The expected degree to which Web-based technologies will impact respondent's future EIS implementations (N=31)						
	Extremely likely	Quite likely	Slightly likely	Uncertain	Slightly unlikely	Quite unlikely	Extremely unlikely
Intranet	17 (54.8%)	7 (22.6%)	3 (9.7%)	2 (6.5%)	0 (0.0%)	1 (3.2%)	1 (3.2%)
Internet	12 (38.8%)	6 (19.3%)	5 (16.1%)	3 (9.7%)	1 (3.2%)	1 (3.2%)	3 (9.7%)
Extranet	6 (19.3%)	7 (22.6%)	3 (9.7%)	8 (25.8%)	0 (0.0%)	1 (3.2%)	6 (19.4%)
E-Commerce: (B2B)	3 (9.7%)	9 (29.0%)	4 (12.9%)	3 (9.7%)	2 (6.5%)	4 (12.9%)	6 (19.3%)
E-Commerce: (B2C)	2 (6.5%)	9 (29.0%)	4 (12.9%)	1 (3.2%)	2 (6.5%)	4 (12.9%)	9 (29.0%)
WAP and other mobile technologies	1 (3.2%)	8 (25.8%)	5 (16.1%)	4 (12.9%)	0 (0.0%)	3 (9.7%)	10 (32.3%)
Portal technologies	3 (9.7%)	2 (6.5%)	1 (3.2%)	1 (3.2%)	1 (3.2%)	2 (6.5%)	21 (67.7%)

that it is unlikely that e-commerce: (B2B) will impact future EIS implementations. Almost half (48.4%) of organisations surveyed reported that it is unlikely that e-commerce: (B2C) will impact future EIS implementations. WAP and other mobile technologies have similar (42.0%) unlikely future levels of impact.

It is striking to note that 21 (67.7%) respondents indicated that it is *Extremely unlikely* that portal technologies will impact future EIS implementations. This result (when combined with the "Slightly unlikely" and "Quite unlikely" degrees) rises to 24 (75.2%) organisations surveyed. This finding is somewhat surprising considering that portal technologies *currently* have the third highest level of impact on EIS implementations in organisations surveyed. An explanation for this finding is that possibly some respondents are not aware of the existence of such technology. Roldán and Leal (2003) report that with the availability of Web-based technologies "together with the need to build something similar to an EIS but focused on all members of the organisation has led to the development of the enterprise information portal (EIP) concept, which, to some extent represents the latest incarnation of EIS." According to Trowbridge (2000), two elements characterise these systems according to the respondents: EIP "acts as a single point of access to internal and external information" and "gives users access to disparate enterprise information systems."

According to Table 4, combining the positive attitude results ("Extremely likely," "Quite likely," and "Slightly likely") for each of the seven Web-based technologies, Table 5 gives a descending ranking order of the expected degree to which Web-based technologies will impact respondents' future EIS implementations.

FUTURE TRENDS AND CONCLUSION

We may notice three significant trends from the data in Table 5. First, this rank order of impact levels of Web-based technologies on *future* EIS implementation matches the current rank order levels of impact of Web-based technologies on EIS implementations (see Table 3). Second, while nearly three quarters (75.2%) of respondents surveyed report that it is unlikely that portal technologies will impact future EIS implementations (see Table 4), seen in the context of the other six Web-based technologies, portals still appear in the top three rankings. This is an important consideration for IS practitioners when planning future EIS implementations. Third, when comparing current and future impact levels of Web-based technologies on EIS, there is a positive impact trend for **all** Web-based technologies. The largest trend increase is the Intranet rising from 32.2% to 87.1%. As Basu, et al. (2000) report, the use of Web-based technologies in the distribution of information is becoming widespread. These technologies will impact future EIS implementations.

The findings of this survey show that while EIS have a significant role in organisations in a large South African metropolitan area, their technological base is not affected considerably by the latest innovations of

Table 5. Descending rank order of impact levels of Web-based technologies on future EIS implementation

Rank	Web-based technology	Tally and level of impact on future EIS implementations
1	Intranet	27 (87.1%)
2	Internet	23 (74.2%)
3	Portal technologies	16 (51.6%)
3	Extranet	16 (51.6%)
5	E-Commerce: (B2C)	15 (48.4%)
6	E-Commerce: (B2B)	14 (45.1%)
7	WAP and other mobile technologies	6 (19.4%)

Web-based technologies, including portals. A potential limitation of the research is the localised sample involved in the investigation, but given the highly developed IT infrastructure of most South African companies, our findings can be cautiously generalised for most other countries. The role of portals is to integrate potential information to the users. IT developers must be aware of emerging trends in the portal technology market to create systems that will be able to incorporate the latest technological developments and new methods of information delivery and presentation for organisations. As the use of Web-based technologies in the distribution of information in organisations becomes more widespread, it is envisaged that the impact level of portal technologies on future EIS implementations will increase significantly.

REFERENCES

Averweg, U., Cumming, G., & Petkov, D. (2003, July 7-10). Development of an executive information system in South Africa: Some exploratory findings. In *Proceedings of a Conference on Group Decision and Negotiation (GDN2003) held within the 5th EURO/INFORMS Joint International Meeting*, Istanbul, Turkey, 7-10 July.

Basu, C., Poindexter, S., Drosen, J., & Addo, T. (2000). Diffusion of executive information systems in organizations and the shift to Web technologies. *Industrial Management & Data Systems, 100*(6), 271-276.

Drakos, N. (2003, August 4-6). *Portalising your enterprise.* Gartner Symposium ITXPO2003, Cape Town, South Africa, 4-6 August.

Eder, L.B. (2000). *Managing healthcare information systems with Web-enabled technologies.* Hershey, PA: Idea Group Publishing.

Hazra, T.K. (2002, May 19-25). Building enterprise portals: Principles to practice. In *Proceedings of the 24th international conference on Software Engineering*, Orlando.

Norwood-Young, J. (2003). The little portal that could. In Wills (Ed.), *Business solutions using technology platform, 1*(4), 14-15.

Pijpers, G.G.M. (2001). Understanding senior executives' use of information technology and the Internet. In Murugan Anandarajan & Claire A. Simmers (Eds.), *Managing Web usage in the workplace: A social, ethical and legal perspective.* Hershey, PA: Idea Group Publishing.

PricewaterhouseCoopers. (2002). Technology forecast: 2002-2004. *Volume 1: Navigating the future of software.* Menlo Park, California.

PricewaterhouseCoopers. (2001). Technology forecast: 2001-2003. *Mobile Internet: Unleashing the power of wireless.* Menlo Park, California.

Rainer, R.K., Jr., & Watson, H.J. (1995). The keys to executive information system success. *Journal of Management Information Systems, 12*(2), 83-98.

Roldán, J.L., & Leal, A. (2003). Executive information systems in Spain: A study of current practices and comparative analysis. In Forgionne, Gupta, & Mora (Eds.), *Decision making support systems: Achievements and challenges for the new decade,* Chapter 18, 287-304. Hershey, PA: Idea Group Publishing.

Smith, M.A. (2004). Portals: Toward an application framework for interoperability. *Communications of the ACM, 47*(10), 93-97.

Sprague, R.H., Jr., & Watson, H.J. (1996). *Decision support for management.* Upper Saddle River, NJ: Prentice-Hall.

Srivihok, A. (1998). *Effective management of executive information systems implementations: A framework and a model of successful EIS implementation.* PhD dissertation. Central University, Rockhampton, Australia.

Statistics South Africa (2001). *Census 2001 digital census atlas.* Retrieved July 5, 2006 from,http://gis-data.durban.gov.za/census/index.html [Accessed on 5 July 2006]

Tang, H., Lee, S., & Yen, D. (1997). An investigation on developing Web-based EIS. *Journal of CIS, 38*(2), 49-54.

Trowbridge, D. (2000). EIP—More profitable for integrators than users? *Computer Technology Review, 20*(5), 20.

Turban, E. (2001). California State University, Long Beach and City University of Hong Kong, USA. *Personal Communication, 7* October.

Turban, E., McLean, E., & Wetherbe, J. (1999). *Information technology for management.* New York: John Wiley & Sons.

Turban, E., Rainer, R.K., & Potter, R.E. (2005). *Introduction to information technology* (3ʳᵈ Ed.). New York: John Wiley & Sons.

Volonino, L., Watson, H.J., & Robinson, S. (1995). Using EIS to respond to dynamic business conditions. *Decision Support Systems, 14*(2), 105-116.

Watson, H.J., Houdeshel, G., & Rainer, R.K., Jr. (1997). *Building executive information systems and other decision support applications.* New York: John Wiley & Sons.

Zimmerman, K.A. (2003). Portals: Not just a one-way street. *KMWorld, Creating and Managing the Knowledge-Based Enterprise, 12*(8), September. Retrieved 27 July, 2007 from http://www.kmworld.com/Articles/PrintArticle.aspx?ArticleID-9496

KEY TERMS

Executive Information System: A computerised system that provides executives with easy access to internal and external information that is relevant to their critical success factors.

Extranet: A private Internet that connects multiple organisations.

Intranet: A private Internet for an organisation.

Portal: Provides access to and interaction with relevant information assets (information/content, applications and business processes), knowledge assets, and human assets, by select target audiences, delivered in a highly personalised manner.

Web-based Technologies: Technologies which are core to the functioning of the World Wide Web.

Wireless Application Protocol (WAP): A collection of standards for accessing online information and applications from wireless devices such as mobile phones, two-way radios, pagers, and personal digital assistants.

World Wide Web: The universe of network-accessible information, supported by a body of software, and a set of protocols and conventions (http://www.w3.org/WWW).

Intellectual Property and the Internet

Alexandra George
University of London, UK

INTRODUCTION

'Intellectual property' (or 'IP') is an umbrella term that is used as shorthand to describe a variety of diverse doctrines that create legally-enforceable monopolies over the use of or access to ideas, information and knowledge. As the Internet is essentially a structure through which such material can be presented, organised, transmitted and disseminated, IP is a key area of law that is used to regulate activity on the Internet. The pervasive significance of this becomes clear when one considers that much of the hardware that forms the framework of computer networks that comprise the Internet, and almost all of the data carried through these networks and linked via the World Wide Web, are—or have been in the past—subject to regulation by IP laws.

IP doctrines that pre-dated the Internet have been co-opted to regulate the online environment. Patent laws have been used to protect monopolies on hardware developments that comprise the Internet's structure and business practices that organize its operation. Copyright laws afford proprietary rights over software and much of the content found on the Internet, while trademark laws regulate the use of the commercial symbols or 'brands' in the virtual shopping mall. In addition, new IP laws have been created, and new alternatives to traditional IP principles are emerging, to meet the challenges presented by the Internet.

BACKGROUND

IP monopolies take the form of 'intellectual property rights' ('IPRs') that can be enforced by proprietors. The particular rights that attach to an object affected by IP law vary according to the type of IP and the jurisdiction. The central doctrines of IP are copyright, patent, trademark and design laws. Examples of the rights created by these laws include the right to reproduce or make copies of, assign (for example, to license or sell)

and the use the subject-matter. By creating artificial scarcity in this way, IP laws create commercial conditions that allow IP proprietors to profit from the ideas, information and knowledge that they control.

Each IP doctrine is a distinct body of law, and many have significant implications for regulation of the Internet. It is important to understand that the specifics of the laws vary from jurisdiction to jurisdiction. A 'jurisdiction' may be a local administrative area (such as a district or state), a national area (such as a country, or federation of countries such as Great Britain), or a multinational area such as the European Union (which incorporates many sovereign nations). Many jurisdictions are also subject to international laws governing IP doctrines, either because they have individually opted to become parties to international treaties or because they are obliged to do so as a condition of membership of an international organisation such as the World Trade Organisation ("WTO"). A consequence is that jurisdictions are commonly covered by several lawyers of legal regulation, many of which contain IP provisions. This makes IP a complicated area of law as several doctrines of several jurisdictions may apply to a single fact situation. This is particularly true in the context of the Internet, whose nature is to transcend territorial borders. The multi-jurisdictional IP laws that are implicated by online activities create a web of legal regulation that potentially affects almost any change or development in the structure of the Internet, and almost any activity on the Internet's World Wide Web ('WWW').

Burgeoning Internet activity since the early 1990s coincides with, and is arguably related to, a period of intense IP law-making. The following definitions concentrate on the main issues involving the core areas of IP law in the Internet.

Copyright Laws

Copyright gives a proprietor a legal monopoly over the copying of artistic, literary, dramatic and musical works, and their derivatives. In most jurisdictions, copyright arises automatically when such works are created.

The ability to digitize data and transmit it over the Internet has created new challenges for copyright law. Much of the material accessible via the Internet is covered by copyright law and is therefore privately owned. The ease with which multiple users in multiple locations and jurisdictions can download perfect but unauthorized copies of copyrighted material has tested the reach of traditional copyright laws.

Internet practices that have caused particular difficulties for copyright proprietors include caching of material viewed on a computer (i.e., making a temporary copy of the material on the local computer), the unauthorized transmission and downloading of computer software, and audio and video recordings through peer-to-peer ('P2P') file-sharing networks, the pirating of copyright material through e-commerce (especially spam, or unsolicited emails), the web-casting of copyright material over Internet radio stations and television channels, and the linking of copyright material online (WIPO, 2002). Questions have also been raised about whether Internet Service Providers should be liable for copyright infringement when those using their services infringe copyright online.

The challenges that the Internet has generated for traditional copyright principles have led to legal changes around the world. Key among these are two 1996 World Intellectual Property Organization ('WIPO') treaties that entered into force in 2002. Collectively known as the 'Internet Treaties', the *WIPO Copyright Treaty* and the *WIPO Performances and Phonograms Treaty* underpin traditional copyright principles by responding (among others) to new practices involving the dissemination of copyright material on the Internet. For example, they contain 'anti-circumvention' clauses that require signatory countries to implement laws making it illegal to circumvent technological protection measures used by copyright proprietors. Similar measures are found in the USA's 1998 *Digital Millennium Copyright Act* ('DMCA') and the EC's 2001 *Copyright Directive*. These measures have prompted much debate about the proper scope of copyright protection, prompting criticisms that the balance between owners and users of copyright material has been pushed too far in favour of the former. Critics fear that, in doing so, these sorts of measures put at risk the production and circulation of ideas, information and knowledge in modern society (Lessig, 2004).

Patent Laws

Patent rights arise when a description of a novel, useful or industrially applicable, inventive or non-obvious invention is registered by a Registry Office. The Registry may be national, such as the UK Patent Office and the United States Patent and Trademark Office, or multinational, such as the European Patent Office. The duration of the patent depends upon the jurisdiction in which it was registered, but registration typically gives proprietors monopoly rights to prevent others from making, using or selling the invention for a period of up to 20 years. Notably, using one's own patented invention might infringe the patent of another proprietor so registration confers only negative rights to exclude others from using – but not positive rights to use – an invention.

Much of the hardware that underpins the Internet's computer structures is, or has been, subject to 'product patent' protection. In some jurisdictions, 'process patents' can be used to monopolise business methods on inventions such as the electronic 'shopping baskets' and online credit card payment systems (WIPO, 2002, p.23). The extension of patent law to cover such processes has been welcomed by some (see analysis in Dreyfuss, 2000), while simultaneously attracting criticisms that these patents grant monopolies over practices that are not novel because they were already commonplace off-line (Krause, 2000).

Trademark Laws

Trademarks are the commercial symbols traders use to distinguish their goods and/or services from those of other traders. In traditional markets and e-commerce alike, trademarks provide a method by which traders can build and protect the brand recognition that attracts customers and inspires consumer confidence about quality and reliability.

Registered trademarks (often marked with the symbol ®) must meet a series of criteria before being registered. There are various registration systems and the appropriate Registry Office may be *national*, such as 'IP Australia', or *multinational*, such as the 'Benelux Trademarks Office' or the European 'Office for Harmonization in the Internal Market'. *International* trademarks registered through the "Madrid System" are filed at a local registry for registration by the International Bureau of WIPO. Unregistered trademarks (sometimes indicated with the symbol ™) are protected by unfair competition or 'passing off' laws in some jurisdictions.

Trademarks traditionally applied in territorially-defined areas, so the supra-jurisdictional nature of the Internet has raised questions about how trademark law operates in cyberspace. For example, the same trademark can be validly registered to quite different proprietors in different jurisdictions. Prior the advent of online commerce, they would have been unlikely to come into competition with one another. However, the Internet makes online businesses easily accessible by consumers from all over the world, thus challenging traditional, territorial trademark principles and practices. Internet marketplaces and auction sites provide a new forum in which such problems can be exacerbated.

Related difficulties arise with the use of confusing Domain Names by different traders, and Domain Names that conflict with the trademarks of other traders.

Using trademarks as keywords in Internet search engines ('metatags') or to link one WWW page to another ('hyperlinking') can raise trademark infringement issues where it involves the unauthorized commercial use of another's mark or where it could prompt consumers to conclude wrongly that a website is connected with an unrelated business.

Concerns about such practices precipitated WIPO guidelines about the use of trademarks on the Internet (WIPO, 2001).

ENFORCEMENT OF INTELLECTUAL PROPERTY RIGHTS ON THE INTERNET

The background just outlined indicates the broad application of IP laws to Internet structures and practices. Expanding on issues introduced above, this section focuses on key legal issues involving IPR enforcement in an Internet environment. It also discusses the related issue of how the law is responding to problems of conflicting rights that have been exacerbated by the Internet's supra-jurisdictional nature.

Sale of Pirated and Counterfeit Goods

The sale of pirated copyright goods and counterfeit trademarked goods through e-commerce has commonplace, and IP proprietors fear that their profits are

being undermined and their brand reputations diluted by this practice.

Meanwhile, consumers accustomed to trusting well-known trademarks in the form of brand-names or logos have become vulnerable to fraud by traders who sell counterfeit rather than genuine goods online. The health and safety implications of the online trade in products such as counterfeit pharmaceuticals raise great anxieties for law enforcement agencies (George, 2003) and governments around the world are introducing laws, such as the EC's *Enforcement Directive* (2004), to prohibit such behaviour. For example, the criminalization of piracy and counterfeiting means offenders can be gaoled rather than just fined.

Transmission and Downloading of Copyright Material

The ease with which copyright-protected material can be digitized and transmitted across the Internet increases the potential audience for that material but makes it simpler for copyright in the material to be infringed.

P2P networks allow users to transfer material such as MP3-format songs to one another. Those who transmit and download the material make copies, and are therefore likely to infringe copyright. This has led to high-profile copyright infringement cases such as *Napster* (2001) and *Grokster* (2005) in the U.S., and *KaZaA* (2005) in Australia, each of which held against P2P network providers. Recording industry litigation against end-users who downloaded infringing copies of songs has been questioned by legal commentators (Groennings, 2005; Sag, 2006).

Liability of Internet Service Providers for Infringement of IPRs

Internet service providers ('ISPs') provide the hardware infrastructure by which individual computers are able to communicate with one another. This raises questions about whether ISPs are liable for IPR infringements by their users (Bently & Sherman, 2004, pp. 149-151).

The EC's *Directive on Electronic Commerce* (2000) limits ISPs' liability for copyright infringements for caching ('automatic, immediate and temporary storage' on a computer for the purpose of accessing the information), or where it acts as a 'mere conduit' or 'hosts' (i.e., stores for a subscriber) copyright-protected material. The ISP is generally protected if it was unaware of illegal activity and acted promptly to remove information when made aware that its use breached copyright. The US's DMCA provides 'safe harbours' with similar effects (Yen, 2000).

Domain Names

The development of Internet domain names introduced the potential for conflicts with trademark law. Whereas trademarks are territorially-based signs that indicate identity in commerce, domain names are international addresses that indicate identity on the Internet. Both can be obtained through registration, but the registration systems are different. Problems arise when trademark proprietors find others have registered their trademarks as domain names. Johnson (2001) suggests that the effect has been to alter IP paradigms.

Courts have been unsympathetic to 'cybersquatters' who register another's trademarked name as a domain name in order to hold the existing trademark proprietor to ransom. For example, in the *One in a Million* cases (1998), a UK court found IP infringement after a company fraudulently and in bad-faith (i.e., intending to sell them to existing trademark proprietors) registered domain names that were confusingly similar to famous trademarks.

More difficult questions arise where trademark proprietors from different jurisdictions wish to register identical or similar domain names, which may be treated as legitimate concurrent use. The Internet Corporation for Assigned Names and Numbers' ('ICANN') *Uniform Domain Dispute Resolution Policy* offers a mechanism for resolving domain name disputes. WIPO operates an Internet-based adjudication service administering these rules (WIPO Arbitration and Mediation Center, 2003). In effect, this has become an international juridical system that bypasses domestic laws because the Internet community has adopted it and usually abides by its findings (rather than having them imposed on it), thus self-regulating the Internet's somewhat anarchic, extra-jurisdictional virtual-world.

FUTURE TRENDS

The complicated nature of contemporary IP regimes has been criticised, as has the high cost of enforcing IPRs and the burdens they place on innovation (Koepsell, 2000, pp. 105-108). However, current IP conceptions seem unlikely to be abandoned in the foreseeable future. Governments have continued to respond to calls from IP-rich industries—such as the software, music, movie and pharmaceutical industries—for increasingly rigorous IPRs (Lessig, 1999, pp. 125-127).

Widespread non-compliance with IP laws does lead to demands for alternatives (Litman, 2001, pp. 194-195), which are taking the form of both more IP law as well as non-IP law approaches.

Structural changes are being made to existing law (e.g., with respect to copyright's evolution, see Menell, 2002/2003). Additional laws, such as those criminalising piracy and counterfeiting, include tougher IP provisions to combat emerging Internet practices that infringe IPRs. In response to the supra-national dimension of the Internet and the globalised society it has helped to usher in, such laws are increasingly harmonised by international treaties to which the majority of nations are signatories. The trend is therefore away from nations making IP law in isolation and in favour of quite uniform IP standards being applied worldwide, thus standardising the rules that regulate IP on the Internet.

Alternative approaches to IP law are also being used. It has become standard for Websites to demand that Internet users accept licenses (contracts) limiting how IP can be used before making their IP available, while technological protection measures are attached to some IP material to prevent it from being transmitted via the internet. Cornish and Llewelyn (2003, pp. 801-815) survey and assess such technical alternatives to IP law, and Lawrence Lessig warns of the threats to the future of ideas generated by locking too much information behind private protection measures (Lessig, 2001). However, some proprietors have adopted business models that recognise commercial benefits in making core aspects of IP-protected products such as software freely available in order to attract customers from whom they will profit in other ways (eg. Shy, 2000, pp.104-112).

Different alternatives that adapt IP laws to new formats are being promoted by those concerned that too much knowledge is being privatised. For example, the 'Creative Commons' project provides licenses that enable proprietors to make their copyright-protected material more widely available on the Internet: a 'some rights reserved' rather than 'all rights reserved' approach. Meanwhile, the 'Free Software' and 'Open Source' software movements allow for computer code and programs to be freely exchanged and used on the Internet and elsewhere.

CONCLUSION

The emergence of the Internet presented clear challenges to traditional IP law doctrines. In turn, IP law has affected the development of Internet practices. The law has responded by playing catch-up, changing to try to meet the competing needs of proprietors and users of IP in cyberspace. This has taken the form of new interpretations of existing laws and the introduction of innovative legal provisions. Meanwhile, IP laws have defined legally-acceptable Internet practices (e.g., the appropriate role of ISPs) and curtailed others (e.g., cybersquatting and P2P file-sharing). Continuation of these trends seems likely to bring an unpredictable and exciting future.

REFERENCES

Bently, L., & Sherman, B. (2004). *Intellectual property law*. Oxford: Oxford University Press.

Dreyfuss, R.C. (2000). Are business method patents bad for business? *Santa Clara Computer and High Technology Law Journal, 16*, 263-280.

George, A. (2003). E-shopping for fakes: The Internet business in trademark counterfeits. *World Internet Law Report, 12*, 7-11.

Groennings, C. (2005). Costs and benefits of the recording industry's litigation against individuals. *Berkeley Technology Law Journal, 20*, 571-601.

Johnson, S.T. (2001). Internet domain name and trademark disputes: shifting paradigms in intellectual property. *Arizona Law Review, 43*, 465-489.

Krause, W. (2000). Sweeping the e-commerce patent minefield: The need for a workable business method exception. *Seattle University Law Review. 24*, 79-105.

Lessig, L. (1999). *Code and other laws of cyberspace*. New York: Basic Books.

Lessig, L. (2001). *The future of ideas: The fate of the commons in a connected world*. New York: Random House.

Lessig, L. (2004). *Free culture: How big media uses technology and the law to lock down culture and control creativity*. New York: Penguin Press.

Litman, J. (2001). *Digital copyright*. New York: Prometheus Books.

Menell, P.S. (2002/2003). Can our current conception of copyright law survive the Internet age? Envisioning copyright law's digital guture. *New York Law School Law Review, 46*, 63-198.

Shy, O., (2000), The economics of copy protection in software and other media. In B. Kahin & H.R. Varian (Eds.), *Internet publishing and beyond: The economics of digital information and intellectual property*. Cambridge, MA: The MIT Press.

Keopsell, D.R. (2000). *The ontology of cyberspace: Philosophy, law and the future of intellectual property*. Chicago: Open Court.

Sag, M. (2006). Twelve year-olds, grandmothers, and other good targets for the recording industry's file sharing litigation. *Northwestern Journal of Technology and Intellectual Property, 4*, 133-155.

WIPO (2001). *The Joint Recommendation Concerning Provisions on the Protection of Marks, and Other industrial Property Rights in Signs, on the Internet*. Geneva: WIPO.

WIPO (2002). *Intellectual Property on the Internet: A Survey of Issues*. Geneva: WIPO.

WIPO Arbitration and Mediation Center (2003). *Guide to WIPO Domain Name Dispute Resolution*. http://arbiter.wipo.int/center/publications/guide-en-web.pdf

Yen, A.C. (2000). Internet service provider liability for subscriber copyright infringement, enterprise liability, and the First Amendment. *Georgetown Law Journal 88*, 1883-1893.

Cases

A&M Records v Napster, 239 F.Supp.3d 1004 (9 Circ, 2001).

Metro-Goldwyn-Mayer Studios Inc v Grokster Ltd, 125 S.Ct. 2764 (2005).

Universal Music Australia Pty Ltd v Sharman License. Holdings Ltd [2005] FCA 1242. ['KaZaA case']

BT & Ors v One in a Million [1999] FSR 1.

Legislation

Digital Millennium Copyright Act, Public Law No. 105-304, 112 Stat. 2860 (28 October 1998).

Directive 2001/29/EC of the European Parliament and of the Council of May 22, 2001, on the Harmonisation of Certain Aspects of Copyright and Related rights in the Information Society. ['Copyright Directive']

Directive 2000/31/EC of the European Parliament and of the Council of 8 June 2000 on certain legal aspects of information society services, in particular electronic commerce, in the Internal Market (Directive on Electronic Commerce)

Directive 2004/48/EC of the European Parliament and of the Council of 29 April 2004 on the enforcement of intellectual property rights ['Enforcement Directive']

KEY TERMS

Copyright Law: An IP doctrine that gives proprietors of artistic, literary, dramatic and musical works, and their derivatives, a legally-enforceable monopoly over the copying of those materials.

ICANN (Internet Corporation for Assigned Names and Numbers): A private, not-for-profit corporation with responsibility for assigning Internet Protocol addresses and other Internet signifiers such as Domain Names. ICANN coordinates the management of Domain Names.

Intellectual Property (IP): 1. The subject-matter monopolised by IP proprietors under IP law. 2. The regulatory system created by IP law.

Intellectual Property Law: A group of legal doctrines (including copyright, trademark and patent laws) that regulate the use of ideas, information and knowledge by creating artificial monopolies around them and providing proprietors with legally-enforceable rights with respect to them.

Intellectual Property Rights (IPRs): Legally-enforceable monopolies that proprietors can use to monopolise use of or access to ideas, information and knowledge.

Patent Law: An IP doctrine that provides a temporary monopoly to exclude others from using a registered invention.

Trademark Law: Trademarks are signs that distinguish the goods and/or services of one trader from those of another. Trademark law is an IP doctrine that allows proprietors to prevent others from using identical or similar signs with respect to identical or similar goods or services in a commercial setting.

World Intellectual Property Organization (WIPO): A United Nations agency that administers international treaties relating to various aspects of IP law in 183 member states. Its stated objectives are the worldwide promotion of IP, and preventing erosion of existing IP law standards.

Internet Gambling

Mark Griffiths
Nottingham Trent University, UK

Adrian Parke
Nottingham Trent University, UK

INTRODUCTION

Technology has always played a role in the development of gambling practices and continues to provide new market opportunities. One of the fastest growing areas is that of *Internet gambling* (also known as *online gambling*). Examples include online lotteries, online casinos, online bookmakers, online betting exchanges, online poker sites, etc. The impact of such technologies should not be accepted uncritically, particularly as there may be areas of potential concern based on what is known about problem gambling off-line. This article therefore has three aims. Firstly, it highlights salient factors in the rise of Internet gambling (i.e., accessibility, affordability, anonymity, convenience, escape immersion/dissociation, disinhibition, event frequency, associability, and simulation). Secondly, it examines whether Internet gambling is "doubly addictive" given research that suggests that the internet can be addictive itself. Finally, it overviews some of the main social concerns about the rise of Internet gambling before examining a few future trends in relation to *remote gambling* more generally.

BACKGROUND

Early prevalence studies of Internet gambling in the UK, Canada, and the U.S. have shown that Internet gambling is not a cause for concern at present in relation to *gambling addiction* (Griffiths, 2001; Ialomiteanu & Adlaf, 2001; Ladd & Petry, 2002). However, the social costs of Internet gambling is beginning to emerge. To date, knowledge and understanding of how the medium of the Internet affects gambling behavior is sparse. Globally speaking, proliferation of Internet access is still an emerging trend and it will take some time before the effects on gambling behavior surface. However, there is strong foundation to speculate on the potential hazards of Internet gambling. For instance, Griffiths (2003) has identified the use of virtual cash, unlimited accessibility, and the solitary nature of gambling on the Internet as potential risk factors for problem gambling development and *Internet gambling addiction*.

THE IMPACT OF TECHNOLOGY ON GAMBLING: SALIENT FACTORS

According to Griffiths (2003), there are a number of factors that make online activities like Internet gambling potentially seductive and/or addictive. Such factors include anonymity, convenience, escape, dissociation/immersion, accessibility, event frequency, interactivity, disinhibition, simulation, and associability. Outlined next are some of the main variables that may account for acquisition and maintenance of some online behaviors (adapted from Griffiths, 2003; Parke & Griffiths, 2005). It would also appear that virtual environments have the potential to provide short-term comfort, excitement, and/or distraction.

- **Accessibility:** Access to the Internet is now commonplace and widespread, and can be done easily from the home and/or the workplace. Given that prevalence of behaviors is strongly correlated with increased access to the activity, it is not surprising that the development of regular online use is increasing across the population. Fundamentally, increased accessibility of gambling activities enables the individual to rationalize involvement in the "risk-behavior" by removing previously restrictive barriers such as time constraints emanating from occupational and social commitments. With reductions in time required to select, place wagers and collect winnings, gambling as a habitual activity appears more viable, as social and occupational commitments are not necessarily compromised (Parke et al., 2005).

- **Affordability:** Given the wide accessibility of the Internet, it is now becoming cheaper and cheaper to use the online services on offer. Parke et al. (2005) concluded that the overall cost of gambling has been reduced significantly through technological developments rendering affordability less of a restrictive force when it comes to rationalizing involvement in the behavior. For example, the saturation of online gambling industry has lead to increased competition, and the consumer is benefiting from the ensuing promotional offers and discounts available on gambling outlay.

- **Anonymity:** The anonymity of the Internet allows users to privately engage in gambling without the fear of stigma. For activities such as gambling, this may be a positive benefit particularly when losing as no one will actually see the face of the loser. Parke et al. (2005) believe that anonymity, like increased accessibility, may reduce social barriers to engaging in gambling, particular skill-based gambling activities such as poker that are relatively complex and often possess tacit social etiquette.

- **Convenience:** Online behaviors will usually occur in the familiar and comfortable environment of home or the workplace thus reducing the feeling of risk and allowing even more adventurous behaviors that may or may not be potentially addictive. For the gambler, not having to move from their home or their workplace may be of great positive benefit.

- **Escape:** For some, the primary reinforcement to engage in Internet gambling will be the gratification they experience online. However, the experience of Internet gambling itself may be reinforced through a subjectively and/or objectively experienced "high." The pursuit of mood-modificating experiences is characteristic of addictions. The mood-modificating experience has the potential to provide an emotional or mental escape and further serves to reinforce the behavior. Excessive involvement in this escapist activity may lead to addiction.

- **Immersion/Dissociation:** The medium of the Internet can provide feelings of dissociation and immersion and may facilitate feelings of escape. Dissociation and immersion can involve lots of different types of feelings. This can include losing track of time, feeling like you're someone else, blacking out, not recalling how you got somewhere or what you did, and being in a trance like state. All of these feelings when gambling on the Internet may lead to longer play either because "time flies when you are having fun" or because the psychological feelings of being in an immersive or dissociative state are reinforcing.

- **Disinhibition:** This is clearly one of the Internet's key appeals as there is little doubt that the Internet makes people less inhibited (Joinson, 1998). Online users appear to open up more quickly online and reveal themselves emotionally much faster than in the off-line world. For the gambler, being in a disinhibited state may lead to more money being gambled, particularly if they are motivated to maintain their initial persona (e.g., as a skillful online poker player).

- **Event frequency:** The event frequency of any gambling activity (i.e., the number of opportunities to gamble in a given time period) is a structural characteristic designed and implemented by the gaming operator. A general rule of thumb is that the higher the event frequency, the more addictive the activity tends to be (Griffiths, 2003). When gambling on the Internet, the event frequency can be very rapid, particularly if the gambler is subscribed or visits several sites. Parke et al. (2005) concluded that the high event frequency in skill-based games like online poker provides increased motivation to participate in such gambling activities. Furthermore, because of technological developments, poker gamblers can participate in several games simultaneously. With reduced time limits for decision making in comparison to traditional poker games, games are also completed at a substantially faster rate.

- **Simulation:** Simulations provide an ideal way in which to learn about something and which tends not to have any of the possible negative consequences. However, Internet gambling simulations may have unthought of effects. Many online gambling sites have a *practice mode* format where a potential customer can place a pretend bet in order to see and practice the procedure of gambling on that site. Although this activity can not be regarded as actual gambling as there is no "real" money involved, it can be accessed by minors and possibly attract an underage player into gambling. Also, gambling in practice modes available within the gambling Web site, may build self-efficacy and potentially increase perceptions of control in determining gambling outcomes motivating participation in their "real cash" counterparts within the site (Parke et al., 2005; Sevigny, Cloutier, Pelletier, & Ladouceur, 2005).

- **Associability:** One of the consequences of technology and the Internet has been to reduce the fundamentally social nature of gambling to an activity that is essentially asocial. Those who experience problems are more likely to be those playing on their own (e.g., those playing to escape).

In addition to these factors, there are many other specific developments that look likely to facilitate uptake of remote gambling services including (1) sophisticated gaming software, (2) integrated e-cash systems (including multi-currency), (3) multi-lingual sites, (4) increased realism (e.g., "real" gambling via Webcams, player and dealer avatars), (5) live remote wagering (for both gambling alone and gambling with others), and (6) improving customer care systems.

INTERNET ADDICTION AND INTERNET GAMBLING ADDICTION

It has been alleged that social pathologies are beginning to surface in cyberspace (i.e., "technological addictions") (Griffiths, 1995). Technological addictions can be viewed as a subset of behavioral addictions and feature all the core components of addiction (e.g., salience, euphoria, tolerance, withdrawal, conflict, and relapse) (see Griffiths, 2005). Young (1999) claims Internet addiction is a broad term that covers a wide variety of behaviors and impulse control problems, and is categorized by five specific subtypes (cybersexual addiction, cyber-relationship addiction, net compulsions, information overload, and computer addiction). Griffiths (2000a) has argued that many of these excessive users are not "Internet addicts" but just use the Internet excessively as a medium to fuel other addictions. Put very simply, a gambling addict who engages in their chosen behavior online is not

addicted to the Internet. The Internet is just the place where they engage in the behavior.

However, in contrast to this, there are case study reports of individuals who appear to be addicted to the Internet itself (Griffiths, 2000b). These are usually people who use Internet chat rooms or play fantasy role playing games—activities that they would not engage in except on the Internet itself. These individuals to some extent are engaged in text-based virtual realities and take on other social personas and social identities as a way of making themselves feel good about themselves. In these cases, the Internet may provide an alternative reality to the user and allow them feelings of immersion and anonymity that may lead to an altered state of consciousness. This in itself may be highly psychologically and/or physiologically rewarding.

To a gambling addict, the Internet could potentially be a very dangerous medium. For instance, it has been speculated that structural characteristics of the software itself might promote addictive tendencies. Structural characteristics promote interactivity and to some extent define alternative realities to the user and allow them feelings of anonymity—features that may be very psychologically rewarding to such individuals. There is no doubt that Internet usage among the general population will continue to increase over the next few years and that if social pathologies exist then there is a need for further research. This area has particular relevance to the area of gambling in the shape of Internet gambling. Despite evidence that both gambling and the Internet can be potentially addictive, there is no evidence (to date) that Internet gambling is "doubly addictive" particularly as the Internet appears to be just a medium to engage in the behavior of choice. What the Internet may do is facilitate social gamblers who use the Internet (rather than Internet users per se) to gamble more excessively than they would have done off-line.

INTERNET GAMBLING: PSYCHOSOCIAL ISSUES

Technological advances in the form of Internet gambling are providing *convenience gambling*. Theoretically, people can gamble all day every day of the year. This will have implications for the social impact of Internet gambling. Griffiths and Parke (2002) previously outlined some of the main social issues concerning Internet gambling. These are briefly described next:

- **Protection of the vulnerable:** There are many groups of vulnerable individuals (e.g., adolescents, problem gamblers, drug/alcohol abusers, the learning impaired, etc.) who in off-line gambling would be prevented from gambling by responsible members of the gaming industry. However, Internet gambling sites provide little in the way of "gatekeeping." In cyberspace, how can you be sure that adolescents do not have access to Internet gambling by using a parent's credit card? How can you be sure that a person does not have access to Internet gambling while they are under the influence of alcohol or other intoxicating substances? How can you prevent a problem gambler who may have been barred from one Internet gambling site, simply clicking to the next Internet gambling link? These are all serious concerns that both regulatory authorities and Internet gambling service providers will have to take on board.

- **Electronic cash:** For most gamblers, it is very likely that the psychological value of electronic cash (e-cash) will be less than "real" cash (and similar to the use of chips or tokens in other gambling situations). This is well known by both those in commerce (i.e., people typically spend more on credit and debit cards because it is easier to spend money using plastic), and by the gaming industry. This is the reason that "chips" are used in casinos. In essence, chips "disguise" the money's true value (i.e., decrease the psychological value of the money to be gambled). Chips are often re-gambled without hesitation as the psychological value is much less than the real value. Evidence would seem to suggest that people will gamble more using e-cash than they would with real cash.

- **Increased odds of winning in practice modes:** One of the most common ways that gamblers can be facilitated to gamble online is when they try out games in the "demo," "practice," or "free play" mode. Recent research carried out by Sevigny et al. (2005) showed it was significantly more commonplace to win while "gambling" on the first few goes on a "demo" or "free play" game. They also reported that it was commonplace for gamblers to have extended winning streaks during prolonged periods while playing in the "demo" modes. Obviously, once gamblers start to play

for real with real money, the odds of winning are considerably reduced.

- **Unscrupulous operators:** Many concerns about the rise of Internet gambling concern unscrupulous practices operated by some Internet gambling sites. A major issue concerns the "trustworthiness" of the site itself. For instance, on a very basic trust level, how can an Internet gambler be sure they will receive any winnings from an unlicensed Internet casino operating out of Antigua or the Dominican Republic? There are, however, other issues of concern including the potentially unscrupulous practices of *embedding* and *circle jerks* and *"pop-ups"* (see Key Terms section).

Perhaps the most worrying concerns over Internet gambling is the way sites can collect other sorts of data about the gambler. Such data can tell commercial enterprises (such as those in the gambling industry) exactly how customers are spending their time in any given financial transaction (i.e., which games they are gambling on, for how long, and how much money they are spending etc.). Many consumers are unknowingly passing on information about themselves that raises serious questions about the gradual erosion of privacy. Customers are being profiled according to how they transact with service providers. Using very sophisticated software, gaming companies can tailor its service to the customer's known interests. When it comes to gambling, there is a very fine line between providing what the customer wants and exploitation. The gaming industry sell products in much the same way that any other business sells things. They are now in the business of brand marketing, direct marketing (via mail with personalized and customized offers), and introducing loyalty schemes (which create the illusion of awareness, recognition, and loyalty).

They know more about the gambler's playing behavior than the gamblers themselves. They are able to send the gambler offers, redemption vouchers, complimentary accounts, and so forth. The industry claims all of these things are introduced to enhance customer experience. However, more unscrupulous operators will be able to entice known problem gamblers back onto their premises with tailored freebies (such as the inducement of "free" bets in the case of Internet gambling). The introduction of Internet gambling has come at a price, and that price is an invasion of the gambler's privacy.

FUTURE TRENDS

The rise and challenges of Internet gambling cannot be seen in isolation particularly as there is ever-increasing multi-media integration between the Internet, mobile phones, and interactive television (i-TV). Griffiths (2003) claimed people are more likely to spend money in particular media. For instance, the Internet can be described as a "lean forward" medium. This means that the user (who is usually alone) takes an active role in determining what they do. Computers are better at displaying text than television and have a wider range of fine-tuning controls through the mouse and keyboards. This makes them more suitable for complex tasks such as obtaining insurance quotations or travel itineraries. In contrast, the television is a "lean back" medium where the viewer (often as part of a group) is more passive and seeks less control over what is going on. The television is better at displaying moving images than computers. This may have implications for the types of gambling done in particular media.

Furthermore, i-TV may also help in one other important area—trust. People appear to trust their television even though it is accessing the Internet in the same way as a computer. However, as previously argued, i-TV is a "lean back" service. If a person is relaxed sitting back on their sofa, it will make television the key to creating a true mass market for online commercial activity (including gambling). In addition, some i-TV services can be linked to actual television programs (such as betting on horse races). Browsing and buying by i-TV are still in its infancy but look set to expand significantly in the future.

CONCLUSION

Analysis of the technological components in gambling activities indicate that situational characteristics impact most on acquisition and that structural characteristics impact most on development and maintenance. Furthermore, the most important of these factors appears to be accessibility of the activity and event frequency. It is when these two characteristics combine that the greatest problems could occur in remote gambling. It can be argued that games that offer a fast, arousing span of play, frequent wins, and the opportunity for rapid replay are associated with problem gambling. There is no doubt that frequency of opportunities to gamble (i.e.,

event frequency) is a major contributory factor in the development of gambling problems (Griffiths, 1999). Addictions are essentially about rewards and the speed of rewards. Therefore, the more potential rewards there are, the more addictive an activity is likely to be. However, there is no precise frequency level of a gambling game at which people become addicted since addiction will be an integrated mix of factors in which frequency is just one factor in the overall equation.

Furthermore, Parke and Griffiths (2004) point out that the most effective way to control the effects of the idiosyncratic features of Internet gambling on development of problematic gambling behavior is to provide individuals with a scrutinized, regulated Internet gambling industry. All over the world, the recognition of the inability to prohibit Internet gambling successfully, has lead various jurisdictions to turn attention to developing harm minimization regulations.

REFERENCES

Griffiths, M. D. (2005). A "components" model of addiction within a biopsychosocial framework. *Journal of Substance Use, 10*, 191-197.

Griffiths, M. D. (2003). Internet gambling: Issues, concerns, and recommendations. *CyberPsychology and Behavior, 6*, 557-568.

Griffiths, M. D. (2001). Internet gambling: Preliminary results of the first UK prevalence study. *Journal of Gambling Issues, 5*. Retrieved November 13, 2005, from http://www.camh.net/egambling/issue5/research/griffiths_article.html

Griffiths, M. D. (2000a). Internet addiction—Time to be taken seriously? *Addiction Research, 8*, 413-418.

Griffiths, M. D. (2000b). Does Internet and computer "addiction" exist? Some case study evidence. *CyberPsychology and Behavior, 3*, 211-218.

Griffiths, M. D. (1999). Gambling technologies: Prospects for problem gambling. *Journal of Gambling Studies, 15*, 265-283.

Griffiths, M. D. (1995). Technological addictions. *Clinical Psychology Forum, 76*, 14-19.

Griffiths, M. D., & Parke, J. (2002). The social impact of Internet gambling. *Social Science Computer Review*, *20*, 312-320.

Ialomiteanu, A., & Adlaf, E. (2001). Internet gambling among Ontario adults. *Electronic Journal of Gambling Issues*, *5*. Retrieved November 13, 2005, from http://www.camh.net/gambling/issue5/research/ialomiteanu_adlaf_articale.html

Joinson, A. (1998). Causes and implications of disinhibited behavior on the Internet. In J. Gackenback (Ed.), *Psychology and the Internet: Intrapersonal, interpersonal, and transpersonal implications* (pp. 43-60). New York: Academic Press.

Ladd, G. T., & Petry, N. M. (2002). Disordered gambling among university-based medical and dental patients: A focus on Internet gambling. *Psychology of Addictive Behaviours*, *16*, 76-79.

Parke, A., & Griffiths, M. D. (2005, July). *Behavioural effects of increased accessibility of remote access gambling in the United Kingdom: A grounded theory theoretical framework*. Paper presented at the 6th European Association for the Study of Gambling Conference, Malmo, Sweden.

Parke, A., & Griffiths, M. D. (2004). Why Internet gambling prohibition will ultimately fail. *Gaming Law Review*, *8*, 297-301.

Sevigny, S., Cloutier, M., Pelletier, M., & Ladouceur, R. (2005). Internet gambling: Misleading payout rates during the "demo" period. *Computers in Human Behavior*, *21*, 153-158.

Young, K. (1999). Internet addiction: Evaluation and treatment. *Student British Medical Journal*, *7*, 351-352.

KEY TERMS

Circle Jerks and "Pop-Ups": Circle jerks are telescoping windows. If someone online accesses a particular type of site and try to get out of it, another box offering a similar type of service will usually "pop up." Many people find that they cannot get out of the never-ending loop of sites except by shutting down their computer. Obviously, those sites that use "circle jerks" hope that a person will be tempted to access a service they are offering while their site is on the screen. This is also related to the continual "pop ups" that appear while surfing the Internet, offering users free bets in online casinos and tempting those who may not have thought about online gambling before. Pop-ups such as these can also be a big temptation for a recovering problem gambler.

Embedding: A common practice referring to the "embedding" of certain words on an Internet gambling site's Web page through the use of "meta-tags." A meta-tag is a command hidden in the Web page to help search engines categorize sites (i.e., telling the search engine how they want the site indexed). Some Internet gambling sites appear to have used the word "compulsive gambling" embedded in their Webpage. In essence, what such unscrupulous sites are saying is "index my casino site in with the other compulsive gambling sites" so people will "hit" this site when they are looking for other information related to compulsive gambling. People looking for help with a gambling problem will get these sites popping up in front of them. This is a particularly unscrupulous practice that at the moment is perfectly legal.

Gambling Addiction: Refers to an addiction to gambling whereby the individual's life is taken over by gambling. Gambling becomes the single most important activity in that person's life that they often do to the neglect of everything else in their life. They build up tolerance over time, use the activity as a mood modifying behavior, and suffer withdrawal symptoms if they are unable to gamble.

Internet Gambling: This is any form of gambling that is done on the Internet and covers many different types. This includes gambling in online casinos (on simulated slot machines, roulette wheels, etc.), gambling in betting exchanges (where gamblers make private bets with other punters and are paired up by the service provider), gambling on lotteries (such as playing the national lotto game via the Internet, or use of an electronic scratchcard), and gambling at online poker sites (where punters play in real time against other real competitors). Also known as online gambling.

Internet Gambling Addiction: An online gambling addiction (see gambling addiction). Here gamblers use the convenient medium of the Internet to facilitate their gambling addiction. These people are not Internet addicts as they are not addicted to the Internet. It is the gambling that they are addicted to.

Online Gambling: See Internet gambling.

Practice Mode: This is "free play" facility offered by numerous online gambling service providers that give players the opportunity to play for free and "practice" the game without spending any money. These are also known as "demonstration" ("demo") or "free play" modes.

Remote Gambling: This is any form of gambling that is provided remotely by gaming operators. This is includes Internet gambling, interactive television gambling, and cell phone gambling.

Internet Measurements

Artur Ziviani

National Laboratory for Scientific Computing (LNCC), Brazil

INTRODUCTION

In the mid-90s, the Internet has started its metamorphosis from a tool restricted to the scientific community into a crucial component of the modern information society. The evolution in the last 15 years from 2,000 to 180,000 active BGP (border gateway protocol) entries as of March 2006 (Smith, 2006) witnesses this metamorphosis and is an indication on how complex Internet has become. Possibly, the most significant consequence of the huge success of the Internet is that the common goal and collaborative spirit that used to guide its players no longer holds because of the large diversity we find in today's Internet. Users, commercial access providers, governments, telecommunication operators, and content providers usually have opposite interests in using the network, commonly leading to a situation where they co-exist in a tussle (Clark, Wroclawski, Sollins, & Braden, 2002). For instance, large network operators need to be interconnected to obtain and offer universal connectivity, even if they are often fierce competitors. As a result, the heterogeneity and fully distributed administration of the Internet, allied to its extensive geographic coverage and to its dynamism in applications and network traffic, impose great challenges to the characterization of the structure and behavior of the Internet as a whole (Floyd & Paxson, 2001; Spring, Wetherall, & Anderson, 2003a).

The seminal work by Paxson (1997) has proposed a measurement-based approach to characterize the workload dynamics of Internet traffic. Afterwards, other measurement-based works have characterized the self-similar nature of network traffic in local networks (Leland, Taqqu, Willinger, & Wilson, 1994), in wide-area networks (Paxson & Floyd, 1995), and for WWW traffic (Crovella & Bestavros, 1997). Taking into account the concepts of long-range dependence and self-similarity has significantly influenced Internet traffic modeling over the last decade (Karagiannis, Molle, & Faloutsos, 2004). Since the mid 90s, many other measurement-based approaches have been proposed to estimate and characterize several different network parameters contributing to render the Internet more observable (Chen, 2001). The introduction of the NIMI (national Internet measurement infrastructure) platform by Paxson, Mahdavi, Adams, and Mathis (1998) has been decisive in this process as it has hosted many of the novel measurement-based tools so far as 2002, when alternative platforms started to show up.

BACKGROUND

The basic operation of the Internet has been conceived from the very beginning with the explicit goal to minimize the complexity at its core and leave the control and adaptation at the edges (Clark, 1988). This design principle has allowed the Internet expansion to its current dimensions, but has also limited the capacity of monitoring the network dynamic behavior (Habib, Khan, & Bhargava, 2004; Mao, 2005). Today, however, there is a need to monitor the network so that we can deal with its increasing complexity, represented by a huge growth in extension, diversity, transmission speeds, and traffic volume.

Network management commonly provides ways to monitor the status of individual nodes. SNMP (simple network management protocol), defined by Case, Fedor, Schoffstall, and Davin (1990), allows a centralized network manager to request data from components of the network (Figure 1). This manager can also be alerted when some pre-defined events happened. The manager is limited to gather simple and individual measurements from each manageable equipment. Although routers are the ideal points to perform traffic measurements, they are in general not equipped for detailed monitoring because router vendors avoid the addition of measurement capacity fearing an eventual

Figure 1. Illustration of SNMP operation

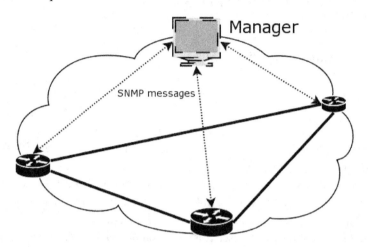

negative impact on packet forwarding performance. Further, administrative privilege is needed to directly collect management data from routers. Moreover, current Internet is composed of a large number of interconnected networks administrated by different organizations that are often competitors and, as a consequence, many domains are uncooperative with external performance measurements.

As a result of the problems with the common methods, several indirect methods are being proposed. The working group IP performance metrics (IPPM) of the IETF (Internet engineering task force) is dedicated to defining relevant metrics for evaluating the quality, performance, and reliability of network services (Uijterwaal & Zekauskas, 2003). There is another working group of IETF called packet sampling (PSAMP) dedicated to the definition of standards to perform packet sampling on network devices (Bierman & Quittek, 2001). Their challenge is to define methods that are simple enough to be ubiquitously implemented without degrading significantly the packet forwarding rates of the current network devices.

INTERNET MEASUREMENTS

Basically, measurement-based approaches use either passive or actives techniques (Barford & Sommers, 2004) to collect measurement data. Passive measurement can provide detailed data about the network

points where the monitoring is carried out and about the traffic in transit in these points (Jaiswal, Iannaccone, Diot, Kurose, & Towsley, 2004). The same process can happen simultaneously in different network vantage points. Nevertheless, a high-performance passive monitoring system needs specialized equipment. An example of passive network measurement points is shown in Figure 2.

In contrast with passive measurements, active measurements obtain in general few information about isolated points within the network, but they can provide a representative view of the path between two points in the network. In Figure 2, active measurement probes sent from node A to node B provide information about the path between these nodes. In this example, it is assumed that the two end nodes are somehow synchronized. From the standpoint of passive measurements, only one of the passive monitoring points is able to register the passage of the probe packets from the active experiment. In performing active measurements, it is important to consider if the additional traffic introduces a bias on the obtained results or not. Hybrid scenarios may also be envisaged to better estimate a certain network characteristic (Ishibashi, Kanazawa, Aida, & Ishii, 2004). Besides being active or passive, measurement-based methods may be differentiated by other features as well such as performed continuously or on demand, direct or indirect, unidirectional or bidirectional, composed of one or multiple data gathering points or probe measurement launching points. Since the early days of

Figure 2. Illustration of passive and active measurements

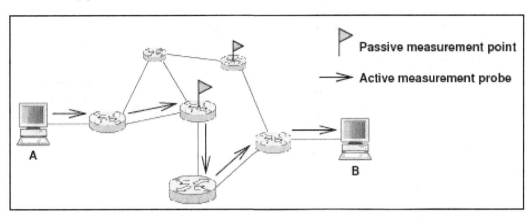

Internet measurement activity, traffic characterization and classification has been a major target. Literature in Internet measurements often makes use of analogies with animals to classify network flows (Brownlee, 2005; Soule, Salamatian, Emilion, Taft, & Papagiannaki, 2004). Considering the flow size, large flows, like file transfers, are called *elephants*. On the other hand, small flows with low volume of data, like Web requests, are called *mice*. The elephant flows may be two to three orders of magnitude larger than the mice flows (Estan & Varghese, 2002; Papagiannaki, Taft, & Diot, 2004). The fundamental difference between elephants and mice refers to the fact that a TCP session characterized as an elephant is affected by the slow start phase of the TCP congestion control mechanism. As a consequence, the behavior of an elephant flow is conditioned by the TCP congestion control. In contrast, mice flows are not controlled by this mechanism because they are totally transmitted *before* TCP is able to apply its congestion control. As an alternative to the flow classification in terms of size, one can also classify flows in terms of their lifetime as suggested by Brownlee and Claffy (2002). In one hand, flows may be identified as very fast, with a duration of less than 2 s. These fast flows, called *dragonflies*, represent at least 45% of the flows in the observed links. Close to 98% of the observed flows are less than 15 minutes long. In the other hand, the remaining 2% of flows reach durations of hours or even days. These long duration flows are called *tortoises*. Although the tortoise flows represent only 2% of the total number of flows, they may carry 40% to 50% of the total volume of traffic. It is also shown by Brownlee and Claffy (2002) that the flow size and

lifetime are independent dimensions, suggesting that both are important to the proper understanding of traffic dynamics and network behavior.

Several measurement-based approaches have been developed in the last decade seeking insight on causes and effects of network issues on Internet dynamics and, as a consequence, on applications and users (Varghese & Estan, 2004). Anderson, Crovella, and Diot (2004) map mainstream measurement-based approaches developed so far onto three large categories: (i) Internet structure and infrastructure, (ii) traffic and network monitoring, and (iii) application properties.

Measurement-based research on Internet structure and infrastructure comprises characterization and inference of Internet topology at different levels—autonomous system (AS) (Dimitropoulos, Krioukov, & Riley, 2005) or router (Spring, Mahajan, Wetherall, & Anderson, 2004) level, for instance. This also includes tools and methods to perform delay, loss, and bandwidth estimation (Mao, 2005; Prasad, Dovrolis, Murray, & Claffy, 2003), as well as approaches to understand how all these properties change over time. Also fall into this category the developments of measurement-based approaches to characterize the BGP interdomain system (Griffin & Premore, 2001), estimate network delay distance (Francis et al., 2001; Ng & Zhang, 2002), or geolocate Internet hosts (Gueye, Ziviani, Crovella, & Fdida, 2004; Padmanabhan & Subramanian, 2001; Ziviani, Fdida, Rezende, & Duarte, 2005), for instance. In traffic and network monitoring, research activities deal with estimating the statistical properties of network traffic to create a basis for traffic matrix estimation (Medina, Taft, Salamatian, Bhattacharyya,

& Diot, 2002; Soule et al., 2005), network traffic prediction for capacity planning (Papagiannaki, Taft, Zhang, & Diot, 2003), and network anomaly detection (Lakhina, Crovella, & Diot, 2004; Roughan, Griffin, Mao, Greenberg, & Freeman, 2004) to support network management and security activities. Finally, the third category, application properties, covers application workload characterization and how to properly map application properties onto network properties (Baset & Schulzrinne, 2004; Moore & Papagiannaki, 2005), thus allowing one to understand how network services may influence the performance perceived by end users of multimedia applications (Ziviani, Wolfinger, Rezende, Duarte, & Fdida, 2005).

FUTURE TRENDS

Despite of the advancements in the Internet measurement area in recent years, the gathering, sampling, anonymization, interpretation, and modeling of empirical Internet data still pose challenging problems that open promising perspectives for novel research activity in the field (Crovella & Krishnamurthy, 2006). A fundamental challenge is that several aspects of the Internet are ever changing. For example, http traffic has grown from zero in 1995 to more than 80% of the total network traffic in the majority of links in 2000. Currently, the proportion of http traffic seems to be decreasing in the majority of links while there is an increasing presence of P2P traffic (Fraleigh et al., 2003). This ever-changing nature of Internet makes it a *moving target* for measurement-based techniques and tools, calling for the development of adaptive tools and prediction methods.

The global scale of the current Internet also imposes great challenges for measurement initiatives, because quite often the composition of network traffic and its behavior are dependent on location and characteristics of particular groups of users. As a consequence, observed results in a single location may not be representative of the Internet as a whole. Therefore, measurements need to be performed from multiple points to obtain a more representative view of the big picture. Recent testbeds like PlanetLab (Peterson, Anderson, Culler, & Roscoe, 2002) and Scriptroute (Spring, Wetherall, & Anderson, 2003b) provide distributed infrastructure that is being applied to carry out large-scale measurement experiments. The potentially huge amount of network data that can be collected calls for better sampling methods and, moreover, the adoption of data mining techniques to find unexpected correlations and derive insights from empirical data. Measurement-based approaches are also gaining momentum in mobile networking as measured data is increasingly being used to characterize real-world behavior of wireless devices and to drive the design of new protocols for wireless networks, in particular with a cross-layer approach.

CONCLUSION

Internet measurement has taken off in the last decade and is receiving increasing research interest. Making the Internet more observable may be the first step in the direction of having a more efficient monitoring of the network. Nevertheless, just collecting huge volumes of measurement data is not efficient without the development of advanced tools to adequately process such a volume of data, extract useful information in order to drive new measurement-based protocols and to provide a basis to the design of more efficient applications and services. Therefore, Internet measurement emerges as a crucial research domain in modern computer networking as its findings and outcomes directly impact other more traditional networking areas, such as network design and capacity planning, traffic engineering, quality of service provisioning, and network management.

REFERENCES

Anderson, T., Crovella, M., & Diot, C. (2004, November). *Internet measurement: Past, present, and future.* Retrieved from http://www.ics.uci.edu/~xwy/ics243c/lec-notes/measurements-survey.pdf

Barford, P., & Sommers, J. (2004, September). Comparing probe-based and router-based packet-loss measurement. *IEEE Internet Computing, 8*(5), 50-56.

Baset, S. A., & Schulzrinne, H. (2004). *An analysis of the Skype peer-to-peer Internet telephony protocol* (Technical Report No. CUCS-039-04). Columbia University.

Bierman, A., & Quittek, J. (2001). *Packet sampling (PSAMP)*. Retrieved from http://www.ietf.org/html. charters/psamp-charter.html

Brownlee, N. (2005, April). Some observations of Internet stream lifetimes. In *Proceedings of the Passive and Active Measurement workshop (PAM)*. Boston.

Brownlee, N., & Claffy, K. C. (2002, October). Understanding Internet traffic streams: dragonflies and tortoises. *IEEE Communications Magazine, 40*(10), 110-117.

Case, J. D., Fedor, M., Schoffstall, M. L., & Davin, J. R. (1990, May). Simple network management protocol (SNMP). *RFC 1157*.

Chen, T. M. (2001, January). Increasing the observability of Internet behavior. *Communications of the ACM, 44*(1), 93-98.

Clark, D. D., (1988, August). The design philosophy of the DARPA Internet protocols. In *Proceedings of the ACM SIGCOMM*. Stanford, CA, USA.

Clark, D. D., Wroclawski, J., Sollins, K. R., & Braden, R. (2002, August). Tussle in cyberspace: Defining tomorrow's Internet. In *Proceedings of the ACM SIGCOMM*. Pittsburgh, PA.

Crovella, M. E., & Bestavros, A. (1997, December). Self-similarity in world wide Web traffic: Evidence and possible causes. *IEEE/ACM Transactions on Networking, 5*(6), 835-846.

Crovella, M. E., & Krishnamurthy, B. (2006, June). *Internet measurement: Infrastructure, traffic, and applications*. John Wiley & Sons, West Sussex, England.

Dimitropoulos, X., Krioukov, D., & Riley, G. (2005, April). Revisiting Internet AS-level topology discovery. In *Proceedings of the Passive and Active Measurement Workshop (PAM)*. Boston.

Estan, C., & Varghese, G. (2002, August). New directions in traffic measurement and accounting. In *Proceedings of the ACM SIGCOMM*. Pittsburgh, PA, USA.

Floyd, S., & Paxson, V. (2001, August). Difficulties in simulating the Internet. *IEEE/ACM Transactions on Networking, 9*(4), 392-403.

Fraleigh, C., Moon, S., Lyles, B., Cotton, C., Khan, M., Moll, D., Rockell, R., Seely, T., & Diot, C. (2003, November). Packet-level traffic measurements from the SprintIP backbone. *IEEE Network, 17*(6), 6-16.

Francis, P., Jamin, S., Jin, C., Jin, Y., Raz, D., Shavitt, Y., Zhang, L. (2001, October). IDMaps: A global Internet host distance estimation service. *IEEE/ACM Transactions on Networking, 9*(5), 525-540.

Griffin, T. G., & Premore, B. J. (2001, November). An experimental analysis of BGP convergence time. In *Proceedings of IEEE International Conference on Network Protocols (ICNP)*. Riverside, CA, USA.

Gueye, B., Ziviani, A., Crovella, M., & Fdida, S. (2004, October). Constraint-based geolocation of Internet hosts. In *Proceedings of the ACM/SIGCOMM Internet Measurement Conference (IMC)*. Taormina, Italy.

Habib, A., Khan, M., & Bhargava, B. (2004, February). Edge-to-edge measurement-based distributed network monitoring. *Computer Networks, 44*(2), 211-233.

Ishibashi, K., Kanazawa, T., Aida, M., & Ishii, H. (2004, June). Active/passive combination-type performance measurement method using change-of-measure framework. *Computer Communications, 27*(9), 868-879.

Jaiswal, S., Iannaccone, G., Diot, C., Kurose, J., & Towsley, D. (2004, March). Inferring TCP connection characteristics through passive measurements. In *Proceedings of the IEEE INFOCOM*. Hong Kong.

Karagiannis, T., Molle, M., & Faloutsos, M. (2004, September). Long-range dependence: Ten years of Internet traffic modeling. *IEEE Internet Computing, 8*(5), 57-64.

Lakhina, A., Crovella, M., & Diot, C. (2004, August). Diagnosing network-wide traffic anomalies. In *Proceedings of the ACM SIGCOMM*. Portland, OR, USA.

Leland, W., Taqqu, M., Willinger, W., & Wilson, D. (1994, February). On the self-similar nature of ethernet traffic. *IEEE/ACM Transactions on Networking, 2*(1), 1-15.

Mao, G. (2005, February). A real-time loss performance monitoring scheme. *Computer Communications, 28*(2), 150-161.

Medina, A., Taft, N., Salamatian, K., Bhattacharyya, S., & Diot, C. (2002, August). Traffic matrix estimation: Existing techniques and new directions. In *Proceedings of the ACM SIGCOMM*. Pittsburgh, PA, USA.

Moore, A., & Papagiannaki, K. (2005, April). Toward the accurate identification of network applications. In *Proceedings of the Passive and Active Measurement Workshop (PAM)*. Boston, MA, USA.

Ng, T. S. E., & Zhang, H. (2002, June). Predicting Internet network distance with coordinates-based approaches. In *Proceedings of the IEEE INFOCOM*. New York, NY, USA.

Padmanabhan, V. N., & Subramanian, L. (2001, August). An investigation of geographic mapping techniques for Internet hosts. In *Proceedings of the ACM SIGCOMM*. San Diego, CA, USA.

Papagiannaki, K., Taft, N., Zhang, Z., & Diot, C. (2003, March). Long-term forecasting of Internet backbone traffic: Observations and initial models. In *Proceedings of the IEEE INFOCOM*. San Francisco.

Papagiannaki, K., Taft, N., & Diot, C. (2004, March). Impact of flow dynamics on traffic engineering design principles. In *Proceedings of the IEEE INFOCOM*. Hong Kong.

Paxson, V., & Floyd, S. (1995, June). Wide area traffic: The failure of Poisson modeling. *IEEE/ACM Transactions on Networking, 3*(3), 226-244.

Paxson, V. (1997). *Measurement and analysis of end-to-end Internet dynamics*. PhD Thesis, University of California-Berkeley.

Paxson, V., Mahdavi, J., Adams, A., & Mathis, M. (1998, August). *An Architecture for Large-Scale Internet Measurement*. IEEE Comunications, 36(8), 48-54.

Peterson, L., Anderson, T., Culler, D., & Roscoe, T. (2002, October). A blueprint for introducing disruptive technology into the Internet. In *Proceedings of the 1st Workshop on Hot Topics in Networks (HOTNETS-I)*. Princeton, NJ, USA.

Prasad, R., Dovrolis, C., Murray, M., & Claffy, K. C. (2003, November). Bandwidth estimation: Metrics, measurement techniques, and tools. *IEEE Network, 17*(6), 27-35.

Roughan, M., Griffin, T., Mao, M., Greenberg, A., & Freeman, B. (2004, August). IP forwarding anomalies and improving their detection using multiple data sources. In *Proceedings of the ACM SIGCOMM Workshop on Network Troubleshooting*. Portland, OR, USA.

Smith, P. (2006, March). *CIDR report*. Retrieved from http://www.cidr-report.org

Soule, A., Lakhina, A., Taft, N., Papagiannaki, K., Salamatian, K., Nucci, A., Crovella, M., & Dior, C. (2005, June). Traffic matrices: Balancing measurements, inference, and modeling. In *Proceedings of the ACM SIGMETRICS*. Banff, Canada.

Soule, A., Salamatian, K., Emilion, R., Taft, N., & Papagiannaki, K. (2004, June). Flow classification by histograms or how to go on safari in the Internet. In *Proceedings of the ACM SIGMETRICS*. New York, NY, USA.

Spring, N., Mahajan, R., Wetherall, D., & Anderson, T. (2004, February). Measuring ISP topologies with Rocketfuel. *IEEE/ACM Transactions on Networking, 12*(1), 2-16.

Spring, N., Wetherall, D., & Anderson, T. (2003a, November). Reverse engineering the Internet. In *Proceedings of the 2nd Workshop on Hot Topics in Networks (HOTNETS-II)*. Cambridge, MA, USA.

Spring, N., Wetherall, D., & Anderson, T. (2003b, March). Scriproute: A public Internet measurement facility. In *Proceedings of the USENIX Symposium on Internet Technologies and Systems (USITS)*. Seattle, WA, USA.

Uijterwaal, H., & Zekauskas, M. (2003). *IP performance metrics (IPPM)*. Retrieved from http://www.ietf.org/html.charters/ippm-charter.html

Varghese, G., & Estan, C. (2004, January). The measurement manifesto. *ACM Computer Communication Review, 34*(1), 9-14.

Ziviani, A., Fdida, S., Rezende, J. F. de, & Duarte, O. C. M. B. (2005, March). Improving the accuracy of measurement-based geographic location of Internet hosts. *Computer Networks, 47*(4), 503-523.

Ziviani, A., Wolfinger, B. E., Rezende, J. F. de, Duarte, O. C. M. B., & Fdida, S. (2005, May). Joint adoption of QoS schemes for MPEG streams. *Multimedia Tools and Applications, 26*(1), 59-80.

KEY TERMS

Active Measurement: An active measurement sends probe packets and the result of the journey of this packets through the network is monitored to estimate network characteristics.

Autonomous System: An autonomous system (AS) corresponds to a routing domain under the control of a single administrative entity (such as a university or a business enterprise, for instance).

BGP: The border gateway protocol (BGP) is a protocol for exchanging routing information between autonomous systems.

Long-Range Dependence: Long-range dependence (LRD) characterizes process that keep statistically significant correlations across large time scales.

P2P Traffic: P2P traffic refers to network traffic generated by distributed applications (i.e. Gnutella, KaZaa, or Skype to name a few) that organize the communication among its participants using the peer-to-peer (P2P) communication model in contrast with the classic client-server model.

Passive Measurement: Passive measurement refers to the process of monitoring network traffic without injecting new traffic or affecting the existing one.

Probe Packet: A packet used in an active measurement experiment to collect knowledge on a given network parameter of interest.

Self-Similarity: A process is said to be self-similar if its behavior is roughly the same across different spacial or time scales.

Traffic Matrix: A traffic matrix (TM) represents the volume of traffic between all possible pairs of sources and destinations in a given IP domain.

IP Multicasting

Robert R. Chodorek

The AGH University of Science and Technology, Poland

INTRODUCTION

The origins of IP multicasting go back to 1986. However, multicasting in its current form was introduced only in 1989. During 20 years of IP multicasting, the service has been evolving continuously—new multicast transport protocols have been designed, new group management protocols have been developed, and new transport protocols and multicast applications have appeared. Nowadays, IP multicast is a mature solution, and concepts and protocols designed for multicasting are also used in non-multicast services.

Introduction of IP multicasting requires changes in hosts and all the Internet infrastructure, including routers and links. Changes in hosts are simple and currently all operating systems support IP multicasting. Changes in the network infrastructure are proceeding slowly because many technical and organisational problems must be solved.

In 1992, the multicast-enabled test network *mbone* (*multicast back*bone) was created. The *mbone* network was established to connect multicast capable subnetworks across the non-multicast Internet. In the nineties, *mbone* was used for transmission of a live coverage from several events (meetings, conferences), radio and TV transmission, conferencing systems, etc. At the turn of the 20th and 21st centuries, the next generation of *mbone* network was build—so-called *m6bone*—based on IPv6. Currently, numbers of IP multicast-enabled networks continue to expand rapidly, but a global multicast Internet is still a thing of the future.

BACKGROUND

Multicast is a many-to-many (M-to-N) transmission scheme, where M senders disseminate information to N receivers. Typically protocols support one-to-many (1-to-N) multicasting (a single transmitter with multiple receivers), and M-to-N transmissions can be emulated using techniques of cloning.

From the end user's point of view, a multicast transmission is an equivalent of N simultaneous unicast (1-to-1) transmissions. The main difference between 1-to-N multicasting and N unicast (1-to-1) transmissions lies in number of packets transmitted for each data block sent. In the case of N simultaneous unicast transmissions, single data block has to be send N times, in N packets sent in the same instant to each destination. A multicast transmitter sends only one packet, and multicast routers provide, if necessary, packet replication. As a result, 1-to-N multicast transmission reduces amount of data transmitted via single path (from the sender to any receiver) to amount of data, which would be transmitted through the same path if the only one unicast transmission is carried out.

The main advantages of multicasting are more effective utilisation of existing infrastructure (links, etc.), reduction of sender performance requirements, and reduction of router load. Application of a multicast transmission allows the introduction on a large scale of a wide spectrum of services, in which the same information is simultaneously transmitted to many recipients. A lot of distribution systems are enabled, in practice, due to IP multicast technology—especially systems, which consist of large and very large (thousands to millions) groups of users. For instance, bandwidth requirements of live Internet Protocol television (IPTV) to a million recipients will be equal to a target bit rate of streaming media when multicast service is used. The same IPTV transmission using unicast service requires bandwidth of the order of terabytes per second.

IP MULTICAST NETWORKING

IP multicast is, in principle, similar to IP broadcast. However, there are some features of multicast transmission, which don't take place in data broadcasting:

- The receiver has to be interested in receiving the disseminated information—there is no compulsory reception.
- The receiver has to demonstrate initiative—the receiver interested in reception has to join the proper multicast group.
- Each receiver, anywhere and anytime, can join the multicast group or leave it.
- Joining and leaving multicast groups does not have an effect on disseminated content—in particular, omitted data is not retransmitted automatically after a new receiver joins the multicast group (sometimes it could be retransmitted on demand).

Multicast transmissions can be acknowledged or unacknowledged, reliable or real-time. Multicast transmissions are addressed to the group of receivers—disseminated data is received only by members of the multicast group. The sender can be (but doesn't have to be) a member of a group. Each host can be a member of one or many multicast groups.

MODELS OF IP MULTICAST DELIVERY

Three models of multicast transmission occur in modern IP networks. There are any-source multicast, source-filtered multicast, and source-specific multicast. Any-source multicast (ASM) and source-filtered multicast (SFM) are typical many-to-many transmission schemes, where *N* senders disseminate information to *M* receivers and any host can send data to the given multicast group. However, in ASM, disseminated information will be always delivered to all members of the group and in the case of SFM, the receiver can filter sources of the received data. Source-specific multicast (SSM) (Holbrook & Cain, 2006) is a one-to-many transmission scheme where receivers receive information from only one source. The SFM and SSM transmission schemes allow one to avoid unintended (and, usually, unauthorised) transmissions. The SSM scheme is intended for data dissemination to large multicast groups (e.g., Internet TV).

MULTICAST ADDRESSING IN IP VERSION 4 AND 6

A multicast group is identified by a multicast addresses, which belong to an IP address space separate from unicast addressing. The IPv4 multicast address space ranges from 224.0.0.0 to 239.255.255.255. IPv6 multicast addresses (Hinden & Deering, 2006) start from prefixes equal to FF (the first octet of IPv6 multicast address contains all ones). Multicast addresses of IPv6 protocol are more flexible and this improves scalability of multicast routing, when compared to IPv4. Each IPv6 multicast address has a strictly defined scope (e.g., link-local scope).

Multicast address may be permanent or transient. The permanent ones are assigned to well-known network services (e.g., IPv4 multicast address 224.2.127.254 is assigned to announce multicast sessions realized by SAP protocols). Transient addresses are typically used by user's applications or services.

MANAGING IP MULTICASTING

Multicast can have both local and global scope. If the scope is local, multicast is used among hosts on a single network in the same way as the "traditional" IP unicast transmission. In this case, no multicast capable routers are necessary on the network. If the scope is global, IP datagrams are multicasted along branches of the optimal delivery tree, from the sender to all receivers belonging to the given multicast group. The sender is a root of the delivery tree, and the receivers are leaves. Any branch of the multicast delivery tree can exist only if it has at least one leaf node. As a result, a change in the group membership may cause the rebuilding of an existing delivery tree.

IP multicasting has a hierarchical management system, based on two mechanisms:

- Local mechanism based on local signalisation
- Inter-router mechanism based on multicast routing

The local mechanism works between a receiver and its nearest (link-local) router. The IP router uses it to discover the presence of multicast receivers in their subnet. The IP host uses it, both:

- To inform the network adapter (network card) that multicast datagrams, addressed to a given group, should be accepted (this function is also used when no multicast capable router is on the network)
- To report multicast group membership (current status of the membership or its change in the case of joining or leaving group) to the nearest multicast router

The local mechanism is based on signalisation via Internet Group Management Protocol (IGMP) in the case of IPv4 or Multicast Listener Discovery (MLD) protocol in the case of IPv6. Older versions of IGMP and MLD protocols were designed for ASM transmission model only. The newest versions of IGMP and MLD (i.e., IGMP version 3 (IGMPv3) (Cain, Deering, Kouvelas, Fenner, & Thyagarajan, 2002) and MLD version 2 (MLDv2) (Vida & Costa, 2004), allow the receiver to filter sources of disseminated information and to use also SFM and SSM transmission. SSM can be treated like the particular case of SFM.

Management of multicast groups on the level of the inter-router mechanism consists largely of (re)building the optimal delivery tree. There are two main types of multicast delivery tree:

- Shortest path tree
- Shared tree

The shortest path trees are formed from a set of shortest paths from the source to all receivers interested in reception of multicast data. As a result, the multicast group has separate delivery trees for each source. The shared tree is a single delivery tree per multicast group, shared among all senders and all receivers. Disseminated data is transmitted from the source to the core of the tree (core router or rendezvous point) and then it is distributed to all receivers. Usage of a shared tree allows improved scalability when there are many active sources in one multicast group.

Functionality of the inter-router mechanism is provided by multicast routing protocols. In respect to assumed receiver density and type of delivery tree, multicast routing protocols can be classified as:

- Dense mode protocols, working with the assumption that receivers are densely located in a given domain and therefore most receivers (or all receivers) are interested in the reception of a given multicast transmission
- Sparse mode protocols, working with the assumption that receivers are sparsely distributed throughout Internet and therefore a small number of receivers (or no receiver) is interested in the reception of a given multicast transmission
- Dense mode protocols (e.g., DVMRP, PIM-DM) are suitable for relatively small networks. "Small network" doesn't mean "small area network," but networks with a limited number of nodes. Usage of these protocols in large networks is disadvantageous, because of flooding (which can lead to congestion) and the weak convergence of routing algorithms in the case of a large number of nodes. Thus, in large networks, sparse mode protocols (e.g., PIM-SM) are used.

IP MULTICAST SUPPORT IN UNDERLYING NETWORKS

Effectiveness of IP multicasting strictly depends on underlying network technologies. Modern networks consist of homogeneous segments (subnets), belonging to one of three main classes:

- Point-to-point networks
- Broadcast networks
- Non-broadcast multi-access networks

The point-to-point networks connect a single pair of end nodes via a single link. IP multicast support in point-to-point networks consists only in the delivery of a multicast datagram (i.e., IP datagram with a multicast destination address) to the other endpoint.

The broadcast network connects several end nodes, and a single frame can reach all destination points. One important feature of broadcast networks (e.g., Ethernet or WLAN 802.11) is their capability of one-to-all transmission. In broadcast networks, realisation of multicast transmission is simple and effective. Usage of multicast addressing of a frame allows all receivers belonging to the multicast group to receive the frame.

The non-broadcast multi-access (NBMA) network (e.g., ATM, Frame Relay) connects several end nodes, but a single physical frame is not able to reach all destination points (although, in some technologies, one frame can reach strictly defined multiple destination points). Because of the absence of broadcast transmission, full implementation of IP multicast requires specialized network services provided by dedicated servers. For instance, in the ATM network, a Multicast Address Resolution Server (MARS) is required when IP multicast is realized using *Classical IP over ATM* service.

MULTICAST TRANSPORT PROTOCOLS

Transport protocols able to take full advantage of IP multicasting are called "multicast transport protocols." Multicast transport protocols must deal with the same problems of end-to-end behaviour as the unicast one—packet losses or damage, reordering of transmitted data, network congestion, receiver's buffer overflow, real-time assurance (if needed), etc. Moreover, multicast transport protocols have to deal with the problem unmet in the case of the unicast one—scalability to large multicast groups. Scalability can be improved using negative acknowledgements instead of positive and applying feedback suppression in receivers and/or feedback aggregation in routers.

Nowadays, the three most representative multicast transport protocols are Real-time Transport Protocol (RTP) (Schulzrinne, Casner, Frederick, & Jacobson, 2003) and User Datagram Protocol (UDP), both for real-time transmission, and Pragmatic General Multicast (PGM) (Speakman et al., 2001) for reliable data transfer.

MULTICAST SESSION MANAGEMENT

A multicast session is established for a given task (e.g., for entertainment purposes or for workgroup's discussion about important questions in large projects). The session can be public or private, encrypted or not encrypted, established on a predetermined time (defined by start and stop time, for example, from 10.30 to 11.15) or infinite time (for permanent sessions, for example, TV broadcasting). Each session utilizes a specified media (e.g., audio, video) transmitted by a suitable transport protocol.

A user who wants to participate in a given multicast session must receive information about the session. This information is described by SDP protocols and can be obtained via SAP, SIP, RTSP, HTTP (WWW), or SMTP (e-mail) protocols (Quinn & Almeroth, 2001).

Session Description Protocols (SDP) give a common description of the multicast session. The Session Announcement Protocol (SAP) is used to propagate advertisement information about multicast sessions. Information about a session should be announced to a large group of receivers in the given scope. Session Initiation Protocol (SIP) is used to initiate a session for explicitly defined users. SIP protocol is commonly used not only for multicast transmission, but also for typical point-to-point services, like IP telephony. Real-time Streaming Protocol (RTSP) is used to control real-time transmission of one or more multimedia streams. RTSP allows users to fully control playback or recording of multimedia stream.

MULTICAST APPLICATIONS

Multicast applications and services use the basic feature of IP multicasting—the ability to simultaneously distribute the same portion of data from multiple sources to multiple receivers (Quinn et al., 2001). Multicast applications and services differ from the unicast one—they are group-oriented and cannot be built according to traditional, user-oriented philosophy.

In respect to their usability, multicast applications and services can be classified into three main groups:

- Real-time multimedia distribution systems
- Teleconferencing systems
- Data dissemination systems

The first two groups are intended for real-time multimedia transmission. Distribution systems, for example, Internet radio or Internet TV, are built usually according to DAVIC specifications. Teleconferencing systems are usually built according to Multiparty Multimedia Session Control (MMUSIC) specification from IETF or H.323 Recommendation from ITU.

The last group is intended mainly for reliable data transfer (including the non-real-time, reliable multimedia distribution). Reliable multicast transmission allows the user to build effective applications for database replication and update, collaborative tools, software upgrade services, Web cache update, and update multihome and multisite Web services.

Although multicast data transfer is still dominated by TCP-based unicast services, multicast technologies are deeply rooted in real-time multimedia transmission. In the case of multimedia, solutions intended for multicasting are also successfully implemented in non-multicast (from their nature) services, as in Video on Demand or IP telephony.

FUTURE TRENDS

IP multicasting is still evolving. Currently, intensive researches in IP multicasting are carried out in many areas of IP multicasting.

MPLS technology gives opportunities to build optimal multicast delivery tree using more sophisticated methods of traffic engineering than provided by current multicast routing protocols (Ooms et al., 2002). Inter-domain multicast routing protocols can enable global multicast routing (Savola, 2006). Interdomain protocols should be massively scalable to support all domains in the Internet.

Research is ongoing into various aspects of massively scalable multicast transport protocols (Luby, Watson, & Vicisano, 2002). Issues include elimination (or, at least, significant reduction) of feedbacks sent to the sender, support of very large multicast groups (in the order of thousands or millions receivers), and new methods of error correction (e.g., using Forward Error Correction) (Watson, Luby, & Vicisano, 2007).

New methods of congestion control (e.g., receiver-driven systems, both for real-time (Chodorek, 2003; Li & Liu, 2003) and reliable (Luby & Goyal, 2004) transmission) also are being developed. Security (Weis, Gross, & Ignjatic, 2002) and QoS (Bless & Wehrle, 2004; Lei, Zhili, & Cruickshank, 2005) issues for IP multicasting, as well as supporting mobility for multicast users (especially through Mobile IP (Garyfalos & Almeroth, 2005)) are now the subject of extensive research.

CONCLUSION

In 1989, RFC 1112 enhanced the best-effort IP service by introducing a new networking paradigm—multicast. Since then, IP multicast becomes a mature solution and many different applications and services have been evolving toward multicasting.

This article describes the most important issues in widely understood IP multicasting, which cover all aspects of this area—from support of underlying networks to utilisation of functionality of IP multicasting in applications. A significant part of the article is devoted to network layer issues—the core of IP multicasting. The critical issues discussed in this article constitute important resource for researchers, developers, service providers, students, and potential users.

REFERENCES

Bless, R., & Wehrle, K. (2004). IP multicast in Differentiated Services (DS) networks. RFC 3754.

Cain, B., Deering, S., Kouvelas, I., Fenner, B., & Thyagarajan, A. (2002). Internet Group Management Protocol, Version 3. RFC 3376.

Chodorek, R. R. (2003). ECN-capable multicast multimedia delivery. *HSNMC'2003*, Lecture Notes in Computer Science, 2720, 62-72.

Garyfalos, A., & Almeroth, K. C. (2005). A flexible overlay architecture for mobile IPv6 multicast. *IEEE Journal on Selected Areas in Communications, 23*(11), 2194-2205.

Hinden, R., & Deering, S. (2006). IP Version 6 Addressing Architecture. RFC 4291.

Holbrook, H., & Cain, B. (2006). Source-specific multicast for IP. RFC 4607.

Lei, L., Zhili, S., & Cruickshank, H. (2005). Relative QoS optimization for multiparty online gaming in DiffServ networks. *IEEE Communications Magazine, 43*(5), 75-83.

Li, B., & Liu, J. (2003). Multirate video multicast over the Internet: An overview. *IEEE Network, 17*(1), 24-29.

Luby, M., & Goyal, V. (2004). Wave and Equation Based Rate Control (WEBRC) Building Block. RFC 3738.

Luby, M., Watson, M., & Vicisano, L. (2007). Asynchronous Layered Coding (ALC) protocol instantiation. Internet-Draft, draft draft-ietf-rmt-pi-alc-revised-04.

Ooms, D., Sales, B., Livens, W., Acharya, A., Griffoul, F., & Ansari, F. (2002). Overview of IP multicast in a Multi-Protocol Label Switching (MPLS) environment. RFC 3353.

Quinn, B., & Almeroth, K. (2001). IP multicast applications: challenges and solutions. RFC 3170.

Savola, P. (2006). Overview of the Internet multicast routing architecture. Internet-Draft, draft-ietf-mboned-routingarch-07.

Schulzrinne, H., Casner, S., Frederick, R., & Jacobson, V. (2003). RTP: A transport protocol for real-time applications. RFC 3550.

Speakman, T., Crowcroft, J., Gemmell, J., Farinacci, D., Lin, S., Leshchiner, D., Luby, M., Montgomery, T., Rizzo, L., Tweedly, A., Bhaskar, N., Edmonstone, R., Sumanasekera, R., & Vicisano, L. (2001). PGM reliable transport protocol specification. RFC 3208.

Vida, R., & Costa, L. (2004). Multicast Listener Discovery Version 2 (MLDv2) for IPv6. RFC 3810.

Watson, M., Luby, M., & Vicisano, L. (2004). Forward Error Correction (FEC) building block. Internet-Draft, draft-ietf-rmt-fec-bb-revised-07.

Weis, B., Gross, G., & Ignjatic, D. (2007). Multicast extensions to the security architecture for the Internet protocol. Internet-Draft, draft-ietf-msec-ipsec-extensions-05.

KEY TERMS

Group Management Protocol: The bottom level of multicast management system hierarchy, responsible for joining and leaving multicast group. Group management protocols operate between receiver ("leaf" of the delivery tree) and nearest multicast router. Nowadays, there are two group management protocols, IGMP for IPv4 and MLD for IPv6.

Multicast: A many-to-many (M-to-N) transmission scheme, where M senders disseminate information to N receivers. Multicast transmissions are not broadcasting to all possible receivers, but they are addressed to the group of receivers--disseminated data is received only by members of the multicast group.

Multicast Address: A single IP address that identifies a group of receivers. Multicast addresses belong to an IP address space separate from other (unicast, anycast, or broadcast) addressing.

Multicast Backbone: Experimental and temporary global multicast network intended to interconnect "multicast islands" over the current (non-multicast) Internet. The first multicast backbone, *mbone*, network was based on IPv4 (IP version 4). The next, *m6bone*, is based on IPv6.

Multicast Delivery Tree: A tree structure, described multicast packets route from the sender to receivers. The sender is a root of the tree, and receivers are leaves.

Multicast Group: A group of zero, one or more receivers, which are interested in receiving the same information sent to the common IP destination address.

Multicast Router: An IP router, which supports IP multicasting. Multicast routers forward IP packets (both unicast and multicast) and provide necessary replication of multicast packets to a set of destinations. To route multicast traffic, additional multicast routing table, separate from the unicast one, is used.

Multicast Routing Protocol: Routing protocol for multicast delivery. Multicast routing protocols function as the upper level of multicast management system hierarchy, responsible for (re)building multicast delivery tree. The best known multicast routing protocols are PIM-SM (a sparse mode protocol, working with the assumption that receivers are sparsely distributed in a given domain) and PIM-DM (a dense mode protocol, working with the assumption that receivers are densely located in a given domain).

Multicast Transport Protocol: Reliable or real-time multicast-enabled transport protocol; all protocol's mechanisms are multicast-oriented. Examples of multicast transport protocols are RTP for real-time multimedia delivery and PGM for reliable data transmission. Note: multicast service is inaccessible when the most popular transport protocol, transmission control protocol (TCP), is used.

Source-Filtered Multicast Service: A model of IP multicast delivery. Current models allow receiver to receive and accept data originating from any sender (any-source multicast, ASM), a specific set of senders (source-filtered multicast, SFM), or one specific sender (source-specific multicast, SSM).

IP Multimedia Subsystem (IMS) for Emerging All-IP Networks

Muhammad Sher
Technical University of Berlin, Germany

Fabricio Carvalho de Gouveia
Technical University of Berlin, Germany

Thomas Magedanz
Technical University of Berlin, Germany

INTRODUCTION AND BACKGROUND

Today the traditional telecommunication technology is declining because of popularity and increasing demand of voice over IP (VoIP) due to the reason that deployment, maintenance, and operation of data networks based on IP infrastructure are less costly than the voice networks. Consequently, it is straightforward to think relaying all types of communications on data networks rather than maintaining in parallel two network technologies. On the other hand, today we see increasing demand of *integrated multimedia services*, bringing together Internet applications with telecommunications. In prospect of these global trends, the mobile communications world has defined an all-IP network vision within the evolution of cellular systems, which integrates cellular networks and Internet. This is the IP multimedia system (IMS) (3GPP, TS 23.228, 2005), namely overlay architecture for provisioning of multimedia services such as VoIP and videoconferencing on top of globally emerging 3G broadband packet networks.

In the face of the IP network vision, namely the use of fixed and mobile IP networks for both data and voice/multimedia information looking for the target service control architecture. The IMS is an approach to provide overlay service delivery platform (SDP) (Magedanz & Sher, 2006) architecture for IP networks, entirely built on Internet protocols defined by the Internet engineering task force (IETF), which have been extended on request of 3GPP (Third Generation Partnership Project) to support telecommunications

requirements such as security, accountability, quality of service, etc. Mobile operators today face the problem that mobile users can gain access to the Internet and make use of Internet services such as *instant messaging, presence*, chat, content download, etc. On the other hand, the operators define a minimum SDP architecture for providing QoS, security, and charging for IP-based services, while providing maximum flexibility for the realization of value added and content services.

EVOLUTION TOWARD CONVERGED NETWORKS

The communication era is passing through the evolutionary phase of fixed-mobile convergence (FMC) and *voice-data integration* as shown in Figure 1, and IMS is considered a common platform for FMC granting convergence and compatibility between fixed/mobile networks, multimedia, and converged services support, and providing key community service enablers such as group management, *presence*, IM/PoC, and generic VoIP/MMoIP support (Magedanz, 2005).

In face of such convergence, the need for universal service delivery platforms (SDPs) supporting integrated services emerged. This means that SDP should, in principle, enable the rapid and uniform programming and provision of seamless multimedia services on top of any network environment. There is no doubt, however, that today two main trends are of pivotal importance for SDPs design, namely the support of mobile users and the support of (mobile) multi media data services.

Figure 1. Toward fixed-mobile-internet convergence

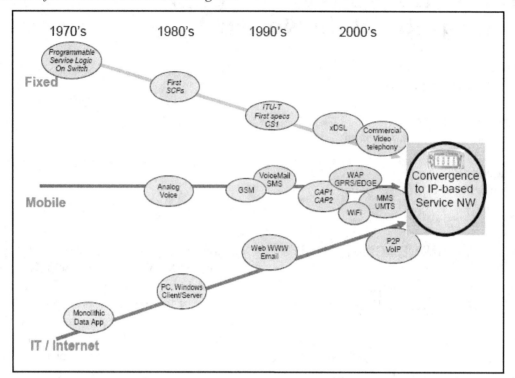

IMS MOTIVATION AND STANDARDIZATION

IMS is designed to provide fancy and attractive Internet services everywhere using mobile networks based on IP protocols and standards with emphasis on QoS, dynamic charging, and integration of different services and roaming facility on reasonable service charges. The IMS provides easy and efficient ways to integrate different services, even from third parties, and enables the *seamless integration* of legacy services and is designed for consistent interactions with circuit switched domains. The IMS manages event-oriented quality of service policies (e.g., use of VoIP and HTTP in a single session—VoIP has QoS, HTTP is best effort). These systems (IMSs) also have event-oriented charging mechanism policies--means change specific events on the appropriate level. If two events need the same IP resources we may charge them differentially for the same user in the same session (Poikselkae, Mayer, Khartabil, & Niemi, 2004). These characteristics make IMS the future technology in a comprehensive service and application-oriented network.

The IMS has been standardized since the beginning of this century within Release 5 and extended in Release 6 within 3GPP and 3GPP2 (Third Generation Partnership Project 2) focus to UMTS/CDMA2000 data packet networks. The Release 5 standards have been driven by the vision to define the IMS for providing multimedia services including VoIP. The IMS is supposed to be standardized access-independent IP-based architecture that interworks with existing voice and data networks for fixed (e.g., PSTN, ISDN) Internet and mobile users (e.g., GSM, CDMA). The IMS architecture makes it possible to establish peer-to-peer IP communications with all types of clients with quality of services and complete service delivery functionalities.

IMS Release 6 is fixing the shortcomings in Release 5 and also contains novel features like *presence*, messaging, conferencing, group managements and local services. Release 6 has optimized the IMS to provide the envisaged IMS killer application push-to-talk (over cellular). The IMS has been planned for deployment in 3G wireless networks around 2006. It also provides additional security features like confidentiality protection of *SIP* messages, usage of public key infrastructure, and subscriber certificates.

In addition, since 2004 ETSI *TISPAN* (Telecommunication and Internet converged Services and Protocols for Advanced Networking) is looking at service

Figure 2. IMS high level functional diagram

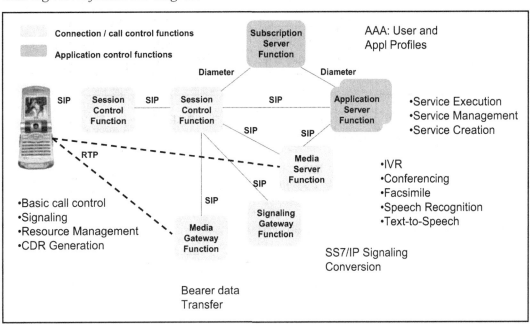

infrastructures for fixed-mobile convergence and next generation networks, which extends the IMS to make it applicable on top of various access networks (i.e., WLANs and particular for fixed Internet (DSL)). The recent IMS Release 7 is a joint cooperation work of 3GPP and TISPAN addressing all IP networks infrastructure.

IMS ARCHITECTURE AND KEY COMPONENTS

The IMS defines service provision architecture and it can be considered as the next generation service delivery platform framework. It consists of modular design with open interfaces and enables the flexibility for providing multimedia services over IP technology. IMS does not standardize specific services but uses standard service enablers (e.g., *presence* inherently supports multimedia over IP and VoIP) (Magedanz et al., 2006). In IMS architecture, SIP protocol (IETF, RFC 3261, 2002) is used as the standard signaling protocol that establishes controls, modifies, and terminates voice, video, and messaging sessions between two or more participants. The related signaling servers in the architecture are referred to as call state control functions (CSCFs) and distinguished by their specific functionalities. It is important to note that an IMS compliant end user system has to provide

the necessary IMS protocol support, namely SIP, and the service related media codecs for the multimedia applications in addition to the basic connectivity support (e.g., GPRS, WLAN, etc.). Figure 2 displays a generic IP-based IMS functional diagram.

The functionality related to authentication, authorization, and accounting (AAA) within the IMS is based on the IETF *diameter* protocol (IETF, RFC 3588, 2003) and is implemented in the home subscriber system (HSS), CSCFs, and various other IMS components in order to allow charging functionality within the IMS. Instead of developing the protocol from scratch, diameter is based on the *remote authentication dial in user service* (RADIUS), which has previously been used to provide AAA services for dial-up and terminal server across environments. The other protocol, which is important for multimedia contents, is *real-time transport protocol* (RTP), which provides end-to-end delivery for real-time data. It also contains end-to-end delivery services like payload-type (codec) identification, sequence numbering, time stamping, and delivering monitoring for real-time data. RTP provides QoS monitoring using the RTP control protocol (RTCP), which conveys information about media session participants.

The IMS entities and key functionalities can be classified in six categories--session management and routing family (CSCFs), databases (HSS, SLF), interworking elements (BGCF, MGCF etc.), serv-

Figure 3. IMS components and architecture

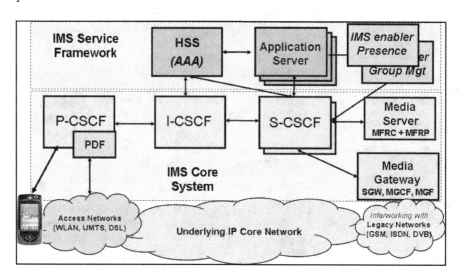

ices (application server, MRCF, MRFP), support entities (THIG, SEG, PDF) and charging (Poik-selkae et al., 2004). Now we describe the most important components and parts of IMS architecture:

- **Proxy Call State Control Function (P-CSCF):** It is the first contact point within IP multimedia core network subsystem. Its address was discovered by UEs following packet data protocol (PDP) context activation. The P-CSCF behaves like a proxy accepting requests and services them internally or forwards them. It performs functions like authorizing the bearer resources for the appropriate QoS level, emergency calls, monitoring, header (de)compression, and identification of I-CSCF.

- **Interrogating Call State Control Function (I-CSCF):** It is the contact point within an operator's network for all connections destined to a subscriber of that network operator, or a roaming subscriber currently located within that network operator's service area. There may be multiple I-CSCFs within an operator's network. I-CSCF performs functions like assigning an S-CSCF to a user performing SIP registration/charging and resource utilization (i.e., generation of charging data records (CDRs)/acting as a topology hiding inter-working gateway (THIG)).

- **Serving Call State Control Function (S-CSCF):** It performs session control services for the end-

point and maintains session state as needed by network operator for support of services. Within an operator's network, different S-CSCFs may have different functionality. The important functions performed by S-CSCF includes user registration/ interaction with services platforms for the support of services. The S-CSCF decides whether an application server is required to receive information related to incoming SIP session request to ensure appropriate service handling. The decision at the S-CSCF is based on filter information received from the HSS. This filter information is stored and conveyed on a per application server basis for each user.

- **Home Subscriber Server:** HSS is equivalent to HLR (home location register) in 2G systems but is extended with two diameter-based reference points. It is the master database of an IMS that stores IMS user profiles including individual filtering information, user status information, and application server profiles.

- **Application Servers:** It provides service platform in IMS environment. It does not address how multimedia/value added applications are programmed but only well defined signalling and administration interfaces (ISC and Sh), and SIP and Diameter protocols are supported. This enable developers to use almost any programming paradigm within a SIP AS such as legacy

Figure 4. IMS as multimedia service enabler

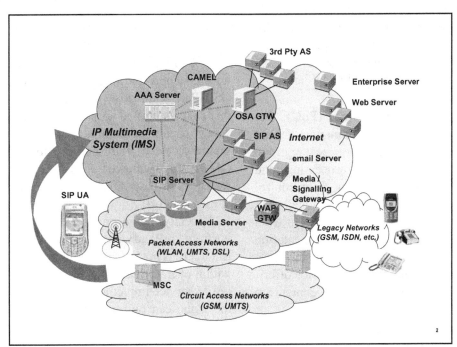

intelligent network servers (i.e., CAMEL support environments), OSA/Parlay servers/gateways, or any proven VoIP SIP programming paradigm like SIP Servlets, call programming language (CPL) and common gateway interface (CGI) scripts, etc. The SIP AS is triggered by the S-CSCF, which redirects certain sessions to the SIP AS based on the downloaded filter criteria or by requesting filter information from HSS in a user-based paradigm. The SIP AS itself comprises filter rules to decide which of the applications deployed on the server should be selected for handling the session. During execution of service logic it is also possible for SIP AS to communicate with HSS to get additional information about a subscriber or to be notified about changes in subscriber profile.

- **Media Processing:** The media resource function (MRF) can be split up into media resource function controller (MRFC) and media resource function processor (MRFP). It provides media stream processing resources like media mixing, media announcements, media analysis, and media transcoding as well speech (Poikselkae et al., 2004). The other three components are border gateway control function (BGCF), media gate control function (MGCF) and Media gate (MG), which perform bearer interworking between RTP/IP and bearers used in the legacy networks.

- **IMS End User System:** It is important to note that an IMS compliant end user system has to provide the necessary IMS protocol support, namely SIP, and service related media codecs for multimedia applications in addition to the basic connectivity support (e.g., GPRS, WLAN, etc.).

IMS FEATURES AND SERVICES

The IMS is designed to provide number of key capabilities required to enable new IP services via mobile and fixed networks. The important key functionalities, which enable new mobile IP services, are:

- Multimedia session negotiation and management
- Quality of service management
- Mobility management
- Service execution, control, and interaction

The IMS services are assumed to be addressed by open mobile alliance (OMA), which was created by

WAP Forum in June 2002 with open mobile architecture objective and consists of more than ten mobile industries. The OMA SIP-based service enablers are specified on top of IMS as common platform (e.g., presence and group management etc.) as shown in Figure 4.

The important services provided by IMS are:

- **Push-to-talk (PTT) over cellular (PoC):** The PoC is *1-to-n* half-duplex communication and the key PTT functions include presence, group list management, PTT media processing, and PTT application logic (including floor control handling). These are bundled tightly together in the vendor-specific PoC deployments, but from 2006 onwards, IMS-based PTT implementation will be deployed. The idea is to enable the reuse of PTT core ingredients for other service offers, such as presence-based services. PoC content are short, instructional, and immediate.
- **Multimedia conferencing and group chat:** It is real time communication providing functionality about reservation and scheduling, document sharing and whiteboard facility, additional group or 1-to-1 chat, and instant messaging availability.
- **Click to dial:** When a user clicks on the screen button, IMS will negotiate and eventually set up automatically a voice session with one or more other users.
- **Dynamic push service:** Allow users to receive disable information based on many factors (e.g., preference, presence, geographic location, device type, and capabilities).

OPEN ISSUES AND FUTURE TRENDS

The new multimedia services are a demanding combination of service capability features. Most likely upcoming services will also rely on features like presence, group-list management, additional logic, and other features on operator network (e.g., location, SMS, MMS). It is obvious that service capability features must be reused for scalability and capital expenses reasons. The future trends are:

- How to manage and orchestrate services
- How to create stringent services that bundle service capability features

- How to operate the network for services in a secure way

As mentioned in 3GPP specifications, the adoption of OSA/Parlay (parlay open service architecture) concepts and technologies can contribute a lot. OSA/Parlay already provides an industry standard that enables unified access with gateway character to service capability features of operators' network. Even secure access by third parties can be handled by the OSA/Parlay framework. This framework may control resources by assuming there is secure access for third parties network.

Recently, there are many IMS pre-products originating from VoIP and wireless telecommunications market. But, there is not yet any commercial IMS deployment within operator networks. However, first push to talk (PTT) service implementations mushrooming around the globe can be regarded as the first big trials for IMS technologies. However, there are still many open issues within IMS architecture and the 3GPP IMS standardization is ongoing, particular in the field of applying the IMS on top of different access networks (i.e., WLAN, WIMAX, and DSL) and IMS evolution toward an all-IP network.

CONCLUSION

The IP multimedia subsystem (IMS) defined by the 3rd Generation Partnership Projects (3GPP) and multimedia domain (MMD) by 3GPP2 is today considered the global service delivery platform (SDP) standard for providing multimedia applications in next generation networks (NGN). IMS defines an overlay service architecture that merges the paradigms and technologies of the Internet with the cellular and fixed telecommunication worlds. Its architecture enables the efficient provision of an open set of potentially highly integrated multimedia services, combining Web browsing, e-mail, instant messaging, presence, VoIP, video conferencing, application sharing, telephony, unified messaging, multimedia content delivery, etc. on top of possibly different network technologies. As such IMS enables various business models for providing seamless business and consumer multimedia applications. IMS platform also supports interworking with Internet and legacy networks.

In this article, we have provided background, motivation, standards, services, and architecture of IP multimedia subsystem (IMS), which is considered the next generation service platform toward all-IP networks. We have also tried to highlight the future trends and open issues in IMS.

REFERENCES

3GPP, Third Generation Partnership Project (3GPP). www.3gpp.org.

3GPP (2005), IP Multimedia Subsystems (IMS); Stage 2, TS 23.228, Version 7.2.0, *Third Generation Partnership Project*. Retrieved December 15, 2005, from www.3gpp.org

3GPP2, Third Generation Partnership Project 2 (3GPP2). www.3gpp2.org.

Calhoun, P., Loughney, J., Guttman, E., Zorn, G., & Arkko, J. (2003). RFC 3588 Diameter Base Protocol. *Internet Engineering Task Force (IETF)*. Retrieved November 28, 2005, from http://www.ietf.org/rfc3588.txt?number=3588

ETSI TISPAN, Telecommunications and Internet converged Services and Protocols for Advanced Networking. http://portal.etsi.org/tispan/TISPAN_ToR.asp.

IETF, RFC 3261 (2002), Rosenberg, J., Schulzrinne, H., Camarillo, G., Johnston, A., Peterson, J., Sparks, R., Handley, M., & Schooler, E., SIP: Session Initiation Protocol.

IETF, RFC 3588 (2003), Calhoun, P., Loughney, J., Guttman, E., Zorn, G., & Arkko, J., Diameter Base Protocol.

Magedanz, T. (2005). Tutorial IEEE ISCC. *IEEE Symposium on Computer and Communications*.

Magedanz, T., & Sher, M. (2006). IT-based open service delivery platforms for mobile networks--From CAMEL to the IP multimedia system. In P. Bellavista & A. Corradi (Eds.), *Mobile middleware* (pp. 1001-1037), Taylor & Francis CRC Press, Florida, USA.

OMA, Open Mobile Alliance, http://www.openmobilealliance.org

OSA/Parlay "Parlay Open Service Architecture", http://www.parlay.org/en/index.asp

Poikselkae, M., Mayer, G., Khartabil, H., & Niemi, A. (2004). *The IMS: IP multimedia concepts and services in the mobile domain*. West Sussex: John Willey & Sons Ltd.

Rosenberg, J., Schulzrinne, H., Camarillo, G., Johnston, A., Peterson, J., Sparks, R., Handley, M., & Schooler, E. (2002). RFC 3261 SIP: Session Initiation Protocol. *Internet Engineering Task Force (IETF)*. Retrieved November 26, 2005, from http://www.ietf.org/rfc/rfc3261.txt?number=3261

Schulzrinne, H., Casner, S., Frederick, R., & Jacobson, V. (2003). RFC 3550 A Transport Protocol for Real-Time Applications. *Internet Engineering Task Force (IETF)*. Retrieved November 28, 2005, from http://www.ietf.org/rfc/rfc3588.txt?number=3588

KEY TERMS

Fixed-Mobile Convergence (FMC): FMC is the merger of fixed and mobile communication paradigms and IMS is considered as common platform for FMC granting convergence and compatibility between fixed/mobile networks, multimedia and converged services support, and providing key community service enablers such as group management, presence, IM/PoC and generic VoIP /MMoIP support.

IP Multimedia Subsystem (IMS): The IP multimedia subsystem (IMS) is standardised by 3GPP & 3GPP2 as next generation network (NGN) architecture to provide mobile and fixed multimedia services. It is based on VoIP, SIP, and IP protocols on the recommendation on 3rd Generation Partnership Project on top of GPRS/UMTS.

Next Generation Network (NGN): A next generation network (NGN) as defined by ITU-T is a packet-based network able to provide services including telecommunication services and able to make use of multiple broadband, QoS-enabled transport technologies and in which service-related functions are independent from underlying transport-related technologies. It offers unrestricted access by users to different service providers. It supports generalized mobility, which will allow consistent and ubiquitous provision of services to users.

Open System Architecture (OSA): The open system architecture (OSA) describes the service architecture for 3rd generation mobile telecommunications network or universal mobile telecommunication networks (UMTS). OSA Standards are being developed and published by as part of 3rd Generation Partnership Project (3GPP) and ETSI. The OSA APIs are developed by parlay group and is called OSA/Parlay service framework.

Service Delivery Platform (SDP): SDP is a foundation for the creation, deployment, provision, control, charging, and management of telecommunication services provided to the end users. The SDPs represent the programming interface enabling programming of the underlying network capabilities and therefore are primarily based in the usage of information technologies (ITs). SDP may apply to many technologies including VoIP, IPTV, HSD (high speed data), Mobile Telephony, Online Gaming, etc.

Third Generation Partnership (3GPP): The 3rd Generation Partnership Project (3GPP) is a collaboration agreement between mobile industries that was established in December 1998 to extend the GSM specifications toward Third Generation (3G) mobile system specifications within the scope of the ITU's IMT-2000 project. 3GPP specifications are generally known as the UMTS system.

Voice Over IP (VoIP): Voice over Internet protocol (VoIP) is the technology for sending voice calls on IP-based network instead of using conventional voice telecommunication networks. VoIP protocol is used to carry voice signals over IP networks.

The IPv6 Protocol

Christos Bouras
Research Academic Computer Technology Institute and University of Patras, Greece

Apostolos Gkamas
Research Academic Computer Technology Institute and University of Patras, Greece

Dimitris Primpas
Research Academic Computer Technology Institute and University of Patras, Greece

Kostas Stamos
Research Academic Computer Technology Institute and University of Patras, Greece

This article provides a description of the IPv6 protocol. It briefly covers the reasons that make IPv6 a necessary upgrade, describes the most important methods for transitioning networks, applications, and hosts from IPv4 to IPv6, and the possibilities that IPv6 opens up. It finally also examines the current status of IPv6 deployment and vendor, protocol, and application support.

INTRODUCTION

In order to address the limited address space of **IPv4** and other concerns regarding its age and ability to support future needs for the Internet, the Internet Engineering Task Force (**IETF**) has developed a suite of protocols and standards known as IP version 6 (IPv6).

The principal problem with IPv4 was the fact that its 32-bit address space allows only about four billion unique addresses, which are not enough to accommodate the rapid growth of the Internet. Moreover, because of inefficient allocation and parts of the address space that cannot be used for unique address allocation, the IPv4 address space is even smaller, and techniques such as NAT, which, however, break the Internet's end-to-end architecture, have to be used. IPv6 solves this problem by providing 128 bits of address space which provides a huge amount of addresses available for every person or device in the world in the foreseeable future.

The design of IPv6 (Deering, 1998) is intentionally targeted for minimal impact on upper- and lower-layer protocols by avoiding the random addition of new features. More than simply increasing the address space, IPv6 offers improvements like built-in security support, plug and play support, no checksum at the IP header, and more flexibility and extensibility than IPv4. IPv6 also facilitates efficient renumbering of sites by explicitly supporting multiple addresses on an interface. The widespread adoption of the new Internet Protocol will fuel innovation and make possible the creation of many new networking applications. It will also allow the replacement of the NAT solutions that have been implemented today in order to work around the lack of IPv4 addresses. NAT introduces a number of problems to network applications that need knowledge of the IP address of the host machine or want to take advantage of Quality of Service mechanisms like VoIP implementations.

BACKGROUND

The proposal for a next generation Internet protocol was first discussed within IETF in 1993, while the final proposal for the IPv6 protocol was defined in 1995. Although in the following years a lot of the parameters of the IPv6 technology were defined, refined, analyzed, and reviewed, the fact that IPv4 is still the dominant protocol well within the 21st century has led many people to either regard IPv6 as a technology that will never gain wide adoption, or has taught them to be cautious in trying to guess when it will start overshadowing IPv4.

However, IPv6 usage is gaining significant support and wide adoption in countries such as China and Japan, where IPv4 address allocation has been scarce because of historical factors (Wang, 2005).

In addition, IPv6 support in most networking vendor equipment, operating systems, and applications has been elevated to a production-quality level, with several years of experimentation, research, and improvement of the product's IPv6 support.

IPV6 DESCRIPTION

The IPv6 protocol has a different header than IPv4, removing some fields and adding others. It also introduces the notion of optional extension headers that are responsible for handling situations that are not always common, in order to spare the forwarding equipment in the network (routers) from complicated processing that would be in most cases unnecessary.

IPv6 has a number of benefits over IPv4, which are explained in more detail.

Enormously Larger Address Space

The number of IP addresses available with IPv6 is huge (2^{128}, which is about 3.4×10^{38} addresses) and will not be exhausted in the foreseeable future. The address space of IPv6 is so enormous that, as a thought experiment, one could allocate 670,000 trillion addresses for each square millimeter of the earth's surface. The large address space of IPv6 opens up new possibilities for easier Internet connectivity to all kinds of devices. Practically, it means that any electronic device, from computers to cell phones, automobiles, and household appliances, can have its own address. As a result, it is no longer required to come up with complex solutions to bypass **NAT** (network access translation) mechanisms which will no longer be necessary. The IPv6 approach of assigning a unique routable address to any device that is connected to the Internet restores the original simplicity of the Internet peer-to-peer architecture. It also makes possible the hassle-free emergence of new

Figure 1. IPv6 header

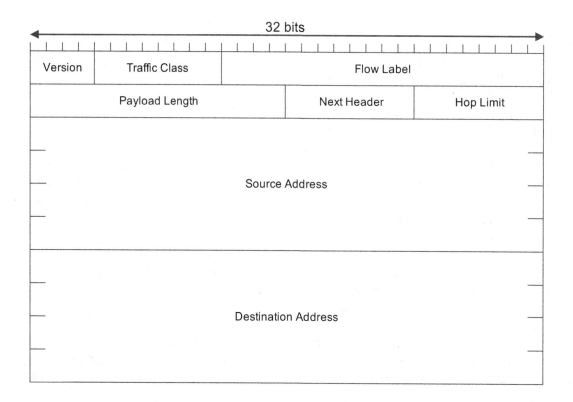

applications, whose deployment is complicated and hindered by NAT's lack of peer-to-peer connectivity.

Furthermore, because of the abundance of IPv6 addresses, their assignment can be made in a hierarchical manner that was not possible for IPv4, and therefore increase the efficiency of routing equipment (Hinden, 2003).

Simplified Packet Header for Routing Efficiency and Performance

IPv6 also improves the efficiency of the Internet by simplifying and optimizing the IP header (Deering, 1998). Unlike IPv4, the IPv6 header has a fixed size, and the 14 header fields of IPv4 have been reduced to eight for IPv6. Simplified packet header information allows for more straightforward and efficient routing of Internet packets. More unusual header fields are handled in a more efficient way through IPv6 header extensions, which combine the benefit of accommodating new features and the efficiency of a fixed and quickly processible standard header. The use of IPv6 also results, as mentioned, in shorter routing tables because most Internet service providers (ISP) can now receive address space in adjacent blocks.

Deeper Hierarchy and Policies for Network Architecture Flexibility

At the enterprise level it is also possible to rapidly define a complete addressing plan (Router Renumbering) by constructing step by step: (1) the prefixes on different router interfaces from the access router, (2) the prefix of the operator network, the service provider network, or that of the network administrator. This approach avoids problems that arise from managing combined private networks on IPv4.

Serverless Autoconfiguration, Easier Renumbering, Multihoming, and Improved Plug and Play Support

IPv6 is "auto-configurable," which means that devices like laptops, PDAs, and mobile phones can be given their own unique IP addresses easily and without delay. This will simplify the installation and maintenance of home, vehicle, and small office networks. IPv6 supports two types of automatic configuration, stateful and stateless. The "stateless" address auto-configuration mechanism that is introduced by IPv6 (Thomson et al., 1998) does away with the need for a **DHCP** server (Droms et al., 2003). With stateless address configuration, hosts on a link automatically configure themselves with IPv6 addresses for the link and with global addresses derived from prefixes advertised by local routers. Even in the absence of a router, hosts on the same link can automatically configure themselves with link-local addresses and communicate without manual configuration.

Security with Mandatory IP Security (IPSec) Support for All IPv6 Devices

IPv6 improves security by facilitating network-level security. It has security services at the IP-layer as a native feature. Also, allowing each communications device to have its own unique IP number facilitates end-to-end security, meaning that an entire communication session can be conducted securely rather than just the parts that use a virtual private network. IPv6 introduces two header extensions (authentication and encapsulating security payload headers) which can be used separately or in combination in order to provide authentication and confidentiality for the data transmitted at the network layer.

Improved Support for Mobile IP and Mobile Computing Devices

Managing **Mobile IP** consists of defining protocols to convey information to a device, wherever it is connected without interruption. Mobile IP solutions exist today on IPv4. However, their implementation creates a number of obstacles that inhibit mass deployment, which is now being addressed by Mobile IPv6. For example, with the use of IPv6 there is need for triangular communication via a home agent. A key factor is the possibility for a mobile node to keep the same unique IPv6 address while moving between different networks.

QoS Support in IPv6

The QoS problems remain the same as IPv4 but IPv6 is a more streamlined protocol (Nichols et al., 1998). Its key benefit over IPv4 is scalability, and many features of IPv6 are IPv4 "add ons." The IPv6 header has two

QoS-related fields, the new 20-bit Flow Label field which can be used for the implementation of IntServ-based QoS schemes, and an 8-bit Traffic Class indicator which can be used for the implementation of DiffServ-based QoS schemes (Bouras et al., 2004). The Flow Label can be used in order to identify specific flows in the network and allows intermediate nodes in the flow path to recognize the flow and treat it appropriately.

Transitioning to IPv6

A large variety of mechanisms have been proposed in order to facilitate the transition from IPv4 to IPv6. The most common approach is the implementation of a dual IPv4/IPv6 stack at hosts, so that they are able to communicate using both protocols. Depending on the network infrastructure used by an IPv6-enabled host (an IPv4 network, an IPv6-enabled network, an MPLS backbone, etc.), several techniques have been developed, such as ISATAP (if the IPv6 host resides in an IPv4 network), 6to4 (if the IPv6 host resides in an IPv6 local network but wants to communicate to another remote host over IPv4 infrastructure), 6PE (if there is available MPLS infrastructure), etc., in order for the IPv6 host to be able to communicate with other IPv6 hosts. These mechanisms are going to be useful for the long period of transitioning from IPv4 to IPv6, when most IPv6 nodes will have to traverse at least part of IPv4-only infrastructure in order to reach each other.

An important part of the proper operation of the dual IPv4/IPv6 stack is the way the DNS service influences whether the IPv4 or the IPv6 host will be used. Upon a DNS request, a DNS server can either return only an IPv6 address, an IPv4 address, or both. It is recommended that the choice of the address used should be made by the requesting host and not the DNS server.

Tunneling mechanisms are used when IPv6 hosts want to communicate over an infrastructure that is partly IPv4. IPv6 packets are then encapsulated as payload in IPv4 packets, transferred over the IPv4 network infrastructure and decoded at the other end of the tunnel for delivery. The encapsulation and the decoding of IPv6 packets can be performed in either a router or a host, and the tunneling procedure can be configured either manually with the intervention of an administrator or automatically.

A widely-used technique for automatic tunneling is called 6to4 (Carpenter et al., 2001), and is particularly useful when an IPv6 host inside a local IPv6 network wants to communicate with another remote host over IPv4 infrastructure. For the 6to4 mechanism to work, the border router at the end of the IPv6 network has to be properly configured in order to support the 6to4 tunneling mechanism.

Another mechanism is 6over4 (Carpenter et al., 1999), which is useful when the underlying IPv4 infrastructure supports multicast. The 6over4 mechanism utilizes the multicast infrastructure in order to make an isolated IPv6 host with no native IPv6 support from its network become a fully functional IPv6 node.

If the IPv4 network provides an **MPLS**-enabled core, it is possible, through the use of the 6PE mechanism (developed by Cisco Systems; Clercq, 2004), to forward IPv6 packets over the MPLS network without enabling IPv6 in the intermediate routers. Furthermore, MPLS also provides the possibility of L2VPNs (Layer 2 Virtual Private Networks) that can connect two remote IPv6 hosts over an intermediate MPLS network, as if they were directly connected at Layer 2.

While 6to4 is suitable for connecting IPv6 hosts in IPv6-enabled local networks over IPv4 infrastructure, another tunneling mechanism called **ISATAP** (Templin et al., 2005) is designed in order to connect isolated IPv6 hosts residing in a network that does not support IPv6.

In cases where none of the above mechanisms is available, a last resort mechanism can be the **Teredo** (Huitema, 2004) mechanism. It is useful when there is no suitable border router with 6to4 support, but there is NAT support available. In such cases, Teredo encapsulates IPv6 packets as IPv4 UDP ones that can traverse NAT.

Apart from communication between IPv6 hosts, there is also a number of translation techniques that enable the communication of hosts using different IP protocols. Techniques such as Bump-in-the-stack (Tsuchiya et al., 2000) or Bump-in-the-API (Lee et al., 2002) are used in order to translate IPv4 traffic generated by an application into IPv6 traffic by the time it reaches the network, and vice versa. Another mechanism called SOCKS, uses an application level gateway (ALG) node, which is responsible for relaying traffic in a TCP or UDP session between an IPv4 and an IPv6 host.

FUTURE TRENDS

IPv6 support is currently widespread among vendors of network equipment and operating systems. All major modern operating systems offer dual stack implementations, and IPv6 support is standard in most new networking equipment and software. Also, the majority of new applications come with a capability to communicate over IPv6, and many legacy applications have been ported to support the new protocol. Overall, the pieces of the transition to IPv6 seem to be in place and the transition is moving forward.

Countries that did not play a large part in the original development of the Internet, such as China and Japan, were not allocated IP addresses proportional to their constantly increasing number of Internet users in the last years. Despite having over half of the world's population, Asia only controls about nine percent of the allocated IPv4 addresses. Therefore, the scarcity of unique routable IP addresses is more intense in these countries than in the U.S., where institutions and enterprises were allocated much larger IP address blocks because of their early adoption of the Internet. As a result, IPv6 adoption in Asia is much larger and growing faster than in Europe and the U.S. (Barnard, 2006).

A significant incentive for the adoption of IPv6 in the United States has been that the U.S. Government has specified that all federal agencies must deploy IPv6 by 2008 (GovExec.com 2005), with the Department of Defense being the most advanced agency in the deployment.

In Europe, the European Union has helped advance IPv6 knowledge and adoption by funding large-scale projects such as 6NET, which have contributed to the promotion of IPv6 as a technology that can be considered at the production stage instead of the research stage.

CONCLUSION

IPv6 has been proposed by IETF in order to overcome the scarcity of unique globally routable addresses in IPv4. It enhances network layer connectivity by offering a number of additional improvements over IPv4. Although techniques such as NAT have reduced the urgency of the situation, most experts in the field foresee a gradual transition to IPv6 within the next years, aided by the maturity of the support for the new

protocol at most new hardware vendor and software implementations coming out today.

REFERENCES

6NET project. (2006). Retrieved March 2006, from http://www.sixnet.org

Barnard, P. (2006). Recent Internet2 land speed records show that IPv6 is almost on par with IPv4. *TMCnet.* Retrieved March 2006, from http://news.tmcnet.com/news/2006/03/09/1444997.htm

Bouras, C., Gkamas, A., Primpas, D., & Stamos, K. (2004). Performance evaluation of the impact of quality of service mechanisms in an IPv6 network for IPv6-capable real time applications. *Journal of Network and Systems Management, 12*(4), 463-483.

Carpenter, B., & Moore, K. (2001). *Connection of IPv6 domains via IPv4 clouds.* RFC 3056.

Carpenter, B., & Jung, C. (1999). *Transmission of IPv6 over IPv4 domains without explicit tunnels.* RFC 2529.

Conta, A., & Deering, S. (1998). *Internet control message protocol (ICMPv6) for the Internet protocol Version 6 (IPv6) Specification.* RFC 2463.

Clercq, J. (2004). *Connecting IPv6 islands over IPv4 MPLS using IPv6 provider edge routers (6PE).* draft-ooms-v6ops-bgp-tunnel-03

Deering, S., & Hinden, R. (1998). *Internet protocol, version 6 (IPv6) specification.* RFC 2460.

Droms, R., Bound, J., Volz, B., Lemon, T., Perkins, C., & Carney, M. (2003). *Dynamic host configuration protocol for IPv6 (DHCPv6).* RFC 3315.

Hinden, R., & Deering, S. (April 2003). *IP version 6 addressing architecture.* RFC 3513.

Huitema, C. (2004). *Teredo: Tunneling IPv6 over UDP through NATs.* draft-huitema-v6ops-teredo-02.

Lee, S., Shin, M-K., Kim, Y-J., Nordmark, E., & Durand, A. (2002). *Dual stack hosts using "Bump-in-the-API" (BIA).* RFC 3338.

Nichols, K., Blake, S., Baker, F., & Black, D. (1998). *Definition of the differentiated services field (DS field) in the IPv4 and IPv6 headers.* RFC 2474.

Rajahalme, J., Conta, A., Carpenter, B., & Deering, S. (2004). *IPv6 flow label specification*. RFC 3697.

Templin, F., Gleeson, T., Talwar, M., & Thaler, D. (2005). *Intra-site automatic tunnel addressing protocol (ISATAP)*. RFC 4214.

Thomson, S., & Narten, T. (1998). *IPv6 stateless address autoconfiguration*. RFC 2462.

Thomson, S., Huitema, C., Ksinant, V., & Souissi, M. (2003). *DNS extensions to support IP version 6*. RFC 3596.

Tsuchiya, K., Higuchi, H., & Atarashi, Y. (2000). *Dual stack hosts using the "Bump-In-the-Stack" technique (BIS)*. RFC 2767.

U.S. government agencies must use advanced Internet by 2008. Retrieved March 2006, from http://www.govexec.com/dailyfed/0605/062905tdpm2.htm

Wang, T. (2005). China is deploying IPv6 to generate enough IP addresses for billions of internet users. Retrieved March 2006, from http://blog.loaz.com/timwang/index.php/2005/04/12/china_is_deploying_ipv6_to_generate_enou

KEY TERMS

DHCP (Dynamic Host Configuration Protocol): A protocol used for dynamic assignment of IP addresses to devices in a network.

DNS (Domain Name Service): A distributed database service developed in order to match IP addresses to human-readable names for easier location and retrieval of Internet services.

Internet Engineering Task Force (IETF): The organization comprised of a large open international community of network designers, operators, vendors, and researchers concerned with the evolution of the Internet architecture and the smooth operation of the Internet.

IPv4 (Internet Protocol, version 4): The version of the Internet protocol that has been used throughout the existence of the Internet.

IPv6 (Internet Protocol, version 6): The new version of the Internet protocol designed to replace IPv4, with the motivation of solving the address scarcity problem and improving protocol efficiency in additional areas.

MPLS (Multi-Protocol Label Switching): A data-carrying mechanism which emulates some properties of a circuit-switched network over a packet-switched network and was designed in order to provide a unified data-carrying service for both circuit-based clients and packet-switching clients which provide a datagram service model.

Quality of Service (QoS): The ability to provide specific guarantees to traffic flows regarding the network characteristics, such as packet loss, delay, and jitter experienced by the flows.

TCP (Transmission Control Protocol): A connection-oriented, reliable protocol of the TCP/IP protocol suite used for managing full-duplex transmission streams.

UDP (User Datagram Protocol): A connectionless, unreliable protocol of the TCP/IP protocol suite used for sending and receiving datagrams over an IP network.

Issues and Applications of Internet Traffic Modelling

Rachel Babiarz
France Telecom R&D Division, France

Jean-Sebastien Bedo
France Telecom R&D Division, France

INTRODUCTION

Traffic modelling has always been the prior to numerous network engineering tasks like network planning or bandwidth yield management. It is still a huge research domain mainly based on advanced signal processing techniques. It can also help to better understand the underlying aspects of the usage of a telecommunication technology as well as to *forecast* its evolutions.

The plain old telephone service (POTS) raised a lot of questions about the best way to deal with the limited rationality underlying the phoning activity (Chemouil & Garnier, 1985; Etève & Passeron, 1983). But Internet has brought much more issues since the IP protocol has become a standard of delivery for very different human activities in terms of bandwidth usage and habits of customers. Furthermore, traffic measures are much more complicated to obtain since no end to end accounting mechanism exists a priori for IP traffic contrary to POTS. However new layer 2 and 2.5 standards like MPLS are bringing some kind of end to end accounting mechanisms. Asymmetrical routing of flows, multi homing and separated management of autonomous systems (AS) (Agarwal, Chuah, & Bhattacharyya, 2004) introduce frequent dynamic changes of routes, which blur the direct measure of IP traffic profiles.

Traffic can be modelled on different network layers and at different time scales but the modelling techniques are dependent on the type of traffic we study and the final application (voice, Web browsing, peer to peer, etc.) of the modelling itself. For example, quality of service test beds are often based on traffic modelling at the network or transport layer at time scales smaller than the second whereas performance tests on databases are based on analysis at the application level and time scales can be larger than a week. In this article, we will focus on the *traffic modelling* of the routing layer (IP) traffic of core networks with hourly time scales. The applications can go from reactive "what if" scenarios to ad hoc contracts for large tunnels of traffic.

BACKGROUND

When considering traffic modelling, one can use different traffic metrics at the same period of time. For example, one could consider the number of bytes, which have transited on the link between Paris and New York (traffic metric 1) or the instantaneous bit rate (traffic metric 2) between 9 and 10 o'clock (time period). But we can also consider different time periods with the same traffic metric (instantaneous bit rate between 9 and 10 o'clock and for the whole day).

The most common way of modelling Internet traffic is to use statistical models. Indeed, the bursty nature of non-aggregated Internet traffic and statistical multiplexing in backbones have put statistical techniques at the forefront of traffic analysis and forecasting. Nevertheless, models have evolved a lot with further analysis of traffic profiles and regularities in the evolution of traffic or regarding the infrastructures. We will not talk about simpler purely static models like gravity models (Kowalski & Warfield, 1995).

At first glance, Internet traffic is often seen as a random variable with a stable distribution: a Poisson process (Vardi, 1996) or a normal distribution (Cao, Davis, Vander Wiel, & Yu, 2000). This modelling can be explained by the fact that Internet traffic in core networks is an aggregation of a large number of individual end to end traffic flows. These individual flows are on-off processes (for example, you download a file and you read it after). If they have similar duration for "on" periods you get a Poisson process otherwise you get a normal distribution. Some approaches have built on this basic framework and modelled Internet traffic as heavy-tailed distributions (like gamma distribution) or mixtures of normal or heavy-tailed distributions (Vaton & Bedo, 2004).

But long range dependencies effects and the fractal nature (self-similar, geometric structuring) of Internet traffic have been raised early (Leland, Taqqu, Willinger, & Wilson, 1994). Indeed, patterns can be isolated in traffic profile traces and traffic distributions are not stable in time. For example, your antivirus downloads its upgrades each day at 8 o'clock but you shut down your computer at midnight and some other persons do it also. However, patterns do not exactly explain Internet traffic (you receive a different number of e-mails each day). As a result, these models have to be improved with statistical methods.

Recently a new field of modelling has opened with the dynamic analysis of traffic and its structure. It has shown that advanced tools like *principal component analysis* (Lakhina, Papagiannaki, Crovella, Diot, & Kolaczyk, 2004), multi resolution wavelet analysis (Papagiannaki, Taft, Lang, & Diot 2003), Markov processes (Vaton & Gravey, 2003; Vaton et al., 2004), and particular filtering (Soule et al., 2005) can be very useful for a more in depth understanding of Internet traffic.

Another important issue in traffic modelling is taking benefit from very different measures in the network (individual flow, use of services, etc.) and learning automatically from these measures some insights, which improve our statistical a priori models and our beliefs. For this purpose, the Bayesian framework (Vardi, 1996) and neural networks (Doulamis, Doulamis, & Kollias, 2003) have been proposed. Bayesian statisticians claim that methods of Bayesian inference are a formalisation of the scientific method involving collecting evidence that points towards or away from a given hypothesis. There can never be certainty, but as evidence accumulates, the degree of belief in a hypothesis changes. On the other hand, neural networks end up in a unique solution: equilibrium. They are non-linear statistical data modelling tools which can be used to model complex relationships between inputs and outputs or to find patterns in data. They represent well the two opposite sides of the models themselves (patterns and confidence levels).

All these traffic modelling techniques have been used for several applications. Indeed, from long-term

(Papagiannaki et al., 2003), mid-term (Babiarz & Bedo, 2006), and short-term (Sang & Li, 2000) forecasting to traffic matrix inference (Bedo, Bouhtou, & Martin 2005; Gunnar, Johansson, & Telkamp, 2004; Vaton, Bedo, & Gravey, 2005; Zhang, Roughan, Lund, & Donoho, 2003). Through "what if" scenarios, the traffic engineering tasks for Internet traffic use traffic modelling as their fundamental principles.

CYCLIC TRENDS IN TRAFFIC MODELLING

There are two main types of measures that can be obtained from a backbone IP network: *end to end traffic demands* (or origin-destination flows or OD flows) and *link counts* (traffic amount exchanged between two adjacent routers). Whereas the end to end traffic demands can be directly measured for telecommunication networks based on circuit-switching, there are more difficult to obtain on Internet networks because they rely on the IP protocol, which does not include an accounting mechanism. Then specific tools like Netflow have been developed to directly measure the end to end traffic demands. These tools are based on sample measures, use a lot of network resources, and then cannot been activated on all routers of a big backbone network of a telecommunications operator. The link counts are easier to obtain thanks to the simple network management protocol (SNMP), which is directly implemented in all routers. There is a strong dependency between the end to end traffic demands and the link counts as these lasts correspond to the superposition or sum of the several end to end traffic users entering the network into one edge router (the origin) and exiting at an other edge router (the destination). The link counts can be directly obtained thanks to the routing matrix and the end to end traffic demands. The problem of estimating OD flows from link counts is an ill-posed inverse problem that can be resolved thanks to traffic matrix inference techniques.

We observe two main types of IP traffic behavior on both links and OD flows stemming from a core network: cyclostationnary and bursty traffic profiles. The cyclostationnary traffic represents the most important volume part of total measured traffic, it exhibits strong daily and weekly periods. The bursty traffic is mainly observed for small links or OD flows. The figures below show examples of cyclostationnary and bursty

Figure 1. Example of a cyclostationnary (left) and bursty (right) OD flow from Abilene

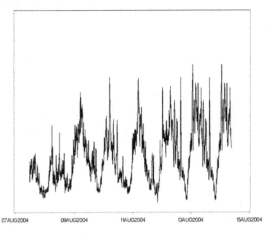

Figure 2. First and second Abilene eigenlinks and eigenflows

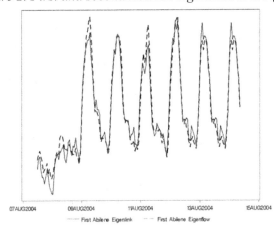
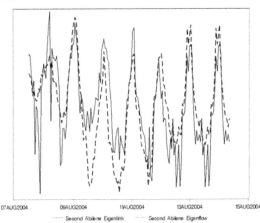

traffic for OD flows from Abilene network. Abilene is a non-commercial Internet backbone network, mainly used by major universities in the USA. The two main types of traffic behavior have also been observed on link counts stemming from the IP international transit network of France Telecom (Babiarz et al., 2006).

Whole-backbone network IP traffic analysis is a difficult task as there are often a high number of OD flows or link counts. For example, in the IP international transit network of France Telecom, there are next to one thousand link counts and even more OD flows. The strong time dependencies that exist between traffic evolutions can be exploited to reduce the number of variables to be studied simultaneously. The most common used technique to do this is the principal component analysis (PCA, Hotelling, 1933). For example, when PCA is applied on OD flows stemming from Abilene or Sprint network, the effective dimension is between

five and ten, much lower than the total number of OD flows (over 100 in each case). The new variables obtained are called the *eigenflows* (when PCA is applied on OD flows, Lakhina et al., 2004) or *eigenlinks* (when PCA is applied on link counts, Babiarz et al., 2006). The first few (between five and ten according to the network and the types of measures) represent the underlying cyclic trends of traffic. We can see in Figure 2 that the underlying structures for OD flows and for link counts are quite the same.

Then, OD flows or link counts of a backbone network can be modelled by only considering the first few eigenlinks or eigenflows. Moreover, the underlying structures are quite stable over time. This nice property allows studying the cycle change of shape by using basic statistical analysis tools such as mean and standard deviation (Babiarz et al., 2006). This technique can be applied to produce forecasts and has the advantage to be fully automated for network planners, contrary to time series models such as SARIMA which need to be fitted manually through the Box-Jenkins methodology (Box & Jenkins, 1996).

It is interesting to complete the underlying cyclostationnary structures to obtain a new basis of time for the traffic profiles. Only the first few components stemming from PCA are quite the same for both link counts and OD flows. The following components are very different since they are bursty. As a consequence, the cyclic trend basis has to be completed with something better than PCA. The Haar wavelets are a good tool for this particular purpose. They are often used to decompose discontinuous signal, very similar to traditional on-off processes. The use of the highest frequency wavelets assures the localisation of the bursts in time. Then, the time basis for the new representation of traffic profiles is obtained by grouping the first cyclostationnary components of PCA and enough of the highest frequency of the Haar wavelets.

This new basis of variations trends constitutes a useful framework for IP traffic matrix estimation as it takes into account sequential time dependency between successive traffic matrices. Thanks to these new basic trends, new temporal constraints are added to the existing SNMP measures classical constraints and reduce the set of feasible matrices (Bedo et al., 2005).

FUTURE TRENDS

The bursty nature of Internet traffic has brought a loss of balance in the business models of telecommunication services. Indeed, it breaks the traditional tariffs schemes since costs-based or usage-based schemes are not natively available with IP. But for the moment small users subsidize big users with flat fees. As a consequence, manufacturers have tried to introduce light ways for accounting in their routers.

Nowadays, more and more traffic measures are available in core routers (link counts, BGP accounting, Netflow, etc.) and MPLS implements natively some rudimental accounting mechanisms. More and more network operators are working on algorithms to find the best places to add probes in their networks in order to obtain more useful traffic measures. These measures are sometimes used to improve statistical

a priori models of traffic. As a result, we would tend to say that more and more measures will be collected directly in the routers (which means some additional expenses for network operators) and less and less statistical methods will be developed. First it will be the case for the lowest layers in the network with the protocols IP and MPLS, and then it will be extended to upper layers (services). This will pave the way for new tariffs schemes and business models.

CONCLUSION

In this manuscript, we have described the most advanced methods to model IP traffic in a core network at the routing level with the minimum measures. We have seen that the structure of traffic over time is regular and that some underlying cyclic trends can be extracted easily. There is still some open issues especially regarding usefulness of additional measures, the optimisation of probing and the extension of traffic modelling at a higher level (toward services).

REFERENCES

Agarwal, S., Chuah, C. N., Bhattacharyya, S., & Diot, C. (2004). Impact of BGP dynamics on intradomain traffic. In *Proceedings of ACM SIGMETRICS*, New York.

Babiarz, R., & Bedo, J. S. (2006). Internet traffic mid-term forecasting: A pragmatic approach using statistical analysis tools. *Networking 2006*, Coimbra, Portugal.

Bedo, J. S., Bouhtou, M., & Martin, V. (2005). Estimating successive traffic matrices in backbone IP networks: A model based on underlying trends of variation. *IPS-MoMe*, Warsaw, Poland.

Brockwell, P., & Davis, R. (1996). *Introduction to time series and forecasting*. Springer.

Cao, J., Davis, D., Vander Wiel, S., & Yu, B. (2000). Time-varying network tomography: Router link data. In Bell Labs Tech. Memo.

Chemouil, P., & Garnier, B. (1985). An adaptive short-term traffic forecasting procedure using kalman filtering. *ITC 11th*, Kyoto, Japan.

Doulamis, A., Doulamis, N., & Kollias, S. (2003). An adaptable neural network model for recursive non-linear traffic prediction and modelling of MPEG video sources. *IEEE Transactions on Neural Networks, 24*(1), 150-166.

Etève, E., & Passeron, A. (1983). Modelling seasonal variations of telephone traffic. *ITC 10th*, Montreal, Canada.

Gunnar, A., Johansson, M., & Telkamp, T. (2004). Traffic matrix estimation on a large IP backbone--A comparison on real data. *IMC'04*, Taormina, Italy.

Hotelling, H. (1933). Analysis of a complex of statistical variables into principal components. *Journal of Educational Psychology, 24*, 417-441.

Kowalski, J., & Warfield, B. (1995). Modeling traffic demand between nodes in a telecommunications network. *ATNAC'95*, Sydney, Australia.

Lakhina, A., Papagiannaki, K., Crovella, M., Diot, C., Kolaczyk, E. D., & Taft, N. (2004). Structural analysis of network traffic flows. In *Proceedings of ACM SIGMETRICS*, New York.

Leland, W., Taqqu, M., Willinger, W., & Wilson, D. (1994). On the self-similar nature of Ethernet traffic. *IEEE/ACM Transactions on Networking, 2*(1), 1-15.

Papagiannaki, K., Taft, N., Lang, Z., & Diot, C. (2003). Long-term forecasting of Internet backbone traffic: Observations and initial models. *IEEE INFOCOM*, San Francisco.

Sang, A., & Li, S. (2000). A predictability analysis of network traffic. *IEEE INFOCOM*, Tel Aviv, Israel.

Soule, A., Lakhina, A., Taft, N., Papagiannaki, K., Salamatian, K., Nucci, A., Crovella, M., & Diot, C. (2005). Traffic matrices: Balancing measurements, inference, and modelling. *SIGMETRICS Perform. Eval. Rev. 33*, 362-373.

Vardi, Y. (1996). Network tomography: Estimating source-destination traffic intensities from link data. *Journal of the American Statistical Association, 91*, 365-377.

Vaton, S., & Bedo, J. S. (2004). Network traffic matrix : How can one learn the prior distributions from the link counts only? *ICC'04*, Paris, France.

Vaton, S., & Gravey, A. (2003). Network tomography: An iterative Bayesian analysis. *ITC 18th*, Charlotte, USA.

Vaton, S., Bedo, J. S., & Gravey, A. (2005). Advanced methods for the estimation of the origin destination traffic matrix. Revue du 25ème anniversaire du GERAD.

Zhang, Y., Roughan, M., Lund, C., & Donoho, D. (2003). An information-theoretic approach to traffic matrix estimation. In *Proceedings ACM SIGCOMM*, Karlsruhe, Germany.

KEY TERMS

Bursty: We say that Internet traffic is bursty in order to explain that the bandwidth used by an IP flow is very irregular. It can go from 1 Mb to 10 Mb in one second. It is closely linked to the concept of sporadicity, which is the ratio of the peak rate and the mean rate of a flow. It reflects the on-off nature of individual connections.

Cyclostationnary: A traffic measure is called to be cyclostationnary if it repeats the same cyclic shape within time. The most important part of the IP traffic is cyclostationnary as it reflects the human periods of activity (daily and weekly period).

Ill-Posed Linear Inverse Problem: A linear inverse problem can be described by the equation: m = A d, where m is the observed data, A is a linear operator and d is the unknown parameter. When the dimension of the kernel of A is greater than zero, the problem is said to be ill-posed.

Long Range Dependency: A self-similar phenomenon behaves the same when viewed at different scales on a dimension (space or time). Self-similar processes are said to exhibit long-range dependency.

Statistical Multiplexing: Statistical multiplexing is a method of making the most efficient use of the bandwidth available. Different flows share the same static resource (e.g. the bandwidth of a central link) and the idea is to allocate the bandwidth to each flow in order to prevent peaks from occurring at the same time on all the flows, which would result in a packet loss.

Traffic Profile: A traffic profile is a sequence of measures over a specific period of time. It can be the traffic profile of a flow or a link count.

Underlying Traffic Structure: New components of traffic stemming from principal component analysis tool constitute the underlying traffic structure of a network. This corresponds to a new basis of traffic trends with a lower dimension that sum up all shapes of traffic evolution observed in a network.

Java Web Application Frameworks

Tony C. Shan
Bank of America, USA

Winnie W. Hua
CTS Inc., USA

INTRODUCTION

In the information systems environment, a framework is a well-defined structural and behavioral model in which applications can be organized and developed. A framework may consist of a variety of artifacts to help design, develop, and glue together various components of an application such as common services, interfaces, reusable modules, code utilities, scripting capability, technology stack, runtime environment, integration, security, platform, process, persistence, storage, communications, and other packages/libraries.

A software framework is a reusable design and building block for a software system and/or subsystem. A software framework can be geared toward constructing applications in different domains such as decision support systems (Gachet, 2003) or financial modeling applications (Birrer & Eggenschwiler, 1993).

A software framework is composed of frozen spots and hot spots (Pree, 1994). The overall architecture of a software application is represented in the frozen spots, which are kept unchanged in the applications, including the basic components and their interrelationships. On the other hand, the application-specific parts in the software framework are defined in the hot spots, which are designed to be generic and extensible so that they can be tailored to the particular requirements of the system to be constructed.

The hot spots of a software framework are specialized in a concrete software system, based on the specific needs of the system. In the object-oriented paradigm, a software framework is composed of abstract and concrete classes. Instantiation of an object-oriented framework involves constructing new classes or extending the existing classes (Buschmann, 1996). Software

frameworks apply the Hollywood Principle: "Don't call us, we'll call you" (Larman, 2002). In other words, the child classes or user-defined classes are invoked by the predefined framework classes. This type of inversion of control is usually realized by implementing the abstract methods of the parent class, in a way similar to the *template method* design pattern.

A Web application framework belongs to the software frameworks.

BACKGROUND

Software Framework Types

In general, there are seven schools of software frameworks in the information systems space:

1. **Conceptual framework:** Overarching architectural model such as the Zachman Framework
2. **Application framework:** Skeletal structure for an application solution such as WebWork
3. **Domain framework:** Representation tailored to specific business sectors such as financial services processes defined in the IBM information framework (IFW)
4. **Platform framework:** Programming model and runtime environment such as .Net and Java EE framework;
5. **Component framework:** Building blocks for an application such as Hibernate and iBatis for object-relational mapping
6. **Service framework:** Business and technical services model for service-oriented computing such as semantic Web services framework

7. **Development framework:** A construction foundation to build a rich client platform, typically for IDEs, such as Eclipse, Netbeans, and OSGi

Definition of Web Application Framework

A Web application framework (WAF) is a reusable, skeletal, semi-complete modular platform that can be specialized to produce custom Web applications, which commonly serve Web browsers via the http(s) protocol. It contains building blocks of services and components that are essential for constructing sophisticated feature-rich business services and collaboration systems. WAF usually implements the model-view-controller (MVC) design pattern, typically in the Model-2 architecture to develop Web-based applications in a request-response mode on the Java EE and .Net models. It also integrates services such as search, authentication/authorization, session management and data validation, which may be leveraged directly by the applications with little or no additional work. WAF in this context is a type of application framework as defined in the preceding section, specifically for http(s)-based communications serving HTML/XML.

Moreover, WAF may also include or integrate with other relevant technologies such as a view template engine, a user interface component library, and an object-relational persistence mapper.

WEB APPLICATION FRAMEWORK SOLUTIONS

Design Philosophy

The key design principles that are applied in developing a Web application framework are listed as follows.

1. **Simplicity:** Less and simpler code should be written by using a framework. XML configuration files should be used as necessary. The plain old Java object (POJO)-centric design should be taken advantage of in a Java WAF.

2. **Consistency:** The design of components and interfaces should be consistent. The conventions should align with the best practices in the organization and industry.

3. **Efficiency:** Applications should perform well and scale with a good use of clustering through sticky sessions for high availability.

4. **Integration:** A framework should have an open and flexible structure to foster a seamless integration.

5. **Reusability:** Constructs in a framework should be fully reusable, reconfigurable, modifiable, and easy to customize and deploy.

6. **Non-intrusive:** HTML or other markup elements should not be polluted with programming semantics. The view rendering part should interoperate with ordinary HTML editors, which enables graphics designs to easily recognize and manipulate the markup elements without being forced to learn the framework-specific tags.

7. **Diagnosis:** In the case of errors and failures, the framework should produce insightful diagnostics and debugging information to help identify the problem points and determine the root causes.

8. **Development tool:** A framework should support seamless plug-in to mainstream development tools with minimum dependency on special tools.

Classification of Web Application Frameworks

Almost all Java Web application frameworks are based on the MVC pattern. Generally speaking, there are five major types of Web application frameworks: *request-based, component-based, hybrid, Meta, and RIA-based framework.*

A *request-based framework* uses a similar design mechanism to that in the traditional CGI architecture. Its controllers and actions deal with incoming requests directly in a stateless fashion. The server- or client-side session management methods add a certain degree of statefulness. The fundamental distinctions among different implementations are the way the logic is mapped to URLs and how the request data is encapsulated and delivered to the business delegate handlers.

A *component-based framework* maximizes the reusability by encapsulating the processing logic into modular components. The implementation details of request handling are abstracted and independent from the incoming request protocols at the transport level. Based on the data in the component instances, the framework deals with the state management and event handling. This programming mechanism is very close to that in desktop GUI toolkits. Different implementations differentiate themselves in the programming interfaces and component integration methods.

A *hybrid framework* makes use of the advantages in both request-based and component-based frameworks. The programming model in a request-based model is leveraged to handle the data and logic flow, where the developers take full control of URLs, request parameters, form actions, path information, and cookies. Instead of a direct mapping of the actions and controllers to the requests, a hybrid framework uses a component object model that manages different artifacts in a consistent fashion, such as incoming requests, individual pages, request filter, page fragments, and control widgets. Compound components can be constructed as packaged groups by assembling other components together, for independent distribution and seamless integration into a new application. A hybrid framework takes advantage of the best-of-breed features from both component-based frameworks and request-based approaches to increase the reusability without losing the raw controls on the data and logic flow.

A *meta framework* contains a set of core interfaces for common services and a highly extensible backbone for integrating components and services. The structure typically implements the *inversion of control* pattern for separation of concerns to flexibly incorporate other concrete frameworks and components. A meta framework is sometimes considered as a framework of frameworks.

Rich Internet application (RIA) refers to a Web page-based application running in a browser with rich user interface features that are common in a fat/thick client, such as drag & drop, tree controls, list sorting, and tabbed panels. A *RIA-based framework* uses a client-side container model to minimize the amount of server communications. Instead of loading an entire HTML page each time a user clicks a link or button on the page, the framework either handles the click locally or requests a smaller block of data from the server in an XML format on demand or asynchronously behind the scene. This means that there is a truly client-side stateful application running inside a browser with a user interaction model--the client is far more than a simple display of Web pages generated by a HTTP server.

Major Frameworks

Request-Based Framework

- WebWork (OpenSymphony, 2006) provides UI themes, dynamic form parameter mapping to JavaBeans, internationalization, robust client/server side validation, and reusable UI templates such as form controls. WebWork was originally developed by Rickard Oberg in 2001, and released as an open source project on SourceForge in March 2002. WebWork joined the OpenSymphony project in the summer of 2002. As of November 2005, WebWork was merged into Struts to become part of Struts Action 2.0 framework.
- Struts (2006) uses and extends the Java Servlet API to adopt the Model-2 architecture, which is an implementation of the classic model-view-controller (MVC) design pattern. In Model-2, a front or application controller manages the business logic execution, while the view logic resides mainly in the JavaServer pages (JSP). The model data is typically handled by a persistence mechanism--JDBC, DAO, EJB, or O/R mappers.
- Craig McClanahan originally developed struts and donated it to the Apache foundation in May 2000. Struts has been a de facto framework with a strong and vibrant user community. The Apache struts project is now divided into two distinct frameworks--the *struts action framework* and the *struts shale framework*. In addition, the

simple Web framework (SWF) is an event-driven framework for developing rich Web applications without migration to JSF.

- Beehive (Apache, 2006) is an extensible framework with an integrated metadata-driven development model for Web services, Web applications, Web page navigation, and resource access. The new features in Java 5 are leveraged in this framework, particularly the JSR 175 metadata annotations. The key components in beehive are NetUI page flow, controls, and Web service metadata. Beehive evolved from a part of the BEA Weblogic workshop product to an Apache project in May 2004.

- Stripes (2006) is a robust yet lightweight presentation framework with no external configuration per page/action. It has a binding engine that builds complex object Webs out of the request parameters, with a built-in support for multiple events per form and transparent file upload capabilities as well as wizard forms. Stripes was initially released in September 2005.

Component-Based Framework

- JavaServer faces (JSF) (JSR-127 2004, JSR-252, 2006) is a server-side user interface component framework. JSF contains a set of APIs that represent UI components, manage component state, handle events, perform server-side data validation and conversion, specify page navigation, support internationalization and accessibility, and provide feature extensibility. A couple of JSP custom tag libraries are included in JSF, to represent UI components in a JSP page and connect UI components to business logic objects. The specification of JSF 1.0 (JSR-127) was initially released in March 2004. The final draft of JSF 1.2 Specification (JSR-252) was released in August 2005, as the next generation of JSF.

- Tapestry (Jakarta, 2006) complements and builds upon the standard Java servlet API. A Web application is decomposed into a set of pages, which are constructed from UI components. The framework deals with key concerns in a consistent structure, such as URL construction and dispatch, user input data validation, client/server-side persistent state storage, exception handling, and localization/internationalization. Tapestry applications use plain HTML templates, combined with small amounts of Java code in XML descriptor files. In Tapestry, an application is developed in an object-oriented style, in terms of objects instead of URLs and query parameters. Tapestry was originally created by Howard Lewis Ship, and the project was moved to the Apache Foundation around early 2004.

- Wicket (2006) is a framework that focuses on separation of concerns, simplicity, and ease of development. Wicket pages can be mocked up, previewed, and modified in standard WYSIWYG HTML design tools. A component model deals with form handling and dynamic content processing. The programming model is supported by POJO data beans, which can be persisted via different technologies. Wicket has a transparent state management with no XML configuration files. The first release of Wicket 1.0 went public in June 2005.

Hybrid Framework

- RIFE (2006) is a full-stack framework with tools and APIs to implement most common Web features. It contains a set of toolkits, which can be integrated together to boost development productivity. RIFE maximizes the reusability by ensuring that every declaration and definition is handled in one place in the code. This kind of design simplifies development, eliminates code duplication, eases maintenance, and enforces consistency. RIFE 1.0 was released in September 2005.

Meta Framework

- Keel (2006) is an extensible skeleton model. Many open source products are incorporated in this framework to form a best-of-breed combination that works right out of the box. The unique component design structure enables an easy swap of existing implementations with new products, with little or no code rewrite in the applications. The first pre-release of Keel was out in January 2003.

- Spring (2006) is a layered Java EE application framework, which includes a lightweight container for automated configuration and wiring of application objects, an abstraction layer for transaction management, a JDBC abstraction layer, aspect-oriented programming functionality, and integration with O-R mappers. The origins of Spring can be traced back to a book by Johnson (2002), who presented his interface 21 framework that was later released into the open source world. The interface 21 framework formed the foundation of the Spring framework. The first official 1.0 release of Spring was available in March 2004.

RIA-Based Framework

- Direct Web remoting (DWR, 2006) is a framework that enables the Javascript in the browser to directly call Java code on the server. DWR contains two major parts: the client-side JavaScript to exchange data with the server and dynamically update the Webpage, and a server-side servlet to process incoming requests and deliver responses to the browser. The unique approach in DWR is that it dynamically generates JavaScript code-based Java classes. Consequently the JavaScript calls the remote Java code like a local method invocation, but has full access to the resources at the Web server. The first release of DWR went public in 2005.

- Echo2 (2005) is a platform for developing Web applications with the rich-client capabilities, as the next-generation of the echo Web framework. The new ajax-based rendering engine brings dramatic performance, capability, scalability, and user-experience improvements. Instead of thinking in terms of Web pages in an application, the user interface development approach is shifted to an object-oriented and event-driven paradigm, with no prerequisite of HTML, HTTP, and JavaScript knowledge. Applications in Echo2 can run in any Java servlet container. The framework is distributed under the terms of the GNU LGPL License and the Mozilla public license. Echo2 initial alpha release became available in March 2005.

- JSON-RPC-Java (JSON, 2006) is a Java implementation of JSON-RPC. A lightweight JSON-RPC JavaScript client enables an application to transparently invoke the Java code at the server side from JavaScript. It can be hosted in a Servlet container like Tomcat or a Java EE application server like JBoss application Server. A JavaScript Web application can call remote plain Java or EJB methods. In JSON-RPC-Java, JavaScript objects are dynamically mapped to and from Java objects via the Java reflection mechanism. As a result, JavaScript can call the existing Java objects at the server side with minimal or no changes required. The reflection on the method signatures makes the exporting of Java objects simple and straightforward in JSON-RPC-Java. The first major release 1.0 was made available in March 2006.

Selection Guidelines

Selecting one of these frameworks depends on the overall architectural decisions as well as the specific functionality of an application. Frameworks are not always required but can significantly reduce the time and efforts needed to develop a Web application from scratch. Other architectural considerations and constraints may drive the use of specific frameworks or the migration from an outdated framework to a mainstream one in the design process.

- Both struts and JSF are supported in IBM WebSphere application server and WebSphere studio application developer (WSAD) IDE as well as the rational application developer, a replacement of WSAD.

Figure 1. Framework classification scheme

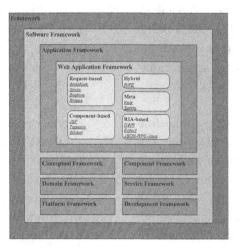

- Sun Microsystems provides a JSF reference implementation, which is free to redistribute in a binary form. In addition, the Apache MyFaces project offers an open source JSF implementation of JSR-127.
- MyEclipse enterprise workbench (version 4.0) supports the Sun JSF reference implementation 1.1.01, and MyFaces 1.0.9. It also provides tapestry integration.
- Use of beehive requires JDK 5. The beehive product supports JSR-175 metadata annotations. Beehive's NetUI page flow is based on struts. Pollinate is an eclipse project to build an IDE and toolset, using the apache beehive framework.
- The flexibility in the struts framework is provided by the controller components, which can be integrated with any presentation technology. JSF and JavaServer standard tag library (JSTL) are complementary to struts, and various extensions are available.
- Spring provides an AOP framework, and unique transaction management abstraction and data access abstractions. Spring modules is an associated project, which extends the reach of the spring platform to areas that are not necessarily integral to the spring core. Spring IDE is a graphical user interface to configure the spring framework. It is built as a set of plug-ins for the eclipse platform.

- As a general implementation guideline in Web application design, Spring may be considered first as a preferred baseline, followed by the selection of an appropriate front-controller implementation such as struts, JSF, wicket, or RIFE. Flexible rendering mechanisms should be evaluated to complement a front-controller framework. Beehive can be used in combination with struts. The PageFlows in beehive is more mature than the WebFlow in spring. Stripes is a good candidate in the scenarios where an application needs Web-based wizard forms. Tapestry may be considered in niche areas at discretion. Echo2 and JSON-RPC-Java are viable options to develop RIA systems.

FUTURE TRENDS

The need for a Web application framework is compelling as there have been dozens of frameworks built in the Java space over the years. Among these competing offerings, a few products have stood out to become the predominant contenders for various reasons such as strong user community, standardization, good documentation, tool integration, vendor endorsement, and ease of use. Some examples are struts/shale, JSF/MyFaces, spring, beehive, and JSON-RPC-Java.

Consolidation has occurred and tends to become stronger, as demonstrated in the recent merger of WebWork and struts (action framework), as well as the incorporation of JSF into struts (shale) and spring (JSF-spring).

A steady stream of new frameworks continues to proliferate, particularly in the evolving RIA field, which is wide open. Virtually all of these RIA frameworks are in the format of open source, even for the vendor-backed products like Echo2. Apparently open source is favored for the future framework development and enhancement.

Use of meta frameworks is growing rapidly, as seen in the adoption of spring. It is expected that more integration and convergence will occur based on meta frameworks, which provide a good foundation to plug and play various components and services, such as Freemaker. The structure tends to become more flexible and loosely coupled, allowing easy swapping of competing technologies to construct best of breed solutions tailored to specific domains.

Simplicity and flexibility will be the critical factors for a framework to sustain in this crowded space. Lightweight technologies like Ruby on Rails and Laszlo pose strong challenges to the traditional programming frameworks in the enterprise computing environment. Other related products and emerging technologies will influence the future outlook of Web application frameworks, such as XUL, general interface, XAML, Ideaburst, and Kanemea.

CONCLUSION

A Web application framework is a critical design element in distributed system development. This article describes various Web application frameworks and related emerging technologies pertinent to the Java EE model from a technical perspective. A definition of "Web application framework" is specified, as this terminology has been widely used and implies drastically distinct meanings in different contexts. The design philosophy of Web application frameworks is articulated. A comprehensive taxonomy is defined to classify various software frameworks and Web application frameworks into appropriate categories. Among dozens of Web application frameworks available as commercial and open source solutions, the predominant Java frameworks are investigated and categorized, followed by the selection guidelines and best-practice recommendations. Relevant technologies and future trends are also discussed in the context. Figure 1 summarizes the framework classification scheme designed in this work.

REFERENCES

Apache. (2006). Beehive framework. Retrieved from http://beehive.apache.org

Birrer, A., & Eggenschwiler, T. (1993). Frameworks in the financial engineering domain: An experience report. In *Proceedings of the European Conference on Object-Oriented Programming* (pp. 21-35). Kaiserslautern, Germany.

Buschmann, F. (1996). *Pattern-oriented software architecture: A system of patterns*. New York: Wiley Publishing.

DWR. (2006). *DWR framework*. Retrieved from http://getahead.ltd.uk/dwr

Echo. (2005). Echo2 framework. Retrieved from http://www.nextapp.com/platform/echo2/echo

Gachet, A. (2003). Software frameworks for developing decision support systems—A new component in the classification of DSS development tools. *Journal of Decision Systems*, *12*(3/4), 271-281.

JSON. (2006). *JSON-RPC-Java framework*. Retrieved from http://oss.metaparadigm.com/jsonrpc

JSR-127. (2004). *JaveServer Faces*. Retrieved from http://www.jcp.org/en/jsr/detail?id=127

JSR-252. (2006). *JaveServer Faces 1.2*. Retrieved from http://www.jcp.org/en/jsr/detail?id=252

Jakarta. (2006). *Tapestry framework*. Retrieved from http://jakarta.apache.org/tapestry

Johnson, R. (2002). *Expert one-to-one J2EE design and development*. Indiana: Wrox Press.

Keel. (2006). *Keel framework*. Retrieved from http://www.keelframework.org

Larman, C. (2002). *Applying UML and patterns: An introduction to object-oriented analysis and design and the unified process*. New Jersey: Prentice Hall PTR.

OpenSymphony. (2006). *WebWork framework*. Retrieved from http://www.opensymphony.com/webwork

Pree, W. (1994). Meta patterns: A means for capturing the essentials of reusable object-oriented design. In *Proceedings of the ECOOP* (pp. 150-160). Bologna, Italy.

Rife. (2006). *RIFE framework*. Retrieved from http://rifers.org

Spring (2006). *Spring framework*. Retrieved from http://www.springframework.org

Stripes (2006). *Stripes framework*. Retrieved from http://www.mc4j.org/confluence/display/stripes/Home

Struts (2006). *Struts framework*. Retrieved from http://struts.apache.org

Wicket (2006). *Wicket framework*. Retrieved from http://wicket.sourceforge.net

KEY TERMS

Component-Based Framework: A Web application framework that encapsulates the processing logic into modular components with the implementation details of request handling abstracted, independent from the incoming request protocols at the transport level.

Design Patterns: Common solutions to common problems in software design.

Hybrid Framework: A Web application framework that makes use of the best-of-breed features from both request-based and component-based frameworks.

The programming model in a request-based model is leveraged to handle the data and logic flow, whereas a component model is used to manage the actions and controllers, which are not directly mapped to the requests.

Meta Framework: A Web application framework that has a set of core interfaces for common services and a highly extensible backbone for integrating components and services. The structure is open and flexible to incorporate other concrete frameworks and components.

Request-Based Framework: A Web application framework that deals with incoming requests via actions and controllers directly in a stateless fashion, similar to the CGI mechanism.

RIA-Based Framework: A Web application framework that uses a client-side container model to minimize the amount of server communications. Instead of loading an entire HTML page each time a user clicks a link or button on the page, the framework either handles the click locally or requests a smaller block of data from the server in an XML format on demand or asynchronously behind the scene.

Rich Internet Application: A Web page-based application running in a browser with rich user interface features that are common in a fat/thick client such as drag & drop, tree controls, list sorting, and tabbed panels.

Software Framework: A reusable design and building block for a software system and/or subsystem.

Web Application: A server-based application that is accessed with a Web browser over a network.

Web Application Framework: A reusable, skeletal, semi-complete modular platform that can be specialized to produce custom Web applications, which commonly serve Web browsers via the Http(s) protocol.

Light-Weight Content-Based Search for File Sharing Systems

Gábor Richly
Budapest University of Technology and Economics, Budapest

Gábor Hosszú
Budapest University of Technology and Economics, Budapest

Ferenc Kovács
Budapest University of Technology and Economics, Budapest

INTRODUCTION

This chapter presents a novel approach to search in shared audio file storages, such as P2P-based systems. The proposed method is based on the recognition of specific patterns in the audio contents in such a way to extend the searching possibility from the description-based model to a content-based one.

The importance of the real-time **pattern recognition** algorithms that are used on audio data for content-based searching in streaming media is rapidly growing (Liu et al., 1998). The main problem of such algorithms is the optimal selection of reference patterns (*sound-prints*) used in the recognition procedure. The proposed method is based on distance maximization, and is able to quickly choose the pattern that later will be used as reference by the pattern recognition algorithms (Richly et al., 2001).

The presented method, called ***EMESE (experimental media-stream recognizer),*** is an important part of a light-weight content-searching method, which is suitable for the investigation of network-wide shared file storage. The efficiency of the proposed procedure is demonstrated in the article.

BACKGROUND

From the development of ***Napster*** (Parker, 2004), Internet-based communication has been developing toward **application level network**s **(ALN)**. On the more and more powerful hosts, various collaborative applications run and create virtual (logical) connections mutually (Hosszú, 2005). They establish virtual **overlay** and, as an alternative of the older **client/server model,** they use the **peer-to-peer (P2P)** communication. The majority of such systems deal with file sharing, requiring the important task of searching in large, distributed shared file storage (Cohen, 2003; Qiu & Srikant, 2004). The ***P2P***-based distributed file-sharing systems can search for specific files, but this search is restricted to some metadata, such as title, length, and key-words about the content. However, an efficient and light-weight pattern recognition-based identification method could improve the effectiveness of finding certain content.

Up to this time, searches have been based on the various attributes of media contents (Yang & Garcia-Molina, 2002). The attributes called metadata can be the name of media file, authors, date of recording, type of media content, or some keywords of descriptive attributes. However, if incorrect metadata were accidentally recorded, the media file may become invisible due to misleading descriptions.

Currently, powerful computers provide the possibility to implement and widely use pattern-recognition methods. Due to the large amount of media files and their very rich content, limited pattern identification should be reached as a realistic goal. This article introduces the problem of media identification based on the recognition of well-defined patterns.

Another problem is introduced if the pattern-based identification method is extended from media files to real-time media streams. The difficulty in this problem is the requirement that the pattern identification system must work in real-time, even in less powerful computing environments as well. For this purpose, full-featured media monitoring methods are not applicable, since they require large processing power in order to run their full-featured pattern recognition algorithms.

The novel system, called ***EMESE,*** is dedicated to solving the special problem, where a small but significant pattern should be found in a large voice stream or bulk voice data file in order to identify known sections of audio. Since this current approach is limited to sound files, the pattern, which serves for identifying the media file, is referred to as a ***soundprint.*** The developed method is light-weight, meaning that its design goals were fast operation and relatively small demand on computing power. In order to reach these goals, the length of the pattern to be recognized should be very limited and the total score is not required.

This article deals mainly with the heart of the EMESE system, the pattern recognition algorithm, especially the selection of the soundprints, in a process called *reference selection.*

THE PROBLEM OF THE PATTERN RECOGNITION

In the field of sound recognition, there are many different methods and applications for specific tasks (Kondoz, 1994; Coen, 1995).

The demand for working efficiently with streaming media on the Internet has increased rapidly. Audio streams may contain artificial sound effects besides the mix of music and human speech. These effects, furthermore, may contain signal fragments that are not audible by the ear. As a consequence, processing this kind of ***audio signal*** is rather different from the already developed methods, as, for example, when the short-term predictability of the signal is not applicable.

The representation of digital audio signals as individual sample values lacks any semantic structure to help automatic identification. For this reason, the audio signal is transformed into several different orthogonal or quasi-orthogonal bases that enable the detection of certain properties.

There are already solutions for classifying the type of broadcast on radio or television using the audio signal. An application (Akihito et al., 1998) makes basically a speech/music decision by examining the spectrum for harmonic content, and the temporal behavior of the spectral-peek distribution. Although it was applied successfully to that decision problem, it cannot be used for generic recognition purposes. Liu et al. (1998) also describe a scheme classifying method where the extracted features are based on the short-time spectral distribution represented by a bandwidth and a central frequency value. Several other features, for example, the volume distribution and the pitch contour along the sound clip, are also calculated. The main difficulty of these methods is their high computation-time demand. That is why their application for real-time or fast monitoring is hardly possible, when taking the great number of references to be monitored into account.

A similar monitoring problem was introduced by Lourens (1990), and the used feature, a section of the energy envelope of the record signal (*reference*), was correlated with the input (*test*) signal. The demand on real-time execution drove the development of a novel recognition scheme (Richly et al., 2000) that is capable of recognizing a pattern of transformed audio signal in an input stream, even in the presence of level-limited noise. This algorithm first selects a short segment of the signal from each record in the set of records to be monitored (Richly et al., 2001).

Carrying out tests on live audio broadcasts showed that the success of an identification process depends on the proper selection of the representative short segment. The position where this representative segment can be extracted is determined by the recognition algorithm of the proposed system called EMESE. The selected references must be non-correlated to avoid false alarms.

The method applied in EMESE is analyzed in the following section in order to explain the synchronization of the monitoring system to the test stream under various conditions. The measured results are also presented.

THE SOUND IDENTIFICATION IN EMESE

The audio signal, sampled at $f_s = 16kHz$, is transformed into a spectral description. It is a block of data, where the columns are feature vectors of the sound corresponding to a ***frame*** of time-domain data ($N_f = 256$ samples, $T_f = 16ms$ long). First, the amplitude of the Fourier spectrum is computed from the frame. Then, averaging is adapted to the neighboring frequency lines to project the spectrum onto the Bark-scale. The reason for this is to speed up the later comparison stage and to include a well-established emphasizing tool used in audio processing, the perceptual modeling of the human auditory system. As a result, $N_B = 20$ values are obtained, building up a vector that is normalized and quantized. Two levels are determined in each transformed frame. The levels are 10 percent and 70 percent of the peak value of the amplitude spectrum. The transformed frame is named a *slice*. In every reference there are $N_S = 50$ slices of non-overlapping consecutive frames; the audio section, from which the reference was made, is called the *soundprint* of that specific record.

The scheme of the recognition algorithm is to grow the already identified parts of the reference patterns continuously, according to the input. This means that the algorithm takes a frame from the input signal, executes the previously described transformation series, and compares the resulting slice to the actual one of every reference. The actual slice is the first one in every initial reference. If it is found to be similar to the slice computed from the input stream (a slice-hit occurs), the next, non-overlapping input slice will be compared to the next slice of that reference. If an input slice is decided to be non-similar, the actual slice of that reference is reset to the first one. The similarity is evaluated by calculating the weighted Manhattan-distance of the two slices that is the sum of the absolute element-vise differences in the slice vectors.

For achieving more accurate alignment between the test and reference signals, the initial slice-hit in a reference is evaluated using a distance buffer. In this circular-memory, the distances of that first reference slice to overlapping test slices are stored and the middle of the buffer is examined to see whether it contains the lowest value in the buffer. In the case that it does, and it also satisfies the threshold criteria, the identification of the reference proceeds to the next reference slice. This method intends to align the identification process to the "distance-pit" described in the next section.

After successfully identifying the last slice of a reference, the system successfully identified that record in the monitored input.

THE METHOD OF SELECTING THE REFERENCE PATTERNS

The selection algorithm also uses the previously described weighted Manhattan-distance for measuring the similarity of the audio segments. In the vicinity of the reference's beginning, there have to be frames that vary a lot in the sense of the applied distance metric. This has to be fulfilled because the pattern recognition algorithm cannot synchronize to the given reference otherwise, since the record may appear anywhere in the monitored signal. This way a robust **synchronization** can be realized that is also successful in the presence of noise.

If a long sound-print (reference candidate) is taken from a record to be monitored, and the distance of this section all along the record is calculated, then it can be observed that the distance function has a local minimum, a *pit* around the candidate's position. This is demonstrated in *Figure 1*, where the x-axis shows which frame of the record is compared with the selected candidate, while the y-axis shows the Manhattan-distance values.

To achieve robust synchronization during the recognition, one must guarantee large Manhattan-distance between the candidate and its vicinity. This is assured if the slope of the pit, as showed on *Figure 1*, is as big as possible. For selecting the best distance-pit and its corresponding candidate section, the steepness of the pit-side should be determined. However, because it is generally not constant, as an alternative, EMESE calculates the width at a given value. *Figure 2* shows pit-width of 100 candidate sections, where the sections are extracted from the same record so that their first samples are consecutive in the record. In *Figure 2*, the

Figure 1. The "distance-pit" around the reference position

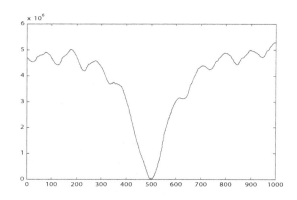

Figure 2. The width of the pits around the sound-print candidate

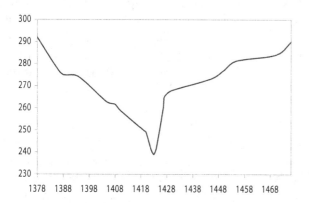

horizontal axis is the sample position of the candidate in the record, while the vertical axis is the width of the pits at a record-adaptive level.

This reference selection algorithm is based on the same principle, but since the pattern recognition method uses the first frame as kernel and grows from the first record, the pit-width for one frame-long candidate is observed. The minimum value has to be found in the above function without calculating every point of it.

It must also be assured that the selected reference does not occur any more in the record again or in any other records. Using database terminology, the reference must be a key. To avoid unambiguous identification, it must try to identify the selected reference in all the other records, and if it is not a unique key then a new reference must be selected.

The exact solution would require comparison of each of the reference-candidates to every other one. This would mean a lot of comparisons, even in the case of a few records, that could not be done in a conceivable time period.

The presented algorithm attempts to keep the number of comparisons tried as low as possible. To do so, only the vicinity is examined of the reference candidate in a region having the width w, where w is expressed in number of samples. Also, not all possible reference candidates are examined, only every 100th. The algorithm is listed in *Table 1*.

Table 1. The reference selection algorithm of the EMESE

1. In the first turn, the reference candidate is selected from the $\frac{w}{2}$ th sample of the first region of the given record (*region* is $w=5000$ samples). The first region begins on the first sample of the record, and it will define the first sample of the frame.
2. The frame is compared to all possible frames in the region, using the distance metric mentioned above. As a result, $d(i)$ is obtained, where $i = 0...w\text{-}N$, as shown in Figure 1.
3. The next region is selected $k*N$ samples forward in the record, and step two is repeated. Further regions are selected the same way and the corresponding $d(i)$ is calculated until we reach the end of the record.
4. The steepest pit and the corresponding i_{opt} frame position in the record are selected, examining all the $d(i)$ functions for the narrowest pit.
5. In the $k*N$ vicinity of position i_{opt}, the frame with the narrowest distance-pit is determined using a gradient search algorithm. This is the lowest point of the function in *Figure 2*.
6. The reference consisting of N_R slices (transformed frames) is extracted from the record beginning with the frame selected in the previous step.
7. This reference is tested for uniqueness using the recognition algorithm. If the reference appears in the record more than once, not only at the correct position, then the next best reference must be selected in the previously described way.
8. The reference is then tried against all the other records, to filter out in-set false alarms. If the reference is found in any other record, step seven is used for reference reselection.
9. The above steps are applied to all other records.

RESULTS

Using this algorithm, references from 69 advertisements were selected that previously had been recorded from a live Internet audio stream. During the tests, these advertisements were broadcast in test Internet stream-media for monitoring. To test the robustness of the system, white noise was added to the input test signal. The duration of the test was 48 hours. The recognition results are shown in *Figure 3*.

Real-time performance of the system was also observed by the number of references handled. The computer used was equipped with a Pentium-II 350 MHz processor and 256 MB of RAM, and the maximum possible number of references was 258. If the record set to be monitored was added to, the reference selection for the added record had to be performed, and the new references had to be checked for false alarms. If a possible false alarm was detected due to representative signal similarity, the selection had to be repeated for the whole set. This took 52.5 minutes in the case of 69 records. This is a worst-case scenario, and it should be very rare. The average selection time for every new record was 10 minutes.

The second test was synchronization test. Fifty frames from the stream were selected, and the dependency of the pit width on the level of noise was observed. The noise level, where the monitoring algorithm cannot synchronize to the correct frame, is shown in *Figure 4*.

Figure 3. Percentage of patterns successfully identified by the recognition algorithm

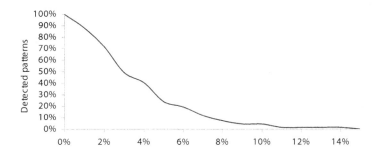

Figure 4. Result of the synchronization test

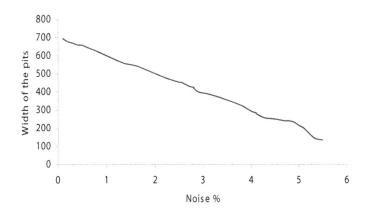

FUTURE TRENDS

Based on the continuous development of the host computers, the **P2P**-based file search systems will have increasing need for content-based media identification, and the enhancements in the hardware will provide the possibility to run light-weight but sophisticated pattern-based identification methods. Using Internet-oriented pattern identification tools as the EMESE, content-based search methods will be inherent parts of e-collaboration systems.

CONCLUSION

A reference selection method has been described and realized for an existing real-time recognition algorithm that was used on live audio streams to identify specific sound signals. The selection algorithm takes the properties of the recognition algorithm into account. The algorithm was tested on Internet media streams with a prerecorded signal set and good results have been reached. Further tests should be carried out to determine the exact effect of the input noise level on the width of the distance-pit.

The experimental results presented in the article and the described algorithms proved that the pattern-fitting based media identification methods can implement, even in Internet-related environment where the computing power and the quality of the media data are limited.

REFERENCES

Adar, E., & Huberman, B.A. (2000). Free riding on Gnutella. *First Monday, 5*(10). Retrieved June 6, 2005, from http://firstmonday.org/issues/issue5_10/adar

Akihito, M.A., Hamada, H., & Tonomura, Y. (1998). Video handling with music and speech detection. *IEEE Multimedia*, July-Sept, 16-25.

Coen, L. (1995). *Time-frequency analysis.* Prentice Hall.

Cohen, B. (2003). *Incentives build robustness in bittorrent.* Retrieved June 6, 2005, from http://bitconjurer.org/BitTorrent/bittorrentecon.pdf

Hosszú, G. (2005). Mediacommunication based on application-layer multicast. In S. Dasgupta (Ed.), *Encyclopedia of virtual communities and technologies* (pp. 302-307). Hershey, PA: Idea Group Reference.

Kondoz, A.M. (1994). *Digital speech.* UK: John Wiley & Sons.

Liu, Z., Wang, Y., & Chen, T. (1998, October). Audio feature extraction and analysis for scene segmentation and classification. *Journal of VLSI Signal Processing Systems for Signal*, Vol. 20, 61-79.

Lourens, J.G. (1990, September). Detection and logging advertisements using its sound. *IEEE Transactions on Broadcasting, 36*(3), 231-233.

Parker, A. (2004). *The true picture of peer-to-peer file sharing.* Retrieved June 8, 2005, from http://www.cachelogic.com

Qiu, D., & Srikant, R. (2004, August 30-September 3). Modeling and performance analysis of bittorrent-like peer-to-peer networks. In *Proceedings of ACM SIGCOMM'04*, 367-378. Portland, Oregon, Agust 30th-September 3rd.

Richly, G., Kozma, R., Kovács, F., & Hosszú, G. (2001). Optimised soundprint selection for identification in audio streams. *IEE Proceedings-Communications, 148*(5), 287-289.

Richly, G., Varga, L., Hosszú, G., & Kovács, F. (2000, May 29-31). Short-term sound stream characterization for reliable, real-time occurrence monitoring of given sound-prints. *MELECON2000, Cyprus* (Vol. 2, pp. 526-529).

Yang, B., & Garcia-Molina, H. (2002, July). Efficient search in peer-to-peer networks. In *Proceedings of IEEE International Conference on Distributed Computing Systems (ICDCS'02)*, 5-14. Vienna, Austria.

KEY TERMS

Application Level Network (ALN): The applications, which are running in the hosts, can create a virtual network from their logical connections. This virtual network is also called *overlay* (*see below*). The operations of such software entities cannot be understood by one another without knowing their logical relations. In most cases, these ALN software entities use the *P2P model* (see below), not the *client/server* one (see below) for the communication.

Audio Signal Processing: The coding, decoding, playing, and content handling of audio data files and streams.

Bark-Scale: A non-linear frequency scale modeling the resolution of the human hearing system. One Bark distance on the Bark-scale equals to the so called critical bandwidth that is linearly proportional to the frequency under 500Hz and logarithmically above that. The critical bandwidth can be measured by the simultaneous frequency masking effect of the ear.

Client/Server Model: A communicating model, where one host has more functionality than the other. It differs from the *P2P model* (see below).

Content-Based Recognition: When media data is identified based on its content and not on the attributes of its file. Its other name is *content-sensitive searching*.

Manhattan-Distance: The L_1 metric for the points of the Euclidean space defined by summing the absolute coordinate differences of two points ($|x2-x1|+|y2-y1|+...$). Also known as "city block" or "taxi-cab" distance; a car drives this far in a lattice-like street pattern.

Overlay: The applications which create an *ALN* (see above) working together; they usually follow the *P2P communication model* (see below).

Pattern Recognition: The procedure of finding a certain series of signals in a longer data file or signal stream.

Peer-to-Peer (P2P) Model: A communication model where each node has the same authority and communication capability. They create a virtual network, overlaid on the Internet. Its members organize themselves into a topology for data transmission.

Synchronization: The name of that procedure which is carried out for finding the appropriate points in two or more streams for the correct parallel playing out.

Malicious Software

Thomas M. Chen
Southern Methodist University, USA

Gregg W. Tally
SPARTA, Inc., USA

INTRODUCTION

Malicious software (malware) allows an intruder to take over or damage a target host without the owner's consent and often without his or her knowledge. Over the past thirty years, malware has become a more serious worldwide problem as Internet-connected computers have proliferated and operating systems have become more complex. Today, the average PC user must be more cognizant of computer security than ever before due to the constant threat of possible infection. Although exact costs are difficult to determine, there is little doubt that malware has widespread impact on equipment damages, loss of data, and loss of productivity. According to surveys, malware is one of the most common and costly types of attack on organizations (CERT, CSO, & ECTF, 2005).

In the early days of computing, malware was predominantly viruses and Trojan horses that spread among computers mainly by floppy disks and shared files (Grimes, 2001). The typical virus writer was a young male experimenting by himself and looking for notoriety. Today, malware is largely worms, viruses, spyware, bots, and Trojans proliferating through computer networks. Worms are a particular concern due to their ability to spread by themselves through computer networks. They can exploit weaknesses in operating systems or common applications such as Web and e-mail clients. They are often used as vehicles to install other types of malware onto hosts. Many thousands of worms and viruses are constantly tracked by the WildList (Wildlist Organization International, 2006) and antivirus companies.

Naturally, host-based and network-based defenses have also evolved in sophistication in response to growing threats. Surveys have found that organizations almost universally use antivirus software, firewalls, intrusion detection systems, and other means of protection (Gordon, Loeb, Lucyshyn, & Richardson, 2005). These defenses certainly block a tremendous amount of malware and prevent global disasters. However, their effectiveness is widely known to be limited by their ability to accurately detect malware. Detection accuracy is critical because malware must be blocked without interfering with legitimate computer activities or network traffic. This difficulty is compounded by the creativity of attackers continually attempting to invent new methods to avoid detection.

BACKGROUND

Self-Replicating Malware

Malware can be classified into self-replicating or non-self-replicating. Self-replicating malware consists of viruses and worms. Fred Cohen originated the term virus after biological viruses for their manner of parasitically injecting their RNA into a normal cell, which then hijack the cell's reproductive process to produce copies of the virus (Cohen, 1994). Analogously, computer viruses attach their code to a normal program or file, which takes over control of execution of the infected program to copy the virus code to another program.

Polymorphism was a major development in virus evolution around 1990. Polymorphic viruses are able to scramble their form to have at most a few bytes in common between copies to avoid detection by virus scanners. In 1991, the dark avenger's mutation engine was an easy to use program for adding polymorphism to any virus. A number of other "mutation engines" were subsequently created by other virus writers.

A new wave of mass-mailing viruses began with Melissa in 1999. It was a macro virus infecting Microsoft Word normal templates. On infected computers, it launched Microsoft Outlook and e-mailed copies of itself to 50 recipients in the address book. It demonstrated the effectiveness of e-mail as a propagation vector, infecting 100,000 computers in 3 days. Since then, e-mail has continued to be a popular vector for viruses and worms because e-mail is used by everyone across different operating systems (Harley, Slade, & Gattiker, 2001). Mass-mailing worms today often carry their own SMTP engines to mail themselves and circumvent security features in e-mail programs.

Whereas viruses are program fragments dependent on execution of a host program, worms are standalone programs capable of spreading by themselves (Nazario, 2004; Skoudis, 2004). A worm searches for potential targets through a computer network and sends a copy of itself if the target is successfully compromised. Worms take advantage of networks and have proliferated as Internet connectivity has become ubiquitous.

One of the earliest and most famous worms was written by Robert Morris Jr. in 1988. Perhaps released accidentally, it disabled 6,000 hosts, which was 10% of the ARPANET (the predecessor to the Internet). A number of fast worms, notably Code Red I, Code Red II, and Nimda appeared in 2001. Two years later, another wave of fast worms included SQL Slammer/Sapphire, Blaster, and Sobig.F. The following year was dominated by MyDoom, Netsky, and Bagle worms (Turner et al., 2006).

Nonself-replicating malware classification of nonself-replicating malware into disjoint subcategories is difficult because many types of nonself-replicating malware share similar characteristics. Perhaps the largest category is Trojan horses defined as programs with hidden malicious functions. A Trojan horse may

be disguised as a legitimate program to avoid detection. For example, a Trojan horse could be installed on a host with the name of a legitimate system file (displacing that file). Alternatively, the intention of the disguise could be to deceive users into executing it. For example, a Trojan horse could appear to be a graphic attachment in an e-mail message but in actuality be a malicious program. Trojans do not replicate by themselves but could spread by file sharing or downloading.

Remote administration or access trojans (RATs) are a well-known type of trojan horse giving covert remote control to attackers. One of the first was Netbus written in 1998. It works in a client-server fashion with the server component installed on the target machine responding to the attacker's client. Another well-known RAT was Back Orifice released by Cult of the Dead Cow in 1998, which was later released as an open source version Back Orifice 2000.

A backdoor is software giving access to a system bypassing normal authentication mechanisms (Skoudis, 2004). Programmers have written backdoors sometimes to allow convenient access for legitimate testing or administrative purposes, but backdoors can be installed and exploited by attackers to maintain covert remote control after a target has been compromised. For example, the Nimda worm dropped a backdoor on infected hosts.

Relatively recently, bots such as Spybot and Gaobot have become a major problem (Turner et al., 2006). Bots installed on a group of hosts act as a large bot net to carry out a remote attacker's instructions which are typically communicated via Internet relay chat (IRC). Bot net sizes in the thousands to hundreds of thousands have been observed. Bot nets have been rented or sold as platforms for spamming, distributed denial of service, and other criminal activities (Lewis, 2005).

A rootkit is low-level software, possibly at the kernel level, designed to conceal certain files and processes. Rootkits are sometimes bundled as part of malware such as worms (Hoglund & Butler, 2006) because the concealment allows attackers to maintain longer control over their targets.

Spyware is software that collects and sends personal information through the network to a remote attacker

(Evans, 2005). Spyware may be bundled with a legitimate program, and its presence may be mentioned in a end user license agreement (EULA). Commonly, a type of spyware called adware is bundled for the purpose of collecting information about user behavior to customize delivery of advertising. Accepting the EULA is considered explicit agreement to installation of the spyware, but many people neglect to read EULAs carefully. More pernicious types of spyware deliberately hide their presence and attempt to steal personal data by recording data to a file which is transmitted to or retrieved by a remote attacker.

MALICIOUS SOFTWARE

Malware involves an ongoing conflict between attackers and defenders. Worms are a prime example of a malware attack. Computers are typically protected by a combination of host-based and network-based defenses.

Self replication basics worms actively select and attack their targets through a network automatically. The capability for self replication is enabled by certain functions in the worm code (Skoudis, 2004). First, a function for target location chooses the next host for attack. The simplest algorithm chooses random IP address as pseudorandomly generated 32-bit numbers. Random target selection is not completely effective because the B and C class address spaces are more populated. Hence, some worms target B and C class addresses more often. Also, some worms favor targets on the same local area network as the victim because they are easier to reach. Another common way to identify targets is to harvest e-mail addresses from the victim host.

Second, a function in the worm code must contain the infection mechanism to compromise a selected target. The most common method is an exploit of a vulnerability. Most operating systems and applications software have vulnerabilities or weaknesses discovered over time. The most common type of vulnerability is a buffer overflow, which can lead to running arbitrary malicious code on a target host if attacked successfully (Foster, Osipov, Bhalla, & Heinen, 2005). When a vulnerability is discovered, the software developer is

usually notified privately and given a chance to develop a patch or update. The vulnerability may be publicly disclosed later along with the patch. Vulnerabilities are regularly published in Microsoft security bulletins, CERT advisories, Bugtraq, MITRE CVEs, and other places. This process allows users to update their systems before attackers can write the exploit code that takes advantage of the vulnerability. Other vulnerabilities may be discovered by attackers but not disclosed, in hopes of catching targets unprotected against so-called zero-day exploits.

Exploits are not the only way for worms to spread. Social engineering takes advantage of human gullibility to trick users into taking an action to help the worm (e.g., opening an e-mail attachment). Password attacks attempt to compromise a target by trying default passwords, easily guessed passwords, or cracking the password file. Another way to spread is to look for backdoors left by other worms.

Worms can easily include multiple exploits to compromise more targets faster. The Morris worm was an example using a combination of different exploits to attack targets: a buffer overflow exploit of the Unix finger daemon; an exploit of the debug mode of the sendmail program; and cracking the password file by a dictionary attack. Another prominent example of a blended threat was Nimda in 2001, using five different vectors.

A third function in the worm code enables replication of the worm to a compromised target. Replication might be combined with the exploit. For example, SQL Slammer/Sapphire carried a buffer overflow exploit and a copy of the worm within a single 404-byte UDP packet.

Finally, worm code may optionally contain a payload. The payload is executed on the target and might be virtually anything such as data theft, data deletion, or installation of other malware.

Host-Based Defenses

The most common suite of host-based defenses includes antivirus software, spyware detection software, and a personal firewall. Antivirus and antispyware software aim to identify specific malware, disinfect, or remove infected files, and prevent new infections if possible. Antivirus and antispyware programs largely work by signatures, which are sets of characteristics that will identify a specific malware (Szor, 2005). Signatures are preferred for their accuracy in identifying known malware, but new malware without a matching signature can escape detection. Antivirus software typically include heuristic rules to detect suspicious new malware based on their behavior or construction. For example, behavior blocking looks at the behavior of programs and raises a warning if the behavior appears suspicious. The disadvantage of heuristics is a possibly high rate of false positives (false alarms).

Another defense against malware is software patching. Software developers often publicize new vulnerabilities along with patches for them. This works for known vulnerabilities but not all vulnerabilities are known by the developers. Also, it can be inconvenient for users to keep up with regular patching.

Host-based intrusion detection systems are processes that observe system activities and raise alarms for suspicious activities. For example, if someone fails several consecutive login attempts, that would be a suspicious activity suggesting that the person does not know the correct password.

Lastly, computers typically include personal firewalls, implemented as software at the network interface. Incoming and outgoing traffic is blocked according to the firewall policies. There might be firewalls on the perimeter of a user's network, but a personal firewall allows packet filtering to be customized to individual preferences.

Network-Based Defenses

Compared to host-based defenses, network-based defenses have the advantage of providing broad protection to groups of users without any special requirements on hosts (Nazario, 2004). Firewalls are perhaps the best known network defense (Northcutt, Zeltser, Winters, Fredrick, & Ritchey, 2002). Firewalls apply filtering rules to block malicious traffic including malware. Rules are often based on fields in packet header fields

such as source and destination addresses, source and destination ports, and protocol.

Routers with access control lists (ACLs) can block traffic similarly to firewalls. Routers must process packet headers for the purpose of forwarding packets along the correct routes. ACLs are simply additional rules to specify which packets are dropped.

Network-based intrusion detection systems (IDS) are specialized equipment to observe and classify traffic as normal, suspicious, or malicious. IDS raise alarms for suspicious traffic but do not take active actions (intrusion prevention systems have that additional capability to block malicious traffic). Like antivirus software, IDS typically work by a combination of signature-based and behavior-based detection (also called misuse and anomaly detection). Signatures are traffic characteristics that unique identify malware traffic and are preferred for accurate detection. However, not all malware traffic is known, and therefore malware might escape signature-based detection (Riordan, Wespi, & Zamboni, 2005). Behavior-based or anomaly detection aims to identify all suspicious traffic that deviates in some sense from normal traffic.

Honeypots are decoy computers intentionally set up to look vulnerable to attackers (Spitzner, 2003). They are not used for legitimate services so all traffic received by a honeypot is unsolicited and inherently suspicious. Their general purpose is to learn about attacker behavior but can be configured to collect malware, particularly worms that choose their targets automatically and randomly. The risks associated with malware impose the necessity for special precautions to limit possibly compromised honeypots from spreading malware to other computers.

CHALLENGES

New vulnerabilities are constantly being discovered in operating systems and applications software, giving rise to new exploits for malware. Turner et al. (2006) reported an average of 10 new vulnerabilities discovered per day. Accurate detection of new exploits requires signatures, but signatures usually takes a few hours to days to develop. In the absence of a signature, the effectiveness of defenses will depend on the accuracy of anomaly (or behavior-based) detection. Anomaly detection based on unique behavioral traits of worms is an active area of research (Al-Hammadi & Leckie, 2005; Gu, Sharif, Qin, Dagon, Lee, & Riley, 2004; Kawaguchi, Azuma, Ueda, Shigeno, & Okada, 2006). For example, random worms might be inferred by the observation of a large number of failed connection messages (Berk, Bakos, & Morris, 2003). Another active research problem is automated defenses after detection such as automatic generation of worm signatures (Newsome, Karp, & Song, 2005; Simkhada, Tsunoda, Waizumi, & Nemoto, 2005) or dynamic quarantine (Moore, Shannon, Voelker, & Savage, 2003).

The situation is complicated by the many means of self-preservation that malware today often use. First, malware attempts to be stealthy through polymorphism or rootkit techniques. Second, malware can actively attack defenses. It is not uncommon for viruses and worms to disable antivirus software on targets by stopping antivirus processes and disabling registry keys. Third, malware has the capability to dynamically download new code or plug-ins, changing its functionality.

FUTURE TRENDS

Malware is always seeking new propagation vectors in addition to the Internet. Recently, malware has begun to spread via wireless networks to mobile devices such as cell phones and PDAs and is increasingly targeting instant messaging (Turner et al., 2006). E-mail and social engineering will continue to be popular propagation vectors.

The changing nature of payloads, increasingly towards remote control and data theft, suggests that malware is become more used for cybercrimes. Malware for profit has been called crimeware. This trend is also suggested by increasing use of stealth techniques.

Finally, worm outbreaks have become faster than humans can respond. For example, SQL Slammer/Sapphire is reported to have infected 90 percent of the vulnerable hosts within 10 minutes. This trend means more dependence on automated defenses in the future. However, the effectiveness of automated

defenses will depend on a solution to the problem of accurate detection.

CONCLUSION

Current defenses based on signatures and anomaly detection are imperfect. Signatures are preferred for accuracy but take time to develop and distribute. On the other hand, anomaly detection has the difficult challenge of differentiating normal from malicious behavior. In the future, malware attacks will be carried out faster, and we will depend more on automated defenses. These defenses will need solutions to automating signature development and making anomaly detection more accurate.

Finally, users are an important part of security. Since malware often use social engineering, user education and awareness of secure practices (such as patching and antivirus updating) are essential. Just as with anything valuable, users must be constantly vigilant to protect their computers and data.

REFERENCES

Al-Hammadi, Y., & Leckie, C. (2005). Anomaly detection for Internet worms. In *Proceedings of IEEE IM 2005* (pp. 133-146).

Berk, V., Bakos, G., & Morris, R. (2003). Designing a framework for active worm detection on global networks. In *Proceedings of the 1st IEEE International Workshop on Info. Assurance* (pp. 13-23).

CERT, CSO, and ECTF. (2005). *2005 e-crime watch survey*. Retrieved April 24, 2006, from http://www.cert.org/archive/pdf/ecrimesummary05.pdf

Cohen, F. (1994). *A short course on computer viruses*. New York: Wiley & Sons.

Evans, G. (2005). *Spyware study and reference guide*. Marina Del Rey, CA: Ligatt Publishing.

Foster, J., Osipov, V., Bhalla, N., & Heinen, N. (2005). *Buffer overflow attacks: Detect, exploit, prevent*. Rockland, MA: Syngress Publishing.

Gordon, L., Loeb, M., Lucyshyn, W., & Richardson, R. (2005). *CSI/FBI computer crime and security survey*. Retrieved April 24, 2006, from http://www.gocsi.com

Grimes, R. (2001). *Malicious mobile code*. Sebastopol, CA: O'Reilly & Associates.

Gu, G., Sharif, M., Qin, X., Dagon, D., Lee, W., & Riley, G. (2004). Worm detection, early warning, and response based on local victim information. In *Proceedings of the 20ᵗʰ IEEE Annual Computer Security Applications Conf*erence (pp. 136-145).

Harley, D., Slade, R., & Gattiker, R. (2001). *Viruses revealed*. New York: McGraw-Hill.

Hoglund, G., & Butler, J. (2006). *Rootkits: Subverting the windows kernel*. Upper Saddle River, NJ: Addison-Wesley.

Kawaguchi, N., Azuma, Y., Ueda, S., Shigeno, H., & Okada, K. (2006). ACTM: Anomaly connection tree method to detect silent worms. In *Proceedings of the 20ᵗʰ IEEE International Conference on Advanced Information Networking and Application* (pp. 901-908).

Lewis, J. (2005). *McAfee virtual criminology report: North American study into organized crime and the Internet*. Retrieved April 24, 2006, from http://www.mcafeesecurity.com/us/local_content/misc/mcafee_na_virtual_criminology_report.pdf

Moore, D., Shannon, C., Voelker, G., & Savage, S. (2003). Internet quarantine: Requirements for containing self-propagating code. In *Proceedings of IEEE INFOCOM 2003*.

Nazario, J. (2004). *Defense and detection strategies against Internet worms*. Norwood, MA: Artech House.

Newsome, J., Karp, B., & Song, D. (2005). Polygraph: Automatically generating signatures for polymorphic worms. In *Proceedings of the 2005 IEEE Symp. on Security and Privacy* (pp. 226-241).

Northcutt, S., Zeltser, L., Winters, S., Fredrick, K., & Ritchey, R. (2002). *Inside network perimeter security: The definitive guide to firewalls, vpns, routers, and intrusion detection systems*. Indianapolis, IN: New Riders.

Riordan, J., Wespi, A., & Zamboni, D. (2005). How to hook worms. *IEEE Spectrum, 42*(5), 32-36.

Simkhada, K., Tsunoda, H., Waizumi, Y., & Nemoto, Y. (2005). Differencing worm flows and normal flows for automatic generation of worm signatures. In *Proceedings of IEEE International Symp. on Multimedia*.

Skoudis, E. (2004). *Malware: Fighting malicious code*. Upper Saddle River, NJ: Prentice-Hall PTR.

Spitzner, L. (2003). *Honeypots: Tracking hackers*. Boston, MA: Pearson Education.

Szor, P. (2005). *The art of computer virus research and defense*. Upper Saddle River, NJ: Addison-Wesley.

Turner, D., Entwisle, S., Friedrichs, O., Ahmad, D., Blackbird, J., & Fossi, M. (2006). *Symantec Internet security threat report: Trends for July 2005-December 2005*. Retrieved April 24, 2006, from http://www.symantec.com.

Wildlist Organization International. (2006). Retrieved April 24, 2006 from http://www.wildlist.org/WildList/.

KEY TERMS

Antivirus: Software to detect viruses and worms, clean infected files, and prevent new infections.

Exploit: Software written to take advantage of a specific vulnerability.

Firewall: A device or software to selectively filter packets.

Intrusion Detection System: A device or software to detect suspicious or malicious activities.

Malware: Software intended to perform a malicious action.

Rootkit: Low-level software designed to avoid detection on a compromised host.

Spyware: A type of malware that collects personal user information and transmits to a remote attacker.

Trojan Horse: A type of malware with a hidden malicious function.

Virus: A type of self-replicating malware that infects other files or programs.

Vulnerability: A security weakness in operating system or application software.

Worm: A standalone program capable of automated replicating itself through a computer network.

Mobility Protocols

Sherali Zeadally
University of the District of Columbia, USA

Farhan Siddiqui
Wayne State University, USA

INTRODUCTION

In recent years, we have witnessed a tremendous growth of wireless networks as well as the emergence of various kinds of devices (personal digital assistants, handhelds, digital cellular phones) with different capabilities and processing power (Perkins, 1998). These technological changes have paved the way for mobile networking and wireless Internet applications. In mobile networking, computing activities are not disrupted when the user changes the computer's point of attachment to the network (e.g., to the Internet). All the needed reconnection occurs automatically and non-interactively (Perkins, 1998). Providing mobile computing capabilities enables users to access the Internet services anytime, anywhere. In this context, there is increasing demand from end-users to support continuous connectivity and uninterrupted service of their Internet applications as they move about across different networking environments.

Several protocols have been proposed (Eddy, 2004; Wanjuin, 1999; Wedlund, 1999) to support mobility. These protocols can be broadly classified according to the level at which they operate in the protocol stack namely, network, transport, or application level:

- **Network layer:** Mobile IP (Perkins, 1998) was proposed by the Internet engineering task force (IETF) to handle mobility at the network layer.
- **Application layer:** The session initiation protocol (SIP) (Rosenberg et al., 2002) is an application layer protocol that keeps mobility support independent of the underlying access technologies.

- **Transport layer:** Another protocol that was recently proposed to handle mobility and operates at the transport layer is the stream control transmission protocol (SCTP) (Stewart et al., 2000). SCTP uses multihoming to support mobility.

In mobile computing environments, the goal is to provide continuous connectivity as a mobile node moves from one network to another—often referred to as *terminal mobility*. All the needed reconnection occurs automatically and non-interactively (Handley, Schulzrinne, Schooler, & Rosenberg, 1999). Terminal mobility can be achieved by exploiting Mobile IP (Perkins, 1998) to provide mobile users the convenience of seamless roaming. Another major requirement for full mobility support is the need of an architecture that enables automatic discovery of the user location, which changes with mobility of the user—a feature often referred as *personal mobility*. New application-layer protocols such as SIP (Handley et al., 1999) can be used to provide this personal mobility.

SESSION INITIATION PROTOCOL (SIP)

SIP is an application-layer control protocol that can establish, modify, and terminate multimedia sessions such as multimedia conferences, Internet telephony calls, and similar applications with one or more participants (Handley et al., 1999). The basic role of SIP is to locate and invite participants to a multimedia session, which could be anything ranging from a VoIP call to text chat, application sharing, video, etc. A participant

Figure 1. SIP-based mobility management

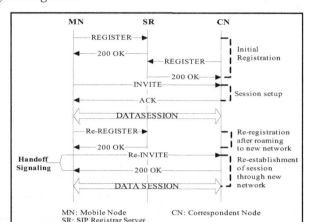

in an SIP session could be a human user or even an automaton such as a media server or a gateway to some other network, such as the public switched telephone network (PSTN). SIP also provides a rich framework of other telephony services including user location, forward, transfer, multiparty, mute, and hold. It also supports certain advanced features such as interactive voice response systems and a form of mobility. The architecture of SIP follows the client-server model and is similar to that of HTTP (Schulzrinne & Rosenberg, 1998) with requests issued by the client and responses returned by the server.

SIP supports various ways to establish and terminate a call (e.g., a voice over IP (VoIP) call):

- **User location:** Discovery of the location of the end-system from where the user wishes to communicate
- **User availability:** Determination of the willingness of the called party to engage in communications
- **User capabilities:** Negotiation and determination of the various media parameters to be used by the caller and the callee
- **Call setup:** Establishment of call parameters and flow of media streams
- **Call handling:** Termination of call sessions, transfer of calls and invocation of other services or modifications in the call parameters

SIP Protocol Characteristics

- **Lower-layer protocol neutral:** SIP makes minimal assumptions about the underlying transport and network-layer protocols. It can directly use any datagram or stream protocol, with reliable or unreliable service. SIP can be used with user datagram protocol (UDP) (Postel, 1980) or transmission control protocol (TCP) (TCP, 1981) in the Internet. Network addresses within SIP are not restricted to be Internet addresses but could be public switched telephone network (PSTN) addresses, open system interconnection (OSI) addresses, or private numbering plans (Schulzrinne et al., 1998).
- **Simple signaling:** Since the design of SIP is expected to handle only basic requirements such as the creation, modification, and termination of sessions, the signaling feature of SIP maintains simplicity and helps in rapid call-setup.
- **Text-based:** SIP is text-based thereby guaranteeing easy implementation in various programming languages along with easy debugging, all of which make SIP flexible and extensible.

Components of SIP Architecture and SIP Messages

A SIP system typically consists of two major components namely, user agents and network servers:

Figure 2. Mobile IPv4 without route optimization

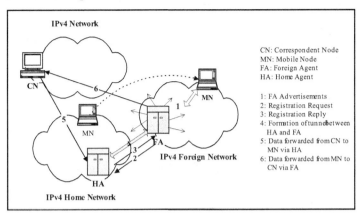

Figure 3. Mobile-IP-based mobility management

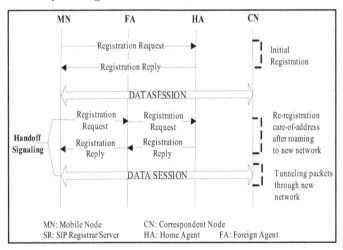

- **SIP User Agents (UA):** A user agent is an end system acting on behalf of a user. There are two parts to a SIP UA—a client and a server. The client portion is called the *user agent client (UAC)* while the server portion is called *user agent server (UAS)*. A UAC is a logical entity to create new SIP requests. A UAS is responsible for receiving SIP requests and sending the corresponding responses along with suitable processing of those SIP requests (Schulzrinne, 2000).
- **SIP Servers:** There are 3 types of servers within a SIP network:
  - **Registrar server:** Receives updates from users about their current addresses and sends an appropriate response message back to the user after the registration process
  - **Proxy server:** Responsible for the routing of SIP messages. A proxy server can be stateful or stateless. A stateless proxy does not maintain any call-related information, thus it is useful for routing of mass traffic in backbone networks. A stateful proxy server is mainly located near a UA and maintains call-related information.
  - **Redirect server:** On receiving requests, a redirect server informs the caller of the next-hop server address.

Figure 4. Mobile IPv4 with route optimization

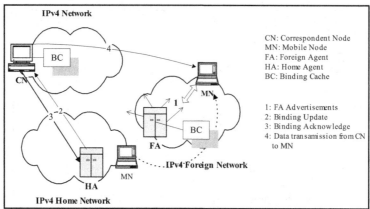

Figure 5. Mobility with mobile IPv6

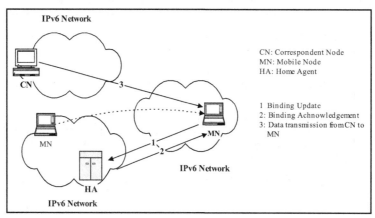

SIP messages are the basic units of SIP communication. The messages are typically requests and responses exchanged between a server and a client. Typical SIP message types used in SIP requests include INVITE, ACK, BYE, OPTIONS, REGISTER, and CANCEL.

Basic SIP Operation

Calls in SIP are uniquely identified by a call identifier, carried in the *CALL-ID* header field in SIP messages. The call identifier is created by the creator of the call and is used by all call participants. The *from* header field names the party that is requesting the connection (call originator—logical connection source). This may not necessarily be the entity that is sending the request as proxies also send requests on behalf of other users. The *to* field indicates the entity whom the originator wishes to contact (call recipient-logical connection destination). The message body provides a description of the session to be established. The type of media and codec, the sampling rate, etc., are included for negotiation by the called party. Currently, the session description protocol (SDP) (Handley & Jacobson, 1998) serves this purpose. SDP expresses lists of capabilities for audio and video and indicates where the media is to be sent to.

Callers and callees in a SIP communication environment are identified by SIP addresses known as SIP uniform resource locators (URLs) so as to enable them to be invited and identified. Each sip host is identified by an address, which is of the form "username@ domain."

The various steps involved in setting up a SIP connection before and after handoff are depicted in Figure 1.

Table 1. A comparison of the features of TCP, UDP, and SCTP

Feature	TCP	UDP	SCTP
Multihoming	No	No	Yes
Framing	No	Yes	Yes
Reliability	Yes	No	Yes
Ordering	Yes	No	Optional and Multi-streaming
Path Maximum Transmission Unit (PMTU) Fragmentation	Yes	No	Yes
Bundling	No	No	Yes
Flow and Congestion Control	Yes	No	Yes

SIP inherently supports personal mobility and can be extended to support service and terminal mobility (Schulzrinne, 2000). Terminal mobility allows a device to move between IP sub-nets, while continuing to be reachable for incoming requests and maintaining sessions across subnet changes. Mobility of hosts in heterogeneous networks is managed by using the terminal mobility support of SIP.

Terminal mobility requires SIP to establish a connection either during the start of a new session, when the terminal or MN has already moved to a different location, or in the middle of a session. The former situation is referred to as *pre-call mobility*, the latter as *mid-call* or *in-session mobility*. Figure 1 shows the messages exchanged for setting up a session between a mobile node and a correspondent node and continuing it after changing the access network.

MOBILE IPv4

When a mobile node is in its home network, in both IPv4 and IP version 6 (IPv6), it behaves just like a stationary node making no use of Mobile IP functionality and following the regular IP routing mechanisms. When a mobile node moves out of its home network it must obtain another IP address because according to the traditional IP protocol a node's address is fixed by geographical location.

So, in mobile IP, a mobile host uses two IP addresses: a fixed home address (a permanent IP address assigned to the host's network) and a care-of address--a temporary address from the new network (i.e., foreign network) that changes at each new point of attachment. Mobile IP also requires the existence of two agents: a home agent (HA) (a router connected to the home network) and a foreign agent (a router connected to the foreign network). When a mobile node moves away from its home network to a foreign network, the home agent makes it possible for the mobile node to continue to receive data on its home network. This is achieved by the home agent receiving all packets destined for the mobile node and arranges to deliver them to the mobile's node actual point of attachment determined by its care-of-address (Perkins, 1997). When the mobile node moves, it discovers its new care-of-address. The care-of-address can be obtained in two ways: by periodic advertising (from the foreign agent as shown in Figure 2) through broadcasting or by means of a "co-located care-of address" acquired by some external means such as from dynamic host configuration protocol (DHCP). The latter occurs when there is no foreign agent available on the foreign network. The mobile node then registers its care-of-address with its home agent by sending a registration request to its home agent via the foreign agent if the mobile node is using the foreign agent's care-of-address. If the mobile node is using a co-located address then it has to register directly with its home agent. The home agent then sends a registration reply either granting or denying the request. If the registration process is successful, the home agent is able to deliver packets to the mobile node at its current point of attachment: the home agent intercepts packets destined for the mobile node and then tunnels them to the mobile node's care-of-address. Tunneling involves doing IP-within-IP (Perkins, 1996) or IP encapsulation

(Perkins, 1998). The home agent encapsulates the packets into its IP packet (IP inside IP). The inner packet is the original, untouched packet; the outer packet is addressed to the care-of address and sent through the usual Internet routing mechanisms. Once the foreign agent receives packets, they are stripped of their outer layer so that the original packet emerges. The mobile node directly replies to the correspondent (sender) node. This gives rise to a problem known as *triangle routing*. The *route optimization* technique (Johnson & Perkins, 1996) is used to solve the triangle routing problem. The route optimization extension adds a conceptual data structure, the binding cache (BC), to the correspondent node and to the foreign agent. The binding cache contains bindings for mobile nodes' home addresses and their current care-of addresses. With the binding the correspondent node can tunnel datagrams *directly* to the mobile node's care-of address.

MOBILE IPv6

IPv6 (Huitema, 1995) is a new network layer protocol designed to address many limitations associated with IPv4. One of the main motivations of IPv6 was to increase the address space available for the Internet hosts. Others motivations include improving routing capabilities, real-time support, security, and multicasting (Deering, 1995).

Support for mobile networking has been considered a mandatory requirement for IPv6, and the design for Mobile IP has been modified to take full advantage of IPv6 features. IPv6 includes many features for mobility support that are missing in IPv4. These features include stateless address auto-configuration and neighborhood discovery. Mobility support in IPv6 follows the design of Mobile IPv4. Mobile IPv6 (Perkins & Johnson, 1998) retains the ideas of a home network, home agent, and the use of encapsulation to deliver packets from the home network to the mobile node's current point of attachment. While we still need discovery of a care-of-address, a mobile node can configure its care-of-address by using stateless address auto-configuration (Thompson & Narten, 1998) (where an address is formed by combining the subnet prefix advertised by the routers and the interface identifier which uniquely identifies

an interface on a subnet) or stateful address auto-configuration (Narten, Nordmark, & Simpson, 1998) (this is the IPv6 equivalent of DHCP where addresses can be obtained from a DHCP server). Thus foreign agents are not required to support mobility in IPv6.

All IPv6 nodes are capable of auto-configuring an IPv6 address appropriate to their current point of attachment to the Internet (Thompson et al., 1998). Since there are plenty of IPv6 addresses available, there is no need for foreign agents to support mobility anymore. Furthermore, since all IPv6 nodes are required to support authentication and privacy protection at the network layer, binding updates can be securely supplied to correspondent nodes that need them. This means that route optimization naturally fits in the IPv6 framework and there is no need for enhancing IPv4-based networks with route optimization support. This significant benefit that IPv6 provides represents a significant reduction in the network load that future IPv6-based networks are expected to support (Perkins, 1998).

In the case of mobile IPv6, when the mobile node (MN) moves, it has to discover a care-of-address. As mentioned previously, the care-of-address can be obtained using stateless or stateful auto-configuration. The mobile node registers its care-of-address with its home agent by sending a *binding update* message. The home agent replies to the mobile node by returning a *binding acknowledgement* message. When the mobile node is not in its home network, and if the sender (i.e., correspondent node) does not know the mobile node's care-of-address, the home agent intercepts (using *proxy neighbor discovery* (Narten et al., 1998)) packets destined for the mobile node. Each intercepted packet is tunneled to the mobile node's care-of address. This tunneling is performed using IPv6 encapsulation. Moreover, it is possible for the correspondent node to communicate directly with the mobile node. For this to happen, the mobile node informs the correspondent node of its current location (care-of address) using the *home address* option. The correspondent node will then use this care-of address as the destination address and will send its packets directly to the mobile node using the IPv6 Routing header. A discussion of other features such as co-existence with Internet ingress filtering, remembering of home networks, automatic home agent discovery supported by IPv6 mobility are beyond the scope of this article but are discussed in (Perkins, 1998).

STREAM CONTROL TRANSMISSION PROTOCOL (SCTP)

The stream control transmission protocol (SCTP) (sctporg; Stewart et al., 2000) is a reliable connection-oriented transport protocol that can operate over a connectionless protocol such as IP (Internet Protocol, 1981). SCTP supports reliable, ordered delivery similar to TCP but preserves message boundaries similar to UDP. The main features of SCTP include multi-homing, multi-streaming, message framing, configurable unordered delivery (where unordered messages can be accepted), and graceful shutdown.

An essential property of SCTP is its support for multi-homed nodes (i.e., nodes that can be reached with several IP addresses). If SCTP nodes are configured in such a way that traffic from one node to another travels on different network paths, the associations become tolerant against physical network failures. SCTP's multi-homing capability makes it a suitable protocol for enabling seamless mobility in heterogeneous network environments.

As mentioned previously, SCTP has been designed to deliver messages reliably between two end-points. These messages may carry sensitive information such as billing or signaling for application such as VoIP. As a result, designers of SCTP have incorporated features into the protocol to enable it to achieve the following security objectives: the availability of reliable and timely delivery of data and ensuring the integrity of the user information (Stewart et al., 2000).

We present a brief comparison of the main features of TCP, UDP, and SCTP in Table 1.

CONCLUSION

Various technologies are being deployed to support mobile computing applications efficiently and cost-effectively. However, one of the significant challenges that still need to be addressed is the ability to provide support for uninterrupted service access for mobile users as they move across highly heterogeneous network environments. To address this challenge, various mobility protocols (operating at application, transport, and network levels) have been implemented and deployed. In this work, we reviewed and discussed some of the most widely used mobility protocols namely, mobile IPv4, mobile IPv6, the session initiation protocol (SIP), and the stream control transmission protocol (SCTP). We argue that these protocols will continue to play a crucial role in emerging mobile computing applications and they will require further optimizations to deliver optimal performances to end-user applications.

ACKNOWLEDGMENT

We would like to thank the anonymous reviewers for their comments and suggestions. We express our gratitude to the editor-in-chief, Mario Freire, for his encouragements and support throughout the preparation of this chapter.

REFERENCES

Deering, S. and Hinden, R. (1995). Internet Protocol Version 6 (IPv6) Specification. IETF RFC 1883, December 1995.

Eddy, W. (2004). At what layer does mobility belong. *IEEE Communications Magazine, 42*(10), 155-159.

Handley, M., & Jacobson, V. (1998). SDP: Session description protocol. RFC2327, IETF, April 1998.

Handley, M., Schulzrinne, H., Schooler, E., & Rosenberg, J. (1999). SIP: Session initiation protocol. IETF RFC 2543, March 1999.

Huitema, C. (1995). *IPv6: The new Internet protocol* (2nd ed.). Prentice Hall.

Internet Protocol. (1981). Internet Protocol-DARPA Internet Program Protocol Specification. IETF, Network Working Group, September 1981.

Johnson, D., & Perkins, C. (1996). Route optimization in mobile IP. Internet Draft, draft-ietf-mobileip-optim-04.txt, February 1996.

Narten, T., Nordmark, E., Simpson, W. (1998). Neighbor discovery for IP version 6 (IPv6). IETF RFC 2461.

Perkins, C. (1996). IP encapsulation within IP. IETF RFC 2003, May 1996.

Perkins, C. (1997). Mobile IP. *IEEE Communications Magazine, 35*(5), pp. 84-99, May 1997.

Perkins, C. (1998). Mobile networking through Mobile IP. *IEEE Internet Computing, 2*(1), 58-69, January-February 1998.

Perkins, C., & Johnson, D. (1998). Mobility support in IPv6. Internet draft, draft-ietf-mobileip-ipv6-07.txt, November 1998.

Postel, J. (1980). RFC 768 - User Datagram Protocol. ISI, August 1980.

Rosenberg, J., Schulzrinne, H., Camarillo, G., Johnston, A., Peterson, J., Sparks, R., Handley, M., Schooler, E. (2002). Session initiation protocol. RFC 3261.

Schulzrinne, H. (2000). Application Layer Mobility with SIP. ACM SIGMOBILE Mobile Computing and Communications, Volume 4, Issue 3, 47-57, July 2000.

Schulzrinne, H., Rosenberg, J. (1998). Signaling for Internet telephony. In *Proceedings of the 6th International Conference on Network Protocols*, October 1998.

Schulzrinne, H., Wedlund, E. (2000). Application Layer Mobility using SIP. *ACM SiGMOBILE Mobile Computing and Communications Review, 4*(3), pp. 47-57, July 2000.

Sctporg. Stream control transmission protocol", www.sctp.org

Stewart, R., Xie, Q., Morneault, K., Sharp, C., Schwarzbauer, H., Taylor, T., Rytina, I., Kalla, M., Zhang, L., Paxson, V. (2000). Stream control transmission protocol. IETF RFC 2960, Network Working Group, October 2000.

Thompson, S., & Narten, T. (1998). IPv6 stateless address auto-configuration. IETF RFC 2462, 1998.

Wanjuin, L. (1999). Mobile Internet telephony protocol: An application layer protocol for mobile Internet telephony services. In *Proceedings of IEEE International Conference on Communications, 1*, 339-343, June 1999.

Wedlund, E., & Schulzrinne, H. (1999). Mobility support using SIP. In *Proceedings of 2nd ACM/IEEE International Conference on Wireless and Mobile Multimedia (WoWMoM'99)* (pp. 76-82), August 1999.

KEY TERMS

Fragmentation: In TCP/IP, fragmentation refers to the process of breaking packets into the smallest maximum size packet data unit (PDU) supported by any of the underlying networks.

IPv6: IPv6 (Internet protocol version 6) is the latest version of the Internet protocol (IP) and is now included as part of IP support in many products including the major computer operating systems. IPv6 has also been called "IPng" (IP next generation).

Mobile IP: Mobile IP is an Internet engineering task force (IETF) standard communications protocol that is designed to allow mobile device users to move from one network to another while maintaining their permanent IP address.

Multi-Homed: Multi-homed describes a computer host that has multiple IP addresses to connected networks. A multi-homed host is physically connected to multiple data links that can be on the same or different networks.

Protocol: A protocol is a special set of rules that end points in a telecommunication connection use when they communicate.

Reliability: Reliability is an attribute of any computer-related component (software, or hardware, or a network, for example) that consistently performs according to its specifications.

Voice Over IP (VoIP): VoIP is an IP telephony term for a set of facilities used to manage the delivery of voice information over the Internet.

Model–Driven Engineering of Distributed Applications

Karim El Guemhioui
University of Quebec in Outaouais, Canada

INTRODUCTION

The information technology (IT) industry has been moving so fast that companies implementing complex distributed software solutions hardly complete a system deployment on a given network middleware before either they are offered a newer version of the middleware technology, or a competing and alleged superior technology appears. This situation raises two somewhat conflicting challenges:

- How to continue to benefit from the state-of-the-art middleware technology?
- How to protect existing investments in current and legacy technological platforms?

The achievement of these two objectives poses difficult problems. On the one hand, acquiring every new middleware technology is costly and unpractical. On the other hand, not embracing the latest technological wave risks the loss of competitive edge and of the potential for innovation. From a scientific viewpoint, the adequacy of existing software development processes for the modeling and design of large systems is also questioned.

The Object Management Group (OMG), a standardization body promoting object-oriented technologies, has introduced a model-driven architecture (MDA) initiative aimed at addressing these issues. The MDA approach proposes to separate the specification of system (or business) functionality from the specification of that functionality on a specific middleware technological platform (CORBA, .NET, J2EE/EJB, XML/SOAP, etc.). Both specifications are expressed as models.

MDA was built on important OMG standards including the unified modeling language (UML) and the meta object facility (MOF). An abstract design constitutes a generic, platform-independent model of a system or business undistorted by any specific middleware idio-syncrasies, but one that will need to be implemented in an actual model for a given computation platform (Miller & Mukerji, 2001).

This activity of modeling the model, or meta-modeling, requires an appropriate infrastructure. This infrastructure should support at least: the concepts that are available for the creation of metamodels, the rules governing the use of these concepts, and a notation for the depiction of the metamodel. The authors of MDA view UML as the language for creating models and MOF as defining the language for creating metamodels.

This central position of UML has been refuted by some stakeholders that argue the need for more specialized and tailored languages for specific domains (Greenfield & Short, 2004). These domain specific languages (DSL) are usually small-sized, easy to manipulate and transform, and aim to overcome the questionable continuity and stability of UML, as well as the lack of rigor surrounding some of its concepts.

Nevertheless, the tenants of this second approach share the same final objective with OMG MDA, which is to improve productivity in middleware-based software development via a model-driven approach that faithfully and unambiguously captures business logic once, and allows for the automatic derivation of multiple platform-specific solutions ("Model once, generate everywhere"). MDA has thus become a special case of a more general approach called model-driven engineering (MDE).

While MDA basically relies on the separation of aspects intrinsic to the domain from aspects related to the underlying platform, MDE goes further by isolating, modeling, and then weaving more general and diverse aspects such as non behavioural requirements (security, network transparency, reliability, etc.).

Keeping up with network middleware evolution requires a clear understanding of the potentialities but also limitations of MDA and MDE.

BACKGROUND

From a historical perspective, the MDA approach is just the latest step in the raising of the abstraction level that has characterized the software engineering discipline from the beginning (Mellor et al., 2004).

The first programs literally consisted of raw machine instructions expressed as 0s and 1s. This tedious and error-prone way of developing software was alleviated by the introduction of assembly languages. Basically, these languages proposed an abstraction of the native machine instructions in the form of a few and simple mnemonics. The programmers could also use a name (another abstraction) to refer to a memory location instead of its binary address. Assemblers took on the task of automatically translating the mnemonics and memory location names into binary representations of native machine instructions and memory addresses. The next step consisted in freeing the developer from thinking in terms of specific processor instruction sets, increasing productivity and reuse since the same high-level program could now be run on multiple hardware platforms, provided appropriate mappings were in place. This became possible thanks to the advent of third-generation programming languages (3GLS) that defined programming abstractions above the concepts of specific processor instruction sets, and compilers that automated the translation of high-level code into targeted machine instructions. The next logical step is to be able to completely define the application logic regardless of any programming language and/or hardware platform technical contingencies, and then automatically generate the appropriate code.

Of course, the whole idea of raising the abstraction level so as to allow the software developers to program in terms of their design intent rather than the underlying computing environment is not new, and several past attempts have been conducted. The best known of these efforts was probably the computer-aided software engineering (CASE) approach that focused on the development of software methods and tools for the expression of designs in terms of general-purpose graphical programming representations, such as state machines, or dataflow diagrams (Schmidt, 2006).

However, CASE failed as a recognized and unified initiative because of the state of the technology at the time: poor mapping of the graphical representations onto the underlying platforms (mostly single-node systems), lack of support for important quality of service properties (distribution transparency, fault tolerance, and security), huge and complex amount of generated code to redress the bareness of the underlying platforms, poor scalability, and lack of effective middleware (Schmidt, 2006).

The main purpose of MDA is to facilitate a software development process that is driven by modeling rather than coding. Indeed, in MDA models are first class entities, and not only used to sketch design ideas and probably be thrown away once the code has been written. A commonly agreed upon definition of a model is that it is a representation of a real system, while being based on semantics and rules that condition its elements. Systems that share the same rules and elements' semantics can be grouped together. Each group defines a domain (or family) and can be endowed with a language for expressing its models; this expression language can be described by a model of a higher level of abstraction called a metamodel.

Thus, metamodeling consists in defining the vocabulary and grammar allowing the realization of a family of models. In other words, a metamodel is a specification model of a class of systems, where each system is itself a valid model expressed in a certain modeling language (Seidewitz, 2003).

For example, in Java (a modeling language for specifying source code), we can use the concepts of "Class," "Interface," "Method," and so on, when defining a Java program, because in the metamodel of Java there are elements that define what is a class, an interface, a method, etc.

Similarly, a metamodel can be written in a language called a meta-language and its model, in turn, will be known as a meta-metamodel. A model is loosely considered an instance of its metamodel since it represents a particular occurrence of the possible concretizations

Figure 1. Raising the abstraction level

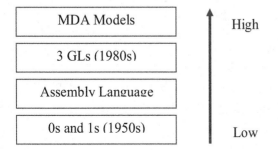

Figure 2. MDA four-layer architecture

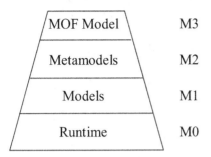

Figure 3. MDA development process

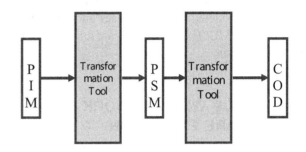

of the metamodel. Atkinson and Kühne (2003) introduce the concept of ontological instance to qualify the link relating a model to its metamodel. However, the exact nature of the relationship between a model and the metamodel to which it must conform is more akin to the relation between a programming language and its grammar.

These concepts help understand the multi-layered architecture used by OMG MDA and are shown in Figure 2. Each layer represents an abstraction level named, respectively, M0, M1, M2, and M3.

Following the same logic, one could define layers of higher levels (e.g., M4 and M5) according to their needs, but the meta-language MOF, belonging to M3 and standardized by OMG, is defined in a self-descriptive way that makes it possible to stop at the fourth layer.

The OMG MDA approach is characterized by the creation of various categories of models of the same system. The development will be driven by the activity of modeling the system in three main steps (see Figure 3):

1. Define a model at a high level of abstraction and independently of any implementation technology. This model is called the platform independent model (PIM).
2. Transform the PIM into one or more models such that each one represents the system by incorporating elements specific to a particular implementation technology. Each one of these models is known as a platform specific model (PSM).
3. Transform each PSM into executable code.

Of course, one of the main challenges of the MDA approach is in the definition of the transformations and the degree of automation that can be achieved. Note that from the beginning, MDA has been interpreted in two rather contrasting ways: an elaborationist view and a translationist vision (McNeile, 2003).

For the elaborationists, once the PIM has been created, a tool automatically generates a rough PSM that the developer must complete (or elaborate on) by adding further information or detail. It is therefore possible that the lower level models get out of step with the higher ones. To overcome this out-of-sync, tools supporting round-trip engineering are necessary. A typical representation of this approach can be found in Kleppe, Warmer, and Bast (2003).

For the translationists, the original PIM is to be directly translated into the final code, though an intermediate PSM can be made available for inspection purposes only. In this approach, the PSM and the final code are not amended by hand. Because changes are made upstream and propagated by regeneration, there is no need for round-trip engineering to keep everything synchronized. This approach derives mainly from works on real-time and embedded systems and is best illustrated in Mellor and Balcer (2002).

As explained in McNeile (2003), both approaches are so far failing in fully modeling behavior which, according to MDA, would permit the execution and test of PIMs. In the first approach, behavior is specified by defining the post and pre-conditions of operations. This means that the PIM is not an executable artifact. In the second approach, behavior is specified using state machines and some action language. However, in business information and transactional systems, state machines are seldom used. In this domain, behavior is normally modeled using use cases and interaction diagrams in UML. These diagrams are not suitable for model execution.

KEEPING UP WITH NETWORK MIDDLEWARE EVOLUTION

Much of the complexity of networked systems is not only due to the volume of code or data, but also to the need to integrate a lot of aspects (reliability, performance, etc.) from the beginning and in a seamless way. Existing systems have evolved very quickly, not because of a change in application requirements, but because of the fast rate at which the underling technological platforms (i.e., the network middleware) have evolved. Finally, as new technologies arrive, old ones do not disappear but become legacy software, thereby exacerbating the heterogeneity problem (Bézivin et al., 2004).

In a model-driven approach to developing distributed systems, the PIMs become the long-lived intellectual assets, instead of the code; and the more automated the transformations, the better the productivity and return on investment.

Increasing the automation of transformations and improving the adequacy and completeness of the generated code depends, at least, on the following factors:

- Ability of the modeling language to accurately and thoroughly render the specifics of the application domain
- Ability to incorporate into the model's non-behavioral requirements that are tantamount to the success of networked applications (transparency, scalability, security, fault tolerance, etc.)
- Availability of a large base of standardized domain and/or technology metamodels from which to build sound models
- Availability of integrated modeling environments and tools for the development, testing, and execution/transformation of the models
- Availability of formal or reliable methods to validate the transformations

Though OMG has undertaken a considerable endeavor to uplift the UML standard to meet MDA

expectations and requirements, the result still suffers from bloat and semantic under-specifications. The latest version (UML 2.0) contains numerous modeling concepts that are related in complex ways, making their learning and application quite difficult.

Several concepts have poorly defined semantics, rendering the automation vain. We will only mention two examples: the concept of variation points that put the burden on the designer for defining and communicating appropriate semantics plugged into a variation point of the model, and the support of the profile mechanism that allows arbitrary extensions to a model but without a means for precisely defining semantics associated with these extensions. For a detailed discussion of the UML 2.0 pitfalls, we refer the reader to France et al. (2006). The UML 2.0 metamodel, very important for defining models and transformations, suffers itself from a high degree of complexity and buries simple but important relationships between some core abstract concepts.

Model-driven engineering (MDE) encompasses MDA and still relies on modeling as a central activity and models as first class entities. However, it acknowledges that UML/MOF may not fit every problem, and that there are technological spaces more appropriate for some domains. A technological space (TS) is a working context with a set of associated concepts, body of knowledge, tools, required skills, and possibilities. It is often associated to a given user community with shared knowhow, educational support, common literature, etc. (Kurtev et al., 2002); for example: the XML TS, or the DBMS TS. UML provides little leverage for a biologist, process control engineer, or hedge-fund analyst whose primary interest is in modeling directly in his or her application domain (Thomas, 2004). Domain-specific languages (DSL) are more adequate in reducing the semantic gap between the application domain and the execution platform. For example, software factories (Greenfield & Short, 2004) provide effective concepts and resources for the model-based design of .NET applications, and could be successfully applied to Web engineering. But for many domains, there is a pressing need for appropriate DSLs that favour the expression of design intent and shield the complexity of the underlying middleware. A noteworthy research effort (Balasubramanian et al., 2006) shows how to create DSLs for the development, deployment, and optimization of component-based distributed real-time and embedded systems.

Separating concerns and supporting the weaving of specific aspects, especially non behavioural requirements, into models is also at the heart of the MDE approach and distinguishes it from the initial MDA. Though the weaving of models follows a simple Y-shaped life cycle, several issues pose complex challenges: merging and alignment of the input models, the model of the weaving itself, the mixing and covering of concerns following a transformation, etc. Aspect-oriented programming approaches do not scale well to model weaving because the former operate at the code level whereas the latter perform at a higher level of abstraction.

Very few domains have standardized and well publicized metamodels on which to build sound PIMs and/or PSMs. A recent contribution (Abd-Ali & El Guemhioui, 2005) targeting the .NET component technology aspires to prompt similar efforts targeting other middleware technologies and/or application domains.

There are several ongoing efforts at developing tools and environments in support of model-based approaches. Because of the lack of theoretical foundations, many of these tools still heavily rely on the CASE experience, which was plagued by proprietary technologies and their poor integration. One of the most promising products that leverage MDE is the eclipse modeling framework (Carlson, 2005).

Finally, we must be able to validate the automated model transformations on which the whole model based approach relies (Selic, 2003). Otherwise, we won't be able to ensure that fundamental properties have been preserved between successive models, or that the running application is consistent with the designer intent. If a transformation is expressed in a language with some mathematical underpinning, it may be possible to prove theoretical properties of the transformation. However, with the exception of very specific and limited areas where formalism, such as finite state machines, is sufficient to describe the behaviour of the system, application dynamics are usually described with semi-formal notations. Küster (2004) considers the validation of model transformations only from the preservation of syntactical properties viewpoint. It is essential that transformations also preserve semantics. A semi-formal approach that can be partially automated is introduced in El Guemhioui and Abd-Ali (2006).

FUTURE TRENDS

For all the issues that we have discussed, we have mentioned on-going research efforts that give a clear indication of the direction in which MDA and MDE are heading.

It is expected that UML will still evolve to better support model-driven development. More DSLs will appear, spurring upstream technology and area-confined metamodels, and downstream tools and transformation rules.

With the advent of sophisticated behaviour modelling, weaving, validation, and round-trip engineering methods and tools, the proportion of generated code should dramatically increase.

CONCLUSION

Model-driven development is still in its infancy. MDA has spawned a paradigm shift from a component-centric to a model-centric approach to software development. Conceptually, MDA is built on the clean and well-defined idea of separating the business model, usually subject to slow changes, from the supporting technologies, historically fast evolving. By doing so, return on investment is increased and productivity is improved. MDE has broadened the scope by covering more of the life cycle.

Nowadays, nobody doubts the benefits of 3GLs over assembly; if MDE delivers on its promises, models will displace 3GLs to where assemblers are today.

REFERENCES

Abd-Ali, J., & El Guemhioui, K. (2005). An MDA .NET metamodel. In *Proceedings of the 9th IEEE International Enterprise Distributed Object Computing Conference* (pp. 142-153). IEEE Computer Press.

Atkinson, C., & Kühne, T. (2003). Model-driven development: A metamodeling foundation. *IEEE Software, 20*(5), 36-41.

Balasubramanian, K., Gokhale, A., Karsai, G., Sztipanovits, J., & Neema, S. (2006). Developing applications using model-driven design environments. *IEEE Computer*, February.

Bézivin, J., Hammoudi, S., Lopes, D., & Jouault, F. (2004). Applying MDA approach for Web service platform. In *Eighth IEEE International Enterprise Distributed Object Computing Conference* (pp. 58-70).

Carlson, D. (2005). *Eclipse distilled.* Addison-Wesley.

El Guemhioui, K., & Abd-Ali, J. (2006). An insight into MDA and model semantics preservation. *WSEAS Transactions on Computers, 5*(10), 2488-2494.

France, R.B., Ghosh, S., & Dinh-Trong, T. (2006). Model-driven development using UML 2.0: Promises and pitfalls. *IEEE Computer*, February, 33-40.

Greenfield, J., & Short, K. (2004). *Software factories.* Wiley.

Kleppe, A., Warmer, J., & Bast, W. (2003). *MDA explained: The model driven architecture: Practice and promise.* Reading, MA: Addison-Wesley.

Kurtev, I., Bézivin, J., & Aksit, M. (2002). *Technological spaces: An initial appraisal.* In *CoopIS, DOA2002 Federated Conferences*, Industrial track, Irvine, CA.

Küster, J.M. (2004). Systematic validation of model transformations. In *Third Workshop in Software Model Engineering* (WiSME@UML 2004).

McNeile, A. (2003). *MDA: The vision with the hole?* Retrieved from http://www.metamaxim.com/download/documents/MDAv1.pdf

Mellor, J.S., & Balcer, M. (2002). *Executable UML: A foundation for model driven architecture.* Addison-Wesley.

Mellor, S.J., Scott, K., Uhl, A., & Weise, D. (2004). *MDA distilled: Principles of model-driven architecture.* Addison-Wesley.

Miller, J., & Mukerji, J. (Eds.). (2001). Model driven architecture. OMG ormsc/2001-07-01. Retrieved from www.omg.com/mda

Schmidt, D.C. (2006). Model driven engineering. *IEEE Computer*, February, 25-31.

Seidewitz, E. (2003). What models mean. *IEEE Software, 20*(5), 26-32.

Selic,B. (2003). The pragmatics of model-driven development. *IEEE Software, 20*(5), 19-25.

Thomas, D. (2004). MDA: Revenge of the modelers or UML utopia? *IEEE Software, 21*(3), 22-24.

KEY TERMS

Meta Object Facility (MOF): A standard for the definition of metamodels in an MDA approach.

Metamodel: The model of a modeling language.

Model: A representation, for a specific purpose, of certain aspects of a real system.

Model-Driven Architecture (MDA): A set of standards that enable the specification of models and their transformation into other models and complete systems.

Model-Driven Engineering (MDE): An emerging technique in software, system, and data engineering, based on the systematic use of models considered as first class entities. MDA is a special case of MDE.

Modeling Language: A notation for expressing models.

Platform Independent Model (PIM): A model that contains no reference to the underlying technological platform.

Platform Specific Model (PSM): A PIM adapted to a specific technological platform.

Unified Modeling Language (UML): A standardized visual language for modeling software systems.

Modeling IP Traffic Behavior through Markovian Models

António Nogueira
University of Aveiro/Institute of Telecommunications Aveiro, Portugal

Paulo Salvador
University of Aveiro/Institute of Telecommunications Aveiro, Portugal

Rui Valadas
University of Aveiro/Institute of Telecommunications Aveiro, Portugal

António Pacheco
Instituto Superior Técnico – UTL, Portugal

INTRODUCTION

It is known for more than a decade that IP traffic may exhibit properties of self-similarity and/or long-range dependence (LRD) (Crovella & Bestavros, 1997; Leland, Taqqu, Willinger, & Wilson, 1994; Paxson & Floyd, 1995), peculiar behaviors that have a significant impact on network performance. However, matching LRD is only required within the time-scales of interest to the system under study (Grossglauser & Bolot, 1999; Nogueira & Valadas, 2001). One of the consequences of this result is that more traditional traffic models such as markov modulated poisson processes (MMPPs) can still be used to model traffic exhibiting LRD (Andersen & Nielsen, 1998; Salvador & Valadas, 2001a; Salvador & Valadas, 2001b; Yoshihara, Kasahara, & Takahashi, 2001).

This article addresses the use of Markovian models based on discrete time MMPPs (dMMPPs) for modeling IP traffic. In order to describe the packet arrival process, we will present three traffic models that were designed to capture self-similar behavior over multiple time scales. The first model is based on a parameter fitting procedure that matches both the autocovariance and marginal distribution of the counting process (Salvador, Valadas, & Pacheco, 2003). The dMMPP is constructed as a superposition of L two-state dMMPPs (2-dMMPPs) designed to match the autocovariance function, and one $M-d$MMPP designed to match the

marginal distribution. The second model is a superposition of MMPPs, each one describing a different time scale (Nogueira, Salvador, Valadas, & Pacheco, 2003a). The third model is obtained as the equivalent to a hierarchical construction process that, starting at the coarsest time scale, successively decomposes MMPP states into new MMPPs to incorporate the characteristics offered by finer time scales (Nogueira, Salvador, Valadas, & Pacheco, 2003b). These two models are constructed by fitting the distribution of packet counts in a given number of time scales.

Accurate modeling of certain types of IP traffic requires matching closely not only the packet arrival process but also the packet size distribution (Gao & Rubin, 1999; Klemm, Lindemann, & Lohmann, 2003). In this way, we also present a discrete-time batch markovian arrival process (dBMAP) (Salvador et al., 2003) that jointly characterizes the packet arrival process and the packet size distribution, while achieving accurate prediction of queuing behavior for IP traffic exhibiting LRD. In this dBMAP, packet arrivals occur according to a dMMPP and each arrival is further characterized by a packet size with a general distribution that may depend on the phase of the dMMPP. This allows having a packet size distribution closely related to the packet arrival process, which is in contrast with other approaches (Gao et al., 1999; Klemm et al., 2003) where the packet size distribution is fitted prior to the matching of the packet arrival rates.

BACKGROUND

The dBMAP is a stochastic process that may be regarded as a Markov random walk whose additive component takes values on the nonnegative integers, N_0 (Lucantoni, 1991, 1993; Pacheco & Prabhu, 1995). Thus, we say that a Markov chain $(X,J) = \{(X_k, J_k), k \in N_0\}$ on the state $N_0 \times S$ is a dBMAP if:

$$P(X_{k+1} = m, J_{k+1} = j \mid X_k = n, J_k = i)$$

$$= \begin{cases} 0 & m < n \\ p_{ij} q_{ij}(m-n) & m \geq n \end{cases}$$

where $P = (p_{ij})_{i,j \in S}$ is a stochastic matrix and, for each pair $(i,j) \in S^2$, $q_{ij} = \{q_{ij}(n), n \in N_0\}$ is a probability function over N_0, and we let $Q(n) = (q_{ij}(n))_{i,j \in S}$. This implies, in particular, that J is a Markov chain, called the *Markov component* or *phase* of (X,J) and S is the set of modulating states or the phase set. When the dBMAP (X,J) is used to model an arrival process, X_K may be interpreted as the total number of arrivals until instant k. We then say that (X,J) is a dBMAP with parameterization $(P, Q(n)_{n \in N_0})$ and if, moreover, S has r states, then we write $(X,J) \sim \text{dBMAP}_r(P, Q(n)_{n \in N_0})$. In this case, with a slight abuse of notation, we also say that the increment process (Y,J), where $Y_K = X_K - X_{K-1}$, is a dBMAP and write $(Y,J) \sim \text{dBMAP}_r(P, Q(n)_{n \in N_0})$.

An important particular case of the dBMAP is the dMMPP. We say that the process (X,J) on the state space $N_0 \times S$ is a dMMPP with parameters (P, Λ), where $P = (p_{ij})_{i,j \in S}$ is a stochastic matrix and $\Lambda = (\lambda_{ij})_{i,j \in S} = (\lambda_i 1_{\{i=j\}})_{i,j \in S}$ is a diagonal matrix with nonnegative entries (i.e., $\lambda_i \geq 0$, $i \in S$), if it is a dBMAP with parameterization $(P, Q(n)_{n \in N})$, where $q_{ij}(n) = e^{-\lambda_j} \frac{\lambda_j^n}{n!}$, for $i,j \in S$ and $n \in N$; (i.e., $q_{ij} = \{q_{ij}(n), n \in N_0\}$) is the probability function of a poisson random variable with mean λ_j. Thus, a dMMPP is a dBMAP for which the number of arrivals in a given instant of time is only a function of the current phase of the dBMAP and when the process is in phase j the number of arrivals at an instant has a poisson distribution with mean λ_j.

The superposition of independent dMMPPs is still a dMMPP. More precisely, if:

$$(X^{(l)}, J^{(l)}) \sim \text{dBMMP}_{r_l}(P^{(l)}, \Lambda^{(l)}), l = 1, 2, \ldots L$$

are independent, then their superposition:

$$(X,J) = \left(\sum_{l=1}^{L} X^{(l)}, \left(J^{(1)}, J^{(2)}, \ldots, J^{(L)} \right) \right)$$

is a $\text{dMMPP}_S(P, \Lambda)$, where:

$$S = \{1, 2, \ldots, r_1\} x \ldots x \{1, 2, \ldots, r_L\},$$
$$P = P^{(1)} \otimes P^{(2)} \otimes \ldots \otimes P^{(L)} \text{ and}$$
$$P = \Lambda^{(1)} \oplus \Lambda^{(2)} \oplus \ldots \oplus \Lambda^{(L)},$$

with $\oplus$ and $\otimes$ denoting the Kronecker sum and product, respectively.

DESCRIPTION OF THE MARKOVIAN TRAFFIC MODELS

$M2^L$ – MMPP Second-Order Self-Similar Model

This section presents a parameter fitting procedure based on MMPPs that matches both the autocovariance and the marginal distribution of the counting process leading to accurate estimates of queuing behaviour for network traffic exhibiting LRD behaviour.

Matching simultaneously the autocovariance and marginal distribution of the counting process is a difficult task since every MMPP parameter influences both characteristics. With the purpose of achieving some degree of decoupling when matching these two statistics, the proposed MMPP $((X,J) \sim M2^L - \text{dMMPP})$ is constructed as a superposition of L independent 2–dMMPPs, $(X^{(l)}, J^{(l)}) \sim \text{dMMPP}_2(P^{(l)}, \Lambda^{(l)}), l = 1, 2, \ldots, L$, that capture the autocovariance function of the increments of the arrival process and one $M - \text{dMMPP}$, $(X^{(L+1)}, J^{(L+1)}) \sim \text{dMMPP}_M(P^{(L+1)}, \Lambda^{(L+1)})$, that approximates the distribution of the increments of the arrival process (Figure 1a). In our approach L and M are not fixed *a priori* but are instead computed as part of the fitting procedure.

Figure 1. (a) Superposition of a M – dMMPP and L 2-dMMPP models; (b) Construction methodology of the superposition model

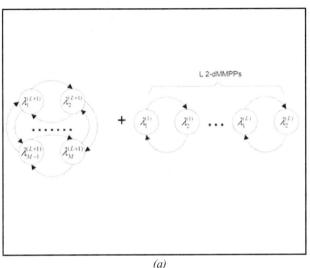

(a)

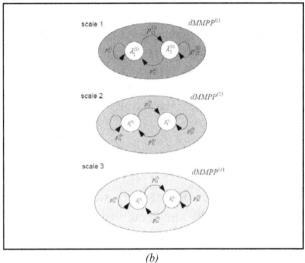

(b)

Let us consider that $Y^{(1)}, Y^{(2)}, ..., Y^{(L+1)}$ and Y are the increment processes associated to $X^{(1)}, X^{(2)}, ..., X^{(L+1)}$ and X, respectively. Since the marginal distribution of $Y^{(l)}, l = 1, 2, ..., L$ is a mixture of two poisson distributions, its autocovariance function exhibits an exponential decay to zero. As we want the $M - dMMPP$ to approximate the distribution of the increments of the arrival process but to have no contribution to the autocovariance function of the increments of the $M2^L$ – dMMPP, we choose to make $J^{(L+1)}$ a Markov chain with no memory whatsoever. In this way, the probability function of $Y^{(L+1)}$ can be easily derived and its autocovariance function is null for all positive lags.

The inference procedure of this process includes four major steps.

1. **Approximation of the empirical autocovariance by a weighted sum of exponentials and identification of the time scales:** Our approach approximates the autocovariance by a large number of exponentials and then aggregates exponentials with a similar decay into the same time-scale, which is close to the approaches considered in Andersen et al. (1998), Feldmann and Whitt (1997), and Yoshihara et al. (2001).

2. **Inference of the $M - dMMPP$ probability function and of the L $2 - dMMPP$ parameters:** In order to simplify the deconvolution operations, the poisson arrival rate in one state of each $2 - dMMPP$ source is assumed as zero; then, the probability function of the $M - dMMPP$ is fitted jointly with the steady-state probabilities of the $2 - dMMPP$s through a constrained minimization process.

3. **Inference of $M - dMMPP$ parameters:** The next step is the inference of the number of states and poisson arrival rates of the $M - dMMPP$ from the fitted probability function of the $M - dMMPP$, $\hat{f}_{L+1}$. To do this, we infer $\hat{f}_{L+1}$ as a weighted sum of poisson probability functions (i.e., as the probability function of a finite poisson mixture with an unknown number of components). The matching is carried out through an algorithm that progressively subtracts a poisson probability function from $\hat{f}_{L+1}$.

4. **$M2^L - dMMPP$ model construction:** Finally, the $M2^L - dMMPP$ process can be constructed using the Kronecker sum and product.

The details of each step of the inference procedure are given in Salvador et al. (2003).

Distributional Self-Similar Models

This section proposes two traffic models based on dMMPPs designed to capture self-similar behaviour over multiple time scales by fitting the empirical distribution of packet counts at each time scale. The number of time scales, L, is fixed *a priori* and the time scales are numbered in an increasing way, from $l = 1$ (corresponding to the largest time scale) to $l = L$ (the smallest time scale).

Superposition Model

This model is based on the superposition of dMMPPs where each dMMPP represents a specific time scale. Figure 1b illustrates the construction methodology of the dMMPP for the simple case of three time scales and two-state dMMPPs in each time scale. The dMMPP associated with time scale l is denoted by dMMPP$^{(l)}$ and the corresponding number of states by $N_{(l)}$. The three most important steps of the inference procedure are:

1. **Computation of the average number of arrivals per time interval at each time scale:** Having defined the time interval at the smallest time scale, Δt, the number of time scales, L, and the level of aggregation, a, the aggregation process computes the data sequences corresponding to the average number of arrivals at each time scale.

2. **For all time scales, calculation of the corresponding empirical probability and mass function (PMF) and inference of a dMMPP that matches the resulting PMF:** Each dMMPP will be inferred from a PMF that represents its contribution to a particular time scale. For the largest time scale, this PMF is simply the empirical one. The traffic components due to time scale l, $l = 2, ...,$ L, are obtained through deconvolution of the empirical PMFs of this and the previous time scales. The number of states, $N_{(l)}$, and the parameters of the dMMPP$^{(l)}$, $\left\{ \left(\pi_j^{(l)}, \lambda_j^{(l)} \right), j = 1, 2, ..., N_{(l)} \right\}$, that

adjusts the empirical PMF of time scale l are calculated using the same procedure described in step 3 of the $M2^L$ – dMMPP inference procedure. The next step associates one of the dMMPP$^{(l)}$ states with each time interval of the arriving process and, finally, the transition probabilities, $p_{ij}^{(l)}$, i, $j = 1, ..., N_{(l)}$ are inferred by counting the number of transitions between each pair of states.

3. **Calculation of the final dMMPP through the superposition of the dMMPPs inferred for each time scale:** The equivalent dMMPP process is constructed using the Kronecker sum and product operations.

The details of each inference procedure step are given in Nogueira et al. (2003a).

Hierarchical Model

This model is constructed using a hierarchical procedure that successively decomposes dMMPP states into new dMMPPs, thus refining the traffic process by incorporating the characteristics offered by finer time scales (Figure 2a). The procedure starts at the largest time scale by inferring a dMMPP that matches the empirical PMF corresponding to this time scale. As part of the parameter fitting procedure, each time interval of the data sequence is assigned to a dMMPP state; in this way, a new PMF can be associated with each dMMPP state. At the next finer time scale, each dMMPP state is decomposed into a new dMMPP that matches the contribution of this time scale to the PMF of the state it descends from. In this way, a child dMMPP gives a more detailed description of its parent state PMF. This refinement process is iterated until a pre-defined number of time scales is integrated. Finally, a dMMPP incorporating this hierarchical structure is derived.

The construction process of the hierarchical model can be described through a tree where, except for the root node, each tree node corresponds to a dMMPP state and each tree level to a time scale. A dMMPP state will be represented by a vector indicating the

Figure 2. Construction methodology of the (a) hierarchical model; (b) BMAP model

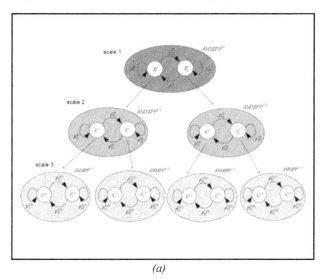

(a)

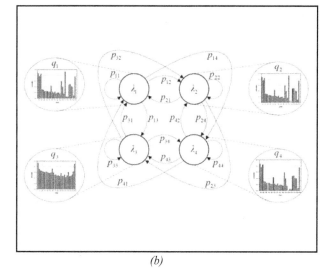

(b)

path in the tree from its higher level ancestor (i.e., the state it descends from at the largest scale, $l = 1$) to itself. Thus, a state at time scale l will be represented by some vector $\vec{s} = (s_1, s_2, ..., s_l)$, $s_i \in N$. Each dMMPP will be represented by the state that generated it (i.e., its parent state), that is, $\text{dMMPP}^{\vec{s}}$ will represent the dMMPP generated by state $\vec{s}$. The root node of the tree corresponds to a virtual state, denoted by $\vec{s} = 0$, that is used to represent the dMMPP of the largest time scale, $l = 1$. This dMMPP will be called the root dMMPP.

The first step of the inference procedure is equal to the one described for the superposition model. The second step of both procedures are very similar: in the hierarchical model the contribution of a dMMPP at time scale l generated from state $\vec{s}$ corresponds also to the deconvolution of empirical PMFs, but now calculated over the set of time intervals corresponding to state $\vec{s}$ at this and the previous time scales. That is, both empirical PMFs are obtained from the same set of time intervals but aggregated at different levels. The final step of the inference procedure is:

1. **Calculation of matrices Λ and P of the dMMPP that incorporates the hierarchical structure:** The goal is to incorporate in the model the level of detail given by the finer time scale, so the equivalent dMMPP will have a number of states equal

to the number of states in smallest time scale of the tree structure, L. The states of the equivalent dMMPP will have Poisson rates which are the sum of the Poisson rates of its ancestors in the tree structure. The transition between each pair of states is determined by the shortest path in the tree structure, passing through the root dMMPP that joins the two states. Note that any pair of states descends from one or more common dMMPPs.

The details of each inference procedure step are given in Nogueira et al. (2003b).

Joint Characterization of Packet Arrivals and Packet Sizes: dBMAP

The proposed dBMAP jointly characterizes the packet arrival process and the packet size distribution, achieving accurate prediction of queuing behaviour for IP traffic exhibiting LRD behaviour. In this process, packet arrivals occur according to a dMMPP (that can be any one of the previously described models) and each arrival is further characterized by a packet size with a general distribution that may depend on the phase of the dMMPP (Figure 2b). This construction process allows having a packet size distribution closely related to the packet arrival process, and is in contrast with the

309

Figure 3. Results for the pAug.TL trace (a) probability function; (b) autocovariance function; (c) packet loss ratio; (d) scaling analysis

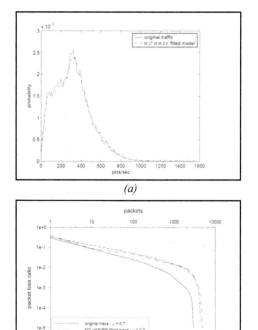

(a)

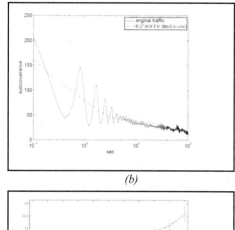

(b)

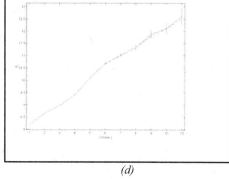

(d)

(c)

approach followed by (Klemm et al., 2003) where the packet size distribution is fitted prior to the matching of the packet arrival rates.

Let's consider that the packets have independent sizes, with the size of packets arriving in phase i having probability function $q_i = \{q_i(n), n \in N\}$. If we let (X,J) denote the dMMPP, on the state space $N_0 \times S$ and having parameterization (P, Λ), that models the packet arrival process, then the byte arrival process (Y,J) is a dBMAP, on the state space $N_0 \times S$, satisfying:

$$P\left(X_{k+1} = m, J_{k+1} = j \mid X_k = n, J_k = i\right)$$

$$= \begin{cases} 0 & m < n \\ p_{ij}q_{ij}\left(m-n\right) & m \geq n \end{cases}$$

with $q_{ij}\left(n\right) = \sum_{l=0}^{+\infty} e^{-\lambda_j} \dfrac{\lambda_j^l}{l!} q_j^{(l)}\left(n\right)$, for $i,j \in S$ and $n \in N_0$,

where $q_j^{(l)}$ denotes the convolution of order l of q_j. Thus, (Y,J) is a dBMAP on the state space $N_0 \times S$, such that, for $n,m \in N_0$:

$$P(Y_{k+1} = m+n, J_{k+1} = j \mid Y_k = m, J_k = i)$$

$$= p_{ij}\sum_{l=0}^{+\infty} e^{-\lambda_j} \dfrac{\lambda_j^l}{l!} q_j^{(l)}\left(n\right)$$

which we express by saying that (Y,J) has *type-II parameterization* $(P, \Lambda, \{q_i, i \in S\})$.

The packet size characterization is carried out in an independent way for each state of the inferred dMMPP and involves two steps: (i) association of each time slot to one of the dMMPP states and (ii) inference, based on histograms, of a packet size distribution for each state of the dMMPP.

The details of the inference procedure are given in Salvador et al. (2003).

RESULTS

We have applied our fitting procedures to several traffic traces: (i) the publicly available August (pAug.TL) Bellcore LAN trace (Leland et al., 1994); (ii) a trace of IP traffic measured on July 10th 2001, from 10.15am to 3.08pm, at University of Aveiro (UA), which is

Figure 4. Results for the Kazaa trace (a) autocovariance function; (b) scaling analysis; (c) PMF at the smallest time scale; (d) PMF at the intermediate time scale; (e) PMF at the largest time scale; (f) packet loss ratio

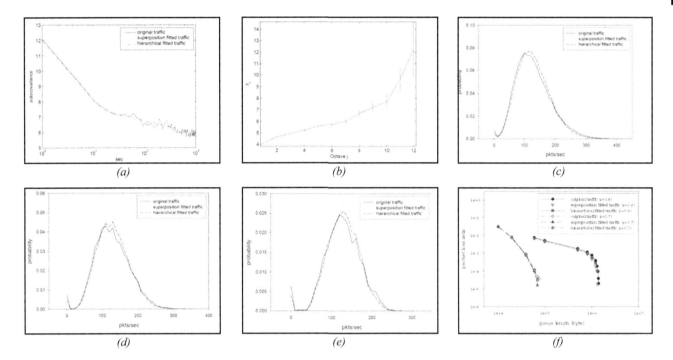

(a)   (b)   (c)

(d)   (e)   (f)

representative of Internet access traffic produced within a University campus environment and (iii) a trace measured on October 18th 2001, from 10.26pm to 11.31pm, at the backbone of a Portuguese ISP network, characterizing the downstream traffic from 10 users of the file sharing application Kazaa. The UA trace has 20 million packets, its mean rate is 1138 packets/s and the mean packet size is 557 bytes, while trace Kazaa has 1 million packets, a mean rate of 131140 packets/s and a mean packet size of 1029 bytes.

The presence of LRD behaviour, in both the original and fitted traces, was analyzed using the method described in Veitch & Abry, 1999. The sampling interval of the counting process was considered as 0.1 seconds.

The performance of the fitting procedures that were proposed to adjust the packet arrival process are evaluated using several evaluation criteria: (i) comparing both the probability and autocovariance functions of the packet arrival counts obtained with the fitted models (theoretical) and with the original data traces; (ii) analyzing queuing behaviour by comparing the packet loss ratio (PLR) obtained, through trace-driven simulation, with the original data traces and simulated traces generated from the fitted models. The results of trace driven simulation for the fitted traces were based on 10 replicas.

$M2^L$ – dMMPP — This fitting procedure was applied to pAug.TL, resulting in a 56 – dMMPP. The empirical autocovariance function was fitted by three exponentials, so three time-scales were identified ($L = 3$). The fitting of the probability function is very good (Figure 3a) but the fitting of the autocovariance function presents some errors that can be explained by the strong oscillatory behaviour of the empirical autocovariance (Figure 3b). The PLR of the original and fitted traces, shown in Figure 3c, are almost coincident for all buffer sizes and link utilizations. The average packet size for this trace is 434 bytes. The fitted trace exhibits LRD, since the y_j values are aligned between octaves 6 and 11, the highest octave present in data (Figure 3d). The estimated Hurst parameter is $\hat{H} = 0.714$.

Superposition and hierarchical — This fitting procedure was applied to the Kazaa trace, that also exhibits self-similar characteristics. Three different time scales were considered: 0.1s, 0.2s and 0.4s. Both fitting approaches are able to capture the traffic LRD behaviour (Figures 4a and 4b): $\hat{H}_{original} = 0.917$, $\hat{H}_{superposition} = 0.897$ and $\hat{H}_{hierarchical} = 0.901$. There is a good agreement between all the PMFs corresponding to the original and dMMPP fitted traces, for all time scales (Figures 4c, 4d,

311

Figure 5. Results for the UA trace (a) scaling analysis for the bytes/s process; (b) packet loss ratio; (c) packet size histogram of the original data; (d) packet size histogram of the fitted trace

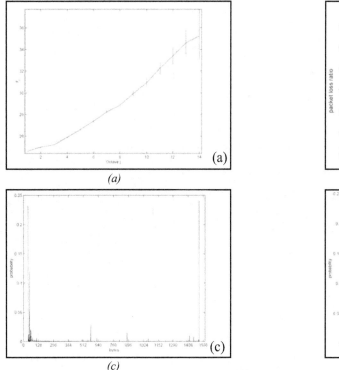

(a)

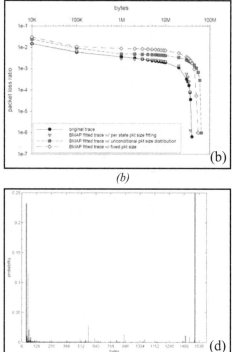

(b)

(c)

(d)

and 4e). This is achieved with the resulting dMMPPs having about 288 states in the superposition model and 38 states in the hierarchical model. Considering queuing performance, Figure 4d shows that PLR behaviour is very well approximated by the equivalent dMMPPs for both utilization ratios.

The computational complexity of both fitting methods is small. This complexity, as well as the number of states of the resulting dMMPPs, is directly related to the level of accuracy used to approximate the empirical PMFs at each time scale by weighted sums of poisson probability functions. The performance of both inference procedures is very similar. Thus, it is not easy to recommend one of approaches over the other based solely on their associated performances. One argument that clearly favours the hierarchical approach is that the numbers of states of the resulting dMMPPs are smaller than the corresponding numbers for the superposition approach. This may be due to the fact that in the hierarchical approach as the time scale increases dMMPPs are fitted to successively smaller sets of intervals whose arrivals characteristics tend to increase in homogeneity and, thus, tend to have

associated a smaller number of states. However, the contribution of each time scale for the characterization of the aggregate traffic characteristics is interpreted in an easier and more natural way through the superposition approach. Note also that, for the same number of states, a smaller number of dMMPPs (and their associated parameters) are needed to compute the final dMMPP using the superposition approach.

dBMAP—The proposed dBMAP models the packet arrival process using the $M2^L - $dMMPP previously described and the packet size process using the procedure described in the dBMAP sub-section. The efficiency of this traffic model is evaluated using the UA trace, which also exhibits LRD behaviour (Figure 5a). The packet size distributions of the original and fitted traces are shown in Figures 5c and 5d, respectively. The distribution is essentially bimodal with two pronounced peaks around 40 and 1500 bytes; it also presents non negligible values at 576 and 885 bytes. Note that the minimum IP packet size is 40 bytes and, in many implementations, the maximum is 1500 bytes. Again, an excellent agreement between the original and fitted distributions was obtained. Note, in particular, the fitting accuracy on the lowest probability packet sizes.

Four types of input traffic are considered in the trace-driven simulation: (i) the original trace, (ii) a trace generated according to the fitted dBMAP, (iii) a trace where the arrival instants were generated according to the fitted dMMPP arrival process and the packet size according to the unconditional packet size distribution of the fitted dBMAP and (iv) a trace where the arrival instants were also generated according to the fitted dMMPP arrival process but the packet size is fixed and equal to the average packet size of the original trace. As it can be observed in Figure 5d, there is a close agreement between the curves corresponding to the original trace and to the trace generated according to the fitted 12 – dBMAP, for all buffer size values. In contrast, for the other two curves corresponding to traces where the packet size is fitted independently of the packet arrival process, significant deviations are obtained. Thus, detailed modelling of the packet size and of the correlations with the packet arrivals is clearly required.

FUTURE TRENDS

There are several potential applications for traffic models, and particularly Markovian models. One of the applications that has been recurrently mentioned is network dimensioning and resource management. However, in this field traffic models can only be applied to simple cases since complex systems generally impose a lot of mathematical challenges. Traffic models can also be used for traffic prediction, enabling the prediction of future values based on the actual state of the traffic process. But we think that traffic models can be really useful when used together with network models that can adequately abstract network behaviour. Having a network model that is able to mimic network functioning, traffic models can be used as inputs to the network or to some of its components in order to evaluate network performance under certain specific scenarios.

CONCLUSION

Accurate modelling of certain types of IP traffic involves the description of the packet arrival process and the packet size distribution. This article presented three traffic models (based on MMPPs) designed to describe the packet arrival process by capturing the self-similar behaviour over multiple time scales. The first model is based on a parameter fitting procedure that matches both the autocovariance and marginal distribution of the counting process and the MMPP is constructed as a superposition of L two-state MMPPs, designed to match the autocovariance function, and one $M - dMMPP$ designed to match the marginal distribution. The second model is a superposition of MMPPs, where each MMPP describes a different time scale of the packet arrival process. The third model is obtained as the equivalent to an hierarchical construction process that, starting at the coarsest time scale, successively decomposes MMPP states into new MMPPs to incorporate the characteristics offered by finer time scales. In order to closely match not only the packet arrival process but also the packet size distribution a dBMAP was also presented: packet arrivals occur according to a dMMPP and each arrival is further characterized by a packet size with a general distribution that may depend on the phase of the dMMPP. This allows having a packet size distribution closely related to the packet arrival process.

REFERENCES

Andersen, A., & Nielsen, B. (1998). A markovian approach for modeling packet traffic with long-range dependence. *IEEE Journal on Selected Areas in Communications, 16,* 5, 719-732.

Crovella, M., & Bestavros, A. (1997). Self-similarity in World Wide Web traffic: Evidence and possible causes. *IEEE/ACM Transactions on Networking, 5,* 6, 835-846.

Feldmann, A., & Whitt, W. (1997). Fitting mixtures of exponentials to long-tail distributions to analyze network performance models. *Performance Evaluation, 31*(3-4), 245-279.

Gao, J., & Rubin, I. (1999). Multifractal analysis and modeling of long-range-dependent traffic. In *Proceedings of ICC'99.*

Grossglauser, M., & Bolot, J. C. (1999). On the relevance of long-range dependence in network traffic. *IEEE/ACM Transactions on Networking, 7,* 5, 629-640.

Klemm, A., Lindemann, C., & Lohmann, M. (2003). Traffic modeling of IP networks using the batch Markovian arrival process. Computer Performance Evaluation, 2002.

Leland, W., Taqqu, M., Willinger, W., & Wilson, D. (1994). On the self-similar nature of Ethernet traffic. *IEEE/ACM Transactions on Networking, 2, 1*, 1-15.

Lucantoni, D. (1991). New results on the single server queue with a batch Markovian arrival process. *Stochastic Models, 7*(1), 1-46.

Lucantoni, D. (1993). The BMAP/G/1 queue: A tutorial. In L. Donatiello & R. Nelson (Eds.), *Models and techniques for performance evaluation of computer and communication systems* (pp. 330-358). London: Springer Verlag.

Nogueira, A., & Valadas, R. (2001). Analyzing the relevant time scales in a network of queues. *Internet performance and control of network systems II, Proceedings SPIE* (Vol. 4523).

Nogueira, A., Salvador, P., Valadas, R., & Pacheco, A. (2003a). Fitting self-similar traffic by a superposition of MMPPs modeling the distribution at multiple time scales. *IEICE Transactions on Communications, E84-B*(8), 2134-2141.

Nogueira, A., Salvador, P., Valadas, R., & Pacheco, A. (2003b). Hierarchical approach based on MMPPs for modeling self-similar traffic over multiple time scales. In *Proceedings of the First International Working Conference on Performance Modeling and Evaluation of Heterogeneous Networks*, 2003.

Pacheco, A., & Prabhu, N. (1995). Markov-additive processes of arrivals. In J. Dshalalow (Ed.), *Advances in queuing: Theory and methods* (pp. 167-194). Boca Raton, FL: CRC.

Paxson, V., & Floyd, S. (1995). Wide-area traffic: The failure of Poisson modeling. *IEEE/ACM Transactions on Networking, 3, 3*, 226-244.

Salvador, P., & Valadas, R. (2001a). A fitting procedure for markov modulated poisson processes with an adaptive number of states. In *Proceedings of the 9th IFIP Working Conference on Performance Modeling and Evaluation of ATM & IP Networks*.

Salvador, P., & Valadas, R. (2001b). Framework based on markov modulated poisson processes for modeling traffic with long-range dependence. *Internet Performance and Control of Network Systems II, Proceedings SPIE* (Vol. 4523).

Salvador, P., Valadas, R., & Pacheco, A. (2003). Multiscale fitting procedure using markov modulated poisson processes. *Telecommunications Systems, 23, 1-2*, 123-148.

Veitch, D., & Abry, P. (1999, April). A wavelet based joint estimator for the parameters of LRD. *IEEE Transactions on Information Theory, 45*(3), 878-897.

Yoshihara, T., Kasahara, S., & Takahashi, Y. (2001). Practical time-scale fitting of self-similar traffic with markov-modulated poisson process. *Telecommunication Systems, 17*(1-2), 185-211.

KEY TERMS

Batch Markovian Arrival Process: The BMAP further extends the MAP by additionally associating rewards (i.e., batch sizes of arrivals) to the corresponding arrival times.

Hurst Parameter: It is an index that quantifies the self-similarity degree. In fact, similarity characteristics of self-similar processes with stationary increments depend only on this parameter.

Long-Range Dependence (LRD): A process is said to be long-range dependent if its autocovariance function decays hyperbolically (slower than exponentially) and the area under it is infinite.

Markov Modulated Poisson Process (MMPP): A process, belonging to the class of markov renewal processes, where arrivals occur according to a state-dependent poisson process with different rates governed by a continuous-time markov chain.

Markovian Arrival Process (MAP): The MAP extends the MMPP model by allowing arrivals not only during holding times in states, but also at state transitions.

Poisson Process: A poisson process is an integer-valued continuous-time stochastic process whose increments are independent random variables following the poisson distribution.

M

Self-Similar: When small parts of an object are qualitatively the same or similar to the whole object. In the context of tele-traffic theory, a self-similar traffic process that presents the same statistical characteristics independently of the considered time scale.

Multicast of Multimedia Data

Christos Bouras
Research Academic Computer Technology Institute and University of Patras, Greece

Apostolos Gkamas
Research Academic Computer Technology Institute and University of Patras, Greece

Dimitris Primpas
Research Academic Computer Technology Institute and University of Patras, Greece

Kostas Stamos
Research Academic Computer Technology Institute and University of Patras, Greece

INTRODUCTION

The heterogeneous network environment that Internet provides to real time applications as well as the lack of sufficient QoS (quality of service) guarantees, many times forces applications to embody adaptation schemes in order to work efficiently. In addition, any application that transmits data over the Internet should have a friendly behaviour toward the other flows that coexist in today's Internet and especially toward the *TCP* flows that comprise the majority of flows. We define as TCP friendly flow, a flow that consumes no more bandwidth than a TCP connection, which is traversing the same path with that flow (Pandhye, Kurose, Towsley, & Koodli, 1999).

During the multicast transmission over the Internet, several aspects need to be considered:

- **Transmission rate adaptation:** The sender must adapt the transmission rate based on the current network conditions.
- **TCP friendliness:** During the multicast transmission over the Internet, the multicasts flows must be TCP-friendly.
- **Scalability:** The performance of the adaptation scheme must not deteriorate with increasing numbers of receivers.

- **Heterogeneity:** The adaptation scheme needs to take into account the heterogeneity of the Internet and must aim at satisfying the requirements of a large part of the receivers if not all possible receivers.

BACKGROUND

When someone multicasts multimedia data over the Internet, he or she has to accommodate receivers with heterogeneous data reception capabilities. To accommodate heterogeneity, the sender application may transmit one multicast stream and determine the transmission rate that better satisfies most of the receivers, may transmit at multiple multicast streams with different transmission rates and allocate receivers at each stream, or may use layered encoding and transmit each layer to a different multicast stream.

The single multicast stream approach has the disadvantage that clients with a low bandwidth link will always get a high-bandwidth stream if most of the other members are connected via a high bandwidth link and vice versa. The previously described problem can be overcome with the use of a multi-stream multicast approach. Single multicast stream approaches have the advantages of easy encoder and decoder implementation and simple protocol operation, due to the fact that

Figure 1. Architecture of a single stream multicast transmission mechanism

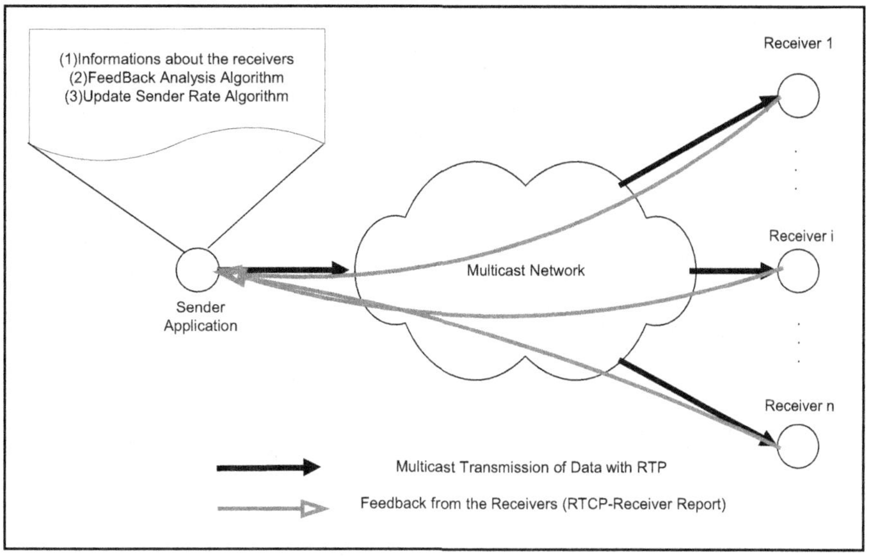

during the single multicast stream approach there is no need for synchronisation of receivers' actions (as is required for the multiple multicast streams and layered encoding approaches).

The methods proposed for the multicast transmission of multimedia data over the Internet can be generally divided in three main categories, depending on the number of multicast streams used:

- The sender uses a single multicast stream for all receivers (Bouras & Gkamas, 2003). This results to the most effective use of the network resources, but on the other hand the fairness problem among the receivers arises, especially when the receivers have very different capabilities. The subject of adaptive multicast of multimedia data over networks with the use of one multicast stream has engaged many researchers. During the adaptive multicast transmission of multimedia data in a single multicast stream, the sender application must select the transmission rate that satisfies most of the receivers with the current network conditions. Three approaches can be found in the literature for the implementation of the adaptation protocol in a single stream multicast mechanism: equation based (Pandhye et al., 1999), network feedback based (Jiang, Ammar, & Zegura, 1998;

Sisalem, 1998) or based on a combination of the previous two approaches (Sisalem & Wolisz, 2000a).

- **Simulcast:** The sender transmits versions of the same video, encoded in varying degrees of quality. This results to the creation of a small number of multicast streams with different transmission rates (Bouras, Gkamas, Karaliotas, & Stamos, 2001). The different multicast streams carry the same video information but in each one the video is encoded with different bit rates, and even different video formats. Each receiver joins in the stream that carries the video quality, in terms of transmission rate, that it is capable of receiving. The main disadvantage in this case is that the same multimedia information is replicated over the network but recent research has shown that under some conditions simulcast has better behavior that multicast transmission of layered encoded video (Kim & Ammar, 2001).

- The sender uses *layered encoded* video, which is video that can be reconstructed from a number of discrete data layers, the basic layer, and more additional layers, and transmits each layer into different multicast stream (Legout & Biersack, 2000; Sisalem & Wolisz, 2000b). The basic layer provides the basic quality and the quality improves

Figure 2. The architecture and the data flow of the server

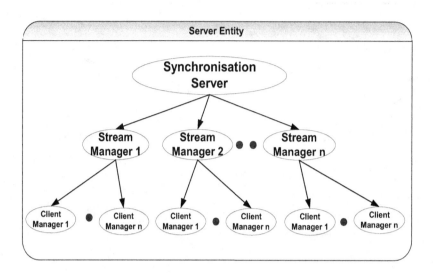

with each additional layer. The receivers subscribe to one or more multicast streams depending on the available bandwidth into the network path to the source.

SINGLE STREAM MULTICAST TRANSMISSION OF MULTIMEDIA DATA

In such mechanism a sender application transmits multimedia data to a group of n receivers with the use of multicast in one stream. The sender application is using *RTP/RTCP* protocols for the transmission of the multimedia data. Receivers receive the multimedia data and inform the sender application for the quality of the transmission with the use of RTCP receiver reports. The sender application collects the RTCP receiver reports, analyses them and determines the transmission rate that satisfy most the group of receivers with the current network conditions.

During the single stream multicast transmission the sender usually runs two algorithms:

- **Feedback analysis algorithm:** Feedback analysis algorithm analyses the feedback information that the receivers sends to the sender application (most mechanisms use RTCP receiver reports for this purpose), concerning the transmission quality of the multimedia data. Every time the sender application receives feedback from a receiver, it runs the feedback analysis algorithm in order to estimate the preferred transmission rate, which will satisfy that receiver. The receiver's preferred transmission rate represents the transmission rate that this receiver will prefer if it was the only one receiver in the multicast transmission of the multimedia data.

- **Update sender rate algorithm:** The sender application in repeated time periods estimates the transmission rate for multicasting the multimedia data with the use of the update sender rate algorithm. The estimation of the sender application transmission rate is aiming to increase the satisfaction of the group of receivers. When the sender application estimates the new transmission rate, it tries to provide to the group of receivers the best satisfaction that the current network conditions allow.

SIMULCAST

In such a mechanism, the server is unique and responsible of:

- Creating the n different multicast streams (in most mechanisms a small number of multicast streams, usually 3 or 4 are enough)

Figure 3. The architecture and the data flow of the sender

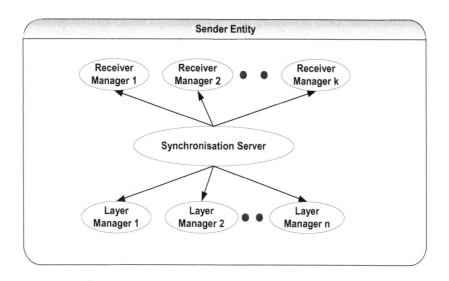

- Setting each stream's bandwidth limits
- Tracking if there are any clients that are not handled with fairness
- Providing the mechanisms to the clients to switch streams whenever they consider that they should be in another stream closer to their capabilities

Figure 2 shows the organisation and the architecture of the server entity. The server generates n different stream managers. In each stream manager, an arbitrary number of client managers is assigned. Each client manager corresponds to a unique client that has joined the stream controlled by this stream manager. The synchronisation server is responsible for the management, synchronisation, and intercommunication between stream managers.

The stream manager entity is responsible for the maintenance and the monitoring of one of the n different multicast streams. Also the stream manager entity has all the intra-stream adaptation mechanisms for the adjustment of the transmission rate. The stream manager periodically gathers the states reported by all client managers belonging to it at the end of a specific, fixed time period. It then uses an appropriate algorithm that tries to improve fairness between clients by determining whether a lower or a higher bit rate is more appropriate. Whenever a client cannot be satisfied by

a stream due to the fact that most of the other clients have much higher or much lower reception capabilities, the stream manager informs it that it has to move to a lower or higher quality stream.

Each client manager corresponds to a unique client (for scalability issues a small representative group of clients may have a corresponding client manager). It processes the RTCP reports generated by the client and can be considered as a representative of the client at the side of the server. It can interact only with one stream manager at a given time, the stream manager controlling the stream from which the client is receiving the video. Client manager receives the RTCP reports from the client and processes them based on packet loss rate and delay jitter information. It then makes an estimation of the state of the client, based on the current and a few previous reports that it stores in a buffer.

LAYERED ENCODING

In such mechanism, the sender transmits multimedia data to a group of m receivers with the use of multicast. The sender is using the layered encoding approach, and transmits the video information in n different layers (the basic layer and n-1 additional layers). The sender transmits each layer into a different RTP/RTCP multicast session. The transmission rate within each layer is adapting within its limits (each layer has an upper and lower limit in its transmission rate) according to the capabilities of the receivers listening up to it. The receivers join the appropriate number of layers which better suit their requirements (available bandwidth between the sender and the receiver, etc) and if during the transmission of multimedia data the network conditions to the path between them and the sender change, the receivers have the capability to receive more or less video layers in order to accomplish better their requirements. The communication between the sender and the receivers is based on RTP/RTCP sessions and the sender is using the RTP protocol to transmit the video layers and the participants (the sender and the receivers) use the RTCP protocol in order to exchange control messages.

Figure 3 shows the organisation and the architecture of the sender entity. The sender generates n different layer managers. Each layer manager is responsible for the transmission of a video layer. The sender creates a new receiver manager every time receives a RTCP report from a new receiver. Each receiver manager corresponds to a unique receiver (for scalability issues a small representative group of receivers may have a corresponding receiver manager). It processes the RTCP reports generated by the receiver and can be considered as a representative of the receiver at the side of the sender. In addition, the synchronisation server is responsible for the management, synchronisation and intercommunication between layer managers and receiver managers. If a receiver manager does not receive RTCP reports from the receiver which it represents for a long time, it stops its operation and releases its resources.

Each receiver measures the characteristics of the path, which connects it with the sender and informs the sender with the use of receiver reports.

EVALUATION PARAMETERS

During the multicast transmission of multimedia data over the Internet the overall target is the optimal usage of the network resources and for this reason an appropriate mechanism is used. In order to evaluate those mechanisms there are the following criteria:

- **Network congestion:** The goal of the multicast transmission mechanisms is to increase the usage of the available bandwidth and decrease the packet losses of all the applications that transmit data in the same network path with the network path of the multicast data.
- **Scalability:** During the multicast transmission of multimedia data, the multimedia data may be received by a large number of receivers. The performance of the selected mechanism must not be downgraded when the number of the receivers of the multicast data is increased. This means that the complexity and the performance of the used mechanism must be acceptable even when a large number of receivers receive the multimedia data through the multicast transmission.
- **Adaptation speed:** With the term adaptation speed we refer to the time needed from the begging of the multicast transmission of the multimedia data until the selected mechanism achieves a stable operation. This time must be relatively small and the performance of the mechanism is better when this time is small.
- **TCP friendliness:** Most of the Internet traffic is TCP traffic. Any application that transmits data over the Internet should have a friendly behaviour toward the other flows that coexist in today's Internet and especially toward the TCP flows that comprise the majority of flows.
- **User satisfaction:** It is difficult to measure the user satisfaction. For example, studies has show that during the transmission of MPEG video, just 3% packet loss can result up to 30% reduction of the presentation quality. As a result the satisfaction of the end user is influenced very much from the packet loss.

TRANSMISSION OF MULTIMEDIA DATA

The transmission of the multimedia data is based on the protocols RTP/RTCP. The protocol RTP is used for the transmission of the multimedia data from the server to the client and the client uses the RTCP protocol, in order to inform the server of the transmission quality.
The RTP/RTCP protocols have been designed

for the transmission of real time data like video and audio. Although the RTP/RTCP protocols were initially designed for multicast transmission, they were also used for unicast transmissions. RTP/RTCP can be used for one-way communication like video on demand or for two-way communication like videoconference. RTP/RTCP offers a common platform for the representation of synchronisation information that real time applications need. The RTCP protocol is the control protocol of RTP. The RTP protocol has been designed to operate in cooperation with the RTCP protocol, which provides information about the transmission quality.

RTP is a protocol that offers end to end transport services with real time characteristics over packet switching networks like IP networks. RTP packet headers include information about the payload type of the data, numbering of the packets and timestamping information.

RTCP offers the following services to applications:

- **QoS monitoring:** This is one of the primary services of RTCP. RTCP provides feedback to applications about the transmission quality. RTCP uses sender reports and receiver reports, which contain useful statistical information like total transmitted packets, packet loss rate and delay jitter during the transmission of the data. This statistical information is very useful, because it can be used for the implementation of congestion control mechanisms.

- **Source identification:** RTCP source description packets can be used for identification of the participants in a RTP session. In addition, source description packets provide general information about the participants in a RTP session. This service of RTCP is useful for multicast conferences with many members.

- **Inter-media synchronisation:** In real time applications it is common to transmit audio and video in different data streams. RTCP provides services like timestamping, which can be used for inter-media synchronisation of different data streams (for example synchronisation of audio and video streams).

More information about RTP/RTCP can be found in RFC 3550 (Schulzrinne, Casner, Frederick, & Jacobson, 2003).

FUTURE TRENDS

The mechanisms described in the previous paragraphs have been proposed for installation and operation over the Internet. One interesting extension of the previous mechanisms is the adaptation of the previous mechanisms to operate over mobile networks. The multicast transmission of multimedia data over mobile networks is a challenge due to the fact the one of the basic characteristics of mobile networks is the continuously changing environment. In order to adapt the previously described mechanisms for usage over mobile networks various issues must be considered such as more efficient encodings.

CONCLUSION

The multicast transmission of real time multimedia data is an important component of many current and future emerging Internet applications such as video-conferencing, distance learning, and video distribution. The heterogeneous nature of the Internet makes the multicast transmission of real time multimedia data a challenge. Different receivers of the same multicast stream may have different processing capabilities, different loss tolerance and different bandwidth available in the paths leading to them.

When multicast multimedia data is transmitted over the Internet, receivers with heterogeneous data reception capabilities have to be accommodated. To accommodate heterogeneity, the sender application may transmit one multicast stream and determine the transmission rate that satisfies most of the receivers, it may transmit at multiple multicast streams with different transmission rates and allocate receivers at each stream or it may use layered encoding and transmit each layer to a different multicast stream.

REFERENCES

Bouras, C., & Gkamas, A. (2003). Multimedia transmission with adaptive QoS based on real time protocols. *International Journal of Communications Systems, 16*(2)*,* 225-248, Wiley InterScience.

Bouras, C., Gkamas, A., Karaliotas, A., & Stamos, K., (2001). Architecture and performance evaluation for redundant multicast transmission supporting adaptive Qos. *International Conference on Software, Telecommunications, and Computer Networks,* Split, Dubrovnik (Croatia) Ancona, Bari (Italy), October 8-11, 2001, pp. 585-592.

Floyd, S., & Fall, K. (1998). Promoting the use of end-to-end congestion control in the Internet. IEEE/ACM Transactions on Networking, Volume 7, Issue 4 (August 1999), pp. 458-472.

Jiang, T., Ammar, M., & Zegura, E. (1998). Inter-receiver fairness: A novel performance measure for multicast ABR sessions. SIGMETRICS, June 22-26, Madison, Wisconsin, USA, pp. 202-211

Kim, T., & Ammar, M. (2001). A comparison of layering and stream replication video multicast schemes. In *Proceedings of the NOSSDAV'01*, Port Jefferson, NY, June 25-26, 2001, pp. 63-72.

Legout, A., & Biersack, E. (2000), PLM: Fast convergence for cumulative layered multicast transmission schemes. In *Proceedings of ACM SIGMETRICS'2000*, Santa Clara, CA, USA, June 17-21, 2000, pp. 13-22.

Pandhye, J., Kurose, J., Towsley, D., & Koodli, R, (1999). A model based TCP-friendly rate control protocol. In *Proceedings of the International Workshop on Network and Operating System Support for Digital Audio and Video*, Basking Ridge, NJ

Schulzrinne, H., Casner, S., Frederick, R., & Jacobson, V. (2003). RTP: A transport protocol for real-time applications, RFC 3550, IETF.

Sisalem, D. (1998). Fairness of adaptive multimedia applications. IEEE International Conference on Communications. Conference Record. Affiliated with SUPERCOMM'98 IEEE,. p.891-5 vol.2. 3 vol. xxxvii+1838 pp

Sisalem, D., & Wolisz, A. (2000a). LDA+TCP-friendly adaptation: A measurement and comparison study. The *10th International Workshop on Network and Operating Systems Support for Digital Audio and Video*, Chapel Hill, NC, USA, June 26-28 2000, pp. 1619-1622.

Sisalem, D., & Wolisz, A. (2000b). MLDA: A TCP-friendly congestion control framework for heterogeneous multicast environments. The *8th International Workshop on Quality of Service*, Pittsburgh, PA, June 5-7, 2000, pp. 65-74.

KEY TERMS

Layered Encoding: Transmission of the multimedia data in n different layers the basic layer and n-1 additional layers.

Multicast: Transmitting data simultaneously to many receivers without the need to replicate the data.

Multimedia Data: Multimedia data refers to data that consist of various media types like text, audio, video, and animation.

Quality of Service (QoS): Quality of service refers to the capability of a network to provide better service to selected network traffic.

RTP/RTCP: Protocol that is used for the transmission of multimedia data. The RTP performs the actual transmission and the RTCP is the control and monitoring transmission.

Simulcast: Transmission of the same multimedia data in multiple multicast streams with different transmission rates.

Multimedia for Mobile Devices

Kevin Curran
University of Ulster, Ireland

INTRODUCTION

Mobile communications is a continually growing sector in industry and a wide variety of visual services such as video-on-demand have been created, which are limited by low-bandwidth network infrastructures. The distinction between mobile phones and personal device assistants (PDA's) has already become blurred with pervasive computing being the term coined to describe the tendency to integrate computing and communication into everyday life. New technologies for connecting devices like wireless communication and high bandwidth networks make the network connections even more heterogeneous. Additionally, the network topology is no longer static, due to the increasing mobility of users. Ubiquitous computing is a term often associated with this type of networking.

BACKGROUND

The creation of low bit rate standards such as H.263 (Harrysson, 2002) allows reasonable quality video through the existing Internet and is an important step in paving the way forward. As these new media services become available, the demand for multimedia through mobile devices will invariably increase. Corporations such as Intel do not plan to be left behind. Intel has created a new breed of mobile chip code named Banias. Intel's president and chief operating officer Paul Otellino states that "eventually every single chip that Intel produces will contain a radio transmitter that handles wireless protocols, which will allow users to move seamlessly among networks. Among our employees this initiative is affectionately referred to as 'radio free Intel.'" Products such as Real Audio and IPCast for streaming media are also becoming increasingly common, however, multimedia, due to its timely nature requires guarantees different in nature with regards to delivery of data from TCP traffic such as HTTP requests. In addition, multimedia applications increase the set of requirements in terms of throughput, end-

to-end delay, delay jitter, and clock synchronisation. These requirements may not all be directly met by the networks therefore end-system protocols enrich network services to provide the quality of service (QoS) required by applications. It is argued here that traditional monolithic protocols are unable to support the wide range of application requirements on top of current networks (ranging from 9600 baud modems up to gigabit networks) without adding overhead in the form of redundant functionality for numerous combinations of application requirements and network infrastructures. In ubiquitous computing, software is used by roaming users interacting with the electronic world through a collection of devices ranging from handhelds such as PDAs (Figure 1a) and mobile phones (Figure 1b) to personal computers (Figure 1c) and laptops (Figure 1d).

The Java language, thanks to its portability and support for code mobility, is seen as the best candidate for such settings (Kochnev & Terekhov, 2003; Román et al., 2002). The heterogeneity added by modern smart devices is also characterised by an additional property, which is that many of these devices are typically tailored to distinct purposes. Therefore, not only memory and storage capabilities differ widely, but local device capabilities, in addition to the availability of resources changing over time (e.g., a global positioning satellite (GPS) system cannot work indoors unless one uses specialised repeaters (Jee, Boo, Choi, & Kim, 2003). Therefore a need exists for middleware to be aware of these pervasive computing properties. With regards to multimedia, applications that use group communication (e.g., video conferencing) mechanisms must be able to scale from small groups with few members, up to groups with thousands of receivers (Tojo, Enokido, & Takizawa, 2003).

The protocols underlying the Internet were not designed for the latest cellular type networks with their low bandwidth, high error losses, and roaming users, thus many "fixes" have arisen to solve the problem of efficient data delivery to mobile resource constrained devices (Saber & Mirenkov, 2003). Mobility requires

Figure 1. (a) PDAs; (b) mobiles; (c) desktops; (d) laptops

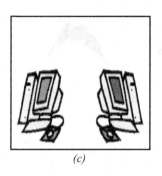

(a)   (b)   (c)   (d)

adaptability meaning that systems must be location-aware and situation-aware taking advantage of this information in order to dynamically reconfigure in a distributed fashion (Matthur & Mundur, 2003; Solon, McKevitt, & Curran, 2003). However, situations, in which a user moves an end-device and uses information services can be challenging. In these situations, the placement of different cooperating parts is a research challenge.

ENABLING TECHNOLOGIES FOR MOBILE MULTIMEDIA

In 1946, the first car-based telephone was set up in St. Louis, MO, USA. The system used a single radio transmitter on top of a tall building. A single channel was used, and therefore a button was pushed to talk and released to listen (Tanenbaum, 2005). This half duplex system is still used by modern day CB-radio systems used by police and taxi operators. In the 60's, the system was improved to a two-channel system called improved mobile telephone system (IMTS). The system could not support many users as frequencies were limited. The problem was solved by the idea of using cells to facilitate the re-use of frequencies. More users can be supported in such a cellular radio system. It was implemented for the first time in the advanced mobile phone system (AMPS). Wide-area wireless data services have been more of a promise than a reality. It can be argued that success for wireless data depends on the development of a digital communications architecture that integrates and interoperates across regional-area, wide-area, metropolitan-area, campus-area, in-building, and in-room wireless networks.

The convergence of two technological developments has made mobile computing a reality. In the last few years, the UK and other developed countries have spent large amounts of money to install and deploy wireless communication facilities. Originally aimed at telephone services (which still account for the majority of usage), the same infrastructure is increasingly used to transfer data. The second development is the continuing reduction in the size of computer hardware, leading to portable computation devices such as laptops, palmtops, or functionally enhanced cell phones. Unlike second-generation cellular networks, future cellular systems will cover an area with a variety of non-homogeneous cells that may overlap. This allows the network operators to tune the system layout to subscriber density and subscribed services. Cells of different sizes will offer widely varying bandwidths: very high bandwidths with low error rates in pico-cells, very low bandwidths with higher error rates in macro-cells as illustrated in Table 1. Again, depending on the current location, the sets of available services might also differ.

Unlike traditional computer systems characterised by short-lived connections that are bursty in nature, Streaming audio/video sessions are typically long lived (the length of a presentation) and require continuous transfer of data. Streaming services will require, by today's standards, the delivery of enormous volumes of data to customer homes. For examples, entertainment NTSC video compressed using the MPEG standards requires bandwidths between 1.5 and 6 Mb/s. Many signalling schemes have been developed that can deliver data at this rate to homes over existing communications links (Forouzan, 2002). Some signalling schemes suitable for high-speed video delivery are:

- **ADSL:** The asymmetrical digital subscriber loop (ADSL) (Bingham, 2000) takes advantage of the advances in coding to provide a customer with a downstream wideband signal, an upstream control. The cost to the end-user is quite low in this

Figure 2. A transcoding proxy

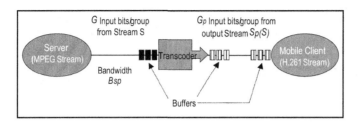

Figure 3. Variations in client-server connectivity

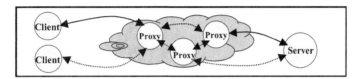

scheme, as it requires little change to the existing equipment.

- **CATV:** Cable TV (CATV) (Forouzan, 2002) uses a broadband coaxial cable system and can support multiple MPEG compressed video streams. CATV has enormous bandwidth capability and can support hundreds of simultaneous connections. Furthermore, as cable is quite widely deployed, the cost of supporting Video-on-demand and other services is significantly lower. However, it requires adaptation to allow bi-directional signalling in the support of interactive services.

A cellular wireless network consists of fixed based stations connecting mobile devices through a wired backbone network where each mobile device establishes contact through their local base stations. The available bandwidth on a wireless link is limited and channels are more prone to errors. It is argued that future evolution of network services will be driven by the ability of network elements to provide enhanced multimedia services to any client anywhere (Harrysson, 2002). Future network elements must be capable of transparently accommodating and adjusting to client and content heterogeneity. There are benefits to filtering IP packets in the wireless network so that minimal application data is carried to the mobile hosts to preserve radio resources and prevent the overloading of mobile hosts with unnecessary information and ultimately wasteful processing. A proxy is an intermediary component between a source and a sink, which transforms

the data in some manner. In the case of mobile hosts, a proxy is often an application that executes in the wired network to support the host. This location is frequently the base station, the machine in the wired network that provides the radio interface. As the user moves, the proxy may also move to remain on the communication path from the mobile device to the fixed network. The proxy hides the mobile from the server, which thinks that it communicates with a standard client (i.e., a PC directly connected to the wired network) (Kammann & Blachnitzky, 2002).

Wireless links are characterised by relatively low bandwidth and high transmission error rates (Chakravorty & Pratt, 2002). Furthermore, mobile devices often have computational constraints that preclude the use of standard Internet video formats on them thus by placing a mobile transcoding proxy at the base station (BS), the incoming video stream can be transcoded to a lower bandwidth stream, perhaps to a format more suitable to the nature of the device, and control the rate of output transmission over the wireless link (Joshi, 2000).

Figure 2 illustrates a scenario where a transcoding gateway is configured to transcode MPEG streams to H.261. In the architecture, the transcoding gateway may also simply forward MPEG or H.261 packets to an alternate session (in both directions) without performing transcoding. Figure 3 illustrates locations in which intelligence about available network services may be placed. Client may utilise this network knowledge to select the most appropriate server and mechanism in order to obtain appropriate content. As an alternative,

Table 1. Characteristics of various wireless networks

Type of Network	Bandwidth Latency	Latency	Mobility	Typical Video Performance	Typical Audio Performance
In-Room/Building (Radio Frequency Infrared)	>> 1 Mbps RF: 2-20 Mbps IR: 1-50 Mbps	<< 10 ms	Pedestrian	2-Way, Interactive, Full Frame Rate (Compressed)	High Quality, 16 bit samples, 22 KHz rate
Campus-Area Packet Relay	Approx. 64 kbps	Approx. 100 ms	Pedestrian	Medium Quality Slow Scan	Medium Quality Reduced Rate
Wide-Area (Cellular, PCS)	19.2 kbps	> 100 ms	Pedestrian/ Vehicular	Video Phone or Freeze Frame	Asynchronous "Voice Mail"
Regional-Area (LEO/VSAT DBS)	Asymmetric Up/ Dn 100 bps to 4.8 kbps 12 Mbps	>> 100 ms	Pedestrian/ Vehicular Stationary	Async Video Playback	Asynchronous "Voice Mail"

this knowledge (and the associated burden) could be entirely or partially transferred to the individual servers or could reside inside the network.

Image transcoding is where an image is converted from one format to another (Vetro, Sun, & Wang, 2001). This may be performed by altering the Qscale (basically applying compression to reduce quality). This is sometimes known as simply resolution reduction. Another method is to scale down the dimensions of the image (spatial transcoding) (Chandra, Gehani, Schlatter Ellis, & Vahdat, 2001) so reduce the overall byte size (e.g., scaling a 160Kb frame by 50% to 32KB). Another method known as temporal transcoding is where frames are simply dropped (this can sometimes be known as simply rate reduction). While another method may be simply to transcode the image to greyscale, which may be useful for monochrome PDA,'s (again this transcoding process results in reduced byte size of the image or video frame). Recently there has been increased research into intelligent intermediaries). Support for streaming media in the form of media filters has also been proposed for programmable heterogeneous networking. Canfora, Di Santo, Venturi, Zimeo, and Zito (2005) propose multiple proxy caches serving as intelligent intermediaries, improving content delivery performance by caching content. A key feature of these proxies is that they can be moved and re-configured to exploit geographic locality and content access patterns thus reducing network server load. Proxies may also perform content translation on static multimedia in addition to distillation functions in order to support content and client heterogeneity (Yu, Katz, & Laksham, 2005). Another example is fast forward networks broadcast overlay architecture where there are media bridges in the network, which can be used in combination with RealAudio or other multimedia streams to provide an application layer multicast overlay network. One could adopt the view at this time that "boxes" are being placed in the network to aid applications.

MOBILE IP

Mobile IP is an extension to IP, which allows the transparent routing of IP datagrams to mobile nodes. In mobile IP, each host has a home agent (i.e., a host connected to the sub network the host is attached to). The home agent holds responsibility for tracking the current point of attachment of the mobile device so when the device changes the network it is connected to it has to register a new care-of address with the home agent. The care-of address can be the address of a foreign agent (e.g., a wireless base station node) that has agreed to provide services for the mobile or the new IP address of the mobile (if one is dynamically assigned by its new network). Traffic to mobiles is always delivered via home agents, and then tunnelled to the care-of address. In the case of a foreign agent care-of address, traffic is forwarded to the mobile via the foreign agent. Traffic from the mobile does not need to travel via the home agent but can be sent directly to (previously) correspondents. Correspondent hosts do not need to be mobile IP enabled or even have to know the location of the mobile if a home agent acts as an intermediary, thus forwarding of packets to the current address of the mobile is transparent for other hosts [Dixit02]. The home agent redirects packets from the home network to the care-of address by creating a new IP header, which contains the mobile's care-of address as the destination IP address. This new header encapsulates the original packet, causing the mobile node's home address to have no effect on the encapsulated packet's routing until it reaches the care-of address. When the mobile leaves the service area of its current foreign agent and registers with a new foreign agent, the home agent must be informed about the change of address. In the process of handoff, the mobile may lose connectivity for a short period of time.

FUTURE TRENDS

Mobile phone technologies have evolved in several major phases denoted by "generations" or "G" for short. Three generations of mobile phones have evolved so far, each successive generation more reliable and flexible than the previous. The first of these is referred to as the first generation or 1G. This generation was developed during the 1980s and early 1990s and only provided an analog voice service with no data services available (Bates, 2002). The second generation or 2G of mobile technologies used circuit-based digital networks. Since 2G networks are digital they are capable of carrying data transmissions, with an average speed o f around 9.6K bps (bits per second). Because 2G networks can support the transfer of data, they are able to support Java enabled phones. Some manufacturers are providing Java 2 Micro Edition (J2ME) (Knudsen & Li, 2005) phones for 2G networks though the majority are designing their Java enabled phones for the 2.5G and 3G networks, where the increased bandwidth and data transmission speed will make these applications more usable (Hoffman, 2002). These are packet based and allow for "always on" connectivity. The third generation of mobile communications (3G) is digital mobile multimedia offering broadband mobile communications

with voice, video, graphics, audio and other forms of information. 3G builds upon the knowledge and experience derived from the preceding generations of mobile communication, namely 2G and 2.5G although 3G networks use different transmission frequencies from these previous generations and therefore require a different infrastructure (Camarillo& Garcia-Martin, 2005). These networks will improve data transmission speed up to 144K bps in a high-speed moving environment, 384K bps in a low-speed moving environment, and 2Mbps in a stationary environment. 3G services see the logical convergence of two of the biggest technology trends of recent times, the Internet and mobile telephony. Some of the services that will be enabled by the broadband bandwidth of the 3G networks include:

- Downloadable and streaming audio and video
- Voice over Internet protocol (VoIP)
- Send and receive high quality colour images
- Electronic agents are self-contained programs that roam communications networks delivering/receiving messages or looking for information or services.
- Downloadable software—Potential to be more convenient than conventional methods of distributing software as the product arrives in minutes
- Capability to determine geographic position of a mobile device using the global positioning system (GPS) (Barnes et al., 2003)

3G will also facilitate many other new services that have not previously been available over mobile networks due to the limitations in data transmission speeds. These new wireless applications will provide solutions to companies with distributed workforces, where employees need access to a wide range of information and services via their corporate intranets, when they are working offsite with no access to a desktop (Camarillo & Camarillo, 2005).

4G technology stands to be the future standard of wireless devices. The Japanese company NTT DoCoMo is testing 4G communication at 100 Mbit/s while moving, and 1 Gbit/s while stationary. NTT DoCoMo plans on releasing the first commercial network in 2010. Despite the fact that current wireless devices seldom utilize full 3G capabilities, there is a basic attitude that if you provide the pipeline then services for it will follow.

CONCLUSION

Flexible and adaptive frameworks are necessary in order to develop distributed multimedia applications in such heterogeneous end-systems and network environments. The processing capability differs substantially for many of these devices with PDA's being severely resource constrained in comparison to leading desktop computers. The networks connecting these devices and machines range from GSM, Ethernet LAN, and Ethernet 802.11 to Gigabit Ethernet. Networking has been examined at a low-level micro-protocol level and again from a high-level middleware framework viewpoint. Transcoding proxies were introduced as a promising way to achieving dynamic configuration, especially because of the resulting openness, which enables the programmer to customize the structure of the system and other issues regarding mobility were also discussed.

REFERENCES

Barnes, J. Rizos, C., Wang, J., Small, D., Voigt, G., & Gambale, N. (2003). LocataNet: A new positioning technology for high precision indoor and outdoor positioning. In *Proceedings of (Institute of Navigation) ION GPS/GNSS 2003,* Oregon Convention Center, Portland, Oregon, September 9-12, 2003

Bates, J. (2002). *Optimizing voice transmission in ATM/IP mobile networks.* McGraw-Hill Telecom Engineering, London, UK.

Bingham, J. (2000). *ADSL, VDSL, and multicarrier modulation* (1st ed.). Wiley-Interscience, Manchester, UK.

Camarillo, G., & Garcia-Martin, M. (2005). *The 3G IP multimedia subsystem (IMS): Merging the Internet and the cellular worlds (2nd ed.).* John Wiley and Sons Ltd, London, UK.

Canfora, G., Di Santo, G., Venturi, G., Zimeo, E., & Zito, M. (2005). Migrating Web application sessions in mobile computing. In *Proceedings of the International World Wide Web Conference*, 2005

Chandra,, S., Gehani, A., Schlatter Ellis, C., & Vahdat, A. (2001). Transcoding characteristics of web images.

In *Proceedings of the SPIE Multimedia Computing and Networking Conference*, January 2001.

Chakravorty, R., & Pratt, I. (2002). WWW Performance over GPRS. The *4th IEEE Conference on Mobile and Wireless Communications Networks (MWCN 2002)*, Stockholm, Sweden, September 9-11, 2002

Dixit, S., & Prasad, R. (2002). *Wireless IP and building the mobile Internet.* Artech House Universal Personal Communications Series, Norwood, MA, USA.

Feng, Y., & Zhu, J. (2001). *Wireless Java programming with J2ME* (1st ed.). Sams Publishing.

Forouzan, B. (2002). *Data communications and networking* (2nd ed.). McGraw-Hill Publishers, London, UK.

Harrysson, A. (2002). Industry challenges for mobile services. The *4th IEEE Conference on Mobile and Wireless Communications Networks (MWCN 2002)*, Stockholm, Sweden, September 9-11, 2002

Hoffman, J. (2002). *GPRS demystified* (1st e.). McGraw-Hill Professional, London, UK.

Jee, G., Boo, S., Choi, J., & Kim, H. (2003). An indoor positioning using GPS repeater. In *Proceedings of (Institute of Navigation) ION GPS/GNSS 2003,* Oregon Convention Center, Portland, Oregon, September 9-12, 2003

Joshi, A. (2000). On Proxy Agents, Mobility and Web Access. *Mobile Networks and Applications, 5*(4), 233-241

Kammann, J., & Blachnitzky, T. (2002). Split-proxy concept for application layer handover in mobile communication systems. The *4th IEEE Conference on Mobile and Wireless Communications Networks (MWCN 2002)*, Stockholm, Sweden, September 9-11, 2002

Knudsen, J., & Li, S. (2005). *Beginning J2ME: From novice to professional.* APress, New York, NY, USA.

Kochnev, D., & Terekhov, A. (2003). Surviving Java for mobiles. *IEEE Pervasive Computing, 2*(2), 90-95.

Matthur, A., & Mundur, P. (2003). Congestion adaptive streaming: An integrated approach. DMS'2003—The *9th International Conference on Distributed Multimedia Systems*, Florida International University Miami, Florida, USA, September 24-26, 2003

Román, M., Hess, C., Cerqueira, R., Ranganathan, A., Campbell, R., & Nahrstedt. K. (2002). A middleware infrastructure for active spaces. *IEEE Pervasive Computing*, *1*(4), 74-83.

Saber, M., & Mirenkov. N. (2003). A multimedia programming environment for cellular automata systems. DMS'2003—The *9th International Conference on Distributed Multimedia Systems*, Florida International University Miami, Florida, USA, September 24-26, 2003

Solon, T., McKevitt, P., & Curran, K. (2003). Telemorph—Bandwidth determined mobile multimodal presentation. *IT&T 2003 – Information Technology and Telecommunications*, Letterkenny Institute of Technology, Co. Donegal, Ireland. 22-23rd October, 2003

Tanenbaum, A. (2005). *Computer networks* (5th ed.). Prentice Hall, New Jersey, USA.

Tojo, T., Enokido, T., & Takizawa, M. (2003). Notification-based QoS control protocol for group communication. DMS'2003—The *9th International Conference on Distributed Multimedia Systems*, Florida International University Miami, Florida, USA, September 24-26, 2003

Vetro, A., Sun, H., & Wang, Y. (2001). Object-based transcoding for adaptable video content delivery. *IEEE Trans. Circuits and System for Video Tech*nology, *11*(2), 387-401, March 2001.

Yu, F., Katz, R., & Laksham, T. (2005). Efficient multi-match packet classification and lookup with TCAM. *IEEE Micro magazine*, *25*(1), 50-59, February 2005.

KEY TERMS

Bandwidth: The amount of data that can be transferred from one point to another, usually between a Web server and a Web browser; It is a measure of the range of frequencies a transmitted signal occupies. In digital systems, bandwidth is the data speed in bits per second. In analog systems, bandwidth is measured in terms of the difference between the highest-frequency signal component and the lowest-frequency signal component.

Broadband: The telecommunication that provides multiple channels of data over a single communications medium.

Cellular Network: A cellular wireless network consists of fixed based stations connecting mobile devices through a wired backbone network where each mobile device establishes contact through their local base stations. The available bandwidth on a wireless link is limited and channels are more prone to errors.

Content: Data that an encoder or server streams to a client or clients. Content can originate from live audio or live video presentation, stored audio or video files, still images, or slide shows. The content must be translated from its original state into a Windows Media format before a Windows Media server can stream it. Windows Media servers can stream live streams or stored Window Media files as content.

Encoding: Encoding accomplishes two main objectives: (1) it reduces the size of video and audio files, by means of compression, making Internet delivery feasible, and (2) it saves files in a format that can be read and played back on the desktops of the targeted audience. Encoding may be handled by a software application or by specialised hardware with encoding software built in.

Media: A term with many different meanings, in the context of *streaming media*, it refers to video, animation, and audio. The term "media" may also refer to something used for storage or transmission, such as tapes, diskettes, CD-ROMs, DVDs, or networks such as the Internet.

Multiple Bit Rate Video: The support of multiple encoded video streams within one media stream. By using multiple bit rate video in an encoder, you can create media-based content that has a variety of video streams at variable bandwidths ranging from, for example, 28.8 Kbps through 300 Kbps, as well as a separate audio stream. After receiving this multiple encoded stream, the server determines which bandwidth to stream based on the network bandwidth available. Multiple bit rate video is not supported on generic HTTP servers.

Streaming Video: A sequence of moving images that are transmitted in compressed form over the Internet and displayed by a viewer as they arrive; is usually sent from pre-recorded video files, but can be distributed as part of a live broadcast feed.

Third Generation Mobile Communications (3G): The third generation of mobile communications (3G) is digital mobile multimedia offering broadband mobile communications with voice, video, graphics, audio, and other forms of information.

Web Casting: The technique of broadcasting media over an intranet, extranet, or the Internet.

Web Server Streaming: Another term for HTTP streaming, pseudo-streaming, or progressive download

ENDNOTES

1   www.realaudio.com

2   www.ipcast.com

3   http://www.3gnewsroom.com

Multimedia Internet Applications over WiMAX Networks: State-of-the-Art and Research Challenges

Nicola Scalabrino
CREATE-NET and Italian National Research Council (CNR) – IIT, Italy

Daniele Miorandi
CREATE-NET, Italy

Enrico Gregori
Italian National Research Council (CNR) – IIT, Italy

Imrich Chlamtac
CREATE-NET, Italy

INTRODUCTION

The IEEE 802.16 standard (IEEE802.16, 2004), promoted by the WiMAX (worldwide interoperability for microwave access) forum (http://www.wimaxforum.org), will be the leading technology for the wireless provisioning of broadband services in wide area networks. Such technology is going to have a deep impact on the way Internet access is conceived, so providing an effective wireless solution for the first mile problem.

The market for conventional first mile solutions (e.g., cable, fiber etc.) presents indeed high entrance barriers, and it is thus difficult for new operators to make their way into the field. This is due to the extremely high impact of labor-intensive tasks (i.e., digging up the streets, stringing cables etc.) that are required to put the necessary infrastructure in place. On the other hand, the market is experiencing an increasing demand for broadband multimedia services (Nokia, 2001), pushing toward the adoption of broadband access technologies. In such a situation, broadband wireless access (BWA) represents an economically viable solution to provide Internet access to a large number of clients, thanks to its infrastructure-light architecture, which makes it easy to deploy services where and when it is needed. Furthermore, the adoption of ad hoc features such as self-configuration capabilities in the subscriber stations (SSs) would make it possible to install customer

premises equipment (CPE) without the intervention of a specialized technician, so boosting the economical attractiveness of WiMAX-based solutions. In this context, WiMAX is expected to be the key technology for enabling the delivery of high-speed services to the end users.

Typical BWA deployments will rely on a point-to-multipoint (PMP) architecture, as depicted in Figure 1(a), consisting of a single base station (BS) wirelessly interconnecting several SSs to an Internet gateway. The standard also supports, at least in principle, mesh-based architectures like the one plotted in Figure 1(b).

In mesh topologies, direct communication among neighboring SSs is allowed so enhancing the network coverage and possibly enabling the deployment of a fully wireless backbone connecting to an Internet gateway.

However, its current version is far from offering a real support to such architecture. Therefore, we intend to restrict the scope of our work to the PMP architecture only.

The fundamental requirements for WiMAX to define itself as a possible winning technology are data reliability and the ability to deliver multimedia contents. Indeed, the provision of quality-of-service (QoS) guarantees will be a pressing need in the next generation of Internet, in order to enable the introduction of novel broadband multimedia applications.

Figure 1. Typical WiMAX system configuration: (a) point-to-multipoint; (b) mesh

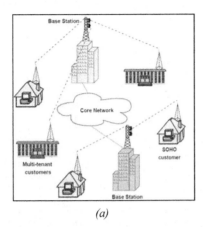

(a)

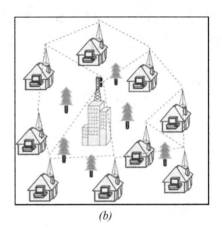

(b)

Users are actually getting more and more interested in broadband applications (e.g., video streaming, video conferencing, online gaming) that require assurances in terms of throughput, packet delay, and jitter, in order to perform well.

This also applies to WiMAX networks, which also has to face all the problems related to the hostile wireless environment, where time-varying channels and power emission mask constraints make it difficult to provide hard QoS guarantees. This entails the definition of a medium access control protocol, which is able to effectively support such multimedia applications while, on the other hand, it efficiently exploits the available radio resources. The IEEE 802.16 standard encompasses four classes of services, with different QoS requirements and provides the basic signaling between the BS and the SSs to support service requests/grants. However, the scheduling algorithms to be employed in the BS and the SSs are not specified and are left open for the manufacturers to compete.

BACKGROUND

WiMAX is the commercial name of products compliant with the IEEE 802.16 standard. Effectively replicating the successful history of IEEE 802.11 and Wi-Fi, an industrial organization, the WiMAX Forum has been set up to promote the adoption of such technology and to ensure interoperability among equipment of different vendors. This forum, which includes all the major industrial leaders in the telecommunication

field, is expected to play a major role in fostering the adoption of IEEE 802.16 as the *de facto* standard for BWA technology.

In terms of raw performance, WiMAX technology can reach a theoretical 50 Km coverage radius and achieve data rates up to *75* Mb/s (Intel, 2005) with a 20 MHz channel. Distances up to 50 km are achievable under optimal conditions and with a reduced data rate (a few Mb/s); the typical coverage will be around 5 km with indoor CPE in non-line-of-sight (NLOS) conditions and around 15 km with a CPE connected to an external antenna in a line-of-sight (LOS) situation. This wide coverage makes it possible, and economically viable to provide broadband connectivity in rural and remote areas, a market that is usually not covered by traditional service providers.

Actual IEEE 802.16 equipments are far from these performance figures. This is, to a wide extent, due to the fact that regulators will often allow only smaller channels (10 MHz or less).

As an example, in Ghosh, Wolter, Andrews, and Chen (2005), the authors report the outcomes of some bit-level numerical simulations performed assuming a channel width of 5 MHz and a multiple-input multiple-output (MIMO) 2x2 system (which reflects the most common actual equipment), showing that, under ideal channel conditions, data rates up to 18 Mb/s are feasible.

The general protocol architecture of the IEEE 802.16 standard is depicted in Figure 2. As can be seen, a common media access control (MAC) is provided to work on top of different physical layers (PHY). The

Figure 2. IEEE 802.16 protocol architecture

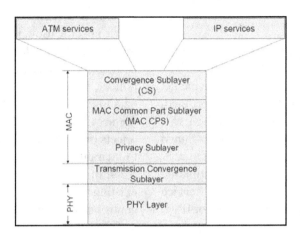

interface between the different PHYs and the MAC is accommodated as a separate sublayer, the transmission convergence sublayer. A convergence sublayer (CS) is provided on top of the MAC, to accommodate both IP as well as ATM-based network technologies. A basic privacy support is provided at the MAC layer.

The transmission convergence sublayer operates on top of the PHY and provides the necessary interface with the MAC. This layer is specifically responsible for the transformation of variable-length MAC PDUs into fixed length PHY blocks (Eklund, Marks, Stanwood, & Wang, 2002).

The necessity to provide secure data transmissions has led to the native inclusion of a privacy sub-layer, at the MAC level. Such protocol is responsible for encryption/decryption of the packet payload, according to the rules defined in the standard.

Since IEEE 802.16 uses a wireless medium for communications, the main target of the MAC layer is to manage the resources of the radio interface in an efficient way, while ensuring that the QoS levels negotiated in the connection setup phase are fulfilled. The 802.16 MAC protocol is connection-oriented and is based on a centralized architecture. All traffic, including inherently connectionless traffic, is mapped into a connection, which is uniquely identified by a *16*-bit address.

The common part sublayer is responsible for the segmentation and the reassembly of MAC service data units (SDUs), the scheduling and the retransmission of MAC PDUs. As such, it provides the basic MAC rules and signaling mechanisms for system access, bandwidth allocation and connection maintenance.

The core of the protocol is bandwidth requests/grants management. A SS may request bandwidth, by means of a MAC message, to indicate to the BS that it needs (additional) upstream bandwidth. Bandwidth is always requested on a per-connection basis to allow the BS uplink scheduling algorithm (which is not specified in the standard) to consider QoS-related issues in the bandwidth assignment process.

Regarding the way bandwidth is granted, the original 2001 standard encompassed two operational modes: grant per connection (GPC) and grant per subscriber station (GPSS). In the latest 2004 release, the term "grant" refers only to the GPSS mode.

In the GPC mode, the BS allocates bandwidth to individual connections. This defines a purely centralized mechanism with all the intelligence placed in the BS, while the SSs act as merely passive stations. On the other hand, the bandwidth, in the GPSS mode, is granted to each individual SS, which is then in charge of allocating the available resources to the currently active flows. This defines a semi-distributed approach to medium access control, in which some intelligence is moved from the BS to the SSs.

As depicted in Fig. 2, the MAC includes a CS, which provides three main functionalities:

1. **Classification:** The CS associates the traffic coming from upper layer with an appropriate *service flow* (SF) and *connection identifier* (CID).
2. **Payload header suppression (PHS):** The CS may provide payload header suppression at the sending entity and reconstruction at the receiving entity.

3. Delivery of the resulting CS PDU to the MAC common part sublayer in conformity with the negotiated QoS levels.

The standard defines two different CSs for mapping services to and from IEEE 802.16 MAC protocol. The ATM CS is defined for ATM traffic, while the packet CS is specific for mapping packet-oriented protocol suites, such as IPv4, IPv6, Ethernet, and virtual LAN. As regards IP, the packets are classified and assigned to the MAC layer connections based on a set of matching criteria, including the IP source and the destination addresses, the IP protocol field, the type-of-service (TOS) or DiffServ code points (DSCP) fields for IPv4, and the traffic class field for IPv6. However, these sets of matching criteria are not in the standard and their implementation is left open to vendors.

MAIN FOCUS OF THE CHAPTER

As previously described, the data packets entering the IEEE 802.16 network are mapped into a connection and a service flow based on a set of matching criteria. These classified data packets are then associated with a particular QoS level, based on the QoS parameters of the service flow they belong to. The QoS may be guaranteed by shaping, policing, and/or prioritizing the data packets at both the SS and BS ends. The BS allocates upstream bandwidth for a particular upstream service flow based on the parameters and service specifications of the corresponding service scheduling class negotiated during connection setup. The IEEE 802.16 standard defines four QoS service classes: Unsolicited grant service (UGS), real-time polling service (rtPS), non-real time polling service (nrtPS), and best effort (BE) (Cicconetti, Lenzini, Mingozzi, & Eklund, 2006).

In order to offer an efficient QoS support to the end user, a WiMAX equipment vendor needs to design and implement a set of protocol components that are left open by the standard. These include traffic policing, traffic shaping, connection admission control, and packet scheduling.

Due to the highly varying nature of multimedia flows, traffic shaping and traffic policing are required by the SS in order to ensure an efficient and fair utilization of network resources. At connection setup, the application requests network resources according to its character-

istics and to the required level of service guarantees. A traffic shaper is necessary to ensure that the traffic generated actually conforms to the pre-negotiated traffic specification. However, traffic shaping may not guarantee such conformance between the influx traffic and service requirements. This is dealt with by a traffic policer, which compares the conformance of the user data traffic with the QoS attributes of the corresponding service and takes corresponding actions (e.g., it rejects or penalizes non conformance flows). In order to guarantee that the newly admitted traffic does not result in network overload or service degradation for existing traffic, a (centralized) connection admission control scheme also has to be provided.

Even though all the aforementioned components are necessary in order to provide an efficient level of QoS support, the core of such a task resides in the scheduling algorithm. An efficient scheduling algorithm is essential for the provision of QoS guarantees, and it plays an essential role in determining the network performance. Besides, a traffic shaper, policer, and connection admission control mechanisms are tightly coupled with the scheduler employed.

Although the scheduling is not specified in the standard, system designers can exploit the existing rich literature about scheduling in wireless ATM (Cao & Li, 2001), from which WiMAX has inherited many features. If this allows one not to start from scratch, existing schemes need to be adapted to match the peculiar features (e.g., traffic classes, frame structure) of the IEEE 802.16 standard.

As an example, the GPSS scheduling mode can be seen as an outcome of the research carried out on hierarchical scheduling (Moorman & Lockwood, 1999). This is rooted in the necessity of limiting the MAC exchange overhead by letting the BS handle all connections of each SS as an aggregated flow. As explained in the previous section, according to the standard, the SSs request bandwidth on per connection-basis; however, the BS grants bandwidth to each individual SS, so that the resources are allocated to the aggregation of active flows at each SS. Each SS is then in charge of allocating the granted bandwidth to the active flows, which can be done in an efficient way since the SS has complete knowledge of its queues status. This, however, requires the introduction of a scheduler at each SS, enhancing the complexity (and consequently the cost) of the SS equipment.

Figure 3. Graphic representation of hierarchical scheduling

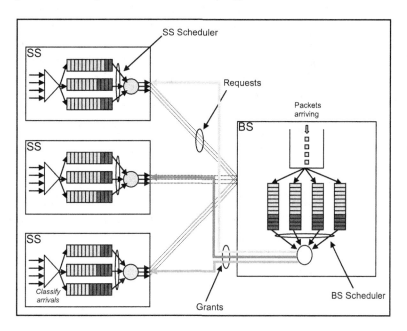

A detailed operational scheme is depicted in Figure 3, outlining the role played by each component and the requests/grants mechanism at the basis of WiMAX QoS support. In downlink, the scheduler has complete knowledge of the queue status, and, thus, may use some classical scheduling schemes such as weighted round robin (WRR), weighted fair queuing (WFQ) etc. (Cao et al., 2001).

Priority-oriented fairness features are also important in providing differentiated services in WiMAX networks. Through priority, different traffic flows can be treated almost as isolated while sharing the same radio resource.

Scheduling uplink flows is more complex because the input queues are located in the SSs and are hence separated from the BS. The UL connections work on a request/grant basis. Using bandwidth requests, the uplink packet scheduling may retrieve the status of the queues and the bandwidth parameters.

The literature is not rich in terms of QoS scheduling schemes specifically designed for WiMAX networks. In the following, we will briefly describe the only two works that address such a topic to the best of author's knowledge.

In Chu, Wang, and Mei (2002), the authors present a GPSS-based QoS architecture for IEEE 802.16 based on priority scheduling and dynamic bandwidth alloca-

tion. In particular, they propose a scheduling process divided into two parts. The first one, executed by the uplink scheduler inside the BS is performed in order to grant resources to the SSs in response to bandwidth requests. This is done by means of a classical WRR (Mezger, Petr, & Kelley, 1994). At each subscriber station, bandwidth assignments are computed by starting from the highest priority class (i.e., UGS flows) and then going down to rtPS, nrtPS, and BE. In this way, a strict priority among service classes is guaranteed. The scheduling schemes employed for the various classes are different. A classical WFQ (Fattah & Leung, 2002) is used for UGS and rtPS, whereas a simpler WRR is used for nrtPS service class. Best Effort traffic is served through a simple FIFO policy. By means of this prioritized approach (which resembles somehow multiclass priority fair queuing (Moorman et al., 1999), the proposed architecture is able to guarantee a good performance level to UGS and rtPS classes, to the detriment of lower priority traffic (i.e., nrtPS and BE flows).

The other work in the literature (Wongthavarawat & Ganz, 2003) presents an approach based on a fully centralized scheduling (GPC-like) scheme, where a global QoS agent collects all the necessary information on traffic flows, and takes decisions on traffic admission, scheduling, and resource allocation. Based on the complete global knowledge of the system, the deterministic quality of service levels can be guaranteed. Their scheme shares some common features with Chu et al. (2002) concerning how the priorities are treated. And even in Wongthavarawat et al. (2003), strict priority among different service classes is provided. In terms of the scheduling discipline used for the various classes, both earliest deadline first (EDF) and WFQ are used.

In particular, EDF is used for rtPS flows that demands the insertion of an additional module in the uplink scheduling for computing the packet deadline. In general, EDF is able to outperform standard WFQ in terms of performance, but the complexity and the cost of this additional module is the price to pay for it. As the authors take into consideration a completely centralized scheme in Wongthavarawat et al. (2003), this cost is negligible. However, this may become a limiting factor in the case of a semi-distributed (i.e., GPSS) scheduling mechanism. WFQ is used to share the bandwidth among the nrtPS schemes, while a simple FIFO mechanisms is encompassed for elastic (e.g., BE) traffic.

FUTURE TRENDS AND CONCLUSION

Though WiMAX is the most promising technology for enabling BWA systems to be widely deployed, many issues need to be addressed in order to make it effectively support the requirements and constraints of end users' multimedia flows. In order to do so, according to the discussion mentioned previously, an efficient QoS-enabled scheduling algorithm has to be designed and implemented. In this section, we point out and briefly describe the most promising, as well as challenging, directions in such a field, by outlining a research roadmap for QoS provisioning in WiMAX networks.

Multiantenna Architectures for WiMAX Networks

In recent years, intensive research efforts have led to the development of spectrally efficient multiuser transmission schemes for wireless communications based on the use of multiple antenna systems. The use of multiple antennas in combination with appropriate signal processing and coding is indeed a promising direction, which aims to provide a high-data-rate and a high-quality wireless communications in the access link. In this sense, multiantenna systems can be seen as a way to enhance the cell capacity while offering a better and more stable link quality at the same time. On the other hand, antennas arrays can be used also to achieve beamforming capabilities, with a remarkable improvement in terms of network performance. Adaptive antenna systems (AAS) are encompassed by the IEEE 802.16 standard to improve the PHY-layer characteristics. However, AAS can also act as enablers of spatial division multiple access (SDMA) schemes. In this way, multiple SSs, separated in space, can simultaneously transmit or receive on the same subchannel. This, obviously, demands the realization of a scheduling algorithm able to effectively exploit the presence of such beamforming capabilities. In this way, through a cross-layer approach, striking results can be obtained in terms of QoS support. An AAS-aware scheduling could indeed profit from the additional degree of freedom (i.e., the spatial dimension provided by the underlying PHY techniques. While this may lead to better performance, it also leads to an increase in the complexity of the scheduler itself. Nonetheless, we believe that the use of this and other related multiantenna techniques (e.g., space-time codes) represent a research direction with big potential in terms of throughput optimization. In order to fully take advantage of the power provided by multiple antenna systems, innovative QoS-enabled scheduling algorithms, able to work in both space and time dimensions, need to be designed and engineered.

Opportunistic Scheduling

In wireless networks, channel conditions may vary over time because of user mobility or propagation phenomena. These effects are usually referred to as shadowing and fading, depending on their typical time-scales. They have been traditionally considered as harmful features of the radio interface due to their potentially negative impact on the quality of communication. However, recent research has shown that the time-varying nature of the radio channel can be used for enhancing the performance of data communications in a multiuser environment. Indeed, time-varying channels in multiuser environments provide a form of diversity, usually referred to as multiuser diversity, that can be exploited by an "opportunistic" scheduler (i.e., a scheduler that selects the next user to be served according to the actual channel status (Liu, Chong, & Shroff, 2001)). This approach may also be applied at the cost of some additional complexity and signaling between PHY and MAC, to WiMAX networks. Opportunistic scheduling schemes do not usually apply to flows that require QoS guarantees, due to the unpredictable delays that may come from the channel dynamics. However, their use may actually lead to an enhanced QoS support. For example, improving the effect of non real-time traffic (i.e., nrtPS and BE traffic) would free some additional resources to higher priority traffic. In this way, opportunistic scheduling schemes may actually help to increase the QoS capabilities of WiMAX networks. Moreover, in this case, novel scheduling schemes are required in order to exploit multiuser diversity while providing QoS guarantees to the active traffic flows at the same time. It may be interesting to note that multiple antenna systems can actually be used to build up multiuser diversity by means of random beamforming mechanisms (usually referred to in the literature as "dumb" antennas (Viswanath, Tse, & Laroia, 2002)). While this direction is somehow orthogonal in nature to the one (based on "smart antennas") previously outlined, it could be worth investigating whether these two techniques may be implemented to coexist (for example, in a time-sharing fashion) in order to obtain the advantages of both approaches.

QoS Support in Mesh-Based Architectures

The techniques we have previously presented as research challenges are aimed at providing a better QoS support in PMP architecture. However, they are still subject to the limits imposed by such an architectural choice in terms of service coverage, network capacity, and system scalability. One possible solution to overcome such problems could be the adoption of a mesh-based architecture (Bruno, Conti, & Gregori, 2005). While mesh-based architectures offer interesting possibilities thanks to its inherent flexibility, they also present many research challenges to be addressed in terms of medium access control and packet routing. This is even more challenging in the case of QoS support for multimedia flows, where reliable levels of services have to be ensured by means of distributed algorithms. In this framework, a "double cross-layer" approach (where information is shared among PHY,

MAC, and NET layers) may lead to potentially dramatic performance improvements compared to conventional layered solutions. This clearly entails the definition of novel scheduling protocols, which are able to work in a distributed and collaborative way, so cooperating with the routing algorithms in order to provide QoS guarantees to service flows based on some PHY information. For example, the integration of scheduling and routing protocols can be based on the actual channel conditions, as well as on the level of interference in the network[1]. The application of these concepts to WiMAX networks is not straightforward, since it would imply some major modifications to the actual standard, in terms of both signaling (necessary for pursuing cross-layer optimization) as well as definition of basic functionalities and interfaces of the routing protocol to be employed.

REFERENCES

Bruno, R., Conti, M., & Gregori, E. (2005, March). Mesh networks: Commodity multihop ad hoc networks. IEEE Communications Magazine, 43(3), 123-131.

Cao, Y., & Li, V. O. (2001, January). Scheduling algorithms in broad-band wireless networks. In Proceedings of the IEEE, 89(1), 76-87.

Chu, G., Wang, D., & Mei, S. (2002, June). A QoS architecture for the MAC protocol of IEEE 802.16 BWA system. IEEE Conference on Communications, Circuits and Systems and West Sino Expositions (Vol. 1, pp. 435-439).

Cicconetti, C., Lenzini, L., Mingozzi, E., & Eklund, C. (2006, March). Quality of service support in IEEE 802.16 networks. IEEE Network Magazine, 20(2), 50-55.

Eklund, C., Marks, R., Stanwood, K., & Wang, S. (2002, June). IEEE standard 802.16: A technical overview of the WirelessMAN air interface for broadband wireless access. IEEE Communications Magazine, 40(6), 98-107.

Fattah, H., & Leung, C. (2002, October). An overview of scheduling algorithms in wireless multimedia networks. IEEE Wireless Communications, 9(5), 76-83.

Ghosh, A., Wolter, D. R., Andrews, J. G., & Chen, R. (2005, February). Broadband wireless access with

WiMax/802.16: Current performance benchmarks and future potential. *IEEE Communications Magazine, 43*(2), 129-136.

IEEE802.16. (2004). IEEE standard for local and metropolitan area networks Part 16: Air interface for fixed broadband wireless access systems. *IEEE Std 802.16-2004.*

Intel. (2005). *Deploying license-exempt WiMAX solutions.* Retrieved from http://www.intel.com/netcomms/technologies/wimax/306013.pdf. (White Paper)

Liu, X., Chong, E., & Shroff, N. (2001, Oct.). Opportunistic transmission scheduling with resource sharing constraints in wireless networks. *IEEE Journal on Selected Areas in Communications, 19*(10), 2053-2064.

Mezger, K., Petr, D. W., & Kelley, T. G. (1994). Weighted fair queueing vs. weighted round robin: A comparative analysis. In *Proceedings of IEEE Wichita Conference on Communications, Networks and Signal Processing.*

Moorman, J., & Lockwood, J. (1999, August). Multiclass priority fair queuing for hybrid wired/wireless quality of service support. In *Proceedings of the 2nd ACM International Workshop on Wireless Mobile Multimedia*, WOWMOM.

Nokia. (2001). *Broadband media services.* Retrieved from http://www.nokia.com/downloads/solutions/operators/broadband_media_services_tutorial_net.pdf. (White Paper)

Viswanath, P., Tse, D., & Laroia, R. (2002, June). Opportunistic beamforming using dumb antennas. *IEEE Transactions on Information Theory, 48*(6), 1277–1294.

Wongthavarawat, K., & Ganz, A. (2003). Packet scheduling for QoS support in IEEE 802.16 broadband wireless access systems. *International Journal of Communication Systems, 16*, 81-96.

KEY TERMS

Broadband Wireless Access (BWA): Technology aimed at providing high-speed wireless access to data networks. WiMAX is expected to be the leading broadband wireless access technology.

Hierarchical Scheduling: Semi-distributed scheduling approach in which some intelligence is moved from the central unit to the mobile stations in order to limit the MAC exchange overhead at the expense of increased complexity of the mobile equipment. This scheduling mechanism is expected to represent a valid base for designing an efficient QoS-enabled scheduler for WiMAX networks.

Mesh Architecture: Consists of several nodes, interconnected via wireless links where each node in the network cooperate to forward packets (by means of store-and-forward operations) to/from the Internet from/to the end node. A recent addition to the WiMAX standard is underway which will add full mesh networking capability.

Multiple-Input Multiple-Output (MIMO): Advanced communication architecture which takes advantage of multipath propagation, exploiting spatial degree of freedom in order to both increase throughput and reduce bit error rates. Such technology is expected to play a key role in boosting the performance of WiMAX systems.

Opportunistic Scheduling: Scheduling technique that exploits the time-varying nature and the spatial diversity of the wireless channel to make an effective use of the available system bandwidth. This approach is very suitable for WiMAX networks, at the cost of some additional complexity and signaling between PHY and MAC.

Point-to-MultiPoint (PMP): Centralized architecture that serves a set of mobile stations within the same antenna sector in a broadcast manner. The PMP is the basic architecture for WiMAX networks.

WiMAX: Acronym that stands for worldwide interoperability for microwave access, a certification mark for products that certify compatibility and interoperability of IEEE 802.16-compliant technologies.

ENDNOTE

[1] Note that this requires the introduction of novel metrics for path selection in routing algorithms (Bruno et al., 2005).

Network Optimization Using Evolutionary Algorithms in Multicast Transmission

Yezid Donoso
Universidad del Norte, Colombia

Ramón Fabregat
Girona University, Spain

INTRODUCTION

The aim of *multicasting* is to be able to send data from a sender to the members of a group in an efficient manner. Many multicast applications, such as audio and videoconferencing or collaborative environments and distributed interactive simulation, have multiple quality-of-service requirements (Striegel & Manimaran, 2002).

To support QoS in today's Internet, several new architecture models have been proposed (Striegel et al., 2002). Traffic engineering has become a key issue within these new architectures, as supporting QoS requires more sophisticated resource management tools. Traffic engineering aims to optimize the performance of operational networks. The main objective is to reduce congestion hot spots and improve resource utilization. This can be achieved by setting up explicit routes through the physical network in such a way that the traffic distribution is balanced across several traffic trunks. This *load balancing* technique can be achieved by multicommodity network flow (Pioro & Medhi, 2004) formulation. This leads to the traffic being shared over multiple routes between the ingress node and the egress nodes in order to avoid link saturation and hence the possibility of congestion, which is the inability to transmit a volume of information with the established capacities for a particular equipment or network.

We can also have per-flow multipath routing where an originating node uses multiple paths for the same flow (i.e., each flow is split into multiple subflows). The split ratio is fed to the routers, which divide the traffic of the same ingress-egress node pair into multiple paths. Several works address this splitting multipath problem of unicast traffic, motivated by its importance in any complete traffic engineering solution (see Donoso, Fabregat, & Marzo, (2004) for a detailed enumeration of these proposals). Traffic splitting is executed for every packet in the packet-forwarding path. In multicast transmission, load balancing consists of traffic being split (using the multipath approach) across multiple *trees*, between the ingress node and the set of egress nodes. Currently, multicast transmissions can be applied using switching technology and in this case, it is possible to use a *MPLS* technology (Rosen, Viswanathan, & Callon, 2001) for this function. In this chapter, we show a multi-objective traffic engineering scheme using different distribution trees to several multicast flows and our proposal solves the traffic split ratio for multiple trees.

BACKGROUND

Various traffic engineering solutions using techniques that balance loads by multiple routes have been designed and analyzed in different studies. Donoso et al. (2004) attempt to optimize a cost function subject to constraints resulting from the application's QoS requirements.

While Sridharan, Guerin, and Diot (2003), Fortz and Thorup (2002), and Song, Kim, Lee, Lee, and Suda (2003) consider unicast flow, in Lee, Seok, Choi, and Kim (2002), Cho, Lee, and Kim (2003), Abrahamsson, Ahlgren, Alonso, Andersson, and Kreuger (2002), and Cetinkaya, and Knightly (2004), this unicast flow is split, and in Seok, Lee, Choi, and Kim, (2002), Roy, Banerjee, and Das (2002), and Cui, Xu, and Wu (2003) the flow is multicast but not split, thus our proposal solves the traffic split ratio for multicast flows. The major differences between our work and the other multicast works are:

- First, in terms of objectives and function, we propose a multi-objective scheme to solve the optimal multicast routing problem with some constraints.
- Second, in relation to how many trees are used, we propose a multitree scheme to optimize resource utilization of the network.
- Third, in relation to traffic splitting, we propose that the traffic split can transmit the multicast flow information through load balancing using several trees for the same flow.

Finally, Muñoz, Martinez, Sorribes, and Junyent (2005) and Yong, and Kuo (2005) consider the *optimization* process in optical (GMPLS) networks.

MULTIOBJECTIVE MULTITREE MODEL FOR MULTICAST TRAFFIC

Although different models have been defined, which fulfil load balancing in unicast transmission, it is necessary to define other models that consider multicast transmission, because in this case, instead of creating multiple paths to transmit the flow from the ingress node to just one egress node, it is necessary to create multiple trees to transport the flow from the ingress node to the egress node set of the multicast group.

In this chapter we show a *multiobjective multitree model* in a pure multiobjective context that considers simultaneously for the first time multicast flow, multitree, and splitting.

Now, this kind of problem can be analyzed as a multi-objective problem (MOP) which can be expressed as:

Optimize	$y = f(x) = \{f_1(x), f_2(x), \dots, f_k(x)\}$
Subject to	$e(x) = \{e_1(x), e_2(x), \dots, e_m(x)\} \geq 0$
Where	$x = \{x_1, x_2, \dots, x_n\} \in X$
	$y = \{y_1, y_2, \dots, y_k\} \in Y$

Where x is the decision factor and y the objective factor. The decision space is denoted by X, and the objective space by Y. Optimizing, depending on the problem, can also mean minimizing or maximizing. For example, the multi-objective problem in multicast transmission of sending several flows doing load balancing can be expressed.

The computer network can be represented as a graph $G(N, E)$, with N denoting the set of nodes and E the set of links. The cardinality of a set is denoted as $|.|$, thus $|N|$ represents the cardinality of N. The set of flows is denoted as F. Each flow $f \in F$ can be split into K_f subflows that after normalization can be denoted as f_k; $k = 1, \dots |K_f|$. In this case, f_k indicates the fraction of $f \in F$ it transports. For each flow $f \in F$ we have a source $s_f \in N$ and a set of destinations or egress nodes $T_f \subset N$. Let t be an egress node (i.e., $t \in T_f$). Let $X_{ij}^{f_k t}$ denote the fraction of subflow f_k to egress node t assigned to link $(i,j) \in E$ (i.e., $0 \leq X_{ij}^{f_k t} \leq 1$. In this way, the n components of decision vector X are given by all $X_{ij}^{f_k t}$. Note that $X_{ij}^{f_k t}$ uses five indexes: i, j, f, k and t for the first time, unlike previous publications that only used a smaller subset of indexes because they did not deal with the same general problem. In particular, the novel introduction of a subflow index k gives an easy way to identify subflows and define LSPs in a MPLS implementation. Let c_{ij} be the capacity (in bps) of each link $(i,j) \in E$. Let b_f be the traffic request (measured in bps) of flow $f \in F$, travelling from source s_f to T_f. Let d_{ij} be the delay (in ms) of each link $(i,j) \in E$. Finally, the binary variables $Y_{ij}^{f_k t}$ represent whether a link (i,j) is being used (value 1) or not (value 0) for transporting subflow f_k to destination node t.

Minimizing for example the following objective functions:

F.1   Maximal link utilization

$$\max\{a_{ij}\}, \text{ where } \alpha_{ij} = \frac{1}{c_{ij}} \sum_{f=1}^{|F|} \sum_{k=1}^{|K_f|} b_f \max_{t \in T_f} \left\{ X_{ij}^{f_k t} \right\}$$

Figure 1. Chromosome representation

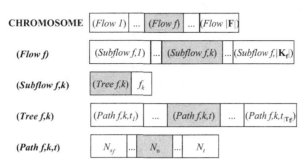

F.2 Hop count average

$$\frac{\sum_{(i,j)\in E}\sum_{f\in F}\sum_{k\in K_f}\sum_{t\in T_f}Y_{ij}^{f_k t}}{\sum_{f\in F}\sum_{k=1}^{|K_f|}\left|T_f\right|}$$

F.3 Maximal delay (useful for QoS assurance)

$$\max_{\substack{\forall f\in F \\ \forall k\in K_f \\ \forall t\in T_f}}\left\{\sum_{(i,j)\in E}d_{ij}\cdot Y_{ij}^{f_k t}\right\}$$

In summary, the objective function follows the general mathematical framework of any MOP. In this context, this model can be considered several objective functions. Clearly, it is not difficult to increment the number of objectives or constraints of the proposed model if new ones appear in the literature or they are useful for a given situation.

At this point, it is important to point out that the mathematical solution of the proposed model is a complete set X^* of Pareto optimal solutions $x^*\in X^*$ (i.e., any solution x' outside the Pareto set $(x'\notin X^*)$ is outperformed by at least one solution x^* of the Pareto set $(\exists x^* \succ x')$); therefore, x' cannot outperform x^* even if not all the objective functions are considered. Now, to solve this problem we use MOEA (*multiobjective evolutionary algorithm*). With this kind of algorithm is possible to give a solution for a combinatorial problem like the multi-objective optimization problem. For this kind of problem is possible to use different techniques such as ant colony, tabu search, simulated annealing, memetic algorithms, etc; but in this work we are using an *evolutionary algorithm* to give a solution.

MULTIOBJECTIVE EVOLUTIONARY ALGORITHM

EAs are interesting given the fact that at first glance they seem especially apt for dealing with the difficulties posed by MOPs. The reason for this is that they can return an entire set of solutions after a simple run and they do not have any of the limitations of traditional techniques. In fact, most recent publications on MOP resolutions using EAs, seem to consider this fact and they have opened the way to a whole new field of research: evolutionary algorithms applied to multi-objective optimization MOEA (Donoso, 2005).

To solve the presented model, a multiobjective evolutionary algorithm (MOEA) approach was selected because of its well recognized advantages when solving MOPs in general and traffic engineering with load balancing in particular (Cui et al., 2003; Roy & Das, 2004; Roy et al., 2002).

At the beginning, an initial population of P_{max} feasible solutions (known as individuals) is created as a starting point for the search. In the next stages (or generations), a performance metric, known as fitness, is calculated for each individual. In general, a modern MOEA calculates fitness considering the dominance properties of a solution with respect to a population. Based on this fitness, a selection mechanism chooses good solutions (known as parents) for generating a new population of candidate solutions, using genetic operators like crossover and mutation. The process continues iteratively, replacing old populations with new ones, saving the best found solutions (a process known as elitism), until a stop condition is reached.

Figure 2. Flow crossover operator

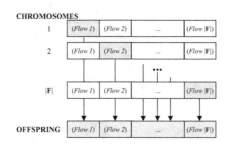

Figure 3. Tree crossover operator

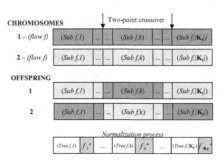

An algorithm based on the *strength pareto evolutionary algorithm* (SPEA) (Donoso, 2005) is used. It has an evolutionary population P and an external set P_{nd} with the best Pareto solutions found. Starting with a random population P, the individuals of P evolve to optimal solutions that are included in P_{nd}. Old dominated solutions of P_{nd} are pruned each time a new solution from P enters P_{nd} and dominates old ones.

ENCODING

Encoding is the process of mapping a decision variable x into a chromosome (the computational representation of a candidate solution). This is one of the most important steps toward solving a TE load balancing problem using evolutionary algorithms. This article proposes an encoding process, as shown in Figure 1, that allows several flows to be represented (unicast and/or multicast) with as many splitting subflows as necessary to optimize a given set of objective functions to be represented.

One interesting advantage of the proposed encoding is that a valid chromosome satisfies restrictions completely, making verifying them unnecessary.

INITIAL POPULATION

To generate an initial population P of valid chromosomes we have considered each chromosome one at a time, building each (*Flow f*) of that chromosome separately. For each (*Flow f*) we first generated a large enough set of different valid paths from source s_f to each destination $t \in T_f$.

In this initialization procedure chromosomes are randomly generated one at a time. A built chromosome is valid (and accepted as part of the initial population) if it also satisfies link capacity constraint; otherwise, it is rejected and another chromosome is generated until the initial population P has the desired size P_{max}.

SELECTION

Good chromosomes of an evolutionary population are selected for reproduction with probabilities that are proportional to their fitness. Therefore, a *fitness function* describes the "quality" of a solution (or individual). An individual with good performance (like the ones in P_{nd}) has a high fitness level, while an individual with bad performance has a low fitness level. In this proposal,

Figure 4. Segment mutation

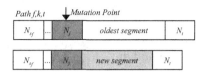

Figure 5. Subflow fraction mutation followed by the normalization process

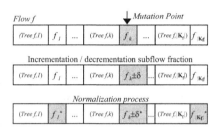

fitness is computed for each individual, using the well-known SPEA procedure.

CROSSOVER

We propose two different crossover operators: *flow crossover* (Figure 2) and *tree crossover* (Figure 3).

MUTATION

A mutation operator is usually used to ensure that an optimal solution can be found with a probability greater than zero. This operator can improve an evolutionary algorithm's performance, given its ability to continue the search for global optimal (or near optimal) solutions even after local optimal solutions have been found. This stops the algorithm from being easily trapped in local sub-optimal solutions. We propose a subflow mutation operator with two phases: *segment mutation* (Figure 4) and *subflow fraction mutation* (Figure 5).

With this scheme, when we have a solution, this solution is a tree set and every tree consists of different path with destination to every egress node. Finally, every path is exactly a LSP in MPLS technology.

FUTURE TRENDS

There are many issues that have been left as future work throughout this work. The most significant ones are the following: This work can be applied in MPLS technology, but it would be interesting to apply these models in GMPLS technology in the photonic label and extend the models to the wireless technology. It could be interesting to probe other kinds of meta-heuristics to look for solutions to the same problem. These kinds of meta-heuristics could be ant colony, memetic algorithms, tabu search, simulated annealing, etc. In the case of multicast optimization as future work would be possible to analyze the new kind of multicast services and their implementation in multicast networks such as multipoint collaborative work, grid computing with multiple destinations, etc.

CONCLUSION

In different networks it is possible to have congestion and many multicast applications, such as audio and videoconferencing or collaborative environments and distributed interactive simulation, and also multiple quality of service requirements on bandwidth, packet delay, packet loss, cost, etc. This work presents a scheme to optimize the network resources through the load balancing technique. It also presents a scheme to transmit multicast flow by more than one tree instead of by just one tree. The model considers three different functions. The computational solution was carried out using MOEA. In this case, it is possible to find the optimal Pareto front.

REFERENCES

Abrahamsson, H., Ahlgren, B., Alonso, J., Andersson, A., & Kreuger, P. (2002). A multi path routing algorithm for IP networks based on flow optimization. LCNS 2511. QoFIS.

Alwayn, V. (2001). Advanced MPLS design and implementation. Cisco Press: Indianapolis, IN, USA.

Cetinkaya, C., & Knightly, E. (2004). Opportunistic traffic scheduling over multiple network paths. *IEEE INFOCOM.*

Cho, H., Lee, J., & Kim, B. (2003). Multi-path constraint-based routing algorithms for MPLS traffic engineering. *IEEE ICC.*

Cui, Y., Xu, K., & Wu, J. (2003). Precomputation for multi-constrained QoS routing in highspeed networks. *IEEE INFOCOM.*

Donoso, Y. (2005). *Multi-objective optimization scheme for static and dynamic multicast flows.* PhD thesis, Universitat de Girona. Retrieved from http://www.tdcat. cesca.es/TDX-0711105-133559/index.html

Donoso, Y. Fabregat, R., & Marzo, J. L. (2004). Multi-objective optimization algorithm for multicast routing with traffic engineering. *Telecommunication Systems Journal.* Kluwer Publisher.

Fortz, B., & Thorup, M. (2002). Optimizing OSPF/IS-IS weights in a changing world. JSAC.

Lee, L., Seok, Y., Choi, Y., & Kim, C. (2002). A constrained multipath traffic engineering scheme for MPLS networks. *IEEE ICC.*

Muñoz, R., Martinez, R., Sorribes, J., & Junyent, G. (2005). Flooding global wavelength information through GMPLS RSVP-TE signaling in unidirectional ring-based networks. *IEEE International Conference on Communications, 2005, 3*(3), 1678-1682.

Pioro, M., & Medhi, D. (2004). Routing, flow, and capacity design in communication and computer networks. Elsevier: San Francisco, CA, USA.

Rosen, E., Viswanathan, A., & Callon, R. (2001). Multiprotocol label switching architecture. RFC 3031.

Roy, A., & Das, S. (2004). QM2RP: A QoS-based mobile multicast routing protocol using multi-objective genetic algorithm. *The Journal of Mobile Communication, Computation, and Information, 10*(3), May 2004, pp. 271-286(16).

Roy, A., Banerjee, N., & Das, S. (2002). An efficient multi-objective qos-routing algorithm for wireless multicasting. *IEEE INFOCOM.*

Seok, Y., Lee, Y., Choi, Y., & Kim, C. (2002). Explicit multicast routing algorithms for constrained traffic engineering. *IEEE ISCC.*

Song, J., Kim, S., Lee, M., Lee, H., & Suda, T. (2003). Adaptive load distribution over multipath in MPLS networks. IEEE ICC.

Sridharan, A., Guerin, R., & Diot, C. (2003). Achieving near-optimal traffic engineering solutions for current OSPF/IS-IS networks. *IEEE INFOCOM.*

Striegel, A., & Manimaran, G. (2002). A survey of QoS multicast issues. *IEEE Communications Magazine.*

Yong, Y., Kuo, G. S. (2005). Label distribution in GMPLS-based wavelength-routed networks. *IEEE International Conference on Communications, 3*(3), 1697-1701.

KEY TERMS

Evolutionary Algorithm (EA): Evolutionary algorithms (EA) are inspired by Darwin's theory of evolution, which is based on the survival of the fittest species. The character of a life is determined by the chromosomes. In a chromosome there are many different genes, which indicate different characters. The EA principle is based on the different combinations of genes in a chromosome. Different combinations will lead to different characters and the more suitable ones will remain in the world.

Load Balancing: A fundamental mechanism for implementing traffic engineering. It concerns the number of overutilized links, which will have low QoS, and underutilized links, which represent a waste to be reduced. It can be achieved by a multicommodity network flow formulation which leads to the traffic being shared over multiple routes between the ingress node and the egress nodes in order to avoid link saturation and hence the possibility of congestion.

Label Switched Path (LSP): It is a path between source node and the egress node in MPLS technology.

Memetic Algorithm: As the evolutionary algorithms are algorithms that can give a solution to combinatorial problems of the same way than the natural behaviour.

Minimize Maximum Link Utilization: When the maximum link utilization is minimized, represented by α in some cases, a new upper bound of the utilization in every link of the network is created. In this way, when this new upper bound is exceeded, the information flow is transmitted by another different path. That is, for all the traffic that exceeds the $(\alpha.u_{ij})$, where u_{ij} is the link capacity, the value will be transmitted by other paths instead of using the total capacity of the links. If the traffic is multicast, instead of paths we consider trees.

Multicast Connections: Transmission from one source to a set of destinations. The aim of multicasting is to be able to send data form a sender to the set of destinations in an efficient manner.

Multiobjective Problem (MOP): A general MOP includes a set of n parameters (decision variables), a set of k objective functions, and a set of m restrictions. The objective and restriction functions are functions of the decision variable. In multiobjective problems, it rarely happens that all the objectives can be optimized simultaneously; it is generally the case that the objectives conflict with each other. Because the multi-objective optimization problem does not always have a single solution and the problem is known to be NP-complete, in several works EA solutions are proposed.

Multipath Routing: Different paths can be used to provide a balanced traffic over the links. Links do not get overused and so do not get congested. Therefore, they have the potential to aggregate bandwidth, allowing a network to support a higher data transfer than is impossible with any single path.

Multiprotocol Label Switching (MPLS): MPLS integrates the label switching forwarding paradigm with network layer routing. MPLS is an approach to packet forwarding whereby short fixed length labels are attached to IP packets by a LSR at the ingress to an MPLS domain. An ingress LSR attaches labels to packets based on the concept of forwarding equivalence classes (FEC), so that packets that belong to the same FEC are assigned the same label value and follow the same LSP.

Quality of Service (QoS): QoS is defined as a collective effect of service performance, which determines the degree of satisfaction of a user of the service. It is the capability of a network to provide better services to selected network traffic over various (heterogeneous) technologies. QoS is a set of service requirements to be met by the network while transporting a flow.

Traffic Engineering (TE): Concerned with performance optimization of operational networks. In general, it encompasses applying technology and scientific principles to measuring, modelling, characterizing, and controlling Internet traffic, and applying the knowledge and techniques to achieve specific performance objectives.

Network Survivability in Optical Networks with IP Prospective

Hongsik Choi
Virginia Commonwealth University, USA

Seung S. Yang
Virginia State University, USA

INTRODUCTION

The explosive growth of the Internet fueled intensive research on high-speed optical networks based on the wavelength-division multiplexing (WDM) technology. WDM technology harnesses the large bandwidth of the optical fiber, which is of the order of several Terabits/s into a few tens of wavelengths, each of which can be operated at electronic rates of a few Gb/s.

Thanks to recent advances in optical routing and switching, wavelength routing techniques becomes reality, where wavelengths can be independently routed from the source to the destination. With the optical switches that are capable of dynamically reconfiguring the routing pattern under electronic control, the flexibility provided by the network is dramatically increased. In a dynamically configurable wavelength-routing network, lightpaths can be provided on a demand basis, depending on traffic requirements.

As wavelength routing paves the way for network throughputs of possibly hundreds of Tb/s, network survivability assumes critical importance. A short network outage can lead to data losses of the order of several gigabits. Hence, protection or dedicating resources in anticipation of faults and rapid restoration of traffic upon detection of faults are becoming increasingly important. According to Gerstel and Ramaswami (2000), the overall availability requirements are of the order of 99.999% or higher.

Survivability is the ability of the network to withstand equipment and link failures. Node equipment failures are typically handled using redundant equipment within the node. On the other hand, link failures, which are by far the most common failures in optical networks, are typically dealt with by allocating redundant capacity on other network links and switching the affected traffic to the redundant capacity. This mechanism in which redundant capacity, or protection capacity, is pre-allocated for use when a link fails is called protection (One may consider restoration for network survivability purpose, but we do not consider the restoration in this article.)

There has been a large amount of work that focuses on protection in optical networks. Protection in optical networks, especially in optical layer, is considered to be fast, partly because of the proximity of the optical layer to the physical layers at which the failure is first detected, partly because of coarse granularity at which protection is done.

However, optical network protection alone does not provide network survivability. Considering that optical WDM network (Murty & Gurusamy, 2002) provides enough bandwidth to accommodate ever increasing traffic and IP network provides proven service on which almost all major network applications are deployed, IP over WDM (The IP network, made of IP routers, built on top of a WDM infrastructure) is considered as the most promising network structure. Therefore, IP network along with optical network should be considered to provide desired network survivability.

In this article, we focused on IP logical topology embedding onto wavelength routing WDM network to provide network survivability desired for IP over WDM network.

Figure 1. Examples of logical IP embedding to optical ring network

(a)	*(b)*	*(c)*	*(d)*

BACKGROUND

Both IP network and WDM optical network has their own protection scheme. While that of IP is implicitly incorporated into the IP routing protocol, protection schemes in WDM network are not standardized yet. However, IP protection and WDM protection are developed independently and deployed, their cooperation is minimal and counters escalating (Doverspike et al., 2000). Therefore, protection should be reconsidered as a inter layer problem between IP logical layer and optical layer with the help of multi-protocol label switching (MPLS). In this section, we will summarize the protection scheme implicitly used in IP network and protection schemes developed for WDM optical network.

Internet protocol (IP) delivers IP packets based on routing information. A router decides the next hop of a packet based on the routing information at a given time (Comer, 2006). A router reorganizes its routing information when a network fault happens. Detection of network faults and update of routing information methods depend on routing protocols. Routing information is updated based on a new network topology, and newly constructed routing information may create unreachable network segments. Because each IP packet is forwarded in a router based on routing information of the router, creation of routing information that maintains network reachability and maintains QoS after a fault is a key issue in IP network survivability.

Popular interior gateway protocols (IGPs) are routing information protocol (RIP) and open shortest path first (OSPF). RIP is a distance vector-based routing protocols and uses a distance metric that contains a list of vectors (Malkin, 1998). Due to the volume of traffic RIP generates, link state-based routing protocols are more preferable in large network (Tanenbaum, 2003).

OSPF is a link state-based routing protocol that each router floods link state information to network and creates routing information by constructing a network topology with the flooded information (Moy, 1998). A router reconstructs its network topology and remakes routing information upon reception of status change message.

As an exterior gateway protocol (EGP), border gateway protocol (BGP) uses a path vector to describe routing information (Rekhter, Li, & Hares, 2006). It creates local and advertising routing information through applying its policies on received routing information. Therefore, depending on each BGP speaker's policy, not all topology changes are engraved in routing information. Aggregation of routing information in BGP should be carefully considered when it detects network fault because aggregation may hide the fault. The impact of change is very critical due to massiveness of the network traffic affected by the routing information change.

Many survivable IP network researches are worked on OSPF. This may be partially affected by the following reasons: Policy takes critical roles in routing information creation in BGP, and RIP is not scalable enough for large network where survivability of IP has more weight on. The knowledge of network topology in each router in OSPF provides more chances to better plan when a fault occurs in a network. Use of evolutionary algorithms in OSPF for single link or single node failure is introduced (Buriol, Resende, & Thorup, 2006). Bifurcated routing in OSPF is studied to provide survivability in IP networks (Bley, Grotschel, & Wessaly, 1998).

Protections in optical network are broadly classified as path protection or link protection, depending on where protection switching is done (Ramaswami & Sivarajan, 1998). In link protection, alternate paths

Figure 2. Logical IP network with optical link failure on link (2,3)

(a)   (b)

called backup or protection paths, between the end points of each link are pre-computed (Ramamurthy, Sahasrabuddhe, & Mukherjee, 2003). Upon link's failure, all of the lightpaths using the link are switched at the end-nodes of the link to their corresponding backup paths. The portion of lightpaths excluding the failed link remains the same. In contrast, path protection entails the end-to-end rerouting of all working lightpaths that use the failed link along pre-computed backup lightpaths (Ou, Zhang, Zang, Sahasrabuddhe, & Mukherjee, 2004). Here, the entire route of working path may be changed. The flexibility of rerouting a lightpath on end-to-end basis in path protection could lead to a lower protection capacity requirement. However, it may require the end-nodes of all failed lightpaths to be notified of a link's failure, if the end-to-end rerouting is failure dependent. On the other hand, link protection may require more protection capacity because of reduced flexibility in routing, but can be much faster as it uses only local knowledge around failed link and perform the switching at lower layer, thus reducing the amount of signaling performed after a failure occurs and providing the potential for much faster recovery than path protection schemes. Both link protection and path protection are highly depends on the routing and wavelength assignment (RWA) algorithm (Zang, Ou, & Mukherjee, 2003) since the lightpath set up is subject to routing and wavelength assignment algorithm. Hybrid scheme to get the virtue of both schemes (Ramamurthy et al. 2003; Xue, Zhang, Tang, & Thulasiraman, 2005; Zheng & Mohan, 2003) and some variations to tolerate several link faults such as shared risk group has been studied.

MAIN FOCUS OF THE CHAPTER

Our main focus is how to provide seamless network service at the IP network level regardless of the fault in the optical network level. Since the optical network layer is hidden from network applications, applications are built on top of the IP logical network. Therefore, network survivability seen by the application is survivability of the IP network. In the IP network, survivability is the ability to route any data from source to destination and it can be achieved as long as the IP logical topology is connected graph.

The survivability issue on the IP/WDM network is fault propagation, meaning a single link fault in WDM optical layer may cause more than one link faults in IP network layer. In the worst case, a single link fault in WDM optical layer makes all links fail in the IP network layer. Therefore, setting up a logical IP link, or lightpath, needs careful coordination between the WDM optical layer and IP layer if the survivability has to be achieved at the IP logical layer.

For example, if the optical network is ring network like SONET, as shown in Figure 1(b), and if the required IP logical topology is two connected graph as in Figure 1(a), we may have two different groups of lightpath set up for the logical IP network as shown in Figure 1(c) and (d). With single link faults in optical network, IP topology in (c) is disconnected and results in service disruption in IP network, while that in (d) is connected and possible to provide continuous service regardless of link fault in optical layer, meaning it is survivable IP embedding onto WDM network. Figure 2 (a) and (b) show IP logical topology after optical link (2,3) fails in Figure 1 (b) when the lightpath setup sued as in Figure 1(c) and (d), respectively.

We now present formulations of our problems as the following.

Survivable Embedding Problem in IP/WDM Network (SEP)

Given a WDM network with n nodes, $Gp(N,Ep)$, and an IP logical network, $Gl(N,El)$ find a route for each lightpath $(i,j) \in E_l$ such that the logical topology, Gl, is connected after the failure of any optical link if possible. If it is not possible, add the minimum number of additional lightpaths and find associates route to make the logical topology survivable.

Survivable Reconfiguration Problem in IP/WDM Network (SRP)

Given a WDM network with n nodes, $Gp(N,Ep)$, and two IP logical networks, $Glc(N,Elc)$ and $Gln(N,Eln)$ finding a sequence of setting up lightpaths and tearing down the lightpaths to reconfigure the network from Glc to Gln while preserving seamless IP network service (i.e., maintaining connected network). Here, we assume that we have survivable embedding for Glc and Gln, respectively.

SEP is whether we can have survivable IP embedding onto WDM network such that we can provide continuous service against single optical link faults. And SRP is whether we can reconfigure IP network from one survivable IP/WDM network to other survivable IP/WDM network while preserving the survivability so that the network provides seamless service even in transition period.

Since the proofs of hardness of the previous problems are beyond the scope of this article, we will present a simple result when the underlying optical network has ring structure like SONET. Interested readers refer to Lee, Choi, Subramaniam, and Choi (2003).

Theorem: Given an arbitrary IP logical network, $Gl(N,El)$, where degree of network is $\lceil 2n/3 \rceil$, meaning every node has to be connected to at least $\lceil 2n/3 \rceil$ other nodes, the IP logical network remains connected in the event of any single optical link failure if each lightpath, or logical IP link, is established using the shortest path route.

Proof: In the following, we assume that n is a multiple of six and proves the theorem. When n is not a multiple of six, similar arguments can be applied to prove the theorem, and we omit the details in this article.

Let $V = \{0,...,n-1\}$ be the set of nodes in the ring network, and assume the lightpaths are assigned using the shortest path route. Suppose $(0, n-1)$ is the failed optical link. Define $L = \{0,1,\cdots,\frac{n}{2}-1\}$ and $R = \{\frac{n}{2},\frac{n}{2}+1,\cdots,n-1\}$. Let S_i be the number of lightpaths (i.e., IP logical links) connecting node i that are not using link $(0, n-1)$. We then observe the following:

$$s_i \geq \begin{cases} \frac{n}{6}+i & if \quad i \in L \\ \frac{n}{6}-i+n-1 & if \quad i \in R \end{cases}$$

Suppose the IP logical topology becomes disconnected after the failure of optical link $(0,n-1)$, and let C denote the smallest component (i.e., a component with the minimum number of nodes) connected via IP logical links after the failure of optical link $(0,n-1)$. Clearly, $|C| \leq \frac{n}{2}$, and assume that $L \cap C \neq 0$. Let t denote the largest index in $L \cap C$. Let t' denote the smallest index in $R \cap C$ if $R \cap C \neq 0$, and t' is not defined if $R \cap C = 0$. Assume without loss of generality that the distance from node 0 to t is no less than the distance from node $n-1$ to t' (i.e., $t \geq n - t' - 1$). In the following, we consider four cases for the value of t and show the contradiction to the existence of C in each case.

Case 1

$$t \leq \frac{n}{4} - 1$$

In this case, the distance in the clockwise from t to t' is larger than $\frac{n}{2}$, and $C \subset L$ (i.e., $R \cap C = 0$). Since t is the largest index in $L \cap C$, it implies that $|C| \leq t + 1$, hence, node t can only be connected to at most t other nodes in C. However, by the definition of S_i, node t must be connected at least $|C| \leq \frac{n}{2}$ nodes all in C, a contradiction.

Case 2

$$t \geq \frac{n}{3}$$

By the definition of S_t, node t must be connected to at least $\frac{n}{6} + t$ (i.e., at least $\frac{n}{2}$) nodes in C. However, $|C| \leq \frac{n}{2}$, a contradiction.

Case 3

$$\frac{n}{4} \leq t \leq \frac{n}{3} - 2$$

For any node $i \in C \cap R$, we then have $n - t - 1 \leq i \leq \frac{n}{2} + t$. This then implies that $|C \cap R| \leq 2t - \frac{n}{2} + 2$, which is $|C \cap R| \leq \frac{n}{6} - 2$. By the definition of S_t, node t must be connected to at least $t + \frac{n}{6}$ nodes in C, where node t can be connected to at most $\frac{n}{6} - 2$ nodes in $C \cap R$. Therefore, node t must be connected to at least $t + 2$ nodes in $C \cap L$, and this is impossible since $|C \cap L| \leq t + 1$.

Case 4

$$t = \frac{n}{3} - 1$$

Since $n - t - 1 \leq i \leq \frac{n}{2} + t$ for any node $i \in C \cap R$, $|C \cap R| \leq \frac{n}{6} - 2$. Again, by the definition of S_t, node t must be connected to at least $t + \frac{n}{6}$ nodes in C. Therefore, node t (i.e., node $\frac{n}{3} - 1$) must be connected to all of the $\frac{n}{6}$ nodes in $C \cap R$ and all of nodes in $(0,1,..., \frac{n}{3} - 2)$. Consequently, we have $C = \{0,1,...,\frac{n}{3} - 1\} \cup \{\frac{2n}{3}, \frac{2n}{3} + 1, \cdots, \frac{5n}{6} - 1\}$ (i.e., $|C| = \frac{n}{2}$). Clearly, any node in C can only be connected to nodes in C, and consider node $j - \frac{2n}{3}$ which is in $C \cap R$. Again, by the definition of S_j, node j must be connected to at least $\frac{n}{2} - 1$ nodes implying that node j must be connected to all nodes (except j itself) in C. However, this is impossible since node 0, for example, cannot be connected to node j without using link $(0, n - 1)$ since the shortest route must be applied.

This completes the proof of the theorem. The result in Theorem shows that the shortest path routing guarantees the survivability of IP logical topology if the minimum degree of the topology (i.e., the minimum number of nodes that each node is connected to) is at least $\lceil 2n/3 \rceil$.

FUTURE TRENDS

When we need to consider network survivability in an IP layer, we have to reconsider the routing and wavelength assignment problem after incorporating the IP network connectivity. That may not only save unnecessary resource reservation for protection, but also provide seamless network service at the IP network layer, which is the most important network service at application point of view. To do so, overlaying network approach should be developed such that WDM layer lightpaths set up should have complete information about the IP network level topology and IP network level routers also need to know underlying optical network structure to utilize the lightpaths efficiently. Alternatively, developing a smart router along with optical switch so that lighpath set up and IP network routing should be considered altogether as we do in integrated routing algorithm.

CONCLUSION

We briefly discussed the survivability issues in WDM network and IP/WDM network. IP and optical networks play vital roles in today's communication system. To provide seamless IP network services, one should consider the WDM network layer and the IP layer together and more close cooperation between the IP network layer and the optical layer. We presented the survivability issues in terms of IP logical topology embedding onto WDM physical network. We proved that the simple shortest path based IP embedding into ring based optical network provides IP survivability when the degree of the IP network is grater than a specific number. Future work may consider the optical network with arbitrary topology.

REFERENCES

Bley, A., Grotschel, M., & Wessaly, R., (1998). Design of broadband virtual private networks: Model and heuristics for the B-WiN. In *Proceedings on DIMACS Workshop on Robust Communication Networks and Survivability* (pp. 1-16). AMS-DIMACS Series 53.

Buriol, L., Resende, M., & Thorup, M., (2004). *Survivable IP network design with OSPF routing*. AT&T Labs Research Technical Report, TD-64KUAW, September.

Choi, H., Subramaniam, S., & Choi, H.-A. (2004). Loopback methods for double-link failure recovery in optical networks. *ACM/IEEE Transactions on Networking*, *12*(6), 1119-1130.

Comer, D. (2006). *Internetworking with TCP/IP* (Vol. 1, 5th ed.). Upper Saddle River, NJ: Prentice Hall.

Doverspike, R. Phillips, S., & Westbrook, J. (2000). Transport network architectures. An IP World. In *Proceedings of INFOCOM2000* (Vol. 1, pp 305-314).

Gerstel, O., & Ramaswami, R. (2000). Optical layer survivability: A services prospective. *IEEE Communications Magazine*, *38*(3), 104-113.

Lee, H., Choi, H., Subramaniam, S., & Choi, H.A. (2003). Survival embedding of logical topology in WDM ring networks. *Information Sciences*, *149*(1-3), 151-160.

Malkin, G. (1998). RIP Version 2, STD 56, RFC 2453.

Moy, J. (1998). OSPF Version, STD 54, RFC 2328.

Murty, C., & Gurusamy, M. (2002). *WDM optical networks*. Upper Saddle River, NJ: Prentice Hall.

Ou, C., Zhang, J., Zang, H., Sahasrabuddhe, L. H., & Mukherjee, B. (2004). New and improved approaches for shared-path protection in WDM mesh networks. *Journal of Lightwave Technology*, *5*(22), 1223-1232.

Ramaswami, R., & Sivarajan, K. (1998). *Optical Networks: A Practical Perspective*. San Francisco: Morgan Kaufmann.

Ramamurthy, S., Sahasrabuddhe, L., & Mukherjee, B. (2003). Establishment of survivable connection in WDM networks using partial protection. *Journal of Lightwave Technology*, *21*(4), 870-883.

Ramamurthy, S., Sahasrabuddhe, L., & Mukherjee, B. (2003). Survivable WDM mesh networks. *Journal of Lightwave Technology*, *4*(21), 870-883.

Rekhter, Y., Li, T., & Hares, S. (2006). A Border Gateway Protocol 4 (BGP-4), RFC 4271.

Tanenbaum, A. (2003). *Computer networks* (4th ed.). Upper Saddle River, NJ: Prentice Hall.

Xue, G., Zhang, W., Tang, J., & Thulasiraman, K.(2005), Hybrid protection in WDM network with shared risk groups. In *Proceedings on International Conference on Communications* (Vol. 3, pp. 1756-1760).

Zang, H., Ou, C., & Mukherjee, B. (2003). Path-protection routing and wavelength assignment (RWA) in WDM mesh networks under duct-layer constraints. *ACM/IEEE Transactions on Networking*, *11*(2), 248-258.

Zheng, Q., & Mohan, G. (2003). An efficient dynamic protection scheme in integrated IP/WDM networks. In *Proceedings on IEEE International Conference of Communications (ICC)* (pp. 1494-1498).

KEY TERMS

Lightpath: Light path is a path from the source to the destination in optical domain, meaning data remains in optical domain without any optical-electronic-optical conversion in between the source and the destination.

Link Protection: Link protection is a link-based protection scheme in optical networks, meaning each link has a protection path it is associated with. Protection is initiated by the end nodes of the fault link, and all the paths over the fault link will be rerouted through the protection path of the fault link. Therefore, link protection takes less protection time than path protection at the cost of fine granularity.

Multi-Protocol Label Switch (MPLS): A combined control plane for networks. It allows using switch level (layer 2) forwarding and IP router level (Layer 3) routing. In follows, it not only improves speeds of networks but also provides scalability and flexibility enough to do traffic engineering.

Path Protection: Path protection is a path based protection scheme, meaning each path has an edge-disjoint protection path associated with it. Protection is initiated by the source node of each path, and each path over the fault link will be rerouted through its own associated protection path. Therefore, path protection takes more protection time than link protection, and provides protection with fine granularity.

Restoration: Restoration does not reserve any resource in advance, rather than it computes a new path from the source to the destination when the existing path becomes unavailable. Therefore, restoration utilizes resources more efficiently than the protection. However, it has much delay associated to compute a new path on the fly when fault occurs.

Routing and Wavelength Assignment (RWA): Means a way to find a route and to select wavelength for the route from the source to the destination. The complexity of the RWA is caused by the wavelength continuity constraint, meaning all the links belong to a route from the source to the destination have to have same wavelength. RWA is most heavily studied in WDM optical network since the network performance in terms of blocking probability, wavelength utilization and etc. is heavily depend on it.

Shared Risk Group (SRG): A group of links where all the links in the group has faults at the same time. For example, a group of links connecting different nodes may be deployed such that they are going through the same conduit at some point. Then all links passing the conduit will have faults when the conduit has been cut.

Wavelength Division Multiplexing (WDM): A way to utilize the huge bandwidth by dividing the bandwidth into multiple channels called wavelength and operating channels in parallel. Theoretically, a single fibre can carry up to 30 Tera bits per second, meaning we can deploy 3000 channels where each channel can carry 10 Giga bit per second. Considering the fact that no electronic device matches with the speed of the optical fibre's data transfer speed, WDM is the only multiplexing method to fully utilize the bandwidth that optical fibre can provide.

Network-Based Intrusion Detection

Gábor Hosszú
Budapest University of Technology and Economics, Budapest

Zoltán Czirkos
Budapest University of Technology and Economics, Budapest

INTRODUCTION

The importance of the network security problems come into prominence by the growth of the Internet, since the network means a breaking point to the intruders (Wang, Jha, Livny, & McDaniel, 2004). This article presents the state of the art of the *P2P* communication technology, the main concepts, and the different classes of the P2P application-level *overlay networks*, including the centralized, decentralized, and unstructured models (Hosszú, 2005).

As an example of the application for non-conventional purposes, a security system is presented in the article that utilizes just the network for protecting the operating system of the computers. The software maintains a database about the experienced intruding attempts. Its entities working on each computer share their experiments among each other on the peer-to-peer (P2P) overlay network created by self organizing on the Internet. In such a way, the security of the participants is increased, and then they can take the necessary steps.

BACKGROUND

Currently the *application-level networking* (ALN) has increasing importance. In this communication technology, the applications running on host directly create connections among them and they use these connections in order to exchange information and packets. Their communication way is different from the more traditional networking model, where the communicating software entities create connections among them for solving certain task (e.g., downloading a file). In case of the ALN, the applications produce more stable virtual network called the *overlay*, which can be used with complex file-management and application level routing functionalities (e.g. making *application-layer multicast* (ALM). The ALN overlays typically use the *peer-to-peer* (P2P) communicating model oppositely to the more traditional *client/server model* (Hosszú, 2005).

The Intrusion Detection

This section describes basic security concepts, dangers threatening user data and resources. We describe different means of attacks and their common features one by one, and the common protection methods for *system and data integrity* will be shown.

Information stored on a computer can be personal or business character, private, or confidential. An unauthorized person can therefore steal it. Stored data can not only be stolen, but changed. Information modified on a host is extremely useful to cause economic damage to a company.

Resources are also to be protected. Resource is not only hardware. Typical type of attack is to gain access to a computer to initiate other attacks from it. This is to make the identification of the original attacker more difficult.

Intrusion attempts, based on their purpose, can be of different methods. But these methods share things in common, scanning networks ports or subnetworks for services, and making several attempts in a short time. This can be used to detect these attempts.

With attempts of downloading data or disturbing the functionality of a host, the network address of the target is known by the attacker. He scans the host for open network ports, in order to find buggy service programs. This is the well-known port scan. The whole range of services is probed one by one. The object of this is to find some security hole, which can be used to gain access to the system (Teo, 2000). The most widely known software application for this purpose is Nmap (Nmap, 2006). It is important to notice that this is not written for bad intention, but (as everything) it can also be used in an unlawful way.

Table 1. The types of information stealth

1.	An unauthorized person gains access to a host.
2.	Network traffic intercepted or monitored by someone.
3.	Abuse by an authorized user.

Unfortunately, not every attack is along with easily automatically detectable signs. For example, the abusing of a system by an assigned user is hard to notice. The oldest way of intrusion detection was the observation of user behavior (Kemmerer & Vigna, 2002). With this, some unusual behavior could be detected. For example, somebody on holiday still logged in the computer. This type of intrusion detection has the disadvantage of being casual and non-scalable for complex systems.

Next generation intrusion detection systems utilized monitoring log files, mainly with Unix-type operating systems. Of course, this is not enough to protect a system, because many types of intrusions can only be detected too late. Supervising a system is only worth this expense if the intrusion detection system also analyzes the collected information. This technology has two main types: anomaly detection and misuse detection.

Anomaly detection has a model of a properly functioning system and well behaving users. Any deviation it founds is considered a problem. The main benefit of anomaly detection is that it can detect attacks in advance. By defining what is normal, every break of the rules can be identified whether it is part of the *threat model* or not. The disadvantages of this method are frequent false alerts and difficult adaptability to fast-changing systems.

Misuse detection systems define what is wrong. They contain intrusion definitions, alias *signatures,* which are compared with the collected supervisory information, searching for the signs of the known threats. Advantage of these systems is that investigation of already known patterns rarely leads to false alerts. At the same times, these can only detect known attack methods, which have a defined signature. If a new kind of attack is found, the developers have to model it and add to the database of signatures.

Protection Methods

Computers connected to networks are to be protected by different means (Kemmerer et al., 2002), described in detail as follows.

The action taken after detecting an intrusion can be of many different types. The simplest of these is an alert, which describes the observed intrusion. But the reaction can be more offensive, like informing an administrator, ringing a bell or initiating a counterstrike.

The counterstrike may reconfigure the gateway to block traffic from the attacker or even attack him. Of course, an offending reaction can be dangerous; it may be against an innocent victim, as the attacker may load the network with spoofed traffic. This appears to come from a given address, but in reality it is generated somewhere else. Reconfiguring the gateways to block traffic from this address will generate a denial of service (DoS) type attack against the innocent address.

No system can be completely secure. The term of a properly skilled attacker (Toxen, 2001) applies to a theoretical person, who by his or her infinite skills can explore any existent security hole. Every hidden bug of a system can be found, either systematically or accidentally.

The more secure a system is, the more difficult the use it (Bauer, 2005). One simple example for this is limiting network usage. A trade-off between security and usability has to be made. Before initiating medium and large sized systems, it is worth making up a so-called *security policy*.

The simplest style of network protection is a *firewall*. This is a host, which provides a strict gateway to the Internet for a subnetwork, checking traffic and maybe dropping some network packets. The three main types of firewalls are listed in the Table 2.

Table 2. Types of firewalls

Firewall type	Description
Packet level	Filtering rules are based on packet hearers, for example the address of the source or the destination.
Application level	Content of network packets are also examined to identify unwanted input.
Personal	Designed for workstations and home computers. With these the user can define, for which applications he grants access to the network.

Host and Network Based Detection and Protection Systems

*Network intrusion detection system*s (NIDS) are capable of supervision and protection of company-scale networks. One commercially available product is RealSecure (RealSecure, 2006), while Snort is an open source solution (Snort, 2006). Snort is based on a description language, which supports investigation of signatures, network application level protocols, anomalies, and even the combination of these. Mainly it realizes a probe being able to attack network traffic. It is a well configurable system, automatically refreshing its signature database regularly through the Internet. New signatures and rules added by developers and users can this way immediately be added to the database of the software.

Investigation of network traffic can sometimes use uncommon methods. One of these is a network card without an IP address (Bauer, 2002). The card, while it is connected to the network (through a hub or a switch), gets all the traffic but generates no output, and therefore can not be detected. The attacker already broken into the subnetwork cannot see that he or she is monitored. Peters (2006) shows a method of special wiring of Ethernet connectors, which makes up a probe that can be put between two hosts. This device is unrecognizable with software methods.

To understand modern intrusion detection, it must be concluded that the detection system does not observe intrusions, but the signs of it. This is the *attack's manifestation* (Vigna et al., 2001). If an attack has no, or only partial manifestation, the system can't detect the intrusion. One good example to help understanding this is a camera with tainted lens, which cannot detect the intruder even if he is in its field of vision.

Information collected by probes installed at different points of the network is particularly important for protection against network scale attacks. Data collected by one probe alone may not be enough, but an extensive analysis of all sensors' information can reveal the fact of an attack (RealSecure, 2006). For the aid of sensors communicating in the network, the intrusion detection working group (*IDWG*) of the Internet engineering task force (*IETF*, 2006) has developed the intrusion detection message exchange format (*IDMEF*).

Attackers are more successful than ever. They share vulnerability information very rapidly, and practice building on others' work. The growth of the Internet works to their advantage. Contrary to this, defenders usually view security as local responsibility, and do not share information outside their organization for privacy and business reasons (Lincoln, Porras, & Shmatikov, 2004).

Research is focused on collaborative systems to handle this situation. Distributed intrusion detection systems like DShield (DShield, 2006) are built to enhance protection of hosts. It is pointed out in (Lincoln, 2004), that system administrators do not yet have the right tools to share information.

Answer to Intrusion

The action taken after detecting an intrusion can be of many different types. The simplest of these is an alert, which describes the observed intrusion. But the reaction can be more offensive, like informing an administrator, ringing a bell or initiating a counterstrike.

The counterstrike may reconfigure the gateway to block traffic from the attacker or even attack him. Of course, an offending reaction can be dangerous; it may be against an innocent victim. For example the attacker can load the network with *spoofed traffic*.

Figure 1. Block diagram of a P2P application

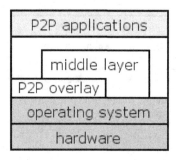

Figure 2. Attack against a Komondor node

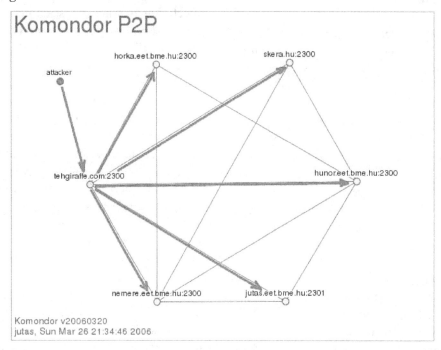

This appears to come from a given address, but in reality it is generated somewhere else. Reconfiguring the gateways to block traffic from this address will generate a *denial of service* (DoS) type attack against the innocent address.

A NOVEL NETWORK-BASED DETECTION SYSTEM

This section introduces a novel system, which uses just the network to protect the hosts and increase their security. The hosts running this software create an *ap-plication level network* (ALN) over the Internet. The clients of the novel software running on individual hosts organize themselves in a network. Nodes connected to this ALN check their operating systems' log files to detect intrusion attempts. Information collected this way is then shared over the ALN, in order to increase the security of all peers, which can then accomplish the necessary protection steps by sharing their own information.

The developed software is named Komondor, which is a famous Hungarian guard dog.

The speed and reliability of sharing the information depends on the network model and the topology. Theory of *peer-to-peer* (P2P) networks has gone through a great

Figure 3. Komondor entity connecting the overlay

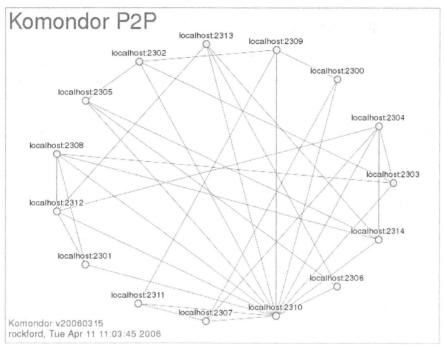

development since the last years. Such networks consist of peer nodes. The parts of an applications realizing a peer-to-peer based network can be seen on *Figure 1* (Hosszú, 2005). The lower layer is responsible for the creation and the maintenance for the overlay network, while the upper one for the communication.

As one host running the Komondor detects an intrusion attempt and shares the address of the attacker on the overlay network, the other ones can prepare and await the *same attacker* in safety. Komondor nodes protect each other this way. If an intrusion attempt was recorded by a node, the other ones can prepare for the attack in advance. This is shown on Figure 2.

Different hosts run the uniform copies of Komondor, monitoring the occurring network intrusion attempts. If one of the peers detects an attempt on a system supervised, takes two actions:

1. Strengthens the protection locally by configuring the firewall to block the offending network address
2. Informs the other peers about the attempt

The first working version of Komondor monitors system log files. These can contain various error messages, which may refer to an intrusion attempt, for example login attempt with an inexistent user name.

Connectivity of the Komondor overlay is important for security. The current version of the software contains two selectable algorithms, which can build the overlay P2P network.

Entities running the first algorithm check their connection counts. Whenever they have less than a specified number of neighbors, for example three, they choose another peer randomly, and connect. The list of active peers can be downloaded from the anchor, similar to other solutions (Gnutella, 2006).

The second algorithm checks the connection count of all peers. An entity joining the overlay connects all other entities. This is shown on *Figure 3*. With this method the newly connecting entity can see, which other ones have little connectivity, and strengthening their participation. Then it shuts down links to peers that have the most neighbors. When a network error occurs, and a peer has lost some of its connections, repeats this process.

The minimum and preferred number of connections can be easily set in a configuration file with both algorithms.

The Komondor network aided security enhancement system is new in principle. It was under extensive testing for months. With its aid not only simulated, but real intrusion attempts were blocked. Effectiveness is determined by the diversity of peers. Intrusion attempts exploiting security holes are software and version specific. The more different peers participate in the network, the more likely is an invulnerable system to protect other vulnerable ones.

It is important to emphasize that the proposed protection system is intended to *mask* the security holes of services provided by the host, not to *repair* them. It can provide protection in advance, but only if somewhere on the network an intrusion was already detected. It does not fix the security hole, but keeps the particular attacker from further activity. The periodical refresh of the *operating system* (OS) of the host and fixing the already know security holes remain important tasks, however, these activities do not give totally protection. That is why the system Komondor has important role to enhance the protection of the host.

FUTURE TRENDS

As software designs get more and more complicated every year, the number of newly discovered flaws in software systems is likely to grow. Present, non-collaborative systems only provide protection for *specific security holes*. A collaborative system can protect hosts against *specific attackers,* which is a powerful way to develop protection faster. That is the reason why research is focused on distributed systems.

As more of these systems emerge, possibilities of collaborative security can be utilized. Several companies offer services already, like the previously mentioned DShield, Symantec DeepSight (Symantec, 2006), and ITR (ITR, 2006). We started developing Komondor, to provide administrators with an easy to use application, which implements a network-sized protection system.

CONCLUSION

The article overviewed the different aspects of host security. Typical attacks were reviewed, along with methods of intrusion detection furthermore, the implemented and widely used host protection methods have been presented.

The article also proposed a novel application, which utilizes the P2P networking model in order to improve the effectiveness of operating system security. The system is easy to use; its clients on different networked nodes organize a P2P overlay automatically, and do not need any user interaction. Months of extensive testing proved the usability of this hybrid design, combining the advantages of P2P and intrusion detection systems. The P2P overlay provides a carrier for sharing security information among peers very effectively.

REFERENCES

Bauer, M. (2002). Stealthful sniffing, intrusion detection and logging. *Linux Journal, October*. Retrieved January 10, 2006, from http://www.linuxjournal.com/article/6222

Bauer, M. (2005). *Linux server security* (2nd ed.). January 2005, O'Reilly and Associates Inc. Cambridge, MA.

Czirkos, Z. (2005). Development of P2P-based security software. In *Proceedings of the Conference of Scientific Circle of Students*, (Second Award), Budapest: November 11, 2005 (in Hungarian).

Dshield. (2006). *Distributed intrusion detection system*. Retrieved March 14, 2006, from http://www.dshield.org/

Gnutella P2P application. (2006). *Protocol draft v0.6*. Retrieved April 29, 2006, from http://rfc-gnutella.sourceforge.net/src/rfc-0_6-draft.html/

Hosszú, G. (2005). Mediacommunication based on application-layer multicast. In S. Dasgupta (Ed.), *Encyclopedia of virtual communities and technologies* (pp. 302-307). Hershey, PA: Idea Group Reference.

IETF IDWG Intrusion Detection Working Group. (2006). Retrieved January 4, 2006, from http://www.ietf.org/

ITR. (2006). *Internet traffic report*. Retrieved March 25, 2006, http://www.internettrafficreport.com/main.htm

Kemmerer, R. A., & Vigna, G. (2002). Intrusion detection: A brief history and overview. *Security & Privacy-2002, Supplement to Computer Magazine*, 27-30.

Lincoln, P., Porras, P., & Shmatikov, V. (2004). Privacy preserving sharing and correlation of information security alerts. SRI International.

Nmap Free Security Scanner, Tools, & Hacking Resources. (2006). Retrieved January 5, 2006, from http://www.insecure.org/

Peters, M. (2006). *Construction and use of a passive Ethernet tap*. Retrieved January 5, 2006, from http://www.snort.org/docs/tap/

RealSecure. (2006). Retrieved January 5, 2006, from http://www.iss.net/

Snort. (2006). *Snort—The de facto standard for intrusion detection/prevention*. Retrieved January 4, 2006, from http://www.snort.org

Symantec. (2006). *Symantec deepsight threat management system*. Retrieved March 20, 2006, http://www.symantec.com

Teo, L. (2000). Network probes explained: Understanding port scans and ping sweeps. *Linux Journal, December*. Retrieved January 10, 2006, from http://www.linuxjournal.com/article/4234

Toxen, B. (2001). *Real World Linux Security*. October 2001, Prentice Hall Professional Technical Reference, Indianapolis, IN, USA.

Vigna, G., Kemmerer, R.A., & Blix, P. (2001). Designing a Web of Highly Configurable Intrusion Detection Sensors. In *Proceedings of Fourth International Symposium on Recent Advances in Intrusion Detection (RAID)* (LNCS 2212, pp. 69-84). New York: Springer Verlag.

Wang, H., Jha, S., Livny, M., & McDaniel, P. D. (2004, June 7-9). Security policy reconciliation in distributed computing environments. *IEEE 5th International Workshop on Policies for Distributed Systems and Networks*. New Yokr: IBM T.J. Watson Research Center, Yorktown Heights.

KEY TERMS

Application Level Network (ALN): The applications, which are running in the hosts, can create a virtual network from their logical connections. This is also called *overlay network*. The operations of such software entities are not able to understand without knowing their logical relations. Most cases this ALN software entities use the *P2P model*, not the *client/server* one for the communication.

Client-Server Model: A communicating way, where one hardware or software entity (server) has more functionalities than the other entity (the client), whereas the client is responsible to initiate and close the communication session towards the server. Usually the server provides services that the client can request from the server. Its alternative is the *P2P model*.

Data Integrity: The integrity of a computer system means that the host behaves and works as its administrator intended it to do so. Data integrity must therefore be always monitored.

Firewall: This is a host or router, which provides a strict gateway to the Internet for a subnetwork, checking traffic and maybe dropping some network packets.

Overlay Network: The applications, which create an *ALN* work together and usually follow the *P2P communication model*.

Peer-to-Peer (P2P) Model: A communication way where each node has the same authority and communication capability. They create a virtual network, overlaid on the Internet. Its members organize themselves into a topology for data transmission. Each peer provides services the others can use, and each peer sends requests to other ones.

Security Policy: It means a set of rules to act, in which the expectations and provisions of accessibility of the computer for the users and the administrators also included. It is worth to be made up before initiating medium or large sized computer networking systems.

Network–Layer Mobility Protocols for IPv6–Based Networks

K. Daniel Wong
Malaysia University of Science and Technology, Malaysia

Ashutosh Dutta
Telcordia Technologies, USA

INTRODUCTION

The Internet is in some ways like the proverbial massive software project whose requirements keep changing, and which is never completed. When the Internet protocols were first designed, there was no concept of the future requirement that IP would need to support mobility. In today's wireless world, mobility support is one of the key requirements for IP. Like the requirements for QoS, security, and multimedia support, the mobility requirement has arisen due to the phenomenal success of the Internet, as a result of which people want to do more and more things over the Internet.

Mobility support in IP was first introduced with mobile IP (Perkins et al., 2002). However, Mobile IP suffered in being an overlay on an existing IPv4-based Internet that was not meant to support mobility. As such, the design requirements were somewhat constraining, leading to non-optimal features. For example, it was required that Mobile IP must work normally with legacy hosts sending packets to a mobile host, where by legacy hosts, we mean hosts that are not aware of Mobile IP, that have not been upgraded in any way to support mobility. A certain non-optimal feature, the "triangular routing" problem, was the result. We will elaborate upon these features shortly.

Meanwhile, IPv6 was introduced as a replacement for IPv4. Since IPv6 was created at a time when the requirement for mobility support was evident, IPv6 is more "mobility friendly" than IPv4. Hence, Mobile IPv6, the mobility support protocol for IPv6, has certain advantages over Mobile IP. Nevertheless, it currently has some weaknesses not found in Mobile IP. We will discuss the pros and cons of Mobile IPv6 shortly.

BACKGROUND

There are actually multiple concepts of mobility management. Schulzrinne and Wedlund (2000) classify them as terminal mobility, session mobility, service mobility, and personal mobility. Perhaps the most prominent, in terms of importance and amount of research done, is terminal mobility. Terminal mobility is the kind of mobility problem which Mobile IPv6 has addressed.

In today's wireless world, machines and terminals (laptops, PDAs, cell phones, and so on) move around often. As they move, they change their point of attachment to the network. *Terminal mobility* is the problem of minimizing disruptions in communications services for these machines and terminals even as they are moving around. For example, cellular systems have ways to minimize disruptions as cell phones switch from base station to base station and the network has to reroute voice circuits to the latest base station. In the IP world, mobile IP, and mobile IPv6 are examples of solutions.

We note that terminal mobility can be handled at layers of the protocol stack other than the network layer. Link layer mobility handling can make it appear that the terminal is on the same link even when it moves between different points of attachment to the network, and the movement thus becomes transparent to the network layer. An example of this is the *extended service set* (ESS) concept in IEEE 802.11 whereby a terminal can move between different access points (APs) in the same ESS and still be in the same local area network (LAN), with no difference in location as far as the IP layer is concerned. Going the other direction, mobility can also be handled higher up the protocol stack. Solutions have been proposed for at the transport layer

Figure 1. Fundamental operations of redirection-based mobility management

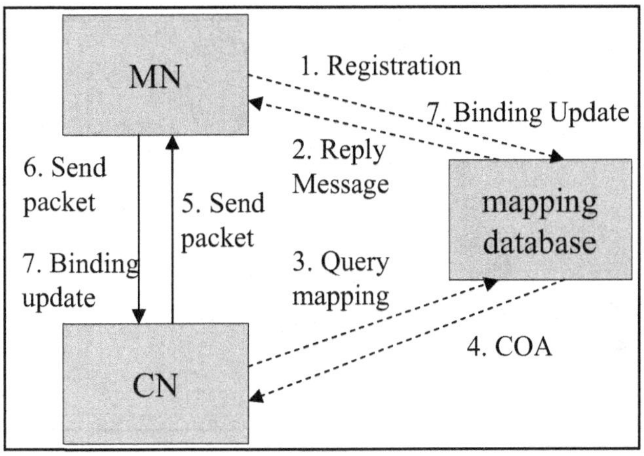

and the application layer. TCP migration (Snoeren & Balakrishnan, 2000) is an example of a transport layer mobility protocol, whereas there have been proposals on how to modify session initiation protocol (SIP) (Rosen et al., 2002), at the application layer to handle mobility.

Returning to the network layer mobility management schemes for IP-based networks, there are two classes of schemes that have been researched in the literature. The first class comprises schemes based on redirection, and the second class comprises schemes based on interception and forwarding. Mobile IP and mobile IPv6 belong to the second class, so we defer discussion to the section, "Mobile IPv6: Strengths and Some Unresolved Issues." Readers who are familiar with SIP may see that these two classes are analogous in some ways to the two kinds of proxies found in SIP, namely the redirection proxies and the forwarding proxies.

Whether we talk about IP mobility protocols based on redirection or based on interception and forwarding, there are some concepts that apply to all the protocols. The mobile node (MN) has a *home address*, an IP address that is assigned to it for the long-term, also referred as a permanent address. The home address is an address in the *home network* of the MN. The MN is identified with its home address, and the task of the IP mobility protocols is to associate the home address with the current location of the MN. The current loca-

tion of the MN is typically specified in terms of an IP address in the network that it is in. We call this IP address its *care-of address* since the MN can be reached at this address.

Probably the earliest IP mobility management protocols based on redirection was *mobile IP with location registers* (MIP-LR) (Jain, Raleigh, Graff, & Bereschinsky, 1998), a protocol developed at Bellcore by Jain and others, that was inspired by the way location registers are used in cellular systems to store and provide location information on subscribers. Since the creation of MIP-LR, there have been a number of other redirection-based protocols that have been proposed in the literature. These include mobile Internet protocol with address translation (MAT) (Inayat, Aibara, Nishimura, Fujita, & Maeda, 2004), location independent network in IPv6 (LIN6) (Ishimaya, Kunishi, Uehara, Esaki, & Teraoka, 2001) and mobility protocol framework to support multiple namespaces (MPF-MN) (Ishimaya, Yasuma, Kunishi, Kohno, & Teraoka, 2004). A comparison of some of these redirection-based IP mobility protocols can be found in Chiam and Wong (2005). Most recently, mobile IP with location registers for IPv6 (MIP-LRv6) has been proposed (Chiam & Wong, 2006).

Generally, these protocols have some common basic operations, as shown in Figure 1. There are *mapping databases* that maintain the location information of the mobile nodes (MNs), in the form of bindings between the MN's home address and the care-of address, together

Figure 2. Mobile IPv6

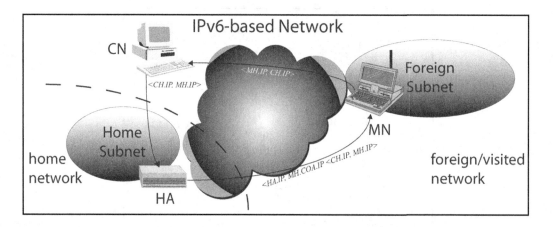

with an associated lifetime (i.e., the binding expires after a period of time). In order to communicate with a MN, first the correspondent node (CN) needs to obtain the IP address of the mapping databases. Each time a MN moves, it will register its care-of IP address at all the databases that it is assigned to.

The CN can start sending packets to an MN after obtaining its care-of address. When the MN moves to a new network, it will either update its new IP address to the mapping databases and all the CNs it is communicating with, or it will only update the mapping databases but alert the CNs to get the new IP address from mapping databases. The CN will cache the mapping information and refresh the cache by querying the databases again before the lifetime expiry.

MOBILE IPV6: FEATURES AND UNRESOLVED ISSUES

The other main class of IP mobility protocols are based on forwarding rather than redirection. In both mobile IP and mobile IPv6, there is a network element called the home agent that plays a pivotal role. The home agent is located in the home network of the MN. It is analogous to the mapping database of redirection-based protocols, in that it maintains the location information of the MN. However, instead of merely responding to queries for the current location of the MN, the home agent also acts as an intercepting agent and forwarding agent. Thus, the CN does not know anything about the mobility of the MN and simply sends packets to its permanent home address as usual. There are two cases to consider:

1. If the MN is roaming in a foreign network, the home agent intercepts the packets when they arrive at the home network (otherwise, the packets would be lost, since the MN is not there to receive them). The home agent then forwards the packets to the care-of address of the MN.

2. If the MN is not roaming in a foreign network, but is in its home network, then the home agent does not intercept the packets, and lets the MN receive them as usual.

Forwarding of packets from home agent to MN is done by tunneling. The original packet from the CN is *encapsulated* in a new IP packet by the home agent. By encapsulation, we mean that a new IP header is appended to the front of the original packet. The source and destination address of the new packet are the home agent address and care-of address, respectively. This is illustrated in Figure 2.

To create the binding between the home address and the care-of address in the first place, the MN sends a binding update message to the home agent. The home agent sends a binding acknowledgment message back

Figure 3. Return routability

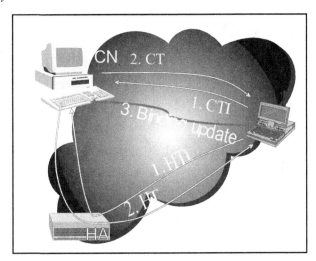

to the MN. Of course, data integrity of these messages is needed. Otherwise, for example, an attacker can send a fake binding update, and cause traffic for a MN to be redirected to an arbitrary address. Indeed, mobile IPv6 uses IPsec ESP to secure these messages.

As mentioned earlier, IPv6 was designed with mobility support in mind. We illustrate this by way of selected comparisons between mobile IPv6 (which takes advantage of the inherent support for mobility provided by IPv6) and mobile IP (which is restricted by the limitations of IPv4).

Route Optimization

In the design of mobile IP, it was decided that there would be too many existing legacy hosts that do not know about mobile IP, so it could not be required that the CN be modified in any way with additional functionality for mobile IP to work. Of course, the MN would need to be mobile IP-aware, but any ordinary IPv4 node could be a CN in the normal operations or mobile IP. Mobile IPv6 is free from such a constraint because IPv6 could (and is) simply designed from the start with the necessary functionality to support mobile IPv6. A consequence of this difference is that *route optimization* is an integral part of mobile IPv6 (whereas it is a non-standard extension to mobile IP (Perkins & Johnson, 2001) that requires changes in a CN).

What is route optimization? It is a solution to the *triangular routing* problem. In mobile IP, the route

taken by packets from CN to MN goes through a home agent, whereas packets from MN to CN go directly to the CN. Thus, a "triangular route" is formed, where the CN, home agent, and MN form three vertexes of a triangle. Thus, the route taken by packets from CN to MN is not optimal. The worst case scenario is where the CN and MN may actually be in the same network while the home agent is on the other side of the world; in this case, the direct path between CN and MN is clearly much shorter.

How does route optimization solve the triangular problem? It allows the MN to inform the CNs with which it is communicating, of its new care-of address directly, whenever it obtains a new care-of address. The CN can then send packets directly to that address. The MN informs the CN of its latest care-of address with a binding update message.

We had mentioned earlier that binding updates sent by a MN to its home agent need to be secure. What about binding updates sent to CNs during route optimization? This issue will be discussed further when we highlight selected issues with Mobile IPv6.

Use of Routing Header

As mentioned earlier, packets are encapsulated by the home agent and thus are forwarded to a MN by way of its care-of address. The routing header is a type of IPv6 extension header that allows for source routing. Mobile IPv6 takes advantage of this feature of IPv6 to

Figure 4. Simultaneous mobility illustrated

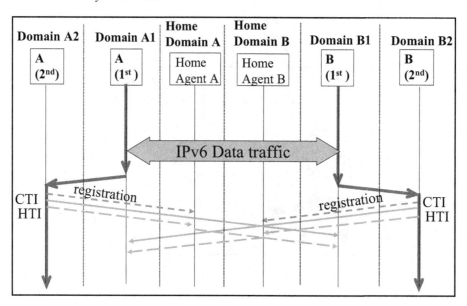

specify a type of routing header (the so-called "Type 2 routing header") that can be used by the CN to send packets directly to the MN at its care-of address, *without* the overhead that comes with encapsulation. Thus, instead of appending a full IPv6 header (40 bytes plus the size of the extension headers) to the front of the packet (i.e., encapsulation), only a 24-byte routing header is appended.

Unresolved Issues

While Mobile IPv6 has attractive features, it is a complex protocol whose kinks have not been completely ironed out. We illustrate with two examples, the security of binding updates for route optimization and simultaneous mobility.

Route Optimization Security

Direct binding updates from the MN to the CNs are an integral part of route optimization for Mobile IPv6. Unfortunately, these pose a security problem. Fake binding updates can be used by an attacker for a variety of purposes (e.g., denial of service to the MN (as its packets are redirected elsewhere)), and so on. Attackers could also launch other attacks such as man-

in-the-middle attacks. In the case of the home agent, it is reasonable to stipulate that the MN and home agent should have some pre-existing security association such as an IPSec security association. However, it may be less reasonable to stipulate that the MN and every potential CN have similar security associations (with a different key for each potential CN). To allow a MN to send binding updates to its CN securely, MIPv6 adopts the so-called return routability procedure as a sub-procedure of the route optimization procedure. This allows the MN and CN to set up a shared key in a somewhat secure manner.

The problem is that "somewhat secure" in this case is not really secure. We briefly explain return routability to point out the issues. The basic return routability procedure, as shown in Figure 3, is as follows: The MN sends two messages to the CN, on two different paths. The care-of test init (CTI) is sent directly to the CN. The other message, the home test init (HTI), however, is reversed tunneled to the home agent from the MN, and then forwarded by the home agent to the CN. The CN responds by sending two messages as well. It sends a care-of test (CT) message sent directly to the MN, addressed to its care-of address. It also sends a home test (HT) message indirectly to the MN, addressed to its home address.

The care-of test message and the home test message each contain one of two tokens, the generation of which involves knowledge known only by the CN. The two tokens are hashed together to form the binding management key used to secure the binding update.

Because the tokens are sent to the MN by two paths, it is most likely only the MN that would also know both tokens. Thus, only the CN and MN can generate the correct binding management key.

Clearly, though, if an attacker can discover both tokens, the attacker can also generate the binding management key. Discovering both tokens should not be too difficult, since they are both sent *in plaintext*. Despite this obvious security weakness, no dominant alternative has emerged in the literature, although several alternatives have been proposed (Wu, Long, & Irwin, 2003). This is because return routability does have its advantages such as not requiring the involvement of external servers.

Simultaneous Mobility

We illustrate the simultaneous mobility problem of mobile IPv6 with an example. Suppose two MNs, A and B, are communicating. A moves, and then initiates the return routability procedure with B. One or both of the home test init and care-of test init messages may be lost because of simultaneous movement by B. Now consider what happens to the registrations that B wishes to initiate with its CNs, including A. Without receiving both the care-of test init and home test init from A, B will not update A's address in its cache, so B will send its care-of test init and home test init messages to A's old care-of-address. More precisely, B will send its care-of test init message directly to A's old care-of-address, and reverse tunnel its home test init to its home agent, which will then forward it to A's old care-of-address. Thus, B will be unable to proceed with its own return routability procedure.

Basically, the scenario is that one of the nodes moves first (say, A), but by the time B moves a little while later, one or both of the home test init messages has not yet reached B, so A's return routability procedure never completes, which implies that B will also be unable to complete its return routability procedure. This scenario is the pictured in Figure 4.

The simultaneous mobility problem for mobile IPv6, plus proposed solutions, are presented in Wong and Dutta (2005), whereas Wong, Dutta, Young, and Schulzrinne (2006) discusses simultaneous mobility more generally for a variety of mobility protocols.

FUTURE TRENDS

As research and development continues, it is expected that the problems with mobile IPv6 will gradually be sorted out. It is unclear, however, if a new and improved specification will be replacing RFC 3775 anytime soon. However, it may be the case, as was with IEEE 802.11 "Wi-Fi", that industry groups moved to plug gaps before changes in the standards occurred (e.g., the Wired Equivalent Privacy, WEP, of 802.11, was considered too weak for commercial usage, so industry groups introduced interim solutions like WPA and WPA2, before IEEE 802.11i emerged; IEEE 802.11i adds significantly better security to 802.11).

Given the trends toward more and more mobile devices and the public's increasing demands for mobile services, network-layer mobility protocols for IPv6, especially Mobile IPv6, look to enjoy a healthy growth in usage.

CONCLUSION

Mobile IPv6 is the dominant network-layer mobility protocol for IPv6 (although we have briefly discussed alternatives). It is still being improved and issues are still being researched and debated, but we expect that most issues would eventually be resolved satisfactorily, leading to a successful deployment in the wireless Internet..

REFERENCES

Chiam, Y., & Wong, K. D. (2005). Redirection-based IP mobility protocols. *China Communications Magazine, 2*(3).

Chiam, Y., & Wong, K. D. (2006). Mobile IPv6 with Location Registers. *ReCSPC.*

Inayat, R., Aibara, R., Nishimura, K., Fujita, T., & Maeda, K. (2004). An end-to-end network architecture for supporting mobility in wide area wireless networks. *IEICE Transactions on Communications, E87-B*(6), 1584-1593.

Ishimaya, M., Kunishi, M., Uehara, K. ,Esaki, H., & Teraoka, F. (2001). LINA: A new approach to mobility support in wide area networks. *IEICE Transactions on Communications, E84-B*(8), 2076-2086.

Ishimaya, M., Yasuma, K., Kunishi, M., Kohno, M., & Teraoka, F. (2004). Design of a mobility protocol framework to support multiple namespaces. *IEICE Transactions on Communications, E87-B*(3), 453-461.

Jain, R., Raleigh, T., Graff, C., & Bereschinsky, M. (1998). Mobile Internet access and QoS guarantees using mobile IP and RSVP with Location Registers. *IEEE ICC*.

Johnson, D., Perkins, C., & Arkko, J. (2004). Mobility support in IPv6. *IETF RFC 3775*.

Perkins, C., et al. (2002). IP mobility support for IPv4. *IETF RFC 3344*.

Perkins, C., & Johnson, D. (2001). Route optimization in mobile IP. IETF draft.

Rosen, J., Schulzrinne, H., Camarillo, G., Johnston, A., Peterson, J., Sparks, R. et al. (2002). Session initiation protocol, *IETF RFC 3261*.

Schulzrinne, H., & Wedlund, E. (2000). Application-layer mobility using SIP. *ACM Mobile Computing and Communications Review, 4*(3), 47-57.

Snoeren, A., & Balakrishnan, H. (2000). An end-to-end approach to host mobility. *ACM MOBICOM*.

Wong, K. D., & Dutta, A. (2005). Simultaneous mobility in MIPv6. *IEEE EIT 2005*.

Wong, K. D., Dutta, A., Young, K., & Schulzrinne, H. (2006). Simultaneous mobility: Solutions and analysis. Accepted for publication in *Journal of Wireless Communications and Mobile Computing*.

Wu, C. H., Long, M., & Irwin, J. D. (2003). Securing binding update in mobile IPv6 using an IP address-based multisignature. *Communication, Network, and Information Security*.

KEY TERMS

Care-Of Address (CoA): The current address of a mobile node, at which it can be reached when it is roaming in a foreign network that is different from its home network.

Correspondent Node (CN): A machine that communicates with a MN; a CN may or may not be mobile.

Forwarding Agent: A network element that forwards packets addressed to a mobile node to the current location of the mobile node. This is a non-standard term introduced by us to represent this concept that is not explicitly defined in the Mobile IPv6 specifications.

Home Address: An IP address that is assigned to a mobile node for a long time, typically in its home network.

Home Agent: A key element in mobile IP and mobile IPv6, where it serves as a combination of an interception agent and forwarding agent.

Home Network: The network where a mobile node can be found whenever it is not roaming in another network. It can be thought of as a default network.

Interception Agent: A network element that intercepts packets addressed to a mobile node, so that they are not lost due to the mobile node having moved elsewhere. This is a non-standard term introduced by us to represent this concept that is not explicitly defined in the Mobile IPv6 specifications.

Mapping Database: In redirection-based IP mobility protocols, the mapping database is where the location information of the MNs are stored (bindings of permanent IP address and care-of address). The term "mapping database" itself is a non-standard term introduced by us to capture a concept common to different redirection-based mobility protocols. It goes by different names in the different protocols (e.g., location register in MIP-LR).

Mobile Node (MN): A machine that moves around and connects to the network through different network attachment points.

Networked Appliances and Home Networking: Internetworking the Home

Madjid Merabti
Liverpool John Moores University, UK

Paul Fergus
Liverpool John Moores University, UK

Omar Abuelma'atti
Liverpool John Moores University, UK

INTRODUCTION

The Internet has revolutionised the way we access and disseminate information and changed the way we communicate with each other. More and more homes are Internet-enabled as people from all walks of life embrace this technology because of the benefits it brings. However, to date Internet usage has predominately focused on personal computing. This said, an interesting technological shift is taking place, whereby any device, irrespective of its capabilities or conventional usage, will form part of the Internet. These devices will reside at the edge of the Internet, thus enabling devices to exploit the power of Internet communications to interoperate devices and utilise the functions they provide.

Researchers believe that this transition mirrors the evolutionary process undertaken within personal computing and wide-area communications, whereby it is difficult to imagine using a computer without Internet access. Given the success of this transition, home networking platforms aim to achieve the same level of acceptance. Already, our homes are populated by numerous electronic computing devices that form part of some network, be they TVs, PCs, set top boxes, or mobile phones, as illustrated in Figure 1.

The difficulty is getting different devices, built to different specifications, to work together without changing their original characteristics or protocols. This will result in more complex systems, which will be a by-product of device heterogeneity and the dynamic nature associated with networks that resist any form of control. Putting complexity aside, there is, however, a need to promote this integration because these developments are too expensive and limiting for innovative applications. The downside is that the proliferation of home appliances and the complex functions they provide make it difficult for a specialist, let alone an ordinary home user, to configure and use them. Therefore, complexity needs to be abstracted using flexible

Figure 1. Networked devices in the future

solutions that allow for better exploitation of devices and the functions they provide.

This new interconnected world will enable devices to automatically integrate and interoperate themselves within the network. It will provide access to a plethora of online services, such as digital radio, programme guides, on-demand TV, online gaming, as well as ad hoc services capable of enhancing or extending the functional capabilities devices support beyond what they where initially designed to do.

What is clear is that we are at a crossroads whereby the ability to effectively manage next generation homes and the interconnected devices they contain will be highly dependent on how we utilise the Internet, Internet technologies, and the IT sector. This is a vision shared by many research communities.

BACKGROUND

There are a number of research initiatives trying to address key requirements for next generation networked appliances and home networking. For example, the ePerSpace project (France Telecom, 2005) aims to develop an end-to-end solution for personalized value-added audiovisual services contained within global environments. It provides distributed multimedia services via open access networks, based on the details defined in personalisation profiles that allow content and devices to be dynamically adapted to specific users. The approach taken creates a trusted and interoperable framework to seamlessly interconnect heterogeneous audio and visual devices. Through this framework, environments are dynamically built to include networked appliances that can be controlled by content creators using rich media object management tools.

It is generally believed that in the future every device will have a network interface that allows it to be connected to the Internet. Given this level of connectivity, we will interact and control the devices we own through global communication channels irrespective of where we physically reside. Basic home automation for heating controllers and security systems are common within most homes, however advances in sensor networks will allow us to monitor and control devices based on real-time environmental changes (Gao et al., 2006).

The Reconfigurable Ubiquitous Networked Embedded Systems (RUNES) project (Koumpis et al., 2005) claims that embedded systems and the Internet will begin to merge to create truly pervasive computing environments. Koumpis et al. argue that environments must be managed using scalable middleware frameworks that provide users, designers, and programmers with the flexibility to interact with services, devices, and sensors, thus easing the overall application development process. Their approach is in the early stages of development and the final product promises to enable the formation of large-scale, distributed, heterogeneous network systems that can interoperate and dynamically self-adapt to environmental changes.

As this highly interconnected world becomes a reality, it will no longer be acceptable to just disperse content and services within and across networking environments. Intelligence needs to be embedded within the network to enable resources to be more accurately discovered, integrated, and managed. Mechanisms need to be developed that automate device configurations and their associated management tasks. One approach is to describe devices, services, and content in such a way that machines can discover, use, and control networked resources in an unambiguous way.

This, in part, has begun, whereby mechanisms are used to describe and discover multimedia services using ontological structures. Figure 2 illustrates, in part, how high-level compositions could be created using concepts semantically related to service ontologies used to expose device functionality, via domain ontologies.

Many approaches have typically relied on attribute-based service matching and discovery, which is inherently restrictive since no universally agreed service description or taxonomy is available to describe services homogeneously. Service and content providers inadvertently use different vocabularies to describe their content and therefore ambiguities between terms are likely. The driving force behind the use of ontology is to reduce this ambiguity through semantic interoperability (Berners-Lee et al., 2001). Building on this approach, the Semantic HiFi project (Jacob, 2004) is trying to address the limitations associated with attribute-based audio processing using semantic descriptions. It allows users to discover music, provided by home users, music labels, and amateur musicians within peer-to-peer networks using a set of libraries, semantic description schemes, specifications, and guidelines.

Looking at device integration through set-top boxes, several research initiatives utilise set-top box technologies to interconnect and control networked appliances.

Figure 2. Using ontology to describe and discover functionality

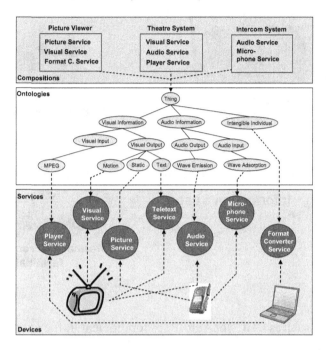

One approach that has extended typical set-top box functionality is the Open Services Gateway Initiative (OSGi) (OSGi Alliance, 2006). This is a well-established middleware standard used to realise the digital home. It has considerable industrial and academic backing from device manufacturers and service providers alike. Its mission is to create open specifications that enable the delivery of multiple services over wide area networks (WANs) to home networks.

Addressing interoperability issues through standardisation, the Digital Living Network Alliance (DLNA) research initiative (DLNA, 2006) has developed interoperability standards to seamlessly interconnect devices and services. DLNA provides a framework that enables internetworking between devices that reside within three domains, these being the Internet, broadcast, and mobile domains. The key to successful integration is to address customer demands where the devices they own work together within and across these domains. This requires design choices constrained through industry consensus to enable better interoperability. It is argued that current open standards are too flexible and consequently interoperability between different vendors fails. As such, standards in conjunction with proprietary manufacturing are used to reduce the time taken to deliver the product to high-street stores. The downside is that such products have no effect on solving the interoperability problem.

Moving away from such solutions, there is considerable interest in ad hoc networking to automatically form networks without the help of third-party services. Devices are seen as the centre of the information space whereby ad hoc networks provide services from the device's immediate vicinity, as illustrated in Figure 3.

Standards such as Bluetooth were designed as cable replacement technologies, however, researchers within the ad hoc networking domain are investigating how such standards can be used to enable new and novel applications. A standard with considerable support that adopts this principle is Universal Plug and Play (UPnP) (Microsoft Corp., 2006). Its sole purpose is to automatically interconnect, discover, and control devices within local area networks. UPnP aims to extend the auto-configuration features of device Plug and Play (PnP) to the entire network, enabling the discovery and control of networked devices and services.

Interoperability and internetworking are achieved by leveraging existing mature standards currently used by the Internet, such as HTTP and XML; a decision to use IP was adopted because it is seen as the de facto standard capable of spanning different physical media. UPnP provides flexible mechanisms that can either use

Figure 3. Information space

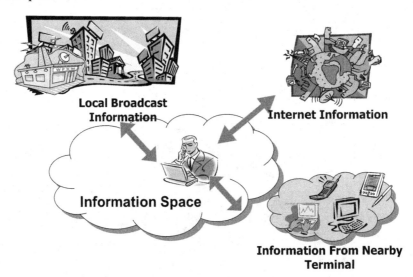

existing addressing schemes such as DHCP or AutoIP functions best suited to simple ad hoc networks.

The Consumer Electronics Powerline Communication Alliance (CEPCA) (CEPCA, 2006) is trying to lead the home networking and ubiquitous computing markets through several high profile initiatives. Matsushita Electric Industrial Co. Ltd (Panasonic), Mitsubishi Electric Corporation, and Sony Corporation have joined forces to create a new alliance to define a new high-speed power line communication (PLC) standard. The consortium aims to provide an interface standard between different devices using electrical power lines for audio, video, and data networking. The consortium believes that bi-directional PLC is a communication channel capable of supporting home networking using existing electrical power lines installed in home environments to enable high-definition video transmissions and IP telephony. Through the consortium and the PLC-based standards it defines, interoperability is addressed between different device manufacturers.

Looking farther ahead, it is believed that hardware will disappear and computing will become ubiquitous. We are already moving towards this vision and Japan is said to be a world leader. One such initiative is the Ubiquitous Network project carried out by the Japan External Trade Organisation (JETRO) project (JETRO, 2006), where wired and wireless network technologies converge to form a society that allows anyone to be connected anytime and anywhere. It provides mechanisms

for efficient traffic congestion management, logistics, and the monitoring and control of networked devices using applications installed on mobile phones.

Mechanisms are in place that allow rail travellers to pay their fares automatically using radio frequency identification (RFID) (Want, 2006) and mobile phone technology. A government initiative is also currently testing large-scale ubiquitous networks aimed at managing transportation systems. In parallel, Japan has launched digital broadcasting within major cities, providing a range of services which includes mobile broadcasting. These advances are a by-product of two major technological advances, that of broadband and mobile devices. Based on the seamless introduction of broadband infrastructure and reduced costs, it has seen large-scale adoption of broadband services.

Another project trying to interconnect heterogeneous products is iReady (Miwa, 2004). It is a framework that has separate data communication components installed within devices known as network adaptors. The framework provides standards for different network adapters, which are dependent on the data exchanged within and across the network. The iReady consortium argues that this makes their framework flexible, because device manufacturers do not have to develop, market, and sell existing products and networked-enabled ones. Users that require network connectivity simply buy the associated adapter.

CHALLENGES

Technology is becoming more pervasive, consequently trying to manage solutions and their associated configurations is becoming more difficult. Several research initiatives in the area of communications and service-oriented computing promise to provide solutions that realise a seamless integration between heterogeneous devices and the functions they provide, however, to date few solutions have produced any convincing results.

Several challenges still need to be addressed, which include networking home appliances, service discovery, dynamic service composition, and self-adaptation. An investigation needs to be performed to determine how technologies can be combined and extended to create new frameworks capable of seamlessly interconnecting devices and automatically managing dynamically created execution paths (Mingkhwan et al., 2006).

Currently, many devices do not have network interfaces, and the numerous functions they provide are operated in isolation using predefined compositions manually created by the user. This problem needs to be debunked. Every device needs to have a network interface and the functions they provide need to be published as independent services. This would permit functions to form an overlay within the network, allowing them to be better utilised (Fergus et al., 2005).

Frameworks capable of exploiting these functions must themselves be comprised of common capabilities dispersed within the network. This will provide flexible mechanisms that allow devices, irrespective of their capabilities, to determine how they use the framework. For example, devices may choose to implement all common capabilities or just some of them and bind to others remotely. Flexibility is of paramount importance, and it is believed that the true power of a service-oriented architecture will present itself through common capabilities and ad hoc services that redundantly coexist. This said, it is important that devices offer services without having to register with third-party providers building on network technologies such as peer-to-peer.

One of the main difficulties is accurately discovering services. Common capabilities that comprise the framework will be predetermined, however, application-specific functions, such as audio and video services, will vary. As such, the discovery mechanism must form part of the common capabilities framework whereby mechanisms allow devices to automatically discover services with little or no human intervention, based on what a device requires and what other devices provide, as illustrated in Figure 4. The output of this process must directly input into dynamic execution path generation mechanisms that allow devices and services to be automatically composed, executed, and managed.

Services will redundantly coexist and devices will be better equipped to provide given services. Consequently, execution-path generation must take into account devices that maintain or surpass predefined quality of service parameters. Given that execution paths can be automatically generated, they must also be automatically managed, whereby configurations must self-adapt to any environmental changes that occur, i.e., if services

Figure 4. Dynamic composition

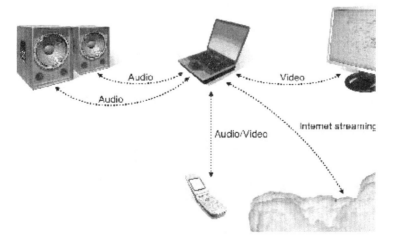

or devices become unavailable then alternative ones need to be discovered and plugged into the execution path with minimal disruption to the end user.

FUTURE TRENDS

While it is difficult to predict what technologies will successfully emerge, based on previous and current trends, an informed guess can be made. We may not see giant leaps in technology that revolutionise the way we live, however, slow incremental changes do tend to build on existing technologies to produce novel applications. For example, the television has been around for some time, however, the next big thing to emerge is watching television on mobile phones. This is not a huge technological shift, but it is novel in that we can now access and watch television while on the move. The same can be said for networking, whereby it is only now that we are seeing networked homes, albeit it is more often than not to share a broadband connection. Nevertheless, it is an incremental change that will revolutionise next generation home networking.

In the short term we will see the research initiatives discussed in this chapter becoming more widespread. The difficulty at present is that not all devices have networking capabilities. However, in the medium term this will not be the case. Once the network infra-structure is in place, research initiatives such as OSGi and UPnP will embrace these new environments and provide internal control as well as external home, network, and device monitoring services offered by third-party providers.

However, the long term challenge is to realise true ubiquitous computing environments that far exceed the capabilities provided by the aforementioned initiatives (Fergus et al., 2005; Mingkhwan et al., 2006). Through intelligent middleware and networked appliances, application behaviours will emerge though the composition of ubiquitous functionality as illustrated in Figure 5.

Functionality will disappear into the fabric of the environments we inhabit. There will be no need for manual configuration and management, as we see devices automatically integrating themselves and self-adapting to environmental changes. This will abstract complexity and leave the end user to only concern themselves with the rudimentary functions needed to perform some given task. However, to date we are far from this vision and much research is still required.

CONCLUSION

Getting devices to seamlessly interconnect is a difficult problem and many global research initiatives are trying

Figure 5. Emergent applications

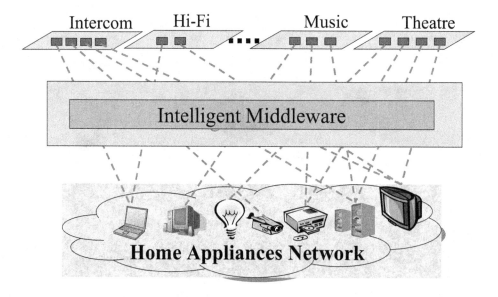

to address this. Projects such as ePerSpace create end-to-end solutions for personalised value-added audio-visual services, while projects like RUNES are trying to manage the complexity associated with combining embedded systems with the Internet. As the proliferation of devices and services become more ubiquitous, and as home networks form part of the Internet, finding and composing services will become paramount and the difficulties associated with this process will mirror those experienced by the World Wide Web in terms of accurately finding content. As such, the Semantic HiFi project is trying to build on advances made within the Semantic Web community to describe and discover content more accurately.

Building on the success of set-top box installations and standardisation, OSGi is trying to provide home monitoring and control services, while UPnP utilises the functions provided by devices within the home, using plug-and-play technologies. Solutions have also been developed to extend these infrastructures to enable users to always be connected so that content can be accessed anywhere and anytime. This is clearly evident in the JETRO project, whereby the transport system automates ticketing using mobile phone technologies and RFID.

Although advances have been made, we are far from solving true interoperability; the reality is that we cannot seamlessly interconnect heterogeneous devices. We are, however, at an exiting technological milestone where technology is becoming more pervasive and the need to interconnect devices is increasing. Consequently, the complexity associated with managing new applications and their associated configurations is becoming more difficult. Alternative solutions are required that automate this process so as not to burden the user with management tasks. There are many challenges that still need to be addressed, and in the short-to-medium term, we will see many of the solutions discussed in this chapter becoming commonplace.

REFERENCES

Berners-Lee, T., Hendler, J., & Lassila, O. (2001). The semantic Web. *Scientific America, 284*(5), 34-43.

CEPCA. (2006). *Consumer electronics powerline communication alliance (CEPCA)*. Retrieved 2006 from http://www.cepca.org/home

DLNA. (2006). *DLNA: Overview and vision*, [White Paper]. Retrieved 2006 from http://www.dlna.org/about/DLNA_Overview.pdf

Fergus, P., Merabti, M., Hanneghan, M. B., Taleb-Bendiab, A., & Mingkhwan, A. (2005). *A semantic framework for self-adaptive networked appliances.* Paper presented at the 2nd IEEE Consumer Communications & Networking Conference (CCNC'05), Las Vegas, Nevada, USA.

France Telecom. (2006). *ePerSpace: Towards the era of personal services at home and everywhere.* Retrieved 2006 from http://www.ist-eperspace.org/

Gao, R. X., & Fan, Z. (2006). Architectural design of a sensory node controller for optimized energy utilisation in sensor networks. *IEEE Transactions on Instrumentation and Measurement, 55*(2), 415-428.

Jacob, M. (2004). *RDF in the semantic hifi European project.* Paper presented at the 1st Italian Workshop on Semantic Web Applications and Perspectives (SWAP), Ancona, Italy.

JETRO. (2005). *Japan external trade organisation—Ubiquitous networks.* Retrieved 2005 from http://www.jetro.org/index.php?option=com_content&task=view&id=237&Itemid=

Koumpis, C., Hanna, L., Anderson, M., & Johansson, M. (2005). *Wireless industrial control and monitoring beyond cable replacement.* Paper presented at the 2nd Profibus International Conference, Warwickshire, UK.

Microsoft Corp. (2006). *UPnP forum.* Retrieved 2006 from http://www.upnp.org/

Mingkhwan, A., Fergus, P., Abuelma'atti, O., Merabti, M., Askwith, B., & Hanneghan, M. (2006). Dynamic service composition in home appliance networks. *Multimedia Tools and Applications: A Special Issue on Advances in Consumer Communications and Networking, 29*(3), 257-284.

Miwa, Y. (2004). *Home appliances get connected.* ECHONET. Retrieved 2006 from http://www.ipv6style.jp/en/netapplnc/20041022/index.shtml

OSGi Alliance. (2005). *The OSGi service platform—Dynamic services for networked devices.* Retrieved 2006 from http://www.osgi.org/

Want, R. (2006). An introduction to RFID technology. *IEEE Pervasive Computing, 5*(1), 25-33.

KEY TERMS

Autonomic Computing: An approach, initially defined by IBM, for designing computer systems that have self-management capabilities. Adopting these principles allows devices to self-configure, self-heal, self-optimise, and self-protect.

Heterogeneity: Devices built by different manufacturers using parts or elements that conform to different standards. This makes inter-device communications difficult.

Home Networking: Residential networks designed to interconnect networked-enabled devices. These networks are typically used in conjunction with Broadband Internet services.

Interoperability: Mechanisms used to overcome heterogeneity. Devices can be made to interoperate and internetwork using agreed upon standards that govern how elements or parts contained within the device are used. This ensures that devices can connect to each other and interoperate in a standardised way.

Networked Appliances: Devices that publish the functions they provide as independent services that can be discovered by other devices in the network to control, monitor, manage, and extend the functionality they support beyond what they where initially designed to do.

Service Discovery: Network protocols used to automatically discover services provided by devices within the network. Standards are used to define how services are described and how queries are formulated in order to find those services.

Ubiquitous Computing: A vision that computers will exist everywhere. Devices with networking and processing capabilities will embed themselves within the fabric of our physical environments, effectively making them invisible to the end user.

Optical Burst Switching

O

Kyriakos Vlachos
University of Patras, Greece

INTRODUCTION

Switching in core optical networks is currently being performed using high-speed electronic or all-optical circuit switches. Switching with high-speed electronics requires optical-to-electronic (O/E) conversion of the data stream, making the switch a potential bottleneck of the network: any effort (including parallelization) for electronics to approach the optical speeds seems to be already reaching its practical limits. Furthermore, the store-and-forward approach of packet-switching does not seem suitable for all-optical implementation due to the lack of practical optical random-access-memories to buffer and resolve contentions. Circuit switching on the other hand, involves a pre-transmission delay for call setup and requires the aggregation of microflows into circuits, sacrificing the granularity and the control over individual flows, and is inefficient for bursty traffic. Optical burst switching (OBS) has been proposed by Qiao and Yoo (1999) to combine the advantages of both packet and circuit switching and is considered a promising technology for the next generation optical internet.

BACKGROUND

An OBS network consists of a set of optical core routers and edge routers. The basic idea is to amortize switching and protocol processing overhead over a larger amount of payload data, and thus enable affordable and less intelligent switches to be employed. An optical burst is constructed at the network edge by aggregating a number of variable size packets of different protocols (IP packets, ATM cells…). The burst is then transmitted in the network and is forwarded transparently (all-optically) to its end destination router. OBS builds upon the tell-and-go protocol (TAG) class developed by Hudek

and Muder (1995). According to this class of protocols, a virtual circuit is set up on the fly for a burst of packets that can go through intermediate switches without buffering and without waiting for acknowledgement of the allocation of the circuit. To this end, a control packet that carries routing and overhead information is transmitted prior to burst transmission. It must be noted here that other signaling schemes exists as well, but OBS was initially designed based on the "*one-way*" reservation concept.

Unlike packet switching, an optical burst can size from a few bytes to multi-giga byte packets, while unlike circuit switching reservation duration is known in advance via the communication to all nodes of the control packet. Thus, reservation is so called *delayed reservation* in the sense that bandwidth is reserved only for time it is actually needed; that is for a time equal to the burst size. Figure 1 illustrates the transmission of two bursts and their associated control packets.

In particular, Figure 1 shows two edge routers that transmit two bursts of data heading for different egress routers. The control packets carry overhead information for the bursts (signaling and routing overhead) and these are communicated to all the *switch control units* of the core routers. The latter process the control packet and signal the optical cross connects (OXCs) to configure their states. In the case of contention, one of the burst is dropped. The control packet precedes the data burst by a time offset to compensate for its processing delay and thus avert the bursts to surpass it. Upon the reception of the burst at the egress router, the latter disassembles the burst and forwards its contents to their end-users.

The success of OBS technology relies on its small control overhead for a large amount of payload data. Data are optically switched in the core and thus there is no need for high-speed electronics, while control packet can be at a significant lower rate. OBS shifts

Figure 1. Optical burst switching network architecture. An edge router is commissioned to assemble the bursts, while the core routers transparently (all-optically) forward the bursts to their end destinations. Control packets carry signaling and routing overhead information.

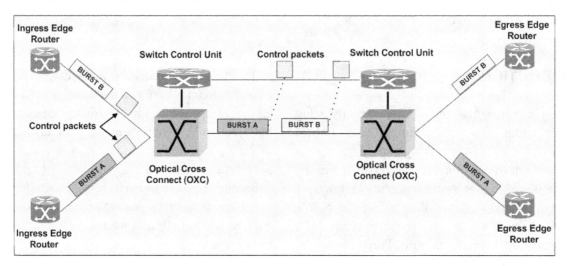

its complexity at the network edge, where the bursts have to be constructed. Figure 2 illustrates a top level architecture of an OBS edge router. The edge router maintains a separate queue per destination, where a separate burst scheduler is responsible for constructing the bursts from packets coming from the access network. Upon completion of the so called *burst assembly* process, a *link scheduler* schedules the burst for transmission. The link scheduler is responsible for wavelength assignment and routing table look up.

RESEARCH AND DEVELOPMENT ISSUES OF OPTICAL BURST SWITCHING

OBS became a hot research topic soon after its introduction. Several issues are under study and some other have been successfully addressed. In particular, issues of pivotal importance include the development of burst assembly algorithms, efficient signaling protocols, contention resolution schemes as well as quality of service provisioning mechanisms. In what follows, we provide an overview of current development and research trends in the aforementioned key areas.

Burst Assembly Algorithms

Burst assembly defines how packets are assembled to form a burst. The burst assembly process starts with the arrival of a packet from a high layer application and continues until a predefined criterion is met. The criterion defines when the burst assembly process stops and the newly generated burst is sent into the network. The assembly process affects, through the assembly criterion, the burst size, the burst duration, as well as the packet delay at the edge router. The packet delay is defined as the time that the packets must wait before burst transmission.

Two distinct burst assembly algorithms have been proposed in the literature: the *timer-based* and the *threshold-based* method. In the timer-based method, also denoted as T_{MAX} in the literature, (Callegati & Tamil, 2000), a time counter starts any time a packet arrives and when the timer reaches a time threshold (T_{MAX}), a burst is created; the timer is then reset to 0 and it remains so until the next packet arrival at the queue. Hence, the ingress router generates periodically bursts, every T_{MAX} time, independently of the yielding burst size. In the second scheme, (Vokkrane, Haridoss, & Jue, 2002), a threshold is used to determine the end of the assembly process. In most cases the threshold used is the burst length denoted in the literature as B_{MAX}.

Figure 2. Optical burst switching edge router architecture. A burst scheduler is commissioned to assemble burst from packets with the same end destination, while a link scheduler is commissioned to assign wavelengths and schedule bursts for transmission

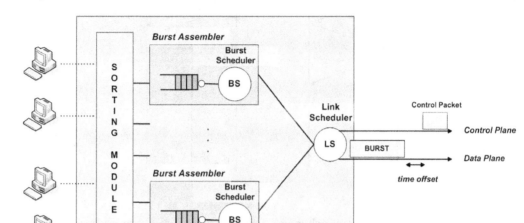

In that case, bursts are thought as containers of a fixed size B_{MAX}, and as soon as the container is completely filled with data, the burst is transmitted.

Apart from the aforementioned assembly schemes, other more complex schemes have been also proposed, which are usually a combination of the *timer -based*, and the *threshold-based* methods. For example the *min-burst length-max-assembly-period (MBMAP)* algorithm, (Cao, Chen, & Qiao, 2002), sends out a burst when its size exceeds a minimum burst length (MBL) or when the assembly period times out. However, all of the above burst assembly criteria do not take into account traffic situation so as to adapt the burst assembly process accordingly. This is very important for higher layer protocols such as TCP, because it limits its effective throughput. To this end, adaptive burst assembly schemes have been also proposed as for example the *adaptive-assembly-period* (AAP) algorithm proposed by Cao, Chen, and Qiao (2002). The AAP algorithm dynamically changes the assembly time at the ingress node according to the length of the burst recently sent. Nevertheless, the proper selection of the timer or threshold parameter is important and is still an open issue. For example, the use of a burst-length threshold may result in long assembly times under light loads while the use of a timer-based method may result to diverse sizes of bursts, making scheduling in the core a difficult task. What is important is to minimize loss ratio in the core

while predicting the assembly expiration time. This will allow transport protocols to predict future round trip times (RTT) and thus minimize time-outs.

Signaling Protocols

A signaling scheme is required for reserving resources and configuring switches in OBS networks. All the signaling schemes developed can be categorized in two main classes: In two-way reservation schemes (also called *tell-and-wait, TAW*) and one-way reservation schemes (also called *tell-and-go, TAG*). Figure 3(a) and (b) illustrate the timing considerations of these two schemes.

In two-way reservation schemes, end-to-end connections are fully established before burst transmission, while resources at intermediate nodes are reserved immediately upon the arrival of the SETUP packet at these nodes. Recent research efforts like the WR-OBS (Dueser & Bayvel, 2002), have shown that such reservation schemes can enable the implementation of a bufferless core network with limited node wavelength conversion capability by moving the processing and buffering functions at the edge.

In one-way reservation schemes, a setup packet is sent in advance over the path, preceding the arrival of the burst by a minor offset. This minimizes the pre-transmission delay, but can result in high burst dropping

Figure 3. Timing considerations of (a) two-way and (b) one-way OBS reservation schemes

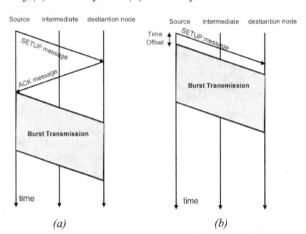

(a)   (b)

probability. A number of one-way reservation schemes have been proposed for OBS networks, including the just-enough-time (JET) (Qiao & Yoo, 1997), the horizon (Turner 1999), the just-in-time (JIT) (Wei & MacFarland Jr., 2000), and the ready-to-go virtual circuit protocol (Varvarigos & Sharma, 1997). The differences among these variances lie mainly in the time instances that determine the allocation and the release of the resources. These can be *implicit* where capacity is freed immediately after burst traversing the OBS node (burst length information is stored in the preceding control packet) or *explicit* with a separate *release* message. Furthermore, for the one-way schemes that employ delayed reservations, sophisticated channel scheduling and void filling algorithms have been proposed to resolve contentions and efficiently utilize the available bandwidth (Xiong, Vandenhoute, & Cankaya, 2000). The use of one-way reservation schemes has introduced a new era for OBS networking and opened new research lines. One-way schemes can guarantee minimum delays at the edge node, on-demand use of bandwidth resources and very low switch setup times. New research lines have emerged on how to avoid burst dropping when contention occurs or how to provision quality of service for bursts carrying packets of a higher priority.

Contention Resolution Schemes

Contention resolution takes place at any of the intermediate nodes upon the reception of two bursts that

request the same outgoing link. Since capacity is not reserved the switch has to resolve contention or otherwise drops one of the bursts. Contention resolution can be performed in one of the following domains:

- In the time domain, employing a fiber-delay-line (FDL) structure for buffering/delaying a burst until the contention situation is resolved. In contrast to electronic RAM based buffers, optical FDLs only provide a fixed delay, which must be long enough to temporary store contending bursts. Under the FDL-based buffering scheme, two prime architectures exist; namely the feed forward and the feedback one. Figure 4 illustrates these two FDL architectures. In the feed-forward method, bursts are fed into fiber delay lines of different lengths and when a burst reaches the output it has to be switched out. In the feedback scheme, a burst may re-circulate from the buffer output to the buffer input until contention is resolved and the requested outgoing link is free.

- In the wavelength domain by means of wavelength conversion, where a burst can be sent on a different wavelength channel of the designated output line.
- In the space domain, where a burst is deflected to a different output line of the OBS switch and follows an alternative route than the predetermined one.

Figure 4. (a) Feed-forward and (b) feedback fiber delay lines schemes for contention resolution in OBS networks

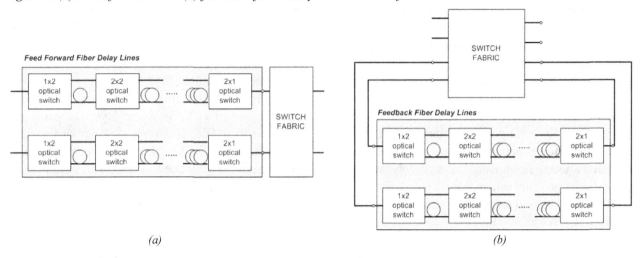

(a)   (b)

Another significant contention resolution strategy relies on the burst segmentation. According to this technique, only the contending part of the two bursts is dropped or routed on another wavelength or deflected (Vokkrane & Jue, 2003).

Most studies on contention resolution in OBS networks focus in the wavelength domain and assume full wavelength conversion at all nodes. For a low to medium load, such an assumption provides a low burst loss ratio. However, for high loads, and in order to achieve a loss ratio of less than 10^{-6}, the number of wavelengths has to be very large and in particular more than >100, making this impractical for a potential deployment.

Similarly, the use of Fiber delay lines is also impractical because of the huge length of fiber needed for an efficient resolution. For example, buffering of a few Mbytes of data requires more than 150km of optical fibre at 10Gb/s. Thus, feedback FDL structures are more attractive. However, the infinite recirculation of the burst data may impair signal quality due to noise accumulation. Further, these schemes increase complexity and size of an OBS node. In particular for an (NxN) switch with L delay lines for burst buffering, instead of (NxN), an $(N+L)$ x $(N+L)$ space switch is required.

To this end, it is not still clear which OBS contention resolution strategy to follow, since all exhibit major drawbacks that lag their commercial implementation. To overcome this drawback, research efforts are focusing to other mechanisms in order to carry high loads

on a per wavelength channel. These techniques include intelligent burst scheduling for load balancing as well as hybrid signaling schemes such as the INI scheme (Karanam et al., 2003).

QoS Provision and Service Differentiation Schemes

Quality of service (QoS) in OBS networks has emerged as an extremely important issue in order to guarantee services to end users. The use of one-way reservation schemes and the absence of an efficient contention resolution mechanism urge the QoS support of optical burst switching. In OBS networks, QoS can be provisioned by introducing service differentiation at any point of the network including for example the burst assembly process, the contention resolution process as well as the burst scheduling process. There are two basic models for QoS provision in optical burst switching networks: relative QoS and absolute QoS. In the relative QoS model, the performance of one class is defined with respect to the other classes. For example it is guaranteed that high priority bursts will exhibit a lower edge delay or lower loss ratio as against other classes. However, its absolute performance still depends on the traffic characteristics of the rest classes. On the other hand, absolute QoS model provides an absolute performance metric of quality as for example defining a worst-case loss ratio for bursts belonging to the same class.

Typical schemes of the first category are the *offset-based* approach, (Qiao & Yoo, 2000), the composite-burst assembly (Vokkrane & Jue, 2003), and the preemptive wavelength reservation (Liao & Loi, 2004). According to the first scheme, an extra offset time is given to higher priority bursts to overcome contention in the core, while the *composite-burst assembly* scheme mixes traffic classes during burst assembly and provides QoS via prioritized burst segmentation. Finally, the third scheme associates each class with a predefined usage limit. Bursts that comply with their usage limits preempt others that do not.

Under the second category of absolute QoS provision, we find two techniques; the *probabilistic preemptive* approach (Yang, Jiang, & Jiang, 2003), according to which high-priority bursts, may preempt lower classes in a probabilistic way and the *early dropping* approach that randomly drops bursts depending on their class (Zhang et al., 2004). This is done on purpose, in order to maintain the required loss ratios of higher priority bursts.

The issue of QoS provision is still under study and is being investigated together with the effect on TCP traffic. The prime target is to provide a guaranteed TCP throughput for end-users, minimizing variance of its performance.

FUTURE RESEARCH LINES

Optical burst switching offers significant advantages when compared to traditional circuit and packet switching. Research effort is now focusing on how to utilize this technology for applications that really depend on huge data exchanges as for examples GRID computing. Currently, GRID networks are using an optical network infrastructure, which is dedicated to a small number of well known organizations with extremely large jobs (e.g., large data file transfers between known users or destinations). OBS has the potential of meeting several important objectives of GRIDS as for example: high bandwidth, low latency as well as transparency (bitrate, protocol, and service) in the transmission of huge data bursts.

Another significant area of research in OBS networks concerns burst scheduling. It is clear that the loss of a large burst that may contain packets from numerous users and applications will have an imminent effect in service delivery. Toward this, research efforts are focusing on multi-constrain burst scheduling techniques that take into account burst size, burst destination, and instant traffic situation.

Finally, research effort is still devoted on assessing the effect of OBS in higher layer protocols and in particular in TCP. In a typical IP network, packet loss probability of each packet is independent of other packets and is largely due to overflow of buffers at the routers. In OBS networks this does not apply. When a burst is lost due to contention, numerous TCP agents will time-out, since numerous clients may have packets in that burst and will not receive an acknowledgement. All these sources will enter a slow start phase, where the congestion window will be set to one and TCP throughput will reset. It is therefore clear that such a situation must be avoided.

To this end, research is focusing towards two directions. The first direction aims to investigate the effect of the burst drop probability in TCP throughput and in particular how this probability depends upon the network load and the level of burst contentions in the network. The second direction involves the investigating of the *burstification* effect and particularly how the burst assembly processes affect TCP throughput. Burst assembly introduces an unpredictable delay that prohibits TCP to predict future round trip times by sampling the behavior of packets sent over a connection and averaging these measurements into a "*smoothed*" round-trip time estimate.

CONCLUSION

Optical burst switching has been proposed as an alternative switching paradigm to combine the strengths of both optical packet and circuit (wavelength-routing) switching. Several issues are still under investigation and even more will emerge as technology continues to mature. Within this context, we have analyzed current research trends in burst assembly algorithms, signaling and contention resolution schemes as well as provided future guidelines on topics like QoS provision and multi-cost burst scheduling, which will be important for a successful deployment of this technology. Two important factors that argue for the success of this technology are that a suitable application has been identified, namely GRID computing, and that OBS can be implemented within the framework of generalized multi-protocol label switching (GMPLS).

REFERENCES

Callegati, F., & Tamil, L., (2000). IEEE Communications Letters, 4(3), 98-100.

Cao, X. Y., Chen, J., Li, & Qiao, C. (2002). IEEE Globecom 2002 (Vol. 3, pp. 2808-2812).

Dueser, M., & Bayvel, P. (2002). IEEE/OSA Journal of Lightwave Technology, 20(4), 574-585.

Hudek, G. C., & Muder, D. J. (1995). IEEE Proceedings of International Conference on Communications (pp. 1206 -1210).

Karanam, R., Vokkarane, V. M., & Jue, J. P. (2003). In *Proceedings, IEEE/OSA Optical Fiber Communication Conference* 2003.

Liao, W., & Loi, C. (2004). IEEE/OSA Journal of Lightwave Technology, 22(7), 1651-1660.

Vokkarane, V.M., Haridoss, K., and Jue, J.P., (2002). In *Proceedings of the Optical Communications Conference* (Vol. 1, pp. 125-136).

Qiao, C. & Yoo, M. (1997). IEEE/LEOS Technology Global Information Infrastructure, 26–27.

Qiao, C. & Yoo, M. (1999). Journal of High Speed Networks, 8, 69-84.

Qiao, C. & Yoo, M. (2000). IEEE Journal on Selected Areas in Communications, 18(10), 2062-2071.

Turner, J. S. (1999). Journal of High Speed Networks, 8(1), 3-16.

Varvarigos, E. A., & Sharma, V. (1997). IEEE/ACM Transactions on Networking, 5 (5), 705-718.

Vokkarane, V., & Jue, J. P. (2003). IEEE Journal on Selected Areas in Communications, 21(7), 1198-1209.

Wei, J. Y., & MacFarland Jr, R. I. (2000). IEEE/OSA Journal of Lightwave Technology, 18(12), 2019-2037.

Xiong, Y., Vandenhoute, M., & Cankaya, H. (2000). IEEE Journal on Selected Areas in Communications, 18(10), 1838-1851.

Yang, L., Jiang, Y., & Jiang, S. (2003). In *Proceedings of the IEEE Global Telecommunication Communication Conference* (pp. 2689-2673).

Zhang, Q., Vokkarane, V. M., Jue, J. P., & Chen, B. (2004). IEEE Journal on Selected Areas in Communications, 22(9), 1781-1795.

KEY TERMS

FDL: Fiber delay line is a fixed length of fibre that is used to induce a given delay in the passing through optical signal.

GMPLS: Generalized multi-protocol label switching protocol allows traffic paths to be set up through a switched network automatically. This involves the configuration of core switches for the transparent forwarding data from a given start to given end point.

GRID: GRID is an emerging computing model that provides the ability to execute complex processing tasks in a number of distributed, inter-networked computers.

Optical Burst Switching (OBS): A new switching concept which lies between optical circuit switching and optical packet switching. In optical burst switching, the switching payload is the aggregation of numerous packets, usually call burst of packets.

OXC: Optical cross-connect is network device (switch fabric) used by network operators to switch high-speed optical signals. It is capable of switching multiple high-speed signals that are not multiplexed together.

Quality of Service (QoS): Refers to the capability of a telecommunication network to meet a requested quality or traffic contract. In many cases quality of service is refered to the probability of a packet succeeding in propagating through a certain link or path in the network, within its delay bounds.

Optical Network Survivability

N. S. C. Correia
University of Algarve, Portugal

M. C. R. Medeiros
University of Algarve, Portugal

INTRODUCTION

The telecommunications world is evolving dramatically toward challenging scenarios where the fast and efficient transportation of information is becoming a key element in today's society. Wavelength division multiplexing (WDM) technology has the potential to satisfy the ever-increasing bandwidth needs of the network users on a sustained basis (Mukherjee, 2000).

Network operators must provide uninterrupted service to their customers, that is, network survivability must be guaranteed. This means that networks must be able to handle link or fiber cuts as well as equipment failures, fact that influences the design and operation of networks (Gerstel & Ramaswami, 2000). When using WDM, survivability becomes even more important because of the huge amount of traffic carried by a single fiber. A single fiber failure, even for few seconds, can be catastrophic (Maier, Pattavina, Patre, & Martinelli, 2002). This issue is actually very important since the optical WDM technology is now being deployed in the field. Network survivability is not just an academic subject. In real networks, failures happen quite frequently (fiber cuts, for example, are very common in terrestrial networks since they share other utility transport conduits such as gas or water pipes and electrical cables, and are considered the least reliable component (Gerstel et al., 2000; Maier et al., 2002). The prevention of service interruption, or the reduction of the service loss when failures occur, must now be an integral part of the network design and operations strategy or otherwise severe service losses can happen.

BACKGROUND

For an easier implementation of optical transport network (OTN) functions, the optical layer has been divided into three sublayers according to the recommendation G.872 of the International Telecommunication Union-Telecommunication Standardization Sector (ITU-T) component (ITU-T Recommendation G. 872, 1999; Gerstel et al., 2000; Maier et al., 2002):

- **Optical channel (OCh):** The managed entity is the lightpath. It takes care of all the end-to-end networking functions such as routing and wavelength assignment, connectivity check, and failure management. Its functions are done at the end-to-end lightpath terminations.
- **Optical multiplex section (OMS):** The managed entity is the multiplex of all the wavelength channels, that is, provides functionality for networking of an aggregate optical signal with multiple wavelengths. Basically, it performs WDM multiplex monitoring. Its functions are done at the link terminations.
- **Optical transmission section (OTS):** The managed entity is the multiplex of all the wavelength channels, as in the OMS, but it manages and supervises optical transmissions devices, such as amplifiers and repeaters, inserted in links. Therefore, it provides functionality for transmitting aggregate optical signals.

Network protection and restoration can be performed by the OCh or OMS sublayers. Schemes at the OCh

Figure 1. Protection and restoration techniques: (a) link-based; (b) path-based

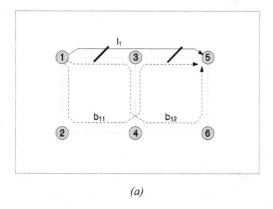

(a)

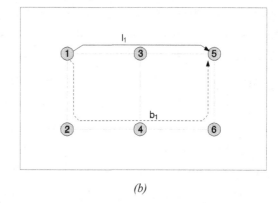

(b)

sublayer protect individual lightpaths while schemes at the OMS sublayer protect all wavelength channels in a link as a group (Gerstel et al., 2000; Mohan & Murthy, 2000).

Besides the link failures, node and channel failures can also occur in a WDM network. A node failure is due to equipment failure at network nodes while a channel failure is due to the failure of transmitting and/or receiving equipment operating at some wavelength. The probability of such failures is much smaller, when compared to link failures, due to the built-in redundancy of most equipment. Besides being more common, link failures have a very high impact on service loss due to the simultaneous failure of several wavelength channels. Therefore, focus will be given to link failures. For more details on node failures, see Wang, Cheng, and Mukherjee (2003).

In non-WDM systems, the protected entity is the link. In WDM systems, due to the availability of multiple wavelength channels in a fiber, the survivability schemes can be more flexible. Either the link (fiber) or the lightpath (wavelength) can be the protected entity at the optical layer. This basically has to do with the sublayer of the WDM layer in which a given survivability mechanism operates. Since more multiplexing/demultiplexing and per-channel switching equipment is necessary for OCh protection, one could think that OCh protection is more expensive than OMS protection. However, this is not true if not all wavelength channels need protection. In this case, OCh protection utilizes capacity more efficiently than OMS protection

and a benefit exists on the number of fibers necessary to provide protection. Since future networks tend to be flexible, providing lightpaths automatically as necessary with a variety of protection levels, and as equipment cost decreases, OCh protection seems to be the choice. For these reasons the focus will be on OCh protection. For more references on OMS protection see Maier et al. (2002).

LIGHTPATH SURVIVABILITY TECHNIQUES

The lightpath survivability techniques used in WDM networks can be broadly classified into protection and restoration (the terms proactive and reactive have also been used) (Mohan, Murthy & Somani, 2001; Sridharan, Salapaka, & Somani, 2002). Protection refers to the fact that recovery from network failures is based on preplanned schemes and uses dedicated resources. These resources are reserved for recovery from failures at either connection setup or network design time, and are kept idle when there is no failure. Thus, the use of capacity is not very efficient but the recovery process is fast.

Restoration implies the dynamic discovery of spare capacity in the network to restore the services affected by the failure. Resources are not reserved at the time of connection establishment but are chosen from available resources when failure occurs. When compared to predesigned protection, dynamic restoration makes

Figure 2. Link-based protection: (a) dedicated; (b) shared

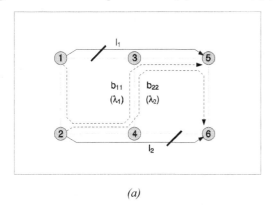

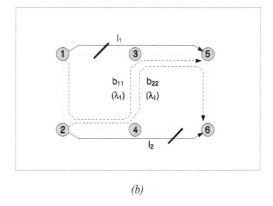

(a)   (b)

a more efficient use of the capacity and provides resilience against different kinds of failures, on the other hand, they are more complex and the restoration time is longer than predesigned protection schemes due to the intense activity of the network management system to set up new connections. Additionally, full recovery is not guaranteed because sufficient spare capacity may not be available at the time of failure. Since restoration time is a key issue in most optical networks, protection is usually used rather than dynamic restoration.

Protection and restoration techniques can be further classified into link-based and path-based, illustrated in Figure 1, according to the kind of rerouting done. In link-based schemes a new path is selected between the end nodes of the failed link. This path along with the working segments of the working lightpath will be used to build the backup lightpath. Therefore, the traffic is rerouted around the failed link. Backup lightpaths used to protect different working lightpaths affected by a link failure may use different paths and/or different wavelengths. In Figure 1a) the backup lightpath b_{11} will replace the primary lightpath l_1 if link 1-3 fails while the backup lightpath b_{12} will replace the primary lightpath l_1 if link 3-5 fails.

In path-based schemes there is a backup lightpath between the end nodes of the failed working lightpath. Thus, the whole path between the source and destination nodes is replaced and there is no need to retain the working segments of the primary lightpath. When compared to link-based, these schemes show better resource utilization but require excessive signalling and

have longer restoration times. In link-based schemes the choice of backup lightpaths is limited and thus a lot of capacity may be required since backup lightpaths are usually longer. Also, link-based schemes can not handle node failures while path-based schemes can. In Figure 1(b) the primary lightpath l_1 is replaced by the backup lightpath b_1 for any link failure affecting l_1.

LINK-BASED LIGHTPATH PROTECTION

Link-based protection can be further classified into dedicated and shared. As illustrated in Figure 2(a), dedicated protection means that all wavelength channels of a backup wavelength path will be dedicated to protect a working wavelength channel of a particular link. That is, if the backup wavelength paths of two working wavelength channels overlap then different wavelengths are required for the backup wavelength paths. This happens even if the working wavelength channels being protected are in different links. In Figure 2(a) the backup lightpaths b_{11} and b_{22} must use different wavelengths. The backup lightpath b_{11} replaces the primary lightpath l_1 if link 1-3 fails while the backup lightpath b_{22} replaces the primary lightpath l_2 if link 4-6 fails. Thus, at least 50% WDM channels cannot be used by working traffic.

Shared protection, illustrated in Figure 2(b), explores the idea that the simultaneous failure of two or more links is a very unlikely event. Backup wavelength paths can share the same wavelength on some overlapping

Figure 3. Path-based protection: (a) dedicated; (b) shared

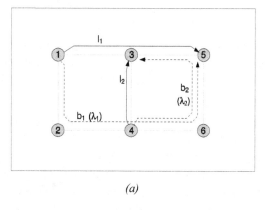

(a)

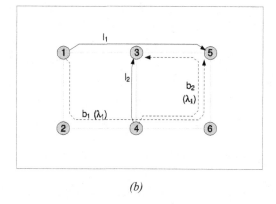

(b)

portion if the working wavelength channels that they are protecting are in different links, meaning that in a single-link failure scenario these will not be activated at the same time. In Figure 2(b) the backup lightpaths b_{11} and b_{22} can use the same wavelength because they are protecting the primary lightpaths l_1 and l_2 against different link failures, 1-3 and 4-6 respectively, not being activated at the same time for a single-link failure scenario. In a single-link failure scenario, the shared protection can provide 100% protection while using capacity more efficiently than dedicated protection. However, multilink failures are less protected than in dedicated protection, which is able to recover from more multilink failure scenarios. Note that dedicated protection can not recover a working lightpath if the multilink failure affects the working and the backup lightpaths simultaneously.

PATH-BASED LIGHTPATH PROTECTION

Upon a link failure, a mechanism must exist to notify the end nodes of the affected working lightpaths so that they can switch to the corresponding backup lightpaths. This requires more network cooperation than in the link-based schemes. Similarly to link-based, path-based protection can be classified into dedicated and shared. In dedicated path-based protection, illustrated in Figure 3a), every wavelength channel assigned to the backup lightpath is reserved to protect a specific working lightpath and cannot be used by other

backup lightpaths even if their corresponding working lightpaths are link-disjoint. In Figure 3(a) the backup lightpaths b_1 and b_2 must use different wavelengths. Thus, at least 50% WDM channels cannot be used by working traffic.

In shared path-based protection, illustrated in Figure 3(b), a wavelength channel in a link can be used for two backup lightpaths if their corresponding working lightpaths are link-disjoint. In Figure 3(b) the backup lightpaths b_1 and b_2 can use the same wavelength because the primary lightpaths l_1 and b_2 do not share links meaning that they will never be activated at the same time in a single-link failure scenario. As in link-based protection, shared path-based schemes can achieve 100% protection from single-link failures whereas dedicated path-based schemes can recover from more multilink failures. In dedicated protection, the resources are kept idle even if no failure occurs, the recovery time is shorter because backup lightpaths are completely set up in advance and only the end nodes will be involved in the recovery process, whereas in shared protection backup resources can be used to protect many working lightpaths. In shared path-based schemes, although the backup lightpaths are preplanned, the configuration of optical crossconnects (OXCs) necessary for backup lightpath activation can only happen after failure occurs, meaning that recovery procedures are more complex and therefore recovery time is longer. In the other hand, dedicated path-based schemes reserve excessive resources, not being recently emphasized in papers, while shared schemes use wavelength channels more efficiently.

Figure 4. Primary-backup multiplexing scheme

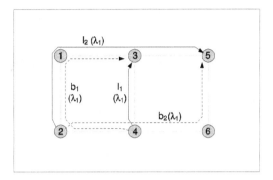

Shared path-based protection schemes can be further classified into failure dependent and failure independent. In failure dependent schemes there is one backup lightpath for each link used by the working lightpath. When a link fails the corresponding backup lightpath is activated. In failure independent schemes there is only one backup lightpath that is be activated for any link failure.

DYNAMIC LIGHTPATH PROTECTION

In dynamic traffic scenarios, slightly different schemes can be used so that blocking probability is reduced. Mohan et al. (2001) proposed a scheme called primary-backup multiplexing, that allows wavelength channels to be shared by a working lightpath and one or more backup lightpaths. The authors sustain this approach arguing that for short-lived lightpaths full protection is a waste. In this scheme working lightpaths are allowed to lose recoverability when a channel used by the corresponding backup lightpath is used by another working lightpath. It regains recoverability when the other working lightpath terminates. This is illustrated in Figure 4. The backup lightpath b_1 shares wavelength channels with the working lightpath l_2 meaning that the working lightpath l_1 lost its recoverability when working lightpath l_2 was created. If lightpath l_2 terminates then l_1 regains its recoverability.

SURVIVABILITY IN MULTILAYER NETWORKS

Current networks have several layers interoperating with each other. At the optical layer, the WDM is the emerging technology that must satisfy connectivity and bandwidth requests from client higher layers. As networks become more Internet protocol (IP) data centric and both the IP and WDM evolve, currently used asynchronous transfer mode (ATM) and synchronous digital hierarchy (SDH) layers will become unnecessary (Colle, Maesschalck, Develder, & et al., 2002; Conte, Listanti, Settembre, & Sabella, 2002). Although higher layers such as ATM and IP have recovery mechanisms, their recovery times are very large when compared to the few milliseconds that the optical layer protection can provide. Besides minimizing data losses, due to faster recovery, optical layer protection can provide protection to higher layers not having this capability.

In IP-over-WDM, fault-tolerance can be provided either by the WDM or the IP layer. At the WDM layer protection is given to lightpaths carrying traffic with protection needs while at the IP client layer fault-tolerance can be provided through IP label-switched path (LSP) protection if multi-protocol label switching (MPLS) is used (Sahasrabuddhe, Ramamurthy, & Mukherjee, 2002; Zheng & Mohan, 2003). The advantages of using WDM lightpath protection are that: protection can be applied to all traffic streams in a lightpath; and the restoration is contained within the network where the failure occurs, improving latency

Figure 5. Primary-shared lightpath protection: (a) network example; (b) Node 4 before backup activation; (c) Node 4 after backup activation

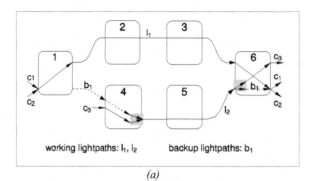

(a)

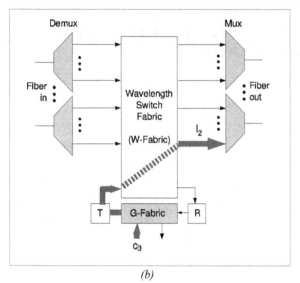

(b)

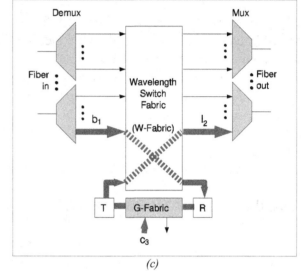

(c)

and stability. However, lightpath protection is inefficient in what concerns to the use of resources. This is because the bandwidth reserved by backup lightpaths is equal to the total bandwidth of the lightpath being protected even if just a small percentage of traffic is being carried, meaning that unused bandwidth is also protected. This tends to aggravate in the future since the bandwidth of channels is expected to grow to OC-768. An alternative to the traditional WDM lightpath protection is the IP LSP protection approach where protection is provided to individual IP LSPs by the IP layer. When using this scheme resources are used efficiently but many signalling messages can be generated for the recovery of every IP LSP (Ye, Assi, Dixit, & Ali, 2001). Survivable traffic grooming (STG) schemes are emerging to solve this problem.

SURVIVABLE TRAFFIC GROOMING

Protection combined with traffic grooming has recently being considered in Correia and Medeiros (2006) and Yao & Ramamurthy (2005), and STG protection schemes have been proposed and analysed. Survivable traffic grooming addresses the survivability of connections together so that resources are better utilized. The STG protection scheme proposed in Correia et al. (2006), called primary-shared lightpath protection, uses resources efficiently while providing optical layer protection. The idea is to use the available bandwidth of working lightpaths, announced as virtual links, for backup purposes thus improving bandwidth utilization when compared with the traditional lightpath protection. This is illustrated in Figure 5(a).

In this example, the low speed streams c_1 and c_2 are delivered using lightpath l_1, connecting nodes 1 and 6, and another traffic stream c_3 is delivered using lightpath l_2. Assuming that only one wavelength channel between nodes 1 and 4 is available on the network, no backup lightpath would be found to protect l_1 if traditional lightpath protection was used. But if lightpath l_2 has available bandwidth then announcing it as a virtual link to the network would mean that backup computation could use it to build backups. Thus, working lightpath l_2 together with the backup lightpath b_1 are able to protect the working lightpath l_1. In case of failure of lightpath l_1, node 4 must groom local traffic of l_2 with traffic from b_1, activated after failure, thus requiring a G-fabric. Figures 5b and 5c illustrate node 4 before and after a link failure affecting the working lightpath l_1, that is, before and after backup activation. This STG protection scheme uses resources efficiently while fast recovery and good scaling are obtained due to optical layer protection. The implementation of this scheme is possible when using generalized multi-protocol label switching (GMPLS) in a peer model.

FUTURE TRENDS

As stated by Yao et al. (2005), network providers are facing the pressure of generating revenues by providing reliable multigranularity connection services while reducing network costs. Therefore, recently proposed schemes employing STG protection, such as those proposed by Correia et al. (2006) and Yao et al. (2005) are expected to play an important role in future optical networks. STG protection remains relatively unexplored and is now gaining attention from researchers.

CONCLUSION

In optical networks, survivability becomes very important because of the huge amount of traffic carried by fibers. Therefore, the prevention of service interruption, or the reduction of the service loss, must now be an integral part of the network design and operations

strategy. In this article, optical network survivability has been discussed and special emphasis has been given to WDM lightpath protection.

REFERENCES

Colle, D., Maesschalck, S., Develder, C., Van Heuven, P., Groebbens, A., Cheyns, J., Lievens, I., Pickavet, M., Lagasse, P., & Demeester, P. (2002). Data-centric optical networks and their survivability. *IEEE Journal on Selected Areas in Communications*, *20*(1), 6-20.

Conte, G., Listanti, M., Settembre, M., & Sabella, R. (2002). Strategy for protection and restoration of optical paths in WDM backbone networks for next-generation internet infrastructures. *IEEE Journal on Lightwave Technology*, *20*(8), 1264-1276.

Correia, N. S. C., & Medeiros, M. C. R. (2006). Protection schemes for IP-over-WDM networks: Throughput and recovery time comparison. *Photonic Network Communications*, *11*(2), 127-149.

Gerstel, O., & Ramaswami, R. (2000). Optical layer survivability: a services perspective. *IEEE Communications Magazine*, *38*(3), 104-113.

ITU-T Recommendation G. 872. (1999). Architecture of Optical Transport Network (OTN).

Maier, G., Pattavina, A., Patre, S., & Martinelli, M. (2002). Optical network survivability: Protection techniques in the WDM layer. *Photonic Network Communications*, *4*(2/4), 251-269.

Mohan, G., & Murthy, C. (2000). Lightpath restoration in WDM optical networks. *IEEE Network*, *14*(6), 24-32.

Mohan, G., Murthy, C., & Somani, A. (2001). Efficient algorithms for routing dependable connections in WDM optical networks. *IEEE/ACM Transactions on Networking*, *9*(5), 553-566.

Mukherjee, B. (2000). WDM optical communication networks: Progress and challenges. *IEEE Journal on Selected Areas in Communications*, *18*(10), 1810-1824.

Sahasrabuddhe, L., Ramamurthy, S., & Mukherjee, B. (2002). Fault management in IP-over-WDM networks: WDM protection versus IP restoration. *IEEE Journal on Selected Areas in Communications, 20*(1), 21-33.

Sridharan, M., Salapaka, M., & Somani, A. (2002). A practical approach to operating survivable WDM networks. *IEEE Journal on Selected Areas in Communications, 20*(1), 34-46.

Wang, Y., Cheng, T., & Mukherjee, B. (2003). Dynamic routing and wavelength assignment scheme for protection against node failure. *IEEE GLOBECOM* (pp. 2585-2589).

Yao, W., & Ramamurthy, B. (2005). Survivable traffic grooming with path protection at the connection level in WDM mesh networks. *Journal of Lightwave Technology, 23*(10), 2846-2853.

Ye, Y., Assi, C., Dixit, S., & Ali, M. (2001). A simple dynamic integrated provisioning/protection scheme in IP over WDM networks. *IEEE Communications Magazine, 39*(11), 174-182.

Zheng, Q., & Mohan, G. (2003). Protection approaches for dynamic traffic in IP/MPLS-over-WDM networks. *IEEE Optical Communications, 41*(5), S24-S29.

KEY TERMS

Generalized Multi-Protocol Label Switching (GMPLS): An extension of the MPLS concept to the circuit switching network and the optical fiber network. GMPLS enables unified control management of the network layers (packet / TDM / wavelength / fiber).

Multi-Protocol Label Switching (MPLS): Circuit-switching based mechanism to carry data over a packet-switched network using the concept of label switching.

Network Survivability: Capacity of the network to provide continuous service in the presence of failures.

Optical Crossconnect (OXC): Optical device used mainly in long-distance networks to switch high-speed optical signals in a fiber optic network.

Survivable Traffic Grooming (STG): Approach that provides multigranularity connections that are reliable and resource-efficient.

Traffic Grooming: Aggregation of different low speed connections into high capacity connections, allowing an efficient utilization of resources, higher throughputs, and minimization of network costs.

Wavelength Division Multiplexing (WDM): Technology which multiplexes multiple optical carrier signals on a single optical fibre by using different wavelengths of laser light to carry different signals. This allows for a multiplication in capacity.

Optimizing Inter-Domain Internet Multicast

Huaqun Guo
Institute for Infocomm Research and National University of Singapore, Singapore

Lek-Heng Ngoh
Institute for Infocomm Research, A*STAR, Singapore

Wai-Choong Wong
National University of Singapore, Singapore

INTRODUCTION

Data communication in the Internet can be performed by any of the following mechanisms: unicast, broadcast, and *multicast*. Unicast is point-to-point communication that takes place over a network between a single sender and a single receiver. Broadcast is when data is forwarded to all the hosts in the network simultaneously. Multicast, on the other hand, is when data is to be transferred to only a group of hosts on a network simultaneously using the most efficient strategy to deliver the data over each link of the network only once and only create copies when the links to the destination hosts split.

In the age of multimedia and high-speed networks, there are many applications that involve sending information to a selective, usually large, number of clients. Common examples of such applications include audio/video conferencing, distance learning, video-on-demand, distributed interactive games, data distribution, service location/discovery, collaborative computing, collaborative visualization, distributed simulation, communicating to dynamic group, and so on. To support such applications, multicast is considered a very efficient mechanism (Lao, Cui, Gerla, & Maggiorini, 2005) since it uses some delivery structures to forward data from senders to receivers, with the aim that the overall utilization of resources in the underlying network is minimized in some sense (Oliveira & Pardalos, 2005). For example, multicast is heavily used for mass media TV distribution, which can be seen from a survey conducted by NAB research and planning (NAB, 2005). NAB research and planning conducted a survey in July 2005 of all U.S. full-power commercial television stations on their plans for DTV (Digital TV) multicast services. Among the 450 response stations, 50% of stations are currently multicasting and 79% among non-multicasting stations are considering multicasting at some point in the future.

First proposed by Steve Deering in 1988 and described as the standard multicast model for IP network (i.e., IP multicast), a single packet transmitted at the source is delivered to an arbitrary number of receivers by replicating the packet within the network routers along a multicast tree rooted at the traffic's source or a router assigned as a rendezvous point (RP). The first experiment of multicast took place during an "audiocast" at the 1992 Internet engineering task force (IETF) meeting in San Diego (Almeroth, 2000). From the first experiment in 1992 to the middle of 1997, standardization and deployment in multicast focused on a single flat topology. This topology is in contrast to the Internet topology, which is based on a hierarchical routing structure. The initial multicast protocol research and standardization efforts were aimed at developing routing protocols for this flat topology. Beginning in 1997, when the multicast community realized the need for a hierarchical multicast infrastructure and *inter-domain* routing, the existing protocols were categorized as intra-domain protocols and work began on standardizing an inter-domain solution (Almeroth, 2000).

ROUTING PROTOCOLS

Many proposals have been made to create technology supporting multicast routing at the network level. Some of the more notable examples of multicast protocols are distance vector multicast routing protocol (DVMRP), protocol independent multicast-dense mode (PIM-DM), multicast open shortest path first (MOSPF), protocol independent multicast-sparse mode (PIM-SM), core based tree (CBT), *multicast source discovery protocol* (MSDP) (Fenner & Meyer, 2003) and *border gateway multicast protocol* (BGMP) (Kumar et al., 1998; Thaler, 2004).

- **DVMRP** is the original IP multicast routing protocol and is based on distance vector or Bellman-Ford technology. It routes multicast datagrams only and does so within a single autonomous system. DVMRP uses a broadcast-and-prune technique to create multicast trees.

- **PIM-DM** is very similar to DVMRP; there are two major differences (Almeroth, 2000). The first is that PIM uses the unicast routing table to perform RPF (reverse path forwarding) checks, while DVMRP maintains its own routing table. The second difference is that DVMRP tries to avoid sending unnecessary packets to neighbors who will then generate prune messages based on a failed RPF check. PIM-DM forwards packets on all outgoing interfaces and floods data packets throughout the network.

- **MOSPF** uses the open shortest path first (OSPF) protocol to provide multicast. Basically, MOSPF floods group membership information to all the routers in an OSPF area so that they can build multicast distribution trees.

- **CBT** uses the basic sparse mode paradigm to create a single shared tree used by all sources. The tree is rooted at a core. All sources send their data to the core and all receivers send explicit join message to the core (Almeroth, 2000).

- **PIM-SM** is similar to PIM-DM in that the underlying unicast routing table is used to make routing decisions, but it uses a different mechanism to construct the multicast tree. PIM-SM uses the similar tree construction algorithm of CBT and has the members explicitly join a multicast distribution tree rooted as a RP.

DVMRP, PIM-DM, and MOSPF rely heavily on broadcasting information and therefore do not scale well to groups that span the Internet (Kumar et al., 1998). CBT and PIM-SM scale better by having the members explicitly join a multicast distribution tree rooted at a core or a RP. However, PIM-SM is an intra-domain multicast protocol and RPs in other domains have no way of knowing about sources located in other domains (Cisco). Internet service providers (ISPs) did not want to rely on a RP maintained by a competing ISP to provide service to their customers. On the other hand, CBT builds a bidirectional tree rooted at a core router and the use of a single core can potentially be subjected to overloading and single-point of failure. Therefore in conclusion, existing solutions DVMRP, PIM-DM, MOSPF, CBT, and PIM-SM are mainly used for intra-domain multicast (Almeroth, 2000).

- **MSDP** was developed for peering between ISPs and presented as one of the inter-domain protocols. The RP in each domain establishes an MSDP peering session using a TCP connection with the RPs in other domains or with border routers leading to other domains. When the RP learns about a new multicast source within its own domain, the RP encapsulates the first data packet in a source-active (SA) message and sends the SA to all MSDP peers. Each receiving peer uses a modified reverse path forwarding (RPF) check to forward the SA, until the SA reaches every MSDP router in the interconnected networks—theoretically the entire multicast Internet. The MSDP speaker periodically sends SAs that include all sources within the domain of the RP. Thus, MSDP allows each ISP to have its own local RP and still forward and receive multicast traffic to other domains. However, MSDP has two drawbacks. First, MSDP requires each multicast router to maintain forwarding state for every multicast tree passing through it and the number of forwarding states grows with the number of groups (Boudani & Cousin, 2002; Boudani, Cousin, & Bonnin, 2004; Fei, Cui, Gerla, & Faloutsos, 2001). Second, MSDP floods source information periodically to all other RPs on the Internet using TCP links between RPs. If there are thousands of multicast sources, the number of SA messages being flooded around the network would increase linearly. Thus, the

MSDP multicast protocol suffers from *scalability* and *control overhead* problems.

- **BGMP** is an attempt to design a true inter-domain multicast routing protocol. However, it is not ready yet. BGMP scales better to large numbers of groups by allowing (*, G-prefix) and (S-prefix, G-prefix) states to be stored at the routers where the list of targets are the same. In order to achieve this, the multicast address-set claim (MASC) protocol must form the basis for a hierarchical address allocation architecture (Kumar et al., 1998). MASC uses a listen and claim with collision detection approach. This approach has two drawbacks. First, this approach is not supported by the present structure of non-hierarchical address allocation architecture. Second, the claimers have to wait for a suitably long period to detect any collision (i.e., 48 hours) (Kumar et al., 1998), hence, it is not suitable for dynamic setup.

SCALABLE MULTICAST SOLUTIONS

Significant research efforts have focused on multicast scalability and controlling overhead problems. Some architectures aim to eliminate forwarding states at routers either completely by explicitly encoding the list of destinations in the data packets, instead of using a multicast address, or partially by using branching node routers in the multicast tree. In aggregated multicast (Fei et al., 2001), multiple multicast groups share one aggregated tree to reduce forwarding state, and a centralized tree manager is introduced to handle aggregated tree management and matching between multicast groups and aggregated trees. Aggregated multicast is targeted for intra-domain multicast and the centralized tree manager is a weakness.

Multi-protocol label switching (MPLS) (Rosen, Viswanathan, & Callon, 2001) has merged as an elegant solution to meet the bandwidth-management and service requirements for next generation Internet protocol (IP) based backbone networks. Multicast and MPLS are two complementary technologies, and merging these two technologies, where multicast trees are constructed in MPLS networks, will enhance performance and present an efficient solution for multicast scalability and control overhead problems (Boudani et al., 2002).

An overview of IP multicast in a MPLS environment is proposed in Ooms et al. (2002). Farinacci, Rekhter, and Qian (2000) explain how to use protocol independent multicast (PIM) to distribute MPLS labels for multicast routes. MPLS multicast tree (MMT) (Boudani et al., 2004) utilizes MPLS label switched paths (LSPs) between multicast tree branching node routers in order to reduce forwarding states and enhance scalability. In MMT, each domain should contain a network information manager system (NIMS) to collect join messages from all group members and have a complete overview about the multicast network. For inter-domain, the border router contacts border routers in other domains with a normal (S, G) join message. Therefore, the centralized NIMS is a weakness too, and the number of forwarding states in inter-domain routers grows with the number of groups.

OPTIMIZING INTER-DOMAIN MULTICAST THROUGH DINLOOP

We introduce DINloop-based multicast to optimize inter-domain multicast through the formation of a DINloop using MPLS (Guo, Ngoh, & Wong, 2005a, 2005b, 2005c). DINloop (data-in-network loop) is a special logical path formed using MPLS LSPs and it consists of multiple DIN nodes, which are core routers that connect to each intra-domain and function as rendezvous points (RP) for that domain respectively. Within a domain, the multicast tree is formed similarly to the bidirectional CBT, rooted at an associated DIN node.

In the core network, first, an explicitly routed LSP is used to form a DINloop, where each DIN node chooses the adjacent DIN node in the DINloop as the next hop. Second, multiple DIN nodes exchange multicast group membership via the DINloop. Third, multiple DIN nodes, which are involved in a particular multicast group, form a Steiner tree for multicast traffic. Finally, traffic for different multicast groups, which share a same path, are aggregated together.

One example of DINloop-based multicast is shown in Figure 1. DIN Nodes A, B, C, and D are the core routers and function as RPs for the associated intra-

Figure 1. DINloop-based multicast

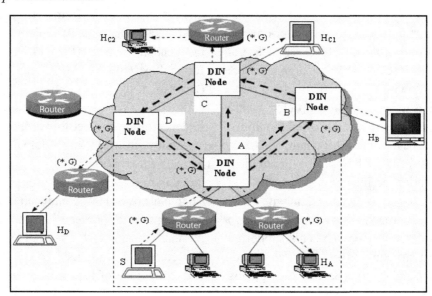

domain (e.g., dot-line square area) respectively. DIN Nodes A, B, C, and D form the DINloop (thick arrow line in Figure 1) in the core network.

The control modules in a DIN node are shown in Figure 2. Intermediate system-to-intermediate system (IS-IS) and open shortest path first (OSPF) are the routing protocols and resource reservation protocol-traffic extension (RSVP-TE) and constraint-based label distribution protocol (CR-LDP) are the signaling protocols for the establishment of LSPs. We use CR-LDP for label distribution and extend it to support explicit routing and resource reservations.

When a multicast packet arrives at the ingress DIN node, the packet processing module looks at the IP header of the multicast packet and identifies the source address and destination address. Next the MPLS manager looks up the label table to assign a label stack with 2-level labels. The top label corresponds to the shared path with the same two end DIN nodes and the bottom label corresponds to the destination address to differentiate the multicast packets.

In order to transmit the label stack along with the packet, the label stack is encoded as a "shim" between the data link layer and network layer headers. Then the multicast packet is fast forwarded in the core network using the top label rather than address matching to determine next hop. When a DIN Node receives a packet, it pops the top label off the label stack and uses the bottom label to examine the multicast packet.

Compared with other inter-domain multicast protocols, our solution has the following advantages:

- DINloop for membership management removes the burden on a single multicast manager and avoids a single point of failure.
- DINloop simplifies the setting up procedures of Steiner tree.
- Only DIN nodes have multicast forwarding state and other core routers do not have it, hence this correspondingly reduces tree maintenance overhead.
- DINloop-based multicast consumes fewer labels with label stacks so as to improve routing scalability, as well as reduce the routing look-up time in the core network.

Figure 2. Control modules in DIN node

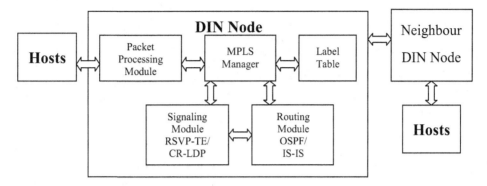

FUTURE TRENDS

Inter-domain multicast is still a challenging research area. Applications such as voice over IP have strong requirement in terms of *quality of service* (QoS). In BGMP & MSDP, data is transmitted with best effort, without considering QoS requirements and constraints. Thus, the future trends for inter-domain multicast will address the issues related to QoS. MPLS/GMPLS (generalized MPLS) may play an important role to support QoS because of their specific techniques.

First, MPLS can direct packet flows along specific LSPs and thus provide a connection-oriented environment that enables traffic engineering (TE) of packet networks (Faucheur, 2002). Because MPLS assigns paths, the vital elements (resource allocation, admission control etc) in the QoS can be addressed. In Yasukawa (2006), point-to-multipoint (P2MP) services will be supported using traffic-engineered LSPs for QoS guarantees.

Second, GMPLS extends MPLS P2MP TE-LSPs to provide the control plane (signaling and routing) for devices that switch in any of these fields: packet, time, wavelength, and fiber. This common control plane promises to simplify network operation and management by automating end-to-end provisioning of connections, managing network resources, and providing the level of QoS that is expected from new, sophisticated applications.

Finally, resource reservation protocol-traffic engineering (RSVP-TE) will be extended for the setup of traffic engineered P2MP LSPs in MPLS and GMPLS networks (Aggarwal, Papadimitriou, & Yasukawa, 2006).

In a brief, the future trends will apply MPLS/GMPLS P2MP TE LSPs techniques into inter-domain multicast to support QoS.

CONCLUSION

This article presents a survey of solutions for today's Internet protocol (IP) inter-domain multicast and discusses their different approaches. Next, we introduce our DINloop-based multicast. DINloop is formed using MPLS LSPs and it consists of multiple DIN Nodes which are core routers that connect to each intra-domain and function as a RP for that domain respectively. An explicitly routed LSP is used to form a DINloop. We then use the DINloop to manage inter-domain multicast group membership and the traffic in the core network. The multicast packet in the ingress DIN node is assigned with a label stack with 2-level labels. Then the multicast packet is fast forwarded in the core network using the top label rather than address matching to determine next hop. DINloop-based multicast has a number of advantages over other solutions. Inter-domain multicast is still a challenging research area. Finally, the future trends will apply MPLS/GMPLS P2MP TE LSPs techniques into inter-domain multicast to support QoS.

REFERENCES

Aggarwal, R., Papadimitriou, D., & Yasukawa, S. (2006). *Extensions to RSVP-TE for point to multipoint TE LSPs*. Network Working Group Internet Draft draft-ietf-mpls-rsvp-te-p2mp-05.txt. May 2006. Retrieved from http://www.ietf.org/internet-drafts/draft-ietf-mpls-rsvp-te-p2mp-05.txt

Almeroth, K. C. (2000). The evolution of multicast: From the MBone to inter-domain multicast to Internet2 Deployment. *IEEE Network*, January/February.

Boudani, A., & Cousin, B. (2002). A new approach to construct multicast trees in MPLS networks. In *Proceedings of the 7th IEEE Symposium on Computers and Communications (ISCC'02)*, Taormina/Giardini Naxos, Italy.

Boudani, A., Cousin, B., & Bonnin, J. M. (2004). An effective solution for multicast scalability: The MPLS multicast tree (MMT). Internet Draft, 2004.

Cisco. IP multicast technology overview. http://www.cisco.com/univercd/cc/td/doc/cisintwk/intolns/mcst_sol/mcst_ovr.htm#53693

Farinacci, D., Rekhter, Y., & Qian, T. (2000). Using PIM to distribute MPLS labels for multicast routes. Internet Draft, 2000.

Faucheur, F.L. (2002). Multi-protocol label switching (MPLS) support of differentiated services. RFC 3270.

Fei, A., Cui, J. H., Gerla, M., & Faloutsos, M. (2001). Aggregated multicast: An approach to reduce multicast state. UCLA CSD Technical Report #010012, 2001.

Fenner, B., & Meyer, D. (2003). Multicast source discovery protocol (MSDP). IETF RFC3618, 2003.

Guo, H. Q., Ngoh, L. H., & Wong, W. C. (2005a). DINloop based inter-domain multicast with MPLS. In *Proceedings of 24th IEEE International Performance Computing and Communications Conference (IPCCC 2005)* (pp. 241-248).

Guo, H. Q., Ngoh, L. H., & Wong, W. C. (2005b). Optimizing inter-domain multicast through DINloop with GMPLS. In *Proceedings of the 4th International Conference on Networking (ICN 2005)* (LNCS 3421, pp. 50-57), Reunion Island, France.

Guo, H. Q., Ngoh, L. H., & Wong, W. C. (2005c). A DINloop-based inter-domain multicast using MPLS. In *Proceedings of the 10th IEEE Symposium on Computers and Communications 2005 (ISCC 2005)* (pp. 406-411), Cartagena, Spain.

Kumar, S., Radoslavov, P., Thaler, D., Alaettinoglu, C., Estrin, D., & Handley, M. (1998). The MASC/BGMP architecture for inter-domain multicast routing. In *Proceedings of ACM SIGCOMM* (pp. 93-104).

Lao, L., Cui, J. H., Gerla, M., & Maggiorini, D. (2005). A comparative study of multicast protocols: Top, bottom, or in the middle? The *8th IEEE Global Internet Symposium (GI'05)* in conjunction with IEEE INFOCOM'05, Miami, Florida.

NAB Research and Planning. (2005). *July 2005 Survey of Television Stations' Multicasting Plans*. Retrieved from http://www.multicasting.com/documents/Multicasting_Plans705.ppt

Oliveira, C. A. S., & Pardalos, P. M. (2005). A survey of combinatorial optimization problems in multicast routing. *Computers and Operations Research*, *32*(8), 1953-1981.

Ooms, D., Sales, B., Livens, W., Acharya, A., Griffoul, F., & Ansari, F. (2002). Overview of IP multicast in a multi-protocol label switching (MPLS) environment. RFC-3353, 2002.

Rosen, E., Viswanathan, A., & Callon, R. (2001). Multiprotocol label switching architecture. RFC-3031, 2001.

Thaler, D. (2004). Border gateway multicast protocol (BGMP): Protocol specification. RFC-3913, 2004.

Yasukawa, S. (2006). Signaling requirements for point-to-multipoint traffic engineered MPLS label switched paths (LSPs). RFC4461. April 2006.

KEY TERMS

Domain: A domain or an autonomous system (AS) is a network or group of networks under a common routing policy, and managed by a single authority.

Inter-Domain Routing: The Internet is an interconnection of multiple networks called domains or autonomous systems (ASes). Inter-domain routing in the Internet takes place between autonomous routing domains and routing information must be exchanged between domains to ensure that a host in one domain can reach another host in a remote domain.

Internet Protocol (IP) Multicast: A routing technique that allows IP traffic to be sent from one source or multiple sources and delivered to multiple destinations. Instead of sending individual packets to each destination, a single packet is sent to a multicast group, which is identified by a single IP destination group address. IP Multicast is a bandwidth-conserving technology aiming that the overall utilization of resources in the underlying network is minimized.

Multi-Protocol Label Switching (MPLS): A data-carrying mechanism which emulates some properties of a circuit-switched network over a packet-switched network. MPLS operates at a OSI model layer that is generally considered to lie between traditional definitions of Layer 2 (data link layer) and Layer 3 (network layer), and thus is often referred to as a "Layer 2.5" protocol. It was designed to provide a unified data-carrying service for both circuit-based clients and packet-switching clients which provide a datagram service model. It can be used to carry many different kinds of traffic, including IP packets, as well as native ATM, SONET, and Ethernet frames.

Quality of Service (QoS): QoS represents the set of techniques necessary to manage network bandwidth, delay, jitter and packet loss. From a business perspective, it is essential to assure that the critical applications are guaranteed the network resources they need, despite varying network traffic load.

Routing: A means of discovering paths in computer networks along which information can be sent. Routing directs forwarding, the passing of logically addressed packets from their source toward their ultimate destination through intermediary nodes, called routers. Forwarding is usually directed by routing tables within the routers, which maintain a record of the best routes to various network destination locations. Thus, the construction of routing tables is important to efficient routing.

Routing Tables: Used to direct forwarding by matching destination addresses to the network paths used to reach them. The construction of routing tables is the primary goal of routing protocols.

Performance of Mobility Protocols

Sherali Zeadally
University of the District of Columbia, USA

Farhan Siddiqui
Wayne State University, USA

INTRODUCTION

In mobile computing environments, the goal is to provide continuous connectivity as a mobile host moves from one network to another—often referred to as *terminal mobility*. All the needed reconnection occurs automatically and non-interactively (Handley et al., 1999). Terminal mobility can be achieved by exploiting mobile IP (Perkins & Johnson, 1998) to provide mobile users the convenience of seamless roaming. Another major requirement for full mobility support is the need of an architecture that enables automatic discovery of the user location, which changes with mobility of the user--a feature often referred as *personal mobility*. New application-layer protocols such as SIP (Handley et al., 1999) can be used to provide this personal mobility.

Several protocols have been proposed (Eddy, 2004; Wanjuin et al., 1999; Wedlund et al., 1999) to support mobility. These protocols can be broadly classified according to the level at which they operate in the protocol stack namely, network (Mobile IP (Perkins et al., 1998)), transport (session initiation protocol (SIP) (Rosenberg, 2002)), or application level (stream control transmission protocol (SCTP) (Stewart et al., 2000)).

SIP AND MOBILE IP INTEGRATION TO SUPPORT SEAMLESS MOBILITY

Design and Implementation of an Architecture Integrating Mobile IP with SIP

We proposed an architecture that incorporates mobile IP functionality into SIP to handle both *personal* and *terminal* mobility. Henceforth, in this article, we refer to this architecture as *SIP*. In this case, we exploit a pure

SIP-based approach that involves only the application layer. We extended the functionality of the SIP user agent (UA) components (that support personal mobility) to provide support for terminal mobility. When the mobile node (MN) moves from the home network to the foreign network, it acquires a new IP address via the dynamic host configuration protocol (DHCP) upon entering the foreign network and registers this address with the LS. Our UA application dynamically detects the change in the IP address (this address is obtained in our implementation by using the "ifconfig" (used to display information about active network interfaces) command. Upon detecting the change in IP address, MN updates the LS with its new IP address by sending a SIP_REGISTER message. When the MN receives an acknowledgement from the LS, it sends a new INVITE message to the correspondent node (CN). The CN then sends a SIP_OK message after which the voice call is re-established between the MN and the CN. Thus, any user wishing to contact the MN can obtain its current address from the LS.

The "pure" SIP-based design approach implemented has the following benefits:

- **Direct communication between MN and CN:** After registering its new IP address with the LS (when the MN moves to a different subnet), the MN sends a re-invite message directly to the CN instead of having to go through the FA and the HA.
- **IP encapsulation is avoided:** In contrast to the SIP-MIP design architecture where IP encapsulations/decapsulations are required, this approach avoids such overheads.
- **Simplicity:** Having the mobility functionality at the application layer eliminates the need for a user to make changes to the IP stack.

Figure 1. Variation of handoff delays over mobile IPv4 and mobile IPv6 for an interleaving distance of 250 meters

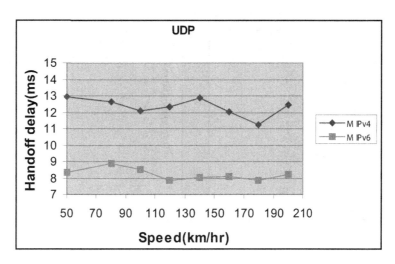

*   **Transparency to the user for both personal and terminal mobility:** With the SIP approach, SIP alone provides support for both types of mobility.

It is worth noting that one drawback of the pure SIP-based solution is that all SIP-based user applications need to incorporate the functionality that takes care of terminal mobility.

Architectural Support for Personal Mobility using SIP and Terminal Mobility using Mobile IP

The main components of our implementation combining SIP and Mobile IP include user agents (UAs) and a SIP location server (LS). Henceforth, in this article, we refer to this architecture as "SIP-MIP." A UA executes on both the mobile node (MN) and the correspondent node (CN). Each user agent consists of a *user agent client (UAC)* and a *user agent server (UAS)*. The UAC is a logical entity to create new SIP requests. The UAS is responsible for receiving SIP requests and sending the corresponding responses. In addition, the UAS is capable of functioning either as a caller or a callee.

Each time a user signs into the system through the UA, a SIP_REGISTER message is immediately sent to the location server, which registers its current location (IP-address) into the database for future lookup requests by potential callers. This feature makes the application independent of the IP-address of the participating users' terminals. When user A moves from one mobile device to another, it registers its new contact address with the LS. When the CN sends an INVITE message to the LS, the latter notifies it of the user A's new contact address. The CN then sends an INVITE request to Node 2 directly and receives an acknowledgement. To achieve terminal mobility, our implementation exploits Mobile IP (Perkins et al., 1998). We implemented the SIP portion of our architecture at the user level and the mobile IP implementation works at the network layer in the kernel.

The disadvantages associated with the SIP-MIP architecture are as follows:

*   **Redundancy of information at the location server (LS) and the home agent (HA):** The mobile node's current address is stored (as duplicate information) at the LS and the HA.
*   **Tunneling delay:** Extra delay is added for voice traffic going towards the mobile node due to encapsulation and decapsulation of packets at the HA and the FA respectively and rerouting of packets through HA and FA.
*   **Separate mechanisms to handle personal and terminal mobility:** There is no integrated

Figure 2. Variation of application throughput with speed of the mobile host for (a) TCP over mobile IPv4, (b) UDP over mobile IPv4, (c) TCP over mobile IPv6, (d) UDP over mobile IPv6 with cell interleaving distances of 250, 500, 750, and 1000 meters

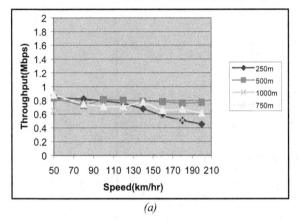

(a)

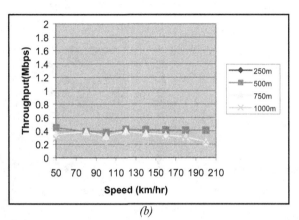

(b)

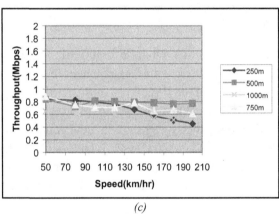

(c)

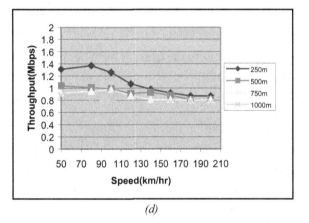

(d)

mechanism to handle ***both*** personal and terminal mobility. The SIP location server handles the personal mobility and mobile IP's HA handles terminal mobility separately.

The benefits of this approach include:

- **Handling TCP connections:** By having mobile IP as a separate mobility mechanism, TCP connections can be maintained as the user moves. This cannot be done with SIP alone (SIP supports only UDP).
- **Transparency in providing personal as well as terminal mobility:** Although these two types of mobility are provided by two different mechanisms, user transparency is still achieved.

PERFORMANCE EVALUATION OF MOBILITY PROTOCOLS

Mobile IPv4 vs. Mobile IPv6 Performance

We conducted several simulation experiments to evaluate the performance of mobile IPv4 and mobile IPv6 using the *ns-2* simulator (Fall & Varadhan, 2000). Sun Microsystems extended *ns* to support mobile IPv4. Motorola laboratories (in collaboration with the INRIA PLANETE Team) extended *ns* to simulate Mobile IPv6 for wide area networks--a the simulation tool is called MobiWan (NS2-Extension). We used IEEE 802.11 MAC layer operating at a rate of 2 Mbits/s at the physical layer. The mobile host and the base stations were configured using the standard mobile node features that the ns simulator provides.

In all tests, we measured the *Handoff delay* for mobile IPv4; this is the time from when the mobile node sends a registration request to the foreign agent to the time when the mobile node receives its first data packet from the corresponding node after moving to the foreign network. For Mobile IPv6, the handoff delay is the time from the time when the mobile node sends a binding update to the home agent till the time when the mobile node receives its first data packet; *Throughput:* the maximum data transfer rate perceived by an end-user application running on the mobile node; *packets loss:* the number of packets dropped.

For all simulation tests, the mobile host moves at a constant speed selected in the range 0 to 200 Km/hr. The motivation for choosing this speed range is to cover application scenarios that typically use these speeds in real life: automobiles, trains (average speed of: Amtrak trains 86 Km/hr (Genesee), French TGV trains 200 Km/hr (TGV), Acela Express 99 to 130 Km/hr (Amtrak), ships 46 to 55 Km/hr (Titanic), automobiles 72 to 92 Km/hr). We used a network topology consisting of four base stations in four cells. Each base station is located at 250, 500, 750, and 1000 meters away from the home agent. The packet size used in all tests was 1024 bytes and we used TCP and UDP transport protocols. For UDP tests, we used a constant bit rate traffic with an interval of 37.5 milliseconds between the packets which translates to a throughput of 218.45 Kbits/s. Tests were repeated for both mobile IPv4 and mobile IPv6. The mobile host moves from the home network towards a destination in a straight line traversing four cells configured such that each is 250 meters.

Handoff Delay

As Figure 1 illustrates, handoff delays with mobile IPv6 remains fairly constant compared to mobile IPv4. The handoff delay for mobile IPv6 is about 50% lower than that of mobile IPv4. This is primarily because when a handoff occurs in mobile IPv6, the mobile host sends a registration request to the home agent directly whereas with mobile IPv4, the mobile host first sends to the foreign agent that forwards it to the home agent. This introduces additional delay for mobile IPv4 leading to an overall increase in the handoff delay.

TCP and UDP Throughput

Figure 2 shows that in the case of UDP, we obtained fairly constant throughput over both mobile IPv4 and mobile IPv6 (especially at high speeds). However, we obtained a *three-fold* increase in UDP throughput over mobile IPv6 (Figure 2d) compared to mobile IPv4 (Figure 3d also shows lower packet loss for UDP over mobile IPv6 leading to higher throughput).

In the case of TCP protocol, we note from Figures 2a and 2c that TCP throughput for a distance of 250 meters is almost the same over both mobile IPv4 and mobile IPv6. This is mainly because at 250 meters the mobile host requires only one handoff thereby causing almost no packet loss (as shown in Figure 3). However, for other distances, (as with UDP) we obtained around *three times* higher throughput with mobile IPv6 compared to mobile IPv4. We also obtained minor TCP throughput degradations as speed increases.

TCP and UDP Packet Loss

Figure 3 shows that the packet loss for distances of 250 and 500 meters is almost 0% for both TCP and UDP over mobile IPv4 and mobile IPv6. However, for distances of 750 and 1000 meters, UDP packet loss increases significantly.

However, there is an increase in packet loss particularly for a cell interleaving distance of 1000 meters. In this case, from Figures 3a and 3b, we obtained 0% to 50% packet loss for TCP and 60 to 80% for UDP. From Figures 3c and 3d, we obtained 0 % to 30% packet loss for TCP, and 20% to 45% for UDP. We argue that the lower packet loss obtained with TCP is due to reliable transmissions, which lead to a higher number of packets that ultimately get delivered compared to UDP. Another observation from Figure 3 is that as the cell interleaving distance increases along with the speed of the mobile host, we note a fairly sharp increase in packet loss. The explanation for this result is that as the distance increases, there are more handoffs (in addition, continuous binding updates are sent by the mobile host) taking place to maintain connectivity.

Figure 3. Variation of packet loss with speed of the mobile host for (a) TCP over mobile IPv4, (b) UDP over mobile IPv4, (c) TCP over mobile IPv6, (d) UDP over mobile IPv6 with cell interleaving distances of 250, 500, 750, and 1000 meters, (e) handoff delay for SIP and SIP-MIP for various VoIP packet sizes

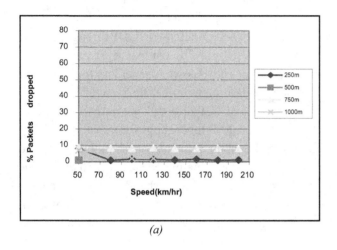

(a)

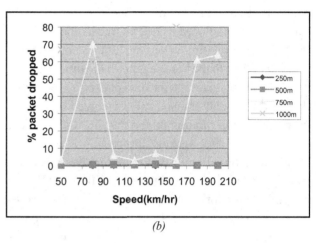

(b)

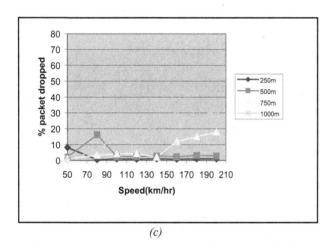

(c)

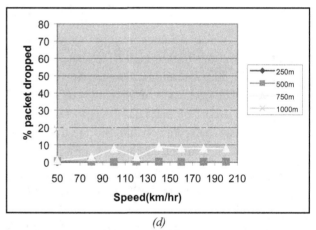

(d)

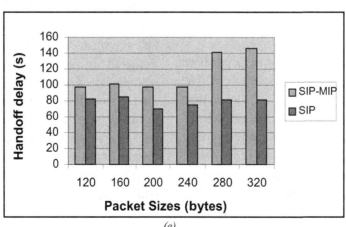

(e)

Table 1. Packet loss for SIP and SIP-MIP

VoIP packet size used = 320 bytes	SIP	SIP-MIP
Total number of packets transmitted	15000	15000
Total number of packets received	10627	8702
Number of packets lost	4373	6298
Percentage of packet loss (%)	29.15	41.09

It is also worthwhile noting that at 1000 meters, UDP incurs 20% to 45% with mobile IPv6 compared to 60% to 80% packet loss over mobile IPv4. With TCP, we obtained 0% to 30% packet loss for mobile IPv6 and 0% to 50% for mobile IPv4. The ability to perform more efficient handoff with mobile IPv6 explains the lower packet loss with mobile IPv6.

PERFORMANCE EVALAUTION OF SIP AND SIP-MIP ARCHITECTURES

Our experimental testbed running the prototype architectures implemented consists of a mobile node (laptop) equipped with an 11 Mbits/s wireless interface card, and several workstations, each acting as a home agent (HA), a foreign agent (FA), and a correspondent node (CN), all of which are connected to an unloaded Ethernet local area network running at 100 Mbits/s. All nodes run Redhat Linux 9.0 and we use the mobile IPv4 implementation from Helsinki University of Technology (HUT)—Dynamics version 0.8.1 (Dynamics HUT) software in our implementation. We conducted our performance evaluation tests on the two implemented design architectures (i.e., SIP and mobile IP and the other SIP only) using a SIP-based VoIP application (which we also developed and capable of delivering linear-PCM encoded voice) and the following performance metrics:

- **Handoff delay:** The time from which MN loses connectivity from its home network and until it receives the first packet from the CH after moving to the foreign network
- **Packet loss:** The number of packets dropped

- **Inter-arrival delay (D_i):** The time delay between the arrival of two consecutive voice packets at the receiver (MN)
- **Jitter (J_i):** The variation in the inter-arrival delay. $J_i = D_{average} - D_i$

Handoff Delay

Figure 3e shows the hand-off delay obtained for the two design approaches (SIP, and SIP_MIP). The hand-off delay results for the pure SIP-based architecture reveal lower delays as compared to the first approach (operating SIP over mobile IP). This is because in the SIP-MIP case, when handoff occurs, the mobile node has to send the registration request to the HA via the FA and also receive a registration reply from the HA. This registration process introduces a larger delay. In the SIP case however, the MN directly sends a registration request to the LS and upon receiving a reply from the LS, MN for the pure SIP-based approach.

Packet Loss

Table 1 shows the packet loss occurrence for the two approaches. We observe that the SIP-MIP implementation yields 41% higher packet loss than with SIP. The higher packet loss is due to the larger handoff delay that occurs with SIP-MIP. In fact, in the case of a VoIP packet size of 320 bytes, we obtained an 81% higher handoff delay with SIP-MIP compared to SIP.

Jitter

We also measured the mean jitter of incoming voice packets at the mobile node as it moves from the home network to the foreign network.

Figure 4. (a) Mean jitter for SIP and SIP-MIP. (b) Percentile distribution (using a packet size of 320 bytes) for jitter: SIP and SIP-MIP. (c) Mean Inter-arrival delay for SIP and SIP-MIP. (d) Percentile distribution (using a packet size of 320 bytes) for Inter-arrival delay: SIP and SIP-MIP

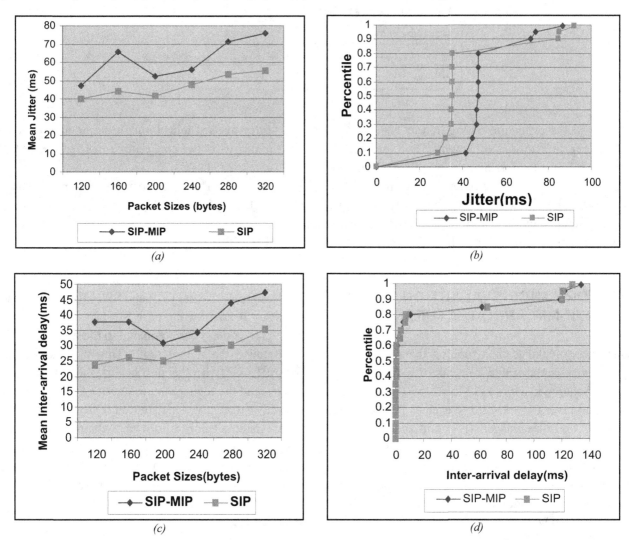

As the results in Figure 4a show, we obtained higher jitter also with the SIP-MIP architecture compared to the SIP design (15% to 44% lower).

The high jitter (greater than 50 milliseconds) associated with the SIP-MIP design also leads to poor voice quality hardly usable in real VoIP applications. Experiencing a voice jitter greater than 50 milliseconds is also considered unacceptable voice quality by authors in Collins (2000). Another interesting observation from figure 4b is that the 80th percentile also reveals lower jitter performance for SIP compared to the SIP-MIP approach. In the case of SIP, we obtained, for the 80th percentile, jitter values within around 36 milliseconds compared to SIP-MIP where the jitter values obtained were within a range of 48 milliseconds, an improvement of about 33% of SIP over SIP-MIP.

Inter-Arrival Delay

We obtained similar trends also in the inter-arrival of voice packets. In this case, SIP yields 17% to 54% lower (from Figure 4c), mean inter-arrival delay compared to SIP-MIP.

However, the percentile distributions shown in Figure 4d did not really show much difference in the inter-arrival delay range. It is also worthwhile pointing out that for both jitter and inter-arrival delay, the smallest packet size (120 bytes) yields the lowest values (i.e., best performance) for the VoIP application used.

The previous results demonstrate that the SIP-based approach performs better when handling both personal and terminal mobility compared to the SIP-MIP design that combines SIP with mobile IP but leaving each protocol to handle personal and terminal mobility respectively. However, one serious drawback of the pure SIP-based approach is that SIP only supports UDP (making it unsuitable for applications that require reliability). We argue that for real-time applications such as video conferencing or IP telephony, and others (many of which use UDP) the pure SIP-based approach shows promise and *outperforms* the SIP-MIP approach in providing seamless, transparent personal and terminal mobility. We demonstrated this fact empirically with our VoIP application.

CONCLUSION

In this work, we presented performance evaluations of mobility protocols such as mobile IPv4 and mobile IPv6. Our performance tests exploited performance metrics such as handoff delay, packet loss, throughput, and jitter. In addition, we also proposed hybrid design architectures that combine features of different mobility protocols such as SIP and mobile IP to enable seamless terminal and user mobility. The design and deployment of efficient mobility protocols have become increasingly important with the rapid proliferation of ubiquitous computing applications.

ACKNOWLEDGMENT

We thank the anonymous reviewers for their comments and suggestions. We express our gratitude to the editor-in-chief, Mario Freire, for his encouragements and support during the preparation of this chapter.

REFERENCES

Amtrak. Amtrak, http://www.amtrak.com/trains/ace-laexpress.html

Collins, D. (2000). *Carrier grade voice over IP.* Mc-Graw-Hill.

Dynamics HUT. Helsinki University of Technology, Dynamics- HUT Mobile IP, http://www.cs.hut.fi/Research/Dynamics/

Eddy, W. (2004). At what layer does mobility belong. *IEEE Communications Magazine, 42*(10), 155-159.

Fall, K., Varadhan, K. (2000). *NS notes and documentation.* The VINT project, LBL, California. Retrieved from http://www.isi.edu/nsnam/ns/

Genesee. Genesee Transportation Council, http://www.gtcmpo.org

Handley. M., Schulzrinne, H., Schooler, E., Rosenberg, J. (1999). SIP: Session Initiation Protocol, IETF RFC 2543.

NS2-Extension. INRIA, MobiWan: NS-2 extensions to study mobility in Wide-Area IPv6 Networks, http://www.inriaples.fr/planete/mobiwan

Perkins, C. and Johnson, D. (1998) Mobility Support in IPv6, Internet draft, draft-ietf-mobileip-ipv6-07.txt.

Perkins, C. (1998). Mobile networking through Mobile IP. *IEEE Internet Computing, 2*(1), 58-69.

Rosenberg, J., Schulzrinne, H., Camarillo, G., Johnston, A., Peterson, J., Sparks, R., Handley, M., & Schooler, E. (2002). RFC 3261 – *Session Initiation Protocol.* IETF Networking Group.

Stewart, R., Morneault, K., Schwarzbauer, H., Taylor, T., Rytina, I., Kalla, M., Zhang, L., Paxson, V. (2000). RFC 2960—Stream Control Transmission Protocol. IETF, Network Working Group.

TGV. TGV Facts, http://trains4u.info

Titanic. The Tiny Titatnic, http://www.rpsoft2000.com/shipsize.htm

Wanjuin, L. (1999). Mobile Internet telephony protocol: An application layer protocol for mobile Internet telephony services. In *Proceedings of IEEE International Conference on Communications* (Vol. 1, pp. 339-343).

Wedlund, E., Schulzrinne, H. (1999). Mobility support using SIP. In *Proceedings of 2ⁿᵈ ACM/IEEE International Conference on Wireless and Mobile Multimedia (WoWMoM'99)* (pp. 76-82).

KEY TERMS

Delay: In a network, delay is an expression of how much time it takes for a packet of data to get from one point to another.

Handoff: Handoff is the transition for any user's signal transmission from one base station to a geographically adjacent base station as the user moves around.

Host: In Internet protocol specifications, the term "host" means any computer that has full two-way access to other computers on the Internet. A host has a specific "local or host number" that, together with the network number, forms its unique IP address.

Internet Protocol: The Internet protocol (IP) is the method or protocol by which data is sent from one computer to another on the Internet.

Jitter: Jitter is the variation in the time between packets arriving, caused by network congestion, timing drift, or route changes. A jitter buffer can be used to handle jitter.

Mobile IP: Mobile IP is an Internet engineering task force (IETF) standard communications protocol that is designed to allow mobile device users to move from one network to another while maintaining their permanent IP address.

Protocol: A protocol is the special set of rules that end points in a telecommunication connection use when they communicate.

TCP: TCP (transmission control protocol) is a set of rules (protocol) used along with the Internet Protocol (IP) to send data in the form of message units between computers over the Internet.

UDP: UDP (user datagram protocol) is a communications protocol that offers a limited amount of service when messages are exchanged between computers in a network that uses the Internet protocol (IP).

VoIP: VoIP (voice over IP) is an IP telephony term for a set of facilities used to manage the delivery of voice information over the Internet.

Positive–Feedback Preference Model of the Internet Topology

Shi Zhou
University College London, UK

INTRODUCTION

This chapter introduces a recently proposed Internet model, namely the positive-feedback preference (PFP) model (Zhou & Mondragón, 2004a). The model is a precise and complete Internet *topology generator*, which accurately reproduces the largest set of important characteristics of the Internet topology at the *autonomous systems* (AS) level.

BACKGROUND

It is vital to obtain a good description of the Internet topology at the AS-level because the delivery of data traffic through the global Internet depends on the complex interactions between ASs that exchange routing information using the border gateway protocol (BGP) (Quoitin et al., 2003). The Internet AS-level topology contains about 10,000 nodes (ASs) and 30,000 links (BGP peering relationships).

Recent measurements show that the Internet topology at the AS-level exhibits an extremely complex structure (Albert & Barabási, 2002; Pastor-Satorras & Vespignani, 2004). First, it is a scale-free network (Barabási & Albert, 1999) because the distribution of node degree, which is the number of links a node has, follows a power-law (Faloutsos et al., 1999). This means that the network has a few very well connected nodes, but the majority of nodes have only a few links. Second, it is also a small-world network (Watts, 1999), in which, on average, any two nodes are separated by a very small number of connections. Third, it shows a rich-club phenomenon (Zhou & Mondragón, 2004b), which describes the fact that the well connected nodes, "rich" nodes, are tightly interconnected with other rich nodes, forming a core group or club. And fourth, it is a "disassortative mixing" network (Newman, 2003), which features a negative correlation between node degree and the nearest-neighbors average degree (Vazquez,

et al., 2003). Other important topology characteristics of the Internet include short cycles (Bianconi et al., 2003) and betweenness centrality (Goh et al., 2003). Each of these topology properties is relevant to some aspect of the Internet engineering.

THE POSITIVE-FEEDBACK PREFERENCE MODEL

Internet research requires a realistic model to correctly generate Internet-like networks (Floyd & Kohler, 2003). A large number of Internet models have been proposed in recent years. As of this writing, one of the most successful Internet models is the Positive-Feedback Preference model (Zhou & Mondragón, 2004a).

Starting from a small random graph, the PFP model generates an Internet-like network by using the following two *evolution mechanisms*.

Mechanism One: Interactive Growth

The interactive growth is described as: (1) at each time step, with probability p, a new node is attached to an old node in the existing system, and at the same time, two new internal links are added, connecting the old node to two other old nodes (see Figure 1-a); and (2) with probability $1-p$, a new node is attached to two old nodes, and a new internal link is added connecting one of the two old nodes to another old node (see Figure 1b).

The interactive growth satisfies observations (Vázquez et al., 2002; Chen et al., 2002; Park et al., 2003) on the Internet historic data. First, the Internet evolution is largely due to two processes: the attachment of new nodes to the existing system and the addition of new internal links between old nodes. Second, the majority of new nodes appearing on the Internet are each attached to no more than two old nodes. The interactive growth emphasizes that new nodes and new internal

Figure 1. Interactive growth (a) with probability p and (b) with probability (1- p)

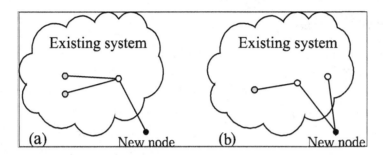

links should be added in an interactive way, that a new internal link starts from an old node to which a new node has just been attached. An intuitive explanation of this interaction is that on the Internet, new customers (new nodes) generate new traffic to service providers (old nodes). This triggers the service providers to construct new connections (new internal links) to other service providers in order to accommodate the increased traffic and improve services.

Mechanism Two: Positive-Feedback Preference

In interactive growth, new links are not attached to randomly selected old nodes. Instead, preference is to be given to old nodes that are already well connected. The probability that a new link is attached to old node i with degree k_i is given as:

$$\Pi(i) = \frac{k_i^{1+\delta \ln k_i}}{\sum_j k_j^{1+\delta \ln k_j}}$$

It is called the positive-feedback preference because a node's ability of acquiring new links increases as a feedback loop of the node's degree. The positive-feed-back preference satisfies the observation on the Internet evolution dynamics (Pastor-Satorras et al., 2001). For low-degree nodes, the positive-feedback preference can be approximated by the linear preference of:

$$\Pi(i) = \frac{k_i}{\Sigma_j k_j}$$

in which the preference probability is proportional to the node degree, i.e., "the rich get richer." For high-degree nodes, the positive-feedback preference grows faster and faster with node degree, and the consequence is that "the rich not only get richer, they get dispropor-tionately richer."

Evaluation results (Zhou & Mondragón, 2004a) have shown that within the two parameters $p = 0.4$ and $\delta = 0.021$, the PFP model accurately reproduces the largest set of important characteristics, including all topology properties mentioned above of the Internet AS-level topology, as collected by the Cooperative Association for Internet Data Analysis (CAIDA) (Mahadevan, et al., 2006).

FUTURE TRENDS

The PFP model is remarkable for its precision and completeness as an Internet topology generator. The generative model achieves this by using only two simple, realistic mechanisms that are designed to resemble the way the Internet evolves.

The PFP model has been used for more representa-tive simulations of the Internet, such as for designing next-generation network routing protocols (CAIDA, 2004). Also the model provides novel insights into the fundamental rules that underlie the evolution of the Internet topology and other complex networks in general.

The PFP model is a phenomenological model. The success of the model in approximating the real topol-ogy is yet to be fully explained. As of this writing, researchers are still searching for an analytical solution for the model.

CONCLUSION

The PFP model is a precise and complete Internet topology generator. The model can be used for more representative simulations of the Internet.

REFERENCES

Albert, R., & Barabási, A. L. (2002). Statistical mechanics of complex networks. *Reviews of Mordern Physics, 74*, 47-97.

Barabási, A. L., & Albert, R. (1999). Emergence of scaling in random networks. *Science, 286,* 509-512.

Bianconi, G., Caldarelli, G., & Capocci, A. (2003). Number of *h*-cycles in the Internet at the autonomous system level. *ArXiv:cond-mat/0310339.*

CAIDA. (2004). Toward mathematically rigourous next-generation routing protocols for realistic network topologies. National Science Foundation (USA) project no. 0434996. Retrived from http://www.caida.org/funding/nets-nr/

Chen, Q., Chang, H., Govindan, R., Jamin, S., Shenker, S. J., & Willinger, W. (2002). The origin of power laws in internet topologies (revisited). In *Proceedings of INFOCOM 2002* (pp. 608-617).

Faloutsos, M., Faloutsos, P., & Faloutsos, C. (1999). On power-law relationships of the Internet topology. *ACM SIGCOMM Computer Communications Reviews, 29*(4), 251-262.

Floyd, S., & Kohler, E. (2003). Internet research needs better models. *ACM SIGCOMM Computer Communications Reviews, 33*(1), 29-34.

Goh, K. I., Oh, E., Kahng, B., & Kim, D. (2003). Betweenness centrality correlation in social networks. *Physical Review E, 67*(017101), 1-4.

Mahadevan, P., Krioukov, D., Fomenkov, M., Huffaker, B., Dimitropoulos, X., Claffy, K., et al. (2006). The Internet AS-level topology: Three data sources and one definitive metric. *ACM SIGCOMM Computer Communications Reviews, 36*(1), 17-26.

Newman, M. E. J. (2003). Mixing patterns in networks. *Physical Review E, 67*(026126), 1-13.

Park, S. T., Khrabrov, A., Pennock, D. M., Lawrence, S., Giles, C. L., & Ungar, L. H. (2003). Static and dynamic analysis of the Internet's susceptibility to faults and attacks. In *Proceedings of IEEE INFOCOM 2003* (pp. 2144-2154).

Pastor-Satorras, R., Vázquez, A., & Vespignani, A. (2001). Dynamical and correlation properties of the Internet. *Physical Review Letter, 87*(258701), 1-4.

Pastor-Satorras, R., & Vespignani, A. (2004). *Evolution and structure of the Internet—A statistical physics approach.* Cambridge University Press.

Quoitin, B., Pelsser, C., & Swinnen, L. (2003). Interdomain traffic engineering with BGP. *IEEE Communications Magazine, 41*(5), 122-128.

Vázquez, A. Boguna, Y., Moreno, R. P.-S., & Vespignani, A. (2003). Topology and correlations in structured scale-free networks. *Physical Review E, 67*(046111), 1-10.

Vázquez, A., Pastor-Satorras, R., & Vespignani, A. (2002). Largescale topological and dynamical properties of Internet. *Physical Review E, 65*(066130), 1-12.

Watts, J. (1999). *Small worlds: The dynamics of networks between order and randomness.* New Jersey: Princeton University Press.

Zhou, S., & Mondragón, R. J. (2004a). Accurately modelling the Internet topology. *Physical Review E, 70*(066108), 1-8,

Zhou, S., & Mondragón, R. J. (2004b). The rich-club phenomenon in the Internet topology. *IEEE Communications Letters, 8*(3), 180-182.

KEY TERMS

Autonomous System: A collection of IP networks and routers under the control of one entity (or sometimes more) that presents a common routing policy to the Internet.

Betweenness Centrality: A measure of a node (or a link) within a graph. Nodes that occur on many of the shortest paths between other nodes have higher betweenness than those that do not.

BGP: Stands for Border Gateway Protocol, which is the core routing protocol of the Internet. It works by maintaining a table of IP networks or "prefixes" which designate network reachability between autonomous systems (AS).

CAIDA: Stands for the Cooperative Association for Internet Data Analysis, which is based at the San Diego Supercomputer Centre, USA. CAIDA is a world-leading organization for Internet measurement and research.

Degree: Is defined, in the graph theory, as the number of connections that a node has, or the number of direct neighbors of the node.

Positive-Feedback Preference Model: A precise and complete Internet topology generator proposed by Zhou and Mondragón in 2004.

Rich-Club Phenomenon: A topology property of some complex networks, which describes the fact that well-connected nodes, "rich" nodes, are tightly interconnected with other rich nodes, forming a core group or club.

Scale-Free Network: A network characterized by a power-law distribution of node degree, where the power-law exponent is invariant to the network size (scale).

Short Cycles: Include triangles and quadrangles, which encode the redundancy information in a network, because the multiplicity of paths between any two nodes increases with the density of short cycles.

Small-World Network: A network in which, on average, any two nodes are separated by a very small number of connections.

Topology: A connectivity graph representing a real network, upon which the network's physical and engineering properties are based.

Privacy in the Digital World

Stefanos Gritzalis
University of the Aegean, Greece

Costas Lambrinoudakis
University of the Aegean, Greece

INTRODUCTION

Recent years have witnessed a significant evolution in the way information and communication systems are utilized, transforming modern communities into modern information societies. Nowadays, personal data are available or/and can be collected at different sites around the world. Even though the utilization of personal information leads to several advantages, including improved customer services, increased revenues, and lower business costs, it can be misused in several ways and may lead to violation of privacy.

Several important legal, regulatory, and ethical issues have emerged, posing the need for urgent and consistent response by modern information societies. It is absolutely essential to raise the awareness of the citizens, provide guidance to online data protection, and apply privacy-related legislation in a coherent and coordinated way. Privacy as a critical, fundamental human right has to be protected in the digital era.

BACKGROUND

The widespread use of various Web-based applications and services has facilitated, as well as promoted, the transition from conventional to electronic transactions. In the framework of e-commerce, several organizations, in order to identify the preferences of their customers, adapt their products accordingly, and thus promote their sales via the Internet, develop new methods for collecting and processing personal data. This is often done during the initial stage (registration phase) of the connection of the client to the seller's Web site. For instance, credit cards leave a trail to the places their holders' visit, regarding where they shop and what they buy. Modern data mining techniques can then be utilized in order to further process the collected data, generating databases of the consumers'

profiles through which each person's preferences can be uniquely identified.

Another example is that of Web sites providing users with medical information and advice. Through the Internet, anyone can address a specific request to a medical Web site and obtain the information he or she wants, provided that they have registered. The organization maintaining the medical Web site can easily generate "user profiles" by monitoring how often a specific user is visiting the site, and furthermore the type of medical information they are interested in.

Therefore, such information can be utilized for invading user's privacy, and thus the 95/46 European Union Directive on the protection of individuals with regard to the processing of personal and sensitive data. Evidently, electronic transactions have raised the major problem of user's privacy protection. In order to avoid confusion, it is important to stress the difference between *privacy* and *security*; a piece of information is secure when its content is protected, whereas it is private when the identity of its owner is protected. It is true that, irrespective of the application domain (i.e., e-commerce, e-health, etc.), the major concern of Internet users is the lack of privacy rather than cost, difficulties in using the service, or undesirable marketing messages.

Considering that conventional security mechanisms, like encryption, cannot ensure privacy protection (encryption, for instance, can only protect the message's confidentiality), new privacy-enhancing technologies (PETs) have been developed. However, the sole use of technological countermeasures is not enough. For instance, even if a company that collects personal data stores it in an ultra-secure facility, the company may at any point in time decide to sell or otherwise disseminate the data, thus violating the privacy of the individuals involved. Therefore, security and privacy are intricately related (Ghosh, 2001). In an information society, privacy is adopted as a fundamental right of the individual and is related to issues like: the type of the information collected, how and for what purpose is this information used, and how is it protected, shared, rented, sold or otherwise disseminated (Data Protection Law, basic articles of the EU 95/46 Directive).

PRIVACY AND LAW

Privacy, as a social and legal issue, has for a long time been the concern of social scientists, philosophers, lawyers, and physicians. The United Nations Declaration of Human Rights, the International Covenant on Civil and Political Rights (Privacy International, 2002), and many other national and international treaties have recognized Privacy as a fundamental human right that must be protected in democratic societies. Two American lawyers, Samuel Warren and Louis Brandeis, defined Privacy as "the right to be alone" (Warren, 1890). In general, the concept of privacy can be applied in three different aspects (Rosenberg, 1992):

- **Territorial privacy:** The protection of the close physical area surrounding a person
- **Privacy of the person:** The protection of a person against undue interference
- **Informational privacy:** The control of whether and how personal data can be gathered, stored, processed, or selectively disseminated

Several researchers have tried to provide alternative definitions for privacy, expressing the above-mentioned "control" of an individual in terms of property, autonomy, and seclusion. Privacy may be understood as property in the sense that a person may give away part of the control over her/his personal information in exchange for some benefit. Furthermore, it may be perceived as autonomy in the sense that each person is free to partially or fully authorize a third party to obtain, process, distribute, share, and use her/his personal information for a specific aim. Finally, privacy may be understood as seclusion in the sense that everyone has the right to remain undisturbed. This article deals with informational privacy and assumes that privacy is the indefeasible right of an individual to control the ways in which personal information is obtained, processed, distributed, shared, and used by any other entity.

As rapid computerization brought fear of a surveillance society, some nations sought to protect, through the appropriate Data Protection Laws, individuals from the misuse of personal data. In the European Union, the Directive 95/46, "On the protection of individuals with regard to the processing of personal data and on the free movement of such data," sets the prerequisites for data owners and processors for collecting, processing, and exchanging personal information. The US government promotes the notion of "self regulation," a set of data protection rules applying to a plurality of market sectors, the content of which has been primarily determined by members of the specific trade sector. Furthermore, telecommunication services, as stipulated in the 97/66 and 2002/58 Directives, are protected by the provisions for the secrecy of telecommunications. Public authorities may be allowed to access secret information, thus compromising this secrecy, only for specific reasons and under specific conditions and procedures provided by the domestic country's legal framework.

IDENTIFYING PRIVACY THREATS AND REQUIREMENTS

Before attempting to identify the potential threats (attacks) to user privacy, it is important to identify the general categories of the actors involved in the electronic transactions realised during various e-commerce applications or/and provision of e-health services. These are:

- **User:** The person utilizing an Internet service
- **Internet service provider (ISP):** The entity providing the infrastructure for facilitating access to the Internet services
- **Telecommunications provider:** The entity providing the physical communication channels
- **End service provider (ESP):** The entity providing the service

Privacy over the Internet is facing many threats in the form of various alternative tactics that have been employed for collecting personal data. The most indicative known threats are the following:

- The user supplies, with his or her consent, personal data during registration to an electronic service
- Personal data are collected without the user's consent, through the appropriate processing of "cookies" left by the user in several Internet sites

With this technique, it is feasible to simulate the "electronic behavior" of the user (i.e., preferences).

- User data are collected by ISPs. Such data may include the Web pages the user visits, the exact time and duration of their navigation, etc.

- Unauthorized persons gain access to the central repositories of the ESP where personal or, in the case of medical services, sensitive client data are stored.

- During an electronic transaction, irrespective of the application domain, users face the man-in-the-middle risk. That means that somebody may act as an eavesdropper and monitor/record all the traffic exchanged through the communication channel.

- The identity of the user can be revealed through a trace-back attack, where someone traces the path back to the initiator along the forward or the reverse path.

- Linking specific communication channels/sequences/sessions with certain client-server pairs can be achieved by tracing the contents and/or the size of a message travelling over a communication link or by attempting to detect and analyse periodically transmitted packets, aiming to discover their source through specific time correlations.

In all the above cases it is evident that if the provisions of the applicable data protection law are not taken into account, the collection and processing of personal information may lead to violations of user's privacy and personal life. It is therefore necessary to identify specific privacy requirements which, when satisfied, can ensure that the possibility of the aforementioned threats occurring and the violation of the user's privacy is minimised. The main privacy requirements that have been identified are: Anonymity, Pseudonymity, Unlikability, and Unobservability.

PRIVACY ENHANCING TECHNOLOGIES AND GUIDELINES

In order to satisfy the aforementioned privacy requirements, new security mechanisms, tools, protocols, and services have emerged (Ghosh, 2001) supporting Internet users to safeguard their rights of anonymity and secrecy. These technologies are known as PET.

An overview of existing PETs is provided in the following section.

In addition to the technological countermeasures, most of the time it is necessary to apply a set of organisational or/and procedural measures that each "*actor category*" should employ for protecting privacy in accordance with existing legislation. These measures are presented in the form of Privacy Enhancing Guidelines for the Users, ISPs, telecommunication providers, and ESPs.

Web Privacy and Anonymity-Enhancing Technologies

Anonymizer: Several tools have been designed for assisting Internet users to maintain their anonymity. The main objective of these tools is to ensure that requests to Web sites cannot be linked to specific IP addresses, thus revealing the identity of the requestor. "Anonymizer" is a typical example of a Web Anonymity tool (Cranor, 1999).

LPWA: The Lucent Personalized Web Assistant (LPWA) (Bleichenbacher, 1998; Gabber, 1999) is a software system designed to support users in browsing the Web in a personalized, private, secure way using LPWA-generated aliases and other related LPWA features. LPWA not only generates secure, consistent, and pseudonymous aliases for Web users, but also offers certain services such as e-mail support and anti-spamming filters.

TRUSTe: A self-regulatory privacy initiative. Its main target is to raise the level of consumer's trust and confidence in the Internet (Benassi, 1999).

P3P: The World-Wide-Web Consortium (W3C) Platform for Privacy Preferences Project (P3P) (W3C, 2003) provides a framework for informed online interactions. The goal of P3P (W3C, 2000) is to enable users to exercise preferences over Web site privacy practices.

Onion Routing (Reed, 1998) can support private communications over public networks. This is achieved through application independent, near real-time and bi-directional anonymous connections that are resistant to both eavesdropping and traffic analysis attacks.

TOR: TOR (Dingledine, 2004) is a circuit-based low-latency anonymous communication service. TOR's architecture is based on the Onion Routing architecture with an improved way of working: It addresses limitations in the original design by adding perfect forward secrecy, congestion control, directory servers, integrity checking, configurable exit policies, and a practical design for location-hidden services. TOR provides a reasonable trade-off between anonymity, usability, and efficiency.

Crowds: (Reiter, 1998) Enables information retrieval over the Web without revealing personal information to a malicious third entity—user or computer system. The design aim of Crowds is to make browsing anonymous. In this way it will be possible to hide information about the user, the Internet sites that he or she visits, and the content that is retrieved from other entities, including Web servers.

Hordes: The Hordes protocol (Shields, 2000) engages multiple proxies for routing in an anonymous way, onepacket to a responder, while it uses anonymous multicast services for routingin reply to the initiator.

Freedom: (Boucher, 2000) has been designed to protect the privacy of users being involved in tasks like sending an e-mail, browsing the Web, posting a message to a news-group, and participating in an Internet chat session.

GAP: GNUnet's Anonymity Protocol GAP (Bennett, 2003) is a protocol claiming to achieve anonymous data transfers. It is important to stress that GAP engages a new perspective on anonymity. Specifically, it is possible for an individual to ignore some of the traditional anonymity requirements and thus allow network nodes to balance anonymity with system efficiency.

Guidelines for Users

It is important that "Users" are informed about PETs and that they focus on issues like:

- **Use of secure technology:** Capitalize on all available means for protecting their personal data and the communication channels they use.
- **Moderate disclosure of personal data:** Be cautious about the information that they disseminate while they navigate through various Web sites during an electronic connection and when using Internet generally.

- **Seeking anonymity:** Evaluate all available mechanisms/procedures that guarantee anonymity to the extent dictated by the applicable law. The best way to safeguard privacy is the employment of anonymous access and settlement of payments.
- **Use of a pseudonym:** The use of nicknames is an extremely effective countermeasure. In cases where full anonymity is legally impossible, the correlation between the nickname and the real person must be disclosed only to trusted entities.
- **Limited purpose disclosure of data:** Reveal only data that are necessary for the attainment of the purposes pursued through the particular communication or transaction.
- **Cautious use of e-mail lists:** The e-mail address constitutes personal information and is protected as all other personal data. Therefore, one should avoid participating in e-mail address lists that do not notify the purpose of collection, the processing duration, the potential recipients of the data, or do not explicitly provide an unsubscribe process.
- **Cautious downloading:** Particular attention should be paid while downloading files/applications through the Internet, as personal data may be processed and transferred to Internet sites unknown to the user.
- **Avoid installation of cookies:** Cookies are files sent to the user's machine by Web sites. They are used for storing personal data, information concerning navigation attributes, the duration of the visit to the specific site, etc. The cookie installation must be disabled through the security adjustments of the Web browser.
- **Be aware of applicable legislation:** Users should be aware of the latest legislation guidelines related to the protection of personal data processing and communication.

Guidelines for Internet Service Providers and Telecommunication Providers

Internet Service Providers (ISPs) and Telecommunication Providers should:

- Use software and hardware of certified quality, capable of ensuring the security of the information transferred.
- Perform a risk analysis study in order to identify all possible threats to the information system; decide

and implement the appropriate security measures and develop a specific security policy.

- Develop an ethics code on the protection of personal data that will be based on the provisions of the 95/46 and 97/66 Directives, and which shall be communicated to the management and all staff.
- Inform users about their rights, as far as the protection of personal life is concerned, and facilitate their access to information security resources. For instance, ISPs should inform users about their right to object to the collection of personal and/or sensitive data affecting them.
- Publicize, through the home page, the privacy policies adopted, pursuant to 95/46 Directive and applicable domestic law.
- Collect the data of the subscribers in a transparent manner. This, in practice, implies that the use of cookies and of technologies of active content should be avoided. The recommended method is the use of electronic application forms. The collected data should be only those that are necessary for the conclusion of the contract between the subscriber and the ISP.
- Provide all appropriate security measures for the protection of personal data required for the conclusion of the contract, when such data are submitted electronically. A suitable technology would be that of digital certificates in conjunction with the use of the SSL protocol.
- Encourage and provide the appropriate technological means for the attainment of anonymous communications. In cases in which full anonymity is legally impossible, the ISP should maintain a file of nicknames.
- Avoid monitoring and recording the communications of users unless this is necessary for pricing purposes. For example, the IP addresses of users in conjunction with usernames communicating with the ISP should not be recorded.
- In cases where recording is necessary for the provision of specific user services, i.e., use of proxies, the inherent risks must be communicated to the users. The use of such services must be allowed only after obtaining the user's explicit consent.
- Control the banners hosted in regard to the personal information that can be intercepted in case the user selects the banner.

Guidelines for End Service Providers

Most of the guidelines for ISPs and telecommunication providers are also applicable to the end service providers. In addition, ESPs should consider the following:

- During the pre-contract stage, the agreement of the user should be secured concerning the transaction due to take place. Furthermore, the online agreement should be clear, understandable by the user, and not lengthy. The user should have the option to download the agreement, read it and then submit it to the ESP in order for the transaction to take place.
- There must be an explicit consent of the user for his/her subscription to e-mail address lists maintained by the ESP and viewing the promotion of its products using the e-mail, or to e-mail address lists maintained by work associates of the ESP or by other traders with the ESP.
- There should be a clear and easy-to-use procedure of opting-out from an e-mail address list for users. Such a procedure should always be available.

FUTURE TRENDS

The rising interest in digital privacy and PETs has driven the production of theoretical, practical, and experimental results, including new architectures and protocols, emerging issues in interdisciplinary areas, case studies and applications, and trend-setting ideas. Based on the existing results and the on-going research work in the area, it is expected that the main stream of future research work will address the following areas: business models with privacy requirements, privacy policies, privacy and medical informatics, privacy economics, privacy and cyber security, computer forensics privacy, and anonymity.

CONCLUSION

In modern digital societies, privacy remains an important value to the human psyche. The protection of personal data within the framework of e-commerce or/and e-health constitutes a crucial factor in the successful attainment of the purposes of the information society. Privacy can be protected through the employment of technical, organizational, and procedural measures that aim to satisfy specific privacy requirements. In fact, each of the actors involved in an electronic transaction—namely the user, the ISP, the telecommunication provider, and the ESP—should adopt specific countermeasures. Within the framework of the continuing development of e-commerce, all actors ought to be constantly informed on technical and legal matters concerning privacy protection. In that way, businesses will provide an impetus to the development of e-transactions, which will respect the citizen in the digital era.

REFERENCES

Benassi, P. (1999). TRUSTe: An online privacy seal program. *Communications of the ACM, 42*(2), 56-59.

Bennett, K., & Grothoff, C. (2003). GAP–Practical anonymous networking. In *Proceedings of the Workshop on PET2003 Privacy Enhancing Technologies*, 1-20. Also available at http://citeseer.nj.nec.com/bennett02gap.html

Bleichenbacher, D., Gabber, E., Gibbons, P.B., Matias, Y., & Mayer, A. (1998). On secure and pseudonymous client relationships with multiple servers. In *Proceedings of the 3rd USENIX Electronic Commerce Workshop* (pp. 99-108).

Boucher, P., Shostack, A., & Goldberg, I. (2000). *Freedom system 2.0 architecture.* Zero-Knowledge Systems Inc.

Cranor, L. (1999). Internet privacy. *Communications of the ACM, 42*(2), 29-31.

Dingledine, R., Mathewson, N., & Syverson, P. (2004). Tor: The second-generator nion router. In *Proceedings of the 13th USENIX Security Symposium,* San Diego, (pp. 303-320).

Gabber, E., Gibbons, P.B., Kristol, D., Matias, Y., & Mayer, A. (1999). Consistent, yet anonymous Web access with LPWA. *Communications of the ACM, 42*(2), 42-47.

Ghosh, A.K. (2001). *Security and privacy for e-business.* John Wiley & Sons.

Privacy International. (2002). *Privacy and human rights– An international survey of privacy laws and developments.* Available at http://www.privacy.org/pi/survey

Reed, M., Syverson, P., & Goldschlag, D. (1998). Anonymous connections and onion routing. *IEEE Journal on Selected Areas in Communications, 16*(4), 482-494.

Reiter, M., & Rubin, A. (1998). Crowds: Anonymity for Web transactions. *ACM Transactions on Information and System Security, 1*(1), 66-92.

Rosenberg, R. (1992). *The social impact of computers.* Academic Press.

Shields, C., & Levine, B. N. (2000). A protocol for anonymous communication over the Internet. In P. Samarati & S. Jajodia (Eds.), *Proceedings of the 7th ACM Conference on Computer and Communications Security* (pp. 33-42). New York:ACM Press.

W3C, World-Wide-Web Consortium. (2000). The platform for privacy preferences 1.0 specification, W3C candidate recommendation 15.

W3C, World-Wide-Web Consortium. (2003). Platform for privacy preferences project—P3P. Available at www.w3.org/P3P

Warren, S., & Brandeis, L. (1890). The rights to privacy. *Harvard Law Review*, 5, 193-220.

KEY TERMS

Anonymity: Anonymity is the state of being not identifiable within a set of subjects (users), known as the anonymity set. To enable anonymity of a subject (user), there always has to be an appropriate set of subjects with potentially the same attributes.

Data Security: The protection of data from disclosure, alteration, destruction, or loss that either is accidental or intentional but unauthorized.

Digital Identity: Any subset of attributes of an individual which are accessible by technical means and identify this individual within any set of individuals. Usually there is no such thing as "a digital identity," but several of them.

P

Privacy: The right of individuals to control or influence what information related to them may be collected and stored, by whom, and to whom that information may be disclosed.

Pseudonymity: Being pseudonymous is the state of using a pseudonym as identification. Therefore, a user can be identified through their pseudonym but remains anonymous as far as their real identity is concerned. Clearly, it is assumed that each pseudonym refers to exactly one holder, invariant over time, being not transferred to other users.

Unlikability: Ensures that a user may make multiple uses of resources or services without others being able to link these uses together. It requires that users are unable to determine whether the same user caused certain specific operations in the system.

Unobesrvability: Ensures that a user may use a resource or service without others, especially third parties, being able to observe that the resource or service is being used. It requires that users cannot determine whether an operation is being performed.

Quality of Service and Service Level Agreements

Christos Bouras
Research Academic Computer Technology Institute and University of Patras, Greece

Apostolos Gkamas
Research Academic Computer Technology Institute and University of Patras, Greece

Dimitris Primpas
Research Academic Computer Technology Institute and University of Patras, Greece

Kostas Stamos
Research Academic Computer Technology Institute and University of Patras, Greece

INTRODUCTION

In order for advanced applications in modern computer networks to function satisfactorily, there is often the need for a guaranteed network performance and guaranteed values for several network parameters. When the provisioning and usage of network services is agreed, relevant specifications for the level of the services are also defined.

The definition of suitable specification for the offered services is very important when these services are provided by external parties. Taking Internet connectivity as an example of a provided service, it is very important that the specifications define the minimum guaranteed capacity of the connection (which affects the speed of the network), the availability of the connection, and other parameters that affect the response time of network applications, so that users do not have to face constant and annoying problems. By specifying the required level of service, the client of the service specifies the required results, but does not specify the way the provider is going to implement the service. A client who tries to specify the way that the provider is going to implement the service cancels the advantage of the provider's specialized technical knowledge.

The specifications guarantee the responsibility on the part of the provider and define the fee for the provided service.

In cases where the buyer assigns the operation of some activities to an external provider (outsourcing), the only way to guarantee a satisfying level of service quality for the buyer is to define the required level of service and then constantly measure the performance of the provider (with regard to the service) in order to decide whether the service is adequately provided and to guarantee that the buyer receives the level of service that is being paid for.

Specifications also affect the cost of the service. Clients who desire very high quality levels create greater resource requirements for the provider and therefore increase the cost of the service. Therefore, proper definition of specifications is vital.

BACKGROUND

The scope of service level agreements is wider than the provisioning of network related services by external providers to clients. It can generally be applied to any service provided by an external party. The term has nevertheless gained acceptance in the Information Technology (IT) field because of the nature of the provided services (Bouras et al., 2002, 2004; Heinanen et al., 1999; Jacobson et al., 1999; Xiao et al., 1999). More specifically, the complexity of the provided services, the difficulty in finding acceptable measurement procedures, and the novel nature of many networking services can easily lead to misunderstandings and disagreements between the parties (Czajkowski, 2002). Therefore, the need for a clear, precise, and unambiguous document detailing such issues has naturally arisen. The following paragraphs of this article briefly explain how this purpose can be reached.

SLA CREATION

A service level agreement (SLA) is a legal document that is included or attached to a more general contract for an agreement of outsourcing activities to an external party. An SLA includes a description of the provided services and determines the specifications for the performance level and the results that the user of the service expects to receive from the provider (Salsano et al., 2000; Singh et al., 2002). The provider has to achieve or exceed these levels of performance.

Although SLAs can be defined for a wide range of services, they are extensively used in the area of network services provisioning.

SLAs can be categorized according to their objective as:

- Technical support
- Networking
- Applications
- Systems infrastructure
- Development environment
- Content
- Process support
- Process execution

The first three categories are the most common ones. A proper SLA has to deal with the following issues:

- What the provider promises
- How the provider will fulfill his or her promises
- Who and how is going to measure the performance
- What happens when the provider fails to reach the promised performance
- How the SLA is modified over time (if that is possible and acceptable)
- What exactly is the service that will be provided
- What is the level of service that the provider expects to reach
- What are the responsibilities of both parties
- How the quality of the service will be measured

- How will the achieved performance be reported
- What corrective measures the provider will take if the desired level of service is not achieved
- What is going to be paid for the service
- What financial compensations are going to be given if the desired levels of service are not reached

The above issues have to be dealt with and agreed upon, so that the SLA can contain the following:

- **Definition of the service:** A description of the service with exact definition of its extent and type.
- **Definition of terms related to the service:** Definition of the terms used in order to avoid misconceptions, especially if these terms are not clearly defined and generally accepted.
- **Specifications of the service and level of quality of the service:** Detailed specification of the service that will allow the verification of the level achieved, and also descriptions related to the service, such as availability and response time.
- **Method that will be used to measure the service, tools to be used, and values calculation:** Description of the way measurements are going to be made, the installations used, the calculation method for statistical quantities, and the method of results interpretation.
- **Compensations and other penalties:** The types and weights of penalties for failure to achieve the desired level of service, and possibly other more direct measures when the level is very low or failures very common.
- **Responsibilities, exceptions, and limits in accountability:** Responsibilities of the parties and exceptions for specific cases, and also compensations that may be paid.
- **Reports and types of documents:** Structure and format of all standardized documents that will be used for the documentation and management of the service.
- **Communication procedures and issue resolving:** Description of all communication procedures between the parties and definition of their relationships. Conflict resolution methods should also be described.
- **Prices and cost:** The cost may be provided as a whole or in parts, or a combination of the two (Wang et al., 2001).

419

The above issues will be organized in a document that will constitute the SLA.

Preparation of an SLA

Description of the Service

Before an organization defines the requirements for the level of service that will be required and who will be the provider, it first has to decide and make clear what the desired results would be, and also the general goal (such as cost reduction, performance increase, flexibility increase, and more choices for the users). The reason is that the metrics that will be defined vary depending on the desired goal. Furthermore, the organization has to clearly define the scope and the limits of the service, which means that the organization has to define not only what will be included in the SLA, but also what will not be.

Each of the above decisions influences the specifications that will be set and therefore the cost of the service. The description of the service will have to focus on what the organization expects to receive from the provider and not how the service will be implemented. The provider is the party that in using its specialized knowledge will implement the service in the most appropriate way. Interference by the organization might lead to non-optimal implementation and might increase the cost.

As an example, if the service is to interconnect two points, the organization has to define, depending on its needs, parameters such as the link capacity, the maximum number of errors, and the round trip time. The organization is not responsible for defining how the interconnection will be achieved, such as whether it will be wireless or wired, whether there will be intermediate nodes, what low level protocols are going to be used, etc.

Nevertheless, the implementation affects the maximum level of service that can be achieved (for example, in order to achieve very high availability, it is necessary to have excess equipment). The organization is therefore justified during the evaluation of offers to require implementation details during the query phase and to examine whether the offered implementation can support the required level of service. It should not, however, generally impose a specific implementation of the service.

Metrics

After the desired service has been described, the parties have to specify what is going to be measured for the duration of the service. The most basic characteristics of the service are determined based on the requirements of the organization. If, for example, the goal is to carry out some procedures quickly and properly, it is wise to study parameters such as speed and quality of the result. A common phenomenon is that the service is provided according to the specification but the users are not satisfied. This means that the parameters measured are not representative of what is acceptable and what is important. A solution to this problem is to define more than one (at least three) parameters for each part of the service and therefore to measure more **metrics**. Even if one of the metrics has not been chosen successfully, the rest of the metrics are likely to capture the "quality" perceived by the users.

The accuracy of the measurements also has to be determined, because too much accuracy is often undesirable because of its cost or complexity. Sometimes a parameter cannot be measured in all cases (or it is not desirable to do so). In such cases there can be a sample measurement and the metrics defined for the service can be obtained from these samples.

Boundaries for the Metrics

After the metrics have been defined, appropriate boundaries for these metrics have to be specified. This can be achieved by studying relevant data in the literature or measuring comparable data from the current situation (the service is provided internally by the organization). These values are then compared to the levels offered by the market, and it is judged whether improvement is necessary, and in what degree. If some of the metrics are statistical in nature, the time period over which the measurement is made has to be taken into account. In order to avoid situations where the service is provided according to the statistical requirements, but in specific cases the service is out of bounds, there have to be additional (more flexible) boundaries for short periods.

There are two kinds of boundaries set for the metrics of the service:

- A level below which the service is no longer considered acceptable; such a violation leads to measures such as compensation of the organization and obligation of the provider to improve the service.

- A level that the service should never fall below, and in which case it is violated, leads to the assumption that the provider is no longer capable of acceptably providing the service and may bring about drastic measures such as termination of the contract or revision of the financial agreement.

Therefore, the boundaries defined should be close to what is acceptable and what is not, and should be realistic. Unnecessarily strict boundaries are costly and can often cause violations that might incur unnecessary burden to both the provider and the organization.

Compensations

It is improbable that a service will always be offered at the specified levels of quality, and therefore cases of violation should be expected. The SLA should provision compensations both because the organization did not receive the proper service (and therefore should not be charged for it) and because the provider should be punished for breaching the SLA. Compensations should be reasonable, because unreasonably high compensations lead to reduced interest by the provider market, while unreasonably low compensations give little motive for the provider to make available the proper levels of service.

Usually, compensations are defined as a percentage of the provider's fee. Continuous or multiple violations of the SLA are undesirable, even if compensated. In order to avoid such violations, the SLA can set limits on the number or duration of violations and provision drastic measures (such as contract termination) if these limits are exceeded.

Measurements

The next step is to determine how the metrics are going to be measured, who is going to perform the measurements, and how they are going to be reported. This is an issue of how the measurements are going to take place, and how the parties are going to agree on the measured quantities. The main problem is that by assigning the service to the provider, the organization often does not have the necessary technical knowledge in order to set up a measurement system. Furthermore, the measurement system should be recognized by the

provider and the measurements have to be accepted as realistic.

In order to deal with such complexities, it is possible that:

- The organization preserves part of the technical knowledge necessary for the implementation and maintenance of a measurement system.
- The measurement system is implemented and used by both the organization and the provider.
- The organization and the provider maintain independent measurement systems, in order to verify each other's credibility. However, this approach introduces the issue of resolving conflicting measurements.
- Measurements are performed by a third party that is credible with both parties. The system is automated and produces results without interference.
- Measurements are performed by the provider, who is, however, supervised by an independent auditor, authorized by the organization.

Regardless of the measurement method chosen and the source of the data, the party responsible for collecting them and the party processing them have to be decided upon and thoroughly described. These data will be used for generating reports containing the measurements of the metrics, violations of the SLA (if any), consequences, measures for avoiding future violations, and any other suggestions. The source, the periodicity, and the scope of circulation for these reports have also to be decided.

Communication Procedures

Defining the **communication** procedures between the organization and the provider is important so that no misunderstandings are created, and in order to have a clear procedure for reporting the appearance and fixing of problems. Furthermore, archived communication data can be used for measuring metrics such as response time and service restoration time.

Other Issues

Finally, the possibility that the SLA should cover issues specific to each case also has to be investigated. In case such issues exist, they should be recorded, along with each party's responsibility for each.

Sample Metrics for Various Services

The metrics presented below are relatively general and can be used for a variety of services. In any case, their usefulness is determined according to the criteria mentioned previously and the levels of service quality should be set according to need.

Some indicative metrics are the following:

- **Availability:** This metric is defined as the percentage of time that the service can be accessed. Usually acceptable values of the availability metric are between 98-100 percent. Common bounds under which drastic measures are taken are 2-3 points lower than the above values (95- 98 percent). In order to avoid prolonged periods of non-availability, the calculation of availability should take place at short intervals (such as daily) or limits set on each period of unavailability (such as half an hour). **Availability** can be measured using an automated system that periodically checks access to the service (for example, for a Web service the check would be the fetching of several pages, for an interconnection service the check would be the transmission and reception of a small message). If the measurement system is outside the provider's network, it might not be able to access the service because of a problem that is not the provider's responsibility. If the measurement system is inside the provider's network, it might not be able to identify connectivity problems for the whole of the provider's network. Therefore, the measurement system should be located at the edge of the provider's network.
- **Capacity:** Capacity is the size of the connection used for some interconnection service (Machiraju, et al., 2002). It influences, along with other parameters, the speed that can be achieved at a network link. Also, in cases of interconnection services to the Internet, capacity only refers to the provider's network. The overall speed of communication with other network nodes might be slow because of reasons outside the provider's responsibility.
- **Number of updates (such as the changes at a Web site's pages):** It defines the responsibility of the provider to update the content related to the service. Alternatively, the rate of updates can be used.

- **Service response time:** Service response time is the time from the moment that a user makes a request to the server until the result of the request comes back. Usually the response time cannot be measured for each individual request, and therefore this metric is the average response time, probably accompanied by its variation. Alternatively, service response time can be defined as the response time for a large number of requests. Service response time can be measured using an automated system that sends requests to the server and calculates the average response time.
- **Number of requests to the server:** This is the number of requests to the server (such as a Web server) in a specific time period, and which have to be served according to the quality level defined by the rest of the metrics. Measurement can be made using the logging service of the server.

FUTURE TRENDS

Networking services have become ever more important in the economy and the everyday operation of most businesses. Together with increased complexity come also increased requirements from the users of these services, as they rely on them for their productivity. These trends make the existence of a properly designed SLA document very important, both for the users and providers of the service, who want to avoid excessive and unpredictable liability. The critical nature of networking services in modern business environment requires strict and unambiguously defined rules and agreements. This evolution is certain to continue in the future, which will result in the greater need for complex but clearly written, usable, and real-world functional SLAs.

CONCLUSION

As SLAs are complex documents, the creation of a proper SLA can be a demanding task. In order to become more manageable, it is common to use a template and other tools for generating the basic document. Because SLAs are usually part of a contract and are considered confidential business information, examples of real-world SLAs are not very easy to find.

A good SLA cannot guarantee customer satisfaction only by having specific objectives and metrics. A good SLA should also include compensations and remedies for situations when the specified service level goals are missed. These compensations should motivate the provider into achieving the objectives, and the remedies should guarantee that the service quality will return to acceptable levels quickly.

REFERENCES

Bouras, C., Campanella, M., & Sevasti, A. (2002), SLA definition for the provision of an EF-based service In *Proceedings of the 16th International Workshop on Communications Quality and Reliability (CQR 2002)* (pp. 17-21).

Bouras, C., & Sevasti, A. (2004). SLA-based QoS pricing in DiffServ networks. In F. Huebner & R. D. van der Mei (Eds.), *Computer Communications Journal, Special Issue, Performance and control of next generation communications networks, 27*(18), 1868-1880.

Coollawyer.com. *Services agreements and services level agreements.* Retrieved 27 July, 2006 from http://www.coollawyer.com/webfront/internet_law_library/articles/law_library_service_level_article.php

Czajkowski, K., Foster, I., Kesselman, C., Sander V., & Tuecke S. (2002, July). SNAP: A protocol for negotiating service level agreements and coordinating resource management in distributed systems. In *Proceedings of 8th Workshop on Job Scheduling Strategies for Parallel Processing* (pp. 153-183). Edinburgh, Scotland.

Darwin Executive Guides. Service level agreements. Retrieved from http://guide.darwinmag.com/technology/outsourcing/sla/

Heinanen, J., Baker, F., Weiss, W., & Wroclawski, J. (1999). *Assured forwarding PHB group.* RFC 2597. Accessed 27 July, 2006.

IEC.org. Visual networks, inc. & telechoice: Carrier service-level agreements (SLAs). Retrieved March, 2006 from, http://www.iec.org/online/tutorials/carrier_sla/index.html

Jacobson, V., Nichols, K., & Poduri, K. (1999). *An expedited forwarding PHB.* RFC 2598. Accessed 27 July 2006.

Machiraju, S., Seshadri, M., & Stoica, I. (2002). A scalable and robust solution for bandwidth allocation. In *Proceedings 10th International Workshop on Quality of Service (IWQoS),* Miami (pp. 148-157).

Salsano, S., et al. (November 2000). *Definition and usage of SLSs in the AQUILA consortium, draft-salsano-aquila-sls-00.txt.* Internet Draft.

Singh, D. M., Garg, R., Singh, R. R., & Saran, H. (2002). A SLA framework for QoS provisioning and dynamic capacity allocation. In *Proceedings of Tenth International Workshop on Quality of Service (IWQoS),* Miami Beach (pp. 129-137).

The SLA Toolkit. http://www.service-level-agreement.net/verizonbusiness.com. ervices agreements and services level agreements. Retrieved 27 July, 2006 from http://www.verizonbusiness.com/terms/us/products/internet/sla/

Wang, X., & Schulzrinne, H. (2001). Pricing network resources for adaptive applications in a differentiated services network. *INFOCOM*, 943-952.

Xiao, X., & Ni, L. M. (1999). Internet QoS: A big picture. *IEEE Network*, 13(2), 8-18.

KEY TERMS

Availability: In the context of this article, availability is the percentage of time that a specific service is operating satisfactorily. The exact definition of the availability (for example, under which circumstances the service is no longer considered available) is a subject of the SLA for the service.

Capacity: In the context of this article, capacity is the bandwidth available for a specific service. The exact definition of the capacity (for example, at which network layer it should be measured) is a subject of the SLA for the service.

Compensations: The possible actions (such as payments or forfeiture of a fee) against a service provider that fails to meet the level of service defined in the SLA.

Metrics: The characteristics that are properly well-defined so that they can be measured and used to evaluate the service and its compliance to the SLA.

Quality of Service (QoS): The ability to provide specific guarantees to traffic flows regarding the network characteristics such as packet loss, delay, and jitter experienced by the flows.

SLA: Service level agreement—a formal agreement between a Service Provider and a Service Client to provide a service with well-defined service levels, accompanied by possible penalty clauses if the SLA is not met.

Service Response Time: Service response time is the time from the moment that a user makes a request to the server, until the result of the request comes back.

Quality of Service Architectures

Christos Bouras
Research Academic Computer Technology Institute and University of Patras, Greece

Apostolos Gkamas
Research Academic Computer Technology Institute and University of Patras, Greece

Dimitris Primpas
Research Academic Computer Technology Institute and University of Patras, Greece

Kostas Stamos
Research Academic Computer Technology Institute and University of Patras, Greece

INTRODUCTION

IP networks are built around the idea of best effort networking, which makes no guarantees regarding the delivery, speed, and accuracy of the transmitted data. While this model is suitable for a large number of applications, and works well for almost all applications when the network load is low (and therefore there is no congestion), there are two main factors that lead to the need for an additional capability of quality of service guarantees. One is the fact that an increasing number of Internet applications are related to real-time and other multimedia data, which have greater service requirements in order to be satisfying to the user. The other is that Internet usage is steadily increasing, and although the network infrastructure is also updated often, it is not always certain that network resource offerings will be ahead of usage demand. In order to deal with this situation, IETF has developed two architectures in order to enable QoS-based handling of data flows in IP networks. This article describes and compares these two architectures.

BACKGROUND

The two main architectures that have been proposed for **quality of service** are IntServ and DiffServ. They follow different philosophies as they approach the topic of Quality of Service from different point of views.

The IntServ architecture tries to provide absolute guarantees via resource reservations across the paths that the traffic class follows. The main protocol that

works with this architecture is the Reservation Protocol (**RSVP**). However, its operation is quite complicated and it also contributes significant network overhead. On the other hand, DiffServ architecture is more flexible and efficient as it tries to provide Quality of Service via a different approach. It classifies all the network traffic into classes and tries to treat each class differently, according to the level of QoS guarantees that each class needs. In the DiffServ architecture, two different types (per hop behaviours in Nichols, 2001) have been proposed, the expedited forwarding (Jacobson et al., 1999) and the assured forwarding (Heinanen et al., 1999); their difference is on the packet forwarding behaviour. **expedited forwarding** (EF) aims at providing QoS for the class by minimizing the jitter and is generally focused on providing stricter guarantees. This type tries to simulate the virtual leased lines and its policy profile should be very tight. **Assured forwarding** (AF) inserts at most four classes with at most three levels of dropping packets. Every time the traffic of each class exceeds the policy criteria, then it is marked as a lower level QoS class.

MAIN QoS ARCHITECTURES

Integrated Services (IntServ)

Integrated Services (IntServ) makes use of the RSVP protocol in order to make reservations for resources across the network. It has been initially developed by IETF in order to extend the traditional "best effort" model that has been used on the Internet. Its basic idea is that it should not be necessary to modify the underlying architecture of the Internet, but simply to add some extensions that can offer additional services beyond the basic "best-effort" service.

Quality of service (QoS) in the IntServ framework refers to the nature of the service being offered by the network, characterized by parameters such as the available bandwidth, packet delay, and packet loss. A network node in the IntServ architecture has the capability to handle packets and subject them to appropriate control. An IntServ-capable node can offer one or more of the IntServ services, while an IntServ-aware node supports the interfaces needed by the IntServ model but cannot offer the required service itself. An IntServ-aware node can simply understand the parameters of the required service and answer negatively.

Resource management is an important aspect of the IntServ architecture, and therefore traffic is subjected to admission control mechanisms. Furthermore, IntServ is responsible for reserving the resources. For that purpose, the RSVP protocol (Resource Reservation Protocol) is used, which aims at specifying the necessary resources for achieving the required quality of service. RSVP (Braden et al., 1997) reserves resources across the whole path used by the packets in a sequential manner. The first router in the path signals to the next router in the path that a resource reservation is required. This process is repeated until the receiving node is reached, and then the same procedure begins in the opposite. The IntServ services that have been currently defined are the "Guaranteed" service, which is the closest service to the dedicated virtual circuits, and the Controlled Load service, which is equivalent to the best-effort service under no congestion.

Differentiated Services (DiffServ)

Differentiated Services (DiffServ) (Blake, 2001) classifies and prioritizes packets depending on the class they belong to. Classes with larger requirements are treated preferentially by the network that supports DiffServ.

DiffServ is the second important effort for providing Quality of Service and was developed in order to overcome some of the disadvantages of IntServ. In particular, IntServ proved to be non-scalable in large networks where a lot of resource reservations are required. DiffServ operation is based on the usage of a field in the IP header called DS, which is contained in the **Type Of Service** (TOS) field in the IPv4 header,

and the Traffic Class field in the IPv6 header (Nichols, 2001). Clients that want to make use of the DiffServ architecture mark the DS field with a specific value. This value specifies the Per-Hop Behavior (PHB) for the client's packets. The possible DS values have to be agreed between the provider and the client in the form of a **service level agreement** (SLA) and they determine the quality of service parameters such as bandwidth, transmission, and rejection priority and queue priority.

DiffServ is a unidirectional and therefore non-symmetrical model. It can also be only used for unicast transmission.

Currently, the following two types of DiffServ services have been proposed:

- **Expedited forwarding (EF):** This service aim at minimizing packet delay and jitter, while providing highest quality of service. Packets that exceed the mutually agreed packet profile of the user are generally rejected. Services of this type emulate the operation of a virtual leased line (Jacobson et al., 1999).
- **Assured forwarding (AF):** This type provides at most four classes of service and at most three levels of rejection per class. AF traffic that exceeds the agreed profile is degraded but not necessarily rejected (Heinanen et al., 1999).

DiffServ operation is based on a number of mechanisms that operate on the traffic flows. These mechanisms are packet classification, marking, metering, and shaping, which are typically applied with this order, although traffic metering can precede marking. The mechanisms only need to be applied at the edge routers of a domain, while no application of the above mechanisms is needed for the core routers of the network. This feature of DiffServ overcomes the scalability problem of IntServ, since the core routers that handle a large number of flows do not have to apply the above mechanisms on these flows.

Packet Classification

Packet classification is the first step in the provisioning of quality of service. Classification of packets entering a network that supports QoS can be done either at a level of flows, or at a level of aggregate flows. This process mainly takes place by checking the header of each packet and using information from some field in order to make the classification. The relevant field is Type of Service (TOS) in IPv4, and the Traffic Class field in IPv6. The classification mechanism has to be very fast in order to be able to follow the rate of incoming packets, and very accurate.

Theoretically flows can be characterized by the following five elements:

• Sender IP address
• Sender port
• Destination IP address
• Destination port
• Protocol used

Classification per flow using these characteristics is called multifield classification and is quite difficult because checking so many fields requires a lot of processing power. Multifield classification is only used when classification based on individual flows is absolutely necessary (which is not a rare occurrence in the input points of DiffServ domains).

On the other hand, classification based on aggregates of flows is called behavior aggregate classification and only a combination of the above characteristics is needed. This classification method is easier and can be performed much faster.

Practically, classification will be done in a limited number of classes, so a single field in the packet header is enough. This is the simplest and most efficient method, and achieves classification at the level of aggregate flows.

Traffic Conditioning

Traffic conditioning includes the marking, metering, and shaping or traffic rejection mechanisms. Usually these mechanisms are applied to the sender's packets as soon as the traffic enters a domain. Nevertheless, the metering mechanism can be applied to the destination, under certain conditions. For this to be possible, all the routers of the network have to support the ECN (Explicit Congestion Notification), which is a congestion control functionality. ECN is a bit at the packets header which is set to 1 when congestion is detected at the network. This enables the rest of the nodes on the path to be notified of congestion.

The traffic control mechanisms presented below are based on the assumption that marking and meter-

ing of packets takes place at the entry points of the network.

Policing

Policing also takes place at the traffic entry points of a DiffServ domain. The policing mechanism controls traffic based on a specified profile that has been agreed upon and then makes certain decisions for handling traffic that exceeds the specified profile. These decisions can be marking the packets at a lower class of service, servicing the packets without guaranteed quality, or even dropping the packets. Which of these policies will be followed has already been agreed upon between the client and the administrator of the network and has been formulated in the form of a service level agreement (SLA). The policing criteria used can depend on the time or day, the source, the destination, or generally any other characteristic of the traffic.

The shaping mechanism aims at shaping the traffic in such a way that bursts (sudden transmission of many packets) are smoothed out and can be configured so that packets out of the specified profile (that would normally be dropped) are temporarily stored and forwarded to the network as soon as the burstiness of their transmission has been eliminated. Therefore, policing and shaping mechanisms can be used simultaneously so that part of the packets that are considered out of profile to be shaped and transmitted.

Queue Management

Queue management is important for the network administrator in order to be able to provide quality of service to the flows as has been agreed. Furthermore, queue management is a basic condition for the time scheduling mechanism that will be presented in the next section. In order for the network to satisfy all quality of service guarantees, it has to be able to handle packets of each class of service at a separate queue, so that the suitable time scheduling mechanism can be applied. Otherwise, the time scheduling mechanism is not able to differentiate between the classes and cannot offer the proper guarantees to the corresponding traffic flows. More specifically, if, for example, no differentiation of classes into separate queues takes place, different flows with different requirements will be accumulated at the same queue, and then packets will either be dropped or delivered with large delay. As a result, the network will not be able to provide the required guarantees and the throughput experienced by the client applications will be significantly downgraded.

The main functions of queue management aim at the proper queue operation and the usage of mechanisms for their control. They are the following:

- Add a packet at the proper queue according to the packet classification by the classification mechanism.
- Reject a packet if the queue that the packet should be added is full.
- Withdraw a packet from the top of the queue when the time scheduler requests so, in order for the packet to be transmitted to the next network node.
- Check the state of the queue. This includes checking the average size of the queue and taking actions in order to keep its size small. Possible actions are the rejection of a packet if the queue is starting to fill and the marking of a packet with the ECN bit when the queue size is large.

As the above functions suggest, queue management does not only deal with the reception and transmission of a packet, but it is also concerned with the efficient operation of the queue through the preservation of small average queue size. By keeping the average queue size small, the queues can easily absorb traffic bursts. If the average queue size gets large, then many packets have to be dropped during traffic bursts. Furthermore, another desired result of the small average queue size is that the average service delay will be small.

Queue management becomes even more critical under network congestion, when queues have to operate quickly and correctly. The main problem in this case is to identify the most appropriate strategies for action. A critical decision is whether packets will be dropped as soon as they reach the queue, or whether it is allowed to drop packets that are already inside the queue, in order to service other, higher priority packets. Another critical aspect is the criteria and information that will determine which packets should be dropped.

The general purpose of the queue management is to handle queues fairly for all classes of service while adhering to the agreements that have been made with the network clients. In order to avoid network congestion (which leads to increased average queue size), TCP at the transport layer offers several mechanisms.

In addition, network administrators have a number of further options, which will be described below. Their purpose is to ease the congestion problem that stems from the transmission of packets with a higher rate than the network can handle, and not congestion that stems from temporary bursts. These mechanisms that can be used by the network administrator are:

- **Dropping packets:** This method achieves two objectives, by directly reducing the network load and also informing the TCP protocol of the congestion condition. This is due to the fact that TCP congestion control mechanism relies on the assumption that each packet loss is due to congestion and therefore the transmission rate is automatically reduced.
- **Packet marking:** This method is less intrusive than the previous one, since it does not directly drop packets, but is also less direct, since the network is not automatically relieved.

Time Scheduler

Time scheduling is the way that the network handles the queues, meaning which queue will send data and for how long. The time scheduling mechanism has all the queues of a router available and decides in what order they are going to transmit packets and for how long.

The role of the time scheduler is critical for a network that wishes to offer quality of service guarantees. The reason is that the time scheduling mechanism determines the delay at each queue and the way that the line is shared between the queues. The time scheduling mechanism actually determines the type of quality of service that will be provided by the network. The parameters that can be affected by the time scheduling mechanism are:

- The throughput of each flow, since the time scheduler can control the intervals that this flow will transmit data.
- The delay of each flow, since the time scheduler controls the transmission rate of the flow and therefore the duration that the packets remain in the queue.
- The jitter.

These parameters determine the quality of service that the network can provide. Therefore, because of the importance of the time scheduler, and because of the fact that there are several time scheduling mechanisms, it is necessary that the proper time scheduling mechanism is chosen according to several criteria. The kind of quality guarantees offered and their level of success should match the nature of applications that will be supported.

Some of the most widely used mechanisms for time scheduling are:

- **First in first out (FIFO):** This is the oldest mechanism, and it assumes there is only one queue. Every packet exits the queue in the order it arrived. As a result, FIFO uses no priorities. It is a simple mechanism, and it is useful for high capacity lines where there is no congestion. On the other hand, it performs badly when there is congestion, or when bursty applications dominate the queue and other applications' packets are rejected.

- **Priority queuing (PQ):** Priority queuing allows different priorities and can handle multiple queues. One queue has strict priority and is always preferentially served. Packets are inserted in the proper queue depending on their classification. The priority queuing mechanism checks the queues sequentially by starting from the highest priority queue, until a non-empty queue is found. The first packet from that queue is then transmitted, and the procedure starts over. Depending on the incoming rate for high priority packets, other queues might be served very slowly or not at all. The latter might occur if high priority traffic arrives at a rate close to or higher than the link capacity, and can be remedied by applying policing or shaping mechanisms to high priority traffic. The main advantage of Priority Queuing is that it achieves very low delay for high priority packets.

- **Modified deficit round robin (M-DRR):** M-DRR is based on deficit round robin (DRR) and round robin (RR) mechanisms. Round robin handles all queues equally and checks them periodically. It transmits any packets that are waiting in a queue, and continues checking other queues. DRR functions similarly, but now queues try to maintain a steady transmission rate. This is achieved by defining for each queue a quantum Q and a deficit D. Q is the maximum number of bytes

that can be transmitted each time. If less bytes are transmitted, the remaining number is stored at D, which increases the maximum number of bytes that can be transmitted next time. M-DRR also introduces a priority queue for achieving low delay. The rest of the queues are served according to the DRR mechanism, and the priority queue is served either alternately with the rest of the queues or in absolute priority. These two variations of M-DRR are correspondingly called Alternate Priority and Strict Priority. M-DRR is flexible and efficient, but only under conditions with not too much congestion. Therefore, it is usually used in conjunction with a mechanism that prevents congestion.

- **Fair queuing (FQ) and weighted fair queuing (WFQ):** Fair queuing is a variation of round robin, with the added goal of serving all queues for a long term equal bandwidth sharing. It schedules packet transmissions in the order that they would have arrived at the other end of the line if an ideal time scheduling mechanism had been used. Its disadvantages are that the computations to achieve such a goal are complex and have to be performed approximately, and that it cannot operate with the aggregate classes model. Weighted Fair Queuing on the other hand, assigns weights to each queue. In case some queues are empty, the excess bandwidth that would be used by these queues is shared among the rest of the queues according to their weights.

FUTURE TRENDS

Nowadays, DiffServ is the most widely used architecture (Grossman, 2002). Its main advantage is its better scalability, since the core network devices only deal with the bulk of flows and not individual flows and reservations. Therefore, core routers are not involved in the complexities of enforcing agreements or collecting payments.

In the framework of the DiffServ architecture, IETF has defined the entity of bandwidth broker (Nichols, et al., 1999). The bandwidth broker is an agent that has some knowledge of an organization's priorities and policies and allocates bandwidth with respect to those policies. In order to achieve an end-to-end allocation of resources across separate domains, the bandwidth broker managing a domain will have to communicate with its adjacent peers, which allows end-to-end services to be constructed out of purely bilateral agreements. bandwidth brokers can be configured with organizational policies, keep track of the current allocation of marked traffic, and interpret new requests to mark traffic in light of the policies and current allocation. Bandwidth brokers only need to establish relationships of limited trust with their peers in adjacent domains, unlike schemes that require the setting of flow specifications in routers throughout an end-to-end path.

The main disadvantage of DiffServ and the architectures for providing quality of service at the network and transport layer is that it is often regarded as a technical solution for a problem (scarcity of network resources) that can be more simply solved by increasing the network's capacity.

Furthermore, the field of policing and shaping mechanisms is still open and various mechanisms can be presented that combine both.

CONCLUSION

While IntServ was the first main architecture for Quality of Service proposed by IETF, its drawbacks led to the development of DiffServ, which has largely substituted IntServ as the main standardized architecture for guaranteed services in IP environments. DiffServ is widely supported in networking equipment and software, and has been implemented, tested, and used in real world environments around the world. It is an important part of the network architecture that has to deal with the real-time and high bandwidth requirements of popular Internet applications.

REFERENCES

Blake, S., Black, D., Carlson, M., Davies, E., Wang, Z., & Weiss, W. (1998). *An architecture for differentiated service.* RFC 2475.

Black, D., Brim, S., Carpenter, B., & Le Faucheur, F. (June 2001). *Per hop behavior identification codes.* RFC 3140.

Braden, R., Zhang, L., Berson, S., Herzog, S., & Jamin, S. (1997). *Resource ReSerVation protocol (RSVP).* RFC 2205.

Crawley, E., Nair, R., Rajagopalan, B., & Sandick, H. (August 1998). *A framework for QoS-based routing in the Internet.* RFC 2386.

Grossman, D. (April 2002). *New terminology and clarifications for Diffserv.* RFC 3260.

Heinanen, J., Baker, F., Weiss, W., & Wroclawski, J. (June 1999). *Assured forwarding PHB group.* RFC 2597.

IETF DiffServ working group. Retrieved 27 July, 2006 from http://www.ietf.org/html.charters/OLD/diffserv-charter.html

IETF IntServ working group. Retrieved 27 July, 2006 from http://www3.ietf.org/proceedings/96mar/area.and.wg.reports/tsv/intserv/intserv.html

Internet2 QoS Working Group. Retrieved 27 July, 2006 from http://qos.internet2.edu/wg/

Jacobson, V., Nichols, K., & Poduri, K. (1999). *An expedited forwarding PHB.* RFC 2598.

Nichols, K., Blake S., Baker F., & Black D. (1998). Definition of the differentiated Services. Field (DS Field) in the IPv4 and IPv6 Headers. RFC 2474.

Nichols, K., & Carpenter, B. (April 2001). *Definition of differentiated services per domain behaviors and rules for their specification.* RFC 3086.

Nichols, K., Jackobson, V., & Zhang, L. (July 1999). *A two-bit differentiated services architecture for the Internet.* RFC 2638.

Shenker, S., Partridge, C., & Guerin, R. (1997). *Specification of guaranteed quality of service.* RFC 2212.

Snir Y., Ramberg, Y., Strassner, J., Cohen, R., & Moore, B. (November 2003). *Policy quality of service (QoS) information model.* RFC 3644. The Internet Engineering Task Force.

Wroclawski, J. (1997). *Specification of the controlled-load network Eeement service.* RFC 2211.

KEY TERMS

Differentiated Services (DiffServ): An architecture that has been defined by IETF in order to provide quality of service in IP networks, which works based on aggregates of flows, by classifying traffic into different types of service, allowing the core routers of the network to deal with only a limited number of aggregated flows.

First-In, First-Out (FIFO): Queue organization method, where each element exits the queue in the order it originally arrived.

Integrated Services (IntServ): An architecture that has been defined by IETF in order to provide Quality of Service in IP networks, which is based on flow-based allocation of resources using RSVP.

Internet Engineering Task Force (IETF): The organization comprised of a large open international community of network designers, operators, vendors, and researchers concerned with the evolution of the Internet architecture and the smooth operation of the Internet.

Per-Hop Behaviour (PHB): The aggregated way packets are forwarded at a differentiated services-compliant node.

Quality of Service (QoS): The ability to provide specific guarantees to traffic flows regarding the network characteristics such as packet loss, delay, and jitter experienced by the flows.

RSVP: Resource Reservation Protocol.

Quality of Service by Way of Path Selection Policy

Wayne Goodridge
Barbados Community College, Barbados

Hadrian Peter
University of the West Indies, Barbados

William Robertson
Dalhousie University, Canada

INTRODUCTION

The pervasive use of the Internet, the world's most extensive public communication system, for services ranging from academic research and e-mail to electronic commerce, necessitates that a policy should be put in place to ensure that such services are delivered in an efficient manner. **Quality of service** (QoS) is the capability of a network to provide better service to selected network traffic over various technologies. In this paper we focus on a specific aspect of QoS–namely, the path selection policy.

The path selection policy of a QoS **routing algorithm** can significantly influence how key resources like bandwidth are allocated. If the QoS routing algorithm chooses a path that is more desirable than the user-specified QoS, the user does not gain any additional utility, and this can lead to network resources being wasted. On the other hand, if a path is not found that meets the user-specified QoS, then this may affect the user application performance.

BACKGROUND

Traditional link state and distance vector routing protocols, such as open shortest path first (OSPF), always forward packets on the shortest path. This can cause problems for flows with a need for QoS guarantees if the shortest path does not have enough resources to meet the requirements. Both IntServ and Diffsev provide mechanisms for flows to reserve resources on the shortest path. However, the shortest path cannot make the reservation if there are not sufficient resources along

the path. What is missing is a framework that can find a path, if one exists, which has the requested resources available. The QoS routing algorithm (1999; Al-Fawaz & Woodward, 2000; Alkahtani et al., 2002; Kuipers et al., 2004) considers the quality of service requirements of a flow when making **routing decisions**.

The QoS routing algorithm optimizes the resource usage in the network as follows :

1. Select feasible routes by avoiding congested nodes or links
2. Offer multiple paths for transferring additional traffic if workload exceeds the limit of existing paths
3. Select alternative paths for quick recovery without seriously degrading the quality if network node failure occurs
4. Let traffic classes with different QoS requirements and identical source and destination travel different paths

The problems of finding a path subject to multiple metrics, and finding an **optimized path** that meets the user constraints are difficult. Many of the solutions proposed are **heuristic algorithms** (Chen & Nahrstedt, 1998; Iwata et al., 1996; Neve & Mieghem, 2000; Korkmaz & Krunz, 2001). There also exist exact solutions like the SAMCRA (Mieghem et al., 2001) and A*Prune (Liu & Ramakrishnan, 2001). QoS algorithms use different techniques to find **feasible paths** in networks. This can lead to QoS algorithms selecting different paths for the same set of QoS requirements. The challenge, therefore, is for the QoS algorithm to select paths that optimize the network resources and at the same time meet the flow requirements of each network user.

This article presents a QoS algorithm called constraint path heuristic routing decision system (CP-H/RDS) that uses the concept of preference functions to address the problem of finding paths in core networks. The paths selected by the popularly used bandwidth-delay-constrained path routing algorithm (BDCR) (1999) are compared to the paths selected by the CP-H/RDS algorithm for a given network topology.

MAIN THRUST

The CP-H/RDS Algorithm

The CP-H/RDS algorithm is a combination of the Constraint Path Heuristic (CP-H) and Routing Decision System (RDS) algorithms. The CP-H algorithm finds a subset C of constraint paths connecting source s and destination t, while the RDS algorithm finds a path $p^* \in C$ based on multi-criteria demands. Figure 1 shows how the two algorithms can be used to find a QoS route from a communication network, given a set of user-specified concave and additive metrics (Tanenbaum, 2002), and a set of policy-based metrics from the network provider. The three-step process is as follows:

1. Prune all links not satisfying the specified concave metric(s)
2. Find a set of feasible constraint paths with respect to the network additive metrics

3. Execute the RDS algorithm with the specified metrics, along with the constraint paths resulting from step (2)

The RDS algorithm calculates a ranking for each path based on the QoS requirements.

We now examine each algorithm in detail.

The CP-H Algorithm

The CP-H algorithm, an improvement on Iwata's algorithm (Iwata et al., 1996), attempts to find a path optimized for one of the metrics and then evaluates whether this path can guarantee other user-specified QoS requirements. If it can, the algorithm is halted and this path is selected. However, if a path optimized for the first metric cannot meet the QoS requirements of all the other user constraints, a path optimized for the second metric is selected, and the procedure repeated. This approach under strict constraints can lead to relatively good running times but poor performance in terms of success rates (Kuipers et al., 2004).

The proposed heuristic finds $\lambda \times m$ paths between source and destination nodes, where λ is a small positive integer and m is the number of QoS additive metrics under consideration. The algorithm in Box 1.

The algorithm accepts a graph G, source node s, destination node t, an empty set C for storage of $\lambda \times m$ paths between s and t, and the set of user constraints L. For a given metric, say m_l, Dijkstra's algorithm is first executed and produces a shortest path P_l with respect to metric m_l. The pruning procedure is then executed and attempts to ensure that distinct paths result from

Figure 1. Using the CP-H and RDS algorithms to find a QoS route

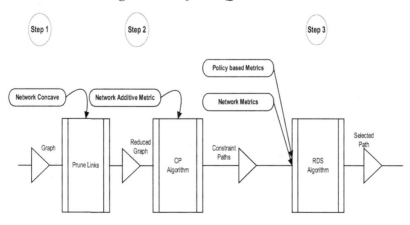

Box 1.

```
Algorithm  CP − H(G,s,t,C,L,λ,m) {
1)    j ← 1
2)    while ( j ≤  m ) {
3)      i ← 1
4)    while ( i ≤ λ ) {
5)       Pᵢ ← Dijkstra(G,s,t,j)
6)      PrunePath( Pᵢ,j )
7)           C ← C ∪ Pᵢ
8)        i ← i + 1
9)    }
10)      j ← j + 1
11) }
12) }

Algorithm PrunePath( P, j ){
For each link  l  in  P {
  τ = maxⱼ(P)
  lⱼ   ← τ +   lⱼ {sets the link weight for the jᵗʰ  metric, where  τ  is a largest value for the jᵗʰ  metric
on path  P .}
}
```

successive runs of Dijkstra's algorithm which, in turn, increases the chance that one of the $\lambda \times m$ paths would satisfy all QoS constraints. The paths are passed to the RDS algorithm which decides which path best satisfies a desired set of objectives.

Simulation results show that a high number of distinct feasible paths in set C is obtained if τ is set to the maximum of link values of path P_1 with respect to a given metric.

The RDS Algorithm

The RDS algorithm is concerned with finding a path that matches the user requests as closely as possible. The algorithm does this by building **preference functions** (Barzilai, 1998) for each metric from the constraint paths produced by the CP-H algorithm. In Goodridge et al. (2004, 2005) introductions to this approach are presented. The basic idea is to use a preference function s that accepts a network metric value, say x, as a parameter and returns a value $s(x)$ between -1 and 1. The pseudocode for the RDS algorithm is given in Box 2.

The algorithm accepts a list of **constraint paths** C, and a vector v of size m containing the user traffic optimization goals for each network metric. The RDS algorithm returns a path P to meet the optimization

goals of the user traffic. The *size()* method returns the number of constraint paths.

The function *BEST* accepts C and metric j, and returns the best value for j among all the paths in C. The best value for a concave metric is the maximum value among all paths, and the best value for an additive metric is the minimum value among all paths. The RDS algorithm will convert multiplicative metrics, to additive metrics as described in Tanenbaum (2002).

The array d_j stores scaled values for the user traffic flow demands. The elements of array *sum* store $\sum_{j=1}^{m} s_j(x_{ij})s_j(d_j)$ for each path. Lines 17-21 are used to set the user demand array d_j to the optimization goals of the network traffic. An optimization goal of 1 means that user traffic wishes to optimize the given metric and a 2 means that no optimization is required.

Simulation Model

To evaluate the CP-H/RDS algorithm in finding a suitable QoS path for a given flow request, we implemented the algorithm in C++/TCL and incorporated it in network simulator *ns-2*. Figure 2 shows the network topology used in the simulation. Each link in the graph is characterized by bandwidth, delay, and

Box 2.

```
Algorithm RDS (C, P, v) {
1)   k  ←  C.size()
2)   if k = 1 then
3)     Return P  ←  C.get(0)
4)   For j  ←  0 to m Do {
5)        a_j  ←  BEST (C, j)
6)        b_j  ←  WORSE (C, j)
7)     For i  ←  0 to k Do {
8)       if a_j ≠  b_j  then
9)              s_j(x_ij) ← 2 (x_j - b_j)/(a_j - b_j) - 1
10)    else
11)            s_j(x_ij) ← 1
12)  }
13) }
14) Let  s_j(d_j) ← -1 , for all  j ∈ [1, m]
15) Let  sum_i ← 0 , for all  i ∈ [1, k]
16) For  j ← 0  to m Do {
17)  If (v[j] = 1) then
18)     s_j(d_j) ← 1
19)  Else
20)  If (v[j] = 2) then
21)        s_j(d_j) ← 0
22)  For  i ← 0  to k Do
23)        sum_i ← sum_i +  s_j(d_j) × s_j(x_ij)
24) }
25) y  ←  LARGEST( sum )
26) return P  ←  C.get(y)
27) }
```

a Traffic Source Link Policy (TSLP). The TSLP link metric is added because it is a well known fact that because of TCP's congestion mechanisms, an increase in UDP (User Datagram Protocol) traffic would affect the performance of TCP traffic. The TSLP is used by the network administrator to help control the degree of TCP and UDP traffic present on a link. TSLP has only two values, 0 and 1. When TSLP is 1, only TCP traffic is encouraged on the link, otherwise only UDP traffic is encouraged.

The TSLP is a concave metric, however; it cannot be pruned since links that are set to 1 can still carry UDP traffic and links that are set to 0 can still carry TCP traffic. This feature demonstrates the power of using the CP-H/RDS algorithm, since the network designer can easily include policy metrics that make it possible to have more control over traffic.

Simulations were performed to study the impact of the dynamic assignment of QoS paths on network and end-user performance for constant bit rate (CBR) and connection-oriented variable bit rate (VBR) traffic with varying demands. The traffic specifications for the flows used in the simulation are summarized in Table 1. Flows 1, 2, 3, 4, 5, and 6 are started at 21, 31, 41, 51, 61, and 71 seconds, respectively, for the BDCR and CP-H/RDS algorithms.

Simulation Results

The main goal of the simulation was to assess the impact that path selection has on receiver throughputs based on existing flows in the network. Table 2 shows the paths calculated when BDCR and CP-H/RDS are used. All six (6) flows were investigated during the simulation exercise. However, because of the requirement that, at most, five (5) figures should be included in this paper, we have only provided below an analysis of receiver throughputs for flows 1, 4, and 6.

Figure 2. Network topology used in the simulation (SCR = source; DES = destination)

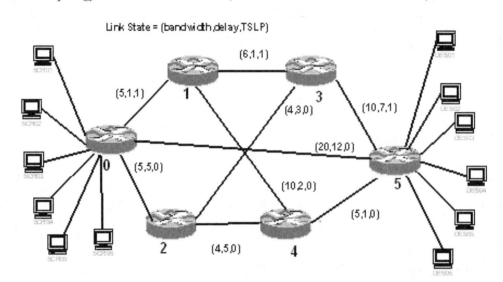

Table 1. Traffic flow configurations

Flow ID	Type	Connection	Capacity
1	CBR UDP	SCR01 to DES01	2 M
2	CBR UDP	SCR02 to DES02	15 M
3	CBR UDP	SCR03 to DES03	5 M
4	TCP	SCR04 to DES04	1 M
5	TCP	SCR05 to DES05	1 M
6	TCP	SCR06 to DES06	1 M

Table 2. Paths selected by CP-H/RDS and BDCR algorithms

Flow ID	Selected Path CP-H/RDS	Selected Path BDCR
1	0_2_3_5	0_1_4_5
2	0_5	0_5
3	0_5	0_5
4	0_2_3_5	0_1_4_5
5	0_1_3_5	0_1_4_5
6	0_1_3_5	0_1_4_5

Flow 1

In Figure 3 as flows are admitted into the network, the graphs show how the throughput of flow 1 is affected. When flows 2 and 3 are started at 31 and 41 seconds, respectively, no change in flow 1 throughput is observed. Neither of the algorithms put flows 2 and 3 on the same path as flow 1. When flow 4 is introduced, both algorithms placed it on the same path as flow 1. However, flow 1 is not affected by flow 4 since enough link bandwidth is present on the path selected for flow 1. When flow 5 is started 40s after flow 1, fluctuations in receiver throughput are observed for both algorithms.

However, the fluctuation of the receiver's throughput in the case of the BDCR algorithm is significantly higher than with RDS. This is because the RDS algorithm selected a path with one link common to the path of flow 1, while BDCR put flow 5 on the same path as flow 1, thus creating an environment where flows have to compete for resources.

Finally, when flow 6 is started 50s after flow 1, an increase in the intensity of the fluctuation of the receiver's throughput is evident. This increase is also present in the case of BDCR but difficult to observe since the receiver's throughput fluctuation is quite intense as a result of flow 5. Note that the BDCR put flow 6 on the same path as flow 1, creating a highly congested path, while RDS selected a path for flow 6 that only has one common link with the path of flow 1.

Flow 4

In Figure 4, since flow 4 is a TCP flow, it transmits until it detects congestion which occurred around 16000 bps. The average receiver throughput for both the CP-H/RDS and BDCR algorithms is equal to the transmitter data rate of 16000bps.

Flow 6

In Figure 5 the RDS selected a path for flow 6 that resulted in the TCP flow having a very high throughput. However, in the case of BDCR, the average throughput of the receiver is less than the transmitter with significant jitter.

FUTURE TRENDS

This chapter provides a framework for QoS routing in a single ISP domain using the CP-H/RDS algorithm. However, extensions of the framework for using the CP-H/RDS algorithm across multiple ISP domains to achieve end-to-end QoS needs to be investigated.

A challenging area is routing in an ad hoc wireless environment which is complicated due to the failing and mobility of nodes. Future work needs to be done to investigate how the CP-H/RDS can be used to help maintain connectivity in such an environment.

Figure 3. Throughputs of source and receiver for flow 1 under the CP-H/RDS algorithm (left) and BDCR algorithm (right)

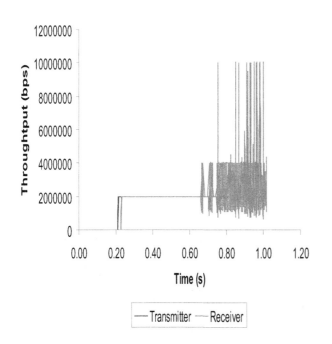
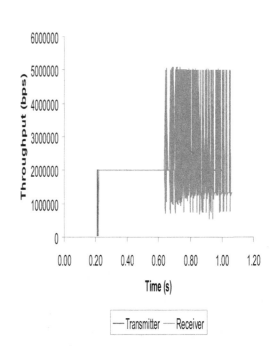

Figure 4. Throughputs of source and receiver for flow 4 under the CP-H/RDS algorithm (left) and BDCR algorithm (right)

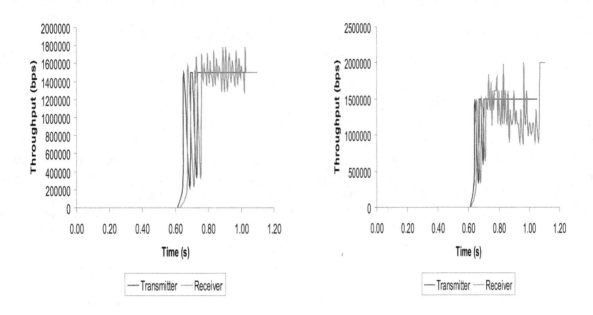

Figure 5. Throughputs of source and receiver for flow 6 under the CP-H/RDS algorithm (left) and BDCR algorithm (right)

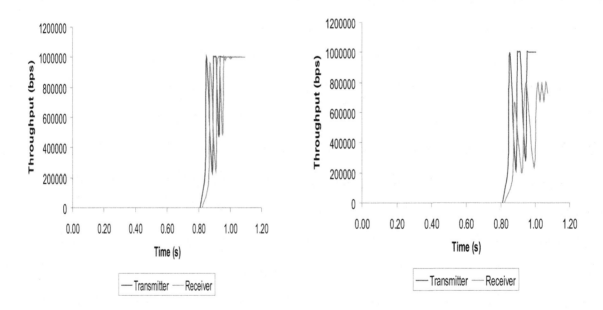

CONCLUSION

The simulation results of this chapter illustrate the importance of having an intelligent path-finding algorithm. By using a simple network path selection policy it was shown that receiver throughput and delay can be significantly improved over a path selection policy that only considered bandwidth and hop count. In addition, the ease with which the TSLP policy was incorporated into the CP-H/RDS illustrates the power of the RDS portion of the CP-H/RDS algorithm.

REFERENCES

Al-Fawaz, M.M.M., & Woodward, M.E. (2000). Fast quality of service routing algorithms with multiple constraints. *Eighth IFIP Workshop on ATM/IP*, Ilkely, UK, pp. 01/1-01/10.

Alkahtani, A.M.S., Woodward, M.E., Al-Begain, K., & Alghannam, A. (2002). QoS routing with multiple and prioritised constraints using the concept of the analytic hierarchy process (ahp). *International Network Conference*, INC2002, UK (pp. 243-251).

Barzilai, J. (1998). On the decomposition of value functions. *Operations Research Letters, 22*(4), 159-170.

Barzilai, J. (1998). Measurement foundations for preference function modeling. In *Proceedings of the IEEE International Conference on Systems, Man, and Cybernetics* (pp. 4034-4044).

Chen, S., & Nahrstedt, K. (1998). On finding multi-constrained paths. In Conference record. *IEEE International Conference on Communications*, 874-879.

Chen, S., & Nahrstedt, K. (1998). An overview of quality-of-service routing for the next generation high- speed networks: Problems and solutions. In *IEEE Network, Special Issue on Transmission and Distribution of Digital Video*, 64-79.

Goodridge, W., Robertson, W., Phillips, W., & Sivakumar, S. (2005). Traffic driven multiple constraint-optimization for qos routing. Inaugural issue of *International Journal of Internet Protocol Technology* (to appear).

Goodridge, W., Robertson, W., Phillips, W., & Sivakumar, S. (2004). Comparing a novel qos routing algorithm to standard pruning techniques used in qos routing algorithms. In *Canadian Conference on Electrical and Computer Engineering* (Vol. 2, pp. 805-808).

Goodridge, W., Robertson, W., Phillips, W., & Sivakumar, S. (2004). Multiple metric qos in differenti-ated services networks using preference functions measurement concepts. In *ICOIN 2004* (LNCS 3090, pp. 390-399). Springer.

Goodridge, W., Robertson, W., Phillips, W., & Sivakumar, S. (2004). Over-constraint qos routing in large networks. In *London Communications Symposium 2004,* Vol. 2, 61-64.

Iwata, A., Izmailov, R., Lee, D.-S., Sengupta, B., Ramamurthy, G., & Suzuki, H. (1996). Atm routing algorithms with multiple qos requirements for multimedia internetworking. *IEICE Transactions Communications*, E79-B, 281-291.

Korkmaz, T., & Krunz, M. (2001). A randomized algorithm for finding a path subject to multiple qos requirements. *Computer Networks*, 36, 251-268.

Korkmaz, T., & Krunz, M. (2001). Multi-constrained optimal path selection. In *Proceedings of the IEEE INFOCOM 2001 Conference*, Alaska (Vol. 2, pp. 834-843).

Kuipers, F., Korkmaz, T., Krunz, M., & Mieghem, P.V. (2004). Performance evaluation of constraint-based path selection algorithms. *IEEE Network*, 18, 16-23.

Liu, G., & Ramakrishnan, K. (2001). A* Prune: An algorithm for finding k shortest paths subject to multiple constraints. *IEEE INFOCOM 2001*, 2, 743-749.

Mieghem, P.V., Neve, H.D., & Kuipers, F. (2001). Hop-by-hop quality of service routing. *Computer Networks*, 37, 407-423.

Neve, H.D., & Mieghem, P.V. (2000). Tamcra: A tunable accuracy multiple constraints routing algorithm. *Computer Communications*, 23, 667-679.

Tanenbaum, A.S. (2002). *Computer networks* (4th ed.). Prentice Hall.

Wang, Z., & Crowcroft, J. (1996). Quality-of-service routing for supporting multimedia applications. *IEEE Journal on Selected Areas in Communications, 14*(7), 1228-1234.

KEY TERMS

Additive Metrics: Let $w(P)$ be the total value for metric w on path P, and let $w(L_i)$ represent the weight of each link with respect to w on path P. Then w is said to be an additive metric if $w(P) = \sum_{i=1}^{l} w(L_i)$, where l is the number of links in the path. Examples are delay and jitter.

Concave Metrics: w is said to be a concave metric if $w(P) = min(w(L_i))$. Example is bandwidth.

Optimization Goal: The user's desire to find a path that minimizes or maximizes the value.

Policy Based Metric: A characteristic of a network link that controls what type of traffic and how that traffic moves across the link. Policy metrics can be used to implement access control and data security of the link.

Preference Function: A preference function f has a domain set D consisting of multiple criteria $x = (x_1, x_2, ..., x_m)$, where x_j represents the jth criterion. Each alternative is a point $q = (q_1, q_2, ..., q_k)$ in the set D.

Building a preference function involves assessment of numerical values of the coordinates $(q_1, q_2, ..., q_k)$ for each alternative. Given $x, y, z \in D$ then the following must hold:

1. x "is preferred to" $y \Leftrightarrow f(x) \geq f(y)$
2. $x - z$ "is preferred to" $y - z \Leftrightarrow f(x) - f(z) \geq f(y) - f(z)$

QoS Routing Algorithm: An algorithm that finds a path that meets a set of user constraints.

Strict User Constraints: Let S be a set of paths, then L_j are strict user constraints if:

$$L_j = w_j(P^*) + \varepsilon_j, \; j = 1, ..., m$$

where P^* is the path for which $\max_{1 \leq j \leq m}(w_j(S))$ is minimum and ε_j are small positive numbers relative to $w_j(P^*)$.

Strict user constraints imply that few paths exist that can meet the demands of the user.

Quality of Service in Mobile Ad Hoc Networks

Winston K. G. Seah
Institute for Infocomm Research, Singapore

Hwee-Xian Tan
National University of Singapore, Singapore

INTRODUCTION

Mobile ad hoc networks (MANETs) form a class of multi-hop wireless networks that can easily be deployed on-the-fly. These are autonomous systems that do not require existing infrastructure; each participating node in the network acts as a host as well as a packet-forwarding router. In addition to the difficulties experienced by conventional wireless networks, such as wireless interference, noise and obstructions from the environment, hidden/exposed terminal problems, and limited physical security, MANETs are also characterized by dynamically changing network topology and energy constraints.

While MANETs were originally designed for use in disaster emergencies and defense-related applications, there are a number of potential applications of ad hoc networking that are commercially viable. Some of these applications include multimedia teleconferencing, home networking, embedded computing, electronic classrooms, sensor networks, and even underwater surveillance.

The increased interest in MANETs in recent years has led to intensive research efforts which aim to provide quality of service (QoS) support over such infrastructure-less networks with unpredictable behaviour. Generally, the QoS of any particular network can be defined as its ability to deliver a guaranteed level of service to its users and/or applications. These service requirements often include performance metrics such as throughput, delay, jitter (delay variance), bandwidth, reliability, etc., and different applications may have varying service requirements. The performance metrics can be computed in three different ways: (i) concave (e.g., minimum bandwidth along each link); (ii) additive (e.g., total delay along a path); and (iii) multiplicative (e.g., packet delivery ratio along the entire route).

While much effort has been invested in providing QoS in the Internet during the last decade, leading to the development of Internet QoS models such as integrated services (IntServ) (Braden, 1994) and differentiated services (DiffServ) (Blake, 1998), the Internet is currently able to provide only best effort (BE) QoS to its applications. In such networks with predictable resource availability, providing QoS beyond best effort is already a challenge. It is therefore even more difficult to achieve a BE-QoS similar to the Internet in networks like MANETs, which experience a vast spectrum of network dynamics (such as node mobility and link instability). In addition, QoS is only plausible in a MANET if it is combinatorially stable, i.e., topological changes occur slow enough to allow the successful propagation of updates throughout the network. As such, it is often debatable as to whether QoS in MANETs is just a myth or can become a reality.

BACKGROUND

The successful deployment of QoS in MANETs is a challenging task because it depends on the inherent properties of the network: node mobility, variable (and limited) capacity links, as well as rapid deployment and configuration. These factors lead to a network with dynamic topology, complex route maintenance, and unpredictable resource availability. It is difficult to implement existing Internet QoS models on MANETs because these mechanisms cannot be efficiently deployed in a network with unpredictable and varying resource availability.

A very critical assumption is made by most, if not all, MANET protocols, which is the willingness of all nodes to participate in the forwarding of packets for other nodes in the network. QoS provisioning in MANETs is therefore a multi-faceted problem which requires the cooperation and integration of the various network layers, which will be discussed in the following subsections.

1. **Physical layer:** The physical layer of any network is used to provide the means to transmit sequences of bits between any pair of nodes joined by a communication channel. In MANETs, the radio channel is used to provide wireless communication between the nodes in the network. In contrast with wired networks, which offer predictability and stability, radio channels are affected by the effects of reflection, diffraction, and scattering from environmental interferences. As such, the wireless medium is often unreliable and subject to drastic variations in signal strength, leading to higher bit rate errors (BER) at the physical layer. Due to node mobility and the erratic behaviour of the wireless channel, the link characteristics of the network experience rapid changes. The effects of large-scale/small-scale fading, shadowing, and path loss may also cause these communication links to be asymmetric. Hence, the physical mechanisms must be able to adapt to the changes and deterioration in link quality during data transmission and change their modulation scheme accordingly to suit the current channel state.

2. **Medium access control (MAC) layer:** The wireless channel in MANETs is a broadcast and shared medium where nodes are often subject to interference from neighbouring nodes within the transmission and interference ranges, and often suffer from hidden/exposed terminal problems. Although many solutions have been proposed to alleviate the exposed/hidden terminal problems, these problems are more pronounced in autonomous, mobile environments; wireless channels are also subjected to errors which are bursty, location-, and mobility-dependent. The MAC layer for MANETs has to cope with these problems, as well as the challenges of minimizing collisions, allowing fair access, and providing reliable data transport under rapidly changing conditions.

3. **Network layer:** The main challenge of the network layer in a MANET is to determine and distribute routing information efficiently under changing link conditions and scarce bandwidth. In addition, it must be able to interoperate with traditional non-ad-hoc networks, such as the Internet and other wireless networks. Existing MANET routing protocols can be broadly grouped under reactive, proactive, or hybrid routing protocols.

If the network topology changes too rapidly due to high node mobility, topology updates in these routing protocols may not propagate fast enough to form stable routes. Most of these protocols are also based on shortest-path algorithms, which may not result in routes that have the required resources to meet the requirements of the applications they support. An ideal QoS routing protocol should be able to adaptively select its paths based on the currently available resources to provide the service desired by a particular application.

4. **Transport layer:** In the wired Internet, there are two transport-layer protocols available to the application layer: (i) UDP (user datagram protocol), which provides unreliable and connectionless service; and (ii) TCP (transmission control protocol), which provides reliable, connection-oriented service to the invoking applications. Besides having to provide logical communication between applications running on mobile hosts, the transport layer in a MANET also needs to handle delay and packet loss arising from conditions unlike wired networks. In TCP (which is used for most applications in the Internet), packet losses are due to congestion, and a back-off mechanism will then be invoked to reduce the sending rate of data packets from the source nodes. However, in wireless media, packet loss is mainly due to transmission errors and current flow control or congestion control techniques that might lead to lowered throughput. There are also large variations in delay when the route changes, which is not addressed by the design of the existing transport layer protocols.

5. **Application layer:** According to Kurose (2003), the service requirements of an application can be broadly classified into data loss, bandwidth, and delay (which can be average end-to-end delay or delay variance). Loss-tolerant applications include multimedia applications such as real-time audio and video, which are not adversely affected by occasional loss of data but are highly sensitive to bandwidth and delay. Other applications involving sensitive data integrity, such as electronic mail and banking transactions, require fully reliable data transfer, but may not be time-sensitive and can work with elastic bandwidth. To cater for QoS in MANETs, the application layer must be designed to handle frequent disconnections and

reconnections caused by the dynamic network topology and varying signal quality of the wireless channel. It must also be able to adapt to widely varying delay and packet losses.

DEVELOPMENTS IN MANET QoS

From the discussion above, we can see that hard QoS in MANET is unlikely to be plausible because of the inherent dynamic nature of a mobile ad hoc environment. It may be more feasible to implement soft QoS, whereby there may exist transient periods of time when the network is allowed to fall short of QoS requirements, up to a permitted threshold. The level of QoS satisfaction is thus quantified by the fraction of total disruption. We can then make QoS a function of the available network resources, and applications should ideally adapt to the quality of the network.

There have been many research efforts to provide QoS support in MANETs. Wu (2001) categorizes these efforts into QoS models, QoS resource reservation signaling, QoS routing, and QoS MAC, and provides an overview of how these different components can work together to deliver QoS in MANETs. In the following subsections, we describe some of the recent developments by the networking community and evaluate their effectiveness in providing QoS in MANET scenarios.

MANET QoS Models

A QoS model defines the methodology and architecture for providing certain types of service in the network, but it does not define the specific protocols, algorithms, or implementations to realize QoS provisioning. An ideal MANET QoS model should take into account the various network dynamics and constraints experienced by the nodes, such as mobility and varying link characteristics, and ensure that the architecture is able to provide some form of QoS guarantees.

Xiao (2000) proposes a flexible QoS model for MANETs (FQMM), which adopts a hybrid provisioning policy by dividing traffic into different classes and applying different QoS handling mechanisms to these classes. IntServ-like per flow provisioning is used for the class with highest priority, while DiffServ-like per aggregate is used for the remaining classes. FQMM is suited for relatively small-sized networks of up to 50

nodes; as in DiffServ, a node can be an ingress node (source node), egress node (destination node), or an interior node which forwards packets for other nodes. Depending on the topology and traffic pattern, the role that each node undertakes changes dynamically.

An integrated MANET QoS (iMAQ) model proposed by Chen (2002) defines a cross-layer architecture for multimedia traffic. The framework is comprised of: (i) an application layer that generates multimedia data, (ii) a middleware layer that uses location information from the network layer to predict network partitioning, and (iii) a network layer that uses predictive location-based routing to select a path to the future location of a node. Information is exchanged among the data advertising, lookup, replication services, and the QoS routing protocol in the form of system profiles, and this helps to achieve a higher quality in data access as well as enhances communications between the respective layers.

A two-layer QoS (2LQoS) model has also been proposed (Nikaein, 2002) which provides differentiated services and soft guarantees to network resources for admitted applications by using class-based weighted fair queuing (CB-WFQ) at the intermediate nodes. The model is comprised of two main phases: (i) path generation, in which the quality of the route is computed based on the network layer quality of intermediate nodes; and (ii) path selection based on the desired QoS class (which are mapped onto various application level metrics). In this architecture, network layer metrics (NLMs), which are used to determine the quality of individual nodes, are separated from the Application Layer Metrics (ALMs). NLMs refer to the hopcount, buffer level, and stability level, whereas ALMs comprise delay, throughput, and enhanced best-effort. The work is extended to include MAC Layer Metrics, such as the signal-to-noise-ratio (SNR) of the link and the coding scheme used.

QoS MAC for MANETs

Medium access control (MAC) protocols for MANETs are non-deterministic and distributed, with no base station of a centralized controller to coordinate the channel access. Therefore, mobile nodes have to contend for access to the shared medium in a random access manner. The industry standard MAC access scheme used in wireless networks is IEEE 802.11, which includes both the point coordination function (PCF) and distributed coordination function (DCF). However, this base standard is not directly applicable to MANETs because of its lack of traffic prioritization mechanism.

A number of contention-based QoS MAC protocols have been proposed, some of which include: (i) priority queuing schemes such as IEEE 802.11e, (ii) multi-channel schemes with separate channels for data and control packets, and (iii) black-burst contention schemes with varying delay for traffic of different priorities.

The IEEE 802.11e MAC standard (and its enhanced distributed coordination function extension) is an enhancement to the original standard which aims to support QoS in wireless networks. Differentiated service is provided to nodes by having four queues with different access categories, each of which corresponds to a different set of channel access parameters. Traffic with higher priority can then contend for channel access more successfully than low priority traffic by modifying parameters such as inter-frame spacing (IFS) and contention window size (He, 2003).

Conventional MAC protocols, such as IEEE 802.11, are single-channel models which experience higher collisions and contention for channel access as the number of nodes in the network increases. Consequently, the network performance degrades significantly because the overall throughput is limited by the bandwidth of the channel. In contrast, multi-channel MAC schemes, such as those proposed by Tian (2003) and Wu (2002), have better throughput performance, decreased propagation delay per channel, and QoS provisioning in MANETs.

The black-burst (BB) contention scheme (Sobrinho, 1999) is a distributed MAC scheme that provides real-time access to ad hoc CSMA wireless networks. The real-time data traffic contend for access to the wireless channel by jamming the media with pulses of energy known as BBs, which have lengths that are functions of the delay being experienced by the nodes. Hence, the BB contention scheme gives priority to real-time traffic, enforces a round-robin discipline among real-time nodes, and results in bounded access delays to real-time packets.

Another MAC protocol that provides multiple priority levels is proposed by Sheu (2004). It adopts the black-burst mechanism, as described earlier, to differentiate between high and low priority stations. This helps to guarantee that the frames with higher priority, such as multimedia real-time traffic, will always be transmitted earlier than frames with lower priority.

Furthermore, stations with the same priority will access the shared channel in a round-robin manner.

MANET QoS Routing

QoS routing is considered by Chakrabarti (2001) to be the most important element in the network because it specifies the process of selecting routes to be used by the packets of a logical connection in attaining the associated QoS guarantee. Crawley (1998) presents a framework for QoS-based routing in the Internet whereby paths for flows are determined based on some knowledge of resource availability in the network as well as the QoS requirements of the connection. There have been significant research efforts on QoS routing in MANETs, some of which include: (i) QoS extensions to existing routing protocols, (ii) AQOR (ad hoc QoS on-demand routing), (iii) CEDAR (core extraction distributed ad hoc routing), (iv) multi-path QoS routing, and (v) QoS-GRID, which uses topology management. Other QoS routing schemes for MANETs are discussed in Jawhar (2004).

As conventional MANET routing protocols implicitly select the shortest paths during route establishment and/or route maintenance, they are unable to offer QoS support to the nodes in the network. As such, many extensions for existing MANET protocols have been proposed to take into account the type of resources desired by the requesting application. Perkins (2003) proposes changes to AODV to provide QoS support by adding extensions to the messages used by the route-discovery process. These extensions specify the service requirements, such as maximum delay and minimum bandwidth, in the route request (RREQ) and route reply (RREP) messages. Badis (2004) has also proposed QOLSR, an extension to the original OLSR. Instead of using the number of hops for route selection, metrics such as the available bandwidth, delay, jitter, loss probability, etc., are also added to the OLSR functionality and control messages format, to be used for multi-point relay (MPR) selection and routing table calculation.

The ad-hoc QoS on-demand routing (AQOR) protocol (Xue, 2003) is another QoS routing protocol that provides end-to-end QoS support in terms of bandwidth and delay. Besides performing accurate admission control and resource reservation via detailed computations, AQOR is also equipped with signaling capabilities to handle temporary reservation and destination-initiated recovery processes.

CEDAR (Sivakumar, 1999) performs QoS routing for small to medium-sized MANETs. It is comprised of three main components: (i) establishment and maintenance of a self-organizing routing infrastructure called the core, by approximating a minimum dominating set, (ii) propagation of the link state of high bandwidth and stable links in the core to all core nodes, and (iii) a QoS-route computation algorithm that is executed at the core nodes using only locally available states. The route is then selected from the dominator of the source node to the dominator of the destination that satisfies the required bandwidth.

In multi-path QoS routing protocols such as Liao (2002), Chen (2004), Leung (2001), and Chen (2004), the route discovery process selects multiple paths (ideally disjoint) from the source to destination. The multiple paths can be used collectively to satisfy the required QoS requirements (such as bandwidth), and in the event of link breakages along the main paths, the backup paths will then take over the routing immediately, thus reducing the time needed for another route-computation process.

QoS-GRID (Liu, 2003) is a location-based routing protocol with QoS provisioning. It uses a two-tier grid system to reduce the transmission power of each node so as to enhance the bandwidth utilization and provide stable bandwidth guarantees.

ALTERNATIVE QoS MECHANISMS

In the previous sections, we have offered a multi-layered overview of the problems and issues that surround QoS provisioning in MANETs. Despite numerous efforts to overcome these challenges and add guarantees to data delivery in autonomous, distributed, and ad hoc environments, it is inherently difficult to provide QoS support in MANETs due to the following factors: (i) unreliable and unpredictable wireless transmission media, (ii) node mobility induced topology and route changes, which lead to inaccurate locality information, and (iii) power control and energy constraints.

In addition, existing algorithms and mechanisms do not provide any form of assurance that routes will be found nor that broken routes will be recovered within a given time. To overcome these uncertainties, tech-

niques like topology control and mobility prediction have been exploited.

In topology control, certain system parameters, such as the transmission radii of the nodes, can be varied using power control. However, this is not straightforward and may increase contention in the nodes. A QoS routing mechanism with mobility prediction has also been proposed by Wang (2001), which uses node movement patterns to determine the future location of nodes. It then selects the most stable path based on mobility prediction and QoS requirements on bandwidth and delay, but this does not eliminate the possibility that link breakages can still occur along the selected paths.

In the following, we propose some key alternatives to overcome the transient and unpredictable characteristics of MANETs and provision for QoS in MANETs.

- **Controlled node movement:** The system/protocols can be empowered with the ability to control the movement of a subset of nodes in the network. This can be done by making use of swarms of mobile robots with sensors and actuators (Seah, 2006), unmanned autonomous vehicles (UAVs), and public transportation (such as buses and trains), which have more predictable mobility patterns.
- **Clustering:** The ad-hoc nature of MANETs, along with their decentralized architecture, poses much difficulty in the coordination and functioning of the network. Clustering techniques enable dynamic hierarchical architectures to be formed and improve the network performance.
- **Vertical coupling (cross layer interactions):** Although traditional networking paradigms promote the usage of a multi-layered protocol stack in which the different layers have minimal impact on each other, this does not lead to optimal performance. Cross layered designs, such as that proposed by Chen (2002) can help to improve network performance by sharing information across the different layers, at the cost of interdependency between adjacent layers.
- **QoS adaptation:** Conventional network protocols have static behavior, i.e., they perform a fixed set of actions at all times, irrespective of the current network conditions. Since a MANET is generally dynamic in nature, QoS adaptation, whereby the protocols adapt to the network conditions at all times, may be able to produce better performance.

FUTURE TRENDS

Although there have been vast amounts of studies in the different aspects of QoS support in MANETs—QoS models, QoS MAC protocols, QoS routing protocols, and QoS signaling techniques, there are currently very few practical deployments of such networks. This is a consequence of the fact that the current research in MANETs is still unable to support the QoS requirements of the envisioned applications.

Future trends in QoS provisioning in MANETs appear to follow a cross-layered approach, with the different protocol layers working together to enhance the reliability, robustness, and overall performance of the network. The dynamic nature of MANETs also necessitates the need for the protocols to adapt their behaviors according to the prevailing network conditions–a mechanism that can generally be defined as QoS adaptation. In addition, the unpredictability and constraints of MANETs push the need for soft QoS to be considered as a compromising principle in MANETs. To provide QoS guarantees in the network, many other issues and assumptions have to be further studied. These include security, node reliability, node misbehaviors, node mobility, and the possible further interoperation of MANETs with the wired Internet.

CONCLUSION

The distributed architecture and autonomous nature of the nodes in MANETs contribute to its attractiveness as a communication network that can be easily deployed on-the-fly. However, the inherent characteristics of MANETs—node mobility, decentralized architecture, multi-hop communications, limited resources, and unstable link quality—contribute to the impediment of network performance. As such, it is difficult to provide QoS support in the network using traditional network techniques (such as resource reservation and traffic differentiation) that are used in the wired Internet. As QoS provisioning in MANETs typically involve the collaboration of various layers of the networking protocol stack, researchers are increasingly considering the use of cross-layered designs, adaptivity, and mobility predictions to achieve QoS guarantees in the network. Nevertheless, there are still several outstanding QoS issues that must be addressed, and alternative forms of mechanisms must be studied in greater depth to facilitate the development of QoS in MANETs.

REFERENCES

Badis, H., Agha, K. A., & Munaretto, A. (2004). *Quality of service for ad hoc optimized link state routing protocol (QOLSR)*. IETF Internet draft, draft-badis-manet-qolsr-00.txt, Work in Progress.

Blake, S., Black, D., Carlson, N., Davies, E., Wang, Z., & Weiss W. (1998). *An architecture for differentiated services*. IETF RFC 2475.

Braden, B., Clark, D., & Shenker, S. (1994). Integrated services in the Internet architecture: An overview. IETF RFC1633, June.

Chakrabarti, S., & Mishra, A. (2001). QoS issues in ad hoc wireless networks. *IEEE Communications Magazine, 39*(2), 142-148.

Chen, K., Shah, S. H., & Nahrstedt, K. (2002). Cross-layer design for data accessibility in mobile ad hoc networks. *Journal of Wireless Personal Communications*, Special Issue on Multimedia Network Protocols and Enabling Radio Technologies, Kluwer Academic Publishers, 21, 49-75, 104-116.

Chen, Y. S., Tseng, Y. C., Sheu, J. P., & Kuo, P. H. (2004). An on-demand, link-state, multi-path QoS routing in a wireless mobile ad-hoc network. *Computer Communications, 27*(1), 27-40.

Chen, Y. S., & Yu, Y. T. (2004). Spiral-multi-math QoS routing in a wireless mobile ad hoc network, *IEICE Transactions on Communications*, E87-B, No. 1.

Crawly, E. S., Nair, R., Rajagopalan, B., & Sandick, H. (1998). *A framework for QoS-based routing in the Internet*. IETF RFC 2386.

He, D., & Shen, C. Q. (2003). Simulation study of IEEE 802.11e EDCF. In *Proceedings of IEEE Vehicular Technology Conference* (VTC 2003, Spring), Seoul, Korea, Vol. 1, 685-689.

Jawhar, I., & Wu, J. (2004). *Quality of service routing in mobile ad hoc networks*. Kluwer Academic Publishers.

Kurose, J. R., & Ross, K. W. (2003). *Computer networking: A top-down approach featuring the Internet* (2nd ed.). Addison Wesley.

Leung, R., Liu, J., Poon, E., Chan, C., & Li, B. (2001). MP-DSR: A QoS-aware multi-path dynamic source routing protocol for wireless ad-hoc networks. In *Proceedings of 26th IEEE Annual Conference on Local Computer Networks (LCN 2001)*, Tampa, Florida, USA, 132-141.

Liao, W. H., Wang, S. L., Sheu, J. P., & Tseng, Y. C. (2002). A multi-path QoS routing protocol in a wireless mobile ad hoc network. *Telecommunications Systems*, 19, 329-347.

Liu, H.,& Li, Y. (2003). A location based QoS routing protocol for ad hoc networks. In *Proceedings of 17th International Conference on Advanced Information Networking and Applications (AINA '03)*, Xi'an, China, 830-833.

Nikaein, N., Bonnet, C., Moret, Y., & Rai, I. A. (2002). 2LQoS–Two-layered quality of service model for reactive routing protocols for mobile ad hoc networks. In *Proceedings of 6th World Multiconference on Systemics, Cybernetics and Informatics (SCI 2002)*, Orlando, Florida, USA.

Perkins, C. E., & Belding-Royer, E. M. (2003). *Quality of service for ad hoc on-demand distance vector routing*. IETF Internet draft, draft-perkins-manet-aodvqos-02.txt, Work in Progress.

Seah, W. K. G., Liu, Z., Lim, J. G., Rao, S. V., & Ang, M. H. Jr. (2006). TARANTULAS: Mobility-enhanced wireless sensor-actuator networks. In *Proceedings of the IEEE International Conference on Sensor Networks, Ubiquitous, and Trustworthy Computing (SUTC2006)*, Taichung, Taiwan, 548-551.

Sheu, J. P., & Liu, C. H. (2004). A priority MAC protocol to support real-time traffic in ad hoc networks. *Wireless Networks*, 10, 61-69.

Sivakumar, R., Sinha, P., & Bharghavan, V. (1999). CEDAR: A core-extraction distributed ad hoc routing algorithm. *IEEE Journal on Selected Areas in Communications*, 17(8), 1454-1465,

Sobrinho, J. L., & Krishnakumar, A. S. (1999). Quality-of-service in ad hoc carrier sense multiple access wireless networks, *IEEE Journal on Selected Areas in Communications*, 17(8), 1353-1368.

Tian, H., Li, Y. Y., Hu, J., & Zhang, P. (2003). A MAC protocol supporting multiple traffic over mobile ad hoc networks. In *Proceedings of 57th IEEE Semiannual Vehicular Technology Conference* (VTC 2003, Spring), Seoul, Korea, Vol. 1, 665-669.

Wang, J., Tang, Y., Deng, S., & Chen, J. (2001). QoS routing with mobility prediction in MANET. In *Proceedings of IEEE Pacific Rim Conference on Communications, Computers and Signal Processing, Victoria, BC, Canada,* Vol. 2, 357-360.

Wu, K., & Harms, J. (2001). QoS support in mobile ad hoc networks. *Crossing Boundaries: The GSA Journal of University of Alberta, 1*(1), 92-106

Wu, S. L., Tseng, Y. C., Lin, C. Y., & Sheu, J. P. (2002). A multi-channel MAC protocol with power control for multi-hop mobile ad hoc networks. *The Computer Journal, 45*(1), 101-110.

Xiao, H., Seah, W. K. G., Lo, A., & Chua, K. C. (2000). A flexible quality of service model for mobile ad-hoc networks In *Proceedings of IEEE 51st Vehicular Technology Conference*, Tokyo, Japan, Vol. 1, 445-449.

Xue, Q., & Ganz, A. (2003). Ad hoc QoS on-demand routing (AQOR) in mobile ad hoc networks. *Journal of Parallel and Distributed Computing, 63*(2), 154-165.

KEY TERMS

Clustering: A networking technique in which nodes in the network group themselves according to some network attributes to form hierarchical architectures.

Cross-Layer Design: A protocol design that leverages on the interactions and dependencies between different layers of the networking protocol stack to achieve better performance. MANET (mobile ad hoc network)—self-configuring and self-maintaining network in which nodes are autonomous and distributed in nature.

QoS (quality of service): The ability of a network to deliver a guaranteed level of service to its users and/or applications.

QoS Adaptation: The adaptation of the behavior of one or more network protocols according to the prevailing network conditions, so as to achieve QoS in the network.

Service Requirements: Performance metrics such as throughput, delay, jitter (delay variance), bandwidth, and reliability which are usually application-specific.

Soft QoS: A compromising principle of QoS support whereby there may exist transient periods of time when the network is allowed to fall short of QoS requirements, up to a permitted threshold. The level of QoS satisfaction is thus quantified by the fraction of total disruption.

UAV (Unmanned Autonomous Vehicle): A machine that can move through the terrain intelligently and autonomously without the need for any human intervention.

Quality of Service Routing

Marília Curado
CISUC/DEI, Portugal

Q

INTRODUCTION

Traditionally, Internet routing is achieved through shortest path protocols that base their decision on the number of hops or administrative metrics. The path computation algorithms belong either to the distance vector or link state families.

Distance vector protocols have been widely used on the Internet since the ARPANET and remain in use today. The protocols of the Distance Vector family are used by routers to exchange routing information with their neighbours and to select the shortest paths to all destinations within the network using the Bellman-Ford algorithm, such as in the routing information protocol (RIP) (Malkin, 1998).

Link-state routing protocol comes as an alternative to distance vector protocols. Open Shortest Path First is a link-state interior gateway protocol that is responsible for routing packets within an autonomous system (Moy, 1998). Link state routing protocols use a flooding mechanism to distribute the information about the state of the links of each node to all nodes in the network and apply the Dijkstra shortest path first algorithm to compute shortest paths to all network destinations.

The routing protocols presented are widely used for Internet routing. However, the inherent shortest-path routing paradigm lacks the potential to support the **quality of service** (QoS) level required by real-time applications. While QoS is provided in actual networks at other levels, such as with queue management and application adaptation mechanisms, **QoS routing** comes up as the missing piece to achieve an interesting level of QoS.

BACKGROUND

The main goal of **quality of service routing** is to select the path that is most suitable according to traffic requirements , based on information about the state of the network, and thus to contribute to the improvement of traffic performance while maximizing the utilization of network resources (Crawley, 1998).

The design of a **QoS routing protocol** needs the definitions of three main building blocks: the metrics used to represent the state of the network, the mechanism used for their distribution, and the QoS path computation algorithm.

Routing metrics include parameters such as bandwidth, loss rate, delay, and jitter. The choice of metrics is one of the main issues that must be addressed in a routing strategy because it determines the characteristics that are offered to traffic and the complexity of the path computation algorithm. **Routing metrics** are classified according to the composition rule used to compute the value of the metric on a path. The composition rule for additive metrics, such as delay and number of hops, is that the value of this metric over a path is the sum of the values at each hop. The composition rule of multiplicative metrics is obtained by the product of its values in each hop, as it is the case of loss rate or reliability. Bandwidth is a concave metric and its composition over a path corresponds to the minimum value observed in all hops of that path.

The distribution of metrics may be done by flooding, signalling protocols, or message probing.

The problem of **QoS routing** when using two additive or multiplicative metrics, or one additive and one multiplicative metric, is a non polynomial complete (NP-complete) problem (Neve, 2002). This definition means that there is not an algorithm that is able to find a feasible solution that satisfies both constraints in polynomial time. There are, however, particular situations concerning the relationship between metrics, the values of metrics, and network topologies that can be solvable by optimal algorithms in pseudo-polynomial time (Kuipers, 2003).

The selection of QoS paths subject to multiple constraints is called a **multi-constrained path** (MCP) **problem**. The MCP problem is to find a path from a source to a destination such that all the QoS constraints are met. The paths that satisfy these constraints are called feasible paths. Since the optimal solution to this type of problem for multiple additive and independent metrics is NP-complete, usually heuristics or approximation algorithms are used. Three of the main solutions for multi-constrained path computation are described next.

First Approach: Bandwidth Restricted Path (BRP)

Metric ordering is the main heuristic used for the solution of the BRP problem. This heuristic requires the identification of the metric that has higher priority and the computation of the best paths according to this measure. Afterwards, it is computed the best path according to the second metric. The algorithms that solve the BRP problem using metric ordering are the widest-shortest path (WSP) (Sobrinho, 2002) and shortest-widest path (SWP) (Shen, 2002). In these families of algorithms, the width of a path is depicted by the available bandwidth and its length can correspond either to the number of hops or to delay.

A compromise between the two performance objectives of WSP and SWP algorithms, minimal resource consumption and improved load balancing, respectively, are achieved by the all hops optimal path algorithm (Guérin, 2002). The AHOP algorithm tries to reduce network cost while achieving load balancing, since a longer path is only used if it has more available bandwidth.

Second Approach: Restricted Shortest Path (RSP)

The MCP problem is when two additive metrics are used. All the paths that satisfy the constraint associated with one of the metrics are computed and then the shortest path according to the second metric is selected.

A widely studied case of the RSP is the delay-constrained least cost problem. The objective of this problem is to find a set of paths that satisfy the delay constraint and then to select the path that minimizes the cost. Even though the DCLC problem is NP-complete, heuristics-based algorithms have been proposed, such as the delay-cost constrained routing (Chen, 1998) and the dual extended bellman-ford (Cheng, 2003).

Third Approach: Metrics Combination (MC)

Metrics combination reduces the complexity of the RSP problem by combining both metrics and then

using a traditional shortest-path algorithm to compute the path that minimizes the resulting metric. There are two main approaches for metrics composition: linear function composition (Cui, 2003) and non-linear function composition (Neve, 2002).

Even tough metrics combinations contribute to the simplification of path computation algorithms; they prevent the provisioning of guarantees regarding the constraints associated with each one of the metrics involved. In order to overcome this problem, there is the need to define the proper weights used in the combination rule of metrics, using, for instance, Lagrange relaxation techniques as in the binary search for Lagrange relaxation algorithm (Korkmaz, 2000) and in the Lagrange relaxation-based aggregated cost algorithm (Jüttner, 2001).

The combination of metrics in a single metric allows for simple and well-known path computation algorithms. However, the rule for combination of the metrics is not always straightforward, and the composition of the resulting metric over a path can also be challenging. Therefore, the choice of the type of heuristic must take into consideration factors such as QoS framework, traffic patterns, and traffic engineering objectives.

QUALITY OF SERVICE ROUTING

The deployment of QoS routing protocols raises several problems that must be assessed in order to guarantee an interesting solution in terms of routing behaviour, traffic performance, and network utilization. The main issues to be addressed in order to achieve successful QoS routing protocols concern the control of **QoS routing overhead**, the treatment of **routing information inaccuracy**, and the avoidance of **routing oscillations**.

QoS Routing Overhead

The objectives of QoS routing protocols may be compromised by the additional burden they impose in the network. The load introduced by QoS routing approaches includes the processing overhead due to more complex and frequent computations and the communication overhead caused by the increase in the amount of routing information exchanged within the network. Signalling and additional storage that are needed to support QoS routing protocols are also of importance when assessing the impact of QoS routing on the network.

Metrics Quantification and Triggering Policies

The advertisement of quantified metrics, instead of the advertisement of instantaneous values, is a common approach to avoid the excessive communication cost of dynamic routing protocols (Apostolopoulos, 1999). Moreover, instead of distributing updates immediately after a change, the instant of distribution is generally controlled by triggering policies. Triggering policies are classified by the type of trigger used, namely, threshold-based, class-based, or time-based.

With threshold-based triggers, a new update is only issued when there is a significant difference between the actual and the previous values of the metrics. Class-based triggers divide the total range of the metrics into intervals, and the emission of updates is triggered when the metric crosses the division between classes. In order to limit the instability due to the successive boundary changes, a hysteresis mechanism can be used, and thus, instead of using the actual transposition of a boundary as trigger, the update is only issued when it reaches the middle value of the new class.

As a complement to the policies described, a hold-down timer ensures a minimum time interval between updates.

Time-based triggers issue routing updates periodically. This type of trigger has the disadvantage of being insensitive to network conditions. On the other hand, it is able to consistently reduce the amount of routing information by a conservative definition of the value of the update period, without influencing traffic patterns.

The solutions described are able to reduce communication and processing overheads, since once routers receive less update messages, they will compute paths less frequently. The utilization of the mechanisms described creates the need for a trade-off between the desired up-to-date state of the network and the burden this imposes in terms of routing overhead (Shaikh, 2001).

Selective Flooding

The flooding mechanism used by Link-State protocols causes a burden that can consume an excessive amount of resources in the network.

The selective flooding protocol uses a combined approach of flooding and probing to avoid the disadvantage of entirely flooding-based approaches (Claypool, 2001). Flooding is used to maintain the topological database of every node, and probing is performed upon the arrival of a connection request. With this approach, the network overhead is reduced and the selection of paths is made based on up-to-date information collected by the probe packets, however, at the expense of connection setup time.

The restricted flooding mechanism limits the distribution of updates among border routers of areas or autonomous systems in hierarchical organized networks (Lee, 2003).

Path Pre-Computation

Most QoS routing proposals use on-demand path computation in order to obtain paths that guarantee the QoS requirements of traffic based on recent information about the state of the network. However, on-demand path computation has two drawbacks, namely, it introduces some delay before the forwarding of traffic starts and it requires the application of the path computation algorithm for each connection request, introducing additional processing overhead on the routers, especially when the arrival rate of connection requests is high. The pre-computation of paths is the alternative approach to handle the problem of the processing overhead associated with on-demand path computation. This comes at the expense of the eventual inaccuracy of the routing decision due to the time frame between path computation and the actual utilization of the path.

Proposals that use path pre-computation to reduce QoS routing overhead include the multi-constrained energy function-based pre-computation (Cui, 2003), the all hops optimal path (Guérin, 2002) algorithms, and the class-based routing QoS routing (Curado, 2003).

Pre-computation is the actual method used for routing in IP networks, and thus becomes an interesting option for a smooth transition to QoS routing. Even though pre-computation schemes can reduce the QoS routing processing overhead when the arrival of requests is high, they have two drawbacks. One is related to the utilization of eventually outdated paths, and the other pertains to the need to pre-compute QoS aware paths to all destinations satisfying all possible QoS requests. The first drawback can be overcome by using suitable path computation algorithm-triggering mechanisms, and the second becomes less important in networks where traffic differentiation has coarser granularity than flow-based, as in the class-based classification style.

QoS Routing Under Inaccurate Information

The main sources of **routing inaccuracy** are the low frequency of the distribution of link-state updates, the information aggregation in hierarchical networks, propagation delay of routing messages in large networks, and the utilization of estimates about the current state of the network. Due to this wide range of factors, the global state that is kept by each router is just an approximation of the actual state. When the path computation algorithms use this inaccurate information as if it was exact, their performance can be highly damaged.

One approach to handle routing information inaccuracy is based on algorithms that use probability functions and random variables, such as the following examples.

The multi-constrained path problem under Inaccurate State Information uses a probabilistic function to find a path that that is the most suitable to accommodate a new request (Mieghem, 2003).

Safety-based routing combines a probabilistic approach with the limitation of the range the metrics can attain between updates to enhance the performance of QoS routing under inaccurate state information, caused by stale link-state information due to large thresholds and hold-down timers (Apostolopoulos, 1999).

The bandwidth-delay-constrained path under inaccurate state information computes delay and bandwidth constrained paths (Korkmaz, 2003).

Message probing is another a technique commonly used to deal with imprecise state information. The utilization of probing avoids the staleness of link-state information because the probes gather the most recent state information. Ticket-based probing (Chen, 1998), the pre-computation based selective probing scheme (Lee, 2000), and the selective flooding protocol (Claypool, 2001) use probes to collect QoS information about paths in order to solve the DCLC problem under inaccurate state information.

QoS Routing Stability

The stability of QoS routing protocols is a determinant factor of their performance. Instability may occur whenever the responsiveness of the protocol becomes exaggerated, introducing unnecessary re-routing of traffic. Specifically, in link-state protocols, the inappropriate flooding of updates may originate route flaps that will degrade traffic performance. This is particularly problematic when the network is congested, since the additional routing messages consume the already scarce bandwidth resources, and the subsequent application of the path computation algorithm imposes even more load on the router processor.

The problem of **routing instability** is influenced by several factors, namely, the type of metrics used to compute the best path, the policy that controls the advertisement of the metrics, and the path computation algorithm. Network topology and traffic patterns also influence routing behaviour and stability.

Control of Metrics Distribution

A common approach to avoid instability is the advertisement of metrics that are quantified in some manner, instead of advertising instantaneous values. The use of metric quantification, while contributing to routing stability, reduces the dynamic nature and the adaptation capabilities of the routing protocol, since it increases the period of routing oscillations.

The limitation of the range of values that the metrics can take is an additional method that can be used to control routing oscillations. This is achieved by the definition of a bias term that is a lower bound of the interval where the metrics values can vary. The upper bound of the interval can also be set in order to limit the range of metrics values. A scaling method can be used to fit the measured metrics values on the range defined by the two bounds.

Any mechanism for metric quantification must preserve an adequate trade-off between route adaptability and routing oscillatory behaviour.

Traffic Characteristics-Aware QoS Routing

Traffic patterns influence the behaviour of QoS routing algorithms, including its stability capability.

In the long-lived-short-lived approach, the resources in the network are dynamically shared between short-lived and long-lived flows (Shaikh, 1999). The paths for long-lived flows are dynamically chosen based on the load level on the network, while the paths for short flows are statically pre-computed. Since the short-lived flows are routed on statically pre-computed paths, the route flaps associated with the dynamic routing of these types of flows are avoided.

In the differentiated routing scheme, a smoothed metric is used to compute the shortest path for long-lived flows, and the most recent value of the metrics to compute the shortest path for short-lived flows (Yang, 2001).

In the enhanced bandwidth-inversion shortest-path, the hop count is included in the cost function in order to avoid oscillations due to the increased number of flows sent over the widest-path (Wang, 2002).

Proactive multi-path routing takes into consideration traffic characteristics and network connectivity (Shen, 2002). The path chosen for long-lived flows is the shortest path that satisfies the requirements of the flow, while short-lived flows use multiple alternate paths.

Class-Pinning

The dynamic selection of paths may cause routing instability and network oscillatory behaviour. The objective of the **class-pinning** mechanism is to limit the number of path shifts due to dynamic changes in the state of the network (Curado, 2005). The class-pinning mechanism addresses the instability problem by controlling the instant when a traffic class shifts to a new path. Normally, when the state of the network changes due to events such as the start of a new flow or a traffic burst, routing messages are sent to all nodes, and new paths are computed. Afterward, traffic of each class will shift to the newer and less congested path, abandoning the path currently used. The next time this process occurs, traffic will eventually go back to the original path, generating an unstable situation. The class-pinning mechanism overcomes this condition by avoiding unnecessary path shifts. When the class-pinning mechanism is active, new paths are also computed upon the arrival of routing messages. However, after path computation, the weight of the path for each *<destination, class>* pair is compared with the weight of the previously installed path. The

new path will only be installed in the routing table if it is significantly better than the path that is currently used by that class.

FUTURE TRENDS

The problem of QoS routing has still many open issues, since there are many trade-offs that must be achieved for a full successful deployment, as was pointed out throughout this discussion. One can expect to see flow-based QoS routing in intra-domain routing, using algorithms to satisfy multiple constraints, and class-based QoS routing in inter-domain routing, using an algorithms base in a single metric resulting from the combination of multiple metrics regarding the characteristics of the classes used within the QoS framework followed.

Moreover, the problem of QoS routing for current and upcoming types of networks, such as wireless, sensor, and ambient, needs further studies due to the specificities of these environments.

CONCLUSION

The need for QoS on the Internet has motivated the development of several mechanisms to evolve actual IP networks. Quality of service routing is one of these components. QoS routing has as its main objective the selection of paths that satisfy the requirements of traffic in the network, while contributing to improved network resource utilization.

The problems addressed show that any QoS routing scheme needs to provide answers to a set of issues that are intertwined and whose implications on the overall performance depend on several, and sometimes unpredictable, factors.

REFERENCES

Apostolopoulos, G., Williams, D., Kamat, S., Guérin, R., Orda, A., & Przygienda, T. (1999). *QoS routing mechanisms and OSPF extensions.* Internet Engineering Task Force, Request for Comments 2676.

Chen, S., & Nahrstedt, K. (1998). On finding multi-constrained paths. *Proceedings of IEEE International*

Conference on Communications (ICC 98) (pp. 874-879). Atlanta, GA.

Cheng, G., & Ansari, N. (2003). A new heuristics for finding the delay constrained least cost path. *Proceedings of IEEE GLOBECOM 2003* (pp. 3711-3715). San Francisco.

Claypool, M., & Kannan, G. (2001). Selective flooding for improved quality-of-service routing. *Proceedings of SPIE Quality of Service over Next-Generation Data Networks* (pp. 33-44). Denver, Colorado.

Crawley, E., Nair, R., Rajagopalan, & Sandick, H. (1998). *A framework for QoS-based routing in the Internet*. Internet Engineering Task Force, Network Working Group, Request for Comments 2386.

Cui, Y., & Wu, J. (2003, March 30-April 3). Precomputation for multi-constrained QoS routing in high-speed networks. *Proceedings of IEEE INFOCOM 2003*, San Francisco.

Curado, M., & Monteiro, E. (2005). A class-pining election scheme for loop-free QoS routing. *Proceedings of IEEE Workshop on High Performance Switching and Routing (HPSR2005)* (pp. 396-400). Hong Kong. IEEE Communications Society

Curado, M., Reis, O., Brito, J., Quadros, G., & Monteiro, E. (2003). Stability and scalability issues in hop-by-hop class-based routing. *Proceedings of the 2nd International Workshop on QoS in Multiservice IP Networks (QoS-IP 2003)* (pp. 103-116). Milano, Italy.

De Neve, H., & Van Mieghem, P. (2002). TAMCRA: A tunable accuracy multiple constraints routing algorithm. *Computer Communications*, 23, 667-679.

Guérin, R., & Orda, A. (2002). Computing shortest paths for any number of hops. *IEEE/ACM Transactions on Networking, 10*(5), 613-620.

Jüttner, A., Szviatovszki, B., Mécs, I., & Rajkó, Z. (2001). Lagrange relaxation based method for the QoS routing problem . *IEEE INFOCOM 2001*, Anchorage, Alaska.

Korkmaz, T., Krunz, M., & Tragoudas, S. (2000). An efficient algorithm for finding a path subject to two additive constraints. Joint international conference on measurement and modeling of computer systems. *Proceedings of the 2000 ACM SIGMETRICS international conference on Measurement and modeling of computer systems table of contents* (pp. 318-327). Santa Clara, California.

Kuipers, F., & Van Mieghem, P., (2003). The impact of correlated link weights on QoS routing. *Proceedings of IEEE INFOCOM 2003*, Vol. 2, pp. 1425-1434, March 30-April 3, San Francisco.

Kuipers, F., Korkmaz, T., Krunz, M., & Van Mieghem, P. (2002). Overview of constraint-based path selection algorithms for QoS routing . *IEEE Communications Magazine*, special issue on IP-Oriented Quality of Service, pp. 16-23.

Lee, S., Das, S., Pau, G., & Gerla, M. (2003). A hierarchical multipath approach to QoS routing: Performance and cost evaluation . *IEEE International Conference on Communications 2003 (ICC 2003)* (pp. 625-630). Anchorage.

Lee, W., & Lee, B. (2000). Pre-computation based selective probing scheme with imprecise state information . *Proceedings of IEEE GLOBECOM 2000*, San Francisco (pp. 460-464).

Malkin, G. (1998). *RIP Version 2* , Internet engineering task force. Network Working Group, Request for Comments 2453.

Moy, J. (1998). *OSPF Version 2* , Internet Engineering Task Force. Network Working Group, Request for Comments 2328.

Shaikh, A., Rexford, J., & Shin, K. (1999). Load-sensitive routing of long-lived IP flows. *Proceedings of ACM SIGCOMM '99* (pp. 215-226). Harvard University Science Center, Cambridge, MA.

Shaikh, A., Rexford, J., & Shin, K. (2001). Evaluating the impact of stale link state on quality-of-service routing. *IEEE/ACM Transactions on Networking, 9*(2), 162-176.

Shen, J., Shi, J., & Crowcroft, J. (2002, Oct 16-18). Proactive multi-path routing . *Proceedings of the International Workshop on Quality of future Internet Services (QofIS 2002)* (pp. 145-156). Zurich, Switzerland.

Sobrinho, J. L. (2002). Algebra and algorithms for QoS path computation and hop-by-hop routing in the Internet. *IEEE Transactions on Networking*, pp. 541-550.

Van Mieghem, P., Kuipers, F., Korkmaz, T., Krunz, M., Curado, M., Monteiro, E., et al. (2003). Quality of service routing. In M. Smirnof, J. Roberts, & J. Crowcroft (Eds.). Springer.

Yang, S., Su, X., Veciana, G. (2001). Heterogeneity-aware shortest path routing: Flow holding time, user demand, and network state. *Proceedings of the IEEE Workshop on High Performance Switching and Routing*, pp. 287-291, Dallas, Texas, USA.

KEY TERMS

Additive Metric: A metric whose value over a path is the sum of the values at each hop.

Concave metric: A metric whose value over a path is the minimum value observed in all hops of that path.

Feasible Paths: The paths that satisfy these constraints are called feasible paths.

Multi-Constrained Path Problem: The selection of QoS paths subject to multiple constraints.

Multiplicative Metric: A metric whose value over a path is the product of the values at each hop.

NP-Complete: This definition means that there is not an algorithm that is able to find a feasible solution that satisfies both constraints in polynomial time.

Quality of Service Routing: The selection, based on information about the state of the network, of the path that can satisfy traffic requirements while maximizing the utilization of network resources

Restricted Shortest Path: A simplification of the original MCP problem, when two additive metrics are used.

Rate Adaptation Mechanisms for Multimedia Streaming

Charalampos Patrikakis
Telecommunications Laboratory School of Electrical and Computer Engineering, NTUA, Greece

P. Fafali
NTUA, Greece

Pantelis N. Karamolegkos
Telecommunications Laboratory School of Electrical and Computer Engineering, NTUA, Greece

Y. Despotopoulos
NTUA, Greece

N. Minogiannis
NTUA, Greece

INTRODUCTION

During the last decade, multimedia streaming has experienced explosive growth. Adaptive video has become a necessity for meeting stringent QoS requirements in non-guaranteed IP networks. Since the user is the final point in the multimedia distribution chain, transmission rate must be adjusted to match the requirements set, the end-to-end effective bandwidth, and the capabilities of the terminals used to access the services offered. In addition, the concept of pervasive and ubiquitous computing has increased the need for rate adaptation so as to fulfill the restrictions posed by mobile terminals (e.g., phones and handhelds). The ultimate goal is the optimization of the subjective audio-visual quality.

BACKGROUND

The need for rate control lies in the diverse user requirements and the variation in bandwidth availability over time. The target is to adapt the transmission rate to the prevailing network conditions. A rate adaptation technique should comprise the following features: seamless modification of the transmission rate, quick response to network dynamics, fairness, ease of deployment, and efficiency. Rate control is strongly related to the employment of congestion control and is inspired by the TCP protocol philosophy. Its fundamental objective is to avoid congestion and optimize the quality of the reproduced signal.

Media streaming popularity is basically attributed to the fact that it promises users live access to content from anywhere and at any time through their desktop PCs, laptops, and handhelds. In fact, recent progress in multimedia communications paves the way for universal multimedia access (UMA) (Pereira & Burnett, 2003). It is apparent that successful content delivery cannot be accomplished by simply meeting quality expectations of the audience. Content must be also tailored to specific features of user devices, such as display size and processing power (Wee et al., 2003).

RATE ADAPTATION MECHANISMS

Currently, there is a broad taxonomy of rate adaptation techniques that are used for multimedia delivery over IP platforms. The most prominent algorithms include:

- **Client buffering:** The challenge for media streaming is to guarantee that data are continuously available at the receiver. This is achieved through a pre-roll (playout) buffer that resides at the player. The buffer is meant to absorb burstiness and compensate for the delay variation experienced. Its size typically ranges between five and 15s. At the beginning of the streaming session, the buffer is filled up so as to be able to combat the case where transmission rate is higher than the available bandwidth. When the buffer is depleted, transmission is temporarily halted until it is refilled. This approach, known as client Buffering (Apostolopoulos et al., 2003) actually complements other rate control mechanisms.

- **Stream thinning:** Another approach suggested when a network is clogged is stream thinning. It refers to the selective elimination of frames from a video feed while protecting the audio feed. This process prevents the loss of the entire signal and re-buffering. Packet dropping stalls when the connection restores its initial bandwidth. Stream thinning is used in conjunction with other rate control mechanisms and it is applied in both multicast and unicast distribution schemes.

- **Individually encoded bit rates:** Initially, streaming information was provided at a single rate. This scheme favored users with connection speeds close to the average media rate. Clients with high access speeds were unable to exploit their transmission facilities. At the other extreme, users with slower connections could not view content at all. Thus, this solution could not scale up to support large numbers of end users.

In order to overcome the obstacles posed by static rate media delivery, a new solution was suggested. The key idea behind this was to offer content at individually encoded bit rates chosen in order to cover the available connection. Although this proposal seemed flexible enough to satisfy the individualities of the Internet population, it failed to meet users' quality standards. The reason is that in most cases traffic travels a long way before it reaches users' Internet access points. Therefore, the bottleneck capacity is not always expressed by the last mile link. Moreover, there is no provisioning for changes in bandwidth availability, and the transmission rate has to be specified at the beginning of the streaming session. This approach is also referred to as bandwidth negotiation.

Offering individually encoded bit rates works more effectively with unicast than multicast. In the case of multicast, due to the heterogeneity of group members, there is no feasible rate selection that can support end-users with different channel conditions and conflicting requirements.

- **Single rate switching:** For unicast communication, single-rate switching is based on the back-channel information provided to the media streaming server. In real-time transport protocol (RTP) streaming (Schulzrinne et al., 1996; Busse et al., 2006), the feedback channel is facilitated by the real-time transport control protocol (RTCP) (Schulzrinne et al., 2003). RTCP specifies periodic receiver report (RR) packets which include information such as the fraction of packets lost, the inter-arrival jitter, the delay, and other quality metrics. Single-rate switching, also known as feedback-based encoder adaptation (Lu, 2000), targets the adaptation of the encoder output bit rate to the network conditions. Many algorithms have been proposed in this direction (Bolot, Turletti, & Wakeman, 1994; Bolot & Turletti, 1994; Bolot & Turletti, 1998; Léannec et al., 1999). However, this technique is not suitable for real-time transmission. Though the encoder can be theoretically configured to adapt the content to the appropriate bit rate with respect to individual client requirements, this solution cannot serve a large scale system because of the overhead imposed by real-time compression.

- **Multi-rate switching:** Multi-rate switching, or stream replication (Li, 2003), is a dynamic extension of the individually encoded bit rates technique. It allows mid-stream switching between different rates according to the detected network conditions. On the basis of this idea, many commercial products have been developed, e.g., RealNetworks-real one player (Birney, 2003), and they already play a significant role in the media streaming market. A representative example is SureStream technology from real networks (Conklin et al., 2001). The innovation of this approach lies in the use of multiple representations of the original content (each encoded at a different bit rate) optimized for various network load conditions. The result is a single file wherein all encoded streams are bundled.

- **TCP-friendly transmission:** TCP traffic dominates the Internet by providing reliable transmission and minimum packet loss. Due to its inherent ability to adapt its sending rate to varying network conditions through the rule of additive increase multiplicative decrease (AIMD), it is considered a scalable solution for data delivery. However, reliability offered through packet retransmission detracts from multimedia applications that require continuous representation of the signal. Furthermore, the AIMD scheme enables rate control over a short time scale and in this way exhibits a variable, sawtooth-like throughput.

- **Layered multicast:** Layered multicast was proposed in order to address the heterogeneity problems of multicast adaptive video. Layered multicast can be further divided into cumulative layering and non-cumulative layering. The fundamental idea behind layered coding is the decomposition of the original media file into a base layer and a number of enhancement layers. The base layer contains the low resolution information and can be decoded into meaningful service. The enhancement layers comprise lower priority, progressive refinements of the video.

- **Cumulative layering:** Cumulative layering can be also seen as a way to cope with the bandwidth deficiency problem of multi-rate switching. The first effort towards this direction was the receiver-driven layered multicast (RLM) protocol (McCanne et al., 1996). As its name denotes, the control responsibility is delegated to the receiver of the content. Each layer is transmitted to a different multicast group. The receiver, according to its capacity constraints, joins or leaves the appropriate number of groups. This way, users' diversified requirements can be successfully met by receiving different numbers of layers.

- **Non-cumulative layering:** Non-cumulative layering is actually implemented through multiple description (MD) coding (Goyal, 2003). MD coding addresses the problem of unreliable channels by means of independent descriptions, while layered coding deals with the problem of heterogeneous clients by means of sequences of layers. In this scheme, the original content is coded into multiple layers which have the next two characteristics as described by Apostolopoulos et al. (2002): First, each description can be independently decoded to give a usable reproduction of the initial content. Second, multiple layers contain complementary information so that the quality of the video is improved with the number of the layers successfully received.

EVALUATION CRITERIA FOR RATE ADAPTATION MECHANISMS

Even though the notion of quality is subjective, it is imperative to define some evaluation criteria that should be fulfilled by each rate adaptation technique. These criteria can be actually extracted from the individual objectives set and pursued by most of the mechanisms examined. We should stress that it is practically impossible for a rate adaptation mechanism to meet all widely accepted optimization criteria. The truth is that some criteria contradict each other. For example, in layered multicasts, fine adaptation granularity, which is achieved by increasing the number of enhancement layers, induces complex processing for the decoding of the original video. The most important criteria for evaluating and selecting the appropriate rate adaptation mechanism are the following:

Content Delivery Mechanism

It is evident that except from the layered approach that applies only to multicast communication, all others can be used in both delivery mechanisms (unicast and multicast). However, not all of them perform well for both distribution schemes (e.g., the single-rate switching approach is prohibitive for the multicast case).

Adaptation Granularity and Fairness

The issues of adaptation granularity and fairness are in a sense quite close (Li, 2003). Adaptation granularity reflects the extent to which the rate assigned to a receiver is commensurate with its available bandwidth. When granularity is coarse, the inter-session fairness is reduced. There is the static and the dynamic way for achieving fine-grained adaptation. In the static approach, it is possible to match the capacity of the end-user either by increasing the number of layers (in layered multicast) or by increasing the number of different encodings (in multi-rate switching). The overhead at the receiver in terms of join/ leave delay and decoding labor in layered encoding and the increase in the file size in multi-rate schema do not favor this solution. The dynamic approach has the prerequisite that the sender and the receiver participate actively in the adaptation process. During the streaming session, the sender has to adjust the rate of layers or streams based on feedback information provided by the receiver.

But this is complex for both sides. It is also desirable that the chosen algorithms should be approximately fair to TCP.

Bandwidth Efficiency

Bandwidth efficiency constitutes another issue that has to be considered for the efficient exploitation of network resources. The need for sophisticated allocation of the available bandwidth depends on the level of users' heterogeneity. For simultaneous transmission to large groups, the layered multicast approach seems quite promising, whereas for unicast distribution, multi-rate switching seems a quite appropriate solution.

Control Responsibility

This aspect refers to the entities responsible for controlling the rate adaptation mechanism. When there is no feedback control, the adaptation is receiver-driven (e.g., for cumulative layering). This scheme is more scalable since a single connection has to be monitored and controlled and the system can react quickly to congestion. However, the downside is that this "one-way" interaction renders the system rather static.

Encoding/Decoding Complexity and Cost

It is widely accepted that best quality is comes in terms of complexity and cost. This holds true in the case of rate adaptation too. Partitioning the media clip into layers or encoding an original signal in multiple presentations (i.e., multi-rate switching and MD coding) entails much complexity and infrastructure cost for both sides: sender and receiver. The situation is further complicated when the best possible signal reconstruction is required. If an encoded stream has to be transcoded on the fly into another bit rate, time becomes a considerable constraint because of the delay introduced. Consequently, a fundamental issue in transcoding is to obtain the expected results without requiring the complete decoding/re-encoding of the content. The ability to reuse discrete cosine transforms (DCT) coefficients and motion vectors provides an aid in this area and makes the process quite fast.

Rate Adjustment Frequency

This is a very critical parameter for providing adaptive rate video. As noted earlier, this is a subject of trade-offs. It reflects the time scale at which control is exerted. Aggressive schemes such as AIMD or the probing mechanism used in layered multicast result in short term adaptation. On the contrary, more conservative, feedback-based schemes such as the model-based TCP-friendliness exhibit smooth rate adaptation over longer time scales. None of these extremes are ideal for the reasons already pointed out. A balance should be achieved between them. The ability to control the frequency of rate adjustments is an interesting alternative.

The frequency adaptation in feedback-based situations depends on the protocols that provide the information. In RTCP, the recommended minimum interval among periodic feedback packets is 5sec (Schulzrinne et al., 2003) and varies according to the media format in use and the size of the session. In addition, the duration of the streaming session can be a determinant decision factor for the rate adjustment frequency. The trade-off among the number of changes and the perceived quality has to be weighted. Maybe this dilemma can be resolved by introducing more comprehensive quality metrics apart from the traditional indicators such as playback buffer starvation or packet loss experienced (Dalal et al., 2003).

Underlying Network Infrastructure

This refers to the infrastructure that hosts the adaptive rate functionality. Information regarding the expansion of the network is important. For example, when dealing with a small-scale network, network-based support (prioritized transmission) can be implemented at an affordable cost.

End System Requirements

Rate adaptation schemes have to be tailored to the clients' potentialities, meaning processing power and decoding functionality, especially if user terminals are mobile devices. As far as the streaming server is concerned, similar issues have to be examined (Wu et al., 2001). In multi-rate switching, the server needs the appropriate software for extracting the streams. Furthermore, the scaling rules for the server capacity when delivering media at different bit rates have to be tested (Cherkasova et al., 2003). To clarify this, the following example is provided: When a server can concurrently deliver streams at 500kbps, it is not certain that it is able to deliver the double number of streams at 250kbps.

TRENDS AND FUTURE DIRECTIONS

An interesting topic for future research regarding rate adaptation is the provision of dynamic rate control on the sender's side. Although some efforts have been done already in this area (Liu et al., 2002), there are still issues that need further investigation. Specifically, the problems in the enforcement of dynamic rate control are mainly the inability of streaming servers to provide complex tasks at the bit stream level (transcoding), and at the same time serve a considerable number of clients. However, in the near future, all critical elements for effective, on-the-fly change of the transmission rate will exist. MPEG-7 has already defined hints that accelerate the transcoding procedure while the produced stream is still of high quality. Therefore, delay is limited and it can be even more tolerable if the temporal depth of the pre-roll buffer is increased. Furthermore, with the recently introduced overlay network architectures (Chu et al., 2000), the servers' workload can significantly decrease through efficient load balancing among streaming access servers.

Another interesting research topic is the dynamic incorporation of history-monitoring information into the media streaming systems. History-monitoring information through well-formulated optimization problems can provide guidelines for the initialization of the rate levels. Throughout a session, feedback from RTCP can be used in order to adjust the rates towards the fulfillment of the objectives set. Furthermore, prior knowledge of the expected number of users and their topological distribution, especially in cases of large events (Patrikakis et al., 2003) such as concerts or major athletic games, can be a priceless asset in the hands of service and access providers. On the basis of this knowledge, architectures such as content delivery networks (CDNs), that assist the media distribution process complementary to the underlying network infrastructure, can be deployed. The result can be a better organized distribution scheme, featuring load balancing and improved resource allocation in terms

of network bandwidth, server processing, and storage capabilities.

CONCLUSION

Rate adaptation comprises one of the major issues that need to be taken into account when designing and implementing a multimedia delivery platform. Currently, there is a variety of proposed and implemented solutions, each one targeted to optimize the user's experience in terms of subjective and/or objective quality. The specific area remains, and will probably continue to be, a highly active area of research, mainly due to the ever-evolving technological landscapes of both multimedia encoding and networking.

REFERENCES

Apostolopoulos, J., Tan, W., & Wee, S. (2002). *Video streaming: Concepts, algorithms, and systems. HP Laboratories report.* HPL-2002-260.

Birney, B. (2003). *Intelligent streaming.* Retrieved March 11, 2006, from http://www.microsoft.com/windows/windowsmedia/howto/articles/intstreaming.aspx

Bolot, J-C., & Turletti, T. (1998). Experience with rate control mechanisms for packet video in the Internet. *Computer Communication Review, 28*(1), 4-15.

Bolot, J-C, & Turletti, T. (1994). A rate control mechanism for packet video in the Internet. In *Proceedings of IEEE INFOCOM* (pp. 1216-1224).

Bolot, J-C., Turletti, T., & Wakeman, I. (1994). Scalable feedback control for multicast video distribution in the Internet. *Computer Communications Review, 24*(4), 58-67

Busse, I., Deffner, B., & Schulzrinne, H. (1996). Dynamic QoS control of multimedia applications based on RT. *Computer Communications, 19*, 49-58

Cherkasova, L., & Staley, L. (2003). Building a performance model of streaming media applications in a utility data center environment. In *Proceedings. of the 3rd IEEE/ACM International Symposium on Cluster Computing and the Grid* (CCGrid 2003), 52-59.

Chu, Y., Rao, S., & Zhang, H. (2000). A case for end system multicast. In *Proceedings of ACM Sigmetrics*, 1456-1471.

Conklin, G. J., Greenbaum, G. S., Lillevold, K. O., Lippman, A. F., & Reznik, Y. A. (2001). Video coding for streaming media delivery on the Internet. *IEEE Transactions on Circuits and Systems for Video Technology, 11*(3), 269-281.

Dalal, A., & Perry, E. (2003). *A new architecture for measuring and assessing streaming media quality. HP Laboratories report.* HPL-2003-28.

Goyal, V. K. (2003). Multiple description coding: Compression meets the network. *IEEE Signal Processing Magazine, 18*, 74-93.

Léannec, F.L., Toutain, F., & Guillemot, C. (1999). Packet loss resilient MPEG-4 compliant video coding for the Internet. *Signal Processing: Image Communications, 15*, 35-56.

Li, B., & Liu, J. (2003). Multirate video multicast over the Internet: An overview. *IEEE Network, 17*(1), 24-29.

Liu, J., Li, B., & Zhang, Y.-Q. (2002). A hybrid adaptation protocol for TCP-friendly layered multicast and its optimal rate allocation. In *Proceedings of IEEE INFOCOM* (pp. 1520-1529).

Lu, J. (2000). Signal processing for Internet video streaming: A review. In *Proceedings of SPIE Image and Video Communications and Processing*, 246-259.

McCanne, S., Jacobson, V., & Vetterli, M. (1996). Receiver-driven layered multicast. In *Proceedings of ACM SIGCOMM* (pp. 117-130).

Patrikakis, Ch., Despotopoulos, Y., Rompotis, A., Lambiris, A., Boukouvalas, C., & Pediaditis, G. (2003). OLYMPIC: Using the Internet for real time coverage of major athletic events. In *Proceedings of International Conference on Cross-Media Service Delivery*, 169-180.

Pereira, F., & Burnett, I. (2003). Universal multimedia experiences for tomorrow. *IEEE Signal Processing Magazine, 20*, 63-73.

RealNetworks. *Introduction to streaming media with RealOne player.* Retrieved March 10, 2006 from, http://service.real.com/help/library/guides/realone/IntroGuide/PDF/ProductionIntro.pdf

Schulzrinne, H., Casner, S., Frederick, R., & Jacobson, V. (2003). *RTP: A transport protocol for real-time applications.* IETF RFC 3550.

Schulzrinne, H., Casner, S., Frederick, R., & Jacobson, V. (1996). *RTP: A transport protocol for real-time applications.* IETF RFC1889.

Wee, S., Apostolopoulos, J., Tan, W., & Roy, S. (2003). Research and design of a mobile streaming media content delivery network. In *Proceedings. of IEEE International Conference on Multimedia & Expo (ICME)*, 5-8.

Wu, D., Hou, Y. T., Zhu, W., Zhang, Y.-Q., & Peha, J. M. (2001). Streaming video over Internet: Approaches and directions. *IEEE Transactions on Circuits and Systems for Video Technology, 11*(3), 282-300.

KEY TERMS

Discrete Cosine Transform (DCT): Transform used in signal and image processing applications. JPEG, MPEG, MJPEG, and DV are video and image formats based on DCT.

Encoding/Decoding: The term "encoding" refers to the process of transforming a raw/uncompressed image and/or video file into a compressed form, through exploitation of spatial-temporal redundancies. Decoding is the reverse process, i.e., the retrieval of the original files through the encoded ones.

Moving Picture Experts Group (MPEG): ISO/IEC working group for developing and standardizing audio/video coding formats. The list of relevant standards includes MPEG-1 (Video CD and MP3 audio format are based on MPEG-1), MPEG-2 (HDTV and DVDs), MPEG-4 (object-based multimedia representations available at a variety of bit rates), MPEG-7 (for multimedia description), and MPEG-21 (multimedia framework).

Real-Time Transport Control Protocol (RTCP): Protocol (complementary to RTP) that is used to convey feedback information to the sender of RTP packets, so as to provide the status of the receiver through reports regarding lost packets and the delay/jitter the stream is experiencing.

Real-Time Transport Protocol (RTP): Application layer protocol that is used for the transmission of multimedia files that need to be displayed in real-time (i.e., streaming applications) through IP-based networking platforms. UDP is usually the transport protocol when RTP packets are sent.

Streaming: Term used to describe the transmission and reproduction of multimedia data. Transmitted data are viewed upon reception of the data packets the media content is encapsulated in. The term contradicts oldest multimedia applications of the download-and-play form.

Transcoding: The term in general refers to the conversion from one encoding scheme to another.

Real-Time Protocols (RTP/RTCP)

Christos Bouras
Research Academic Computer Technology Institute and University of Patras, Greece

Apostolos Gkamas
Research Academic Computer Technology Institute and University of Patras, Greece

Dimitris Primpas
Research Academic Computer Technology Institute and University of Patras, Greece

Kostas Stamos
Research Academic Computer Technology Institute and University of Patras, Greece

INTRODUCTION

Real-time protocols cover specific needs by applications with real-time characteristics. Real-time applications, such as voice over IP (VoIP), videoconferencing applications, video on demand, continuous data applications, and control and measurement applications have specific requirements from the lower layers, mainly in terms of packet loss, delay, and jitter. Traditional transport protocols such as **TCP** and **UDP** have been designed for general use and are not specialized for such specific purposes. In particular, real-time protocols have to be able to deliver high throughput, handle multicast, manage the transmission quality, and be friendly to the rest of the traffic, and, more importantly, to the congestion-sensitive TCP traffic.

BACKGROUND

An early attempt at a protocol designed for transferring real-time data was **NVP** (Cohen, 1981). It was first implemented in 1973 by Danny Cohen of the Information Sciences Institute (ISI), University of Southern California. The project's stated goals (Cohen, 1976) were "to develop and demonstrate the feasibility of secure, high-quality, low-bandwidth, real-time, full-duplex (two-way) digital voice communications over packet-switched computer communications networks…[and to] supply digitized speech which can be secured by existing encryption devices. The major goal of this research is to demonstrate a digital high-quality, low-bandwidth, secure voice handling capability as part of the general military requirement for worldwide secure voice communication." NVP was used to send speech between distributed sites on the ARPANET, using several different voice-encoding techniques.

RTP/RTCP protocol was first defined in RFC 1889 (Schulzrinne et al., 1996), which was later updated with RFC 3550 (Schulzrinne et al., 2003). The discussions on the rationale and design choices behind RTP were summarized in Schulzrinne (1993), which provides a good reference to the desired characteristics for an efficient and flexible real-time protocol.

REAL TIME PROTOCOLS DESCRIPTION

Desired Characteristics of Real-Time Protocols

High Throughput

Multimedia data and especially video require continuous high-rate transmission. The real-time protocol that takes over the transport of data has to be fast enough to support the application requirements, and in particular the protocol throughput has to be faster than the network access speed, otherwise the bandwidth will not be used efficiently and the transport protocol will be a bottleneck.

Another approach to the throughput requirements for a transport protocol is the total communications system view. The throughput of a transport protocol has to be higher than the access speed of the network, otherwise it would not be possible to fully utilize the bandwidth offered by the network access points, and the transport protocol would become a bottleneck of the whole communications system (Rosenberg et al. 1998).

Multicast Capability

Multicast support is also essential, because many applications specify multiple recipients and transmitting the same large amount of data over multiple unicast connections wastes available network resources.

Transmission Quality Management

Multimedia data flows require quality of service guarantees regarding bandwidth, delay, and jitter. In order to satisfy these requirements, a transport system has to provide the applications with a mechanism for determining and negotiating their **quality of service** (QoS) requirements. These QoS requirements are transferred by the transport layer to the network layer, which is responsible for propagating them and for making the necessary reservations of resources over a network connection. This network connection often supports multicast functionality which is useful for many multimedia applications. In order to support QoS guarantees, the cooperation of all the subsystems of a transport system is necessary, which includes resource management, network access control, and queue management at network devices. The operating system should also be able to support multimedia applications.

In the case that the network is not able to provide quality of service guarantees, the real-time protocol has to be able to adapt the transmitted multimedia data to the current network conditions. Although this technique does not offer specific QoS guarantees, as in Jacobson et al. (1999) and Heinanen et al. (1999), it can improve the network performance as a whole because of the reduction in congestion and packet losses.

TCP Friendliness

The TCP protocol implements a congestion avoidance mechanism that is best suited to the transmission of non real-time data such as HTTP or FTP. Real-time applications have to be based on UDP, which is faster and offers no reliability or congestion control. The lack of congestion control mechanism in UDP can lead to congestion problems if a UDP sender exceeds the transmission rate that can be handled by the network. TCP traffic is very sensitive to congestion because of TCP's congestion avoidance mechanism, and therefore the UDP traffic rate has to be somehow controlled. These mechanisms should not only aim at avoiding network overload, but also transmiting TCP-friendly traffic. TCP-friendly traffic is a traffic stream that does not consume more bandwidth than a TCP stream would consume on the same network path (Bouras et al., 2005).

Extensibility

Real-time multimedia services are still a field of research where new ideas and implementations occur often, and therefore, a real-time protocol should be able to incorporate additional services as practical experience with the protocol is gathered and as applications that were not originally anticipated use its services. Furthermore, experimental applications should be able to exchange application-specific information without jeopardizing interoperability with other applications (Schulzrinne et al., 2003).

Multiple Content

Real-time protocols are mainly motivated by audio and video for conferences (Basso et al., 1997). However, other applications, such as distribution of voice/video, distributed simulations, and loss-tolerant remote data acquisition may also use the services provided by such a protocol. Also, new formats of established media, for example, high-quality multi-channel audio or combined audio and video sources, should be anticipated (Rosenberg et al., 1996).

The RTP/RTCP Protocol

The RTP/RTCP protocols have been specifically created for transferring multimedia data such as voice and video. Initially designed for multicast communication, they have also been widely used for unicast communications. They can be used for one-direction communication, such as for video on demand services, but also for full-duplex communication, such as for videoconferencing and VoIP applications. They provide a common platform for data transfer and synchronization of information.

RTCP (real-time control protocol) is the control protocol for RTP (real-time protocol). RTP operates in cooperation with RTCP, which provides the information regarding the connection quality and the participants in the RTP **session**.

RTP offers end-to-end transport services for data with real-time characteristics. In particular, RTP enables the specification and identification of the payload type, sequential numbering of packets, timestamps, and control of the transport procedures. RTP offers end-to-end services, but does not offer the complete functionality of a transport layer protocol. An application can use RTP over TCP or UDP in order to take advantage of multiplexing and checksum functions of the TCP or UDP protocol, but any other suitable transport protocol can also be used. RTP is not aware of the connection and can therefore operate over both connection-oriented and connectionless lower level protocols.

RTP offers no mechanism for guaranteeing the delivery of data in specific time intervals, and no quality of service guarantees for the transmission, because that is an issue for the lower level protocols. For an application that requires such guarantees, RTP can be accompanied by mechanisms such as **RSVP**, which can provide resource reservation and reliable services.

Multimedia applications usually pose strict time constraints regarding transmission of data, which does not fit very well with the architecture of the Internet. The RTP protocol provides several mechanisms that take into account these issues. Such mechanisms are timestamps and sequential numbering of packets.

Timestamps provide useful information to real-time applications. The sender inserts a timestamp into each packet, which is used by the receiver in order to determine how the data should be presented to the end user. In other words, timestamps provide the synchronization signals so that the receivers can properly reconstruct the initial data. Timestamps are also used for the synchronization of separate data flows, such as audio and video (RTP/RTCP transmits audio and video using separate data flows). RTP is not accountable for this synchronization, which is the responsibility of the applications.

UDP, which is typically used for the transmission of RTP/RTCP packets, does not deliver packets in the order they were transmitted. Therefore, RTP packets are sequentially numbered upon transmission, so

that the receiver can properly arrange them. These sequence numbers are also used in order to detect packet losses.

Since RTP is often used for multicast communication, an RTP data packet contains the identity of the information sender, so that the session group can identify which member of the session transmits data. The sender's identity is provided in the source identification field.

RTP is typically used over the UDP transport protocol. TCP and UDP are the most widely used transport protocols on the Internet. While TCP offers connection-oriented services and reliable data transmission, UDP offers connectionless services and no reliability. UDP is preferable as the transport protocol for RTP because:

- RTP is mainly designed for multicast transmissions which do not fit well with the connection-orientated TCP.
- Especially for multimedia data, reliability is not as important as timely transmission. Reliable transmission is usually achieved through retransmission of lost packets, which might not be desirable, since it can lead to network overloading and can hinder the steady transmission of data.

The idea behind the control protocol RTCP is that applications that have recently transmitted multimedia data generate a sender report which is sent to all the participants in the RTP session. This report includes counters for the packet data and the bytes sent, and the receivers can use them to estimate the actual data transmission rate.

In order to establish an RTP session, an application determines a pair of destination addresses (which is comprised of an IP network address and two ports, one for RTP and one for RTCP). The address can be either a unicast or a multicast network address. During a multimedia session, each medium is transmitted in a separate RTP session, and RTCP packets report the transmission quality for each separate session. This means that audio and video are transmitted at separate RTP during a videoconference.

Although RTP/RTCP packets are transferred inside UDP packets, data packets and control packets use two sequential ports, with the RTP port always being the lower one and with an odd number. In the case of other protocols below RTP at the protocol stack (such as the case of having RTP directly over AAL5: ATM Adaptation Layer type 5), it is possible to transfer both data (RTP) and control information (RTCP) within a single data unit of the lower layer protocol, with data following the control information.

Therefore, an RTP session is characterized by the following parameters:

- **IP address of participants:** This can be either a multicast IP address, which corresponds to the multicast session of the participants group, or a set of unicast addresses
- **RTP port:** The port number used by all participants in the session for sending data
- **RTCP port:** The port number used by all participants in the session for sending RTCP control messages

The RTP header provides the synchronization information necessary for synchronizing and presenting audio and video data, and also for determining whether any packets have been lost or arrived out of order. Furthermore, the header determines the data type and therefore allows multiple types of data and compression. RTP can be tuned to meet the specific requirements of each application by using auxiliary data structure and shape specifications.

In order to allow a higher level of synchronization or to synchronize non-periodical data flows, RTP uses a clock that increments monotonically. This clock is usually increased in time units smaller than the smallest block size of the data flow, and its initial value is random. An application does not use the RTP timestamps directly but it rather uses the NTP (network time protocol) timestamps and the RTP timestamps from the transmitted RTCP packets for each flow that needs synchronization.

Session participants produce receiver reports for all the senders—sources of audio and video data from which they have recently received data. The reports contain information regarding the highest sequence number received, the number of lost packets, the jitter, and the timestamps needed for calculating an estimate of the transmission **round trip time** (RTT).

As RTP and RTCP create separate sessions for separate data streams, an RTCP sender report contains an indication of the actual time, and an RTP timestamp which can be used for synchronizing multiple data flows at the receiver.

RTP data packets identify their source only through a 32-bit randomly generated number, while RTCP messages include a source description (SDES) which contains relevant information. Such a body of information is the canonical name, a globally unique identification code of the session participant. Other possible SDES objects are the user's name, e-mail address, telephone number, and application information.

RTCP offers feedback capabilities related to the current network conditions and the reception quality, allowing the applications to automatically adapt to changing network conditions. For example, a slowdown by many receivers could possibly be due to a network problem (for example a faster link has failed and has been substituted by a slower backup link) and are not due to a specific participant. In such a case, the sender could choose to immediately switch to another codec with lower bandwidth requirements, or temporarily stop transmitting video, or use some other technique to reduce the multimedia transmission rate.

In other cases, the network administrators can use information from RTCP packets in order to evaluate the performance of their networks. Since RTCP sends feedback information not only to the sender, but also to all other receivers of a multicast stream, it enables a user to realize whether a problem is due to the local node or is more general to the network.

The basis for traffic and congestion control is offered by the RTCP sender and receiver reports. By analyzing the jitter field, which is included in the RTCP sender report, the fluctuation during a certain time period can be measured and the possibility of congestion can be identified and dealt with before it appears and causes packet losses.

FUTURE TRENDS

Since RTP contains no specific assumptions about the capabilities of the lower layers, except the fact that they provide framing, it is capable of running over **IPv6** (Deering et al., 1998), the new Internet protocol that is expected to gradually replace the currently used IPv4 in the near future. RTP contains no network-layer addresses, so it is not affected by address changes. IPv6 includes enhanced support for lower-layer capabilities such as security or quality-of-service guarantees, and these features can be used by applications employing RTP. This combination makes RTP an attractive option for new multimedia applications that can benefit from both RTP support for real-time data and enhancements from IPv6 and other emerging Internet technologies

CONCLUSION

This article presented the main design characteristics for real-time protocols and a detailed presentation of RTP/RTCP, the most widely implemented and used protocol for transportation of real-time data. Real-time protocols should be extensible, provide for high throughput, be able to operate over multicast, and transfer multiple types of content. Naturally, no end-to-end protocol can ensure in-time delivery, since this always requires the support of lower layers that actually have control over resources in switches and routers. RTP/RTCP satisfactorily covers the above requirements and provides functionality suited for carrying real-time content, e.g., a timestamp and control mechanisms for synchronizing different streams with timing properties.

REFERENCES

Basso, A., Cash, G.L., & Civanlar, M.R. (1997). Transmission of MPEG-2 streams over non-guaranteed quality of service networks. In *Picture Coding Symposium*, 419-425.

Bouras, Ch., Gkamas, A., Karaliotas, & An., Stamos, K. (2005), Architecture and performance evaluation for redundant multicast transmission supporting adaptive QoS. *Multimedia Tools and Applications Archive, 25*(1), 85-110.

Cohen, D. (1981). *A network voice protocol: NVP-II.* Technical report. University of Southern California/ISI, Marina del Ray.

Cohen, D. (January 1976). *Specifications for the network voice protocol (NVP).* RFC 741.

Deering, S., & Hinden, R. (December 1998). *Internet protocol, Version 6 (IPv6) Specification.* RFC 2460.

Heinanen J., Baker, F., Weiss, W., & Wroclawski, J. (1999). *Assured forwarding PHB group.* RFC 2597.

Jacobson,V., Nichols, K., & Poduri, K. (1998, June). An expedited rorwarding PHB. RFC 2598.

Rosenberg, J., & Schulzrinne, H. (1998). Timer reconsideration for enhanced RTP scalability. In *Proceedings of IEEE Infocom*, San Francisco (pp. 233-241).

Rosenberg, J., & Schulzrinne, H. (1006, Nov). *Issues and options for an aggregation service within RTP.* Draft, Work in Progress, IETF AVT Working Group.

Schulzrinne, H., (1996). *RTP profile for audio and video conferences with minimal control.* RFC 1890.

Schulzrinne, H. (October 1993). *Issues in designing a transport protocol for audio and video conferences and other multiparticipant real-time applications.* Expired Internet Draft.

Schulzrinne, H., & Casner, S. (July 2003). *RTP profile for audio and video conferences with minimal control.* RFC 3551.

Schulzrinne, H., Casner, S., Frederick, R., & Jacobson, V. (July 2003). *RTP: A transport protocol for real-time applications.* RFC 3550.

Schulzrinne, H., Casner, S., Frederick, R., & Jacobson, V. (January 1996). *RTP: A transport protocol for real-time applications.* RFC 1889.

The Internet Engineering Task Force..Retrieved 27 July, 2006 from http://www.ietf.org

KEY TERMS

Delay Jitter: Delay jitter is defined to be the mean deviation (smoothed absolute value) of the difference in packet spacing at the receiver compared to the sender for a pair of packets.

Internet Engineering Task Force (IETF): The organization comprised of a large open international community of network designers, operators, vendors, and researchers concerned with the evolution of Internet architecture and the smooth operation of the Internet.

Multimedia Data: Multimedia data refers to data that consist of various media types like text, audio, video, and animation.

NVP (Network Voice Protocol): A pioneering network protocol for transporting human speech over packetized communications networks.

Packet Loss Rate: Packet loss rate is defined as the fraction of the total transmitted packets that did not arrive at the receiver.

Quality of Service (QoS): The ability to provide specific guarantees to traffic flows regarding the network characteristics, such as packet loss, delay, and jitter experienced by the flows.

TCP (Transmission Control Protocol): A connection-oriented, reliable protocol of the TCP/IP protocol suite used for managing full-duplex transmission streams.

UDP (User Datagram Protocol): A connection-less, unreliable protocol of the TCP/IP protocol suite used for sending and receiving datagrams over an IP network.

Rich–Club Phenomenon of the Internet Topology

Shi Zhou
University College London, UK

INTRODUCTION

This chapter introduces a recently discovered structure of the Internet, namely the rich-club phenomenon (Zhou & Mondragón, 2004a). The significance of this discovery is that an appreciation of the rich-club phenomenon is essential for a proper examination of global Internet characteristics, such as routing efficiency, network flexibility, and robustness (Zhou & Mondragón, 2004b). Today, rich-club connectivity has been adopted by the networks research community as a topology metric to characterise the Internet structure (Mahadevan et al., 2005).

BACKGROUND

The Internet contains millions of routers, which are grouped into thousands of subnetworks, called *autonomous systems* (AS). Internet topology can be considered at the router level or the autonomous systems (AS) level. The architecture of the Internet is characterised by the AS-level topology, not the router level topology, because network structure inside an AS only affects local properties, whereas the delivery of data traffic through the global Internet depends on the complex interactions between AS that exchange routing information using the border gateway protocol (BGP) (Quoitin et al., 2003). In this chapter we focus on the Internet AS-level topology, which contains many thousands of nodes (AS) and tens of thousands of links (BGP peering relations).

Only recently did measurement data of the Internet topology begin to emerge. Projects and institutions that map and publish the Internet AS graphs include the National Laboratory for Applied Network Research (NLANR, http://moat.nlanr.net/), Route Views Project of the University of Oregon (http://www.routeviews.org/), Internet Mapping Project of Lumeta (http://research.lumeta.com/ches/map/), and the Cooperative Association For Internet Data Analysis (CAIDA, http://www.caida.org/).

Researchers use the statistical physical approach to characterise the structure of such a large network. In graph theory, degree k is defined as the number of connections or links a node has. Faloutsos, et al. (1999) discovered that the Internet AS graph did not have an even distribution of node degree. Instead, a very few network nodes were far more connected than other nodes. In general, they found that the probability that a node in the network has degree k was proportional to $k^{-\gamma}$, where the power-law exponent $\gamma = -2.2$. This discovery was significant because it effectively invalidated all previous Internet models that were based on random network theories and assumed a Poisson degree distribution (Erdös & Rényi, 1960). Graphs with a power law degree distribution are also called "scale-free" networks (Barabási & Albert, 1999), because the degree distribution is characterised not by the average degree, but by the power-law exponent, which is invariant to the network size (scale).

RICH-CLUB PHENOMENON

Zhou and Mondragón (2004a) discovered a new hierarchical structure of the Internet, called the rich-club phenomenon, which describes the fact that high-degree nodes, "rich" nodes, are tightly interconnected between themselves, forming a core group or club (see Figure 1). Subgraphs formed by richer nodes are progressively more interconnected.

The quantity of interconnectivity among members of a rich-club is measured by the metric of rich-club connectivity. If rank of a node, r, denotes a node's position on the non-increasing degree list of a network, i.e., $r = 1 \ldots N$, where N is the total number of nodes contained in the network, then the rich-club membership is defined as "the r best connected nodes," and the rich-club connectivity, $\varphi(r)$, is defined as the ratio of the actual number of links to the maximum pos-

Figure 1. (a) Non rich-club core; (b) rich-club core

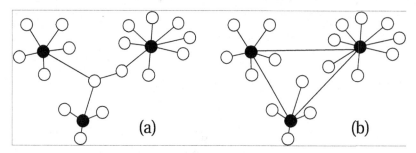

Figure 2. Rich-club connectivity vs. normalised rank, φ (r/N)

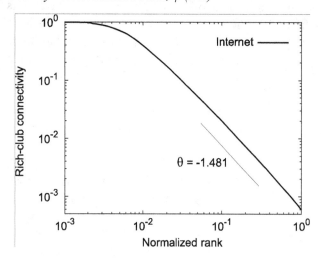

sible number of links, i.e., $r(r-1)=2$, between the rich-club members. Rich-club connectivity indicates how well club members "know" each other, e.g., φ = 1 means that all the members have a direct link to any other member, i.e., they form a fully connected mesh, a clique. The top clique size of a network, n_{clique}, is defined as the maximum number of highest-ranked nodes still forming a clique.

Figure 2 illustrates the Internet's rich-club connectivity as a function of the increasing rich-club membership, r/N, which is measured as the node rank normalised by the total number of nodes on a log-log scale. The rich-club connectivity φ (r/N) follows a power law $\varphi(r/N) \sim r^{\theta}$, with $\theta \approx -1.481$, in the area of medium and large r/N, i.e., $0.1<r/N<1$, which accounts for 90 percent of the nodes. The top clique size of the Internet is 16.

The rich-club phenomenon fundamentally affects the Internet's functions. Members of the rich-club are tightly interconnected. If two club members do not have a direct connection, they are very likely to share a neighbouring club member. Thus, the rich-club provides a large amount of shortcuts and together functions as a super traffic hub. This makes the Internet a "small-world" network (Watts, 1999), in which, on average, any two nodes are separated by a very small number of connections. Today, the average shortest path length of the Internet AS graph is only 3.12 hops.

The tight interconnections among rich-club members also forms a large number of short cycles (Bianconi et al., 2003) and consequently construct a large quantity of alternative paths, which increase the flexibility of network routing. This, in a sense, also alleviates the vulnerability of the Internet as a scale-free network, because the redundant interconnections between the rich-club members provide a cushion against targeted attacks, until the rich-club is broken apart and then the network suddenly splinters.

The Internet also exhibits a so-called disassortative mixing behaviour (Newman, 2003), which describes the fact that on the Internet, high-degree nodes statistically tend to connect with low-degree nodes, and vice versa. The rich-club phenomenon does not conflict with the disassortative mixing behaviour because the rich-club phenomenon does not imply that the majority of rich node links are directed to other rich-club members. Indeed, rich nodes have very large numbers of links and only a few of them are enough to provide the interconnectivity to other club members, whose number is small anyway (Pastor-Satorras & Vespignani, 2004). In fact, the rich club phenomenon and the disassortative mixing behaviour work together to make the network a small-world: the rich-club functions as a super traffic hub while the disassortative mixing makes sure that poorly connected, peripheral nodes are always close to the hub. The above analysis on the rich-club phenomenon suggests that the Internet is more dependent on its richest nodes than previously thought.

FUTURE TRENDS

There are a number of ongoing works related to the rich-club phenomenon. Researchers are measuring the rich-club connectivity of complex networks in other domains. They are trying to model and explain the formation of rich-club phenomena (Zhou & Mondragón, 2004c), and to understand its implication for future systems.

CONCLUSION

We introduce the rich-club phenomena observed on the AS-level Internet topology. This topology property has a far-reaching impact on our understanding of the Internet structure and functions. The rich-club phenomenon is also useful for characterising and modelling other real complex networks.

REFERENCES

Albert, R., Jeong, H., & Barabási, A. L. (2000). Error and attack tolerance of complex networks. *Nature, 406*, 378-381.

Barabási, A. L., & Albert, R. (1999). Emergence of scaling in random networks. *Science, 286*, 509-512.

Bianconi, G., Caldarelli, G., & Capocci, A. (2003). Number of *h*-cycles in the Internet at the autonomous system level. *ArXiv:cond-mat/0310339*. Retrieved 1 June, 2006 from http://arxiv.org/abs/cond-mat/0310339

Erd"os, P., & R´enyi, A. (1960). On the evolution of random graphs. *Publications of the Mathematics Institute of the Hungarian Academy of Scences, 5*, 17.

Faloutsos, M., Faloutsos, P., & Faloutsos, C. (1999). On power-law relationships of the Internet topology. *ACM SIGCOMM Computer Communications Reviews, 29*(4), 251-262.

Mahadevan, P., Krioukov, D., Huffaker, B., Dimitropoulos, X., K.C., & Vahdat, A. (2005). *Lessons from three views of the Internet topology*. Technical report, CAIDA. Retrieved 1 June, 2006 from http://www.caida.org/outreach/papers/2005/tr-2005-02/

Newman, M. E. J. (2003). Mixing patterns in networks. *Physical Review E, 67*(026126), 1-13.

Pastor-Satorras, R., & Vespignani, A. (2004). *Evolution and structure of the Internet: A statistical physics approach*. Cambridge University Press.

Quoitin, B., Pelsser, C., & Swinnen, L. (2003). Interdomain traffic engineering with BGP. *IEEE Communications Magazine, 41*(5), 122-128.

Watts, J. (1999). *Small worlds: The dynamics of networks between order and randomness*. NJ: Princeton University Press.

Zhou, S., & Mondragón, R. J. (2004a). The rich-club phenomenon in the Internet topology. *IEEE Communications Letters, 8*(3), 180-182.

Zhou, S., & Mondragón, R. J. (2004b). Redundancy and robustness of the AS-level Internet topology and its models. *IEE Electronics Letters, 40*(2), 151-152.

Zhou, S., & Mondragón, R. J. (2004c). Accurately modelling the Internet topology. *Physical Review E, 70*(066108), 1-8.

KEY TERMS

Autonomous System: A collection of IP networks and routers under the control of one entity (or sometimes more) that presents a common routing policy to the Internet.

BGP: Border gateway protocol, which is the core routing protocol of the Internet. It works by maintaining a table of IP networks or "prefixes" which designate network reachability between autonomous systems (AS).

CAIDA: Cooperative Association for Internet Data Analysis, which is based at the San Diego Supercomputer Center, U.S. CAIDA is a world-leading organisation for Internet measurement and research.

Degree: Is defined, in the graph theory, as the number of connections that a node has, or the number of direct neighbours of the node.

Disassortative Mixing: Describes a statistic behaviour where high-degree nodes tend to connect with low-degree nodes and visa versa. It is found in biological and telecommunications networks, such as the Internet.

Rich-Club Phenomenon: A topology property of some complex networks, which describes the fact that well-connected nodes, "rich" nodes, are tightly interconnected with other rich nodes, forming a core group or club.

Scale-Free Network: A network characterised by a power-law distribution of node degree, where the power-law exponent is invariant to the network size (scale).

Short Cycles: Include triangles and quadrangles, which encode the redundancy information in a network, because the multiplicity of paths between any two nodes increases with the density of short cycles.

Small-World Network: A network in which, on average, any two nodes are separated by a very small number of connections.

Statistical Physics: One of the fundamental theories of physics. It uses methods of statistics in solving physical problems. It can describe a wide variety of fields with an inherently stochastic nature.

Topology: A connectivity graph representing a real network, upon which the network's physical and engineering properties are based.

Scalable Reservation–Based QoS Architecture (SRBQ)

Rui Prior
Institute of Telecommunications – University of Porto, Portugal

Susana Sargento
Institute of Telecommunications – University of Aveiro, Portugal

INTRODUCTION

Having its roots in the military ARPANET, conceived as a data transport network with a focus on resilience, the Internet supports only a best-effort service model, where all packets are treated the same way, therefore providing a single level of service. Now that the Internet is becoming a ubiquitous global communication infrastructure, new applications are emerging with more demanding and diversified requirements than data transport. Internet telephony, for example, has much stricter delay requirements than remote terminal, the most demanding of the original applications. The deployment of other service models providing better quality of service (QoS) is of great importance for the transport of these new applications.

While many approaches to providing QoS on the Internet have been proposed, none has gained enough acceptance to be deployed across the Internet at large. One important reason for this is the difficulty in conciliating strict QoS guarantees with the required scalability and with good resource utilization.

The realization that the scalability limitations of the existing per-flow reservation QoS architectures are not intrinsic to the per-flow approach itself, but rather to the employed algorithms, led to the development of the scalable reservation-based QoS (SRBQ) architecture (Prior et al., 2003a).

BACKGROUND

Two main architectures have been standardized by the IETF for the introduction of QoS and traffic differentiation on the Internet. The Integrated Services (IntServ) architecture (Braden, Clark, & Shenker,

1994), commonly used with the Resource Reservation Protocol (RSVP) (Braden et al., 1997), provides strict QoS guarantees and efficient resource usage, but suffers from scalability problems concerning the per-flow scheduling, classification, and reservation procedures. The differentiated services (DiffServ) architecture (Blake et al., 1998), conceived as a solution to the limitations of IntServ, is free from these scalability concerns, since flows are aggregated in classes according to specific characteristics, but without admission control mechanisms, all the flows from a given class may receive degraded quality of service due to excessive traffic at the link.

Aiming at the introduction of QoS support without the aforementioned problems, several other architectures have been proposed in the literature. All of these architectures, however, suffer from one or more of the following problems: lack of strict QoS guarantees, underutilization of network resources, or scalability limitations stemming from the complexity of the algorithms and procedures used. For example, the SCORE architecture (Stoica, 2000) keeps the stateless character of the network by carrying state information in data packet headers, but imposes a scheduling discipline on all routers with a computational complexity that is still high. In the Egress Admission Control architecture (Cetinkaya & Knightly, 2000), only the egress routers perform admission control, based on passive monitoring, but it cannot provide strict QoS guarantees. With probing schemes (Almesberger, Ferrari, & Le Boudec, 1998; Bianchi, Capone, & Petrioli, 2000; Elek, Karlsson, & Ronngren, 2000; Breslau, et al., 2000; Sargento, Valadas, & Knightly, 2001; Key & Massoulié, 2003) no network control is required, but no firm QoS guarantees are possible, among other problems. In Bernet et al. (2000) a framework is proposed for the operation of IntServ over DiffServ networks, avoiding signaling processing inside the domain, but it may have sub-optimal resource allocation and imprecise admission control. The RSVP Reservation Aggregation architecture (Baker et al., 2001) achieves scalability by aggregating reservations in core domains, but it implies a tradeoff between resource utilization and signaling scalability, leading to underutilization in high-speed networks. Westberg et al. (2002) proposed the resource management in DiffServ (RMD), based on similar principles.

Centralized approaches have also been proposed (Nichols, Jacobson, & Zhang, 1999; Schelen, & Pink, 1998; Terzis et al., 1999; Chimento et al., 2002; Sargento et al., 2004) which offload the (core) routers from the need to maintain state and perform signaling by moving resource management and admission control to bandwidth brokers (BB), with per-flow or aggregate reservations. While the routers are simplified, BBs are subject to scalability limitations, particularly severe in per-flow approaches, and become single points of failure. Aggregate BBs, on the other hand, share some of the problems of distributed aggregation-based architectures, namely, lower resource utilization.

The Next Steps in Signaling (NSIS) Working Group has proposed a two-layer extensible signaling architecture that addresses many limitations of RSVP, having QoS signaling as one of the first applications (Fu et al., 2005). NSIS concerns signaling only, and was designed to support any QoS model; therefore, its characteristics in terms of QoS, resource utilization, and scalability are largely dependent on the underlying QoS model.

In the scalable reservation-based QoS (SRBQ) architecture, scalability is achieved by lowering the computational complexity of all the tasks associated with a per-flow, reservation-based architecture for QoS provisioning, namely those related to packet scheduling, reservation signaling, and admission control. This approach is able to conciliate scalability with a good utilization of network resources (Prior et al., 2003b, 2004a, 2004b, 2004c).

THE SRBQ ARCHITECTURE

SRBQ combines the strict end-to-end QoS guarantees of a signaling-based approach with per-flow reservations subject to admission control, both in terms of bounded delay and minimal loss, with the efficiency and scalability provided by flow aggregation and by several mechanisms and algorithms. The next sub-sections describe some aspects of the architecture. A detailed description is provided in Prior et al. (2003a).

General System Architecture

The underlying architecture of the proposed model is strongly based on DiffServ (with which it may coexist) with the addition of signaling-based reservations subject to admission control. The network is partitioned into domains, consisting of core and edge nodes. In addition, access domains also have access nodes. Individual flows are aggregated according to service classes, mapped to DiffServ (DS) compatible per-hop behaviors (PHBs), and aggregate classification is performed based on the DS field of the packet header.

Besides best effort (BE), SRBQ provides two additional service classes: (1) the guaranteed service (GS) class that is characterized by hard QoS assurance in terms of both delivery guarantee and maximum delay, based on the same principles as the EF (expedited forwarding) PHB in DiffServ; and (2) one or more controlled load (CL) classes that emulate the behavior of lightly-loaded best effort networks, based on the AF (assured forwarding) PHB. The simplest queuing model for the routers is depicted in Figure 1(a). There are up to four different controlled load service classes using DiffServ code points (DSCP) from other AF classes, provided these are not used by DiffServ. In this case, the CL queuing block is replaced by the one shown in Figure 1(b). Reservations for traffic flows using the GS class are characterized by a token bucket. Reservations for traffic flows using CL classes are characterized by three average rate watermarks: packets exceeding the first two watermarks will receive a degraded service in terms of drop probability; packets exceeding the third watermark will be dropped.

Admission control is performed at every node along the flow path. A GS flow i, characterized by the token-bucket (r_i, b_i), is admitted in a link with j GS flows already accepted if:

$$r_i + \sum_j r_j \le R_{GS\max}$$

and

Figure 1. Queuing model

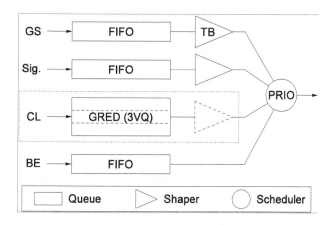

a) Single CL class

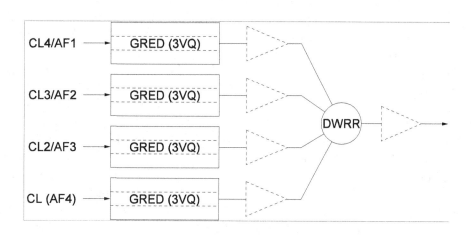

b) Multiple CL classes

$$b_i + \sum_j b_j \leq B_{GS\,max},$$

where $R_{GS\,max}$ and $B_{GS\,max}$ are the bandwidth and buffer space assigned to the GS class. A CL flow i is admitted if:

$$r_{i,w} + \sum_j r_{j,w} \leq R_{w\,max}, \forall w,$$

where $R_{w\,max}$ is the configured maximum rate for watermark w. Admission control in the GS class must be parameter-based (PBAC), whereas in the CL class it may be parameter- or measurement-based (MBAC).

As illustrated in Figure 1, the highest priority queue, corresponding to the GS traffic class, is subject to a token-bucket type traffic shaper in order to avoid packet dropping at the next policing node. Since the shaper curve is the summed token bucket, an upper bound to the arrival curve of the aggregate, this shaper does not degrade the QoS guarantees of the GS class (Le Boudec & Thiran, 2001). The signaling/routing traffic, though not subject to admission control, must be shaped in order to prevent starvation of the CL class. This class may also be shaped, but this is only required if the network administrator wants to ensure that the best effort class does not starve. Contrary to the GS shaper, these are work-conserving.

All nodes in the architecture perform signaling and support the previously described queuing model. The

475

access nodes perform per-flow policing for the CL class and per-flow ingress shaping for the GS class. Edge nodes perform aggregate policing and DSCP remarking. Core nodes perform no policing.

Label Switching

In other protocols, one of the scalability-limiting tasks for the core routers, especially in terms of worst case, is the lookup of the stored flow information, based on the 5-tuple parameters that specify the flow, usually implemented using hash tables. In order to efficiently access the reservation structures, SRBQ employs a label-switching mechanism which allows direct access to these structures without any need for hash lookups. These labels are 32-bit values, whose meaning is externally opaque, but internally may be an index to a table of reservation structures or the memory address of the reservation structure. Three label fields are stored in this structure: B, T, and F. The T (this) label, which may be implicit, is the label for the node itself, directly mapped to the memory address of the reservation structure; the B label, to be used in messages sent backwards (upstream), corresponds to the T label of the previous hop; the F label, to be used in messages sent forwards (downstream), corresponds to the T label of the next hop. Labels are installed at reservation setup time.

The label switching mechanism is also advantageous in all per-flow processing, like policing performed at the access routers. The labels may also be used to improve route change detection: A mismatch between the next hop assigned by the routing tables with the one stored in the reservation structure of the flow means that the route has changed. In order to profit from these advantages on per-flow processing, all packets would need to carry the label information. Notice that in spite of these advantages, labels are not used for packet classification (except perhaps at the access routers), since it is performed on an aggregate basis using just the DS field of the IP header.

Signaling Protocol

The signaling protocol works on a hop-by-hop basis, providing unidirectional, soft state, sender-initiated reservations. Though implemented as an extension to the RSVP protocol, SRBQ is much more scalable,

since (1) the access to the flows' information is direct by using the labels, (2) timers for the expiration of soft reservations are implemented in a very efficient way, and (3) it uses simple reservation identification in order to decrease the length of the refresh and explicit tear down messages. As RSVP is meant to perform receiver-initiated reservations, SRBQ extends it by adding three new message types (see Figure 2): SResv (sender reservation), used to establish, refresh, and modify reservations; SResvStat (sender reservation status), used for reservation confirmation and error reporting; and SResvTear (sender reservation tear down), used to explicitly terminate a reservation.

Full SResv messages include flow identification, reservation quantification, a LABEL_SETUP object (used to install the label), an identifier of the service class, and a reservation expiration timeout value. The last two are conveyed by a SRESV_PARMS object. Upon receiving an initial SResv message, the request is subject to admission control; if accepted, the router updates the resource reservation of the flow's class, creates an entry for the flow in the reservation structure list, stores the label at the B field for this reservation, and forwards the SResv message to the next router after changing the LABEL_SETUP to the reservation entry assigned to this flow. If the flow cannot be accepted (anywhere in the path), a SResvStat message is sent towards the sender reporting the error. This message already makes use of the B labels in order to access to the flow reservation structure. When the SResv reaches the destination, all routers along the path have reserved resources for the new flow and all labels required for backward message processing are installed in the reservation state. The receiver acknowledges the successful reservation by sending a SResvStat message towards the sender, making use of the labels already installed in the opposite direction. The LABEL object in this message is used to access the memory structure for this reservation and the LABEL_SETUP object is stored in the F field of each node. Each node switches the LABEL to the value installed at the B field and forwards the message to the next node upstream, until the sender is reached. The SResvStat message will also trigger the commitment of the resource reservation to both the policing and the queuing modules at the routers if the reservation succeeded, or the removal from the admission control module if it failed.

Figure 2. Message flow

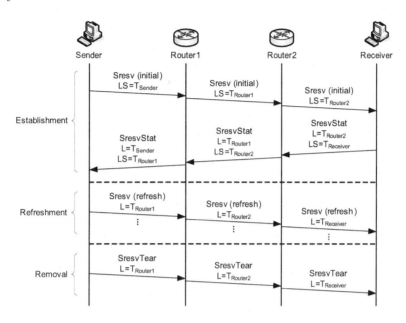

Soft State Timers

In SRBQ, reservations are soft state: If no SResvTear message is received and the reservation is not refreshed, the associated timer expires and is removed. Having a good range of reservation expiration timer values means that short-lived flows will not remain stale for long periods whenever something unusual occurs (such as an application lockup or premature termination, or an undetected route change) but longer-lived flows will not generate too much signaling traffic just to refresh the reservation.

The basic implementation concept for timers is a sorted event queue: The processor waits until the first timer value in the list expires, dequeues it, performs the appropriate processing, then goes on waiting for the next timer value to expire. While dequeuing an event is trivial, inserting an event with a random expiration time is a very expensive operation, highly dependent on the total number of events queued. Contrasting to the complexity of generic timers, fixed delay timers are very simple and efficient to implement (a single FIFO queue). As a compromise between the two types, SRBQ uses an algorithm with trivial timer queuing and low and constant cost timer dequeuing, providing eight possible timer delays in a base-2 logarithmic scale with a range of 1:128. The implementation is based on eight different queues, each of which has

an associated fixed delay. Internally, therefore, these queues are served using a FIFO discipline. Enqueuing an event is a simple matter of adding it to the tail of the corresponding queue, which is trivial. Dequeuing an event means choosing one of the eight possible queues (the one whose timers expires first) and taking the first event from that queue.

Applications should use timer values representing a good tradeoff between signaling traffic and fast recovery from faults for the expected flow lifespan. When the lifespan cannot be estimated a priori, the application may use a short timer at first and increase it using the SRESV_PARMS objects in refresh messages.

PERFORMANCE OF SRBQ

The SRBQ architecture has been thoroughly evaluated (Prior et al., 2003b, 2004b), using both synthetic flows and real-word multimedia streams. It has been demonstrated that SRBQ is able to provide strict and soft QoS guarantees in the GS and the CL classes, respectively, and that adequate isolation is achieved between the traffic classes and between flows in the same class (particularly in GS).

A comparative analysis of SRBQ and RSVP aggregation (RSVPRAgg) was presented in Prior et al. (2004a, 2004c). Both models aim at providing QoS levels comparable to RSVP/IntServ, but in a scalable manner. Both of them make use of flow aggregation in order to achieve scalability in packet classification and scheduling; the main differences stem from the different approaches to signaling. With RSVPRAgg, reservations at the core are performed in an aggregate basis and their bandwidth is updated in bulk quantities. However, per-flow signaling is performed at edge routers of transit domains (and also classification and scheduling, at the deaggregators). In SRBQ, the end-to-end character of reservation signaling is preserved without scalability issues; the amount of stored state is not a problem (Prior, 2003b), and resource usage is always optimal.

The next paragraphs describe some results from Prior (2004b), obtained by simulation in ns-2 (Version 2.26) using the dumbbell topology of Figure 3. All the information about the simulation setup is summarized in the figure. The mean time between calls is adjusted to vary the offered load between 0.8 and 1.2 times the bandwidth allocated to the CL class at the core link. The results from this set of simulations are presented in Figure 4.

In all models, the mean delay is not much larger than the sum of transmission and propagation delays (12.08 ms), meaning that the time spent in queues is low. Nevertheless, it is lower in SRBQ, as is jitter (not shown), probably due to the use of WFQ in RSVP and in RSVPRAgg outside the aggregation region. In all models presented there are no losses. Regarding the utilization of bandwidth allocated to the CL class, it is much higher in SRBQ (similar to standard RSVP) than in RSVPRAgg. In the latter, the utilization decreases noticeably with the increase in the bulk size: The use of larger bulk sizes in order to increase the scalability would lead to very poor network resource utilization. Corresponding to the lower utilization figures, the blocked bandwidth in RSVPRAgg is higher than in SRBQ. The blocked bandwidth figures are similar in SRBQ and regular RSVP, since end-to-end reservations are accepted up to the bandwidth reserved for the CL class in both models, contrasting to the RSVPRAgg model in which end-to-end reservations are only accepted up to the reserved rate of the corresponding aggregate. The number of signaling messages processed at C1 (see Figure 3) was also evaluated. This number

Figure 3. Topology used in comparison simulations

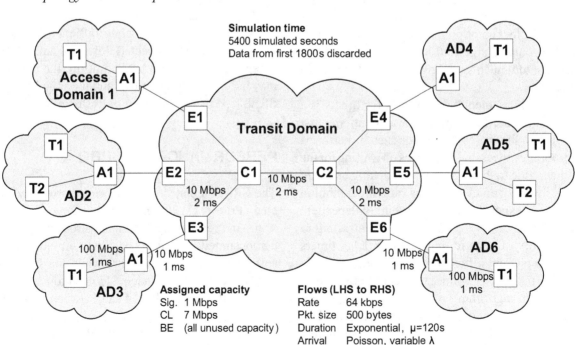

9 possible aggregates in RSVPRAgg from left hand side (LHS) to right hand side (RHS)

Figure 4. Performance of SRBQ, RSVPRAgg, and RSVP with a single type of flow

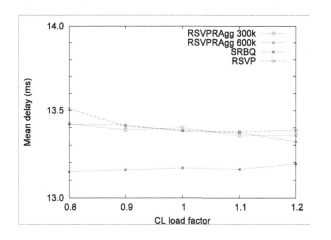

a) Delay

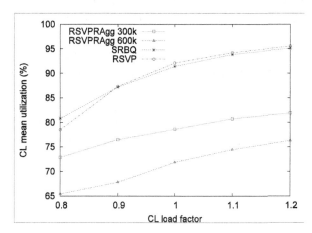

b) CL class utilization

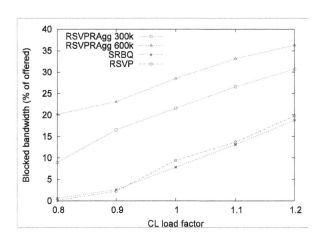

c) Blocking probability

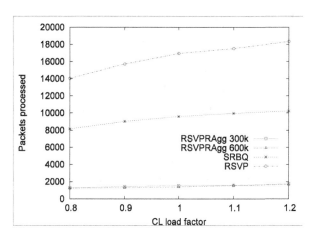

d) Signaling packets processed at the core

is much lower in RSVPRAgg than in SRBQ or RSVP. This is an obvious result, since at interior nodes only aggregate messages are processed in RSVPRAgg. The almost twofold difference between SRBQ and RSVP is due to the fact that in RSVP both Path and Resv refreshes are needed. Though from the number of processed messages at the core nodes alone RSVPRAgg looks more scalable, the SRBQ model makes use of low complexity, highly efficient algorithms which use much less CPU time to process each message.

FUTURE TRENDS

The future of QoS on the Internet is still unclear. In order for operators to deploy QoS mechanisms, they must regard them as an opportunity for increased revenue, by charging a premium for connections with QoS. Given the ever-increasing number of services provided over the Internet, many with real-time and other QoS requirements, the demand is there, but it is currently cheaper for operators to increase the core capacity than to deploy QoS mechanisms. However, the ratio of core-to-access capacity, currently at a peak, has historically oscillated as a result of the evolution of core and access technologies, and the need for QoS mechanisms becomes evident at the troughs (Crowcroft et al., 2003). On the other hand, there is a case for end-to-end QoS mechanisms inside administrative domains, where it is much easier to deploy a single mechanism in every node: For example, many broadband ISPs provide content-oriented and other value-added services only to their customers. SRBQ may certainly find application in this field, even if it will not be implemented in the whole Internet.

CONCLUSION

The SRBQ architecture emerged as a scalable alternative to RSVP/IntServ. It is able to provide both IntServ service models—guaranteed service with strict QoS guarantees and controlled load with soft QoS guarantees—with an underlying DiffServ-like architecture. The use of aggregate packet classification and scheduling mechanisms combined with the use of efficient algorithms (label switching, etc.) minimizes the processing load at each network element, allowing SRBQ to scale to a very large number of simultaneous flows. Compared with the RSVP reservation aggregation architecture proposed by the IETF, SRBQ provides comparable (and usually more favorable) QoS values, while allowing for a substantially higher utilization of the network resources, therefore reducing the amount of blocked reservations.

REFERENCES

Almesberger, W., Ferrari, T., & Le Boudec, J.-Y. (1998). SRP: A scalable resource reservation protocol for the Internet. *Computer Communications, 21*(14), Special issue on "Multimedia Networking," 1200-1211.

Baker, F., Iturralde, C., Le Faucheur, F., & Davie, B. (2001). *Aggregation of RSVP for IPv4 and IPv6 reservations*. IETF RFC-3175.

Bernet, Y., et al. (2000). *A framework for integrated services operation over Diffserv networks*. IETF RFC-2998.

Bianchi, G., Capone, A., & Petrioli, C. (2000). Throughput analysis of end-to-end measurement-based admission control in IP. *Proceedings of IEEE INFOCOM 2000*, 1461-1470.

Blake, S., Black, D., Carlson, M., Davies, E., Wang, Z., & Weiss, W. (1998). *An architecture for differentiated services*. IETF RFC-2475.

Braden, R., Clark, D., & Shenker, S. (1994). *Integrated services in the Internet architecture: An overview*. IETF RFC-1633.

Braden, R., Zhang, L., Berson, S., Herzog, S., & Jamin, S. (1997). *Resource reservation protocol (RSVP)–Version 1 functional specification*. IETF RFC-2205.

Breslau, L., Knightly, E. W., Shenker, S., Stoica, I., & Zhang, H. (2000). Endpoint admission control: Architectural issues and performance. *Proceedings of ACM SIGCOMM 2000*, 57-69.

Cetinkaya, C., & Knightly, E. (2000). Egress admission control. *Proceedings of IEEE INFOCOM 2000*, 1471-1480.

Chimento, P., et al. (2002). *QBone signaling design team*. Final report. Retrieved 27 July, 2007 from http://qos.internet2.edu/wg/documents-informational/20020709-chimento-etal-qbone-signaling/

Crowcroft, J., Hand, S., Mortier, R., Roscoe, T., & Warfield, A. (2003). QoS's downfall: At the bottom, or not at all! *Proceedings of the ACM SIGCOMM 2003 Workshops*, 109-114.

Elek, V., Karlsson, G., & Ronngren, R. (2000). Admission control based on end-to-end measurements. *Proceedings of IEEE INFOCOM 2000*, 623-630.

Fu, X., Schulzrinne, H., Bader, A., Hogrefe, D., Kappler, C., Karagiannis, G., Tschofenig, H., et al. (2005). NSIS: A new extensible IP signaling protocol suite. *IEEE Communications Magazine, 43*(10), 133-141.

Key, P., & Massoulié, L. (2003). Probing strategies for distributed admission control in large and small scale systems. *Proceedings of the IEEE INFOCOM 2003*, 608-618.

Le Boudec, J.-Y., & Thiran, P. (2001). Network calculus: A theory of deterministic queuing systems for the Internet. *Lecture Notes in Computer Science, 2050.* Springer-Verlag.

Nichols, K., Jacobson, V., & Zhang, L. (1999). *A two-bit differentiated services architecture for the Internet.* IETF RFC-2638.

Prior, R., Sargento, S., Brandão, P., & Crisóstomo, S. (2004a). Comparative evaluation of two scalable QoS architectures. *Networking-2004: Lecture Notes in Computer Science, 3042,* 1452-1457. Springer-Verlag.

Prior, R., Sargento, S., Brandão, P., & Crisóstomo, S. (2003b). Efficient reservation-based QoS architecture: Interactive multimedia on next generation networks. *Lecture Notes in Computer Science, 2899,* 168-181. Springer-Verlag.

Prior, R., Sargento, S., Crisóstomo, S., & Brandão, P. (2003a). End-to-end QoS with scalable reservations. *Proceedings of the 11th International Conference on Telecommunication Systems, Modeling and Analysis (ICTSM11),* 21-34.

Prior, R., Sargento, S., Brandão, P., & Crisóstomo, S. (2004b). Evaluation of a scalable reservation-based QoS architecture. *Proceedings of the Ninth IEEE International Symposium on Computers and Communications (ISCC-2004),* 993-999.

Prior, R., Sargento, S., Brandão, P., & Crisóstomo, S. (2004c). SRBQ and RSVPRAgg: A comparative study. *Telecommunications and Networking. ICT 2004, 11th International Conference on Telecommunications. Lecture Notes in Computer Science, 3124* (pp. 1210-1217). Springer-Verlag.

Sargento, S., et al. (2004). *QoS architecture and protocol design specification.* IST-DAIDALOS project deliverable D321.

Sargento, S., Valadas, R., & Knightly, E. (2001). Resource stealing in endpoint controlled multi-class networks. *Proceedings of IWDC 2001* (invited paper), 195-211.

Schelen, O., & Pink, S. (1998). Aggregating resource reservations over multiple routing domains. *Proceedings of the 6th International Workshop on Quality of Service (IWQoS'98),* 29-32.

Stoica, I. (2000). *Stateless core: A scalable approach for quality of service in the Internet.* PhD thesis, Carnegie Mellon University.

Terzis, A., Wang, L., Ogawa, J., & Zhang, L. (1999). A two-tier resource management model for the Internet. *Proceedings of GLOBECOM'99,* Vol. 3, 1779-1791,

Westberg, R., Császár, A., Karagiannis, G., Marquetant, A., Partain, D., Pop, O., et al. (2002). Resource management in Diffserv (RMD): A functionality and performance behavior overview. *Protocols for High Speed Networks – 7th IFIP/IEEE International Workshop, PfHSN. Lecture Notes in Computer Science, 2334* (pp. 17-34). Springer-Verlag.

KEY TERMS

Arrival Curve: The arrival curve of a flow is a wide-sense increasing function α defined for $t \geq 0$, such that the amount of data flowing in any time interval of length t is less than or equal to $\alpha(t)$. It is used to place a constraint on the flow's arrival process.

Flow Aggregation: Merging of multiple flows, possibly sharing common characteristics, in order to treat them as a single flow in the use of a given resource.

Label Switching: Technique used in protocols whereby a short identifier (label) is carried in signaling messages and/or data packets in order to allow for easy and efficient classification or access to a given data structure or state information. Along the path, labels may be kept intact, exchanged, or stacked, according to the protocol.

Quality of Service (QoS): Subjectively defined in Recommendation E.800 of the ITU-T as "The collective effect of service performance which determines the degree of satisfaction of a user of the service," QoS refers to the probability of the network meeting a given traffic contract, which may be quantitatively expressed by parameters such as transfer delay and jitter and probability of packet loss, error, or out-of-order delivery.

Scalability: The ease with which a system or component can handle increased dimensions of the problem it is designed to solve.

Soft State: Technique whereby the state information is automatically deleted if not refreshed for a given period. It is used to improve the resilience of protocols by providing automatic recovery from faults and changing conditions.

Traffic Policing: Forcing an input flow to have an output that conforms to a given traffic envelope σ by discarding non-conformant bits (or packets) of the flow or reclassifying them to a different flow or aggregate.

Traffic Shaping: Forcing an input flow to have an output that conforms to a given traffic envelope σ by delaying the non-conformant bits (or packets) of the flow in a buffer. At the output of the traffic shaper, the flow has σ as an arrival curve.

Scaling Properties of Network Traffic

David Rincón
Technical University of Catalonia (UPC), Spain

Sebastià Sallent
Technical University of Catalonia (UPC), Spain

INTRODUCTION

The availability of good stochastic models of network traffic is the key to developing protocols and services. A precise statistical characterization of packet interarrival time, size distribution, and connection arrival rate help network engineers to design network equipment and evaluate its performance.

The classical models developed for the telephone network more than a century ago, such as the Erlang-B and C models, are based on exponential distributions, Poisson arrival processes, and Markov chains. These models are *memoryless*, meaning that past events do not influence the future behaviour of the process and that the traffic process is therefore uncorrelated. These assumptions are quite accurate for telephony traffic.

In the early days of computer networks and packet switching, new models were developed and gave rise to queuing theory (Kleinrock, 1975). These models generally assumed uncorrelated, independent arrivals and were used for network dimensioning and performance evaluation. However, as networks and protocols grew in complexity, the results obtained with these models started to diverge from reality. Modern network services and applications, such as the World Wide Web, FTP, P2P, and video and audio streaming exhibit strong correlation and differentiated traffic patterns on various time scales.

In a paper that shook the teletraffic community, Leland et al. (1994) analyzed the traffic on the Ethernet network of Bellcore Laboratories and found *fractal* or *scaling* properties. Fractals are objects whose main property is that they have the same appearance when they are observed on finer and coarser scales (Mandelbrot, 1983). The same effect was detected in the Bellcore traces: The intrinsic variability (burstiness) observed on the finer time scales is the same as on coarser time scales (see Figure 1). This is contrary to classical, Pois-

Figure 1. Throughput (bytes arrived per time slot) of the Bellcore BC_pAug89 trace, seen at different time scales. Burstiness is maintained.

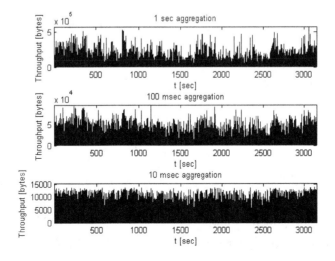

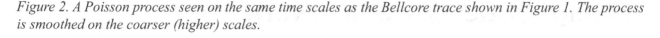

Figure 2. A Poisson process seen on the same time scales as the Bellcore trace shown in Figure 1. The process is smoothed on the coarser (higher) scales.

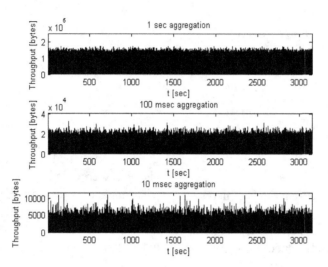

son-based models, in which traffic is smoothed on the coarser scales by the effect of statistical multiplexing. Figure 2 illustrates this effect.

Scaling phenomena can be understood in terms of the variability, or burstiness, of network traffic, i.e., the fact that long packet bursts are followed by long periods of inactivity. The novelty is that this happens on a wide range of time scales, while classical models can only capture the burstiness on a certain "natural" scale.

The scaling properties of traffic have a major impact on network performance. Norros (1994) found that Poisson-based models greatly underestimate the probability of buffer overflow. Not all of the effects are bad; for example, correlation can help in long-term traffic prediction (Papagiannaki et al., 2003).

BACKGROUND

This section defines the fractal models, together with some estimation techniques. A deeper mathematical treatment can be found in Park and Willinger (2000).

Traffic Traces

Traffic traces include at least two columns: a timestamp (the time at which the packet was captured) and packet size. Further information, such as the port or the origin and destination addresses can be useful for filtering different flows. In traffic studies, the series of interest

are usually the packet interarrival time (the difference between consecutive timestamps) and the instantaneous bit rate (the number of bytes that arrive during time slots of a constant length, such as the example shown in Figure 1). In both cases, we get a one-dimensional time series over which scaling estimation methods can be applied.

Traffic traces are studied on different time scales though aggregation. Given a stochastic process $Z(t)$, we define its aggregated version $Z^{(m)}(t)$ at aggregation level m as the average of $Z(t)$ in non-overlapping blocks of size m, as:

$$Z^{(m)}(k) = \frac{1}{m}\left[\sum_{t=km+1}^{(k+1)m} Z(t)\right] \qquad k = 0, 1, 2\dots \quad (1)$$

Self-Similarity

A stochastic process $Y(t)$ is considered *self-similar* with Hurst parameter H if, when it is studied on different time scales, it has exactly the same (rescaled) statistical distribution, as shown in (2).

$$Y(t) \stackrel{d}{=} a^{-H} Y(ta) \qquad (2)$$

Self-similarity is linked with fractality; the process is observed on different scales, and its appearance (in the statistical sense) is maintained. The Hurst parameter

H ($0.5 < H < 1$) measures the degree of self-similarity. One example of a self-similar process is Fractional Brownian Motion (FBM), which is the only Gaussian self-similar process (Park & Willinger, 2000).

A self-similar process cannot be stationary, so we are usually more interested in its (stationary) increment process $X(t)=Y(t+1)-Y(t)$, which is related to the concept of long-range dependence.

Long-Range Dependence (LRD)

A stochastic process $X(t)$ is *long-range dependent* if its autocorrelation $\rho(k)$ decays so slowly with time lag k that it is not summable (3). These processes are said to have *long memory*, due to the non-negligible autocorrelation, even for large lags.

$$\sum_{k=-\infty}^{\infty} \rho(k) \to \infty \qquad (3)$$

An equivalent definition in the frequency domain states that the spectral density of the process has strong low-frequency components and follows (4), where c_f is a constant and $0 < \alpha < 1$.

$$S_x(f) \sim \frac{c_f}{|f|^a} \quad \text{when } |f| \to 0 \qquad (4)$$

The scaling parameter α is related to the intensity of LRD and is understood as a qualitative measure, while c_f has dimensions of variance and can be interpreted as a quantitative measure. The increment process of a self-similar process whose Hurst parameter is in the range $0.5 < H < 1$ is LRD. This is why the scaling parameter α is usually expressed as a rewritten version of H: $\alpha = 2H-1$. One example of a LRD process is Fractional Gaussian noise (FGN), the increment process of FBM. FGN has been proposed as a good model for LRD traffic.

Heavy Tails

The distribution of a random variable X is said to be heavy-tailed if its tail decays hyperbolically:

$$\Pr[X > x] \sim cx^{-\alpha} \qquad (5)$$

where c is a positive constant and $0 < \alpha < 2$ is the tail index or shape parameter. The Pareto distribution is an example of heavy-tailed distribution, while exponential and Gaussian distributions are light-tailed distributions. The main property of a heavy-tailed distribution is the non-negligible probability of taking very high values.

Heavy tails have been found in network-related variables (HTTP or FTP file sizes, TCP, and HTTP connection durations, for example) and have been identified as being responsible for the associated traffic's burstiness and long-range dependence.

Estimators for Fractal Processes

There are several estimators of the scaling and Hurst parameters: the wavelet-based LogScale Diagram, the variance-time analysis, the rescaled adjusted range statistic (also known as the R/S plot), the periodogram-based method, and Whittle's method, among others (Molnár, 2004).

The wavelet-based method seems to be the most efficient and accurate method available to date. The discrete wavelet transform (DWT) provides a multi-resolution analysis of a process x(n). The output is a low-pass approximation of the original signal on scale J, $a_x(J,k)$, and a set of high-pass details $d_x(j,k)$ for each scale j=1…J, k being the time variable. Abry and Veitch developed the *LogScale Diagram* (Abry et al., 2000), an unbiased and efficient estimator of LRD parameters. It computes the second moment of the wavelet coefficients in each subband (octave) of the DWT decomposition and represents it in a log-log diagram. LRD processes show a straight line with slope α and an offset related to c_f. Both parameters can be estimated by performing a weighted linear regression.

Multifractals

Self-similar and LRD processes fall into the class of monofractal processes. Multifractals are a generalization in which the small time-scale behaviour of the process exhibits local variations of the scaling parameter, i.e., $\alpha(t)$ is no longer constant and depends on time. More details of multifractal formalism can be found in Riedi and Willinger (2000). The authors of the LogScale Diagram also developed an extension for multifractal processes, the Multiscale Diagram (Abry et al., 2000).

One multifractal process, the multiplicative generated multifractal (also known as cascades), fragments a given set into smaller pieces according to a geometric or random rule. This process has been proposed as a traffic model because it mimics the fragmentation performed by the protocol stack (Feldmann et al., 1998).

SCALING PROPERTIES OF NETWORK TRAFFIC

This section provides an overview of the measurements that have found fractal properties in almost all of the networks and services available today, and discusses the origins of such phenomena and the impact of fractal traffic on the performance of computer networks.

Fractal Properties in Network Traffic

After the seminal paper by Leland et al. (1994) on self-similarity in Ethernet networks, other networks and traffic sources were studied. Garrett and Willinger (1994) studied LRD in variable-bit-rate (VBR) video and found strong low-frequency components. Self-similarity was found by Duffy et al. (1994) in the signalling network of telephone operators. Paxson and Floyd (1995) found fractal properties in wide-area network traffic, specifically in TCP, FTP, and Telnet. Crovella and Bestavros (1997) found self-similarity in World Wide Web (WWW) traffic. Finally, Joo et al. (2004) recently found that peer-to-peer (P2P) file sharing systems are much burstier than Web traffic.

The Origins of Traffic Fractality

The traffic research community advocates physically understandable models—that is, models that not only provide a mathematical description but also try to explain what is happening in the network and identify the physical causes of self-similarity (Park & Willinger, 2000). Three main scenarios have been identified, based on whether the cause is user behaviour, traffic source statistics, or network protocol dynamics.

Regarding how users can be a source of fractality, it has been shown that FTP and Telnet packet interarrival times are not exponential (Paxson & Floyd, 1995), while Web users seem to follow heavy-tailed usage patterns (Crovella and Bestavros, 1997). Actually, the behaviour of a WWW user is intrinsically bursty on various scales due to the transitions between page download and inactivity (reading time), which translate into con-

nections and packet bursts that inherit fractality.

The second cause of fractality, also called *structural causality* by Park et al. (1996), is related to an empirical property inherent to distributed systems: the heavy-tailedness of the file-size distribution found in UNIX disk systems (Park et al., 1996) and Web objects (Crovella & Bestavros, 1997). The transfer of these files through networks generates heavy-tailed packet bursts and connections, and multiplexing at the network core generates self-similarity. In one of the fundamental results of modern traffic modelling, Willinger et al. (1997) proved that the superposition of a large number of independent on/off sources with heavy-tailed on or off periods leads to long-range dependence in the aggregated process. VBR video is another case in which the traffic source is intrinsically LRD, according to Garrett and Willinger (1994), and transfers this property to the traffic flow.

Finally, protocol dynamics have been identified as the source, or propitiator, of scaling in certain situations. Network traffic exhibits long bursts of packets followed by long silences. This property is found on several time scales (packets can be aggregated in bursts, bursts in connections, and connections in user sessions). The fragmentation induced by the protocol stack may be the cause of traffic multifractality because it is similar to cascades and multiplicative processes. The congestion-control algorithms implemented in TCP also seem to affect the short-time structure of traffic and induce multifractality (Feldmann et al., 1999) or at least some degree of scaling (Jiang & Dovrolis, 2005).

Impact of Scaling Properties on Network Performance

Norros (1994) studied the performance of a single server queue under monofractal FBM traffic and analytically showed that self-similar traffic causes higher buffer overflow probability and/or an increase in packet delay than classical Poisson-based models (see Figure 3).

The queue length follows a subexponential tail, while in the case of short-range dependent arrivals (such as the M/M/1 and M/D/1 models), the tail decays exponentially. This phenomenon has important implications for network resource planning, since the smoothing effect of buffers is no longer valid with self-similar traffic unless we incur prohibitive buffer sizes. Some authors advocate the truncating effect of finite (and short) buffers (Heyman & Lakshman, 1996)

Figure 3. Mean queue size versus normalized traffic (utilization) ρ for Poisson-based queue models M/M/1 and M/D/1, and FBM with H = 0.7 and H = 0.9.

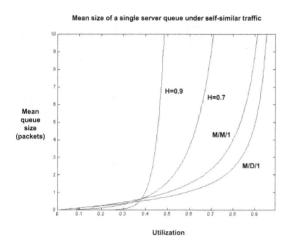

that destroy the memory of the process and therefore its correlation. However, this is only possible if we assume a certain degree of loss, and it may not work if retransmission mechanisms repeat the lost packets, which causes longer delays. Grossglauser and Bolot (1996) propose a simple resource-provisioning approach based on the combination of small buffers and large bandwidth.

Regarding multifractal traffic, Dang et al. (2003) provided analytical results for the case of a single-server, infinite-capacity queue with a constant service rate that are coherent with those of Norros for monofractal traffic. The authors conclude that multifractal processes behave even worse (in terms of queue length) than monofractal input processes.

DISCUSSION

Though it is clear that Poisson-based models fail to incorporate the intrinsic burstiness of traffic sources on several scales, it is still under discussion whether, and which, models proposed in the literature provide a good characterization of the complex processes found in real traces. This is an ill-posed problem, since Internet traffic is constantly evolving in terms of both volume and structure. Network applications and services in the

early 1990s, when self-similarity was first described, had nothing to do with the predominant position of Web traffic seen later; and since 2000, P2P file sharing applications have been responsible for the biggest share of bytes transferred in the Internet. Furthermore, Internet infrastructure is constantly growing due to the demand from existing and new users, which makes it even more difficult to compare past results and new traces.

Just to provide an overview of the latest trends in traffic modelling, we will mention some of the newest contributions, in which network researchers seem to advocate simpler, more physical models. Karagiannis et al. (2004) recently showed that modern aggregated wide-area traffic can be well modelled by Poisson processes on sub-second scales, while piecewise-linear non-stationarity and long-range dependence seem to fit well on higher scales. Veitch et al. (2005) consider that the physical evidence for multifractality in TCP traffic is weak and provide a case against it, in which multifractal behaviour can be explained as a misinterpretation due to the limitations of current statistical methods. Finally, interest is growing in the role of non-stationarity in the statistical properties of traffic. For example, Uhlig (2004) studied the high-order scaling and non-stationarity present in TCP flow arrivals using the wavelet transform.

FUTURE TRENDS

The scaling paradigm is firmly established as the foundation of modern teletraffic modelling, though it is still unclear which specific model is the most appropriate. Given the complexity of Internet traffic, probably no model—either known or yet to be devised—will ever be found to be definitive. However, more research is needed on this topic. There are important network performance issues, and protocols and algorithms should be aware of the scaling properties of traffic. Some steps have been taken in this direction, with the development of a fractal-aware version of TCP congestion control (He, 2002) and the novel resource-control algorithm for IP over WDM networks developed by Elbiaze and Cherkaoui (2005). A promising field for research is the development of estimation algorithms that can adapt to the non-stationarity of traffic, which is a challenging task.

CONCLUSION

Several studies have proved that network traffic exhibits scaling properties that cannot be captured by traffic models based on Poissonian or Markovian stochastic processes. Traffic fractality has been detected in almost every network service, including FTP, P2P, HTTP, and video-over-IP. The implications for network performance are serious: higher delays and loss ratios at router queues than have been predicted by Poissonian models. However, the correlation induced by scaling opens the opportunity for new fractal-aware mechanisms such as traffic predictors, congestion control, and resource-provisioning algorithms. The inherent non-stationary nature of Internet traffic makes traffic characterization more difficult and highlights the need for algorithms capable of adapting to the evolution of traffic.

REFERENCES

Abry, P., Flandrin, P., Taqqu, M.S., & Veitch, D. (2000) Wavelets for the analysis, estimation and synthesis of scaling data. In K. Park & W. Willinger (Eds.) *Self-similar network traffic and performance evaluation*. New York: Wiley.

Crovella, M.E., & Bestavros, A. (1997). Self-similarity in World Wide Web traffic: Evidence and possible causes. *IEEE/ACM Transactions on Networking, 5*(6), 835-846.

Dang, T. D, Molnár, S., & Maricza, I. (2003). Some results on multiscale queueing analysis. *Proceedings of IEEE International Conference on Telecommunications (ICT)* (pp. 1631-1638). Tahiti, French Polynesia.

Duffy, D.E., McIntosh, A.A., Rosenstein, M., & Willinger, W. (1994). Statistical analysis of CCSN/SS7 traffic data from working CCS subnetworks. *IEEE Journal on Selected Areas in Communications, 12*(3), 544-551.

Elbiaze, H., & Cherkaoui, O. (2005, October). Exploiting self-similar traffic analysis in network resource control: The IP over WDM networks case. *Proceedings of IEEE ICAS/ICNS*, pp. 65-70, Papeete, Tahiti.

Feldmann, A., Gilbert, A.C., & Willinger, W. (1998). Data networks as cascades: Iinvestigating the multifractal nature of Internet WAN traffic. *ACM SIGCOMM Computer Communication Review, 28*(4), 42-55.

Feldmann, A., Gilbert, A.C., Huang, P., & Willinger, W. (1999). Dynamics of IP traffic: A study of the role of variability and the impact of control. *Proceedings of ACM SIGCOMM 1999* (pp. 301-313).

Garrett, M., & Willinger, W. (1994). Analysis, modeling, and generation of self-similar VBR video traffic. *Proceedings of ACM SIGCOMM,* Londo (pp. 269-280).

Grossglauser, M., & Bolot, J.C. (1996). On the relevance of long-range dependence in network traffic. *IEEE/ACM Transactions on Networking, 7*(5), 629-640.

He, G., Gao, Y., Hou, J., & Park, K. (2002, November). A case for exploiting self-similarity of network traffic in TCP congestion control. *Proceedings of the 10th IEEE International Conference on Network Protocols*, pp. 34-43, Paris.

Heyman, D., & Lakshman, T. (1996). What are the implications of long-range dependence for VBR-video traffic engineering? *IEEE/ACM Transactions on Networking, 4*(3), 301-317.

Jiang, H., & Dovrolis, C. (2005). Why is the Internet traffic bursty in short time scales? *ACM SIGMETRICS Performance Evaluation Review, 33*(1), 241-252.

Joo, S., Lee, C., & Chung, Y. (2004). Analysis and modeling of traffic from residential high speed Internet subscribers. *Proceedings of ICOIN 2004*, Busan, Korea (pp. 410-419).

Karagiannis, T., Molle, M., Faloutsos, M., & Broido, A. (2004, March). A nonstationary Poisson view of Internet traffic. *Proceedings of IEEE Infocom*, pp. 1558-1569, Hong-Kong.

Kleinrock, L. (1975). *Queueing systems*. New York: John Wiley & Sons.

Leland, W., Taqqu, M., Willinger, W., & Wilson, D. (1994). On the self-similar nature of ethernet traffic (Extended Version). *IEEE/ACM Transactions on Networking, 2*(1), 1-15.

Mandelbrot, B. B. (1983). *The fractal geometry of nature (updated)*. San Francisco: W.H. Freeman.

Molnár, S. (2004). *Traffic analysis and modeling* [Tutorial]. EuroNGI Summer School, University of Bamberg, Germany, October.

Norros, I. (1994). A storage model with self-similar input. *Queueing Systems,* (16), 387-396.

Papagiannaki, K., Taft, N., Zhang, Z., & Diot, C. (2003). Long-term forecasting of Internet backbone traffic: Observations and initial models. *Proceedings of IEEE Infocom*, pp. 1110-1124, San Francisco.

Park, K., & Willinger, W. (2000). Self-similar network traffic: An overview. In K. Park & W. Willinger (Eds.), *Self-similar network traffic and performance evaluation*. New York: Wiley.

Park, K., Kim, G. & Crovella, M. (1996, October-November). On the relationship between file sizes, transport protocols, and self-similar network traffic. *Proceedings of IEEE International Conference on Network Protocols,* pp. 171-180, Columbus, Ohio.

Paxson, V., & Floyd, S. (1995). Wide area traffic: The failure of Poisson modeling, *IEEE/ACM Transactions on Networking, 3*(3), 226-244.

Riedi, R.H., & Willinger, W. (2000). Toward an improved understanding of network traffic dynamics. In K. Park & W. Willinger (Eds.), *Self-similar network traffic and performance evaluation*. New York: Wiley.

Uhlig, S. (2004). High-order scaling and non-stationarity in TCP flow arrivals: A methodological analysis. *ACM SIGCOMM Computer Communication Review, 34*(2) 9-24.

Veitch, D., Hohn, N., & Abry, P. (2005). Multifractality in TCP/IP traces: The case against. *Computer Networks, 48*, 293-313.

Willinger, W., Taqqu, M., Sherman, R., & Wilson, D. (1997). Self-similarity through high variability: Statistical analysis of ethernet LAN traffic at the source level. *IEEE/ACM Transactions on Networking, 5*(1), 71-86.

KEY TERMS

S

Aggregation (of a time series): The action of averaging the time series over non-overlapping blocks of constant size.

Fractals: Objects (in particular, figures) that have the same appearance when they are seen on fine and coarse scales.

Heavy-Tailed Distribution: A statistical distribution with tails that decay subexponentially.

Hurst Parameter: A qualitative measure of self-similarity related to the scaling parameter α defined for long-range dependent processes.

Long-Range Dependence (also known as long memory): A property found in stochastic processes with strong low-frequency components.

Multifractality: A generalization of self-similarity in which the small time-scale behaviour of the process shows local variations in the scaling parameter.

Self-Similarity: When applied to stochastic processes, it indicates that the process follows the same distribution on all time scales.

Seamless Multi-Hop Handover in IPv6-Based Hybrid Wireless Networks

Tonghong Li
Universidad Politécnica de Madrid, Spain

INTRODUCTION

Mobile ad hoc networks (MANETs) are becoming popular due to the abundance of mobile devices, the speed and the convenience of deployment, and the independence of network infrastructure (Chin, 2002; Royer, 1999). It is desired that MANETs be interconnected to fixed IP networks so that the Internet services can be offered to MANET nodes. In such scenarios, commonly known as **hybrid ad hoc networks**, mobile nodes (MNs) are viewed as an easily deployable extension to the existing infrastructure. Gateways (GWs) are installed, which can be used by MNs to communicate with nodes in the fixed network.

BACKGROUND

Recently, much work has been done on providing Internet connectivity for mobile nodes in hybrid ad hoc networks (Lee, 2003; Jönsson, 2000; Ratanchandani, 2003; Sun, 2002; Tseng, 2003; Wakikawa, 2002; Xi, 2002). Although different aspects, including the global address configuration, gateway discovery, and communication in different scenarios, are addressed, the multi-hop handover is still an open issue. Considering multiple GWs in hybrid networks, many proposals extended mobile IP to achieve seamless handover for MNs one hop away from GWs; however, work on handover for MNs multi-hop away from GWs is very limited.

Typpö (2001) proposed an integrated protocol for IPv6-based hybrid wireless multi-hop networks based on Cellular IP and AODV (Perkins, 2003). This protocol extends micro-mobility management into an ad hoc network. Two different handover schemes, proxy-based and proxy-disabled, are included to allow the protocol to adapt to different networking requirements. However, its handover schemes are designed

for intra GW handover, where MNs still use the same GW when changing its base station due to its movement. The network architecture used is different from the scenario studied here, as there are base stations between MANETs and GWs.

Ghassemian (2004) compared different gateway discovery approaches for IPv4-based hybrid ad hoc networks in various scenarios by means of simulation. Multi-hop handover is performed if MNs change their GW while communicating with a corresponding node (CN) in the Internet, which is categorized into forced handover and route optimization handover. Forced handover occurs whenever the path between the MN and the GW is disrupted during data transmission. The following GW discovery process may result in the detection of a new GW, which will consequently result in a handover. On the other hand, if the MN detects that a shorter path to the Internet becomes available while communicating with a CN, the active path will be optimized. In case the shorter path is via a different GW, a route optimization handover occurs. Though the performance of multi-hop handover under different gateway discovery approaches is evaluated, no scheme is proposed to provide smooth multi-hop handover.

This paper studies multi-hop handover in IPv6-based hybrid ad hoc networks. Our hybrid ad hoc network architecture is constructed by integrating Mobile IPv6 (MIPv6) with MANET, which is very similar to the architecture used in Ghassemian (2004). We assume the routing protocol for MANET is AODV, though our handover scheme can be applied to any other on-demand MANET protocol. The main contribution of this paper is a seamless multi-hop handover scheme to reduce the packet loss and handover delay without incurring too much signaling overhead during the handover. For the purpose of studying the performance, we also developed extensions to NS2 for simulating hybrid networks based on Hierarchical MIPv6 (HMIPv6) (Soliman, 2003) and AODV. To our knowledge, this is the first simulation tool that integrates HMIPv6 and AODV in hybrid ad hoc network.

SEAMLESS MULTI-HOP HANDOVER IN IPV6-BASED HYBRID WIRELESS NETWORKS

In this section, we first introduce our hybrid network architecture, and its gateway discovery and registration procedure. Afterwards, we describe our seamless multi-hop handover scheme in detail. Finally, we show the simulation results.

IPv6-Based Hybrid Ad Hoc Network

Figure 1 shows our **IPv6-based hybrid network** architecture. MNs use AODV to communicate with each other. GWs are installed, which connect MANETs and wired networks. HMIPv6 is used in access networks due to its smooth local mobility management feature. We assume each MN has a unique IP address to be identified in wireless and wired networks; this address is called the home address, conforming to mobile IP. MNs and GWs understand HMIPv6 and AODV, and they identify each other by their home addresses.

Hybrid Gateway Discovery

To connect with the Internet, a MN must find a GW. In our hybrid network, we use a **hybrid GW discovery** scheme to realize GW discovery. Each GW broadcasts the router advertisement (RA) messages within N hops in a fixed advertisement interval. N is called the **flood-ing range**, which can be adjusted by setting the TTL field in the IP header of the RA message.

For each MN in the flooding range, it records the address of the mobility anchor point (MAP), the address of the GW, the advertisement sequence number, and advertisement lifetime in its GW table upon receiving RA messages. It also sets up a route to the GW. This route allows a MN to update its routes to the GW if the RA message arrives along a shorter path or to refresh the route entries if the route is already known.

For each MN beyond the flooding range, it will broadcast a solicitation for GW discovery if Internet access is required, as it cannot receive RA messages. Upon receiving the solicitation, the GW will unicast a RA message to the MN. Solicitation also sets up a reverse route to the MN, ensuring that unicast RA messages sent out in response do not generate unnecessary RREQ messages. When a MN receives this RA message, the procedure will be the same as the MN in the flooding range.

Registration

After a MN receives an RA message, the MN will add an entry in its GW table and choose one of <*MAP, GW*> to register with. The choice can be based on criteria such as distance, cost, or other information contained in RA messages. In our scheme, we select the GW with the shortest hop count. Afterwards, the MN auto-configures a unique RCoA (regional care of address) and LCoA (local care of address) which will be contained in Binding Update (BU) messages.

When GW receives a BU from a MN, it will record the MN at its MN table, which is used to keep track of

Figure 1. Hybrid multi-hop wireless network

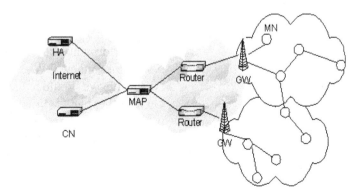

registered MNs for making routing decisions. When MAP receives a BU message, it will create an entry in its binding cache to bind the MN's RCoA to LCoA, and set a registration time for this entry. Similarly, the HA will create an entry to bind the MN's home address to RCoA, and set a registration time for this entry as well. MNs must periodically register with the HA and the MAP to refresh the entries. GWs forward BU acknowledgements they receive from the MAP back to the MN. Once the MN receives the acknowledgement, it will set the lifetime field in the entry. To maintain the registration, the mobile node must re-register before the lifetime expires. Through periodical registrations, the bi-directional path to the registered GW from the MN can be refreshed periodically.

For each MN beyond the flooding range, it registers with the current GW until there is no path to this GW. In this case, its GW table is checked in order to find an alternative GW for registration. If it fails, the GW discovery is initiated to discover a new GW for registration.

Seamless Multi-Hop Handover

In a traditional wireless access network, MNs have link-layer connections with access points, and handover is normally defined as the service disruption period between the disconnection with a previous access point and establishing connection with a new access point. For MNs multi-hop away from GWs, as in our hybrid wireless network, the handover issue is much more complicated. We define the multi-hop handover as a route change from MN to the registered GW, which may occur when a MN itself, or any of the intermediate MNs, moves and breaks the active route to the registered GW during the MN's communication with a CN in the wired network. In mobile IP, the handover process includes Layer-2 handover and Layer-3 handover. In our hybrid wireless network, MNs that are multi-hop away from a GW do not have link-layer connections with the GW, and thus handover is only performed at Layer 3.

Multi-Hop Handover Type

Considering different situations, multi-hop handover can be classified as follows:

- **Intra-GW handover and Inter-GW handover:** Intra-GW handover occurs when MN still registers with the same GW although the route to the current GW is broken; while Inter-GW handover occurs when the MN registers with a new GW. When Intra-GW handover happens, no mobile IP operation is involved. However, for Inter-GW handover, mobile IP operations like BU are required.
- **Compulsory handover and optimized handover:** A compulsory handover occurs when MN detects that the route to its current GW is broken. The optimized handover occurs when the MN's route to its current GW is still active, but a better (more optimized) route is available and selected.

Combining the above two categories of handovers, we can classify the handover into four types:

1. **Compulsory intra-GW handover:** When the route to the current GW breaks, but there is an alternative path to the current GW. This type of handover is handled by AODV's recovery procedure.
2. **Compulsory Inter-GW handover:** When there is no path to the current GW and the subsequent GW discovery process results in the detection of a new GW.
3. **Optimized intra-GW handover:** No route break, but a MN uses a shorter path to the current GW when a new RA message from the current GW arrives from a shorter path. This type of handover is completely handled by the RA message-processing in GW discovery procedure.
4. **Optimized inter-GW handover:** no route break, a MN uses a shorter path to another GW when it receives a new RA message with less hop count from another GW.

Type 2 handover has a bad impact on communications performance because the delay and overhead of discovering a new GW and a route to it are very high. As a result, we should reduce the rate of its occurrence. On the other hand, a timely type four handover is very useful. In multi-hop scenarios, using shorter paths can reduce the packet end-to-end delay; moreover, a shorter path to a new GW may indicate a potential future compulsory Inter-GW handover, thus using optimized Inter-GW handover can prevent a future route break.

Our Enhanced Multi-Hop Handover Scheme

The objective of our handover scheme is to achieve low handover latency and low packet loss without incurring excessive overhead. For this purpose, we propose the following approaches:

1. Proactively maintain a bi-directional route between a MN and its registered GW.

   In AODV, when the path to the current GW is broken, the source node does not reinitiate the route discovery unless there is traffic to the current GW, which leads to the long delay for packet transmission. To solve this problem, we proactively maintain a bi-directional route between the MN and its registered GW, which can be realized as follows: the bi-directional route can be refreshed each registration through BU and BU acknowledgement messages. Between two consecutive registrations, the route discovery is initiated immediately upon receiving Route Error message for the bi-directional route irrespective of the presence of traffic between the GW and a MN.

2. Dependant Notifying Mechanism

   For a MN at the *N*th hop from its current GW, it will immediately inform its dependants with <*previous GW, new GW*> information by broadcasting a handover notification message when performing an optimized Inter-GW handover. To be a MN's **dependant** two conditions must be satisfied: (1) it is registered in the same GW as the MN; (2) it uses this MN as the next hop in the route to its registered GW. When its dependant receives the message, the MN constructs a route to the new GW and registers with it; a new notification message is also broadcasted. In this way, future compulsory Inter-GW handovers can be avoided.

   A MN beyond the *N*th hop from its GW will immediately notify its dependants by using a new type of Route Error message called "GW_Error" when performing a compulsory Inter-GW handover. The GW_Error also includes the <*previous GW, new GW*> information. When a dependant receives this error message, it will construct a route to the new GW and register with it if no alternative path to the previous GW can be discovered by AODV's repair process. Similarly, a new "GW_Error" message is broadcasted again if a dependant decides to switch to the new GW. In this way, the dependants can perform compulsory Inter-GW handover without the start of GW discovery, which results in the reduction of handover delay and overhead.

3. Intermediate nodes reply to solicitation request for the GW if they have active routes to the GW.

   When a MN outside the RA flooding range wants to connect to the Internet, it will send out a solicitation. When a GW receives the solicitation, it will unicast a RA message to the MN. Previously, the intermediate node just forwarded the solicitation. To let intermediate nodes reply to solicitation can reduce the GW discovery latency and overhead.

4. Intermediate nodes hear the RA message unicasted by GW.

   When the intermediate node forwards a unicasted RA message, it can update its GW table's entry with respect to this GW.

5. Optimized Inter-GW handover stability management.

   This is to prevent high frequent oscillations and decrease the probability of a MN registering with a GW that is only temporarily better. A MN will not start an optimized Inter-GW handover immediately, even if the new GW is nearer than the original one. Instead, it will only perform this type of handover after receiving at least two consecutive RA messages about the new GW.

We name the handover scheme with the above approaches, "**enhanced HMIPAODV** (E-HMIPAODV)," and the scheme without these approaches, "**plain HMIPAODV** (P-HMIPAODV)." We compare the two schemes through simulation.

Simulation Results

MobiWan (MOTOROLA Labs Paris, 2002) is a simulation tool based on NS2 (version ns-2.1b6), meant to simulate Mobile IPv6 under large wide area networks (both local-area mobility and global-area mobility). In order to enable it to support AODV and HMIPv6, we modify the Network and MIPv6 agent. The Network agent is replaced by an AODV agent, which integrates our seamless handover scheme. The MIPv6 agent is responsible for tasks like maintaining binding cache and sending Binding Update.

The purpose of the simulation is to study the performance of our enhanced multi-hop handover scheme in a hybrid network. The protocol metrics used are: (1) handover latency; (2) packet loss ratio; and (3) control overhead. These metrics have been examined under different network scale (small and large), mobility level (changing pause time), and other related network parameters (e.g., RA interval, RA flooding range, etc.).

Figure 2 shows our simulation scenario, where the wired network consists of a cloud of five CNs (CN0 to CN4), HA for all MNs, one MAP, and four GWs. In the wireless network, we study two topologies, a small network with 30 MNs over 600x600m area and a large network with 50 MNs over 1000x1000m area. To simplify the simulation, we make the entire wireless network belong to one MAP, thus there is no handover between MAPs. Five of the MNs are CBR sources, and the five CNs are CBR sinks. Each source node sends constant bit rate (CBR) traffic with sending rate 10 packet/s (packet size is 50 bytes). A MN's movement complies with the random waypoint mobility model. All the simulations are done with the maximum speed set to 10m/s, the pause time is changed to simulate different level of mobility.

Figure 2. Simulation scenario

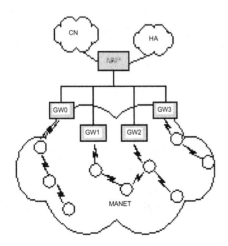

Impact of Mobility on Performance

Each MN moves randomly with speed uniformly distributed in the range (0, 10) m/s, the pause time is set to [5, 10, 20, 100, 200, 300, 400s] in each simulation respectively. RA flooding range is set to one and RA interval is set to 10s for all simulations in this set.

For a small network with 30 MNs, Figure 3(a) shows that E-HMIPAODV has less average handover latency than P-HMIPAODV. For both schemes, the handover latency decreases with increasing pause time. Figure 3(b) shows that E-HMIPAODV has less packet loss than P-HMIPAODV under different mobility levels. We also noticed that its improvement is more significant when pause time is shorter. Figures 3(c) and 3(d) show both schemes' overhead, which is measured as the total number of transmissions of control packet during simulation times. E-HMIPAODV reduces AODV control overhead because of its notification mechanism and allowing intermediate nodes to reply with GW route information. However, it introduces more HMIPv6 control messages because E-HMIPAODV performs more Inter-GW handover than P-HMIPADOV.

Figure 4(a)~4(d) show the results in a large network with 50 MNs, which are similar to the results in the small network with 30 MNs. However, we note that performance improvement of E-HMIPAODV is greater in larger networks and under higher mobility.

Impact of Frequency of RA

To examine both schemes' performance against the frequency of RA messages, we use the large network topology with the flooding range set to one and the MN's pause time set to 10s.

We find that the handover performance of both schemes has little difference when the sending rate of RA is very high or a node's mobility is very low. We also observe that the RA sending rate has impact on the performance of both schemes. The higher the RA sending rate is, the lower the handover delay is. However, a high RA sending rate causes high protocol overhead. There is an optimal value of RA interval considering both handover delay and protocol overhead, which depends on the node mobility and traffic pattern. In our scenario, the optimal value of RA interval is 10s.

Figure 3. Performance of both schemes in a small network with 30 MNs

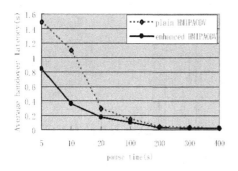

(a) Average handover latency

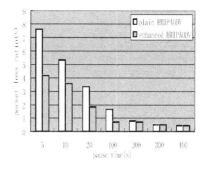

(b) Packet loss ratio

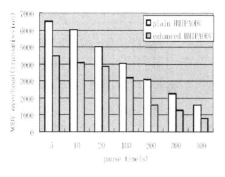

(c) AODV overhead

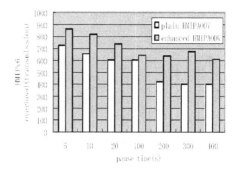

(d) HMIPv6 overhead

Impact of RA Flooding Range

We also study the impact of RA flooding range on both schemes' performance. We use the large network topology with RA interval set to 10s and the MN's pause time set to 10s.

We observe that E-HMIPAODV outperforms P-HMIPAODV at lower N. However when N is large, both schemes have similar results. That is because the entire area is likely to be covered by the flooding area of RA messages when N is large. Under the pure proactive GW discovery approach, there is no difference between schemes.

On the other hand, packet loss and handover delay can decrease dramatically as N increases in both schemes. This can be explained as follows: When N is small, there is only a small area in which the MN can receive GW information. Other MNs use the on-demand approach to discover GWs. Hence, when handover occurs, these MNs need longer time to reestablish the GW route compared with MNs in the flooding range. By increasing N, more MNs are covered by the flooding range. As a result, handover due to route failures reduces, while handover due to route optimization, which does not incur packet loss, becomes more frequent.

However, when N is large, the overhead of RA broadcasting is high, which leads to heavy protocol overhead. Therefore, RA flooding range should be adjusted according to different network scenarios in a similar approach to Tan (2004) to keep the overhead at a reasonable level while maintaining low delay and packet loss.

FUTURE TRENDS

Our proposed multi-hop handover scheme is only concerned with the uplink communication from the

Figure 4. Performance of both schemes in a big network with 50 MNs

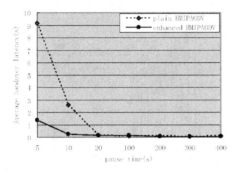

(a) Average handover latency

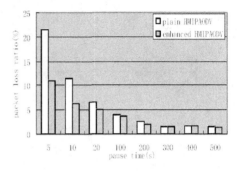

(b) Packet loss ratio

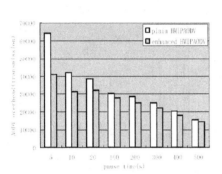

(c) AODV overhead

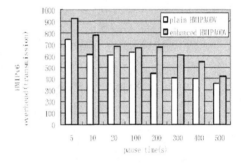

(d) HMIPv6 overhead

MN to the node in the fixed network; the downlink handover is still an open issue. One way to achieve seamless handover for downlink communication is to predict the movement of the MN so that the packet can be forwarded to the new GW before the MN is going to perform a handover. A detailed algorithm for the next GW prediction is being designed and implemented as an extension of our proposed scheme.

CONCLUSION

This paper studies multi-hop handover in an IPv6-based hybrid ad hoc network. We define multi-hop handover in a hybrid network and propose approaches to reduce multi-hop handover latency while minimizing protocol overhead. The key to provide a smooth handover for MNs in a hybrid network is to reduce the occurrence rate of compulsory Inter-GW handover as well as its handover latency. We propose several methods to solve this problem. Through simulation, we show our handover scheme can reduce the handover latency and packet loss without incurring too much overhead.

REFERENCES

Chin, K.W., Judge, J., Williams, A., & Kermode, R. (2002, November). Implementation experience with MANET routing protocols. ACM *SIGCOMM Computer Communications Review, 32*(5), 49-59.

Ghassemian, M., Hofmann, P., Prehofer, C., Friderikos, V., & Aghvami, H. (2004, April). Performance analysis of Internet gateway discovery protocols in ad hoc networks. WCNC 2004, Atlanta, USA.

Jönsson, U., Alriksson, F., Larsson, T., Johansson, P., & Magure, G. Q. (2000, August). MIPMANET—mobile

IP for mobile ad hoc networks. *ACM MobiHoc 2000*, Boston.

Lee, J., et al. (2003, April). Hybrid gateway advertisement scheme for connecting mobile ad hoc networks to the internet. *VTC 2003*-Spring, Jeju, Korea.

MOTOROLA Labs Paris, & INRIA PLANETE (2002, May). MobiWan: NS-2 extensions to study mobility in Wide-Area IPv6 Networks. http://www.inrialpes.fr/planete/pub/mobiwan.

Perkins, C.E., Belding-Royer, E.M., & Das, S. (2003, July). Ad hoc on-demand distance vector (AODV) routing. IETF, RFC 3561.

Ratanchandani, P., & Kravets, R. (2003, March). A hybrid approach to Internet connectivity for mobile ad hoc networks. WCNC 2003, New Orleans, Louisiana, USA.

Royer, E. M., & Toh, C.-K. (1999, April). A review of current routing protocols for ad-hoc mobile wireless networks. *IEEE Personal Communications, 6*(2), 46-55.

Soliman, H., Castelluccia, C., El-Malki, K., & Bellier, L. (2003, June). *Hierarchical MIPv6 mobility management* (HMIPv6). IETF, Internet Draft.

Sun, Y., Belding-Royer, E.M., & Perkins, C.E. (2002). Internet connectivity for ad hoc mobile networks. *International Journal of Wireless Information Networks special issues on mobile ad hoc networks, 9*(2), 75-88.

Tan, Hwee-Xian, & Seah, Winston K.G. (2004, September). Dynamically adapting mobile ad hoc routing protocols to improve scalability. In *the IASTED International Conference on Communication Systems and Networks (CSN2004)*, Marbella, Spain.

Tseng, Y.C., Shen.C.C., & Chen, W.T. (2003). Mobile IP and ad hoc networks: an integration and implementation experience. *IEEE Computer, 36*(5), 48-55.

Typpö, V. (2001). *Micro-mobility within wireless ad hoc networks: Towards hybrid wireless multihop networks.* Diploma thesis, Department of Electrical Engineering, University of Oulu, Finland.

Wakikawa, R., Malinen, J. T., Perkins, C. E., Nilsson, A., & Tuominen, A. J. (2002, November). *Global connectivity for IPv6 mobile ad hoc networks.* IETF, Internet draft.

Xi, J., & Bettstetter, C. (2002, May). Wireless multihop Internet access: gateway discovery, routing, and addressing. *International Conference on Third Generation Wireless and Beyond (3Gwireless'02)*, San Francisco.

KEY TERMS

Compulsory Handover: It means a handover when the MN detects that the route to its current GW is broken. Hybrid gateway discovery. An approach used by the MN to discover available GWs. In this approach, the periodical router advertisements are not flooded throughout the entire ad hoc network but only sent to MNs that are in the vicinity of the GW. MNs that are further away solicit advertisements reactively.

Hybrid Wireless Network: A type of network, which interconnects MANETs to fixed IP networks. In such networks, MNs are viewed as an easily deployable extension to the existing infrastructure. GWs are installed, which can be used by MNs to communicate with nodes in the fixed network.

MANET: A type of mobile wireless network. In contrast to an infrastructure wireless network, a MANET is an infrastructure-less network. In a MANET, there is no fixed router. Instead, each MN can serve as a router that discovers and maintains routes to other nodes.

Multi-Hop Handover: A route change from a MN to its registered GW, which may occur when the MN itself or any of the intermediate MNs moves and breaks the active route to the registered GW during the MN's communication with a CN in the wired network.

Optimized Handover: It means a handover when a MN's route to its current GW is still active, but a better (more optimized) route is available and selected. Seamless. In our paper, it means to reduce the packet loss and handover delay without incurring too much protocol overhead during multi-hop handover.

Security Issues with Wi-Fi Networks

Kevin Curran
University of Ulster, Ireland

Elaine Smyth
University of Ulster, Ireland

INTRODUCTION

On the surface, WLANs act the same as their wired counterparts, transporting data between network devices. However, there is one fundamental, and quite significant, difference: WLANs are based upon radio communications technology as an alternative to structured wiring and cables. Data is transmitted between devices through the air by utilizing radio waves. Devices that participate in a WLAN must have a network interface card (NIC) with wireless capabilities. This essentially means that the card contains a small radio device that allows it to communicate with other wireless devices within the defined range for that card, for example, the 2.4-2.4853 GHz range. For a device to participate in a wireless network, it must firs be permitted to communicate with the devices in that network and, second, it must be within the transmission range of the devices in that network. To communicate, radio-based devices take advantage of electromagnetic waves and their ability to be altered in such a manner that they can carry information, known as modulation (Vines, 2002). Here we discuss wireless security mechanisms.

WIRELESS NETWORKS BACKGROUND

Wired networks have always presented their own security issues, but wireless networks introduce a whole new set of rules with their own unique security vulnerabilities. Most wired security measures are just not appropriate for application within a WLAN environment; this is mostly due to the complete change in transmission medium. However, some of the security implementations developed specifically for WLANs are also not terribly strong. Indeed, this aspect could be viewed as a "work-in-progress"; new vulnerabilities are being discovered just as quickly as security measures are being released. Perhaps the issue that has received the most publicity is the major weaknesses in WEP, and, more particularly, the use of the RC4 algorithm and relatively short initialisation vectors (IVs). WLANs suffer from all the security risks associated with their wired counterparts; however, they also introduce some unique risks of their own. The main issue with radio-based wireless networks is signal leakage. Due to the properties of radio transmission, it is impossible to contain signals within one clearly defined area. In addition, because data is not enclosed within cable, it makes it very easy to intercept without being physically connected to the network (Hardjono, 2005). This puts it outside the limits of what a user can physically control; signals can be received outside the building and even from streets away. See below for a view of just how far leakage can go. Signal leakage may not be a huge priority when organisations are implementing their WLAN, but it can present a significant security issue, as demonstrated below. The same signals that are transmitting data around an organisation's office are the same signals that can also be picked up from streets away by an unknown third party. This is what makes WLANs so vulnerable (Sundaralingham, 2004). Before WLAN's became common, someone wishing to gain unauthorised access to a wired network had to physically attach themselves to a cable within the building. This is why wiring closets needed to be kept locked and secured. Any potential hacker had to take great risks to penetrate a wired network. Today potential hackers do not have to use extreme measures, there's no need to smuggle equipment on site when it can be done from two streets away. It is not difficult for someone to obtain the necessary equipment; access can be gained in a very discrete manner from a distance.

WIRELESS SECURITY MECHANISMS

To go some way towards providing the same level of security the cable provides in wired networks, the wired equivalent protocol (WEP) was developed. WEP was designed to provide the security of a wired LAN by encryption through use of the RC4 (Rivest Code 4) algorithm. Its primary function was to safeguard against eavesdropping ("sniffing"), by making the data that is transmitted unreadable by a third party who does not have the correct WEP key to decrypt it. RC4 is not specific to WEP, it is a random generator, also known as a keystream generator or a stream cipher, and was developed in RSA Laboratories by Ron Rivest in 1987 (hence the name Rivest code (RC)). It takes a relatively short input and produces a somewhat longer output, called a pseudo-random key stream. This key stream is simply added modulo two that is exclusive ORed (XOR), with the data to be transmitted, to generate what is known as ciphertext (Briere, 2005).

WEP is applied to all data above the 802.11b WLAN layers (physical and data link layers, the first two layers of the OSI reference model) to protect traffic such as transmission control protocol/Internet protocol (TCP/IP), Internet packet exchange (IPX), and hyper text transfer protocol (HTTP). It should be noted that only the frame body of data frames are encrypted and the entire frame of other frame types are transmitted in the clear, unencrypted (Karygiannis & Owens, 2003). To add an additional integrity check, an initialisation vector (IV) is used in conjunction with the secret encryption key. The IV is used to avoid encrypting multiple consecutive ciphertexts with the same key, and is usually 24 bits long. The shared key and the IV are fed into the RC4 algorithm to produce the key stream. This is XORed with the data to produce the ciphertext, the IV is then appended to the message. The IV of the incoming message is used to generate the key sequence necessary to decrypt the incoming message. The ciphertext, combined with the proper key sequence, yields the original plaintext and integrity check value (ICV) (Hardjono, 2005). The decryption is verified by performing the integrity check algorithm on the recovered plaintext and comparing the output ICV to the ICV transmitted with the message. If it is in error, an indication is sent back to the sending station. The IV increases the key size; for example, a 104-bit WEP key with a 24-bit IV becomes a 128-bit RC4 key. In general, increasing the key size increases the security of a cryptographic technique. Research has shown that key sizes of greater than 80 bits make brute force[1] code breaking extremely difficult. For an 80-bit key, the number of possible keys is 10^{24}, which puts computing power to the test; but this type of computing power is not beyond the reach of most hackers. The standard key in use today is 64-bit. However, research has shown that the WEP approach to privacy is vulnerable to certain attacks regardless of key size (Karygiannes & Owens, 2003). Although the application of WEP may stop casual "sniffers," determined hackers can crack WEP keys in a busy network within a relatively short period of time.

WEP's Weaknesses

When WEP is enabled in accordance with the 802.11b standard, the network administrator must personally visit each wireless device in use and manually enter the appropriate WEP key. This may be acceptable at the installation stage of a WLAN or when a new client joins the network, but if the key becomes compromised and there is a loss of security, the key must be changed. This may not be a huge issue in a small organisation with only a few users, but it can be impractical in large corporations, that typically have hundreds of users (Gavrilenko, 2004). As a consequence, potentially hundreds of users and devices could be using an identical key for long periods of time. All wireless network traffic from all users will be encrypted using the same key; this makes it a lot easier for someone listening to traffic to crack the key as there are so many packets being transmitted using the same key. Unfortunately, there were no key management provisions in the original WEP protocol.

A 24 bit initialisation vector WEP is also appended to the shared key. WEP uses this combined key and IV to generate the RC4 key schedule; it selects a new IV for each packet, so each packet can have a different key (Walker, 2002). Mathematically there are only 16,777,216 possible values for the IV. This may seem like a huge number, but given that it takes so many packets to transmit useful data, 16 million packets can easily go by in hours on a heavily used network. Eventually the RC4 algorithm starts using the same IVs over and over. Thus, someone passively "listening" to encrypted traffic and picking out the repeating IVs can begin to deduce what the WEP key is. Made easier by the fact that there is a static variable (the shared key), an attacker can eventually crack the WEP key (Nakhjiri, 2005). For example, a busy AP, which constantly sends 1500 byte packets at 11Mbps, will exhaust the space of IVs after 1500 x 8/(11 x 10^6) x 2^24 = 18,000 seconds, or 5 hours. (The amount of time may actually be smaller since many packets are less than 1500 bytes.) This allows an attacker to collect two ciphertexts that are encrypted with the same key stream. This reveals information about both messages. By XORing two ciphertexts that use the same key stream would cause the key stream to be cancelled out and the result would be the XOR of the two plaintexts (Vines, 2002).

War-Driving

So called "war-driving" is a term used to describe a hacker who, armed with a laptop, a wireless NIC, an antenna, and sometimes a GPS device, travels, usually by car, scanning or "sniffing" for WLAN devices, or, more specifically, unprotected or "open" and easily accessed networks. The name is thought to have come from another hacking technique called War-Dialling, where a hacker programs their system to call hundreds of phone numbers in search of a poorly protected computer dial-up (Nakhjiri, 2005). Due to the increased use of WLANs in recent years, it is quite possible that the number of unsecured devices has also risen in tandem, thus providing potential hackers with more choice. After all that has been written about the insecurities of WLAN, some users/organisations still insist on implementing them with their default settings and no encryption (Ulanoff, 2003). There is a plethora of hacking tools widely available to download from the Internet for any potential war-driver to use. There has been a lot of press globally, and many articles and papers written about wireless networks and their security vulnerabilities. However, despite all the literature, some enterprises still make the mistake of believing that they don't have to worry about wireless security if they are running non-critical systems with non-sensitive information across their WLANs. All information is sensitive information, and what an enterprise may class as being non-sensitive to them may be very useful to a hacker. In addition, most WLANs will connect with the wired enterprise backbone at some point, thus providing hackers with a launch pad to the entire network. The havoc an unwelcome third party could cause from here would be unlimited and very difficult to trace. Aside from the various attacks they could

instigate (DoS and viruses); the loss of confidentiality, privacy, and integrity that would occur if someone were able to steal, alter, or delete information on your customer database is damaging enough. Access to sensitive information, perhaps even customer's credit card details, would be made relatively easy. This could have an un-quantifiable affect on business, perhaps resulting in the loss of customers/clients and future revenue (AirDefense, 2003).

WIRELESS ATTACK METHODS

A passive attack is an attack on a system that does not result in a change to the system in any way; the attack is purely to monitor or record data. Passive attacks affect confidentiality, but not necessarily authentication or integrity. Eavesdropping and traffic analysis fall under this category. When an attacker eavesdrops, they simply monitor transmissions for message content. It usually takes the form of someone listening into the transmissions on a LAN between stations/devices.

Eavesdropping is also known as "sniffing" or wireless "footprinting." There are various tools available for download which allow the monitoring of networks and their traffic, developed by hackers, for hackers. Netstumbler, Kismet, Airsnort, WEPCrack, and Ethereal are all well known names in wireless hacking circles, and all are designed specifically for use on wireless networks, with the exception of Ethereal, which is a packet analyser and can also be used on a wired LAN. NetStumbler and Kismet can be used purely for passive eavesdropping; they have no additional active functions, except perhaps their ability to work in conjunction with global positioning systems (GPSs) to map the exact locations of identified wireless LANs. NetStumbler is a Windows-based sniffer, where Kismet is primarily a Linux-based tool. NetStumbler uses an 802.11 Probe Request sent to the broadcast destination address, which causes all APs in the area to issue an 802.11 Probe Response containing network configuration information, such as their SSID, WEP status, the MAC address of the device, name (if applicable), the channel the device is transmitting on, the vendor and the type, either peer or AP, along with a few other pieces of information. Using the network information and GPS data collected, it is then possible to create maps with tools such as StumbVerter and MS Mappoint.

Kismet, although not as graphical or user friendly as NetStumbler, is similar to its Windows counterpart, but it provides superior functionality. While scanning for APs, packets can also be logged for later analysis. Logging features allow for captured packets to be stored in separate categories, depending upon the type of traffic captured. Kismet can even store encrypted packets that use weak keys separately in order to run them through a WEP key cracker after capture, such as Airsnort or WEPCrack (Sundaralingham, 2005). Wireless network GPS information can be uploaded to a site called Wigle (http://www.wigle.net). Therefore, if Wigle data exists for a particular area, there is no need to drive around that area probing for wireless devices; this information can be obtained in advance from the Wigle Web site. All that remains is to drive to a location where known networks exist to observe traffic. Wigle currently has a few hundred thousand networks on its database.

Traffic Analysis gains intelligence in a more subtle way by monitoring transmissions for patterns of communication. A considerable amount of information is contained in the flow of messages between communicating parties. Airopeek NX, a commercial 802.11 monitoring and analysis tool for Windows, analyses transmissions and provides a useful node view, which groups detected stations and devices by their MAC addresses and will also show IP addresses and protocols observed for each. The peer map view, within Airopeek NX, presents a matrix of all hosts discovered on the network by their connections to each other. This can make it very easy to visualise AP and client relationships, which could be useful to hackers in deciding where to try and gain access or target for an attack (McClure, 2003). Some attacks may begin as passive, and then cross over to active as they progress. For example, tools such as Airsnort or WEPCrack may passively monitor transmissions, but their intent is to crack the WEP key used to encrypt data being transmitted. Ultimately the reasons for wanting to crack the key are so that an unauthorised individual can access a protected network and then launch an active attack of some form or another. These types of attacks are classed as passive decryption attacks.

An active attack, also referred to as a malicious attack, occurs when an unauthorised third party gains access to a network and proceeds to perform a denial of service (DoS) attack to disrupt the proper operation of a network, to intercept network traffic and either modify or delete it, or inject extra traffic onto the network. There are many active attacks that can be launched against wireless networks; the following few paragraphs outline almost all of these attacks, how they work, and what affect they have (Karygiannis, 2003). DoS attacks are easily the most prevalent type of attack against 802.11 networks, and can be waged against a single client or an entire WLAN. In this type of attack the hacker usually does not steal information, they simply prevent users from accessing network services, or cause services to be interrupted or delayed. Consequences can range from a measurable reduction in performance to the complete failure of the system. Some common DoS attacks are outlined below.

A man in the middle attack is carried out by inserting a malicious station between the victim station and the AP, thus the attacker becomes the "man in the middle"; the station is tricked into believing that the attacker is the AP, and the AP into believing that the attacker is the legitimate station. To begin the attack, the perpetrator passively monitors the frames sent back and forth between the station and the AP during the initial association process with an 802.11 analyser. As a result, information is obtained about both the station and the AP, such as the MAC and IP address of both devices, association ID for the station, and SSID of the network. With this information a rogue station/AP can be set up between the two unsuspecting devices. Because the original 802.11 does not provide mutual authentication, a station will happily re-associate with the rogue AP. The rogue AP will then capture traffic from unsuspecting users; this, of course, can expose information such as user names and passwords (Gavrilenko, 2004).

An association flood is a resource starvation attack. When a station associates with an AP, the AP issues an associate identification number (AID) to the station in the range of 1-2007. This value is used for communicating power management information to a station that has been in a power-save state. This attack works by sending multiple authentication and association requests to the AP, each with a unique source MAC address. The AP is unable to differentiate the authentication requests generated by an attacker and those created by legitimate clients, so it is forced to process each request. Eventually, the AP will run out of AIDs to allocate and will be forced to de-associate stations to reuse previously allocated AIDs. In practice, many APs will restart after a few minutes of authentication flooding, however this attack is effective in bringing down entire networks or network segments if repeatedly carried out, and can cause a noticeable decrease in network uptime (Wright, 2003). The final issue is a threat posed by the simple network management protocol (SNMP). Some APs can be managed via wireless link, usually with a proprietary application, replying on SNMP. Executing these operations can represent a frightening vulnerability for the whole LAN because eavesdroppers can decipher the password to access read/write mode on the AP using a packet analyser; this means that they share the same administration privileges with the WLAN administrator and can manage the WLAN in a malicious manner (Me, 2003). The sheer number of attacks, and their affects, would seem to put WLANs at a severe disadvantage over their wired counterparts. However, there are just as many, if not more, security measures that users can utilise to counteract most of the above attacks. Layering one security measure on top of another, strengthens the overall system in order to deter any potential attackers, or to make their task more difficult, if not impossible.

FUTURE TRENDS

The IEEE specifies basically two categories of WLAN standards: those that specify the fundamental protocols for the complete wireless system and those that address specific weaknesses or provide additional functionality (3Com Corporation, 2006). Here we mention just three of the latter standards which may have a significant influence in coming days.

The 802.11i standard is a major extension because it was intended to improve WLAN security on 802.11a and 802.11b networks, which were in tatters. It adds two main blocks of improvements—improved security for data in transit, and better control network users. It covers key management and distribution, encryption, and authentication, the three main components of security (Briere, 2005). The 802.11i specification can be viewed as consisting of three main sections, organised into two layers. On the lower level are improved encryption algorithms in the form of the temporal key

integrity protocol (TKIP) and the counter mode with cipher block chaining-message authentication code, CBC-MAC protocol (CCMP). Both of these provide enhanced data integrity over WEP, with TKIP being targeted at legacy equipment and CCMP being targeted at future WLAN equipment (Nakhjiri, 2005).

The goal of the 802.11k standard is to make measurements from layers one and two of the OSI protocol stack—physical and data link layers—available to the upper layers. It is expected that the upper layers will then be able to make decisions about the radio environment. It is called radio resource management. One feature is better traffic distribution. Normally a wireless device will connect to whatever AP gives it the strongest signal. However, this can lead to an overload on some APs and under-load on others, resulting in an overall lowered service level. The 802.11k standard will allow network management software to detect this situation and redirect some of the users to under-utilised APs. The 802.11n standard is a high-performance standard that would boost both 802.11b and 802.11a 11Mbps and 54Mbps, respectively. Proposals say it could go to 108Mbps or beyond, to as much as 320Mpbs.

Community 802.11b networks will continue to grow as people realize they can share their high-speed, high-cost Internet connections, turning them into high-speed, low- or no-cost connections for a larger group of people (Imai, 2005).

CONCLUSION

Wireless networks have a number of security issues. Signal leakage means that network communications can be picked up outside the physical boundaries of the building in which they are being operated, thus, a hacker can operate from the street outside or discretely from blocks away. In addition to signal leakage, wireless networks have various other weaknesses. WEP, the protocol used within WLANs to provide the equivalent security of wired networks, is inherently weak. The use of the RC4 algorithm and weak IVs makes WEP a vulnerable security measure. In addition to WEPs' weaknesses, there are various other attacks that can be initiated against WLANs, all with detrimental effects.

REFERENCES

3COM (2006). Retrieved 2 May, 2006 from http://www.3com.com/whitepapers.html

AirDefense. (2003) *Wireless LAN security–What hackers know that you don't.* Retieved 7 May, 2006 from http://ssl.salesforce.com/servlet.Email/AttachmentDownload?q=00m0000000003Pr00D00000000hiyd00500000005k8d5

Briere, D. (2005). *Wireless network hacks and mods for dummies.* Hungrey Minds Inc.

Gavrilenko, K. (2004). *WI-FOO: The secrets of wireless hacking.* Addison Wesley.

Hardjono, T., & Lakshminath, R.D. (2005). *Security in wireless LANs and MANs.* Artech House Books.

Harte, L., Kellog, S., Dreher, R., & Schaffinit, T. (2000). *The comprehensive guide to wireless technologies: Cellular, PCS, paging, SMR and satellite.* NC: APDG Publishing.

Imai, H. (Ed.). (2005). *Wireless communications security.* Artech House Books.

Karygiannis, T., & Owens, L. (2003). National institute of standards and technology, Special Publication, 800-48, Draft. Retrieved 4 March, 2006 from http://csrc.nist.gov/publications/drafts/draft-sp800-48.pdf

McClure, S., Scambray, J., & Jurtz, G. (2003). *Hacking exposed: Network security secrets and solutions* (4th ed.). Osbourne, McGraw-Hill.

Me, G. (2003). *A threat posed by SNMP use over WLAN.* Retrieved 7 May, 2006 from http://www.wi-fitechnology.com/Wi-Fi_Reports_and_Papers/SNMP_use_over_WLAN.html

Nakhjiri, M. (2005). *AAA and network security for mobile access: Radius, diameter, EAP, PKI and IP Mobility.* John Wiley & Sons.

Sundaralingham, S. (2004). *Cisco wireless LAN security.* Cisco Press.

Ulanoff, L. (2003, July). Get free Wi-Fi, while it's hot. *PC Magazine*, 52: Ziff Davis.

Vines, R.D. (2002). *Wireless security essentials: Defending mobile systems from data piracy.* Wiley Publishing.

Walker, J. (2002). *Unsafe at any key size: An analysis of the WEP encapsulation.* Retrieved 6 May, 2006 from http://www.dis.org/wl/pdf/unsafe.pdf

Wright, J. (2003). *Detecting wireless LAN MAC address spoofing.* http://home.jwu.edu/jwright/papers/wlan-mac-spoof.pdf

KEY TERMS

Denial of Service: A denial of service (DoS) attack is an incident in which a user or organization is deprived of the services of a resource they would normally expect to have. Typically, the loss of service is the inability of a particular network service to be available or the temporary loss of all network connectivity and services

Direct Sequence Spread Spectrum (DSSS): DSSS combines a data signal with a higher data rate bit sequence, referred to as a "chipping code.". The data are exclusive ORed (XOR) with a PRS which results in a higher bit rate, This increases the signal's resistance to interference.

IEEE 802.11 Standards: IEEE has developed several specifications for WLAN technology, the names of which resemble the alphabet. There are basically two categories of standards: those that specify the fundamental protocols for the complete wireless system, these are called 802.11a, 802.11b, and 802.11g; and those that address specific weaknesses or provide additional functionality, these are 802.11d, e, f, h, I, j, k, m, and n.

Jamming: Jamming is a simple, yet highly effective method of causing a DoS on a wireless LAN. Jamming, as the name suggests, involves the use of a device to intentionally create interfering radio signals to effectively "jam" the airwaves, resulting in the AP and any client devices being unable to transmit.

Frequency Hopping Spread Spectrum (FHSS): Here the signal hops from frequency to frequency over a wide band of frequencies. The transmitter and receiver change the frequency they operate on in accordance with a pseudo-random sequence (PRS) of numbers. To properly communicate, both devices must be set to the same hopping code.

War Driving: War-driving is a term used to describe a hacker, who, armed with a laptop, a wireless NIC, an antenna, and sometimes a GPS device, travels, usually by car, scanning or "sniffing" for WLAN devices, or more specifically, unprotected or "open" and easily accessed networks.

Wireless Access Point (AP): An access point (AP) is a piece of hardware that connects wireless clients to a wired network. It usually has at least two network connections and the wireless interface is typically an onboard radio or an embedded PCMCIA wireless card.

Wireless Network Interface Cards (NICs): Each NIC has a unique media access control (MAC) address burned into it at manufacture, to uniquely identify it; it also contains a small radio device and an antenna. However, the NIC must be compatible with the AP before communication can occur. For example, an 802.11b card needs an 802.11b AP.

Wired Equivalent Privacy: WEP was designed to provide the security of a wired LAN by encryption through use of the RC4 (Rivest Code 4) algorithm. Its primary function was to safeguard against eavesdropping ("sniffing"), by making the data that are transmitted unreadable by a third party who does not have the correct WEP key to decrypt the data

ENDNOTE

[1]   A method that relies on sheer computing power to try all possibilities until the solution to a problem is found. It usually refers to cracking passwords by trying every possible combination of a particular key space.

The Semantic Web

Kevin Curran
University of Ulster, Ireland

Gary Gumbleton
University of Ulster, Ireland

INTRODUCTION

Tim Berners-Lee, director of the World Wide Web Consortium (W3C), states that, "The Semantic Web is not a separate Web but an extension of the current one, in which information is given well-defined meaning, better enabling computers and people to work in cooperation" (*Berners-Lee, 2001*). The Semantic Web will bring structure to the meaningful content of Web pages, creating an environment where software agents, roaming from page to page, can readily carry out sophisticated tasks for users. The Semantic Web (SW) is a vision of the Web where information is more efficiently linked up in such a way that machines can more easily process it. It is generating interest not just because Tim Berners-Lee is advocating it, but because it aims to solve the problem of information being hidden away in HTML documents, which are easy for humans to get information out of but are difficult for machines to do so. We will discuss the Semantic Web here.

BACKGROUND

Knowledge representations (KR) are need for the Semantic Web to function; the computers and software agents using it need to have access to structured information and inference rules in order to perform some reasoning. The rules and information must also be powerful enough to describe complex terms (Glassey, 2004). Languages like the extensible mark-up language (XML) and resource description framework (RDF) are already in place and helping to make this happen, along with newer languages such as here and here, which shall all be described in more detail later on. Ontologies are a document or file that formally defines the relationship between terms. On the Web, the most commonly used type of ontology is the taxonomy (subclass-super class)

hierarchy, though it may not just be limited to this form. These taxonomies work on classes and describe the relationship between them; together with their inference rules, they play a vital part in the semantic Web. For example, if a salary class is associated with a currency class, and the currency class is then associated with a county class, the inference rules could then say that if an employee gets paid in British pounds then they work in the UK. Also, you could have different ontologies pointing to each other so your ontology for "person" could point to someone else's that is describing the same thing but using different terminology. This would then increase the scope of the inference rules and make them more reliable. Agents are the programs that will gather the contents of the semantic Web, process them, and exchange them with other agents. Of course, for the agents to exchange information with each other there will have to be some degree of proof between them that the information they gathered is true. Digital signatures and proofs can overcome this.

THE SEMANTIC WEB

The Semantic Web is built upon the current WWW. The bottom layer is made up of uniform resource identifier (URI). URIs are a fundamental component of the Web and are also the foundation of the Semantic Web. URIs are a compact string of characters for identifying an abstract or physical resource. Because anyone can create a URI, and their ownership is clearly delegated, they are the ideal building blocks for the Web; and because URIs are not tied to a specific protocol, they can be used to access different ones. So when a new protocol is invented, the same URI can be used to address the same resource.

XML is a system for defining specialized markup languages that are used to transmit formatted data. This markup is used to encode instructions that can tell applications what to do with the information it refers to (Vizine-Goetz, 2005). It was created to make a version of SGML (standard generalized mark-up language) that would be as widely-used on the Internet as HTML. The problem with HTML being that it did not allow machines to easily extract information from it as it was mainly designed to present information to humans, and SGML was considered too difficult to implement just for a Web browser. XML, however, is a text-based language; it is platform- and software-independent, and this also has the added effect of making XML documents transmittable over networks using existing protocols. In addition, because it is a hierarchical structure, it allows for powerful data constructs from databases and other applications.

The syntax of XML is similar to that of HTML; this is because both of them are derived from SGML, with the exception that in XML we are describing the data not the format of the document (Howarth, 2004). XML allows authors of documents to create their own mark-up language, where the meaning of the information is placed in the document. The information placed into the document is called "elements"; these elements are encapsulated by start (<) and end tags (/>). Tag names are the word inside the start and end tags of elements. Since XML cannot express the meaning of the tags, it can cause problems for machine processing, as most processing applications require tag sets whose meanings have been agreed to by some standard or convention.

DTDs specify elements, the context of elements, and which attributes in elements can be changed. Although DTDs allow for syntax in XML documents, the semantics are still implicit. This means that a human infers the meaning of a DTD element by the name given to it as a comment in the DTD, or it is described in a separate document. This makes it easy to exchange XML documents between people on a small scale, as they can get together beforehand and design DTDs that will meet their combined needs. But it runs into problems when you scale it up, and, for example, you want to integrate your DTD with similar ones from multiple sources. One of these problems is exchanging representations of the same idea structure. XML allows the author of the document to represent that data in their own way. This can lead to a simple thing like a name structure being represented in different ways, causing a lack of semantics. XML Schema is an XML language for describing and constraining the content of XML documents (Thompson, 2003). This gives us greater flexibility when defining an XML document.

In this new version, the mark-up elements have been uniquely identified by use of a URL; doing so is called XML Namespacing. An XML namespace is a collection of names identified by a URI reference. XML namespaces differ from the "namespaces" conventionally used in computing disciplines in that the XML version has internal structure and is not, mathematically speaking, a "set." By using namespaces, everyone can create their own tags for XML documents and mix and match them with others created by different people. But XML Schema still suffers from the same semantic flaws as DTD.

Resource Development Language (RDF)

Though XML is good at letting one invent tags, it can have problems with scalability. For example, often the

Figure 1. Example XML structure version 2

```
<? Xml version="1.0" encoding="utf-8"? >
<xs: schema xmlns: xs="http://www.w3.org/2001/XMLSchema">
<dataBaseFootball>
  <team>
<Xs: element team="character" minOccurs="0" maxOccurs="unbounded'
    <manager> Ferguson </manager>
    <name>Manchester United</name>
    <leagueposition>3</leagueposition>
  </team>
</dataBaseFootball>
</xs: schema>
```

order in which elements appear in XML is significant, so keeping the correct order of data items on something as extensive as the Web could prove impractical. To help solve this, RDF was developed by a number of different metadata communities under the umbrella flagship of the W3C, with the aim to develop a flexible architecture for supporting Metadata on the Web (Chen, 2005). Its history derives from 1995 when the W3C developed PICS (platform for Internet content selection), which was a mechanism for communicating the ratings of Web pages from a server to a client (mainly with the aim to tell the client if a particular Web page was or wasn't suitable for children) by using metadata. However, for whatever reason, PICS did not take off, but it was clear that other metadata communities could use some of the infrastructure that had been developed. So the W3C created a working group to bring together the requirements of several different metadata groups and, in 1998, they released these recommendations. In its essence, RDF is a method to express and process a series of simple assertions, such as "Ora Lassila created this page (Home/Lassila)." This is called an RDF statement and illustrated, it looks like Figure 2, comprising nodes, labeled arcs, and values. It consists of three parts: a subject (Resource), predicate (Property), and an object (Literal), as shown in Table 1 with their corresponding values (Baumgartner, 2005).

RDF provides also provides a model for describing resources The basic concept behind it is that an object (a resource) is described through a collection of properties called an RDF description, which itself consists of a property type and value, as long as that object has a unique URL address. In RDF, values may be text, strings, numbers, and so on, but they may also be other resources which themselves can have properties of their own.

Figure 3 shows Figure 2 as an RDF description with some additional descriptive information.

Because more descriptive information is provided in Figure 2, a unique identifier has to be provided about Ora Lassila; in

Figure 3, Ora Lassila is given a staff number. This can be something like an employee number. This is needed for the unambiguous association of properties on resources. As the person, Ora Lassila may be the value of different property types, e.g., he may be the creator of index.html but may also be a value in a table "employees" for a company. This allows for the reuse of descriptive information. RDF Schema is needed

Figure 3. An RDF graph[2]

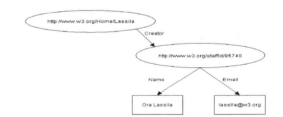

Figure 2. An example of an RDF diagram (Triple)[1]

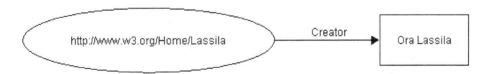

Table 1. Figure 2 broken up into consistence parts

Subject (Resource)	http://www.w3.org/Home/Lassila.html
Predicate (Property)	Creator
Object (literal)	Ora Lassila

for the creation of controlled, sharable, and extensible vocabularies. It extends RDF to include a larger reserved vocabulary with more complex semantic constraints allowing users to create schemas of classes and properties using RDF. RDF then uses XML Namespaces in order to avoid confusion between two separate definitions of the same term, which could have conflicting meaning. RDF can easily be marked up into XML. The use of XML namespaces, such as RDF, relies heavily on XML namespaces for disambiguating names.

Ontologies

The next Layer proposed for the SW is ontologies. Ontologies, as already mentioned, are fundamental to the SW, providing the mechanisms for the interchange of data between different Knowledge representations. Ontologies are a specification of a representational vocabulary for a shared domain of discourse—definitions of classes, relations, functions, and other objects (McClelland, 2004). Today, there is a great deal of research going on into this area, carried out by such groups as DAML, who in conjunction with the European initiative, came up with DAML + OIL, which is an extension of the RDF language. Other ontology languages include Simple HTML ontology extensions (SHOE) and the Ontology Exchange Language (XOL). The reasons for developing ontologies are:

- To share common understanding of the structure of information between people or machines
- To enable the reuse of knowledge
- To make , , , domain assumptions clear
- To separate domain knowledge from operational knowledge
- To analyze domain knowledge

To share common understanding of the structure of information is one of the more common reasons for developing ontologies. Doing so will allow computer software agents to extract information from different sites that share the same ontologies and then go on to possibly use this information to answer queries or to use them as inputs to other queries. Enabling the reuse of knowledge allows us to save time in developing our own ontology. For example, if a group of researchers develop a complex ontology and publish it, other researchers can simply copy it, saving both time and money. Also, if a large ontology needs to be built, the researchers

developing it may be able to group together several smaller ones in order to achieve their goal. There are already lots of reusable ontologies on the Web, such as the DAML ontology library (DAML, 2006) or Dublin core (Dublin, 2006). By making clear the domain assumptions made about knowledge and its structure, it is easier to change these assumptions if our knowledge about the domain changes. This also makes it easier for newcomers to the area that the ontology was written about to pick it up and continue the work.

DAML + OIL

RDF was developed at about the same time as XML with the aim to provide a language for modeling semi-structured metadata and enabling knowledge management systems (Baumgartner, 2005) and it has proved to be successful because of its simplicity (Shvaiko, 2005). But as RDF scope has expanded to include things like SW, the limitations of its RDF Schema have become clear, as it lacks for catering to data typing and a consistent expression for enumerations, as well as other facilities. In response, the DAML (DARPA Agent Mark-up Language) was set up and grouped its efforts with OIL (Ontology Inference Layer), another group working in the same area, to provide a more sophisticated classification, using constructs from frame-based AI (Artificial Intelligence). This resulted in a language that was able to express far more sophisticated classifications and properties of resources than RDFS. The W3C is making the DAML + OIL specifications and its relationship with RDF and RDFS a series of notes, and have commissioned the WOWG (Web Ontology Working Group) to produce a new ontology language which is to be based upon DAML + OIL. DAML + OIL makes separates properties that relate object-to-object (called Object properties) and those that relate objects to datatype values (Datatype properties) (McGuinness, 2005). There are also some changes to the semantics of rdfs: domain and rdfs: range, such as: now a property can have multiple value ranges. In RDF and RDFS there is limited expression allowed on property declarations. Properties in DAML + OIL can also be defined as being identical to each other by using daml: equivalentTo or daml: samePropertyAs. Other more expressive terms can be obtained with properties such as daml: UniqueProperty, daml: TransitiveProperty and daml: UnambiguousProperty. The most important facility DAML + OIL provides is allowing designers to increase the expressivity in classifying resources. The daml: Class is defined as being a subclass of rdfs: Class and it new facilities. An example of this is the built-in support for enumerations, which was lacking in RDF. An enumeration defines a class by giving an explicit list of its members. In RDFS you could define a class and then have instances of this class. But the problem was that someone could come along and add new instances. An example of one such enumeration in DAML + OIL is shown in Figure 4.

In Figure 4 a DAML + OIL agent will be able to interpret the body of a property element as a special form of list, which is made up of each of the instances that appear in the element body. In this type of list you cannot add an item without replacing another. With DAML + OIL it is possible to say that one class

is disjointed from another, so that the two classes will have no instances in common. This is achieved by using daml: disjointWith. DAML + OIL also allows for property restrictions, which is a way to restrict classes to a set of resources based on particular properties of theirs, the number or the value of these properties. An example of this is shown in Figure 5.

Figure 5 defines the fish class as a subclass of another class that is defined as a DAML + OIL restriction. These types of classes are defined by rules that specify what conditions of a resource's properties have to be met for a resource to be a member of that class. Daml: onProperty identifies which property is to be checked. Daml: hasValue then declares that the property in question must have a particular value. So Figure 5 says that a fish is a subclass of all resources, which has at least one-piece anatomy property whose value is fins. A number of companies got together to define a standard for electronic business cards, which was later developed by the International Mail Consortium and standardized by the IETF in RFC 2426 and became known as VCards. VCards consist of different property types describing different properties a person may want to put on a business card. The majority of these properties have strings or numbers as their values. Some of these include: First Name, Last Name, Full Name (FN), Birthday (BDAY), Role, Title, Phone number, E-Mail Address and URI. RDF uses XML name spaces to uniquely identify the metadata schema and version. Using a prefix, which contains the current version number, has the advantage that there is no need to provide a special version number among the property tags. It also means that there is no need for the "begin" and "end" types, as XML encoding of

Figure 4. An example DAML + OIL enumeration

```
<daml:Class ID="Position">
 <daml:oneOf parseType="daml:collection">
  <daml:Thing rdf:ID="1st">
   <rdfs:label>1st position</rdfs:label>
  </daml:Thing>
  <daml:Thing rdf:ID="2nd">
   <rdfs:label>2nd position</rdfs:label>
  </daml:Thing>
  <daml:Thing rdf:ID="3rd">
   <rdfs:label>3rd position</rdfs:label>
  </daml:Thing>
 </daml:oneOf>
</daml:Class>
```

Figure 5. Example DAML + OIL property restriction

```
<daml:Class rdf:ID="Fish">
 <rdfs:label>Types of Fish</rdfs:label>
 <rdfs:comment>A type of animal that lives in water</rdfs:comment>
 <rdfs:subClassOf>
  <daml:Restriction>
   <daml:onProperty rdf:resource="#anatomy"/>
   <daml:hasValue rdf:resource="#Fins"/>
  </daml:Restriction>
 </rdfs:subClassOf>
</daml:Class>
```

RDF automatically tells when the description starts and ends (Nair, 2004).

FUTURE TRENDS

Many businesses are now using XML metadata to tag content so that computers can readily find, identify, and manipulate information much as an intelligent agent would (Nee, 2005). RSS feeds, based on XML, also allow individuals to have specific content sent directly to them, and they are one of the newer trends on the Web. In early 2006, Google introduced three services, Google Marketplace Search, Google Personal Agent, and Google Verification Manager, and a software product, Google Marketplace Manager. These are all basically following the Semantic Web model as vsualized by Paul Ford in his "August 2009: How Google beat Amazon and Ebay to the Semantic Web" visionary article[3]. We can expect more of the same from giants such as eBay and Yahoo.

Searching for information online and learning about a subject will be made much easier in the future. Frameworks such as mSPace (Schraefel, 2005) can gather information sources and present them to the user in a single window. It can potentially be applied to any subject, provided the basic information is available. The semantic Web interface brings together audio, text, links, and images about the domain, in this case classical music, in a way that allows people to explore the subject more fully. Wrapping an mSpace around the data allows the user to preview music, learn about the history of each composer, and so on (Sherriff, 2005).

The net result of all this activity is that Berners-Lee's dream for the next stage of the Web is slowly unfolding, but possibly not in the way he envisioned. We are likely to end up less with a not so neatly constructed Semantic Web, but rather a patchwork quilt of home-grown solutions and standards (Nee, 2005).

CONCLUSION

The Semantic Web is a vision of what the Web of the future will be. Offering a Web which is not just designed for navigation by humans but also by machines, where information will not just be hidden away on text documents but will be structured in a manner that will make the discovery of documents and facts far easier. To support the metadata describing the resources, the authors of the Semantic Web proposed the use of ontologies, with the aim of providing the "semantics" for this Semantic Web.

REFERENCES

Baumgartner, R., Henze, N., & Herzog, M. (2005, May 29-June 1). The personal publication reader: Illustrating Web data extraction, personalization and reasoning for the semantic Web. In A. Gómez-Pérez, J. Euzenat, & Heraklion (Eds.), *The Semantic Web: Research and Applications. 2nd European Semantic Web Conference, ESWC 2005*, 34-43. Heraklion, Greece, May 29-June 1.

Berners-Lee, T., Hendler, J., & Lassila, O. (2001). *Scientific American, 5*(1), 34-43.

Chen, Y-N., & Chen, S-J. (2005, May 25-26). A study of metadata developments and trends in library and information science. *Conference of Information Organization & Archive Technology in the New Century*, 102-108. National Chengchi University, Taipei, Taiwan, May 25-26.

DAML ontology library (2006). Retrieved 20 June, 2006 from http://www.daml.org/ontologies/

Dublin Core. (2006). Dublin core metadata element set, Version 1.1: Reference Description. (2004). *Dublin Core Metadata Initiative*. Retrieved April 18, 2005, from http://dublincore.org/documents/dces/

Glassey, O. (2004). Developing a one-stop government data model. *Government Information Quarterly, 21*(2), 156-169.

Howarth, L. C. (2004). Metadata schemas for subject gateways. *International Cataloguing and Bibliographic Control, 33*(1), 8-12.

McClelland, M. (2004). Distributed learning metadata standards. *Journal of Computing in Higher Education, 16*(1), 93-105.

McGuinness, D. (2005, July). Why should you trust answers from the Web? In *Proceedings of the Joint Conference on Information Sciences, Web Intelligence and Security Track*, 55-65. Salt Lake City, Utah.

Shvaiko, P., Giunchiglia, F., Silva, P., & McGuinness, D. (2005, May 29-June 1). Web explanations for semantic heterogeneity discovery. In *Proceedings of the 2ⁿᵈ European Semantic Web Conference (ESWC 2005)*, 22-29. Heraklion, Greece, May 29ᵗʰ-June 1ˢᵗ.. Springer.

Nair, S. S., & Jeevan, V. K. J. (2004). A brief overview of metadata formats. *DESIDOC Bulletin of Information Technology*, *24*(4), 3-11.

Nee, E. (2005). Web future is not semantic, or overly orderly, *CIO Insight*.

Schraefel, M.C., Smith, D.A., Owens, A., Russell, A., Harris, C., & Wilson, M. L. (2005). The evolving mSpace platform: Leveraging the Semantic Web on the trail of the Memex. In *Proceedings of Hypertext*, 102-112. Salzburg, Austria.

Sherriff, L. (2005). University launches semantic Web interface, *The Register*, February 17.

Thompson, H., & Tobin, R. (2003). *XML schema validator*. W3C & University of Edinburgh.

Vizine-Goetz, D., Childress, E., & Houghton, A. (2005, September 12-14). Web services for genre vocabularies. In *Proceedings of the International Conference on Dublin Core and Metadata Applications*, 2-5. Madrid, Spain.

KEY TERMS

Document Type Definition (DTD): A DTD is a metadocument containing information about how a given set of SGML tags can be used. In the XML world this role will be taken over by a schema.

Dublin Core: A set of basic metadata properties (such as title) for classifying Web resources.

Metadata: Data about data on the Web, including, but not limited to, authorship, classification, endorsement, policy, distribution terms, IPR, etc. Some metadata, such as file dates and sizes, can easily be seen by users; other metadata can be hidden or embedded and unavailable to users who are not technically adept. Metadata is generally not reproduced in full form when a document is printed.

The Resource Description Framework (RDF): The resource description framework is a markup language for describing information and resources on the Web. The RDF metadata model is based upon the idea of making statements about resources in the form of a subject-predicate-object expression, called a triple in RDF terminology. The subject is the resource, the "thing" being described. The predicate is a trait or aspect about that resource, and often expresses a relationship between the subject and the object. The object is the object of the relationship or value of that trait.

Semantic Web: The Semantic Web is a Web that is able to describe things in a way that computers can understand such as U" being a rock band from Dublin, Ireland. Statements are built with syntax rules. The syntax of a language defines the rules for building the language statements.

Standard Generalized Markup Language (SGML): An international standard in markup languages, a basis for HTML, and a precursor to XML. SGML is both a language and an ISO standard for describing information embedded within a document.

Universal Resource Identifier (URI): The string (often starting with http) comprising a name or address that can be used to refer to a resource. It is a fundamental component of the World Wide Web.

Web Ontology Language (OWL): OWL is a semantic markup language for publishing and sharing ontologies on the World Wide Web. OWL developed as a vocabulary extension of RDF (the resource description framework) and is derived from the DAML+OIL Web ontology language.

World Wide Web Consortium (W3C): A neutral meeting of those to whom the Web is important, with the mission of leading the Web to its full potential. It was established in 1994 to lead the Web to its full potential by developing common standards.

ENDNOTES

1. http://www.w3.org/TR/1999/REC-rdf-syntax-19990222/
2. http://www.w3.org/TR/1999/REC-rdf-syntax-19990222/
3. http://www.ftrain.com/google_takes_all.html

Semantic Web Languages and Ontologies

Livia Predoiu
University of Mannheim, Germany

Anna V. Zhdanova
University of Surrey, UK

INTRODUCTION

On the current World Wide Web, most of the information is stored syntactically, i.e., only as data. The information that lies within the data can only be understood by humans and not automatically by computer programs. In order to overcome this issue, the idea of encoding the information not just syntactically but also with semantics has created a new notion of the Web called *Semantic Web*. This notion emerged together with developments of semi-structured languages like SGML and XML.

As the Web is a "many-to-many data-interchange medium," it works only if the exchange format provides interoperability at various levels (Decker et al., 2000). The first requirement is *universal expressive power,* which means that any type of data is expressible. The second requirement is *syntactic interoperability,* which means that data and information modelling languages have a wide implementation support. The third, and last, requirement is *semantic interoperability*, which means that mappings between terms within the data can be discovered automatically.

It has been agreed in research that the best way to represent semantics is to use formal ontologies. This agreement is due to the fact that ontologies can be seen as formal and structured representations of the concepts and relationships a domain exposes and thus of the data within as information. There exist different kinds of ontologies (e.g., lightweight and heavyweight) and different languages for describing them. Currently, XML-based W3C recommendations, such as RDF(S) and OWL, are the most widely-exploited ontology languages. However, new extensions and usages of existing ontology languages, as well as new ontology languages, continue to appear. The amount of domain-dependent ontologies also expands rapidly over time. Following the successes of RSS, FOAF, vCard, and Dublin Core, ontologies are now being constructed to describe practically every side of human life. Therefore, methods for ontology discovery and reuse gain further importance. Dynamicity of Semantic Web development makes it difficult for Internet application developers to be aware of existing initiatives and trends in ontologies and ontology languages. Choosing and adopting Semantic Web core components thus remains a challenge. To assist in addressing this challenge, we provide an overview of leading ontology languages and ontologies in this paper.

The paper is organized as follows. In the second section we present a background to the topic. State of the art and trends in the area of languages and ontologies on the Web are discussed in the third section. In the fourth section we identify challenges in this area and, finally, the fifth section concludes the article.

BACKGROUND

Semantic Web languages and ontologies are strongly related. While a Semantic Web Language can be used to specify an ontology, a Semantic Web language can also be seen as a an ontology with its modelling primitives being ontological entities. In this chapter we first describe the evolution of Semantic Web languages and then clarify the meaning of the term ontology.

HTML (Ragett et. al., 1999) was the promoter of the World Wide Web because it provided a standard for structuring documents such that browsers were able to display them in a uniform way. The first Web-based Ontology Language, SHOE, was based on HTML. The main disadvantage of HTML, namely being a very rigid and inflexible language by not allowing adaptation to different types of documents, was overcome by the standardization of XML (Bray et. al., 2004) and XML Schema.

However, syntactic interoperability is not enough for the purpose of automatic processing of queries posed to the huge amount of data available on the Internet. In order to enable information sharing, information integration, and retrieval of semantically similar documents available on the Web, languages offering means to model semantics are required. XML is not appropriate for semantic interoperability because it "just describes grammars" and therefore it is not able "to recognize a semantic unit from a particular domain because XML aims at document structure and imposes no common interpretation of the data contained in the document" (Decker et. al, 2000).

A first step to syntactic and semantic interoperability has been reached by means of the standardization of RDF/RDF schema. RDF has been attached to an XML syntax but it has a different and much richer data model. RDF is designed to provide "a basic object-attribute-value data model." By this means, chaining (i.e., any object can play the role of a value) and reification (any RDF statement can be the object or value of a triple) can be modelled. However, "this intentional semantics is described only informally in the standard" and "apart from that, RDF does not make any data-modelling commitments" (Decker et al., 2000). But RDF Schema introduces "some simple ontological concepts" (McBride 2004) and provides means for defining more complex and formal Ontology Languages on top of it.

The first full-fledged ontology languages to be defined on top of RDF/RDF Schema and standardized by the W3C were OIL and DAML+OIL. They correspond to some Description Logics variants and thus provide well-known algorithms for automatic reasoning and, therefore, the automatic handling of information by software tools.

The term ontology originates from philosophy where it denotes *"the theory or study of being as such, i.e., the basic characteristics of all reality."*[1] In computer science, different views of the meaning of the term "ontology" exist (Guarino & Giaretta, 1995). Studer et al. (1998) have merged different definitions and set up the following one which has been adopted by the Semantic Web community:

An ontology is a formal, explicit specification of a shared conceptualization. Conceptualization refers to an abstract model of some phenomenon in the world by having identified the relevant concepts of that phenomenon. Explicit means that the type of concepts used, and the constraints on their use are explicitly defined. Formal refers to the fact that the ontology should be machine-readable. Shared reflects the notion that an ontology captures consensual knowledge, that is, it is not private of some individual, but accepted by a group.

Ontologies can be categorized according to different criteria. Guarino (1998) classifies ontologies according to their usage and application field. He distinguishes between top-level, domain, task, and application ontologies. Lassila and McGuiness (2002) classify ontologies according to their expressivity and internal structure. They mainly distinguish between *lightweight ontologies* and *heavyweight ontologies*. For heavyweight ontologies, a proof theory can be defined and thus automatic reasoning is possible. Automatic reasoning means that the computer can deduce new information that is encoded implicitly in the ontology. Automatic deduction of information implicitly encoded in the ontology leads to powerful means of querying these so-called knowledge bases. Ontologies are also used for Information Integration purposes as the semantics of different, seemingly disconnected, knowledge bases or ontologies as specified by means of the ontologies.

LANGUAGES AND ONTOLOGIES ON THE WEB

In this section we describe state of the art in Semantic Web languages and typical widespread ontologies lying in the core area of current Web applications. Furthermore, we identify domains where the Semantic Web is present factually, though not formally, or not standardized, and outline further areas of use for ontology languages.

Semantic Web Languages on the Web

RDF(S)

RDF (Lassila & Swick, 1999; Manola & Miller, 2004) became a W3C recommendation in 1999. It is a general-purpose language for representing resources on the Web in terms of named properties and values (McBride, 2004). With RDF, it is not possible to define the relationships between properties and resources. For this purpose, RDF Schema (Brickley & Guha, 2004) has been specified. It became a W3C recommendation in 2004 and is basically an extension of RDF. More specifically, it is a formal description language for eligible RDF expressions. In particular, a schema defines the kinds of properties available for resources (e.g., title, author, subject, size, colour, etc.) and the kind of resource classes being described (e.g., books, Web pages, people, companies, etc.). RDF Schema is a simple ontology and a simple ontology definition language. RDF and RDF Schema are usually denoted RDF(S).

RDF(S) is based on some syntactical principles of XML (e.g., URIs) and has been equipped with an XML syntax as well. The most basic Semantic Web language which provides the syntactical basis for all other Semantic Web languages is RDF(S). RDF(S) is not provided completely with a formal logical semantics, and thus reasoning is only possible in part.

Topic Maps

Topic maps are a data modelling language that became an ISO standard (ISO/IEC 13250) in 2000. A Topic Map offers a means to create an index of information which resides *outside* of that information. It describes the information in documents and databases by linking into them using URIs. A topic map consists of topics, associations (relationships between topics), and occurrences (information resources relevant to a topic). Topics and occurrences can be typed. Types in topic maps are themselves topics and thus there is no real difference between a topic and a type.

There exists SGML, XML, and RDF language support for Topic Maps. However, they are very simple and do not have a formal semantics and thus no sophisticated inference support. Nonetheless, because of their simplicity, they are often used in industry applications.

OWL

OWL (Dean et al., 2004) became a W3C recommendation in 2004. OWL is mainly based on OIL and DAML+OIL, which are obsolete Semantic Web languages and therefore not mentioned further here. OWL is equipped by an RDF syntax and includes three sub languages:

- *OWL-Lite* roughly consists of RDF(S) plus equality and 0/1-cardinality. It is intended for

classification hierarchies and simple constraints. OWL-Lite corresponds semantically to the formal Description Logic *SHIF(D)* and cannot express the whole RDF vocabulary.
- *OWL-DL* contains the language constructs of OWL-Lite. OWL-DL corresponds semantically to the Description Logic *SHOIN*(D). Although strictly more expressive than OWL-Lite, it still provides computational completeness and decidability.
- *OWL Full* does not correspond to a formal logic anymore as it builds upon the complete RDF(S) vocabulary which also lacks a correspondence to a formal logic. The language incorporates maximum expressive power and syntactic freedom, but offers no computational guarantees.

Semantic Web Languages not Yet Standardized

In this subsection, we consider Semantic Web languages which have been submitted to the W3C and thus have communities promoting them. At least some of them can be expected to become W3C recommendations.

Examples of such languages are:

- **Languages based on the logic programming knowledge representation paradigm:** The trend to the aforementioned paradigm exists already since the year 2000 when the development of RuleML[2] was started. RuleML is a set of languages revolving around the Logic Programming paradigm and equipped with an RDF syntax. Other examples of Semantic Web Languages with Logic Programming semantics are WRL[3], a set of three-layered rule languages of increasing expressivity, and SWRL[4], a language which combines OWL and RuleML but is computationally intractable. Furthermore, a W3C working group[5] has been formed to establish standards for Semantic Web rule languages.
- **Semantic Web service modelling languages:** Semantic Web services will play an important role in the Semantic Web as they combine Web Services with semantics. Examples for Semantic Web Services Languages are WSML[6] and SWSL[7]. The languages serve for the specification of ontologies describing Semantic Web services. E.g., WSML is used to describe WSMO[8] and SWSL is used to describe SWSO[9].

The advantage of rule languages is that role chaining can be expressed and, thus, also the transitive hull of a relation can be computed. This is not possible in languages based on description logics. Furthermore, databases can be integrated much easier to the Web by means of rule languages. However, description logics have advantages as well, e.g., negation is based on the Open World Assumption (OWA) and thus seems to be more suitable for the Web in which Web sites providing information can become available or unavailable at any time.

Ontologies on the Web

vCard, FOAF, Dublin Core, and RSS

There are several examples of ontologies that became widely accepted and reused for the purpose of distributed data exchange and integration for semantic community portals. Very often these ontologies were organically grown and quickly found a large number of creative users, even though for a long time they were not endorsed by any of the popular standards committees. Two examples of the most often described domains are represented by ontologies describing a *person* and ontologies describing a *document*. Below, we provide typical examples of the person and document ontologies that gained a high degree of popularity.

Person ontologies:

1. **VCard**[10] is a schema to specify electronic business card profiles. Factually, vCard is a simple ontology to describe a person with 14 attributes, such as Family Name, Given Name, Street Address, Country, etc. The ontology provides a precise way to describe the instance data using RDF.

2. **FOAF** (Friend of a Friend) is a schema which is similar to VCard in a way that FOAF also is a wide-spread ontology to describe a person. FOAF schema provides 12 core attribute types that are similar to the attribute vCard provides: First Name, Last Name, E-mail address, etc., and the precise way to describe the instance data using RDF is also proposed by the FOAF-project.

Document/Web publication ontologies:

1. **Dublin Core**[11] stands for a vocabulary aimed to be used to semantically annotate Web resources and documents. The core vocabulary consists of 15 attributes to describe a document or a Web resource and contains parameters that express the primary characteristics of the documents, e.g., Title, Creator, Subject, Description, Language, etc.

2. **RSS**[12] is variably used as a name by itself and as an acronym for "RDF Site Summary," "Rich Site Summary," or "Really Simple Syndication." The RSS ontology specifies the model, syntax, and syndication feed format and consists of four concepts: "channel," "image," "item," and "textinput," each of them having some attributes like "title," "name," and "description."

Internet Ontologies not Formalized Semantically

In this subsection, we consider popular schemata which are most typical for the Web, and are used for representation of information commonly found on the Web. Currently there exist a large number of schemata that are shared among people and applications and could be ontologies, but they do not employ common Semantic Web languages.

Examples of such shared schemata include:

*   RSS, this aforementioned format is more successful and widespread in its XML version rather than in the Semantic RDF version;
*   WSDL[13], which is a current W3C candidate recommendation, and most other acknowledged Web service specification formalisms are based purely on XML technologies;
*   EMMA[14] is a shared format facilitating interoperation and information exchange between fixed and mobile terminals supporting different modality. It is designed as an XML schema and the instance data are exchanged duly in the XML format.

Bringing these and new appearing schemata for information sharing to the use of a Semantic Web language will grant benefits. Such benefits would include:

- Improved interoperability between different knowledge domains (e.g., services and applications addressing the same topic)
- Integration of information arriving from different platforms (e.g., seamless switch of data stream from a mobile device to a fixed terminal, roaming)
- More accurate/expressive representation of the information entities (e.g., knowledge engineers have an opportunity to unambiguously define and share arbitrary datatypes—whereas XML schema formalism is not sufficient for this)

At the moment, transition from shared schemata to ontologies on the Web is hindered by the fact that currently XML has a larger community behind it than any Semantic Web language does. Thus, XML is used more widely due to the fact many developers share experience with this technology. Another barrier to transition to the Semantic Web is complexity of Semantic Web formalisms: Even the simplest Semantic languages are more complex than XML schema.

FUTURE TRENDS

In addition to the trend towards migration to the Semantic Web in knowledge representation, future trends in the area of Semantic Web languages and ontologies include addressing the following challenges.

Integrated Semantics for Monotonic and Nonmonotonic Negation

The languages that potentially seem to be prevalent in the Semantic Web will revolve around logic programming paradigms, and thus nonmonotonic negation under the CWA and description logic paradigms and monotonic negation under the OWA. These different kinds of negation need to be integrated semantically in order to enable a coherent and valid reasoning mechanism. Different preliminary ideas have been manifested, like scoped negation (Polleres et al., 2006) or Open Answer Set Programming (Heymans et al., 2005). However, these ideas are at a very preliminary stage and it still remains a big challenge to integrate monotonic and nonmonotonic negation properly into a Semantic Web language and provide tractable reasoning algorithms for such a language.

Representation of Context, Mappings, and Information Integration

The Internet forms a huge network of peers where each peer employs an independent set of ontologies, with each peer possibly using different knowledge representation formalisms. In this setting, the context or the mappings that connect the different ontologies needs to be represented in order to enable a coherent reasoning mechanism for the distributed information in the network. Approximation to a solution includes C-OWL (Bouquet et al., 2004) and community-driven ontology matching (Zhdanova & Shvaiko, 2006).

Convergence of Mobile and the Web: Adoption of Semantics

Mobile environments and the Web converge forming a shared communication sphere. Convergence of mobile and the Web causes the appearance of new settings to be supported, such as when the user utilizes mobile and fixed devices to interact with systems, and mobile applications become increasingly connected with the Internet. To ensure interoperation of mobile and Web applications, and tools in such a sphere, developers need to have a shared specification of objects belonging to the sphere and their roles. Certain ontologies have already been developed for the mobile communications area with employment of Semantic Web formalisms (Pfoser et al., 2002; Korpipää et al., 2004). However, widespread and global adoption of such ontologies remains a challenge.

CONCLUSION

State of the art and trends in Semantic Web languages and ontologies are presented in this article. Languages and ontologies in general are detailed, and the contributions of Semantic Web technologies to the Web have been discussed. Specific attention is paid to semantic languages recommended by W3C. Future challenges in this area have been outlined, including the development of an integrated semantics for monotonic and nonmonotonic negation, the representation of context and mappings, and the convergence of mobile and the Wweb.

REFERENCES

Bouquet, P., Giunchiglia, F., van Harmelen, F., Serafini, L., & Stuckenschmidt, H. (2004). Contextualizing ontologies. *Journal of Web Semantics, 1*(4), 325-343.

Bray, T., Paoli, J., Sperberg-McQueen, C.M., Maler, E., & Yergeau, F. (2004) Extensible markup language (XML) 1.0. W3C Recommendation, http://www.w3.org/TR/REC-xml/

de Bruijn, J., Lara, J. R., Polleres, A., & Fensel, D. (2005). OWL-DL vs. OWL flight: Conceptual modelling and reasoning for the semantic Web. In *Proceedings of the 14ᵗʰ International Conference on World Wide Web.*

Decker, S., Melnik, S., van Harmelen, F., Fensel, D., Klein, M., Broekstra, J., et al. (2000). The Semantic Web: The roles of XML and RDF. *IEEE Internet Computing, 4*(5), 63-67.

Ding, L., Zhou, L., Finin, T., & Joshi, A. (2005). How the semantic Web is being used: An analysis of FOAF documents. In *Proceedings of the 38th International Conference on System Sciences.*

Guarino, N. (1998). Formal ontology in information systems. In N. Guarino (Ed.), *First international conference on formal ontology in information systems.*

Guarino, N., & Giaretta, P. (1995). Ontologies and knowledge bases: Towards a terminological clarification. In N. Mars (Ed.), *Towards very large knowledge bases* (pp. 25-32).

Heymans, S., Van Nieuwenborgh, D., & Vermeir, D. (2005). Guarded open answer set programming. In *Proceedings of the 8ᵗʰ International Conference on Logic Programming and Non Monotonic Reasoning.*

Korpipää, P., Häkkilä, J., Kela, J., Ronkainen, S., & Känsälä I. (2004). Utilising context ontology in mobile device application personalization. *ACM International Conference Proceeding Series*, Vol. 83 (pp. 133-140).

Lassila, O., & McGuiness, D. (2002). The role of frame-based representation on the Semantic Web. *Electronic Transactions on Artificial Intelligence.*

Lassila, O., & Swick, R. (1999). *Resource description framework (RDF) model and syntax specification.*

W3C Recommendation. http://www.w3.org/TR/REC-rdf-syntax/

Manola, F., & Miller, E. (2004). RDF Primer. W3C Recommendation. http://www.w3.org/TR/rdf-primer/

Pfoser, D., Pitoura, E., & Tryfona, N. (2002). Metadata modeling in a global computing environment. In *The 10ᵗʰ ACM International Symposium on Advances in Geographic Information Systems.*

Polleres, A., Feier, C., & Harth, A. (2006). Rules with contextually scoped negation. In *Proceedings of the 3ʳᵈ European Semantic Web Conference.* Springer-Verlag. LNCS 4011.

Ragett, D., le Hors, A., & Jacobs, I. (1999). HTML 4.01 Specification. W3C Recommendation. http://www.w3.org/TR/REC-html40/

Studer, R., Benjamins, V.R., & Fensel, D. (1998). Knowledge engineering: Principles and methods. *IEEE Transactions on Data and Knowledge Engineering 25*(1-2),161-197.

Zhdanova, A. V., & Shvaiko, P. (2006). Community-driven ontology matching. In *Proceedings of the 3ʳᵈ European Semantic Web Conference.* Springer-Verlag. LNCS 4011.

KEY TERMS

Closed World Assumption (CWA): The presumption that what is not currently known to be true is false. This assumption introduces nonmonotonicity if the world is not closed, i.e., new information can be introduced or deleted. The opposite of the CWA is the OWA, stating that lack of knowledge does not imply falsity.

Heavyweight Ontology: An ontology of different, but rather higher expressivity, which bases on a formal logic. With such an ontology, it is possible to perform formal reasoning.

Lightweight Ontology: An ontology which corresponds rather to a vocabulary and usually does not base on a formal logic.

Ontology: A data model that represents the objects, sets of similar objects (i.e., classes), and their interrelations within a domain of discourse.

Ontology Language: A formal language used to encode an ontology.

Open World Assumption (OWA): The presumption that what is not stated true is unknown and thus cannot be assumed to be either true or false. The OWA is considered being implicit in the Web as new Web sites can be connected and disconnected to the Web at any time.

Semantic Interoperability: Applications can understand the meaning of representations and thus can setup automatically mappings between different representations by content analysis.

Semantic Web: The next evolutionary step of the World Wide Web. It bases on language standards that provide not only universal expressive power and syntactic interoperability, but also semantic interoperability.

Syntactic Interoperability: Applications can take advantage of parsers and APIs providing syntactical manipulation facilities. If a language is standardized, it is used actively and required parsers and APIs are implemented.

ENDNOTES

[1] This definition has been taken from the Encyclopaedia Britannica.

[2] http://www.ruleml.org

[3] http://www.w3.org/Submission/WRL/

[4] http://www.w3.org/Submission/SWRL/

[5] http://www.w3.org/2005/rules/wg

[6] http://www.w3.org/Submission/WSML/

[7] http://www.w3.org/Submission/SWSF-SWSL/

[8] http://www.w3.org/Submission/WSMO/

[9] http://www.w3.org/Submission/SWSF-SWSO/

[10] http://www.w3.org/TR/vcard-rdf

[11] http://dublincore.org

[12] http://web.resource.org/rss/1.0

[13] http://www.w3.org/TR/wsdl20/

[14] http://www.w3c.org/TR/emma/

Semantic Web Services: A Technology for Service-Oriented Computing

Dumitru Roman
DERI Innsbruck, Austria

Ioan Toma
DERI Innsbruck, Austria

Dieter Fensel
DERI Innsbruck, Austria

INTRODUCTION

Service-oriented computing (SOC) is the new emerging paradigm for distributed computing, especially in the area of e-business and e-work processing, that has evolved from object-oriented and component-based computing to enable the building of scalable and agile networks of collaborating business applications distributed within and across organizational boundaries; services will count for customers and not the specific software or hardware component that is used to implement the services. In this context, services become the next level of abstraction in the process of creating systems that would enable automation of e-businesses and e-works.

SOC is the computing paradigm that utilizes services—heterogeneous, autonomous, and distributed systems—as fundamental elements for developing applications and solutions. To build the service model, SOC relies on the *service-oriented architectures (SOA)*—a way and methodology of reorganizing and building software applications and infrastructure into a set of meaningful interacting services. SOA aims at providing a methodology and framework for documenting enterprise functionalities and behaviours and can support integration activities.

Although significant advances in terms of technical results, standards, and worldwide research have been achieved since the 1999 declaration by IBM, Microsoft, and Sun of SOA in terms of Web services, computing in service oriented environments is still in its infancy. The major problem still to be overcome is scalability—SOA will not scale without significant mechanization of service discovery, adaptation, negotiation, composition,

invocation, and monitoring, as well as data, protocol, and process mediation. This mechanization can only be achieved if explicit, formal descriptions of services are provided. In consequence, machine processable semantics need to be added to bring service oriented computing to its full potential. *Semantic Web services (SWS)* technology has recently emerged as a new technology based on Semantic Web and Web services technologies, with the aim of providing support for automation of service discovery, adaptation, negotiation, composition, invocation, and monitoring, as well as data, protocol, and process mediation.

In this context, this chapter provides an overview of SWS as a key technology to support SOC/SOA. First, we provide background information on SWS and a short overview of different approaches to these services. Then we highlight an emerging proposal to integrate SWS with SOA/SOC under the term Semantically-enabled service-oriented architectures (SESA). At the end, we provide some insights about the future of SWS in service-oriented environments, and conclude this chapter with some challenges.

BACKGROUND

Web services (Alonso et al., 2004) are proposing a uniform and standardized way to access functionality over the Web. They address stringent business problems like integration and automation of business processes. Their fundaments rely on standards like SOAP (2003), WSDL (2006), and UDDI (2005). However, these standards operate at a syntactic level and, therefore, a scalable solution for business problems cannot be achieved without human support. Realizing such a solution will require richer descriptions that can be processed by machines in a meaningful manner, thus enabling the automation of service-related tasks like service discovery, composition, and execution.

With current research around the *Semantic Web* (Berners-Lee et al., 2001) the means to provide such richer descriptions for services are developed. Ontologies, the core building blocks of the Semantic Web, are used to share a common understanding of a particular domain in terms of concepts, relations between them, and constraints. Such terms are further used when building semantic descriptions of services. Having such descriptions in place, the automation of tasks for Web services like discovery, compositions and invocation should be achievable, thus enabling seamless interoperation between them while keeping human intervention to a minimum.

Based on the two previously described technologies, *Semantic Web services* aim to describe the various aspects of a Web service using explicit, machine-understandable semantics, enabling the automatic location, combination, and use of Web Services (McIlraith et al., 2001; Fensel & Bussler, 2002). Semantic mark-up can be exploited to automate the tasks of discovering services, executing them, composing them, and enabling seamless interoperation between them, thus providing what are also called intelligent Web Services. The description of Web services in a machine-understandable fashion is expected to have great impact in the areas of e-commerce and enterprise application integration, as it can enable dynamic, scalable, and reusable cooperation between different systems and organizations.

Considerable research has been completed and is under way to realize the potential of semantically enabled SOA. Some of the most prominent research initiatives are: OWL-S (OWL-based Web service ontology), SWSF (Semantic Web services framework), IRS-III (Internet Reasoning Service III), WSDL-S (Web service semantics), and WSMO (Web service modeling ontology), each of which has gained some momentum and addresses specific pragmatic aspects. Below we briefly introduce these initiatives in terms of the conceptual model they employ, the languages that provide the means to realize their conceptual models, and their execution environments.

OWL-S (2004) is an ontology Web language (OWL) for Web services which aims at providing the building blocks for encoding rich semantic service descriptions.

As top level entities for a semantic service description, OWL-S considers the following elements: *profile, process model, and grounding*. The *profile* is used to express "what a service does" for purposes of advertising, constructing service requests, and matchmaking; the *process model* describes "how it works," to enable invocation, enactment, composition, monitoring, and recovery; and the *grounding* maps the constructs of the process model onto detailed specifications of message formats, protocols, and so forth (normally expressed in WSDL). These elements are further described using finer constructs. Finally, they are all grouped under a common top-level element called *service*. Thus, OWL-S ontology can be seen as a service related vocabulary that can be used together with the other aspects of the OWL language to create service descriptions.

SWSF (2005) incorporates two major components: an ontology for SWS called Semantic Web services ontology (SWSO), and a language used to formally specify the semantic descriptions called Semantic Web services language (SWSL). The conceptual model followed by SWSF and materialized in SWSO is a refinement of the OWL-S conceptual model. Building blocks like *service descriptor, process model,* and *grounding* can be easily mapped to their correspondents from OWL-S, namely: *profile, process model,* and *grounding*. Although SWSF and OWL-S share much of their conceptual model, the difference between these two approaches relies on different languages (with their corresponding expressivity) used to formalize the semantic descriptions. SWSO is represented in the associated language, SWSL, which comes in two variants: SWSL-FOL, based on first-order logic formalism, and SWSL-RL, based on logic programming formalism.

IRS-III (Domingue et al., 2004) is a framework and implemented platform which acts as a broker mediating between the goals of a user or client, and available deployed Web services. The IRS uses WSMO as its basic ontology and follows the WSMO design principles with respect to SWS descriptions. Some principles promoted by IRS-III are: *supporting capability-based invocation, ease of use* by hiding the complexity of service-related tasks like service creation, *one click publishing,* which allows easy incorporation of legacy functionality as a Web service, *agnostic to service implementation platform, connected to the external environment*—external systems which provide additional requested information can be integrated, *open*—the modularity of the IRS-III broker allows components to be plug-in or plug-out, *inspectibility*—easy to check and monitor the status of the service life cycle.

WSDL-S (Akkiraju et al., 2005) is another framework for SWS which takes an augmentative approach in defining a solution for semantic service description. The starting point is WSDL, as the standard for service-functional descriptions, which is further enriched with light semantics. WSDL-S adheres to the following principles: *build on existing Web service standards, annotate agnostically to the semantic representation languages*, and *support annotation of XML Schema data types*.

The WSMO approach (Roman et al., 2006) represents a unifying framework for conceptually modeling, formally representing, and executing SWS. Since the WSMO approach to SWS is the most compressive approach to date[1], in tackling many aspects of SWS (at least compared to the other existing approaches), we focus in the next section on the role and integration of WSMO with service-oriented environments, thus highlighting an emerging proposal to integrate SWS with SOA/SOC.

SEMANTIC WEB SERVICES IN SERVICE-ORIENTED ENVIRONMENTS

The role of SWS in service-oriented environments has been discussed in detail, under the term semantically-enabled service-oriented architectures (SESA) in Brodie et al. (2005), where three main elements of a semantically enabled SOA (the problem-solving layer, the common service layer, and the resource layer) have been introduced (also depicted in Figure 1).

In the following, we briefly describe these layers and point out the place of SWS, in particular the WSMO approach to SWS, in the overall picture.

Figure 1. Three layers of SESA (Brodie et al., 2005)

Problem-Solving Layer
Common Services Layer
Resource Layer

The objective of the **problem-solving layer (PSL)** is to turn a SOA into a domain-specific, problem-solving environment. Following the "layered" approach of our vision, the problem-solving layer represents the transparent interface to the user(s), where we assume that all computing resources are turned into or expressed as services.

The **common services layer (CSL)** provides an adaptive execution environment and supporting infrastructure that maps the problem descriptions generated at the problem-solving layer to the services that can solve the problems.

Resources are used to solve problems or, more conventionally, to execute applications. The **resource layer (RL)** deals with resource discovery, selection, and negotiation for advanced or on-the-fly reservation of resources. The RL also covers the deployment and provisioning of *physical resources* (e.g., computers, data servers, and networks), which are commonly connected to form a grid of computing and storage platforms and logical resources, and *logical resources*, such as application components, or common services, enabling more advanced composition of applications.

The core of SESA is the semantic enrichment of SOAs that implement the *common service layer capabilities*. This enrichment aims to automate service discovery, adaptation, negotiation, composition, invocation, and monitoring, as well as data, protocol, and process mediation. This automation is a prerequisite for SOA scalability. SWS represent an attractive technology to be placed at the level of the CSL. To this end, the WSMO approach to SWS can be considered as an enabler technology that combines the following three major building blocks: *the Web service modeling ontology* (basic concepts of SWS), *the Web service modeling language* (formal syntax and semantics for WSMO), and *the Web service modelling execution environment* (a reference implementation for WSMO). In the following we briefly overview them and highlight the relation between them.

The Web Service Modeling Ontology (WSMO)

The WSMO (Roman et al., 2005) provides three main categories to structure semantic descriptions. First, it provides means to describe *Web services*; second, it provides means to describe user *goals* referring to the problem-solving aspect of our architecture; and third, it provides means to ensure interoperability between the various semantic descriptions of heterogeneous environments: *ontologies* and *mediators*.

Goals provide means to characterize user requests in terms of functional and non-functional requirements. For the former, a standard notion of pre- and post-conditions has been chosen and the latter provides a predefined Ontology of generic properties.

Web service descriptions enrich this by an interface definition that defines access patterns of a service as well as means to express services as being composed from other services. More concretely, a Web service presents:

- A *capability* that is a functional description of a Web service, describing constraints on the input and output of a service through the notions of preconditions, assumptions, post conditions, and effects;
- *Interfaces* that specify how the service behaves in order to achieve its functionality. A service interface consists of a *choreography* that describes the interface for the client-service interaction required for service consumption, and an *orchestration* that describes how the functionality of a Web service is achieved by aggregating other Web services.

Ontologies provide a first and important means to achieve interoperability between goals and services as well as between various services themselves. By reusing standard terminologies, different elements can be either link directly or indirectly via predefined mapping and alignments.

Mediators provide additional procedural elements to specify further mappings that cannot be captured directly through the usage of ontologies. Using ontologies provides real-world semantics to our description elements as well as machine processable formal semantics through the formal language used to specify them. The concept of mediation in WSMO addresses the handling of heterogeneities occurring between elements that shall interoperate by resolving mismatches between different terminologies used (data level), on communicative behaviour between services (protocol level), and on the business process level. A WSMO Mediator connects the WSMO elements in a loosely coupled manner, and provides mediation facilities for resolving mismatches that might arise in the process of connecting different elements defined by WSMO.

The Web Service Modeling Language (WSML)

WSML (de Bruijn, 2005) provides a formal Web language for the WSMO conceptual model. WSML brings together different well-known logical language paradigms in order to enable the description of SWS. More specifically, Description Logics, Logic Programming, and First Order Logic are taken as starting points for the development of a number of WSML language variants, namely WSML-Core, WSML-DL, WSML-Flight, WSML-Rule, and WSML-Full.

The core language—*WSML-Core*—corresponds to the intersection of Description Logic and Horn Logic (without function symbols and without equality), extended with datatype support in order to be useful in practical applications. WSML-Core is fully compliant with a subset of OWL. This core language is extended, both in the direction of Description Logics and in the direction of Logic Programming, to WSML-DL and WSML-Flight. *WSML-DL* extends WSML-Core to an expressive Description Logic, namely, *SHIQ*, thereby covering that part of OWL which is efficiently implementable. *WSML-Flight* extends WSML-Core in the direction of Logic Programming. WSML-Flight has a rich set of modeling primitives for modeling different aspects of attributes, such as value and integrity constraints. Furthermore, WSML-Flight incorporates a fully-fledged rule language, while still allowing efficient decidable reasoning. *WSML-Rule* extends WSML-Flight to a fully-fledged Logic Programming language, including function symbols.

The final WSML variant—*WSML-Full*—unifies the Description Logic and Logic Programming paradigms under a common First-Order umbrella with non-monotonic extensions which allows the capture of a nonmonotonic negation of the WSML-Rule.

Syntax-wise, WSML takes the user point of view, on the one hand with its syntax for conceptual modeling and on the other hand allowing full flexibility to specify arbitrary logical axioms and constraints using the logical expression syntax.

The Web Service Modeling Execution Environment (WSMX)

WSMX (Cimpian et al., 2005) is an execution environment for the dynamic discovery, selection, mediation, invocation, and inter-operation of the SWS, providing a reference implementation for an SOA that uses semantic annotation in all of its major elements. Therefore, a general architecture as well as necessary components have been defined and the interfaces and communication of components have been standardized. WSMX is a reference implementation for WSMO. The development process for WSMX includes defining its conceptual model (which is WSMO), standardizing the execution semantics for the environment, describing the architecture and a software design, and building a working implementation. WSMX is not only a reference implementation based on a conceptual model of WSMO, it will become a reference implementation of SESA. This goal has driven the following design and architectural decisions:

- **Dynamics:** WSMX embarked on the principle of dynamics by interpreting WSML for SWS definitions as opposed to a compilation approach.
- **Interface vs. implementation:** WSMX ensured that SWS could be implemented in any language or on any platform by clearly supporting the difference between interface and implementation. While SWS interfaces are described in WSML, they can be implemented using any language or technology.
- **Grounding:** WSMX recognizes existing base technology such as operating systems, databases, and remote communication mechanisms.
- **Dynamic architecture:** All functionality is implemented in dedicated components; all components are dynamically configured. New components can be added dynamically and existing components can be exchanged or removed.

FUTURE TRENDS

Although in a very early stage of development, standardization organizations such as OASIS, OMG, and W3C have established several groups or technical committees to develop and standardize aspects of SWS and SOA. While some of these groups, such as SEE TC[2], directly focus on the development of the CSL layer of the SESA architecture highlighted in this chapter, other groups are working on other important related aspects (e.g., the W3C Semantic Annotations for the WSDL Working Group[3]). Standards are still evolving in this area: After

year 2000 standards grew enormously in number and complexity with few reference technologies.

According to Brodie et al. (2005), in industry, service-orientation is recognized not only as the next generation of computing, but also as the technology that will largely replace or encapsulate current technologies.

CONCLUSION

SWS constitute one of the most promising research directions to improve the integration of applications within and across enterprise boundaries. In this chapter we provided an overview of SWS, highlighted the most important approaches to SWS, and pointed out an emerging proposal to integrate SWS with SOA/SOC, under the term of semantically-enabled service oriented architectures (SESA).

Although SWS is a widely recognized technology with the potential to enable scalability in service-oriented computing, many challenges lie ahead. Among these challenges, the most important can be considered to be the movement to service-orientation and the semantic enablement of industrial scale infrastructures and applications. Achieving such a goal will require collaboration not only within the research community, but also within the industrial community; this will require research to understand the state and nature of the relevant industrial problems, products, and solutions, as well as industry to understand the relevant challenges and opportunities to which research can contribute.

REFERENCES

Akkiraju, R., Farrell, J., Miller J, Nagarajan, M., Schmidt, M., Sheth, A., et al. (2005). *Web service semantics–WSDL-S*. Technical note. Retrieved February 2006 from http://lsdis.cs.uga.edu/library/download/WSDL-S-V1.html

Alonso, G., Casati, F., Kuno, H., & Machiraju, V. (2004). *Web services: Concepts, architecture and applications.* Springer-Verlag.

Berners-Lee, T., Hendler, J., & Lassila, O. (2001). The Semantic Web. *Scientific American, 284*(5), 34-43.

Brodie, M.L., Bussler, C., de Bruijn, J., Fahringer, T., Fensel, D., Hepp, et al. (n.d.). *Semantically enabled service-*

oriented architectures: A manifesto and a paradigm shift in computer science. Technical Report TR-2005-12-26.

Cimpian, E., Vitvar, T., & Zaremba, M. (Eds.). (2005). *Overview and scope of WSMX*. WSMX Deliverable D13.0 v0.2. Retrieved February 2006 from http://www. wsmo.org/TR/d13/d13.0/v0.2/

de Bruijn, J. (Ed.). *The Web aervice modeling language WSML*. (2005). WSML Deliverable D16 v0.2. Retrieved February 2006 from http://www.wsmo. org/TR/d16/d16.1/v0.2/

Domingue, J., Cabral, L., Hakimpour, F., Sell, D., & Motta, E. (2004). IRS-III: A Ppatform and infrastructure for xreating WSMO-based aemantic Web aervices. In *Proceedings of the Workshop on WSMO Implementations*. CEUR, September 29-30, Frankfurt, Germany.

Fensel, D., & Bussler, C. (2002). The Web service modeling framework WSMF. *Electronic Commerce Research and Applications, 1*(2), 113-137.

McIlraith, S., Son, T.C., & Zeng, H. (2001). Semantic Web services. *IEEE Intelligent Systems,* Special Issue on the Semantic Web, *16*(2), 46-53.

OWL-S (OWL-based Web service ontology) 1.1. (2004). Retrieved February 2006 from http://www. daml.org/services/owl-s/1.1/

Roman, D., Keller, U., Lausen, H., de Bruijn, J., Lara, R., Stollberg, M., et al. (2005). Web service modeling ontology. *Applied Ontology, 1*(1), 77-106.

Roman, D., de Bruijn, J., Mocan, A., Lausen, H., Domingue, J., Bussler, et al. (2006). WWW: WSMO, WSML, and WSMX in a nutshell. In *Proceedings of the 1ˢᵗ Asian Semantic Web Conference*, 516-522, Springer-Verlag, Beijing, China.

Roman, D., de Bruijn, J., Mocan, A., Toma, I., Lausen, H., Kopecky, J., et al. (2006a). Semantic web services—Approaches and perspectives. In P. Warren, J. Davies, & R. Studer (Eds.), *Semantic Web technologies: Trends and research in ontology-based systems*. John Wiley & Sons.

SOAP (Simple Object Access Protocol) 1.2. (2003). Available at http://www.w3.org/TR/soap12

SWSF (Semantic Web Services Framework) 1.0. (2005). Available from http://www.daml.org/services/swsf/1.0/

UDDI (Universal Description, Discovery, and Integration) 3.0. (2005). Retrieved February 2006 from http://www.uddi.org/

WSDL (Web Services Description Language) 2.0. (2006). Retrieved February 2006 from http://www. w3.org/TR/wsdl20/

KEY TERMS

Semantic Web Services (SWS): An emerging technology that combines Web services and Semantic Web technologies in order to allow for a higher level of automation when dealing with Web services.

Semantically Enabled Service-Oriented Architectures (SESA): A comprehensive framework that augments existing SOA frameworks to incorporate semantic solutions to address the SOA semantic gap.

Service-Oriented Architectures (SOA): A methodology for reorganizing and building software applications and infrastructure into a set of meaningful interacting services.

Service-Oriented Computing (SOC): The new emerging paradigm for distributed computing in which services become the next level of abstraction in the process of creating systems.

Web Service Modeling Environment (WSMX): An execution environment and a reference implementation for WSMO.

Web Service Modeling Language (WSML): A language that formalizes the WSMO conceptual model.

Web Service Modeling Ontology (WSMO): A conceptual model which defines the basic concepts of SWS.

ENDNOTES

[1] For a detailed comparison of SWS approaches, we refer the reader to Roman et al. (2006a).
[2] www.oasis-open.org/committees/semantic-ex/
[3] http://www.w3.org/2005/10/sa-ws-charter.html

Service Provisioning in the IP Multimedia Subsystem

Adetola Oredope
University of Essex, UK

Antonio Liotta
University of Essex, UK

INTRODUCTION

The IP multimedia subsystem (IMS) specifies a service-centric framework for converged, all-IP networks. This promises to provide the long awaited environment for deploying technology-neutral services over fixed, wireless, and cellular networks, known as third generation (3G) networks. Since its initial proposal in 1999, the IMS has gone through different stages of development, from its initial Release 5 up to the current Release 7.

The IMS is also known as a domain for easily integrating and customising different services offering a new range of applications which aim at increasing the end-user experience. The IMS architecture will deploy both current and future Internet services on multi-access, 3G Networks (Camarillo & Garcâia-Martâin, 2006). These services include voice over IP (VoIP), instant messaging, video conferencing, online gaming, push-to-talk, and whiteboard sharing, to mention a few.

Service provisioning in the IMS offers the required mechanisms for execution, control, and integration of these services, including better and more efficient billing, accounting, quality of service (QoS), and interoperability across different administrative domains. All present and future Internet services will be deployed on a multi-access, all-IP overlay network via the IMS.

This version is based on the session initiation protocol (SIP) (Rosenberg et al., 2002) for its core functionality. SIP is used to create, modify and terminate sessions within the framework. SIP is also used to deliver sessions descriptions between SIP entities using the session description protocol (SDP) (Handley & Jacobson, 1998). The IMS provides an open interface for third-party services, such as the open service access (OSA) (3GPP-TS29.198, 2001) to be easily integrated, providing an opportunity for end-users to experience rich and personalized services (Liotta et al., 2002).

In this paper, the second section provides a brief description of the IMS network and service architectures required for deploying advanced IP services over converged networks. It also explains the IMS services capabilities standardization efforts and collaboration between the Third Generation Partnership Project (3GPP), 3GPP2, and the Open Mobile Alliance (OMA). The third section describes service provisioning in the IMS, providing the key elements for service execution (session and presence management), service quality control (quality control and billing), and service integration (open service access and converged billing), which are basic enablers for IMS service provisioning. The fourth section describes the future trends for service provisioning, outlining both academic and industrial opportunities in these areas. Finally, in the fifth section we draw key conclusions about service provisioning in the IMS.

IMS SERVICE ARCHITECTURE

IMS is based on a service oriented architecture (SOA) in which different services and applications from different vendors can easily communicate and be integrated to develop new services. In the IMS, service capabilities are standardised and not services. To help understand the IMS Service architecture, a brief description of the IMS network architecture (3GPP-TS23.002, 2006) and the standardisation service capabilities are first provided.

IMS Network Architecture

The IMS network architecture is built on a layered approach with open and standard interfaces to allow for seamless interconnection of standardized functions. In the IMS, nodes are not standardized, allowing vendors to combine as many functions as they wish into a particular node (Camarillo & Garcâia-Martâin, 2006). The horizontal layered approach of the IMS allows for lower layers to be transparent to the upper layers, enabling operators and service developers to use different underlying networks. This advantage allows interoperability and roaming. The IMS network architecture is divided in three basic layers as explained below (Figure 1).

A full description of the IMS network architecture can be found in 3GPP-TS23.002, 2006). From Figure 1, the Access Layer is an access-independent interface that allows users to connect to the IMS network via existing fixed or wireless networks, The session control layer is made up of SIP servers and proxies for controlling and managing sessions within the IMS. This is made up of the Proxy CSCF (P-CSCF), interrogating CSCF (I-CSCF), and the serving CSCF (S-CSCF). The service/application layer is also made up of different application servers for the execution of various IMS services and the provision of end user service logic.

Standardisation of Service Capabilities

Service capabilities are mechanisms needed to realise services within the IMS network and under the network control (3GPP-TS22.105, 2006). They are usually standardised to allow for service differentiation and system continuity. Service capabilities include descriptions for bearer services, teleServices, and supplementary services.

The standardisation of service capabilities exists in other systems such as GPRS, but in the IMS, 3GPP, 3GPP2, and OMA are responsible for the standardisation of the service capabilities.

Figure 1. The IMS network architecture

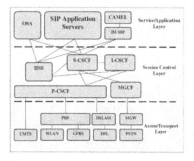

Some of OMA works are based on the IMS platform, and this leads to the proposals to extend the IMS in order to support additional requirements or service. This is the basis of the agreement between OMA, 3GPP, and 3GPP2 in which OMA generates the requirements for the IMS and the 3GPP and 3GPP2 extend the IMS to support the specified requirement (Camarillo & Garcâia-Martâin, 2006).

Due to this collaboration, OMA and 3GPP work on similar specifications at times and they aim to have compatible specifications. Examples of similar specifications being worked on by OMA and 3GPP include presence, messaging, and push-to-talk/push-over-cellular (PTT/PoC).

IMS Service Architecture

Based on the standardisation of service capabilities in Section 2.2, an IMS service architecture is developed to allow easy deployment and management of services. From the diagram, the Wired and Wireless sub networks provide interfaces that allow the IMS services to be transparent to the access network. These interfaces are explained below.

Bearer Control

Bearers allow information to be efficiently transferred to teleservices and applications via sub networks providing different levels of quality of service (QoS). They are usually classified with parameters such as "throughput," "delay tolerance," "maximum bit error rate," "symmetry," etc. (3GPP-TS22.105 2006). The bearer control plays a major role during interworking of functions and content adaptation.

Call Control

Call control allows the network operator to have total control of all information in the IMS network. This is achieved via a SIP proxy server known as a back-to-back user agent (B2BuA) placed in the signal and media path of end-to-end services between users. The B2BUA is based on an architecture that modifies the SIP messages (headers and bodies), generates and responds to requests (Camarillo & Garcâia-Martâin, 2006). The B2BUA allows the network operator full control of the traffic in the network, which in return allows for proper session management, resource reservation, internetwork billing, signalling interworking, protocol adaptation, and provision of integrated services. In the IMS, the B2BUA plays the major role of interconnecting the IMS with external networks (3GPP-TR29.962, 2005).

Mobility Management

Mobility is a key issue in the IMS because a large percentage of terminals in the network are mobile devices such as 3G phones, PDAs, laptops, and portable games. In fact, one of the most important challenges IP networks face is mobility support. Mobile IPv4 (MIPv4) (Perkins, 2002) and Mobile IPv6 (MIPv6) (Johnson, Perkins, et al., 2004) are the result of IETF mobility support efforts. These protocols enhance the network layer, so that IP hosts can change location while retaining their communicating sessions. Due to the limitation of Mobile IP, the IMS manages mobility through GPRS, providing layer two tunnelling mechanisms. This allows for a successful handover to be made without the session or application breaking. Terminal Mobility also allows for roaming, which is led by the CSCF and the HSS to allow the access to the subscribed services either in a home or visited network (Camarillo & Garcâia-Martâin, 2006).

SERVICE PROVISIONING IN THE IMS

Why is IMS Service Provisioning Important?

The IMS aims to provide specialized end-user experience, better billing systems, enhanced security

Figure 2. IMS service architecture (3GPP-TS22.105, 2006)

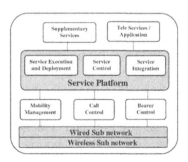

mechanisms, better mobility management (roaming), improved quality of service, and, most importantly, the integration of various services which cannot be found in present 3G networks. The IMS is viewed as a service-centric platform for endless development of new, rich, and exciting services. The IMS has put in place various mechanisms for the execution, control, and integration of theses services as shown in Figure 2. This process is known as service provisioning as explained in the following sections.

Service Execution and Deployment

The services offered in the IMS are hosted on application servers whereby some application servers may host multiple services. When a user registers with the network, the subscriber service profile (SSP) of the user is downloaded by the CSCF from the HSS. The SSP contains unique user-specific information such as:

- The services needed to be executed and the information on the order in which multiple services should be executed
- The location information of the application servers required to execute the services, and the order in which multiple services should be executed when they are on the same application server

The SSP information is used to deliver user-specific or personalized services to the end-users. These services are built on the various service enablers as explained below.

Presence Services

The presence service (PS) is the foundation of service provisioning in the IMS because it allows the collection of various forms of information on the characteristics of the network, users, and terminals. This service enabler allows users to subscribe for certain information (watchers) about other elements (presentities). Presentities can then decide to publish this information, which could include capabilities of terminals, locations, communication addresses, or user availability. Moreover, the IMS can also make the published information available to other services to allow for easy creation of new services and integration with existing services. For example, the IMS terminal plays the role of both a watcher and a presence user agent (PUA). The application server in the home network also plays the role of the presence server (PS), also known as presence agent (PA).

In order to allow for proper service execution in the IMS, the PA needs to get all relevant information from the necessary elements in the network, such as the home location register (HLR) in circuit networks, the gateway GPRS support node (GGSN) in GPRS networks, and the S-CSCF in the IMS network. This allows for proper service logics to be computed in order to deliver personalized services to the user.

Session Management

Sessions management is based on creation, modification, integration, and modification of conventional SIP messages as described in RFC-3261 (Rosenberg, Schulzrinne, et al., 2002). This allows end-users and operators to manage different sessions in the IMS, and also create new services. The CSCF (Figure 1) is at the heart of session management routing. The CSCF is basically a SIP server, and is divided in three major categories: P-CSCF, I-CSCF, and S-CSCF, as described earlier in the second section. IMS also supports SIP extensions in which "required" and "supported" headers are used. This also allows for the creation of new services such as presence (Roach, 2002) and instant messaging (Campbell, Rosenberg, et al., 2002).

The IMS terminal can send a REGISTER request via the P-CSCF to the I-CSCF and then the S-CSCF. If the registration is successful, a 200 OK message is replied back to the terminal via the same route. Once registration is complete, sessions to User Agents can be easily managed by invoking new or existing services using various SIP messages such as INVITE, SUBSCRIBE, NOTIFY, and PRACK to mention a few.

Application Servers and Gateways

As described earlier in the second section, application servers are used to host and execute the services used in the IMS network. An application server can host more than a single service. There are three different application servers: namely, the SIP application servers for IMS services, the open service access-service capability server (OSA-SCS), a gateway to execute OSA in the IMS, and the IMS switching function (IM-SSF)—a gateway between the IMS and CAMEL, which is deployed in GSM networks.

Gateways, on the other hand, are used to interconnect other standardized formats to the standards supported in the IMS. Examples include: the Media Gateway, which interfaces the media plane in the circuit-switched network, converting between PCM and RTP. Also, the media gateway controller function (MGCF) is used as call-control protocol conversion between SIP and ISUP (integrated services digital network user part). The latter defines the procedures used to setup, manage, and release trunk circuits that carry voice and data calls over the public switched telephone network (PSTN).

Group List Management

This enabler is part of the presence service (PS). It allows users to create and manage network-based groups using definitions of the services deployed in the IMS. It allows the users to have access to information on, and receive notifications about, the groups. This is used in the development of buddy lists, contact lists, blogs, public/private chat groups, and new services where identities are required. This enabler can also be used for roaming purposes, where the users need access to the usual customized services.

IMS Service Control

Service control (Figure 2) plays a major role in IMS service provisioning due to the fact that it allows the synchronization needed for session establishment and quality of service (QoS) management. In this way, the end-users can have a predictable experience at a reasonable charge as compared to present 3G networks. Service control also allows the service platform to be reusable by allowing proper control and management of complex functions such as service filtering, triggering, and interaction. The main enablers for service control are: quality control, mobility management, security, and billing, as described below.

Quality Control

Quality control in the IMS is described in terms of end-to-end QoS, aiming at a predictable user experience. All steps are taken to ensure that all necessary policies are enforced to guarantee the assigned QoS (Dong, 2005).

In order to allow end-to end QoS, QoS is managed within each domain. The IMS supports various end-to-

S

end QoS models in which the basic reservation protocols are used. The terminals can use either the Integrated Services—including the resource reservation protocol (RSVP)—or differentiated services (DiffServ) codes, as long as they are mapped to the DiffServ codes in the network (Borosa, Marsic, et al., 2003). The link-layer resource reservation is made over a policy decision point (PDP) context and is assigned to the appropriate DiffServ code point (DSCP), which is possibly in the same domain, and is then sent into the DiffServ-enabled Network.

Security

Security in the IMS is based on the IP security protocol (IPSec) (Kent & Atkinson, 1998) in which extensions have been created to manage IPSec security associations for SIP in the IMS. IPSec is also the preferred choice for IPv6. It is an extension of IP which allows security to be removed from the network and placed on the endpoints by applying encryption to either the entire IP payload (tunnel mode) or only to the upper-layer protocols of the IP payload (transport mode). IPSec allows for security services such as data integrity protection, data origin authentication, anti-replay protection, and confidentiality, also offering protection to the upper layers. This allows the security mechanism in the IMS to be divided into Access Security (for users and the network) and Network Security (for the protection of traffic between network elements).

Billing

The IMS is built on multimedia messages requiring large file transfers to ensure good quality. By contrast to the billing approach used in conventional Telecom systems, in the IMS the end-users are charged for the services offered rather than by the bytes transferred. This allows, for example, chat sessions to be charged based on duration rather than by the amount of messages transferred. Each session carries a unique IMS charging identifier (ICID) per session and also an inter-operator identifier (IOI) defining the originating and termination networks. There are basically two categories of billing, which are offline for post-paid users, and online charging for prepaid users.

IMS Service Integration

Service integration in the IMS is the element of service provisioning that allows new and rich services to be easily developed. This also allows for an inexpensive integration of both real time and non-real time services to easily construct more complex and attractive "bundled services." The basic enablers for service integration are explained below.

Open Service Architecture (OSA)

The OSA is the defined architecture that allows operators and third-party service providers to make use of the underlying network functionalities through the standardised open standard interface as described in the second section. The OSA also makes the application independent of the underlying network technology (Figure 3) (3GPP-TS23.127 2002). Service capability servers (SCS) provide the application with service capability features (SCF), which are abstractions from the underlying network functionality. SCS implement SCF and interact with the core network. Example SCF are call control, session control, terminal capability, charging, account management, and user location.

The framework provides applications with basic mechanisms that enable them to make use of service capabilities in the network. Example framework functions include service discovery and registration, authentication, trust and security management, and service factory.

The main aim of OSA is to provide an extensible and scalable architecture that allows for inclusion of new service capability features and SCS with a minimum impact on the applications, using the OSA interface.

Figure 3. OSA architecture

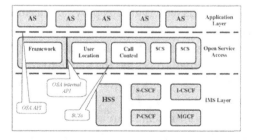

While SCS provide a first, low-level of support aimed at facilitating application development, the application layer offers a second, higher-level of support aimed at speeding up application development. Applications are implemented in one or more application servers (AS), which hide distributional aspects and offer a standard programming environment, application-oriented APIs (e.g., JAIN), and reusable components (e.g., Java Beans) that realise SCF functionality.

Converged Billing

The concept of converged billing allows the operator to charge on the basis of service, content, volume, or an integration of the services in a prepaid or post-paid manner (the modes of payment were discussed under billing earlier on). Converged billing also allows the user to use the operator as their converging point for all their billing, even if some of their services are offered by third-party service providers. This is possible via the single sign on feature in the IMS that allows the user to register with the network, and does not need any form of re-authentication for subsequent services. This gives users the assurance that all their billing is handed by a centrally secure source and gives them enough confidence to spend on the services.

FUTURE TRENDS

The IMS core network architecture is being deployed by various vendors and operators. A lot of end-to-end interoperability testing has been carried out, for instance by Nokia and NEC (Nokia & NEC, 2004). IBM and Swisscom have conducted proof-of-concept tests (IBM, 2006). Also, new services are staring to appear, for instance the proposed mobile gaming architecture (Akkawi, Schaller, et al., 2004) and the platform for mobile TV (Faria, Henriksson, et al., 2006). There also are various tools available to develop IMS services. An example is the Java API for integrated networks (JAIN) in which various expert groups provide reusable APIs that are easily assessed.

The enormous interest surrounding the IMS indicates that this may really become the standard framework for deploying advanced, ubiquitous services over converged, all-IP networks, i.e., the "domain of services." However, not all research areas have been fully explored yet, especially in the area of distributed session management. Many approaches have been developed to eliminate (or reduce) the number of centralized servers from the IMS, aiming at a better level of scalability. Another promising area of research is looking at the deployment of peer-to-peer services in the IMS (Liotta, 2005). This requires coming up with solutions as to how SIP sessions can be managed via distributed signalling protocols (Bryan, 2005).

CONCLUSION

Service provisioning in the IMS enables network operators, service providers, and end-users to benefit from the advantages of an open architecture which relies on a solid framework for service execution, control, and integration. These provisioning enablers include presence and location services, quality control, security, and billing (to mention a few).

The IMS as a whole has great potential and has been developing rapidly over the years, offering a solution to the all-IP vision of rich, multi-access multimedia services accessible anywhere, at any time, with the required quality, and at the right price.

The IMS is now widely considered as the future service-centric platform of preference, although several researchers are still arguing that the benefits of IMS come with a high cost linked to its layered approach (complexity). Only a large-scale deployment of the IMS and a wide adoption by operators and service providers will allow a full assessment of its benefits and shortcomings. These will hopefully be unveiled in the next few years.

REFERENCES

3GPP-TR29.962 (2005). *Signalling interworking between the 3GPP profile of the Session Initiation Protocol (SIP) and non-3GPP SIP usage (Release 6).* (3GPP TR 29.962).

3GPP-TS22.105 (2006). *Services and service capabilities.* (3GPP-TS22.105 version 8).

3GPP-TS23.002 (2006). *Network architecture (Release 7).* (3GPP-TS23.002).

3GPP-TS23.127 (2002). *Virtual home environment/ Open service access.* (3GPP-TS23.127).

3GPP-TS29.198 (2001). *Open service architecture (OSA).* (3GPP TS 29.198).

Akkawi, A., et al. (2004). *Networked mobile gaming for 3G-networks.* Entertainment Computing, ICEC 2004, 457-467.

Borosa, T., B. Marsic, et al. (2003). *QoS support in IP multimedia subsystem using DiffServ.* Vol. 2. 669-672.

Camarillo, G., & Garcâia-Martâin, M.A. (2006). *The 3G IP multimedia subsystem (IMS): Merging the Internet and the cellular worlds.* Chichester, West Sussex; Hoboken, NJ: J. Wiley.

Campbell, B., J., et al. (2002). *Session initiation protocol (SIP) extension for instant messaging.* Internet Engineering Task Force (IETF RFC 3428).

Dong, S. (2005). *End-to-end QoS in IMS enabled next generation networks.* WOCC, 28.

Faria, G., et al. (2006). DVB-H: digital broadcast services to handheld devices. *Proceedings of the IEEE, 94*(1), 194-209.

Handley, M., & Jacobson, V. (1998). *SDP: Session description protocol.* Internet Engineering Task Force (IETF RFC 2327).

IBM. (2006). *Service architecture for 3GPP IP multimedia subsystem–The IBM and Swisscom proof-of-concept experience.* Retrieved 31 July, 2007 from http://www-03.ibm.com/industries/telecom/doc/content/bin/swisscomm_02.09.06a.pdf

Johnson, D., et al. (2004). *Mobility support in IPv6.* Internet Engineering Task Force (IETF RFC 3775).

Kent, S., & Atkinson, R. (1998). *Security architecture for the Internet protocol.* Internet Engineering Task Force (IETF RFC 2401).

Liotta, A., et al. (2002). *Delivering service adaptation with 3G Technology,* 108-120.

Nokia and NEC (2004). Nokia and NEC successfully test interoperability of IP multimedia subsystem (IMS) for richer communications. Retrieved 31 July, 2007 from http://press.nokia.com/PR/200409/960657_5.html

Perkins, C. (2002). *IP mobility support for IPv4.* Internet Engineering Task Force (IETF RGC 3344).

Roach, A. B. (2002). *Session initiation protocol (SIP)-Specific event notification.* RFC 3265—Internet Engineering Task Force (IETF RFC 3265).

Rosenberg, J., et al. (2002). *SIP: Session initiation protocol.* Internet Engineering Task Force (IETF RFC 3261).

KEY TERMS

Application Servers: Application servers are used to host and execute the services used in the IMS network.

IMS Service Provisioning: Service provisioning in the IMS offers the required mechanisms for execution, control, and integration of services in the IMS.

IMS Session Management: Sessions management is based on creation, modification, integration, and modification of conventional SIP messages.

Open Service Architecture (OSA): The OSA is the defined architecture that allows operator and third party applications to make use of the underlying network functionalities through standardized, open interface.

Presence Service: This allows for the collection of various forms of information on the characteristics of the network, users, and terminals. Users can subscribe or be notified of this information.

Services Capabilities: These are standardised mechanisms needed to realise services within the IMS network and under the network control.

Service Integration: This is the integration of both real-time and non-real time services to more complex and attractive "bundled services."

Session Initiation Protocol

Ilija Basicevic
Faculty of Technology Sciences, Novisad, Serbia

Miroslav Popovic
Faculty of Technology Sciences, Novisad, Serbia

INTRODUCTION

With the appearance of the Internet as an important communications medium for widespread everyday use, which can be dated to the mid 90s, a need to establish a signalization protocol for *multimedia communications* was recognized. There were two major proposals: SIP by the Internet community, and *H.323* by ITU-T.

SIP is the result of work in IETF. As of today, it is one of the most important protocols for signalization in *VoIP telephony*. Work on SIP began in 1995 in the IETF MMUSIC working group. Later, in 1999, the SIP working group was formed. That was the first, primary working group dedicated to the development of SIP protocol, but later several other working groups related to this protocol were formed. These were dedicated to: applications of SIP, mechanisms for support of *presence service*, and interactions of PSTN/IN networks with the Internet for the realization of services.

SIP is defined in a series of RFC documents. The first RFC document defining SIP is RFC 2543 (Handley, Schulzrinne, Schooler, & Rosenberg, 1999), but it was replaced with RFC 3261 (Rosenberg, Schulzrinne, Camarillo, Johnston, Peterson, Sparks, Handley, & Schooler, 2002). There is a group of RFC documents defining extensions to SIP.

BACKGROUND

The two proposals were influenced by two technical traditions. ITU-T has been the most important regulation body in the area of telecommunications for a long time. During the '90s, most of the services that were available earlier in communications networks regulated by ITU-T—multimedia sessions being one of them—became available to customers on the Internet. ITU-T approached this problem based on their long experience in the area of telecommunication networks. Thus, H.323 accumulates many solutions already used in other ITU-T standards (ASN.1 is one example). On the other hand, experts responsible for the development of SIP applied many solutions proven during the development and use of other Internet protocols.

SESSION INITIATION PROTOCOL

Among the solutions that SIP inherited from earlier work on Internet protocols, the most important is certainly a distributed architecture, with intelligence dominantly located at the end points. Other SIP features following below are adopted from earlier protocols:

- It is media independent
- Protocol syntax is text-based
- It uses *URL* addressing scheme
- It uses *SDP*, for its offer-answer model in session establishment
- It uses a *three-way handshake* for session establishment
- It uses a client-server model

Distributed intelligence is a characteristic of Internet networks, and it has been proven as successful. Thus, its use in the development of protocol that represents another level on the top of the Internet protocol stack is a logical step. On the other hand, networks of fixed telephony, PSTN/ISDN, are based on centralized logic: "intelligent network and dumb terminals." The Internet proved that distributed intelligence that lies mostly at end points allows far more flexibility for the development of new services. In a centralized model, the introduction of a new service is an arduous task, since the complex logic of internal network nodes has to be changed. Along the time-scale, this logic becomes more and more complex, so introducing a new service turns out to be an even more complicated task. In the distributed model it is easier to add a new service, as it does not require significant changes in the implementation of existing nodes. This approach to the design of SIP can be seen in early papers by SIP researchers (Schulzrinne & Rosenberg, 1998; Schulzrinne, 1997).

Designers of SIP implemented the same principle already present in existing Internet architecture in the next step of Internet evolution. We have to remark that since Internet structure has grown significantly richer, internal nodes have become more complex, but still its architecture provides the advantages of a distributed intelligence approach.

SIP protocol syntax is text-based. It inherited some characteristics of HTTP syntax. These are:

- It uses self-identifying attribute-value pairs (AVP), followed by separators
- Processing is best-effort. Receivers ignore unknown AVP pairs and skip to the next AVP
- Some header fields are inherited from HTTP
- Classification of status codes is inherited from HTTP

SIP uses the UTF-8 standard. There are two types of SIP messages: requests and responses. Requests are sent from a client to a server, and responses in the opposite direction. Both requests and responses begin with a start line, have one or more header fields, and end-of-header fields indicated by an empty line and an optional message body.

In the case of a request, the start line carries, besides other elements, the request method. RFC 3261, (Rosenberg et al., 2002) defined the following methods:

- **INVITE:** Request for the initiation of multimedia session
- **ACK:** Request that completes the three-way handshake in session establishment
- **CANCEL:** For cancelling the INVITE request. INVITE is the only request that can be cancelled
- **BYE:** For terminating a session
- **OPTIONS:** For capabilities query

Extensions of SIP, published in several other RFC documents, specified several additional methods. In the case of a response, the start line is known as a status line and it carries, besides other elements, status code.

All responses have similar structure. Generally, responses are divided into six groups:

- 100-199- provisional
- 200-299 -success. Most important response code in this group is 200 (OK)
- 300-399 - redirect
- 400-499 - client error
- 500-599 - server error
- 600 and greater - general error (failure)

Roughly, these are divided into two classes: provisional (100-199) and final (all the rest). Final responses terminate the SIP transaction, while provisional responses do not.

An alphabetical list of header field types contains more than 40 items so it is not presented here.

The successful use of several URL addressing schemes (the current standard is RFC 3986, Berners-Lee, Fielding, & Masinter, 2005) on the Internet continued its way in the case of SIP. Generally, SIP URI identifiers have two types:

- **Email-like form:** user@host. Host is a fully qualified domain name that can be resolved to an IP address using the DNS system.
- **Telephone number form:** number@host. The Host part is optional and may indicate a server that can reach this phone number. Today processing is done mostly based on number part only.

During the signalling required for the establishment of a multimedia session, negotiation of characteristics of the session is realized. This negotiation follows an offer/answer model. Basically, one of the sides makes the first proposal—the "offer," which is followed by the other side sending its proposal—the—"answer." Upon analysing the contents of the offer, this side decides what is the closest match to the offered characteristics among those it can support, and thus it compiles the "answer." Both offer and answer contain session descriptions in SDP language (RFC 2327, Handley & Jacobson, 1998).

SIP uses a three-way handshake for the establishment of a session. This sequence consists of the client side sending an INVITE request, which is answered with a 200 (OK) response; after receiving the 200 (OK) response, the initiating side concludes the handshake by sending an ACK message (see Figure 1; the terms UAC and UAS are explained).

For the modification of an existing session, the same message is used as for the initiation, namely an INVITE request. In SIP terminology, this is known as re-INVITE. The same offer/answer model is used in re-INVITE as in the initial INVITE. One difference from the initial INVITE is that re-INVITE cannot fork, and for that reason it will result in only one response.

Using the OPTIONS request, a SIP client can learn about methods, content types, extensions, coding/decoding rules, and other characteristics that the remote side supports. This request can be sent before dialogue is established, and it does not create a dialogue, or it can be sent within a dialogue. An OPTIONS request can be forked, but will result in only one response, due to proxy procedures that are applied to it.

Every implementation of SIP must support UDP and TCP. However, SIP can rely on any other transport protocol. In RFC 3261 (Rosenberg et al., 2002), names used in message headers are defined for UDP, TCP, SCTP, and TLS. Proxy servers, redirect servers, and registrars must implement TLS. TLS is assumed to be TLS over TCP.

Communication paths taken by SIP messages can differ, depending on the case, but the general case of two endpoints in different domains is referred to as the "SIP trapezoid" (see Figure2). In this case, if we assume that the endpoint that actively initiates the session is A, and the other one B, we have the following route: the A's SIP client sends an INVITE request to the proxy in its own domain. A's proxy routes the request to proxy of B's domain. B's proxy consults the location service, and forwards the request to B. The path of the responses and further requests depends on several factors, and in the general case does not have to follow the same route.

Important concepts of SIP are transaction and dialogue. A transaction is a request sent by a client to the server, followed by all responses to that request, sent from the server to the requesting client. There can be zero or more provisional responses, and one or more final responses for each request. An exception is the INVITE transaction, which in some cases includes the ACK request as well. There are two types of transactions: INVITE and non-INVITE. The main difference

Figure 2. SIP trapezoid

Figure 1. Typical message exchange during the lifetime of one session

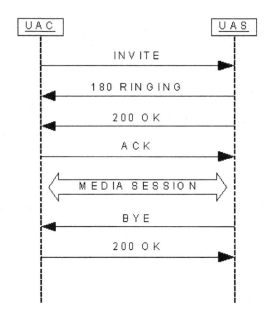

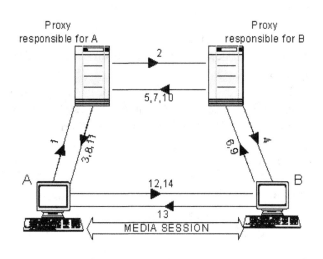

MESSAGES EXCHANGED:

1,2,4: INVITE
3,5: 100 TRYING
6,7,8: 180 RINGING
9,10,11,14: 200 OK
13: BYE
12: ACK

is in the structure—INVITE consists of a three-way handshake, while others consist of a two-way one (see Figure 1). The duration is also different, since the duration of INVITE transactions often depends on human reaction, while other transactions are managed automatically. Interaction between two SIP endpoints is realized as a series of transactions. A peer-to-peer relationship established between two endpoints with a successful INVITE transaction is a dialogue. The possibility of starting a dialogue with a SUBSCRIBE transaction has been added later.

When speaking about roles in SIP, each side in the communication can have a client or server role. This distinction changes during the duration of the session. The side that initiated the session, as a client, can later become a server when the other side initiates a new transaction (for example, a re-INVITE).

Event notification mechanism has been introduced as an extension to SIP protocol, in RFC 3265 (Roach, 2002). There are two types of entities in this mechanism: publisher and subscribers. The latter subscribe for publishing at a publisher entity. The Publisher sends event notifications (publishes its state changes) to subscribed entities. Subscriptions can be added or revoked dynamically. In SIP implementation, confirmed SUBSCRIBE messages start a new subscription association. State changes are transmitted using NOTIFY messages. The subscription mechanism in SIP is generic. For each specific use of this mechanism, an event package should be developed. Event packages are published in separate RFC documents. Some already existing event packages are:

- **Presence:** Publishing of presence state changes, used for the development of presence services (RFC 3856, Rosenberg, 2004). Presence notification messages use *PIDF* format (RFC 3863, Sugano, Fujimoto, Klyne, Bateman, Carr, & Peterson, 2004), based on XML.
- **Registration:** Publishing of registration state changes (RFC 3680, Rosenberg, 2004).
- **Refer:** Used in session transfer (RFC 3515, Sparks, 2003). In this case, a REFER request, which triggers session transfer to another endpoint, also implicitly begins subscription. NOTIFY messages carry results of invoked session transfers.

The introduction of event-notification has also changed the notion of dialogue in the SIP protocol. Now, both INVITE and SUBSCRIBE are dialogue-creating requests. Each dialogue can contain several subscriptions, and to terminate the dialogue all those associations have to be terminated.

Logical elements of a SIP network are user agents and proxy, redirection, and registrar servers. User agents (UA) are systems that represent endpoints. It is said that each UA has two parts, user agent client (UAC) and user agent server (UAS), based on the roles defined above. Each UA takes the roles of both client and server during the communication, so both parts are necessary.

A SIP proxy is an intermediary system whose primary function is that of routing messages between endpoints (or other proxies). It acts as a server on one side, and as a client on the other. It makes requests as a client on behalf of the other client, to whom it appears as a server. Another important function of a proxy is the enforcement of policy in its responsible domains. Based on the type of processing it does on the messages it receives from client user agents, or other proxies, there are two types of proxies:

- **Stateless:** Basically forward messages that they may modify.
- **Stateful:** Store information that contains transaction and/or dialogue processing states. This provides the possibility for the implementation of more complex functions in session processing.

A redirection server can support one user in locating another. Upon receiving a client request, it generates a response in class (300-399) containing a set of URI identifiers where the requested user could be reached.

When processing requests, the registrar server accepts requests that add, refresh, or delete address bindings stored in location services and queried by proxies. These bindings map SIP addresses to network level addresses.

Though not explicitly supported in most important RFC documents defining SIP (RFC 2543, Handley et al., 1999 and RFC 3261, Rosenberg et al., 2002), there has been significant work to provide for the realization of conferencing functions in the SIP protocol. Elements of SIP infrastructure for conferencing are defined in

RFC 4245 (Levin & Even, 2005). Support for instant messaging has been introduced into SIP in RFC 3428 (Campbell, 2002).

There are some security services that are required for the successful function of a SIP network. These are identified in (RFC 3261, Rosenberg et al., 2002) as:

- Confidentiality and integrity of SIP messages
- Support for authentication and privacy of the participants in sessions
- Prevention of denial-of-service (DOS) attacks

At this point, SIP again reuses some mechanisms from other Internet protocols. SIP needs low-layer security mechanisms like hop-by-hop encryption, since end-to-end encryption of SIP messages is not feasible. Intermediate systems en route, namely proxies, need to parse and modify some header fields. SIP also needs cryptographic authentication mechanisms. In order to solve these problems, the following solutions have been introduced: SIP provides a stateless, challenge-based mechanism for authentication that is based on authentication in HTTP. Any SIP element, client, or proxy, may challenge the sender of request it has received to determine its authenticity. This authentication can be realized on either a user-to-user or user-to-proxy basis. The possible use of secure *MIME* in order to secure message bodies is also provided. Also, in order to provide a variant of end-to-end authentication, tunnelling of SIP messages when the entire SIP message is encapsulated within a MIME and afterwards a secure MIME is applied, is possible. Additionally, the SIPS URI scheme has been introduced. Use of a SIPS scheme allows users to specify that they want to be reached securely. If a target URI is a SIPS URI, each hop on the route to target domain has to be secured with TLS.

IP telephony services are often accessed by end users using *softphone* applications. Most softphone applications as of this moment are based on SIP protocol. In this case, softphones are used for first-party call control. Besides first-party call control functions, where one entity controls session which it participates directly in, SIP supports development of third-party call control services too. In this case, one entity controls the session which it does not participate in. An example of such service is click-to-dial (RFC 3725, Rosenberg et al., 2004). In this service, a Web server

creates a call (which a customer requests by clicking on a Web page) between the customer and customer service representative. Another service in this class is mid-call announcement (RFC 3725, Rosenberg et al., 2004). This service can be used to interrupt a call that has been initiated using a pre-paid calling card and play an announcement to the caller. There are other types of services in this class. In traditional telephony, third-party call control is used for operator services–for example, when an operator creates a call between two participants. It is also used for conferencing.

FUTURE TRENDS

Today, SIP has become the de facto standard for signalization in multimedia communications over the Internet. The list of applications is not exhausted with voice and video sessions but includes others, such as instant messaging, network gaming, or virtual reality.

It has been chosen as the signalling protocol for IP telephony in the next generation of wireless networks by 3GPP.

Work in SIP-related IETF working groups continues in several areas: interoperation with circuit-switched networks, conferencing, instant messaging, and interaction with firewalls. There is also ongoing research in other institutions related to the application of SIP in the next generation of networks (Banerjee, Das, & Acharya, 2005;Blum, & Magedanz, 2005) and other issues in this area.

CONCLUSION

SIP is a signalling protocol used for establishment, modification, and termination of multimedia sessions. Besides this primary function, SIP can support other features, including registration, user location, redirection, instant messaging, and presence. SIP is a component that can be used with other components to build a multimedia communications system. It does not determine which other protocols will be used in such a system. Successful application of some concepts, already proven in the design of Internet protocols, and innovative solutions have made SIP the most important protocol in this area.

REFERENCES

Banerjee N., Das, S. K., & Acharya, A. (2005). SIP-based mobility architecture for next generation wireless networks. In *Third IEEE International Conference on Pervasive Computing and Communications (PerCom'05).*

Berners-Lee, T., Fielding, R., & Masinter, L. (2005, January). Uniform resource identifier (URI): Generic syntax. RFC 3986. Internet Engineering Task Force.

Blum, N., & Magedanz, T. (2005). PTT + IMS = PTM. Towards community/presence-based IMS multimedia services. *Seventh IEEE International Symposium on Multimedia (ISM'05)*, 337-344. Irvine, CA, USA.

Campbell, B., Ed., Rosenberg J., Schulzrinne H., Huitema C. & Gurle D. (2002, December). Session initiation protocol (SIP) extension for instant messaging. Internet Engineering Task Force. RFC 3428.

Handley, M., & Jacobson, V. (1998, April). *Session description protocol (SDP)*. RFC 2327. Internet Engineering Task Force.

Handley, M., Schulzrinne, H., Schooler, E., & Rosenberg, J. (1999, March). *SIP: Session initiation protocol* RFC 2543, Internet Engineering Task Force.

Levin, O., & Even, R. (2005, November). *High-level requirements for tightly coupled SIP conferencing*. RFC 4245, Internet Engineering Task Force.

Roach, A. B. (2002, June). *SIP-Specific event notification*. RFC 3265. Internet Engineering Task Force.

Rosenberg, J. (2004, March). *A session initiation protocol (SIP) event package for registrations*. RFC 3680, Internet Engineering Task Force.

Rosenberg, J. (2004, August). *A presence event package for the SIP protocol*. RFC 3856, Internet Engineering Task Force.

Rosenberg, J. Peterson J., Schulzrinne H., & Camarillo G., (2004, April). *Best current practices for third party call control (3pcc) in the session initiation protocol (SIP)*. RFC 3725, Internet Engineering Task Force.

Rosenberg, J. Schulzrinne, H., Camarillo, G., Johnston, A., Peterson, J., Sparks R., et al. (2002, June). *SIP: Session initiation protocol*. RFC 3261. Internet engineering task force.

Schulzrinne, H., & Rosenberg, J. (1998). A comparison of SIP and H.323 for Internet telephony, network and operating system support for digital audio and video (NOSSDAV). Cambridge, UK ACM.

Schulzrinne, H. (1997). A comprehensive multimedia control architecture for the Internet, Proceedings *International Workshop on Network and Operating System Support for Digital Audio and Video (NOSSDAV)*, St. Louis, Missouri ACM.

Singh, A., & Acharya, A. (2004). Using SIP to build context-aware VoIP support for multiplayer networked games. *Proceedings of 3rd ACM SIGCOMM workshop on Network and system support for games*, 98-105. Portland, Oregon.

Sparks, R. (2003, April). *The session initiation protocol (SIP) refer method*. RFC 3515. Internet Engineering Task Force.

Sugano, H., Fujimoto, S., Klyne, G., Bateman A., Carr, W., & Peterson, J. (2004, August). *Presence information data format (PIDF)*. RFC 3863, Internet Engineering Task Force.

KEY TERMS

3GPP (Third Generation Partnership Project): An organization that develops and promotes standards for third generation mobile phone systems.

H.323: The name refers to a set of protocols adopted by ITU-T, aimed at providing multimedia communications in packet networks.

IN: Telecommunications network architecture standardized by ITU-T.

ITU-T: International Telecommunication Union (ITU) Standardization Sector.

MIME (Multipurpose Internet Mail Extensions): Message representation protocol.

PSTN/ISDN: Standards of fixed telephony adopted by ITU-T.

SCTP: Transport level protocol, used on the Internet.

TLS (Transport Layer Security): Protocol that provides privacy and data integrity.

UTF-8: 8-bit Unicode Transformation Format. Encoding standard used in Internet.

XML (Extensible Markup Language): Restricted form of Standard Generalized Markup Language (SGML, ISO 8879).

Sharing Protected Web Resources

Sylvia Encheva
Stord-Haugesund University College, Norway

Sharil Tumin
University of Bergen, Norway

INTRODUCTION

Role-based access control (RBAC) is a security mechanism that can lower the cost and complexity of security administration for large networked applications. RBAC simplifies security administration by using roles, hierarchies, and constraints to organize privileges (Ferraiolo et al., 1992).

Earlier ways of defining access control are access control lists, a discretionary access control, and a mandatory access control. RBAC has a clear advantage over these alternative approaches in that it addresses the security needs of different organizations. The RBAC model defines three kinds of separation of duties—static, dynamic, and operational. Separation of duties, various time-constrained cardinality, and control-flow dependency were discussed in Bertino et al. (2001). Permissions in RBAC are associated with roles, and users are made members of appropriate roles, thereby acquiring the roles' permissions (Schwoon et al., 2003). In RBAC, access decisions are based on an individual's roles and responsibilities within the organization or user base (Andress, 2001; Joshi et al., 2005).

The model presented in this paper is intended to improve user management in networked systems. An automated addition or removal of users from roles simplifies maintaining their membership appropriate groups. Group-role relations are used to facilitate users with an access control and permissions to different resources. In such a system, users' and group data are shared across organizations.

BACKGROUND

Use of groups in UNIX, privilege grouping in database systems, and separation of duty concepts has been discussed in Ferraiolo et al. (2001), and a summary of traditional access controls and security models, such as Mandatory and Discretionary Access Controls, Clark-Wilson, Biba, Chinese Wall security models, and the reference monitor concept is presented in Ferraiolo et al. (2003).

At present, a delegation in computer systems may be presented as human-to-human, human-to-machine, and machine-to-machine. A framework for modeling the delegation of roles from one user to another is proposed in Barka et al. (2004). The model focuses on the human-to-human form of delegation using roles. A multiple-leveled RBAC model for protecting privacy in object-oriented systems is presented by Chou (2004). It offers multiple levels of control granularity. A multi-domain environment employing RBAC policies is described by Shafiq et al. (2005). The design and implementation of an integrated approach to engineering and enforcing context constraints in RBAC environments is described in Strembeck et al. (2004) and Al-Kahtani (2004) presents a rule-based RBAC model with negative authorization. Furthermore, the authors provide detailed analysis of different aspects of negative authorization in an RBAC context. A RBAC approach to XML security is discussed by Zhang et al. (2003) and Bhatti et al. (2004). A location and time-based RBAC model is constructed by Chandran et al. (2005), and although quite interesting, the paper does not address industry related problems.

While RBAC provides a formal implementation model, Shibboleth defines standards for implementation based on OASIS security assertion markup language (SAML) (shibbolethinternet2.edu). Our work differs from Shibboleth in modeling implementation and user/group/role management. Our model is more open-ended, based on XML-RPC written in Python.

USER-GROUP MANAGEMENT IN INDEPENDENT ORGANIZATIONS

The user-group management in an organization provides a centralized account identity database from which users who belong to that organization authenticate themselves. The management system must also provide a centralized database for the user-group membership. The group membership of a user can be queried at any time by service providers.

The role-resource management in another organization (i.e., a service provider) provides a centralized permissions' database where an action is defined. The management system must also provide a database for the group role memberships. Collaboration among organizations entails that all must agree on group names to be used in user-group and group-role relations. A group name acts as a bridge in an inter-organization authorization mechanism. All users and groups are identified using the domain-name of their organization.

STATIC AND DYNAMIC SEPARATION OF DUTIES

This collaborative management model can be used by a security administrator to enforce a policy of separation of duties. Separation of duties appears to be of great value in a case of collaboration among various job-related capabilities where, for example, two roles have been specified as mutually exclusive and cannot both be included in a user's set of authorized roles. Separation of duty also requires that for any particular set of transactions, no single user is allowed to execute all the transactions within the set. A system administrator can control access at a level of abstraction that is natural to the way those enterprises typically conduct business. This is achieved by statically and dynamically regulating users' actions through the establishment, and the definition of roles, relationships, and constraints.

A static separation of duty enforces all mutually exclusive roles at the time an administrator sets up role authorizations, while a dynamic separation of duty enforces all rules at the time a user selects roles for a session. The dynamic separation of duty places constraints on a simultaneous activation of roles. A user can become active in a new role only if the proposed role is not mutually exclusive with any of the roles in which the user is currently active.

When an XML-RPC communication mechanism is presented. It determines a domain user's authentication and authorization where, in a collaborative independent management among organization's role, data in a service provider domain contain references to an external group's data from clients' domains. Defining disjoint groups' permissions is a duty of role managers at service provider domains, and assigning users to proper groups is a duty of group managers at service client domains. These managers need to cooperate very closely. Policies and rules governing a resource's usage must be documented and understood by all parties. The managers at service provider domains have the right and the means to block any user in an event of a conflict. A dynamic separation of duty requires that a user cannot hold two conflicting roles in the same session, e.g., an examinee and an examiner of the same subject. A role with less permissions has lower rank than a role with more permissions. A conflict of interests constraint must be checked by the application. An audit track of user-assigned roles can be used to expose conflicts. Roles can be ranked in such a way that a higher-ranked role also contains all the rights of lower-ranked roles. The ranking order of roles on a resource depends on operations. Thus, a role with "read-only" permission is ranked lower than a role with "read-write" permission. Role managers define a ranking order of roles on a resource. Role managers need to work very closely with the service implementers. Role conflicts appear when a user simultaneously has both a higher ranked role and lower-ranked roles on a resource. In such cases, the user will get the role with the least rank, and, therefore, receives minimum permission on that resource.

The service provider administrators have the right to place a user and/or an external group in a "quarantine group" in relation to a protected resource. Users and groups placed in a quarantine group lose all their rights on the corresponding resource as long as they are in that quarantine group. The following three management areas are of interest:

- User-group management enforces a static separation of duty by defining a set of disjoint groups for conflicting roles. Thus, a user cannot be a member of several disjoint groups for conflicting roles.
- Group-role management enforces a dynamic separation of duty by defining a set of disjoint roles for a particular resource. A user cannot be

granted permission to have more than one role for the same resource.

- Role-resource management assigns permissions to roles on resources and adds groups to appropriate roles.

FRAMEWORK

Assume that there are two organizations in a collaborative agreement, service-client organization (*org1*) and service-provider organization (*org2*). Organization *org2* provides services that any authorized users, compounded by the agreement, can use. At organization *org1*, a specific user identified by *user1@org1* is a member of a specific group *group1@org1*, while organization *org2* provides a specific service *service1@org2* related to a role *role1@org2*. The *user1@org1* is permitted to use the resource provided by *service1@org2* if *group1@org1* is a member of *role1@org2*.

Users' managers at each organization manage a centralized users and groups database, which should be done centrally at an ICT center. Local department managers manage group memberships of centrally-defined users and groups. Resources managers at each organization manage a centralized services, roles, and group authorizations database. A service provider at the local departmental level provides resource names and data. Collaboration managers between organizations manage roles memberships of remotely-defined groups.

To participate in this framework, the service-client organization must have a domain *authentication server* on which the domain users can be authenticated and to provide users' authorization based on their domain group memberships. This model suggests a Web form authentication, which also provides a single-sign-on mechanism, based on session number and cookies. Any service-provider organization server can access an authenticated domain user's valid session number and group memberships on demand from an organization's *authentication server*. Any authenticated domain user within this framework can access any of the shared services, defined by group-role relations at other organizations, if he/she belongs to the proper groups at his/her home organization. Within this framework, the service-provider organizations must provide a *portal server,* through which all services published by this organization can be reached by users. This portal ac-

cepts authenticated domain users applying the agreed single-sign-on mechanism from their own organization and other participating organizations.

Once a *portal server* accepts a user, the user can then access any services accessible by the user's home domain group, defined by a corresponding role membership of the group on the service-provider organization. Each time an authenticated user wants to access a protected resource, the *portal server* needs to connect to the *authentication server* of the user's home organization in order to query the user group membership of a particular domain group, depending on the domain group's role membership for that particular resource.

A simple and secure XML-RPC communication mechanism between a *portal server* and an authentication *server* is proposed. The *portal server* knows which *authentication server* to connect to by the fact that the groups in roles data at the service-provider organization contain server references to service-client organizations. Thus, in a collaborative independent management among organizations, where group management assigns users membership to a group at an organization and role management assigns a group membership to a role at another organization, the hooks for cooperation among organizations are provided.

SYSTEM ARCHITECTURE

We assumed that each organization has a centralized user management system, and that users' authentication data and group memberships can be accessed from an enterprise identities repository. Such a repository can be a directory in a lightweight directory access protocol server.

The framework needs to support at least two servers, an *authentication server* and a *portal server*. These servers are Web-based servers with database back-ends. Each server is composed of the following four main components:

- **Web server:** Web servers provide users' interaction with the system. A user is authenticated when a correct credential (user-identifier, password) is given in a sign-on Web form. A Web server can set and read client's (Web browser) cookies.
- **System support run-time environment:** A communication module provides peer-to-peer,

541

request/respond communication between servers based on secure XML-RPC. A resource domain server can send a request to a user domain server for a user's authorization data (user and group membership). A resource domain acts as a client to a user domain for users' data. Users' credentials never leave the user domain server—a database module provides scriptable structured query language (SQL) operations on databases– and a lightweight directory access protocol module provides connectivity functions to a directory server.

- **Database:** Servers are supported by relational database management systems (DBMS). Operational data are stored in these databases.
- **Server-side scripts:** These scripts are responsible for enforcing resource protection policies and providing users with dynamic HTML pages.

In this collaborative user/resource system architecture, a *portal server* provides a Web portal entry point for all resources and applications offered to Web clients. An *authentication server* maintains users/resources authentication and authorization policies and provides a Web-based single sign-on application for domain users. A *portal server* will assign a Web browser with a unique portal session identifier (*PSID*) the first time an unauthenticated user is trying to access a protected Web resource controlled by that particular *portal server*. This generated portal session identifier is used as a cookie name with an empty value and is saved in the Web browser's cookie by the *portal serve'*s session controller. The user is then asked to provide his/her home domain name for authentication. The portal session identifier, the Web browser's IP addresses (*BIP*), and the home domain name are saved in a session database connected to the *portal server*. The portal session identifier is associated with the *BIP* for the session but is not yet associated with a valid user.

The *portal server* will then redirect the user's browser to his/her home domain's *authentication server*. The portal session identifier, the originator *portal server*'s IP address (*RIP*) and URI, are sent as "GET"-request parameters in the redirection. A logon Web-form is then displayed on the user's Web browser by the *authentication server*. The user is authenticated if he/she provides a valid credential (user-identifier (*ID*), or password) pair. The *authentication server* will then create a unique authentication session identifier (*ASID*)

associated with the session {*PSID*, *RIP*, *BIP*, *ID*}-quadruplet. The session-quadruplet and the {authentication session identifier, timestamp}-pair are saved in the session database connected to the *authentication server*. The portal session identifier is then associated with an authenticated *ID* for this particular session. The session is valid as long as the session-quadruplet exists in the *authentication server*'s session database.

The *authentication server* redirects the user's browser back to the originating *portal server*. The authentication session identifier is sent as a "GET"-request parameter in the redirection. Using the given authentication session identifier as a parameter, the *portal server* makes an XML-RPC call to an authentication service at the user home domain *authentication server*. If the authentication session identifier is still valid, the *ID* associated with the authentication session identifier is returned. The portal session identifier is then associated with an authenticated user *ID* at the *portal server*. A user is authenticated if both a session cookie portal session identifier and a session entry exist for that particular *portal server*.

An authentication session identifier is a short-term, one-time (i.e., having a limited period of validity and only one use) session identifier, and is used between a *portal server* and an *authentication server* for the initial session control. At any time, the *portal server* can obtain a new authentication session identifier by calling the *authentication server* and using a valid (*PSID*, *RIP*, *BIP*) parameter. The newly obtained authentication session identifier can be used to check a user's authorization from the *authentication server*'s group data, for example.

The architecture allows two types of logoff methods, local sign-off and global sign-off. On the local level a user is logged off from a specific *portal server* when the *portal server* disables the user's session cookie portal session identifier and deletes its local session (*PSID*, *BIP*) from its database. The *portal server* sends an XML-RPC call to the *authentication server* with the (*PSID*, *RIP*, *BIP*) parameters. The *authentication server* deletes the session-quadruplet from its database. The user is then invalid for that *portal server*.

The global sign-off signifies the inability of the *authentication server* to provide new authentication session identifiers to a particular {*PSID*, *RIP*, *BIP*}-triplet. When a *portal server* requests an *authentication server* for global user sign-off, the *authentication server* will perform the following sequence of actions:

- Select all session-quadruplets containing a *PSID*, *BIP*, and *ID*. Then do an XML-RPC call to the *portal server* for each *RIP* in the selection. Each *portal server* will delete its local session (*PSID*, *BIP*) from its database.
- Delete each session listed in the selection from the database.

Using a short-term authentication session identifier and a long-term portal session identifier, a simple security mechanism for a user's session can be maintained between *portal* and *authentication servers*. The portal session identifier is bound to a *BIP* at the *portal server*'s domain side and to the *ID* after a valid user logon at the *authentication server*'s domain side. The two initial URI-redirections (logon redirect and response redirect) are done over HTTPS. By using a peer-to-peer secure XML-RPC call over a HTTPS, an authentication session identifier is used to map the validity of an *ID* for user authentication and authorization. All *authentication servers* maintain a list of valid *portal servers* that are allowed to make XML-RPC calls to them.

A user never discloses his/her user-identifier and password in a foreign domain. Both HTTPS and XML-RPC have to be compromised in order for a rouge user or application to gain illegal access to resources. The risk for illegal access is minimized by using two calls, the first to obtain the short-term, one-time authentication session identifier associated with {*PSID*, *BIP*}, and the second to obtain the user authentication and authorization associated with the authentication session identifier.

FUTURE TRENDS

The work introduced here represents early stages towards the safe use of protected Web resources among independent educational organizations working in collaboration. A future goal is to develop a complete model, based on the proposed framework.

CONCLUSION

A policy of duty separation can be implemented by system administrators applying the model introduced in this paper. The model provides a solution to the question of how to guarantee the uniqueness of us-

ers across organizational boundaries. In addition, it minimizes the risk of illegal access by using one call to obtain a short-term, one-time authentication session identifier and another for obtaining authentication and authorization associated with the authentication session identifier.

REFERENCES

Al-Kahtani, M., & Sandhu, R. (2004). Rule-based RBAC with negative authorization. In *Twentieth Annual Computer Security Applications Conference*, Arizona. 405-415.

Andress, M. (2001) Access control. *Information Security Magazine 4*(4), 1-9.

Barka, E., & Sandhu, R. (2004). Role-based delegation model/hierarchical roles In *Twentieth Annual Computer Security Applications Conference*, Arizona. 396-404.

Bertino, E., Bonatti, P.A., & Ferrari, E. (2001). TRBAC: A temporal role-based access control model. *ACM Transactions on Information and System Security, 3*(3), 191-223.

Bhatti, R., Bertino E., Ghafoor A., & Joshi, J.B.D. (2004). XML-based specification for Web services document security. *IEEE Computer, 37*(4), 41-49.

Chandran, S.M., & Joshi, J.B.D. (2005). LoT RBAC: A location and time-based RBAC model. In *Proceedings of the Sixth International Conference on Web Information Systems Engineering*, New York. 361-375.

Chou, S-C. (2004). A multiple-leveled role-based access control model for protecting privacy in object-oriented systems. *Journal of Object Technology, 3*(3), 91-120.

Ferraiolo, D., & Kuhn, D. R. (1992). Role-based access control. In *15th National Computer Security Conference*, Gaithersburg, MD. 554-563.

Ferraiolo, D., Sandhu, R., Gavrila, S., Kuhn R.D., & Chandramouli, R. (2001). Proposed NIST standard for role-based access control. *ACM Transactions on Information and System Security, 4*(3), 224-274.

Ferraiolo, D., Kuhn., D. R., & Chandramouli, R. (2003). Role-based access control. Artech House. Computer Security Series.

http://shibbolethinternet2.edu

Joshi, J.B.D., Bertino, E., Latif, U., & Ghafoor, A. (2005). Generalized temporal role based access control model. *IEEE Transactions on Knowledge and Data Engineering, 7*(1), 1557-1577.

Schwoon, S., Jha, S., Reps, T., & Stubblebine, S. (2003). On generalized authorization problems. In *Proceedings of the 16th IEEE Computer Security Foundations Workshop*, Pacific Grove, CA.

Shafiq, B., Joshi, J.B.D., Bertino, E., & Ghafoor, A. (2005). Secure interoperation in a multi-fomain rnvironment rmploying RBAC policies. *IEEE Transactions on Knowledge and Data Engineering, 7*(1), 4-23.

Strembeck, M., & Neumann, G. (2004). An integrated approach to engineer and enforce context constraints in RBAC environments. *ACM Transactions on Information and System Security, 7*(3), 392-427.

Zhang, X., Park, J., & Sandhu, R.(2003). Schema based XML security: RBAC approach. In *Seventeenth IFIP 11.3 Working Conference on Data and Application Security*, Colorado. 330-343.

KEY TERMS

Action: A matrix of operations on objects.

Domain Identity: A human being, a machine, or an intelligent autonomous agent.

Group: A set of users.

Permission: Defines a right of a role to perform an action on a resource.

Resource: Defines a set of protected Web objects.

Role: Contains a set of groups associated with similar duty and authority.

User: Defined as a valid domain identity at a particular organization.

Social and P2P Networks on the Internet

Milica Stojmenovic
Carleton University, Canada

INTRODUCTION

This article studies *social networks* on the Internet created by popular applications such as *e-mails, Web, chat, file sharing* via *peer-to-peer interaction*, and *online gaming*.

The Internet has its roots in military and academia. Connections are available around the world at academic institutions, military installations, government agencies, commercial enterprises, commercial information providers (AOL, CompuServe, and MSN), and Internet service providers. The Internet offers the following services: sending and receiving e-mail (electronic mail), transferring files between computers, participating in discussion groups through newsgroups and mailing lists, searching and retrieving information, chat, Internet relay chat, instant messaging, Internet telephony (voice chat), and on-line shopping. Newsgroups contain databases of messages on topics. They are similar to mailing lists, except that e-mail messages are posted to newsgroup sites. Bulletin boards and discussion groups offer similar services. People "surf the net" to find information and download files and connect directly to other computers. Web pages are used to communicate with customers and suppliers, describe organizations and products, tender documents, and provide services (banking, stocks, and software).

Similar to most other communication breakthroughs before it, the initial media and popular reaction to the Internet has been mostly negative. For example, it has been described as "awash in pornography," and as making people "sad and lonely." Yet, counter to the initial claim that Internet use causes depression and social isolation, the body of evidence is mainly to the contrary. It is argued that like the telephone and television before it, the Internet by itself is not a main-effect cause of anything. Research in psychology investigates how social identity, social interaction, and relationship formation may be different on the Internet than in real life.

File sharing is emerging as an important use of the Internet. The widely-recognized peer-to-peer (*P2P*) file-sharing applications (e.g., Napster, Kazaa, and Emule) have gained their reputation due to the large number of people using them and because of the public controversy that has been created about whether or not their use is legal. They also have a similar impact in the research community. File-sharing applications have demonstrated that from basic peer-to-peer interactions, it is possible to dynamically create social networks within which people can collaborate by sharing and retrieving information.

Because of the popularity of Napster and its successors (Gnutella, Kazaa, Morpheus, and E-Donkey), file sharing has become the killer P2P application. Gnutella addressed Napster's shortfall of complete decentralization, but its unstructured nature raised concerns over its search mechanism's efficiency and scalability. In 2001, P2P applications started to use *superpeers* (a set of more powerful nodes in a heterogeneous network) to transform the existing flat topology of these networks into a hierarchical one. Superpeers are considered faster and more reliable than normal peers and take on server-like responsibilities. For example, in the case of file sharing, a superpeer builds an index of the files shared by its client peers and participates in the search protocol on their behalf. This improves scalability by limiting the flood of search traffic.

The most successful peer-to-peer application appears to be BitTorrent. In BitTorrent, groups of peers with the same interest in downloading a specific files cooperate to accelerate the process. Essentially, a tracker node stores a list of peers in the group, thus letting new peers join. Each peer stores pieces of the file. Cooperating peers download and upload required pieces. If a peer stops uploading, other peers will likely block it; that is, they stop uploading to it. This implements the tit-for-tat-like process. Seeders, peers that store the whole file, are crucial to a group's functioning. If a group contains no seeders, eventually some pieces of the file might be completely missing from the group. Because peers gain nothing themselves by being seeders, the system requires some *altruistic behavior* from peers. This requirement is reflected by the mantra often repeated on BitTorrent Web sites: leave your download running for a little while after you've got the entire file.

BACKGROUND

McKenna and Bargh (2000) identified four major differences between relationship formation on the Internet and in real life, and their implications for self and identity, social interaction, and relationships: one's greater anonymity, the greatly reduced importance of physical appearance and physical distance as "gating features" to relationship development, and one's greater control over the time and pace of interactions.

Anolli, Villani, and Riva (2005) considered psychological and social features of a particular electronic environment, the chat room. Their results highlighted that chat room users were not a homogeneous group, but were composed of different personality types. This specific virtual environment is crowded with similar individuals, who were looking for independence but who needed also to be supported and encouraged. They created deep on-line relationships, but these remained limited to the virtual world. Anolli et al. (2005) also point out that the access age in chat is remarkably low. It is likely that chat is combined with the desire for independence, as well as with the need to raise self-esteem, peculiar to teenagers who are looking for autonomy.

Peris et al. (2002) argue that relationships developed online are healthy and a complement to face-to-face relationships. Previous research has been largely silent about what precisely influences online friendship formation and has ignored motives for online communication as potential explanations. Peter et al. (2005) tested a path model of adolescent friendship formation including, as predictors introversion/extraversion, online self-disclosure, motive for social compensation, and frequency of online communication. Their path analysis showed that extraverted adolescents self-disclosed and communicated online more frequently, which, in turn, facilitated the formation of online friendships. "*Extraverts* would be expected to use online chats to strike up new acquaintances given their high levels of sociability" (Peris et al., 2002). *Introverted* adolescents

were more strongly motivated to communicate online to compensate for lacking social skills. This increased their chances of making friends online. Among them, a stronger motive for social compensation also led to more frequent online communication and online self-disclosure, resulting in more online friendships.

Users can become addicted to the Internet. Addiction to the Internet shares some of the negative aspects of substance addiction and can lead to consequences such as failing school, and family and relationship problems. Ng and Wiemer-Hastings (2005) show that online games are, for most users, an alternative to other forms of social entertainment. If online games did not exist, then these users would not seek friends or social situations such as parties, bars, or clubs, but perhaps other forms of socializing online in the form of e-mail, chat rooms, or instant messenger.

According to Nagaraya et al. (2006), P2P has democratized the way people use computing. It links people irrespective of their location and affiliation and raises numerous possibilities of interaction and collaboration, not only in social activities but also in commercial ones. It presents an opportunity for sharing digital content, computing, and other resources, and enables unbounded social interaction and collaboration without depending on centralized facilities. Applications such as communication, conferencing, network gaming, voting, opinion polling, and synchronized viewing of video streams can leverage this P2P feature. Existing applications such as NetMeeting and some features in today's instant-messaging systems give us glimpses of what is possible. A few P2P applications support collaboration between people in an enterprise, but they are specialized to deal with data and processes in a work setting.

De Bruijn and Stathis (2003) define socio-cognitive grids as the term which embraces the fields of grid, pervasive, and peer-to-peer computing. This includes applications which are composed of computer resources together with seamlessly integrated and interacting intelligences, both computational processes (e.g., software agents) and human processors (i.e., people). Ramirez-Cano and Pitt (2005) describe the properties of peer-to-peer networks in various scenarios, including sharing distributed resources, customer-to-customer interaction, mass user support, and digital rights management. They study the use of classical sociological theory of social structures and interpersonal relations for analyzing social networks on the Internet. Finally, they address the issue of psychological impacts of peer-to-peer networks on human behavior.

Hales and Patarin (2005) analyze why some peer-to-peer systems work. Predicting the complex interactions between nodes due to the constantly changing user topology is almost impossible. Essentially, if users move between groups (leave one group and enter another) on the basis of the quality of the service they receive, groups containing many freeloaders will tend to "die," as peers leave the group for better groups. Groups that contain altruists will tend to grow because they support a quality service. Users might choose unconditional altruism rather than the more restrictive reciprocal approach in order to select peers acting for the group's benefit at their own individual cost.

Hughes et al. (2005) study the deviant behavior on P2P file sharing networks. However, the activities of P2P community members are sometimes at odds with what real-world authorities consider acceptable. One example is the use of P2P networks to distribute illegal pornography. Empirical evidence suggests that a small subset of the peer-to-peer community produces the majority of P2P-mediated illegal pornography.

SOCIAL NETWORKS ON THE INTERNET

People use the Internet primarily because of all the benefits it provides, including greatly reduced cost, increased speed, and ease of use compared to other means of communication. Users can naturally become addicted to it. Our discussion in this section concentrates on three Internet applications that have significant social aspects associated with them: chat, file sharing, and online games.

Chat interaction may or may not be accompanied with face-to-face meetings. Chat users seem to be people who constantly need support and approval. They may reach a high degree of disclosure, saying everything that they have in mind, without strict emotional control. For this intrinsically gratifying condition, they likely look for others who are similar to them, as Bonebrake (2002) pointed out. In opposition to the perspective of Mckenna and Bargh (2000), anxiety and loneliness are not peculiar features of those who have the inclination to form online relationships. As a matter of fact, individuals who form online relationships appear to be no less socially skilled than others (Bonebrake, 2002).

One of the factors leading to beginning and maintaining socially satisfying relationships via chat lies in the familiarity principle. According to this principle, we find people who we are familiar with to be nicer, friendlier, and more trustworthy. Because familiarity does not necessarily require direct interaction, people can use online chats to satisfy their need for social contacts with friendly people, at least at the beginning of the chat interaction. One can access an online chat room without actually saying anything (by only monitoring ongoing conversations), until one becomes familiar with a number of chat users. By listening and/or reading conversations, chat users are able to form impressions about other people's personalities and values through their exposure. Interaction increases the sense of niceness attributed to other people. The familiarity, the frequency of interaction, or a nickname's appeal contributes to the feel that people are nicer. Chatters often comment that virtual online friends are as familiar as face-to-face friends. Online chats allow the discovery of the nice people so that one can choose how and when to interact with them without necessarily self-exposing. "Chatting" reinforces the feeling of self-sufficiency, and minimizes efforts and social risks during the interaction. The perceived quality of the satisfaction in the relationship with another person is decisive for maintaining interpersonal relationships, whether face-to-face or online. The Internet facilitates the development of relationships, but this does not necessarily imply satisfaction. There is a wide range of possibilities as far as Internet relationships are concerned, such as short online chats, long-lasting friendships, or love affairs that can remain in the virtual world or can be transferred to the real world. Studies (e.g., Anolli et al., 2005) however, show that most relationships developed online are weak.

Peer-to-peer file-sharing systems are massively deployed and appear to support high levels of desirable emergent functionality, such as cooperation and altruism. However, these systems generally aren't engineered according to certain methodologies. Rather, these systems are implemented informally within open-source communities and essentially tested "in the wild." Systems that work will tend to be adopted, resulting in millions of users downloading and running the P2P client software on their machines and connecting over the Internet, which becomes a node in the system.

P2P (peer-to-peer) file-sharing has led to many disputes about copyright laws and has become "a worldwide problem." Given the difficulties in implementing copyright laws, Lu (2006) analyzed the impact of P2P on music production, and some other general economic, social, and ethical implications of this technology. The paper recognizes, on the one hand, the significance of P2P as an advanced technology for popularizing music and sharing human and spiritual values with more people; on the other hand, it points to several critical issues caused by the current illegal use of this technology for sharing copyrighted music files, e.g., the serious damage to music production and the infringement on copyright holders' interests. The technological conditions, social demands, and problems with the current type of music production have deepened the present crisis and suggest that a new type of music production is needed. Legislation should enhance such a new development, support P2P technology in the interests of the public, protect copyrights, and regulate P2P stakeholders' interests in a balanced manner according to the ethics of law.

Researchers have studied how anonymity affects computer-mediated communication. Some have argued that anonymity generally increases the likelihood of engaging in deviant online behavior. Such findings suggest that when online, people might engage in behaviors that would ordinarily incur strong social disapproval or sanction. Other researchers, however, have suggested that anonymity's consequences in computer-mediated communication can be better understood in terms of group-specific social norms. If, however, this behavior is due to the influence of pre-inscribed group norms, it might be that sharing illegal sexual material on P2P file-sharing networks merely reflects deeper societal issues, requiring more subtle approaches to discouraging such behavior.

Social aspects of online games draw users into them. These gamers seek social experiences that are not available elsewhere in their lives. Even with high usage times, research shows users normally cannot be categorized as addicted, because they do not exhibit the behaviors of addicts. Since it is apparent that most users in online games are not addicted, determining how they spend their time while gaming could explain their attraction to the games. These social aspects and in-game activities need an in-depth exploration.

FUTURE TRENDS

The model by Peter et al. (2005) suggests that the antecedents of online friendship formation are more complex than previously assumed and that motives for online communication should be studied more closely.

Future research should address new forms of social networking on Internet. The first example is compromising peer-to-peer interactions with digital rights. For instance twenty second music samples can be made available in a music store or on the Internet, allowing users to buy whole songs with the right to share them, fully or partially, with friends on a peer-to-peer network. In a mass user-support scenario, a user's software agents may contact those of other users in a peer-to-peer network in order to get information of interest, such as data about the neighborhood of a house considered for purchase. In customer-to-customer scenarios, agents are matching their customers in scenarios such as finding a roommate for renting an apartment.

The field of P2P has seen significant advances over the last five years. The set of core structures, algorithms, and mechanisms developed in this community have helped address various issues, including scale, performance, availability, security, and trust within these networks. However, despite these advances, the field has yet to realize its full potential in the application domain. It's time to move beyond file-sharing applications and fill this void.

The ultimate test for P2P's success will be its ability to support applications of commercial value over the network. Establishing marketplaces and auctions in a P2P setting would create the equivalent of today's Amazon and eBay without the negatives associated with centralization. Current research is certainly targeting a broader P2P application space. Several proposals exist to build more complex applications using the existing base of efficient, scalable core services. Examples include: a digital library (Stribling et al., 2005) a complex, massively multiplayer online game that uses Chord for object location (Douglas et al., 2005), and a commercial content distribution network that assumes the presence of neutral superpeers to perform bookkeeping for downloads between the provider and consumer (Wierzbicki & Goworek, 2005). Research is also ongoing to construct network-wide infrastructures, such as a P2P-based Domain Name System (Park et al., 2004) and a spam-filtering service (Zhou et al., 2003) that can improve overall performance of legacy and P2P applications alike.

CONCLUSION

Empirical evidence confirms that interpersonal communication is the dominant use of the Internet. People's reasons to initiate and maintain interpersonal relationships vary. Regardless of personal reasons, social reasons may also motivate people to seek social contacts through appropriate communication media. However, conflicting claims have been presented in the literature about online management of personal relationships. For example, as computer and Internet use become attached to everyday life, the potential for overuse is introduced, which may lead to addiction. E-mail, chat, and the Web are examples of applications used on the Internet with natures that have addictive properties.

REFERENCES

Anolli, L., Villani, D., & Riva, G. (2005). Personality of people using chat: An on-line research. *CuberPsychology & Behavior, 8*(4), 89-95.

Bonebrake, K. (2002). College student's Internet use, relationship formation, and personality correlates. *CyberPsychology & Behavior 5,*551-557.

De Bruijn, O., & Stathis, K. (2003). Socio-cognitive grids: The net as a universal human resource. *Workshop at Tales of the Disappearing Computing.* Santorini, Greece.

Douglas, S., et al. (2005). Enabling massively multiplayer online gaming applications on a P2P architecture. In *Proceedings of the International Conference on Information and Automation* (pp. 7-12). Colombo, Sri Lanka: IEEE Press.

Hales, D., & Patarin, S. (2005). Computational sociology for systems 'in the wild': The case of BitTorrent. *IEEE Distributed Systems Online, 6*(7), 1-6.

Hughes, D., Walkerdine, J., Coulson, G., & Gibson, S. (2006). Is deviant behavior the norm on P2P file-sharing networks? *IEEE Distributed Systems Online, 7,* 2.

Lu, X. (2006). On P2P file-sharing: A major problem. A Chinese perspective. *Journal of Business Ethics, 63,* 63-73.

McKenna, K., & Bargh, J. (2000). Plan 9 from cyberspace: The implications of the Internet for personality and social psychology. *Personality and Social Psychology Review, 4,* 57-75.

Nagaraja, K., Rollins, S., & Khambatti, M. (2006). Looking beyond the legacy of Napster and Gnutella. *IEEE Distributed Systems Online, 7,* 3.

Ng, B.D., & Wiemer-Hastings, P. (2005). Addiction to the Internet and online gaming. *CyberPsychology & Behavior, 8*(2), 110-113.

Park, K., et al. (2004). CoDNS: Improving DNS performance and reliability via cooperative lookups. In *Proceedings of the Sixth Symposium on Operating Systems Design and Implementation* (OSDI 04), Usenix (pp. 199-214). San Francisco, CA, USA.

Peris, R., Gimeno, M.A., Pinazo, D., et al. (2002). On-line chat rooms: Virtual spaces of interaction for socially oriented people. *CyberPsychology & Behavior, 5,* 43-51.

Peter, J., Valkenburg, P.M., & Schouten, A.P. (2005). Developing a model of adolescent friendship formation on the Internet. *CyberPsychology & Behavior, 8*(5), 423-430.

Ramirez-Cano, D., & Pitt, J. (2005). *Emergent structures of social exchange in socio-cognitive grids.* AP2PC 2004, LNAI 3601 (pp. 74-85). Springer.

Stribling, J., et al. (2005). OverCite: A cooperative digital research library In *Proceedings Fourth International Workshop on Peer-to-Peer Systems (IPTPS 05)* (LNCS 3640, pp. 69-79). Ithaca, NY, USA: Springer.

Wierzbicki, A., & Goworek, K. (2005). Peer-to-peer direct sales. In *Proceedings of the Fifth International Conference On Peer-to-Peer Computing (P2P 05)* (pp. 106-113). Washington, DC, USA: IEEE CS Press.

Zhou, F., et al. (2003). Approximate object location and spam filtering on peer-to-peer systems. In *Proceedings of the ACM/IFIP/Usenix International Middleware Conference (Middleware 03) Rio De Janeiro, Brazil* (LNCS 2672, pp. 1-20). Springer.

KEY TERMS

Altruism: Unselfish regard for the welfare of others.

Chat: Synchronous, computer-mediated communication when two or more actors are present on the Internet at the same time during the interaction.

E-Mail: Asynchronous, computer-mediated communication on the Internet, normally from a sender to a receiver, or from a sender to a group of receivers.

Extrovert: A person whose emotions express themselves readily in external actions and events

Instant Messenger: Service that enables a short message sent from the Internet or a mobile phone to be immediately delivered to receiver on his/her phone.

Internet: A worldwide collection of computer networks ("information highway").

Introvert: A self-centered, introspective individual.

Peer-to-Peer Interactions: Dynamically created social networks on the Internet within which people can collaborate by sharing and retrieving information.

Socio-Cognitive Grid: An application of resources from many networked computers and people at the same time to the same single problem.

Web: A large set of distributed pages created by individual users, which contain links (called hyperlinks) between them and textual and pictorial information.

Software Modernization of Legacy Systems for Web Services Interoperability

Chia-Chu Chiang
University of Arkansas at Little Rock, USA

INTRODUCTION

Software maintenance is an inevitable process due to program evolution (Lehman & Belady, 1985). Adaptive maintenance (Schenidewind, 1987) is an activity used to adapt software to new environments or new requirements due to the evolving needs of new platforms, new operating systems, new software, and evolving business requirements. For example, companies have been adapting their legacy systems to Web-enabling environments of doing business that could not have been imagined even a decade ago (Khosrow-Pour & Herman, 2001; Werthner & Ricci, 2004).

To understand software modernization of legacy systems for Web services, it is necessary to address how legacy integration has evolved from centralized computing to distributed, component-based computing due to the advent and widespread use of object-oriented and client-server technologies. Legacy systems were typically developed on a centralized, terminal-to-host architecture. Users usually accessed their legacy systems through terminals that included character-based menus and data entry screens. Consequently, legacy systems built on the central mainframe are inaccessible remotely without adaptations.

Component-based middleware technologies, such as Java RMI, common object request broker architecture (CORBA), and component object model/distributed component object model (COM/DCOM), provide solutions to support the interoperability of legacy systems in a heterogeneous and distributed environment (Chiang, 2001). Unfortunately, the technologies have proved to be insufficient in application integration solutions for several reasons (Stal, 2002). Although the technologies share common communication architectural foundations, the implementation of each technology differs in several aspects, including the object models provided, the communication protocols, and data marshaling/demarshaling. Due to the proprietary implementations of the technologies, they do not interoperate well with each other. Obviously, existing component-based middleware only partially solves the interoperability problems of legacy systems. More effort is still required to make the legacy systems totally interoperable in a heterogeneous and distributed environment.

BACKGROUND

Web services have been widely considered as a better solution to legacy integration for software interoperability using open standards that include extensible markup language (XML), the simple object access protocol (SOAP), the Web services description language (WSDL), and the universal description, discovery, and integration (UDDI) (Chung, Lin, & Mathieu, 2003; Stal, 2002; Zhang & Yang, 2004). Service requesters and providers follow the Web service standards for message exchanges. When a service provider has a service for public exposure, it must write a description of the service in WSDL and register the service description with UDDI to a global repository. A service requester can then query the repository using UDDI to retrieve the service description. The service requester uses the service description in WSDL to send requests, and the service provider replies to the requests under SOAP.

LEGACY MODERNIZATION FOR WEB SERVICES AND CHALLENGES

There are three main reasons for modernizing legacy systems: to reduce the system evolution risk, to recoup the investment on the systems, and to make the system distributed and scalable for business-to-consumer and business-to-business, as well as making it highly available to Web users.

Companies usually have two approaches to turn their legacy systems into Web services: wrapping and reengineering. Wrapping provides a cost-effective way to integrate legacy systems with Web services into a heterogeneously distributed computing environment. Unfortunately, the wrapping approach requires the whole legacy system to be exposed to the public as a Web service, which fails to properly abstract the system (Vinoski, 2002; Vogels, 2003). Furthermore, the wrapping approach increases the difficulty of maintaining the legacy system in the long run. Thus, the wrapping approach is generally a temporary solution, rather than a strategic one. The reengineering approach applies reverse engineering techniques to legacy systems to recover business rules, and develop Web services from the extracted business rules. This approach streamlines legacy systems but is highly dependent on the success of recovery on the business rules from legacy systems.

Wrapping legacy systems for Web services can be performed through wrappers or adapters. A wrapper is built to encapsulate a legacy system and provide access to the legacy system through the encapsulation layer. This layer exposes only the methods with parameter attributes to remote service requesters. In addition, the wrapper must resolve the incompatible communication issues between the legacy systems and the Web server using SOAP/XML messaging. Therefore, programmers are required to write a wrapper to reconcile the issues, as well as a WSDL for public exposure. Unfortunately,

a wrapper is difficult to maintain, inefficient, and error-prone (Engelen, Gupta, & Pant, 2003). A sample Web service architecture via a wrapper is shown in Figure 1.

Turning legacy systems in middleware-based components into Web services is slightly different from the technique described above. Because the legacy system has already been wrapped in middleware, companies may be unwilling to un-wrap their systems in order to turn the system into a Web service. Fortunately, there are Web services toolkits available to turn middleware-based componentized legacy systems into Web services (Engelen, Gupta, & Pant, 2003). First, the toolkits translate the interface definition of a component in the interface definition language (IDL) into a service description in WSDL for public exposure. These toolkits then provide a wrapper component that enables distributed access to the component as a Web service through SOAP. A service requester can then find the WSDL in the registry and interact with the component as a Web service. Using the Web services toolkits, the creation of a wrapper component can be simplified. However, the technique could quickly reach design limitations as legacy systems continue to evolve. One limitation is that the operating system and programming language support in middleware is

Figure 1. A Web service architecture to access legacy systems via wrappers

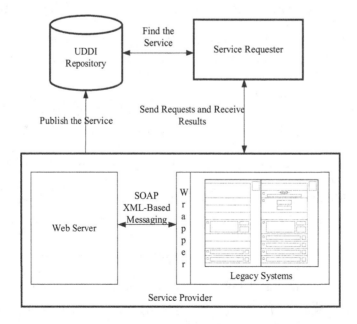

totally dependent on the development and deployment platforms that are offered by middleware vendors. In many situations, the platforms supporting the legacy systems may not be available for the development of middleware. An alternative to solve this problem is to create an adapter on an available platform and use some other strategy.

An adapter can resolve the language and platform dependency through inter-language binding, inter-process communications, and network communications. Compared to a wrapper, the adapter provides a better and more flexible solution to encapsulate legacy systems by reducing some degree of platform, operating system, and programming language dependency. However, an adapter may create an additional point of failure introduced by a service provider. A sample architecture of using an adapter is shown in Figure 2, and an application of this architecture is the IBM Web Services Technologies (Barcia, Hines, Alcott, & Botzum, 2004; Kreger, 2001).

In Figure 2, a Web service adapter is developed for each service invocation. The connection between the legacy systems and the adapter can be any communication protocol that includes TCP/IP and CICS supported by the backend server hosting the legacy system. The Web service adapter may call one single backend system per SOAP service request. It is also possible for the adapter to transform one SOAP request to multiple requests to one or more backend systems. The combined results of the backend requests are composed into one SOAP response, which is then passed back to the server requester.

Unlike the wrapping approach, the reengineering approach develops business rules from legacy systems into Web services. Legacy systems are first thoroughly analyzed for understanding. Code corresponding to the business rules is identified and extracted into a library for the creation of Web services as shown in Figure 3.

Next, the interface of the extracted code as a Web service is constructed for creating the Web service in WSDL. The WSDL specification is then compiled into a skeleton of a service provider as shown in Figure 4. Whenever a service requester sends a request message to the service provider, the skeleton automatically demarshals the request and invokes the service. When the service provider returns the results, the skeleton marshals the results into a response message and sends the response back to the service requester.

The WSDL specification of a service provider is also used to create a stub of a service requester for the invocation of the service remotely. The WSDL specification is retrieved from a UDDI repository, and

Figure 2. A Web service architecture to access legacy systems via adapters

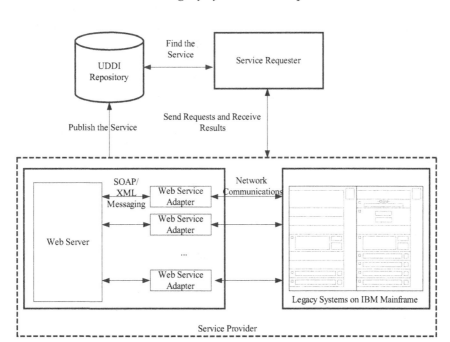

Figure 3. Code extraction from legacy systems

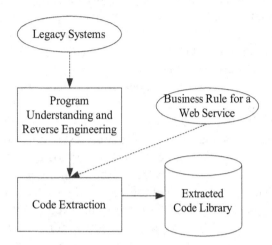

Figure 4. Creation of skeletons via a WSDL compiler

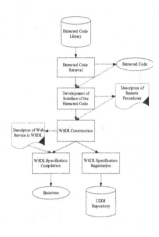

a description of the remote procedures is created from the WSDL specification. The description of the remote procedures is then compiled into a stub of the service requester for marshaling and demarshaling request and response messages at runtime. The development strategy of constructing executable files of a service requester and provider for Web services is illustrated in Figure 5.

In this approach, a WSDL specification does not define any language bindings. This allows stubs and skeletons to be constructed in any programming languages, such as C, C++, Visual Basic, Perl, and Python. Because a service provider's skeleton leaves

Figure 5. Construction of service requester and provider executables

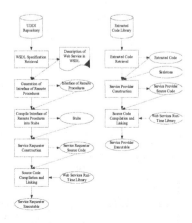

the implementation of the service unspecified, the extracted code from the legacy system can be inserted into the skeleton to make the concrete implementation of the service. This approach is more than just converting code from one language to another. It is the conversion of an entire system architecture into a Web services architecture, including the user interfaces and database structures. The approach to developing Web services takes the same development strategy as the middleware approach for the development of distributed applications. The proxies are automatically generated from a WSDL specification describing the interface of the service. The extracted code from the legacy system fills in the concrete implementation of the service. Samples of the reengineering approach can be found in references (Engelen, Gupta, & Pant, 2003; Graveley, 2001). Two primary Web services architectures supporting the reengineering approach are the Java 2 platform Enterprise Edition (J2EE) and the .NET platform (Erl, 2005). The J2EE platform is a development and runtime environment based on the Java programming language. The .NET platform (MacDonald, 2003) is a proprietary development and runtime environment developed for use with Windows operating systems. The .NET platform provides unified support for a set of programming languages including Visual Basic, C, C++, and C#.

Web services identification plays an important role in the reengineering approach. It starts with program understanding. Program understanding via reverse engineering provides different views of abstraction of legacy systems which are helpful for identifying services. The code corresponding to the services is extracted from the legacy systems in terms of the business rules defined in the systems. Several techniques used for supporting reverse engineering and design recovery activities have been cataloged in various collections and surveys (Arnold, 1994; Bellay & Gall, 1997; Zvegintzov, 1997). Program slicing techniques (Huang et al., 1996; Sneed & Erdos, 1996; Wang, Sun, Yang, He, & Maddineni, 2004) are used to extract source code corresponding to the business rules from legacy systems. The extracted code may be used as a candidate for Web services. Due to the inherent complexity of the system and the language in which it is written, existing program slicing techniques cannot be fully automated yet. Therefore, human interventions are required to filter the candidates and should be kept to a minimum. Clustering techniques (Wiggerts, 1997) can be used to group the relevant extracted code into classes in terms of the attributes that provide promising candidates for Web services.

Despite all its promises and glories (Arsanjani, Hailpern, Martin, & Tarr, 2003), software modernization of legacy systems for Web services is not free of associated risks and challenges (Tilley et al., 2002). From a business perspective, there are issues of cost, manpower, management, maintenance, personnel pressure, and return on investment that must be examined when considering the integration of legacy systems to a Web services computing environment. The immaturity of these technologies may also offer technical challenges. The current generation of Web services infrastructures and tools has problems of large space consumption and performance degradation. Tools of reverse engineering and program slicing are not mature enough to be fully automated. These issues need to be addressed as these technologies evolve. In order to make a rational decision on the potential of each technology, one must assess the costs, limitations, and risks (Seacord, Plakosh, & Lewis, 2003; Ulrich, 2002). The issues, problems, and limitations of modernizing legacy systems for Web services interoperability are summarized as follows:

- **Economics of modernizing legacy systems:** Inability to assess the costs of each approach

- **Security:** Maintaining secure and safe systems and keeping unauthorized user access out
- **Performance:** Degrading the system's performance due to the migration from one environment to another or from one language to another
- **Quality:** Failing to attain the quality of the system due to a poorly designed quality plan or unforeseen results from the migration
- **Acceptance:** Rejection of the system by users due to lack of knowledge of the Internet and its usefulness
- **Exposure points:** Risks associated with accessing the firm's systems remotely
- **Privacy and confidentiality agreements:** Addressing an individual's right to privacy and the sharing of confidential information
- **Automated tools:** Effective tools that reduce user intervention during the migration

FUTURE TRENDS

Companies will continuously modernize their legacy systems from centralized to distributed and Web-enabled environments due to the needs of evolving business requirements. Companies may choose to outsource the legacy modernization process for Web services to another company that specializes in such tasks. Automated tools used for extracting business rules from legacy systems will be continuously required for construction of Web services. Web service support tools that migrate middleware-based components into Web services will continue to improve the technology for reliability and transactional guarantees.

CONCLUSION

The applications of the World Wide Web (WWW) are used not only for information gathering, but also as an exciting technological breakthrough providing companies with new opportunities for conducting their businesses. Business applications must respond to changing business requirements quickly to combat conflicts resulting from having heterogeneous computing environments. Modernizing legacy systems for Web services plays a key role for companies to achieve their system integration. The critical issues discussed in this paper provide many implications and challenges to the companies. These issues must be dealt with before new issues arise as Web services technologies continue to evolve.

REFERENCES

Arnold, R. S. (1994). *Software reengineering.* Los Altimos, CA: IEEE Computer Society Press.

Arsanjani, A., Hailpern, B., Martin, J., & Tarr, P. (2003). Web services: Promises and compromises. *ACM Queue, 1*(1). Retrieved March 27, 2006, from http://www.acmqueue.org/modules.php?name=Content&pa=showpage&pid =31

Barcia, R., Hines, B., Alcott, T., & Botzum, K. (2004). *IBM WebSphere: Development and advanced configuration.* New York: Prentice Hall PTR.

Bellay, B., & Gall, H. (1997). A comparison of four reverse engineering tools. *Proceedings of the 4th Working Conference on Reverse Engineering* (pp. 2-11).

Chiang, C-C. (2001). Wrapping legacy systems for use in heterogeneous computing environments. *Information and Software Technology, 43*(8), 497-507.

Chikofsky, E. J., & Cross II, J. H. (1990). Reverse engineering and design recovery: A taxonomy. *IEEE Software, 7*(1), 13-17.

Christensen, E., Curbera, F., Meredith, G., & Weerawarana, S. (2001). *Web services description language (WSDL) 1.1.* Retrieved March 27, 2006, from http://www.w3.org/TR/wsdl

Chung, J.-Y., Lin, K.-J., & Mathieu, R. G. (2003). Web services computing: Advancing software interoperability. *Computer, 36*(10), 35-37.

Engelen, R., Gupta, G., & Pant, S. (2003). Developing Web services for C and C++. *IEEE Internet Computing, 7*(2), 53-61.

Erl, T. (2005). *Service-oriented architecture: Concepts, technology, and design.* New York: Prentice Hall PTR.

Graveley, A. (2001). Making SOAP with soup. *Proceedings of Ottawa Linux Symposium.* Retrieved from http://lwn.net/2001/features/OLS/pdf/pdf/soup.pdf

Haas, H., & Brown, A. (2004). *Web services glossary.* Retrieved March 27, 2006, from http://www.w3.org/TR/ws-gloss/

Huang, H., Tsai, W. T., Bhattacharya, S., Chen, X. P., Wang, Y., & Sun, J. (1996). Business rule extraction from legacy code. *Proceedings of IEEE 20th Computer Software and Applications* (pp. 162-167).

Institute of Electrical and Electronics Engineering. (1993). *IEEE standard for software maintenance* (IEEE Publication No. IEEE STD 1219). Los Altimos, CA: IEEE Computer Society Press.

Khosrow-Pour, M., & Herman, N. (2001). Web-enabled technologies assessment and management: critical issues. In Khosrow-Pour & Herman (Eds.), *Managing Web-enabled technologies in organizations: A global perspective* (pp. 1-22). Hershey, PA: Idea Group Publishing.

Kreger, H. (2001). *Web services conceptual architecture (WSCA 1.0).* Retrieved March 27, 2006, from http://www-306.ibm.com/software/solutions/webservices/pdf/WSCA.pdf

Lehman, M. M., & Belady, L. (1985). *Program evolution: Processes of software change.* London: Academic Press.

MacDonald, M. (2003). *Microsoft .NET distributed applications: Integrating XML Web services and .NET remoting.* Redmond, NY: Microsoft Press.

Schneidewind, N. F. (1987). The state of software maintenance. *IEEE Transactions on Software Engineering, 13*(3), 303-310.

Seacord, R. C., Plakosh, D., & Lewis, G. (2003). *Modernizing legacy systems: Software technologies, engineering processes, and business practices.* Boston: Addison-Wesley.

Sneed, H. M., & Erdos, K. (1996). Extracting business rules from source code. *Proceedings of IEEE 4th International Workshop on Program Comprehension* (pp. 240-247).

Stal, M. (2002). Web services: Beyond component-based computing. *Communications of the ACM, 45*(10), 71-76.

Tilley, S., Gerdes, J., Hamilton, T., Huang, S., Müller, H., & Wong, K. (2002). Adoption challenges in migrating to Web services. *Proceedings of the Fourth International Workshop on Web Site Evolution.*

Ulrich, W. M. (2002). *Legacy systems: Transformation strategies.* New York: Prentice Hall PTR.

Vinoski, S. (2002). Web services interaction model. *IEEE Internet Computing, 6*(3), 89-91.

Vogels, W. (2003). Web services are not distributed objects. *IEEE Internet Computing, 7*(6), 59-66.

Wang, X., Sun, J., Yang, X., He, Z., & Maddineni, S. R. (2004). Business rules extraction from large legacy systems. *Proceedings of IEEE Eighth European Conference on Software Maintenance and Reengineering* (pp. 249-254).

Werthner, H., & Ricci, F. (2004). E-commerce and tourism. *Communication of the ACM, 47*(12), 101-105.

Wiggerts, T. A. (1997). Using clustering algorithms in legacy systems remodularization. *Proceedings of the Fourth Working Conference on Reverse Engineering* (pp. 33-43).

Zhang, Z., & Yang, H. (2004). Incubating services in legacy systems for architectural migration. *Proceedings of the 11th Asia-Pacific Software Engineering Conference* (pp. 196-203).

Zvegintzov, N. (1997). A resource guide to year 2000 tools. *Computer, 30*(3), 58-63.

KEY TERMS

Reverse Engineering: Reverse engineering is the process of discovering the functions and their interrelationships of a software system as well as creating representations of the system in another form or at a higher level of abstraction.

SOAP: The W3C definition of SOAP is "a set of protocols governing the format and processing rules of SOAP messages."

Software Maintenance: Software maintenance is the process of enhancing and adapting a software product after delivery as well as correcting faults.

Software Reengineering: Chikofsky and Cross define software reengineering as "the examination and alternation of a software system to reconstitute it in a new form and subsequent implementation of that form."

UDDI: UDDI is a Web services registry and discovery technology for strings and retrieving Web services interfaces.

Web Services: The W3C definition of a Web service is "a software system designed to support interoperable machine-to-machine interaction over a network. It has an interface described in WSDL. Other systems interact with the Web services using SOAP messaging defined in the WSDL specification."

WSDL: The W3C definition of WSDL is "an XML format for describing Web services interfaces, message types, operations, and protocol mappings."

The Speech-Enabled Web

L. E. Moser
University of California, Santa Barbara, USA

P. M. Melliar-Smith
University of California, Santa Barbara, USA

INTRODUCTION

Speech recognition and synthesis technology has advanced to the point where the use of voice input and output is now feasible for Web-based applications over the Internet. This article describes applications, standards, and architectures for a speech-enabled Web, or SpeechWeb.

The ready availability of mobile devices, such as cell phones and PDAs with wireless access to the Internet but without a conventional desktop keyboard, mouse, and large display, make voice input and output very compelling. Voice input and output for small screen/keyboard devices, and for hands-/eyes-free situations, is essential to enable the user's interaction with the device and to make it more user friendly.

Voice can be used to provide access to Web-based services from a mobile device, making it practical to access the Web anytime and anywhere, whether at work, at home, or on the go. Voice can also be used as an adjunct to desktop browsers with high-resolution graphical displays, providing an alternative means of interaction for the user.

Many everyday applications used by millions of people can benefit from a speech-enabled Web. Such applications include those that provide travel directions, weather information, restaurant and hotel reservations, appointments and reminders, voice mail, and e-mail. Particular groups of users, and particular sectors of the economy, can benefit substantially from a speech-enabled Web.

Standards for the speech-enabled Web, such as the voice extensible markup language, also known as VoiceXML (VoiceXML Forum, 2006), and the speech application language tags, also known as SALT (SALT Forum, 2006), aim to allow people to access Web-based services via key pads, spoken commands, listening to pre-recorded speech, and synthetic speech.

Such speech-enabled and multi-modal standards support interoperability and portability of the Web-based applications.

Various architectures for the speech-enabled Web have been investigated (Eurescom, 2000; Frost, 2005). In the speech-enabled Web, the Web page provides the means to scope the dialog with the user, limiting interactions to navigating the page, traversing links, and filling in forms. Speech recognition grammars are derived from speech-enabled Web pages, and are used to direct speech recognition software.

As speech recognition software improves, as the processing power, memory capacity, and battery life of mobile devices increase, and as Web accessibility becomes more pervasive, speech-enabled mobile devices that provide access to the Web will become readily available and, indeed, eventually ubiquitous. The economic impact is likely to be substantial.

BACKGROUND

Much progress has been made in creating the speech-enabled Web, allowing it to support not only keyboard and mouse navigation but also voice input and output.

In the mid 1990s, the Speech-Aware Multimedia (SAM) system (Hemphill & Thrift, 1995) made the Mosaic browser speech-aware, and thus demonstrated the ability to surf the Web by voice. It implemented the notion of a *speakable hotlist*, by which the user could associate a grammar or a language with a URL. Correspondingly, the user could speak an underlined hypertext link on a Web page. It also implemented the idea of a *smart page*, which associates a grammar with a Web page. The SAM system knows the language for the Web page, recognizes sentences using that language, and passes the results back to the Web page for interpretation.

In March 2000, the VoiceXML Forum released VoiceXML 1.0 for Web-based distributed conversational applications (Lucas, 2000). It was accepted by the World Wide Web Consortium (W3C) two months later as the basis of a W3C dialogue markup language. The VoiceXML Forum continues to produce new versions of the VoiceXML specification (VoiceXML Forum, 2006). In July 2002, the SALT Forum published the SALT specification 1.0 (SALT Forum, 2006). SALT is based on XML and HTML, and supports both multi-modal and pure telephony (speech) input and output.

The Eurescom P923-PF project has investigated various architectures and tools that enable speech access to the Web (Eurescom, 2000). Studies (Zhang, He, Chow, Yang, & Su, 2000) have shown that, with server-only processing, pure voice transmission requires high-speed network bandwidth, and that low-bandwidth connections result in significant degradation of speech recognition quality. Recently, Frost has proposed a possible architecture for the speech-enabled Web in which the speech processing takes place on the client device and the application processing takes place on the server (Frost, 2005). We discuss below alternative architectures, including an architecture in which both the speech and application processing are on the client device and the client applications access server applications and Web pages remotely (Hu, Davis, Prasad, Schuricht, Melliar-Smith, & Moser, 2006). We summarize the advantages and disadvantages of five alternative architectures, which managers might want to consider before committing to a particular architecture.

SPEECH AND THE WEB

Applications

For many applications, such as Web search and on-line shopping, keyboard and mouse are appropriate input media, and a large high-resolution display is desirable. For small screen/keyboard mobile devices and for hands-/eyes-free situations, such as automobiles, voice input and output are more suitable.

Speech technology is useful in many sectors of the economy, including call centers, retail sales, transportation, travel, healthcare, manufacturing, government, banking, and other financial services.

Particular groups of users for which a speech-enabled Web is particularly useful include disabled persons,

military personnel, transportation workers, manufacturing workers, and emergency response personnel.

Many kinds of applications can benefit from a speech-enabled Web. In particular, a speech-enabled Web is useful for:

- Providing operator services, such as asking callers who or what they want, catalog ordering, support and help desks, order tracking, airline departure and arrival information, theater and sports ticket booking, hotel and restaurant reservations, and banking and other financial transactions
- Accessing weather, traffic conditions, maps and directions for hotels, gas stations, banks, restaurants, and the latest news and sports scores
- Maintaining personal calendars, contact lists with names, addresses and telephone numbers, to-do lists, and shopping lists
- Assisting the user in communicating with other people via voice mail, e-mail, SMS and MMS messages.

Standards

The benefit of developing Web pages and applications based on standards is that standards promote portability and interoperability of the applications. The W3C Speech Interface Framework (W3C, 2006) is a suite of markup specifications that includes speech recognition, voice dialogs, pre-recorded speech, and speech synthesis. Some of these specifications are discussed below.

Voice Extensible Markup Language

The Voice Extensible Markup Language (VoiceXML) supports interactive voice applications, and controls the dialog between the applications and the user. VoiceXML pages are downloaded from HTTP servers in the same way as HTML pages.

A simple example of a VoiceXML document that contains a *menu* element and a *form* element is the following:

```
<vxml version="2.0">
<menu>
 <prompt>Say one of:<enumerate/></prompt>
  <choice next="http://www.weather.example/
              weather:vxml">
```

```
    Weather information
  </choice>
  <choice next="http:/wwww.traffic.example/traffic.
              vxml">
    Traffic conditions
  </choice>
</menu>

<form id="login">
  <field name="phone_number" type="phone">
    <prompt>"Please say your phone number
              including area code"
    </prompt>
  </field>
  <field name="pin" type="digits">
    <prompt>"Please say your pin"</prompt>
  </field>
  <block>
    <submit next="/servlet/login"/>
  </block>
</form>
</vxml>
```

This VoiceXML document enables a dialogue such as the following in which a device (D) supplies a prompt and a human (H) provides an item from the menu:

D: Say one of: Weather information, Traffic conditions, Log in

H: Traffic conditions

The device then retrieves and interprets a VoiceXML document from the Web site at www.traffic.example/ traffic.vxml, containing a specification of the next part of the dialogue (in this case, traffic conditions). This particular dialogue uses the *menu* element, but not the *form* element.

The basic dialogue unit of VoiceXML is the *form* element. The *form* element describes a set of *fields* (inputs) needed from the user to complete an interaction between the user's browser and a Web server. Each *field* includes a prompt and a specification of what the user is allowed to say in order to provide the required input. The *form* element also specifies what the server is to do with the set of fields that the user supplies.

The following dialogue uses both the *menu* element and the *form* element.

D: Say one of: Weather information, Traffic conditions, Log in

H: Log in
D: Please say your phone number including area code
H: 805-893-9876
D: Please say your pin
H: 1234

When the browser has the *fields* it needs for log in, it executes the code block containing a submit command, causing the information to be submitted to the Web server for processing.

Interpreters for VoiceXML provide support for common *field* types, such as numbers, digits, telephone numbers, dates, and times. VoiceXML applications may also specify their own *field* types using grammars. VoiceXML enables relatively natural dialogues by allowing grammars to be specified at the *form* level, rather than only the *field* level.

Speech Application Language Tags

The Speech Application Language Tags (SALT) specification (SALTforum, 2006) enables multi-modal and telephony access to the Web by providing access to information, applications, and Web services from PCs, telephones, and PDAs. SALT is an extension of XML, HTML, and other markup languages that adds a speech and telephony interface to Web applications.

The tags defined by SALT are intended to be added to HTML pages, so that they can be browsed via speech, by extending existing browsers. In contrast, VoiceXML is an independent language that can be used to create and hyperlink speech applications.

The W3C Voice Browser Working Group is considering the use of SALT, as it develops the requirements and specifications for the next version of VoiceXML.

Speech Recognition Grammar Specification

The Speech Recognition Grammar Specification (SRGS) (W3C, 2006) allows applications to specify the words and phrases that users are prompted to speak. It provides a way to define the phrases that an application recognizes, including words that may be spoken, patterns in which words may occur, and the spoken language for each word. SRGS aims to enable robust speaker-independent speech recognition.

Speech Synthesis Markup Language

The Speech Synthesis Markup Language (SSML) specification (W3C, 2006) defines an XML-based markup language for creating synthetic speech within an application. SSML enables the control of synthetic speech that includes pronunciation, volume, pitch, and rate of speech. SSML is used in conjunction with VoiceXML to prompt the user and to provide responses to the user.

Standards such as those described above promote interoperability and portability of the applications. However, not many Web pages currently use those standards, and so alternative technologies and architectures must be considered.

Architectures

Several different kinds of architectures have been proposed for the speech-enabled Web (Eurescom, 2000; Frost 2005). These architectures include:

- Speech interfaces to existing HTML pages
- Hyperlinked VoiceXML pages
- Speech application servers, such as those in call centers
- Local recognition remote processing
- Local recognition local processing.

Hybrid architectures that combine one or more of these strategies are also possible. General principles for the design of modern Web architectures can be found in Fielding and Taylor (2002).

Speech Interfaces to Existing HTML Pages

The speech interfaces to existing HTML pages architecture, shown in Figure 1, provides speech access to information already available on the Web. Local speech recognition allows the user to provide training for his/her own voice to improve recognition accuracy.

The advantages of the speech interfaces to existing HTML pages architecture are that:

- Existing HTML pages can be used without modification.
- Multiple Web pages and applications can be integrated, as when a conventional keyboard, mouse, and display are used.

The disadvantages of the speech interfaces to existing HTML pages architecture are that:

- HTML pages are not designed for speech browsing. Rather, HTML pages use icons and other visual graphics to convey information about how

Figure 1. Speech interfaces to existing HTML pages

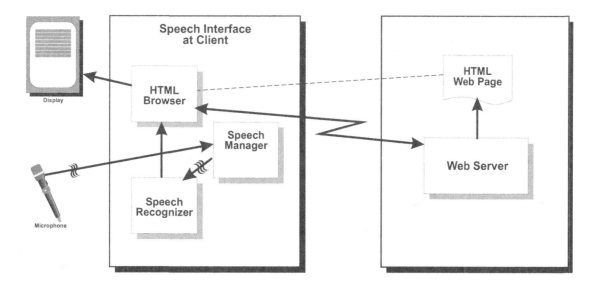

the pages are structured to exploit the user's ability to scan the pages in two dimensions.

- Speech recognition grammars can't be derived from HTML pages.
- Speech recognition accuracy is not good, because of the large number of words and phrases that a user might input.
- The client handsets must be powerful enough to perform speech processing and must provide speech recognition software.

Hyperlinked VoiceXML Pages

The hyperlinked VoiceXML pages architecture is shown in Figure 2. An architecture based on SALT would be similar. VoiceXML pages are executed on VoiceXML browsers on the client device, and include commands for prompting user speech input, invoking recognition grammars, outputting synthesized voice, iterating through blocks of code, and hyperlinking to other VoiceXML pages.

The advantages of the hyperlinked VoiceXML pages architecture are that:

- VoiceXML supports interoperability and portability of speech-enabled Web applications.

- Speech recognition is made more accurate through the use of small recognition grammars derived from the VoiceXML pages.
- Web pages and applications can be designed to accommodate the limited capabilities of speech and the speech recognizer.

The disadvantages of the hyperlinked VoiceXML pages architecture are that:

- The client handsets must be powerful enough to perform speech processing and must provide speech-processing software.
- Developers most supply VoiceXML pages for their speech applications.
- Users must adhere to the limited forms of expression and vocabulary offered by the VoiceXML pages.
- Users are limited to the relatively small number of specially designed VoiceXML pages that exist today. Standard HTML pages cannot be used.

Speech Application Servers

The speech application servers architecture, shown in Figure 3, supports telephone access to remote speech

Figure 2. Hyperlinked VoiceXML pages

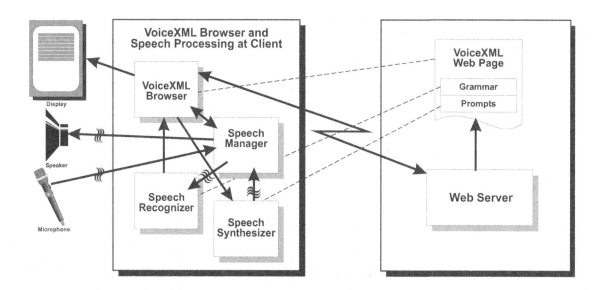

Figure 3. Speech application servers as used in call centers

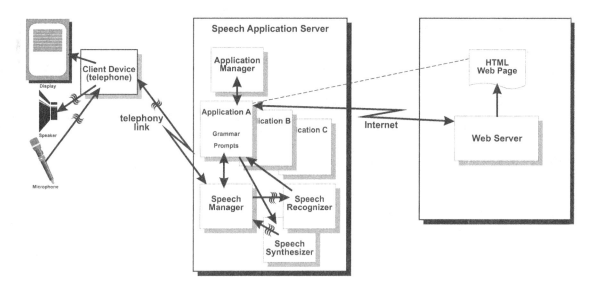

applications, and is based on speech application servers, such as those in call centers, that allow users to telephone in and speak to their applications. Speech and application processing are carried out by the remote speech application servers.

The advantages of the speech application server architecture are that:

- Existing unmodified cell phones, or telephones, can be used to access the applications.
- The applications reside on conventional servers, and can be written in any language.
- Sophisticated applications that require powerful processing and extensive databases can be supported.

The disadvantages of the speech application server architecture are that:

- User voice profiles must be stored at the speech application server provider, or transferred from the client to the server each time they are accessed, to achieve speech recognition accuracy. Most call centers do not maintain individual user profiles.
- Many concurrent users must be supported by the speech application server.
- For security and privacy reasons, some users might not want to store their personal information, such as calendars, contact lists, and health

information, on a remote server provided by a speech application server provider.

Local Recognition Remote Processing

In the Local Recognition Remote Processing (LRRP) architecture (Frost, 2005), shown in Figure 4, the speech applications and their associated recognition grammars are stored on the server, with LRRP browsers on the client devices. Speech recognition is local to the client device, and application processing is remote. When a user accesses a remote application, a grammar is downloaded to the user's browser, where it is used to tailor the speech recognizer for the application. Following recognition of a user's request, the request is sent to the remote application for processing and, finally, the result is returned to the user in the form of synthesized speech.

A user can ask to be connected to other speech applications by uttering a speech hyperlink (e.g., "Can I talk to the weather service?" or "I would like to talk to the weather service.") The Web address of the application is then returned to the browser, which downloads a new recognition grammar from that address and subsequently sends recognized requests to that application.

The advantages of the LRRP architecture are that:

Figure 4. Local recognition remote processing architecture

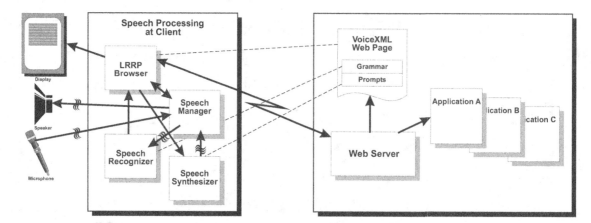

Recognition accuracy is improved because speech is not degraded by a low quality telephony connection.

- The applications reside on conventional servers, and can be written in any language.
- Sophisticated applications, that require powerful processing and extensive databases, can be supported.
- Recognition accuracy is improved by using voice profiles that are maintained locally on the client devices and application-specific grammars that are downloaded to the client devices.
- The LRRP architecture uses VoiceXML pages, which support interoperability and portability of the applications.

The disadvantages of the LLRP architecture are that:

- The client devices must be powerful enough to perform speech processing and must have speech-processing software on them.
- For security and privacy reasons, some users might not want to store their personal information, such as calendars, contact lists and health information, on a remote server.
- Most existing Web pages use HTML, and not VoiceXML, which the architecture requires.

Local Recognition Local Processing

In the Local Recognition Local Processing (LRLP) architecture, shown in Figure 5, both the speech applications and their associated recognition grammars are stored on the client device. The applications running on the client may access remote applications and Web pages on Web servers.

The advantages of the LRLP architecture are that:

- Recognition accuracy is improved by using application-specific grammars and user voice profiles on the client device.
- Applications can support larger vocabularies and more flexibility in sentence structure than VoiceXML pages can.
- Clients and servers communicate by means of text and conventional protocols, for greater efficiency and lower costs.
- Because applications execute on the client's device, the user has greater confidence in the security and privacy of his/her personal information.
- Applications can access a wide range of existing HTML pages and Web services.

The disadvantages of the LRLP architecture are that:

Figure 5. Local Recognition Local Processing architecture

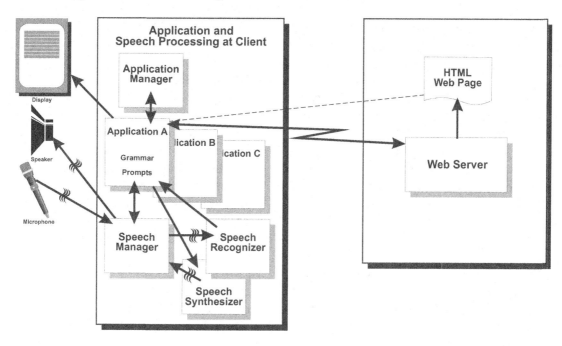

- The client devices must be powerful enough to perform speech processing and must have speech-processing software on them.
- The client device must have a powerful processor and ample memory to run the applications.
- Powerful processors and ample memory might impact battery life.

- Some speech applications require access to large knowledge bases, and are best executed on powerful remote servers, rather than on a client device.

A comparison of the speech-enabled Web architectures is shown in Table 1.

Table 1. Comparison of the speech-enabled Web architectures

	Speech Technology	Application Execution	Specific Grammars	Web Page Design	Application Design
Speech Interfaces to HTML Pages	Local	Remote	None	Standard HTML pages	Not designed for speech
Hyperlinked VoiceXML Pages	Remote	Remote	Defined by VoiceXML pages	VoiceXML pages	Invoked from VoiceXML pages
Speech Application Servers	Remote	Remote	Defined by application	Standard HTML pages	Designed for speech
Local Recognition Remote Processing	Local	Remote	Defined by VoiceXML pages	VoiceXML pages	Invoked from VoiceXML pages
Local Recognition Local Processing	Local	Local	Defined by application	Standard HTML pages	Designed for speech

FUTURE TRENDS

To enable the widespread adoption and use of speech technology on the Web, a number of challenges remain, some of which have been identified in Deng and Huang (2004). As mobile devices acquire more powerful processors and more memory capacity, the Local Recognition Local Processing architecture will become more feasible.

Currently, speech-enabled applications typically use short commands from the human that are translated into navigational or functional operations. What is needed is speech recognition technology that supports a more natural, conversational style similar to that which humans use to communicate with one another.

The accuracy of the speech recognition system can be increased by training the speech recognizer to the voice of the particular user. It can also be increased by employing adaptations of the vocabulary of the speech recognizer to the current and recent past context of interactions with the individual user.

Background noise remains a problem for speech recognition systems, particularly in noisy environments. The quality of the microphone, and the use of a headset to decrease the distance between the microphone and the speaker's mouth, can improve recognition accuracy. Moreover, the speech recognition and application software can be designed to seek confirmation from the user or to ask questions of the user when the response is below an acceptable threshold of confidence scores.

A challenging problem is the use of speech input and output for services that involve multiple applications or multiple Web pages. An example is, "Find a Chinese restaurant near Susan's house." This request involves both a contact service to obtain the address of Susan's house and a local search service to obtain the name, address, and telephone number of a Chinese restaurant near that address.

Integration of multiple applications, and multiple grammars, is not too difficult for a small number of applications that have been designed and programmed to work together. However, future systems will need to support tens or hundreds of applications, many of which will be designed and programmed independently. Integration of those applications and their grammars will be a challenge.

For hand-held devices, battery life is a problem, particularly when speech recognition software or applications require powerful processors. Novel battery technologies, or possibly fuel cells, might solve the battery life problem.

CONCLUSION

The use of voice input and output, in addition to text and graphics, as a human interface for accessing the Web, increases ease of use and provides substantial benefits to the user. It allows individuals to access information, applications, and services on the Web more readily, particularly from their mobile devices. Standards for speech-enabled Web pages, such as VoiceXML and SALT, promote interoperability and portability of voice-enabled applications on the Web; however, standard HTML pages are more readily available. The choice of architecture for the speech-enabled Web depends on a number of factors, including the processing power of the mobile device, network bandwidth and latency considerations, and the need or desire to use existing HTML pages.

REFERENCES

Deng, L., & Huang, X. (2004). Challenges in adopting speech recognition. *Communications of the ACM, 47*(1), 69-75.

Eurescom. (2000). The European institute for research and strategic studies in telecommunications. Report EDIN 0010-0923 of Project P923–PF. MultiLingual Web sites. Best practice, guidelines and architectures. Retrieved 27 July, 2007 from http://www.eurescom. de/~pub-deliverables/P90D-series/P923/D1Vol4/ P923D1Vol4.pdf

Fielding, R.T., & Taylor, R.N. (2002). Principled design of the modern Web architecture. *ACM Transactions on Internet Technology, 2*(2), 115-150.

Frost, R.A. (2005). Call for a public-domain Speech-Web. *Communications of the ACM, 48*(11), 45-49.

Grasso, M.A., Ebert, D.S., & Finin, T.W. (1998). The integrality of speech in multi-modal interfaces. *ACM Transactions on Computer-Human Interaction, 5*(4), 303-325.

Hemphill, C.T., & Thrift, P.R. (1995). Surfing the Web by voice. *Proceedings of the ACM Multimedia '95 Electronic Conference*. San Francisco, 215-222.

Hu, M., Davis, Z., Prasad, S., Schuricht, M., Melliar-Smith, P. M., & Moser, L.E. (2006). Speech-enabled Web services for mobile devices. *Proceedings of the 2006 International Conference on Semantic Web and Web Services,* Las Vegas, NV (pp. 103-109).

Knight, S., Gorrell, G., Rayner, M., Milward, D., Koeling, R., & Lewin, I. (2001). Comparing grammar-based and robust approaches to speech understanding: A case study. *Proceedings of Eurospeech 2001, Seventh European Conference of Speech Communication and Technology,* Aalborg, Denmark (pp. 1779-1782).

Lucas, B. (2000). VoiceXML for Web-based distributed conversational applications. *Communications of the ACM, 43*(9), 53-57.

McTear, M. (2002). Spoken dialogue technology: Enabling the conversational user interface. *ACM Computing Surveys, 34*(1), 90-169.

Oviatt, S., & Cohen, P. (2000). Multi-modal interfaces that process what comes naturally. *Communications of the ACM, 43*(3), 45-53.

SALT Forum. (2006). *Speech application language tags (SALT) specification 1.0.* Retrieved 27 July, 2007 from http://www.saltforum.org/saltforum/downloads/SALTTechnicalWhitePaper.pdf

VoiceXML Forum. (2000). VoiceXML Specification. Retrieved 27 July, 2007 from http://www.voicexml.org/specs/VoiceXML-100.pdf

W3C. (2006). *Voice browser activity.* Retrieved 27 July, 2007 from http://www.w3.org/Voice

Zhang, W., He, L., Chow, Y., Yang, R., & Su, Y. (2000). The study on distributed speech recognition system.

Proceedings of the IEEE International Conference on Acoustical Speech and Signal Processing, Istanbul, Turkey (pp. 1431-1434).

S

KEY TERMS

Speech Application Language Tags (SALT): A standard that enables multi-modal and telephony access to the Web by providing access to information, applications, and Web services from PCs, telephones, and PDAs.

Speech Recognition: The process of interpreting human speech for transcription or as a method of interacting with a computer, using a computer equipped with a source of speech input, such as a microphone.

Speech Recognition Grammar Specification (SRGS): A standard that allows applications to specify the words and phrases that users are prompted to speak.

Speech Synthesis: The artificial production of human speech. Speech synthesis systems are also called text-to-speech systems in reference to their ability to convert text into speech.

Speech Synthesis Markup Language (SSML): A standard that specifies the rendering of synthesized speech to the user.

SpeechWeb: A collection of hyper-linked applications that are distributed over the Internet and are accessible by spoken commands and queries that are input through remote end-user devices.

Voice Extensible Markup Language (VoiceXML): A standard that is used for defining dialogs and for specifying the exchange of information between a user and a speech application.

Standards in Asynchronous E-Learning Systems

Sergio Gutiérrez
University Carlos III of Madrid, Spain

Abelardo Pardo
University Carlos III of Madrid, Spain

Carlos Delgado Kloos
University Carlos III of Madrid, Spain

INTRODUCTION

E-learning has evolved very rapidly in recent years, from a first stage in which a set of documents were simply made available to the students in an electronic platform, to current tools that integrate not only academic but also administrative aspects in educational institutions. Today, learning is possible virtually anywhere, anytime and new scenarios are possible thanks to the technological support available. The so-called "learning management systems" (LMS) or "learning content management systems" (LCMS) now must handle aspects ranging from tuition fees to personalized pedagogical approaches or collaborative activities.

But this widespread presence of learning activity requires its material to be interoperable among different platforms. A course that can only be used in one single platform is bound to be accessed by a very small percentage of its potential users. Also, learning material for this new scenario includes a much wider variety of resources, and as a consequence the production stage has also increased its complexity. E-learning platforms, then, need to be able to guarantee interoperability, and the production of material could be greatly improved by accessing and reusing learning objects from other courses.

The answer to these needs are international standards to define a common framework to make learning software adaptable, interoperable, and reusable. But e-learning is so wide and touches so many aspects that the task of defining such standards is being done gradually. Vendors and tools are adopting them gradually by providing, in some cases, partial compliance.

STANDARDS, INTEROPERABILITY AND REUSE

With the current education landscape, standards are needed to cover at least two crucial aspects when having access to as much information as offered on the Internet. The first of these needs is interoperability. The introduction of technology in a context as complex as education has translated into a wide variety of LMSs. Also, since most of the simple tasks involved in this context are suitable for computer support, an even larger number of tools appeared to fill this gap.

As happened in other fields, most of these tools started manipulating data stored in their proprietary formats. For example, a tool from a particular vendor for producing quizzes would store questions, answers, feedback, etc., in a format that only such a product would be able to understand. So the need for common descriptions and data representation became immediately apparent. The rationale behind this need is that content can be manipulated by more than one platform, thus extending its use.

But a second aspect in which standards are perceived as crucial is to facilitate the reuse of educational material. Due to the presence of technology in the learning process, producing effective educational material has become an even more complex task. The possibility of reusing parts of learning material is identified as a departure from typical inflexible training material to a scenario in which large databases are populated with granular objects written independently from the delivery media.

The metaphor used to explain the use of learning objects is based on building blocks that, with the right shapes, allow the construction of arbitrarily complex structures. A learning object is informally defined as a set of generic information objects with its own description suitable to be reused in multiple learning scenarios. But producing learning material from learning objects is feasible if they are thoroughly annotated with information including identification, description of their content, information on how they were created, contextualization data, access requirements, etc.

It is precisely in this aspect where the largest standardization effort has been made. The Learning Object Metadata Standard (IEEE 1484.12.1-2002) was conceived to define the information that must accompany each learning object to facilitate its reuse. A more detailed description of this standard is provided in the following sections.

The vision of a large pool of databases containing perfectly documented learning objects capable of adapting to multiple LCMS has been partially fulfilled. First, there is a need for critical mass in the amount of available objects for it to be fully incorporated into content production methodology. Second, the more detailed information a learning object has about itself, the easier the reuse in multiple learning scenarios, but including such information may be tedious and users are usually reluctant to do it. Techniques for automatic metadata acquisition have been studied as an alternative to alleviate the problem, but their success is highly dependent on the context, This example reflects the difficulties faced by the standardization process.

But the goal of fully interoperable e-learning platforms and material is not restricted only to content, but to all aspects involved in the process: content organization, tests, student profiles, content sequencing, etc. A more detailed account of the most relevant initiatives is given in the following sections.

Figure 1. Standardization process

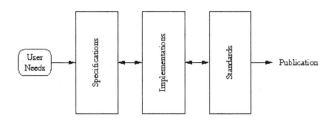

In the e-learning community, there is a very significant amount of activity in this context covering virtually every aspect of the learning process from simple content organization to administrative aspects. Figure 1 illustrates how this type of activity is related to the standardization process.

This process is the last of a set of steps, at the beginning of which are the users of the e-learning technologies (learners, teaching staff, content developers, administrative personnel, etc.). There are numerous institutions that actively participate in providing specifications as well as implementing some of them. It is in this context where users usually perceive the advances in e-learning. All these specifications, models, and guidelines may become what is informally called a *de facto* standard meaning that, even though there is no international standard published, there is a somewhat large community of users.

CURRENT STANDARDS AND SPECIFICATIONS

Given the important role taken by the specifications, models, and guidelines, their study is fundamental for understanding what could be called a broader standard landscape in e-learning. It is for this reason that a description follows of not only the most relevant standards in the context of e-learning, but also of the most significant specifications, models, and guidelines being used in e-learning tools.

IEEE Learning Technology Standards Committee: Learning Object Metadata

The Institute of Electrical and Electronics Engineers (IEEE) is a non-profit organization offering technical and professional information, resources, and services to a large portion of the engineering community. The Learning and Technology Standards Committee (LTSC) within the institute is focused on developing and publishing technical standards as well as recommending practices and guides for learning technology. Its tasks are organized in work groups specializing in different aspects of the e-learning spectrum.

Probably the most relevant contribution of this institute so far is the publication of the IEEE Standard for Learning Object Metadata (1484.12.1-2002), a conceptual data schema that defines the structure of a metadata instance for learning objects. In this context, a learning object is simply any entity that is used for learning.

The goal of this standard is to define the minimum set of attributes to be attached to these objects in order for them to be managed, located, and evaluated efficiently. These attributes try to capture not only simple administrative aspects but also pedagogical grade level prerequisites as well. One key feature of this standard is that it contemplates the possibility of extending the set of attributes for specific purposes.

Attributes are divided into the following categories:

General: It includes generic information about the object, such as its title, identifier, catalog number, description, keywords, structure, etc.

Life cycle: This category contains attributes related to the evolution of the object such as version, contributor, status, etc.

Meta-metadata: A description of the metadata attached to the object. It contains information about the contributors to the marking, language, etc.

Technical: These attributes are oriented toward how the object needs to be manipulated in a platform on aspects such as requirements, type of object, versions, duration, how to install the resource, etc.

Educational: This is the category containing pedagogical aspects such as type and level of interactivity in the object, semantic density, intended use, level of difficulty, etc.

Rights: This is legal information to manipulate the object.

Relation: These attributes capture how the object relates to others. There might be multiple instances of these attributes to capture arbitrarily complex relations.

Annotation: Information about how the object has been used in a learning environment to allow the exchange of assessments, suggestions, etc.

Classification: Attributes to locate this object within a pre-defined classification system. There might be multiple instances of these attributes if the object needs to be classified according to different criteria.

Nowadays, tools have an uneven adoption of LOM. Some authoring tools such as RELOAD do include

extensive support for both an e-learning object-based approach as well as metadata. But due to the large variety of possible production flows of learning material, metadata for learning objects are not yet fully adopted.

Instructional Management Systems Global Consortium (IMS)

The Instructional Management Systems Global Consortium (henceforth IMS) is a non-profit organization oriented toward facilitating the adoption of e-learning technology worldwide. Its members include vendors, content providers, educational institutions, publishers, government organizations, and other consortia from more than 50 countries.

Rather than publishing international standards, IMS focuses more on promoting the adoption of "open technical specifications" to achieve fully interoperable learning technology at all levels. The impact of this consortium in e-learning is beyond any doubt, because several of these specifications have become *de facto* standards for e-learning products and services.

IMS specifications address interoperability in the following e-learning aspects: accessibility, competency definition, content packaging, digital repositories, enterprise services, e-portfolios, learner information, learning design, learning object metadata, question and tests, resource list interoperability, simple sequencing, etc. Among these, and for the sake of brevity, there follows a brief description of the most relevant:

Content Packaging

When designing learning material, on top of having a detailed description of all learning objects, there is a need to define how this material is organized so that it can be moved from one platform to another and reused. This aspect is especially important because it determines how content can be produced once and used in multiple platforms. The problem then is how to produce and organize platform-independent material.

The IMS Content Packaging Specification defines how material should be organized in order for it to be imported, exported, aggregated, and disaggregated. The key component for this description is an XML file called *imsmanifest.xml*, containing the collection of assets used in a package and how are they organized.

Question and Test

An important aspect of designing learning material is that of evaluation. In general, evaluation is a fairly complex task and has numerous variants. The Question and Test Interoperability specification (QTI) defines a data model specifically oriented toward the design and reuse of tests. This type of evaluation is suitable to offer automatic grading and feedback production.

The model provides definitions for the most commonly used questions, such as multiple choice, true/false, fill in the blanks, multimedia-based, etc. It also allows for the definition of grading schemes, question organization in sections, randomization, and automatic feedback production.

There are numerous authoring tools that already support the model proposed by QTI, so they are capable of importing/exporting documents from different sources. However, due to the large number of aspects considered in the specification, complete support is rarely provided (although often claimed) by these tools.

Simple Sequencing

Sequencing of learning material is another important aspect that needs to be addressed by technology. The Simple Sequencing specification defines the representation needed to capture how a set of discrete learning activities must be sequenced within a learning system.

It is assumed that all activities are organized in a tree-like structure with rules to transfer control to the following activity depending on a set of conditions evaluated over a set of properties that can be modified by the activities. The goal of this framework is to provide some degree of content adaptation based on the evaluation of previously defined rules. It does not have enough expressive power to provide intelligent tutoring.

The main feature of this specification is that it provides sequencing of activities for a single learner. But current learning management systems also facilitate collaboration among learners, which translates to a larger number of learning scenarios. The following specification, also developed by IMS, tries to extend content sequencing to cover these scenarios.

Learning Design

Learning Design tries to support a wide range of pedagogical approaches to learning. It provides a language by which a learning experience can be described at the level of actor participation, which roles are considered, how activities are organized, etc. Ideally, any run-time environment must be capable of organizing a set of resources and services as to provide a specific pedagogical approach described in this language. This specification derived from previous work (mainly at the Open University of the Netherlands) on pedagogical languages.

Using Learning Design, an author may define how the activities and resources of a course can be organized, sequenced, and activated to provide a generic pedagogical scenario. The specification offers a flexible sequencing mechanism. At a first level, a learning design description may have an arbitrary number of concurrent *plays*, each one of them containing a fixed sequence of *acts,* with a concurrent set of *roles* respectively. At a second level it provides access to properties and conditions to modify the flow of events within plays, acts, and roles. The third level introduces the concept of notification on events.

Both Learning Design and Simple Sequencing contain sequencing constructs, but learning design offers a much more flexible language capable of accommodating both sequential sequencing for single learners (as Simple Sequencing) and arbitrarily complex group-based activities.

Learners Information

This specification addresses the issue of collecting information about a learner, group of learners, or producer of learning content. The main objective is to facilitate the import/export of these types of data among platforms. Nowadays, learning activity is expanding over the entire life of an individual into what is called life long learning. An individual then learns over a larger time period and with a large number of organizations. Sharing learner information would facilitate the adaptation of the overall learning process.

The specification is organized around the following broad structures: accessibility, activities, affiliations, competencies, goals, identifications, interests, qualifications, security keys, transcripts, etc.

Accessibility

This specification is closely related to the previous one. The AccessForAll meta-data specification is intended to provide the required information to identify the resources that match the preferences stated by a user in the learner information package. Such implementation includes only the preferences, whereas this AccessForAll defines the required metadata to attach to resources in order to be properly selected.

The specification is conceived in a generic context in which disability is just a concrete instance. E-learning material should be produced with multiple user requirements. When a resource is offered to a user, there needs to be a process of adaptation from the e-learning environment to the user requirements. The goal is then to provide a specification capable of describing the level of flexibility in the e-learning environments to adapt to the user's needs. These needs typically include multiple presentation means, control resources, resource types, and resource enhancements.

Advanced Distributed Learning Initiative (ADL)

The Advanced Distributed Learning Initiative (ADL) is an organization initially created by the United States Department of Defense to work with federal agencies, academia, and industry to develop specifications for technology-based learning. ADL works together with standard and specification organizations such as ISO, IEEE, or IMS to collaboratively develop guidelines oriented toward defining the guidelines for making learning software accessible, adaptable, interoperable, and reusable. More than playing a particular role developing standards, this institution acts more as a guide toward such process.

Shareable Content Object Reference Model (SCORM)

The best known contribution of ADL is the shareable content object reference model (SCORM). It defines how learning systems should handle Web-based learning content and serve it to learners. Due to the wider scope of its goal, SCORM refers to specifications and guidelines proposed by other institutions (like IMS) but within the umbrella of its defined model.

The main contribution of this model is not in any specific aspect of the overall e-learning process but on how all of them must be combined to achieve an effective online learning system. Ideally, if both content and system developers follow this model, learning material would seamlessly integrate in any platform.

The underlying idea in this model is to consider a Web-based course as a collection of content objects that are interconnected. But for this idea to translate into usable platforms, a large number of aspects needs to be considered, some of them already mentioned in this document: content organization, metadata, content sequencing, etc.

SCORM is divided into three sub-modules, each focusing on different aspects:

1. Content aggregation model
2. Runtime environment
3. Sequencing and navigation

The content aggregation model defines how content is assembled, labeled, and packaged. SCORM is an object-based model, thus a detailed description on how these objects are connected is clearly needed. The components that make up a learning experience are assets, sharable content objects (henceforth SCOs), and content organization.

An SCO is made of several assets, and several SCOs create a content organization. Examples of assets are HTML documents, audio/video files, figures, animations, etc. SCOs contain a set of assets and should be *launchable* by the learning management system. A content organization describes how a set of SCOs are organized in a tree-like structure with arbitrary branching. The leaves of this tree must have either SCOs or launchable assets.

The Runtime environment (henceforth RTE) describes the launch procedure performed by a learning management system over an SCO as well as the communication between them. Each learner may have only one SCO active at any given time. The model does not specify how navigational controls are presented to the learner in order to select different material, they should be part of the SCO. The communication between SCOs and the system is achieved by an application programming interface that is part of the model.

SCORM uses multiple IMS specifications as well as the IEEE LOM standard. The proposed model describes how e-learning material has to be managed. For most of the concrete aspects of this management, these specifications are adopted as part of the model. Let us consider content sequencing as an example. It is only one of multiple aspects considered by the SCORM model. The model describes how such sequencing interacts with the rest of the RTE, but the description of the sequencing is done using the IMS Simple Sequencing specification.

It is very likely that, as new specifications appear for additional aspects related to e-learning, future SCORM versions will integrate some of them as part of the proposed model. For example, again in the context of content sequencing, two IMS specification have been described: simple sequencing and learning design. SCORM 2004 uses the former, but a later version could consider including the latter to provide a more flexible sequencing capability.

SCORM is probably the most widely adopted model among current learning management systems. Current tools support the import/export of courses in SCORM, translating into a certain degree of reusability. The main problem when effectively designing a course with one tool and importing it into several platforms is the level of compliance. SCORM is an extensive model based on fairly complete specifications, so vendors usually support a subset of its functionality.

Due to the variations in these subsets, it not uncommon to have SCORM compliant material in one platform that does not preserve all its aspects when imported into a second one. This issue has been addressed by ADL by publishing a set of conformance requirements critical for vendors to know so they can include these critical aspects in the tools to claim being SCORM 2004 compliant.

APPLICATION PROFILES

Application profiles appear as a consequence of the way designers and implementers use existing specifications and models to produce e-learning tools. Rather than exploiting the full potential of one single specification, typical solutions involve concrete subsets of multiple specifications mixed in an *ad hoc* solution.

These solutions typically have specific requirements derived from the context in which they must operate. This translates into refinements and extensions of current specification as well as the combination of several of them into a brand new specification.

Application profiles were introduced by Heery and Patel as a mechanism to formalize the combination of multiple schemas from different specifications. They include data elements obtained from multiple namespaces combined to optimize their usage in a concrete application and cannot create new elements.

Ideally, application profiles allow for easier sharing of e-learning content, since they combine the power of standards and specifications with the flexibility required by concrete applications and contexts.

As standards and specifications evolve, so do application profiles. There are a large number of application profiles derived for the most relevant standards, such as LOM, as well as specifications, such as Content Packaging and Simple Sequencing (both from IMS), to mention a few.

CONCLUSION

The deployment of technology in learning activities has been shown to be promising and challenging at the same time. With the new scenarios offered by technology, learning can take place anywhere, anytime, and therefore learning management systems and learning material require high levels of adaptation, accessibility, interoperability, and reuse.

Standards are a way to foster and promote these requirements at international levels. Several international institutions have procedures to deliver the best possible technical solutions to current technological problems. E-learning is one of the areas in which the effect of these standards is perceived not only as beneficial but also crucial.

Institutions such as IEEE and ISO have numerous working groups elaborating standards to guarantee that learning management systems offer a common set of functionality and a data representation framework so that learning material can be considered platform independent.

An example of such effort is the Learning Object Metadata standard. But there is a very important set of specifications and models aimed at providing a common background upon which to build truly reusable material.

Vendors have quickly adopted these proposals, but after this first stage, due to the complexity of the models, new problems appear with the level of compliance that could reduce the level of interoperability. Despite this, an e-learning landscape with fully compliant tools achieving complete interoperability is definitively possible in the near future.

REFERENCES

Abdullah, N. A., & Davis, H. (2003). Is simple sequencing simple adaptive hypermedia? In HYPERTEXT '03: Proceedings of the 14th ACM Conference on Hypertext and Hypermedia (pp. 172-173). New York: ACM Press.

ADL (2006). *Advanced distributed learning.* www.adlnet.gov

Cardinaels, K., Meire, M., & Duval, E. (2005). Automating metadata generation: The simple indexing interface. In *Proceedings of the World Wide Conference.*

Dodds, P. (2001). *The SCORM content aggregation model.* ADL.

Godby, J. (2004). What do application profiles reveal about the learning object metadata standard? In *Ariadne Issue 41.* Retrieved December 2006 from www.ariadne.ac.uk

Heery, R., & Patel, M. (2000). Application profiles: Mixing and matching metadata schemas. In *Ariadne Issue 25.* Retrieved December 2006 from www.ariadne.ac.uk

IMS. (2006). IMS: Instructional management systems global consortium. Retrieved December 2006 from www.imsglobal.org

Koper, R., & Tattersall, C. (Eds.). (2005). *Learning design: A handbook on modelling and delivering networked education.* Springer Verlag.

Silva Muñoz, & J. P. M. d. O. (2004). Adaptive Web-based courseware development using metadata standards and ontologies. In *Proceedings of the 16th International Conference on Advanced Information Systems Engineering* (LNCS 084, pp. 414-428). Springer Verlag.

Learning, A. D. (2004). *SCORM 2004 sharable content object reference model.* Specification.

Learning, A. D. (2006). *SCORM 2004 conformance requirement.* Published draft.

LOM (2002). *IEEE Standard for Learning Object Metadata 1484.12.1-2002.* Retrieved December 2006 from ltsc.ieee.org/wg12

LTSC (2006). IEEE Learning and Technology Standards Committee. ieeeltsc.org

Olivié, H., Cardinaels, K., & Duval, E. (2002). Issues in automatic learning object indexation. In *Proceedings of the World Conference on Educational Multimedia, Hypermedia and Telecommunications* (pp. 239-240).

RELOAD. (2006). *RELOAD: Reusable elearning object authoring and delivery.* Retrieved December 2006 from www.reload.ac.uk

KEY TERMS

Application Profile: The description of how a set of data elements from different namespaces are combined together to support a particular e-learning application.

Asynchronous E-Learning: A computer-assisted learning experience in which interaction takes place at different instances of time.

Interoperability: Ability of e-learning systems to exchange data and resources transparently to the user.

Learning Management System: A platform that provides an online learning environment for students and that allows the management of classes, group interaction, documents, administrative aspects, etc.

Learning Object: Any entity, digital or non-digital, which can be used, re-used, or referenced during technology-supported learning.

Metadata: In the e-learning context, the set of data describing a resource.

Runtime Environment: Description of a virtual machine which allows the execution of all tasks related with an e-learning application.

Stream Control Transmission Protocol (SCTP)

Farhan Siddiqui
Wayne State University, USA

Sherali Zeadally
University of the District of Columbia, USA

INTRODUCTION

The proliferation of wired and wireless technologies has given rise to the possibility of multi-access options for mobile, multi-homed hosts. Enabling multi-access techniques improves fault tolerance by adding redundancy to network connections. For example, if a host is enabled with two network interfaces connected to the Internet via two different Internet service providers (ISPs), the failure of one network will not stop data transmission. The host will be capable of continuing the data transfer by switching over to the other network. Furthermore, if both networks are active at the same time, but packets experience higher delay and congestion on one path, multihoming facilitates the possibility of switching over to the network path offering better performance. However, the key factor in attaining the benefits of multihoming is to ensure that the handoff or switch over from one network interface (or a network path) to the other active interface should take place with minimal interruption. Stream control transmission protocol (SCTP) provides support for multihoming by allowing a single connection between two nodes to hold several IP addresses simultaneously.

RELATED WORK

The SCTP protocol is in a phase of development and evaluation for the purpose of attaining seamless mobility for multi-homed hosts in heterogeneous network environments. Several research works have dealt with the proposal and evaluation of SCTP as a transport protocol for mobility in wired and wireless networks. Shi et al. (2003) presented a performance evaluation of SCTP in wireless environments, and they found that SCTP-multihoming can provide better throughput performance and more robustness in wireless multi-access scenarios. Liu et al. (2004) proposed a new

approach to improve the performance of SCTP in wired-wireless environments by avoiding unnecessary congestion window decreases. Fracchia et al. (2005) proposed a modification to the SCTP protocol to support the selection of the best available path based upon available bandwidth and packet losses. Ye et al. (2004) proposed a per-path congestion-control principle for SCTP to support efficient multihoming. Funansak, et al. (2005) proposed a new path switching strategy for SCTP to improve the switching delay.

In this work we present an overview of the SCTP features and mechanisms. We also present a comparison of SCTP implementations at the user and kernel levels. Finally, we discuss the applicability of the protocol and its future trends.

OVERVIEW OF SCTP

SCTP (Stream control transmission protocol) (Stewart & Xie, 2000) is a reliable connection-oriented transport protocol that operates on top of a potentially unreliable connectionless packet service, such as IP. It was designed by the signaling transport (SIGTRAN) group of the Internet Engineering Task Force (IETF) to serve as a reliable signaling and control transport protocol for telecommunications traffic to run on IP networks via a number of proposed adaptation layers. However, SCTP also has potential for traditional data applications as a result of a number of desirable features, including message framing, multi-homed connection association, disassociation of reliable transfer from in-order delivery, and multiple logical streams multiplexed over a single physical connection.

The expedient and reliable exchange of control information is vital for the success of modern telecommunication networks, and influences the user perceived quality of service substantially. The evolution of modern heterogeneous networks further requires that signaling transport is provided via pure IP networks with satisfactory reliability and performance (Mexiner et al., 2001). Currently, the exchange of signaling messages in IP-based networks is typically performed by either UDP (Postel, 1980) or TCP. However, both of these protocols have a number of limitations when used for signaling and control. For example, UDP only provides unreliable datagram service. TCP, on the other hand, provides reliable data transfer. However, the abstraction of a single reliable and in-order byte stream is not always a perfect match for telecommunication and certain classes of data applications. The byte-oriented nature of TCP requires explicit delineation of messages by the end application. TCP's coupling of reliable and in-order delivery can cause a *head of line* blocking problem. Here, application data is buffered in the kernel waiting for the delivery of earlier packets. This can cause unnecessary delays for applications that are able to move forward with processing of later packets (Mexiner et al., 2001). Another limitation of TCP for certain applications is that TCP connections are strictly identified by a pair of transport addresses (IP address + port number). This prevents transparent support of multi-homed hosts. Next, TCP is not robust against certain denial of service attacks, for example, SYN flooding. Finally, TCP protocol extensions are limited by a pre-defined maximum size. SCTP differs from UDP by providing a reliable transfer of datagrams. At the same time, it overcomes some of the limitations of TCP enumerated above.

Features of SCTP

The following are some of the important features of SCTP (Hakkinen):

1. **Optional reliability and ordering in a stream:** The SCTP protocol provides both reliable as well as partially reliable transfer of data along a full duplex communication channel. Messages sent along a stream may be ordered or can be assigned as "unordered."
2. **Multihoming:** Multihoming is a significant feature of SCTP. Multihoming allows a single end-point to be associated with more than one IP address or a single connection to have several IP addresses, each assigned to a different network interface. In the base version of SCTP, multihoming was supported such that all IP addresses

associated with a SCTP connection should be indicated during the association setup phase. It did not allow dynamic addition of IP addresses during an ongoing association. Later, extensions to the base SCTP protocol were introduced which defined two new functions, ADDIP and DELETE-IP, which support dynamic addition of IP addresses to an ongoing association.

3. **Multi-streaming:** SCTP allows each association to be made up of several streams, each of which is a logical connection between the two end-points. Due to the division of data into streams, single packet losses among messages of one stream do not block other streams.
4. **Protection against SYN attacks:** SCTP uses a cookie-based four-way handshake mechanism to ward off SYN flood attacks. Each time a connection request is initiated, the receiver sends back a SYN cookie that has to be ACKed by the sender before the receiver allocates space for the connection.
5. **Use of SACK/fast retransmit:** Use of SACK (Selective ACK) is mandatory in SCTP. This helps in efficient notification of missing packets to the sender, who can then use the fast retransmit algorithm to send the missing packets.
6. **No half closed connection:** SCTP does not allow a half-open connection. A disconnection by one end leads to the termination of the connection on the whole.

SCTP Packet Structure

An SCTP packet is composed of a common header and chunks. A chunk contains either user information or data. Each SCTP packet contains at least one chunk. Multiple chunks may be multiplexed into one packet depending upon the path's maximum transmission unit (MTU). If a user message does not fit into one SCTP packet, it can be fragmented into multiple packets.

SCTP packets start with a common 12-byte header. The header contains source and destination port numbers. The verification tag is used to ensure that the packet is not fabricated. The tag is specific to an association and is exchanged between endpoints at association startup. The checksum is used by the error detection functions. Following the common header are the control and data chunks. Control chunks are present before the data chunks.

Each chunk begins with a type field, followed by chunk-specific flags and the length field. The value field contains the actual payload and the actual format id dependent of the chunk type. The value may be omitted. There are 14 chunk types. Type 0 is reserved for data chunks and remaining types are for the following SCTP phases including: connection establishment, initiation, data transfer, heartbeat, shutdown, and explicit congestion notification.

The control chunk values consist of a type specific header followed by zero or more parameters. The chunks value follows a common type-length-value (TLV) structure.

SCTP Operation

Before peer SCTP users can send data to each other, a connection must be established between two endpoints. This connection is called association in SCTP context. A cookie mechanism is employed during the initialization to provide protection against security attacks. Figure 1 shows a sample SCTP message flow. A SCTP

client initiates an association by sending a SCTP sever an INIT message.

Once an association is successfully established, the SCTP client can send its user data using a SCTP DATA message. The server acknowledges the receipt of the user data by returning a SCTP SACK message. SCTP monitors the reachability of the peer by periodically sending HEARTBEAT messages. A user can shut down the association by sending a SHUTDOWN message and the peer acknowledges the shutdown request by returning a SHUTDOWN_ACK message.

SCTP MULTIHOMING

An essential property of SCTP is its support of multihomed nodes, i.e., nodes that can be reached under several IP addresses. If the SCTP nodes are configured in such a way that traffic from one node to another travels on different network paths, associations become tolerant against physical network failures. SCTP implements multihoming (SCTPBEG) in the following ways:

Figure 1. Phases of SCTP operation: (a) SCTP association establishment; (b) SCTP data transfer; (c) SCTP heartbeat mechanism; and (d) SCTP association shutdown

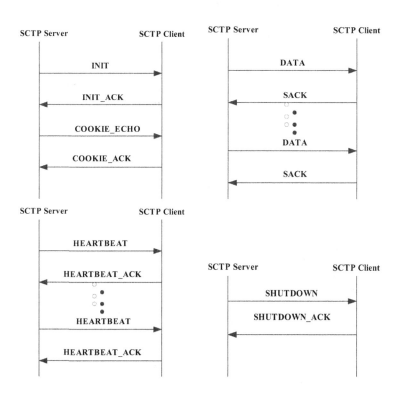

Address Management at Association Setup

If a client is multi-homed, it informs the server about all its IP addresses with the INIT chunk's address parameters. If no explicit IP addresses are contained in the INIT or INIT-ACK chunk, the source IP address of the IP packet which carries the SCTP datagram is used. An extension to the SCTP, called mSCTP (mobile SCTP), also allows dynamic addition and deletion of IP addresses from an association, even if these addresses were not present during association startup.

Path and Peer Monitoring

A SCTP instance monitors all transmission paths to the peer instance of an association. To this end, HEARTBEAT chunks are sent over all paths which are currently not used for the transmission of data chunks. Each HEARTBEAT chunk has to be acknowledged by a HEARTBEAT-ACK chunk. If transmissions on a certain path seem to fail repeatedly, the path is regarded as *inactive*.

Path Selection

At the setup of an SCTP association, one of the IP addresses from the returned list is selected as initial *primary path*. Data chunks are transmitted over this primary transmission path by default. For retransmissions, however, another active path may be selected if available.

SCTP IMPLEMENTATIONS

There are several implementations of the SCTP protocol which are currently available. Some of these implementations are open-source and available for free (SCTPLIB and LKSCTP) while others are proprietary. Details of different types of SCTP implementations can be found in SCTPORG, USRSCTP.

SCTPLIB and LKSCTP are two free and publicly available implementations of SCTP. They are both designed to operate on the Linux operating system and conform to the standard SCTP features described in RFC 2960 (Stewart & Xie, 2000).

USER-LEVEL SCTP IMPLEMENTATION

SCTPLIB is a user-level implementation of SCTP. It is a collaborative effort between Siemens AG, and the Computer Networking Technology Group at the University of Essen, Germany (SCTPIMPL).

In SCTPLIB (Figure 3), the socket API is a wrapper of the Upper Layer Protocol (ULP). SCTPLIB operates on top of IP and opens a raw socket to catch all incoming packets with the IP protocol id byte set to 132 (= SCTP), indicating SCTP messages. A memory copy occurs every time a packet crosses the user-kernel space boundary. If an application on a sender machine wants to transmit a packet to the server machine using SCTP, it passes the packet to be transmitted to SCTPLIB. SCTPLIB pushes the packet via a raw socket to the IP stack in the kernel. This involves a memory copy from user space to the kernel space (Pang, 2003). At the receiver side, SCTPLIB collects the packet

Figure 2. SCTP multihoming

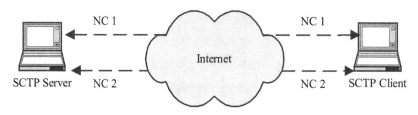

SCTP: Stream Control Transmission Protocol   NC: Network Connection

S

Figure 3. Architecture of user-level SCTP implementation (SCTPLIB)

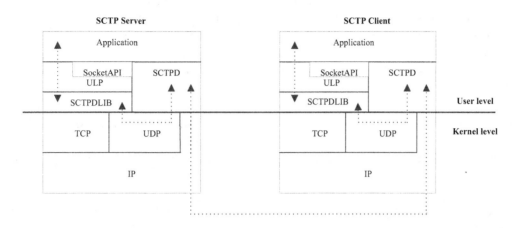

via a raw socket from the IP stack in the kernel. This involves another memory copy from kernel space to user space. SCTPLIB then passes the packet to the application. Since all the SCTP messages are processed at the user space, many memory copies are expected to take place between the user and kernel spaces. This may impact the performance of an application that uses SCTP as the transport protocol. In SCTPLIB, all SCTP messages, including control messages such as HEARTBEAT, COOKIE_WAIT, COOKIE_ECHO, and SACK acknowledgment messages, are processed by the application at the user level.

KERNEL-LEVEL SCTP IMPLEMENTATION

LKSCTP is a kernel-level implementation of SCTP. It was developed by researchers in the industry, including Motorola, Cisco, and Nortel Networks. Its design is similar to the existing TCP and UDP stack in the Linux kernel (Figure 4). User applications access LKSCTP using either upper layer protocol (ULP) or socket API. Not all the SCTP messages received by LKSCTP from the network are passed to the application. SCTP control messages, such as INIT, INIT_ACK, HEARTBEAT,

Figure 4. Architecture of kernel-level SCTP implementation (LKSCTP)

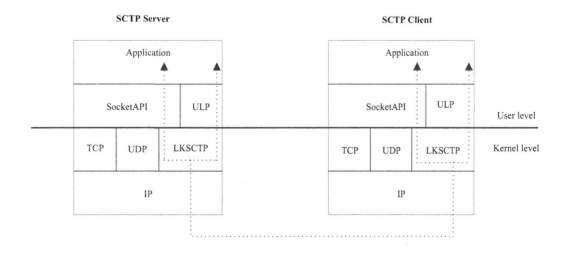

COOKIE_WAIT, etc., are not passed to the application unless they are explicitly requested. This can reduce unnecessary memory copies between the user and the kernel spaces. The LKSCTP architecture allows multiple processes to access the SCTP stack without going through an intermediary (such as the SCTP daemon in SCTPLIB). LKSCTP supports a socket-like API similar to TCP/UDP. This makes developing an application for SCTP similar to writing applications for TCP or UDP. It also allows quick adoption of SCTP by the users who have TCP/UDP socket programming experience.

BENEFITS AND DRAWBACKS OF IMPLEMENTING SCTP IN USER AND KERNEL SPACES

Table 1 summarizes the major benefits and limitations of SCTPLIB (user-level SCTP) and LKSCTP (kernel-level SCTP) implementations.

APPLICABILITY OF SCTP

SCTP was originally designed to transport PSTN signaling messages over IP networks, but it is capable of supporting a broader range of applications. It is designed to address the limitations and complexity of TCP while transporting real time signaling and data such as PSTN signaling over IP networks. SCTP can also run above the UDP layer.

SCTP offers the following services:

- Acknowledged error-free transfer of user data
- Sequenced delivery of user messages within multiple streams
- Optional bundling of multiple user messages into a single SCTP packet
- Network resilience by providing multihoming

The design of SCTP also includes appropriate congestion avoidance control and resistance to flooding and masquerade attacks.

The applications that would benefit most from SCTP are as follows:

- Applications that have sufficient traffic levels to justify the overhead of association establishment and congestion and flow control measures
- Applications that require framing of reliable data streams
- Applications that transfer multiple independent message sequences
- Applications that require network redundancy

FUTURE TRENDS

The stream control transmission protocol is a suitable protocol for next generation IP communication networks. Its multihoming capability improves its resilience and makes it a right candidate for enabling continuous network connectivity in future multi-access network environments. The multi-streaming capabilities of SCTP further distinguish it from other existing

Table 1. A comparison of user (SCTPLIB) and kernel (LKSCTP) level SCTP implementations

SCTPLIB		LKSCTP	
Benefits	**Limitations**	**Benefits**	**Limitations**
Easy implementation	Lack of scalability: intermediary process called SCTPD is required to run more than one instance of the SCTP library simultaneously	High Scalability: several instances of the SCTP library can run without the need for any intermediary process	Difficult implementation
Easy debugging and maintenance	Poor performance: high data transmission and handoff delay due to processing of all control messages by the application and interaction with SCTPD	Competitive performance: low data transfer times and handoff delays	Difficult debugging and maintenance
		Socket-based API similar to TCP and UDP	

transport protocols such as TCP and UDP. SCTP also avoids the head-of-line blocking of TCP. The dynamic address reconfiguration mechanism of SCTP makes it a useful protocol for handling real-time applications in mobile environments by gracefully handling service re-configuration without interrupting ongoing sessions. One of the outstanding issues that still needs to be addressed is the performance of SCTP in wireless networking environments. The base-SCTP protocol was designed for wireline networks and therefore cannot distinguish packet losses occurring due to congestion from those due to wireless communication. Research is in progress to extend SCTP to provide better support for wireless environments. It is envisioned that these improvements, together with features of multihoming and multi-streaming, will make SCTP the transport protocol of choice for the next generation of mobile multimedia systems.

CONCLUSION

SCTP's multihoming capability makes it a suitable protocol for the implementation of seamless mobility in heterogeneous network environments. In this work we presented and discussed the main features of the SCTP protocol. We compared the salient architectural features of the user-level and kernel-level SCTP implementations that are available to designers and application developers. We also discussed some application areas that can exploit SCTP. Finally, we highlighted some future trends of SCTP.

ACKNOWLEDGMENT

We thank the anonymous reviewers for their comments and suggestions. We express our gratitude to the editor-in-chief, Mario Freire, for his encouragements and support during the preparation of this chapter.

REFERENCES

Fracchia, R., Casetti, C., et al. (2005). A WiSE extension of SCTP for wireless networks. *Proceedings of IEEE International Conference on Communications, 3*, 1448-1453, Seoul, Korea.

Fuanhua, Y., Saadawi, T., et al. (2004). IPCC-SCTP: An enhancement to the standard SCTP to support multi-homing efficiently. In *Proceedings of IEEE International Conference on Performance, Computing and Communication*, pp. 523-530, Phoenix, Arizona.

Funasaka, J., Ishida, K., et al. (2005). A study on the primary path switching strategy of SCTP. In *Proceedings of Autonomous Decentralized Systems* (pp. 536-54).

Hakkinen, A. *SCTP: Stream control transmission protocol*. Retrieved April 2006 from http://www.cs.helsinki.fi/u/ahakkine/sctp.pdf

Liu S., Yang, S., et al. (2004). Collaborative SCTP: A collaborative approach to improve the performance of SCTP over wired-cum-wireless networks. In *Proceedings of the 29th Annual IEEE International Conference on Local Computer Networks*, pp. 276-283, Tampa, Florida.

Mexiner, A., Onyango, et al. (2001). *Design and evaluation of a kernel-level SCTP implementation*. Duke University. Retrieved April 2006 from http://www.cs.duke.edu/~py/paper/miscPaper/sys-sctp.tech.2001.pdf

Pang, T. (2003). *Stream control transmission protocol support in session initiation protocol proxy server*. Retrieved April 2006 from http://www.ensc.sfu.ca/~ljilja/cnl/pdf/thomas.pdf

Postel, J. (1980). *User Datagram Protocol*. RCC 768. Retrieved April 2007 from http://www.faqs.org/rfcs/rfc768.html

SCTPBEG. *SCTP for beginners*. Retrieved April 2006 from http://tdrwww.exp-math.uni-essen.de/inhalt/forschung/sctp_fb/sctp_multihoming.html

SCTPIMPL. *Documentation of SCTP-implementation*. Retrieved April 2006 from tdrwww.exp-math.uni-essen.de/inhalt/forschung/sctp_fb/sctp-api.pdf

SCTPORG. *Stream control transmission protocol*. Retrieved April 2006 from www.sctp.org

Shi, J., Jin, Y., et al. (2003). Experimental performance of SCTP in wireless access networks. In *Proceedings of International Conference on Communication Technology*, Vol. 1, pp. 392-195, Beijing, China.

Stewart, R., Xie, Q., et al. (2000). *Stream Control Transmission Protocol*. RFC 2960. IETF, Network Working Group, October.

USRSCTP. *User level SCTP implementation*. http://www.sctp.de

KEY TERMS

Cookie: A cookie is information for future use that is stored by the server on the client side of a client/server communication.

Fragmentation: In TCP/IP, fragmentation refers to the process of breaking packets into the smallest maximum size packet data unit (PDU) supported by any of the underlying networks.

MTU: A maximum transmission unit (MTU) is the largest size packet or frame, specified in octets (eight-bit bytes), that can be sent in a packet- or frame-based network such as the Internet.

Multi-Homed: Multi-homed describes a computer host that has multiple IP addresses to connected networks. A multi-homed host is physically connected to multiple data links that can be on the same or different networks.

NAT (Network Address Translation): Translation of an Internet protocol address (IP address) used within one network to a different IP address known within another network. One network is designated the *inside* network and the other is the *outside*.

Network: In information technology, a network is a series of points or nodes interconnected by communication paths. Networks can interconnect with other networks and contain sub-networks.

Packet: A packet is the unit of data that is routed between an origin and a destination on the Internet or any other packet-switched network.

Protocol: A protocol is a special set of rules that end points in a telecommunication connection use when they communicate.

Reliability: Reliability is an attribute of any computer-related component (software, hardware, or a network, for example) that consistently performs according to its specifications.

SCTP (Stream Control Transmission Protocol): A protocol for transmitting multiple streams of data at the same time between two end points that have established a connection in a network.

Survey: Pricing Ubiquitous Network Services

Jairo A. Gutiérrez
University of Auckland, New Zealand

INTRODUCTION

One of the keys for the success of ubiquitous network services is the issue of assigning prices to those services. Furthermore, ubiquitous services based on a network of complementary technologies, both fixed and wireless, have created the expectation of services that can be obtained dynamically and automatically with the minimum possible of interaction between the users and potentially complex network systems. Intelligent agents would negotiate the best conditions to make sure the user obtains the best possible connection always (Voinov & Valladares, 2003). This best possible connection would be selected by comparing the different services, quality of the services offered, and prices, then reaching a decision based on the policies the user has configured in his or her intelligent agent and in conjunction with the policies being presented by the different service providers.

It is clear that from the technical point of view, the scenario depicted above is feasible. There has been continued progress on the integration of technologies such as WiFi, "Mesh," and "Ad-Hoc" networks with the traditional phone networks and fixed sub-networks based on the TCP/IP family of protocols. Telecommunication companies have exploited the popularity of WiFi "hot spots" as access ramps to their 3G services (Legard, 2003). However, there is work to be done in the area of agreeing how to price network services, especially when that "network" is supplied by different organizations, and potential users may not have contractual agreements with all the players involved.

The current telecommunications environment, in which virtual operators re-sell network services, and some firms are customers of a traditional "Telco" while at the same time offering services to many other smaller organizations, forces us to redefine many of the business models that had been used so far. Long-term contracts are being challenged by many other arrangements that give more flexibility to the users. These changes, in most cases promoted by users' requirements and further "pushed" by competitive, and innovative, entrants into the telecommunications arena, have resulted in a profound transformation in the way services are acquired and billed. This fact will always clash with the tendency of traditional "Telcos" to keep billing as simple as possible (Meyer, 2003).

It is entirely possible that the much vaunted convergence of the Internet and Telco worlds will push companies competing in that field to adjust the way they do business (Panagiotakis, et al., 2005). An optimistic view of these changes argues that network operators will be able to obtain additional revenues by pricing quality services (with guaranteed levels of performance or guaranteed security) at a premium and that selected customers will be more than willing to foot the bill for a better service.

MAIN FOCUS OF THE CHAPTER

The field of pricing Internet-based network services has been an active area of research and development ever since the "MIT Workshop on Internet Economics" took place in March of 1995. The papers presented in the workshop were later compiled in McKnight and Bailey (1997). There had been some contributions to the field before the MIT workshop (Shenker et al., 1991, 1993; Parris, et al., 1992; Cocchi et al., 1993; MacKie-Mason & Varian, 1994, enhanced later as a book chapter [see 1995b]), however, the basis of the current state-of-the-art has been developed during the last 10 years or so. This paper has also excluded some pre- and post-1995 contributions that deal mainly with pricing of ATM networks (for example, Murphy et al., 1994; Lazar et al., 1995), since it is generally agreed that services based on wireless ATM networks are no longer in contention as candidates for ubiquitous services. There is another set of contributions that clearly specify fixed networks or core networks, usually working with QoS (quality of service) frameworks, such as differentiated services (DiffServ). That type of research is also excluded from this survey (for example, Rizzo et al., 1999; Paschalidis & Tsitsiklis, 2000 [this paper discusses interesting aspects of the problem of optimizing the aggregated social welfare of a service by using mechanisms that permit differential billing]; Stiller et al., 2001; La & Anantharam, 2002; Başar & Srikant, 2002; Savagaonkar et al., 2002; He & Walrand, 2003; Jin et al., 2003; Li et al., 2004; Fulp & Reeves, 2004; Wang & Schulzrinne, 2004; Bouras & Sevasti, 2004; Hayel & Tuffin, 2005). In general, the schemes discussed in this paper are: (1) the classic, well-known network pricing mechanisms found in the literature, or (2) they are mechanisms that can be used with wireless ubiquitous services.

ECONOMIC FACTORS ASSOCIATED WITH NETWORK SERVICES

Economics is a key discipline in the quest to understand the pricing of network services. These services have some characteristics that make them different from the great majority of products and services commercialized in the traditional economy. With no congestion in the network, the marginal cost of sending another packet is practically zero. That's why network services are more comparable to products such as movies, music, and other digital offerings that require a large initial investment and subsequently, very low marginal cost to produce one more CD or DVD. The other important factor is the so-called "network externalities," where the value of the good changes with the number of people using that good. Those effects could be positive (an example of Metcalf's law: the more users on e-mail the more useful that system of communications become; let's forget about spam for a second!) or the effects could be negative (for instance: causing congestion in the network). The other fundamental difference between network services and common market goods is that the latter can be easily described using a couple of parameters, such as size and weight, while we often need much more than that to describe a network service (for instance, bandwidth requirements, maximum delay, security parameters, jitter characteristics). This range of required factors makes it hard to compare offerings from different providers and complicates the production of pricing strategies for these services (Courcoubetis & Weber, 2003).

Economic theory is the foundation of all the schemes that attempt to distribute resources among consumers competing in the marketplace. The market can be described with a Utility function $Ur(dr)$ for consumer r demanding d resources and a Cost function $Cn(s_n)$, which describes the monetary value of the resources s supplied by provider n.

We can describe the market by assuming that a consumer with a Utility function U receives d resource units and pays w for them. The net payoff for the consumer is $Gc = U(d) - w$

For the provider, the net payoff is $Gp = w - C(s)$, assuming that s units are supplied at a cost $C(s)$ and a payment w is received. The net payoff, therefore, describes the monetary benefit for both parties (Courcoubetis & Weber, 2003). Finally, it is necessary to introduce the concept of *Pareto efficiency*: This is used to measure the efficiency of the distribution of resources among several consumers. A distribution is Pareto efficient if the net benefit for one participant cannot be improved without decreasing the benefit of another participant in that transaction. Once you reach that condition, the prices for the products or services are equal to the marginal utility of the participants in the transaction. For the simple case of two participants, this optimisation problem can be described as:

Maximise U1(d1) + U2(d2)
with d1 + d2 <=S
and d1, d2 >= 0

In this simple case, a market mechanism is able to generate a single price that would be equal for all consumers. To figure out what that price is at the point of equilibrium is sufficient to know what the aggregated demand and supply functions are (Dr and Sn respectively) for all consumers (r) and all providers (n). The market mechanism is able to calculate a price (p^*) in such a way that the aggregate demand equals the aggregate supply.

PRICING NETWORK SERVICES

The literature offers different ways of classifying pricing schemes. Perhaps the most common of those ways is to divide the schemes into two categories: static versus dynamic. However, the reader may also encounter classifications based on how the prices are calculated, i.e., per flow, packet, contract, etc.

- **Flat rate:** With a flat-rate system, the client pays a monthly fee that covers all the services. This system had some early champions (Anania & Solomon, 1997; Odlyzko, 1998, 2001) and its main advantage lies in the simplicity of the scheme, for both providers (easy to bill) and users (easy to understand). However, flat-rate systems have been criticized because they do not help to alleviate congestion (which will continue to be a challenge for wireless networks) and do not permit providers to obtain extra revenues for premium (with QoS guarantees) or innovative services.

- **Expected capacity pricing:** With this model, introduced by David Clark in the MIT Workshop of 1995, the clients get billed according to the capacity of the network that they hope to utilize, not by the peaks that they may reach during actual usage. This simplifies the measurements required to implement the mechanism. In the case of congestion, the user can only utilize the agreed upon capacity.

- **Edge pricing:** This system, introduced by Shenker et al. (1996), aims to provide a useful way of dealing with very large, decentralized networks (such as the Internet). Their model charges usage at the edge of the network rather than trying to calculate prices node by node along the entire route used. The edge price can also be used so that different providers are able to exchange payments according to the portions or services of the different networks utilized by the clients. All the billing information is kept local, and this scheme is suitable to be used in combination with other mechanisms, such as flat-rate pricing.

- **Paris Metro pricing (PMP):** PMP adds the concept of *traffic classes* in order to provide different qualities of service. This mechanism was developed by Odlyzko (1997, 1999) and coincided with the then popular DiffServ quality of service framework introduced as an enhancement to TCP/IP. The main idea is to divide the available capacity among several logical networks which are then assigned different prices. Users pay higher prices when they deem it necessary, and thus automatically classify the traffic among the several available networks. (This is turn cre-

ates the different levels of service that can be mapped to DiffServ classes.) The system is easy to understand from the users' point of view but additional resources are needed to keep track of the different classes of services, and additional overhead is required to perform the calculations in every node. In Ercetin and Tassiulas (2005), the authors present a variety of PMP, where users can be billed according to the resources consumed rather that just taking into consideration the class assigned to the traffic generated by them. The key to this enhancement is that users don't need to examine the status of the network to determine which class to select, therefore making the scheme simpler to implement. However, the scenario discussed involves subscription to an ISP and it is not so easily applied to cases where the control and cooperation in the network is distributed, as is the case with most ubiquitous services.

- **Priority pricing:** The key to these systems (Shenker et al., 1993; Gupta et al., 1997) is the use of priorities when requesting services. The charges are calculated according to those priorities. With this type of scheme, it is crucial to have an effective price strategy, because otherwise users are tempted to label most traffic with the highest priority possible. One of the great advantages of this scheme is that IP has been equipped to deal with priorities since its early days: Version 4 of the protocol has a priority field for each packet transmitted; the use of that field has been included in all the important QoS frameworks proposed by the Internet community (IntServ, DiffServ) and can be used in conjunction with technologies that support QoS, such as MPLS (multi-protocol label switching).

- **Effective bandwidth pricing:** This system is designed to motivate the user to use real values when describing the traffic they plan to transmit through the network. The user gets charged according to a function that models the traffic specified in the most accurate way, and users get fined if they underestimate the amount of traffic they plan to transmit. This allows the network to receive more precise information about the expected load. It is possible to use connection admission control (CAC) mechanisms to regulate access, and users have monetary incentives to be as truthful as possible when estimating factors such as the mean and peaks expected during transmission (Kelly, 1994, 1997a).

- **Proportional fairness pricing:** In this scheme, *Fair* means the distribution of resources is proportional to the willingness of users to pay for those resources (Gibbens & Nelly, 1998; Kelly, 1997b; Kelly et al., 1998). In other words, the resources (bandwidth, usually) are assigned to the users that value them the most. The mechanism is based on a double optimization system: on one hand there is optimization from the point of view of the users: resources assigned according to the offers; on the other hand, there is optimization from the point of view of the network operator: All the available resources, without compromising on quality, are sold, although different prices for different portions of the divisible resource are accepted. A number of researchers in this sub-field have used game theory to propose systems that provide resources in a fair way based on user-selected priorities. This is usually done by using specific scenarios (games) between the service provider and its clients (DaSilva et al., 1997; Marbach, 2001, 2002, 2004; Cao et al., 2002). Another related work also uses game theory to examine different strategies; for example: how does the behavior of users change if the most important criterion is price? What happens if the most important issue is quality of service (Sairamesh & Kephart, 2000)? What are the incentives for a provider to operate the network with very high capacity links, and what's the strategy that maximizes revenue (Başar & Srikant, 2002)?

- **Smart-market pricing** (aka Generalised *Vickrey* Auctions): This mechanism was proposed by MacKie-Mason and Varian (1995a, 1995b) to alleviate the problem of (expected) congestion in the Internet. This is one of the schemes that works at the packet level: Each one of those units carries an estimate of how much the user is willing to pay for its transmission. The node that receives the packets sorts them according to those estimates (from highest to lowest). The system has clear advantages in terms of economic efficiency and "fair" use of the available resources, but its great weakness lies in its lack of scalability: Remember that a central node has to arbitrate the offered prices and assign the resources according to the results of each auction.

- **Auctions at different levels of service:** Shu and Varaiya (2003) also adopted the generalized *Vickrey* auctions by adding the capacity of carrying out several auctions according to the different levels of service that an operator may wish to offer. With DiffServ-capable networks, the traffic that fulfills its contractual agreement (*in-profile*) can pay a fixed price while the traffic that violates the agreement (*out-profile*) is obliged to participate in an auction and negotiate price and access with a connection admission control (CAC) module.

- **The progressive second-price [PSP] auction:** Semret and Lazar (2003; Semret et al., 2000) have used game theory to propose an auction system that produces a more efficient and fair result when dealing with scarce resources. Additionally, the scheme can be used in a distributed manner, and it relies on intelligent agents that negotiate resources on behalf of their users. The PSP auctions are also derived from the generalized *Vickrey* auctions, used to distribute divisible resources among the bidders. The PSP auction lets the participants bid using two values: the percentage of the resource they wish to obtain and the price they are willing to pay for it. The efficiency of PSP guarantees that the resources are allocated to the agents with the best offers (but charging the "second-price," i.e., the price offered in the second-highest bid) and the scheme rewards the use of real values in the bids. Users gain nothing with offer strategies that are overly complex resulting in an easier-to-implement system. However, it is still necessary to equip each user with an intelligent agent to act on his or her behalf and participate in the auctions, and service providers have to be willing to participate in the scheme (this is, of course, the hardest part!).

Finally, the articles by DaSilva (2000) and Falkner, et al. (2000) contain good, and relatively recent, discussions about the pricing of network services.

PRICING IN WIRELESS NETWORKS

This section contains a review, arranged chronologically, of the most important contributions to the sub-field of network pricing that deals with wireless networks. This is particularly important when attempting to deliver ubiquitous services over multi-owner, multi-operator networks.

Although the article by Kephart et al. (2000) is not specifically about pricing in wireless networks (their work takes into account all types of networks), it is important for the purpose of this paper because it discusses aspects linked to intelligent agents that act on behalf of their "owners." The authors discuss how a market of thousands of agents would operate, from a macroeconomic point of view, when acting autonomously (but based on rules specified by the owner) in the process of selling and buying services with dynamic prices.

Viterbo and Chiasserini (2001) discussed dynamic pricing on a wireless network that offers connection-oriented services. The authors modeled the demand of the users and the duration of each connection (call) as functions of the service price and they proved (analytically) that their proposed solution results in better quality of service for the users and improved revenue for the service providers.

Saraydar et al. (2002) introduced a design for power control based on pricing mechanisms for wireless networks. The scheme uses a model based on game theory, in which the participants act in a selfish manner (there is no collaboration among the players). However, the price function used has a linear behavior in relation to the available transmission power and, in this manner, it is able to distribute the available power at the same time as maximizing the aggregated social welfare of the system. The efficiency of the scheme depends on the location and utility function of the users.

Marbach and Berry (2002) have investigated the use of a price system to control access to a WiFi access point. The focus of the study is to find a way to maximize the revenue of the access point operator. The authors used an auction system based on the best price offered. In the scenario presented, users can obtain a better channel if they are willing to pay a bit more. The system promotes economic efficiency given that the scarce resources are allocated to the users that value them most. Another consequence of the scheme is that the network operator can charge different prices according to the location and contextual conditions of the user (noise, interference, etc.).

Zhou et al. (2002) have developed a model for the distribution of resources of the "uplink" connection of a wireless network that combines data and voice services. The authors use two different utility functions:

one for voice communications (inelastic) and the other for data transmissions, which is elastic and that can be further qualified with user-provided priorities. These priorities are to be decided by each user according to their particular mix of applications. The authors discuss several possible combinations of applications and provide simulation results for some of them.

Qiu and Marbach (2003) utilize a price system that rewards cooperation among nodes of an "ad-hoc" wireless network. These types of networks are characterized by their dynamic nature and lack of structure. Without incentives, it is quite possible for the nodes to act selfishly and not cooperate with nearby nodes. In the system proposed by Qiu and Marbach, users obtain the largest benefit by maximizing their utility function, but also by transmitting in-transit packets as a service to other nodes. The authors also show that this local optimization produces a global benefit for the entire network.

The work presented in Leloup (2003) is not explicitly dedicated to wireless networks, however it is included in this survey since it deals with some of the key characteristics of dynamic network pricing. The scenario modeled in this paper is that of a seller agent that interacts with several buyer agents and, by using simulation, the author studies some of the properties of interest when using that type of configuration. Some key aspects are: the use of multiple autonomous agents that negotiate on behalf of the users, and the use of dynamic programming rules in order to obtain the required resources.

Chen and Nahrstedt (2004) propose a system of incentives based on an auction mechanism. The generalized *Vickrey* auction is once again used as a basis to support this scheme in which each flow contains an estimate of how much the user is willing to pay for the service. An auction takes place in each node participating, and the flows with the best bids are transmitted (this is similar to *smart-market pricing* but the unit is the flow and not each packet). The authors show that with their proposed system, the users have incentives to use real estimates in their bids, and that the scheme is economically efficient.

Sun et al. (2004) introduce an "everyone pays" auction mechanism to distribute bandwidth in the form of time slots during which transmitters can use the channel. To demonstrate the scheme, the authors suggest a scenario that consists of one transmission cell, two users on it, and no interference between them. For each "time slot," a mini-auction is held in which users behave according to a pre-defined demand function (in other words there are no surprises). The authors also study the case in which users can change their demand function (e.g., they can vary their demand strategy), and they show that this second case results in a Nash equilibrium which is no worse than three quarters of the maximum possible throughput when fairness constraints are not imposed and all slots are allocated to users with the best channel quality.

Heikkinen (2004) is another researcher who uses game theory to tackle the issue of dynamic network pricing. She introduced the scenario of a bandwidth allocation game in which the participants are a set of intelligent agents acting on behalf of their owners (the users). The agents do not cooperate (the scheme is implemented with a "selfish" algorithm); nevertheless, the author proves analytically that the game quickly reaches a Pareto-efficient distribution. The network used for the sample scenario is a W-CDMA cellular network and each agent is installed in the users' mobile device.

Crowcroft et al. (2004) present a model that takes into consideration the special characteristics of Mobile ad-hoc networks (MANETs) in which power plays a crucial role (besides the bandwidth cost). Using simulation techniques, the researchers examine the type of incentives that can be added, via pricing mechanisms, to improve the operation of these kinds of networks.

Altman et al. (2004) studied, from the point of view of game theory, two alternatives (with and without cooperation) used to select the probability of re-transmission in a wireless network that uses the *slotted Aloha* access mechanism. Their work showed that if the probability of re-transmission is increased, then the behavior of the mobile devices becomes more aggressive and the overall performance of the network suffers. The option in which the devices cooperate resulted in better performance, even though there was an increase in the number of re-transmissions.

Das, Lin, and Chatterjee (2004) also utilize game theory to introduce an econometric model that allows several wireless users to participate in a competitive services environment. The goal of the service provider is to maximize its revenue while the goal of the users is to obtain an adequate connection (quality) at the best possible price. The mechanisms—resource management, admission, and control—were designed for a CDMA network, and one of the main motivations of the researchers is to try and minimize the tendency of users to switch network operators, which is an acute problem in countries that have legislated number portability. Curiously, the most detailed explanations in that paper relate to the case of a single operator and multiple clients.

Ileri et al. (2005) have proposed a scheme, again based on game theory, for the pricing of MANETs. Basically, the scheme provides incentives for the nodes to cooperate by rewarding nodes for forwarding messages among them (this is a key requirement for this type of network to function). The authors examine a number of different configurations of the game that reach Nash equilibriums and are economically efficient.

In Roggendorf et al. (2006), the authors present a simulation environment that allows experimentation with multiple intelligent agents which participate in wireless resource (bandwidth) auctions using a mechanism based on the Progressive Second-Price [PSP] auction (see Section 3). The simulation environment gives researchers the option of studying different price strategy options and, potentially, to work with multiple service providers.

CONCLUSION

The accumulated work produced in this area, and surveyed in this paper, makes it possible to elaborate a wish list of the characteristics required in a mechanism for the pricing of ubiquitous services. A mechanism that operates on a wireless environment, with dynamic pricing and relying on a heterogeneous mix of networks, operators, and service providers are what many researchers envision as necessary for the success and adoption of ubiquitous services. Those characteristics are:

1. **Operator/operators:** The mechanism should be able to work with several service providers, giving the users flexibility and choice when selecting ubiquitous services. It is clear that sometimes this goal may not be feasible (geographical coverage, market size, etc.) but it is a fundamental requirement for competitive markets.
2. **Implementation:** The mechanism should be technically feasible and should be compatible with existing major technologies (such as IP).

One of the key aspects to accomplish this, then, is the level of complexity of the mechanism in question. An otherwise attractive but overly complex scheme will not be welcome by the industry (which will face the challenge of implementing it). Complexity also raises the issue of scalability: Simpler schemes have a much better chance of being adopted by networks that connect thousands (or millions) of nodes.

3. **Pricing scheme:** Apparently, there is no system among those surveyed (static, dynamic, and hybrid) that would be ideal in every situation. It is possible that the mechanism would be forced to work with a number of pricing schemes in an integrated fashion, and according to the contextual circumstances. To satisfy this requirement, it is important for the chosen decision to take into account the user context in the network at the time of the request, and that means the mobile device has to be able to capture and transmit contextual information that would be needed at the moment of assigning the price.

4. **Information exchange:** This requirement deals with the way in which users and devices exchange information during the process that will result in the allocation of prices and resources. The ideal mechanism would have to operate in an autonomous, or at least distributed, fashion. This condition rules out any centralized solution, which by its very nature contradicts the fundamental philosophy of ubiquitous services.

5. **Multi-service/multi-technology:** The selected mechanism should work across a wide range of wireless network technologies: Wi-Fi, 3 and 4G, Bluetooth, etc. It is now evident that a number of technologies will be competing against each other in the near term and the proposed mechanism should function with the main networks in widespread use.

6. **Business models:** New business models need to take on board innovative ways of billing for ubiquitous services. The pricing allocation for these services could be more complex and would typically involve a larger number of participants. Instead of a traditional client-provider relationship, it is realistic to think about situations where several entities have a role to play (content provider, traditional fixed-telephony operator, mobile network operator, ISP, application hosting provider, virtual private network [VPN] provider, etc.)

7. **Efficient use of resources:** This is of particular importance for ubiquitous services since, quite often, the available resources are scarce and must be utilized in the most efficient manner. This is a requirement that applies not only to bandwidth but also to resources of the ubiquitous device itself: battery life, memory, and processing capabilities.

8. **Economic benefit:** In particular, from the point of view of the users, the selected mechanism should benefit economically the target community of users. In other words, the requirement is to focus on the overall utility level (or user benefit) of the user community.

ACKNOWLEDGMENT

I'd like to thank Matthias Roggendorf for the useful discussions and sharing of ideas that assisted me in producing this paper.

REFERENCES

Altman, E., El Azouzi, R., & Jiménez, T. (2004). Slotted Aloha as a game with partial information. *Computer Networks 45*, 701-713.

Anania, L., & Solomon, R.J. (1997). Flat: The minimalist price. In L.W. McKnight & J.P. Bailey (1997). *Internet economics*. Cambridge, MA: MIT Press.

Başar, T., & Srikant, R. (2002). Revenue-maximizing pricing and capacity expansion in a many-users regime. *Proceedings of the IEEE INFOCOM 2002 Conference.*

Bouras, C., & Sevasti, A. (2004). SLA-based QoS pricing in DiffServ networks. *Computer Communications 27*, 1868-1880.

Cao, X. R., Shen, H.X., Milito, R., & Wirth, P. (2002). Internet pricing with a game theoretical approach: Concepts and examples. *IEEE/ACM Transactions on Networking, 10(2)*, 208-16.

Chen, K., & Nahrstedt, K. (2004). ipass: An incentive compatible auction scheme to enable packet forwarding service in MANETs. *Proceedings of the 24th International Conference on Distributed Computing Systems* (pp. 534-542).

Clark, D. (1997). A model for cost allocation and pricing in the Internet. In L.W. McKnight & J.P. Bailey (1997). *Internet economics*. Cambridge, MA: MIT Press.

Cocchi, R., Shenker, S., Estrin, D., & Zhang, L. (1993). Pricing in computer networks: Motivation, formulation, and example. *IEEE/ACM Transactions on Networking, 1*(6), 614-627.

Courcoubetis, C., & Weber, E. (2003). *Pricing communication networks: Economics, technology and modelling*. Wiley-Interscience series in systems and optimization.

Crowcroft, J., Gibbens, R., Kelly, F., & Östring, S. (2004). Modelling incentives for collaboration in mobile ad hoc networks. *Performance Evaluation, 57*, 427-439.

Das, S.K., Lin, H., & Chatterjee, M. (2004). An econometric model for resource management in competitive wireless data networks. *IEEE Network, 18*(6), 20-26.

DaSilva, L.A., Petr, D. W., & Akar, N. (1997). Equilibrium pricing in multiservice priority-based networks. *Proceedings of the IEEE GLOBECOM*, Phoenix, AZ (pp. S38.6.1-5).

DaSilva, L.A. (2000). Pricing for QoS-enabled networks: A survey. *IEEE Communications Surveys, Second Quarter.* Available at http://www.comsoc. org/pubs/surveys

Ercetin, O., & Tassiulas, L. (2005). Pricing strategies for differentiated services content delivery networks. *Computer Networks, 49*, 840-855.

Flakner, M., Devetsikiotis, M., & Lambadaris, I. (2000). An overview of pricing concepts for broadband IP networks. *IEEE Communications Surveys, Second Quarter.* Available at http://www.comsoc.org/pubs/surveys

Fulp, E.W., & Reeves, F.S. (2004). Bandwidth provisioning and pricing for networks with multiple classes of service. *Computer Networks, 46*(1), 41-52.

Gibbens, R. J., & Kelly, F. (1998). *Resource pricing and the evolution of congestion control*. Available from URL http://www.statslab.cam.ac.uk/~frank/evol.html

Gupta, A., Stahl, D., & Whinston, A. (1997). Priority pricing of integrated services networks. In L.W. McKnight & J.P. Bailey (1997). *Internet economics*. Cambridge, MA: MIT Press.

Hayel, Y., & Tuffin, B. (2005). A mathematical analysis of the cumulus pricing scheme. *Computer Networks, 47*(6), 907-921.

He, L., Walrand, J. (2003, Oct). Pricing Internet services with multiple providers. *Proceedings of the 41st Annual Allerton Conference on Communication, Control and Computing*, Monticello, IL. Available at http://www. eecs.berkeley.edu/

Heikkinen, T. (2004). Distributed scheduling and dynamic pricing in a communication network. *Wireless Networks, 10*, 233-44.

Ileri, O., Mau, S.-C., & Mandayam, N. B. (2005). Pricing for enabling forwarding in self-configuring Ad Hoc Networks. *IEEE Journal on selected Areas in Communications, 23*(1), 151-162.

Jin, N., Venkitachalam, G., & Jordan, S. (2003). Dynamic pricing of network resources. *Proceedings of the GLOBECOM 2003 Conference.*

Kelly, F. (1994). On tariffs, policing, and admission control for multiservice networks. *Operations Research Letters, 15*.

Kelly, F. (1997a). Charging and accounting for bursty connections. In L.W. McKnight & J.P. Bailey (1997). *Internet economics*. Cambridge, MA: MIT Press.

Kelly, F. (1997b). Charging and rate control for elastic traffic. *European Transactions on Telecommunications, 8*, 33-37.

Kelly, F., Maulloo, A.K., & Tan, D.K.H. (1998). Rate control for communication networks: Shadow prices, proportional fairness, and stability. *Journal of the Operational Research Society, 49*, 237-52.

Kephart, J.O., Hanson, J.E., & Greenwald, A.R. (2000). Dynamic pricing by software agents. *Computer Networks. 32*, 731-752.

La, R.J., & Anantharam, V. (2002). Utility-based rate control in the Internet for elastic traffic. *IEEE Transactions on Networking, 10*(2), 272-286.

Lazar, A. A., Orda, A., & Pendarakis, D.E. (1995). Virtual path bandwidth allocation in multi-user net-

S

works. *Proceedings of the IEEE INFOCOM*, Boston (pp. 312-20).

Lazar, A. A., & Semret, N. (2003). Design and analysis of the progressive second price auction for network bandwidth sharing. *Telecommunications Systems, Special Issue on Network Economics*, Apr. 24

Legard, D. (2003). SingTel, NTT DoCoMo tie up to push 3G. IDG News Service.

Leloup, B. (2003). Pricing with local interactions on agent-based electronic marketplaces. *Electronic Commerce Research and Applications, 2*, 187-198.

Li, T., Iraqi, Y., & Boutaba, R. (2004). Pricing and admission control for QoS-enabled Internet. *Computer Networks, 46*(1), 87-110.

MacKie-Mason, J. K., & Varian, H. R. (1994, March). Pricing the internet. *International Conference on Telecommunication Systems Modelling*, Nashville, TN (pp. 378-393).

MacKie-Mason, J.K., & Varian, H.R. (1995a). Pricing congestible network resources. *IEEE Journal on selected Areas in Communications, 13*(7), 1141-1149.

MacKie-Mason, J. K., & Varian, H. R. (1995b). *Pricing the Internet: Public access to the Internet*. Cambridge, MA: MIT Press.

Marbach, P. (2001). Pricing differentiated services networks: Bursty traffic. In the *Proceedings of the IEEE INFOCOM 2001 Conference*.

Marbach, P. (2002). Priority service and max-min fairness. In *Proceedings of the IEEE INFOCOM 2002 Conference*. Also available at shttp://citeseer.ist.psu.edu/marbach02priority.html

Marbach, P. (2004). Analysis of a static pricing scheme for priority services. *IEEE/ACM Transactions on Networking, 12*(2), 312-325.

Marbach, P., & Berry, R. (2002). Downlink resource allocation and pricing for wireless networks. *Proceedings of the IEEE INFOCOM 2002*.

McKnight, L.W., & Bailey, J.P. (1997). *Internet economics*. Cambridge, MA: MIT Press.

Meyer, D. (2003). AT&T wireless tries simple rate plans, fewer freebies. *RCR Wireless News, 22*(7).

Murphy, L., Murphy, J., & Posner, E.C. (1994, June). Distributed pricing for embedded ATM networks. *Proceedings of the International Teletraffic Congress ITC-14,* Antibes, France (pp. 1053-1063).

Odlyzko, A. (1997). *A modest proposal for preventing Internet congestion*. Retrieved from http://www.research.att.com/~amo/doc/modest.proposal.ps

Odlyzko, A. (1998). *The economics of the Internet: Utility, utilization, pricing, and quality of service*. Retrieved from URL http://www.research.att.com/~amo

Odlyzko, A. (1999). Paris metro pricing for the Internet. In *First ACM Conference on Electronic Commerce*, Denver, Colorado (pp. 140-147).

Odlyzko, A. (2001). Internet pricing and the history of communications. *Computer Networks, 36*(5/6), 493-517.

Panagiotakis, S., Koutsopoulou, M., & Alonistioti, A. (2005). Business models and revenue streams in 3G market. *IST Mobile Communication Summit 2005*, Dresden, Germany.

Paschalidis, I.Ch., & Tsitsiklis, J.N. (2000). Congestion-dependent pricing of network services. *IEEE/ACM Transactions on Networking, 8*(2), 171-184.

Parris, C., Keshav, S., & Ferrari, D. (1992). *A framework for the study of pricing in integrated networks*. ICSI Technical Report TR-92-016 y. AT&T Bell Labs Technical Memorandum TM-920105-03, January.

Qiu, Y., & Marbach, P. (2003). Bandwidth allocation editor. *Proceedings of the Twenty-Second Annual Communications Joint Conference of the IEEE Computer and Communications Societies (INFOCOM 2003)* (pp. 797-807).

Rizzo, M., Briscoe, B., Tassel, J., & Damianakis, K. (1999). A dynamic pricing framework to support a scalable, usage-based charging model for packet-switched networks. *Proceedings of the First International Working Conference on Active Networks, Lecture Notes in Computer Science, Vol. 1653* (pp. 48-59). London: Springer-Verlag.

Roggendorf, M., Beltrán, F., & Gutiérrez, J. (2006). Architecture and implementation of an agent-based simulation tool for market-based pricing in next-generation wireless networks. *Proceedings of the 2nd International Conference on Testbeds & Research Infrastructures for the Development of Networks and Communities (IEEE TridentCOM2006)*, March, Barcelona, Spain.

Sairamesh, J., & Kephart, J. O. (2000). Price dynamics and quality in information markets. *Decision Support Systems, 28*, 35-47.

Saraydar, C., Mandayam, N., & Goodman, D. (2002). Efficient power control via pricing in wireless data networks. *IEEE Transactions on Communications, 50*(2), 291-303.

Savagaonkar, U., Givan, R.L., & Chong, E.K.P. (2002). Dynamic pricing for bandwidth provisioning. *Proceedings of the 2002 Conference on Information Sciences and Systems*, Princeton University.

Semret, N., Liao, R.F., Campbell, A.T., & Lazar, A.A. (2000). Pricing, provisioning and peering: Dynamic markets for differentiated Internet services and implication for network interconnections. *IEEE Journal: Selected Areas in Communications,* Special Issue on Quality of Service on the Internet, December.

Shenker, S., Cocci, R., Estrin, D., & Zhang, L. (1991). A study of priority pricing in multiple service class networks. *Proceedings of SIGCOMM 91*, September. Oxford University Press.

Shenker, S., Cocci, R., Estrin, D., & Zhang, L. (1993). Pricing in computer networks: Motivation, formulation and example. *ACM/IEEE Transactions on Networking, 1*, 614-627.

Shenker, S., Clark, D., Estrin, D., & Herzog, S. (1996). Pricing in computer networks: Reshaping the research agenda. *ACM Computer Communications Review, 26*(2), 19-43.

Shu, J., & Varaiya, P. (2003). Pricing network services. *Proceedings of the IEEE INFOCOM Conference*, San Francisco.

Stiller, B., Gerke, J., Reichl, P., & Flury, P. (2001). Management of differentiated services usage by the cumulus pricing scheme and a generic Internet charging system. *IM 2001 - IFIP/IEEE International Symposium on Integrated Network Management* (pp. 93-106).

Sun, J., Modiano, E., & Zheng, L. (2004). A novel auction algorithm for fair allocation of a wireless fading channel. *Proceedings of the Conference on Information Science and Systems*.

Viterbo, E., & Chiasserini, C. F. (2001). Dynamic pricing in wireless networks. In *International Symposium on Telecommunications*, September (pp. 385-388).

Voinov, I. A., & Valladares, T. R. (2003). An enhanced socket interface for next generation systems. In *First International Workshop on Wireless, Mobile & Always Best Connected*, University of Strathclyde, Glasgow, UK (pp. 73-85).

Wang, X., & Schulzrinne, H. (2004). Comparative study of two congestion pricing schemes: Auction and tâtonnement. *Computer Networks, 46*(1), 111-31.

Wikipedia (2006). Retrieved July 20, 2006, from, http://en.wikipedia.org/wiki/Category:Game_theory

Zhou, C., Honig, M., Jordan, S., & Berry, R. (2002). Utility-based resource allocation for wireless networks with mixed voice and data services. *Proceedings of the IEEE International Conference on Computer Communications and Networks*, Miami, Florida (pp. 485-488).

KEY TERMS

Charge: Amount of money billed for a particular service (Courcoubetis & Weber, 2003).

Game Theory: Branch of mathematics that uses models to study interactions with formalized incentive structures or "games" (Wikipedia, 2006).

Pareto Efficiency: A distribution is Pareto efficient if the net benefit for one participant cannot be improved without decreasing the benefit of another participant in that transaction.

Price: In the context of this paper, a *price* represents the monetary value associated with one unit of a specific service.

Price Strategy: Covers the entire range of factors utilized to determine the price of a product or service.

Survivability Mechanisms of Generalized Multiprotocol Label Switching

M. C. R. Medeiros
University of Algarve, Portugal

N. S. C. Correia
University of Algarve, Portugal

INTRODUCTION

Internet protocol (IP) over optical (IP-over-optical) networks is the widely accepted solution to meet the ever increasing demands of IP traffic. In an IP-over-optical network, the IP routers are attached to an optical core network, composed by optical cross-connects (OXC) that are interconnected by dynamically established optical wavelength channels called lighpaths (Rajagopalan, Pendarakis, Saha, Ramamoorthy, & Bala, 2000). To control such lightpaths in a dynamic, efficient, and real-time manner, generalized multiprotocol label switching (GMPLS) based control plane has been proposed by the Internet engineering task force (IETF) in the RFC 3945 edited by Mannie (2003).

BACKGROUND

GMPLS is a suite of control and signaling plane protocols that are being defined within the IETF, based on their expertise on multiprotocol label switching (MPLS) (Rosen, Viswanathan, & Callon, 2001). The MPLS protocol has been defined to support the forwarding of packets based on a label. MPLS allows multiple data packets to be bundled onto the same label switch path (LSP) if they share a common path and common resource requirements. At the ingress of an MPLS controlled network, a label edge router (LER) examines the incoming IP data packets and assigns the label associated with the LSP it belongs to. The labeled packets are forwarded along an LSP where each label switched router (LSR) makes a switching decision based only on the label of the packet. GMPLS extends the capabilities offered by MPLS to network elements that have a nonpacket-based forwarding mechanism. GMPLS can support multitype of LSPs

such as packet-switched capable (PSC), time division multiplex (TDM), lambda-switched capable (LSC), and fiber-switched capable (FSC). This enables the implementation of a single control plane able to handle a whole multilayer network. With GMPLS, service providers are able to build a hierarchy of MPLS-based networks where LSPs of lower level networks see higher layer LSPs as links. Therefore, it is possible to tunnel a set of lower level LSPs with the same source and destination through a higher level LSP (Dutta & Rouskas, 2002) as is illustrated in Figure 1.

IP-OVER-OPTICAL NETWORK ARCHITECTURE

An IP-over-optical network is a two layers network. The optical layer is composed by OXCs connected by fibers as illustrated in Figure 2.

The optical layer provides lightpaths to the IP network, which has a collection of LSRs that establish IP LSP connections. That is, the optical core network is the serving entity providing end-to-end optical connections, while the IP layer acts as a client. The IP/MPLS layer and the optical layer can cooperate in several ways at the convenience of the manufacturers and operators, including overlay, peer, and augmented models proposed in GMPLS architecture document edited by Mannie (2003). The key difference among these models is the amount of information that can be shared between the two layers.

- **Overlay model:** The IP/MPLS layer and the optical layer are controlled separately, each layer having a distinct control plane. The layers communicate between themselves by means of a standard user network interface (UNI). The IP/

Figure 1. GMPLS switching hierarchy

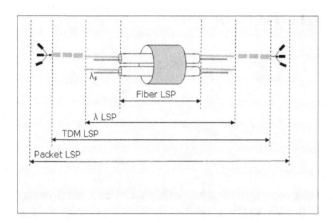

Figure 2. Schematic representation of an IP-over-optical network

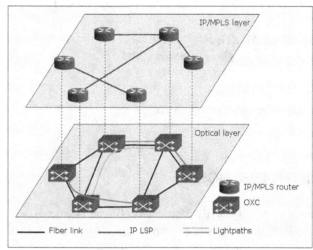

MPLS network requests services such as lightpath creation and deletion to the optical layer, which satisfies these requests according to the service level agreement (SLA). The UNI concentrates and hides all the details such as addressing, topology, and routing of the optical layer from the IP/MPLS layer. This operation model is suitable for network scenarios where optical transport and IP/MPLS service networks belong to different domains and the service providers want to operate and manage their networks independently.

- **Peer model:** The IP/MPLS and the optical network are treated as a single integrated network from the control plane view. All the network nodes, IP/MPLS nodes, and optical nodes act as peers sharing the same complete network topological information. Under this scenario, naming, addressing, topology, and routing information are common for all types of resources in the network. The GMPLS signaling, routing, and link management protocols can be used to implement a common control plane in such a network. The advantages of the peer model are that, it allows seamless interconnection between the IP/MPLS and the optical network. Its main drawback is the amount of information that has to be handled by any network element.

- **Augmented model:** This model assumes separate routing instances in the two layers, but information from one routing instance can be passed through to the other routing instance. Augmented model is suitable for a scenario, where optical transport

and IP/MPLS service networks administrated by different entities would like to maintain separation between IP/MPLS and optical layers and at the same time have the benefits of the integrated model approach.

SURVIVABILITY OPTIONS: SINGLE-LAYER AND MULTILAYER

Survivability can be provided by single-layer or multilayer survivability schemes. In the single-layer approach, the following options are possible:

- **Survivability at the optical layer:** In this case, protection is given to lightpaths carrying traffic. Every lightpath carrying IP traffic must have a link-disjoint backup lightpath, which can be calculated using several approaches (Zhang & Mukherjee, 2004). Advantages of this method are that recovery actions are performed at coarse granularity and failures do not propagate to the upper layers. However, lightpath protection is inefficient in what concerns to the use of resources. This is because the bandwidth reserved by backup lightpaths is equal to the total bandwidth of the lightpath being protected even if just a small percentage of traffic is being carried. Furthermore, failures in

Figure 3. Network architecture with peer model

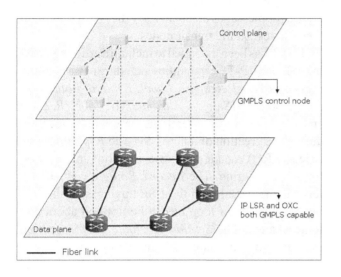

upper layers may not be resolved and in case of lower layer node failure, the upper layer nodes might be left in isolation.

- **Survivability at the IP layer:** In MPLS-based IP networks, survivability can be provided through protection or restoration (Sahasrabuddhe, Rama-murthy, & Mukherjee, 2002). Protection at the IP layer can be provided through the creation of a primary IP LSP and a backup IP LSP, both with the required bandwidth and link-disjoint. This approach can use the shared risk link groups (SRLGs) concept, which identifies groups of lightpaths sharing a common physical resource (Rajagopalan, Luciani, & Awduche, 2003). Advantages of this method are that recovery actions are performed at a fine granularity, IP LSP, which allows for differentiation of flows for recovery speeds/priority classes, as well as may lead to better capacity utilization. A disadvantage is that several recovery actions and notification messages may be needed because of the finer flow granularity.
- **Survivability provided by the IP layer and the optical layer:** When both layers are allowed to provide survivability, the choice of which layer will provide survivability is a key issue. The following two options can be identified: (1) Survivability at the lowest detecting layer and (2) survivability at the highest possible layer. An advantage of using the first technique is that

upper layer failures are easily handled, although the isolated upper layer node problem is still persistent. An advantage of using the second technique is that it addresses properly the situation when traffic flows are injected on different layers, but many recovery actions may be needed in a case of lowest layer link failure.

The following strategies were identified by Pickavet et al. (2006):

- **Uncoordinated approach:** Recovery mechanisms are installed on several layers. All of them try to recover from failure, but there is no coordination between them. Although simple, this strategy has negative consequences on efficiency, capacity requirements, and network stability.
- **Sequencial approach:** In this approach if the recovery process of the current layer is not able to recover within the predefined time, the recovery process escalates for the next layer, which then tries the network recovery. Although the sequential approach can be used with any sequence of layers, two obvious strategies are: (1) bottom-up: the lowest detecting layer starts the recovery, and recovery actions on the upper layers follow. An advantage of this approach is that recovery is performed at the appropriate granularity; (2) top-down: the upper layer starts the recovery. An obvious disadvantage of sequential recovery approach is that recovery actions on the next layers are delayed, independently of the failure. When implementing sequential recovery mechanism coordination between the layers is essential. The sequential approach has been implemented recently by Ratnam, Zhou, and Gurusamy (2006).
- **Integrated approach:** Multilayer survivability techniques can be achieved by allowing survivability mechanisms of several layers to cooperate in recovering from failures. It allow for better network resource utilization, due to the sharing of the spare capacity among recovery mechanisms in the different layers. In such scenario, the peer network model is the most appropriate and the GMPLS protocol suite can provide the necessary control plane for the implementation of multilayer integrated protection strategies as discussed by Puype et al., (2005).

MULTILAYER RECOVERY AND GMPLS

GMPLS relies on the peer model to provide a single unified GMPLS control plane to IP-over-optical networks. The transport plane of the network is formed by nodes interconnected by fibers. The nodes in the network are GMPLS LSRs. The nodes consist of IP LSRs and OXC both controlled by GMPLS as represented in Figure 3.

The network nodes are able to perform ordinary IP routing, packet-oriented switching as well as lambda-oriented switching. The switching decision depends on the information associated with the generalized label (GL), which can consist in labels added to packets, cells, frames, as well as wavelength and interfaces of the incoming signal.

The control plane manages and supervises the transport plane. Signaling and routing protocols extended with traffic engineering (TE) capabilities are used for configuration and control of LSPs. The two signaling protocols used are the reservation protocol (RSVP-TE) (Awduche et al., 2001) and the constrained label distribution protocol (CR-LDP) (Andersson et al., 2002). Two routing protocols, extended with TE capabilities that are used are open shortest path first (OSPF-TE) (Katz, Kompella, & Yeung, 2003) and intersystem to intersystem (ISIS-TE) (Smit & Li, 2004).

GMPLS TOOLS AND TECHNIQUES

Since GMPLS is built on the foundation of MPLS, first we consider the MPLS features, which can be applied to GMPLS. Resource reservation protocol (RSVP) and constraint routing-label distribution protocol (CR-LDP) are the two signaling protocols used by GMPLS in order to exchange the necessary control information among nodes to set up lightpaths. Only RSPV is considered here. RSVP signaling relies on two fundamental message types: *Path* and *Resv. Path* messages travel downstream toward the egress while *Resv* messages travel upstream toward the ingress. Both messages are processed by all transit nodes along the data path.

The *Path* and *Resv* messages create "path state" and "resv state" in each transit nodes, respectively. These states are periodically refreshed and updated by the *Path* and *Resv* messages. Both states may also be deleted by *PathTear* and *ResvTear* messages. Furthermore, errors in the "path state" and the "resv state" are reported by *PathErr* and *ResvErr* messages, respectively. Unless a "state_removed" flag is set in *PathErr* and ResvErr, both error messages do not modify the "path state" and "resv states" in the transit nodes.

RSVP has been extended to include traffic engineering (TE) RSVP-TE capabilities including new signaling messages *Label_Request*, *Label*, *Explicit_Route*, *Record_Route*, and *Session_Attribute*. The *Label_Request* and the *Label* objects facilitate new label allocation during the creation of a new LSP. The *Explicit_Route* object (ERO) encodes end-to-end routing information for source routing. The *Record_Route* object (RRO) records the actual path the LSP traverses so that the ingress can detect loop or can be notified about any route change. The *Session_Attribute* aids in session identification and diagnosis. In addition, the RSVP-TE protocol introduces a *Hello* mechanism. This *Hello* extension enables RSVP nodes to detect when a neighboring node is not reachable either because of a control channel failure or because of a node failure. The RSVP protocol extensions under the GMPLS framework retain all of the setup, teardown, and error reporting mechanisms in RSVP-TE under MPLS, but add features necessary to work in the TDM and optical domains (Berger, 2003). The added GMPLS features which enable efficient multilayer operational strategies for survivable IP-over-optical networks GMPLS are the following:

- **Multitype of switching and transfer layer:** GMPLS can support multi-type LSPs such as packet-switched-capable (PSC), time division multiplex (TDM), lambda-switched-capabable (LSC), and fiber-switch- capable (FSC). A connection can be established only between, or through, interfaces of the same type.

- **LSP hierarchy:** LSP hierarchy is a notion that LSPs can be nested inside other LSPs. The nesting can also occur between interface types. At the top of the hierarchy are FSC interfaces, followed by LSC interfaces, followed by TDM interfaces, followed by LSC, and followed by PSC interfaces. Therefore, an LSP that starts and ends on a PSC interface can be nested, together with other LSPs, into an LSP that starts and ends on a LSC interface.

- **Forwarding adjacencies:** The use of forwarding adjacencies (FA) provides a mechanism that can improve bandwidth utilization when bandwidth allocation can be performed only in discrete units. It offers also a mechanism to aggregate forwarding state, thus allowing the number of required labels to be reduced. Once a lightpath is established between two LSRs, the lightpath can be advertised as a FA in a link state protocol, such as open shortest path first (OSPF). In this way, a node when performing route computation is able to use conventional and virtual links since they both appear in the OSPF routing table.

- **Out-of-band signaling:** Non-packet LSPs tend to require out-of-band control channels. This is because the large bandwidth granularity of the TDM or wavelength channels makes it wasteful to use a whole time-slot or wavelength as a signaling channel. In order to support the use of a distinct, out-of-band control network (e.g., Ethernet), GMPLS introduces the concepts of signaling message encapsulation and data interface identification. The message encapsulation allows each signaling message to be addressed to the adjacent node on the data path. Originally, RSVP messages are addressed to either ingress or egress nodes. The interface identification allows the node to distinguish the data interface indicated by the signaling message.

- **Notify message:** Although effective, the RSVP error report based on *PathErr/ResvErr* messages is slow. This is because all nodes along the path must process *PathErr/ResvErr* messages. In addition, if failure affects many LSPs at the same time, multiple *PathErr/ResvErr* messages could congest the network. GMPLS introduces a *Notify* message, which is sent directly from the point of failure detection to the point of repair (PoR), without being intercepted by transit nodes. The recipient of the *Notify* message must be specified by the *Path* or *Resv* message during the connection setup or the state refresh. In order to reduce the load in the control network, the *Notify* message is defined so that it can report errors for multiple LSPs as long as they fail with the same error code and have the same PoR.

- **Bidirectionality:** The ability to set up bidirectional connections becomes essential for connections in the optical domain. Typically, bidirectional setup requires two unidirectional setup signals.

GMPLS introduces the *"upstream_label"* object to the *Path message*. This object indicates the label that should be used by the adjacent downstream node to forward data in the reverse direction. The addition of the *upstream_label* object allows the setup of both directions to complete within one *Path-Resv* roundtrip.

- **Graceful deletion:** To delete a connection, GMPLS requires an additional signaling roundtrip before a *PathTear* or a *ResvTear* message can be issued. This additional signaling consists of transmissions of *Path* and *Resv* messages with a "Delete (D)" flag set. The purpose of this extra signaling is to notify transit nodes the intention to teardown. Without this extra notification, the transit nodes may not see the out-of-band *PathTear* or *ResvTear* in time to turn off the loss-of-light alarm. As a result, the management system at these nodes may raise the alarm because it mistakes the teardown of a lightpath for a failed connectivity.

- **Graceful restart/control state recovery:** Since the GMPLS control plane could be physically diverse from the data plane, a recovery mechanism is needed to ensure the operation of the data plane when the control plane has failed. To guarantee that an LSP will not be turn down just because the control plane has failed, GMPLS introduces the "Restart_cap" object. This object advertises the capability of a node to recover GMPLS states after a control plane has failed or restarted.

EMERGING TRENDS

GMPLS integrating traffic engineering (TE) capabilities allows traffic grooming techniques to be applied to solve the survivability problem of IP-over-optical networks as proposed by Correia and Medeiros (2006) and Yao and Ramamurthy (2005). This research area remains relatively unexplored and several key issues need to be considered.

The practical implementation of GMPLS control planes able to provide multilayer survivability such as in Habib, Song, Li, and Rao (2006) is another actual issue, which will continue to provide many research challenges.

CONCLUSION

In IP-over-optical networks, various survivability strategies are possible. This article presented an overview of various survivability strategies and how they can be implemented in GMPLS IP-over-optical networks.

REFERENCES

Andersson, L., Callon, R., Dantu, R., Wu, L., Doolan, P., Worster, T., et al. (2002). *Constraint-based LSP setup using LDP.* IETF Internet RFC 3212.

Awduche, D., Berger, L., Gan, D., Li, T., Srinivasan, V., & Swallow. G. (2001). *RSVP-TE: extensions to RSVP for LSP tunnels.* IETF Internet Draft RFC 3209.

Berger, L. (2003). Generalized multi-protocol label switching (GMPLS) signaling resource reservation protocol-traffic engineering (RSVP-TE) Extensions. IETF Internet RFC 2473.

Correia, N. S. C., & Medeiros, M. C. R. (2006). Protection schemes for IP-over-WDM networks: Throughput and recovery time comparison. *Photonic Network Communications, 11*(2), 127-149.

Dutta, R., & Rouskas, G. N. (2002). Traffic grooming in WDM networks: Past and future. *IEEE Network, 16*(6), 46-56.

Habib, I. W., Song, Q., Li, Z., & Rao, N. R. V. (2006). Deployment of the GMPLS control plane for grid applications in experimental high-performance networks. *IEEE Communications Magazine, 44*(3), S65-S73.

Katz, D., Kompella, K., & Yeung. D. (2003). *Traffic engineering (TE) extensions to OSPF.* IETF Internet RFC 3630.

Mannie, E. (2003). *Generalized multi-protocol label switching architecture.* IETF Internet Draft RFC 3945.

Muñoz, R., Rivera, R. V. M., Sorribes, J., & Giralt, G. J. (2005). Experimental GMPLS-based provisioning for future all-optical DPRing-based MAN. *IEEE Journal of Lightwave Technology, 33*(10), 3034-3045.

Pickavet, M., Demeester, P., Cole, D., Staessens, D., Puype, B., Depré, L., & Lievens, I. (2006). Recovery in multilayer optical networks. *IEEE Journal of Lightwave Technology, 24*(1), 122-134.

Puype, B., Vasseur, J., Groebbens, A., Maesschalck, S., Colle, D., Lievens, I., et al. (2005). Benefits of GMPLS for multilayer recovery. *IEEE Communications Magazine, 43*(7), 51-59.

Rajagopalan, B., Luciani, J., & D. Awduche, D. (2003). *IP over optical networks: A Framework.* IETF Internet Draft RFC 3717.

Rajagopalan, B., Pendarakis, D., Saha, D., Ramamoorthy, R. S., & Bala, K. (2000). IP over optical networks: Architectural aspects. *IEEE Communications Magazine, 38*(9), 94-102.

Ratnam, K., Zhou, L., & Gurusamy, M. (2006). Efficient multilayer operational strategies for survivable IP-over-WDM networks. *IEEE Journal on Selected Areas in Communications, 24*(8), 16-31.

Rosen, E., Viswanathan, A., & Callon, R. (2001). *Multiprotocol label switching architecture.* IETF Internet Draft RFC 3031.

Sahasrabuddhe, L., Ramamurthy, S., & Mukherjee, B. (2002). Fault management in IP-over-WDM networks: WDM protection versus IP restoration. *IEEE Journal on Selected Areas in Communications, 20*(1), 21-23.

Smit, H., & Li., T. (2004). *Intermediate system to intermediate system (IS-IS) extensions for traffic engineering (TE).* IETF Internet RFC 3784.

Yao, W., & Ramamurthy, B. (2005). Survivable traffic grooming with path protection at the connection level in WDM mesh networks. *Journal of Lightwave Technology, 23*(10), 2846-2853.

Zhang, J., & Mukherjee, B. (2004). A review of fault management in WDM mesh

networks: Basic concepts and research challenges. *IEEE Network, 18*(2), 41-48.

KEY TERMS

Generalized Multiprotocol Label Switching (GMPLS): Extends the capabilities offered by MPLS to network elements that have non-packet-based forwarding mechanism.

Label Edge Router (LER): An ingress router of a MPLS controlled network.

Label Switch Path (LSP): A specific traffic path through an MPLS network.

Label Switched Router (LSR): A core router of a MPLS controlled network.

Lightpath: An all-optical wavelength channel between two nodes, it may span more than one fiber link.

Multiprotocol Label Switching (MPLS): Supports the forwarding of data based on a label.

Network Survivability: The capacity of the network to provide continuous service in the presence of failures.

S

Swarm Intelligence Applications for the Internet

Sergio Gutiérrez
University Carlos III of Madrid, Spain

Abelardo Pardo
University Carlos III of Madrid, Spain

Carlos Delgado Kloos   `
University Carlos III of Madrid, Spain

INTRODUCTION

A **swarm** may be defined as a population of interacting elements that is able to optimize some global objective through collaborative search of a space (Kennedy, 2001). The elements may be very simple machines or very complex living beings, but there are two restrictions to be observed: They are limited to *local* interactions; usually the interaction is not performed directly but indirectly through the environment. The property that makes swarms interesting is their ***self-organizing* behaviour**; in other words, it is the fact that a lot of simple processes can lead to complex results.

The behaviour of ants is the best-known example of swarm intelligence. In many ant species, ants deposit a chemical substance called pheromone as they move from a food source to the nest. Ants do not communicate directly with each other, but they follow pheromone trails (leaving their own pheromones, so the trail is reinforced). The path connecting the food source and the nest is optimized without any global knowledge of the problem by any of the agents. This process of indirect communication in a swarm is called ***stigmergy***. The possibility that a system gets stuck in a locally better but not optimal solution is called ***stagnation*** (Bonabeau, 1999).

BACKGROUND

Swarm intelligence is a growing field of active research, and its applications outside the Internet are manifold. Swarm intelligence techniques have been applied to many different kinds of problems. Examples range

from the very general, like graph coloring (Costa, 1995) or constraint satisfaction (see Zlochin, 2002, for a survey on this topic), to those applied to very particular problems, like allocating tasks for robots in a factory (Morley, 1996), routing a fleet of trucks (Gambardella, 1999), or even designing the timetable for a set of university courses (Socha, 2002). There is a good survey of robotic applications, along with explanations of the varying ant behaviours that inspired them (from food foraging to collective transport or nest building) in Bonabeau (1999).

SWARM INTELLIGENCE APPLICATIONS BASED ON VIRTUAL AGENTS

Most applications based on **swarm intelligence** phenomena are based on groups of **virtual agents**. They show good results when applied to problems that are spatially distributed and change over time. As many Internet problems are distributed and time-varying by nature, swarm-based optimization and problem-solving techniques show good results when applied to them.

If we focus on network-oriented applications, most are related to **routing** problems. Although there has been a lot of research on this topic (see Steenstrup, 1995 for a good survey), swarm intelligence techniques are specially suited for these families of problems as they are inherently dynamic and distributed.

In packet networks like the Internet, every packet may follow a different route towards its destination. The main function of a packet network (sometimes called data network) is to assure efficient distribution of information among its users. There are three main issues to be taken into account: congestion control, security of communication, and routing. There have been many swarm-based approaches to the **routing** problem (see Dorigo, 2004 for a survey). We will focus here on the AntNet algorithm in the form it is explained in Dorigo (2004), as it is a representative example and shows all the main characteristics of swarm-based approaches (simple agents, indirect communication, and emergent swarm behaviour). Interested readers will find more applications in Bonabeau (1999) and Dorigo (2004).

The AntNet algorithm is a *distributed, adaptive, distance-vector* **routing algorithm**. It is a special case of **ACO** algorithm based on artificial **ants** and **pheromones** deposition. In AntNet, every node keeps two different tables (apart from the routing table): a *pheromone* table, T, and a *traffic model* network, M. Their construction and update mechanism is explained below.

AntNet uses two types of **artificial agents** or **ants**: *forward* ants and *backward* ants. Ants are all independent and there is neither coordination nor direct communication between them. Forward ants are generated at each node, and are directed to other nodes in relation to the node's generated traffic: More forward ants are generated towards those nodes where more traffic is being sent. They share the normal queues used by data packets, so they experience the same traffic load. They store the path they travel until they get to their destination. Backward ants are generated when a forward ant arrives at its destination, and follow the path stored by the corresponding forward ant. Not all forward ants arrive at their destination, as those ants that perform a cycle (visit an already-visited node) that is longer than half the ant's age are discarded. Backward ants use high-priority queues on their way back.

After arriving at each node, forward ants select their next hop probabilistically according to the pheromones matrix (avoiding, if possible, already visited nodes). The pheromone matrix has a number of columns equal to the number of nodes in the network, and a number of rows equal to the number of outgoing links (neighbours) of the node. All columns sum up to one and, for any given destination, they show the (uncorrected) probability that a forward ant will follow that link. This probability is corrected using a heuristic rule that gives a higher probability to those links with emptier outgoing queues, so the system is reactive to network load fluctuations. The mission of forward ants is to store the path followed to their destination and to record the time needed to reach every node along it.

The mission of backward ants is to update the **pheromone** and the traffic model matrices. The traffic model matrix has three rows, and for every possible destination stores the mean (μ_d) and variance (σ_d) time to arrive there, as well as the best time during the last M_{max} iterations. When a backward ant arrives at a node, the node's M matrix is updated with the values stored in the ant's memory (collected by the corresponding forward ant). The mean and the average are updated in a way so that more recent values have more weight than older ones. The update of the pheromone matrix T is done in a way that depends on a measure of goodness associated with the trip time experienced by the forward ant. The pheromone value that corresponds to the destination node and the outgoing link of that ant is increased (small pheromone values are increased proportionally more). The other values are decreased accordingly (virtual **pheromone evaporation**) in order for the column to sum up to one.

Finally, data packets in an AntNet scenario are sent probabilistically. Routing tables are calculated from pheromone tables by elevating each probability to a factor, thus boosting high probabilities and neglecting low ones.

AntNet has been simulated and compared to some state-of-the-art routing algorithms like the distributed Bellman-Ford (Bertsekas, 1992) and the Predictive Q-routing (Choi, 1996), with positive results (Dorigo, 2004).

SWARM INTELLIGENCE APPLICATIONS BASED ON SOCIAL GROUPS

There are several applications that are based on real people instead of virtual agents, but nevertheless show **swarm-like behaviour** characteristics: a large amount of interacting persons with no direct communication between them, indirect communication through some kind of environment, and **emergent patterns** not immediately related to individual behaviour.

Collaborative Filtering

Collaborative filtering is based on the premise that people looking for information should be able to make use of what others have already found and evaluated.

Traditional collaborative filtering systems (Dron, 1999) stored preferences and evaluations of users with respect to several items (from novels and songs, to learning resources in a class). Those preferences allowed other users to see what their peers preferred, and use this information as a guide for their actions.

In the last years, the growth of e-commerce has stimulated the use of collaborating filtering systems as recommender systems. Thus, the goal of a modern collaborative filtering system may be stated as predicting the utility of a certain item for a particular user based on the user's previous likings and the opinions of other like-minded users.

Modern collaborative filtering systems can be classified into *memory-based* and *model-based*. The first ones employ a user-item database to generate a prediction. These systems use statistical techniques to find a set of users (*neighbours*) that have a similar profile of agreeing with the target user (Pennock, 2000). Model-based collaborative filtering algorithms provide item recommendation by first developing a model of user ratings. Algorithms in this category take a probabilistic approach and envision the collaborative filtering process as computing the expected value of a user prediction, given his/her ratings on other items. The model-building process is performed by different techniques, such as bayesian networks (Miyahara, 2000), latent semantic analysis (Hofmann, 2003), and rule-based approaches (Boley, 2003).

Collaborative Adaptive Sequencing

Adaptive sequencing is one of the main challenges nowadays in the field of **Web-based education**. It can be stated as the problem of selecting the order in which a set of units are presented to the student (in a sequence) in order to make his or her learning as successful as possible, taking into account the capabilities and needs of every student. Different students maximize their learning with different sequences of activities: Some will benefit from a sequence with a top-bottom approach, while others will prefer the opposite; longer sequences of exercises for those topics that they find especially difficult may be preferred, as well as shorter sets for those topics they already know; some will prefer activities with a lot of written text, while others will learn more with graphical resources, etc.

Although different students will prefer different learning sequences, their preferences will show some degree of correlation, as in the previous case. Moreover, the sequencing problem is one of path optimization ("find the path that maximizes the learning"). Thus, swarm-intelligence techniques may be used for it.

Semet (2003) used the following approach for Paraschool (a leading French e-learning company), where he took advantage of the large number of system users (around 10.000). A **graph** of exercises was created: Every node was an exercise and every arc determined a transition from one node to another according to some probabilities (set *a priori* by a pedagogical team). Every student left pheromones in the arcs after trying an exercise in a node: Successful students left positive pheromones while failures led to the deposit of negative pheromones. After every exercise, the next node (and thus the sequencing) was selected according to the probabilities on every outgoing arc, and these were increased or decreased according to the positive or negative pheromones deposited on them. This work has shown its capacity to correct incorrectly-set probabilities on the arcs. Further research has shown some difficulties of using real people in the same way as artificial ants for path optimization processes, and has led to the concept of pheromone erosion instead of **pheromone diffusion** (Valigiani, 2005).

Tattersall (2005) takes another approach. The goal is the creation of paths in a Learning Network (Koper, 2005), a network made of learning activities. The success of the students when pursuing different activities is recorded, and that information is used to make a recommendation to other students as to which is the best activity for them to continue with. Preliminary results show an improvement in the effectiveness of the students' learning process (Janssen, 2005).

FUTURE TRENDS

In the field of packet-switching networks, the field of **ad-hoc networks** is the most promising one for the development of swarm-based applications. It is still a growing field, and its inherently distributed nature makes ACO-type algorithms very appropriate for their application there. There have been many results in the preceding years (Baras, 2003; Heissenbüttel, 2003), and it is clear that others will follow in the near future.

Another field that has been scarcely explored is that of WDM networks and protocols like GMPLS (Yamanaka, 2005). The possibility of applying algorithms like ABC (Schoodenboerd, 1997) or CAF (Heusse, 2001) to these networks could bring interesting results (Chin, 2005).

In any case, many of the most promising applications of swarm intelligence techniques to the Internet come from the ***social swarm*** field. Collaborative filtering is an active field with well known commercial applications, such as the Amazon.com recommender system (Linden, 2003), while the research on collaborative sequencing may lead to a better understanding of the way the user navigates through the Web (Wu, 2003; Ramos, 2004).

Although the **sequencing** problem brings similarities to other path optimization problems, there are differences to be taken into account. First, the path has to be optimized for every user. The path that is "optimal" for everybody may not be optimal for each student. This is specially critical for e-learning systems. The approach taken by Gutiérrez (2006) is a mixture of both traditional collaborative filtering and collaborative sequencing systems, giving the students information about the performance of their peers and the actions taken by them (as a group, not individually). This approach puts the student in a meta-cognitive state when confronted with his or her peers' results, and brings some similarities to the method suggested in Valigiani (2006), although in that case the comparison is made between the students' level and the exercises' level.

CONCLUSION

In AntNet, any pair of forward-backward ants can make an approximation to solve the shortest-path problem between two nodes, but it is only the swarm of ants that solves the general routing problem. In a Learning Network, every student goes their own way, but it is only the swarm of students that finds the best pedagogical sequencing of learning units. Both examples illustrate the features of swarm-intelligence applications: flexibility, robustness, indirect and/or local communication, decentralized control, self-organization, and adaptability.

In recent years many steps have been made towards the understanding of swarms and how swarm-based systems can be engineered (Dorigo, 2004). However, there is still a lack of knowledge on the theoretical part, especially for those systems based on social swarms. Thus, it is difficult to predict how these systems will behave when confronted with unexpected events. That may be the reason that there are few applications in the field of Economics, where they could find many interesting applications. Meanwhile, more applications will appear in years to come, both in the context of the Internet and in other fields, especially robotics.

REFERENCES

Baras, J.S., & Mehta, H. (2003). A probabilistic emerging routing algorithm for mobile ad hoc networks. In *Proceedings of Modelling and Optimization in Mobile, Ad-Hoc and Wireless Networks*.

Bertsekas, D., & Gallager, R. (1992). *Data networks*. Prentice Hall.

Boley, H. (2003). RACOFI: A rule-applying collaborative filtering system. *Proceedings of 2003 IEEE/WIC International Conference on Web Intelligence/Intelligent Agent Technology*.

Bonabeau, E., & Dorigo. M., & Theraulaz, G. (1999). *Swarm intelligence: From natural to artificial systems*. MIT Press.

Chin, T.S. (2005). An ant algorithm for single-hop wavelength assignment in WDM mesh network. *Proceedings of the 17th IEEE International Conference on Tools with Artificial Intelligence (ICTAI'05)* (pp. 111-117).

Choi, S., & Yeung, D. (1996). Predictive Q-outing: A memory-Bbased reinforcement learning approach to adaptive traffic control. *Advances in Neural Information Processing Systems, 8* (NIPS 8), 945-951.

Costa, D., Hertz, A., & Dubious, O. (1995). Embedding of a sequential algorithm within an evolutionary algorithm for coloring problems in graphs. *Journal of Heuristics, 1*, 105-128.

Dorigo, M., & Stützle, T. (2004). *Ant colony optimization*. MIT Press.

Dron, J., Mitchell, R., Siviter, P,& Boyne, C. (1999). CoFIND: Experiment in n-dimensional collaborative filtering. In *Proceedings of WebNet 99*.

Gambardella, L.M., Taillard, E., & Agazzi, G. (1999). MACS-VRPTW: A multiple ant colony system for vehicle routing problems with time windows. *New Ideas in Optimization,* 63-76.

Gutiérrez, S., Pardo, A., Delgado, & Kloos, C. (2006). Some ideas for the collaborative search of the optimal learning path. *Proceedings of Adaptive Hypermedia 2006.*

Heissenbüttel, M., & Braun, T. ((2003). Ant-based routing in large-scale mobile ad-hoc networks. *Machine Learning, 20*(3), 197-244.

Heusse, M. (2001). *Routage et équilibrage de charge par agents dans les réseaux de communication.* PhD thesis, École des Hautes Études en Sciences Sociales, Paris.

Hofmann, T. (2003). Collaborative filtering via Gaussian probabilistic latent semantic analysis. *Proceedings of the 26th ACM SIGIR Conference on Research in Information Retrieval.*

Janssen, J., Tattersall, C., Waterink, W.,Van den Berg, B.,Van Es, R., & Bolman, C., et al. (2005). Self-organizing navigational support in lifelong learning: How predecessors can lead the way. *Computers & Education.*

Kennedy, J., & Eberhart, R. (2001). *Swarm intelligence.* Morgan Kauffman.

Koper, R. (2005). Designing learning networks for lifelong learners. In: R.Koper & C. Tattersall (Eds.), *Learning design: A handbook on modelling and delivering networked education and training* (pp. 239-252).

Linden, G., Smith, B., & York, J. (2003). Amazon.com recommendations: Item-to-item collaborative filtering. *IEEE Internet Computing, 7*(1), 76-80.

Maniezzo, V., & Carbonaro, A. (2000). An ANTS heuristic for the frequency assignment problem. *Future Generation Computer Systems, 16,* 927-935.

Miyahara, K., & Pazzani, M. (2000). Collaborative filtering with the simple Bayesian classifier. In *Pacific Rim International Conference on Artificial Intelligence* (pp. 679-689).

Morley, R. (1996). Painting trucks at General Motors: The effectiveness of a complexity-based approach. *Embracing complexity: Exploring the application of complex adaptive systems to business,* 53-58.

Navarro, Varela, G., & Sinclair, M.C. (1999). Ant colony optimization for virtual-wavelength-path routing and wavelength allocation. *Proceedings of Congress on Evolutionary Computation (CEC'99)* (pp. 1809-1816).

Pennock, D., Horvitz, E., Lawrence, S., & Lee Giles, C. (2000). Collaborative filtering by personality diagnosis: A hybrid memory- and model-based approach. *Proceedings of the 16th Conference on Uncertainty in Artificial Intelligence (UAI 2000).*

Ramos, V., & Abraham, A. (2004). Evolving a stigmergic self-organized data-mining. *Proceedings of the 4th International Conference on Intelligent Systems, Design and Applications.*

Schoodenboerd, R., Holland, O., & Bruten, J. (1997). Ant-like agents for load balancing in telecommunication networks. In *Proceedings of the First International Conference on Autonomous Agents* (pp. 209-216).

Semet, Y., Lutton, E., & Collet, P. (2003). Ant colony optimization for e-learning: Observing the emergence of pedagogic suggestions. In *Proceedings of IEEE Swarm Intelligence Symposium 2003.*

Socha, K., Knowles, J., & Sampels, M. (2002). A MAX-MIN ant system for the University Timetabling Problem. In *Proceedings of the Third International Workshop on Ant Algorithms (ANTS 2002)* (pp. 1-13).

Steenstrup, M. (1995). *Routing in communication networks.* Prentice Hall.

Tattersall, C., Manderveld, J., Van den Berg, B.,Van Es, R., Janssen, J., & Koper, R. (2005). Swarm-based wayfinding support in open and distance learning. In E.M. Alkhalifa (Ed). *Cognitively informed systems: Utilizing practical approaches to enrich information presentation and transfer* (pp. 166-183).

Valigiani, G.,Jamont, Y., Biojout, R.,Lutton E., & Collet, P. (2005). Experimenting with a real-size man-hill to optimize pedagogical paths. In *Proceedings of the ACM Symposium on Applied Computing (SAC'05).*

Valigiani, G., Lutton, E., Jamont, Y., Biojout, R., & Collet, P. (2006). Automatic rating process to audit a man-hill. *WSEAS Transactions on Advances in Engineering Education, 3*(1), 1-7.

Wu, J., & Aberer, K. (2003) Swarm intelligent surfing in the Web. In *Proceedings of the Third International Conference on Web Engineering (ICWE03).*

Yamanaka, M. (2005). *GMPLS technologies: Broadband backbone networks and systems*. CRC Publishers.

Zlochin, M., & Dorigo, M. (2002). Model-based search for combinatorial optimization: A comparative study. In *Proceedings of the Seventh International Conference on Parallel Problem Solving from Nature* (pp. 651-661).

KEY TERMS

ACO (Ant Colony Optimization): A swarm intelligence-based optimization heuristic in which small ant-like agents interact indirectly only through changes to the environment and reacting to those changes.

Collaborative Filtering: An application in which different users express their individual preferences about some items, and the emerging result is the possibility of making predictions about items not rated or for new users.

Collaborative Sequencing: An application in which the sequences of activities followed by some users is used to infer the best sequence for other users.

Distance Vector Routing: A routing algorithm that requires that each router simply inform its neighbours of its routing table. The opposite is a link-state routing algorithm.

Link-State Routing Algorithm: A routing protocol that requires each router to maintain at least a partial map of the network. The opposite is a distance-vector routing algorithm.

Routing: The distributed activity of building and using tables at the nodes of a packet network that state the path to be followed by packets going from a source to a not-directly-connected destination.

Stagnation: Situation in which a system does not evolve towards a better solution because it has found a local optimum. For example, sometimes ant colonies stick to existing trails to food even if better, new ones appear because the pheromone trail is so strong they cannot leave it.

Stigmergy: Indirect communication process in which the individual parts of a system communicate with one another, not directly but by modifying their local environment.

A Taxonomy of Online Game Security

Kuen Park
Korea University, South Korea

Heejo Lee
Korea University, South Korea

INTRODUCTION OF ONLINE GAME SECURITY

People enjoy playing games for simple pleasure. Recently, since the emergence and advance of the computer technologies, especially in terms of graphic and networking, which enables people to experience virtual world with a computer network they couldn't ever have imagined (Smed & Hakonen, 2003). In this respect, the popularity of games has roared, which builds up the cultural phenomenon because numerous people are involved in the game forming community.

The online game market scale amounted to $19 billion by 2011 (Gamasutra, 2006), which shows that games are not a negligible industry but a Midas's hand, which relates to the other industries such as cinema and music. For instance, the famous game character "Lara Croft" of the game "Tomb Raider" was converted to Hollywood cinema, which was greatly successful.

However, online games face many threats (Chen, Hwang, Song, Yee, & Korba, 2005). An attacker who comprehends the mechanism of online games attempts to lead a game to his favor with malicious actions. This generates unfair advantage for fun or profit (Pritchard, 2001). Online game cheating has not been a simple problem because it is the primary reason an honest player quits the game if he or she had experienced unfair playing from a cheater. Therefore, an online game designer should consider online game security seriously (Yan & Choi, 2002).

This article is constituted as follows. A classification of online games and the associated brief explanations are described with the viewpoint of security. Afterward, a taxonomy of online game attacks and the respective countermeasures are provided. The next section demonstrates how to prepare for predictable game attacks. This article concludes in the final section.

BACKGROUND: ONLINE GAME CLASSIFICATION

Online games have various types of how to attack the game. Thus, game designers should consider the game type about what factors are vulnerable in its game type. Figure 1 represents our classification of online games. Online games can be divided in five categories: abstraction, action, simulation, story-driven, and strategy. The characteristics and security consideration of each game are as follows.

Abstraction Games

Abstraction games represent the game, which is abstracted by the computer programming and its respective design for online gaming. Classical board games and gambling games are often made with some modifications for new rules or fun. Go and chess are good examples of this category. The characteristic of this game type is that it is easy to learn to play than any other game type. Typically, game portal sites such as http://www.hangame.com and http://www.netmarble. com are providing this type of game collectively. In addition, Internet Chess Club (http://www.chessclub. com) is a case for providing this type of game category. A good security analysis of this site is released in 2006 (Black, Cochran, & Gardner, 2006).

Action Games

Action games have genres such as classical arcade, fighting, sports, and FPS games. These kinds of games need fast reactions in the virtual environment. An attacker attempts to modify the related values such as the number of bullets or energy status.

Figure 1. A classification of online games

Story-Driven Games

Story-driven games have two main categories: adventure games and role-playing games. Adventure games focus on resolving specific missions such as quest, mission, or mystery. In role-playing games, the user should make an effort to build his or her character to be stronger with activities. Diablo, Final Fantasy, and World of Warcraft are the representative cases (Griffiths, Davies, & Chappell, 2003).

Simulation Games

Simulation games can be divided into two categories: real-time strategy games and turn-based strategy game. Simulation games focus on careful planning and skillful resource management to achieve victory. In simulation games, resource is the indispensable factor so an attacker tries to alter the amount of resources.

ONLINE GAME SECURITY

Online game attacks can be classified into the following four categories: server attacks, network attacks, client attacks, and user attacks. The respective attacks are briefly introduced in the follow section. Figure 2 shows the classification as a tree format. In the viewpoint of generally accepted security principals and models, we can enumerate online game attacks with respect to three security factors:

- **Confidentiality:** Confidentiality ensures that computer-related assets are accessed only by authorized parties. In this respect, game data attacks harm confidentiality. For maintaining fair online games, confidential information exchange between client and server is necessary.
- **Integrity:** Integrity means that assets can be modified only by authorized parties or in authorized ways. In this context, packet attack and client's four attacks--memory, file, time, and event attacks—are purposed to damage game integrity. If someone can manage packet, memory, file, time, and event, he or she is able to take control of the game on his or her purpose. To protect these values controlled by an attacker, integrity checks should be realized during game play.
- **Availability:** Availability means that assets are accessible to authorized parties at appropriate times. Therefore, DDoS and user attacks damage availability. Someone who transmits overwhelming service requests to the game server can interrupt normal gaming services. In addition, kinds of user attacks disrupt normal item usage of an honest user.

Server Attacks

Game servers contain sensitive data such as ID, password, and game record, which is the main target for an attacker. Game information leakage can be serious damage to the game vendor.

Network Attacks

Online games must interact between server and host via network infrastructure. An attacker can use this property on attack. An attacker can sniff the game packet and fabricate it in his or her favor. Furthermore, he or she can interrupt normal game play with the use of a great number of botnet agents that generate high volumes of traffic.

Figure 2. A classification of online game attacks

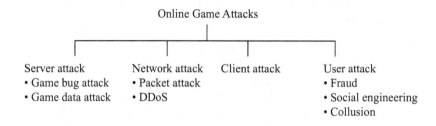

Client Attacks

Transforming software file and local environment values such as memory, OS time, and event are the good attacking strategy for an attacker. In addition, numerous auxiliary game hack programs help attackers attack games. These kinds of hack programs have been devised and distributed by hackers for fun or profit.

User Attacks

Because of invisible network gaming environments between users, an attacker can deceive an honest player. For instance, an attacker can obtain an honest user's game information or items by fraud.

SERVER ATTACKS

Game bug attacks represent a game server that has design bugs. An attacker can use it for his or her advantage effectively. For instance, an attacker found a place where he or she may be invisible to an honest user in a certain FPS game. An attacker could kill an honest player only keeping his or her position in the place and shooting the gun when an honest player appeared. In this respect, game server bugs harm the fairness of the game. Therefore, game designers should make effort to cover this kind of vulnerability. Since game data can be transformed into real money, an attacker attempts to fulfill game data attacks. Therefore, an attacker tries to gather items the malicious way. If he or she can take control of server information, he or she is able to transmit items to his or her account and make a profit.

To protect game data attacks, the following set of countermeasures can be adopted. First, data encryption using HTTPS and registry key encryption are recommended prevention. In addition, access control policies should be regularly examined and enforced. Second, OS and DB vulnerability should be checked with OS and DB security tools, which can further check the patch status. Real time backdoor monitoring systems and vulnerability scanning activity can be a good way to protect server attacks. In particular, a trial vulnerability examination is a good way to check and cover the potential threat.

NETWORK ATTACKS

Network attacks to game systems can be divided into two categories: packet manipulation attacks and DDoS. Packet manipulation attacks (Baughman & Levine, 2001) have an objective to reveal the content of game packets. Once an attacker knows its specific meaning, he or she can design packets for his or her favor and transmit them to game server. DDoS attacks are closely coupled with availability that is a main component of computer security. An attacker can attack game systems in order to interrupt normal service using a large number of botnet (Hussain, Heidemann, & Papadopoulos, 2003; Smed, Kaukoranta, & Hakonen, 2001). To prepare for the network attacks, IPS (intrusion prevention system) and its management equipments are dedicated to prevention. Furthermore, network firewall and ACL on router and switch should be examined for DDoS attacks (Dietrich, 2004). SSL VPN and the separation of an internal network with respect to roles can diminish network threats (Merabti & Rhalibi, 2004).

CLIENT ATTACKS

Once an online game is released and it gains popularity, an attacker may start to analyze the game software on the client. After analyzing the software, related auxiliary hacking tools emerge. The hacking tools can be classified as follows:

- **Speedhack (Yan, 2005):** Modifying the time of an game
- **Maphack (wallhack):** Enabling to see game status
- **Memoryhack:** Altering the memory value of an game
- **Packeteditor:** Editing game packets
- **Trainermaker:** Enabling to build customizing hacking functions
- **File patcher:** Replacing game files with hacked files
- **File packer:** Unpacking game files for hacking files
- **Debugger:** Disassembling files to analyze files (Debray, 2005)
- **Gamebot:** Launching programs for automatic item harvesting (Kim, Hong, & Kim, 2005)
- **Bug hack:** Exploits bugs in the game

Secure game designs (Yan, 2003) fundamentally decrease security threats of online gaming. Typically, attackers can analyze game files with reverse engineering. To protect reverse engineering attacks, the code sequence can be obfuscated in a file. In other ways, the integrity checking of game files are highly recommended as an effective defense. In addition, monitoring client game values such as memory, file, time, and event should be required to protect the game variable modification attack. For game client security, various countermeasures can be used. Anti-hack solution is a good way to prevent malicious process communications, which aim to capture targeted memory event. Thus, anti-hack solution can monitor the anomaly situations of game files and game time modification. In addition, the installation of a Web application firewall, which monitors covert channels and traffics for data theft and application disruption, can be an effective countermeasure.

USER ATTACKS

An attacker deceives an honest user to obtain virtual assets using fraud, social engineering, and collusion. Fraud often occurs when exchanging or trading virtual assets. Hence, game designers need to consider the development of a fair trading system that does not allow illegal trading such as taking items but no giving proper rewards. In addition, even if an illegal trading or transaction may occur, a set of procedures that trace swindled items such as a unique ID number for each virtual asset and transaction record system should be prepared. Social engineering represents an attackers' psychological trick on game users in an effort to obtain profitable information or assets (White, 2003). For example, an attacker sends an e-mail disguised as a game administrator requesting a new password and an old password of a user. Collusion occurs when an attacker collaborates with other attackers for the purpose of deceiving honest users to acquire unfair advantages (Murdoch & Zielinski, 2004). In order to avoid collusion, user reputation and reporting systems can be used effectively.

PREPARING FUTURE ATTACKS AND DEFENSES

Anti-Hack Solution File Attack

An attacker tries to modify or delete anti-hack files so that anti-hack cannot operate properly. Some anti-hack solution vendors verify files' integrity; however, the checking module may not always operate correctly. The solution is to check whether anti-hack solution files are impaired during game play.

Skipping Attack

Some anti-hack solutions adopt the policy to check whether an auxiliary client hacking program exists on client with signature-based detection. However, an attacker can skip this check procedure using hot-key based or time-based usage. In particular, delicately devised hacking files are overwritten to real files. Therefore, the anti-hack solution requires monitoring the execution of auxiliary programs during game playing with anomaly detection.

Hardware-Based Gamebot

Current anti-hack solutions are able to distinguish software-based keyboard events and mouse events in order to detect a gamebot for automatic item harvesting. However, hardware-based gamebots can avoid such a detection mechanism. Currently, some gamebot-related vendors distribute many types of hardware-based gamebots for profit, and such commercialized gamebots have gained popularity recently in South Korea. To protect this kind of gamebot, anti-hack solution should encompass the ability to recognize hardware-based gamebots.

CONCLUSION

Online game security is the indispensable factor to determine the market penetration of a game. The pervasive nature of the online game coupled with recent threats makes online game security an area of significant importance. In this article, we have presented a classification of online game attacks and discussed the defense mechanism for four main types of attack. This article confirms that there are several important issues, which requires long-term research attention. The ultimate goal of online game security is to protect games against both known and unknown online game attacks. This ambitious goal cannot be achieved in a single stroke. Therefore, we need to continue the enhancement of online game security in various aspects.

REFERENCES

Baughman, N. E., & Levine B, N. (2001). Cheat-proof playout for centralized and distributed online games. *IEEE INFOCOM.*

Baxter, I. D., & Mehlich, M. (2000). Reverse engineering network: Professional resources for reverse code engineering. *Science of Computer Programming, 2-3,* 131-147.

Black, J., Cochran, M., & Gardner, R. (2006). A security analysis of the internet chess club. *IEEE Security & Privacy Magazine, 4,* 46-52.

Carless, S. (2006). Analyst: Online Game Market $13 Billion by 2011. *Gamasutra Industry News.* Retrieved May 17, 2007, from http://www.gamasutra.com/php-bin/news_index.php?story=9610

Chen, Y. C., Hwang J. J., Song, R., Yee, G., & Korba, L. (2005). Online gaming cheating and security issue. In *International Conference on Information Technology: Coding and Computing.*

Griffiths, M, D., Davies, M. N. O., & Chappell, D. (2003). Breaking the stereotype: The case of online gaming. *Cyber Psychology & Behavior, 6*(1).

Hussain, A., Heidemann, J., & Papadopoulos, C. (2003). A framework for classifying denial of service attacks. *SIGCOMM.*

John, B., Martin, C., & Ryan, G. (2006). A security analysis of the Internet chess club. *Security & Privacy Magazine, IEEE.*

Kim, H., Hong, S., & Kim, J. (2005). Detection of auto programs for MMORPGs. *Advances in Artificial Intelligence, 3809, 1281-1284.*

Merabti, M., & Rhalibi, A. E. (2004). Peer-to-peer architecture and protocol for a massively multiplayer online game. *IEEE Globecom Workshops.*

Mirkovic, J., Dietrich, S., Dittrich, D., & Reiher, P. (2004). *Internet denial of service.* Prentice Hall.

Murdoch, S, J., & Zielinski, P. (2004). Covert channels for collusion in online computer games. *Information Hiding, 3200, 355-367.*

Pritchard, M. (2000). How to hurt the hackers: The scoop on Internet cheating and how you can combat it. *Information Security Bulletin.* Retrieved May 17, 2007 from http://www.gamasutra.com/features/20000724/pritchard_pfv.htm

Ruggles, C., Wadley, G., & Gibbs, M. R. (2005). *Online community building techniques used by video game developers.* International Federation for Information Processing.

Smed. J., & Hakonen. H. (2003). *Towards a definition of a computer game.* Turku Centre for Computer Science.

Smed, J., Kaukoranta, T., & Hakonen, H. (2001). Aspects of networking in multiplayer computer games. In

International Conference on Application and Development of Computer Games.

Udupa, S., Debray, S., & Matias, M. (2005). Deobfuscation: Reverse engineering obfuscated code. In *Working Conference on Reverse Engineering.*

White, S, M. (2003). Social engineering. *Engineering of Computer-Based Systems, 1109, 261-267.*

Yan, J. J. (2003). Security design in online games. In *Annual Computer Security Applications Conference.*

Yan, J. J. (2005). A systemic classification of cheating in online games. *Workshop on Network & System Support for Games.*

Yan, J. J., & Choi, H. J. (2002). Security issues in online games. *The Electronic Library, 20*(2).

KEY TERMS

Anomaly-Based Detection: Anomaly-based detection detects abnormal states, which an attacker provokes.

Anti-Hack Solution: The solution for prevention, detection, and response to the game cheating.

Collusion: An malicious activity between two or more persons to defraud another game user.

Encryption: A procedure that renders the contents of a message or file unintelligible to anyone not authorized to read it.

Gamebot: A program for item harvesting automatically.

Keylogger: A computer program that captures the keystrokes of a computer user and stores them. Modern keyloggers can store additional information, such as images of the user's screen. Most malicious keyloggers send this data to a third party remotely (such as via e-mail).

MMORPG: A massively (or massive) multiplayer online role-playing game or MMORPG is a multiplayer computer role-playing game that enables thousands of players to play in an evolving virtual world at the same time over the Internet.

Online Game: Multiple clients connect a host server through the Internet so that they may play network game.

Signature-Based Detection: Signature-based detection represents a detection method distinguishing the distinctive bit stream from an auxiliary program.

TCP and TCP–Friendly Protocols

Agnieszka Chodorek
Kielce University of Technology, Poland

INTRODUCTION

One of the most popular transport protocols—Transmission Control Protocol (TCP)—has a long history. The first document describing TCP protocol in early stages was published in 1974. Since then, TCP specification was changed several times, and finally in 1981 was standardised by RFC 793 (Postel, 1981). Two years later TCP, together with Internet Protocol (IP), became the official protocol suite of the Internet. In the same year the first widely available implementation of TCP in the 4.2 BSD operating system was built.

In the eighties, the Internet grew rapidly and some problems with TCP congestive collapse were observed. Therefore, in 1988 the next version of TCP was introduced in 4.3 BSD Tahoe. In this version significant changes were made, including introduction of congestion control and improvement of error control. After 4.3 BSD, this version of TCP was named TCP Tahoe. Certain problems with congestion control in TCP Tahoe caused a 1990 release of a new version of TCP, called TCP Reno, which was implemented in 4.3 BSD Reno. This version had a more aggressive congestion control mechanism, which significantly improved TCP performance in a congested environment. TCP Reno was used in almost all popular operating systems.

In the final decade of the 20th century, several versions of TCP were proposed. The most widely applied were TCP New Reno (TCP Reno with modified action taken when exiting via Fast Recovery) and TCP SACK (TCP Reno with selective acknowledgements). The last one, at the end of nineties, has replaced TCP Reno in the most popular operating systems.

In the second half of nineties, rapid development of real-time multimedia weakened the monopolist position of TCP. As a result, TCP has had to compete for bandwidth with more aggressive, streaming traffic. The new term—TCP-friendly—to describe fair behaviour toward competing TCP connections appeared in the work of Floyd and Fall (1999). The first TCP-friendly protocol standardized by an RFC document was TCP-Friendly Rate Control (TFRC). Nowadays, TCP-friendliness is one of the features expected from modern congestion control.

BACKGROUND

TCP is a general-purpose, connection-oriented unicast transport protocol, designed to provide reliable end-to-end transmission over potentially unreliable networks. It is the best known transport protocol and the primary transport protocol of the current Internet. The protocol is used by data transfer applications, such as e-mail, WWW, file transfer (ftp), etc.

Effective congestion control, elaborated error control, full duplex transmission, and a long history of implementations (that led to good verification of both algorithms and code) makes TCP a good solution for point-to-point reliable data transmission. As a result, for about 25 years since the RFC 793 was published, there was no necessity of replacing TCP with other reliable transport protocols, and TCP's mechanisms were only improved or supplemented. The first specification of TCP was supplemented by slow start, congestion avoidance and fast retransmit (TCP-Tahoe), fast recovery (TCP-Reno) and selective acknowledgements option (TCP-SACK). Moreover, several improvements have been introduced by consecutive RFCs only, without a separate version—as ECN-capability, window scalability, or delayed ACK.

The TCP protocol isn't the perfect solution for all network applications and services. Its strong optimisation for point-to-point connection, unicast-oriented mechanisms, and elastic adjustment to network circumstances means that TCP isn't (and probably will not be in the future) multicast-enabled or suitable to use with real-time applications. Therefore, in such situations other transport protocols are applied.

The multi-protocol Internet must be fair for all Internet traffic. Because many authors associate the fair nature of TCP with its congestion-control mechanism, transport protocols that under congestion behave like TCP (so-called TCP-friendly protocols), are believed to be able to co-exist with TCP on the Internet. Rapid growth of non-TCP applications, such as multicast data transfer, VoIP, IPTV, and audio- and videoconferencing has resulted in TCP-friendliness–a relatively new term in traffic engineering–quickly becoming one of the more important aspects of a protocol's design and implementation.

TCP AND TCP-FRIENDLINESS

In this section, three main mechanisms of modern TCP are described (error control, flow control, and congestion control) as well as the most important properties of TCP transmission.

Error Control

Error control is aimed at reliability assurance of TCP connections. It consists of error detection, signalling by acknowledgements, and error correction. Damaged or lost packets are detecting by both end systems. The sender detects errors by expiration of retransmission timeout, and the receiver detects errors by using the checksum service (packet damage) or by detection of a gap in sequence space (packet losses).

The receiver confirms the proper reception of delivered data using positive acknowledgement (ACK). If the transmission error was detected by the receiver, the sender learns of it by reception of three replications of ACK packet with the same acknowledged data segment (so-called "fast retransmit"). TCP confirms reception of continuous sequence space. The SACK version also enables confirmation of discontinuous sequence space.

Packets detected as lost or damaged are retransmitted. The sender performs retransmission of undelivered data in two manners–using selective retransmission (only undelivered data is retransmitted) or go-back-N retransmission (all packets in the current wnd window are retransmitted). Usually, selective retransmission is used and go-back-N is utilised only in the case of severe errors.

Flow Control

The flow control mechanism prevents the receiver's buffer from overflowing. Flow control slows down the data sending rate to adjust it to receiver's reception ability. TCP implements end-to-end window-based flow control, where the so-called receiver window (rwnd) represents the current receiver buffer space.

The well-known definition of window, taken from RFC 793, is: "*the window indicates an allowed number of octets that the sender may transmit before receiving further permission*" (Postel, 1981, p. 3). In other words, the sender is able to send without prior acknowledgement an amount of data only equal to window size. In some networks, especially high-speed or long-distance, flow control can cause unintended limitation of achieved throughput. In such a situation, the Window Scale Option introduced by RFC 1323 can be used.

Congestion Control

Congestion—a temporary or permanent loss of stability of a packet network—is observed in the network as output buffer overflows. Therefore, transport protocols typically interpret packet drops as implicit congestion notification.

TCP's congestion control mechanism can work both with implicit (using packet losses) and explicit (using ECN bits) congestion signalling. The mechanism introduces an additional window—the congestion window (cwnd). As a consequence, TCP flow is controlled by the resultant TCP window (wnd), equal to minimum cwnd and rwnd.

TCP's congestion control consists of four algorithms (Allman, Paxson, & Stevens, 1999): slow start, congestion avoidance, fast retransmit, and fast recovery. The last two algorithms define congestion signalling (fast retransmit) and recovery procedure (fast recovery). The first two algorithms use the congestion window to limit transfer rate of the protocol and are directly responsible for congestion avoidance.

In the case of severe danger of congestion, the slow start algorithm is used. During the slow start, the congestion window is incremented one full-sized segment after the reception of each acknowledgement. The behaviour of slow start can be observed as the exponential growth of the congestion window in time. Slow start introduces congestion control at the initial stages of transmission. The mechanism is also used for congestion avoidance after a severe congestion has been detected.

If danger of congestion is less severe, the congestion avoidance algorithm will be used. During congestion avoidance, the congestion window is incremented by one full-sized segment after reception of each round (non-overlapping window). The behaviour of congestion avoidance can be observed as linear growth of the congestion window in time.

To identify "severe" and "less severe" danger of congestion, a slow start threshold (ssthresh) state variable is used. When the window cwnd is less than ssthresh, the danger of congestion is considered "severely dangerous," otherwise it is considered less severe. The initial value of ssthresh is, usually, set to rwnd. When congestion is detected, the cwnd is reduced and a new value of ssthresh is set (typically to one half wnd).

The reduction of cwnd depends on the detection of congestion. When a TCP sender detects segment loss using the retransmission timer, the value of cwnd is reduced to one MSS and the slow start begins. When a TCP sender is informed about congestion via the Fast Retransmit algorithm or ECN signalling, the new value of cwnd is set to ssthresh. As a result, a slow start is omitted.

TCP over Wireless Channels

TCP mechanisms are optimized for a relatively small error rate, and TCP's congestion control works under the assumption that packet loss occurs in routers and packet loss (damage) in links is negligible. In the case of wireless networks, characterized by relatively high bit error rates (BER), implicit congestion signaling is open to misinterpretation. In addition, if the wireless transmission is carried out via the long-distance link, TCP's mechanisms must face the challenge of great latency (satellite transmission), as well as bandwidth asymmetry (UMTS transmission and satellite transmission), which result in rate and delay variability.

Although a lot of research has been carried out to improve TCP throughput in wireless environments, this problem still remains an important subject of research. Research generally falls under three main categories: improving TCP mechanisms, applying TCP/IP proxies or accelerators (also known as TCP/IP spoofing), and improving the underlying wireless network. Interesting discussions about TCP in wireless environments were presented in Tian, Xu, and Ansari (2005). Some solutions worth noticing (in the Author's opinion) are mentioned in Section Four.

It's worth remarking that the TCP-SACK is more suitable for wireless transmission than previous versions of TCP. The TCP-SACK, which enables confirmation of discontinuous sequence space, better deals with (typical for wireless channels) multiple packet losses from a current window.

Properties of TCP Transmission

One of the most important features of TCP protocol is its ability for fair bandwidth allocation between competing TCP flows. Measure of a flows' fairness is the so-called fairness coefficient, F, usually defined as follows:

$$F = \frac{1}{N}\left(\sum_{i=1}^{N} \text{Thr}_i\right)^2 \cdot \left(\sum_{i=1}^{N} \left(\text{Thr}_i\right)^2\right)^{-1} \quad (1)$$

where N is a number of competing TCP flows and Thr_i is a throughput of ith TCP connection, $i = 1, 2, \ldots, N$.

The TCP usually achieves $F \approx 1$ (competing TCP flows connections utilise network resources in an approximately equal fashion). Fair bandwidth allocation is a result of applying a congestion control scheme. However, there are three main phenomena which degrade TCP connections: phase effect, global synchronisation, and TCP-unfriendliness.

Phase effect and global synchronisation occur in networks with a homogeneous transport layer. The phase effect—delay-dependent unfairness toward competing flows—is a phenomenon observed in a system where two or more flows, characterized by different round-trip-times (RTT), compete for shared network resources. A relatively small difference in RTT has strong impact on throughput and flow with the larger RTT achieving lower throughput than flow with the smaller ones.

Global synchronisation is the tendency to synchronously drop packets belonging to many TCP connections during congestion. As a consequence, these connections reduce the congestion window approximately at the same time. It results in weak utilisation of the bottleneck link, as well as in traffic fluctuations in delivery paths.

TCP-unfriendliness occurs typically in networks with a heterogeneous transport layer. It is an especially serious problem in shared networks, where bulk data carried by TCP is transmitted in the same link with inelastic (real-time) traffic. In such networks, we can observe strong degradation of TCP connections when TCP competes for bandwidth with streaming traffic.

TCP-Friendly Protocols

The problem of TCP-unfriendliness can be resolved using so-called TCP-friendly protocols. The well-known definition of TCP-friendliness goes: *"We say a flow is TCP-friendly if its arrival rate does not exceed the arrival of a conformant TCP connection in the same circumstances"* (Floyd & Fall, 1999). Because lack of congestion control in real-time transport protocols is blamed for TCP-unfriendliness, TCP-friendly protocols use congestion control mechanisms similar to the one implemented in TCP. According to the applied method of congestion avoidance, the TCP-friendly protocols can be classified into one of two groups:

- Protocols which implement TCP's congestion control
- Protocols which emulate TCP's congestion control

The modern TCP-friendly protocols emulate TCP's congestion control, and the similarity between TCP and TCP-friendly protocol is based on the same behavior in the presence of packet losses. Because this behavior is modeled by the so-called "TCP throughput equation," these protocols also are known as "equation-based" TCP-friendly protocols.

A model of TCP behaviour assumes that the throughput of a TCP connection is directly proportional to TCP's maximum segment size (MSS) and inversely proportional to both RTT and a certain function of packet error rate (PER). The form of this function depends on required model accuracy (Figure 1). Typically, the loss function is given as a square root of PER (Mathis et al., 1997):

$$T\left(PER\right) = \frac{MSS}{RTT} \cdot \frac{C_1}{\sqrt{PER}} \tag{2}$$

or as a polynomial (Handley et al., 2003):

$$T\left(PER\right) = \frac{MSS}{RTT} \cdot C_2 \cdot \left(\begin{matrix} \sqrt{\frac{2}{3}PER} + \\ +12 \cdot PER \cdot \sqrt{\frac{3}{8} \cdot PER} \cdot \left(1 + 32 \cdot PER^2\right) \end{matrix} \right)^{-1} \tag{3}$$

where T is a TCP throughput, and C_1, C_2 are scale coefficients.

The most popular of TCP-friendly protocols is the TCP Friendly Rate Control protocol (TFRC), described in RFC 3448 (Handley et al., 2003). The TFRC is a unicast-oriented protocol which varies sending rate in response to congestion. The protocol sends data at a rate calculated from the TCP throughput equation. Typically, equation (3) is used, although any equation giving TCP throughput as a function of loss event rate and RTT can be applied. TFRC does not implement either flow control or retransmissions. Moreover, the protocol has a much lower variation of throughput over time compared with TCP, so RFC 3448 suggests that TFRC is suitable for applications such as telephony or streaming media.

Figure 1. Accuracy of TCP models: TCP throughput (x's), equation (2) (+'s),and equation (3) (o's)

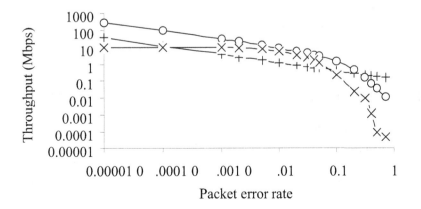

The Wave and Equation Based Rate Control (WEBRC) (Luby & Goyal, 2004) is a multi-purpose multicast transport protocol. WEBRC applies receiver-driven congestion control, that allows the protocol to be massively scalable toward large and very large multicast groups. Each WEBRC receiver computes target reception rate according to a TCP throughput equation, which comes from an equation used by TFRC. The sender sends packets to one base channel and multiple wave channels. The transmission rate of a channel starts at a high rate and the rate decreases over a long period of time. The receiver joins the base channel and a consecutive set of wave channels to achieve the computed rate, resulting in the achievement of TCP-friendliness.

FUTURE TRENDS

TCP development will focus on the successful deployment of the protocol in future networks (both wired and wireless). To improve TCP behavior at high speed (e.g., optical) or over long distance (e.g., satellite) networks, limited slow start (Floyd, 2004) and Quick-Start (Floyd, Alman, Jain, & Sarolahti, 2007) mechanisms, as well as HSTCP (Floyd, 2003) and H-TCP (Leith & Shorten, 2007) versions of TCP are being introduced. To solve typical wireless ad hoc network problems such as congestion indication, changing routes, and frequent routes failure, new TCP versions are being proposed (Al Hanbali, Allman, & Nain, 2005), such as TCP Westwood+ (Grieco & Mascolo, 2004). It's worth remarking that a new version of TCP's congestion control standard is being prepared now (Allman, Paxson, & Blanton, 2007). The new RFC will specify TCP behavior after a relatively long idle period.

At the same time as the TCP protocol is being enhanced, new TCP-friendly protocols are being proposed. A multicast variant of the TFRC protocol (Widmer & Handley, 2006) is being designed, as well as a PGMCC protocol for PGM congestion control (Rizzo, Iannaccone, Vicisano, & Handley, 2004). TCP-like congestion control has been introduced to the Datagram Congestion Control Protocol (Floyd & Kohler, 2006) and to the RTP protocol (Gharai, 2007). Finally, a new variant of TFRC has been designed for applications that send small packets (Floyd & Kohler, 2007).

CONCLUSION

The TCP protocol has been around for a quarter of a century and it's more than likely that it will be used on the future Internet. In current networks, as well as in the future, TCP must share resources with the other transport protocols. To achieve fairness (understood as equal bandwidth share) toward competing TCP flows, TCP-friendly protocols are suggested.

This chapter is roughly divided into two parts. In the first part, TCP's protocol mechanisms as well as some aspects of TCP transmission are presented. The second part of this chapter discusses the problem of TCP-friendliness and overviews two TCP-friendly transport protocols: the unicast TFRC protocol and the multicast WEBRC protocol.

REFERENCES

Al Hanbali, A., Altman E., & Nain, P. (2005). A survey of TCP over ad hoc networks. *IEEE Communications Surveys & Tutorials, 7*(3), 22-36.

Allman, M., Paxson, V., & Blanton, E. (2007). *TCP congestion control*. Internet-Draft, draft-ietf-tcpm-rfc2581bis-02

Allman, M., Paxson, V., & Stevens, W. (1999). *TCP congestion control*. RFC 2581.

Floyd, S, Allman, M., Jain, A., & Sarolahti, P. (2007). *Quick-start for TCP and IP*. RFC 4782.

Floyd, S. (2003). *HighSpeed TCP for large congestion windows*. RFC 3649.

Floyd, S. (2004). *Limited slow-start for TCP with large congestion windows*. RFC 3742.

Floyd, S., & Fall, K. (1999). Promoting the use of end-to-end congestion control in the Internet. *IEEE/ACM Transactions on Networking*, 458-472.

Floyd, S., & Kohler, E. (2006). *Profile for DCCP congestion control ID 2: TCP-like congestion control*. RFC 4341.

Floyd, S., & Kohler, E. (2007). *TCP friendly rate control (TFRC): The small-packet (SP) variant*. RFC 4828.

Gharai, L. (2007). *RTP profile for TCP friendly rate control*. Internet-Draft, draft-ietf-avt-tfrc-profile-10.

Grieco, L. A., & Mascolo, S. (2004). Performance evaluation and comparison of Westwood+, New Reno and Vegas TCP congestion control. *ACM Computer Communication Review, 34*(2), 25-38.

Handley, M., Floyd S., Padhye J., & Widmer, J. (2003). *TCP Friendly Rate Control (TFRC): Protocol specification*. RFC 3448.

Leith, D.J., & Shorten, R.N. (2007). *H-TCP: TCP congestion control for high bandwidth-delay product paths*. Internet-Draft, draft-leith-tcp-htcp-04.

Luby, M., & Goyal, V. (2004). *Wave and Equation Based Rate Control (WEBRC) building block*. RFC 3738.

Mathis, M., Semke, J., Mahdavi, J., & Ott, T. (1997). The macroscopic behavior of the TCP congestion avoidance algorithm. *Computer Communication Review, 27*(3), 67-82.

Postel, J. (1981). *Transmission Control Protocol*. RFC 793.

Rizzo, L., Iannaccone, G., Vicisano, L., & Handley, M., (2004). *PGMCC single rate multicast congestion control: Protocol specification*. Internet-Draft, draft-ietf-rmt-bb-pgmcc-03.

Tian, Y., Xu, K., & Ansari, N. (2005). TCP in wireless environments: Problems and solutions. *IEEE (Radio) Communications Magazine, 43*(3), 27-32.

Widmer, J., & Handley, M. (2006). *TCP-friendly Multicast Congestion Control (TFMCC): Protocol specification*. RFC 4654.

KEY TERMS

Congestion: A temporary or permanent loss of network stability. Congestion appears in network node when the traffic offered to a given resource exceeds its output capacity, that leads to saturation of buffers and, in result, to packet drops.

Congestion Control: Methods and algorithms aimed at counteracting existing congestions and avoiding approaching congestions.

Error Control: A generic name of a set of intertwined methods and algorithms for detection, signalling, and correction of damaged or lost packets. Typically, error detection is based on checksum, packet sequence numbering, or retransmission timers; error signalling is based on acknowledgements (positive or negative) or receiver reports, and error correction is based on retransmission (go-back-N or selective) or forward error correction (FEC).

Flow Control: Methods and algorithms aimed at prevention of the receiver's buffer overflow.

Port Number: The transport address (the third, apart from IP, and MAC, addressing usage in Internet technology). Port numbers range from 0 to 65535 and identify transport-level endpoints. Port numbers of endpoints (source and destination), together with IP addresses of endpoints and a protocol identifier, identify a single connection (e.g., single TCP flow).

TCP-Friendliness: The ability of a system to behave under congestion like the TCP protocol. Lack of TCP-friendliness manifests itself in a strong degradation of TCP connections when TCP competes for bandwidth with one or more TCP-unfriendly flows.

TCP-Friendly Protocol (System): A protocol (system), which applies TCP-like congestion control. TCP-friendly protocols (systems) directly apply TCP's congestion control mechanism or emulate it using the TCP throughput equation. The main properties of TCP-friendly protocols (systems) are avoidance of TCP connections collapse and fairness toward competing flows.

TCP Throughput Equation: An analytical model of TCP protocol behaviour in the presence of packet losses. It describes throughput of a single TCP connection as a function of packet error rate (PER).

Transmission Control Protocol (TCP): The connection-oriented, multi-purpose transport protocol, designed for reliable data transfer. Since the beginning of the eighties, the primary transport protocol of the Internet. It's used by such applications, as e-mail, WWW, file transfer (ftp), etc.

Transport Protocol: The protocol functionally located at the fourth (transport) layer of the OSI reference model of communication network. It provides end-to-end service (in contrast to chained service of lower layers), connection-oriented or connectionless, reliable or real-time. Internet technologies treat the transport protocol as an interface between a network (usually seen as Internet Protocol, IP) and an application. Applications utilize the functionality of IP via the transport service given by transport protocols.

TCP Enhancements for Mobile Internet

Bhaskar Sardar
Jadavpur University, India

Debashis Saha
Indian Institute of Management (IIM) Calcutta, India

INTRODUCTION

Transmission Control Protocol (TCP), the most popular transport layer communication protocol for the Internet, was originally designed for wired networks, where bit error rate (BER) is low and congestion is the primary cause of packet loss. Since mobile access networks are prone to substantial noncongestive losses due to high BER, host motion and handoff mechanisms, they often disturb the traffic control mechanisms in TCP. So the research literature abounds in various TCP enhancements to make it survive in the mobile Internet environment, where mobile devices face temporary and unannounced loss of network connectivity when they move. Mobility of devices causes varying, increased delays and packet losses. TCP incorrectly interprets these delays and losses as sign of network congestion and invokes unnecessary control mechanisms, causing degradation in the end-to-end goodput rate. This chapter provides an in-depth survey of various TCP enhancements which aim to redress the above issues and hence are specifically targeted for the mobile Internet applications.

BACKGROUND

As wireless devices are becoming the fastest growing segments of the computer industry, the networking picture has changed radically in the last decade. Millions of people now want to access the Internet at any time from wherever in the world they may be. To allow this, mobile IP [PER96] has been developed to route packets to these mobile users. As a best effort type of protocol, mobile IP has fulfilled its task fairly well; but TCP [POS81] has to glue well to the mobile IP in order to provide the applications with an end-to-end

and connection-oriented packet transport mechanism that ensures reliable and the ordered delivery of data. However, in the absence of wireless enhancements for TCP to work over mobile Internet, several known problems affect its performance [CAC95]. Nevertheless, most of the wireless data applications (e.g., FTP, Web, telnet, multicasting, etc.) use TCP as the default ***transport layer protocol,*** as they want to achieve reliable and guaranteed delivery of data. But TCP, having faced several problems specific to this network, poses a huge bottleneck to reaching a high goodput rate.

As a result, over the years TCP has been modified several times to improve its performance, and, hence, several important TCP versions have emerged, such as TCP-Tahoe [FAL96], TCP-Reno [FAL96], TCP-Vegas [BRA95], TCP-New Reno [FLO99], and TCP-SACK [FAL96],[MAT96]. However, all these mechanisms and various versions do not work the same, when called to work in diverse environments such as satellite networks, last hop wireless networks, and mobile ad-hoc networks. In [TSA02], [TIA05] authors have compared several TCP enhancing schemes for mobile/wireless networks. In [TSA02], Tsaoussidis and Matta have considered the effect of high BER, unexpected disconnection, and battery power for comparing various TCP enhancing schemes. They are of the opinion that the error detection mechanism must be able to classify different types of errors (e.g., congestion, transient wireless error, persistent wireless error, and handoff), and, based on the error classification, an appropriate recovery strategy must be employed that differs from congestion-oriented mechanisms employed by TCP. They argued for the importance of defining a new performance metric (e.g., energy efficiency) to measure protocol stability and fairness in last hop wireless networks. In [TIA05], Tian et al., have considered different application areas (e.g., cellular, satellite, ad-hoc, and heterogeneous networks) for TCP. But they concentrated on the effect of high BER and channel asymmetry on the performance of TCP in all four application areas.

TCP IN MOBILE INTERNET

Problem of Running TCP in Mobile Internet

The following characteristics have major impact on the performance of TCP in Mobile Internet [SAR06]:

- **High BER:** The bit error rate in wireless networks is much higher than those experienced in traditional wired networks. High BER results in a large number of packet drops. TCP treats these drops as congestion loss and starts congestion control procedures resulting in a degraded performance.
- **Limited spectrum:** Bandwidth is a scarcer resource in wireless networks than its wireline counterparts (e.g., the bandwidth of fast Ethernet is 100 Mbps, whereas GPRS has a bandwidth of 384 Kbps). So, sharing wireless bandwidth efficiently between mission critical and non-critical traffic is a very important task.
- **Handoff:** When a user leaves a cell and enters a new one, handoff takes place. During handoff, a mobile host may lose connection to the base station, and any data transmitted for the mobile host are lost. TCP treats this packet loss as congestion and slows down transmission rate resulting.
- **Unpredictable delay:** As a mobile user moves randomly, distance from a BS varies, resulting in

temporally varied delay. This unpredictable delay is difficult for TCP to handle gracefully.

- **Frequent disconnection:** Mobile hosts often get disconnected (when in motion and/or discharged battery) without any warning. Transmission during this period causes huge packet drops leading to pseudo-congestion and hence degraded performance.
- **Limited energy:** Mobile devices are battery powered, and, hence, cannot afford too many retransmissions, unlike electrically powered devices. In other words, TCP is not designed as an energy-efficient protocol.

Classification of TCP Enhancements

At first approximation, TCP enhancements for mobile Internet can be divided into two main categories as shown in the Figure 1.

In this section we will describe notable proposals which have been made in the literature to improve the performance of TCP in both *3G* cellular networks and *WLAN*. We will provide a comprehensive comparison of these proposals and show which problems are solved by these proposals and which have not yet been solved.

TCP for 3G Cellular Networks

Freeze-TCP [GOF00]

Freeze-TCP was designed mainly to deal with frequent disconnection and handoff. The main idea is to move the onus of signaling an impending disconnection to the Mobile Host (MH). It avoids timeouts at the sender

Figure 1. Classification of TCP enhancements

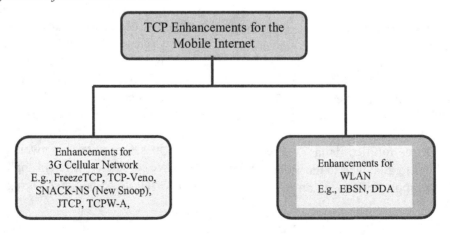

during periodic disconnection and handoff, since a timeout shrinks the sending window and reduces the performance. It exploits the ability of the MH to advertise a window of zero. Based on the signal strength, the MH detects the handoff and advertises a zero window adjustment (ZWA). The sender then freezes transmission and timeout value and enters the persist mode. Once the MH is reconnected, it advertises a non-zero window, so that the sender resumes with their window and timeout values unaffected due to handoff. To implement Freeze-TCP, the network stack needs to be aware of mobility (at least to some extent). In essence, some cross-layer (layers of the protocol stack) efforts and information exchange are needed. It is also necessary for the MH to predict impending disconnection within the round-trip time. If a disconnection cannot be predicted, the behavior and performance will be exactly that of standard TCP.

TCP-Veno [FU03]

TCP-Veno is a novel end-to-end congestion control mechanism and effective for dealing with random packet loss. TCP-Veno exploits a mechanism similar to Vegas [BRA95] to estimate the state of the connection and applies the AIMD schemes of TCP-Reno. Specifically: (1) it refines the multiplicative decrease algorithm of TCP-Reno by adjusting the slow start threshold according to the perceived network congestion level rather than a fixed drop factor, and (2) it refines the linear increase algorithm so that the connection can stay longer in an operating region in which the network bandwidth is fully utilized. It calculates the number of backlog packets as in Vegas but uses this value as an indication whether the connection is in a congestive state. If packet loss is detected when the connection is in the congestive state, it will be considered as congestion loss; otherwise, it is assumed as random loss. TCP-Veno can reduce the amount of window size degradation but might not have good behavior when the random loss is high. It does not deal with disconnection and handoff.

SNACK-NS (New snoop) [SUN04]

SNACK-NS is a link layer retransmission protocol with the ability to overcome the limitations of batched ACK used by TCP. SNACK-NS consists of two protocol components: SNACK-Snoop and SNACK-TCP. The SNACK-Snoop is deployed at the base station (BS) and SNACK-TCP is deployed at the MH. SNACK

mechanism is designed to provide explicit information on multiple packet losses over wireless link. In SNACK, explicit loss information is conveyed by several loss blocks, and each block stores the sequence number of the lost packets.

Figure 2 shows the recovery steps after the drops of packets three and four. During transmission from MH to fixed host (FH), SNACK-Snoop does not require the storage of arriving packets. It only stores the sequence number of the received packets to determine the losses. When an ACK arrives at the BS, whether new or duplicate, SNACK-Snoop can detect the wireless losses, if any, and piggyback all their sequence numbers to the ACK as primary multiple wireless loss information. For data transmission from fixed host to mobile host (see Figure 3), SNACK-Snoop stores all the packets received by the base station. These packets are used to judge whether a loss is due to congestion or wireless error, and supports fast local retransmission over wireless links. The protocol fails when IP payload is encrypted.

JTCP [WU04]

JTCP is a Jitter-based, end-to-end, robust, and fair protocol for the heterogeneous wireless networks. It was designed to identify the causes of packet lose and react accordingly. To differentiate between congestion and wireless losses, the protocol uses jitter ratio, which is the loss predictor formulated by the inter-arrival jitter. A congestion event is defined as when the timer expires or three DUPACKs are received and the jitter ratio is significant. As three DUPACKs are received, JTCP determines if these DUPACKs arrive within a RTT. If the period for DUPACKs has been extended to the next RTT and jitter ratio is significant, the protocol treats it as one congestion event and enters into fast recovery phase as TCP-Reno. Otherwise it enters the immediate recovery phase as it assumes that losses are due to wireless error. After a timeout, if the jitter ratio is significant, it enters slow start phase, otherwise it assumes burst losses caused the timer expiration and enters fast recovery phase because of the non-congestion event. As multi-losses occur in the same RTT, it considers them as one congestion event and reduces the sending rate once. It performs poorly in the presence of frequent disconnection and handoff. It reduces the sending rate even if there were no congestion or wireless errors.

Figure 2. Recovery from two losses in MH to FH direction

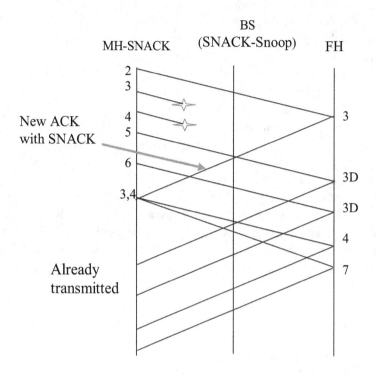

Figure 3. Recovery from two losses in FH to MH direction

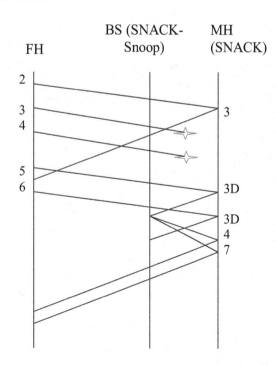

TCP-Westwood with Agile Probing (TCPW-A) [WAN05]

TCPW-A is a sender-side only enhancement of TCPW [GER01] that deals with highly dynamic bandwidth, large propagation time/bandwidth, and random loss. Along with eligible rate estimate (ERE) mechanism of TCPW, TCPW-A uses two more mechanisms: agile probing and persistent non-congestion detection (PNCD). The PNCD mechanism is concerned with how to detect extra unused bandwidth. PNCD identifies the availability of persistent extra bandwidth in congestion avoidance, and invokes agile probing accordingly. Agile probing adaptively and repeatedly resets slow start threshold-based ERE. Each time the slow start threshold is reset to a value higher than the current one, the congestion window climbs exponentially to the new value. The result is fast convergence of the congestion window to a more appropriate slow start threshold value. Even if the PNCD algorithm can accurately detect non-congestion, there is always the possibility that the network becomes congested immediately after the connection switches to agile probing phase. One such scenario is after a buffer overflow at the bottleneck router. Many of the TCP connections may decrease their congestion window after a buffer overflow, and congestion is relieved in a short time period.

TCP for WLAN

The protocols described in this section are mainly designed to work in 3G cellular networks. But it has been seen that these protocols (e.g., [WAN98]) perform better when called to work in a WLAN environment.

Explicit Bad State Notification (EBSN) [BAK97]

[BAK97] proposed the EBSN scheme. When the wireless link is in bad state, BS sends an EBSN to the source, which causes the previous time out to be cancelled and a new time out put in place based on an existing estimate of round trip time. The major downside of this scheme is that end-to-end semantic is violated.

Delayed Duplicate Acknowledgement (DDA) [VAI99]

DDA scheme attempts to mimic the behavior of Snoop protocol [BAL95]. In this scheme, the BS does not need to look into the TCP header. This scheme may be preferred when encryption is used. The BS implements a link level retransmission scheme for packets those are lost on wireless link. This scheme uses link level ACK to trigger retransmissions. The TCP receiver attempts to reduce interference between TCP and link level retransmission by delaying the third and subsequent DUPACKs for some interval d. If d is chosen large enough to allow time for link level retransmission of the lost packet, then the retransmitted packet would reach the receiver before the third and subsequent DUPACKs could be sent. Since the TCP sender does not receive more than two DUPACKs, it will not fast retransmit. In the presence of real congestion, the performance of this scheme is degraded compared to standard TCP. Standard TCP will send the third DUPACK without any delay, thus initiating fast retransmission sooner than this scheme.

Overall Comparison of the Protocols

It is extremely difficult to do a comprehensive comparison of the proposals because each aims to solve a different problem (e.g., high BER, handoff, frequent disconnection, battery constraint, etc.) of the wireless link. Nevertheless, we make a bold attempt in Table 1 to compare the protocols against the issues discussed earlier. We add two more issues here: end-to-end TCP semantic and encrypted TCP payload. Although these two are not typical issues for Mobile Internet only, we believe that these two features must not be violated in any TCP enhancement scheme.

It is clear from Table 1 [SAR06] that most the proposals try to maintain end-to-end semantics and are effective in dealing with high BER, but none of the proposals provides real-time handoff and roaming facility. However, only Freeze-TCP effectively deals with frequent disconnection and handoff. It is interesting to note that none of the proposals satisfies the criteria of efficient sharing of wireless bandwidth, which is very important in real life.

FUTURE TRENDS

Although the existing protocols provide some possible solutions to alleviate the problems of TCP in mobile networks, a careful scrutiny of the protocols indicates that, none of the protocols solves all the wireless specific issues of TCP. To design an efficient TCP for mobile Internet, the desirable properties of the protocol must include the solutions for all wireless specific problems of TCP. But we believe that it is difficult to create a "one size fits all" TCP for Mobile Internet. Also 3G cellular networks have substantially higher uplink rates. The channel interference characteristic on the uplink is very different from downlink. Uploading is becoming more and more important. So, TCP enhancement schemes must perform equally well in the case of transmission from MH to FH direction.

CONCLUSION

When TCP encounters packet drop, it usually invokes congestion control and avoidance procedures. Due to the characteristics specific to wireless networks, such as signal fading and mobility, packets may be lost due to congestive and noncongestive losses. So it might mistake a channel loss or losses due to temporal disconnection and handoff as congestion event, and reduce the window size immediately. This makes TCP a bad

Table 1. General comparison of TCP enhancement schemes for mobile Internet

	Intermed-iate node TCP mod?	End-to-End TCP semantic	Handing High BER	Frequent disconnect-tion	Handoff	Real time handoff	Wireless bandwidth sharing	Encrypted TCP payload	Energy efficiency
Freeze-TCP	No	Yes	No	Yes	Yes	No	No	Yes	Medium
TCP-Veno	No	Yes	No	No	No	No	No	Yes	Medium
SNACK-NS	Yes	Yes	Yes	No	No	No	No	No	Medium
JTCP	No	Yes	Yes	No	No	No	No	Yes	Medium
TCPWA	No	Yes	Yes	No	No	No	No	Yes	Medium
EBSN	Yes	No	Yes	No	No	No	No	No	Medium
DDA	No	Yes	Yes	No	No	No	No	Yes	Low

choice for Mobile Internet (cellular or WLAN). In this chapter, we have provided a comprehensive and in-depth survey on recent research in TCP for mobile Internet. The taxonomy and characteristics of TCP enhancements for mobile wireless access networks are introduced, and a categorized analysis of different existing solutions show that researchers are yet to find an elegant technique to detect the exact cause of packet loss.

REFERENCES

Bakshi, B. S., Krishna, P., Vaidya, N. & Pradhan, D. K. (1997). Improving performance of TCP over wireless networks. *ICDCS*, 365-373.

Balakrishnan, H., Seshan, S., & Katz, R. H. (1995). Improving reliable transport and handoff performance in cellular wireless networks *ACM Wireless Networks, 1*(4), 469-481.

Brakmo, L., & Peterson, L. (1995). TCP Vegas: End to end congestion avoidance on a global Internet. *IEEE JSAC, 13*(8), 1465-1480.

Caceres, R., & Iftode, L. (1995). Improving the performance of reliable transport protocol in mobile computing environment. *IEEE Journal of Selected Areas in Communications, 13*(5), 850-857.

Fall, K., & Floyd, S. (1996). Simulation-based comparisons of Tahoe, Reno, and SACK TCP. *Computer communication review, 26*(3), 5-21.

Floyd, S., & Henderson, T. (1999). *The new-Reno modification to TCP's fast recovery algorithm.* RFC 2582.

Fu, C. P., & Liew, S. C. (2003). TCP Reno: TCP enhancement for transmission over wireless access networks. *IEEE JSAC, 21*(2), 216-228.

Gerla, M., Sanadidi, M., Wang, R., Zanella, A., Casetti, C., & Masco, S. (2001). TCP Westwood: Congestion window control using bandwidth estimation. *IEEE GLOBECOM*, 3, 1698-1702.

Goff, T., Moronski, J., Phatak, D.S., & Gupta, V. (2000). Freeze-TCP: A true end-to-end TCP enhancement mechanism for mobile environments. *IEEE INFOCOM*, 3, 1537-545.

Ka-Cheong, L., & Li, V. O. K., (2006). Transmission Control Protocol (TCP) in Wireless Networks: Issues, Approaches and Challenges. *IEEE Communications Surveys & Tutorials*, 8(4), pp. 64-79.

Mathis, M., Mahdavi, J., Floyd, S., & Romanow, A. (1996). *TCP selective acknowledgement options*. RFC 2018.

Perkins, C. (1996). *IP mobility support*. RFC 2002.

Postel, J. (1981). *Transmission control protocol*. RFC 793.

Sardar, B., & Saha, D., (2006). A Survey of TCP Enhancements for Last-Hop Wireless Networks. *IEEE Communications Surveys & Tutorials*, 8(3), pp. 20-34.

Sun, F., Soung, V. L., & Liew, C. (2004). Design of SNACK mechanism for wireless TCP with New Snoop. *IEEE WCNC*, 5(1), 1046-1051.

Tian, Y., Xu, K., & Ansari, N. (2005). TCP in wireless environments: Problems and solutions. *IEEE Communication Magazine*, 43(3), S27-S32.

Tsaoussidis, V., & Matta, I. (2002). Open issues on TCP for mobile computing. *Journal on Wireless Communication and Mobile Computing*, 2(1), 3-20.

Vaidya, N., & Mehta, M. (1999). *Delayed duplicate acknowledgements: A TCP-unaware approach to improve performance of TCP over wireless*. Technical Report 99-003.

Wang, R., Yamada, K., Sanadidi, M. Y., & Gerla, M. (2005). TCP with sender-side intelligence to handle dynamic, large, leaky pipes. *IEEE JSAC*, 23(2), 235-248.

Wang, T. S. (1998). Mobile-end transport protocol: An alternative to TCP/IP over wireless links. *IEEE INFOCOM*, 3, 1046-1053.

Wu, E. H. K., & Chen, E. H. K. (2004). JTCP: Jitter-based TCP for heterogeneous wireless networks. *IEEE JSAC*, 22(4), 757-766.

Xu, K., Tian, Y., & Ansari, N. (2004). TCP-Jersey for wireless IP communications. *IEEE JSAC*, 22(4), 747-756.

KEY TERMS

Congestion Window: The maximum number of TCP packets that a sender is allowed to send at a time to the network, or in other words, it is the maximum carrying capacity of the network.

DUPACK: An acknowledgement packet that contains the sequence number of last acknowledged packets.

Energy Efficiency: The ratio of minimum energy consumption required to transmit a certain amount of data to that of actual energy consumption.

Goodput: The ratio of number of packets successfully transmitted to number of packets actually transmitted.

Mobile IP: A modified IP protocol to allow users on the move to access the backbone network like the Internet.

TCP: A true end-to-end, connection-oriented protocol for providing reliable and ordered delivery of packets to the application, bypassing the unreliable nature of the Internet.

Throughput: The ratio of number of packets successfully transmitted to amount of time required to complete the communication.

ENDNOTES

[1] Portions reprinted, with permission, from (B. Sardar, and D. Saha, "A Survey of TCP Enhancements for Last-Hop Wireless Networks", IEEE Communications Surveys & Tutorials, Vol. 8, No. 3, pp. 20-34, 2006) ©2006 IEEE".

TCP for High-Speed Networks

Nelson Luís Saldanha da Fonseca
State University of Campinas, Brazil

Neila Fernanda Michel
State University of Campinas, Brazil

In response to a series of collapses due to congestion on the Internet in the mid-'80s, congestion control was added to the transmission control protocol (TCP) (Jacobson, 1988), thus allowing individual connections to control the amount of traffic they inject into the network. This control involves regulating the size of the **congestion window** (cwnd) to impose a limit on the size of the transmission window. In the most deployed TCP variant on the Internet, TCP Reno (Allman, Floyd, & Partridge, 2002), changes in congestion window size are driven by the loss of segments. **Congestion window** size is increased by 1/cwnd for each acknowledgement (ack) received, and reduced to half for the loss of a segment in a pattern known as additive increase multiplicative decrease (AIMD). Although this congestion control mechanism was derived at a time when the line speed was of the order of 56 kbs, it has performed remarkably well given that the speed, size, load, and connectivity of the Internet have increased by approximately six orders of magnitude in the past 15 years. However, the AIMD pattern of **window growth** seriously limits efficienct operation of TCP-Reno over high-capacity links, so that the transport layer is the network bottleneck. This text explains the major challenges involved in using TCP for high-speed networks and briefly describes some of the variations of TCP designed to overcome these challenges.

BACKGROUND

In long distance and **high-speed networks**, very large window sizes are required for the complete utilization of the transmission pipe. The window size should be roughly equal to the **bandwidth delay product**. The conservative approach of TCP Reno congestion control restrains the speed of growth of the **congestion window**, thus, preventing efficient use of the high bandwidth available. Moreover, the drastic reduction in window size after each loss event prolongs the process of achieving an efficient window size. For instance, it takes roughly one and a half hours for the TCP Reno transmitting 1500-byte packets to reach a window size which fully utilizes a 10Gbps link with 100ms of propagation delay (Floyd, Ratnasamy, & Shenker, 2002). The error free transmission period required for this window growth involves a packet loss rate on the order of 10^{-11}, which is lower than the theoretical limit of bit error rates of optical links.

Current practices for the utilization of high bandwidth availability involve the opening of multiple TCP connections as well as the transmission of large packets, known as jumbo packets. However, such practices are neither scalable nor flexible. Therefore, numerous **TCP variants** for **high-speed networks** have recently been proposed. The common goals of these proposals are:

- **Friendliness:** TCPs for high-speed networks should not jeopardize TCP-Reno. The ideal goal would be that this protocol obtain the same amount of bandwidth that it would if it was competing with TCP-Reno;
- **Efficiency:** A TCP protocol for high-speed networks should strive to utilize the available bandwidth efficiently. This requires sustainable high transmission rates, as well as rapid achievement of these rates;
- **Intra-protocol fairness:** Fairness should exist among competing flows generated by the same TCP variant, even though it may have different RTTs;
- **Responsiveness**: Connections should react rapidly to traffic changes, such as the starting and stopping of other flows;
- The deployment of TCP for high-speed networks should not require changes in the network core.

The **TCP variants** differ to the extent they achieve these goals. However, none of the proposals so far has fulfilled all the objectives, due mainly to the difficulty of balancing efficiency and fairness.

VARIANTS OF TCP FOR HIGH-SPEED NETWORKS

Variants of TCP for high-speed networks differ in relation to the congestion signal used to define the dynamics of the window size changes. Some proposals are loss driven, whereas others are driven by delay. Still others take both loss and delay into consideration. Loss-based approaches use AIMD-like window dynamics to make **window growth** more aggressive than the TCP-Reno. Delay-based approaches identify congestion by variation in the RTT values and reduce the sending rate when RTT increases. The major proposals are described. Variants which require changes on network core routers are out of the scope of this text (Katabi, Handley, & Rohrs, 2002).

HighSpeed-TCP

HighSpeed-TCP (HSTCP) (Floyd, 2003), one of the first variants proposed, operates in two different modes. In scenarios with loss rate higher than 10^{-3}, HSTCP operates like TCP-Reno. When congestion events are rare, it adopts a more aggressive window growth function to scale to the available bandwidth. This function is based on three parameters. The first of these is actually a threshold for changing the mode of operation, while the second establishes an upper bound for the congestion window size, and the third specifies a packet drop rate to achieve an upper bound to the window size. These parameters are set in a way that establishes a linear relationship in a log-log scale between the sending rate and that of congestion events.

FAST-TPC

Fast active management scalable transmission control protocol (**FAST-TCP**) (Jin, Low, & Wei, 2004) has a congestion control mechanism composed of four functionally independent components: estimation, data control, window control, and burstiness control. The estimation component provides estimations of the parameters to be used by the other three. For each acknowledgement received, the RTT value is computed and used to calculate an exponentially smooth average RTT value and a minimum RTT value. When a loss is detected, the estimation component notifies the data component. The congestion control component computes the size of the congestion window on the basis of both delay estimations and packet loss events by using the formula:

$$cwnd \leftarrow \min\{2cwnd, (1-\gamma)cwnd + \gamma\frac{baseRTT}{RTT}cwnd + \alpha\}$$

where: γ is a constant between 0 and 1, baseRTT is the minimum RTT value found, RTT is the average RTT value, and α is a parameter for controlling fairness and number of packets.

The data control component is responsible for the selection of the next packet to be transmitted. In general, packets are transmitted in the same sequence acks are received. When a loss occurs, the next packet to be transmitted is selected from the new packets, those deemed lost and those transmitted but not yet acknowledged. This choice is especially important in the avoidance of exacerbation of congestion and a consequent loss of packets.

The burstiness control smoothes out packet transmission in a fluid-like fashion. Transmission may be too bursty due to the reception of cumulative acks or to CPU availability, but this component tries to limit the size of a burst on a time scale smaller than one RTT. However, considerable overhead is necessary to reduce this burstiness.

Scalable-TCP

Scalable-TCP (Kelly, 2003, 2004) was developed to utilize link capacity efficiently regardless of its size. The recovery time from a loss with a Scale-TCP connection depends entirely on the RTT values and is not affected by the link capacity. Scalable-TCP adopts a simple variation of TCP window update mechanism. Upon reception of an ack, the congestion window is updated according to the formula $cwnd \leftarrow cwnd + \alpha$ but when a loss occurs, this updating is based on the following: $cwnd \leftarrow cwnd - [cwnd * \beta]$. Suggested values for α and β in the establishment of friendliness and stability would bc 0.01 and 0.125, respectively.

BIC/CUBIC

Binary increase congestion control (**BIC-TCP**) (Xu, Harfoush, & Rhee, 2004) defines the transmission rate to be used on the basis of a binary search. Given a maximum window size, the minimum window value would be that for which no packet loss would occur at the sending rate involved. For each step, the window is increased to a value that is the midpoint between minimum and maximum window sizes, if the increase is less than a pre-defined threshold value. Otherwise, this threshold determines the increase. If no packet loss occurs with the updated window size, this value becomes the minimum window size for a new binary search. If, however, the updated window size leads to packet loss, it becomes the maximum target value, and a minimum size is determined on the basis of a multiplicative decrease factor. This search process is repeated until the difference between the minimum and maximum values is lower than a different threshold value. After this, BIC employs a "slow-start" algorithm to determine a new maximum window size.

CUBIC-TCP (Rhee & Xu, 2005) is a variant designed to simplify BIC window control, as well as to enhance TCP-friendliness, yet maintaining scalability. Congestion window size with this variant is determined by the following equation:

$$cwnd \leftarrow c(t - K)^3 + W_{max}.$$

where t is the time elapsed since the last window reduction, W_{max} is the window size just before the last window reduction, $K = \sqrt[3]{W_{max}\,\beta/C}$, and β is a multiplicative reduction factor. The increase in window size as a function of t assures RTT friendliness, since competing flows with different RTTs will all have the same value of t after a synchronized packet loss.

Compound-TCP

Compound-TCP (Tan, Song, Zhang, & Sridharan, 2006) uses both delay and loss as criteria for managing the transmission window. The idea here is that the window should grow aggressively upon the indication of the availability of bandwidth obtained by measuring the delay experienced by transmitted packets. The size of the transmission window is determined by both *cwnd* and the value of a variable, *dwnd*, which indicates how

much the window can grow based on the estimated delay. The value of *dwnd* increases multiplicatively when bandwidth is available and also decreases multiplicatively in the case of packet loss. The parameters used for the degrees of scalability (α) are TCP friendliness (β) and responsiveness (k) in calculating changes in window size. By setting different values for these parameters, one can obtain different dynamics for window changes, emphasizing one aspect or the other. The window size in Compound-TCP is governed by the following equations:

$$Ack : cwnd \leftarrow cwnd + \alpha \times cwnd^k$$
$$Loss : cwnd \leftarrow cwnd \times (1 - \beta)$$

$$dwnd = \begin{cases} dwnd + (\alpha \cdot cwnd^k)^+ & diff < \gamma \\ (dwnd - \zeta \cdot diff)^+ & diff \geq \gamma \\ (cwnd \cdot (1 - \beta) - cwnd/2)^+ & if\ loss \end{cases}$$

where $(.)^+$ is defined as $\max(.,0)$; ζ is a parameter that defines how rapidly the delay based component should reduce this window when early congestion is detected, and γ is the number of packets backlogged in the bottleneck queue to detect early congestion that can be a fixed value (30 packets) or dynamically adjusted based on the network configuration.

TCP-AFRICA

Adaptive and fair rapid increase congestion avoidance mechanism (King, Riedi, & Baraniuk, 2005) adopts a two-mode congestion avoidance rule. Switching between modes is dictated by the delay experienced by transmitted packets. By using samples of the RTT, **TCP-Africa** estimates the number of packets in bottleneck queue. Whenever a queue builds up, TCP-Africa switches to slow growth mode, similar to the congestion avoidance algorithm of TCP-Reno. The rationale of this mode is that once a connection has reached a reasonable percentage of its maximum rate, there is no need for fast window growth. Conversely, when a limited availability of bandwidth inferred from low sample delay values is identified, TCP-Africa adopts an aggressive window growth approach borrowed from HSTCP. Window dynamics are determined by the following equations:

$$\begin{cases} \text{cwnd} \leftarrow \text{cwnd} + \text{fastInc(cwnd)} / \text{cwnd} & \text{for cwnd(aRTT} - \min \text{RTT)} < \alpha \times \text{aRTT} \\ \text{cwnd} \leftarrow \text{cwnd} + 1/\text{cwnd} & \text{otherwise} \end{cases}$$

where the function *fastInc(cwnd)* is specified by a set of modified increase rules for TCP and α is a multiplicative increase parameter.

H-TCP

The AIMD pattern for congestion window change promotes rapid convergence to the equilibrium of the bandwidth shared by competing flows. Two key features underpin this convergence: The windows of the connection increase at the same rate, and a multiplicative decreasing assures that connections with larger windows reduce window size more, in absolute terms, than do those with smaller windows. Thus, connections with small windows seize bandwidth from those with large windows, leading to a rapid convergence to fair bandwidth share. Since TCP variants which adopt an increase factor that is a function of the *cwnd* value unbalancing the competition between new and ongoing flows, new flows tend to take longer periods to converge to their share of the bandwidth. To overcome this deficiency, **H-TCP** (Shorten & Leith, 2003) uses an increase parameter, which is a function of the time elapsed since the previous congestion event Δ. This parameter is set to yield the desired rate of increase. The definition of decrease factor considers both duration and number of congestion events in such a way that the queues at the routers diminish with a decrease in the congestion window. The window dynamics of H-TCP are defined by:

$$\overline{\alpha}(\Delta) = \begin{cases} 1 & \Delta \leq \Delta_L \\ \overline{\alpha}(\Delta) & \Delta > \Delta_L \end{cases}$$

with

$$\overline{\alpha}(\Delta) = 1 + 10(\Delta - \Delta_L) + \left(\frac{\Delta - \Delta_L}{2}\right)^2$$

where Δ_L is the threshold for switching from standard/legacy operation to the new increase function $\overline{\alpha}(\Delta)$.

TCP-Libra

TCP-Libra (Marfia, Palazzi, Pau, Gerla, Sanadidi, & Roccetti, 2005) approaches the issues involved in TCP over high-speed networks by focusing on the fairness of RTT and TCP. It uses RTT estimations to evaluate the available capacity and control the rate of increase in size of the transmission window. It has a modular design including capacity estimation and control of fairness, scalability, stability, and burstiness. The capacity control component estimates the capacity available at the beginning of new sessions. The fairness control is responsible for equalizing the throughput of heterogeneous RTT flows by controlling the throughput variance, as well as the rate of convergence to equilibrium rate. The scalability control component obtains the estimated capacity of the bottleneck link from the capacity estimation module and uses it to determine the rate of window increase. This component has been introduced to ensure that TCP-Libra scales to any bandwidth delay product value without the need for retrofitting or replacement that characterizes TCP-Reno. Stability control acts as a gauge for the control of scalability, which can be too aggressive when there are too many competing flows. This component plays with the trade-off between scalability and efficiency. Burstiness control determines how the sending of packets should be timed to avoid the injection of long bursts. Pacing strategies are adopted to avoid synchronization of losses from competing flows and consequent multiple reduction of the size of the congestion window. The equations governing window growth in TCP-Libra are the following:

$$\text{Ack} : \text{cwnd} \leftarrow \text{cwnd} + \frac{1}{\text{cwnd}} \times \frac{\alpha \cdot T^2}{T + T_0}$$

$$\text{Loss} : \text{cwnd} \leftarrow \text{cwnd} - \frac{T_1 \cdot \text{cwnd}}{2(T + T_0)}$$

$$\alpha = k_1 \cdot c \cdot e^y \qquad y = -k_2 \frac{T - T_{min}}{T_{max} - T_{min}}$$

where k_1 and k_2 are fixed parameters, c is the capacity of the bottleneck link seen by the source, and T_{min} and T_{max} are the minimum and the maximum round trip times experienced during the connection up.

Table 1 summarizes the main characteristics of TCP variants presented in this paper.

Table 1. Main characteristics of TCP variants

TCP Variant	Main Characteristics	Pattern of Congestion Window Changes
HS-TCP	Linear relationship between the rate of sending and congestion events in a log-log scale	Two modes of operation: TCP-Reno AIMD and Fast Increase
FAST-TCP	Four functionally independent components: estimation, data control, window control, and burstiness control	Delay based
Scalable-TCP	Utilizes the link efficiently regardless of its capacity	Multiplicative increase Multiplicative decrease (MIMD)
BIC	Dynamic search to establish window size	Additive increase and binary search increase, multiplicative decrease (AIBIMD)
CUBIC	Dynamic search to establish window size	Additive increase and cubic increase function, multiplicative decrease (AICIMD)
Compound-TCP	Hybrid approach	AIMD and delay based control
TCP-Africa	Delay based	Two modes: AIMD and Fast increase
H-TCP	Fast convergence to the bandwidth share at equilibrium	Two modes: AIMD and Fast Increase
TCP-Libra	RTT friendliness, five components: fairness control, capacity estimation, burstiness control, scalability control, and stability control	AIMD

FUTURE TRENDS

While the conception of TCP variants has received a great deal of attention, far less attention has been paid to the systematic evaluation of these variants. Although simulations and experimental evaluations have been conducted by the proponents of these variants, these results are difficult to compare due to the diversity of scenarios investigated. Experimental evaluations conducted up to now involve a wide range of scenarios, from experiments using intercontinental links to network setting in laboratories using dummynet software (which allows the variation of several network parameters such as RTT) (Rizzo, 1997). However, these experiments have neglected several relevant aspects, such as the use of non-responsive background traffic and mixes of long- and short-lived flows. The use of different network stack implementations also leads to difficulties in comparing the results since it may reveal

the efficiency of the stack implementation, rather than the congestion mechanism. Moreover, there is no agreement on a relevant set of representative performance measures and the same aspects may be measured differently in different experiments. Consequently, there is a clear need for the adoption of a TCP benchmark and a specific set of performance measures so that the interpretation of results will provide conclusions about the efficacy of the variants. The investigation of this efficacy under uniform and realistic settings should provide a challenge for years to come.

CONCLUSION

TCP-Reno has scaled remarkably well to the ever-increasing size and line speed of the Internet so far. However, it does not work efficiently in networks with high bandwidth delay product due to the AIMD pattern used for changes in congestion window, thus, becoming a bottleneck for the network. To overcome this inefficiency, several TCP variants have been proposed, differing in the ways they try to achieve not only scalability and fairness, but also friendliness to TCP-Reno. These proposals use different strategies for changing the congestion window, some using the delay as a signal for change, while others adopt the loss of a packet, and even a hybrid approach. Although numerous TCP variants have been proposed, there is no report that any have successfully fulfilled all the desired objectives. Moreover, there is a clear need to adopt meaningful benchmarks, including realistic Internet traffic for the evaluation of such protocols.

REFERENCES

Allman, M., Floyd, S., & Partridge, C. (2002). *Increasing TCP's initial window*. RFC 3390.

Floyd, S. (2003). *HighSpeed TCP for large congestion windows*. RFC 3649.

Floyd, S., Ratnasamy, S., & Shenker, S. (2002). *Modifying TCP's congestion control for high speeds*. Unpublished manuscript.

Jacobson, V. (1988). Congestion avoidance and control. *Computer Communication Review, 18*(4), 314-329.

Jin, C., Low, S., & Wei, D. (2004). FAST TCP: Motivation, architecture, algorithms and performance. *Proceedings of the IEEE INFOCOM 2004* (Vol. 4, pp. 2490-2501). Hong Kong.

Katabi, D., Handley, M., & Rohrs, C. (2002). Congestion control for high bandwidth-delay product networks. *ACM SIGCOMM Computer Communication Review, 32*(4), 89-102.

Kelly, T. (2003). Scalable TCP: Improving performance in highspeed wide area networks. *ACM SIGCOMM Computer Communication Review, 33*(2), 83-91.

Kelly, T. (2004). *Engineering flow controls for the Internet*. PhD thesis, Department of Engineering, University of Cambridge. http://www-lce.eng.cam. ac.uk/~ctk21/papers/

King, R., Riedi, R., & Baraniuk, R. (2005). TCP-Africa: An adaptive and fair rapid increase rule for scalable TCP. *Proceedings of IEEE INFOCOM 2005* (Vol. 3, pp. 1838-1848). Miami, Florida.

Leith, D. J., Shorten, R. N., & Li, Y. (2005). *H-TCP: A framework for congestion control in high-speed and long-distance networks*. Technical Report, Hamilton Institute.

Marfia, G., Palazzi, C., Pau, G., Gerla, M., Sanadidi, M., & Roccetti, M. (2005). *TCP-Libra: Exploring RTT fairness for TCP*. UCLA Computer Science Department. Technical Report # UCLA-CSD TR-050037.

Rhee, I., & Xu, L. (2005). CUBIC: A new TCP-friendly high-speed TCP variant. *Proceedings of PFLDnet 2005*, Lyon, France.

Rizzo, L. (1997). Dummynet: A simple approach to the evaluation of network protocols. *ACM SIGCOMM Computer Communication Review, 27*(1), 31-41.

Shorten, R. N., & Leith, D. J. (2003) H-TCP: TCP for high-speed and long-distance networks. *Proceedings of PFLDnet 2003*, Argonne, Illinois.

Tan, K., Song, J., Zhang, Q., & Sridharan, M. (2006) A compound TCP approach for high-speed and long distance networks. *IEEE INFOCOM 2006*, Barcelona, Catalunya, Spain.

Xu, L., Harfoush, K., & Rhee, I. (2004, March). Binary increase congestion control for fast, long distance networks. *Proceedings of IEEE INFOCOM 2004*, Hong Kong (Vol. 4, pp. 2514-2524).

KEY TERMS

Acknowledgment (ACK): A packet sent by the receiver to the sender to notify the successful reception of a packet.

Bandwidth Delay Product: Product of the link capacity and the round trip time (RTT).

Congestion: State of the network characterized by the demand of traffic transmission exceeding its transport capacity.

Congestion Control: Traffic control mechanisms to avoid network congestion.

Flow Control: A traffic control mechanism which aims at equalizing the rate of transmission of a sender with the reception capacity of a receiver.

Round Trip Time: Time elapsed between the transmission of a packet and the reception of the corresponding acknowledgement.

Segment: Protocol data unit used by transport protocols.

Transmission Window: Range of packets that can be transmitted by a sender.

Towards Autonomic Infrastructures via Mobile Agents and Active Networks

Stamatis Karnouskos
SAP Research, Germany

ABSTRACT

As we move towards service-oriented complex infrastructures, what is needed, security, robustness, and intelligence distributed within the network. Modern systems are too complicated to be centrally administered; therefore, the need for approaches that provide autonomic characteristics and are able to be self-sustained is evident. We present here one approach towards this goal, i.e., how we can build dynamic infrastructures based on mobile agents (MA) and active networks (AN). Both concepts share common ground at the architectural level, which makes it interesting to use a mix of them to provide a more sophisticated framework for building dynamic systems. We argue that by using this combination, more autonomous systems can be built that can effectively possess at least at some level of self-* features, such as self-management, self-healing, etc., which, in conjunction with cooperation capabilities, will lead to the deployment of dynamic infrastructures that autonomously identify and adapt to external/internal events. As an example, the implementation of an autonomous network-based security service is analyzed, which proves that denial of service attacks can be managed by the network itself intelligently and in an autonomic fashion.

INTRODUCTION

Systems and services are becoming more ubiquitous, which calls for sophisticated solutions to be in place. As we move towards the "Internet of things" (Dolin, 2006), it can be expected that millions of devices of different size and capability will be connected and interact with each other over IP, e.g., sensor networks (Marsh, 2004). Therefore, any approach will have to take into consideration that:

- Complexity will increase
- Heterogeneity in devices, software platforms, online services, etc., will increase
- A large proportion of end-nodes will be connected wirelessly to the backbone infrastructure (the line of wired vs. wireless systems will blur more)
- Bandwidth and computing power will increase
- Ad-hoc computing, collaboration, task delegation, and environmental adaptation will be basic necessities
- On-demand software and service deployment will be vital
- Security and its satellite services will gain importance

In such an assumed future infrastructure, autonomic systems are expected to be of considerable help, since they will be able to be at a great degree self-sustained and also react to a dynamic changing environment.

Autonomic computing (Sterritt et Al., 2005) was introduced by IBM as a means to target increasing computer system complexity, and aimed initially at automating management of enterprise computational systems. In *The Vision of Autonomic Computing* (Kephart & Chess, 2003) it is stated that the dream of interconnectivity of computing systems and devices could become the "nightmare of pervasive computing," in which architects are unable to anticipate, design, and maintain the complexity of interactions. The essence of autonomic computing is system self-management, freeing administrators from low-level task management whilst delivering an optimized system. In a self-managing system, or Autonomic System, the human operator does not control the system directly, but only defines general policies and rules that serve as an input for the self-management process. For this process, IBM has defined the following four functional areas:

- **Self-configuration:** Automatic configuration of components
- **Self-healing:** Automatic discovery, and correction of faults
- **Self-optimization:** Automatic monitoring and control of resources to ensure the optimal functioning with respect to the defined requirements
- **Self-protection:** Proactive identification and protection from arbitrary attacks

There are two strategies in achieving autonomic behavior, i.e., through adaptive learning and via integral engineering into systems (Sterritt, 2004). Our approach focuses on how to engineer such an autonomous system, while adaptive learning, or self-learning, is seen as an ad-hoc component that can be imported from the domain of intelligent agents.

AMALGAMATION OF ACTIVE NETWORKS AND MOBILE AGENTS

Active and programmable networks (Karnouskos & Denazis, 2004) introduce a new network paradigm where network-aware applications and services can be not only distributed, but also can configure the heterogeneous network to optimally respond to task-specific requirements. We are able to utilize within the network: (a) computation, as we are able to compute on data received from active nodes, and (b) programmability, as we can inject user code into the network nodes in order to realize customized computation. Being able to achieve the above, we succeed in decoupling network services from the underlying hardware, deploy fine-grained customized services, relax the dependencies on network vendors and standardization bodies, and generally open the way for higher-level. network-based application programming interfaces.

Agents are software components that act alone or in communities on behalf of an entity and are delegated to perform tasks under some constraints or action plans (Jennings & Wooldridge, 1996). One key characteristic of agents is mobility (mobile agents), which allows them to transport themselves from node to node and continue their execution there. Additionally, autonomy, independent decision-making, goal-directed behavior, and social ability are also key characteristics agents may possess (Genesereth & Ketchpel, 1994). Mobile agent technology has established itself as an improvement

of today's distributed systems due to its benefits, such as dynamic, on-demand provision and distribution of services, reduction of network traffic and dependencies, fault tolerance, etc. The number of mobile agent platforms coming from the commercial sector, as well as academia, is increasing day by day.

Active networks and Mobile Agent technology are very close to each other, sharing common ground on theoretical/conceptual and implementational levels. From the viewpoint of mobile agent research, existing active network approaches take mobile active code very close to the mobile agent paradigm:

- **Capsule:** A typical code mobility paradigm, i.e., a single mobile agent
- **Active/programmable node:** Instantiation of code on-demand

From the active network research viewpoint, the mobile agent technology is one of the possible technologies that can be used to build active networks. Mobile agents are regarded as specific types of active code and a MA-based node as a specific type of active network node. Due to the fact that the MA research arena has existed more than a decade now, it is far more advanced in active code-related matters, therefore, it could provide a boost to specific AN matters at conceptual and implementation levels.

The right side of Figure 1 depicts the architecture of a legacy active node, while the mobile agent based implementation is depicted on the right side. We can clearly distinguish the following levels:

- Active applications/services which exist as a result of the execution of active code within an EE. An active code can: (a) provide a standalone service, or (b) cooperate with other active codes residing on the same EE (EE-based service), on different EEs in the same node (multi-EE service), or even on different EEs in different nodes (network multi-EE service).
- Execution environments where the active code executes. As an active node is expected to host multiple execution environments, these environments must have the ability to communicate with each other and to group in order to ease interactions. There are several functional types of EE aggregation, such as node virtual environment (NVE), node virtual environment network

Figure 1.The agent-based AN node versus the legacy one

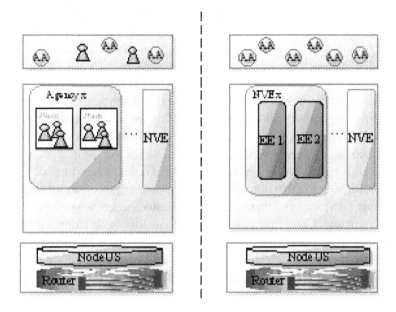

(NVEN), execution environment network (EEN), etc.

- NodeOS, which is an operating system for active nodes. The nodeOS provides generic services to the hosted Ees, e.g., inter-EE communication (at the EE, NVE, or Active Application level), router resource management, EE isolation, etc. The nodeOS offers these services based on several facilities, such as resource control, security, management, demultiplexing facilities, etc.

As shown in Figure 1, one of the execution environments is the agent execution environment. This is the agency as described within the MASIF (OMG-MASIF, 1998) standard. The agent system consists of Places. A Place is a context within an agent system in which an agent is executed. This context can provide services/functions such as access to local resources, etc. Cooperating agents reside in the agent-based Ees, and via the facilities offered to them (re)-program the node. These can be either mobile agents (e.g., visiting agents) or even stationary intelligent ones that reside permanently in the EE, implementing various services. The integrated approach of agents and active networks allows us to apply several security techniques at the network programming level (Karnouskos, 2001) that promote service and network security. Further information on this architecture and its security issues can be found in Karnouskos (2002). The mobile agent framework is able to realize the abstract functions of the EE, NVE, etc. The AAs are considered, for implementation reasons, to be mobile agents, but could also be applications that partially depend on them.

APPLICATION SCENARIO

An autonomic computing system (ACS) is able to (re)-configure itself in response to varying environmental conditions. Such a dynamic system can deal with unknown intrusions or attacks and is event-able to recover from malfunctions or heal itself. The scenario presented here deals with a network-based security system that is able to depict at some degree the characteristics of an ACS.

Securing a network nowadays is synonymous with hardening of its services. However, this approach makes the network inflexible and blurs the line between security and usability. Furthermore, each node has its own requirements on security which may also be varying in time. Within the vision of "Internet of things," such per-node or even per-task modification of security would be impossible to manage due to the large number and complexity of devices. Furthermore, those devices will build ad-hoc, short-lived networks, where the burden of taking such actions may not be justified. Additionally, no common base exists among various security solutions available in the market. In other words, available products do not communicate with each other (interoperate), and work alone for their own and their distribution company's good, not necessarily for the user's network. A collaborative approach must be considered; however, due to the nature of the future networks, this must be done on-demand and customized to the specific context. Community-aware tactics on the other side may offer a better alternative. Adopting modeling approaches from the evolution of biological systems (Forrest et al., 1997), they are seen as networks formed from cooperating living parts that

interoperate at various levels and share information. ACS systems seem a promising approach towards that direction, mainly due to their self-* characteristics.

We assume a typical denial of service (DoS) attack scenario. As depicted in Figure 2, the network topology consists of various active nodes (e.g., nodes A, B,and C) and legacy nodes (e.g., node D). In normal operation, the agents that implement our system reside within the agencies and filter the flow that is directed to the node. At some point, the attacker initiates the DoS attack via the compromised hosts against the AN node C. One agent in node C detects the attack. This can be a result of an attack signature recognition (if the attack is known and exists in the system database) or a result of a dynamic correlation of events received by the system. Once the attack is detected, several security guards (SG) are released within the network (dynamic lookup of the neighboring nodes) and the attack information is disseminated towards the other

Figure 2. DoS threat management

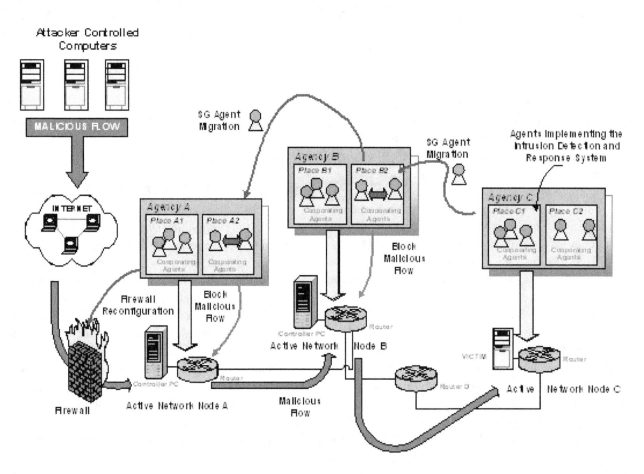

nodes that reside within the path of the attack. In this way, the agents continue in an autonomic way to roam the network, identify the nodes that are prone to this attack, and share information which eventually lead to a policy change and blocking of the specific malicious traffic within that node. At the end, the malicious flow is blocked towards the borders of the domain, and the network nodes are protected from this attack. Further detailed information about this approach can be found in Karnouskos (2004).

The engines behind the data analysis and event correlation, as well as decision and action management, can be standalone; however, it is much more interesting if they act in a collaborative manner. . Therefore, at each domain, central analysis points (CAP) exist which have an overview of what is happening in the domain, thereby making it easier to recognize attacks that include multiple nodes in different parts of the network. CAPs have the global view, and therefore are more efficient in attack recognition and decision making, while the action is done locally on each node; this tactic allows thin components to be deployed even to devices that do not feature high computational capabilities.

The result of this approach is that we have a network that features, at some degree, characteristics if autonomic systems. More specifically:

- **Self-configuration:** Automatic configuration of the different components that recognize the attacks is done. The agents are goal-driven and are able to reconfigure themselves based on the environmental context they act on.
- **Self-healing:** Automatic discovery and correction of faults for network parts is done. Once this is detected, the specific sub-network part can be isolated in order to avoid network misbehavior, and classical solutions to the problem can be applied.
- **Self-optimization:** Automatic monitoring and control of resources of the network can be done. In that case, early indicators can be correlated and emerging problems are easier to pinpoint.
- **Self-protection:** The network is protected from well-known attacks, including those that can be dynamically identified based on the correlation of events or even with "socializing" (i.e., information exchange) with other networks.

As presented, our approach deals with some aspects of ACS; in the future, more specific research should be invested towards a fine-grain exploitation of each of the features in detail. Self-managing mechanisms can have several instantiations: self-government, self-correction, self-organization, self-scheduling, self-planning, self-administration, self-optimization, self-monitoring, self-adjusting, self-tuning, self-configuration, self-diagnosis of faults, self-protection, self-healing, self-recovery, self-learning, self-sensing/perceiving, self-modeling, self-evolution, self-assessment of risks, etc. (Tianfeld & Unland, 2004).

CONCLUSION

We have presented an approach that is based on the amalgamation of active networks and mobile agents. We merge specific capabilities from each domain, e.g., the network programmability from active networks and the autonomic, goal-driven social characteristics of mobile agents, in order to create a powerful combination and implement a system that depicts, at some degree, behavior that characterizes autonomic systems. The approach taken is open and can be seen as a platform to further integrate research results coming from the two domains. Furthermore, we have not yet touched issues like self-learning mechanisms, which however, initially could be imported from the work already done by the research community on intelligent software agents. Security, trust, and privacy issues as identified by Cardoso and Freire (2005) need to be further examined, especially because our collaborative approach taken here heavily depends on them. Finally, other approaches that move towards the usage of agents for implementing specific scenarios also exist, e.g. (Soldatos et al., 2006).

The essence of autonomic computing systems is the creation of dynamic infrastructures that can deal in a proactive way with changing environmental contexts; this is a fact that is gaining importance as we move towards a complex heterogeneous infrastructure, e.g., as depicted in the "Internet of things," where all interconnected devices will also form ad-hoc networks for even task-specific goals. Without such approaches, large-scale complex computing systems will be unmanageable.

REFERENCES

Cardoso, R., & Freire, M. (2005, October 23-28). Towards autonomic minimization of security vulnerabilities exploitation in hybrid network environments. In P. Dini & P. Lorenz (Eds.), *Proceedings of the Joint International Conference on Autonomic and Autonomous Systems and International Conference on Networking and Services (ICAS/ICNS 2005)*, Papeete, Tahiti, French Polynesia. Los Alamitos, CA: IEEE Computer Society Press.

Dolin, R. A. (2006, January 23-27). Deploying the "Internet of things." In *Proceedings of the International Symposium on Applications on the Internet* (pp. 216-219). Washington, DC: IEEE Computer Society.

Forrest, S., Hofmeyr, S., & Somayaji, A. (1997). Computer immunology. *Communications of the ACM, 40*(10), 88-96.

Genesereth, M. R., & Ketchpel, S. P. (1994). Software agents. *Communications of the ACM 37*, 7, 48ff.

Jennings, N., & Wooldridge, M. (1996). Software agents. *IEE Review, 42*(1), 17-21. http://www.csc.liv.ac.uk/~mjw/pubs/iee-review96.pdf

Karnouskos, S. (2001). Security implications of implementing active network infrastructures using agent technology. *Computer Networks Journal*, Special Issue on Active Networks and Services, *36*(1), 87-100.

Karnouskos, S. (2002). Realization of a secure active and programmable network infrastructure via mobile agent technology. *Computer Communications Journal*, Special Issue on Computational Intelligence in Telecommunications Networks, *25*(16), 1465-1476.

Karnouskos, S. (2004). Community-aware network security and a DDoS response system. *Annals of Telecommunications* (Annales des Télécommunications), Special Issue on Active Networks, *59*(5-6).

Karnouskos, S., & Denazis, S. (2004). Programmable networks: Background. In A. Galis, S. Denazis, C. Brou, & C. Klein (Eds.), *Programmable networks for IP service deployment*. Artech House Books.

Kephart, J. O., & Chess, D. M. (2003). The vision of autonomic computing. *Computer 36*, 1(January), 41-50.

Marsh, D., Tynan, R., O'Kane, D., & O'Hare, G. (2004). Autonomic wireless sensor networks. *Engineering Applications of Artificial Intelligence, Autonomic Computing Systems, 17*(7), 741-748.

OMG-MASIF, (1998). *Mobile agent system interoperability facility, OMG.* http://www.omg.org/docs/orbos/98-03-09.pdf

Soldatos, J., Pandis, I., Stamatis, K., Polymenakos, L., & Crowley, J. (2006). Agent based middleware infrastructure for autonomous context-aware ubiquitous computing services. *Computer Communications*. Available online January 17, 2006.

Sterritt, R. (2004) Autonomic networks: Engineering the self-healing property. *Engineering Applications of Artificial Intelligence, Autonomic Computing Systems, 17*(7), 727-739.

Sterritt, R., Parashar, M., Tianfield, H., & Unland, R. (2005). A concise introduction to autonomic computing. *Advanced Engineering Informatics, Autonomic Computing, 19*(3), 181-187.

Tianfield, H., & Unland, R. (2004). Towards autonomic computing systems. *Engineering Applications of Artificial Intelligence, Autonomic Computing Systems, 17*(7), 689-699.

KEY TERMS

Active Application: This is the code that is actually executed in the Execution Environment of the node. Via its execution in the EE, the code programs the node according to the user's preferences.

Active Networks: Active networks are a communication paradigm that allows packets flowing through a communication network to dynamically modify the operation of the network.

Autonomic Computing: An initiative started by IBM in 2001. Its ultimate aim is to create self-managing computer systems to overcome their rapidly growing complexity and to enable their further growth.

DoS: Denial of service attacks result in computers consuming their resources for malicious events without being able to further process legitimate user requests

Execution Environment: This is the place where the active code executes. The EE offers access to the core node resources via a policy-controlled scheme. This can be, for instance, a mobile agent system that takes care of the execution of an agent.

Mobile Agents: A mobile agent is a composition of computer software and data which is able to migrate (move) from one computer to another autonomously and continue its execution on the destination computer.

Sensor Networks: Sensor networks are computer networks of many, spatially distributed devices using sensors to monitor conditions at different locations, such as temperature, sound, vibration, pressure, motion, or pollutants. Usually these devices are small and inexpensive, so that they can be produced and deployed in large numbers, and so their resources in terms of energy, memory, computational speed, and bandwidth are severely constrained.

Towards Formulation of Principles for Engineering Web Applications

Pankaj Kamthan
Concordia University, Canada

INTRODUCTION

The last decade has seen remarkable changes in the way Web applications are developed and the services that are expected from them. The desire to control and manage the size and complexity of Web applications has led to a systematic approach for creating them that is known as *Web engineering* (Ginige & Murugesan, 2001).

A focus on the "essence" rather than "accidents" is crucial to any engineering (McConnell, 1999). The engineering environment of Web applications is in a constant state of technological and social flux. New implementation languages, variations in user agents, demands for new services, and user classes from different cultural backgrounds and age groups, are faced by the Web engineers on a regular basis. For sustainability and evolvability of Web applications, it is critical that they be based upon domain, time- and technology-independent bodies of knowledge. One such invariant is the set of principles that forms the foundation of Web engineering.

The rest of the article is organized as follows: we first outline the background necessary for later discussion. This is followed by the introduction of principles governing Web engineering that address both social and technical concerns, along with concrete suggestions for their realization. Next, challenges and directions for future research are outlined. Finally, concluding remarks are given.

BACKGROUND

There are various characteristics that make Web applications uniquely challenging compared to other forms of software development: The user has little control over the application, which is not packaged and distributed to run on a user's desktop; user context (agent, processing power, computer settings, and cognitive and physiological abilities) can be very diverse, and often difficult to predict; for their effective use, applications often require (usually nonlinear) navigation and searching skills on the part of the user, are document- rather than data- oriented and hence the design focus needs to be on both information and software architecture: The need for frequent maintenance, whether it is fixing a spelling error across documents (corrective maintenance), adding a daily news item (perfective maintenance), or porting the system across servers (adaptive maintenance).

The notion that the increasing size and complexity of Web applications needs to be managed and a planned development is necessary was realized in the late 1990s (Powell, Jones, & Cutts, 1998). Since then, there have been various approaches towards a systematic development of Web applications (Suh, 2005; Kappel et al., 2006; Mendes & Mosley, 2006; Rossi et al., 2008).

However, these efforts lack a theoretical basis in the form of principles that underlie the development of Web applications similar to software engineering principles (Parnas, 1978; Boehm, 1983; Davis, 1994; Borque et al., 2002; Ghezzi, Jazayeri, & Mandrioli, 2003). If introduced, these principles could also be useful in other contexts, such as forming the basis for guidelines, patterns, or frameworks for these applications.

WEB ENGINEERING PRINCIPLES AND THEIR IMPLICATIONS

In this section, we propose ten Web engineering principles (WEP) that address both social and technical concerns. Although we will restrict ourselves primarily to the product aspect, WEP apply to Web application projects, processes, and people.

The first seven technically-inclined principles that we propose are inspired by established software engineering principles (Ghezzi, Jazayeri, & Mandrioli, 2003), namely *Separation of Concerns*, *Abstraction*,

Modularity, *Anticipation of Change*, *Incrementality*, *Generality*, and *Rigor and Formality*. Then, we have added to this list the socially-inclined principles of *Universality*, *Trustworthiness*, and *Ethical Conduct*.

The principles are in general at a high level of abstraction, which can make their appreciation difficult, particularly for novice users. Therefore, we provide example means for realization of each of these principles in a typical Web application process. We also highlight relevant relationships among these principles where needed.

Principle 1. Separation of Concerns

The principle of Separation of Concerns is perhaps the most fundamental of all technical principles. It is based on the premise that there are various concerns in production and delivery of Web applications, and to manage them effectively, each of these semantically different concerns needs to be addressed separately. In particular, separation by parts, time, quality, and views are of special interest.

Realization. This principle could be applied to a project team by a clear "division of labor" and allocation of responsibilities. It can also be applicable to the product. For example, by adopting separation by parts, we can separate information presentation (rendering) and user interaction (processing) concerns, improve the delivery of documents via the "single source approach," deal with design and implementation by separating them by time, deal with correctness of documents before addressing their efficiency, or separate transaction data flow from control flow in conceptual modeling. For example, the HyperText Markup Language (HTML) in its definition blurred the distinction between structure (the use of <p>) and presentation (the use of <font>). The Extensible Markup Language (XML), when strictly following the philosophy of descriptive markup, provides means for separating structure, presentation, and logic in a document.

Principle 2. Abstraction

The principle of Abstraction is based on the idea that it is often necessary to highlight only the essentials while suppressing the details.

Realization. The key to abstraction is to provide a metadata perspective of information as well as to present information on a viewer's need-to-know basis. For instance, the same information identically rendered may not be of interest to every user, and therefore it is of interest to "personalize" it by providing different views of it. A Web application can take advantage of abstraction in many ways. One example of this is user agents (browsers) providing a rendered view (for a general user) and a source view (for a document engineer) of the same HTML document. A provider supplying news could include only the news headlines on the home page, which could be linked to a separate resource for access by a user who is interested in more details. A navigation system in general, and the Fly-Out Menu (Figure 1) in particular, is another example of the use of abstraction.

Principle 3. Modularity

The principle of Modularity is based on the notion that things that are semantically similar (different) should stay together (apart). It is a special case of *Principle 1. Separation of Concerns* (Parts) but is significant enough to be included separately here. *Principle 2. Abstraction* is a prerequisite for modularity, which is essential for flexibility of future documents (Malloy, 2005). Many of the ideas behind modular and object-oriented programming are based on this principle.

Realization. In authoring a document, one could attain modularity by selecting and following a "theme" for each document. In information architecture, modularity is realized by "chunking" information. For example, HTML and XML provide opportunities for modular

Figure 1. A Fly-Out Menu only exposes (renders) a part of the overall menu while suppressing other items

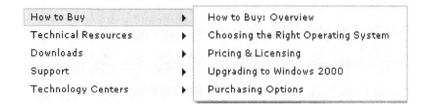

documents by supporting the concept of entities (such as " for "). In the following, we illustrate how separation by parts and modularity work together. In many dynamically-generated Web applications, common information is first isolated and then included on-demand. The Server-Side Includes (SSI) (Kamthan, 1999) is a classical implementation of this idea. This avoids physical repetition of the same code in each document, which in turn supports maintenance. For example, similar style declarations and logical rules could be aggregated and isolated in a style sheet file and the script file, respectively, and included dynamically. In HTML, this could, for example, be achieved by placing

```
<link type="text/css" rel="stylesheet" href="path/to/styles/mystyle.css" />
<script type="text/javascript" src="path/to/scripts/myscript.js"></script>
```

in the head element.

Principle 4. Anticipation of Change

The principle of Anticipation of Change is based on the premise that change in a (nontrivial) Web application is inevitable, and to accommodate change, adequate preparation is necessary.

Realization. There can be various sources that lead to changes in a Web application's environment: change in organizational vision or financial standing, change in team dynamics (member entering or exiting the team in the middle of a project), change in technology (obsolescence or discontinuation of support), and so on. As an example, for marketing purposes, organizations like to change the presentation ("look and feel") of their Web applications from time to time. If not planned in advance, or if the techniques used are resistant to modifications, this can be an arduous task. Keeping the presentation layer of the Web application separated from other aspects makes changes to it relatively simpler. As another example, "cutting edge" technology coming off a nightly build may be attractive to the engineers as a novelty but is against this principle: it poses higher risk compared to those that have stood the test of time and of users, and therefore its use in public Web applications should be discouraged.

Principle 5. Incrementality

The principle of incrementality is related to *Principle 1. Separation of Concerns* and *Principle 4. Anticipation of Change* and is based on the notion that creation of a Web application in increments should be encouraged.

Realization. Incrementality is important, as it is risky to develop large interactive applications without reflection. One of most common approaches for creating Web applications, particularly those that are heavily interactive, is prototyping. Prototyping usually proceeds via increments, where increments are added after user feedback and testing. Google's GMail is an example of a Web application that followed this principle: It started with the introduction of basic e-mail features that were essential for sending and receiving emails. It then added other features such as RSS Feeds, GMail Mobile, and chat over the time. We note that incrementality is not automatic or merely a sequential addition of components: Making increments to a Web application whose sub-systems are heavily coupled could prove to be costly.

Principle 6. Generality

The principle of Generality is based on the assertion that the more general a Web application is, the broader the audience it can reach and the more reusable in different situations it is.

Realization. A Web application can be made general by making it sensitive to a wide range of user contexts, or by basing it on the lowest common denominator of the user environment. XML attempts to be general by being neutral to user context, vendor, domain, device, network, programming language, and by supporting the largest character set currently available, namely the Universal Character Set (UCS)/unicode. Generality is neither given nor automatic; it takes concerted effort to make a Web application general. For example, Web applications that make assertions of the type "best viewed by browser XYZ," or use color to imply meaning, are not general.

Principle 7. Rigor and Formality

The principle of Rigor and Formality aims to reduce the potential of ambiguity, contradictions, or misinterpretations, and to enable a more precise description of the process or products related to Web applications. It does so by requiring predictability in development or a formal (logical) syntax and semantics of the language deployed.

Realization. There are various ways of being rigorous or formal. The process underlying the development of Web applications could be rigorous if it is based on a well-investigated process model, such as the spiral model or the Unified Process (UP). The process documents could be rigorous if they are based on, say, ISO or IEEE Standards. Web applications will typically be implemented in a formal language such as HTML and XML documents that have well-defined syntax and semantics.

Principle 8. Universality

The principle of universality is based on the premise that the Web was invented based on the philosophy of delivery of information and services to anybody, at any time, anywhere, and on any device. The goal of universality is inclusion. It is related to the *Principle 1. Separation of Concerns* and *Principle 6. Generality*, both of which can help attain universality. It is also related to *Principle 10. Ethical Conduct* as, grounded in the philosophy of Immanuel Kant, universality is seen as an ethical consideration (Tavani, 2004).

Realization. This is one of the most challenging principles to strive for. From a practical viewpoint, this principle is crucial to a business's bottom line: If a remote user cannot even access the information provided, it is unlikely that he/she will become a potential customer. There are means to approach universality. Open access reduces the cost barrier for accessing information. The language used to express the content should be syntactically correct to assure proper processing and rendering in conforming to user agents. The Web Content Accessibility Guidelines (WCAG) of the Web Accessibility Initiative (WAI) of the World Wide Web (W3C) Consortium and the Section 508 mandate of the U.S. Government Federal Access Board provide detailed guidelines for assuring accessibility. These guidelines not only assist those with some form of disability or special requirements, but also help others in need for a lowest common denominator. Tools such as A-Prompt or Bobby are freely available (at least for non-commercial use) and can automatically test for conformance to these guidelines. If a Web application needs to be shut down temporarily, it is incumbent upon the provider to announce publicly the reasons for doing

so (such as maintenance) and the associated schedule (else it violates the notion of "any time").

Principle 9. Trustworthiness

The principle of Trustworthiness is based on the notion that prior to the use of a Web application, a user should be able to establish a trusting relationship with the provider.

Realization. There are various opportunities where a user needs to trust information and/or service provided. For example, a user may need to agree to security certificates or allow the download/installation of cookies to his/her computer in order to use a Web application. As another example, a customer may need to provide his/her personal information (such as social security number) in order to register to a restricted portal. It is in general difficult to obtain sufficient conditions (guarantees) for trust; however, the more open the provider is with the user, the higher the possibility of the establishment of trust. Making available contact information, including physical address, announcing policies related to accessibility, privacy, security, legality, and usage of user-supplied data, and providing clear terms and conditions of using the Web application, are some of the ways to do that. The structure, presentation, and quality of information (including its novelty) in a Web application are considered the most important facets for it to be viewed as credible (Fogg, 2003). Indeed, trustworthiness has been labeled (Fogg, 2003) as one of the principles for computer credibility in general.

Principle 10. Ethical Conduct

The principle of Ethical Conduct is founded on the view that ethical behavior and practices form the basis of any engineering profession (Reynolds, 2003) and the same applies to Web Engineering. It is closely related to the *Principle 9. Trustworthiness*.

Realization. Ethical conduct is all-encompassing and perhaps the most important among all the principles. Ethics is an ever-increasing concern in information technology-based networked applications in general (Reynolds, 2003; Tavani, 2004), and Web applications in particular (Johnson, 1997). Web applications these days can be easily set-up without any clear evidence of authority, accountability, or degree of testing before a launch. The use of domain names such as InternationalE-Business can give an (often false) impression of the "depth" of ownership and .com or .org can "hide" provider location. Much like infomercials, a large and attractive Web application can be set-up to give the perception of legitimacy where the users could be lured into the world of "faceless" commerce. To bolster public confidence, it is important that organizations set up and follow a code of ethics and make that publicly available.

Applicability of Web Engineering Principles

The WEP are related to other forms of knowledge (Figure 2), some of which we have alluded to in the foregoing. In this section, we restrict ourselves to a brief discussion of the relationship of the WEP to quality.

We contend that WEP are the first theoretical choice in the toolkit of an engineer for achieving the quality goals of a Web application. This is because the other instruments at our disposal, such as guidelines, patterns (Van Duyne, Landay, & Hong, 2003), methodologies/ methods/techniques, or tools are themselves, explicitly or implicitly, based upon established principles (Ghezzi, Jazayeri, & Mandrioli, 2003).

The WEP can be related to either *internal* (intrinsic to the software product and directly an engineer's concern) or *external* (extrinsic to the software product and directly a user's concern) product quality attributes (Fenton & Pfleeger, 1997). As an example, the principles of *Separation of Concerns*, *Modularity*, *Anticipation of Change*, and *Incrementality* support maintainability (an

external quality attribute). The principle of *Modularity* supports readability (an external quality attribute) as well as structural complexity (an internal quality attribute). The principle of *Rigor and Formality* helps achieve syntactic and semantic correctness (an internal quality attribute).

FUTURE TRENDS

In this section, we outline challenges and directions for future work. We first note that a natural extension of the work presented here would be to revisit WEP with respect to other software engineering principles (Boehm, 1983; Davis, 1994; Bourque et al., 2002) that focus on four dimensions, namely project, process, people, and product.

One of the main reasons for establishing principles for Web Engineering is to be able to address quality concerns in all four dimensions. For instance, we would like to optimize (minimize) the cost of developing a Web application (project-level concern), like the engineers to be productive (process-level concern), improve employee satisfaction in a changing work environment (people-level concern), or like the system to be maintainable (product-level concern). A detailed and precise mapping from quality attributes to relevant WEP would be of interest.

To create awareness, and for a widespread acceptance of the proposed WEP, it will be crucial that they be adopted in some form in initiatives for standardizing the development of Web applications (IEEE, 2003),

Figure 2. Principles form the basis of other entities of knowledge in the discipline of Web engineering

the Web engineering body of knowledge (Navarro et al., 2005), and aligned with the models of Web Engineering teaching strategies and learning theories (Hadjerrouit, 2005).

There is also an urgent need for a Web engineering code of ethics similar to those for other disciplines, namely the Software Engineering Code of Ethics and Professional Practice (SECEPP) put forth by ACM/IEEE.

Finally, a natural extension of the WEP is to the next generation of Web applications, namely Semantic Web applications, Web services, and Semantic Web services.

CONCLUSION

The engineering of large-scale Web applications is more than a mere application of technologies or an exercise in skills. By addressing prevention rather than cure, the WEP form the first line of defense in dealing with the quality of Web applications. Therefore, it is crucial that they become an integral part of methodologies for engineering Web applications.

We recognize that there is a cost factor associated with any activity, and a consideration of WEP is not immune to it. However, we contend that the long-term benefits do outweigh the costs.

In conclusion, although WEP may seem "ideal" in nature, it does not preclude us from making efforts to attain them. Indeed, Web applications with high goals or ambitious objectives need to, even implicitly, demonstrate what makes them unique, and WEP could be one measure.

REFERENCES

Boehm, B. W. (1983). Seven Basic Principles of Software Engineering. Journal of Systems and Software, 3(1), 3-24.

Bourque, P., Dupuis, R., & Abran, A., Moore, J. W., Tripp, L., & Sybille, W. (2002). Fundamental Principles of Software Engineering - A Journey. Journal of Systems and Software, 62(1), 59-70.

Davis, A. M. (1994). Fifteen Principles of Software Engineering. IEEE Software, 11(6), 94-96.

Fenton, N. E., & Pfleeger, S. L. (1997). *Software metrics: A rigorous & practical approach*. International Thomson Computer Press.

Fogg, B. J. (2003). *Persuasive technology: Using computers to change what we think and do*. Morgan Kaufmann Publishers.

Ghezzi, C., Jazayeri, M., & Mandrioli, D. (2003). *Fundamentals of software engineering* (2nd ed.). Prentice-Hall.

Ginige, A., & Murugesan, S. (2001). Web engineering: An introduction. *IEEE Multimedia, 8*(1), 14-18.

Hadjerrouit, S. (2005). Designing a Pedagogical Model for Web Engineering Education: An Evolutionary Perspective. Journal of Information Technology Education, 4, 115-140.

IEEE. (2003). *IEEE Standard 2001-2002. IEEE recommended practice for the Internet: Web site engineering, Web site management, and Web site life cycle*. Internet Best Practices Working Group, IEEE Computer Society.

Johnson, D. G. (1997). Ethics online. *Communications of the ACM, 40*(1), 60-65.

Kamthan, P. (1999). *Server-side includes and its extensions*. Internet Related Technologies (IRT.ORG).

Kappel, G., Pröll, B., Reich, S., & Retschitzegger, W. (2006). *Web engineering*. John Wiley & Sons.

Keller, D. (1990). A guide to natural naming. *ACM SIGPLAN Notices, 25*(5), 95-102.

McConnell, S. C. (1999). Software Engineering Principles. IEEE Software, 16(2), 6-8.

Mendes, E., & Mosley, N. (2006). *Web engineering*. Springer.

Navarro, A., Sierra, J. L., Fernández-Valmayor, A., & Fernández-Manjón, B. (2005). A First Step Towards the Web Engineering Body of Knowledge. The Fifth International Conference on Web Engineering (ICWE 2005), Sydney, Australia, July 27-29, 2005.

Parnas, D. L. (1978). Some Software Engineering Principles. In: State of the Art Report on Structured Analysis and Design, INFOTECH International, 237-247.

Powell, T. A., Jones, D. L., & Cutts, D. C. (1998). *Web site engineering*. Prentice-Hall.

Rossi, G., Pastor, O., Schwabe, D., & Olsina, L. (2008). Web Engineering: Modelling and Implementing Web Applications. Springer.

Reynolds, G. (2003). *Ethics in information technology*. Thompson Publishing Group.

Suh, W. (2005). *Web engineering: Principles and techniques*. Idea Group Inc.

Tavani, H. T. (2004). *Ethics and technology*. John Wiley & Sons.

Van Duyne, D. K., Landay, J., & Hong, J. I. (2003). *The design of sites: Patterns, principles, and processes for crafting a customer-centered Web experience*. Addison-Wesley.

KEY TERMS

Delivery Context: A set of attributes that characterizes the capabilities of the access mechanism, the preferences of the user, and other aspects of the context into which a resource is to be delivered.

Descriptive Markup: A model of text that focuses on the description of information using markup delimiters for consumption by both humans and machines.

Formal Specification: A software representation with well-defined syntax and semantics that is usually used to express software requirements or detailed software design.

Natural Naming: A technique for using full names based on the terminology of the application domain that consists of one or more words of the natural language instead of acronyms or abbreviations for elements in a software representation.

Semantic Web: An extension of the current Web that adds technological infrastructure for better knowledge representation, interpretation, and reasoning.

Single Source Approach: A technique that encourages once-only-creation of a resource, such as a document, in a manner that it could be reused or repurposed for different contexts.

Web Engineering: A discipline concerned with the establishment and use of sound scientific, engineering, and management principles and disciplined and systematic approaches to the successful development, deployment, and maintenance of high quality Web applications.

Traffic Control

Thomas M. Chen
Southern Methodist University, USA

INTRODUCTION

Networks are designed to handle a certain amount of traffic with an acceptable level of network performance. Network performance will deteriorate if the offered traffic exceeds the given network capacity. Packets will suffer long queuing delays at congested nodes and possibly packet loss if buffers overflow.

Traffic control within the network regulates traffic flows for the purpose of maintaining adequate network performance during conditions of congestion. The Internet currently has a simple approach—dropping IP packets during congestion—but will evolve to more sophisticated traffic controls in the future.

BACKGROUND

Quality of service (QoS) is closely related to network performance, but QoS metrics are oriented towards a user's end-to-end experience (Chao & Guo, 2002). Network performance is measured mainly from the network provider's viewpoint, which may not be that meaningful to users concerned with their application's requirements. QoS parameters quantify the end-to-end network performance seen from the viewpoint of a user's particular connection (Gozdecki, Jajszczyk, & Stankiewicz, 2003). QoS parameters are directly relevant to an application's requirements (Seitz, 2003). For example, a real-time application might require QoS guarantees for a maximum end-to-end packet delay of 0.1 sec and packet loss rate of 10^{-6}. A different user may require a different QoS at the same time.

QoS may be classified as absolute or relative. Absolute, or "hard," QoS parameters are guaranteed in measurable and verifiable terms. An example of hard QoS is a guarantee that no more than one percent of packets will experience a delay of 100 msec. In contrast, relative, or "soft," QoS involves some assurance but not verifiable guarantees. Relative QoS is often defined for one service in comparison with another. An example is a high priority service that will always have a shorter average packet delay than a low priority service, but there are no absolute guarantees for either high or low priority service.

To support QoS, networks rely on a combination of various traffic controls (Wang, 2001). Routers and switches are programmed with packet scheduling and buffer management (selective packet discarding). Routers and switches could support resource reservations and admission control, and ingress nodes then perform access policing. Nodes may be capable of explicit congestion notification. At the higher level, transport or application layer protocols can be adaptive to the congestion level in the network.

TRAFFIC CONTROL

In practice, a variety of preventive and reactive traffic controls can be employed at different points in the networks (El-Gendy, Bose, & Shin, 2003). Admission control and access policing are preventive methods that reserve resources to avoid congestion and guarantee QoS. Reactive congestion control methods take remedial action after congestion is detected.

Admission Control. Admission control gives the network an opportunity to make a decision whether to accept or reject a new traffic flow to limit the total amount of carried traffic. Admission control can be quite effective in preventing congestion (Firoiu, Le Boudec, Towsley, & Zhang, 2002). Traditionally, admission control relies on a signaling protocol such as RSVP (resource reservation protocol) that allows applications to explicitly request a QoS or service class (Braden, Zhang, Berson, Herzog, & Jamin, 1997). Information about the new traffic flow (e.g., peak rate, average rate, and burstiness) must be provided to the network at the same time so that sufficient resources can be allocated. Based on the information provided, the network estimates the amount of bandwidth and buffer resources needed for a new traffic flow and compares the estimate with available resources. The network also estimates the potential impact of the new traffic flow on the current network performance. There must be assurance that the new flow will not cause the QoS for other flows to drop below acceptable levels.

The admission decision can be made by nodes in a deterministic, stochastic, or measurement-based manner (Perros & Elsayed, 1996). Deterministic approaches use worst-case bounds which can result in inefficient utilization. For better utilization, stochastic approaches assume a random traffic model to accurately estimate required resources. However, the accuracy of stochastic approaches depends greatly on the choice of traffic models. Traffic modeling is a difficult problem due to the dynamic nature of network traffic (Adas, 1997; Michiel & Laevens, 1997). Measurement-based approaches attempt to avoid the modeling problem by using measurements of actual traffic statistics (Shiomoto, Yamanaka, & Takahashi, 1999).

Endpoint admission control is an alternative to the traditional signaling approach. The idea is to leave the admission decision to the source host or ingress router (Elek, Karlsson, & Ronngre, 2000). Thus, a signaling protocol is not needed, and routers do not need to keep track of traffic reservations. The source can estimate whether sufficient resources are available by sending probe packets through the network (Ganesh, Key, Polis, & Srikant, 2006).

Another alternative is the concept of a centralized bandwidth broker (Nichols, Jacobson, & Zhang, 1999). Within a DiffServ domain, a bandwidth broker keeps track of allocated and available resources, makes all admission decisions, and configures the access routers to regulate incoming traffic. The bandwidth broker has a domain-wide view that should enable optimal resource allocation decisions. This is an open area of research (Zhang, Duan, Gao, & Hou, 2000).

Access Policing. When an admission control decision is made, that decision is based on traffic descrip-tors and QoS parameters provided by traffic sources. If the network admits a packet flow, it might be said that the user and network have agreed upon an implicit traffic contract. Sources are obligated to conform to the traffic descriptors that they provided for the admission decision. Excessive traffic will consume more network resources and degrade the QoS seen by all users.

Access policing refers to a mechanism at the network boundary to enforce the ingress traffic rate parameters. A traffic policer differentiates between conforming and non-conforming packets (according to the traffic contract). Conforming packets should be allowed immediate entrance into the network as if the traffic policer was transparent. Non-conforming packets may be discarded immediately or admitted with some kind of packet marking to lower their priority. If congestion is encountered anywhere, marked packets should be discarded first.

The leaky bucket algorithm is widely used for access control. The leaky bucket is virtual and easily implemented by a counter. The leaky bucket algorithm simply determines whether a packet is conforming or not. The basic version consists of a buffer (bucket) of size B and a leak rate R, as shown in Figure 1. Packets are conforming if they can increment the buffer content without overflowing. The contents of the buffer are emptied at the leak rate R. A larger bucket size allows greater variations from the rate R. A burst at higher rate can still be conforming as long as the burst is not long enough to overflow the bucket. Hence, the maximum burst length is directly related to the bucket size.

In the DiffServ framework, access control includes packet classification, policing, and marking according to a traffic conditioning agreement (TCA) (Longsong, Tianji, & Lo, 2000). The TCA defines out of profile (non-conforming) packets and the actions taken for them (dropping or marking).

Packet Scheduling. Packet scheduling is an essential element of traffic control because it recognizes that

Figure 1. Leaky bucket algorithm

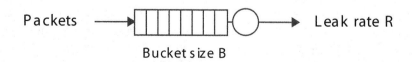

packets have different forwarding requirements (Jha & Hassan, 2002). Packet scheduling should recognize different service priorities and give preferential treatment to packets with more stringent delay requirements (El-Gendy et al., 2003). A packet flow may require a minimum throughput, maximum end-to-end delay, or maximum packet delay variation.

A simple and intuitive packet schedule gives preferential treatment according to static priorities, as shown in Figure 2. Each packet belongs to one of priority levels one to N, where priority one is always transmitted first, priority two is transmitted when there is no priority 1 packet, and so on. The advantage of static priorities is simple implementation. A disadvantage of static priorities is the possibility of starvation of low priorities. Because low priority packets are serviced only in the absence of high priority packets, low priority packets have no assurance of receiving any service.

Round robin is another simple and intuitive scheduling algorithm. Each packet flow is queued in a separate buffer, the head of line one is transmitted, then head of line two, and so on, eventually back to line one. Round robin seems intuitively fair because each packet flow takes equal turns. However, it may not be entirely fair because packets could be unequal in size. A flow with longer packets will consume more bandwidth compared to flows with shorter packets. In addition, certain flows may require more bandwidth than other flows. Weighted round robin accounts for bandwidth requirements assign weights $w_1, w_2, ..., w_N$, to each flow. A larger weight means that more packets are transmitted from that buffer in each turn.

Fair queuing might be viewed as an approximation to bit-by-bit round robin. It is obvious that bit-by-bit round robin cannot be implemented in actuality because packets must be transmitted in their entirety, not piecemeal as separate bits. In fair queuing, the hypothetical finishing time of each packet under bit-by-bit round robin is calculated and associated with that packet (Demers, Keshav, & Shenker, 1989). The next packet chosen to transmit is always the packet waiting with the earliest hypothetical finishing time.

Along the same idea, weighted fair queuing (WFQ) is a packet-by-packet approximation to bit-by-bit weighted round robin. It is fair in the sense that the i-th packet flow is guaranteed a fraction of bandwidth equal to at least $w_i/(w_1 + ... + w_N)$. As a consequence of the guaranteed bandwidth, it may be expected that if a traffic source is rate limited, then the delay through a queuing system with WFQ would be bounded (Parekh & Gallager, 1993). The bounded delay makes WFQ very appealing because it means that admission control can guarantee a maximum end-to-end packet delay.

A widely known class of scheduling algorithms is based on deadlines (Conway, Maxwell, & Miller, 2003). When a packet arrives at the buffer, it is assigned a deadline d, which is the time when it should be transmitted. For example, a real-time packet might have a deadline that is a short time after its arrival time, whereas a nonreal-time packet might have a deadline much farther in the future. A packet's lateness l is computed as the difference between its finishing time and deadline, $l = f - d$. A packet with positive lateness has not met its deadline, whereas a packet with negative lateness is considered early. Typically, a penalty is associated with lateness but not earliness. A number of optimal schedules are known, such as earliest due date (EDD), depending on the criterion to optimize.

Figure 2. Static priorities

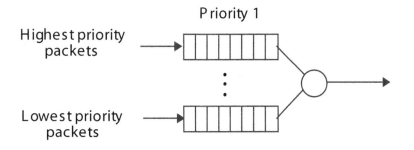

Buffer Management. Buffer management involves preferential access to limited buffer space. Packets may be denied access or pushed out of the queue, and hence buffer management is the problem of selective packet discarding (Labrador & Banerjee, 1999).

In theory, packets may be marked with an explicit loss priority. Although the type of service (TOS) field in the IP packet header has a bit to maximize reliability (or presumably minimize dropping), the TOS field has ambiguous interpretations and has been preempted by Diffserv (Carpenter & Nichols, 2002). IP does not allow explicit loss priorities, but strategies for discarding IP packets are an active area of research because packet loss effects TCP performance. These strategies are usually called active queue management (AQM) (Ryu, Rump, & Qiao, 2003).

The most important example is random early detection (RED). Normally, packets are dropped from the tail of a full buffer. However, the simple tail drop strategy causes global synchronization of TCP flows. TCP sources search for the proper sending rate by gradually increasing their rate until they detect a dropped packet by a retransmission time-out, then they will drop their rates (Jacobson, 1988). When a buffer overflows, it takes some time for TCP sources to detect a packet loss. In the meantime, the buffer continues to overflow, and packets will be discarded from multiple TCP flows. Thus, many TCP sources will detect packet loss and slow down at the same time. Even if the TCP sources were initially out of phase, they will become synchronized. The synchronization phenomenon causes underutilization and large queues. Underutilization occurs when all sources slow down at the same time, then large queues are accumulated when all sources simultaneously increase their transmission rates.

RED eliminates the synchronization phenomenon and thereby achieves better utilization and smaller queues (Floyd & Jacobson, 1993). A great advantage is that RED can be implemented in routers without any change to the existing TCP protocol. Instead of waiting for the buffer to overflow, RED drops a packet randomly from the queue so that multiple TCP flows will lose packets at different times. Therefore, the TCP flows slow down and ramp up at different times. Since the flows are out of phase, their aggregate rate is smoother than when the flows are synchronized. From a queuing theory viewpoint, smooth traffic achieves the best utilization and shortest queue.

Although RED has been widely accepted, it has been difficult to determine the proper parameters for effective performance (Bohacek, Shah, Arce, & Davis, 2004). Also, several problems have been seen under certain traffic conditions (Zhu, Wang, Aweya, Ouellette, & Montuno, 2002). Numerous variations have been proposed, and active queue management continues to be an ongoing area of research.

Explicit Congestion Notification. Instead of simply discarding packets during congestion, it is better to avoid congestion entirely if possible. The most effective way to avoid congestion is explicit congestion notification by the network, which acts as a method of "early warning." This advance warning can give sufficient time for traffic sources to reduce their rates before congestion occurs.

Protocols such as ATM and frame relay allow switches to mark packets when congestion appears to be imminent. The current version of IP does not include a capability for explicit congestion notification, but it has been proposed to borrow the last two bits from the TOS field in the IP packet header (Ramakrishnan & Floyd, 1999). One bit for ECN-capable transport (ECT) would allow hosts to signal whether they are capable of making use of ECN. The second bit for congestion experienced (CE) would allow routers or switches to signal a state of congestion to hosts. ECN and active queue management can effectively improve the performance of TCP (Yan, Gao, & Ozbay, 2005).

OPEN RESEARCH PROBLEMS

All areas of traffic control continue to attract researchers. The difficulty in traffic control always lies in balancing competing objectives. On the one hand, network resources should be completely shared on demand to achieve a high efficiency. But since random demand can exhaust resources at times, it is difficult (if not impossible) to guarantee QoS without reservations. On the other hand, it is well known that QoS can be guaranteed by reserving worst-case resources for each traffic flow. Reservations isolate resources for each traffic flow so that flows do not have to compete for resources. However, reservations can lead to inefficient utilization.

FUTURE TRENDS

The IETF's IntServ framework (Braden, Clark, & Shenker, 1994) was found to suffer from two serious drawbacks. First, routers would have to support a resource reservation protocol, RSVP. Second, the framework is not scalable. Routers are traditionally stateless but resource reservations would require some memory (state) to be maintained for each flow reservation. The amount of state increases with the number of flows.

IntServ has been supplanted by the DiffServ framework (Carpenter & Nichols, 2002). DiffServ avoids the need for stateful routers in the core network and moves complexity to access routers. Also, traffic is classified into different service classes, each defined by per-hop behaviors (PHBs). So far, only a few service classes have been defined. It is not clear how absolute QoS can be guaranteed without reservations.

CONCLUSION

Traffic control is essential to the future Internet which will support a broad diversity of applications. Many applications will demand absolute QoS guarantees which were not designed in the current Internet. The problem is not the lack of traffic control mechanisms. As seen in this chapter, many approaches to traffic control have been studied. However, implementation of traffic controls is constrained by several factors including cost, effectiveness, fairness, stability, scalability, and compatibility with existing infrastructure.

REFERENCES

Adas, A. (1997). Traffic models in broadband networks. *IEEE Communicatoins Magazine, 35,* 82-89.

Bohacek, S., Shah, K., Arce, G., & Davis, M. (2004). Signal processing challenges in active queue management. *IEEE Signal Processing Magazine, 21*(5), 69-79.

Braden, R., Zhang, L., Berson, S., Herzog, S., & Jamin, S. (1997). *Resource reservation protocol (RSVP) – version 1 functional specification.* IETF RFC 2205.

Braden, R., Clark, D., & Shenker, S. (1994). *Integrated services in the Internet architecture: an overview.* IETF RFC 1633.

Carpenter, B., & Nichols, K. (2002). Differentiated services in the Internet. *Proceedings of the IEEE, 90*(9), 1479-1494.

Chao, J., & Guo, X. (2002). *Quality of service control in high speed networks.* NY: Wiley & Sons.

Conway, R., Maxwell, W., & Miller, L. (2003). *Theory of scheduling.* Dover Publications.

Demers, A., Keshav, S., & Shenker, S. (1989). Analysis and simulation of a fair queueing algorithm. In *Proceedings of ACM SIGCOMM 89,* 1-12.

El-Gendy, A., Bose, A., & Shin, K. (2003). Evolution of the Internet QoS and support for soft real-time applications. *Proceedings of the IEEE, 91*(7), 1086-1104.

Elek, V., Karlsson, G., & Ronngre, R. (2000). Admission control based on end-to-end measurements. In *Proceedings of IEEE INFOCOM 2000,* 623-630.

Firoiu, V., Le Boudec, J-Y., Towsley, D., & Zhang, Z-L. (2002). Theories and models for Internet quality of service. *Proceedings of the IEEE, 90*(9), 1565-1591.

Floyd, S., & Jacobson, V. (1993). Random early detection gateways for congestion avoidance. *IEEE/ACM Transactions on Networking, 1*(4), 397-413.

Ganesh, A., Key, P., Polis, D., & Srikant, R. (2006). Congestion notification and probing mechanisms for endpoint admission control. *IEEE/ACM Transactions on Networking, 14*(3), 568-578.

Gozdecki, J, Jajszczyk, A., & Stankiewicz, R. (2003). Quality of service terminology in IP networks. *IEEE Communications Magazine, 41*(3), 153-159.

Jacobson, V. (1988). Congestion avoidance and control. In *Proceedings of ACM SIGCOMM'88,* 314-329.

Jha, S., & Hassan, M. (2002). *Engineering Internet QoS.* Norwood, MA: Artech House.

Labrador, M. & Banerjee, S. (1999). Packet dropping policies for ATM and IP networks. *IEEE Communication Surveys, 2,* 2-14.

Longsong, L., Tianji, J., & Lo, J. (2000). A generic traffic conditioning model for differentiated services. In *Proceedings of IEEE ICC 2000*, 1305-1309.

Michiel, H., & Laevens, K. (1997). Teletraffic engineering in a broadband era. *Proceedings of the IEEE, 85*(12), 2007-2033.

Nichols, K., Jacobson, V., & Zhang, L. (1999). *A two-bit differentiated services architecture for the Internet.* IETF RFC 2638.

Parekh, A., & Gallager, R. (1993). A generalized processor sharing approach to flow control in integrated services networks: The single node case. *IEEE/ACM Trans. on Networking, 1*(3), 344-357.

Perros, H., & Elsayed, K. (1996). Call admission control schemes: A review. *IEEE Communications Magazine, 34*(11), 82-91.

Ramakrishnan, K., & Floyd, S. (1999). *A proposal to add explicit congestion notification (ECN) to IP.* IETF RFC 2481.

Ryu, S., Rump, C., & Qiao, C. (2003). Advances in Internet congestion control. *IEEE Communications and Surveys, 5,* 28-39.

Seitz, N., (2003). ITU-T QoS standards for IP-based networks. *IEEE Communications Magazine, 41*(6), 82-89.

Shiomoto, K., Yamanaka, N., & Takahashi, T. (1999). Overview of measurement-based connection admission control schemes. *IEEE Communication Surveys, 2,* 2-13.

Wang, Z. (2001). *Internet QoS: Architectures and mechanisms for quality of service.* San Francisco: Morgan Kaufmann.

Yan, P., Gao, Y., & Ozbay, H. (2005). A variable structure control approach to active queue management for TCP with ECN. *IEEE Transactions on Control Systems Technology, 13*(2), 203-215.

Zhang, Z-L., Duan, Z., Gao, L., & Hou, Y. (2000). Decoupling QoS control from core routers: A novel bandwidth broker architecture for scalable support of guaranteed services. In *Proceedings of ACM SIG-COMM'00,* 71-83

Zhu, C., Wang, O., Aweya, J., Ouellette, M., & Montuno, D. (2002). A comparison of active queue management algorithms using the OPNET modeler. *IEEE Communications Magazine, 40*(6), 158-167.

KEY TERMS

Access Policing: Regulation of ingress traffic at the network boundary, usually by a leaky bucket algorithm.

Active Queue Management (AQM): Intelligent buffer management strategies, such as random early detection (RED), enabling traffic sources to respond to congestion before buffers overflow.

Admission Control: A procedure for the network to accept or block new traffic flows before the flows start, usually by means of a signaling or resource reservation protocol.

Congestion: a state of the network where an excessive amount of offered traffic causes serious degradation of network performance.

Differentiated Services (DiffServ): An IETF framework supporting QoS classes by means of Diffserv code point marking, per hop behaviors (PHBs), and stateless core routers.

Explicit Congestion Notification: A proactive congestion avoidance method involving routers or switches conveying congestion information to hosts via fields in packet headers.

Integrated Services (IntServ): An IETF framework supporting QoS based on RSVP reservations per flow.

Quality of Service (QoS): End-to-end network performance defined from the perspective of a specific user's connection.

Transporting TDM Service on Metropolitan Bus–Based Optical Packet Switching Networks

Viet Hung Nguyen
Institut National des Télécommunications, France

Tülin Atmaca
Institut National des Télécommunications, France

INTRODUCTION

Today's telecommunication world is seeing dramatic changes in network infrastructures and services. These changes are mainly driven by the ever-growing rate of network traffic. Global Internet traffic is doubling each year due to both tremendous growth in the number of users and rapid increase of bandwidth accessible by each user (e.g., the Global Internet Geography report (2004) stated that in Asia, Internet traffic growth was about 400 percent in the year 2004). Not only is network traffic growing at an unprecedented speed, but the traffic mix is changing greatly. The traditional voice traffic volume has now become very small relative to the huge volume of data and video traffic, due to the deployment of Gigabit technologies in the access part of the service providers' networks.

These changes in traffic will cause service providers to rethink the way they build their networks. Traditional **circuit switching** networks, which were specifically designed for transporting voice traffic, are becoming inappropriate for fulfilling new user demands, both in terms of bandwidth and value-added services. In this context, to offer service providers more flexibility in allocating bandwidth to users, **optical packet switching** (OPS) technology is being studied and gradually introduced into next generation networks. By combining data, video, and voice over the same high-speed OPS network infrastructure, service providers are increasingly creating new value-added services, spurring the user's bandwidth consumption, hence maximizing their revenues.

On the global telecommunication networks map, the **Metropolitan Area Network** (MAN) is mostly influenced by the rapid evolution of traffic and advanced networking technologies. The traffic pattern changes much more rapidly in metro networks than in long-haul backbone networks. Moreover, in a metro area, a business corporation might need several types of service: leased line private services for voice and video communication, fiber channel or Gigabit Ethernet for data storage purposes, and high speed xDSL for Internet applications. The implication is that a MAN service provider should handle a set of overlay networks to fulfill this mix of services. Therefore, it should be beneficial for MAN service providers to replace these overlay networks by a single new MAN infrastructure.

This paper introduces a particular metropolitan bus-based OPS network for future MANs. As explained above, the main technological challenge for MAN service providers today is to handle all types of service, such as data, voice, and video over a single packet-based network infrastructure. Recall that voice traffic has been traditionally transported by **time division multiplexing** (TDM)-based networks, which provide high quality of service (QoS) for voice. In order to ensure the same QoS for voice service when it is mixed with bursty data service over the bus-based OPS network, we will need a specific mechanism. More specifically, this work investigates the **circuit emulation service** (CES) technology aiming at transporting **TDM service** over a packet-based network. Recently, CES was standardized by a number of organisms, such as the Internet Engineering Task Force (IETF), International Telecommunication Union (ITU), Metro Ethernet Forum (MEF), etc. This standard-based technology promises to be a good candidate for the convergence of circuit and packet services over future packet-based MANs.

BACKGROUND

Bus-Based OPS Architecture

The concept of the bus-based OPS network studied here is mainly based on a recent experimental architecture, the dual bus optical ring network (DBORN) (Le Sauze, Dotaro, Dupas, et al., 2002). The idea is to design an optical network that satisfies requirements for the next generation MANs, while reducing the network cost by employing advanced technologies in optical networking.

As shown in Figure 1(a), the bus-based OPS network considered consists of two unidirectional buses: a transmission bus that provides a shared transmission medium for carrying traffic from several access point (AP) nodes to a point of presence (POP) node, and a reception bus carrying traffic from the POP node to all AP nodes. Thus, an AP node always "writes" to the POP node employing the transmission bus and "listens" for the POP node using the reception bus. The traffic emitted on the transmission bus by an AP node is first received by the POP node, then is either switched to the reception bus to reach its destination node, or is

routed to other MANs or backbone networks. Thus, on the transmission bus, *transit* optical packets flowing from upstream AP nodes pass through downstream AP nodes optically (i.e., without O/E/O conversion), thanks to the use of passive optical couplers. This is the well-known concept of a passive optical network (PON), which highly reduces the number of transmitters and receivers at AP nodes.

Since the transmission bus is a shared transmission medium, AP nodes need a MAC protocol to control the access to the medium. The optical unslotted carrier sense multiple access with collision avoidance (OU-CSMA/CA) protocol is used for this purpose (Figure 1(b)). In addition to the simplicity property inherited from the well-known CSMA protocol, the OU-CSMA/CA protocol provides more efficient resource utilization thanks to avoidance of collision. It is worth mentioning that the network that uses OU-CSMA/CA protocol obviously supports variable length packets (e.g., Internet packets) thanks to the asynchronous nature of this access protocol. Briefly, thanks to a fiber-delay line (FDL) at each node, the OU-CSMA/CA protocol operates based on the detection of idle periods (*voids*) on the transmission wavelength.

Figure 1(a). Metropolitan double-bus network architecture

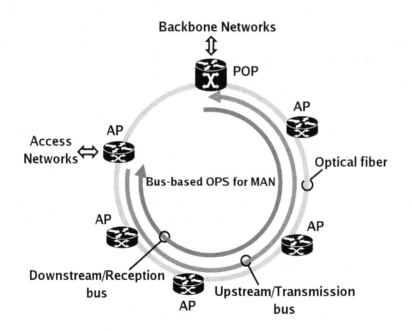

Figure 1(b). Access node architecture

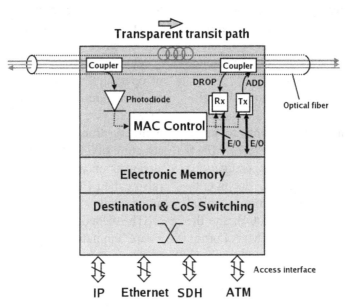

Circuit Emulation Service Technology

CES is a technology aiming at transporting TDM service such as PDH (E1/T1/E3/T3), as well as SONET/SDH circuits over **packet switching** networks. The main intention of CES is to make the packet switching network behave as a standard TDM-based SONET/SDH and/or PDH network as seen from the customer's point of view. Thus, CES should allow customers to be able to use the same existing TDM equipment, regardless of whether their traffic is carried by standard SONET/SDH and/or PDH network or a packet-switching network using CES.

Historically, circuit emulation originally comes from the asynchronous transfer mode (ATM) world (ATM Forum, 1997). This technology emerged due to the demand for carrying certain types of constant bit rate (CBR) or TDM traffic over ATM networks. Service providers were starting to upgrade their circuit switching networks to ATM networks, but they needed to maintain the support of customers using TDM equipment. Therefore, the ATM forum proposed CES technology for emulating TDM circuits across an ATM network so that customers at the two end points of the ATM network receive the same TDM service as though the

TDM circuit was transmitted over a traditional TDM network. At that time CES over ATM had specifically covered some low bit rate PDH circuits, such as E1/T1/E3/T3 services.

The idea of CES has been recently taken up in the packet switching world by a number of organisms, including the IETF, the MEF, the ITU-T, and the multi-protocol label switching frame relay and ATM alliance (MFA forum). There are no important differences between the CES standards being defined by these organisms. They actually address different layers within the network (e.g., IP, MPLS, Ethernet, etc.), and emphasize different aspects of the CES, depending on the specific services they are concerned with.

Within the IETF, the **pseudo-wire emulation edge to edge** (PWE3) working group is chartered to develop methods to carry Layer-1 and Layer-2 services across a packet-switched network (principally IP or MPLS). The group has proposed three standards for CES over packet-switching networks, namely the structured-agnostic TDM over packet (Vainshtein & Stein, 2005), the structure-aware CES over packet-switched network (Vainshtein, Sasson, Metz, Frost, & Pate, 2006), and the TDM over IP (Stein, Shashoua, Insler, & Anavi, 2005) standards. Similarly, the ITU recommendation Y.1413

(ITU-T, 2004) has defined the formats that support all encapsulation methods for carrying CES across MPLS networks. The Y.1413 supports both structure-agnostic and structure-aware TDM emulations. These standards mainly describe the protocols without specific reference to any implementation requirements.

In comparison with the above standards, the MEF and MFA forum are looking to propose CES standards with specific implementation agreements to make it applicable to metropolitan Ethernet and/or MPLS contexts. They provide more detailed specifications that are not covered by IETF and ITU documents. For instance, the MEF has produced the technical specification (Metro Ethernet Forum, 2004), and the MFA forum has released two standards (MFA Forum, 2003 and MFA Forum, 2004) supporting the various inter-working functions of CES.

CES OVER METROPOLITAN BUS-BASED OPS NETWORK

CES Global Reference Model

The reference model for CES on the metro bus-based OPS network is based on the global model for circuit emulation described in IETF RFC3985 (Bryant & Pate, 2005) and the MEF3 specification (Metro Ethernet Forum, 2004). Figure 2 presents the reference model of CES for a metro bus-based OPS network. Generally, we have two TDM customers' edges (CE) communicating via the network considered. One CE is connected to an AP node (ingress CE), the other CE is connected to the POP node (egress CE). TDM service

generated by ingress CE is emulated across the network to egress CE. The emulated TDM service between two CEs is managed by two inter-working functions (IWF) implemented at appropriate nodes.

Operation Modes. CES has two principal modes of operation. In the first one, called "unstructured" or "structure-agnostic" emulation mode, the entire TDM service bandwidth is emulated transparently, including framing and overhead present. The frame structure of TDM service is ignored. The ingress bit stream is encapsulated into an emulated TDM flow (also called *CES flow*) and is identically reproduced at the egress side.

The second mode, called "structured" or "structure-aware" emulation, requires the knowledge of the TDM frame structure being emulated. In this mode, individual TDM frames are visible and are byte aligned in order to preserve the frame structure. "Structured" mode allows frame-by-frame treatment, permitting overhead stripping, and flow multiplexing/demultiplexing. This means that a single "structured" TDM service may be decomposed into two or more CES flows, or two or more "structured" TDM services may be combined to create a single CES flow as well.

Service Interfaces. There are two basic service interfaces in the architecture of CES. The first one is the TDM service interface where the original TDM service is terminated (at the ingress side) or reconstructed (at the egress side). The second one is the CES interface where the emulated TDM circuit starts (at the ingress side) or ends (at the egress side).

Functional Blocks. In the reference model of CES, the native service processing (NSP) block performs some necessary operations (in TDM domain) on native

Figure 2. Reference model for CES on metropolitan bus-based OPS network

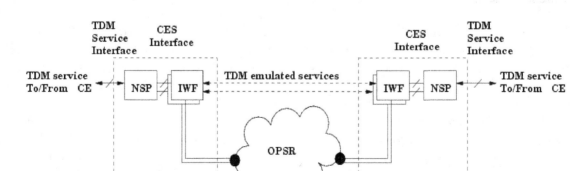

TDM service such as overhead treatment or flow multiplexing/demultiplexing, terminating the native TDM service coming/going from/to CE. For instance, as the "unstructured" TDM service does not need framing treatment, it might not be handled by the NSP and can pass directly to the IWF block for emulation. However, the "structured" TDM service should be treated by the NSP block before going to the IWF block. Actually, the NSP could be the standard SONET/SDH framer or mapper, or other propriety products.

The inter-working function (IWF) block could be considered as an adaptation function that interfaces the CES application to the bus-based OPS layer. This means that the CES technology could be considered as an application service that uses the bus-based OPS network as a virtual wire between two TDM networks. Thus, the IWF block is responsible for ensuring a good operation of the emulated service. The main functions of IWF are to encapsulate TDM service in transport optical packets, to perform TDM service synchronization, sequencing, signaling, and also to monitor performance parameters of emulated TDM service. Each TDM emulated service requires a pair of IWF installed, respectively, at the ingress and egress sides.

CES Optical Packet Format

Figure 3 shows the example of optical packet format for CES, inspired from Vainshtein et al. (2005) and Vainshtein et al. (2006), in the bus-based OPS network using Ethernet technology.

A CES control word is added to each TDM payload to differentiate the network outage and the emulated service outage, to signal problems detected at the IWF egress to the IWF ingress, to save bandwidth by not transferring invalid data, and to perform packet sequencing if a Real-time Transport Protocol (RTP) header is not used.

An optional RTP header may be added to the resulting packet for synchronization and sequencing purposes. The CES control word and RTP header form the CES header. Additional multiplexing headers could be added to the resulting packet in order to multiplex many emulated TDM flows over the same transmission channel.

Finally, the new resulting packet is encapsulated in the transmission unit of the used transmission protocol (e.g., in this case, the standard ethernet PDU). The final optical packet is then built by adding optical

Figure 3. Optical packet format and CES encapsulation in metro bus-based OPS network using Ethernet technology

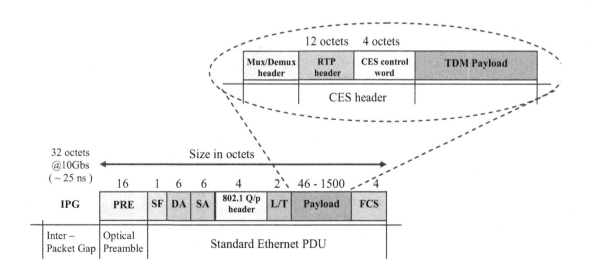

overhead to the new resulting packet. All details about the structure of CES control word and RTP header are described in Vainshtein et al. (2005) and Vainshtein et al. (2006).

Segmentation Mechanisms for TDM Frames

A TDM frame would ideally be relayed across the emulated TDM service as a single unit. However, when the combined length of the TDM frame and its associated header exceeds the maximum transmission unit (MTU) length of the used transmission protocol, a segmentation and re-assembly process should be performed in order to deliver TDM service over the network considered.

By this consideration, therefore, Nguyen, Ben Mamoun, Atmaca, et al. (2004) and Nguyen and Atmaca (2004) have proposed two segmentation mechanisms. The first one, called *dynamic segmentation*, fragments a TDM frame into smaller segments according to void length detected on the transmission wavelength. This approach promises a good use of wavelength bandwidth, but is technically complex to implement. The second segmentation method is *static segmentation*, which segments the TDM frame according to a predefined threshold. This technique is simple to implement, and it provides resulting TDM segments with predictable size. Thus, current TDM monitoring methods could be reused, simplifying the management of CES.

Segmentation threshold for TDM frames is a parameter to be determined. Vainshtein et al. (2006) have recommended some rules to determine this segmentation threshold.

First, the segmentation threshold should be either an integer multiple or an integer divisor of the TDM payload size. For example, for unstructured SONET/SDH services, the segmentation threshold could be an integer multiple of an STS-1 (or STM-0) frame of 810 bytes.

Second, for unstructured E1 and DS1 services, the segmentation threshold for E1 could be 256 bytes (i.e., multiplexing of eight native E1 frames), and for DS1 could be 193 bytes (i.e., multiplexing of eight native DS1 frames).

Besides, Nguyen et al. (2004) have identified that a threshold of 810 bytes is good for the transport of all unstructured SONET/SDH flows across the bus-based OPS network.

Performance Parameters and Requirements for CES

Generally, many performance requirements must be met in order to transport emulated TDM circuits across a packet switching network. The Metro Ethernet Forum (2004) defines some main performance parameters for each CES flow.

The CES Packet Loss Rate (*CPLR*) is defined as the ratio of lost packets carrying TDM service among total sent packets carrying TDM service.

The CES end-to-end Packet Delay (*CPD*) is the maximum end-to-end delay measured for a percentile *P* (superior to 99.999%) of successfully delivered packets carrying TDM service over a measured interval *T*. According to the Metro Ethernet Forum (2004), the percentile *P* is required to be equal to 99.999 percent or higher. This means that the measured CPD must satisfy the following condition: 99.999 percent of the observed delays during *T* are less than or equal to CPD.

The CES Packet Jitter (*CPJ*) is derived from the CPD measured over the same measurement interval T and percentile P. CPJ is obtained by subtraction of the lowest end-to-end packet delay from CPD measured for the same percentile P and interval T. CPJ is typically used to size the Jitter buffer at the egress side of emulated circuit.

All the aforementioned parameters must meet the requirements for CES defined in the Metro Ethernet Forum (2004). Specifically, *the CPLR and CPD of each CES flow shall be kept to a minimum, and the CPJ of each CES flow shall not exceed 10 ms.*

Quality of Service Architecture for Metro Bus-Based OPS Network

Of course, the CES technology must be used in combination with QoS architecture and enhanced access schemes in order to deliver satisfying QoS to TDM customers and other services across the bus-based OPS network. The global metropolitan traffic can be divided into two main categories: real-time traffic (e.g., TDM) and non-real-time traffic (e.g., data). The non-real-time traffic can be divided, in turn, into QoS-guarantee traffic (e.g., loss-sensitive data applications) and QoS-non-guarantee traffic (e.g., Internet best-effort traffic). These three traffic categories (or classes of service (CoS)) seem enough for covering all types of traffic that a MAN might be supposed to transport. Table 1

Table 1. QoS architecture for bus-based OPS network

CoS Type	Priority	Network performance		
		Packet Loss Rate	**Delay**	**Jitter**
CoS1 (real-time)	High	10^{-9}	Strictly limited	Strictly limited
CoS2 (loss-sensitive)	Medium	10^{-9}	Limited	Limited
CoS3 (best-effort)	Low	No guarantee	No guarantee	No guarantee

summarizes assumptions about the QoS architecture, including traffic classification, priority, and expected network performance requirements for the metropolitan bus-based OPS network under study.

Some Performance Results

Nguyen (2006) has pointed out that from a logical performance perspective, the realization of CES across a bus-based OPS network is feasible. Figures 4(a), 4(b), 4(c), and 4(d) illustrate performance parameters

of the bus-based OPS network measured at the offered network load of 0.80 using different access schemes. The TCARD (Bouabdallah, Dotaro, Ciavaglia, et al., 2004) and Di-MAC (Nguyen & Atmaca, 2006) schemes are fairness-aware mechanisms aiming at improving the performance of the OU-CSMA/CA protocol. The detailed technical description of those access schemes are out of the scope of this paper. Readers are invited to refer to Nguyen (2006) for more information. Globally, OU-CSMA/CA and TCARD schemes may provide satisfying QoS for TDM service, but at the expense

Figure 4. Performance results on CES: offered ring load = 0.80, TDM segmentation threshold = 810 bytes

Figure 4(a). Packet loss rate of CoS2 and CoS3

Figure 4(b). Average access delay of CoS1

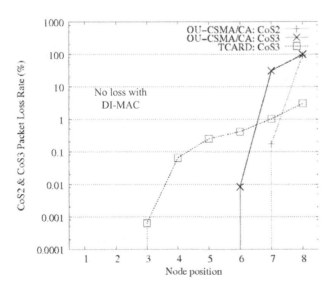

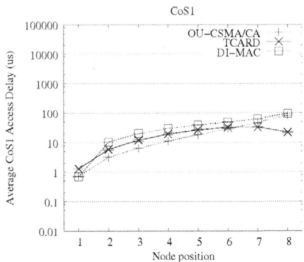

Figure 4(c). Average access delay of CoS2

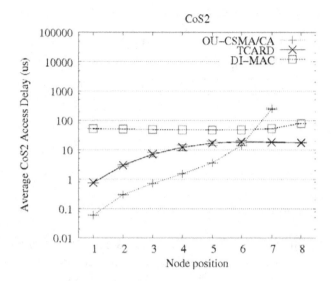

Figure 4(d). Average access delay of CoS3

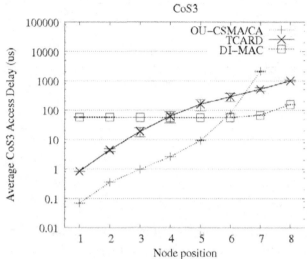

of degrading or even losing low priority traffic, such as best-effort traffic. However, the Di-MAC scheme seems to be a better support of all types of service. It effectively guarantees expected QoS for TDM service and, at the same time, provides low loss and low packet delay for lower priority services.

FUTURE TRENDS

CES is a standard supported by many international organizations. Therefore, the use of CES for the transport of circuit service (e.g., voice) across an OPS network promises to be a good candidate for the next generation OPS networks. However, voice over IP (VoIP) technology is now widely deployed in current packet switching network infrastructures, and also guarantees QoS for voice traffic. Thus, a possible work in the future will be the comparison in terms of performance and cost between CES and VoIP technologies in supporting voice service across OPS networks.

CONCLUSION

The need of creating common packet-based network infrastructures that support multiple services with guaranteed QoS (e.g., traditional TDM service, new video and data services, etc.) becomes more and more urgent due to the proliferation of multimedia and data applications of today. We have presented in this work a bus-based OPS network which has been proposed for the next generation MAN. This bus-based OPS network should be able to deliver services with guaranteed quality to metropolitan users. We have described the proposed QoS architecture for the bus-based OPS network, including three classes of services covering delay-sensitive, loss-sensitive, and best-effort applications. In order to provide TDM-like QoS for traditional TDM service (delay-sensitive), we have introduced CES technology into the network. The main advantage of CES is that it is a cost-efficient solution for transporting TDM across a packet-switching network, and it is also a standard supported by the IETF, MEF, ITU, and MFA forums. The feasibility of performing CES across the bus-based OPS network has been also demonstrated. The comparison of CES versus VoIP is supposed to be the topic of future work.

REFERENCES

ATM Forum. (1997). *Circuit emulation service interoperability specification 2.0* (af-vtoa-0078.000). Retrieved 1 November, 2005 from http://www.atmforum.com

Bouabdallah, N., Dotaro, E., Ciavaglia, L., et al. (2004). Resolving the fairness issue in bus-based optical access networks. *IEEE Communications Magazine, 42*(11), S12-S18.

Bryant, S., & Pate, P. (2005). *Pseudo wire emulation edge-to-edge (PWE3) architecture*. Retrieved 13 March, 2005 from http://www.ietf.org/rfc/rfc3985.txt?number=3985

Global Internet Geography. (2004). *TeleGeography report*. Retrieved 7 October, 2004 from http://www.telegeography.net

IEEE Standard 802. (1990). IEEE standards for local and metropolitan area networks: Overview and architecture. *IEEE Std 802-1990*.

Le Sauze, N., Dotaro, E., Dupas, A., et al. (2002). DBORN: A shared WDM Ethernet bus architecture for optical packet metropolitan network. In *Proceedings of th Photonic in Switching Conference, 21-25 July, 2002*, pp. 89-91.

Metro Ethernet Forum. (2004). Circuit emulation service definitions, framework and requirements in metro Ethernet networks. *Technical specification MEF3*. Available at http://www.metroethernetforum.org/PDFs/Standards/MEF3.pdf

MFA Forum. (2003). *TDM transport over MPLS using AAL1 implementation agreement*. Retrieved 12 December, 2005 from http://www.mfaforum.org/tech/MFA4.0.pdf

MFA Forum. (2004). *Emulation of TDM circuits over MPLS using raw encapsulation implementation agreement*. Retrieved 12 December, 2005 from http://www.mfaforum.org/tech/MFA8.0.0.pdf

Nguyen, V.H. (2006). *Performance study on multi-service optical metropolitan area network: MAC protocols and quality of service*. PhD dissertation at Institut National des Télécommunications, Evry, France.

Nguyen, V.H., & Atmaca, T. (2006). Dynamic intelligent MAC protocol for metropolitan optical packet switching ring networks. In *IEEE International Conference on Communications – ICC 2006*, Istanbul, Turkey, Vol. 6, pp. 2661-2668.

Nguyen, V.H., & Atmaca, T. (2004). Integrating circuit emulation service and modified packet bursting technologies in metropolitan optical network. In *2e Performance Modelling and Evaluation of Heterogeneous Networks (Het-Nets '04)*. Technical Proceeding, p34/1-34/10.

Nguyen, V.H., Ben Mamoun, M., Atmaca T., et al. (2004). Performance evaluation of circuit emulation service in a metropolitan optical ring architecture. *Telecommunications and Networking – ICT 2004* (LNCS 3124, pp. 1173-1182).

Stein, Y.J., Shashoua, R., Insler, R., & Anavi, M. (2005). *TDM over IP (TDMoIP)*. Retrieved 5 December, 2005 from http://www.ietf.org/internet-drafts/draft-ietf-pwe3-tdmoip-05.txt

Vainshtein, A., Sasson, I., Metz, E., Frost, T., & Pate, P. (2006). *Structure-aware TDM circuit emulation over packet switched network (CESoPSN)*. Retrieved 1 June, 2006 from http://www.ietf.org/internet-drafts/draft-ietf-pwe3-cesopsn-07.txt

Vainshtein, A., & Stein, Y.J. (2005). *Structure-agnostic TDM over packet (SAToP)*. Retrieved 15 June, 2006 from http://www.rfc-editor.org/rfc/rfc4553.txt

KEY TERMS

Circuit Emulation Service: A technology allowing the transport of TDM service such as PDH (E1/T1/E3/T3) as well as SONET/SDH circuits over packet-switching networks.

Circuit Switching: A communication technology in which a dedicated circuit (channel) is established for the duration of a transmission. In circuit-switching networks, network resources are static and remain dedicated to the circuit during the entire transmission. This technology, combined with TDM technology, is mostly used in the well-known telephony and SONET/SDH networks for transporting voice traffic.

Metropolitan Area Network: A set of computer networks or telecommunication networks that work together to provide access and services in a metro region such as a large campus or a city (IEEE Standard 802, 1990).

Optical Network: A high capacity telecommunication network operating based on optical technologies and components (e.g., optical transmission, optical fiber, lasers, optical amplifiers, etc.). Optical networks allow for the transmitting of user data at very high bit rates at single wavelength (e.g., 10 Gbits/s, 40 Gbits/s, etc.).

Optical Packet Switching Network: an optical network in which packets are switched optically without being converted to electrical signal.

Packet Switching: A communication technology in which a message is broken into packets, each of which can take a different route to the destination where

packets are recompiled into the original message. In packet-switching networks, network resources are not static, but are dynamically shared by several packet streams. Packet-switching technology was usually used for transporting enterprise data traffic, but nowadays it is gradually introduced into optical networks for transporting both voice and data traffic.

Time Division Multiplexing: A technology that increases transmission bit rate by multiplexing many lower rate data streams into a higher rate data stream. The multiplexer herein typically interleaves (in time domain) the lower rate streams to obtain the higher rate stream.

Voice Over Internet Protocol: A New Paradigm in Voice Communication

Indranil Bose
The University of Hong Kong, Hong Kong

Fong Man Chun
The University of Hong Kong, Hong Kong

INTRODUCTION

One of the hottest technologies these days is voice communication over packet-switched data networks. This is known as voice over Internet protocol (VoIP). Hardy (2003) defines VoIP as "the interactive voice exchange capability carried over packet switched transport employing the Internet protocol." With VoIP, voice signal from the sender is digitized into packets that are transmitted to the receiver through a network, which often includes the Internet. As the Internet is a free resource, the communication cost of VoIP is much lower than that of traditional telephone systems. This is a major advantage of VoIP. VoIP system also increases the efficiency and service quality of businesses. As a result of VoIP, many advanced applications can be built and these include unified messaging, video

conferencing, and ring list. But VoIP is not without its limitations. Its main drawback is low reliability. It also suffers from uncertain quality of voice transmission. In addition, it cannot guarantee security because it uses public networks. Although the idea of VoIP was known from the 1970s, it did not become commercially viable until 1995, when Vocaltec became the first company to produce the first commercially available VoIP product (Varshney et al., 2002).

BACKGROUND

Voice over Internet protocol (VoIP) is a technology which digitizes the analog voice signal using an encoder. The digitized data is transmitted as a stream of packets from the sender to the receiver. When the packets reach

Figure 1. Scenario of VoIP transmission

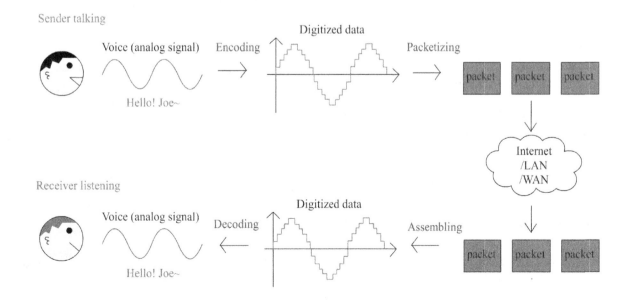

Figure 2. Components of a VoIP system

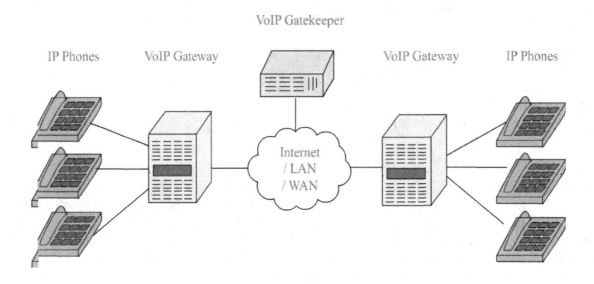

the receiver they are reassembled and decoded using a decoder. The decoder constructs the voice signal so that the receiver can hear what the sender said. The principle of action of VoIP can be illustrated with the help of Figure 1.

A VoIP system consists of IP phones, VoIP gateways, VoIP gatekeeper, and also the network (Internet, LAN, or WAN). IP phone provides the user with the same user interface as the traditional phone. However, it has advanced features embedded in it which allow VoIP transmission. VoIP Gateway is a device which provides communication between the IP phone and the VoIP Gatekeeper that records the number of users connected to the VoIP system and keeps track of the traffic condition of the network. Inside an office, an IP PBX is also required. It is used for internal switching of VoIP calls. When a user calls within the office, the IP PBX sends the call to the corresponding office IP Phone. If a user calls outside the company, the IP PBX directs the call to the VoIP Gateway which then makes the connection with the receiver. Figure 2 shows the essential components of a VoIP system.

BENEFITS AND LIMITATIONS OF VoIP

The benefits of VoIP are many. They can be described under the following sub-headings:

New Services and Applications

One major advantage of VoIP over public switched telephone network (PSTN) or the traditional circuit switched telephone network is that it provides flexibility to add new features to telephone systems. Examples of such features include unified messaging and video conferencing. With unified messaging, companies can use a common interface to get all types of messages, like voice mail, fax, e-mail, and SMS. Also, these messages can be subjected to different kinds of operations like retrieve, forward, save, and broadcast. VoIP-based video conferencing can help cut down travel costs and enhance real-time face-to-face conversations. With the help of these advanced features, quality and efficiency of services of businesses can be enhanced. Moreover, unlike the traditional telephone system, where equipment is usually incompatible at different locations, VoIP is not affected by different equipment used by PSTN vendors in different locations. This increases the flexibility of the communication system because users at different locations can use the same equipment and do not need to buy new equipments or adapters.

Flexibility in Communication

When traveling to other countries, businessmen sometimes forget to bring their mobile phones with them.

This causes them much inconvenience because there is no way to contact others. VoIP provides a useful alternative in such situations. Since the Internet is available everywhere, the business traveler can make use of their VoIP phones, or even a personal computer (PC) equipped with a speaker and a microphone, to keep in touch with their home base and their clients throughout the world who may be using either an ordinary phone or a PC. Thus, with VoIP, flexibility of communication is increased to a great extent. In addition to phone-to-phone calls, VoIP allows users to make PC-to-phone calls, phone-to-PC calls, and PC-to-PC calls. Vonage and Skype are two VoIP service providers who provide Internet-based voice services. They have different and competitive charging schemes for travelers who want to talk for long periods with customers or family members from distant locations.

Lower Communication Cost

Traditionally, businesses maintain two infrastructures, one for voice system (PSTN) and one for data system (Internet). Therefore, they pay the setup, maintenance, and upgrade costs for both infrastructures. These kinds of double setup, maintenance, and upgrade costs constitute a large overhead for companies, especially small and medium enterprises. In addition to the infrastructure, two kinds of specialists are needed for the normal operations of the voice and data systems. With VoIP, the two infrastructures can be merged. Since both voice and data transmission takes place through the Internet, only one kind of setup, maintenance, and upgrade cost is incurred and only one type of specialist is needed for the normal operation of the merged system. This can greatly reduce the operating cost of a company. At the same time, there are savings in the cost of voice calls because the Internet is a free resource. VoIP service providers are able to support calls at a much lower rate compared to long distance telephone service providers. Although the setup cost of a VoIP system is higher than a traditional phone system, it is likely that there will be a break even after use for a short time, and with continued use of the system, the investment will prove to be cost effective in the long run.

Improvement in Service Quality

For any business, efficiency and service quality are the two pillars of success. VoIP can increase the efficiency

and service quality of businesses due to the advanced applications that can be developed on top of it. These applications include, among others, voicemail, call redialing, ring list, and call transfer. Many VoIP service providers, such as SunRocket and Vonage, have already provided these advanced services. By providing the Voicemail service, VoIP allows voicemail messages to be retrieved online or via e-mail. They can be downloaded to the users' computers and saved for future reference. Moreover, voicemail notifications can be sent to users' cell phones or e-mail addresses so that users become aware of any important missed calls. With call redialing, users can redial a phone number automatically until there is a connection with the other party. It can save time when there is a need to redial the same phone number a number of times. The ring list allows users to get their online address books with names and corresponding phone numbers, sort the contacts by categories, and also click any contact number to call without dialing. Avaya's director of IP telephony and mobility, Lawrence Byrd, has commented that the future of VoIP depends on its applications. When more applications evolve that need support of this technology, the market for VoIP services will automatically become large and profitable (Ascierto, 2006).

At the same time it must be remembered that there are several shortcomings of VoIP systems which can be categorized under the following sub-headings:

Lower Reliability of Service

Users feel comfortable with PSTN because users perceive that its reliability is high. In fact, it is a known fact that PSTNs can achieve the five nines reliability (99.999%) and have about five minutes service downtime each year. In contrast to that, VoIP can achieve only 98 percent reliability with about 175 hours as service downtime each year (Kos et al., 2005). This low reliability of VoIP systems is usually not acceptable for any business. The two main causes of this unreliability are jitter and packet loss (Kurose & Ross, 2004). Jitter is the phenomenon that causes the time between generation of a packet at the source and its reception at the receiver to vary with the degree of network congestion. As VoIP systems often use the Internet as the medium of transmission, they suffer from the problem of jitter, which increases with the increase in the degree of network congestion. Also, as the Internet is a best-effort model, packets are dropped in the network when there is traffic congestion. Although packet losses do not significantly affect the quality of data transmission, their effect on voice transmission is not insignificant. Loss in voice packets can lead to inability of the receiver to correctly reconstruct the voice signal, and this can also contribute to the lower reliability of the VoIP service.

Inferior Security

The security issue of the communication system is very important for most businesses. There are two major security issues for VoIP systems, namely, eavedropping and denial of service (DoS). Eavesdropping is listening to others' conversations secretly without getting their consent. As VoIP uses the Internet for transmitting voice packets to the receiver, the voice packets suffer the risk of being eavesdropped at the routers. Packet sniffer software can be used for eavesdropping voice packets. VOMIT and Ethereal Network Analyzer are two such examples of eavesdropping (Bradley, 2006). VOMIT, which stands for Voice Over Misconfigured Internet Telephone, is a software which converts a Cisco IP phone conversation into a .wav file (VOMIT, 2006). On the other hand, Ethereal Network Analyzer is a packet sniffer which captures and decodes packets. It can capture usernames, passwords, and sensitive information. Denial of service (DoS) is an attack on a computer system which causes loss of network connectivity or loss of services to users. It is done by flooding servers, proxy servers, or gateway servers with huge amounts of dummy or malignant packets. Examples of DoS attacks are ICMP flood and IP spoof, SYN flood. Systems under ICMP flood may crash, freeze, or reboot themselves, ending with DoS, while those under IP spoof may exhaust memory, crash, or become inoperative. It is reported that if a DoS attack can prevent only five percent of packets from reaching their destination on time, then the effect is catastrophic for the VoIP system (Walsh & Kuhn, 2005).

Uncertain Quality of Voice Signalling

The quality of voice in VoIP is uncertain. It is due to several reasons. First, the voice encoding affects the quality of speech. When the analog voice is digitized into voice packets, there may be a loss of data during encoding. Second, when voice packets are traveling through the network, there is always a chance for

packet loss due to congestion in the network. This can degrade the quality of speech. Third, there are unpredictable packet delays suffered by voice packets inside the network. In fact, it has been shown that the delay performance of VoIP packets is dependent on the adoption of a specific queuing discipline (Han et al., 2002). When the receiver plays out the packets, those packets that come in late cannot be played out and are assumed to be lost. Last, in some situations there may be echo in the system which causes great degradation of quality (echo is a signal reflection of a speakers' voice). Although echo is acceptable in the PSTN (because the round-trip delay through the PSTN is smaller than 50 msec and there is masking on the echo by the normal tone of telephone), it is not acceptable for the VoIP system. This is because round-trip delays in the Internet are typically more than 50 msec. Therefore, echos can degrade the quality of speech in VoIP system to a great extent.

INDUSTRY BEST PRACTICES FOR VoIP

Companies who lead the way in the mass adoption of VoIP systems in the current consumer marketplace are Skype, SunRocket, Vonage, and 8x8 (Packet 8). They have been developing the VoIP solutions early and have been marketing VoIP aggressively during 2005. Other companies that have joined the VoIP bandwagon include Bellsouth, Verizon, SBC, and Qwest Communications, among others. More and more companies are entering the VoIP market. This is because the future of VoIP is bright and the revenue potentials are high. In fact, it is estimated that the number of VoIP subscribers will reach 10 million by the end of 2006 (2005). In the following section we discuss two VoIP service providers in some detail.

Skype

Skype is a global peer-to-peer telephony company which offers their customers free but superior quality calling around the world. It provides a software called Skype, same as the company name, for VoIP services. The software is available in 27 languages and has advanced features like advanced voicemail, personalization, video calling, and call forwarding. Skype is regarded as one of the most innovative firms in the technology sector, and has recently been acquired by the auction giant eBay. The Skype software doesn't charge any money from users for PC-to-PC calls. However, if the user makes a PC-to-phone call, or the receiver makes a phone-to-PC call, Skype charges a small amount to the users. For PC-to-phone calls, Skype presently charges 0.017 euro cent per minute. Unlike other service providers, such as Vonage and SunRocket, Skype doesn't require any specialized equipment other than a PC with a microphone and speaker. Its ease in installation has attracted millions of users, and it is definitely the most popular VoIP service provider in the world.

Vonage

Vonage is one of the largest VoIP players who have led the way towards mass adoption of VoIP in the U.S., UK, and Canada (Woolley, 2006). According to a recent study in which data were collected and analyzed by Sandvine's North American and European broadband customer networks, Vonage occupied a 21.7 percent share of North American minutes and was rated as the most popular third-party VoIP service provider (Sims, 2006). Vonage provides services like Emergency 911, 3-way calling, call forwarding, call blocking, and call waiting. In January 2006, Vonage announced that it had turned on the emergency 911 service in over 2,200 call centers in the U.S. (Torres, 2006). However, unlike Skype, it charges for VoIP services on a monthly basis. The charges for service plans vary from US$14.99-49.99 per month. For using Vonage, users need special equipment, like a broadband Ethernet connection, a Vonage phone adapter (a device which connects the phone and fax machines to the network router or gateway), and any touch-tone phone (corded or cordless).

FUTURE TRENDS

Although VoIP has become more and more commercially viable for business and residential markets, traditional telephone systems are competitive because of their high quality of service. The cost advantages provided by VoIP systems are not substantial as yet because of the low rates already offered by traditional telephone service providers. For example, City Telecom, a company based in Hong Kong that provides IDD service, charges only 0.18 Hong Kong cents for calling Australia (City Telecom Hong Kong, 2006).

Although VoIP calling is cheap, the savings only become substantial for calls made in large volumes. However, VoIP's future is bright. Based on a recent survey of 1000 North American and European firms, the Forrester Group has predicted that by the end of 2008 about 40 percent of the firms would adopt VoIP (Paulson, 2005). The single setup, maintenance, and upgrade cost of VoIP is an attractive feature for most businesses. In the future, many business opportunities will develop based entirely on VoIP systems. Fax over IP is one such service which will use the Internet for fax services using a VoIP system. The currently developed advanced features include: advanced voice mail features, international call blocking, ring list, and so on. More and more, such features will continue to be developed and VoIP will become so attractive that all businesses would use it without any doubt.

CONCLUSION

VoIP technology is becoming more and more important in today's world. In this chapter various advantages and limitations of VoIP systems are discussed and the business models of two VoIP service providers are stated as well. VoIP is a promising technology because of its high flexibility, low cost advantage, and ability to integrate with new applications. There is no denying that this technology will flourish even more in the future. The main drawback of VoIP systems currently is their low reliability and security. QoS for VoIP is already being developed for the commercial world and this promises to overcome the limitations of reliability for VoIP systems (Fineberg, 2005; Wang et al., 2006). It remains to be seen when VoIP systems will be able to overtake PSTN as the primary technology for voice communication in this world.

REFERENCES

Ascierto, R. (2006). Avaya says VoIP value lies beyond the network. *Computer Business Review Online*. Retrieved March 20, 2006, from http://www.cbronline.com/article_news.asp?guid=ED52441B-4462-4A47-94E5-FF033CDA59FA

Bradley, T. (2006). Ethereal network protocol analyzer. *About.com*. Retrieved February 26, 2006, from http://

netsecurity.about.com/od/securitytoolprofiles/p/aapre-thereal.htm

City Telecom Hong Kong. Retrieved March 10, 2006, from http://www.ctihk.com/index_c.html

Fineberg, V. (2005, January). A practical architecture for implementing end-to-end QoS in an IP network. *IEEE Communications Magazine, 40*(1), 122-130.

Han, J-S., Ahn, S-J., & Chung, J-W. (2002, September/October). Study of delay patterns of weighted voice traffic of end-to-end users on the VoIP network. *International Journal of Network Management, 12*(5), 271-280.

Hardy, W. C. (2003). *VoIP service quality: Measuring and evaluating packet-switched voice.* New York: Mc-Graw Hill.

Kos, A., Klepec, B., & Tomaxic, S. (2005). *Challenges for VoIP technologies in corporate environments.* Laboratory for Communication Devices, University of Ljubljana, Slovenia. Retrieved February 15, 2006, from http://www.lkn.fe.unilj.si/lknpub/Clanki/2004/Anton%20Kos%20%20ICN04%20%20Challenges%20for%20VoIP%20Technologies%20in%20Corporate%20Environments.pdf

Kurose, J. F., & Ross, K. W. (2004). *Computer networking: A top-down approach featuring the Internet* (3rd ed.). Addison Wesley.

Paulson, L. D. (2005, July-August). Is it time you considered VoIP? *IT Professional, 7*(4), 7-10.

Sims, D. (2006). *Vonage: Kicks butt in US, butt kicked in Europe.* Retrieved March 15, 2006, from http://news.tmcnet.com/news/-voip-growth-vonage-skype-/2006/01/31/1327932.htm

Torres, J. (2006, January 27). Vonage offers VoIP E911 service in over 2200 calling centers. *TMCNet.* Retrieved March 9, 2006, from http://news.tmcnet.com/news/-vonage-voip-e911-service-over-2200-call-ing-centers-/2006/01/27/1320650.htm

UK News (2005). *Rise of VoIP could be last call for phones.* Retrieved March 10, 2006, from http://www.lse.co.uk/ShowStory.asp?story=FD2921102X&news_headline=rise_of_voip_could_be_last_call_for_phones

Varshney, U., Snow, A., McGivern, M., & Howard, C. (2002, January). Voice over IP. *Communications of the ACM, 45*(1), 89-96.

VOMIT. (2006). Retrieved March 10, 2006, from http://vomit.xtdnet.nl

Walsh, T. J., & Kuhn, D. R. (2005, May-June). Challenges in securing voice over IP. *IEEE Security and Privacy Magazine, 3*(3), 44-49.

Wang, S., Mai, Z., Xuan, D., & Zhao, W. (2006, March). Design and implementation of QoS-provisioning system for voice over IP. *IEEE Transactions on Parallel and Distributed Systems, 17*(3), 276-288.

Woolley, S. (2006, February 8). The trouble with VoIP. *Forbes.com.* Retrieved March 12, 2006, from http://www.forbes.com/home/wireless/2006/02/08/ipo-von-age-voip-cz_sw_0208vonage.html

KEY TERMS

Best-Effort Model: Best-effort model is a network model in which the network does not provide any resource guarantee to the data delivery. It only provides the "best effort" which means "try its best to serve the user."

Circuit Switched Network: Circuit switched network is a network in which a dedicated connection exists between two end-users. It is typically used for voice communication.

Internet Session: Internet session is a connection between a client and a server computer. It is essential for exchange of information between two computers.

LAN (Local Area Network): It is a computer network connecting computers in a small local area, such as home, office, campus, or building.

Packet-Switched Network: Packet-switched network is a network which allows data packets to flow through it using the store and forward method.

PSTN (Public Switched Telephone Network): It provides traditional telephone service to residential customers.

QoS (Quality of Service): It refers to the capability to provide resource guarantee and service differentiation to applications. Resource guarantee implies that an application can get the amount of network resource it requests. Service differentiation provides higher priority to those applications with stringent time constraints. For example, when using QoS, video conferencing can be given higher priority than activities like file sharing.

Round-Trip Delay: Round-trip delay is the total time taken for a packet to go from a client to the server and then return from the server to the client.

WAN (Wide Area Network): It is a computer network connecting computers in a large geographical area that may be a country or region. One example of WAN is the Internet.

Waking Up Sensor Networks

Yew-Fai Wong
Institute for Infocomm Research, A*STAR, Singapore

Trina Kok
Institute for Infocomm Research, A*STAR, Singapore

Lek-Heng Ngoh
Institute for Infocomm Research, A*STAR, Singapore

Wai-Choong Wong
National University of Singapore, Singapore

Winston K. G. Seah
Institute for Infocomm Research, Singapore

INTRODUCTION

Our natural world is an environment that is highly dynamic and constantly changing. Such environmental changes may impact lives on a large scale, such as those caused by a Tsunami, global warming, or global dimming phenomena. Monitoring technologies have improved tremendously over the years in the hope of predicting such events. The manmade world today is also highly complex, and has become increasingly sophisticated. In the same spirit as monitoring systems for the natural world that save lives, technology has also made it possible to monitor structural stress and instabilities within buildings. Target tracking systems (Wong, 2004) using acoustics, passive infra-red, and even other modes, such as chemical compound analysis, are capable of warning against possible attacks by terrorists on our civilized world.

At the same time, collecting information about the environment can lead to significant economic benefits. The seismic imaging of both on-land and underwater oil wells (Heidemann, 2005) undertaken by energy companies has long been a direct and indirect source of wealth generation for many. Yet, in another application, collecting temperature and humidity information in vineyards (Burrell, 2003) predicts the grade of wine quality that directly affects pricing of wine for a particular year. By controlling such factors that are known through environmental monitoring, strategies for quality improvement and subsequently revenue upgrades are enabled.

In the past, and in many of today's systems, such monitoring devices are almost certainly of large form-factor and costly. For instance, underwater oilfield seismic imaging is achieved by a seismic vessel towing an array of streamers every time a geological area needs to be surveyed. Tsunami warning systems of today rely on large seismic stations and tide monitoring stations to furnish the necessary data. As such, they remain expensive and difficult to scale up for widespread usage. This tradition is set to change with the dawn of a new class of networks that are dominated by small and cheap device nodes that are capable of sensing the environment, performing computations, possessing memory for storage, and communicating with each other within reasonable range (about ten to a couple of hundred meters). To achieve longer distance communication, information is multi-hopped from one node to another. This is the world of "sensor networks."

THE ENERGY PROBLEM IN SENSOR NETWORKS

Sensor nodes are usually small, compact, and powered only by batteries, and thus have a limited lifetime. The most commonly known sensor node platform is the Berkeley family of motes (Crossbow Technology Inc.).

Other existing platforms include Cricket (Priyantha, 2000) and Specknet (Arvind, 2004).

The energy issue has a direct economic impact on deployment feasibility. Numerous topology management schemes that conserve energy in sensor networks have been proposed, widely ranging from selection methods of a subset of nodes to put to sleep, energy-efficient routing of information from one part of the network to another, and energy-aware data aggregation and collection techniques to reduce unnecessary data transmissions. This paper focuses on one aspect of energy conservation–sensor wakeup schemes.

TRADEOFFS IN SENSOR NETWORKS

Part of a sensor network is often put to sleep when not all of them are required for operation by the requested application. This is possible because sensor nodes are relatively cheap and can be deployed in abundance. As such, they are usually denser than traditional networks, in contrast to those of the Internet, peer-to-peer networks, and even mobile ad-hoc networks. There are exceptions, of course, such as in the underwater context where nodes are more costly (Crossbow Technology Inc., Vasilescu, 2005) and usually deployed more sparsely. Sensor nodes are also often available in several working modes, thereby allowing them to switch off selected parts of their operation modules to save energy when not in use. Capitalizing on this feature, a sensor network may continue to provide reasonable performance in one or more of the following:

- Sensing coverage
- Network connectivity
- Delay or delivery requirements of the application
- Robustness of the network in case of node failures

These are often the tradeoffs that a sensor network exchanges for battery life, thus extending the useful lifespan of the network. These are also the technical challenges that the researchers address in an attempt to optimize one or more of these tradeoffs with energy. The next section discusses some of these possible solutions and their relationships with these tradeoffs.

WAKEUP SCHEMES FOR SENSOR NETWORKS

Unfortunately, classification of wakeup solutions is not a simple exercise, since many of these schemes are seemingly suitable for several categories. However, in this discourse, schemes are organized under the best-representative category according to the listing below. We investigate six categories of wakeup methods.

The Connected Dominating Set Solution

In a connected dominating set (CDS), sensor nodes are either in the set or are neighbour nodes of this set. The CDS in a network therefore acts as a "backbone" of nodes, where information may be sent from one node to another across the network in a relatively short time. To reduce energy consumption as much as possible, many algorithms aim to elect a minimum connected dominating set (MCDS), i.e., a CDS with minimum cardinality. Election of nodes to form the MCDS is an NP-complete problem, but in practice, heuristics may be used to form a CDS that approximates the MCDS. Centralized CDS election algorithms, such as that by Guha and Khuller (Guha, 1998) can theoretically be implemented in a distributed manner, albeit with higher control overhead in exchanging neighbour information. There are many ways of electing a CDS, and the energy consumption rate varies with each. Topology management by priority ordering, or TMPO (Bao, 2003), is a distributed algorithm that elects nodes for an energy-aware CDS. Nodes are assigned randomized priorities based on their node identifiers, mobility, and battery life. Nodes are required to wake periodically and exchange topology information with their neighbors. After this update, TMPO computes a CDS of the network using only two-hop information in three separate stages of clusterhead, and doorway and gateway election. The clusterheads form a dominating set, and the doorways and gateways connect the clusterheads to form a CDS. TMPO addresses a load-balancing problem amidst a connectivity problem to reduce delays, but not a coverage problem. SPAN (Chen, 2001) is a distributed, randomized algorithm that maintains the original connectivity of the network via the "backbone" of nodes. A node expresses willingness to be a coordinator if it discovers that two of its neighbors cannot communicate with each other directly or through an existing coordinator. The willingness factor depends on the node's remaining energy and the number of neighbors it can potentially connect, and is updated periodically using broadcasted HELLO messages. Each node also periodically checks if it should withdraw as a coordinator, by determining if its neighbor nodes could be connected via other coordinators or neighbors. Wu and Li (Wu, 1999) proposed an algorithm similar to SPAN that incorporates additional pruning rules to reduce the size of the elected CDS. TMPO, SPAN, and Wu and Li require periodic broadcasts, which limit the possible energy savings.

The Neighbour-Configured Solution

There are many schemes that configure their wakeup schedules based on information received from neighbouring nodes. The probing environment and adaptive sleeping (PEAS) algorithm (Ye, 2003) for sensor networks is one where nodes configure their wakeup times based on counting the number of neighbouring nodes that they discover after deployment. It is assumed that nodes wake up asynchronously after they are first deployed, after which sensor nodes that operate in Awake Mode send PROBE messages to neighbours. If no replies were received, the node stays in the Awake Mode until it is completely depleted of its energy. If at least one reply is received, the node operates in the Sleep Mode. Nodes in the Sleep Mode regularly wake up to send PROBE messages. The probing range may also be chosen to meet certain sensing coverage criterion. PEAS is time-asynchronous and assumes a very dense network deployment scenario. Since nodes in PEAS permanently operate in the Awake Mode and subsequently deplete of all their energies once they discover no PROBE replies, energy consumption in the network is unbalanced and may cause network partitioning. PECAS (Gui, 2004) improved upon PEAS with additional features that allow a sensor node that is already in the Awake Mode to go back into Sleep Mode beyond some energy threshold limit measured within that node.

While PEAS and PECAS are all configured by neighbour count, the coverage configuration protocol (CCP) (Xing, 2005) configures the wakeup times of a sensor node by the degree of sensing coverage of its neighbour nodes. The scheme establishes a relationship between sensing coverage and network connectivity,

where a k-covered network implies a k-connectivity network, for as long as the communication range is twice its sensing range (double range property). With this, CCP strives to maximize the number of sleeping nodes, while maintaining both k-coverage and k-connectivity in the network at the same time. Each node first evaluates if its coverage area is k-covered, and this computational complexity is $O(N^3)$ (Wang, 2005), where N is the number of sensors within a distance of two times their sensing range. If the node is k-covered, it is also k-connected and goes into Idle Mode, and subsequently into the Sleep Mode after expiration of a random timer. Nodes in the Sleep Mode periodically enter the Idle Mode to monitor the channel to check if the area is still k-covered. If not, they enter the Awake Mode; otherwise, they go back to Sleep Mode. CCP operates together with SPAN (Chen, 2001) for the case when the double range property fails. SPAN is a connectivity-preserving scheme, and some nodes working under CCP+SPAN remain in Awake Mode, even if they are redundant in sensing coverage, so that desired connectivity is maintained.

The Combinatorics Solution

Combinatorics is a branch of mathematics concerned with the selection, arrangement, and operation of elements in a set. In a sensor wakeup schemes context, they represent the arrangement of a number of wakeup time slots in a set of all available time slots within one time cycle. Each sensor is assigned one time schedule based on this arrangement. Zheng (2003) proposed a cyclic symmetric block design (CSBD), where every sensor schedule has exactly one active wakeup slot overlap with any other sensor schedule in the set. The existence of such a design is not trivial and implies that any sensor node using any schedule from this set is always guaranteed to be able to communicate multi-hop to any other node in the set within bounded time. Moreover, this design is time-asynchronous, requiring no expensive synchronization of clocks amongst the sensor nodes. This solution was originally proposed for mobile ad hoc networks where nodes are mobile. Regardless of node mobility, nodes are still connected in finite time because every schedule in the set has one active slot overlap with any other schedule. In most sensor network context, such a solution becomes extravagant in terms of energy expenditure since sensor nodes are usually static. The symmetry of the design can be viewed as a form of "over-provisioning" for node mobility. In fact, according to Wong (2005), such symmetry creates the "Lonely Node" problem where nodes wake up to find no communicable neighbours, and this wastes sensor energy. This phenomenon becomes more pronounced when the network density is sparse.

The adaptive wakeup schedule function or AWSF (Wong, 2005) adapts the cyclic symmetric design to the deployed network topology without requiring geographical location information. This is done in two stages, the pruning stage (PNS) and the reconstruction stage (RCS). PNS removes those active wakeup slots that nodes find themselves in when waking up to no communicable neighbours, thereby eliminating the "lonely node problem." RCS reallocates the pruned-off active slots to other time slots to improve the local connectivity of the network. In such an implementation, the symmetry of the design is broken in exchange for more efficient energy usage. AWSF is highly suitable for underwater sensor networks (Wong, 2006) where node density is sparse and time-synchronization is very difficult to achieve because of the slow data transfer rates using acoustic modems. Underwater communication is typically three orders slower (Freitag, 2005) than communication over the air. AWSF inherits the bounded communication delay property from CSBD and remains time asynchronous with some added control overheads. In the lucrative underwater oilfield imaging industry, where a surveyed area need not be re-surveyed, possibly for durations of months to years (hibernation period), clock drifts do not affect CSBD. For AWSF, clock drifts may have an impact during the long hibernation period since control overheads cannot be exchanged to ensure that the time-asynchronism property holds. Fortunately, AWSF is based on CSBD, and it may easily switch back to the CSBD mode before the long hibernation period and re-adapts to solve the "lonely node" problem when it next wakes up. Most research works are focused on providing a 1-connected network even when some nodes are put to Sleep Mode. Nevertheless, a 1-connected network graph still implies that the entire network graph of Awake nodes is connected in one connected component. In the underwater world where the data transmission rates are slow, having a 1-connected network may not be entirely ideal since information does not usually have the opportunity to traverse many hops at a time,

owing to the larger propagation delays. AWSF, in this case, does not guarantee 1-connectivity, but rather 1-neighbour connectivity.

Another added advantage of these combinatorics solutions is that the communication modules of those sensor nodes that are not required can be completely shut off. This is largely different from the paging solution that we shall also describe shortly. Allowing nodes to be completely shut off when not in use theoretically conserves about three orders of energy more (Cross-Bow. Mica2 data sheet) compared to schemes that only put nodes to the Idle Mode, where nodes continue to consume energy for monitoring or "data snooping" the communication channel. Of course, the overall routing network delay of such solutions over many hops can become large even though these delays are bounded in finite time.

The Paging Solution

The sparse topology and energy management (STEM) protocol (Schurgers, 2002) for sensor networks proposes the use of two channels, one for data transmission and the other as a control or paging channel to wake up neighbouring sensor nodes. When a sensor node has data to send, it uses a wakeup tone or beacon message to wake up the necessary neighbouring nodes using the paging channel and transmits actual data on the channel. In this manner, sensors are reactively being turned on as and when required. The drawback of such a solution is that it requires the cost of two channels and the energy savings could be minimal because the paging channel is required to be always at the "monitoring" state, or in Idle Mode (in contrast to Sleep Mode) to receive possible wakeup beacons. However, connectivity of the network is equivalent to one that is fully awake and delays incurred in data transmission are minimized, less the time to wakeup neighbouring sensors.

While STEM uses a separate channel to page neighbouring nodes into the Awake Mode, the power aware multi-access protocol with signaling (PAMAS) (Singh, 1998) proposed the use of a separate signaling channel that conserves energy by turning off the sensor node if it has no data to send and a neighbour node is transmitting at the same time. The context at that time was Ad Hoc Networks, and it was claimed that delay or throughput performance is not compromised as a direct consequence of the manner in which nodes are powered off. Again, the added cost is the extra channel and its maintenance.

The Data-Aided Wakeup Solution

Wakeup schemes may also be configured by information other than neighbour count or neighbour-sensing coverage. The adaptive self-configuring sensor networks topologies (ASCENT) (Cerpa, 2002) protocol measures neighbour connectivity as well as data loss rate to configure wakeup times. Each node keeps track of monotonically increasing sequence numbers in packets and infers the data loss rate. Nodes also infer the number of active neighbours by keeping track of packets received from each neighbour. Therefore, there is no periodic probing required to discover neighbours. ASCENT aims to achieve optimal and maximum connectivity that minimizes collision rate. ASCENT assumes a very dense network scenario so that network partitioning is not a key issue.

The Random Solution

Paruchuri (2004) proposed the random asynchronous wakeup (RAW) scheme where each node wakes up once in every time slot, is awake for a predetermined fixed time, and then sleeps again. The exact time at which each node wakes up in any particular time slot is random. Data is sent from a node N to a forwarding set of neighbouring nodes so that delay can be minimized. The forwarding set includes all nodes that lie in the area intersection of the circular transmission range of node N and the circular range of a certain radius centred about the destination node. This solution assumes an extremely dense network. It is reported that for 10 nodes in the forwarding set, a per-hop packet loss rate of 18 percent is expected. This also represents the frequency at which the "Lonely Node" problem occurs. However, wakeup schedules are time-asynchronous owing to the randomness their solution. Delays incurred are small because of numerous choices in forwarding nodes in the forwarding sets, a direct consequence of a dense network deployment.

Kumar (2004) proposed random independent scheduling (RIS), where time is divided into cycles using a time synchronization method. At the start of each cycle, every node independently takes on an Awake Mode with probability p and Sleep Mode with probability $(1 - p)$. Therefore, RIS uses this parameter p to control network

lifetime. RIS also determines how nodes should be initially deployed to ensure asymptotic k-coverage. However, although RIS has no communication overheads and requires no location information, it does not address connectivity issues and the "Lonely Node" problem is obvious. The scheme is also not robust against node failures and requires expensive time-synchronization techniques that inhibit scalability.

SUMMARY OF SOLUTIONS

Each sensor wakeup scheme has its pros and cons. Some may have more requirements than others, while some may be more suited for certain classes of sensor network applications. Table 1 summarizes our discussion.

FUTURE TRENDS

The problems of connectivity and sensing coverage under the constraint of energy have been major issues of research in recent years. As these connectivity and coverage metrics become standardized and more widely adopted, new schemes based on the optimization of such metrics will be developed. One challenge is to reduce the complexity of such schemes so that their ease of implementation and scalability are justified. Energy balancing, even without traffic influence, is a major research interest because this inevitably leads to undesirable network partitioning, thereby limiting the usefulness of the sensor network. A widely accepted energy balancing metric, or a reasonably realistic metric to define network lifetime, shall propel sensor network research to the next level of standardization.

While connectivity, coverage, and network lifetime are important factors to consider for designing wakeup schemes, other performance issues, such as information delays and network robustness must be taken into account. While sensor network research is very focused primarily on land systems thus far, more challenging deployment environments, such as an underwater sensor networks, will progressively form a more significant part of research efforts within the community. Yet, with greater technological advancements in even smaller "speck-sized" sensor nodes, sensor network research will continue to be as vibrant and exciting as it is today, if not more.

Table 1.

		Requirements				Performance				
		Dense Deployment	Dual Channel	TS*	C/O^	Sensing Coverage	NC†	Delay	Robustness	Energy Balance
CDS	TMPO	No	No	No	High	N.A.	CDS	Small	N.A.	Yes
	SPAN	No	No	No	High	N.A.	Original conn	Small	N.A.	Yes
	WuLi	No	No	No	High	N.A.	CDS	Small	N.A	Yes.
Neighbour-Configured	PEAS	Yes	No	No	Low	Indirect	Indirect	N.A.	N.A.	No
	PECAS	Yes	Optional	No	Depends	Indirect	Indirect	N.A.	N.A.	Yes
	CCP	Yes	Yes	No	High	k-cov.	k-conn.	Small	N.A.	No
Combinatorics	CSBD	Yes	No	No	Low	k-cov.	Connected in bounded time	Bounded	N.A.	Yes
	AWSF	No	No	No	Low	N.A.	1-Nconn.	Bounded	N.A.	Yes
Paging	STEM	No	Yes	No	High	N.A.	Full	Small	N.A.	N.A.
	PAMAS	No	Yes	No	High	N.A.	Full	Small	N.A.	N.A.
Data-Aided	ASCENT	Yes	No	No	Low	N.A.	Indirect	N.A.	Yes	N.A.
Random	RAW	Yes	No	No	Low	N.A.	Indirect	Small	Yes	N.A.
	RIS	Yes	No	Yes	Low	Ak-cov.	N.A.	N.A.	N.A.	N.A.

* TS: Time Synchronization   N.A.: Not Addressed k-cov.: k-covered

^ C/O: Complexity / Cost / Overheads k-conn.: k-connected   Ak-cov.: Asymptotic k-covered

† NC: Network Connectivity k-Nconn.: k-Neighbor-connected

CONCLUSION

Many wakeup strategies have been devised to solve the energy scarcity problem widely known in battery-powered sensor networks. This is possible because advances in hardware technologies are capable of switching different node components to several work-ing modes, including Awake, Idle, and Sleep. In sensor networks, deployed for a wide variety of purposes from monitoring, imaging, research, and security enhance-ment to target tracking operations, network connectivity, sensing coverage issues, data access delays, delivery ratios, and robustness of network-to-node failures (such as energy depletion in nodes) are amongst the considerations that research is progressing to trade off with energy consumption. This paper has provided an overview of several wakeup schemes organized in six categories. Different wakeup schemes may be suitable for different needs of an application.

REFERENCES

Arvind, D. K., & Wong, K. J. (2004). Speckled computing: Disruptive technology for networked information appliances. In *Proceedings of the IEEE International Symposium on Consumer Electronics* (pp. 219-223).

Bao, L., & Garcia-Luna-Aceves, J. J. (2003). Topology management in ad hoc networks.

Burrell, J., Brooke T., & Beckwith, R. (2003). Vineyard computing: Sensor networks in agricultural production. *IEEE Pervasive Computing, 3*, 38-45.

Cerpa, A., & Estrin, D. (2002). Ascent: Adaptive self-configuring sensor networks topologies. In *Proceedings of IEEE INFOCOM, 3*, 1278-1287.

Chen, B., Jamieson, K., Balakrishnan, H., & Morris, R. (2001). Span: An energy-efficient coordination algorithm for topology maintenance in ad hoc wireless networks. In *ACM/IEEE International Conference on Mobile Computing and Networking* (pp. 16-21).

Crossbow. Mica2 data sheet. Retrieved 30 July, 2007 from http://www.xbow.com/Products/Product_pdf_files/wireless_pdf/MICA2_Datasheet.pdf

Crossbow Technology Inc. Retrieved 30 July, 2007 from http://www.xbow.com

Freitag, L., Grund, M., Singh, S., Partan, J., et al. (2005). The WHOI micro-modem: An acoustic communications and navigation system for multiple platforms. In *IEEE Oceans Conference.*

Guha, S., & Khuller, S. (1998). Approximation algorithms for connected dominating sets, *Algorithmica, 20*(4), 374-387.

Gui, C., & Mohapatra, P. (2004). Power conservation and quality of surveillance in target tracking sensor networks. In *Proceedings of the 10th Annual International Conference on Mobile Computing and Networking* (pp. 129-143).

Heidemann, J., Li, Y., & Syed, A. (2005). *Underwater sensor networking: Research challenges and potential applications.* USC/ISI Technical Report ISI-TR-2005-603.

Kumar, S., Lai, T. H., & Balogh, J. (2004). On k-coverage in a mostly sleeping sensor network. In *Proceedings of the 10th Annual International Conference on Mobile Computing and Networking* (pp. 144-158).

Paruchuri, V., Basavaraju, S., Durresi, A., Kannan, R., & Iyengar, S. S. (2004). Random asynchronous wakeup protocol for sensor networks. In *Proceedings of the First International Conference on Broadband Networks* (pp. 710-717).

Priyantha, N. B., Chakraborty, A., & Balakrishnan, H. (2000). The cricket location-support system. In *Proceedings of the Sixth ACM MOBICOM* (pp. 32-43).

Singh, S., & Raghavendra, C. S. (1998). PAMAS: Power aware multi-access protocol with signalling for ad hoc networks. *ACM Computer Communications Review, 28*(3), 5-26.

Schurgers, C., Tsiatsis, V., & Srivastava, M. (2002). STEM: Topology management for energy efficient sensor networks. In *IEEE Aerospace Conference* (pp. 78-89).

Vasilescu, I., Kotay, K., Rus, D., Dunbabin, M., et al. (2005). Data collection, storage, and retrieval with an underwater sensor network. In *Proceedings of ACM Sensys.* (pp. 154-165).

Wang, L., & Xiao, Y. (2005). A survey of energy saving mechanisms in sensor networks. In *Proceedings of the IEEE Broadnets* (Vol. 1, pp. 724-732).

Wong, Y. F., Wu, J. K., Ngoh, L. H., & Wong, W. C. (2004). Collaborative data fusion tracking in sensor networks using Monte Carlo methods. In *29th Annual IEEE International Conference on Local Computer Networks* (pp. 563-564).

Wong, Y. F., Ngoh, L. H., & Wong, W. C. (2005). An adaptive wakeup scheme to support fast routing in sensor networks. In *Second ACM Performance Evaluation in Wireless Sensor and Ubiquitous Networks* (pp. 18-24).

Wong, Y. F., Ngoh, L. H., Wong, W.C., & Seah, W. (2006). Wakeup scheme for ocean monitoring underwater sensor networks (UWSN). In *IEEE Oceans Conference*.

Wu, J., & Li, H. (1999). On calculating connected dominating sets for efficient routing in ad hoc wireless networks. In *Proceedings of the Third ACM International Workshop Discrete Algorithms and Methods for Mobile Computing and Communications* (pp. 7-17).

Xing, G. L., Wang, X. R., Zhang, Y. F., Lu, C. Y., et al. (2005). Integrated coverage and connectivity configuration for energy conservation in sensor networks. *ACM Transactions on Sensor Networks, 1*(1), 36-72.

Ye, F., Zhong, G., Cheng, J., Lu, S., & Zhang, L. (2003). Peas: A robust energy conserving protocol for long-lived sensor networks. In *Proceedings of the 23rd International Conference on Distributed Computing Systems* (pp. 28-37).

Zheng, R., Hou, J. C., & Sha, L. (2003). Asynchronous wakeup for ad hoc networks. In *Proceedings of the Fourth ACM International Symposium on Mobile Ad Hoc Networking & Computing* (pp. 35-45).

KEY TERMS

Asymptotic *k*-Covered Area: Assuming that there are an infinite number of sensors deployed, a network area is Asymptotic *k*-covered if at any instant in time, *k* sensors are in the Awake Mode to monitor that area.

Combinatorics: A branch of mathematics that is concerned with selection, arrangement, and operation of elements in a set. It is sometimes also referred to as the science of counting.

Connected Dominating Set: A dominating set; any two nodes in the set can communicate, possibly through other nodes via multihop broadcasting.

Cyclic Symmetric Block Design: A combinatorial arrangement solution that imposes a time-shifted pre-determined wake-up schedule onto the nodes in a network, so that there is/are always overlap(s) between any two schedules in the design.

Dominating Set: A subset of network nodes in which each node is either in this subset or is a neighbour of a node in this subset.

Forwarding Set: The set of nodes in the routing table of a node in which information or data packets are forwarded to.

***k*-Covered Area:** Given a finite number of sensors deployed, a network area is *k*-covered if at any instant in time, *k* sensors are in the Awake Mode to monitor that area.

***k*-Connected Network:** A network is *k*-connected if all nodes in the network remain connected to each other when *k* nodes are removed (or switched to the Sleep Mode, in our context).

***k*-Neighbour Connected Network:** A *k*-neighbour connected network is one where all nodes have at least *k* neighbouring nodes for communication.

Lonely Node Problem: The lonely node problem happens when a network node wakes up to find no other communicable neighbouring nodes.

Web Accessibility

Gregory R. Gay
University of Toronto, Canada

Paola Salomoni
University of Bologna, Italy

Silvia Mirri
University of Bologna, Italy

INTRODUCTION

The explosive growth of Internet services has greatly impacted people's lives. The Internet is making distances smaller and smaller, connecting people anytime and anywhere, reaching to the far corners of the earth. But is the Internet for everyone? More specifically, is it also for people with **disabilities**?

Technologies have been developed to make personal computers accessible to people with disabilities, important for promoting **inclusion** in everyday life, education, and work. In the 90s, the spread of Internet applications, and specifically of the Web, created a new issue: Would the Web be accessible to people with disabilities? Web **accessibility** is partially dependent on **assistive technologies** used by people with disabilities to access their PCs. But, it also depends on whether people with various disabilities can perform specific tasks on their PCs with the help of their assistive technologies. Another dimension of Web accessibility is the responsibility of Web authors, developers, designers, and technologies they use to develop Web content.

Many organizations have been working on defining **guidelines** that ensure that Web content will be accessible, and their efforts have resulted in a Web accessibility specification created by the **Web Accessibility Initiative** (WAI) of the World Wide Web Consortium (W3C). They produced the first set of accessibility principles to be accepted worldwide.

BACKGROUND

The term "*accessibility*" in computer science generally refers to the capability of computer systems to provide information and services to people using assistive technologies or special computer configurations often required to accommodate a disability. By referring specifically to the Web, "*Web accessibility means that people with disabilities can perceive, understand, navigate and interact with the Web, and that they can contribute to the Web*" (WAI, 2005a).

Access to Internet and Web resources is becoming a part of everyday life for a large portion of the population in the developed world: in employment, education, health care, commerce, and recreation. As such, "*an accessible Web can also help people with disabilities more actively participate in society*" (Pilgrim, 2002). Together with the obvious need to offer people with disabilities an equal opportunity to access information and services, there are some other challenging aspects of promoting and enforcing equal access. For example, printed information or content that is delivered through audio or video **media** will often be inaccessible for some groups of people with sensory **impairments**. The Web can make media available to these individuals through alternative formats such as text, captioning, and descriptive audio. Furthermore, the availability of services and information on the Web can help people with mobility impairments overcome difficulties of physically reaching onsite services. The Web often allows these individuals to bypass the limits of their disabilities (Bohman, 2003).

Web accessibility also provides benefits to other groups of individuals in addition to those with disabilities, including older people with age-related changes in ability, people using non-conventional devices, such as PDAs (personal data assistants) or smart phones, to access the Internet, as well as people in areas of the world where Web access bandwidth is limited. These groups represent a rich market and potential motivation to produce accessible content. Such aspects are generally considered an important "lever" for promoting accessibility, softening the imposition of guidelines and legal requirements that are often viewed as a burdensome duty by Web developers and content authors. Web accessibility is not limited to people with disabilities but "*provides improved access, and thus can increase social inclusion, for other groups of people that are often a focus of corporate social responsibility*" (WAI, 2005b). Additionally, accessibility can help people who are working in situations where their senses or hands are busy, while driving or watching a video in noisy surroundings, for instance. Benefits to the population at large are often referred to as "*curb cuts,*" the analogy being not only do those in wheelchairs benefit from curb cuts, but so do those pushing a baby carriage, a shopping cart, or riding a bicycle.

Frequently the terms Web accessibility and Web **usability** are confused, mainly because these two concepts are not mutually exclusive. Though they are often referred to as independent topics, accessibility and usability are interrelated. The goal of accessibility is the removal of barriers for people with disabilities, while the aim of usability (Nielsen, 1999) is to offer a better experience for users in terms of efficiency, effectiveness, and satisfaction. Accessibility is an integral part of usability, as better access results in more usable products, programs, or services.

MAIN FOCUS OF WEB ACCESSIBILITY

How People with Disabilities Use the Web

To introduce how people with disabilities access the Web, we can consider a few examples of specific disabilities and the assistive technologies that might be used. The examples here are obviously not an exhaustive list, but are intended to offer a short overview of some of the more relevant cases, where the type of disability has a significant affect on a person's ability to access information on the Web.

First, we consider people who are blind, who will likely use a *screen reader* to access their computers. A screen reader gathers information from a computer screen and outputs that information as synthesized speech. While accessing the Web, a screen reader may encounter a variety of barriers, such as uncommented images or information whose meaning depends on colour or its position on the screen. Visual information without text alternatives that can be read by a screen reader will otherwise not be accessible to a blind person.

Similarly, people who have poor vision may use an assistive technology that enhances their residual sight, such as a *screen magnifier.* This tool enlarges the information displayed on the screen and helps the user by appropriately modifying some of its characteristics such as font size, contrast, or colours. The resulting display from a screen magnification tool shows only a portion of the whole screen, which often creates a loss of context. To accommodate those using a screen magnifier, authors need to create content that can be easily resized, using relative measures (e.g., em and %) instead of absolute measures (e.g., pt and px) to define the size characteristics of their content. This allows the content to be resized to fit any size browser window without losing or distorting the information being presented.

Mobility-related difficulties range from simply being unable to grasp or handle a mouse, to disabilities that require the use of voice input to control a computer, instead of the traditional keyboard and mouse. Generally, people with mobility impairments need Web pages that can be fully accessed by using a keyboard- or mouse-equivalent input device. A head mouse and single-click switches might be used in place of a traditional mouse, controlling the cursor with head movement, and controlling mouse clicks by leaning on a large button like switch. Alternative mouse input devices might be used together with an onscreen keyboard or voice recognition system for navigating and entering content.

Finally, consider the less obvious, or hidden, disabilities, such as learning disabilities and dyslexia, disabilities that impact on a user's ability to read, write, navigate, comprehend, and recall relevant information. People who have such disabilities may use a text-to-speech system that reads text on the screen aloud using synthesized speech. Consistency in presentation is often important for improving accessibility and usability for those with learning disabilities, such as navigation tools that remain the same throughout a Web site, a consistent look-and-feel, and page layouts that do not change from screen to screen.

Accessibility Standards, Guidelines, and Laws

Many guidelines and requirements have been written to support the production of accessible Web applications and Web content. The W3C has led the Web Accessibility Initiative (WAI) since 1997, which develops guidelines and resources specifically devoted to Web accessibility. The best-known document authored by this group is the Web Content Accessibility Guidelines (WCAG), which defines a collection of authoring guidelines related to several main themes associated with accessible design (W3C, 1999). The guidelines make recommendations that foster the development of accessible Web content, such as providing equivalent alternatives to non-textual content and using appropriate markup and style sheet elements. This document references a second practical techniques document that explains how to design and implement accessible HTML- and CSS-based content. The next version of WCAG (2.0), in development when this article was written, is based on four main principles of Web content accessibility (W3C, 2005b):

1. Content must be perceivable
2. Interface elements in the content must be operable
3. Content and controls must be understandable
4. Content must be robust enough to work with current and future technologies

Other WAI guideline documents make recommendations for developing:

- Accessible user agents, including Web browsers, media players, and assistive technologies (User Agent Accessibility Guidelines "UAAG") (W3C, 2002)
- Accessible authoring tools that produce accessible content (Authoring Tool Accessibility Guidelines, "ATAG") (W3C, 2000)

All the W3C recommendations could be considered as a worldwide reference for Web accessibility, though their use has been primarily voluntary. In order to promote the ethics associated with inclusion, accessibility is frequently encouraged, and often compelled by law. Many countries have added to existing accessibility laws, including chapters related specifically to Web ac-

cessibility. In 1998 the United States government added ICT (information and communication technologies) accessibility through **Section 508** of the Rehabilitation Act (U.S. Rehabilitation Act, 1998), imposing hardware, software, and Web accessibility constraints upon federal agencies and their suppliers. Similarly, the Canadian Government made accessibility mandatory for federal government Web sites by enacting The Common Look and Feel for the Internet legislation (Treasury Board of Canada Secretariat, 2000) in 2000. In the same year, the European Community raised the profile of accessibility in information technologies with the e-Inclusion policy, one of seven "eEurope policy priorities" intended to sustain participation of all those in the knowledge-based society (European Union, 2006). In addition, several European countries, like Italy (Italian Law n. 4, January 9, 2004), UK, Germany, Portugal, and Spain, have enacted their own rules or guidelines to ensure accessibility of Web content. The number of countries that are addressing Web accessibility issues continues to grow, and is being monitored by W3C (WAI, 2006).

Creating Accessible Web Content

All the above mentioned guidelines, laws, and requirements are based on (X)HTML-accessible authoring practices. Seven such practices are presented below. This is not a comprehensive list, but does presents the main practices associated with accessible Web content authoring:

1. Provide alternative formats for all non-text content, including graphical information, multimedia, and programmed objects. A user may be unable to use a specific media format due to a sensory disability (e.g., a blind user cannot see an image) or may have difficulties in accessing a resource that requires the use of a specific plug-in or helper application. Audio tracks should be supplemented with synchronized captioning or a transcript, and video should include captioning and descriptive audio, the latter used to describe information that cannot be deduced from the audio track of a video. Interface elements in plug-in or add-on software must include a text label so they can be read by assistive technologies. The most common alternative format is the (X)HTML Alt attribute, used to provide a short text description of something visual.

2. Explicitly define table structure by associating header cells with data cells. Properly associated column headings using the TH element, along with the scope or headers attributes, can greatly improve comprehension of (X)HTML-based tabular information for screen reader users.

3. Provide contextual information for frames, tables, lists, and links to aid comprehension. For example, use a table summary attribute to describe a complex layout and use link text that is meaningful when read on its own.

4. Create accessible forms by explicitly associating labels with form elements using the (X)HTML Label element, and by grouping related form fields together.

5. Separate presentation from content by using cascading style sheets (CSS) (W3C, 1998) rather than using inline (X)HTML attributes. This will allow users to personalize Web content by overriding an author style sheet, perhaps increasing font sizes or colour contrast with their own personal style sheet.

6. Design for device independence, creating Web pages that are accessible both with a mouse and a keyboard. Some people with disabilities may have difficulties using a keyboard perhaps due to mobility impairment, and some others such as blind users may be unable to use a mouse. Plug-in or add-on software used to play multimedia content must also be usable in a device independent manner. A good test is to use the Tab key repeatedly to see if all Web site or interface elements can accessed.

7. Validated (X)HTML markup. Assistive technologies, and particularly screen readers, may function incorrectly when they encounter poorly-formed markup. The W3C provides an online (X)HTML validator that can be used to quickly check markup validity (see: http://validator.w3.org).

Accessibility Evaluation

Web accessibility has to be kept in mind throughout the life-cycle of Web applications or Web content. It can be added as a new feature for existing services (i.e., retrofitting), or it could be considered during the design phase, planned into a project from the beginning. In both cases, accessibility needs to be verified regularly where content is changing. Many tools have now been created that help developers verify the accessibility of their content. Such automated tools, and user-centered techniques, can be used to assess the accessibility of Web content or services. Most tools are able to confirm some accessibility errors, but they are limited in what they can identify with certainty, hence a human operator will usually have to inspect and address some accessibility issues manually.

One component of an accessibility evaluation is validating the compliance of a page or Web site with a defined markup specification. Web pages that comply with Web standards can easily and correctly be interpreted by a wide range of Web browsers and assistive technologies. Similarly, appropriate use of semantic markup, such as headings, lists, and metadata, that can be understood independently of the visual effects of markup, help assistive technology users comprehend information more easily by organizing Web content in meaningful structures (e.g., sections, groupings, and hierarchies) Many tools, including the Web-based W3C HTML validator described earlier, are available to help Web authors create technically correct markup. The latest developments in this field are devoted to standardizing results generated by automated accessibility evaluation tools. To such an end, W3C is developing EARL (Evaluation and Report Language), a standardized markup language used to express test results (W3C, 2005a).

CURRENT AND FUTURE TRENDS

Current pursuits in Web accessibility are focused on developing guidelines that will be applicable to all content delivered through the Web (not just to Web pages), on the promotion of public awareness of Web accessibility, and also on introducing accessibility guidelines into national laws. Future trends in Web development are being driven by the increasing use of mobile devices, the accessibility to which shares much in common with Web accessibility issues associated with assistive technologies. This "curb cut" effect will widely influence future improvements in Web accessibility, and the "*anytime, anywhere, any device*" Web will strongly promote an "*anyone*" dimension.

With the recent introduction of transformation standards, such as the IMS accessibility learner information profile specification (ACCLIP) (IMS, 2005), Web content, and electronic information in general, will be customisable to each individual user. By entering an XML profile string when entering an ACCLIP-aware Web site or application, a blind user viewing a video, for example, will automatically receive that video with descriptive audio. A deaf user will receive the same video but with captioning instead. A user on a cell phone may use an ACCLIP profile to display the video at a lower resolution. A typical user will receive just the video without any transformations. Similarly, an ACCLIP profile can be used to configure a computer work station with the appropriate assistive technologies, or reconfigure a Web application perhaps simplifying it for a person with a learning disability or a cognitive impairment, all simply by inserting a USB memory stick, or swiping a smart card with an ACCLIP profile on it.

CONCLUSION

Web accessibility has become a fundamental element of social inclusion and an essential aspect in fighting against a "*digital divide.*" A wide range of tools and specifications are now available to guide developers in the creation of accessible Web content. Legislation more frequently compels Web content developers to meet specific Web accessibility requirements. By following a few relatively simple accessible authoring principles, Web site designers, content authors, and administrators can support a diverse range of user needs. Those needs are not necessarily related to disability, but are governed by the context of the information being accessed, the goals a person has for that information once acquired, as well as the means through which a person navigates the Web to obtain that information. Moving away from accommodating *special needs,* to accommodating the specific requirements of the technologies accessing the information instead, is key to removing Web barriers and creating a fully-accessible Web. The experience gained in making the Web accessible will have a positive influence on the accessibility of emerging technologies and on the development of more general access policies.

REFERENCES

Bohman, P. (2003). *Introduction to Web accessibility*. Retrieved 30 July, 2007 from http://www.webaim.org/intro/

European Union (2006). *eInclusion & eAccessibility*. Retrieved 30 July, 2007 from http://europa.eu.int/information_society/policy/accessibility/index_en.htm

IMS (2005). *AccessForAll Meta-data specification 1.0*. IMS Global Learning Consortium. http://www.imsglobal.org/accessibility/index.html

ISO (1998). *ISO 9241-11: Guidance on usability*. 30 July, 2007.

Italian Law n. 4, January 9, 2004 (2004). Provisions to support the access to information technologies for the disabled (English version). Retrieved 30 July, 2007 from http://www.pubbliaccesso.it/normative/law_20040109_n4.htm, 2004

Nielsen, J. (1999). *Designing web usability: The practice of simplicity*. New Riders Press.

Pilgrim, M. (2002). *Dive into accessibility*. Retrieved 30 July, 2007 from http://diveintoaccessibility.org/

Treasury Board of Canada Secretariat, Chief Information Officer (2000). Common look and feel for the Internet – Accessibility Section. Retrieved 30 July, 2007 from http://www.tbs-sct.gc.ca/clf-nsi/index_e.asp

U.S. Rehabilitation Act (1998). Section 508. Retrieved 30 July, 2007 from http://www.section508.gov

W3C (2000). Authoring tool accessibility guidelines 1.0. W3C Recommendation Retrieved 3 February, 2000, from http://www.w3.org/TR/WAI-AUTOOLS/.

W3C (1998). Cascading style sheets, level 2. CSS2 Specification, W3C Recommendation May 12,1998. Retrieved 30 July, 2007 from http://www.w3.org/TR/CSS2/

W3C (2005a). *Evaluation and report language (EARL) 1.0 Schema*. W3C Working Draft . http://www.w3.org/TR/EARL10/

W3C (2002). *User agent accessibility guidelines 1.0*. W3C Recommendation 17 December 2002. Retrieved 30 July, 2007 from http://www.w3.org/TR/WAI-USERAGENT/

W3C (1999). *Web content accessibility guidelines 1.0.* W3C Recommendation May 5. Retrieved 30 July, 2007 from http://www.w3.org/TR/1999/WAI-WEBCONTENT-19990505/

W3C (2005b). *Web content accessibility guidelines 2.0.* W3C Working Draft. Retrieved 30 July, 2007 from http://www.w3.org/TR/WCAG20/

WAI (2005a). *Introduction to Web wccessibility.* Retrieved 30 July, 2007 from http://www.w3.org/WAI/intro/accessibility.php

WAI (2005b). *Social factors in developing a Web accessibility business case for your organization.* Retrieved 30 July, 2007 from http://www.w3.org/WAI/bcase/soc

WAI (2006). *Policies relating to Web accessibility.* Retrieved 30 July, 2007 from http://www.w3.org/WAI/Policy/

KEY TERMS

Assistive Technologies: Assistive, adaptive, and rehabilitative devices and technologies that promote independence for people with disabilities by enabling them to perform tasks that otherwise they are unable to achieve, or may have difficulty accomplishing.

Device Independence: The most common computer "input devices" are the keyboard and mouse. In most cases, device independence means a function or feature can be accessed by some means other than using a mouse, though ultimately it means they can be accessed by any device. The phrase implies that Web content will be accessible to anyone, including people with disabilities that frequently use non-conventional devices and access methods.

Digital Divide: This expression denotes the socio-economic differences between communities or groups and their ability to access information technology. A digital divide is created when network infrastructure, computing technology, or computer literacy is lacking. At one end of the divide are those "with" technology: They advance and grow. At the other end of the divide are those "without" technology: They stagnate and fall behind those who have access to technology.

Markup Language: A formal language that describes a document by combining text with information about the structure and presentation of the text, and about the relationships between documents. The most widely-known markup language is HTML (hypertext markup language) used to format Web content.

Style Sheet: A "style sheet" is a mechanism (supported by desktop publishing programs) used to apply display formatting to text, separating the presentation from content. Custom style sheets can be created by individuals that may include a wide variety of formatting properties that dictate how particular documents are displayed. The use of style sheets in Web documents is based on the CSS (cascading style sheet) language, used to apply formatting to (X)HTML Web pages.

Text Equivalents: This expression indicates text-based information used to communicate meaning contained in visual (images, video, and animations) or audio media. Text equivalents include text transcript of audio information, synchronous captioning of speech, as well as text descriptions of images, charts, graphics, and videos.

Usability: According to an ISO (ISO, 1998) definition, this term indicates "the extent to which a product can be used by specified users to achieve specified goals with effectiveness, efficiency, and satisfaction in a specified context of use." More generally, "usability" denotes the ease with which people can employ a particular tool or object in order to achieve a particular goal. The term also refers to techniques for testing ease-of-use of existing products as well as methods for improving simplicity of usage during the design process of new ones.

Web Mining: A Conceptual Overview on Intelligent Information Retrieval Systems

Henrik Hanke
University of Duisburg-Essen, Germany

Alf Neumann
University of Cologne, Germany

INTRODUCTION

The scale and scope of information on the Internet has been extended enormously over the past decade. The growth of more and more intelligent Web-based services and applications has resulted in an enormous growth of potentially useful data of both commercial and non-commercial interest. While this rise has brought a great amount of positive impact on global economic, social, and political development, it also implies an enormous flood of information into an increasingly complex information space. This is to be found on a vast variety of topics originating from a vast variety of sources, which range from private Web sites containing different kinds of information, to business-to-business B2B platforms. In most cases, these data are of an unsorted and unstructured kind, making efficient and target-oriented information retrieval very hard, if not nearly impossible. Coping with the challenge of a lack of transparency can be remedied by intelligent software agents, also referred to as softbots, which guide users through finding, sorting, and filtering this accruing data on the Internet like commonly used search engines.

Current research focuses in principle on more sophisticated software implementations, like high-quality Web interfaces. Generally, such systems fall back on techniques known from statistics, machine learning, and *data mining*. The mining concept is commonly targeted at finding, extracting, processing, and preparing non-lucid information in traditional databases, commonly referred to as finding answers to non-asked questions. *Web mining* focuses on finding and extracting data to be found on the Internet (Fürnkranz, Holzbaur, & Temel, 2002; Lin, Alvarez, & Ruiz, 2002).

The following overview presents the three major directions and concepts showing the way for Web research and development in this field: *Web structure mining*, with its specificities in intra-page and inter-page analysis, *Web content mining* on Web page content and search results, and *Web usage mining* by access pattern tracking or customized usage tracking systems (Chakrabarti, 2002).

WEB STRUCTURE MINING

Web structure mining is of special importance to Web mining in general, and its subtopics in particular. Within this field of mining for Web *intelligence,* is the foundation for extraction, exploration, and analysis of Web information data (Han & Chang, 2002). There are several integral subtopics dealing with the way in which the Web is built, such as graph structures, search methods, content categorization, and classification concepts.

Directed Graphs

The Internet is, as far as it is lucid, built up by a huge amount of documents. However, these documents are not to be seen as standalone objects, but rather as a collection that is connected through hyperlinks. In contrast to conventional information retrieval, but focussing primarily on information that is provided by the text of Web documents, hyperlinks provide additional information through their own structure, namely the way in which different documents are connected to each other.

Defining Web sites or documents as nodes and hyperlinks as edges, the Web may be seen as a directed graph. There have been a vast amount of studies and research conducted in order to analyze the exact properties and structure of this graph. The awareness of such hyperlink structures enables efficient Web searching opportunities, as their analysis draws a figure of the relations within these structures (Broder et al., 2000).

Web Search

The resulting relations from the structure of nodes and edges mentioned above presents the opportunity to utilize information immanent in this structure, respectively hidden within the hyperlinks. As this might support to sorting query results from a search engine, it might be a somewhat distracting result. In order to get a qualitative measure of a search result, both incoming and outgoing connections should be considered in ranking techniques. It seems useful to substructure pages into *authorities* and *hubs* (Kleinberg, 1999). While authorities represent useful information about the searched topic, hubs enclose pointers to high quality information sources. Hence, hubs and authorities are closely connected by being self-conditioned to each other, as hubs point to authorities and authorities are being pointed to by hubs.

However, such parallel research on query topics implies an algorithm, which measures the probability a page is visited or left randomly as well as existing page ranks according to referenced or referent sites. The main advantage of a page rank over the hubs and authority logic is reasoned because of its high searching performance (Han & Chang, 2002).

Text Categorization

Text categorization can be defined as classing documents into a number of categories. The main problems occur due to the questions of efficiency. The use of sensible categories should be assured in order to present a usable classification result, hence to cope with the high degree of freedom immanent in Internet data. Therefore, a suitable set of features is needed: a clear basis for machine learning systems and special sets of words and phrases, so-called *training classifiers,* in first hand, non-automatic manner (Sebastiani, 2002). In this sense, different approaches have been developed to classify text in absolute and relative measures. First, two properties can be alternatively or collectively assigned to each word. Second, words can be engaged with specific weights, indicating the priority assigned to a term.

An ever-emerging field has received increased attention in the past years, namely automated filtering

of spam. Again, training classifiers are substantial, but also a particularly challenging problem for machine learning in this context. In most cases, these so-called *spam-filters* are based on Bayesian learning, tangential to this special problem and capable of building useful solutions (Androutsopoulos, Paliouras, & Michelakis, 2004). The special task in this context is, however, to cope with misclassification issues and skewed example distribution.

Hypertext Classification

In order to provide a more efficient search-engine logic, hypertext classification can help to sort and analyze pairs of hyperlinks. A common analysis procedure is manifested in the combination of certain key-parts of predecessor pages and the contents of the page to categorize, but also with developing different feature sets for the referent site and the successor page (Yang, Slattery, & Ghani, 2002). However, the research results are not very lucid on this point, so far. A major problem, for example, exists in the selection of fitting predecessor pages, specifically, the partial content the referred sites' key-phrases are to be combined with.

Recently, several approaches to overcome this issue have been developed, most notably a classification of hyperlinks themselves. Contrasting with previously mentioned methods, classification takes place concerning the hyperlink's target page, hence switching the focus from successor to predecessor pages. This categorization is based on the terms found in the context of the link, hence the sourcecode of the referring page, therefore providing a classification for each hyperlink (Fürnkranz, 2002).

WEB CONTENT MINING

Mining the Web structure can be seen as a function serving prerequisite actions to further Web mining applications, such as retrieving specific content from the vast variety of information to be found on the Web. Content mining is concerned with the extraction of certain information items from unstructured text or from raw data of an unknown structure, such as stock exchange data from different Web resources and online broker Web sites. While Web crawlers and sophisticated search techniques can be used to find the relevant Web content and pages, information extraction tools are needed to identify and collect particular content items (Pazienza, 2003).

Text Extraction

There are numerous algorithms to analyse unstructured text based on domain-specific extraction patterns, which employ natural language processing. Therefore, a set of noun phrases is required that constitutes the information to be extracted. Syntactic heuristics create linguistic patterns that can extract the interesting information. Other systems that work with unstructured text are based on inductive rule learning algorithms that can make use of a multitude of features, including linguistic and mark-up language tags, etc. Such systems learn a set of extraction rules that specify which combination of features indicates an appearance of the target information (Califf & Mooney, 2003).

Wrapper Induction

While the systems mentioned above work on unstructured text, a recently emerging direction of technology development focuses on the extraction of items from structured HTML or XML content through so-called wrappers. Wrappers assume a highly regular source page that allows a mapping of its content by learning delimiters for each content attribute. A significant problem of inducing such wrappers is the inconsistency of tags, as wall as Web content that does not perfectly comply to Web development standards (Kushmerick, 2000).

Semantic Web

The Semantic Web concept is supposed to facilitate and foster the access to information towards a more efficient automation of Web data processing (Berendt, Hotho, & Stumme, 2002). Therefore, the concept is based on freely accessible ontologies, like Web documents, which define certain types of content objects and the relations between them so that Web applications for content mining can easily draw inferences about the information provided on, and structures of, Web sites (Li & Zhong, 2006).

In this context, an essential technology issue is to annotate the information available on the Web through semantic tags. Hypertext classifications and information extraction techniques can be used to assign Web page content as entities within an ontology (Fensel,

2001). A typical application of this approach would be a consistent backbone for Web catalogues (Staab & Maedche, 2001).

WEB USAGE MINING

The approaches presented above deal with the analysis of content, or content structures, in the Web. Additional commercially valuable information can be obtained from the interaction of users with Web sites, i.e., for personalizing Web services and optimizing search engines (Srivastava, Cooley, Deshpande, & Tan, 2000; Tan & Kumar, 2002).

Simple usage mining systems rely solely on active user interventions, such as search requests or user feedback. More advanced systems have overcome the necessity of user feedback and work with Web logs that track and trace user activities on a Web site. Special methods, such as click streams, are used to monitor such browsing behaviour of individual users, also referred to as browsing paths (Mobasher, Cooley, & Srivastava, 2000).

Collaborative Filtering

Collaborative filtering is an important concept of usage mining. The information on previous recommendations or user preferences obtained through the Web site is used to propose content items to other users that also likely reflect their preferences (Kim, Im, & Atluri, 2005). Therefore, collaborative filtering systems follow the idea that recommendations can be based on similarity of preferences, and that user preferences can in turn be defined by the similarity of their recommendations (Chakrabarti, 2002).

Recommender Systems

Alternatively, recommender systems can also be based on the similarity of content, which is defined via the recommendations of the users that recommended the items in question (Sarwar, Karypis, Konstan, & Riedl, 2001).

Recommender systems store data on pairs of content items and the analysis of correlations of user recommendations for such pairs. In this context, recommendation means both an explicit user feedback, for example, by rating a product, or an implicit evaluation, for example, by buying a product. The analytical methodology of the recommender system concept has been advancing significantly over the past years, from memory-based to model-based approaches, clustering methods, latent semantic models, and association rules (Lin, Alvarez, & Ruiz, 2002).

Artificial Users

The concept of artificial users in the context of Web usage mining extends the basic ideas of collaborative filtering and recommender systems, and emphasizes the interdependence of content and user behaviour. Analyzing the behaviour of artificial users as models of real user groups within a given framework of Web content can provide an essential check that Web resources are correctly implemented and tailored to the specific behavioural patterns of an artificial user (Joseph, Jospeh, & Joseph, 2004). Furthermore, this analysis is an eligible approach to verify the inter-relatedness of content items in an ideal test environment, prior to the implementation of a real-life application or content resource, i.e., for predicting correlations of preferences (Manzotti & Tagliasco, 2005).

CONCLUSION

The current stage of research and development in the field of Web technologies and the Internet, as well as its unabated growth, hence inducing unabated generation of structure, content, and usage information data, confirm that the concepts of Web mining are, and will more and more be, the key to uncovering and cataloging valuable information, traversal patterns, and semantic structures of Web resources. These are likely to bring intelligence and direction to Web interactions. Three major points of interest can be identified, inducing further growth of Web mining's influence.

First, mining for information will have a certain role in the field of e-commerce. Hence, further potential is located within the identification of patterns concerning decision-making processes. Click-stream data and enhanced analysis-technologies provide the potential to gain valuable information in aligning Web site appearance and content with the relevant user.

Second, correlating to their ever-evolving growth, Web services architecture needs to be robust and effective. In this case, Web mining can provide behav-

ioural information on the data explored and extracted through its techniques. Hence, further research brings forward an opportunity to improve Web services in various aspects.

Third, the anonymity of the Internet, as well as its mass of users, are nutrient opportunities to criminal actions, such as credit card betrayal and various other kinds of fraud. This provides a perfectly shaped starting point for Web mining actions. Hence, in this respect research needs to concentrate on fraud-recognition- and fraud-characterization-methods as well as techniques to identify new frauds.

Thus, Web mining will not only stay, but gain influence as an important driver for Web transparency and facilitated access to the immense information available, and vice-versa for more efficient ways to share and explore meaningful content in the information economy and society.

REFERENCES

Androutsopoulos, I., Paliouras, G., & Michelakis E. (2004). *Learning to filter unsolicited commercial e-mail.* Technical Report 02.2004, NCSR Demokritos, March.

Berendt, B., Hotho, A., & Stumme, G. (2002). Towards Semantic Web mining. In I. Horrocks & J. Hendler (Eds.), *Proceedings of the 1st International Semantic Web Conference, ISWC-02.* Berlin, Germany: Springer Verlag.

Broder, A., Kumar, R., Maghoul, F., Raghavan, P., Rajagopalan, S., Stata, R., et al. (2000). Graph structure in the Web. *Proceedings of the 9th International World Wide Web Conference, WWW-9. Computer Networks, 33*(1- 6), 309-320.

Califf, M.E., & Mooney, R.J. (2003). Bottom-up relational learning of pattern matching rules for information extraction. *Journal of Machine Learning Research, 4*(6), 177-210.

Chakrabarti, S. (2002). *Mining the Web: analysis of hypertext and semi-structured data.* Morgan Kaufmann.

Fensel, D. (2001). *Ontologies: Silver bullet for knowledge management and electronic commerce.* Berlin, Germany: Springer Verlag.

Fürnkranz, J., Holzbaur C., & Temel, R. (2002). User profiling for the Melvil knowledge retrieval system. *Applied Artificial Intelligence, 16*(4), 243-281.

Han, J., & Chang, K.C.C. (2002). Data mining for Web intelligence. *Computer, 35*(11), 64-70.

Joseph, S.R.H., Joseph, S.H., & Joseph, M.H. (2005, July 18-22). Sequencing vocabulary instruction: Artificial vs. real users. Paper presented at the *International Conference on Artificial Intelligence in Education AIED05 Workshop 12 on Student Modeling for Language Tutors*, Amsterdam, Netherlands, 29-38.

Kim, D.H., Im, I., & Atluri, V. (2005). A clickstream-based collaborative filtering recommendation model for e-commerce. In *Proceedings of the 17th IEEE International Conference on E-Commerce Technology, CEC05*, 84-91.

Kleinberg, J. M. (1999). Authoritative sources in a hyperlinked environment. *Journal of the ACM, 46*(5), 604-632.

Kushmerick, N. (2000). Wrapper induction: Efficiency and expressiveness. *Artificial Intelligence, 118*, 15-68.

Li ,Y., & Zhong, N. (2006). Mining ontology for automatically acquiring Web user information needs. *Knowledge and Data Engineering, 18*(4), 554-568.

Lin, W., Alvarez, S.A., & Ruiz, C. (2002). Efficient adaptive support association rule mining for recommender systems. *Data Mining and Knowledge Discovery, 6*(1), 83-105.

Manzotti, R., & Tagliasco, V. (2005). Towards an artificial user: The "what" problem for an architecture capable of developing new goals. In M. Negrotti (Ed.), *Yearbook of the artificial* (Vol. 3, pp. 249-256). New York: Peter Lang Publishing Group.

Mobasher, B., Cooley, R., & Srivastava, J. (2000). Automatic personalization based on Web usage mining. *Communications of the ACM, 43*(8), 142-151.

Pazienza, M. T. (Ed.). (2003). Information extraction in the Web era: Natural language communication for knowledge acquisition and intelligent information agents. *Summer Convention on Information Extraction, SCIE 2002*, Frascati, Italy. Berlin, Germany: Springer Verlag, 129-147.

Sarwar, B.M., Karypis, G., Konstan, J.A., & Riedl J. (2001, May). Item-based collaborative filtering recommendation algorithms. In *Proceedings of the 10th International World Wide Web Conference, WWW-10*, Hong Kong, 285-295.

Sebastiani, F. (2002). Machine learning in automated text categorization. *ACM Computing Surveys, 34*(1), 1-47.

Srivastava, J., Cooley, R., Deshpande, M., & Tan, P.N. (1999) Web usage mining: Discovery and applications of usage patterns from Web data. *SIGKDD Explorations, 1*(2), 12-23.

Staab, S., & Maedche, A. (2001). Knowledge portals: Ontologies at work. *AI Magazine, 21*(2), 63-75.

Tan, P.N., & Kumar, V. (2002). Discovery of Web robot sessions based on their navigational patterns. *Data Mining and Knowledge Discovery, 6*(1), 9-35.

Yang, Y., Slattery, S., & Ghani, R. (2002). A study of approaches to hypertext categorization. *Journal of Intelligent Information Systems, 18*(2-3), Special Issue: Automatic Text Categorization, 219-241.

KEY TERMS

Authorities and Hubs: Based on an information-centric view that the Internet in general can be sub-structured into two main kinds of Web-pages: authorities who represent useful information about the topic searched on, and hubs that enclose pointers to high quality information sources

Data Mining: (Semi-)Automatic and systematic exploration and extraction of unknown information which accrues within large data-pools.

Training Classifier: In order to cope with the high degree of freedom immanent in Internet data, the use of sensible categories to present a clear basis for machine learning systems, such as special sets of words and phrases (training classifiers) is needed. Also, training classifiers are substantial within the task of automated spam filtering

Web Content Mining: The extraction of certain information from the unstructured raw data text of unknown structures is referred to as Web content mining.

A set of information extraction tools is brought forward in order to identify and collect content items, such as Text Extraction and Wrapper Induction.

Web Intelligence: Web intelligence represents extraction, exploration, and utilization of unstructured data accruing on the Internet by using techniques known from Web Mining, which is subdivided into Web structure mining, Web content mining, and Web usage mining.

Web Structure Mining: Web structure mining presents several integral subtopics, such as graph structures and searching, as well as content categorization and classification techniques to set a sound foundation in order to explore, extract, and analyze Web information data.

Web Usage Mining: Based on the interaction of Internet-users with Web sites, Web usage mining copes with the identification of commercially valuable information in order to create personalized Web-pages or provide enhanced search engines.

Wrapper: Based on highly standardized, regular, validated, and tag-consistent source pages, wrappers can map content provided in the pages' source code to certain content attributes, and therefore extract items from structured HTML or XML content.

Web Services

Kevin Curran
University of Ulster, Ireland

Padraig O'Kane
University of Ulster, Ireland

INTRODUCTION

The term "Web services" was initially employed by Bill Gates, chairman of Microsoft, at the Microsoft Professional Developers Conference in Orlando, Florida on July 12, 2000. Fundamentally, the term refers to automated resources accessed via an Internet URL. However, a more comprehensive definition is that of the World Wide Web Consortium (W3C)[1], which declare Web services as *"providing a standard means of interoperating between different software applications, running on a variety of platforms and/or frameworks."* An Internet connection allows retrieval of software-powered resources or functional components and is therefore regarded as an extension of the World Wide Web infrastructure. Web services represent the evolution of a human-oriented utilization of the Web to a technology that is application driven. It attempts to replace human-centric searches for information with searches that are primarily application based (Staab, 2003).

The primary elements associated with Web services are repositories (i.e., a location for storage) and messaging. Web service applications can perform a range of requests or processes, yet several characteristics found are common throughout. All Web service applications connect over a network, i.e., a medium that allows users to share information and resources (Kodali, 2005). The networks frequently associated with Web services are an intranet (within an organisation), extranet (within an organisation including controlled outside partners), or the Internet (within the global community). Communication between the applications within the network is performed using a set of standardised protocols; those used include hypertext transport protocol (HTTP) and the secure hypertext transport protocol (HTTPS).

Another common characteristic associated with Web services is that the connection between applications is standardized, yet it is operating system and language independent so that disparate or varying systems can benefit. The principal language that conveys the information distributed across the network is extensible mark-up language (XML). Web services are often called XML Web services to emphasize the importance of XML as the underlying language, while distinguishing such services for other types commonly available on the Web. The interfaces of a Web service are often defined using the Web services description language (WSDL). XML is used in describing network services as collections of endpoints capable of exchanging messages (Goldfarb, 2005). Through the use of WSDL, Web services can enable applications to use its services once they have found and interpreted its definition. Characteristics of a Web service including its existence, location, and purpose can be published and discovered using universal description, discovery, and integration (UDDI). Web service descriptions and the methods for publishing and discovering them are stored in a repository that implements the UDDI specification. No one can deny that there exists at present a progression from a human-oriented use of the Web to an application-driven concept referred to as Web services. Here we discuss the factors leading to this development and the inspiration behind Web services, and detail the languages, platforms, and systems involved in these services.

BACKGROUND

Web services derived from the efforts of a number of businesses that shared a mutual interest in developing and maintaining an "electronic marketplace." In 1975, electronic data interchange (EDI) was launched and was deemed the first attempt to create a medium where businesses could communicate over a network. However, EDI was difficult to implement due to its complexity and cost constraints, and in the 25 years since its introduction, numerous efforts at a global business network technology have been introduced, e.g., distributed component object model, UNIX remote procedure call, and Java remote method invocation. Each of the applications failed to gain significant market status or enough momentum to succeed. Although all of them exist today and are still useful, they failed to generate broad industry support. A combination of factors has contributed to the failure of these previous technologies and it was imperative that software vendors accepted this and concentrated on implementing a technology where an "electronic marketplace" was a realisation. Before the introduction of the Web, the possibility of ensuring that all major software vendors agreed on a transport protocol for communication across network application services was unrealistic. But when the Web was a reality, lower level transports for standardized communication was specified. The standards TCP/IP and HTTP where already integrated by the time the Web went global in 1994, all that was required was a messaging and data encapsulation standard and it was essential that software vendors co-operated fully.

The introduction of extensible mark-up language (XML) was instrumental in the rise of Web services. It officially became a recognised standard in February 1998 when the World Wide Web Consortium announced that XML 1.0 was suitable for integration into software applications. XML is described as a *"widely heralded, platform independent standard for data description"* (Levitt, 2001). It provided the means of communicating between standardized applications, and by early 1998, a number of attempts where made at an XML protocol encouraging interprocess communication. One such protocol, SOAP, is regarded as the basis for Web services. It proved popular, considering the consensus among certain individuals who appeared a little dubious at first, due to the fact that Microsoft developed the protocol. SOAP was advantageous in that it was by flexible and general purpose, and its compatibility across platforms meant that its acceptance was widespread. Surprisingly, after private meetings, IBM publicly backed Microsoft's SOAP and in March 2000 both companies began to develop SOAP 1.1. Both companies also began to work individually on protocols, which encouraged connectivity to a Web service. They emerged with IBM's network accessible service specification language and Microsoft's service description language and SOAP contract language.

During the autumn of 2000, the protocol proposals were merged and Web Services Description Language (WSDL) was announced. Companies could therefore create and describe their Web services using SOAP and WSDL, yet a means of locating and advertising Web services was still required. IBM, Microsoft, and now Ariba began working on a solution in March 2000, and their efforts produced the standard universal description, discovery and integration (UDDI), which was announced in September 2000.

With SOAP, WSDL, and UDDI in place, it was apparent that the standards to create, locate, and advertise Web services had arrived. However, Software Infrastructure Vendors remained defiant and it was not until the end of 2000 that Oracle, HP, Sun, IBM, and Microsoft revealed their intention to support and incorporate the standards into their products.

WEB SERVICES

Web services use a number of interrelated technologies and languages. However, we intend to focus on those that have aided the growth of Web services and those that were established in an effort to maximize their potential, namely XML, SOAP, and WSDL.

XML

In order to understand XML (Goldfarb, 2005), it is important to realise that it is an outgrowth of standard generalized mark-up language (SGML), which became a standard of the International Organization for Standardization (ISO) in 1986. SGML had its early origins in IBM, they realised the importance of publishing content in a number of different ways. With a number of organizations struggling with similar problems, IBM seized the opportunity to create a standard for document mark-up. The resulting rich document mark-up language allowed authors to separate the logical content of a document from its presentation. This approach involved the introduction of metadata. Metadata describes the attributes of an information bearing-object (IBO), e.g., document, dataset, database, image, etc. It is more commonly referred to as *"Data about Data"* (Dick, 2001). Another definition states *"Metadata usually includes information about the intellectual content of the image, digital representation data and security or rights management information"* (Nayak, 2002). With

SGML, metadata was added to indicate the logical structure and to provide shared context. HTML is also a descendant of SGML. When companies began to develop a standard addressing the problems associated with these languages, they naturally looked at SGML as a starting point. As mentioned previously, the World Wide Web Consortium formed a working group to study the issue. Their primary goal was to establish a simplified subset of SGML suitable for use on the Web, as SGML is extremely complex and poses problems for automated processing of large volumes of Internet documents. A subset of SGML that would be simple enough for people to understand yet expressive enough to meet the need for shared context on the Internet was what was required. The resulting specification was XML 1.0. The XML approach to metadata and shared context is simple to grasp. Programmers add Metadata through tags, the syntax is similar to that of HTML, with angled brackets (<>) commonplace throughout (see Code Example 1).

Document designers add shared context through document type definitions (DTDs). A DTD uses a collection of rules to specify the allowable order, structure, and attributes of tags for a particular type of document; in simpler terms, the DTD handles the mark-up language and therefore specifies what tags are valid. Using an Internet uniform resource locator (URL), a document can reference the DTD. XML offers a standard, flexible data format that is extensible, which therefore reduces the burden of organizing a number of technologies needed to ensure that Web services are a success. The XML syntax is an extremely important aspect, as are the concepts of the XML Infoset, XML Schema, and XML Namespaces. XML Infoset is a formal set of information items and associated properties that provide an abstract description of an XML document. It attempts to define a set of terms that specifications can use to refer to information within an XML document. The concept of XML Namespaces is extremely important in that it ensures XML documents remain recognizable and are free from "collisions" that occur when other software packages use similar attribute-or element-naming conventions. The XML Namespaces mechanism is a collection of names identified by a URL reference, they differ from other naming conventions in that the XML version has an internal structure and uses families of reserved attributes. The XML Schema is a concept that allows machines to process work based on a series of rules developed by people. The structure and content of an XML document can be defined using such a schema (Rusty, 2004).

SOAP

SOAP is a protocol that uses XML to encode the information in Web service request and response messages before they can be sent over a network. SOAP is used to gain access to services, objects, and servers in a standard way. Its main goal is to facilitate interoperability, i.e., the ability of software and hardware located in multiple machines to communicate. SOAP is independent of any operating system and/or protocol and can be sent using

Figure 1. Transfer of XML messages using SOAP

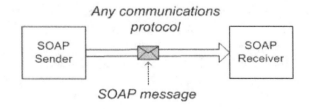

Code Example 1. XML document detailing a letter regarding an order

```
<to>Padraig</to>
<from>Ruairi</from>
<re><customer-name>Joe Bloggs</customer-name>
    <customer-number>0101-0101-010</customer-number>
    <document-type-request>order form</document-type-request>
</re>
<p>Joe Bloggs wants to complain about his order. He feels he has been overcharged.</p>
```

a range of Internet protocols, however, the underlying communication protocol is that of HTTP.

When SOAP was first introduced, programmers/authors focused on accessing objects, a medium specific to technologies that recognised an object-oriented approach. Over time it was felt that SOAP was too restricted and that a wider audience was required, and therefore the specification moved away from an object-centric one to a generalized XML Messaging framework (Verma, 2005). As mentioned previously, SOAP defines a method of transferring XML messages from one point to the next (see Figure 1).

The messaging framework carries this out, as it is extensible, usable over a variety of underlying protocols and independent of programming models. The key to SOAP is its extensibility. Simplicity still remains one of SOAP's primary design goals as is often witnessed with software. SOAP lacks in a number of various distributed system features, such as security, routing, and reliability, however, IBM, Microsoft, and other software vendors are working continually on SOAP. Second, SOAP can be used over any transport protocol, such as TCP; however, a standard protocol, such as HTTP, needed to be required in order to outline rules governing the environment. The SOAP specification encourages the definition of concrete protocols by providing such a flexible framework. The third characteristic of SOAP is that it doesn't conform to only one programming model. SOAP defines a model for processing individual, single path messages, however, it is possible to combine multiple messages into an overall message exchange; SOAP therefore allows for any number of message exchange patterns (Verma,

2005). The SOAP messaging framework consists of a number of core elements: Envelope, Header, Body, and Fault. The Envelope element is the root element of a SOAP message, making it easy for applications to identify a message by simply looking at the name of the root element. The version of SOAP being used can also be identified from information stated in the Envelope element. The Envelope element contains an optional Header element, which is followed by a Body element, which represents the majority of the message. The body element can contain varying numbers of elements from any namespace. The data that a user wants to send is placed within the body element. The Fault element indicates errors within the body element in the event that something goes wrong. A standard error representation is paramount in that it ensures that applications refrain from inventing their own, therefore making it impossible for the general infrastructure to differentiate between success and failure.

WSDL

WSDL provides an XML grammar and supplies a means of grouping messages into operations, and operations into interfaces. WSDL is essential to the Web services architecture, as it describes the complete contract for application communication. WSDL is a machine-readable language and therefore tools and infrastructure can be easily built around it. Developments within this technology have ensured that programmers can use WSDL definitions to generate code that interacts with Web services precisely. Code generation like this encapsulates details concerned with the sending

Code Example 2. Basic structure of a WSDL definition

```
<!-- WSDL definition structure -->
<definitions
        name="MathService"
        targetNamespace="http://example.org/math/" xmlns=http://schemas.xmlsoap.org/wsdl/
>
        <!-- abstract definitions -->
        <types> ...
        <message> ...
        <portType> ...
        <!-- concrete definitions -->
        <binding> ...
        <service> ...
</definition>
```

and receiving of SOAP messages over different protocols and makes Web services more approachable. Regardless of the programming language in use, be it JAVA, C++, etc., the classes generated from the same WSDL definition should be able to communicate with each other through the WSDL-provided interfaces. A WSDL definition contains several elements, including types, messages, port Type, binding, and service (see Code Example 2), all of which come from the same namespace. It is therefore important that that a qualified name is used when referencing something in a WSDL file (Goldman, 2004).

The element type, message, and portType are abstract definitions of the Web service interface. These three elements make up the programmatic interface with which one. The last two elements (binding and service) describe the concrete details of how the interface translates messages onto the wire. The underlying infrastructure handles these details rather than the application code. Several editors are now available, allowing the generation of WSDL and thus making the authoring of such definitions a lot easier.

FUTURE TRENDS FOR WEB SERVICES

Web services have established themselves and have found a critical mass. In order to maintain this momentum, Web service standards need to progress quickly and efficiently and the concept of interoperability must be achieved. The choices evident within the world of Web services are of an extremely delicate nature, especially during such a formative period. The factors that will determine the success of Web services technology are those concerned with the variety of scales and whether the technology can be used with simple, small projects as well as more complex developments (Graham, 2004). Both SOAP and WSDL are complementary to projects of varying sizes, and it is these technologies that will ensure continued support from businesses and organizations as these standards are now globally accepted. Integrated environments, such as Microsoft Visual Studio.NET, already provide a framework to create and control Web services in a seamless fashion. Other Web service product developers, such as IBM, are extending their environments to encourage an easy to use development platform. It is predicted that as the number of businesses publishing Web services grows, they will seek to provide services alternatives

to guarantee 24/7 availability and aid in the monitoring of Web services as well as validating service providers and offering one-stop shopping for Web services. It is also felt that a centralised Web services repository will be created to encourage real time processing of data from multiple systems in the correct format, and this may be a fundamental stage in ensuring the future of Web services (Binstock, 2005).

CONCLUSION

Since the introduction of XML in 1998, Web service technology has steadily gathered momentum. Both Microsoft and IBM were pioneering forces behind its implementation, and their work together has seen a number of developments, most notably SOAP and WSDL, gain global status in an effort to firmly establish Web services as the key in developing an electronic marketplace. It is, however, imperative that companies, vendors, and the World Wide Web Consortium agree on standards, and that the factors contributing to successful Web service growth are harnessed in order to ensure that the future for Web services is prosperous.

REFERENCES

Binstock, A. (2005, July). Middleware finds its mojo again: SOAs and ESBs key to advancing middleware in 2005. *Infoworld*, 11-12.

Dick, K. (2001). *XML: A manager's guide.* Wiley Publishers.

Goldfarb, C., & Prescod, P. (2005). *The XML handbook* (3rd ed.). Prentice Hall.

Goldman, O. (2004, November). Taking on XML's bandwidth and memory constraints. *Dr. Dobb's Journal,* 21-26.

Graham, S. (2004). *Building Web services with Java: Making sense of XML, SOAP, WSDL and UDDI.* Pearson Education.

Harold, E.R., & Means, W.S. (2004). *XML in a nutshell* (3rd ed.). O'Reilly Publishers.

Kodali, R. (2005, June). What is service-oriented architecture? An introduction to SOA. *Javaworld,* 32-36.

Levitt, J. (2001, October). From EDI to XML and UDDI: A brief history of Web services. *Information Week*, 28-32.

Nayak, R., Witt, R., & Tonev, A. (2002). Data mining and XML documents. In *Proceedings of the International Conference on Internet Computing, IC2002*, 660-666. Las Vegas, NV.

Staab, S., van der Aalst, W., Benjamins, R., & Sheth, A. (2003). Web services: Been there, done that? *IEEE Intelligent Systems, 18*(1), 72-73.

Verma, K. (2005). METEOR-S WSDI: A scalable P2P infrastructure of registries for semantic publication and discovery of Web services information technology and management. *Springer Science+Business Media B.V, 6*(1).

KEY TERMS

Binding: An association between an interface, a concrete protocol, and a data format. A binding specifies the protocol and data format to be used in transmitting messages defined by the associated interface.

Discovery: The act of locating a machine-processable description of a Web service-related resource that may have been previously unknown and that meets certain functional criteria.

Message: A message is the basic unit of data sent from one Web services agent to another in the context of Web services.

Proxy: An agent that relays a message between a requester agent and a provider agent, appearing to the Web service to be the requester.

Service-Oriented Architecture: A collection of services that communicate with each other. The services are self-contained and do not depend on the context or state of the other service. They work within a distributed systems architecture.

SOAP: A means for allowing a program running in one kind of operating system to communicate with a program in the same or another kind of an operating system by using the World Wide Web's hypertext transfer protocol and its extensible mark-up language (XML) as the mechanisms for information exchange.

Web Service: A Web service is a software component that is described via WSDL and is capable of being accessed via standard network protocols such as (but not limited to) SOAP over HTTP. It has an interface described in a machine-processable format (specifically WSDL).

ENDNOTE

[1]   www.webservices.org

Web-Based Commerce Applications: Adoption and Evaluation

Chad Lin
Curtin University of Technology, Australia

Helen Cripps
Edith Cowan University, Australia

Yu-An Huang
National Chi Nan University, Taiwan

INTRODUCTION

The transaction of business via the Web is becoming an imperative for organizations aiming at improving their competitiveness. The Web-based commerce applications allow organizations to access potential customers and suppliers via the Internet. Expected benefits include: expanded marketplaces, potential cost reductions, productivity improvements, customization of products and services, 24-hour trading and information exchange, and management (McIvor & Humphreys, 2004; Raisinghani et al., 2005). This expansion of Web-based commerce has led to growing research into the impact of investments made by organisations in this field (Raisinghani et al., 2005).

Small-to-medium enterprises (SMEs) play a crucial role in national economies and are estimated to account for 80 percent of global economic growth (Jutla et al., 2002). In addition, the importance of Web-based commerce to SMEs is growing as globalization and rapid technological changes have brought new opportunities, as well as risks. In order to minimize the problems in adopting Web-based commerce, a number of adoption issues in SMEs have been identified, which include: a lack of organisational resources, technical expertise and experience, management support or awareness of opportunities, customer demand for online services, usage of Web-based commerce, and concerns with the security of online transactions (Buhalis & Deimezi, 2003; Chau, 2004; Lawson et al., 2003). Despite these issues, there are many drivers and benefits for SMEs in adoption of Web-based commerce, and it has been shown that recognition and anticipation of achievable benefits motivates SMEs to adopt it (Chau, 2004).

Most of the studies on Web-based commerce applications investment evaluation and benefits realization (benefits management) that have been done to date have been carried out in large organizations (e.g., Lin & Pervan, 2003; Lin et al., 2005). Very little research has been published in relation to SMEs in Australia.

BACKGROUND

IT Investment Evaluation and Benefits Realization

The major benefits organizations can gain from e-commerce investments are inherently qualitative and cannot be easily assessed beforehand and calculated in monetary terms (Torkzadeh & Dhillon, 2002). The problem becomes more evident as IT is used to link the supply chain or to change the structure of industries, and costs and benefits have to be tracked across functional and organizational boundaries (Love et al., 2005). This is because the less precisely bounded environment of e-commerce technology adds more complexity to the IT measurement problem, as this type of investment is physically distributed between suppliers and customers (Straub et al., 2002).

Doherty and King (2001) suggest that the recent IT project failure rate ranged from 30 to 70 percent. Among recent research on IT investments in e-commerce initiatives by Australian organizations, Marshall and McKay (2002) indicate that nearly half of the respondents had no measures of success, and most did not carry out post-implementation reviews for their investments. Thus, failure to plan for and derive the benefits from, an IT investment can have detrimental consequences on organizational performance.

Evaluation of E-Commerce Investment in SMEs

Despite the competitive advantages offered by e-commerce, SMEs are reluctant to adopt e-commerce, which may be partly due to difficulties in identifying and measuring costs, benefits, and risks associated with their IT adoption and investments (Marshall & McKay, 2002). There is also some evidence that the IT adoption by SMEs has directly or indirectly motivated further IT investments, such as Internet and e-commerce initiatives (Marshall & McKay, 2002). According to Lee and Runge (2001), SMEs that evaluate their IT adoption and investments are better able to exploit the Internet's potential for their organization, and thus create short-term competitive advantages.

Considering its importance, very few recent studies of IT evaluation by SMEs have been published. Most of the studies carried out indicate a lack of strategy for evaluation and limited access to capital resources as the two inhibitors for SMEs to undertake IT investment evaluation (e.g., Hilam & Edwards, 2001 [UK]; Love et al., 2005 [Australia]). Research conducted by Laitinen (2002) in Finland argues that employee motivation, customer satisfaction, and organizational financial position should be considered in the evaluation processes for SMEs. However, some research indicates that most SMEs rely on ad hoc evaluation approaches (e.g., ROI, and gut feeling) and hence, not surprisingly, most SMEs were not satisfied with their evaluation practices (Marshall & McKay, 2002 [Australia]). According to the research by Marshall and McKay (2002), there was virtually no proactive management of IT benefits realization or benefits management by SMEs. With such a diversity of views suggested by the research, further research needs to be undertaken into the evaluation practices of e-commerce adoption for SMEs (Daniel & Wilson, 2002).

SMEs are still lagging behind larger organizations in the adoption and evaluation of e-commerce, despite the benefits it offers. SMEs experience a number of difficulties in their adoption and evaluation of e-commerce as a result of their limited financial, technical, and managerial resources. Considering the complexity of the decisions and the large expenditure required for

SMEs to engage in e-commerce projects, a better understanding of the adoption and evaluation practices of IT investment in e-commerce in Australian SMEs will assist them in their involvement in e-commerce.

RESEARCH METHODOLOGIES AND FINDINGS

This paper presents the preliminary findings of a study conducted with the main purpose of addressing the following two research objectives:

1. To identify the key issues faced by Australian SMEs in their adoption of Web-based commerce applications
2. To determine the current evaluation practices by Australian SMEs adopting Web-based commerce applications

Case studies utilizing semi-structured interviews, observation, and document review were employed for this research. Multiple sources of data were used to address the ethical need to increase the reliability and validity of the research processes (Yin, 1994). According to Remenyi and Williams (1996), case study is one of the most frequently used research methods in information systems research. For this paper, the authors have used the European Commission definition of SMEs as employing less than 250 people (EC, 2004).

After having reviewed the literature on IT adoption and evaluation in SMEs, a series of exploratory, semi-structured interviews were conducted in Australia with senior managers and key personnel from several organizations to gain an overview of their IT adoption issues and the evaluation practices of their IT and e-commerce investments. Twenty interviews were carried out within eight organizations in Australia that were involved in IT and e-commerce projects. The industries represented the following: travel (3 SMEs), hotel (1 SME), service industry (2 SMEs), and housing industry (2 SMEs).

A number of key issues and results emerged from the analysis of the text data which are presented below in some detail. Some of the results listed below were consistent with the findings in the literature while others were not.

Key Issues in IT and E-Commerce Adoption

All of the organizations interviewed had Internet access and agreed that the further adoption of IT will be an important factor for the future success of the organization. The participating organizations indicated that they had used e-mail to communicate with their customers and suppliers and to increase internal efficiencies. All but one of the organizations interviewed had a Web site. However, half of these organizations failed to utilize their Web sites to conduct business effectively with their customers and suppliers. Many organizations indicated that they had insufficient technical and financial resources to implement and maintain the sort of Web sites that they required to effectively conduct their business online. Most users were not satisfied with the e-commerce projects that had been adopted by their organizations.

Adoption of E-Commerce by SMEs

All but two of the organizations interviewed had attempted to improve their ability to conduct their business online. Several of them had invested in e-commerce applications, such as business-to-business (B2B) e-commerce systems, electronic customer relationship management (eCRM) applications, and electronic accounting and payment systems.

The relevant literature has stressed that there is a direct relationship between users' involvement and system success (Lin & Shao, 2000). However, the adoption and use of the e-commerce systems by the Australian SMEs interviewed were generally forced upon the employees by the senior management. Many stakeholders and users within the organizations interviewed said they were not extensively consulted beforehand and were not involved in the designing and adoption of these systems. For example, when asked about her involvement in the eCRM project, one account manager said: *"I am really not involved in the initial adoption of the system....I am not very knowledgeable about the system. The best person to speak to is probably our sales manager...our IT person is responsible for implementing the system. I am responsible for maintaining the system as an account manager."* It is surprising that the account manager was responsible for maintaining the system but was not involved in the adoption and implementation of the project.

Those organizations which kept the users and customers in the dark tend to have low usage for their systems. Furthermore, many benefits expected from the adoption of these systems were mainly tailored for the customers and the senior managers. Very seldom were the benefits for the users considered thoroughly. For example, although usability of the system was mentioned by almost all of the organizations interviewed as one of the most important factors considered before implementing an e-commerce application, the applications were often considered from the perspective of the top management, not the employees.

Objectives of Implementing E-Commerce Projects

There appeared to be a lack of obvious linkage between the expected outcomes of the e-commerce projects' adoption and organizational goals. Alignment with stated organizational goals has a key bearing on how investment is organized and conducted. Objectives for adopting the e-commerce systems by organizations varied greatly. The objectives mentioned by most organizations were basically those benefits that were expected to be delivered by the e-commerce systems. They were all related to the improved customer services and cost and time savings. However, many SMEs simply failed to establish a linkage between the reasons for adopting an e-commerce system and their organizational goals. These systems were often installed without linking the benefits to their organizational goals. For example, the owner of a service chain said: *"The system is not a critical part of our business and it is just an add-on sort of thing to our business. It works sometimes and it does not work some other times. We can still function as it is without the system if it is down. It is just more inconvenience. That's all."*

IT Investment Evaluation Processes

Evaluation happens in many ways (e.g., formally or informally), uses diverse criteria (e.g., financial, technical, and social), follows rigorous methodologies or "gut" feelings, often becomes a political instrument that influences the balance of organizational power and stimulates organizational changes (Serafeimidis & Smithson, 2003). As mentioned earlier, evaluation for any e-commerce initiatives (e.g., eCRM) is difficult and requires a much more rigorous evaluation process (Straub et al., 2002).

Less than one-third of the organizations interviewed had carried out some sort of IS/IT investment evaluation process. For example, two organizations had developed their own key performance indicators (KPIs) (e.g., number of orders and customer complaints) to assess the effectiveness of their projects. However, these indicators were not benchmarked against the industry indicators and there were no formal procedures for the evaluators to determine whether or not the numbers from these indicators were satisfactory.

The other organizations either did not evaluate at all or simply relied on their senior management's gut feeling or intuition. When asked about the evaluation process, one senior manager admitted that there was no formal evaluation process and said: *"I guess the system has been tried and proven over and over again for a long period of time ....The accounting department is actively monitoring the whole situation to see if the system is working ok, I meant, in terms of number of sales."* Most organizations indicated that they did not have the capability and resources to do so or they did not know they had no evaluation process. While almost all of the senior managers interviewed thought it would be worthwhile to have such a process, most of them simply did not do it or relied on their intuition.

IT Benefits Realization Processes

All participants readily admitted that there was no formal benefits realization methodology or process within their organizations. Those who indicated some process existed were actually referring to the informal evaluation mechanisms such as KPIs. No formal IT benefits realization methodology, such as the Cranfield process model of benefit management (Ward & Daniel, 2006) technique, or process was mentioned or specified by any of the participants or in any available documents. The fact that no organization had a benefits management methodology or process is not really surprising as much attention is paid to ways of justifying investments, with little effort being extended to ensuring that the benefits expected are realized (Ward & Daniel, 2006).

The lack of resources and expertise available to SMEs due to their size seems to hamper the adoption and evaluation of Web-based commerce applications.

FUTURE TRENDS

Due to the limited IT sophistication between SMEs and their suppliers and business partners, SMEs are lagging behind the bigger players in using Web-based commerce applications to create competitive business networks. However, these applications are transforming industries by shifting business focus from physical stores to the virtual business. They are creating a more level playing field for SMEs. It is expected that future Internet applications will bring about faster and more efficient business to SMEs by providing customers convenience and variety.

Future Web-based commerce applications are expected to assist SMEs in obliterating the "production focused economy" of the industrial age and extend the information age to new heights, resulting in competitive markets, leading to specialization of products and concluding in higher profits and enhanced service.

CONCLUSION

The research was conducted as an exploratory case study with the results showing that most organizations appeared to fail in some ways to conduct a proper assessment of business needs before the adoption of Web-based commerce applications. Pre-project planning and justification processes were not properly carried out to assess the needs and feasibility of these projects. Most users were not involved in the initial phases of adopting and implementing the applications, and the use of these systems was generally forced upon them by senior management. In addition, there appeared to be a lack of obvious linkage between the expected outcomes of the Web-based commerce applications adoption and organizational goals.

Furthermore, it was disappointing to see that less than one-third of the organizations interviewed had evaluated their Web-based commerce applications. No formal IT benefits realization methodology or process was carried out to ensure that the expected benefits were eventually delivered.

The results here are really a cause for concern as successful Web-based commerce applications require that organizations allocate sufficient resources for improving business processes, continuously evaluating e-commerce initiatives and ensuring that expected benefits are delivered. The evaluation and benefits realization mechanisms can expedite the organizational learning process and help make Web-based commerce applications work to the benefit of all customers, suppliers, and the organizations themselves, whether viewed from a narrow buyer/seller perspective or a broader supply-chain perspective (McGaughey, 2002). Therefore, SMEs should ensure that appropriate evaluation practices are put in place for their Web-based commerce applications.

REFERENCES

Buhalis, D., & Deimezi, O. (2003). Information technology penetration and e-commerce developments in Greece, with a focus on small to medium-sized enterprises. *Electronic Markets, 13*(4), 309-324.

Chau, S. (2004). The use of e-commerce amongst 34 Australian SMEs: An experiment or a strategic business tool. *Journal of Systems and Information Technology, 7*(1), 49-66.

Daniel, E., & Wilson, H. (2002). Adoption intentions and benefits realised: A study of e-commerce in UK SMEs. *Journal of Small Business and Enterprise Development, 9*(4), 331-348.

Doherty, N. F., & King, M. (2001). An investigation of the factors affecting the successful treatment of organizational issues in systems development projects. *European Journal of Information Systems, 10*, 147-160.

European Commission (EC) (2004). SME Definition, European Commission. Retrieved 16 January, 2006 from http://europa.eu.int/comm/enterprise/enterprise_policy/sme_definition/index_en.htm

Hillam, C. E., & Edwards, H.M. (2001). A case study approach to evaluation of information technology/information systems (IT/IS) investment evaluation processes within SMEs. *The Electronic Journal of Information Systems Evaluation, 4*(1). Retrieved 30 July, 2007 from http://www.ejise.com/volume-4/volume4-issue1/issue1-art.html

Jutla, D., Bodorik, P., & Dhaliqal, J. (2002). Supporting the e-business readiness of small and medium-sized enterprises: Approaches and metrics. *Internet Research: Electronic Networking Applications and Policy, 12*(2), 139-164.

Laitinen, E.M. (2002). A dynamic performance system: Evidence from small Finnish technology companies. *Scandinavian Journal of Management, 18*, 65-99.

Lawson, R., Alcock, C., Cooper, J., & Burgess, L. (2003). Factors affecting adoption of electronic technologies by SMEs: An Australian study. *Journal of Small Business and Enterprise Development, 10*(3), 265-276.

Lee, J., & Runge, J. (2001). Adoption of information technology in small business: Testing drivers of adoption for entrepreneurs. *The Journal of Computer Information Systems, 42*(1), 44-57.

Lin, C., & Pervan, G. (2003). The practice of IT benefits management in large Australian organizations. *Information and Management, 41*(1), 13-24.

Lin, C., Pervan, G., & McDermid, D. (2005) IS/IT investment evaluation and benefits realization issues in Australia. *Journal of Research and Practices in Information Technology, 37*(3), 235-251.

Lin, W.T., & Shao, B.B.M. (2000). The relationship between user participation and system success: A simultaneous contingency approach. *Information and Management, 37*, 283-295.

Love, P.E.D., Irani, Z., Standing, C., Lin, C., & Burn, J. (2005). The enigma of evaluation: Benefits, costs and risks of IT in small-medium sized enterprises. *Information and Management, 42*(7), 947-964.

Marshall, P., & McKay, J. (2002). Evaluating the benefits of electronic commerce in small and medium enterprises. *The Australian Journal of Information Systems, 9*(2).

Martin, L.M., & Matlay, H. (2001). Blanket approaches to promoting ICT in small firms: Some lessons from the DTI ladder adoption model in the UK. *Internet Research: Electronic Networking Applications and Policy, 11*(5), 399-410.

McGaughey, R. E. (2002). Benchmarking business-to-business electronic commerce. *Benchmarking: An International Journal, 9*(5), 471-484.

McIvor, R., & Humphreys, P. (2004). The implications of electronic B2B intermediaries for the buyer-supplier interface. *International Journal of Operations & Production Management, 24*(3), 241-269.

McKay, J., & Marshall, P. (2004). *Strategic management of eBusiness*. Queensland, Australia: John Wiley & Sons Australia.

Raisinghani, M. S., Melemez, T., Zhou, L., Paslowski, C., Kikvidze, I., Taha, S., & Simons, K. (2005). E-business models in B2B: Process based categorization and analysis of B2B models. *International Journal of E-Business Research, 1*(1), 16-36.

Remenyi, D., & Williams, B. (1996). The nature of research: Qualitative or quantitative, Narrative or paradigmatic? *Information Systems Journal, 6*, 131-146.

Serafeimidis, V., & Smithson, S. (2003). Information systems evaluation as an organisational institution: Experience from a case study. *Information Systems Journal, 13*(2), 251-274.

Straub, D. W., Hoffman, D. L., Weber, B. W., & Steinfield, C. (2002). Measuring e-commerce in net-enabled organizations: An introduction to the special issue. *Information Systems Research, 13*(2), 115-124.

Torkzadeh, G., & Dhillon, G. (2002). Measuring factors that influence the success of Internet commerce. *Information Systems Research, 13*(2), 187-204.

Ward, J., & Daniel, E. (2006). *Benefits management: Delivering value from IS & IT investments*. Chichester, UK: John Wiley & Sons.

Yin, R.K. (1994). *Case study research: Design and methods*. Applied Social Research Methods Series. Sage.

KEY TERMS

Benefits Management: A managed and controlled process of checking, implementing, and adjusting expected results and continuously adjusting the path leading from investments to expected business benefits.

Electronic Commerce: A business model that is conducted over the Internet in which clients are able to participate in all phases of a purchase decision. Electronic commerce can be between two businesses transmitting funds, goods, or services or between a business and a customer.

IT Benefits Realization Methodologies: Approaches that are used to ensure that benefits expected in the IT investments by organizations are eventually delivered.

IT Investment Evaluation: The weighing up process to rationally assess the value of any in-house IT assets and acquisition of software or hardware which are expected to improve business value of an organization's information systems.

Methodology: An organized, documented set of guidelines and procedures for one or more phases of the systems development life cycle, such as analysis or design.

SMEs (Small-to-medium enterprises): The European Commission has defined SMEs as organizations which employ less than 250 people.

Web-Based Commerce Applications: Web-based commerce applications provide an organization with a mechanism to access potential customers and suppliers via the Internet.

Web–Based Information Systems in Construction Industry: A Case Study for Healthcare Projects

Alaa Abdou
United Arab Emirates University (UAEU), UAE

John Lewis
University of Liverpool, UK

Moh'd A. Radaideh
HR General Directorate, UAE

Sameera Al Zarooni
United Arab Emirates University (UAEU), UAE

INTRODUCTION

The construction industry is fragmented in nature due to the many stakeholders with different professional backgrounds involved in different phases developing the project. According to Nitithamyong and Skibniewski (2004), this fragmentation has led to well-documented problems with communication and information processing and sharing, and often is seen as one of the major contributors to low productivity in the construction industry.

The evolving Internet technologies, with their potential for communication, collaboration, and information sharing, provide a unique platform for decision support systems (DSSs). With the level of competitive pressures in the current market, the construction organizations are rapidly realizing the needs for integrating Internet technologies into their daily activities in order to maintain profitability.

This paper describes the development and construction of a Web-based system for the appraisal stage of public healthcare construction projects in the United Arab Emirates. The system is implemented on the World Wide Web. PHP and MySQL were selected as the scripting language and database management system to build this system prototype. Its main objectives focus on assisting decision-makers in examining different function program alternatives and their associated conceptual budgets. In addition, the system facilitates reflecting uncertainty and risk factors associated with healthcare space programming into cost estimating and forecasting processes.

BACKGROUND

With the introduction of the Internet, which provides an infrastructure that best facilitates communication and information sharing among different project stakeholders, many research projects have been recently generated investigating the potential benefits of integrating the Internet in the development and management of construction projects. According to Abdou et al. (2005b), the first wave of Web-based systems-facilitated document management and collaboration activities among project participants in order to save time, communication cost, and paper. For example, Tam (1999) developed a system that comprised document management and collaboration functions such as data exchange and remote login, white-boarding chat, video cam, e-mail, and a search engine.

Moving construction procurement and project control processes into an online Internet environment was the subject of the following wave of research work and system development. Abudayyeh, Temel, Al-Tabtabai, and Hurley (2001) suggest the use of an Intranet-based project management system, focusing on cost control as a mechanism for improving the quality and timeliness of information. The authors highlight the potential benefits of using Web technology for project control, such as the instant, automated online reports that could be produced up-to-the-minute and on-demand, which will lead to improvements in decision-making processes. Another example of an Internet-based project control system has been developed by Moselhi, Li, and Alkass (2004). They developed the integrated time and cost control system (IT/CC). This takes advantage of the Internet to provide an efficient data-sharing environment and accordingly provides timely generation and dissemination of site progress reports. Other example cases for project procurement and control include the work of Tserng and Lin (2002) and Chau, Cao, Anson, and Zhang (2003).

The integration of electronic-commerce in construction material procurement, as well as supply chain management, into construction processes has received a great deal of attention recently. Kong et al. (2004) developed a Web services-based prototype system named "E-Union." It utilizes Web services technology to provide information sharing between different construction material e-commerce systems. According to Abdou et al. (2005b), the construction industry, with its huge materials marketplace, is expected to witness more application of DSSs in the area of electronic commerce, supply chain management, and inventory management, with more intelligent agents applications. It is also expected that the DSSs will be more integrated with enterprise resource planning (ERP) to provide better supply chain management for construction projects.

THE DEVELOPMENT OF THE HEALTHCARE DECISION SUPPORT SYSTEM (HCDSS)

The analysis stage is the early and most important stage in any decision support system (DSS) development; its main objective is to produce a detailed set of requirements for its development. According to Holsapple et al. (1993), three preliminary categories of the system requirements can be established: (1) function requirements, (2) interface requirements, and (3) coordination requirements. These different system requirements were assessed prior to starting the design and construction of the proposed system, and this process is described in the coming paragraphs.

Preliminary system architecture was developed in order to analyze and develop basic function requirements of the system, including the relation between the main parts of the system, knowledge storage, recall, and production issues. To identify the interface requirements, possible menus, different report structure, and the formats of outputs and reports were investigated. To determine the coordination requirements of the system, different flow charts investigating the sequence of events associated with processes carried out by the

Figure 1. Basic system architecture for the healthcare decision support system (HCDSS)

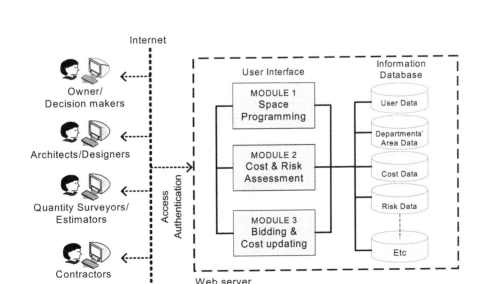

different parts of the proposed system were developed and refined. Following that, the system architecture was refined to include three functional modules: (a) a space programming module, (b) a risk assessment and cost estimating module, and (c) a cost bidding/updating module. Figure 1 shows the basic system architecture for the proposed system.

Programming Language and Database Selection

The PHP Hypertext processor was selected as the programming language for building the system prototype. PHP is a server-side scripting language; it is a widely-used open source, general-purpose scripting language that is especially suited for Web development and can be embedded into HTML codes. Its script is processed by the Web server which translates the PHP code and returns conventional HTML code back to the browser. This kind of interaction allows for some complex operations (PHP Group, 2005). PHP also supports a large number of databases, including Informix, Oracle, Sybase, Solid, and PostgreSQL and ODBC. An open-source database management system known as MySQL was selected as well. It is one of the most popular open-source database management systems. According to Cheung et al. (2004), MySQL can handle large databases, e.g., it is capable of handling

databases with 50 million records, 60,000 tables, and 5,000,000,000 rows.

The PHP-MySQL combination is also cross-platform, which means you can develop in Windows and serve on a UNIX platform. Also, PHP can be run as an external CGI process, a stand-alone script interpreter, or an embedded Apache module. With the above-mentioned advantages of PHP and MySQL, both were selected to build the proposed system prototype. It was the preliminary intention of the authors to use free shareware due to limited resources for this research. It is the authors' opinion that interchange between work environments might not be particularly critical to the success of this research project, as the outcome of the research can be used in different work environments.

SYSTEM DESIGN AND CONSTRUCTION

After the selection of required tools and techniques, the design and construction stage commenced, which took advantage of the strengths and features of those tools. During this stage, continuous refinement processes were carried out in order to achieve and maintain the original prototype objectives. The prototype design and construction, as well as its detailed components, are described in the following sections.

The proposed HCDSS can be operated through a user interface, which is accessed via the Internet through a

Figure 2. Users' types and classification

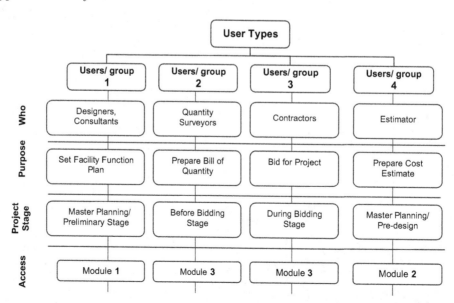

user name and a password. The system is a three-tier client/server system. It involves a presentation-tier, an application logic-tier, and a data-tier. The developing of the proposed system went through continuous refinement processes in order to achieve the original system objectives.

One of the early studies that were conducted during system design and construction was the detailed user description and classification, which was taken into consideration in both the authentication access mechanism and the user interface development. Figure 2 illustrates the classification of different users accessing the system.

The Authentication Mechanism

The authentication mechanism is designed in a way that the user, upon accessing the system, will be directed to the page that he/she is allowed to access, according to the classification shown in Figure 2. This is achieved by setting an access level during the creation of a certain user account. For example, a consultant can access the space-programming page, or a quantity surveyor can access the bill of quantity (BOQ) page. The Administrator has the highest authority in relation to system main activities: He or she can add/delete projects which can be accessed by a consultant to conduct a space program, a quantity surveyor to build the BOQ, or by a contractor to bid for the project. The Administrator can add/delete, activate/deactivate, or modify users and groups and assign access level for each user that allows the user to access his or her target module/page. The user then can accept/modify their password.

The User Interface Development

The user interface (UI) is simply what the user sees and interacts with. It is a layer imposed on the core functionality of the system which makes it more accessible to the user. According to Lewis (1998), the UI basically does three things. First, it allows the user to see the data in various ways, second, it allows user input to alter data, and finally, it allows user input to initiate actions supported by the program.

It is important that the design of the interface be user friendly. Many modern development tools provide visual ways for developing and manipulating user interfaces. For the proposed system, the user interaction and data input are carried out via Web browser pages.

DreamWeaver as well as Microsoft PageMaker software packages were used for the developing the proposed system UI. A login password is required for the access. A Web-based "wizard" style interface will guide users throughout the different parts of the system. The following paragraphs will provide a detailed description of the basic three functional modules of the proposed system and their main components.

THE SPACE PROGRAMMING MODULE

In this functional module, the approved projections of procedures, outpatient visits, or workload inputs are utilized to calculate needed space requirements for the facility's preliminary function plan. The different departments were categorized and structured. A total of twenty departments were identified and classified into four groups, namely: (1) patient-care services; (2) diagnostics and treatment services; (3) administrative services; and (4) support services.

When prompted by the module, the user can select the department/s needed to be studied/ investigated from four drop-menu lists using the four group classifications mentioned earlier. This will direct him or her to the selected department main page where the user can feed the system with values for factors that affect space programming of the department under investigation, such as: patient days, a procedure's time, etc. The user then determines the function planning unit size by selecting minimum, average, or maximum, as well as the required support spaces size for these units. The values/ranges for different function planning units' sizes, as well as different grossing factors, which were established before through analysis of different case studies, were utilized and integrated in the module's modeling criteria. The output result will be saved/updated in the associated database table. It will be also shown in the same page, which includes tabulation for the room numbers along with their net area, support areas, and the gross area ranges (minimum, average, and maximum) for the investigated department. Figure 3 provides a detailed description of the user interface processes chart used in this module.

Generally, the user interface for any department is divided into two main sections: first, the "Key Input" section, where users can enter/select space programming values, and second, the "Space Summary" section, where the details of calculated results are presented.

Figure 3. Flowchart of main processes for space programming user interface-Module One

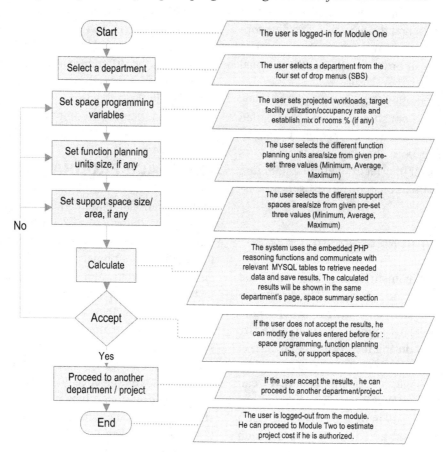

As a sample of the proposed system prototype, two departments have been constructed with their detailed programming factors. They were coded by PHP and linked to MySQL database tables to update, modify, and save records for each department. The user can print the investigated department page, which includes both space programming assumptions and their calculated spaces, in the same page which can provide early needed information for other members of the professional planning/design team of the project.

This information can also be used as a tool for scope management during the project design stage, as it provides guidance to the architect/designer in charge of facility design as well as a control mechanism for the client over the architect/designer. Figure 4 illustrates the main page for the inpatient nursing units department with its two sections: "Key input" and "Space summary."

THE COST ESTIMATING AND RISK ASSESSMENT MODULE

In this module, uncertainty and risk factors are analyzed and assessed in order to forecast the facility's total conceptual cost estimate. The proposed risk assessment criteria for this system suggest that the cost estimate consists of two main parts: a building base estimate and a risk allowance. Furthermore, it classifies the risk allowance part into two more parts: fixed risk and variable-risk allowances. The project total cost can be assessed through three processes.

1. **Prediction client:** In this part, the user feeds the system with a cost index to develop real-time forecasted cost per sq/m values for each hospital department. Values will be calculated based on stored price records for January 2006. (These

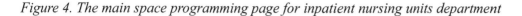

Figure 4. The main space programming page for inpatient nursing units department

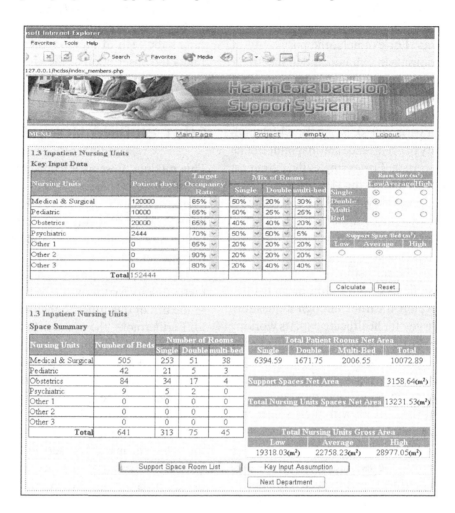

values were developed based on historical cost data analysis for several healthcare case studies with adjustment using the Delphi method from experts' points-of-view.)

2. **Building base estimate:** In this part, the user selects the examined/investigated departments from a drop menu listing all hospital departments. Upon selecting a department, the system calls the forecasted value for the department's cost/m2 from the previous step as its average value (the uncertainty associated with department's cost/m2 is presented by three values—minimum, average, and maximum). The estimator/user can accept/modify the proposed average value and assume its minimum and maximum values. He or she also adds the department net and gross areas ranges that were developed from Module One (the Space Programming module). Circulation areas (in the case of more than one department), can be included in the cost estimate as a separate department. All departments' data are shown in the main page. They can be edited, modified, or deleted. A mathematical model using the central limit theorem is integrated to calculate the expected building-base estimate for all examined/investigated departments. Figure 5, right part, illustrates the main page for building base estimate parts.

3. **Project risk allowance:** In this part, the uncertainty/risk factors associated with healthcare project environment that are expected to affect its

cost are identified and categorized as either "fixed" or "variable" risks. The fixed risk is viewed as one that, if it happens, happens in full, so the total cost will occur. For example, the possibility of the client requiring an extra operating theatre or nursing station. The probabilistic component of fixed risk resides in the expression of the probability that such a requirement may arise. On the other hand, a variable risk is one for which both the probability of occurrence and magnitude of its effect are uncertain. For example, the extra cost that might occur due to the slow process of the government approval system or the cost resultant due to unforeseen soil conditions. For both types, a range or probability values can be assumed and included in this model.

o   *Variable risk*: the estimator can select possible risk factors from a drop-menu list that was developed earlier through a questionnaire survey for healthcare experts working in UAE. More details can be found in Abdou et al. (2005a). Then, the estimator assigns the best estimate for their allowance values (minimum, average, and maximum). All selected risk factors with their values will be shown tabulated on the same page which can be edited /deleted.

o   *Fixed risk:* the estimator can select possible departments that expected to have an additional area (the list will include only departments that were considered/ examined earlier in the previous building-base estimate section). The estimator feeds the system with their possible expected area and probability of occurrence. The system will recall the stored selected average cost/m2 for every department, developed earlier by the prediction client part, and calculate the possible cost allowance ranges. All selected risk factors with their data will show on the same page and could be edited /deleted. At the end of the risk assessment page, final values of variable and fixed risk allowances will be calculated and shown.

Project Cost Summary

In the main estimator page, the final calculated values for building-base estimate and total risk allowance will be summarized as the project total cost estimate with risk assessment. A mathematical model using the central limit theorem is integrated to calculate the total values for each of previous steps. Figure 5 provides a detailed description of the User Interface processes chart used in Module Two.

COST BIDDING MODULE

This module presents a mechanism for using the recurring bidding process during the bidding stage as a source of a reliable, in-house cost index that can assist the estimator for the conceptual cost estimating process which was conducted in Module Two. It also enables the bidding process to be online to improve its timeline and its document management process. The proposed methodology for this part is to link each item included in the bill of quantities to the department they belong to. Furthermore, the system, following mathematical formulae, quantifies and calculates every department's cost as well as its square meter cost for every project. This information is used in updating the inner cost database, which can be used in Module Two as an advisory in developing the building-base estimate.

A password is needed for quantity surveyor/estimator as well as invited bidders to access the Web-based bidding process. The quantity surveyor/estimator first builds the BOQ, and then contractors can later bid and estimate their best prices for BOQ. The system can then generate cost summaries/analyses for review.

CONCLUSION AND FUTURE WORK

The development of a Web-based information system prototype for healthcare construction projects is presented and described in this paper. The underlying philosophy of the approach used is to integrate space programming and cost estimating processes with a risk/uncertainty assessment approach in order to obtain a more realistic cost estimate, along with a clear scope of work for the preliminary function plan of the healthcare facility. The system has a number of interesting features: (1) it takes advantages of the Internet to provide an effective data-sharing environment and improve the timeline for space programming, cost estimating, and bidding processes; (2) it examines different preliminary function program alternatives

Figure 5. Flowchart of main processes for cost and risk assessment user interface-Module Two

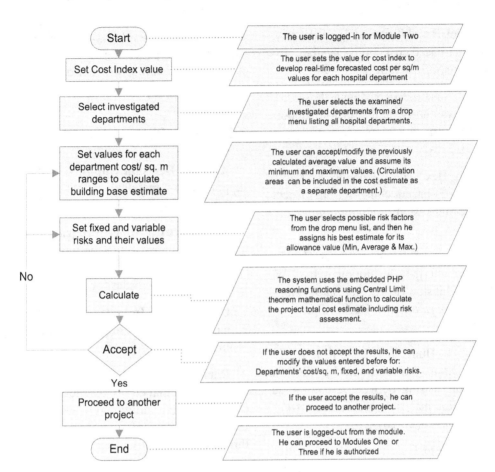

and their associated conceptual budgets during the healthcare project appraisal stage; (3) it integrates uncertainty/risk factors into the estimating processes in order to determine more realistic conceptual cost estimates for the project; (4) it utilizes a recurring tendering process to construct a source of a reliable, in-house cost index that can assist the estimator in the conceptual cost estimating process.

Future development of the presented system may focus on extending the system's scope to integrate a healthcare workload projection module and also investigate the integration of a neuro-fuzzy component to improve the cost forecasting mechanism.

ACKNOWLEDGMENT

The authors would like to express their appreciation to the Scientific Research Affairs Sector, UAE University for funding the individual research project number 01-04-9-11/04, which partially supported the database execution and code scripting of this prototype. Special thanks go to Engineers Tarek Shehabeldin and Saleh Alwahaishi for their effort during the database implementation and code scripting of this prototype.

REFERENCES

Abdou, A., Al Zarooni, S., & Lewis, J. (2005a). *Risk identification and rating for public healthcare projects in the United Arab Emirates.* Paper presented at the COBRA 2005: The Construction Research Conference of the RICS Foundation, Brisbane, Australia.

Abdou, A., Radaideh, M., & Lewis, J. (2005b). Decision support systems and their application in construction. In A. Kazi (Ed.), *Knowledge management in the con-*

struction industry: A socio-technical perspective (pp. 274-296). Hershey, PA: IDEA Group Inc.

Abudayyeh, O., Temel, B., Al-Tabtabai, H., & Hurley, B. (2001). An Intranet-based cost control system. *Advances in Engineering Software, 32*(2), 87-94.

Chau, K. W., Cao, Y., Anson, M., & Zhang, J. (2003). Application of data warehouse and decision support system in construction management. *Automation in Construction, 12*(2), 213-224.

Cheung, S. O., Suen, H. C. H., & Cheung, K. K. W. (2004). PPMS: A Web-based construction project performance monitoring system. *Automation in Construction, 13*(3), 361-376.

Holsapple, C. W., Park, S., & Whinston, A. B. (1993). A framework for DSS interface development. In C. W. Holsapple & A. B. Whinston (Eds.), *Recent developments in decision support systems*. Berlin: Springer-Verlag.

Kong, S. C. W., Li, H., Hung, T. P. L., Shi, J. W. Z., Castro-Lacouture, D., & Skibniewski, M. (2004). Enabling information sharing between e-commerce systems for construction material procurement. *Automation in Construction, 13*(2), 261-276.

Lewis, S. (1998). *How to build an application*. Retrieved August 5, 2005, from http://www.lordjoe.com/UIHandling.html

Moselhi, O., Li, J., & Alkass, S. (2004). Web-based integrated project control system. *Construction Management & Economics, 22*(1), 35-46.

Nitithamyong, P., & Skibniewski, M. J. (2004). Web-based construction project management system: How to make them successful. *Automation in Construction, 13*(4), 491-506.

PHP Group. (2005). Introduction chapter. *PHP Manual*. Retrieved April 1, 2006, from http://www.php.net/manual/en/introduction.php

Tam, C. M. (1999). Use of the Internet to enhance construction communication: Total Information Transfer System. *International Journal of Project Management, 17*(2), 107-111.

Tserng, H. P., & Lin, P. H. (2002). An accelerated subcontracting and procuring model for construction projects. *Automation in Construction, 11*(1), 105-125.

KEY TERMS

Ad Hoc Decision Support System: A decision support system that deals with a specific problem and is typically developed for one-time use.

Architectural Space Programming: The architect's first task and often the most important one. Its main objective is to determine the internal space required for the building in order for it to function properly.

Construction Industry: The industry associated with designing, executing, and maintaining buildings or infrastructure projects.

Decision Support System (DSS): A computer-based system that combines models and data with the aim of assisting individual or group decision-makers in solving unstructured and semi-structured problems through an interactive user interface.

Hyper (Integrated) DSS: A computer system that integrates two or more types of programs or decision support systems in order to solve a particular problem.

Intelligent Decision Support Systems: A type of decision support system that includes one or more artificial intelligence components such as: expert systems, intelligent agents, or artificial neural networks and are thus designed to employ reasoning based on expertise or case-based knowledge in order to solve complex problems

Risk Management: A form of decision-making technique that involves identification and assessment of possible risk events, then generating a response plan to reduce and/or control these risks to an acceptable level.

Wi-Fi Technology

Antonios Alexiou
Research Academic Computer Technology Institute and University of Patras, Greece

Dimitrios Antonellis
Research Academic Computer Technology Institute and University of Patras, Greece

Christos Bouras
Research Academic Computer Technology Institute and University of Patras, Greece

INTRODUCTION

Wi-Fi, short for "wireless fidelity," is a term for certain types of **wireless local area network (WLAN)** that use specifications in the 802.11 family. In general, the wireless technologies are used for the replacement or the expansion of the common wired **networks**. They possess all the functionality of wired LANs but without the physical constraints of the wire itself. The wireless nature inherently allows easy implementation of broadcast/multicast services. When used with portable computing devices (e.g., notebook computers), wireless LANs are also known as cordless LANs because this term emphasizes the elimination of both power cord and network cable (Tanenbaum, 2003).

Wi-Fi sprang into existence as a result of a decision in 1985 by the Federal Communications Commission (FCC) to open several bands of the wireless spectrum for use without a government license. To operate in these bands though, devices would be required to use "spread spectrum" technology. This technology spreads a **radio signal** out over a wide range of frequencies, making the signal less susceptible to interference and difficult to intercept. In 1990, a new IEEE committee, called 802.11, was set up to look into getting a standard started. It was not until 1997, that this new standard was published (though pre-standard devices were already shipping).

Two variants were ratified over the next two years—802.11b, which operates in the Industry, Medical, and Scientific (ISM) band of 2.4 GHz and 802.11a, which operates in the Unlicensed National Information Infrastructure bands of 5.3 GHz and 5.8 GHz. Wi-Fi's popularity really took off with the growth of high-speed broadband Internet access in the home. It was,

and remains, the easiest way to share a broadband link between several computers spread over a home. The growth of hotspots, free and fee-based public access points, have added to Wi-Fi's popularity. The latest variant was 802.11g (WiFi-Forum, 2006).

The first version of **IEEE 802.11** provides data rates up to 2 Mbps, while now there is a set of relevant protocols such as IEEE 802.11a, IEEE 802.11b, IEEE 802.11e, IEEE 802.11f, IEEE 802.11g, and IEEE 802.11i. The most popular of these are the 802.11b and the 802.11g that use the frequency of 2.4 GHz, and the 802.11a, which uses the frequency of 5GHz. Additionally, the 802.11b specification provides a bandwidth rating of 11 Mbps, while 802.11a and 802.11g offer higher performance, providing a maximum bandwidth of 54Mbps, almost five times that of 802.11b. Furthermore, the performance of both the 802.11 families decreases as the distance from the antenna increases.

The 802.11 standard specifies wireless connectivity for fixed, portable, and moving clients in a limited geographic area. Specifically, it defines an interface between a wireless client and an access point, as well as among wireless clients. As in any 802 LAN standard, such as 802.3 (Ethernet) and 802.5 (Token Ring), the 802.11 standard specifies data rates of at least 1 Mbit/s and defines only the **physical (PHY)** and **medium access control (MAC) layers**, which correspond to the first two layers of the Open System Interconnect (OSI) network hierarchy. However, the 802.11 MAC layer also performs functions that are usually associated with higher-layer protocols. These additional functions allow the 802.11 MAC layer to conceal the unique characteristics of the wireless PHY layer from higher layers.

BACKGROUND

As Wikipedia LAN (2006) refers, a local area network (LAN) is a computer network covering a small local area, like a home, office, or small group of buildings, such as a home, office, or college. Current LANs are most likely to be based on switched Ethernet or Wi-Fi technology, running at 10 to 10000 Mbit/s. The defining characteristics of LANs, in contrast to WLANs, are: (a) much higher data rates, (b) smaller geographic range—at most a few kilometers—and (c) the fact that they do not involve leased telecommunication lines. "LAN" usually does not refer to data running over local analog telephone lines, as on a private branch exchange (PBX).

Additionally, in the wireless LANs (WLANs), there is the opportunity for the wireless transfer of the data. More specifically, as Wikipedia WLAN (2006) mentions, a wireless LAN, or WLAN, is a wireless local area network that uses radio waves as its carrier: The last link with the users is wireless, to give a network connection to all users in the surrounding area. Areas may range from a single room to an entire campus. The backbone network usually uses cables, with one or more wireless access points connecting the wireless users to the wired network.

As mentioned above, the Wi-Fi is one of the technologies that are used in the WLANs. Therefore, the three most popular protocols of the 802.11 technology have a number of differences that are presented in Table 1.

WI-FI TECHNOLOGY

Like all IEEE 802 standards, the 802.11 standards focus on the bottom two levels: the OSI model, the Physical Layer, and Data Link Layer (Figure 1). Any LAN application, network operating system, or protocol will run on an 802.11-compliant WLAN as easily as they run over Ethernet (IEEE 802.11 (2006)).

The 802.11-based networks consist of the following logical units:

- **Access point (AP):** The AP functions as a gateway between the wired and the wireless network.
- **Distribution system (DS):** The distribution system merges the APs of the network and users that are served from different APs and are reachable by the entire network.
- **Wireless medium:** Many physical layers have been assigned that use microwaves for the transmission of the packets among the APs.
- **Stations:** The stations that exchange information through the wireless network are mostly mobile devices.

More specifically, when two or more stations come together to communicate with each other, they form a basic service set (BSS). The minimum BSS consists of two stations; 802.11 LANs use the BSS as the standard building block. A BSS that stands alone and is not connected to a base is called an Independent Basic Service Set (IBSS), or is referred to as an ad-hoc network. An ad-hoc network is a network where stations communicate only peer-to-peer. There is no base and no one gives permission to talk. Mostly these networks are spontaneous and can be set up rapidly. Ad-hoc or IBSS networks are characteristically limited, both temporally and spatially (Wikipedia Wi-Fi Technology (2006)).

When BSSs are interconnected, the network becomes one with infrastructure. The 802.11 infrastructure has several elements. Two or more BSSs are intercon-

Table 1. Comparison of Wi-Fi technologies

Wireless Standard	802.11b	802.11g	802.11a
Max speed	11 Mbps	54 Mbps	54 Mbps
Max encryption	128 bit WEP	128 bit WEP	152 bit WEP 256 bit AES
Discrete channels	3	3	8
Max range full throughput	~30 ft.	~20 ft.	~10 ft.
Natively compatible	802.11b, 802.11g	802.11b, 802.11g	802.11a
Potential user	Entry level and home networks	Larger networks, small business	Large businesses concerned with security

Figure 1. IEEE 802.11 and the OSI model

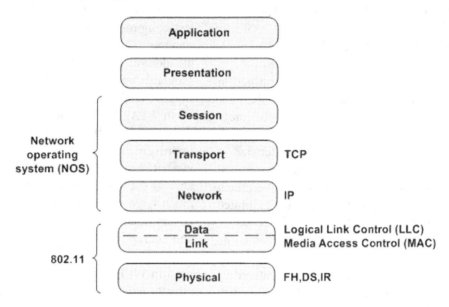

nected using a distribution system (DS). This concept of a DS increases network coverage. Each BSS becomes a component of an extended, larger network. Entry to the DS is accomplished with the use of access points. An access point is a station, thus addressable. So, data moves between the BSS and the DS with the help of these access points. Creating large and complex networks using BSSs and DSs leads us to the next level of hierarchy, namely extended service set (ESS). The interesting point in the ESS is that the entire network looks like an independent basic service set to the Logical Link Control layer (LLC). This means that stations within the ESS can communicate or even move between BSSs transparently to the LLC.

Unless adequately protected, a Wi-Fi network can be susceptible to access by unauthorized users who use the access as a free Internet connection. The first, and most commonly used, wireless encryption standard, wired equivalent privacy (WEP), has been shown to be easily breakable even when correctly configured. Most wireless products now on the market support the Wi-Fi protected access (WPA) encryption protocol, which is considered much stronger, though some older access points have to be replaced to support it. The adoption of the 802.11i standard (marketed as WPA2) makes available a rather better security scheme—when properly configured. The new versions of the popular operating systems support the WPA2. While waiting for better standards to be available, many enterprises have chosen to deploy additional layers of encryption

(such as VPNs) to protect against interception. Some report that interference of a closed or encrypted access point with other open access points on the same or a neighboring channel can prevent access to the open access points by others in the area. This can pose a problem in high-density areas, such as large apartment buildings where many residents are operating Wi-Fi access points (Wi-Fi Technology, 2006).

WI-FI NETWORK SECURITY

Much attention has been focused recently on the **security aspects** of existing 802.11b wireless LAN systems. This occurs because unlike cables, radio signals are easily exposed and cannot be physically contained. Additionally, the broadcast nature of wireless LANs makes it difficult to protect such LANs from unauthorized access. Thus, many ways to prevent unauthorized access are applied (Benny, 2002).

Service Set Identifier (SSID)

One commonly used wireless LAN feature is a naming handle called a service set identifier (SSID), which provides a primitive level of access control. More specifically, before associating with a particular access point (AP), users are required to enter the AP's SSID together with a password. Unfortunately, the SSID is regularly broadcast by the AP and can easily be detected. Thus, better approaches to the issue of the wireless networks' security have been adopted (Tan & Bing, 2003).

Wired Equivalent Privacy (WEP)

WEP is part of the IEEE 802.11 standard ratified in September 1999. It uses the stream cipher RC4 for confidentiality and the CRC-32 checksum for integrity. Standard 64-bit WEP uses a 40-bit key, to which a 24-bit initialization vector (IV) is concatenated to form the RC4 traffic key. At the time that the original WEP standard was being drafted, U.S. Government export restrictions on cryptographic technology limited the key size. Once the restrictions were lifted, all of the major manufacturers eventually implemented an extended 128-bit WEP protocol using a 104-bit key size. A 128-bit WEP key is almost always entered by users as a string of 26 Hexadecimal (Hex) characters (0-9 and A-F). Each character represents four bits of the key (4 * 26 = 104 bits). Adding the 24-bit IV brings us what we call a "128-bit WEP key." A 256-bit WEP system is available from some vendors, and as with the above-mentioned system, 24 bits of that is for the IV, leaving 232 actual bits for protection. This is typically entered as 58 Hexadecimal characters (58 * 4 = 232 bits) + 24 IV bits = 256 bits of WEP protection (Wikipedia WEP (2006)).

Key size is not the major security limitation in WEP. Cracking a longer key requires interception of more packets, but there are active attacks that stimulate the necessary traffic. There are other weaknesses in WEP, including the possibility of IV collisions and altered packets that are not helped at all by a longer key. Thus, WEP is said to be easily broken, although a substantial amount of data have to be collected before a wireless network can be cracked successfully. Note, however, that using readily-available and downloadable tools, WEP networks can be cracked within minutes (Webopedia WEP, 2006).

Wi-Fi Protected Access (WPA)

Certifications for implementations of WPA started in April 2003 and became mandatory in November 2003. The full 802.11i was ratified in June 2004. WPA is designed for use with an 802.1X authentication server, which distributes different keys to each user; however, it can also be used in a less secure "pre-shared key" (PSK) mode (Wi-Fi Alliance, 2006). The newer version of WPA is the WPA2, whose product certification is available through the Wi-Fi Alliance certifying wireless equipment as being compatible with the 802.11i standard. The goal of WPA2 certification is to support the additional mandatory security features of the 802.11i standard that are not already included for products that support WPA.

In WPA, data are encrypted using the RC4 stream cipher, with a 128-bit key and a 48-bit IV. One major improvement in WPA over WEP is the temporal key integrity protocol (TKIP), which dynamically changes keys as the system is used. When combined with the much larger IV, this defeats the well-known key recovery attacks on WEP. In addition to authentication and encryption, WPA also provides vastly improved payload integrity. The cyclic redundancy check (CRC) used in WEP is inherently insecure; it is possible to alter the payload and update the message CRC without knowing the WEP key.

WPA was formulated as an intermediate step towards improved 802.11 security for two reasons: first, 802.11i's work lasted far longer than originally anticipated, spanning four years, during a period of ever-increasing worries about wireless security; second, it encompasses as a subset of 802.11i-only elements that were backwards compatible with WEP for even the earliest 802.11b adopters. WPA firmware upgrades have been provided for the vast majority of wireless network interface cards shipped; 802.11 access points sold before 2003 generally needed to be replaced. By increasing the size of the keys and IVs, reducing the number of packets sent with related keys, and adding a secure message verification system, WPA makes breaking into a wireless LAN far more difficult (Wi-Fi Planet, 2006).

FUTURE TRENDS

Even with the progress in the wireless technology, what has been missing is a universal wireless technology with the performance to connect consumer electronic multimedia products. To actually deliver on consumer expectations, wireless technologies need to be significantly faster than what is currently available today, while at the same time managing to be power-efficient during operation (UWB Forum, 2006).

To meet these demands, pioneers in the industry, working through the IEEE, turned to **ultra wideband**

(UWB) technology. Scalable in performance from 100Mbps to over 2Gbps, certain UWB systems will deliver secure wireless connections between high-quality multimedia products that are not susceptible to interference and breaks in performance. The usefulness of UWB will not just end with high-quality multimedia. Its raw high-speed performance will enable wireless to finally deliver on true device synchronization. Unlike conventional wireless systems which use narrowband modulated carrier waves to transmit information, UWB transmits over a wide swath of radio spectrum, using a series of very narrow and low-power pulses. The combination of broader spectrum, lower power, and pulsed data means that UWB causes significantly less interference than conventional narrowband radio solutions while safely coexisting with other wireless technologies on the market (Intel UWB, 2006).

Another technology that is related to the Wi-Fi technology and is currently evolved is the **WiMAX** technology. From a technical perspective, WiMAX and Wi-Fi are two different things. Unlike Wi-Fi, WiMAX requires a network plan and sites for base-station antennas. Additionally, WiMAX offers not only more range, but also more bandwidth. While Wi-Fi solutions can broadcast up to 100 meters (330 feet) with a maximum of 54 megabits per second (Mbps), WiMAX has a range of up to 50 kilometers (30 miles) with a transmission speed of about 70 Mbps—under certain conditions. WiMAX is a shared medium, which means that the capacity is spread over all users in a radio cell. The speed also drops as the user's distance from the base station increases.

CONCLUSION

In this article, the Wi-Fi technology was presented. As has been shown, wireless technologies are used for the replacement or the expansion of the common wired networks. The first version of IEEE 802.11 provides data rates up to 2 Mbps, while there is a set of available relevant protocols such as IEEE 802.11a, IEEE 802.11b, IEEE 802.11e, IEEE 802.11f, IEEE 802.11g, IEEE 802.11i. The most popular of these are the 802.11b and the 802.11g that use the frequency of 2.4 GHz, and the 802.11a, which uses the frequency of 5GHz (IEEE 802.11, 2006).

Additionally, much attention has been focused recently on the security aspects of existing 802.11 wireless LAN systems. This occurs because unlike cables, radio signals are easily exposed and cannot be physically contained. One commonly used wireless LAN feature is a naming handle called a service set identifier (SSID), which provides a primitive level of access control. Unfortunately, the SSID is regularly broadcast by the AP and can easily be detected. Similarly, the wired equivalent privacy (WEP) is unsecured, and hence the Wi-Fi protected access (WPA) was designed so as to improve the security of the wireless networks. As was presented, the future of the wireless networks is the WiMAX and the ultra wideband (UWB) technology, which aims to provide from 100Mbps to over 2Gbps secure wireless connections between high-quality multimedia products that are not susceptible to interference and breaks in performance.

REFERENCES

Bing, B. (2002). *Wireless local area networks: The new wireless revolution.* John Wiley & Sons.

IEEE 802.11 (2006). The working group setting the standards for wireless LANs. Retrieved March 15, 2006, from http://www.ieee802.org/11/Wikipedia

Local Area Network (LAN) (2006). Retrieved March 11, 2006, from http://en.wikipedia.org/wiki/LAN/

Tan, T.K., & Bing, B. (2003). *World wide Wi-Fi: Technological trends and business strategies.* John Wiley & Sons.

Tanenbaum, A.S. (2003). *Computer networks* (4th ed.). Prentice Hall.

UWB (2006). Retrieved March 9, 2006 from, http://www.intel.com/technology/comms/uwb/

UWB Forum (2006). Retrieved March 10, 2006, from http://www.uwbforum.org/Intel

Webopedia WEP (2006). Retrieved March 15, 2006 from, http://www.webopedia.com/TERM/W/WEP.html

WiFi-Forum (2006). Retrieved March 9, 2006, from http://www.wifi-forum.com/Wikipedia Wireless

Wikipedia Wired Equivalent Privacy (WEP) (2006). Retrieved March 10, 2006 from, http://en.wikipedia.org/wiki/Wired_Equivalent_Privacy

Wi-Fi Alliance (2006). Retrieved March 15, 2006, from http://www.wi-fi.org/

Wi-Fi Planet (2006). Retrieved March 15, 2006, from http://www.wi-fiplanet.com/tutorials/article.php/1368661

Wi-Fi Technology (2006). Retrieved March 10, 2006, from http://www.wi-fitechnology.com/

Wikipedia Wi-Fi Technology (2006). Retrieved March 11, 2006 from, http://en.wikipedia.org/wiki/WiFi/

KEY TERMS

IEEE 802: Standards for the interconnection of LAN computer equipment. They deal with the Data Link Layers of the ISO Reference Model for OSI.

IEEE 802.11: 802.11 refers to a family of specifications developed by the IEEE for wireless LAN technology. 802.11 specifies an over-the-air interface between a wireless client and a base station or between two wireless clients.

LAN: A local area network (LAN) is a computer network covering a small local area, like a home, office, or small group of buildings such as a home, office, or college.

Ultra Wideband (UWB): Ultra wideband (UWB) systems transmit signals across a much wider frequency than conventional systems and are usually very difficult to detect.

WEP: Wired-equivalent privacy (WEP) protocol was specified in the IEEE 802.11 standard and attempts to provide a wireless LAN (WLAN) with a minimal level of security and privacy comparable to a typical wired LAN. WEP encrypts data transmitted over the WLAN to protect the vulnerable wireless connection between users (clients) and access points (APs).

Wi-Fi: Abbreviation of wireless fidelity, standard technology for wireless access to local networks.

WiMAX: The Worldwide Interoperability for Microwave Access (WiMAX) is a certification mark for products that pass conformity and interoperability tests for the IEEE 802.16 standards. IEEE 802.16 is working group number 16 of IEEE 802, specialising in point-to-multipoint broadband wireless access.

WPA: WiFi protected access (WPA) is a fairly new standard for wireless networks and is more secure than WEP.

Index

Symbols

.NET platform 554
3G cellular networks 620
3GPP (third generation partnership project) 537

A

access control list (ACL) 287
AccessForAll meta-data specification 572
accessibility 678
accessibility laws 680
accessible authoring tools 680
accessible user agents 680
accessible Web content 680
access point (AP) 504
access point (AP) nodes 654
access policing 652
ACK-clocking 60
acknowledgment (ACK) 88, 626, 632
action 544
active/programmable node 634
active and programmable networks 634
active application 638
active networks (AN) 633, 638
active queue management (AQM) 1–6, 153, 155, 650, 652
active server page (ASP) 135
ad-hoc computer network 87
ad-hoc multicast 87
ad-hoc multicasting 88
ad-hoc networks 87, 602
ad-hoc QoS on-demand routing (AQOR) 444
adaptive maintenance 551
adaptive self-configuring sensor networks topologies (ASCENT) 674
adaptive wakeup schedule function (AWSF) 673
A DDA scheme 623

addiction 230
additive increase multiplicative decrease (AIMD) 60, 107, 457, 626
ad hoc decision support system 710
ad hoc network 92, 673
admission control 652
ADSL 29
ADSL2+ Technology 31
Advanced Distributed Learning Initiative (ADL) 572
Advanced Lab for Bioinformatics Agencies (ALBA) 52–58
aggregation 489
Ajax 134
ALM routing protocol 92
altruism 549
anomaly detection 354
anonymity 413
anonymous gossip routing 88
ant colony optimization (ACO) 605
antivirus software 286
AntNet algorithm 601
ants 601
ants, artificial 601
ants, backward 601
ants, forward 601
ants-routing approach 12
application-level multicast (ALM) 86, 92, 157
application-level multicast properties 86
application-level network (ALN) 92, 283
application-level networking (ALN) 353
application-level networking (ALN) technology 87
application level networks (ALN) 277
application profile 574
application servers 528, 531
application servers (AS) 530
architectural space programming 710